COMPUTER ORGANIZATION
AND ARCHITECTURE
Designing for Performance
SIXTH EDITION

COMPUTER ORGANIZATION AND ARCHITECTURE

Designing for Performance

SIXTH EDITION

William Stallings

Prentice Hall

Pearson Education International

Vice President and Editorial Director, ECS: *Marcia J. Horton*
Publisher: *Alan R. Apt*
Project Manager: *Jake Warde*
Associate Editor: *Toni D. Holm*
Editorial Assistant: *Patrick Lindner*
Vice President and Director of Production and Manufacturing, ESM: *David W. Riccardi*
Executive Managing Editor: *Vince O'Brien*
Assistant Managing Editor: *Camille Trentacoste*
Production Editor: *Rose Kernan*
Director of Creative Services: *Paul Belfanti*
Creative Director: *Carole Anson*
Art Director: *John Christiana*
Art Editor: *Greg Dulles*
Cover Designer: *John Christiana*
Manufacturing Manager: *Trudy Pisciotti*
Manufacturing Buyer: *Lisa McDowell*
Senior Marketing Manager: *Jennie Burger*

 © 2003 by Pearson Education, Inc.
Upper Saddle River, New Jersey 07458

The author and publisher of this book have used their best efforts in preparing this book. These efforts include the development, research, and testing of the theories and programs to determine their effectiveness. The author and publisher make no warranty of any kind, expressed or implied, with regard to these programs or the documentation contained in this book. The author and publisher shall not be liable in any event for incidental or consequential damages in connection with, or arising out of, the furnishing, performance, or use of these programs.

Printed in the United States of America

10 9 8 7 6 5 4 3 2

ISBN 0-13-049307-4

Pearson Education Ltd.
Pearson Education Australia Pty. Limited
Pearson Education Singapore, Pte. Ltd.
Pearson Education North Asia Ltd.
Pearson Education Canada, Inc.
Pearson Educacíon de Mexico, S.A. de C.V.
Pearson Education—Japan
Pearson Education Malaysia, Pte. Ltd.
Pearson Education, *Upper Saddle River, New Jersey*

As always
For A. T. S.

WEB SITE FOR COMPUTER ORGANIZATION AND ARCHITECTURE
Sixth Edition

The Web site at WilliamStallings.com/COA6e.html provides support for instructors and students using the book. It includes the following elements.

Course Support Materials

The course support materials include

- Copies of figures from the book in PDF format
- Copies of tables from the book in PDF format
- A set of PowerPoint slides for use as lecture aids
- A set of PDF course notes suitable for student handout or for use as viewgraphs
- Computer Science Student Resource Site: contains a number of links and documents that students may find useful in their ongoing computer science education. The site includes a review of basic, relevant mathematics; advice on research, writing, and doing homework problems; links to computer science research resources, such as report repositories and bibliographies; and other useful links
- An errata sheet for the book, updated at most monthly

COA Courses

The COA5e Web site includes links to Web sites for courses taught using the book. These sites can provide useful ideas about scheduling and topic ordering, as well as a number of useful handouts and other materials.

Useful Web Sites

The COA6e Web site includes links to relevant Web sites. The links cover a broad spectrum of topics and will enable students to explore timely issues in greater depth.

 # Internet Mailing List

An Internet mailing list is maintained so that instructors using this book can exchange information, suggestions, and questions with each other and the author. Subscription information is provided at the book's Web site.

 # Simulation Tools for COA Projects

The Web site includes links to the SimpleScalar and SMPCache Web sites. These are two software packages that serve as frameworks for project implementation. Each site includes downloadable software and background information. See Appendix C for more information.

CONTENTS

APPENDICES

PREFACE

This book is about the structure and function of computers. Its purpose is to present, as clearly and completely as possible, the nature and characteristics of modern-day computer systems.

This task is challenging for several reasons. First, there is a tremendous variety of products that can rightly claim the name of computer, from single-chip microprocessors costing a few dollars to supercomputers costing tens of millions of dollars. Variety is exhibited not only in cost, but in size, performance, and application. Second, the rapid pace of change that has always characterized computer technology continues with no letup. These changes cover all aspects of computer technology, from the underlying integrated circuit technology used to construct computer components, to the increasing use of parallel organization concepts in combining those components.

In spite of the variety and pace of change in the computer field, certain fundamental concepts apply consistently throughout. The application of these concepts depends on the current state of the technology and the price/performance objectives of the designer. The intent of this book is to provide a thorough discussion of the fundamentals of computer organization and architecture and to relate these to contemporary design issues.

The subtitle suggests the theme and the approach taken in this book. It has always been important to design computer systems to achieve high performance, but never has this requirement been stronger or more difficult to satisfy than today. All of the basic performance characteristics of computer systems, including processor speed, memory speed, memory capacity, and interconnection data rates, are increasing rapidly. Moreover, they are increasing at different rates. This makes it difficult to design a balanced system that maximizes the performance and utilization of all elements. Thus, computer design increasingly becomes a game of changing the structure or function in one area to compensate for a performance mismatch in another area. We will see this game played out in numerous design decisions throughout the book.

A computer system, like any system, consists of an interrelated set of components. The system is best characterized in terms of structure—the way in which components are interconnected—and function—the operation of the individual components. Furthermore, a computer's organization is hierarchical. Each major component can be further described by decomposing it into its major subcomponents and describing their structure and function. For clarity and ease of understanding, this hierarchical organization is described in this book from the top down:

- **Computer System:** Major components are processor, memory, and I/O.
- **Processor:** Major components are control unit, registers, ALU, and instruction execution unit.
- **Control Unit:** Major components are control memory, microinstruction sequencing logic, and registers.

The objective is to present the material in a fashion that keeps new material in a clear context. This should minimize the chance that the reader will get lost and should provide better motivation than a bottom-up approach.

Throughout the discussion, aspects of the system are viewed from the points of view of both architecture (those attributes of a system visible to a machine language programmer) and organization (the operational units and their interconnections that realize the architecture).

EXAMPLE SYSTEMS

This book uses examples from a number of different machines to clarify and reinforce the concepts being presented. Many, but by no means all, of the examples are drawn from two computer families: the Intel Pentium 4, and the IBM/Motorola PowerPC. These two systems together encompass most of the current computer design trends. The Pentium 4 is essentially a complex instruction set computer (CISC) with some RISC features, while the PowerPC is essentially a reduced instruction set computer (RISC). Both systems make use of superscalar design principles and both support multiple processor configurations.

PLAN OF THE TEXT

The book is organized into five parts:

Part One—Overview: This part provides a preview and context for the remainder of the book.

Part Two—The Computer System: A computer system consists of processor, memory, and I/O modules, plus the interconnections among these major components. With the exception of the processor, which is sufficiently complex to be explored in Part Three, this part examines each of these elements in turn.

Part Three—The Central Processing Unit: The CPU consists of a control unit, registers, the arithmetic and logic unit, the instruction execution unit, and the interconnections among these components. Architectural issues, such as instruction set design and data types, are covered. Part Three also looks at organizational issues, such as pipelining.

Part Four—The Control Unit: The control unit is that part of the processor that activates the various components of the processor. This part looks at the functioning of the control unit and its implementation using microprogramming.

Part Five—Parallel Organization: This final part looks at some of the issues involved in multiple processor and vector processing organizations.

The book also includes an extensive glossary, a list of frequently used acronyms, and a bibliography. Each chapter includes homework problems, review questions, a list of key words, suggestions for further reading, and recommended Web sites.

A more detailed, chapter-by-chapter summary of each part appears at the beginning of that part.

INTENDED AUDIENCE

The book is intended for both an academic and a professional audience. As a textbook, it is intended as a one- or two-semester undergraduate course for computer science, computer engineering, and electrical engineering majors. It covers all the topics in *CS 220 Computer Architecture*, which is one of the core subject areas in the *IEEE/ACM Computer Curricula 2001* [JTF01].

For the professional interested in this field, the book serves as a basic reference volume and is suitable for self-study.

INTERNET SERVICES FOR INSTRUCTORS AND STUDENTS

There is a Web site for this book that provides support for students and instructors. The site includes links to other relevant sites, copies of the figures and tables from the book in PDF (Adobe Acrobat) format, and sign-up information for the book's Internet mailing list. The Web page is at WilliamStallings.com/COA6e.html; see the section, "Web Site for Computer Organization and Architecture, Sixth Edition", preceding this Preface, for more information. An Internet mailing list has been set up so that instructors using this book can exchange information, suggestions, and questions with each other and with the author. As soon as typos or other errors are discovered, an errata list for this book will be available at WilliamStallings.com. In addition, the Computer Science Student Resource site, at WilliamStallings.com/StudentSupport.html, provides documents, information, and useful links for computer science students and professionals.

PROJECTS FOR TEACHING COMPUTER ORGANIZATION AND ARCHITECTURE

For many instructors, an important component of a computer organization and architecture course is a project or set of projects by which the student gets hands-on experience to reinforce concepts from the text. This book provides an unparalleled degree of support for including a projects component in the course. The instructor's manual not only includes guidance on how to assign and structure the projects, but also includes a set of suggested projects that covers a broad range of topics from the text:

- **Research projects:** The manual includes a series of assignments that instruct the student to research a particular topic on the Web or in the literature, and write a report.
- **Simulation projects:** The manual provides support for the use of the two simulation packages: SimpleScalar can be used to explore computer organization and architecture design issues. SMPCache provides a powerful educational tool for examining cache design issues for symmetric multiprocessors.
- **Reading/report assignments:** The manual includes a list of papers in the literature, one or more for each chapter, that can be assigned for the student to read and then write a short report.

See Appendix C for details.

WHAT'S NEW IN THE SIXTH EDITION

In the three years since the fifth edition of this book was published, the field has seen continued innovations and improvements. In this new edition, I try to capture these changes while maintaining a broad and comprehensive coverage of the entire field. To begin this process of revision, the fifth edition of this book was extensively reviewed by a number of professors who teach the subject. In addition, a number of professionals working in the field reviewed individual chapters. The result is that, in many places, the narrative has been clarified and tightened, and illustrations have been improved. Also, a number of new "field-tested" problems have been added.

Beyond these refinements to improve pedagogy and user friendliness, there have been substantive changes throughout the book. Roughly the same chapter organization has been retained, but much of the material has been revised and new material has been added. Some of the most noteworthy changes are the following:

- **IA-64/Itanium architecture:** This new architecture includes such important concepts as predicated execution and speculative loading. This edition features a chapter-length description and analysis.

- **Cache memory:** Cache memory is a central element in the design of high-performance processors, and cache design has become increasingly complex. An entire chapter is devoted to this issue in the new edition.
- **Optical memory:** The material on optical memory has been expanded and updated.
- **Advanced DRAM architecture:** More material has been added to cover this topic, including an updated discussion of SDRAM and RDRAM.
- **SMPs, clusters, and NUMA systems:** The chapter on parallel organization has been expanded and updated.
- **Expanded instructor support:** As mentioned previously, the book now provides extensive support for projects. Support provided by the book Web site has also been expanded.

ACKNOWLEDGMENTS

This new edition has benefited from review by a number of people, who gave generously of their time and expertise. The following people reviewed all or a large part of the manuscript: Willis King (University of Houston), Albert Heaney (California State University), A. S. Pandya (Florida Atlantic University), Yaser Khalifa (University of North Dakota), and Sanjeev Baskiyar (Auburn University).

Thanks also to the many people who provided detailed technical reviews of a single chapter: Nicole Kaiyan, Terje Mathisen, Daniel M. Pressel, Jeff Deifik, Bill Todd, Charlie Cassidy, Andy Isaacson, Alex Potemkin, Michael Spratte, Hatem Yassine, Grzegorz Mazur, Alan Lehotsky, Jonathan Hall, Sophie Wilson, Alan Alexander, David Vickers, Pete Smoot, and Erik Seligman.

Professor Cindy Norris of Appalachian State University contributed some homework problems.

Professor Miguel Angel Vega Rodriguez, Prof. Dr. Juan Manuel Sánchez Pérez, and Prof. Dr. Juan Antonio Gómez Pulido, all of University of Extremadura, Spain prepared the SMPCache problems in the instructors manual and authored the SMPCache User's Guide.

Todd Bezenek of the University of Wisconsin and James Stine of Lehigh University prepared the SimpleScalar problems in the instructors manual, and Todd also authored the SimpleScalar User's Guide.

ABOUT THE AUTHOR

WILLIAM STALLINGS has made a unique contribution to understanding the broad sweep of technical developments in computer networking and computer architecture. He has authored 17 titles, and counting revised editions, a total of 35 books on various aspects of these subjects. For five years in a row, he has been the recipient of the award for the best Computer Science and Engineering textbook of the year from the Textbook and Academic Authors Association.

In over 25 years in the field, Dr. Stallings has been a technical contributor, technical manager and an executive with several high-technology firms. He is an independent consultant whose clients have included computer and networking manufacturers and customers, software development firms and leading-edge government research institutions. He created and maintains the Computer Science Student Resource Site at:
WilliamStallings.com/StudentSupport.html.

Dr. Stallings holds a Ph.D. from MIT in computer science and a B.S. from Notre Dame in electrical engineering.

COMPUTER ORGANIZATION AND ARCHITECTURE

Designing for Performance

SIXTH EDITION

PART ONE Overview

ISSUES FOR PART ONE

The purpose of Part One is to provide a background and context for the remainder of this book. The fundamental concepts of computer organization and architecture are presented.

ROAD MAP FOR PART ONE

Chapter 1 Introduction

Chapter 1 introduces the concept of the computer as a hierarchical system. A computer can be viewed as a structure of components and its function described in terms of the collective function of its cooperating components. Each component, in turn, can be described in terms of its internal structure and function. The major levels of this hierarchical view are introduced. The remainder of the book is organized, top down, using these levels.

Chapter 2 Computer Evolution and Performance

Chapter 2 serves two purposes. First, a discussion of the history of computer technology is an easy and interesting way of being introduced to the basic concepts of computer organization and architecture. The chapter also addresses the technology trends that have made performance the focus of computer system design and previews the various techniques and strategies that are used to achieve balanced, efficient performance.

CHAPTER 1

INTRODUCTION

This book is about the structure and function of computers. Its purpose is to present, as clearly and completely as possible, the nature and characteristics of modern-day computers. This task is a challenging one for two reasons.

First, there is a tremendous variety of products, from single-chip microcomputers costing a few dollars to supercomputers costing tens of millions of dollars, that can rightly claim the name *computer*. Variety is exhibited not only in cost, but also in size, performance, and application. Second, the rapid pace of change that has always characterized computer technology continues with no letup. These changes cover all aspects of computer technology, from the underlying integrated circuit technology used to construct computer components to the increasing use of parallel organization concepts in combining those components.

In spite of the variety and pace of change in the computer field, certain fundamental concepts apply consistently throughout. To be sure, the application of these concepts depends on the current state of technology and the price/performance objectives of the designer. The intent of this book is to provide a thorough discussion of the fundamentals of computer organization and architecture and to relate these to contemporary computer design issues. This chapter introduces the descriptive approach to be taken and provides an overview of the remainder of the book.

1.1   ORGANIZATION AND ARCHITECTURE

In describing computers, a distinction is often made between *computer architecture* and *computer organization*. Although it is difficult to give precise definitions for these terms, a consensus exists about the general areas covered by each (e.g., see [VRAN80], [SIEW82], and [BELL78a]).

Computer architecture refers to those attributes of a system visible to a programmer or, put another way, those attributes that have a direct impact on the logical execution of a program. Computer organization refers to the operational units and their interconnections that realize the architectural specifications. Examples of architectural attributes include the instruction set, the number of bits used to represent various data types (e.g., numbers, characters), I/O mechanisms, and techniques for addressing memory. Organizational attributes include those hardware details transparent to the programmer, such as control signals, interfaces between the computer and peripherals, and the memory technology used.

As an example, it is an architectural design issue whether a computer will have a multiply instruction. It is an organizational issue whether that instruction will be implemented by a special multiply unit or by a mechanism that makes repeated use of the add unit of the system. The organizational decision may be based on the anticipated frequency of use of the multiply instruction, the relative speed of the two approaches, and the cost and physical size of a special multiply unit.

Historically, and still today, the distinction between architecture and organization has been an important one. Many computer manufacturers offer a family of computer models, all with the same architecture but with differences in organization. Consequently, the different models in the family have different price and performance characteristics. Furthermore, a particular architecture may span many years and encompass a number of different computer models, its organization changing with changing technology. A prominent example of both these phenomena is the IBM System/370 architecture. This architecture was first introduced in 1970 and included a number of models. The customer with modest requirements could buy a cheaper, slower model and, if demand increased, later upgrade to a more expensive, faster model without having to abandon software that had already been developed. Over the years, IBM has introduced many new models with improved technology to replace older models, offering the customer greater speed, lower cost, or both. These newer models retained the same architecture so that the customer's software investment was protected. Remarkably, the System/370 architecture, with a few enhancements, has survived to this day as the architecture of IBM's mainframe product line.

In a class of computers called microcomputers, the relationship between architecture and organization is very close. Changes in technology not only influence organization but also result in the introduction of more powerful and more complex architectures. Generally, there is less of a requirement for generation-to-generation compatibility for these smaller machines. Thus, there is more interplay between organizational and architectural design decisions. An intriguing example of this is the reduced instruction set computer (RISC), which we examine in Chapter 12.

This book examines both computer organization and computer architecture. The emphasis is perhaps more on the side of organization. However, because a computer organization must be designed to implement a particular architectural specification, a thorough treatment of organization requires a detailed examination of architecture as well.

1.2 STRUCTURE AND FUNCTION

A computer is a complex system; contemporary computers contain millions of elementary electronic components. How, then, can one clearly describe them? The key is to recognize the hierarchical nature of most complex systems, including the computer [SIMO69]. A hierarchical system is a set of interrelated subsystems, each of the latter, in turn, hierarchical in structure until we reach some lowest level of elementary subsystem.

The hierarchical nature of complex systems is essential to both their design and their description. The designer need only deal with a particular level of the system at a time. At each level, the system consists of a set of components and their interrelationships. The behavior at each level depends only on a simplified, abstracted characterization of the system at the next lower level. At each level, the designer is concerned with structure and function:

- **Structure:** The way in which the components are interrelated
- **Function:** The operation of each individual component as part of the structure

In terms of description, we have two choices: starting at the bottom and building up to a complete description, or beginning with a top view and decomposing the system into its subparts. Evidence from a number of fields suggests that the top-down approach is the clearest and most effective [WEIN75].

The approach taken in this book follows from this viewpoint. The computer system will be described from the top down. We begin with the major components of a computer, describing their structure and function, and proceed to successively lower layers of the hierarchy. The remainder of this section provides a very brief overview of this plan of attack.

Function

Both the structure and functioning of a computer are, in essence, simple. Figure 1.1 depicts the basic functions that a computer can perform. In general terms, there are only four:

- Data processing
- Data storage
- Data movement
- Control

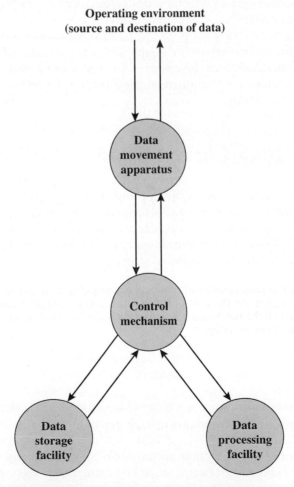

Figure 1.1 A Functional View of the Computer

The computer, of course, must be able to *process data.* The data may take a wide variety of forms, and the range of processing requirements is broad. However, we shall see that there are only a few fundamental methods or types of data processing.

It is also essential that a computer *store data.* Even if the computer is processing data on the fly (i.e., data come in and get processed, and the results go out immediately), the computer must temporarily store at least those pieces of data that are being worked on at any given moment. Thus, there is at least a short-term data storage function. Equally important, the computer performs a long-term data storage function. Files of data are stored on the computer for subsequent retrieval and update.

The computer must be able to *move data* between itself and the outside world. The computer's operating environment consists of devices that serve as either sources or destinations of data. When data are received from or delivered to a device that is directly connected to the computer, the process is known as *input–output* (I/O), and the device is referred to as a *peripheral.* When data are moved over longer distances, to or from a remote device, the process is known as *data communications.*

Finally, there must be *control* of these three functions. Ultimately, this control is exercised by the individual(s) who provides the computer with instructions. Within the computer, a control unit manages the computer's resources and orchestrates the performance of its functional parts in response to those instructions.

At this general level of discussion, the number of possible operations that can be performed is few. Figure 1.2 depicts the four possible types of operations. The computer can function as a data movement device (Figure 1.2a), simply transferring data from one peripheral or communications line to another. It can also function as a data storage device (Figure 1.2b), with data transferred from the external environment to computer storage (read) and vice versa (write). The final two diagrams show operations involving data processing, on data either in storage (Figure 1.2c) or en route between storage and the external environment (Figure 1.2d).

The preceding discussion may seem absurdly generalized. It is certainly possible, even at a top level of computer structure, to differentiate a variety of functions, but, to quote [SIEW82],

> There is remarkably little shaping of computer structure to fit the function to be performed. At the root of this lies the general-purpose nature of computers, in which all the functional specialization occurs at the time of programming and not at the time of design.

Structure

Figure 1.3 is the simplest possible depiction of a computer. The computer interacts in some fashion with its external environment. In general, all of its linkages to the external environment can be classified as peripheral devices or communication lines. We will have something to say about both types of linkages.

But of greater concern in this book is the internal structure of the computer itself, which is shown at a top level in Figure 1.4. There are four main structural components:

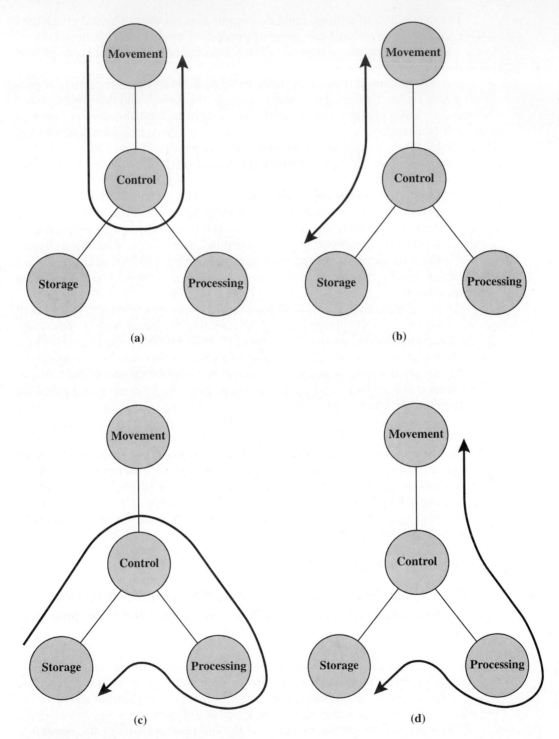

Figure 1.2 Possible Computer Operations

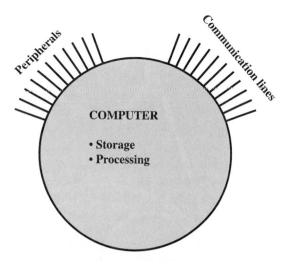

Figure 1.3   The Computer

- **Central processing unit (CPU):** Controls the operation of the computer and performs its data processing functions; often simply referred to as *processor*
- **Main memory:** Stores data
- **I/O:** Moves data between the computer and its external environment
- **System interconnection:** Some mechanism that provides for communication among CPU, main memory, and I/O

There may be one or more of each of the aforementioned components. Traditionally, there has been just a single CPU. In recent years, there has been increasing use of multiple processors in a single computer. Some design issues relating to multiple processors crop up and are discussed as the text proceeds; Part Five focuses on such computers.

Each of these components will be examined in some detail in Part Two. However, for our purposes, the most interesting and in some ways the most complex component is the CPU; its structure is depicted in Figure 1.5. Its major structural components are as follows:

- **Control unit:** Controls the operation of the CPU and hence the computer
- **Arithmetic and logic unit (ALU):** Performs the computer's data processing functions
- **Registers:** Provides storage internal to the CPU
- **CPU interconnection:** Some mechanism that provides for communication among the control unit, ALU, and registers

Each of these components will be examined in some detail in Part Three, where we will see that complexity is added by the use of parallel and pipelined organizational techniques. Finally, there are several approaches to the implementation of the control unit, but the most common is a *microprogrammed* implementation. In essence,

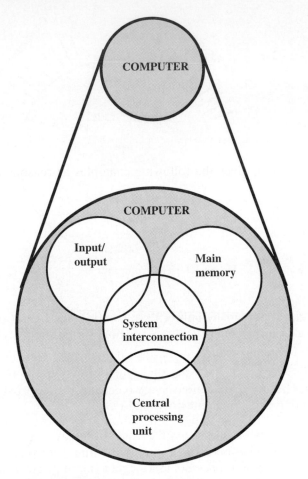

Figure 1.4 The Computer: Top-Level Structure

a microprogrammed control unit operates by executing microinstructions that define the functionality of the control unit. With this approach, the structure of the control unit can be depicted as in Figure 1.6. This structure will be examined in Part Four.

1.3 WHY STUDY COMPUTER ORGANIZATION AND ARCHITECTURE?

The *IEEE/ACM Computer Curricula 2001* [JTF01], prepared by the Joint Task Force on Computing Curricula of the IEEE (Institute of Electrical and Electronics Engineers) Computer Society and ACM (Association for Computing Machinery), lists computer architecture as one of the core subjects that should be in the curriculum of all students in computer science and computer engineering. The report says the following:

The computer lies at the heart of computing. Without it most of the computing disciplines today would be a branch of theoretical mathematics. To be a professional in any field of computing today, one should not regard the computer as just a black box that executes programs by magic. All students of computing should acquire some understanding and appreciation of a computer system's functional components, their characteristics, their performance, and their interactions. There are practical implications as well. Students need to understand computer architecture in order to structure a program so that it runs more efficiently on a real machine. In selecting a system to use, they should to able to understand the tradeoff among various components, such as CPU clock speed vs. memory size.

[CLEM00] gives the following examples as reasons for studying computer architecture:

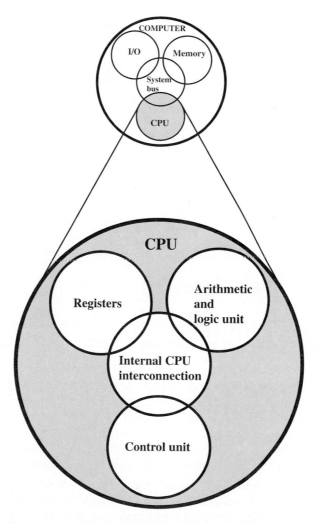

Figure 1.5 The Central Processing Unit (CPU)

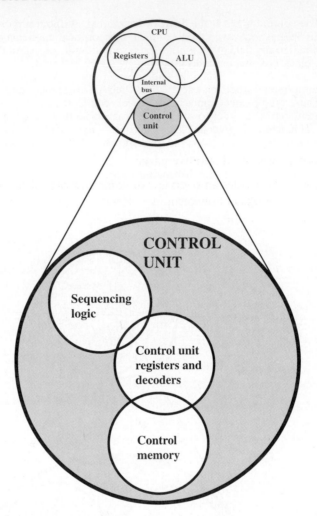

Figure 1.6 The Control Unit

1. Suppose a graduate enters the industry and is asked to select the most cost-effective computer for use throughout a large organization. An understanding of the implications of spending more for various alternatives, such as a larger cache or a higher processor clock rate, is essential to making the decision.

2. Many processors are not used in PCs or servers but in embedded systems. A designer may program a processor in C that is embedded in some real-time or larger system, such as an intelligent automobile electronics controller. Debugging the system may require the use of a logic analyzer that displays the relationship between interrupt requests from engine sensors and machine-level code.

3. Concepts used in computer architecture find application in other courses. In particular, the way in which the computer provides architectural support for programming languages and operating system facilities reinforces concepts from those areas.

As can be seen by perusing the table of contents of this book, computer organization and architecture encompasses a broad range of design issues and concepts. A good overall understanding of these concepts will be useful both in other areas of study and in future work after graduation.

1.4 OUTLINE OF THE BOOK

The book is organized into five parts:

Part One: Provides an overview of computer organization and architecture and looks at how computer design has evolved.

Part Two: Examines the major components of a computer and their interconnections, both with each other and the outside world. This part also includes a detailed discussion of internal and external memory, and of I/O. Finally, the relationship between a computer's architecture and the operating system running on that architecture is examined.

Part Three: Examines the internal architecture and organization of the processor. This part begins with an extended discussion of computer arithmetic. Then we look at the instruction set architecture. The remainder of the part deals with the structure and function of the processor, including a discussion of RISC and superscalar approaches, as well as a detailed look at the IA-64 architecture.

Part Four: Discusses the internal structure of the processor's control unit and the use of microprogramming.

Part Five: Deals with parallel organization, including symmetric multiprocessing and clusters.

1.5 INTERNET AND WEB RESOURCES

There are a number of resources available on the Internet and the Web to support this book and to help one keep up with developments in this field.

Web Sites for This Book

A special Web page has been set up for this book at WilliamStallings.com/ COA6e.html. See the two-page layout at the beginning of this book for a detailed description of that site.

An errata list for this book will be maintained at the Web site and updated as needed. Please e-mail any errors that you spot to me. Errata sheets for my other books are at WilliamStallings.com.

I also maintain the Computer Science Student Resource Site, at WilliamStallings.com/StudentSupport.html; the purpose of this site is to provide documents, information, and useful links for computer science students and professionals. Links are organized into four categories:

- **Math:** Includes a basic math refresher, a queuing analysis primer, a number system primer, and links to useful math Web sites
- **How-to:** Advice and guidance for solving homework problems, writing technical reports, and preparing technical presentations
- **Research resources:** Links to important collections of papers, technical reports, and bibliographies
- **Miscellaneous:** A variety of useful documents and links

Other Web Sites

There are numerous Web sites that provide information related to the topics of this book. In subsequent chapters, pointers to specific Web sites can be found in the "Recommended Reading and Web Sites" section. Because the URLs for Web sites tend to change frequently, I have not included these in the book. For all of the Web sites listed in the book, the appropriate link can be found at this book's Web site. Other links will be added when appropriate.

 The following are Web sites of general interest related to computer organization and architecture:

- **WWW Computer Architecture Home Page:** A comprehensive index to information relevant to computer architecture researchers, including architecture groups and projects, technical organizations, literature, employment, and commercial information
- **CPU Info Center:** Information on specific processors, including technical papers, product information, and latest announcements
- **ACM Special Interest Group on Computer Architecture:** Information on SIGARCH activities and publications
- **IEEE Technical Committee on Computer Architecture:** Copies of TCAA newsletter

USENET Newsgroups

A number of USENET newsgroups are devoted to some aspect of computer organization and architecture. As with virtually all USENET groups, there is a high noise to signal ratio, but it is worth experimenting to see if any meet your needs. The most relevant are as follows:

- **comp.arch.:** A general newsgroup for discussion of computer architecture. Often quite good.
- **comp.arch.arithmetic:** Discusses computer arithmetic algorithms and standards.
- **comp.arch.storage:** Discussion ranges from products to technology to practical usage issues.
- **comp.parallel:** Discusses parallel computers and applications.

CHAPTER 2

COMPUTER EVOLUTION AND PERFORMANCE

KEY POINTS

◆ The evolution of computers has been characterized by increasing processor speed, decreasing component size, increasing memory size, and increasing I/O capacity and speed.

◆ One factor responsible for the great increase in processor speed is the shrinking size of microprocessor components; this reduces the distance between components and hence increases speed. However, the true gains in speed in recent years have come from the organization of the processor, including heavy use of pipelining and parallel execution techniques and the use of speculative execution techniques, which results in the tentative execution of future instructions that might be needed. All of these techniques are designed to keep the processor busy as much of the time as possible.

◆ A critical issue in computer system design is balancing the performance of the various elements, so that gains in performance in one area are not handicapped by a lag in other areas. In particular, processor speed has increased more rapidly than memory access time. A variety of techniques is used to compensate for this mismatch, including caches, wider data paths from memory to processor, and more intelligent memory chips.

We begin our study of computers with a brief history. This history is itself interesting and also serves the purpose of providing an overview of computer structure and function. Next, we address the issue of performance. A consideration of the need for balanced utilization of computer resources provides a context that is useful throughout the book. Finally, we look briefly at the evolution of the two systems that serve as key examples throughout the book: Pentium and PowerPC.

2.1 A BRIEF HISTORY OF COMPUTERS

The First Generation: Vacuum Tubes

ENIAC

The ENIAC (Electronic Numerical Integrator And Computer), designed by and constructed under the supervision of John Mauchly and John Presper Eckert at the University of Pennsylvania, was the world's first general-purpose electronic digital computer.

The project was a response to U.S. wartime needs during World War II. The Army's Ballistics Research Laboratory (BRL), an agency responsible for developing range and trajectory tables for new weapons, was having difficulty supplying these tables accurately and within a reasonable time frame. Without these firing tables, the new weapons and artillery were useless to gunners. The BRL employed more than 200 people who, using desktop calculators, solved the necessary ballistics equations. Preparation of the tables for a single weapon would take one person many hours, even days.

Mauchly, a professor of electrical engineering at the University of Pennsylvania, and Eckert, one of his graduate students, proposed to build a general-purpose computer using vacuum tubes for the BRL's application. In 1943, the Army accepted this proposal, and work began on the ENIAC. The resulting machine was enormous, weighing 30 tons, occupying 1500 square feet of floor space, and containing more than 18,000 vacuum tubes. When operating, it consumed 140 kilowatts of power. It was also substantially faster than any electromechanical computer, being capable of 5000 additions per second.

The ENIAC was a decimal rather than a binary machine. That is, numbers were represented in decimal form and arithmetic was performed in the decimal system. Its memory consisted of 20 "accumulators," each capable of holding a 10-digit decimal number. A ring of 10 vacuum tubes represented each digit. At any time, only one vacuum tube was in the ON state, representing one of the 10 digits. The major drawback of the ENIAC was that it had to be programmed manually by setting switches and plugging and unplugging cables.

The ENIAC was completed in 1946, too late to be used in the war effort. Instead, its first task was to perform a series of complex calculations that were used to help determine the feasibility of the hydrogen bomb. The use of the ENIAC for a purpose other than that for which it was built demonstrated its general-purpose nature. The ENIAC continued to operate under BRL management until 1955, when it was disassembled.

The von Neumann Machine

The task of entering and altering programs for the ENIAC was extremely tedious. The programming process could be facilitated if the program could be represented in a form suitable for storing in memory alongside the data. Then, a computer could get its instructions by reading them from memory, and a program could be set or altered by setting the values of a portion of memory.

This idea, known as the *stored-program concept,* is usually attributed to the ENIAC designers, most notably the mathematician John von Neumann, who was a consultant on the ENIAC project. Alan Turing developed the idea at about the same time. The first publication of the idea was in a 1945 proposal by von Neumann for a new computer, the EDVAC (Electronic Discrete Variable Computer).

In 1946, von Neumann and his colleagues began the design of a new stored-program computer, referred to as the IAS computer, at the Princeton Institute for Advanced Studies. The IAS computer, although not completed until 1952, is the prototype of all subsequent general-purpose computers.

Figure 2.1 shows the general structure of the IAS computer. It consists of the following:

- A main memory, which stores both data and instructions
- An arithmetic and logic unit (ALU) capable of operating on binary data
- A control unit, which interprets the instructions in memory and causes them to be executed
- Input and output (I/O) equipment operated by the control unit

Figure 2.1 Structure of the IAS Computer

This structure was outlined in von Neumann's earlier proposal, which is worth quoting at this point [VONN45]:

> 2.2 **First:** Because the device is primarily a computer, it will have to perform the elementary operations of arithmetic most frequently. These are addition, subtraction, multiplication and division. It is therefore reasonable that it should contain specialized organs for just these operations.
>
> It must be observed, however, that while this principle as such is probably sound, the specific way in which it is realized requires close scrutiny. . . . At any rate a *central arithmetical* part of the device will probably have to exist and this constitutes *the first specific part: CA.*
>
> 2.3 **Second:** The logical control of the device, that is, the proper sequencing of its operations, can be most efficiently carried out by a central control organ. If the device is to be *elastic,* that is, as nearly as possible *all purpose,* then a distinction must be made between the specific instructions given for and defining a particular problem, and the general control organs which see to it that these instructions—no matter what they are—are carried out. The former must be stored in some way; the latter are represented by definite operating parts of the device. By the *central control* we mean this latter function only, and the organs which perform it form *the second specific part: CC.*
>
> 2.4 **Third:** Any device which is to carry out long and complicated sequences of operations (specifically of calculations) must have a considerable memory . . .
>
> (b) The instructions which govern a complicated problem may constitute considerable material, particularly so, if the code is circumstantial (which it is in most arrangements). This material must be remembered . . .
>
> At any rate, the total *memory* constitutes *the third specific part of the device: M.*
>
> 2.6 The three specific parts CA, CC (together C), and M correspond to the *associative* neurons in the human nervous system. It remains to discuss the equivalents of the *sensory* or *afferent* and the *motor* or *efferent* neurons. These are the *input* and *output* organs of the device . . .

The device must be endowed with the ability to maintain input and output (sensory and motor) contact with some specific medium of this type. The medium will be called the *outside recording medium of the device: R* . . .

2.7 **Fourth:** The device must have organs to transfer . . . information from R into its specific parts C and M. These organs form its *input,* the *fourth specific part: I.* It will be seen that it is best to make all transfers from R (by I) into M and never directly from C . . .

2.8 **Fifth:** The device must have organs to transfer . . . rom its specific parts C and M into R. These organs form its *output, the fifth specific part: O.* It will be seen that it is again best to make all transfers from M (by O) into R, and never directly from C.

With rare exceptions, all of today's computers have this same general structure and function and are thus referred to as von Neumann machines. Thus, it is worthwhile at this point to describe briefly the operation of the IAS computer [BURK46]. Following [HAYE98], the terminology and notation of von Neumann are changed in the following to conform more closely to modern usage; the examples and illustrations accompanying this discussion are based on that latter text.

The memory of the IAS consists of 1000 storage locations, called *words,* of 40 binary digits (bits) each. Both data and instructions are stored there. Hence, numbers must be represented in binary form, and each instruction also has to be a binary code. Figure 2.2 illustrates these formats. Each number is represented by a sign bit and a 39-bit value. A word may also contain two 20-bit instructions, with each instruction consisting of an 8-bit operation code (opcode) specifying the operation to be performed and a 12-bit address designating one of the words in memory (numbered from 0 to 999).

The control unit operates the IAS by fetching instructions from memory and executing them one at a time. To explain this, a more detailed structure diagram is needed, as indicated in Figure 2.3. This figure reveals that both the control unit and the ALU contain storage locations, called *registers,* defined as follows:

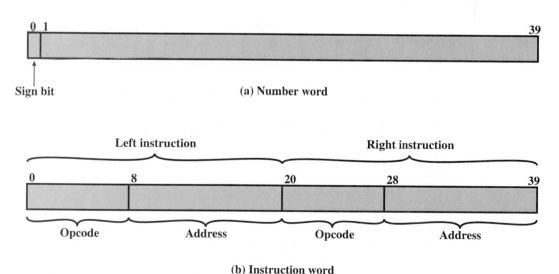

Figure 2.2   IAS Memory Formats

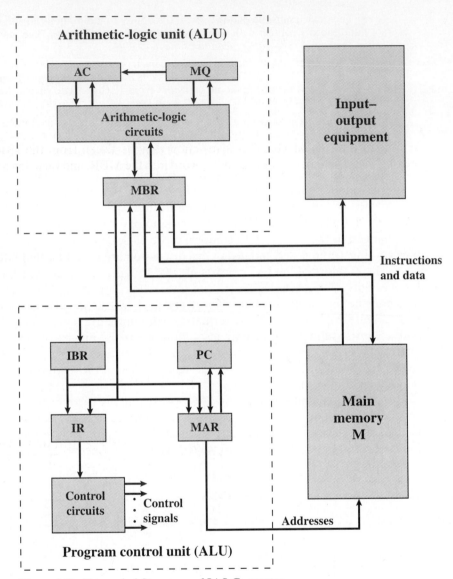

Figure 2.3 Expanded Structure of IAS Computer

- **Memory buffer register (MBR):** Contains a word to be stored in memory, or is used to receive a word from memory.
- **Memory address register (MAR):** Specifies the address in memory of the word to be written from or read into the MBR.
- **Instruction register (IR):** Contains the 8-bit opcode instruction being executed.
- **Instruction buffer register (IBR):** Employed to hold temporarily the right-hand instruction from a word in memory.
- **Program Counter (PC):** Contains the address of the next instruction-pair to be fetched from memory.

- **Accumulator (AC) and multiplier quotient (MQ):** Employed to hold temporarily operands and results of ALU operations. For example, the result of multiplying two 40-bit numbers is an 80-bit number; the most significant 40 bits are stored in the AC and the least significant in the MQ.

The IAS operates by repetitively performing an *instruction cycle,* as shown in Figure 2.4. Each instruction cycle consists of two subcycles. During the *fetch cycle,* the opcode of the next instruction is loaded into the IR and the address portion is loaded into the MAR. This instruction may be taken from the IBR, or it can be obtained from memory by loading a word into the MBR, and then down to the IBR, IR, and MAR.

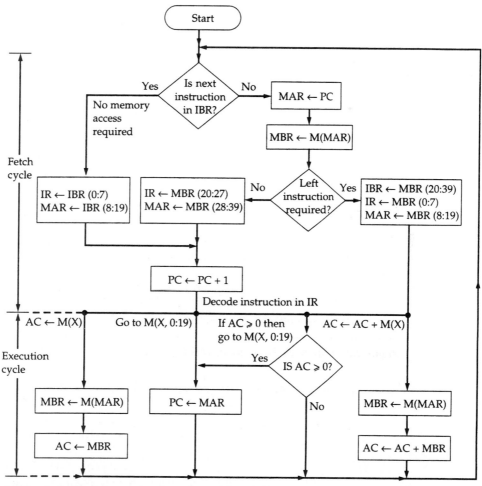

M(X) = contents of memory location whose address is X
(X : Y) = bits X through Y

Figure 2.4 Partial Flowchart of IAS Operation

Why the indirection? These operations are controlled by electronic circuitry and result in the use of data paths. To simplify the electronics, there is only one register that is used to specify the address in memory for a read or write, and only one register to be used for the source or destination.

Once the opcode is in the IR, the *execute cycle* is performed. Control circuitry interprets the opcode and executes the instruction by sending out the appropriate control signals to cause data to be moved or an operation to be performed by the ALU.

The IAS computer had a total of 21 instructions, which are listed in Table 2.1. These can be grouped as follows:

- **Data transfer:** Move data between memory and ALU registers or between two ALU registers.
- **Unconditional branch:** Normally, the control unit executes instructions in sequence from memory. This sequence can be changed by a branch instruction. This facilitates repetitive operations.
- **Conditional branch:** The branch can be made dependent on a condition, thus allowing decision points.
- **Arithmetic:** Operations performed by the ALU.
- **Address modify:** Permits addresses to be computed in the ALU and then inserted into instructions stored in memory. This allows a program considerable addressing flexibility.

Table 2.1 presents instructions in a symbolic, easy-to-read form. Actually, each instruction must conform to the format of Figure 2.2b. The opcode portion (first 8 bits) specifies which of the 21 instructions is to be executed. The address portion (remaining 12 bits) specifies which of the 1000 memory locations is to be involved in the execution of the instruction.

Figure 2.4 shows several examples of instruction execution by the control unit. Note that each operation requires several steps. Some of these are quite elaborate. The multiplication operation requires 39 suboperations, one for each bit position except that of the sign bit!

Commercial Computers

The 1950s saw the birth of the computer industry with two companies, Sperry and IBM, dominating the marketplace.

In 1947, Eckert and Mauchly formed the Eckert-Mauchly Computer Corporation to manufacture computers commercially. Their first successful machine was the UNIVAC I (Universal Automatic Computer), which was commissioned by the Bureau of the Census for the 1950 calculations. The Eckert-Mauchly Computer Corporation became part of the UNIVAC division of Sperry-Rand Corporation, which went on to build a series of successor machines.

The UNIVAC I was the first successful commercial computer. It was intended, as the name implies, for both scientific and commercial applications. The first paper describing the system listed matrix algebraic computations, statistical problems, premium billings for a life insurance company, and logistical problems as a sample of the tasks it could perform.

Table 2.1 The IAS Instruction Set

Instruction Type	Opcode	Symbolic Representation	Description
Data transfer	00001010	LOAD MQ	Transfer contents of register MQ to the accumulator AC
	00001001	LOAD MQ,M(X)	Transfer contents of memory location X to MQ
	00100001	STOR M(X)	Transfer contents of accumulator to memory location X
	00000001	LOAD M(X)	Transfer M(X) to the accumulator
	00000010	LOAD −M(X)	Transfer −M(X) to the accumulator
	00000011	LOAD |M(X)|	Transfer absolute value of M(X) to the accumulator
	00000100	LOAD −|M(X)|	Transfer −|M(X)| to the accumulator
Unconditional branch	00001101	JUMP M(X,0:19)	Take next instruction from left half of M(X)
	00001110	JUMP M(X,20:39)	Take next instruction from right half of M(X)
Conditional branch	00001111	JUMP+M(X,0:19)	If number in the accumulator is nonnegative, take next instruction from left half of M(X)
	00010000	JUMP+M(X,20:39)	If number in the accumulator is nonnegative, take next instruction from right half of M(X)
Arithmetic	00000101	ADD M(X)	Add M(X) to AC; put the result in AC
	00000111	ADD |M(X)|	Add |M(X)| to AC; put the result in AC
	00000110	SUB M(X)	Subtract M(X) from AC; put the result in AC
	00001000	SUB |M(X)|	Subtract |M(X)| from AC; put the remainder in AC
	00001011	MUL M(X)	Multiply M(X) by MQ; put most significant bits of result in AC, put least significant bits in MQ
	00001100	DIV M(X)	Divide AC by M(X); put the quotient in MQ and the remainder in AC
	00010100	LSH	Multiply accumulator by 2 (i.e., shift left one bit position)
	00010101	RSH	Divide accumulator by 2 (i.e., shift right one position)
Address modify	00010010	STOR M(X,8:19)	Replace left address field at M(X) by 12 right-most bits of AC
	00010011	STOR M(X,28:39)	Replace right address field at M(X) by 12 right-most bits of AC

The UNIVAC II, which had greater memory capacity and higher performance than the UNIVAC I, was delivered in the late 1950s and illustrates several trends that have remained characteristic of the computer industry. First, advances in technology allow companies to continue to build larger, more powerful computers. Second, each company tries to make its new machines *upward compatible* with the older machines. This means that the programs written for the older machines can be executed on the new machine. This strategy is adopted in the hopes of retaining the customer base; that is, when a customer decides to buy a newer machine, he or she is likely to get it from the same company to avoid losing the investment in programs.

The UNIVAC division also began development of the 1100 series of computers, which was to be its major source of revenue. This series illustrates a distinction that existed at one time. The first model, the UNIVAC 1103, and its successors for many years were primarily intended for scientific applications, involving long and complex calculations. Other companies concentrated on business applications, which involved processing large amounts of text data. This split has largely disappeared, but it was evident for a number of years.

IBM, which was then the major manufacturer of punched-card processing equipment, delivered its first electronic stored-program computer, the 701, in 1953. The 701 was intended primarily for scientific applications [BASH81]. In 1955, IBM introduced the companion 702 product, which had a number of hardware features that suited it to business applications. These were the first of a long series of 700/7000 computers that established IBM as the overwhelmingly dominant computer manufacturer.

The Second Generation: Transistors

The first major change in the electronic computer came with the replacement of the vacuum tube by the transistor. The transistor is smaller, cheaper, and dissipates less heat than a vacuum tube but can be used in the same way as a vacuum tube to construct computers. Unlike the vacuum tube, which requires wires, metal plates, a glass capsule, and a vacuum, the transistor is a *solid-state device,* made from silicon.

The transistor was invented at Bell Labs in 1947 and by the 1950s had launched an electronic revolution. It was not until the late 1950s, however, that fully transistorized computers were commercially available. IBM again was not the first company to deliver the new technology. NCR and, more successfully, RCA were the front-runners with some small transistor machines. IBM followed shortly with the 7000 series.

The use of the transistor defines the *second generation* of computers. It has become widely accepted to classify computers into generations based on the fundamental hardware technology employed (Table 2.2). Each new generation is characterized by greater processing performance, larger memory capacity, and smaller size than the previous one.

Table 2.2 Computer Generations

Generation	Approximate Dates	Technology	Typical Speed (operations per second)
1	1946–1957	Vacuum tube	40,000
2	1958–1964	Transistor	200,000
3	1965–1971	Small- and medium-scale integration	1,000,000
4	1972–1977	Large-scale integration	10,000,000
5	1978–	Very-large-scale integration	100,000,000

But there are other changes as well. The second generation saw the introduction of more complex arithmetic and logic units and control units, the use of high-level programming languages, and the provision of *system software* with the computer.

The second generation is noteworthy also for the appearance of the Digital Equipment Corporation (DEC). DEC was founded in 1957 and, in that year, delivered its first computer, the PDP-1. This computer and this company began the minicomputer phenomenon that would become so prominent in the third generation.

The IBM 7094

From the introduction of the 700 series in 1952 to the introduction of the last member of the 7000 series in 1964, this IBM product line underwent an evolution that is typical of computer products. Successive members of the product line show increased performance, increased capacity, and/or lower cost.

Table 2.3 illustrates this trend. The size of main memory, in multiples of 2^{10} 36-bit words, grew from 2K ($1K = 2^{10}$) to 32K words, while the time to access one word of memory, the *memory cycle time,* fell from 30 μs to 1.4 μs. The number of opcodes grew from a modest 24 to 185.

The final column indicates the relative execution speed of the central processing unit (CPU). Speed improvements are achieved by improved electronics (e.g., a transistor implementation is faster than a vacuum tube implementation) and more complex circuitry. For example, the IBM 7094 includes an Instruction Backup Register, used to buffer the next instruction. The control unit fetches two adjacent words from memory for an instruction fetch. Except for the occurrence of a branching instruction, which is typically infrequent, this means that the control unit has to access memory for an instruction on only half the instruction cycles. This prefetching significantly reduces the average instruction cycle time.

The remainder of the columns of Table 2.3 will become clear as the text proceeds.

Figure 2.5 shows a large (many peripherals) configuration for an IBM 7094, which is representative of second-generation computers [BELL71a]. Several differences from the IAS computer are worth noting. The most important of these is the use of *data channels.* A data channel is an independent I/O module with its own processor and its own instruction set. In a computer system with such devices, the CPU does not execute detailed I/O instructions. Such instructions are stored in a main memory to be executed by a special-purpose processor in the data channel itself. The CPU initiates an I/O transfer by sending a control signal to the data channel, instructing it to execute a sequence of instructions in memory. The data channel performs its task independently of the CPU and signals the CPU when the operation is complete. This arrangement relieves the CPU of a considerable processing burden.

Another new feature is the *multiplexor,* which is the central termination point for data channels, the CPU, and memory. The multiplexor schedules access to the memory from the CPU and data channels, allowing these devices to act independently.

The Third Generation: Integrated Circuits

A single, self-contained transistor is called a *discrete component.* Throughout the 1950s and early 1960s, electronic equipment was composed largely of discrete components—transistors, resistors, capacitors, and so on. Discrete components were

Table 2.3 Example Members of the IBM 700/7000 Series

Model Number	First Delivery	CPU Tech-nology	Memory Tech-nology	Cycle Time (μs)	Memory Size (K)	Number of Opcodes	Number of Index Registers	Hardwired Floating Point	I/O Overlap (Channels)	Instruction Fetch Overlap	Speed (relative to 701)
701	1952	Vacuum tubes	Electro-static tubes	30	2–4	24	0	no	no	no	1
704	1955	Vacuum tubes	Core	12	4–32	80	3	yes	no	no	2.5
709	1958	Vacuum tubes	Core	12	32	140	3	yes	yes	no	4
7090	1960	Transistor	Core	2.18	32	169	3	yes	yes	no	25
7094 I	1962	Transistor	Core	2	32	185	7	yes (double precision)	yes	yes	30
7094 II	1964	Transistor	Core	1.4	32	185	7	yes (double precision)	yes	yes	50

26

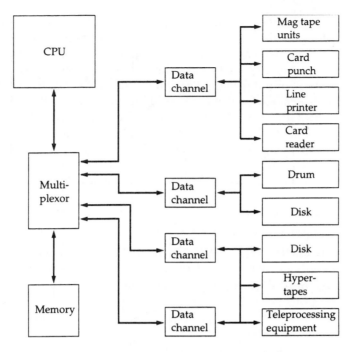

Figure 2.5 An IBM 7094 Configuration

manufactured separately, packaged in their own containers, and soldered or wired together onto masonite-like circuit boards, which were then installed in computers, oscilloscopes, and other electronic equipment. Whenever an electronic device called for a transistor, a little tube of metal containing a pinhead-sized piece of silicon had to be soldered to a circuit board. The entire manufacturing process, from transistor to circuit board, was expensive and cumbersome.

These facts of life were beginning to create problems in the computer industry. Early second-generation computers contained about 10,000 transistors. This figure grew to the hundreds of thousands, making the manufacture of newer, more powerful machines increasingly difficult.

In 1958 came the achievement that revolutionized electronics and started the era of microelectronics: the invention of the integrated circuit. It is the integrated circuit that defines the third generation of computers. In this section we provide a brief introduction to the technology of integrated circuits. Then we look at perhaps the two most important members of the third generation, both of which were introduced at the beginning of that era: the IBM System/360 and the DEC PDP-8.

Microelectronics

Microelectronics means, literally, "small electronics." Since the beginnings of digital electronics and the computer industry, there has been a persistent and consistent trend toward the reduction in size of digital electronic circuits. Before examining the implications and benefits of this trend, we need to say something about the nature of digital electronics. A more detailed discussion is found in Appendix A.

The basic elements of a digital computer, as we know, must perform storage, movement, processing, and control functions. Only two fundamental types of components are required (Figure 2.6): gates and memory cells. A gate is a device that implements a simple Boolean or logical function, such as IF *A* AND *B* ARE TRUE THEN *C* IS TRUE (AND gate). Such devices are called gates because they control data flow in much the same way that canal gates do. The memory cell is a device that can store one bit of data; that is, the device can be in one of two stable states at any time. By interconnecting large numbers of these fundamental devices, we can construct a computer. We can relate this to our four basic functions as follows:

- **Data storage:** Provided by memory cells.
- **Data processing:** Provided by gates.
- **Data movement:** The paths between components are used to move data from memory to memory and from memory through gates to memory.
- **Control:** The paths between components can carry control signals. For example, a gate will have one or two data inputs plus a control signal input that activates the gate. When the control signal is ON, the gate performs its function on the data inputs and produces a data output. Similarly, the memory cell will store the bit that is on its input lead when the WRITE control signal is ON and will place the bit that is in the cell on its output lead when the READ control signal is ON.

Thus, a computer consists of gates, memory cells, and interconnections among these elements. The gates and memory cells are, in turn, constructed of simple digital electronic components.

The integrated circuit exploits the fact that such components as transistors, resistors, and conductors can be fabricated from a semiconductor such as silicon. It is merely an extension of the solid-state art to fabricate an entire circuit in a tiny piece of silicon rather than assemble discrete components made from separate pieces of silicon into the same circuit. Many transistors can be produced at the same

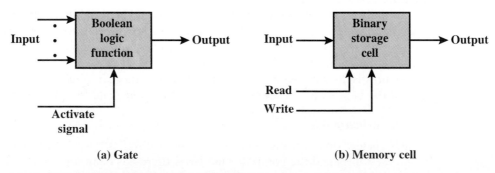

(a) Gate   (b) Memory cell

Figure 2.6   Fundamental Computer Elements

Figure 2.7 Relationship between Wafer, Chip, and Gate

time on a single wafer of silicon. Equally important, these transistors can be connected with a process of metallization to form circuits.

Figure 2.7 depicts the key concepts in an integrated circuit. A thin *wafer* of silicon is divided into a matrix of small areas, each a few millimeters square. The identical circuit pattern is fabricated in each area, and the wafer is broken up into *chips*. Each chip consists of many gates and/or memory cells plus a number of input and output attachment points. This chip is then packaged in housing that protects it and provides pins for attachment to devices beyond the chip. A number of these packages can then be interconnected on a printed circuit board to produce larger and more complex circuits.

Initially, only a few gates or memory cells could be reliably manufactured and packaged together. These early integrated circuits are referred to as *small-scale integration* (SSI). As time went on, it became possible to pack more and more components on the same chip. This growth in density is illustrated in Figure 2.8; it is one of the most remarkable technological trends ever recorded. This figure reflects the famous Moore's law, which was propounded by Gordon Moore, cofounder of Intel, in 1965 [MOOR65]. Moore observed that the number of transistors that could be put on a single chip was doubling every year and correctly predicted that this pace would continue into the near future. To the surprise of many, including Moore, the pace continued year after year and decade after decade. The pace slowed to a doubling every 18 months in the 1970s, but has sustained that rate ever since.

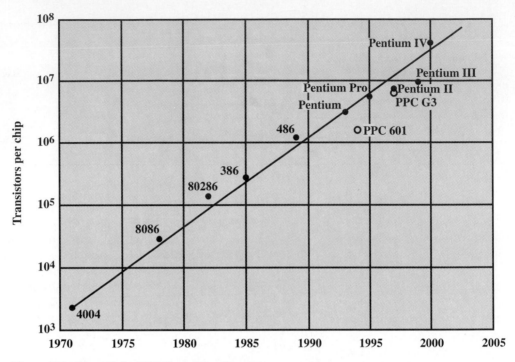

Figure 2.8 Growth in CPU Transistor Count

The consequences of Moore's law are profound:

1. The cost of a chip has remained virtually unchanged during this period of rapid growth in density. This means that the cost of computer logic and memory circuitry has fallen at a dramatic rate.

2. Because logic and memory elements are placed closer together on more densely packed chips, the electrical path length is shortened, increasing operating speed.

3. The computer becomes smaller, making it more convenient to place in a variety of environments.

4. There is a reduction in power and cooling requirements.

5. The interconnections on the integrated circuit are much more reliable than solder connections. With more circuitry on each chip, there are fewer inter-chip connections.

IBM System/360

By 1964, IBM had a firm grip on the computer market with its 7000 series of machines. In that year, IBM announced the System/360, a new family of computer products. Although the announcement itself was no surprise, it contained some unpleasant news for current IBM customers: The 360 product line was incompat-

Table 2.4 Key Characteristics of the System/360 Family

Characteristic	Model 30	Model 40	Model 50	Model 65	Model 75
Maximum memory size (bytes)	64K	256K	256K	512K	512K
Data rate from memory (Mbytes/s)	0.5	0.8	2.0	8.0	16.0
Processor cycle time (μs)	1.0	0.625	0.5	0.25	0.2
Relative speed	1	3.5	10	21	50
Maximum number of data channels	3	3	4	6	6
Maximum data rate on one channel (Kbytes/s)	250	400	800	1250	1250

ible with older IBM machines. Thus, the transition to the 360 would be difficult for the current customer base. This was a bold step by IBM, but one IBM felt was necessary to break out of some of the constraints of the 7000 architecture and to produce a system capable of evolving with the new integrated circuit technology [PADE81, GIFF87]. The strategy paid off both financially and technically. The 360 was the success of the decade and cemented IBM as the overwhelmingly dominant computer vendor, with a market share above 70%. And, with some modifications and extensions, the architecture of the 360 remains to this day the architecture of IBM's mainframe[1] computers. Examples using this architecture can be found throughout this text.

The System/360 was the industry's first planned family of computers. The family covered a wide range of performance and cost. Table 2.4 indicates some of the key characteristics of the various models in 1965 (each member of the family is distinguished by a model number). The models were compatible in the sense that a program written for one model should be capable of being executed by another model in the series, with only a difference in the time it takes to execute.

The concept of a family of compatible computers was both novel and extremely successful. A customer with modest requirements and a budget to match could start with the relatively inexpensive Model 30. Later, if the customer's needs grew, it was possible to upgrade to a faster machine with more memory without sacrificing the investment in already-developed software. The characteristics of a family are as follows:

- **Similar or identical instruction set:** In many cases, the exact same set of machine instructions is supported on all members of the family. Thus, a program that executes on one machine will also execute on any other. In some cases, the lower end of the family has an instruction set that is a subset of that of the top end of the family. This means that programs can move up but not down.

---

[1]The term *mainframe* is used for the larger, most powerful computers other than supercomputers. Typical characteristics of a mainframe are that it supports a large database, has elaborate I/O hardware, and is used in a central data processing facility.

- **Similar or identical operating system:** The same basic operating system is available for all family members. In some cases, additional features are added to the higher-end members.
- **Increasing speed:** The rate of instruction execution increases in going from lower to higher family members.
- **Increasing number of I/O ports:** In going from lower to higher family members.
- **Increasing memory size:** In going from lower to higher family members.
- **Increasing cost:** In going from lower to higher family members.

How could such a family concept be implemented? Differences were achieved based on three factors: basic speed, size, and degree of simultaneity [STEV64]. For example, greater speed in the execution of a given instruction could be gained by the use of more complex circuitry in the ALU, allowing suboperations to be carried out in parallel. Another way of increasing speed was to increase the width of the data path between main memory and the CPU. On the Model 30, only 1 byte (8 bits) could be fetched from main memory at a time, whereas 8 bytes could be fetched at a time on the Model 70.

The System/360 not only dictated the future course of IBM but also had a profound impact on the entire industry. Many of its features have become standard on other large computers.

DEC PDP-8

In the same year that IBM shipped its first System/360, another momentous first shipment occurred: PDP-8 from Digital Equipment Corporation (DEC). At a time when the average computer required an air-conditioned room, the PDP-8 (dubbed a minicomputer by the industry, after the miniskirt of the day) was small enough that it could be placed on top of a lab bench or be built into other equipment. It could not do everything the mainframe could, but at $16,000, it was cheap enough for each lab technician to have one. In contrast, the System/360 series of mainframe computers introduced just a few months before cost hundreds of thousands of dollars.

The low cost and small size of the PDP-8 enabled another manufacturer to purchase a PDP-8 and integrate it into a total system for resale. These other manufacturers came to be known as original equipment manufacturers (OEMs), and the OEM market became and remains a major segment of the computer marketplace.

The PDP-8 was an immediate hit and made DEC's fortune. This machine and other members of the PDP-8 family that followed it (see Table 2.5) achieved a production status formerly reserved for IBM computers, with about 50,000 machines sold over the next dozen years. As DEC's official history puts it, the PDP-8 "established the concept of minicomputers, leading the way to a multibillion dollar industry." It also established DEC as the number one minicomputer vendor, and, by the time the PDP-8 had reached the end of its useful life, DEC was the number two computer manufacturer, behind IBM.

Table 2.5   Evolution of the PDP-8 [VOEL88]

Model	First Shipped	Cost of Processor + 4K 12-bit Words of Memory ($1000s)	Data Rate from Memory (words/μs)	Volume (cubic feet)	Innovations and Improvements
PDP-8	4/65	16.2	1.26	8.0	Automatic wire-wrapping production
PDP-8/5	9/66	8.79	0.08	3.2	Serial instruction implementation
PDP-8/1	4/68	11.6	1.34	8.0	Medium-scale integrated circuits
PDP-8/L	11/68	7.0	1.26	2.0	Smaller cabinet
PDP-8/E	3/71	4.99	1.52	2.2	Omnibus
PDP-8/M	6/72	3.69	1.52	1.8	Half-size cabinet with fewer slots than 8/E
PDP-8/A	1/75	2.6	1.34	1.2	Semiconductor memory; floating-point processor

In contrast to the central-switched architecture (Figure 2.5) used by IBM on its 700/7000 and 360 systems, later models of the PDP-8 used a structure that is now virtually universal for minicomputers and microcomputers: the bus structure. This is illustrated in Figure 2.9. The PDP-8 bus, called the Omnibus, consists of 96 separate signal paths, used to carry control, address, and data signals. Because all system components share a common set of signal paths, their use must be controlled by the CPU. This architecture is highly flexible, allowing modules to be plugged into the bus to create various configurations.

Later Generations

Beyond the third generation there is less general agreement on defining generations of computers. Table 2.2 suggests that there have been a fourth and a fifth generation, based on advances in integrated circuit technology. With the introduction of large-scale integration (LSI), more than 1000 components can be placed on a single integrated circuit chip. Very-large-scale integration (VLSI) achieved more than 10,000 components per chip, and current VLSI chips can contain more than 100,000 components.

Figure 2.9   PDP-8 Bus Structure

With the rapid pace of technology, the high rate of introduction of new products, and the importance of software and communications as well as hardware, the classification by generation becomes less clear and less meaningful. It could be said that the commercial application of new developments resulted in a major change in the early 1970s and that the results of these changes are still being worked out. In this section, we mention two of the most important of these results.

Semiconductor Memory

The first application of integrated circuit technology to computers was construction of the processor (the control unit and the arithmetic and logic unit) out of integrated circuit chips. But it was also found that this same technology could be used to construct memories.

In the 1950s and 1960s, most computer memory was constructed from tiny rings of ferromagnetic material, each about a sixteenth of an inch in diameter. These rings were strung up on grids of fine wires suspended on small screens inside the computer. Magnetized one way, a ring (called a *core*) represented a one; magnetized the other way, it stood for a zero. Magnetic-core memory was rather fast; it took as little as a millionth of a second to read a bit stored in memory. But it was expensive, bulky, and used destructive readout: The simple act of reading a core erased the data stored in it. It was therefore necessary to install circuits to restore the data as soon as it had been extracted.

Then, in 1970, Fairchild produced the first relatively capacious semiconductor memory. This chip, about the size of a single core, could hold 256 bits of memory. It was nondestructive and much faster than core. It took only 70 billionths of a second to read a bit. However, the cost per bit was higher than for that of core.

In 1974, a seminal event occurred: The price per bit of semiconductor memory dropped below the price per bit of core memory. Following this, there has been a continuing and rapid decline in memory cost accompanied by a corresponding increase in physical memory density. This has led the way to smaller, faster machines with memory sizes of larger and more expensive machines with a time lag of just a few years. Developments in memory technology, together with developments in processor technology to be discussed next, changed the nature of computers in less than a decade. Although bulky, expensive computers remain a part of the landscape, the computer has also been brought out to the "end user," with office machines and personal computers.

Since 1970, semiconductor memory has been through 11 generations: 1K, 4K, 16K, 64K, 256K, 1M, 4M, 16M, 64M, 256M, and, as of this writing, 1G bits on a single chip ($1K = 2^{10}$, $1M = 2^{20}$, $1G = 2^{30}$). Each generation has provided four times the storage density of the previous generation, accompanied by declining cost per bit and declining access time.

Microprocessors

Just as the density of elements on memory chips has continued to rise, so has the density of elements on processor chips. As time went on, more and more elements were placed on each chip, so that fewer and fewer chips were needed to construct a single computer processor.

A breakthrough was achieved in 1971, when Intel developed its 4004. The 4004 was the first chip to contain *all* of the components of a CPU on a single chip: The microprocessor was born.

The 4004 can add two 4-bit numbers and can multiply only by repeated addition. By today's standards, the 4004 is hopelessly primitive, but it marked the beginning of a continuing evolution of microprocessor capability and power.

This evolution can be seen most easily in the number of bits that the processor deals with at a time. There is no clear-cut measure of this, but perhaps the best measure is the data bus width: the number of bits of data that can be brought into or sent out of the processor at a time. Another measure is the number of bits in the accumulator or in the set of general-purpose registers. Often, these measures coincide, but not always. For example, a number of microprocessors were developed that operate on 16-bit numbers in registers but can only read and write 8 bits at a time.

The next major step in the evolution of the microprocessor was the introduction in 1972 of the Intel 8008. This was the first 8-bit microprocessor and was almost twice as complex as the 4004.

Neither of these steps was to have the impact of the next major event: the introduction in 1974 of the Intel 8080. This was the first general-purpose microprocessor. Whereas the 4004 and the 8008 had been designed for specific applications, the 8080 was designed to be the CPU of a general-purpose microcomputer. Like the 8008, the 8080 is an 8-bit microprocessor. The 8080, however, is faster, has a richer instruction set, and has a large addressing capability.

About the same time, 16-bit microprocessors began to be developed. However, it was not until the end of the 1970s that powerful, general-purpose 16-bit microprocessors appeared. One of these was the 8086. The next step in this trend occurred in 1981, when both Bell Labs and Hewlett-Packard developed 32-bit, single-chip microprocessors. Intel introduced its own 32-bit microprocessor, the 80386, in 1985 (Table 2.6).

Table 2.6   Evolution of Intel Microprocessors

(a) 1970s Processors

	4004	**8008**	**8080**	**8086**	**8088**
Introduced	11/15/71	4/1/72	4/1/74	6/8/78	6/1/79
Clock speeds	108 KHz	108 KHz	2 MHz	5 MHz, 8 MHz, 10 MHz	5 MHz, 8 MHz
Bus width	4 bits	8 bits	8 bits	16 bits	8 bits
Number of transistors (microns)	2300 (10)	3500	6000 (6)	29,000 (3)	29,000 (3)
Addressable memory	640 bytes	16 KBytes	64 KBytes	1 MB	1 MB
Virtual memory	—	—	—	—	—

Table 2.6 *(continued)*

(b) 1980s Processors

	80286	386TM DX	386TM SX	486TM DX CPU
Introduced	2/1/82	10/17/85	6/16/88	4/10/89
Clock speeds	6 MHz– 12.5 MHz	16 MHz–33 MHz	16 MHz–33 MHz	25 MHz–50 MHz
Bus width	16 bits	32 bits	16 bits	32 bits
Number of transistors (microns)	134,000 (1.5)	275,000 (1)	275,000 (1)	1.2 million (0.8–1)
Addressable memory	16 metabytes	4 gigabytes	4 gigabytes	4 gigabytes
Virtual memory	1 gigabyte	64 terabytes	64 terabytes	64 terabytes

(c) 1990s Processors

	486TM SX	Pentium	Pentium	Pentium II
Introduced	4/22/91	3/22/93	11/01/95	5/07/97
Clock speeds	16 MHz– 133 MHz	60 MHz– 166 MHz	150 MHz– 200 MHz	200 MHz– 300 MHz
Bus width	32 bits	32 bits	64 bits	64 bits
Number of transistors (microns)	1.185 million (1)	3.1 million (.8)	5.5 million (0.6)	7.5 million (0.35)
Addressable memory	4 gigabytes	4 gigabytes	64 gigabytes	64 gigabytes
Virtual memory	64 terabyte	64 terabytes	64 terabytes	64 terabytes

(d) Recent Processors

	Pentium III	Pentium 4
Introduced	2/26/99	11/2000
Clock speeds	450–660 MHz	1.3–1.8 GHz
Bus width	64 bits	64 bits
Number of transistors (microns)	95 million (0.25)	42 million
Addressable memory	64 gigabytes	64 gigabytes
Virtual memory	64 terabytes	64 terabytes

Source: Intel Corp. http://www.intel.com/intel/museum/25anniv/hof/tspecs.htm

2.2   DESIGNING FOR PERFORMANCE

Year by year, the cost of computer systems continues to drop dramatically, while the performance and capacity of those systems continue to rise equally dramatically. At a local warehouse club, you can pick up a personal computer for less than $1000 that packs the wallop of an IBM mainframe from 10 years ago. Inside that personal computer, including the microprocessor and memory and other chips, you get 100s of millions of transistors. You cannot buy 100 million of anything else for so little. That many sheets of toilet paper would run more than $100,000.

Thus, we have virtually "free" computer power. And this continuing technological revolution has enabled the development of applications of astounding complexity and power. For example, desktop applications that require the great power of today's microprocessor-based systems include

- Image processing
- Speech recognition
- Videoconferencing
- Multimedia authoring
- Voice and video annotation of files
- Simulation modeling

Workstation systems now support highly sophisticated engineering and scientific applications, as well as simulation systems, and have the ability to support image and video applications. In addition, businesses are relying on increasingly powerful servers to handle transaction and database processing and to support massive client/server networks that have replaced the huge mainframe computer centers of yesteryear.

What is fascinating about all this from the perspective of computer organization and architecture is that, on the one hand, the basic building blocks for today's computer miracles are virtually the same as those of the IAS computer from over 50 years ago, while on the other hand, the techniques for squeezing the last iota of performance out of the materials at hand have become increasingly sophisticated.

This observation serves as a guiding principle for the presentation in this book. As we progress through the various elements and components of a computer, two objectives are pursued. First, the book explains the fundamental functionality in each area under consideration, and second, the book explores those techniques required to achieve maximum performance. In the remainder of this section, we highlight some of the driving factors behind the need to design for performance.

Microprocessor Speed

What gives the Pentium or the PowerPC such mind-boggling power is the relentless pursuit of speed by processor chip manufacturers. The evolution of these machines continues to bear out Moore's law, mentioned previously. So long as this law holds, chipmakers can unleash a new generation of chips every three years—with four times as many transistors. In memory chips, this has quadrupled the capacity of dynamic random-access memory (DRAM), still the basic technology for computer main memory, every three years. In microprocessors, the addition of new circuits, and the speed boost that comes from reducing the distances between them, has improved performance four- or fivefold every three years or so since Intel launched its x86 family in 1978.

But the raw speed of the microprocessor will not achieve its potential unless it is fed a constant stream of work to do in the form of computer instructions. Anything that gets in the way of that smooth flow undermines the power of the processor. Accordingly, while the chipmakers have been busy learning how to fabricate chips of greater and greater density, the processor designers must come up with ever more elaborate techniques for feeding the monster. Among the techniques built into contemporary processors are the following:

- **Branch prediction:** The processor looks ahead in the instruction code fetched from memory and predicts which branches, or groups of instructions, are likely to be processed next. If the processor guesses right most of the time, it can prefetch the correct instructions and buffer them so that the processor is kept busy. The more sophisticated examples of this strategy predict not just the next branch but multiple branches ahead. Thus, branch prediction increases the amount of work available for the processor to execute.

- **Data flow analysis:** The processor analyzes which instructions are dependent on each other's results, or data, to create an optimized schedule of instructions. In fact, instructions are scheduled to be executed when ready, independent of the original program order. This prevents unnecessary delay.

- **Speculative execution:** Using branch prediction and data flow analysis, some processors speculatively execute instructions ahead of their actual appearance in the program execution, holding the results in temporary locations. This enables the processor to keep its execution engines as busy as possible by executing instructions that are likely to be needed.

These and other sophisticated techniques are made necessary by the sheer power of the processor. They make it possible to exploit the raw speed of the processor.

Performance Balance

While processor power has raced ahead at breakneck speed, other critical components of the computer have not kept up. The result is a need to look for performance balance: an adjusting of the organization and architecture to compensate for the mismatch among the capabilities of the various components.

Nowhere is the problem created by such mismatches more critical than in the interface between processor and main memory. Consider the history depicted in Figure 2.10. While processor speed and memory capacity have grown rapidly, the speed with which data can be transferred between main memory and the processor has lagged badly. The interface between processor and main memory is the most crucial pathway in the entire computer, because it is responsible for carrying a constant flow of program instructions and data between memory chips and the processor. If memory or the pathway fails to keep pace with the processor's insistent demands, the processor stalls in a wait state, and valuable processing time is lost.

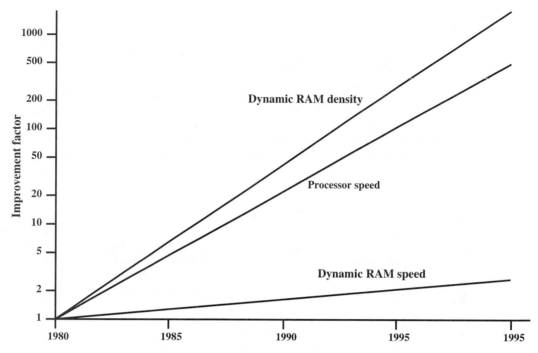

Figure 2.10   Evolution of DRAM and Processor Characteristics

The effects of these trends are shown vividly in Figure 2.11. The amount of main memory needed is going up, but DRAM density is going up faster. The net result is that, on average, the number of DRAMs per system is going down. The solid black lines in the figure show that, for a fixed-size memory, the number of DRAMs needed is declining. But this has an effect on transfer rates, because with fewer DRAMs, there is less opportunity for parallel transfer of data. The shaded bands show that for a particular type of system, main memory size has slowly increased while the number of DRAMs has declined.

There are a number of ways that a system architect can attack this problem, all of which are reflected in contemporary computer designs. Examples include the following:

- Increase the number of bits that are retrieved at one time by making DRAMs "wider" rather than "deeper" and by using wide bus data paths.
- Change the DRAM interface to make it more efficient by including a cache or other buffering scheme on the DRAM chip.
- Reduce the frequency of memory access by incorporating increasingly complex and efficient cache structures between the processor and main memory. This includes the incorporation of one or more caches on the processor chip as well as on an off-chip cache close to the processor chip.
- Increase the interconnect bandwidth between processors and memory by using higher-speed buses and by using a hierarchy of buses to buffer and structure data flow.

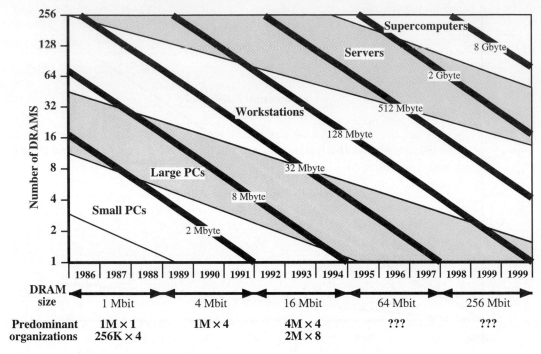

Figure 2.11 Trends in Dram Use [PRZY94]

Another area of design focus is the handling of I/O devices. As computers become faster and more capable, more sophisticated applications are developed that support the use of peripherals with intensive I/O demands. Table 2.7 gives some examples of typical peripheral devices in use on personal computers and workstations. These devices create tremendous data throughput demands. While the current generation of processors can handle the data pumped out by these devices, there remains the problem of getting that data moved between processor and peripheral. Strategies here include caching and buffering schemes plus the use of higher-speed interconnection buses and more elaborate structures of buses. In addition, the use of multiple-processor configurations can aid in satisfying I/O demands.

Table 2.7 Typical Bandwidth Requirements for Various Peripheral Technologies

Peripheral	Technology	Required Bandwidth (Mbytes/s)
Graphics	24-bit color	30
Local area network	100 BASEX or FDDI	12
Disk controller	SCSI or P1394	10
Full-motion video	1024 × 768@30 fps	67+
I/O peripherals	Other miscellaneous	5+

The key in all this is balance. Designers constantly strive to balance the throughput and processing demands of the processor components, main memory, I/O devices, and the interconnection structures. This design must constantly be rethought to cope with two constantly evolving factors:

- The rate at which performance is changing in the various technology areas (processor, buses, memory, peripherals) differs greatly from one type of element to another.
- New applications and new peripheral devices constantly change the nature of the demand on the system in terms of typical instruction profile and the data access patterns.

Thus, computer design is a constantly evolving art form. This book attempts to present the fundamentals on which this art form is based and to present a survey of the current state of that art.

2.3 PENTIUM AND POWERPC EVOLUTION

Throughout this book, we rely on many concrete examples of computer design and implementation to illustrate concepts and to illuminate trade-offs. Most of the time, the book relies on examples from two computer families: the Intel Pentium and the PowerPC. The Pentium represents the results of decades of design effort on complex instruction set computers (CISCs). It incorporates the sophisticated design principles once found only on mainframes and supercomputers and serves as an excellent example of CISC design. The PowerPC is a direct descendant of the first RISC system, the IBM 801, and is one of the most powerful and best-designed RISC-based systems on the market.

In this section, we provide a brief overview of both systems.

Pentium

In terms of market share, Intel has ranked as the number one maker of microprocessors for decades, a position it seems unlikely to yield. The evolution of its flagship microprocessor product serves as a good indicator of the evolution of computer technology in general.

Table 2.6 shows that evolution. Interestingly, as microprocessors have grown faster and much more complex, Intel has actually picked up the pace. Intel used to develop microprocessors one after another, every four years. But Intel hopes to keep rivals at bay by trimming a year or two off this development time, and has done so with the most recent Pentium generations.

It is worthwhile to list some of the highlights of the evolution of the Intel product line:

- **8080:** The world's first general-purpose microprocessor. This was an 8-bit machine, with an 8-bit data path to memory. The 8080 was used in the first personal computer, the Altair.

- **8086:** A far more powerful, 16-bit machine. In addition to a wider data path and larger registers, the 8086 sported an instruction cache, or queue, that prefetches a few instructions before they are executed. A variant of this processor, the 8088, was used in IBM's first personal computer, securing the success of Intel.

- **80286:** This extension of the 8086 enabled addressing a 16-MByte memory instead of just 1 MByte.

- **80386:** Intel's first 32-bit machine, and a major overhaul of the product. With a 32-bit architecture, the 80386 rivaled the complexity and power of mini-computers and mainframes introduced just a few years earlier. This was the first Intel processor to support multitasking, meaning it could run multiple programs at the same time.

- **80486:** The 80486 introduced the use of much more sophisticated and power-ful cache technology and sophisticated instruction pipelining. The 80486 also offered a built-in math coprocessor, offloading complex math operations from the main CPU.

- **Pentium:** With the Pentium, Intel introduced the use of superscalar tech-niques, which allow multiple instructions to execute in parallel.

- **Pentium Pro:** The Pentium Pro continued the move into superscalar organi-zation begun with the Pentium, with aggressive use of register renaming, branch prediction, data flow analysis, and speculative execution.

- **Pentium II:** The Pentium II incorporated Intel MMX technology, which is designed specifically to process video, audio, and graphics data efficiently.

- **Pentium III:** The Pentium III incorporates additional floating-point instruc-tions to support 3D graphics software.

- **Pentium 4:** The Pentium 4 includes additional floating-point and other en-hancements for multimedia.[2]

- **Itanium:** This new generation of Intel processor makes use of a 64-bit organi-zation with the IA-64 architecture, which is discussed in detail in Chapter 15.

PowerPC

In 1975, the 801 minicomputer project at IBM pioneered many of the architecture concepts used in RISC systems. The 801, together with the Berkeley RISC I pro-cessor, launched the RISC movement. The 801, however, was simply a prototype intended to demonstrate design concepts. The success of the 801 project led IBM to develop a commercial RISC workstation product, the RT PC. The RT PC, intro-duced in 1986, adapted the architectural concepts of the 801 to an actual product. The RT PC was not a commercial success, and it had many rivals with comparable or better performance. In 1990, IBM produced a third system, which built on the lessons of the 801 and the RT PC. The IBM RISC System/6000 was a RISC-like superscalar machine marketed as a high-performance workstation; shortly after its introduction, IBM began to refer to this as the POWER architecture.

---

[2]With the Pentium 4, Intel switched from Roman numerals to Arabic numerals for model numbers.

For its next step, IBM entered into an alliance with Motorola, developer of the 68000 series of microprocessors, and Apple, which used the Motorola chip in its Macintosh computers. The result is a series of machines that implement the PowerPC architecture. This architecture is derived from the POWER architecture. Changes were made to add key missing features and to enable more efficient implementation by eliminating some instructions and relaxing the specification to eliminate some troublesome special cases. The resulting PowerPC architecture is a superscalar RISC system. The PowerPC is used in millions of Apple Macintosh machines and in numerous embedded chip applications. An example of the latter is IBM's family of network management chips, which can be embedded in network equipment to provide common management access for users with multivendor platforms.

The following are the principal members of the PowerPC family (Table 2.8):

- **601:** The purpose of the 601 was to bring the PowerPC architecture to the marketplace as quickly as possible. The 601 is a 32-bit machine.
- **603:** Intended for low-end desktop and portable computers. It is also a 32-bit machine, comparable in performance with the 601, but with lower cost and a more efficient implementation.
- **604:** Intended for desktop computers and low-end servers. Again, this is a 32-bit machine, but it uses much more advanced superscalar design techniques to achieve greater performance.
- **620:** Intended for high-end servers. The first member of the PowerPC family to implement a full 64-bit architecture, including 64-bit registers and data paths.
- **740/750:** Also known as the G3 processor. This processor integrates two levels of cache in the main processor chip, providing significant performance improvement over a comparable machine with off-chip cache organization.
- **G4:** This processor increases the parallelism and internal speed of the processor chip.

Table 2.8 PowerPC Processor Summary

	601	**603/603e**	**604/604e**	**740/750 (G3)**	**G4**
First ship date	1993	1994	1994	1997	1999
Clock speeds (MHz)	50–120	100–300	166–350	200–366	500
L1 cache	—	16 Kbyte inst 16 Kbyte data	32 Kbyte inst 32 Kbyte data	32 Kbyte instr 32 Kbyte data	32 Kbyte instr 32 Kbyte data
Backside L2 cache support	—	—	—	256 Kbyte –1 Mbyte	256 Kbyte –1 Mbyte
Number of transistors (10^6)	2.8	1.6–2.6	3.6–5.1	6.35	—

2.4 RECOMMENDED READING AND WEB SITES

A description of the IBM 7000 series can bc found in [BELL71a]. There is good coverage of the IBM 360 in [SIEW82] and of the PDP-8 and other DEC machines in [BELL78a]. These three books also contain numerous detailed examples of other computers spanning the history of computers through the early 1980s. A more recent book that includes an excellent set of case studies of historical machines is [BLAA97]. A good history of the microprocessor is [BETK97].

One of the best treatments of the Pentium is [SHAN98]. The Intel documentation itself is also good [INTE01]. [BREY00] provides a good survey of the Intel microprocessor line, with emphasis on the 32-bit machines.

[IBM94] is a thorough treatment of the PowerPC architecture. [SHAN95] provides similar coverage. [WEIS94] treats both the POWER and PowerPC architectures.

For interesting discussions of Moore's law and its consequences, see [HUTC96], [SCHA97], and [BOHR98].

BELL71a   Bell, C., and Newell, A. *Computer Structures: Readings and Examples.* New York: McGraw-Hill, 1971.

BELL78a   Bell, C.; Mudge, J.; and McNamara, J. *Computer Engineering: A DEC View of Hardware Systems Design.* Bedford, MA: Digital Press, 1978.

BETK97   Betker, M.; Fernando, J.; and Whalen, S. "The History of the Microprocessor." *Bell Labs Technical Journal*, Autumn 1997.

BLAA97   Blaauw, G., and Brooks, F. *Computer Architecture: Concepts and Evolution.* Reading, MA: Addison-Wesley, 1997.

BOHR98   Bohr, M. "Silicon Trends and Limits for Advanced Microprocessors." *Communications of the ACM*, March 1998.

BREY00   Brey, B. *The Intel Microprocessors: 8086/8066, 80186/80188, 80286, 80386, 80486, Pentium, Pentium Pro and Pentium II Processors.* Upper Saddle River, NJ: Prentice Hall, 2000.

HUTC96   Hutcheson, G., and Hutcheson, J. "Technology and Economics in the Semiconductor Industry." *Scientific American*, January 1996.

IBM94   International Business Machines, Inc. *The PowerPC Architecture: A Specification for a New Family of RISC Processors.* San Francisco, CA: Morgan Kaufmann, 1994.

INTE01   Intel Corp. *IA-32 Intel Architecture Software Developer's Manual* (2 volumes). Document 245470 and 245471. Aurora, CO, 2000.

SCHA97   Schaller, R. "Moore's Law: Past, Present, and Future." *IEEE Spectrum*, June 1997.

SHAN95   Shanley, T. *PowerPC System Architecture.* Reading, MA: Addison-Wesley, 1995.

SHAN98   Shanley, T. *Pentium Pro and Pentium II System Architecture.* Reading, MA: Addison-Wesley, 1998.

SIEW82   Siewiorek, D.; Bell, C.; and Newell, A. *Computer Structures: Principles and Examples.* New York: McGraw-Hill, 1982.

WEIS94   Weiss, S., and Smith, J. *POWER and PowerPC.* San Francisco: Morgan Kaufmann, 1994.

Recommended Web Sites:

- **Intel Developer's Page:** Intel's Web page for developers; provides a starting point for accessing Pentium information. Also includes the Intel Technology Journal.
- **PowerPC:** Two Web sites, one by Motorola and one by IBM, for the PowerPC.
- **Top500 Supercomputer Site:** Provides brief description of architecture and organization of current supercomputer products, plus comparisons.
- **Charles Babbage Institute:** Provides links to a number of Web sites dealing with the history of computers.

2.5 KEY TERMS, REVIEW QUESTIONS, AND PROBLEMS

Key Terms

accumulator (AC)	instruction register (IR)	Opcode
arithmetic and logic unit (ALU)	instruction set	original equipment manufacturer (OEM)
chip	integrated circuit (IC)	program control unit
data channel	main memory	program counter (PC)
execute cycle	memory address register (MAR)	stored program computer
fetch cycle	memory buffer register (MBR)	upward compatible
Input/output (I/O)	microprocessor	von Neumann machine
instruction buffer register (IBR)	multiplexor	wafer
instruction cycle		word

Review Questions

2.1 What is a stored program computer?

2.2 What are the four main components of any general-purpose computer?

2.3 At the integrated circuit level, what are the three principal constituents of a computer system?

2.4 Explain Moore's law.

2.5 List and explain the key characteristics of a computer family.

2.6 What is the key distinguishing feature of a microprocessor?

Problems

2.1 Let $\mathbf{A}$ = A(1), A(2), . . , A(1,000) and $\mathbf{B}$ = B(1), B(2) . . . B(1000) be two vectors (one-dimensional arrays) comprising 1000 numbers each that are to be added to form an array C such that C(I) = A(I) + B(I) for I = 1, 2, . . . , 1000. Using the IAS instruction set, write a program for this problem.

2.2 In the IBM 360 Models 65 and 75, addresses are staggered in two separate main memory units (e.g., all even-numbered words in one unit and all odd-numbered words in another). What might be the purpose of this technique?

PART TWO

The Computer System

ISSUES FOR PART TWO

A computer system consists of a processor, memory, I/O, and the interconnections among these major components. With the exception of the processor, which is sufficiently complex to devote Part Three to its study, Part Two examines each of these components in detail.

ROAD MAP FOR PART TWO

Chapter 3 A Top-Level View of Computer Function and Interconnection

At a top level, a computer consists of a processor, memory, and I/O components. The functional behavior of the system consists of the exchange of data and control signals among these components. To support this exchange, these components must be interconnected. Chapter 3 begins with a brief examination of the computer's components and their input–output requirements. The chapter then looks at key issues that affect interconnection design, especially the need to support interrupts. The bulk of the chapter is devoted to a study of the most common approach to interconnection: the use of a structure of buses.

Chapter 4 Cache Memory

Computer memory exhibits a wide range of type, technology, organization, performance, and cost. The typical computer system is equipped with a hierarchy of memory subsystems, some internal (directly accessible by the processor) and some external (accessible by the processor via an I/O module). Chapter 4 begins with an overview of this hierarchy. Next, the chapter deals in detail with the design of cache memory, including separate code and data caches and two-level caches.

Chapter 5 Internal Memory

The design of a main memory system is a never-ending battle among three competing design requirements: large storage capacity, rapid access time, and low cost. As memory technology evolves, each of these three characteristics is changing, so that the design decisions in organizing main memory must be revisited anew with each new implementation. Chapter 5 focuses on design issues related to internal memory. First, the nature and organization of semiconductor main memory is examined. Then, recent advanced DRAM memory organizations are explored.

Chapter 6 External Memory

For truly large storage capacity and for more permanent storage than is available with main memory, an external memory organization is needed. The most widely used type of external memory is magnetic disk, and much of Chapter 6 concentrates on this topic. First, we look at magnetic disk technology and design considerations. Then, we look at the use of RAID organization to improve disk memory performance. Chapter 6 also examines optical and tape storage.

Chapter 7 Input/Output

I/O modules are interconnected with the processor and main memory, and each controls one or more external devices. Chapter 7 is devoted to the various aspects of I/O organization. This is a complex area, and less well understood than other areas of computer system design in terms of meeting performance demands. Chapter 7 examines the mechanisms by which an I/O module interacts with the rest of the computer system, using the techniques of programmed I/O, interrupt I/O, and direct memory access (DMA). The interface between an I/O module and external devices is also described.

Chapter 8 Operating System Support

A detailed examination of operating systems (OSs) is beyond the scope of this book. However, it is important to understand the basic functions of an operating system and how the OS exploits hardware to provide the desired performance. Chapter 8 describes the basic principles of operating systems and discusses the specific design features in the computer hardware intended to provide support for the operating system. The chapter begins with a brief history, which serves to identify the major types of operating systems and to motivate their use. Next, multiprogramming is explained by examining the long-term and short-term scheduling functions. Finally, an examination of memory management includes a discussion of segmentation, paging, and virtual memory.

CHAPTER 3

A TOP-LEVEL VIEW OF COMPUTER FUNCTION AND INTERCONNECTION

KEY POINTS

◆ An instruction cycle consists of an instruction fetch, followed by zero or more operand fetches, followed by zero or more operand stores, followed by an interrupt check (if interrupts are enabled).

◆ The major computer system components (processor, main memory, I/O modules) need to be interconnected in order to exchange data and control signals. The most popular means of interconnection is the use of a shared system bus consisting of multiple lines. In contemporary systems, there typically is a hierarchy of buses to improve performance.

◆ Key design elements for buses include arbitration (whether permission to send signals on bus lines is controlled centrally or in a distributed fashion); timing (whether signals on the bus are synchronized to a central clock or are sent asynchronously based on the most recent transmission); and width (number of address lines and number of data lines).

A t a top level, a computer consists of CPU (central processing unit), memory, and I/O components, with one or more modules of each type. These components are interconnected in some fashion to achieve the basic function of the computer, which is to execute programs. Thus, at a top level, we can describe a computer system by (1) describing the external behavior of each component, that is, the data and control signals that it exchanges with other components; and (2) describing the interconnection structure and the controls required to manage the use of the interconnection structure.

This top-level view of structure and function is important because of its explanatory power in understanding the nature of a computer. Equally important is its use to understand the increasingly complex issues of performance evaluation. A grasp of the top-level structure and function offers insight into system bottlenecks, alternate pathways, the magnitude of system failures if a component fails, and the ease of adding performance enhancements. In many cases, requirements for greater system power and fail-safe capabilities are being met by changing the design rather than merely increasing the speed and reliability of individual components.

This chapter focuses on the basic structures used for computer component interconnection. As background, the chapter begins with a brief examination of the basic components and their interface requirements. Then a functional overview is provided. We are then prepared to examine the use of buses to interconnect system components.

3.1 COMPUTER COMPONENTS

As discussed in Chapter 2, virtually all contemporary computer designs are based on concepts developed by John von Neumann at the Institute for Advanced Studies,

Princeton. Such a design is referred to as the *von Neumann architecture* and is based on three key concepts:

- Data and instructions are stored in a single read–write memory.
- The contents of this memory are addressable by location, without regard to the type of data contained there.
- Execution occurs in a sequential fashion (unless explicitly modified) from one instruction to the next.

The reasoning behind these concepts was discussed in Chapter 2 but is worth summarizing here. There is a small set of basic logic components that can be combined in various ways to store binary data and to perform arithmetic and logical operations on that data. If there is a particular computation to be performed, a configuration of logic components designed specifically for that computation could be constructed. We can think of the process of connecting the various components in the desired configuration as a form of programming. The resulting "program" is in the form of hardware and is termed a *hardwired program.*

Now consider this alternative. Suppose we construct a general-purpose configuration of arithmetic and logic functions. This set of hardware will perform various functions on data depending on control signals applied to the hardware. In the original case of customized hardware, the system accepts data and produces results (Figure 3.1a). With general-purpose hardware, the system accepts data and control signals and produces results. Thus, instead of rewiring the hardware for each new program, the programmer merely needs to supply a new set of control signals.

How shall control signals be supplied? The answer is simple but subtle. The entire program is actually a sequence of steps. At each step, some arithmetic or logical operation is performed on some data. For each step, a new set of control signals is needed. Let us provide a unique code for each possible set of control signals, and let us add to the general-purpose hardware a segment that can accept a code and generate control signals (Figure 3.1b).

Programming is now much easier. Instead of rewiring the hardware for each new program, all we need to do is provide a new sequence of codes. Each code is, in effect, an instruction, and part of the hardware interprets each instruction and generates control signals. To distinguish this new method of programming, a sequence of codes or instructions is called *software.*

Figure 3.1b indicates two major components of the system: an instruction interpreter and a module of general-purpose arithmetic and logic functions. These two constitute the CPU. Several other components are needed to yield a functioning computer. Data and instructions must be put into the system. For this we need some sort of input module. This module contains basic components for accepting data and instructions in some form and converting them into an internal form of signals usable by the system. A means of reporting results is needed, and this is in the form of an output module. Taken together, these are referred to as *I/O components.*

One more component is needed. An input device will bring instructions and data in sequentially. But a program is not invariably executed sequentially; it may jump around (e.g., the IAS jump instruction). Similarly, operations on data may require access to more than just one element at a time in a predetermined sequence.

(a) Programming in hardware

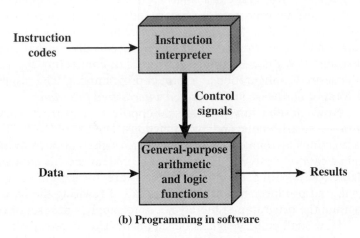

(b) Programming in software

Figure 3.1 Hardware and Software Approaches

Thus, there must be a place to store temporarily both instructions and data. That module is called *memory,* or *main memory* to distinguish it from external storage or peripheral devices. Von Neumann pointed out that the same memory could be used to store both instructions and data.

Figure 3.2 illustrates these top-level components and suggests the interactions among them. The CPU exchanges data with memory. For this purpose, it typically makes use of two internal (to the CPU) registers: a memory address register (MAR), which specifies the address in memory for the next read or write, and a memory buffer register (MBR), which contains the data to be written into memory or receives the data read from memory. Similarly, an I/O address register (I/OAR) specifies a particular I/O device. An I/O buffer register (I/OBR) is used for the exchange of data between an I/O module and the CPU.

A memory module consists of a set of locations, defined by sequentially numbered addresses. Each location contains a binary number that can be interpreted as either an instruction or data. An I/O module transfers data from external devices to CPU and memory, and vice versa. It contains internal buffers for temporarily holding these data until they can be sent on.

Having looked briefly at these major components, we now turn to an overview of how these components function together to execute programs.

Figure 3.2 Computer Components: Top-Level View

3.2 COMPUTER FUNCTION

The basic function performed by a computer is execution of a program, which consists of a set of instructions stored in memory. The processor does the actual work by executing instructions specified in the program. This section provides an overview of the key elements of program execution. In its simplest form, instruction processing consists of two steps: The processor reads (*fetches*) instructions from memory one at a time and executes each instruction. Program execution consists of repeating the process of instruction fetch and instruction execution. The instruction execution may involve several operations and depends on the nature of the instruction (see, for example, the lower portion of Figure 2.4).

The processing required for a single instruction is called an *instruction cycle.* Using the simplified two-step description given previously, the instruction cycle is depicted in Figure 3.3. The two steps are referred to as the *fetch cycle* and the *execute cycle.* Program execution halts only if the machine is turned off, some sort of unrecoverable error occurs, or a program instruction that halts the computer is encountered.

Instruction Fetch and Execute

At the beginning of each instruction cycle, the processor fetches an instruction from memory. In a typical processor, a register called the program counter (PC) holds the address of the instruction to be fetched next. Unless told otherwise, the processor always increments the PC after each instruction fetch so that it will fetch the next instruction in sequence (i.e., the instruction located at the next higher memory address). So, for example, consider a computer in which each instruction occupies one 16-bit word of memory. Assume that the program counter is set to location 300. The processor will next fetch the instruction at location 300. On succeeding instruction cycles, it will fetch instructions from locations 301, 302, 303, and so on. This sequence may be altered, as explained presently.

The fetched instruction is loaded into a register in the processor known as the instruction register (IR). The instruction contains bits that specify the action the processor is to take. The processor interprets the instruction and performs the required action. In general, these actions fall into four categories:

- **Processor-memory:** Data may be transferred from processor to memory or from memory to processor.
- **Processor-I/O:** Data may be transferred to or from a peripheral device by transferring between the processor and an I/O module.
- **Data processing:** The processor may perform some arithmetic or logic operation on data.
- **Control:** An instruction may specify that the sequence of execution be altered. For example, the processor may fetch an instruction from location 149, which specifies that the next instruction be from location 182. The processor will remember this fact by setting the program counter to 182. Thus, on the next fetch cycle, the instruction will be fetched from location 182 rather than 150.

An instruction's execution may involve a combination of these actions.

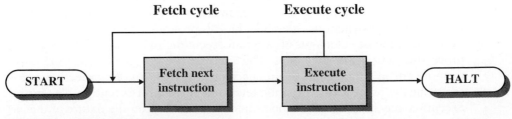

Figure 3.3 Basic Instruction Cycle

(a) Instruction format

(b) Integer format

Program counter (PC) = Address of instruction
Instruction register (IR) = Instruction being executed
Accumulator (AC) = Temporary storage

(c) Internal CPU registers

0001 = Load AC from memory
0010 = Store AC to memory
0101 = Add to AC from memory

(d) Partial list of opcodes

Figure 3.4 Characteristics of a Hypothetical Machine

Consider a simple example using a hypothetical machine that includes the characteristics listed in Figure 3.4. The processor contains a single data register, called an accumulator (AC). Both instructions and data are 16 bits long. Thus, it is convenient to organize memory using 16-bit words. The instruction format provides 4 bits for the opcode, so that there can be as many as $2^4 = 16$ different opcodes, and up to $2^{12} = 4096$ (4K) words of memory can be directly addressed.

Figure 3.5 illustrates a partial program execution, showing the relevant portions of memory and processor registers.[1] The program fragment shown adds the contents of the memory word at address 940 to the contents of the memory word at address 941 and stores the result in the latter location. Three instructions, which can be described as three fetch and three execute cycles, are required:

1. The PC contains 300, the address of the first instruction. This instruction (the value 1940 in hexadecimal) is loaded into the instruction register IR and the PC is incremented. Note that this process involves the use of a memory address register (MAR) and a memory buffer register (MBR). For simplicity, these intermediate registers are ignored.

---

[1]Hexadecimal notation is used, in which each digit represents 4 bits. This is the most convenient notation for representing the contents of memory and registers when the word length is a multiple of 4. See Appendix B for a basic refresher on number systems (decimal, binary, hexadecimal).

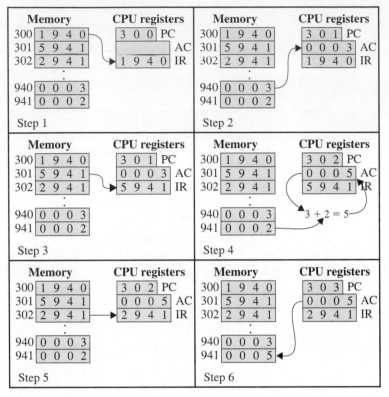

Figure 3.5 Example of Program Execution (contents of memory and registers in hexadecimal)

2. The first 4 bits (first hexadecimal digit) in the IR indicate that the AC is to be loaded. The remaining 12 bits (three hexadecimal digits) specify the address (940) from which data are to be loaded.

3. The next instruction (5941) is fetched from location 301 and the PC is incremented.

4. The old contents of the AC and the contents of location 941 are added and the result is stored in the AC.

5. The next instruction (2941) is fetched from location 302 and the PC is incremented.

6. The contents of the AC are stored in location 941.

In this example, three instruction cycles, each consisting of a fetch cycle and an execute cycle, are needed to add the contents of location 940 to the contents of 941. With a more complex set of instructions, fewer cycles would be needed. Some older processors, for example, included instructions that contain more than one memory address. Thus the execution cycle for a particular instruction on such processors could involve more than one reference to memory. Also, instead of memory references, an instruction may specify an I/O operation.

For example, the PDP-11 instruction expressed symbolically as ADD B,A stores the sum of the contents of memory locations B and A into memory location A. A single instruction cycle with the following steps occurs:

- Fetch the ADD instruction.
- Read the contents of memory location A into the processor.
- Read the contents of memory location B into the processor. In order that the contents of A are not lost, the processor must have at least two registers for storing memory values, rather than a single accumulator.
- Add the two valuue.
- Write the result from the processor to memory location A.

Thus, the execution cycle for a particular instruction may involve more than one reference to memory. Also, instead of memory references, an instruction may specify an I/O operation. With these additional considerations in mind, Figure 3.6 provides a more detailed look at the basic instruction cycle of Figure 3.3. The figure is in the form of a state diagram. For any given instruction cycle, some states may be null and others may be visited more than once. The states can be described as follows:

- **Instruction address calculation (iac):** Determine the address of the next instruction to be executed. Usually, this involves adding a fixed number to the address of the previous instruction. For example, if each instruction is 16 bits long and memory is organized into 16-bit words, then add 1 to the previous address. If, instead, memory is organized as individually addressable 8-bit bytes, then add 2 to the previous address.
- **Instruction fetch (if):** Read instruction from its memory location into the processor.
- **Instruction operation decoding (iod):** Analyze instruction to determine type of operation to be performed and operand(s) to be used.
- **Operand address calculation (oac):** If the operation involves reference to an operand in memory or available via I/O, then determine the address of the operand.

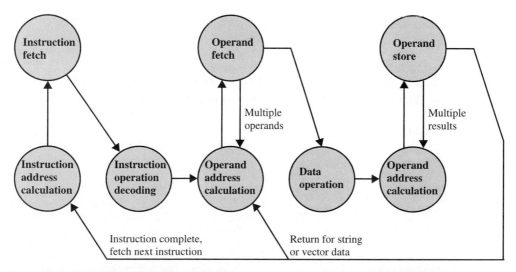

Figure 3.6   Instruction Cycle State Diagram

- **Operand fetch (of):** Fetch the operand from memory or read it in from I/O.
- **Data operation (do):** Perform the operation indicated in the instruction.
- **Operand store (os):** Write the result into memory or out to I/O.

States in the upper part of Figure 3.6 involve an exchange between the processor and either memory or an I/O module. States in the lower part of the diagram involve only internal processor operations. The oac state appears twice, because an instruction may involve a read, a write, or both. However, the action performed during that state is fundamentally the same in both cases, and so only a single state identifier is needed.

Also note that the diagram allows for multiple operands and multiple results, because some instructions on some machines require this. For example, the PDP-11 instruction ADD A,B results in the following sequence of states: iac, if, iod, oac, of, oac, of, do, oac, os.

Finally, on some machines, a single instruction can specify an operation to be performed on a vector (one-dimensional array) of numbers or a string (one-dimensional array) of characters. As Figure 3.6 indicates, this would involve repetitive operand fetch and/or store operations.

Interrupts

Virtually all computers provide a mechanism by which other modules (I/O, memory) may interrupt the normal processing of the processor. Table 3.1 lists the most common classes of interrupts. The specific nature of these interrupts is examined later in this book, especially in Chapters 7 and 12. However, we need to introduce the concept now to understand more clearly the nature of the instruction cycle and the implications of interrupts on the interconnection structure. The reader need not be concerned at this stage about the details of the generation and processing of interrupts, but only focus on the communication between modules that results from interrupts.

Interrupts are provided primarily as a way to improve processing efficiency. For example, most external devices are much slower than the processor. Suppose that the processor is transferring data to a printer using the instruction cycle scheme of Figure 3.3. After each write operation, the processor must pause and remain idle until the printer catches up. The length of this pause may be on the order of many hundreds or even thousands of instruction cycles that do not involve memory. Clearly, this is a very wasteful use of the processor.

Table 3.1 Classes of Interrupts

Program	Generated by some condition that occurs as a result of an instruction execution, such as arithmetic overflow, division by zero, attempt to execute an illegal machine instruction, or reference outside a user's allowed memory space.
Timer	Generated by a timer within the processor. This allows the operating system to perform certain functions on a regular basis.
I/O	Generated by an I/O controller, to signal normal completion of an operation or to signal a variety of error conditions.
Hardware failure	Generated by a failure such as power failure or memory parity error.

Figure 3.7a illustrates this state of affairs. The user program performs a series of WRITE calls interleaved with processing. Code segments 1, 2, and 3 refer to sequences of instructions that do not involve I/O. The WRITE calls are to an I/O program that is a system utility and that will perform the actual I/O operation. The I/O program consists of three sections:

- A sequence of instructions, labeled 4 in the figure, to prepare for the actual I/O operation. This may include copying the data to be output into a special buffer and preparing the parameters for a device command.
- The actual I/O command. Without the use of interrupts, once this command is issued, the program must wait for the I/O device to perform the requested function (or periodically poll the device). The program might wait by simply repeatedly performing a test operation to determine if the I/O operation is done.
- A sequence of instructions, labeled 5 in the figure, to complete the operation. This may include setting a flag indicating the success or failure of the operation.

Because the I/O operation may take a relatively long time to complete, the I/O program is hung up waiting for the operation to complete; hence, the user program is stopped at the point of the WRITE call for some considerable period of time.

Interrupts and the Instruction Cycle

With interrupts, the processor can be engaged in executing other instructions while an I/O operation is in progress. Consider the flow of control in Figure 3.7b. As before, the user program reaches a point at which it makes a system call in the form of a WRITE call. The I/O program that is invoked in this case consists only of the preparation code and the actual I/O command. After these few instructions have been executed, control returns to the user program. Meanwhile, the external device is busy accepting data from computer memory and printing it. This I/O operation is conducted concurrently with the execution of instructions in the user program.

When the external device becomes ready to be serviced, that is, when it is ready to accept more data from the processor, the I/O module for that external device sends an *interrupt request* signal to the processor. The processor responds by suspending operation of the current program, branching off to a program to service that particular I/O device, known as an interrupt handler, and resuming the original execution after the device is serviced. The points at which such interrupts occur are indicated by an asterisk in Figure 3.7b.

From the point of view of the user program, an interrupt is just that: an interruption of the normal sequence of execution. When the interrupt processing is completed, execution resumes (Figure 3.8). Thus, the user program does not have to contain any special code to accommodate interrupts; the processor and the operating system are responsible for suspending the user program and then resuming it at the same point.

To accommodate interrupts, an *interrupt cycle* is added to the instruction cycle, as shown in Figure 3.9. In the interrupt cycle, the processor checks to see if any interrupts have occurred, indicated by the presence of an interrupt signal. If no interrupts are pending, the processor proceeds to the fetch cycle and fetches the next instruction of the current program. If an interrupt is pending, the processor does the following:

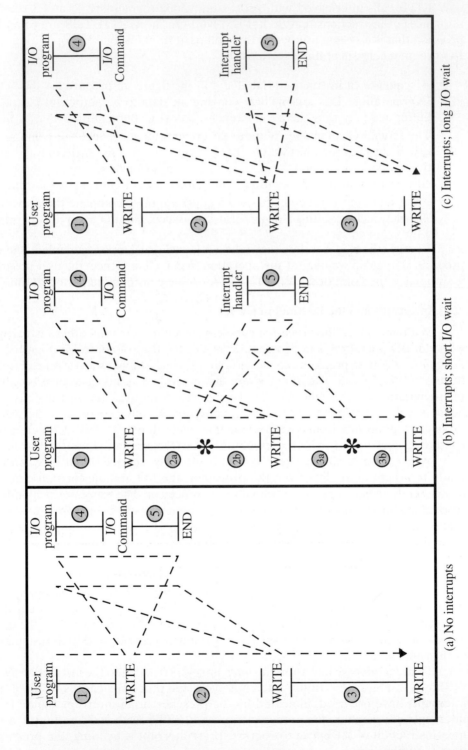

Figure 3.7 Program Flow of Control without and with Interrupts

(a) No interrupts

(b) Interrupts; short I/O wait

(c) Interrupts; long I/O wait

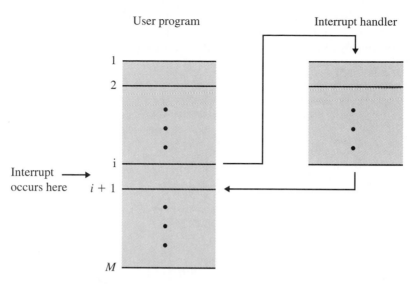

Figure 3.8 Transfer of Control via Interrupts

- It suspends execution of the current program being executed and saves its context. This means saving the address of the next instruction to be executed (current contents of the program counter) and any other data relevant to the processor's current activity.
- It sets the program counter to the starting address of an *interrupt handler* routine.

The processor now proceeds to the fetch cycle and fetches the first instruction in the interrupt handler program, which will service the interrupt. The interrupt handler program is generally part of the operating system. Typically, this program determines the nature of the interrupt and performs whatever actions are needed. In the example we have been using, the handler determines which

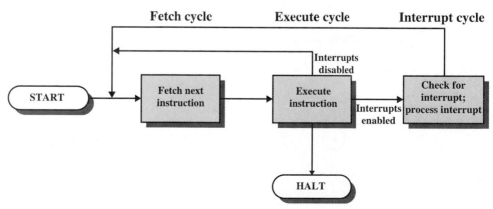

Figure 3.9 Instruction Cycle with Interrupts

I/O module generated the interrupt, and may branch to a program that will write more data out to that I/O module. When the interrupt handler routine is completed, the processor can resume execution of the user program at the point of interruption.

It is clear that there is some overhead involved in this process. Extra instructions must be executed (in the interrupt handler) to determine the nature of the interrupt and to decide on the appropriate action. Nevertheless, because of the relatively large amount of time that would be wasted by simply waiting on an I/O operation, the processor can be employed much more efficiently with the use of interrupts.

To appreciate the gain in efficiency, consider Figure 3.10, which is a timing diagram based on the flow of control in Figures 3.7a and 3.7b. Figures 3.7b and 3.10 assume that the time required for the I/O operation is relatively short: less than the time to complete the execution of instructions between write operations in the user program. The more typical case, especially for a slow device such as a printer, is that

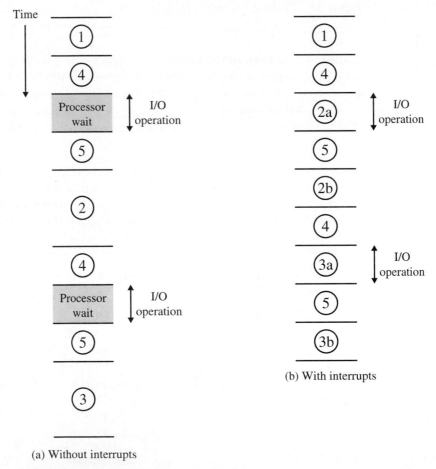

(a) Without interrupts

(b) With interrupts

Figure 3.10   Program Timing: Short I/O Wait

the I/O operation will take much more time than executing a sequence of user instructions. Figure 3.7c indicates this state of affairs. In this case, the user program reaches the second WRITE call before the I/O operation spawned by the first call is complete. The result is that the user program is hung up at that point. When the preceding I/O operation is completed, this new WRITE call may be processed, and a new I/O operation may be started. Figure 3.11 shows the timing for this situation with and without the use of interrupts. We can see that there is still a gain in efficiency because part of the time during which the I/O operation is underway overlaps with the execution of user instructions.

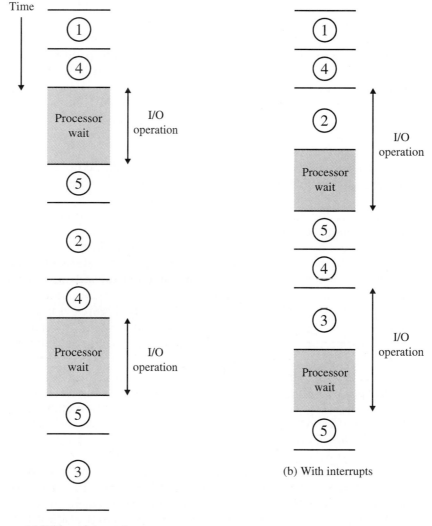

(a) Without interrupts

(b) With interrupts

Figure 3.11 Program Timing: Long I/O Wait

Figure 3.12 shows a revised instruction cycle state diagram that includes interrupt cycle processing.

Multiple Interrupts

The discussion so far has focused only on the occurrence of a single interrupt. Suppose, however, that multiple interrupts can occur. For example, a program may be receiving data from a communications line and printing results. The printer will generate an interrupt every time that it completes a print operation. The communication line controller will generate an interrupt every time a unit of data arrives. The unit could either be a single character or a block, depending on the nature of the communications discipline. In any case, it is possible for a communications interrupt to occur while a printer interrupt is being processed.

Two approaches can be taken to dealing with multiple interrupts. The first is to disable interrupts while an interrupt is being processed. A *disabled interrupt* simply means that the processor can and will ignore that interrupt request signal. If an interrupt occurs during this time, it generally remains pending and will be checked by the processor after the processor has enabled interrupts. Thus, when a user program is executing and an interrupt occurs, interrupts are disabled immediately. After the interrupt handler routine completes, interrupts are enabled before resuming the user program, and the processor checks to see if additional interrupts have occurred. This approach is nice and simple, as interrupts are handled in strict sequential order (Figure 3.13a).

The drawback to the preceding approach is that it does not take into account relative priority or time-critical needs. For example, when input arrives from the communications line, it may need to be absorbed rapidly to make room for more input. If the first batch of input has not been processed before the second batch arrives, data may be lost.

A second approach is to define priorities for interrupts and to allow an interrupt of higher priority to cause a lower-priority interrupt handler to be itself interrupted (Figure 3.13b). As an example of this second approach, consider a system with three I/O devices: a printer, a disk, and a communications line, with increasing priorities of 2, 4, and 5, respectively. Figure 3.14 illustrates a possible sequence. A user program begins at $t = 0$. At $t = 10$, a printer interrupt occurs; user information is placed on the system stack and execution continues at the printer interrupt service routine (ISR). While this routine is still executing, at $t = 15$, a communications interrupt occurs. Because the communications line has higher priority than the printer, the interrupt is honored. The printer ISR is interrupted, its state is pushed onto the stack, and execution continues at the communications ISR. While this routine is executing, a disk interrupt occurs ($t = 20$). Because this interrupt is of lower priority, it is simply held, and the communications ISR runs to completion.

When the communications ISR is complete ($t = 25$), the previous processor state is restored, which is the execution of the printer ISR. However, before even a single instruction in that routine can be executed, the processor honors the higher-priority disk interrupt and control transfers to the disk ISR. Only when that routine is complete ($t = 35$) is the printer ISR resumed. When that routine completes ($t = 40$), control finally returns to the user program.

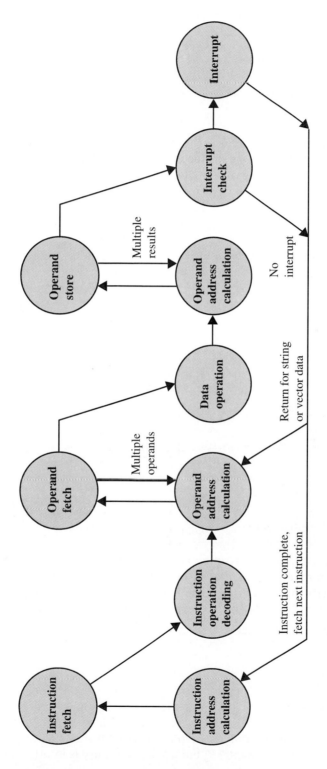

Figure 3.12 Instruction Cycle State Diagram, with Interrupts

65

(a) Sequential interrupt processing

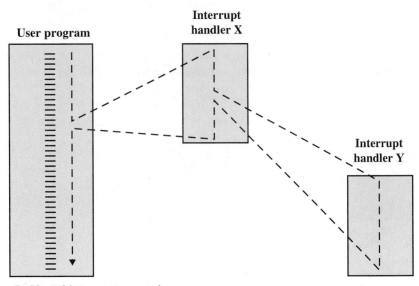

(b) Nested interrupt processing

Figure 3.13 Transfer of Control with Multiple Interrupts

I/O Function

Thus far, we have discussed the operation of the computer as controlled by the processor, and we have looked primarily at the interaction of processor and memory. The discussion has only alluded to the role of the I/O component. This role is discussed in detail in Chapter 7, but a brief summary is in order here.

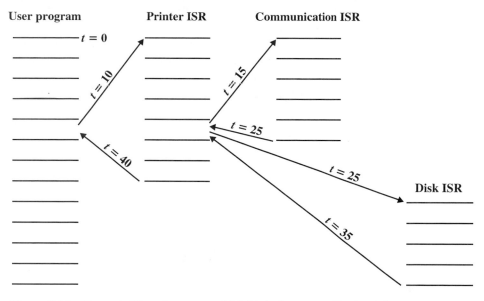

Figure 3.14 Example Time Sequence of Multiple Interrupts [TANE90]

An I/O module (e.g., a disk controller) can exchange data directly with the processor. Just as the processor can initiate a read or write with memory, designating the address of a specific location, the processor can also read data from or write data to an I/O module. In this latter case, the processor identifies a specific device that is controlled by a particular I/O module. Thus, an instruction sequence similar in form to that of Figure 3.5 could occur, with I/O instructions rather than memory-referencing instructions.

In some cases, it is desirable to allow I/O exchanges to occur directly with memory. In such a case, the processor grants to an I/O module the authority to read from or write to memory, so that the I/O-memory transfer can occur without tying up the processor. During such a transfer, the I/O module issues read or write commands to memory, relieving the processor of responsibility for the exchange. This operation is known as direct memory access (DMA) and is examined Chapter 7.

3.3 INTERCONNECTION STRUCTURES

A computer consists of a set of components or modules of three basic types (processor, memory, I/O) that communicate with each other. In effect, a computer is a network of basic modules. Thus, there must be paths for connecting the modules.

The collection of paths connecting the various modules is called the *interconnection structure*. The design of this structure will depend on the exchanges that must be made between modules.

Figure 3.15 suggests the types of exchanges that are needed by indicating the major forms of input and output for each module type:

- **Memory:** Typically, a memory module will consist of N words of equal length. Each word is assigned a unique numerical address $(0, 1, \ldots, N - 1)$. A word of data can be read from or written into the memory. The nature of the operation is indicated by read and write control signals. The location for the operation is specified by an address.
- **I/O module:** From an internal (to the computer system) point of view, I/O is functionally similar to memory. There are two operations, read and write. Further, an I/O module may control more than one external device. We can refer to each of the interfaces to an external device as a *port* and give each a unique address (e.g., $0, 1, \ldots, M - 1$). In addition, there are external data paths for the input and output of data with an external device. Finally, an I/O module may be able to send interrupt signals to the processor.

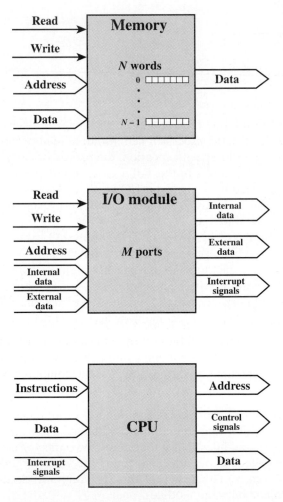

Figure 3.15 Computer Modules

- **Processor:** The processor reads in instructions and data, writes out data after processing, and uses control signals to control the overall operation of the system. It also receives interrupt signals.

The preceding list defines the data to be exchanged. The interconnection structure must support the following types of transfers:

- **Memory to processor:** The processor reads an instruction or a unit of data from memory.
- **Processor to memory:** The processor writes a unit of data to memory.
- **I/O to processor:** The processor reads data from an I/O device via an I/O module.
- **Processor to I/O:** The processor sends data to the I/O device.
- **I/O to or from memory:** For these two cases, an I/O module is allowed to exchange data directly with memory, without going through the processor, using direct memory access (DMA).

Over the years, a number of interconnection structures have been tried. By far the most common is the bus and various multiple-bus structures. The remainder of this chapter is devoted to an assessment of bus structures.

3.4 BUS INTERCONNECTION

A bus is a communication pathway connecting two or more devices. A key characteristic of a bus is that it is a shared transmission medium. Multiple devices connect to the bus, and a signal transmitted by any one device is available for reception by all other devices attached to the bus. If two devices transmit during the same time period, their signals will overlap and become garbled. Thus, only one device at a time can successfully transmit.

Typically, a bus consists of multiple communication pathways, or lines. Each line is capable of transmitting signals representing binary 1 and binary 0. Over time, a sequence of binary digits can be transmitted across a single line. Taken together, several lines of a bus can be used to transmit binary digits simultaneously (in parallel). For example, an 8-bit unit of data can be transmitted over eight bus lines.

Computer systems contain a number of different buses that provide pathways between components at various levels of the computer system hierarchy. A bus that connects major computer components (processor, memory, I/O) is called a *system bus.* The most common computer interconnection structures are based on the use of one or more system buses.

Bus Structure

A system bus consists, typically, of from about 50 to hundreds of separate lines. Each line is assigned a particular meaning or function. Although there are many different bus designs, on any bus the lines can be classified into three functional groups

(Figure 3.16): data, address, and control lines. In addition, there may be power distribution lines that supply power to the attached modules.

The *data lines* provide a path for moving data between system modules. These lines, collectively, are called the *data bus*. The data bus may consist of from 32 to hundreds of separate lines, the number of lines being referred to as the *width* of the data bus. Because each line can carry only 1 bit at a time, the number of lines determines how many bits can be transferred at a time. The width of the data bus is a key factor in determining overall system performance. For example, if the data bus is 8 bits wide and each instruction is 16 bits long, then the processor must access the memory module twice during each instruction cycle.

The *address lines* are used to designate the source or destination of the data on the data bus. For example, if the processor wishes to read a word (8, 16, or 32 bits) of data from memory, it puts the address of the desired word on the address lines. Clearly, the width of the address bus determines the maximum possible memory capacity of the system. Furthermore, the address lines are generally also used to address I/O ports. Typically, the higher-order bits are used to select a particular module on the bus, and the lower-order bits select a memory location or I/O port within the module. For example, on an 8-bit address bus, address 01111111 and below might reference locations in a memory module (module 0) with 128 words of memory, and address 10000000 and above refer to devices attached to an I/O module (module 1).

The *control lines* are used to control the access to and the use of the data and address lines. Because the data and address lines are shared by all components, there must be a means of controlling their use. Control signals transmit both command and timing information between system modules. Timing signals indicate the validity of data and address information. Command signals specify operations to be performed. Typical control lines include the following:

- **Memory write:** Causes data on the bus to be written into the addressed location.
- **Memory read:** Causes data from the addressed location to be placed on the bus.
- **I/O write:** Causes data on the bus to be output to the addressed I/O port.
- **I/O read:** Causes data from the addressed I/O port to be placed on the bus.
- **Transfer ACK:** Indicates that data have been accepted from or placed on the bus.
- **Bus request:** Indicates that a module needs to gain control of the bus.

Figure 3.16 Bus Interconnection Scheme

- **Bus grant:** Indicates that a requesting module has been granted control of the bus.
- **Interrupt request:** Indicates that an interrupt is pending.
- **Interrupt ACK:** Acknowledges that the pending interrupt has been recognized.
- **Clock:** Used to synchronize operations.
- **Reset:** Initializes all modules.

The operation of the bus is as follows. If one module wishes to send data to another, it must do two things: (1) Obtain the use of the bus, and (2) transfer data via the bus. If one module wishes to request data from another module, it must (1) obtain the use of the bus, and (2) transfer a request to the other module over the appropriate control and address lines. It must then wait for that second module to send the data.

Physically, the system bus is actually a number of parallel electrical conductors. In the classic bus arrangement, these conductors are metal lines etched in a card or board (printed circuit board). The bus extends across all of the system components, each of which taps into some or all of the bus lines. The classic physical arrangement is depicted in Figure 3.17. In this example, the bus consists of two vertical columns of conductors. At regular intervals along the columns, there are attachment points in the form of slots that extend out horizontally to support a printed circuit board. Each of the major system components occupies one or more boards and plugs into the bus at these slots. The entire arrangement is housed in a chassis. This scheme can still be used for some of the buses associated with a computer system. However, modern systems tend to have all of the major components on the same board with more elements on the same chip as the processor. Thus, an on-chip bus may connect the processor and cache memory, whereas an on-board bus may connect the processor to main memory and other components.

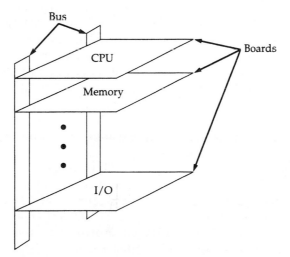

Figure 3.17   Typical Physical Realization
of a Bus Architecture

This arrangement is most convenient. A small computer system may be acquired and then expanded later (more memory, more I/O) by adding more boards. If a component on a board fails, that board can easily be removed and replaced.

Multiple-Bus Hierarchies

If a great number of devices are connected to the bus, performance will suffer. There are two main causes:

1. In general, the more devices attached to the bus, the greater the bus length and hence the greater the propagation delay. This delay determines the time it takes for devices to coordinate the use of the bus. When control of the bus passes from one device to another frequently, these propagation delays can noticeably affect performance.
2. The bus may become a bottleneck as the aggregate data transfer demand approaches the capacity of the bus. This problem can be countered to some extent by increasing the data rate that the bus can carry and by using wider buses (e.g., increasing the data bus from 32 to 64 bits). However, because the data rates generated by attached devices (e.g., graphics and video controllers, network interfaces) are growing rapidly, this is a race that a single bus is ultimately destined to lose.

Accordingly, most computer systems use multiple buses, generally laid out in a hierarchy. A typical traditional structure is shown in Figure 3.18a. There is a local bus that connects the processor to a cache memory and that may support one or more local devices. The cache memory controller connects the cache not only to this local bus, but to a system bus to which are attached all of the main memory modules. As will be discussed in Chapter 4, the use of a cache structure insulates the processor from a requirement to access main memory frequently. Hence, main memory can be moved off of the local bus onto a system bus. In this way, I/O transfers to and from the main memory across the system bus do not interfere with the processor's activity.

It is possible to connect I/O controllers directly onto the system bus. A more efficient solution is to make use of one or more expansion buses for this purpose. An expansion bus interface buffers data transfers between the system bus and the I/O controllers on the expansion bus. This arrangement allows the system to support a wide variety of I/O devices and at the same time insulate memory-to-processor traffic from I/O traffic.

Figure 3.18a shows some typical examples of I/O devices that might be attached to the expansion bus. Network connections include local area networks (LANs) such as a 10-Mbps Ethernet and connections to wide area networks (WANs) such as a packet-switching network. SCSI (small computer system interface) is itself a type of bus used to support local disk drives and other peripherals. A serial port could be used to support a printer or scanner.

This traditional bus architecture is reasonably efficient but begins to break down as higher and higher performance is seen in the I/O devices. In response to these growing demands, a common approach taken by industry is to build a high-

(a) Traditional bus architecture

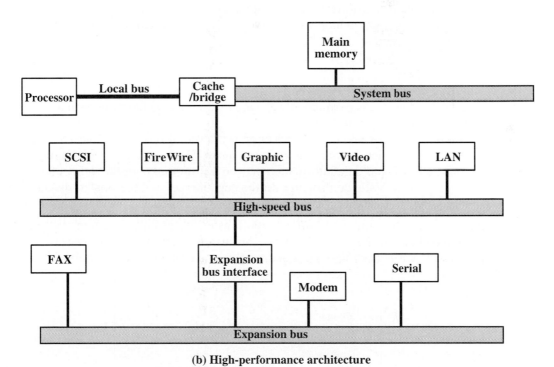

(b) High-performance architecture

Figure 3.18 Example Bus Configurations

speed bus that is closely integrated with the rest of the system, requiring only a bridge between the processor's bus and the high-speed bus. This arrangement is sometimes known as a mezzanine architecture.

Figure 3.18b shows a typical realization of this approach. Again, there is a local bus that connects the processor to a cache controller, which is in turn connected to a system bus that supports main memory. The cache controller is integrated into a bridge, or buffering device, that connects to the high-speed bus. This bus supports connections to high-speed LANs, such as Fast Ethernet at 100 Mbps, video and graphics workstation controllers, as well as interface controllers to local peripheral buses, including SCSI and FireWire. The latter is a high-speed bus arrangement specifically designed to support high-capacity I/O devices. Lower-speed devices are still supported off an expansion bus, with an interface buffering traffic between the expansion bus and the high-speed bus.

The advantage of this arrangement is that the high-speed bus brings high-demand devices into closer integration with the processor and at the same time is independent of the processor. Thus, differences in processor and high-speed bus speeds and signal line definitions are tolerated. Changes in processor architecture do not affect the high-speed bus, and vice versa.

Elements of Bus Design

Although a variety of different bus implementations exist, there are a few basic parameters or design elements that serve to classify and differentiate buses. Table 3.2 lists key elements.

Bus Types

Bus lines can be separated into two generic types: dedicated and multiplexed. A dedicated bus line is permanently assigned either to one function or to a physical subset of computer components.

An example of functional dedication is the use of separate dedicated address and data lines, which is common on many buses. However, it is not essential. For example, address and data information may be transmitted over the same set of lines using an Address Valid control line. At the beginning of a data transfer, the address is placed on the bus and the Address Valid line is activated. At this point, each module has a specified period of time to copy the address and determine if it is the

Table 3.2   Elements of Bus Design

Type	Bus Width
Dedicated	Address
Multiplexed	Data
Method of Arbitration	**Data Transfer Type**
Centralized	Read
Distributed	Write
Timing	Read-modify-write
Synchronous	Read-after-write
Asynchronous	Block

addressed module. The address is then removed from the bus, and the same bus connections are used for the subsequent read or write data transfer. This method of using the same lines for multiple purposes is known as *time multiplexing*.

The advantage of time multiplexing is the use of fewer lines, which saves space and, usually, cost. The disadvantage is that more complex circuitry is needed within each module. Also, there is a potential reduction in performance because certain events that share the same lines cannot take place in parallel.

Physical dedication refers to the use of multiple buses, each of which connects only a subset of modules. A typical example is the use of an I/O bus to interconnect all I/O modules; this bus is then connected to the main bus through some type of I/O adapter module. The potential advantage of physical dedication is high through-put, because there is less bus contention. A disadvantage is the increased size and cost of the system.

Method of Arbitration

In all but the simplest systems, more than one module may need control of the bus. For example, an I/O module may need to read or write directly to memory, without sending the data to the processor. Because only one unit at a time can suc-cessfully transmit over the bus, some method of arbitration is needed. The various methods can be roughly classified as being either centralized or distributed. In a cen-tralized scheme, a single hardware device, referred to as a *bus controller* or *arbiter,* is responsible for allocating time on the bus. The device may be a separate module or part of the processor. In a distributed scheme, there is no central controller. Rather, each module contains access control logic and the modules act together to share the bus. With both methods of arbitration, the purpose is to designate one device, either the processor or an I/O module, as master. The master may then ini-tiate a data transfer (e.g., read or write) with some other device, which acts as slave for this particular exchange.

Timing

Timing refers to the way in which events are coordinated on the bus. Buses use either synchronous timing or asynchronous timing.

With **synchronous timing**, the occurrence of events on the bus is determined by a clock. The bus includes a clock line upon which a clock transmits a regular sequence of alternating 1s and 0s of equal duration. A single 1–0 transmission is referred to as a *clock cycle* or *bus cycle* and defines a time slot. All other devices on the bus can read the clock line, and all events start at the beginning of a clock cycle. Figure 3.19 shows a typical, but simplified, timing diagram for synchronous read and write operations (see Appendix 3A for a description of timing diagrams). Other bus signals may change at the leading edge of the clock signal (with a slight reaction delay). Most events occupy a single clock cycle. In this simple example, the processor places a memory address on the address lines during the first clock cycle, and may assert various status lines. Once the address lines have stabilized, the processor issues an address enable signal. For a read operation, the processor issues a read command at the start of the second cycle. A memory module recog-nizes the address and, after a delay of one cycle, places the data on the data lines.

Figure 3.19 Timing of Synchronous Bus Operations

For a write operation, the processor puts the data on the data lines at the start of the second cycle, and issues a write command after the data lines have stabilized. The memory module copies the information from the data lines during the third clock cycle.

With **asynchronous timing**, the occurrence of one event on a bus follows and depends on the occurrence of a previous event. In the simple read example of Figure 3.20a, the processor places address and status signals on the bus. After pausing for these signals to stabilize, it issues a read command, indicating the presence of valid address and control signals. The appropriate memory decodes the address and responds by placing the data on the data line. Once the data lines have stabilized, the memory module asserts the acknowledged line to signal the processor that the data are available. Once the master has read the data from the data lines, it deasserts the read signal. This causes the memory module to drop the data and acknowledge lines. Finally, once the acknowledge line is dropped, the master removes the address information.

Figure 3.20b shows a simple asynchronous write operation. In this case, the master places the data on the data line at the same time that is puts signals on the status and address lines. The memory module responds to the write command by copying the data from the data lines and then asserting the acknowledge line. The master then drops the write signal and the memory module drops the acknowledge signal.

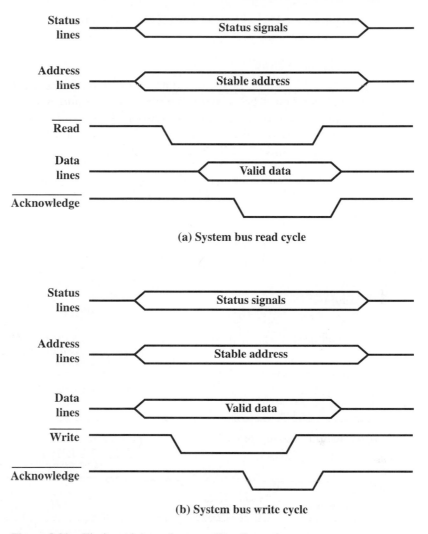

(a) System bus read cycle

(b) System bus write cycle

Figure 3.20 Timing of Asynchronous Bus Operations

Synchronous timing is simpler to implement and test. However, it is less flexible than asynchronous timing. Because all devices on a synchronous bus are tied to a fixed clock rate, the system cannot take advantage of advances in device performance. With asynchronous timing, a mixture of slow and fast devices, using older and newer technology, can share a bus.

Bus Width

We have already addressed the concept of bus width. The width of the data bus has an impact on system performance: The wider the data bus, the greater the number of bits transferred at one time. The width of the address bus has an impact on system capacity: The wider the address bus, the greater the range of locations that can be referenced.

Data Transfer Type

Finally, a bus supports various data transfer types, as illustrated in Figure 3.21. All buses support both write (master to slave) and read (slave to master) transfers. In the case of a multiplexed address/data bus, the bus is first used for specifying the address and then for transferring the data. For a read operation, there is typically a wait while the data is being fetched from the slave to be put on the bus. For either a read or a write, there may also be a delay if it is necessary to go through arbitration to gain control of the bus for the remainder of the operation (i.e., seize the bus to request a read or write, then seize the bus again to perform a read or write).

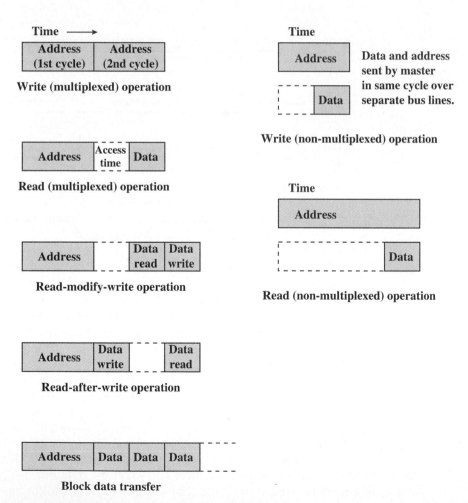

Figure 3.21   Bus Data Transfer Types [GOOR89]

In the case of dedicated address and data buses, the address is put on the address bus and remains there while the data are put on the data bus. For a write operation, the master puts the data onto the data bus as soon as the address has stabilized and the slave has had the opportunity to recognize its address. For a read operation, the slave puts the data onto the data bus as soon as it has recognized its address and has fetched the data.

There are also several combination operations that some buses allow. A read-modify-write operation is simply a read followed immediately by a write to the same address. The address is only broadcast once at the beginning of the operation. The whole operation is typically indivisible to prevent any access to the data element by other potential bus masters. The principal purpose of this capability is to protect shared memory resources in a multiprogramming system (see Chapter 8).

Read-after-write is an indivisible operation consisting of a write followed immediately by a read from the same address. The read operation may be performed for checking purposes.

Some bus systems also support a block data transfer. In this case, one address cycle is followed by n data cycles. The first data item is transferred to or from the specified address; the remaining data items are transferred to or from subsequent addresses.

3.5 PCI

The peripheral component interconnect (PCI) is a popular high-bandwidth, processor-independent bus that can function as a mezzanine or peripheral bus. Compared with other common bus specifications, PCI delivers better system performance for high-speed I/O subsystems (e.g., graphic display adapters, network interface controllers, disk controllers, and so on). The current standard allows the use of up to 64 data lines at 66 MHz, for a raw transfer rate of 528 MByte/s, or 4.224 Gbps. But it is not just a high speed that makes PCI attractive. PCI is specifically designed to meet economically the I/O requirements of modern systems; it requires very few chips to implement and supports other buses attached to the PCI bus.

Intel began work on PCI in 1990 for its Pentium-based systems. Intel soon released all the patents to the public domain and promoted the creation of an industry association, the PCI SIG, to develop further and maintain the compatibility of the PCI specifications. The result is that PCI has been widely adopted and is finding increasing use in personal computer, workstation, and server systems. As of this writing, the current version is PCI 2.2. Because the specification is in the public domain and is supported by a broad cross section of the microprocessor and peripheral industry, PCI products built by different vendors are compatible.

PCI is designed to support a variety of microprocessor-based configurations, including both single- and multiple-processor systems. Accordingly, it provides a general-purpose set of functions. It makes use of synchronous timing and a centralized arbitration scheme.

Figure 3.22a shows a typical use of PCI in a single-processor system. A combined DRAM controller and bridge to the PCI bus provides tight coupling with the

(a) Typical desktop system

(b) Typical server system

Figure 3.22 Example PCI Configurations

processor and the ability to deliver data at high speeds. The bridge acts as a data buffer so that the speed of the PCI bus may differ from that of the processor's I/O capability. In a multiprocessor system (Figure 3.22b), one or more PCI configurations may be connected by bridges to the processor's system bus. The system bus supports only the processor/cache units, main memory, and the PCI bridges. Again, the use of bridges keeps the PCI independent of the processor speed yet provides the ability to receive and deliver data rapidly.

Bus Structure

PCI may be configured as a 32- or 64-bit bus. Table 3.3 defines the 49 mandatory signal lines for PCI. These are divided into the following functional groups:

- **System pins:** Include the clock and reset pins.
- **Address and data pins:** Include 32 lines that are time multiplexed for addresses and data. The other lines in this group are used to interpret and validate the signal lines that carry the addresses and data.
- **Interface control pins:** Control the timing of transactions and provide coordination among initiators and targets.
- **Arbitration pins:** Unlike the other PCI signal lines, these are not shared lines. Rather, each PCI master has its own pair of arbitration lines that connect it directly to the PCI bus arbiter.
- **Error reporting pins:** Used to report parity and other errors.

In addition, the PCI specification defines 51 optional signal lines (Table 3.4), divided into the following functional groups:

- **Interrupt pins:** These are provided for PCI devices that must generate requests for service. As with the arbitration pins, these are not shared lines. Rather, each PCI device has its own interrupt line or lines to an interrupt controller.
- **Cache support pins:** These pins are needed to support a memory on PCI that can be cached in the processor or another device. These pins support snoopy cache protocols (see Chapter 18 for a discussion of such protocols).
- **64-bit bus extension pins:** Include 32 lines that are time multiplexed for addresses and data and that are combined with the mandatory address/data lines to form a 64-bit address/data bus. Other lines in this group are used to interpret and validate the signal lines that carry the addresses and data. Finally, there are two lines that enable two PCI devices to agree to the use of the 64-bit capability.
- **JTAG/boundary scan pins:** These signal lines support testing procedures defined in IEEE Standard 1149.1.

PCI Commands

Bus activity occurs in the form of transactions between an initiator, or master, and a target. When a bus master acquires control of the bus, it determines the type of

Table 3.3 Mandatory PCI Signal Lines

Designation	Type	Description
System Pins		
CLK	in	Provides timing for all transactions and is sampled by all inputs on the rising edge. Clock rates up to 33 MHz are supported.
RST#	in	Forces all PCI-specific registers, sequencers, and signals to an initialized state.
Address and Data Pins		
AD[31::0]	t/s	Multiplexed lines used for address and data.
C/BE[3::0]#	t/s	Multiplexed bus command and byte enable signals. During the data phase, the lines indicate which of the four byte lanes carry meaningful data.
PAR	t/s	Provides even parity across AD and C/BE lines one clock cycle later. The master drives PAR for address and write data phases; the target drive PAR for read data phases.
Interface Control Pins		
FRAME#	s/t/s	Driven by current master to indicate the start and duration of a transaction. It is asserted at the start and deasserted when the initiator is ready to begin the final data phase.
IRDY#	s/t/s	Initiator Ready. Driven by current bus master (initiator of transaction). During a read, indicates that the master is prepared to accept data; during a write, indicates that valid data are present on AD.
TRDY#	s/t/s	Target Ready. Driven by the target (selected device). During a read, indicates that valid data are present on AD; during a write, indicates that target is ready to accept data.
STOP#	s/t/s	Indicates that current target wishes the initiator to stop the current transaction.
IDSEL	in	Initialization Device Select. Used as a chip select during configuration read and write transactions.
DEVSEL#	in	Device Select. Asserted by target when it has recognized its address. Indicates to current initiator whether any device has been selected.
Arbitration Pins		
REQ#	t/s	Indicates to the arbiter that this device requires use of the bus. This is a device-specific point-to-point line.
GNT#	t/s	Indicates to the device that the arbiter has granted bus access. This is a device-specific point-to-point line.
Error Reporting Pins		
PERR#	s/t/s	Parity Error. Indicates a data parity error is detected by a target during a write data phase or by an initiator during a read data phase.
SERR#	o/d	System Error. May be pulsed by any device to report address parity errors and critical errors other than parity.

Table 3.4 Optional PCI Signal Lines

Designation	Type	Description
Interrupt Pins		
INTA#	o/d	Used to request an interrupt.
INTB#	o/d	Used to request an interrupt; only has meaning on a multifunction device.
INTC#	o/d	Used to request an interrupt; only has meaning on a multifunction device.
INTD#	o/d	Used to request an interrupt; only has meaning on a multifunction device.
Cache Support Pins		
SBO#	in/out	Snoop Backoff. Indicates a hit to a modified line.
SDONE	in/out	Snoop Done. Indicates the status of the snoop for the current accent. Asserted when snoop has been completed.
64-bit Bus Extension Pins		
AD[63::32]	t/s	Multiplexed lines used for address and data to extend bus to 64 bits.
C/BE[7::4]#	t/s	Multiplexed bus command and byte enable signals. During the address phase, the lines provide additional bus commands. During the data phase, the lines indicate which of the four extended byte lanes carry meaningful data.
REQ64#	s/t/s	Used to request 64-bit transfer.
ACK64#	s/t/s	Indicates target is willing to perform 64-bit transfer.
PAR64	t/s	Provides even parity across extended AD and C/BE lines one clock cycle later.
JTAG/Boundary Scan Pins		
TCK	in	Test Clock. Used to clock state information and test data into and out of the device during boundary scan.
TDI	in	Test Input. Used to serially shift test data and instructions into the device.
TDO	out	Test Output. Used to serially shift test data and instructions out of the device.
TMS	in	Test Mode Select. Used to control state of test access port controller.
TRST#	in	Test Reset. Used to initialize test access port controller.

in   Input-only signal
out   Output-only signal
t/s   Bidirectional, tri-state, I/O signal
s/t/s   Sustained tri-state signal driven by only one owner at a time
o/d   Open drain: allows multiple devices to share as a wire-OR
Signal's active state occurs at low voltage

transaction that will occur next. During the address phase of the transaction, the C/BE lines are used to signal the transaction type. The commands are

- Interrupt Acknowledge
- Special Cycle
- I/O Read
- I/O Write
- Memory Read
- Memory Read Line
- Memory Read Multiple
- Memory Write
- Memory Write and Invalidate
- Configuration Read
- Configuration Write
- Dual Address Cycle

Interrupt Acknowledge is a read command intended for the device that functions as an interrupt controller on the PCI bus. The address lines are not used during the address phase, and the byte enable lines indicate the size of the interrupt identifier to be returned.

The Special Cycle command is used by the initiator to broadcast a message to one or more targets.

The I/O Read and Write commands are used to transfer data between the initiator and an I/O controller. Each I/O device has its own address space, and the address lines are used to indicate a particular device and to specify the data to be transferred to or from that device. The concept of I/O addresses is explored in Chapter 7.

The memory read and write commands are used to specify the transfer of a burst of data, occupying one or more clock cycles. The interpretation of these commands depends on whether or not the memory controller on the PCI bus supports the PCI protocol for transfers between memory and cache. If so, the transfer of data to and from the memory is typically in terms of cache lines, or blocks.[2] The three memory read commands have the uses outlined in Table 3.5. The Memory Write command is used to transfer data in one or more data cycles to memory. The Memory Write and Invalidate command transfers data in one or more cycles to memory. In addition, it guarantees that at least one cache line is written. This command supports the cache function of writing back a line to memory.

The two configuration commands enable a master to read and update configuration parameters in a device connected to the PCI. Each PCI device may include up to 256 internal registers that are used during system initialization to configure that device.

---

[2]The fundamental principles of cache memory are described in Chapter 4; bus-based cache protocols are described in Chapter 18.

Table 3.5   Interpretation of PCI Read Commands

Read Command Type	For Cachable Memory	For Noncachable Memory
Memory Read	Bursting one-half or less of a cache line	Bursting 2 data transfer cycles or less
Memory Read Line	Bursting more than one-half a cache line to three cache lines	Bursting 3 to 12 data transfers
Memory Read Multiple	Bursting more than three cache lines	Bursting more than 12 data transfers

The Dual Address Cycle command is used by an initiator to indicate that it is using 64-bit addressing.

Data Transfers

Every data transfer on the PCI bus is a single transaction consisting of one address phase and one or more data phases. In this discussion, we illustrate a typical read operation; a write operation proceeds similarly.

Figure 3.23 shows the timing of the read transaction. All events are synchronized to the falling transitions of the clock, which occur in the middle of each clock cycle. Bus devices sample the bus lines on the rising edge at the beginning of a bus cycle. The following are the significant events, labeled on the diagram:

a. Once a bus master has gained control of the bus, it may begin the transaction by asserting FRAME. This line remains asserted until the initiator is ready to complete the last data phase. The initiator also puts the start address on the address bus, and the read command on the C/BE lines.

b. At the start of clock 2, the target device will recognize its address on the AD lines.

c. The initiator ceases driving the AD bus. A turnaround cycle (indicated by the two circular arrows) is required on all signal lines that may be driven by more than one device, so that the dropping of the address signal will prepare the bus for use by the target device. The initiator changes the information on the C/BE lines to designate which AD lines are to be used for transfer for the currently addressed data (from 1 to 4 bytes). The initiator also asserts IRDY to indicate that it is ready for the first data item.

d. The selected target asserts DEVSEL to indicate that it has recognized its address and will respond. It places the requested data on the AD lines and asserts TRDY to indicate that valid data is present on the bus.

e. The initiator reads the data at the beginning of clock 4 and changes the byte enable lines as needed in preparation for the next read.

Figure 3.23 PCI Read Operation

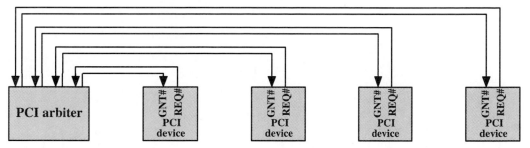

Figure 3.24 PCI Bus Arbiter

f. In this example, the target needs some time to prepare the second block of data for transmission. Therefore, it deasserts TRDY to signal the initiator that there will not be new data during the coming cycle. Accordingly, the initiator does not read the data lines at the beginning of the fifth clock cycle and does not change byte enable during that cycle. The block of data is read at beginning of clock 6.

g. During clock 6, the target places the third data item on the bus. However, in this example, the initiator is not yet ready to read the data item (e.g., it has a temporary buffer full condition). It therefore deasserts IRDY. This will cause the target to maintain the third data item on the bus for an extra clock cycle.

h. The initiator knows that the third data transfer is the last, and so it deasserts FRAME to signal the target that this is the last data transfer. It also asserts IRDY to signal that it is ready to complete that transfer.

i. The initiator deasserts IRDY, returning the bus to the idle state, and the target deasserts TRDY and DEVSEL.

Arbitration

PCI makes use of a centralized, synchronous arbitration scheme in which each master has a unique request (REQ) and grant (GNT) signal. These signal lines are attached to a central arbiter (Figure 3.24) and a simple request–grant handshake is used to grant access to the bus.

The PCI specification does not dictate a particular arbitration algorithm. The arbiter can use a first-come-first-served approach, a round-robin approach, or some sort of priority scheme. A PCI master must arbitrate for each transaction that it wishes to perform, where a single transaction consists of an address phase followed by one or more contiguous data phases.

Figure 3.25 is an example in which devices A and B are arbitrating for the bus. The following sequence occurs:

a. At some point prior to the start of clock 1, A has asserted its REQ signal. The arbiter samples this signal at the beginning of clock cycle 1.

b. During clock cycle 1, B requests use of the bus by asserting its REQ signal.

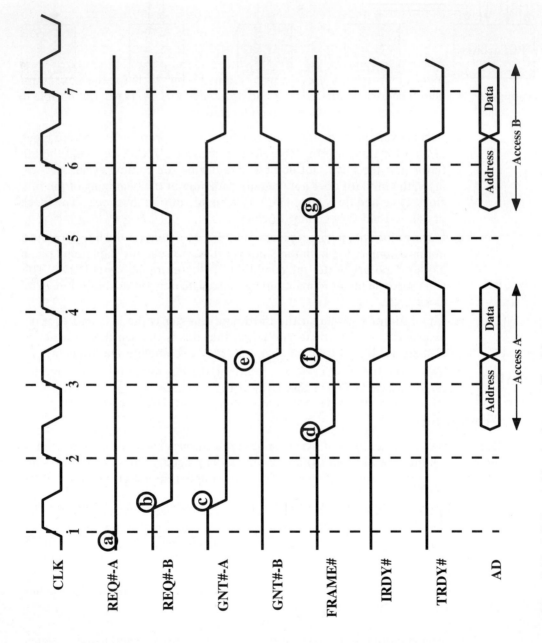

Figure 3.25 PCI Bus Arbitration between Two Masters

c. At the same time, the arbiter asserts GNT-A to grant bus access to A.

d. Bus master A samples GNT-A at the beginning of clock 2 and learns that it has been granted bus access. It also finds IRDY and TRDY deasserted, indicating that the bus is idle. Accordingly, it asserts FRAME and places the address information on the address bus and the command on the C/BE bus (not shown). It also continues to assert REQ-A, because it has a second transaction to perform after this one.

e. The bus arbiter samples all REQ lines at the beginning of clock 3 and makes an arbitration decision to grant the bus to B for the next transaction. It then asserts GNT-B and deasserts GNT-A. B will not be able to use the bus until it returns to an idle state.

f. A deasserts FRAME to indicate that the last (and only) data transfer is in progress. It puts the data on the data bus and signals the target with IRDY. The target reads the data at the beginning of the next clock cycle.

g. At the beginning of clock 5, B finds IRDY and FRAME deasserted and so is able to take control of the bus by asserting FRAME. It also deasserts its REQ line, because it only wants to perform one transaction.

Subsequently, master A is granted access to the bus for its next transaction.

Notice that arbitration can take place at the same time that the current bus master is performing a data transfer. Therefore, no bus cycles are lost in performing arbitration. This is referred to as *hidden arbitration*.

3.6 RECOMMENDED READING AND WEB SITES

The literature on buses and other interconnection structures is, surprisingly, not very extensive. [ALEX93] includes an in-depth treatment of bus structures and bus transfer issues, including accounts of several specific buses.

The clearest book-length description of PCI is [SHAN95]. [ABBO00] also contains a lot of solid information on PCI.

ABBO00 Abbot, D. *PCI Bus Demystified.* Eagle Rock, VA: LLH Technology Publishing, 2000.

ALEX93 Alexandridis, N. *Design of Microprocessor-Based Systems.* Englewood Cliffs, NJ: Prentice Hall, 1993.

SHAN95 Shanley, T., and Anderson, D. *PCI Systems Architecture.* Richardson, TX: Mindshare Press, 1995.

Recommended Web Sites:

- **PCI Special Interest Group:** Information about PCI specifications and products.
- **PCI Pointers:** Links to PCI vendors and other sources of information.

3.7 KEY TERMS, REVIEW QUESTIONS, AND PROBLEMS

Key Terms

address bus	distributed arbitration	memory address register
asynchronous timing	instruction cycle	(MAR)
bus	instruction execute	memory buffer register
bus arbitration	instruction fetch	(MBR)
bus width	interrupt	peripheral component
centralized arbitration	interrupt handler	interconnect (PCI)
data bus	interrupt service routine	synchronous timing
disabled interrupt		system bus

Review Questions

3.1 What general categories of functions are specified by computer instructions?

3.2 List and briefly define the possible states that define an instruction execution.

3.3 List and briefly define two approaches to dealing with multiple interrupts.

3.4 What types of transfers must a computer's interconnection structure (e.g., bus) support?

3.5 What is the benefit of using a multiple-bus architecture compared to a single-bus architecture?

3.6 List and briefly define the functional groups of signal lines for PCI.

Problems

3.1 The hypothetical machine of Figure 3.4 also has two I/O instructions:

$$0011 = \text{Load AC from I/O}$$
$$0111 = \text{Store AC to I/O}$$

In these cases, the 12-bit address identifies a particular I/O device. Show the program execution (using the format of Figure 3.5) for the following program:

1. Load AC from device 5.

2. Add contents of memory location 940.

3. Store AC to device 6.

Assume that the next value retrieved from device 5 is 3 and that location 940 contains a value of 2.

3.2 The program execution of Figure 3.5 is described in the text using six steps. Expand this description to show the use of the MAR and MBR.

3.3 Consider a hypothetical 32-bit microprocessor having 32-bit instructions composed of two fields: The first byte contains the opcode and the remainder the immediate operand or an operand address.

a. What is the maximum directly addressable memory capacity (in bytes)?

b. Discuss the impact on the system speed if the microprocessor bus has

1. a 32-bit local address bus and a 16-bit local data bus, or

2. a 16-bit local address bus and a 16-bit local data bus.

c. How many bits are needed for the program counter and the instruction register?

Source: [ALEX93]

3.4 Consider a hypothetical microprocessor generating a 16-bit address (for example, assume that the program counter and the address registers are 16 bits wide) and having a 16-bit data bus.

a. What is the maximum memory address space that the processor can access directly if it is connected to a "16-bit memory"?

b. What is the maximum memory address space that the processor can access directly if it is connected to an "8-bit memory"?

c. What architectural features will allow this microprocessor to access a separate "I/O space"?

d. If an input and an output instruction can specify an 8-bit I/O port number, how many 8-bit I/O ports can the microprocessor support? How many 16-bit I/O ports? Explain.

Source: [ALEX93]

3.5 Consider a 32-bit microprocessor, with a 16-bit external data bus, driven by an 8-MHz input clock. Assume that this microprocessor has a bus cycle whose minimum duration equals four input clock cycles. What is the maximum data transfer rate that this microprocessor can sustain? To increase its performance, would it be better to make its external data bus 32 bits or to double the external clock frequency supplied to the microprocessor? State any other assumptions you make, and explain.

Source: [ALEX93]

3.6 Consider a computer system that contains an I/O module controlling a simple keyboard/printer teletype. The following registers are contained in the processor and connected directly to the system bus:

INPR: Input Register, 8 bits

OUTR: Output Register, 8 bits

FGI: Input Flag, 1 bit

FGO: Output Flag, 1 bit

IEN: Interrupt Enable, 1 bit

Keystroke input from the teletype and printer output to the teletype are controlled by the I/O module. The teletype is able to encode an alphanumeric symbol to an 8-bit word and decode an 8-bit word into an alphanumeric symbol.

a. Describe how the processor, using the first four registers listed in this problem, can achieve I/O with the teletype.

b. Describe how the function can be performed more efficiently by also employing IEN.

3.7 Figure 3.26 indicates a distributed arbitration scheme that can be used with an obsolete bus scheme known as Multibus I. Agents are daisy-chained physically in priority order. The left-most agent in the diagram receives a constant *bus priority in* (BPRN) signal indicating that no higher-priority agent desires the bus. If the agent does not wish the bus, it asserts its *bus priority out* (BPRO) line. At the beginning of

Figure 3.26 Multibus I Distributed Arbitration

a clock cycle, any agent can request control of the bus by lowering its BPRO line. This lowers the BPRN line of the next agent in the chain, which is in turn required to lower its BPRO line. Thus, the signal is propagated the length of the chain. At the end of this chain reaction, there should be only one agent whose BPRN is asserted and whose BPRO is not. This agent has priority. If, at the beginning of a bus cycle, the bus is not busy (BUSY inactive), the agent that has priority may seize control of the bus by asserting the BUSY line.

It takes a certain amount of time for the BPR signal to propagate from the highest-priority agent to the lowest. Must this time be less than the clock cycle? Explain.

3.8 The VAX SBI bus uses a distributed, synchronous arbitration scheme. Each SBI device (i.e., processor, memory, I/O module) has a unique priority and is assigned a unique transfer request (TR) line. The SBI has 16 such lines (TR0, TR1, . . . , TR15), with TR0 having the highest priority. When a device wants to use the bus, it places a reservation for a future time slot by asserting its TR line during the current time slot. At the end of the current time slot, each device with a pending reservation examines the TR lines; the highest-priority device with a reservation uses the next time slot.

A maximum of 17 devices can be attached to the bus. The device with priority 16 has no TR line. Why not?

3.9 Paradoxically, the lowest-priority device usually has the lowest average wait time. For this reason, the processor is usually given the lowest priority on the SBI. Why does the priority 16 device usually have the lowest average wait time? Under what circumstances would this not be true?

3.10 Draw and explain a timing diagram for a PCI write operation (similar to Figure 3.23).

APPENDIX 3A TIMING DIAGRAMS

In this chapter, timing diagrams are used to illustrate sequences of events and dependencies among events. For the reader unfamiliar with timing diagrams, this appendix provides a brief explanation.

Communication among devices connected to a bus takes place along a set of lines capable of carrying signals. Two different signal levels (voltage levels), representing binary 0 and binary 1, may be transmitted. A timing diagram shows the signal level on a line as a function of time (Figure 3.27a). By convention, the binary 1 signal level is depicted as a higher level than that of binary 0. Usually, binary 0 is the default value. That is, if no data or other signal is being transmitted, then the level on a line is that which represents binary 0. A signal transition from 0 to 1 is frequently referred to as the signal's *leading edge;* a transition from 1 to 0 is referred to as a *trailing edge.* Such transitions are not instantaneous, but this transition time is usually small compared with the duration of a signal level. For clarity, the transition is usually depicted as an angled line that exaggerates the relative amount of time that the transition takes. Occasionally, you will see diagrams that use vertical lines, which incorrectly suggests that the transition is instantaneous. On a timing diagram, it may happen that a variable or at least irrelevant amount of time elapses between events of interest. This is depicted by a gap in the time line.

Signals are sometimes represented in groups (Figure 3.27b). For example, if data are transferred a byte at a time, then eight lines are required. Generally, it is not important to know the exact value being transferred on such a group, but rather whether signals are present or not.

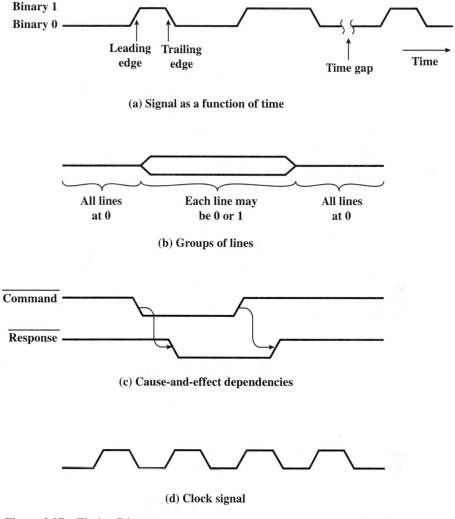

Figure 3.27   Timing Diagrams

A signal transition on one line may trigger an attached device to make signal changes on other lines. For example, if a memory module detects a read control signal (0 or 1 transition), it will place data signals on the data lines. Such cause-and-effect relationships produce sequences of events. Arrows are used on timing diagrams to show these dependencies (Figure 3.27c).

In Figure 3.27c, the overbar over the signal name indicates that the signal is active low as shown. For example, $\overline{Command}$ is active, or asserted, at 0 volts. This means that $\overline{Command} = 0$ is interpreted as logical 1, or true.

A clock line is often part of a system bus. An electronic clock is connected to the clock line and provides a repetitive, regular sequence of transitions (Figure 3.27d). Other events may be synchronized to the clock signal.

CHAPTER 4

CACHE MEMORY

KEY POINTS

- Computer memory is organized into a hierarchy. At the highest level (closest to the processor) are the processor registers. Next comes one or more levels of cache. When multiple levels are used, they are denoted L1, L2, etc. Next comes main memory, which is usually made out of dynamic random-access memory (DRAM). All of these are considered internal to the computer system. The hierarchy continues with external memory, with the next level typically being a fixed hard disk, and one or more levels below that consisting of removable media such as ZIP cartridges, optical disks, and tape.

- As one goes down the memory hierarchy, one finds decreasing cost/bit, increasing capacity, and slower access time. It would be nice to use only the fastest memory, but because that is the most expensive memory, we trade off access time for cost by using more of the slower memory. The trick is to organize the data and programs in memory so that the memory words needed are usually in the faster memory.

- In general, it is likely that most future accesses to main memory by the processor will be to locations recently accessed. So the cache automatically retains a copy of some of the recently used words from the DRAM. If the cache is designed properly, then most of the time the processor will request memory words that are already in the cache.

Although seemingly simple in concept, computer memory exhibits perhaps the widest range of type, technology, organization, performance, and cost of any feature of a computer system. No one technology is optimal in satisfying the memory requirements for a computer system. As a consequence, the typical computer system is equipped with a hierarchy of memory subsystems, some internal to the system (directly accessible by the processor) and some external (accessible by the processor via an I/O module).

This chapter and the next focus on internal memory elements, while Chapter 6 is devoted to external memory. To begin, the first section examines key characteristics of computer memories. The remainder of the chapter examines an essential element of all modern computer systems: cache memory.

4.1 COMPUTER MEMORY SYSTEM OVERVIEW

Characteristics of Memory Systems

The complex subject of computer memory is made more manageable if we classify memory systems according to their key characteristics. The most important of these are listed in Table 4.1.

Table 4.1 Key Characteristics of Computer Memory Systems

Location	**Performance**
Processor	Access time
Internal (main)	Cycle time
External (secondary)	Transfer rate
Capacity	**Physical Type**
Word size	Semiconductor
Number of words	Magnetic
Unit of Transfer	Optical
Word	Magneto-optical
Block	**Physical Characteristics**
Access Method	Volatile/nonvolatile
Sequential	Erasable/nonerasable
Direct	**Organization**
Random	
Associative	

The term **location** in Table 4.1 refers to whether memory is internal and external to the computer. Internal memory is often equated with main memory. But there are other forms of internal memory. The processor requires its own local memory, in the form of registers (e.g., see Figure 2.3). Further, as we shall see, the control unit portion of the processor may also require its own internal memory. We will defer discussion of these latter two types of internal memory to later chapters. Cache is another form of internal memory. External memory consists of peripheral storage devices, such as disk and tape, that are accessible to the processor via I/O controllers.

An obvious characteristic of memory is its **capacity**. For internal memory, this is typically expressed in terms of bytes (1 byte = 8 bits) or words. Common word lengths are 8, 16, and 32 bits. External memory capacity is typically expressed in terms of bytes.

A related concept is the **unit of transfer**. For internal memory, the unit of transfer is equal to the number of data lines into and out of the memory module. This may be equal to the word length, but is often larger, such as 64, 128, or 256 bits. To clarify this point, consider three related concepts for internal memory:

- **Word:** The "natural" unit of organization of memory. The size of the word is typically equal to the number of bits used to represent a number and to the instruction length. Unfortunately, there are many exceptions. For example, the CRAY C90 has a 64-bit word length but uses a 46-bit integer representation. The VAX has a stupendous variety of instruction lengths, expressed as multiples of bytes, and a word size of 32 bits.
- **Addressable units:** In some systems, the addressable unit is the word. However, many systems allow addressing at the byte level. In any case, the relationship between the length in bits A of an address and the number N of addressable units is $2^A = N$.

- **Unit of transfer:** For main memory, this is the number of bits read out of or written into memory at a time. The unit of transfer need not equal a word or an addressable unit. For external memory, data are often transferred in much larger units than a word, and these are referred to as blocks.

Another distinction among memory types is the **method of accessing** units of data. These include the following:

- **Sequential access:** Memory is organized into units of data, called records. Access must be made in a specific linear sequence. Stored addressing information is used to separate records and assist in the retrieval process. A shared read/write mechanism is used, and this must be moved from its current location to the desired location, passing and rejecting each intermediate record. Thus, the time to access an arbitrary record is highly variable. Tape units, discussed in Chapter 6, are sequential access.
- **Direct access:** As with sequential access, direct access involves a shared read–write mechanism. However, individual blocks or records have a unique address based on physical location. Access is accomplished by direct access to reach a general vicinity plus sequential searching, counting, or waiting to reach the final location. Again, access time is variable. Disk units, discussed in Chapter 6, are direct access.
- **Random access:** Each addressable location in memory has a unique, physically wired-in addressing mechanism. The time to access a given location is independent of the sequence of prior accesses and is constant. Thus, any location can be selected at random and directly addressed and accessed. Main memory and some cache systems are random access.
- **Associative:** This is a random-access type of memory that enables one to make a comparison of desired bit locations within a word for a specified match, and to do this for all words simultaneously. Thus, a word is retrieved based on a portion of its contents rather than its address. As with ordinary random-access memory, each location has its own addressing mechanism, and retrieval time is constant independent of location or prior access patterns. Cache memories may employ associative access.

From a user's point of view, the two most important characteristics of memory are capacity and **performance**. Three performance parameters are used:

- **Access time (latency):** For random-access memory, this is the time it takes to perform a read or write operation, that is, the time from the instant that an address is presented to the memory to the instant that data have been stored or made available for use. For non-random-access memory, access time is the time it takes to position the read–write mechanism at the desired location.
- **Memory cycle time:** This concept is primarily applied to random-access memory and consists of the access time plus any additional time required before

a second access can commence. This additional time may be required for transients to die out on signal lines or to regenerate data if they are read destructively. Note that memory cycle time is concerned with the system bus, not the processor.

- **Transfer rate:** This is the rate at which data can be transferred into or out of a memory unit. For random-access memory, it is equal to 1/(cycle time).

For non-random-access memory, the following relationship holds:

$$T_N = T_A + \frac{N}{R}$$

where

T_N = Average time to read or write N bits
T_A = Average access time
N = Number of bits
R = Transfer rate, in bits per second (bps)

A variety of **physical types** of memory have been employed. The most common today are semiconductor memory, magnetic surface memory, used for disk and tape, and optical and magneto-optical.

Several **physical characteristics** of data storage are important. In a volatile memory, information decays naturally or is lost when electrical power is switched off. In a nonvolatile memory, information once recorded remains without deterioration until deliberately changed; no electrical power is needed to retain information. Magnetic-surface memories are nonvolatile. Semiconductor memory may be either volatile or nonvolatile. Nonerasable memory cannot be altered, except by destroying the storage unit. Semiconductor memory of this type is known as *read-only memory* (ROM). Of necessity, a practical nonerasable memory must also be nonvolatile.

For random-access memory, the **organization** is a key design issue. By *organization* is meant the physical arrangement of bits to form words. The obvious arrangement is not always used, as will be explained presently.

The Memory Hierarchy

The design constraints on a computer's memory can be summed up by three questions: How much? How fast? How expensive?

The question of how much is somewhat open ended. If the capacity is there, applications will likely be developed to use it. The question of how fast is, in a sense, easier to answer. To achieve greatest performance, the memory must be able to keep up with the processor. That is, as the processor is executing instructions, we would not want it to have to pause waiting for instructions or operands. The final question must also be considered. For a practical system, the cost of memory must be reasonable in relationship to other components.

As might be expected, there is a trade-off among the three key characteristics of memory: namely, cost, capacity, and access time. At any given time, a variety of technologies are used to implement memory systems. Across this spectrum of technologies, the following relationships hold:

- Faster access time, greater cost per bit
- Greater capacity, smaller cost per bit
- Greater capacity, slower access time

The dilemma facing the designer is clear. The designer would like to use memory technologies that provide for large-capacity memory, both because the capacity is needed and because the cost per bit is low. However, to meet performance requirement, the designer needs to use expensive, relatively lower-capacity memories with short access times.

The way out of this dilemma is not to rely on a single memory component or technology, but to employ a **memory hierarchy**. A typical hierarchy is illustrated in Figure 4.1. As one goes down the hierarchy, the following occur:

a. Decreasing cost per bit

b. Increasing capacity

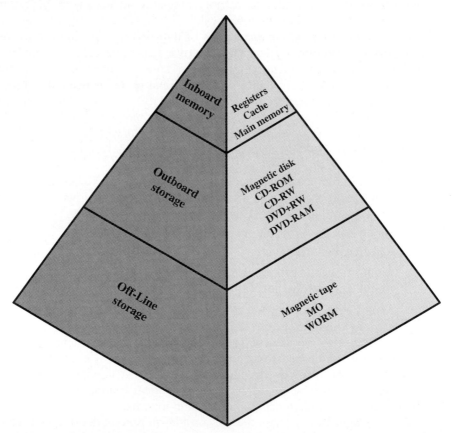

Figure 4.1 The Memory Hierarchy

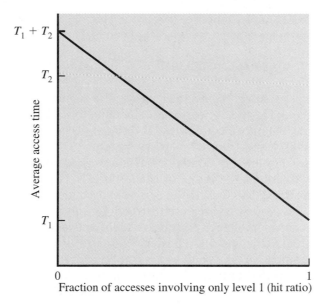

Figure 4.2 Performance of a Simple Two-Level Memory

c. Increasing access time

d. Decreasing frequency of access of the memory by the processor

Thus, smaller, more expensive, faster memories are supplemented by larger, cheaper, slower memories. The key to the success of this organization is item (d): decreasing frequency of access. We examine this concept in greater detail when we discuss the cache, later in this chapter, and virtual memory in Chapter 8. A brief explanation is provided at this point.

Suppose that the processor has access to two levels of memory. Level 1 contains 1000 words and has an access time of 0.01 μs; level 2 contains 100,000 words and has an access time of 0.1 μs. Assume that if a word to be accessed is in level 1, then the processor accesses it directly. If it is in level 2, then the word is first transferred to level 1 and then accessed by the processor. For simplicity, we ignore the time required for the processor to determine whether the word is in level 1 or level 2. Figure 4.2 shows the general shape of the curve that covers this situation. The figure shows the average access time to a two-level memory as a function of the hit ratio H, where

$$H = \text{fraction of all memory accesses that are found}$$
$$\text{in the faster memory (e.g., the cache)}$$
$$T_1 = \text{access time to level 1}$$
$$T_2 = \text{access time to level 2}$$

As can be seen, for high percentages of level 1 access, the average total access time is much closer to that of level 1 than that of level 2.

In our example, suppose 95% of the memory accesses are found in the cache. Then the average time to access a word can be expressed as

$$(0.95)\ (0.01\ \mu s) + (0.05)\ (0.01\ \mu s + 0.1\ \mu s) = 0.0095 + 0.0055 = 0.015\ \mu s$$

In this example, the average access time is much closer to 0.01 μs than to 0.1 μs, as desired. The use of two levels of memory to reduce average access time works in principle, but only if conditions (a) through (d) apply. By employing a variety of technologies, a spectrum of memory systems exists that satisfies conditions (a) through (c). Fortunately, condition (d) is also generally valid.

The basis for the validity of condition (d) is a principle known as **locality of reference** [DENN68]. During the course of execution of a program, memory references by the processor, for both instructions and data, tend to cluster. Programs typically contain a number of iterative loops and subroutines. Once a loop or subroutine is entered, there are repeated references to a small set of instructions. Similarly, operations on tables and arrays involve access to a clustered set of data words. Over a long period of time, the clusters in use change, but over a short period of time, the processor is primarily working with fixed clusters of memory references.

Accordingly, it is possible to organize data across the hierarchy such that the percentage of accesses to each successively lower level is substantially less than that of the level above. Consider the two-level example already presented. Let level 2 memory contain all program instructions and data. The current clusters can be temporarily placed in level 1. From time to time, one of the clusters in level 1 will have to be swapped back to level 2 to make room for a new cluster coming in to level 1. On average, however, most references will be to instructions and data contained in level 1.

This principle can be applied across more than two levels of memory, as suggested by the hierarchy shown in Figure 4.1. The fastest, smallest, and most expensive type of memory consists of the registers internal to the processor. Typically, a processor will contain a few dozen such registers, although some machines contain hundreds of registers. Skipping down two levels, main memory is the principal internal memory system of the computer. Each location in main memory has a unique address. Main memory is usually extended with a higher-speed, smaller cache. The cache is not usually visible to the programmer or, indeed, to the processor. It is a device for staging the movement of data between main memory and processor registers to improve performance.

The three forms of memory just described are, typically, volatile and employ semiconductor technology. The use of three levels exploits the fact that semiconductor memory comes in a variety of types, which differ in speed and cost. Data are stored more permanently on external mass storage devices, of which the most common are hard disk and removable media, such as removable disk, tape, and optical storage. External, nonvolatile memory is also referred to as secondary or auxiliary memory. These are used to store program and data files and are usually visible to the programmer only in terms of files and records, as opposed to individual bytes or words. Disk is also used to provide an extension to main memory known as virtual memory, which is discussed in Chapter 8.

Other forms of memory may be included in the hierarchy. For example, large IBM mainframes include a form of internal memory known as Expanded Storage. This uses a semiconductor technology that is slower and less expensive than that of main memory. Strictly speaking, this memory does not fit into the hierarchy but is a side branch: Data can be moved between main memory and expanded storage but not between expanded storage and external memory. Other forms of secondary memory include optical and magneto-optical disks. Finally, additional levels can be effectively added to the hierarchy in software. A portion of main memory can be used as a buffer to hold data temporarily that is to be read out to disk. Such a technique, sometimes referred to as a disk cache,[1] improves performance in two ways:

- Disk writes are clustered. Instead of many small transfers of data, we have a few large transfers of data. This improves disk performance and minimizes processor involvement.
- Some data destined for write-out may be referenced by a program before the next dump to disk. In that case, the data is retrieved rapidly from the software cache rather than slowly from the disk.

Appendix 4A examines the performance implications of multilevel memory structures.

4.2 CACHE MEMORY PRINCIPLES

Cache memory is intended to give memory speed approaching that of the fastest memories available, and at the same time provide a large memory size at the price of less expensive types of semiconductor memories. The concept is illustrated in Figure 4.3. There is a relatively large and slow main memory together with a smaller, faster cache memory. The cache contains a copy of portions of main memory. When

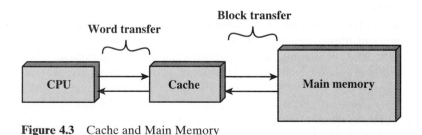

Figure 4.3 Cache and Main Memory

---

[1]Disk cache is generally a purely software technique and is not examined in this book. See [STAL01] for a discussion.

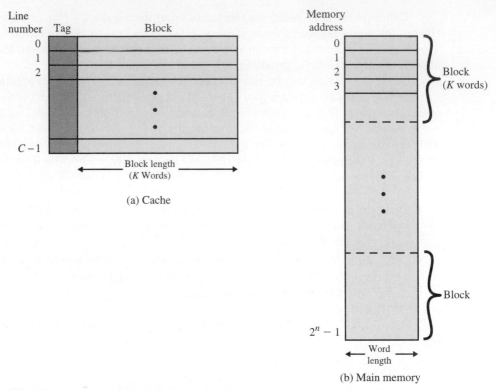

Figure 4.4 Cache/Main Memory Structure

the processor attempts to read a word of memory, a check is made to determine if the word is in the cache. If so, the word is delivered to the processor. If not, a block of main memory, consisting of some fixed number of words, is read into the cache and then the word is delivered to the processor. Because of the phenomenon of locality of reference, when a block of data is fetched into the cache to satisfy a single memory reference, it is likely that there will be future references to that same memory location or to other words in the block.

Figure 4.4 depicts the structure of a cache/main-memory system. Main memory consists of up to 2^n addressable words, with each word having a unique n-bit address. For mapping purposes, this memory is considered to consist of a number of fixed-length blocks of K words each. That is, there are $M = 2^n/K$ blocks. Cache consists of C **lines** of K words each, and the number of lines is considerably less than the number of main memory blocks ($C \ll M$). At any time, some subset of the blocks of memory resides in lines in the cache. If a word in a block of memory is read, that block is transferred to one of the lines of the cache. Because there are more blocks than lines, an individual line cannot be uniquely and permanently dedicated to a particular block. Thus, each line includes a **tag** that identifies which particular block is currently being stored. The tag is usually a portion of the main memory address, as described later in this section.

Figure 4.5 illustrates the read operation. The processor generates the address, RA, of a word to be read. If the word is contained in the cache, it is delivered to the processor. Otherwise, the block containing that word is loaded into the cache, and the word is delivered to the processor. Figure 4.5 shows these last two operations occurring in parallel and reflects the organization shown in Figure 4.6, which is typical of contemporary cache organizations. In this organization, the cache connects to the processor via data, control, and address lines. The data and address lines also attach to data and address buffers, which attach to a system bus from which main memory is reached. When a cache hit occurs, the data and address buffers are disabled and communication is only between processor and cache, with no system bus traffic. When a cache miss occurs, the desired address is loaded onto the system bus and the data are returned through the data buffer to both the cache and the processor. In other organizations, the cache is physically interposed between the processor and the main memory for all data, address, and control lines. In this latter case, for a cache miss, the desired word is first read into the cache and then transferred from cache to processor.

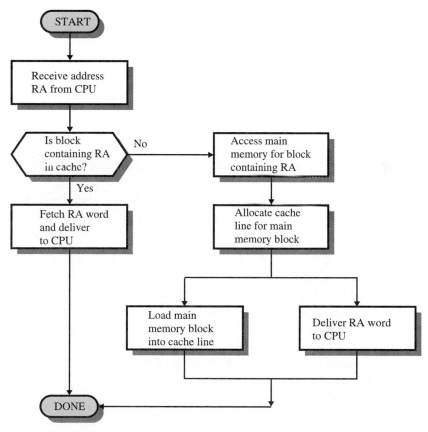

Figure 4.5 Cache Read Operation

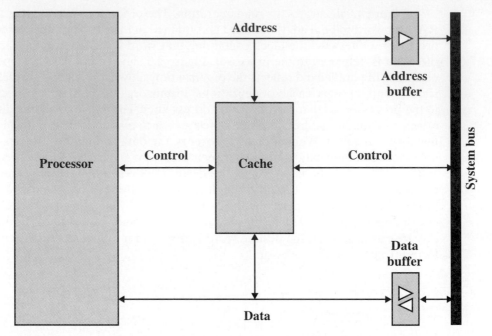

Figure 4.6 Typical Cache Organization

A discussion of the performance parameters related to cache use is contained in Appendix 4A.

4.3 ELEMENTS OF CACHE DESIGN

This section provides an overview of cache design parameters and reports some typical results. We occasionally refer to the use of caches in high-performance computing (HPC). HPC deals with supercomputers and supercomputer software, especially for scientific applications that involve large amounts of data, vector and matrix computation, and the use of parallel algorithms. Cache design for HPC is quite different than for other hardware platforms and applications. Indeed, many researchers have found that HPC applications perform poorly on computer architectures that employ caches [BAIL93]. Other researchers have since shown that a cache hierarchy can be useful in improving performance if the application software is tuned to exploit the cache [WANG99, PRES01].[2]

Although there are a large number of cache implementations, there are a few basic design elements that serve to classify and differentiate cache architectures. Table 4.2 lists key elements.

----

[2]For a general discussion of HPC, see [DOWD98].

Table 4.2 Elements of Cache Design

Cache Size	**Write Policy**
Mapping Function	Write through
Direct	Write back
Associative	Write once
Set associative	**Line Size**
Replacement Algorithm	**Number of caches**
Least recently used (LRU)	Single or two level
First in first out (FIFO)	Unified or split
Least frequently used (LFU)	
Random	

Cache Size

The first element, cache size, has already been discussed. We would like the size of the cache to be small enough so that the overall average cost per bit is close to that of main memory alone and large enough so that the overall average access time is close to that of the cache alone. There are several other motivations for minimizing cache size. The larger the cache, the larger the number of gates involved in addressing the cache. The result is that large caches tend to be slightly slower than small ones—even when built with the same integrated circuit technology and put in the same place on chip and circuit board. The available chip and board area also limits cache size. Because the performance of the cache is very sensitive to the nature of the workload, it is impossible to arrive at a single "optimum" cache size. Table 4.3 lists the cache sizes of some current and past processors.

Mapping Function

Because there are fewer cache lines than main memory blocks, an algorithm is needed for mapping main memory blocks into cache lines. Further, a means is needed for determining which main memory block currently occupies a cache line. The choice of the mapping function dictates how the cache is organized. Three techniques can be used: direct, associative, and set associative. We examine each of these in turn. In each case, we look at the general structure and then a specific example. For all three cases, the example includes the following elements:

- The cache can hold 64 KBytes.
- Data is transferred between main memory and the cache in blocks of 4 bytes each. This means that the cache is organized as $16K = 2^{14}$ lines of 4 bytes each.
- The main memory consists of 16 Mbytes, with each byte directly addressable by a 24-bit address ($2^{24} = 16M$). Thus, for mapping purposes, we can consider main memory to consist of 4M blocks of 4 bytes each.

The simplest technique, known as **direct mapping**, maps each block of main memory into only one possible cache line. Figure 4.7 illustrates the general mechanism. The mapping is expressed as

Table 4.3 Cache Sizes of Some Processors

Processor	Type	Year of Introduction	L1 cache[a]	L2 cache	L3 cache
IBM 360/85	Mainframe	1968	16 to32 KB	—	—
PDP-11/70	Minicomputer	1975	1KB	—	—
VAX 11/780	Minicompterer	1978	16 KB	—	—
IBM 3033	Mainframe	1978	64 KB	—	—
IBM 3090	Mainframe	1985	128 to 256 KB	—	—
Intel 80486	PC	1989	8 KB	—	—
Pentium	PC	1993	8 KB/8 KB	256 to 512 KB	—
PowerPC 601	PC	1993	32 KB	—	—
PowerPC 620	PC	1996	32 KB/32 KB	—	—
PowerPC G4	PC/server	1999	32 KB/32 KB	256 KB to 1 MB	2 MB
IBM S/390 G4	Mainframe	1997	32 KB	256 KB	2 MB
IBM S/390 G6	Mainframe	1999	256 KB	8 MB	—
Pentium 4	PC/server	2000	8 KB/8 KB	256 KB	—
IBM SP	High-end server/ supercomputer	2000	64 KB/32 KB	8 MB	—
CRAY MTA[b]	PC/server	2001	16 KB/16 KB	96 KB	4 MB
Itanium	PC/server	2001	16 KB/16 KB	96 KB	4 MB
SGI Origin 2001	High-end server	2001	32 KB/32 KB	4 MB	—

[a]Two values separated by a slash refer to instruction and data caches.
[b]Both caches are instruction only; no data caches.

$$i = j \text{ modulo } m$$

where

i = cache line number
j = main memory block number
m = number of lines in the cache

The mapping function is easily implemented using the address. For purposes of cache access, each main memory address can be viewed as consisting of three fields. The least significant w bits identify a unique word or byte within a block of main memory; in most contemporary machines, the address is at the byte level. The remaining s bits specify one of the 2^s blocks of main memory. The cache logic interprets these s bits as a tag of $s - r$ bits (most significant portion) and a line field of r bits. This latter field identifies one of the $m = 2^r$ lines of the cache. To summarize,

Figure 4.7 Direct-Mapping Cache organization [HWAN93]

109

- Address length $= (s + w)$ bits
- Number of addressable units $= 2^{s+w}$ words or bytes
- Block size $=$ line size $= 2^w$ words or bytes
- Number of blocks in main memory $= \dfrac{2^{s+w}}{2^w} = 2^s$
- Number of lines in cache $= m = 2^r$
- Size of tag $= (s - r)$ bits

The effect of this mapping is that blocks of main memory are assigned to lines of the cache as follows:

Cache line	Main memory blocks assigned
0	$0, m, 2m, \ldots, 2^s - m$
1	$1, m + 1, 2m + 1, \ldots, 2^s - m + 1$
$\vdots$	$\vdots$
$m - 1$	$m - 1, 2m - 1, 3m - 1, \ldots, 2^s - 1$

Thus, the use of a portion of the address as a line number provides a unique mapping of each block of main memory into the cache. When a block is actually read into its assigned line, it is necessary to tag the data to distinguish it from other blocks that can fit into that line. The most significant $s - r$ bits serve this purpose.

Figure 4.8 shows our example system using direct mapping.[3] In the example, $m = 16K = 2^{14}$ and $i = j$ modulo 2^{14}. The mapping becomes as follows:

Cache line	Starting memory address of block
0	000000, 010000, \ldots, FF0000
1	000004, 010004, \ldots, FF0004
$\vdots$	$\vdots$
$2^{14} - 1$	00FFFC, 01FFFC, \ldots, FFFFFC

Note that no two blocks that map into the same line number have the same tag number. Thus, blocks with starting addresses 000000, 010000, \ldots, FF0000 have tag numbers 00, 01, \ldots, FF, respectively.

Referring back to Figure 4.5, a read operation works as follows. The cache system is presented with a 24-bit address. The 14-bit line number is used as an index into the cache to access a particular line. If the 8-bit tag number matches the tag

---

[3]In this and subsequent figures, address and memory values are represented in hexadecimal notation. See Appendix B for a basic refresher on number systems (decimal, binary, hexadecimal).

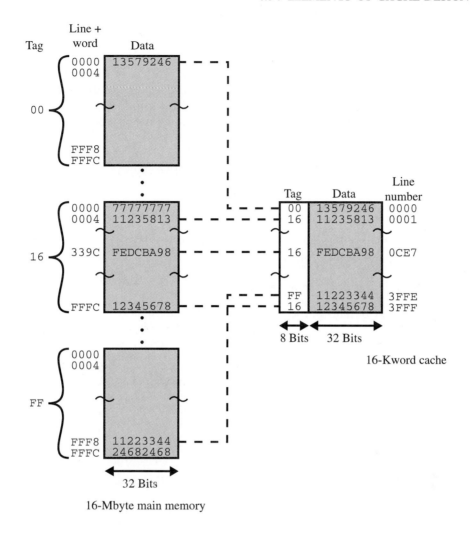

Figure 4.8 Direct Mapping Example

number currently stored in that line, then the 2-bit word number is used to select one of the four bytes in that line. Otherwise, the 22-bit tag-plus-line field is used to fetch a block from main memory. The actual address that is used for the fetch is the 22-bit tag-plus-line concatenated with two 0 bits, so that 4 bytes are fetched starting on a block boundary.

The direct mapping technique is simple and inexpensive to implement. Its main disadvantage is that there is a fixed cache location for any given block. Thus, if a program happens to reference words repeatedly from two different blocks that map into the same line, then the blocks will be continually swapped in the cache, and the hit ratio will be low (a phenomenon known as *thrashing*).

Associative mapping overcomes the disadvantage of direct mapping by permitting each main memory block to be loaded into any line of the cache. In this case, the cache control logic interprets a memory address simply as a tag and a word field. The tag field uniquely identifies a block of main memory. To determine whether a block is in the cache, the cache control logic must simultaneously examine every line's tag for a match. Figure 4.9 illustrates the logic. Note that no field in the address corresponds to line number, so that the number of lines in the cache is not determined by the address format. To summarize,

- Address length = $(s + w)$ bits
- Number of addressable units = 2^{s+w} words or bytes
- Block size = line size = 2^w words or bytes
- Number of blocks in main memory = $\dfrac{2^{s+w}}{2^w} = 2^s$
- Number of lines in cache = undetermined
- Size of tag = s bits

Figure 4.10 shows our example using associative mapping. A main memory address consists of a 22-bit tag and a 2-bit byte number. The 22-bit tag must be stored with the 32-bit block of data for each line in the cache. Note that it is the leftmost (most significant) 22 bits of the address that form the tag.[4] Thus, the 24-bit hexadecimal address 16339C has the 22-bit tag 058CE7. This is easily seen in binary notation:

memory address	0001	0110	0011	0011	1001	1100	(binary)
	1	6	3	3	9	C	(hex)

tag (leftmost 22 bits)	00	0101	1000	1100	1110	0111	(binary)
	0	5	8	C	E	7	(hex)

With associative mapping, there is flexibility as to which block to replace when a new block is read into the cache. Replacement algorithms, discussed later in this section, are designed to maximize the hit ratio. The principal disadvantage of associative mapping is the complex circuitry required to examine the tags of all cache lines in parallel.

Set associative mapping is a compromise that exhibits the strengths of both the direct and associative approaches while reducing their disadvantages. In this case, the cache is divided into v sets, each of which consists of k lines. The relationships are

---

[4]In Figure 4.10, the 22-bit tag is represented by a 6-digit hexadecimal number. The most significant hexadecimal digit in fact is only 2 bits in length.

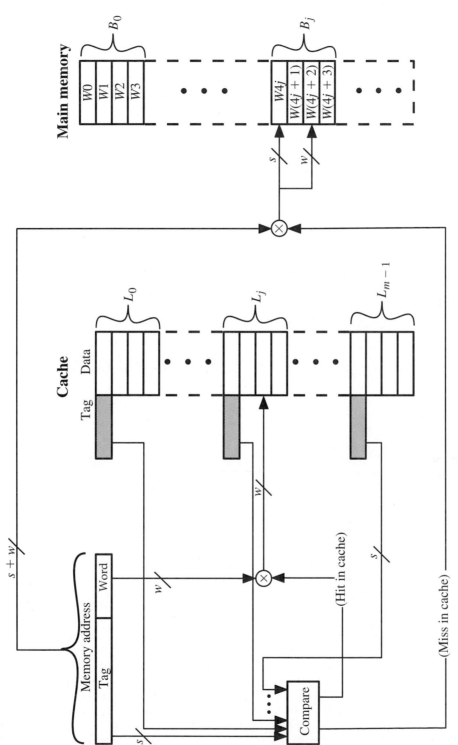

Figure 4.9 Fully Associative Cache Organization [HWAN93]

113

$$m = v \times k$$
$$i = j \text{ modulo } v$$

where

i = cache set number
j = main memory block number
m = number of lines in the cache

This is referred to as k-way set associative mapping. With set associative mapping, block B_j can be mapped into any of the lines of set i. In this case, the cache control logic interprets a memory address simply as three fields: tag, set, and word. The d

Figure 4.10 Associative Mapping Example

set bits specify one of $v = 2^d$ sets. The s bits of the tag and set fields specify one of the 2^s blocks of main memory. Figure 4.11 illustrates the cache control logic. With fully associative mapping, the tag in a memory address is quite large and must be compared to the tag of every line in the cache. With k-way set associative mapping, the tag in a memory address is much smaller and is only compared to the k tags within a single set. To summarize,

- Address length $= (s + w)$ bits
- Number of addressable units $= 2^{s+w}$ words or bytes
- Block size $=$ line size $= 2^w$ words or bytes
- Number of blocks in main memory $= \dfrac{2^{s+w}}{2^w} = 2^s$
- Number of lines in set $= k$
- Number of sets $v = 2^d$
- Number of lines in cache $= kv = k \times 2^d$
- Size of tag $= (s - d)$ bits

Figure 4.12 shows our example using set associative mapping with two lines in each set, referred to as two-way set associative.[5] The 13-bit set number identifies a unique set of two lines within the cache. It also gives the number of the block in main memory, modulo 2^{13}. This determines the mapping of blocks into lines. Thus, blocks 000000, 008000, . . . , FF8000 of main memory map into cache set 0. Any of those blocks can be loaded into either of the two lines in the set. Note that no two blocks that map into the same cache set have the same tag number. For a read operation, the 13-bit set number is used to determine which set of two lines is to be examined. Both lines in the set are examined for a match with the tag number of the address to be accessed.

In the extreme case of $v = m$, $k = 1$, the set associative technique reduces to direct mapping, and for $v = 1$, $k = m$, it reduces to associative mapping. The use of two lines per set ($v = m/2$, $k = 2$) is the most common set associative organization. It significantly improves the hit ratio over direct mapping. Four-way set associative ($v = m/4$, $k = 4$) makes a modest additional improvement for a relatively small additional cost [MAYB84, HILL89]. Further increases in the number of lines per set have little effect.

Replacement Algorithms

When a new block is brought into the cache, one of the existing blocks must be replaced. For direct mapping, there is only one possible line for any particular block, and no choice is possible. For the associative and set associative techniques, a replacement algorithm is needed. To achieve high speed, such an algorithm must be implemented in hardware. A number of algorithms have been tried: We mention four of the most common. Probably the most effective is least recently used (LRU): Replace that block in the set that has been in the cache longest with no reference to

---

[5]In Figure 4.12, the 9-bit tag is represented by a 3-digit hexadecimal number. The most significant hexadecimal digit in fact is only 1 bit in length.

Figure 4.11 *k*-Way Set Associative Cache Organization

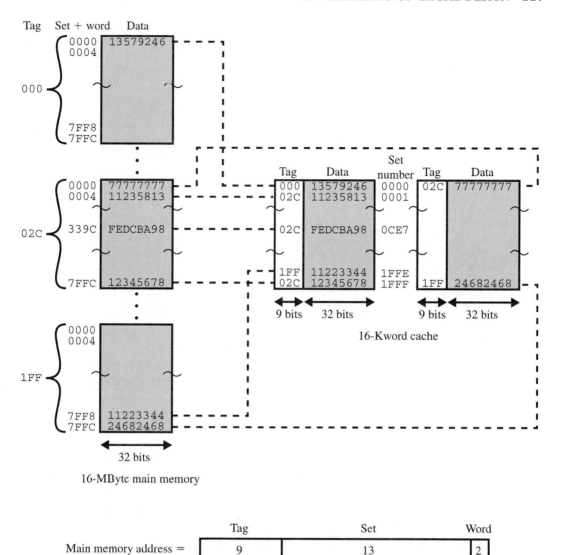

Figure 4.12   Two-Way Set Associative Mapping Example

it. For two-way set associative, this is easily implemented. Each line includes a USE bit. When a line is referenced, its USE bit is set to 1 and the USE bit of the other line in that set is set to 0. When a block is to be read into the set, the line whose USE bit is 0 is used. Because we are assuming that more recently used memory locations are more likely to be referenced, LRU should give the best hit ratio. Another possibility is first-in-first-out (FIFO): Replace that block in the set that has been in the cache longest. FIFO is easily implemented as a round-robin or circular buffer technique. Still another possibility is least frequently used (LFU): Replace that block in the set that has experienced the fewest references. LFU could be implemented by associating a counter with each line. A technique not based on usage is to pick a line at random from among the candidate lines. Simulation studies have shown that random replacement provides only slightly inferior performance to an algorithm based on usage [SMIT82].

Write Policy

Before a block that is resident in the cache can be replaced, it is necessary to consider whether it has been altered in the cache but not in main memory. If it has not, then the old block in the cache may be overwritten. If it has, that means that at least one write operation has been performed on a word in that line of the cache, and main memory must be updated accordingly. A variety of write policies, with performance and economic trade-offs, is possible. There are two problems to contend with. First, more than one device may have access to main memory. For example, an I/O module may be able to read/write directly to memory. If a word has been altered only in the cache, then the corresponding memory word is invalid. Further, if the I/O device has altered main memory, then the cache word is invalid. A more complex problem occurs when multiple processors are attached to the same bus and each processor has its own local cache. Then, if a word is altered in one cache, it could conceivably invalidate a word in other caches.

The simplest technique is called *write through*. Using this technique, all write operations are made to main memory as well as to the cache, ensuring that main memory is always valid. Any other processor–cache module can monitor traffic to main memory to maintain consistency within its own cache. The main disadvantage of this technique is that it generates substantial memory traffic and may create a bottleneck. An alternative technique, known as *write back*, minimizes memory writes. With write back, updates are made only in the cache. When an update occurs, an UPDATE bit associated with the line is set. Then, when a block is replaced, it is written back to main memory if and only if the UPDATE bit is set. The problem with write back is that portions of main memory are invalid, and hence accesses by I/O modules can be allowed only through the cache. This makes for complex circuitry and a potential bottleneck. Experience has shown that the percentage of memory references that are writes is on the order of 15% [SMIT82]. However, for HPC applications, this number may approach 33% (vector-vector multiplication) and can go as high as 50% (matrix transposition).

In a bus organization in which more than one device (typically a processor) has a cache and main memory is shared, a new problem is introduced. If data in one cache are altered, this invalidates not only the corresponding word in main memory, but also that same word in other caches (if any other cache happens to have that same word). Even if a write-through policy is used, the other caches may contain invalid data. A system that prevents this problem is said to maintain cache coherency. Possible approaches to cache coherency include the following:

- **Bus watching with write through:** Each cache controller monitors the address lines to detect write operations to memory by other bus masters. If another master writes to a location in shared memory that also resides in the cache memory, the cache controller invalidates that cache entry. This strategy depends on the use of a write-through policy by all cache controllers.
- **Hardware transparency:** Additional hardware is used to ensure that all updates to main memory via cache are reflected in all caches. Thus, if one proces-

sor modifies a word in its cache, this update is written to main memory. In addition, any matching words in other caches are similarly updated.

- **Noncacheable memory:** Only a portion of main memory is shared by more than one processor, and this is designated as noncacheable. In such a system, all accesses to shared memory are cache misses, because the shared memory is never copied into the cache. The noncacheable memory can be identified using chip-select logic or high-address bits.

Cache coherency is an active field of research. This topic is explored further in Chapter 18.

Line Size

Another design element is the line size. When a block of data is retrieved and placed in the cache, not only the desired word but also some number of adjacent words are retrieved. As the block size increases from very small to larger sizes, the hit ratio will at first increase because of the principle of locality, which states that data in the vicinity of a referenced word are likely to be referenced in the near future. As the block size increases, more useful data are brought into the cache. The hit ratio will begin to decrease, however, as the block becomes even bigger and the probability of using the newly fetched information becomes less than the probability of reusing the information that has to be replaced. Two specific effects come into play:

- Larger blocks reduce the number of blocks that fit into a cache. Because each block fetch overwrites older cache contents, a small number of blocks results in data being overwritten shortly after they are fetched.
- As a block becomes larger, each additional word is farther from the requested word, and therefore less likely to be needed in the near future.

The relationship between block size and hit ratio is complex, depending on the locality characteristics of a particular program, and no definitive optimum value has been found. A size of from 8 to 32 bytes seems reasonably close to optimum [SMIT87, PRZY88, PRZY90, HAND98]. For HPC systems, 64 and 128 byte cache line sizes are most frequently used.

Number of Caches

When caches were originally introduced, the typical system had a single cache. More recently, the use of multiple caches has become the norm. Two aspects of this design issue concern the number of levels of caches and the use of unified versus split caches.

Multilevel Caches

As logic density has increased, it has become possible to have a cache on the same chip as the processor: the on-chip cache. Compared with a cache reachable via an external bus, the on-chip cache reduces the processor's external bus activity and therefore speeds up execution times and increases overall system performance. When the requested instruction or data is found in the on-chip cache, the bus access is eliminated. Because of the short data paths internal to the processor, compared with bus lengths, on-chip cache accesses will complete appreciably faster than would even zero-wait state bus cycles. Furthermore, during this period the bus is free to support other transfers.

The inclusion of an on-chip cache leaves open the question of whether an off-chip, or external, cache is still desirable. Typically, the answer is yes, and most contemporary designs include both on-chip and external caches. The resulting organization is known as a two-level cache, with the internal cache designated as level 1 (L1) and the external cache designated as level 2 (L2). The reason for including an L2 cache is the following. If there is no L2 cache and the processor makes an access request for a memory location not in the L1 cache, then the processor must access DRAM or ROM memory across the bus. Due to the typically slow bus speed and slow memory access time, this results in poor performance. On the other hand, if an L2 SRAM (static RAM) cache is used, then frequently the missing information can be quickly retrieved. If the SRAM is fast enough to match the bus speed, then the data can be accessed using a zero-wait state transaction, the fastest type of bus transfer.

Two features of contemporary cache design for multilevel caches are noteworthy. First, for an off-chip L2 cache, many designs do not use the system bus as the path for transfer between the L2 cache and the processor, but use a separate data path, so as to reduce the burden on the system bus. Second, with the continued shrinkage of processor components, a number of processors now incorporate the L2 cache on the processor chip, improving performance.

The potential savings due to the use of an L2 cache depends on the hit rates in both the L1 and L2 caches. Several studies have shown that, in general, the use of a second-level cache does improve performance (e.g., see [AZIM92], [NOVI93]. [HAND98]). However, the use of multilevel caches does complicate all of the design issues related to caches, including size, replacement algorithm, and write policy; see [HAND98] and [PEIR99] for discussions.

Unified versus Split Caches

When the on-chip cache first made an appearance, many of the designs consisted of a single cache used to store references to both data and instructions. More recently, it has become common to split the cache into two: one dedicated to instructions and one dedicated to data.

There are two potential advantages of a unified cache:

- For a given cache size, a unified cache has a higher hit rate than split caches because it balances the load between instruction and data fetches automatically. That is, if an execution pattern involves many more instruction fetches than data fetches, then the cache will tend to fill up with instructions, and if an execution pattern involves relatively more data fetches, the opposite will occur.
- Only one cache needs to be designed and implemented.

Despite these advantages, the trend is toward split caches, particularly for superscalar machines such as the Pentium and PowerPC, which emphasize parallel instruction execution and the prefetching of predicted future instructions. The key advantage of the split cache design is that it eliminates contention for the cache between the instruction fetch/decode unit and the execution unit. This is important in any design that relies on the pipelining of instructions. Typically, the processor will fetch instructions ahead of time and fill a buffer, or pipeline, with instructions to be executed. Suppose now that we have a unified instruction/data cache. When the execution unit performs a memory access to load and store data, the request is submitted to the unified cache. If, at the same time, the instruction prefetcher issues a read request to the cache for an instruction, that request will be temporarily blocked so that the cache can service the execution unit first, enabling it to complete the currently executing instruction. This cache contention can degrade performance by interfering with efficient use of the instruction pipeline. The split cache structure overcomes this difficulty.

4.4 PENTIUM 4 AND POWERPC CACHE ORGANIZATIONS

Pentium 4 Cache Organization

The evolution of cache organization is seen clearly in the evolution of Intel microprocessors. The 80386 does not include an on-chip cache. The 80486 includes a single on-chip cache of 8 KBytes, using a line size of 16 bytes and a four-way set associative organization. All of the Pentium processors include two on-chip L1 caches, one for data and one for instructions. For the Pentium 4, the L1 data cache is 8 KBytes, using a line size of 64 bytes and a four-way set associative organization. The Pentium 4 instruction cache is described subsequently The Pentium 4 also includes an L2 cache that feeds both of the L1 caches. The L2 cache is eight-way set associative with a size of 256KB and a line size of 128 bytes.

Figure 4.13 provides a simplified view of the Pentium 4 organization, highlighting the placement of the three caches. The processor core consists of four major components:

- **Fetch/decode unit:** Fetches program instructions in order from the L2 cache, decodes these into a series of micro-operations, and stores the results in the L1 instruction cache.
- **Out-of-order execution logic:** Schedules execution of the micro-operations subject to data dependencies and resource availability; thus, micro-operations may be scheduled for execution in a different order than they were fetched from the instruction stream. As time permits, this unit schedules speculative execution of micro-operations that may be required in the future.
- **Execution units:** These units executes micro-operations, fetching the required data from the L1 data cache and temporarily storing results in registers.
- **Memory subsystem:** This unit includes the L2 cache and the system bus, which is used to access main memory when the L1 and L2 caches have a cache miss, and to access the system I/O resources.

Unlike the organization used in all previous Pentium models, and in most other processors, the Pentium 4 instruction cache sits between the instruction decode logic and the execution core. The reasoning behind this design decision is as follows. As discussed more fully in Chapter 14, the Pentium process decodes, or translates, Pentium machine instructions into simple RISC-like instructions called micro-operations. The use of simple, fixed-length micro-operations enables the use of superscalar pipelining and scheduling techniques that enhance performance. However, the Pentium machine

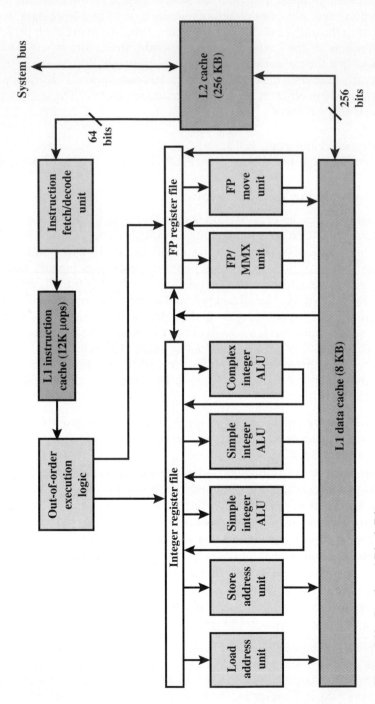

Figure 4.13 Pentium 4 Block Diagram

Table 4.4 Pentium 4 Cache Operating Modes

Control Bits		Operating Mode		
CD	NW	Cache Fills	Write Throughs	Invalidates
0	0	Enabled	Enabled	Enabled
1	0	Disabled	Enabled	Enabled
1	1	Disabled	Disabled	Disabled

Note: CD = 0; NW = 1 is an invalid combination.

instructions are cumbersome to decode; they have a variable number of bytes and many different options. It turns out that performance is enhanced if this decoding is done independently of the scheduling and pipelining logic. We return to this topic in Chapter 14.

The data cache employs a write-back policy: Data are written to main memory only when they are removed from the cache and there has been an update. The Pentium 4 processor can be dynamically configured to support write-through caching.

The L1 data cache is controlled by two bits in one of the control registers, labeled the CD (cache disable) and NW (not write-through) bits (Table 4.4). There are also two Pentium 4 instructions that can be used to control the data cache: INVD invalidates (flushes) the internal cache memory and signals the external cache (if any) to invalidate. WBINVD writes back and invalidates internal cache, then writes back and invalidates external cache.

PowerPC Cache Organization

The PowerPC cache organization has evolved with the overall architecture of the PowerPC family, reflecting the relentless pursuit of performance that is the driving force for all microprocessor designers.

Table 4.5 shows this evolution. The original model, the 601, includes a single code/data 32-KByte cache that is eight-way set associative. The 603 employs a more sophisticated RISC design but has a smaller cache: 16 KBytes divided into separate instruction and data caches, both using two-way set associative organization. The result is that the 603 gives approximately the same performance as the 601 at lower cost. The 604 and 620 each doubled the size of the caches from the preceding model. The G3 and G4 models has the same size L1 caches as the 620.

Figure 4.14 provides a simplified view of the PowerPC G4 organization, highlighting the placement of the two caches. The core execution units are two integer

Table 4.5 PowerPC Internal Caches

Model	Size	Bytes/Line	Organization
PowerPC 601	1 32-Kbyte	32	8-way set associative
PowerPC 603	2 8-Kbyte	32	2-way set associative
PowerPC 604	2 16-Kbyte	32	4-way set associative
PowerPC 620	2 32-Kbyte	64	8-way set associative
PowerPC G3	2 32-Kbyte	64	8-way set associative
PowerPC G4	2 32-Kbyte	32	8-way set associative

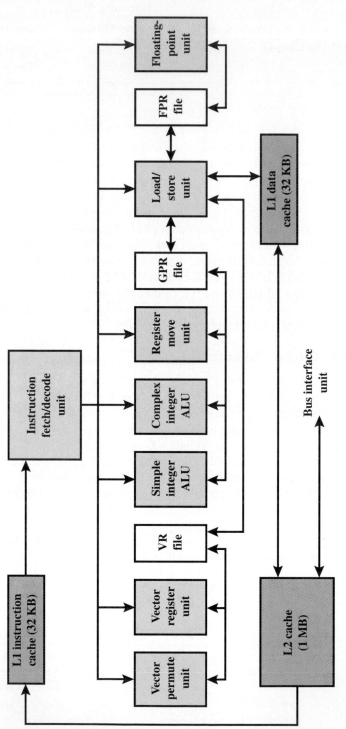

Figure 4.14 PowerPC G4 Block Diagram

124

arithmetic and logic units, which can execute in parallel, and a floating-point unit with its own registers and its own multiply, add, and divide components. The data cache feeds both integer and floating-point operations via a load/store unit. The instruction cache, which is read only, feeds into an instruction unit, whose operation is discussed in Chapter 14.

The L1 caches are eight-way set associative. The L2 cache is a two-way set associative cache with 256K, 512K, or 1MB of memory.

4.5 RECOMMENDED READING

A thorough treatment of cache design is to be found in [HAND98]. A discussion of Pentium 4 cache organization can be found in [HINT01] and of PowerPC G4 cache organization in [MOTO01]. A classic paper that is still well worth reading is [SMIT82]; it surveys the various elements of cache design and presents the results of an extensive set of analyses. [AGAR89] presents a detailed examination of a variety of cache design issues related to multiprogramming and multiprocessing. [HIGB90] provides a set of simple formulas that can be used to estimate cache performance as a function of various cache parameters.

AGAR89   Agarwal, A. *Analysis of Cache Performance for Operating Systems and Multi-programming.* Boston: Kluwer Academic Publishers, 1989.

HAND98   Handy, J. *The Cache Memory Book.* San Diego: Academic Press, 1993.

HIGB90   Higbie, L. "Quick and Easy Cache Performance Analysis." *Computer Architecture News,* June 1990.

HINT01   Hinton, G., et al. "The Microarchitecture of the Pentium 4 Processor." *Intel Technology Journal,* Q1 2001. http://developer.intel.com/technology/itj/

MOTO01   Motorola, Inc. *PowerPC MPC7410 RISC Microprocessor Hardware Specifications.* Denver, CO: 2001. www.motorola.com

SMIT82   Smith, A. "Cache Memories." *ACM Computing Surveys,* September 1992.

4.6 KEY TERMS, REVIEW QUESTIONS, AND PROBLEMS

Key Terms

access time	hit ratio	sequential access
associative mapping	instruction cache	set-associative mapping
cache hit	L1 cache	spatial locality
cache line	L2 cache	split cache
cache memory	L3 cache	tag
cache miss	locality	temporal locality
cache set	memory hierarchy	unified cache
data cache	multilevel cache	write back
direct access	random access	write once
direct mapping	replacement algorithm	write through
high performance computing (HPC)		

Review Questions

4.1 What are the differences among sequential access, direct access, and random access?

4.2 What is the general relationship among access time, memory cost, and capacity?

4.3 How does the principle of locality relate to the use of multiple memory levels?

4.4 What are the differences among direct mapping, associative mapping, and set-associative mapping?

4.5 For a direct-mapped cache, a main memory address is viewed as consisting of three fields. List and define the three fields.

4.6 For an associative cache, a main memory address is viewed as consisting of two fields. List and define the two fields.

4.7 For a set-associative cache, a main memory address is viewed as consisting of three fields. List and define the three fields.

4.8 What is the distinction between spatial locality and temporal locality?

4.9 In general, what are the strategies for exploiting spatial locality and temporal locality?

Problems

4.1 A set associative cache consists of 64 lines, or slots, divided into four-line sets. Main memory contains 4K blocks of 128 words each. Show the format of main memory addresses.

4.2 For the hexadecimal main memory addresses 111111, 666666, BBBBBB, show the following information, in hexadecimal format:

    a. Tag, Line, and Word values for a direct-mapped cache, using the format of Figure 4.8.

    b. Tag and Word values for an associative cache, using the format of Figure 4.10.

    c. Tag, Set, and Word values for a two-way set associative cache, using the format of Figure 4.12.

4.3 List the following values:

    a. For the direct cache example of Figure 4.8: address length, number of addressable units, block size, number of blocks in main memory, number of lines in cache, size of tag.

    b. For the associative cache example of Figure 4.10: address length, number of addressable units, block size, number of blocks in main memory, number of lines in cache, size of tag.

    c. For the two-way associative cache example of Figure 4.12: address length, number of addressable units, block size, number of blocks in main memory, number of lines in set, number of sets, number of lines in cache, size of tag.

4.4 Consider a 32-bit microprocessor that has an on-chip 16 KByte four-way set-associative cache. Assume that the cache has a line size of four 32-bit words. Draw a block diagram of this cache showing its organization and how the different address fields are used to determine a cache hit/miss. Where in the cache is the word from memory location ABCDE8F8 mapped?

Source: [ALEX93]

4.5 Given the following specifications for an external cache memory: four-way set associative; line size of two 16-bit words; able to accommodate a total of 4K 32-bit words from main memory; used with a 16-bit processor that issues 24-bit addresses. Design the cache structure with all pertinent information and show how it interprets the processor's addresses.

Source: [ALEX93]

4.6 The Intel 80486 has an on-chip, unified cache. It contains 8 KBytes and has a four-way set associative organization and a block length of four 32-bit words. The cache is organized into 128 sets. There is a single "line valid bit" and three bits, B0, B1, and

B2 (the "LRU" bits), per line. On a cache miss, the 80486 reads a 16-byte line from main memory in a bus memory read burst. Draw a simplified diagram of the cache and show how the different fields of the address are interpreted.

Source: [ALEX93]

4.7 Consider a machine with a byte addressable main memory of 2^{16} bytes and block size of 8 bytes. Assume that a direct mapped cache consisting of 32 lines is used with this machine.

   a. How is a 16-bit memory address divided into tag, line number, and byte number?

   b. Into what line would bytes with each of the following addresses be stored?

   0001 0001 0001 1011
   1100 0011 0011 0100
   1101 0000 0001 1101
   1010 1010 1010 1010

   c. Suppose the byte with address 0001 1010 0001 1010 is stored in the cache. What are the addresses of the other bytes stored along with it?

   d. How many total bytes of memory can be stored in the cache?

   e. Why is the tag also stored in the cache?

4.8 For its on-chip cache, the Intel 80486 uses a replacement algorithm referred to as **pseudo least recently used**. Associated with each of the 128 sets of four lines (labeled L0, L1, L2, L3) are three bits B0, B1, and B2. The replacement algorithm works as follows: When a line must be replaced, the cache will first determine whether the most recent use was from L0 and L1 or L2 and L3. Then the cache will determine which of the pair of blocks was least recently used and mark it for replacement. Figure 4.15 illustrates the logic.

   a. Specify how the bits B0, B1, and B2 are set and then describe in words how they are used in the replacement algorithm depicted in Figure 4.15.

   b. Show that the 80486 algorithm approximates a true LRU algorithm. *Hint:* Consider the case in which the most recent order of usage is L0, L2, L3, L1.

   c. Demonstrate that a true LRU algorithm would require 6 bits per set.

4.9 A set associative cache has a block size of four 16-bit words and a set size of 2. The cache can accommodate a total of 4048 words. The main memory size that is cacheable is 64K × 32 bits. Design the cache structure and show how the processor's addresses are interpreted.

Source: [ALEX93]

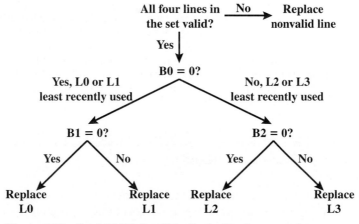

Figure 4.15   Intel 80486 On-Chip Cache Replacement Strategy

4.10 Consider a memory system that uses a 32-bit address to address at the byte level, plus a cache that uses a 64-byte line size.

   a. Assume a direct mapped cache with a tag field in the address of 20 bits. Show the address format and determine the following parameters: number of addressable units, number of blocks in main memory, number of lines in cache, size of tag.

   b. Assume an associative cache. Show the address format and determine the following parameters: number of addressable units, number of blocks in main memory, number of lines in cache, size of tag.

   c. Assume a 4-way set associative cache with a tag field in the address of 9 bits. Show the address format and determine the following parameters: number of addressable units, number of blocks in main memory, number of lines in set, number of sets in cache, number of lines in cache, size of tag.

4.11 Describe a simple technique for implementing an LRU replacement algorithm in a four-way set associative cache.

4.12 Consider the following code:

```
for (i = 0; i < 20; i++)
    for (j = 0; j < 10; j++)
        a[i] = a[i] * j
```

   a. Give one example of the spatial locality in the code.

   b. Give one example of the temporal locality in the code.

4.13 Generalize Equations (4.1) and (4.2), in Appendix 4A, to N-level memory hierarchies.

4.14 A computer system contains a main memory of 32K 16-bit words. It also has a 4K-word cache divided into four-line sets with 64 words per line. Assume that the cache is initially empty. The processor fetches words from location s $0, 1, 2, \ldots, 4351$ in that order. It then repeats this fetch sequence nine more times. The cache is 10 times faster than main memory. Estimate the improvement resulting from the use of the cache. Assume an LRU policy for block replacement.

4.15 Consider a memory system with the following parameters:

$$T_c = 100 \text{ ns} \qquad C_c = 0.01 \text{ ¢/bit}$$
$$T_m = 1,200 \text{ ns} \qquad C_m = 0.001 \text{ ¢/bit}$$

   a. What is the cost of 1 MByte of main memory?

   b. What is the cost of 1 MByte of main memory using cache memory technology?

   c. If the effective access time is 10% greater than the cache access time, what is the hit ratio H?

4.16 A computer has a cache, main memory, and a disk used for virtual memory. If a referenced word is in the cache, 20 ns are required to access it. If it is in main memory but not in the cache, 60 ns are needed to load it into the cache, and then the reference is started again. If the word is not in main memory, 12 ms are required to fetch the word from disk, followed by 60 ns to copy it to the cache, and then the reference is started again. The cache hit ratio is 0.9 and the main memory hit ratio is 0.6. What is the average time in ns required to access a referenced word on this system?

APPENDIX 4A   PERFORMANCE CHARACTERISTICS OF TWO-LEVEL MEMORIES

In this chapter, reference is made to a cache that acts as a buffer between main memory and processor, creating a two-level internal memory. This two-level architecture provides improved performance over a comparable one-level memory, by exploiting a property known as locality, which is explored in this appendix.

Table 4.6 Characteristics of Two-Level Memories

	Cache	Virtual Memory (Paging)	Disk Cache
Typical access time ratios	40/1 (on-chip cache to main memory) 10/1 (off ship cache to main memory)	10,000/1 (main memory to disk)	10,000/1 (main memory to disk)
Memory management system	Implemented by special hardware	Combination of hardware and system software	System software
Typical block size	4 to 128 bytes	64 to 4096 bytes	64 to 4096 bytes
Access of processor to second level	Direct access	Indirect access	Indirect access

The main memory cache mechanism is part of the computer architecture, implemented in hardware and typically invisible to the operating system. There are two other instances of a two-level memory approach that also exploit locality and that are, at least partially, implemented in the operating system: virtual memory and the disk cache (Table 4.6). Virtual memory is explored in Chapter 8; disk cache is beyond the scope of this book but is examined in [STAL01]. In this appendix, we look at some of the performance characteristics of two-level memories that are common to all three approaches.

Locality

The basis for the performance advantage of a two-level memory is a principle known as *locality of reference* [DENN68]. This principle states that memory references tend to cluster. Over a long period of time, the clusters in use change, but over a short period of time, the processor is primarily working with fixed clusters of memory references.

From an intuitive point of view, the principle of locality makes sense. Consider the following line of reasoning:

1. Except for branch and call instructions, which constitute only a small fraction of all program instructions, program execution is sequential. Hence, in most cases, the next instruction to be fetched immediately follows the last instruction fetched.
2. It is rare to have a long uninterrupted sequence of procedure calls followed by the corresponding sequence of returns. Rather, a program remains confined to a rather narrow window of procedure-invocation depth. Thus, over a short period of time references to instructions tend to be localized to a few procedures.
3. Most iterative constructs consist of a relatively small number of instructions repeated many times. For the duration of the iteration, computation is therefore confined to a small contiguous portion of a program.
4. In many programs, much of the computation involves processing data structures, such as arrays or sequences of records. In many cases, successive references to these data structures will be to closely located data items.

Table 4.7   Relative Dynamic Frequency of High-Level Language Operations

Study	[HUCK83]	[KNUT71]	[PATT82]		[TANE78]
Language	Pascal	FORTRAN	Pascal	C	SAL
Workload	Scientific	Student	System	System	System
Assign	74	67	45	38	42
Loop	4	3	5	3	4
Call	1	3	15	12	12
IF	20	11	29	43	36
GOTO	2	9	—	3	—
Other	—	7	6	1	6

This line of reasoning has been confirmed in many studies. With reference to point 1, a variety of studies have analyzed the behavior of high-level language programs. Table 4.7 includes key results, measuring the appearance of various statement types during execution, from the following studies. The earliest study of programming language behavior, performed by Knuth [KNUT71], examined a collection of FORTRAN programs used as student exercises. Tanenbaum [TANE78] published measurements collected from over 300 procedures used in operating-system programs and written in a language that supports structured programming (SAL). Patterson and Sequein [PATT82a] analyzed a set of measurements taken from compilers and programs for typesetting, computer-aided design (CAD), sorting, and file comparison. The programming languages C and Pascal were studied. Huck [HUCK83] analyzed four programs intended to represent a mix of general-purpose scientific computing, including fast Fourier transform and the integration of systems of differential equations. There is good agreement in the results of this mixture of languages and applications that branching and call instructions represent only a fraction of statements executed during the lifetime of a program. Thus, these studies confirm assertion 1.

With respect to assertion 2, studies reported in [PATT85a] provide confirmation. This is illustrated in Figure 4.16, which shows call-return behavior. Each call is represented by the line moving down and to the right, and each return by the line moving up and to the right. In the figure, a *window* with depth equal to 5 is defined. Only a sequence of calls and returns with a net movement of 6 in either direction causes the window to move. As can be seen, the executing program can remain within a stationary window for long periods of time. A study by the same analysts of C and Pascal programs showed that a window of depth 8 will need to shift only on less than 1% of the calls or returns [TAMI83].

The principle of locality of reference continues to be validated in more recent studies. For example, Figure 4.17 illustrates the results of a study of Web page access patterns at a single site.

A distinction is made in the literature between spatial locality and temporal locality. **Spatial locality** refers to the tendency of execution to involve a number of memory locations that are clustered. This reflects the tendency of a processor to access instructions sequentially. Spatial location also reflects the tendency of a program to access data locations sequentially, such as when processing a table of data. **Temporal locality** refers to the tendency for a processor to access memory locations

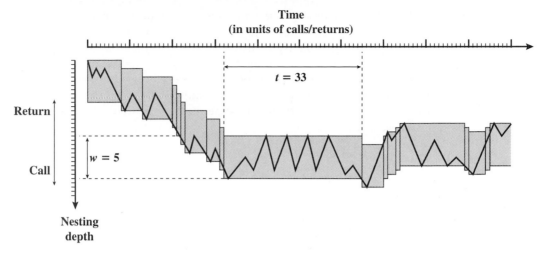

Figure 4.16 Example Call-Return Behavior of a Program

that have been used recently. For example, when an iteration loop is executed, the processor executes the same set of instructions repeatedly.

Traditionally, temporal locality is exploited by keeping recently used instruction and data values in cache memory and by exploiting a cache hierarchy. Spatial locality is generally exploited by using larger cache blocks and by incorporating prefetching mechanisms (fetching items of anticipated use) into the cache control logic. Recently, there has been considerable research on refining these techniques to achieve greater performance, but the basic strategies remain the same.

Operation of Two-Level Memory

The locality property can be exploited in the formation of a two-level memory. The upper-level memory (M1) is smaller, faster, and more expensive (per bit) than the lower-level memory (M2). M1 is used as a temporary store for part of the contents

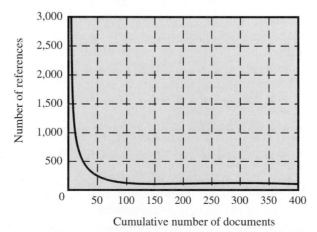

Figure 4.17 Locality of Reference for Web Pages [BAEN97]

of the larger M2. When a memory reference is made, an attempt is made to access the item in M1. If this succeeds, then a quick access is made. If not, then a block of memory locations is copied from M2 to M1 and the access then takes place via M1. Because of locality, once a block is brought into M1, there should be a number of accesses to locations in that block, resulting in fast overall service.

To express the average time to access an item, we must consider not only the speeds of the two levels of memory, but also the probability that a given reference can be found in M1. We have

$$T_s = H \times T_1 + (1 - H) \times (T_1 + T_2)$$
$$= T_1 + (1 - H) \times T_2 \qquad (4.1)$$

where

T_s = average (system) access time
T_1 = access time of M1 (e.g., cache, disk cache)
T_2 = access time of M2 (e.g., main memory, disk)
H = hit ratio (fraction of time reference is found in M1)

Figure 4.2 shows average access time as a function of hit ratio. As can be seen, for a high percentage of hits, the average total access time is much closer to that of M1 than M2.

Performance

Let us look at some of the parameters relevant to an assessment of a two-level memory mechanism. First consider cost. We have

$$C_S = \frac{C_1 S_1 + C_2 S_2}{S_1 + S_2} \qquad (4.2)$$

where

C_s = average cost per bit for the combined two-level memory
C_1 = average cost per bit of upper-level memory M1
C_2 = average cost per bit of lower-level memory M2
S_1 = size of M1
S_2 = size of M2

We would like $C_s \approx C_2$. Given that $C_1 \gg C_2$, this requires $S_1 \ll S_2$. Figure 4.18 shows the relationship.

Next, consider access time. For a two-level memory to provide a significant performance improvement, we need to have T_s approximately equal to T_1 ($T_s \approx T_1$). Given that T_1 is much less than T_2 ($T_1 \ll T_2$), a hit ratio of close to 1 is needed.

So we would like M1 to be small to hold down cost, and large to improve the hit ratio and therefore the performance. Is there a size of M1 that satisfies both requirements to a reasonable extent? We can answer this question with a series of subquestions:

- What value of hit ratio is needed so that $T_s \approx T_1$?
- What size of M1 will assure the needed hit ratio?
- Does this size satisfy the cost requirement?

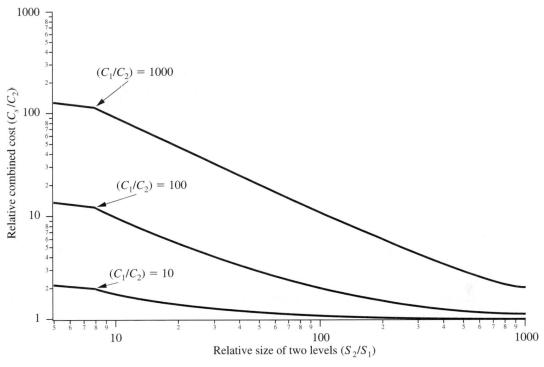

Figure 4.18 Relationship of Average Memory Cost to Relative Memory Size for a Two-Level Memory

To get at this, consider the quantity T_1 / T_s, which is referred to as the *access efficiency*. It is a measure of how close average access time (T_s) is to M1 access time (T_1). From Equation (4.1),

$$\frac{T_1}{T_s} = \frac{1}{1 + (1 - H)\dfrac{T_2}{T_1}} \tag{4.3}$$

In Figure 4.19, we plot T_1 / T_s as a function of the hit ratio H, with the quantity T_2 / T_1 as a parameter. Typically, on-chip cache access time is about 25 to 50 times faster than main memory access time (i.e., T_2 / T_1 is 5 to 10), off-chip cache access time is about 5 or 15 times faster than main memory access time (i.e., T_2 / T_1 is 5 to 15),[6] and main memory access time is about 1000 times faster than disk access time $(T_2 / T_1 = 1000)$. Thus, a hit ratio in the range of near 0.9 would seem to be needed to satisfy the performance requirement.

---

[6]For example, at the time of this writing, for the Pentium 4, on-chip cache access time is 1 ns for data cache, 2 ns for instruction cache, and 3.5 ns for L2 cache; main memory access time is 30 ns. For the Itanium, on chip cache access time is 2 ns for L1 cache and 6 ns for L2 cache; off-chip access time for L3 cache is 21 ns; main memory access time is 50 ns.

We can now phrase the question about relative memory size more exactly. Is a hit ratio of, say, 0.8 or better reasonable for $S_1 << S_2$? This will depend on a number of factors, including the nature of the software being executed and the details of the design of the two-level memory. The main determinant is, of course, the degree of locality. Figure 4.20 suggests the effect that locality has on the hit ratio. Clearly, if M1 is the same size as M2, then the hit ratio will be 1.0: All of the items in M2 are always stored also in M1. Now suppose that there is no locality; that is, references are completely random. In that case the hit ratio should be a strictly linear function of the relative memory size. For example, if M1 is half the size of M2, then at any time half of the items from M2 are also in M1 and the hit ratio will be 0.5. In practice, however, there is some degree of locality in the references. The effects of moderate and strong locality are indicated in the figure.

So if there is strong locality, it is possible to achieve high values of hit ratio even with relatively small upper-level memory size. For example, numerous studies have shown that rather small cache sizes will yield a hit ratio above 0.75 *regardless of the size of main memory* (e.g., [AGAR89], [PRZY88], [STRE83], and [SMIT82]). A cache in the range of 1K to 128K words is generally adequate, whereas main memory is now typically in the multiple-megabyte range. When we consider virtual memory and disk cache, we will cite other studies that confirm the same phenomenon, namely that a relatively small M1 yields a high value of hit ratio because of locality.

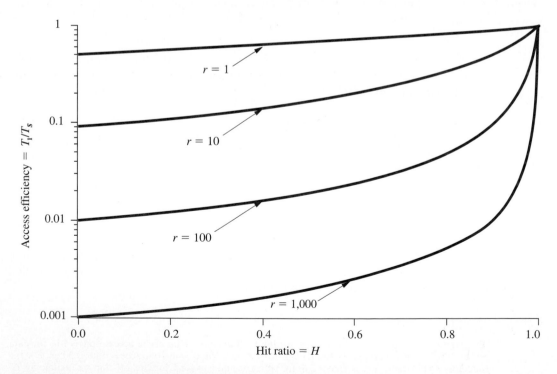

Figure 4.19 Access Efficiency as a Function of hit Ratio ($r = T_2/T_1$)

Figure 4.20   Hit Ratio as a Function of Relative Memory Size

This brings us to the last question listed earlier: Does the relative size of the two memories satisfy the cost requirement? The answer is clearly yes. If we need only a relatively small upper-level memory to achieve good performance, then the average cost per bit of the two levels of memory will approach that of the cheaper lower-level memory.

Please note that with L2 cache, or even L2 and L3 caches, involved, analysis is much more complex. See [PEIR99] and [HAND98] for discussions.

CHAPTER **5**

INTERNAL MEMORY

KEY POINTS

◆ The two basic forms of semiconductor random-access memory are dynamic RAM (DRAM) and static RAM (SRAM). SRAM is faster, more expensive, and less dense than DRAM, and is used for cache memory. DRAM is used for main memory.

◆ Error correction techniques are commonly used in memory systems. These involve adding redundant bits that are a function of the data bits to form an error-correcting code. If a bit error occurs, the code will detect and, usually, correct the error.

◆ To compensate for the relatively slow speed of DRAM, a number of advanced DRAM organizations have been introduced. The two most common are synchronous DRAM and RamBus DRAM. Both of these involve using the system clock to provide for the transfer of blocks of data.

This chapter begins with a survey of semiconductor main memory subsystems, including ROM, DRAM, and SRAM memories. Then we look at error control techniques used to enhance memory reliability. Following this, we look at more advanced DRAM architectures.

5.1   SEMICONDUCTOR MAIN MEMORY

In earlier computers, the most common form of random-access storage for computer main memory employed an array of doughnut-shaped ferromagnetic loops referred to as *cores*. Hence, main memory was often referred to as *core,* a term that persists to this day. The advent of, and advantages of, microelectronics has long since vanquished the magnetic core memory. Today, the use of semiconductor chips for main memory is almost universal. Key aspects of this technology are explored in this section.

Organization

The basic element of a semiconductor memory is the memory cell. Although a variety of electronic technologies are used, all semiconductor memory cells share certain properties:

- They exhibit two stable (or semistable) states, which can be used to represent binary 1 and 0.
- They are capable of being written into (at least once), to set the state.
- They are capable of being read to sense the state.

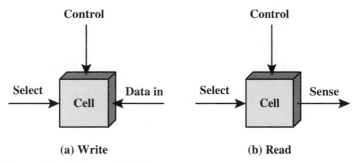

Figure 5.1 Memory Cell Operation

Figure 5.1 depicts the operation of a memory cell. Most commonly, the cell has three functional terminals capable of carrying an electrical signal. The select terminal, as the name suggests, selects a memory cell for a read or write operation. The control terminal indicates read or write. For writing, the other terminal provides an electrical signal that sets the state of the cell to 1 or 0. For reading, that terminal is used for output of the cell's state. The details of the internal organization, functioning, and timing of the memory cell depend on the specific integrated circuit technology used and are beyond the scope of this book, except for a brief summary. For our purposes, we will take it as given that individual cells can be selected for reading and writing operations.

DRAM and SRAM

All of the memory types that we will explore in this chapter are random access. That is, individual words of memory are directly accessed through wired-in addressing logic.

Table 5.1 lists the major types of semiconductor memory. The most common is referred to as *random-access memory* (RAM). This is, of course, a misuse of the term, because all of the types listed in the table are random access. One distinguishing characteristic of RAM is that it is possible both to read data from the memory and to write new data into the memory easily and rapidly. Both the reading and writing are accomplished through the use of electrical signals.

The other distinguishing characteristic of RAM is that it is volatile. A RAM must be provided with a constant power supply. If the power is interrupted, then the data are lost. Thus, RAM can be used only as temporary storage. The two traditional forms of RAM used in computers are DRAM and SRAM.

Dynamic RAM

RAM technology is divided into two technologies: dynamic and static. A dynamic RAM (DRAM) is made with cells that store data as charge on capacitors. The presence or absence of charge on a capacitor is interpreted as a binary 1 or 0. Because capacitors have a natural tendency to discharge, dynamic RAMs require periodic charge refreshing to maintain data storage. The term *dynamic* refers to this tendency of the stored charge to leak away, even with power continuously applied.

Table 5.1   Semiconductor Memory Types

Memory Type	Category	Erasure	Write Mechanism	Volatility
Random-access memory (RAM)	Read-write memory	Electrically, byte level	Electrically	Volatile
Read-only memory (ROM)	Read-only memory	Not possible	Masks	Nonvolatile
Programmable ROM (PROM)				
Erasable PROM (EPROM)	Read-mostly memory	UV light, chip level	Electrically	
Electrically Erasable PROM (EEPROM)		Electrically, byte level		
Flash memory		Electrically, block level		

Figure 5.2a is a typical DRAM structure for an individual cell that stores one bit. The address line is activated when the bit value from this cell is to be read or written. The transistor acts as a switch that is closed (allowing current to flow) if a voltage is applied to the address line and open (no current flows) if no voltage is present on the address line.

For the write operation, a voltage signal is applied to the bit line; a high voltage represents 1, and a low voltage represents 0. A signal is then applied to the address line, allowing a charge to be transferred to the capacitor.

For the read operation, when the address line is selected, the transistor turns on and the charge stored on the capacitor is fed out onto a bit line and to a sense amplifier. The sense amplifier compares the capacitor voltage to a reference value and determines if the cell contains a logic 1 or a logic 0. The read out from the cell discharges the capacitor, which must be restored to complete the operation.

Although the DRAM cell is used to store a single bit (0 or 1), it is essentially an analog device. The capacitor can store any charge value within a range; a threshold value determines whether the charge is interpreted as 1 or 0.

Static RAM

In contrast, a static RAM (SRAM) is a digital device, using the same logic elements used in the processor. In a SRAM, binary values are stored using traditional flip-flop logic-gate configurations (see Appendix A for a description of flip-flops). A static RAM will hold its data as long as power is supplied to it.

Figure 5.2b is a typical SRAM structure for an individual cell. Four transistors (T_1, T_2, T_3, T_4) are cross connected in an arrangement that produces a stable logical state. In logic state 1, point C_1 is high and point C_2 is low; in this state, T_1 and T_4 are off and T_2 and T_3 are on.[1] In logic state 0, point C_1 is low and point C_2 is high; in

---

[1]The circles at the head of T_3 and T_4 indicate signal negation.

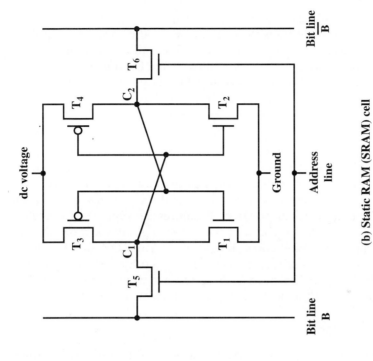

(b) Static RAM (SRAM) cell

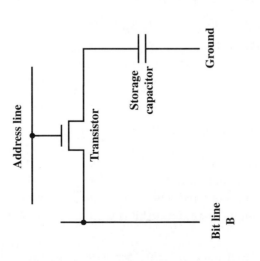

(a) Dynamic RAM (DRAM) cell

Figure 5.2 Typical Memory Cell Structures

this state, T_1 and T_4 are on and T_2 and T_3 are off. Both states are stable as long as the direct current (dc) voltage is applied. Unlike the DRAM, no refresh is needed to retain data.

As in the DRAM, the address line is used to open or close a switch. The address line controls two transistors (T_5 and T_6). When a signal is applied to this line, the two transistors are switch on, allowing a read or write operation. For a write operation, the desired bit value is applied to line B, while its complement is applied to line $\bar{B}$. This forces the four transistors (T_1, T_2, T_3, T_4) into the proper state. For a read operation, the bit value is read from line B.

SRAM versus DRAM

Both static and dynamic RAMs are volatile; that is, power must be continuously supplied to the memory to preserve the bit values. A dynamic memory cell is simpler and smaller than a static memory cell. Thus, a DRAM is more dense (smaller cells = more cells per unit area) and less expensive than a corresponding SRAM. On the other hand, a DRAM requires the supporting refresh circuitry. For larger memories, the fixed cost of the refresh circuitry is more than compensated for by the smaller variable cost of DRAM cells. Thus, DRAMs tend to be favored for large memory requirements. A final point is that SRAMs are generally somewhat faster than DRAMs. Because of these relative characteristics, SRAM is used for cache memory (both on and off chip), and DRAM is used for main memory.

Types of ROM

As the name suggests, a **read-only memory** (ROM) contains a permanent pattern of data that cannot be changed. A ROM is nonvolatile; that is, no power source is required to maintain the bit values in memory. While it is possible to read a ROM, it is not possible to write new data into it. An important application of ROMs is microprogramming, discussed in Part Four. Other potential applications include

- Library subroutines for frequently wanted functions
- System programs
- Function tables

For a modest-sized requirement, the advantage of ROM is that the data or program is permanently in main memory and need never be loaded from a secondary storage device.

A ROM is created like any other integrated circuit chip, with the data actually wired into the chip as part of the fabrication process. This presents two problems:

- The data insertion step includes a relatively large fixed cost, whether one or thousands of copies of a particular ROM are fabricated.
- There is no room for error. If one bit is wrong, the whole batch of ROMs must be thrown out.

When only a small number of ROMs with a particular memory content is needed, a less expensive alternative is the **programmable ROM** (PROM). Like the ROM, the PROM is nonvolatile and may be written into only once. For the PROM, the writing process is performed electrically and may be performed by a supplier or customer at a time later than the original chip fabrication. Special equipment is required for the writing or "programming" process. PROMs provide flexibility and convenience. The ROM remains attractive for high-volume production runs.

Another variation on read-only memory is the read-mostly memory, which is useful for applications in which read operations are far more frequent than write operations but for which nonvolatile storage is required. There are three common forms of read-mostly memory: EPROM, EEPROM, and flash memory.

The optically **erasable programmable read-only memory** (EPROM) is read and written electrically, as with PROM. However, before a write operation, all the storage cells must be erased to the same initial state by exposure of the packaged chip to ultraviolet radiation. Erasure is performed by shining an intense ultraviolet light through a window that is designed into the memory chip. This erasure process can be performed repeatedly; each erasure can take as much as 20 minutes to perform. Thus, the EPROM can be altered multiple times and, like the ROM and PROM, holds its data virtually indefinitely. For comparable amounts of storage, the EPROM is more expensive than PROM, but it has the advantage of the multiple update capability.

A more attractive form of read-mostly memory is **electrically erasable programmable read-only memory** (EEPROM). This is a read-mostly memory that can be written into at any time without erasing prior contents; only the byte or bytes addressed are updated. The write operation takes considerably longer than the read operation, on the order of several hundred microseconds per byte. The EEPROM combines the advantage of nonvolatility with the flexibility of being updatable in place, using ordinary bus control, address, and data lines. EEPROM is more expensive than EPROM and also is less dense, supporting fewer bits per chip.

Another form of semiconductor memory is **flash memory** (so named because of the speed with which it can be reprogrammed). First introduced in the mid-1980s, flash memory is intermediate between EPROM and EEPROM in both cost and functionality. Like EEPROM, flash memory uses an electrical erasing technology. An entire flash memory can be erased in one or a few seconds, which is much faster than EPROM. In addition, it is possible to erase just blocks of memory rather than an entire chip. Flash memory gets its name because the microchip is organized so that a section of memory cells are erased in a single action or "flash." However, flash memory does not provide byte-level erasure. Like EPROM, flash memory uses only one transistor per bit, and so achieves the high density (compared with EEPROM) of EPROM.

Chip Logic

As with other integrated circuit products, semiconductor memory comes in packaged chips (Figure 2.7). Each chip contains an array of memory cells.

In the memory hierarchy as a whole, we saw that there are trade-offs among speed, capacity, and cost. These trade-offs also exist when we consider the organization of memory cells and functional logic on a chip. For semiconductor memories, one of the key design issues is the number of bits of data that may be read/written at a time. At one extreme is an organization in which the physical arrangement of cells in the array is the same as the logical arrangement (as perceived by the processor) of words in memory. The array is organized into W words of B bits each. For example, a 16-Mbit chip could be organized as 1M 16-bit words. At the other extreme is the so-called one-bit-per-chip organization, in which data is read/written one bit at a time. We will illustrate memory chip organization with a DRAM; ROM organization is similar, though simpler.

Figure 5.3 shows a typical organization of a 16-Mbit DRAM. In this case, 4 bits are read or written at a time. Logically, the memory array is organized as four square arrays of 2048 by 2048 elements. Various physical arrangements are possible. In any case, the elements of the array are connected by both horizontal (row) and vertical (column) lines. Each horizontal line connects to the Select terminal of each cell in its row; each vertical line connects to the Data-In/Sense terminal of each cell in its column.

Address lines supply the address of the word to be selected. A total of $\log_2 W$ lines are needed. In our example, 11 address lines are needed to select one of 2048 rows. These 11 lines are fed into a row decoder, which has 11 lines of input and 2048 lines for output. The logic of the decoder activates a single one of the 2048 outputs depending on the bit pattern on the 11 input lines ($2^{11} = 2048$).

An additional 11 address lines select one of 2048 columns of 4 bits per column. Four data lines are used for the input and output of 4 bits to and from a data buffer. On input (write), the bit driver of each bit line is activated for a 1 or 0 according to the value of the corresponding data line. On output (read), the value of each bit line is passed through a sense amplifier and presented to the data lines. The row line selects which row of cells is used for reading or writing.

Because only 4 bits are read/written to this DRAM, there must be multiple DRAMs connected to the memory controller to read/write a word of data to the bus.

Note that there are only 11 address lines (A0–A10), half the number you would expect for a 2048 × 2048 array. This is done to save on the number of pins. The 22 required address lines are passed through select logic external to the chip and multiplexed onto the 11 address lines. First, 11 address signals are passed to the chip to define the row address of the array, and then the other 11 address signals are presented for the column address. These signals are accompanied by row address select ($\overline{RAS}$) and column address select ($\overline{CAS}$) signals to provide timing to the chip.

The write enable ($\overline{WE}$) and output enable ($\overline{OE}$) pins determine whether a write or read operation is performed. Two other pins, not shown in Figure 5.3, are ground (Vss) and a voltage source (Vcc).

As an aside, multiplexed addressing plus the use of square arrays result in a quadrupling of memory size with each new generation of memory chips. One more pin devoted to addressing doubles the number of rows and columns, and so the size of the chip memory grows by a factor of 4.

Figure 5.3 also indicates the inclusion of refresh circuitry. All DRAMs require a refresh operation. A simple technique for refreshing is, in effect, to disable the DRAM chip while all data cells are refreshed. The refresh counter steps through all of the row values. For each row, the output lines from the refresh counter are supplied to the row decoder and the RAS line is activated. The data are read out and written back into the same location. This causes each cell in the row to be refreshed.

Chip Packaging

As was mentioned in Chapter 2, an integrated circuit is mounted on a package that contains pins for connection to the outside world.

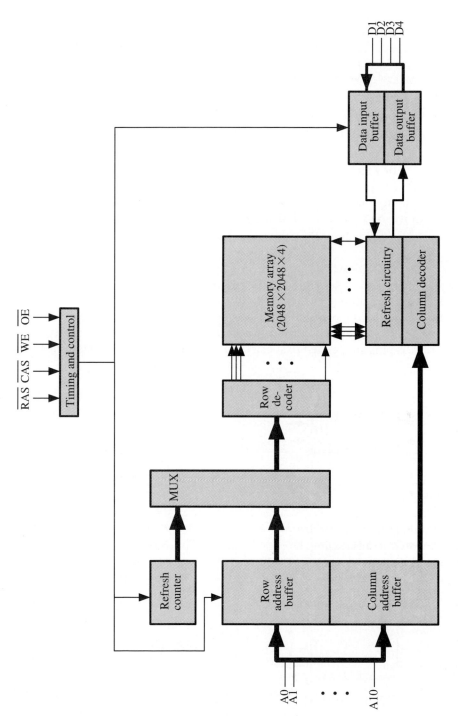

Figure 5.3 Typical 16 Megabit DRAM (4M × 4)

145

Figure 5.4a shows an example EPROM package, which is an 8-Mbit chip organized as 1M × 8. In this case, the organization is treated as a one-word-per-chip package. The package includes 32 pins, which is one of the standard chip package sizes. The pins support the following signal lines:

- The address of the word being accessed. For 1M words, a total of 20 ($2^{20} = 1M$) pins are needed (A0–A19).
- The data to be read out, consisting of 8 lines (D0–D7).
- The power supply to the chip (Vcc).
- A ground pin (Vss).
- A chip enable (CE) pin. Because there may be more than one memory chip, each of which is connected to the same address bus, the CE pin is used to indicate whether or not the address is valid for this chip. The CE pin is activated by logic connected to the higher-order bits of the address bus (i.e., address bits above A19). The use of this signal is illustrated presently.
- A program voltage (Vpp) that is supplied during programming (write operations).

A typical DRAM pin configuration is shown in Figure 5.4b, for a 16-Mbit chip organized as 4M × 4. There are several differences from a ROM chip. Because a RAM can be updated, the data pins are input/output. The write enable (WE) and output enable (OE) pins indicate whether this is a write or read operation. Because the DRAM is accessed by row and column, and the address is multiplexed, only 11 address pins are needed to specify the 4M row/column combinations ($2^{11} \times 2^{11} =$

(a) 8-Mbit EPROM   (b) 16-Mbit DRAM

Figure 5.4 Typical Memory Package Pins and Signals

$2^{22} = 4M$). The functions of the row address select (RAS) and column address select (CAS) pins were discussed previously. Finally, the no connect (NC) pin is provided so that there are an even number of pins.

Module Organization

If a RAM chip contains only 1 bit per word, then clearly we will need at least a number of chips equal to the number of bits per word. As an example, Figure 5.5 shows how a memory module consisting of 256K 8-bit words could be organized. For 256K words, an 18-bit address is needed and is supplied to the module from some external source (e.g., the address lines of a bus to which the module is attached). The

Figure 5.5 256-Kbyte Memory Organization

Figure 5.6 1-Mbyte Memory Organization

address is presented to 8 256K × 1-bit chips, each of which provides the input/output of 1 bit.

This organization works as long as the size of memory equals the number of bits per chip. In the case in which larger memory is required, an array of chips is needed. Figure 5.6 shows the possible organization of a memory consisting of 1M word by 8 bits per word. In this case, we have four columns of chips, each column containing 256K words arranged as in Figure 5.5. For 1M word, 20 address lines are needed. The 18 least significant bits are routed to all 32 modules. The high-order 2 bits are input to a group select logic module that sends a chip enable signal to one of the four columns of modules.

5.2 ERROR CORRECTION

A semiconductor memory system is subject to errors. These can be categorized as hard failures and soft errors. A **hard failure** is a permanent physical defect so that the memory cell or cells affected cannot reliably store data, but become stuck at 0 or 1 or switch erratically between 0 and 1. Hard errors can be caused by harsh environmental abuse, manufacturing defects, and wear. A **soft error** is a random, nondestructive event that alters the contents of one or more memory cells, without damaging the memory. Soft errors can be caused by power supply problems or alpha particles. These particles result from radioactive decay and are distressingly common because radioactive nuclei are found in small quantities in nearly all materials.

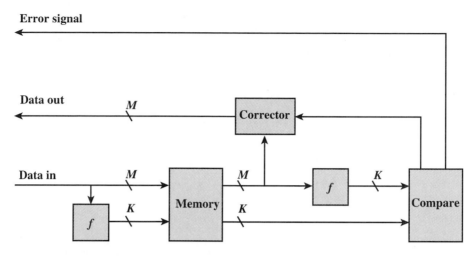

Figure 5.7   Error-Correcting Code Function

Both hard and soft errors are clearly undesirable, and most modern main memory systems include logic for both detecting and correcting errors.

Figure 5.7 illustrates in general terms how the process is carried out. When data are to be read into memory, a calculation, depicted as a function f, is performed on the data to produce a code. Both the code and the data are stored. Thus, if an M-bit word of data is to be stored, and the code is of length K bits, then the actual size of the stored word is $M + K$ bits.

When the previously stored word is read out, the code is used to detect and possibly correct errors. A new set of K code bits is generated from the M data bits and compared with the fetched code bits. The comparison yields one of three results:

- No errors are detected. The fetched data bits are sent out.
- An error is detected, and it is possible to correct the error. The data bits plus error correction bits are fed into a corrector, which produces a corrected set of M bits to be sent out.
- An error is detected, but it is not possible to correct it. This condition is reported.

Codes that operate in this fashion are referred to as *error-correcting codes.* A code is characterized by the number of bit errors in a word that it can correct and detect.

The simplest of the error-correcting codes is the *Hamming code* devised by Richard Hamming at Bell Laboratories. Figure 5.8 uses Venn diagrams to illustrate the use of this code on 4-bit words ($M = 4$). With three intersecting circles, there are seven compartments. We assign the 4 data bits to the inner compartments (Figure 5.8a). The remaining compartments are filled with what are called *parity bits.* Each parity bit is chosen so that the total number of 1s in its circle is even (Figure 5.8b). Thus, because circle A includes three data 1s, the parity bit in that circle is set to 1. Now, if an error changes one of the data bits (Figure 5.8c), it is easily found.

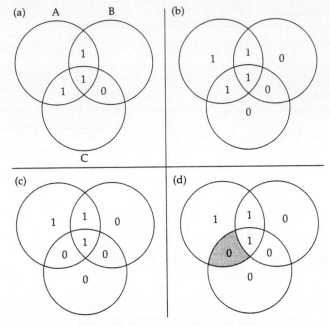

Figure 5.8 Hamming Error-Correcting Code

By checking the parity bits, discrepancies are found in circle A and circle C but not in circle B. Only one of the seven compartments is in A and C but not B. The error can therefore be corrected by changing that bit.

To clarify the concepts involved, we will develop a code that can detect and correct single-bit errors in 8-bit words.

To start, let us determine how long the code must be. Referring to Figure 5.7, the comparison logic receives as input two K-bit values. A bit-by-bit comparison is done by taking the exclusive-or of the two inputs. The result is called the *syndrome word*. Thus, each bit of the syndrome is 0 or 1 according to if there is or is not a match in that bit position for the two inputs.

The syndrome word is therefore K bits wide and has a range between 0 and $2^K - 1$. The value 0 indicates that no error was detected, leaving $2^K - 1$ values to indicate, if there is an error, which bit was in error. Now, because an error could occur on any of the M data bits or K check bits, we must have

$$2^K - 1 \geq M + K$$

This inequality gives the number of bits needed to correct a single bit error in a word containing M data bits. For example, for a word of 8 data bits ($M = 8$), we have

- $K = 3$: $2^3 - 1 < 8 + 3$
- $K = 4$: $2^4 - 1 > 8 + 4$

Thus, eight data bits require four check bits. The first three columns of Table 5.2 lists the number of check bits required for various data word lengths.

Table 5.2   Increase in Word Length with Error Correction

	Single-Error Correction		Single-Error Correction/ Double-Error Detection	
Data Bits	Check Bits	% Increase	Check Bits	% Increase
8	4	50	5	62.5
16	5	31.25	6	37.5
32	6	18.75	7	21.875
64	7	10.94	8	12.5
128	8	6.25	9	7.03
256	9	3.52	10	3.91

For convenience, we would like to generate a 4-bit syndrome for an 8-bit data word with the following characteristics:

- If the syndrome contains all 0s, no error has been detected.
- If the syndrome contains one and only one bit set to 1, then an error has occurred in one of the 4 check bits. No correction is needed.
- If the syndrome contains more than one bit set to 1, then the numerical value of the syndrome indicates the position of the data bit in error. This data bit is inverted for correction.

To achieve these characteristics, the data and check bits are arranged into a 12-bit word as depicted in Figure 5.9. The bit positions are numbered from 1 to 12. Those bit positions whose position numbers are powers of 2 are designated as check bits. The check bits are calculated as follows, where the symbol $\oplus$ designates the exclusive-or operation:

$$
\begin{aligned}
C1 &= D1 \oplus D2 \oplus D4 \oplus D5 \oplus D7 \\
C2 &= D1 \oplus D3 \oplus D4 \oplus D6 \oplus D7 \\
C4 &= D2 \oplus D3 \oplus D4 \oplus D8 \\
C8 &= D5 \oplus D6 \oplus D7 \oplus D8
\end{aligned}
$$

Bit position	12	11	10	9	8	7	6	5	4	3	2	1
Position number	1100	1011	1010	1001	1000	0111	0110	0101	0100	0011	0010	0001
Data bit	D8	D7	D6	D5		D4	D3	D2		D1		
Check bit					C8				C4		C2	C1

Figure 5.9   Layout of Data Bits and Check Bits

Each check bit operates on every data bit whose position number contains a 1 in the same bit position as the position number of that check bit. Thus, data bit positions 3, 5, 7, 9, and 11 (D1, D2, D4, D5, D7) all contain a 1 in the least significant bit of their position number as does C1; bit positions 3, 6, 7, 10, and 11 all contain a 1 in the second bit position, as does C2; and so on. Looked at another way, bit position n is checked by those bits C_i such that $\Sigma i = n$. For example, position 7 is checked by bits in position 4, 2, and 1; and $7 = 4 + 2 + 1$.

Let us verify that this scheme works with an example. Assume that the 8-bit input word is 00111001, with data bit D1 in the rightmost position. The calculations are as follows:

$$C1 = 1 \oplus 0 \oplus 1 \oplus 1 \oplus 0 = 1$$
$$C2 = 1 \oplus 0 \oplus 1 \oplus 1 \oplus 0 = 1$$
$$C4 = 0 \oplus 0 \oplus 1 \oplus 0 = 1$$
$$C8 = 1 \oplus 1 \oplus 0 \oplus 0 = 0$$

Suppose now that data bit 3 sustains an error and is changed from 0 to 1. When the check bits are recalculated, we have

$$C1 = 1 \oplus 0 \oplus 1 \oplus 1 \oplus 0 = 1$$
$$C2 = 1 \oplus 1 \oplus 1 \oplus 1 \oplus 0 = 0$$
$$C4 = 0 \oplus 1 \oplus 1 \oplus 0 = 0$$
$$C8 = 1 \oplus 1 \oplus 0 \oplus 0 = 0$$

When the new check bits are compared with the old check bits, the syndrome word is formed:

	C8	C4	C2	C1
	0	1	1	1
$\oplus$	0	0	0	1
	0	1	1	0

The result is 0110, indicating that bit position 6, which contains data bit 3, is in error.

Figure 5.10 illustrates the preceding calculation. The data and check bits are positioned properly in the 12-bit word. Four of the data bits have a value 1 (shaded in the table), and their bit position values are XORed to produce the Hamming code 0111, which forms the four check digits. The entire block that is stored is 001101001111. Suppose now that data bit 3, in bit position 6, sustains an error and is changed from 0 to 1. The resulting block is 001101101111. The resulting Hamming code is still 0111. An XOR of the Hamming code and all of the bit position values for nonzero data bits results in 0110. The nonzero result detects an error and indicates that the error is in bit position 6.

The code just described is known as a *single-error-correcting* (SEC) code. More commonly, semiconductor memory is equipped with a single-error-correcting, double-error-detecting (SEC-DED) code. As Table 5.2 shows, such codes require one additional bit compared with SEC codes.

Bit position	12	11	10	9	8	7	6	5	4	3	2	1
Position number	1100	1011	1010	1001	1000	0111	0110	0101	0100	0011	0010	0001
Data bit	D8	D7	D6	D5		D4	D3	D2		D1		
Check bit					C8				C4		C2	C1
Word stored as	0	0	1	1	0	1	0	0	1	1	1	1
Word fetched as	0	0	1	1	0	1	1	0	1	1	1	1
Position number	1100	1011	1010	1001	1000	0111	0110	0101	0100	0011	0010	0001
Check bit					0				0		0	1

Figure 5.10 Check Bit Calculation

Figure 5.11 illustrates how such a code works, again with a 4-bit data word. The sequence shows that if two errors occur (Figure 5.11c), the checking procedure goes astray (d) and worsens the problem by creating a third error (e). To overcome the problem, an eighth bit is added that is set so that the total number of 1s in the diagram is even. The extra parity bit catches the error (f).

An error-correcting code enhances the reliability of the memory at the cost of added complexity. With a one-bit-per-chip organization, an SEC-DED code is generally considered adequate. For example, the IBM 30xx implementations use an 8-bit SEC-DED code for each 64 bits of data in main memory. Thus, the size of main memory is actually about 12% larger than is apparent to the user. The VAX computers use a 7-bit SEC-DED for each 32 bits of memory, for a 22% overhead. A number of contemporary DRAMs use 9 check bits for each 128 bits of data, for a 7% overhead [SHAR97].

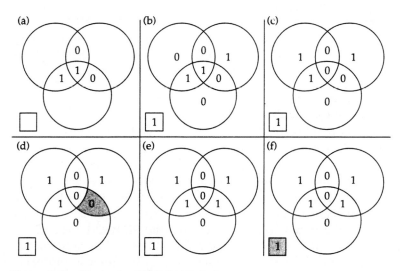

Figure 5.11 Hamming SEC-DEC Code

5.3 ADVANCED DRAM ORGANIZATION

As was discussed in Chapter 2, one of the most critical system bottlenecks when using high-performance processors is the interface to main internal memory. This interface is the most important pathway in the entire computer system. The basic building block of main memory remains the DRAM chip, as it has for decades; until recently, there had been no significant changes in DRAM architecture since the early 1970s. The traditional DRAM chip is constrained both by its internal architecture and by its interface to the processor's memory bus.

We have seen that one attack on the performance problem of DRAM main memory has been to insert one or more levels of high-speed SRAM cache between the DRAM main memory and the processor. But SRAM is much costlier than DRAM, and expanding cache size beyond a certain point yields diminishing returns.

In recent years, a number of enhancements to the basic DRAM architecture have been explored, and some of these are now on the market. The two schemes that currently dominate the market are SDRAM and RDRAM. CDRAM has also received considerable attention. We examine each of these approaches in this section.

Synchronous DRAM

One of the most widely used forms of DRAM is the synchronous DRAM (SDRAM) [VOGL94]. Unlike the traditional DRAM, which is asynchronous, the SDRAM exchanges data with the processor synchronized to an external clock signal and running at the full speed of the processor/memory bus without imposing wait states.

In a typical DRAM, the processor presents addresses and control levels to the memory, indicating that a set of data at a particular location in memory should be either read from or written into the DRAM. After a delay, the access time, the DRAM either writes or reads the data. During the access-time delay, the DRAM performs various internal functions, such as activating the high capacitance of the row and column lines, sensing the data, and routing the data out through the output buffers. The processor must simply wait through this delay, slowing system performance.

With synchronous access, the DRAM moves data in and out under control of the system clock. The processor or other master issues the instruction and address information, which is latched by the DRAM. The DRAM then responds after a set number of clock cycles. Meanwhile, the master can safely do other tasks while the SDRAM is processing the request.

Figure 5.12 shows the internal logic of IBM's 64 Mb SDRAM [IBM01], which is typical of SDRAM organization, and Table 5.3 defines the various pin assignments. The SDRAM employs a burst mode to eliminate the address setup time and row and column line precharge time after the first access. In burst mode, a series of data bits can be clocked out rapidly after the first bit has been accessed. This mode is useful when all the bits to be accessed are in sequence and in the same row of the array as the initial access. In addition, the SDRAM has a multiple-bank internal architecture that improves opportunities for on-chip parallelism.

The mode register and associated control logic is another key feature differentiating SDRAMs from conventional DRAMs. It provides a mechanism to customize the SDRAM to suit specific system needs. The mode register specifies the

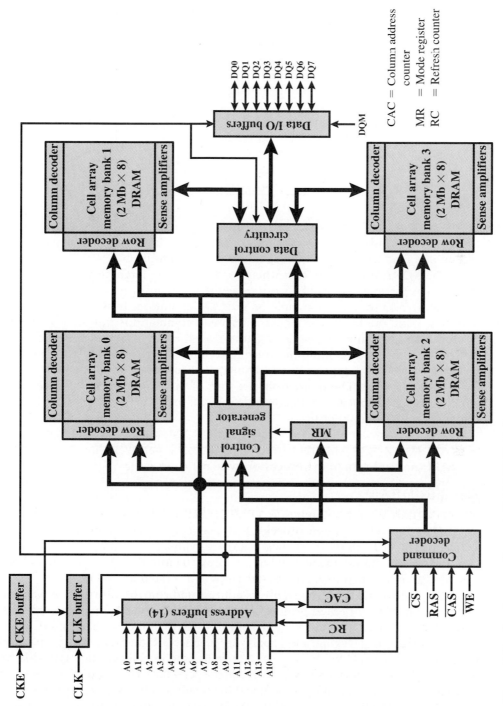

Figure 5.12 Synchronous Dynamic RAM (SDRAM)

155

Table 5.3 SDRAM Pin Assignments

A0 to A13	Address inputs
CLK	Clock input
CKE	Clock enable
$\overline{\text{CS}}$	Chip select
$\overline{\text{RAS}}$	Row address strobe
$\overline{\text{CAS}}$	Column address strobe
$\overline{\text{WE}}$	Write enable
DQ0 to DQ7	Data input/output
DWM	Data mask

burst length, which is the number of separate units of data synchronously fed onto the bus. The register also allows the programmer to adjust the latency between receipt of a read request and the beginning of data transfer.

The SDRAM performs best when it is transferring large blocks of data serially, such as for applications like word processing, spreadsheets, and multimedia.

Figure 5.13 shows an example of SDRAM operation. In this case, the burst length is 4 and the latency is 2. The burst read command is initiated by having $\overline{\text{CS}}$ and $\overline{\text{CAS}}$ low while holding $\overline{\text{RAS}}$ and $\overline{\text{WE}}$ high at the rising edge of the clock. The address inputs determine the starting column address for the burst, and the mode register sets the type of burst (sequential or interleave) and the burst length (1, 2, 4, 8, full page). The delay from the start of the command to when the data from the first cell appears on the outputs is equal to the value of the $\overline{\text{CAS}}$ latency that is set in the mode register.

There is now an enhanced version of SDRAM, known as double data rate SDRAM (DDR-SDRAM) that overcomes the once-per-cycle limitation. DDR-SDRAM can send data to the processor twice per clock cycle.

Rambus DRAM

RDRAM, developed by Rambus [FARM92, CRIS97], has been adopted by Intel for its Pentium and Itanium processors. It has become the main competitor to SDRAM. RDRAM chips are vertical packages, with all pins on one side. The chip exchanges data with the processor over 28 wires no more than 12 centimeters long. The bus can address up to 320 RDRAM chips and is rated at 1.6 GBps.

The special RDRAM bus delivers address and control information using an asynchronous block-oriented protocol. After an initial 480 ns access time, this produces the 1.6 GBps data rate. What makes this speed possible is the bus itself, which defines impedances, clocking, and signals very precisely. Rather than being controlled by the explicit RAS, CAS, R/W, and CE signals used in conventional DRAMs, an RDRAM gets a memory request over the high-speed bus. This request contains the desired address, the type of operation, and the number of bytes in the operation.

Figure 5.14 illustrates the RDRAM layout. The configuration consists of a controller and a number of RDRAM modules connected together via a common

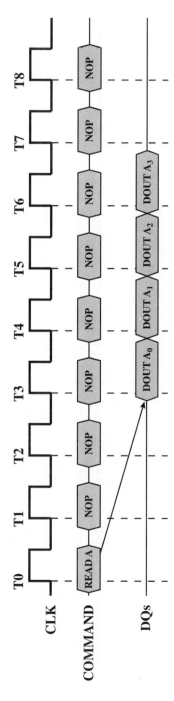

Figure 5.13 SDRAM Read Timing (burst length = 4, $\overline{CAS}$ latency = 2)

157

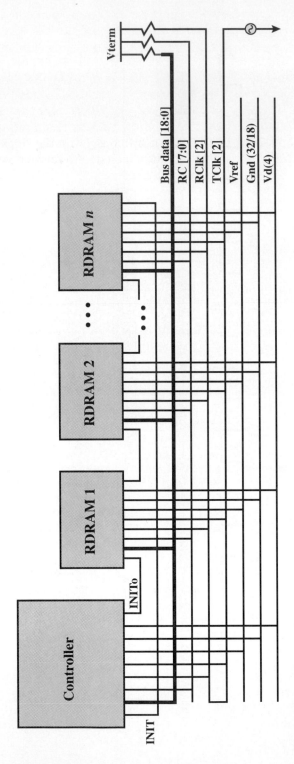

Figure 5.14 RDRAM Structure

bus. The controller is at one end of the configuration, and the far end of the bus is a parallel termination of the bus lines. The bus includes 18 data lines (16 actual data, two parity) cycling at twice the clock rate; that is, one bit is sent at the leading and following edge of each clock signal. This results in a signal rate on each data line of 800 Mbps. There is a separate set of 8 lines (RC) used for address and control signals. There is also a clock signal that starts at the far end from the controller propagates to the controller end and then loops back. A RDRAM module sends data to the controller synchronously to the clock to master, and the controller sends data to an RDRAM synchronously with the clock signal in the opposite direction. The remaining bus lines include a reference voltage, ground, and power source.

Cache DRAM

Cache DRAM (CDRAM), developed by Mitsubishi [HIDA90, ZHAN01], integrates a small SRAM cache (16 Kb) onto a generic DRAM chip.

The SRAM on the CDRAM can be used in two ways. First, it can be used as a true cache, consisting of a number of 64-bit lines. The cache mode of the CDRAM is effective for ordinary random access to memory.

The SRAM on the CDRAM can also be used as a buffer to support the serial access of a block of data. For example, to refresh a bit-mapped screen, the CDRAM can prefetch the data from the DRAM into the SRAM buffer. Subsequent accesses to the chip result in accesses solely to the SRAM.

5.4 RECOMMENDED READING AND WEB SITES

[PRIN91] provides a comprehensive treatment of semiconductor memory technologies, including SRAM, DRAM, and flash memories. [SHAR97] covers the same material, with more emphasis on testing and reliability issues. [PRIN99] focuses on advanced DRAM and SRAM architectures. For an in-depth look at DRAM, see [KEET01].

A good explanation of error-correcting codes is contained in [MCEL85]. For a deeper study, worthwhile book-length treatments are [ADAM91] and [BLAH83]. [SHAR97] contains a good survey of codes used in contemporary main memories.

ADAM91   Adamek, J. *Foundations of Coding.* New York: Wiley, 1991.

BLAH83   Blahut, R. *Theory and Practice of Error Control Codes.* Reading, MA: Addison-Wesley, 1983.

KEET01   Keeth, B., and Baker, R. *DRAM Circuit Design: A Tutorial.* Piscataway, NJ: IEEE Press, 2001.

MCEL85   McEliece, R. "The Reliability of Computer Memories." *Scientific American,* January 1985.

PRIN91   Prince, B. *Semiconductor Memories.* New York: Wiley, 1991.

PRIN99   Prince, B. *High Performance Memories: New Architecture DRAMs and SRAMs, Evolution and Function.* New York: Wiley, 1999.

SHAR97   Sharma, A. *Semiconductor Memories: Technology, Testing, and Reliability.* New York: IEEE Press, 1997.

Recommended Web Sites:

- **The RAM Guide:** Good overview of RAM technology plus a number of useful links
- **RambusSite:** Useful collection of documents and pointers to RDRAM vendors
- **RDRAM:** Another useful site for RDRAM information

5.5 KEY TERMS, REVIEW QUESTIONS, AND PROBLEMS

Key Terms

cache DRAM (CDRAM)	Hamming code	single-error-correcting
dynamic RAM (DRAM)	hard failure	(SEC) code
electrically erasable	nonvolatile memory	single-error-correcting,
programmable ROM	programmable ROM	double-error-detecting
(EEPROM)	(PROM)	(SEC-DED) code
erasable programmable	RamBus DRAM	soft error
(EPROM)	(RDRAM)	static RAM (SRAM)
error-correcting code	read-mostly memory	synchronous DRAM
(ECC)	read-only memory	(SDRAM)
error correction	(ROM)	syndrome
flash memory	semiconductor memory	volatile memory

Review Questions

5.1 What are the key properties of semiconductor memory?
5.2 What are two senses in which the term *random-access memory* is used?
5.3 What is the difference between DRAM and SRAM, in terms of application?
5.4 What is the difference between DRAM and SRAM, in terms of characteristics such as speed, size, and cost?
5.5 Explain why one type of RAM is considered to be analog and the other digital.
5.6 What are some applications for ROM?
5.7 What are the differences among EPROM, EEPROM, and flash memory?
5.8 Explain the function of each pin in Figure 5.4b.
5.9 What is a parity bit?
5.10 How is the syndrome for the Hamming code interpreted?
5.11 How does SDRAM differ from ordinary DRAM?

Problems

5.1 Suggest reasons why RAMs traditionally have been organized as only one bit per chip whereas ROMs are usually organized with multiple bits per chip.

5.2 Consider a dynamic RAM that must be given a refresh cycle 64 times per ms. Each refresh operation requires 150 ns; a memory cycle requires 250 ns. What percentage of the memory's total operating time must be given to refreshes?

5.3 Design a 16-bit memory of total capacity 8192 bits using SRAM chips of size 64 × 1 bit. Give the array configuration of the chips on the memory board showing all required input and output signals for assigning this memory to the lowest address space. The design should allow for both byte and 16-bit word accesses.
Source: [ALEX93]

5.4 For the Hamming code shown in Figure 5.10, show what happens when a check bit rather than a data bit is in error.

5.5 Suppose an 8-bit data word stored in memory is 11000010. Using the Hamming algorithm, determine what check bits would be stored in memory with the data word. Show how you got your answer.

5.6 For the 8-bit word 00111001, the check bits stored with it would be 0111. Suppose when the word is read from memory, the check bits are calculated to be 1101. What is the data word that was read from memory?

5.7 How many check bits are needed if the Hamming error correction code is used to detect single bit errors in a 1024-bit data word?

5.8 Develop an SEC code for a 16-bit data word. Generate the code for the data word 0101000000111001. Show that the code will correctly identify an error in data bit 5.
Source: [ALEX93]

CHAPTER 6

EXTERNAL MEMORY

KEY POINTS

♦ Magnetic disks remain the most important component of external memory. Both removable and fixed, or hard, disks are used in systems ranging from personal computers to mainframes and supercomputers.

♦ To achieve greater performance and higher availability, a popular scheme on servers and larger systems is the RAID disk technology. RAID refers to a family of techniques for using multiple disks as a parallel array of data storage devices, with redundancy built in to compensate for disk failure.

♦ Optical storage technology has become increasingly important in all types of computer systems. While CD-ROM has been widely used for many years, more recent technologies, such as writable CD and DVD, are becoming increasingly important.

This chapter examines a range of external memory devices and systems. We begin with the most important device, the magnetic disk. Magnetic disks are the foundation of external memory on virtually all computer systems. The next section examines the use of disk arrays to achieve greater performance, looking specifically at the family of systems known as RAID (Redundant Array of Independent Disks). An increasingly important component of many computer systems is external optical memory, and this is examined in the third section. Finally, magnetic tape is described.

6.1 MAGNETIC DISK

A disk is a circular platter constructed of nonmagnetic material, called the substrate, coated with a magnetizable material. Traditionally, the substrate has been an aluminum or aluminum alloy material. More recently, glass substrates have been introduced. The glass substrate has a number of benefits, including the following:

- Improvement in the uniformity of the magnetic film surface to increase disk reliability
- A significant reduction in overall surface defects to help reduce read–write errors
- Ability to support lower fly heights (described subsequently)
- Better stiffness to reduce disk dynamics
- Greater ability to withstand shock and damage

Magnetic Read and Write Mechanisms

Data are recorded on and later retrieved from the disk via a conducting coil named the head; there are in many systems two heads, a read head and a write head. During a read or write operation, the head is stationary while the platter rotates beneath it.

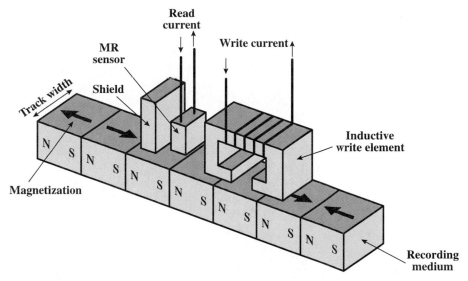

Figure 6.1   Inductive Write/Magnetoresistive Read Head

The write mechanism is based on the fact that electricity flowing through a coil produces a magnetic field. Pulses are sent to the write head, and magnetic patterns are recorded on the surface below, with different patterns for positive and negative currents. The write head itself is made of easily magnetizable material and is in the shape of a rectangular doughnut with a gap along one side and a few turns of conducting wire along the opposite side (Figure 6.1). An electric current in the wire induces a magnetic field across the gap, which in turn magnetizes a small area of the recording medium. Reversing the direction of the current reverses the direction of the magnetization on the recording medium.

The traditional read mechanism is based on the fact that a magnetic field moving relative to a coil produces an electrical current in the coil. When the surface of the disk passes under the head, it generates a current of the same polarity as the one already recorded. The structure of the head for reading is in this case essentially the same as for writing and therefore the same head can be used for both. Such single heads are used in floppy disk systems and in older rigid disk systems.

Contemporary rigid disk systems use a different read mechanism, requiring a separate read head, positioned for convenience close to the write head. The read head consists of a partially shielded magnetoresistive (MR) sensor. The MR material has an electrical resistance that depends on the direction of the magnetization of the medium moving under it. By passing a current through the MR sensor, resistance changes are detected as voltage signals. The MR design allows higher-frequency operation, which equates to greater storage densities and operating speeds.

Data Organization and Formatting

The head is a relatively small device capable of reading from or writing to a portion of the platter rotating beneath it. This gives rise to the organization of data on the platter in a concentric set of rings, called **tracks**. Each track is the same width as the head. There are thousands of tracks per surface.

Figure 6.2 Disk Data Layout

Figure 6.2 depicts this data layout. Adjacent tracks are separated by **gaps**. This prevents, or at least minimizes, errors due to misalignment of the head or simply interference of magnetic fields.

Data are transferred to and from the disk in **sectors** (Figure 6.2). There are typically hundreds of sectors per track, and these may be of either fixed or variable length. In most contemporary systems, fixed-length sectors are used, with 512 bytes being the nearly universal sector size. To avoid imposing unreasonable precision requirements on the system, adjacent sectors are separated by intratrack (intersector) gaps.

A bit near the center of a rotating disk travels past a fixed point (such as a read–write head) slower than a bit on the outside. Therefore, some way must be found to compensate for the variation in speed so that the head can read all the bits at the same rate. This can be done by increasing the spacing between bits of information recorded in segments of the disk. The information can then be scanned at the same rate by rotating the disk at a fixed speed, known as the **constant angular velocity (CAV)**. Figure 6.3a shows the layout of a disk using CAV. The disk is divided into a number of pie-shaped sectors and into a series of concentric tracks. The advantage of using CAV is that individual blocks of data can be directly addressed by track and sector. To move the head from its current location to a specific address, it only takes a short movement of the head to a specific track and a short wait for the proper sector to spin under the head. The disadvantage of CAV is that the amount of data that can be stored on the long outer tracks is the same as what can be stored on the short inner tracks.

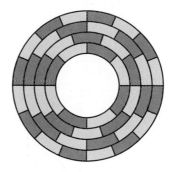

(a) **Constant angular velocity**   (b) **Multiple zoned recording**

Figure 6.3   Comparison of Disk Layout Methods

Because the **density**, in bits per linear inch, increases in moving from the outermost track to the innermost track, disk storage capacity in a straightforward CAV system is limited by the maximum recording density that can be achieved on the innermost track. To increase density, modern hard disk systems use a technique known as **multiple zone recording**, in which the surface is divided into a number of zones (16 is typical). Within a zone, the number of bits per track is constant. Zones farther from the center contain more bits (more sectors) than zones closer to the center. This allows for greater overall storage capacity at the expense of somewhat more complex circuitry. As the disk head moves from one zone to another, the length (along the track) of individual bits changes, causing a change in the timing for reads and writes. Figure 6.3b suggests the nature of multiple zone recording; in this illustration, each zone is only a single track wide.

Some means is needed to locate sector positions within a track. Clearly, there must be some starting point on the track and a way of identifying the start and end of each sector. These requirements are handled by means of control data recorded on the disk. Thus, the disk is formatted with some extra data used only by the disk drive and not accessible to the user.

An example of disk formatting is shown in Figure 6.4. In this case, each track contains 30 fixed-length sectors of 600 bytes each. Each sector holds 512 bytes of data plus control information useful to the disk controller. The ID field is a unique identifier or address used to locate a particular sector. The SYNCH byte is a special bit pattern that delimits the beginning of the field. The track number identifies a track on a surface. The head number identifies a head, because this disk has multiple surfaces (explained presently). The ID and data fields each contain an error-detecting code.

Physical Characteristics

Table 6.1 lists the major characteristics that differentiate among the various types of magnetic disks. First, the head may either be fixed or movable with respect to the radial direction of the platter. In a **fixed-head disk,** there is one read–write head per track. All of the heads are mounted on a rigid arm that extends across all tracks; such systems are rare today. In a **movable-head disk,** there is only one read–write head. Again, the head is mounted on an arm. Because the head must be able to be positioned above any track, the arm can be extended or retracted for this purpose.

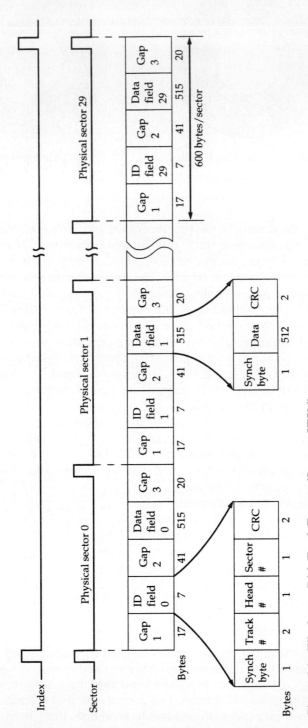

Figure 6.4 Winchester Disk Track Format (Seagate ST506)

168

Table 6.1   Physical Characteristics of Disk Systems

Head Motion	**Platters**
Fixed head (one per track)	Single platter
Movable head (one per surface)	Multiple platter
Disk Portability	**Head Mechanism**
Nonremovable disk	Contact (floppy)
Removable disk	Fixed gap
Sides	Aerodynamic gap (Winchester)
Single sided	
Double sided	

The disk itself is mounted in a disk drive, which consists of the arm, a shaft that rotates the disk, and the electronics needed for input and output of binary data. A **nonremovable disk** is permanently mounted in the disk drive; the hard disk in a personal computer is a nonremovable disk. A **removable disk** can be removed and replaced with another disk. The advantage of the latter type is that unlimited amounts of data are available with a limited number of disk systems. Furthermore, such a disk may be moved from one computer system to another. Floppy disks and ZIP cartridge disks are examples of removable disks.

For most disks, the magnetizable coating is applied to both sides of the platter, which is then referred to as **double sided**. Some less expensive disk systems use **single-sided** disks.

Some disk drives accommodate **multiple platters** stacked vertically a fraction of an inch apart. Multiple arms are provided (Figure 6.5). Multiple-platter disks

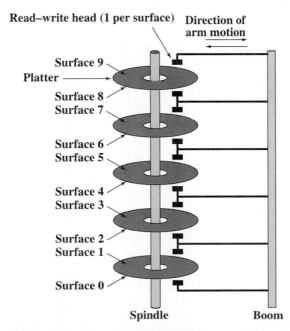

Figure 6.5   Components of a Disk Drive

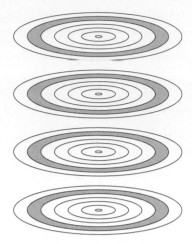

Figure 6.6 Tracks and Cylinders

employ a movable head, with one read–write head per platter surface. All of the heads are mechanically fixed so that all are at the same distance from the center of the disk and move together. Thus, at any time, all of the heads are positioned over tracks that are of equal distance from the center of the disk. The set of all the tracks in the same relative position on the platter is referred to as a **cylinder**. For example, all of the shaded tracks in Figure 6.6 are part of one cylinder.

Finally, the head mechanism provides a classification of disks into three types. Traditionally, the read-write head has been positioned a fixed distance above the platter, allowing an air gap. At the other extreme is a head mechanism that actually comes into physical contact with the medium during a read or write operation. This mechanism is used with the **floppy disk**, which is a small, flexible platter and the least expensive type of disk.

To understand the third type of disk, we need to comment on the relationship between data density and the size of the air gap. The head must generate or sense an electromagnetic field of sufficient magnitude to write and read properly. The narrower the head is, the closer it must be to the platter surface to function. A narrower head means narrower tracks and therefore greater data density, which is desirable. However, the closer the head is to the disk, the greater the risk of error from impurities or imperfections. To push the technology further, the Winchester disk was developed. Winchester heads are used in sealed drive assemblies that are almost free of contaminants. They are designed to operate closer to the disk's surface than conventional rigid disk heads, thus allowing greater data density. The head is actually an aerodynamic foil that rests lightly on the platter's surface when the disk is motionless. The air pressure generated by a spinning disk is enough to make the foil rise above the surface. The resulting noncontact system can be engineered to use narrower heads that operate closer to the platter's surface than conventional rigid disk heads.[1]

---

[1]As a matter of historical interest, the term Winchester was originally used by IBM as a code name for the 3340 disk model prior to its announcement. The 3340 was a removable disk pack with the heads sealed within the pack. The term is now applied to any sealed-unit disk drive with aerodynamic head design. The Winchester disk is commonly found built in to personal computers and workstations, where it is referred to as a hard disk.

Table 6.2 Typical Hard Disk Drive Parameters

Characteristics	Seagate Barracuda 180	Seagate Cheetah X15-36LP	Seagate Barracuda 36ES	Toshiba HDD1242	IBM Microdrive
Application	High-capacity server	High-performance server	Entry-level desktop	Portable	Handheld devices
Capacity	181.6 GB	36.7 GB	18.4 GB	5 GB	1 GB
Minimum track-to-track seek time	0.8 ms	0.3 ms	1.0 ms	—	1.0 ms
Average seek time	7.4 ms	3.6 ms	9.5 ms	15 ms	12 ms
Spindle speed	7200 rpm	15K rpm	7200	4200 rpm	3600 rpm
Average rotational delay	4.17 ms	2 ms	4.17 ms	7.14 ms	8.33 ms
Maximum transfer rate	160 MB/s	522 to 709 MB/s	25 MB/s	66 MB/s	13.3 MB/s
Bytes per sector	512	512	512	512	512
Sector per track	793	485	600	63	—
Tracks per cylinder (number of platter surfaces)	24	8	2	2	2
Cylinders (number of tracks on one side of platter)	24,247	18,479	29,851	10,350	—

Table 6.2 gives disk parameters for typical contemporary high-performance disks.

Disk Performance Parameters

The actual details of disk I/O operation depend on the computer system, the operating system, and the nature of the I/O channel and disk controller hardware. A general timing diagram of disk I/O transfer is shown in Figure 6.7.

When the disk drive is operating, the disk is rotating at constant speed. To read or write, the head must be positioned at the desired track and at the beginning of the desired sector on that track. Track selection involves moving the head in a movable-head system or electronically selecting one head on a fixed-head system. On a movable-head system, the time it takes to position the head at the track is known as **seek time**. In either case, once the track is selected, the disk controller waits until the appropriate sector rotates to line up with the head. The time it takes for the beginning of the sector to reach the head is known as **rotational delay**, or rotational latency. The sum of the seek time, if any, and the rotational delay equals the **access time**, which is the time it takes to get into position to read or write. Once the head is in position, the read or write operation is then performed as the sector moves under the head; this is the data transfer portion of the operation; the time required for the transfer is the **transfer time**.

In addition to the access time and transfer time, there are several queuing delays normally associated with a disk I/O operation. When a process issues an I/O request, it must first wait in a queue for the device to be available. At that time, the device is assigned to the process. If the device shares a single I/O channel or a set of I/O channels with other disk drives, then there may be an additional wait for the channel to be available. At that point, the seek is performed to begin disk access.

In some high-end systems for servers, a technique known as rotational positional sensing (RPS) is used. This works as follows: When the seek command has been issued, the channel is released to handle other I/O operations. When the seek is completed, the device determines when the data will rotate under the head. As that sector approaches the head, the device tries to reestablish the communication path back to the host. If either the control unit or the channel is busy with another I/O, then the reconnection attempt fails and the device must rotate one whole revolution before it can attempt to reconnect, which is called an RPS miss. This is an extra delay element that must be added to the time line of Figure 6.7.

Seek Time

Seek time is the time required to move the disk arm to the required track. It turns out that this is a difficult quantity to pin down. The seek time consists of two key components: the initial startup time, and the time taken to traverse the tracks that have to be crossed once the access arm is up to speed. Unfortunately, the traversal time is not a linear function of the number of tracks, but includes a startup time and a settling time (time after positioning the head over the target track until track identification is confirmed).

Much improvement comes from smaller and lighter disk components. Some years ago, a typical disk was 14 inches (36 cm) in diameter, whereas the most common size today is 3.5 inches (8.9 cm), reducing the distance that the arm has to travel. A typical average seek time on contemporary hard disks is under 10 ms.

Rotational Delay

Disks, other than floppy disks, rotate at speeds ranging from 3600 rpm (for handheld devices such as digital cameras) up to, as of this writing, 15,000 rpm; at this latter speed, there is one revolution per 4 ms. Thus, on the average, the rotational

Figure 6.7   Timing of a Disk I/O Transfer

delay will be 2 ms. Floppy disks typically rotate at between 300 and 600 rpm. Thus the average delay will be between 100 and 50 ms.

Transfer Time

The transfer time to or from the disk depends on the rotation speed of the disk in the following fashion:

$$T = \frac{b}{rN}$$

where

$$
\begin{aligned}
T &= \text{transfer time} \\
b &= \text{number of bytes to be transferred} \\
N &= \text{number of bytes on a track} \\
r &= \text{rotation speed, in revolutions per second}
\end{aligned}
$$

Thus the total average access time can be expressed as

$$T_a = T_s + \frac{1}{2r} + \frac{b}{rN}$$

where T_s is the average seek time. Note that on a zoned drive, the number of bytes per track is variable, complicating the calculation.

A Timing Comparison

With the foregoing parameters defined, let us look at two different I/O operations that illustrate the danger of relying on average values. Consider a disk with an advertised average seek time of 4 ms, rotation speed of 15,000 rpm, and 512-byte sectors with 500 sectors per track. Suppose that we wish to read a file consisting of 2500 sectors for a total of 1.28 Mbytes. We would like to estimate the total time for the transfer.

First, let us assume that the file is stored as compactly as possible on the disk. That is, the file occupies all of the sectors on 5 adjacent tracks (5 tracks × 500 sectors/ track = 2500 sectors). This is known as *sequential organization*. Now, the time to read the first track is as follows:

$$
\begin{array}{ll}
\text{Average seek} & 4 \text{ ms} \\
\text{Rotational delay} & 4 \text{ ms} \\
\text{Read 500 sectors} & \underline{8 \text{ ms}} \\
& 16 \text{ ms}
\end{array}
$$

Suppose that the remaining tracks can now be read with essentially no seek time. That is, the I/O operation can keep up with the flow from the disk. Then, at most, we need to deal with rotational delay for each succeeding track. Thus each successive track is read in 4 + 8 = 12 ms. To read the entire file,

$$\text{Total time} = 16 + 4 \times 12 = 64 \text{ ms} = 0.064 \text{ seconds}$$

Now let us calculate the time required to read the same data using random access rather than sequential access; that is, accesses to the sectors are distributed randomly over the disk. For each sector, we have

Average seek	4	ms
Rotational delay	4	ms
Read 1 sectors	0.016	ms
	8.016	ms

Total time = $500 \times 8.016 = 4008$ ms = 4.008 seconds

It is clear that the order in which sectors are read from the disk has a tremendous effect on I/O performance. In the case of file access in which multiple sectors are read or written, we have some control over the way in which sectors of data are deployed, and we shall have something to say on this subject in the next chapter. However, even in the case of a file access, in a multiprogramming environment, there will be I/O requests competing for the same disk. Thus, it is worthwhile to examine ways in which the performance of disk I/O can be improved over that achieved with purely random access to the disk. This leads to a consideration of disk scheduling algorithms, which is the province of the operating system and beyond the scope of this book (see [STAL01] for a discussion).

6.2 RAID

As discussed earlier, the rate in improvement in secondary storage performance has been considerably less than the rate for processors and main memory. This mismatch has made the disk storage system perhaps the main focus of concern in improving overall computer system performance.

As in other areas of computer performance, disk storage designers recognize that if one component can only be pushed so far, additional gains in performance are to be had by using multiple parallel components. In the case of disk storage, this leads to the development of arrays of disks that operate independently and in parallel. With multiple disks, separate I/O requests can be handled in parallel, as long as the data required reside on separate disks. Further, a single I/O request can be executed in parallel if the block of data to be accessed is distributed across multiple disks.

With the use of multiple disks, there is a wide variety of ways in which the data can be organized and in which redundancy can be added to improve reliability. This could make it difficult to develop database schemes that are usable on a number of platforms and operating systems. Fortunately, industry has agreed on a standardized scheme for multiple-disk database design, known as RAID (Redundant Array of Independent Disks). The RAID scheme consists of seven levels,[2] zero through six.

---

[2]Additional levels have been defined by some researchers and some companies, but the seven levels described in this section are the ones universally agreed on.

These levels do not imply a hierarchical relationship but designate different design architectures that share three common characteristics:

1. RAID is a set of physical disk drives viewed by the operating system as a single logical drive.
2. Data are distributed across the physical drives of an array.
3. Redundant disk capacity is used to store parity information, which guarantees data recoverability in case of a disk failure.

The details of the second and third characteristics differ for the different RAID levels. RAID 0 does not support the third characteristic.

The term *RAID* was originally coined in a paper by a group of researchers at the University of California at Berkeley [PATT88].[3] The paper outlined various RAID configurations and applications and introduced the definitions of the RAID levels that are still used. The RAID strategy replaces large-capacity disk drives with multiple smaller-capacity drives and distributes data in such a way as to enable simultaneous access to data from multiple drives, thereby improving I/O performance and allowing easier incremental increases in capacity.

The unique contribution of the RAID proposal is to address effectively the need for redundancy. Although allowing multiple heads and actuators to operate simultaneously achieves higher I/O and transfer rates, the use of multiple devices increases the probability of failure. To compensate for this decreased reliability, RAID makes use of stored parity information that enables the recovery of data lost due to a disk failure.

We now examine each of the RAID levels. Table 6.3 summarizes the seven levels. Of these, levels 2 and 4 are not commercially offered and are not likely to achieve industry acceptance. Nevertheless, a description of these levels helps to clarify the design choices in some of the other levels.

Figure 6.8 is an example that illustrates the use of the seven RAID schemes to support a data capacity requiring four disks not counting redundancy. The figure highlights the layout of user data and redundant data and indicates the relative storage requirements of the various levels. We refer to this figure throughout the following discussion.

RAID Level 0

RAID level 0 is not a true member of the RAID family, because it does not include redundancy to improve performance. However, there are a few applications, such as some on supercomputers in which performance and capacity are primary concerns and low cost is more important than improved reliability.

---

[3] In that paper, the acronym RAID stood for Redundant Array of Inexpensive Disks. The term *inexpensive* was used to contrast the small relatively inexpensive disks in the RAID array to the alternative, a single large expensive disk (SLED). The SLED is essentially a thing of the past, with similar disk technology being used for both RAID and non-RAID configurations. Accordingly, the industry has adopted the term *independent* to emphasize that the RAID array creates significant performance and reliability gains.

Table 6.3 RAID Levels

Category	Level	Description	I/O Request Rate (Read/Write)	Data Transfer Rate (Read/Write)	Typical Application
Striping	0	Nonredundant	Large strips: Excellent	Small strips: Excellent	Applications requiring high performance for noncritical data
Mirroring	1	Mirrored	Good/fair	Fair/fair	System drives; critical files
Parallel access	2	Redundant via Hamming code	Poor	Excellent	
	3	Bit-interleaved parity	Poor	Excellent	Large I/O request size applications, such as imaging, CAD
Independent access	4	Block-interleaved parity	Excellent/fair	Fair/poor	
	5	Block-interleaved distributed parity	Excellent/fair	Fair/poor	High request rate, read intensive, data lookup
	6	Block-interleaved dual distributed parity	Excellent/poor	Fair/poor	Applications requiring extremely high availablity

For RAID 0, the user and system data are distributed across all of the disks in the array. This has a notable advantage over the use of a single large disk: If two different I/O requests are pending for two different blocks of data, then there is a good chance that the requested blocks are on different disks. Thus, the two requests can be issued in parallel, reducing the I/O queuing time.

But RAID 0, as with all of the RAID levels, goes further than simply distributing the data across a disk array: The data are *striped* across the available disks. This is best understood by considering Figure 6.9. All of the user and system data are viewed as being stored on a logical disk. The disk is divided into strips; these strips may be physical blocks, sectors, or some other unit. The strips are mapped round robin to consecutive array members. A set of logically consecutive strips that maps exactly one strip to each array member is referred to as a *stripe*. In an n-disk array, the first n logical strips are physically stored as the first strip on each of the n disks, forming the first stripe; the second n strips are distributed as the second strips on each disk; and so on. The advantage of this layout is that if a single I/O request consists of multiple logically contiguous strips, then up to n strips for that request can be handled in parallel, greatly reducing the I/O transfer time.

Figure 6.9 indicates the use of array management software to map between logical and physical disk space. This software may execute either in the disk subsystem or in a host computer.

(text continues on page 180)

(a) RAID 0 (Nonredundant)

(b) RAID 1 (Mirrored)

(c) RAID 2 (Redundancy through Hamming code)

Figure 6.8 RAID Levels (page 1 of 2)

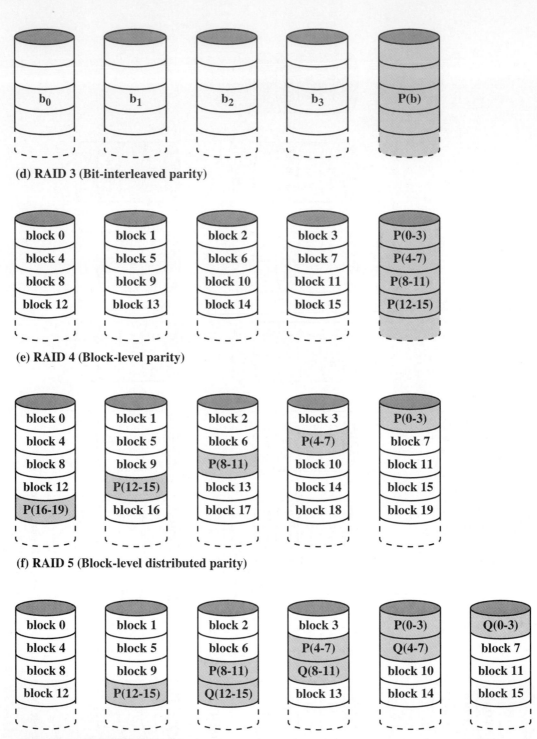

(d) RAID 3 (Bit-interleaved parity)

(e) RAID 4 (Block-level parity)

(f) RAID 5 (Block-level distributed parity)

(g) RAID 6 (Dual redundancy)

Figure 6.8   RAID Levels (page 2 of 2)

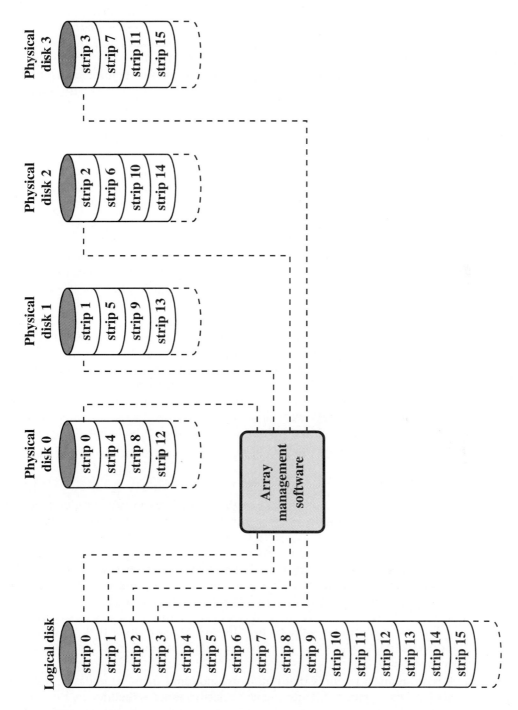

Figure 6.9 Data Mapping for a RAID Level 0 Array

RAID 0 for High Data Transfer Capacity

The performance of any of the RAID levels depends critically on the request patterns of the host system and on the layout of the data. These issues can be most clearly addressed in RAID 0, where the impact of redundancy does not interfere with the analysis. First, let us consider the use of RAID 0 to achieve a high data transfer rate. For applications to see a high transfer rate, two requirements must be met. First, a high transfer capacity must exist along the entire path between host memory and the individual disk drives. This includes internal controller buses, host system I/O buses, I/O adapters, and host memory buses.

The second requirement is that the application must make I/O requests that drive the disk array efficiently. This requirement is met if the typical request is for large amounts of logically contiguous data, compared to the size of a strip. In this case, a single I/O request involves the parallel transfer of data from multiple disks, increasing the effective transfer rate compared to a single-disk transfer.

RAID 0 for High I/O Request Rate

In a transaction-oriented environment, the user is typically more concerned with response time than with transfer rate. For an individual I/O request for a small amount of data, the I/O time is dominated by the motion of the disk heads (seek time) and the movement of the disk (rotational latency).

In a transaction environment, there may be hundreds of I/O requests per second. A disk array can provide high I/O execution rates by balancing the I/O load across multiple disks. Effective load balancing is achieved only if there are typically multiple I/O requests outstanding. This, in turn, implies that there are multiple independent applications or a single transaction-oriented application that is capable of multiple asynchronous I/O requests. The performance will also be influenced by the strip size. If the strip size is relatively large, so that a single I/O request only involves a single disk access, then multiple waiting I/O requests can be handled in parallel, reducing the queuing time for each request.

RAID Level 1

RAID 1 differs from RAID levels 2 through 6 in the way in which redundancy is achieved. In these other RAID schemes, some form of parity calculation is used to introduce redundancy, whereas in RAID 1, redundancy is achieved by the simple expedient of duplicating all the data. As Figure 6.8b shows, data striping is used, as in RAID 0. But in this case, each logical strip is mapped to two separate physical disks so that every disk in the array has a mirror disk that contains the same data.

There are a number of positive aspects to the RAID 1 organization:

1. A read request can be serviced by either of the two disks that contains the requested data, whichever one involves the minimum seek time plus rotational latency.
2. A write request requires that both corresponding strips be updated, but this can be done in parallel. Thus, the write performance is dictated by the slower of the two writes (i.e., the one that involves the larger seek time plus rota-

tional latency). However, there is no "write penalty" with RAID 1. RAID levels 2 through 6 involve the use of parity bits. Therefore, when a single strip is updated, the array management software must first compute and update the parity bits as well as updating the actual strip in question.

3. Recovery from a failure is simple. When a drive fails, the data may still be accessed from the second drive.

The principal disadvantage of RAID 1 is the cost; it requires twice the disk space of the logical disk that it supports. Because of that, a RAID 1 configuration is likely to be limited to drives that store system software and data and other highly critical files. In these cases, RAID 1 provides real-time backup of all data so that in the event of a disk failure, all of the critical data are still immediately available.

In a transaction-oriented environment, RAID 1 can achieve high I/O request rates if the bulk of the requests are reads. In this situation, the performance of RAID 1 can approach double of that of RAID 0. However, if a substantial fraction of the I/O requests are write requests, then there may be no significant performance gain over RAID 0. RAID 1 may also provide improved performance over RAID 0 for data transfer intensive applications with a high percentage of reads. Improvement occurs if the application can split each read request so that both disk members participate.

RAID Level 2

RAID levels 2 and 3 make use of a parallel access technique. In a parallel access array, all member disks participate in the execution of every I/O request. Typically, the spindles of the individual drives are synchronized so that each disk head is in the same position on each disk at any given time.

As in the other RAID schemes, data striping is used. In the case of RAID 2 and 3, the strips are very small, often as small as a single byte or word. With RAID 2, an error-correcting code is calculated across corresponding bits on each data disk, and the bits of the code are stored in the corresponding bit positions on multiple parity disks. Typically, a Hamming code is used, which is able to correct single-bit errors and detect double-bit errors.

Although RAID 2 requires fewer disks than RAID 1, it is still rather costly. The number of redundant disks is proportional to the log of the number of data disks. On a single read, all disks are simultaneously accessed. The requested data and the associated error-correcting code are delivered to the array controller. If there is a single-bit error, the controller can recognize and correct the error instantly, so that the read access time is not slowed. On a single write, all data disks and parity disks must be accessed for the write operation.

RAID 2 would only be an effective choice in an environment in which many disk errors occur. Given the high reliability of individual disks and disk drives, RAID 2 is overkill and is not implemented.

RAID Level 3

RAID 3 is organized in a similar fashion to RAID 2. The difference is that RAID 3 requires only a single redundant disk, no matter how large the disk array. RAID 3 employs parallel access, with data distributed in small strips. Instead of an error-correcting code, a simple parity bit is computed for the set of individual bits in the same position on all of the data disks.

Redundancy

In the event of a drive failure, the parity drive is accessed and data is reconstructed from the remaining devices. Once the failed drive is replaced, the missing data can be restored on the new drive and operation resumed.

The data reconstruction is quite simple. Consider an array of five drives in which X0 through X3 contain data and X4 is the parity disk. The parity for the ith bit is calculated as follows:

$$X4(i) = X3(i) \oplus X2(i) \oplus X1(i) \oplus X0(i)$$

Suppose that drive X1 has failed. If we add $X4(i) \oplus X1(i)$ to both sides of the preceding equation, we get

$$X1(i) = X4(i) \oplus X3(i) \oplus X2(i) \oplus X0(i)$$

Thus, the contents of each strip of data on X1 can be regenerated from the contents of the corresponding strips on the remaining disks in the array. This principle is true for RAID levels 3 through 6.

In the event of a disk failure, all of the data are still available in what is referred to as reduced mode. In this mode, for reads, the missing data are regenerated on the fly using the exclusive-OR calculation. When data are written to a reduced RAID 3 array, consistency of the parity must be maintained for later regeneration. Return to full operation requires that the failed disk be replaced and the entire contents of the failed disk be regenerated on the new disk.

Performance

Because data are striped in very small strips, RAID 3 can achieve very high data transfer rates. Any I/O request will involve the parallel transfer of data from all of the data disks. For large transfers, the performance improvement is especially noticeable. On the other hand, only one I/O request can be executed at a time. Thus, in a transaction-oriented environment, performance suffers.

RAID Level 4

RAID levels 4 through 6 make use of an independent access technique. In an independent access array, each member disk operates independently, so that separate I/O requests can be satisfied in parallel. Because of this, independent access arrays are more suitable for applications that require high I/O request rates and are relatively less suited for applications that require high data transfer rates.

As in the other RAID schemes, data striping is used. In the case of RAID 4 through 6, the strips are relatively large. With RAID 4, a bit-by-bit parity strip is calculated across corresponding strips on each data disk, and the parity bits are stored in the corresponding strip on the parity disk.

RAID 4 involves a write penalty when an I/O write request of small size is performed. Each time that a write occurs, the array management software must update not only the user data but also the corresponding parity bits. Consider an array of five drives in which X0 through X3 contain data and X4 is the parity disk. Suppose that a write is performed that only involves a strip on disk X1. Initially, for each bit i, we have the following relationship:

$$X4(i) = X3(i) \oplus X2(i) \oplus X1(i) \oplus X0(i)$$

After the update, with potentially altered bits indicated by a prime symbol,

$$\begin{aligned} X4'(i) &= X3(i) \oplus X2(i) \oplus X1'(i) \oplus X0(i) \\ &= X3(i) \oplus X2(i) \oplus X1'(i) \oplus X0(i) \oplus X1(i) \oplus X1(i) \\ &= X4(i) \oplus X1(i) \oplus X1'(i) \end{aligned}$$

To calculate the new parity, the array management software must read the old user strip and the old parity strip. Then it can update these two strips with the new data and the newly calculated parity. Thus, each strip write involves two reads and two writes.

In the case of a larger size I/O write that involves strips on all disk drives, parity is easily computed by calculation using only the new data bits. Thus, the parity drive can be updated in parallel with the data drives and there are no extra reads or writes.

In any case, every write operation must involve the parity disk, which therefore can become a bottleneck.

RAID Level 5

RAID 5 is organized in a similar fashion to RAID 4. The difference is that RAID 5 distributes the parity strips across all disks. A typical allocation is a round-robin scheme, as illustrated in Figure 6.8f. For an n-disk array, the parity strip is on a different disk for the first n stripes, and the pattern then repeats.

The distribution of parity strips across all drives avoids the potential I/O bottleneck found in RAID 4.

RAID Level 6

RAID 6 was introduced in a subsequent paper by the Berkeley researchers [KATZ89]. In the RAID 6 scheme, two different parity calculations are carried out and stored in separate blocks on different disks. Thus, a RAID 6 array whose user data require N disks consists of $N + 2$ disks.

Figure 6.8g illustrates the scheme. P and Q are two different data check algorithms. One of the two is the exclusive-OR calculation used in RAID 4 and 5. But the other is an independent data check algorithm. This makes it possible to regenerate data even if two disks containing user data fail.

The advantage of RAID 6 is that it provides extremely high data availability. Three disks would have to fail within the MTTR (mean time to repair) interval to cause data to be lost. On the other hand, RAID 6 incurs a substantial write penalty, because each write affects two parity blocks.

6.3   OPTICAL MEMORY

In 1983, one of the most successful consumer products of all time was introduced: the compact disk (CD) digital audio system. The CD is a nonerasable disk that can store more than 60 minutes of audio information on one side. The huge commercial success of the CD enabled the development of low-cost optical-disk storage technology that has revolutionized computer data storage. A variety of optical-disk systems have been introduced (Table 6.4). We briefly review each of these.

Compact Disk

CD-ROM

Both the audio CD and the CD-ROM (compact disk read-only memory) share a similar technology. The main difference is that CD-ROM players are more rugged and have error correction devices to ensure that data are properly transferred from disk to computer. Both types of disk are made the same way. The disk is formed from a resin, such as polycarbonate. Digitally recorded information (either music or computer data) is imprinted as a series of microscopic pits on the surface of the polycarbonate. This is done, first of all, with a finely focused, high-intensity laser to create a master disk. The master is used, in turn, to make a die to stamp out copies onto polycarbonate. The pitted surface is then coated with a highly reflective surface, usually aluminum or gold. This shiny surface is protected against dust and scratches by a top coat of clear acrylic. Finally, a label can be silkscreened onto the acrylic.

Table 6.4   Optical Disk Products

CD
Compact Disk. A nonerasable disk that stores digitized audio information. The standard system uses 12-cm disks and can record more than 60 minutes of uninterrupted playing time.
CD-ROM
Compact Disk Read-Only Memory. A nonerasable disk used for storing computer data. The standard system uses 12-cm disks and can hold more than 650 Mbytes.
CD-R
CD Recordable. Similar to a CD-ROM. The user can write to the disk only once.
CD-RW
CD Rewritable. Similar to a CD-ROM. The user can erase and rewrite to the disk multiple times.
DVD
Digital Video Disk. A technology for producing digitized, compressed representation of video information, as well as large volumes of other digital data. Both 8- and 12-cm diameters are used, with a double-sided capacity of up to 17 Gbytes. The basic DVD is read-only (DVD-ROM).
DVD-R
DVD Recordable. Similar to a DVD-ROM. The user can write to the disk only once. Only one-sided disks can be used.
DVD-RW
DVD Rewritable. Similar to a DVD-ROM. The user can write to the disk multiple times. Only one-sided disks can be used.

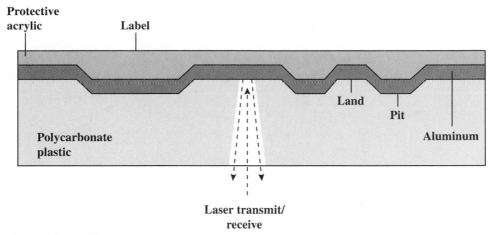

Figure 6.10 CD Operation

Information is retrieved from a CD or CD-ROM by a low-powered laser housed in an optical-disk player, or drive unit. The laser shines through the clear polycarbonate while a motor spins the disk past it (Figure 6.10). The intensity of the reflected light of the laser changes as it encounters a pit. Specifically, if the laser beam falls on a pit, which has a somewhat rough surface, the light scatters and a low intensity is reflected back to the source. The areas between pits are called *lands*. A land is a smooth surface, which reflects back at higher intensity. The change between pits and lands is detected by a photosensor and converted into a digital signal. The sensor tests the surface at regular intervals. The beginning or end of a pit represents a 1; when no change in elevation occurs between intervals, a 0 is recorded.

Recall that on a magnetic disk, information is recorded in concentric tracks. With the simplest constant angular velocity (CAV) system, the number of bits per track is constant. An increase in density is achieved with multiple zoned recording, in which the surface is divided into a number of zones, with zones farther from the center containing more bits than zones closer to the center. Although this technique increases capacity, it is still not optimal.

To achieve greater capacity, CDs and CD-ROMs do not organize information on concentric tracks. Instead, the disk contains a single spiral track, beginning near the center and spiraling out to the outer edge of the disk. Sectors near the outside of the disk are the same length as those near the inside. Thus, information is packed evenly across the disk in segments of the same size and these are scanned at the same rate by rotating the disk at a variable speed. The pits are then read by the laser at a **constant linear velocity (CLV)**. The disk rotates more slowly for accesses near the outer edge than for those near the center. Thus, the capacity of a track and the rotational delay both increase for positions nearer the outer edge of the disk. The data capacity for a CD-ROM is about 680 MB.

Data on the CD-ROM are organized as a sequence of blocks. A typical block format is shown in Figure 6.11. It consists of the following fields:

- **Sync:** The sync field identifies the beginning of a block. It consists of a byte of all 0s, 10 bytes of all 1s, and a byte of all 0s.
- **Header:** The header contains the block address and the mode byte. Mode 0 specifies a blank data field; mode 1 specifies the use of an error-correcting code and 2048 bytes of data; mode 2 specifies 2336 bytes of user data with no error-correcting code.
- **Data:** User data.
- **Auxiliary:** Additional user data in mode 2. In mode 1, this is a 288-byte error-correcting code.

With the use of CLV, random access becomes more difficult. Locating a specific address involves moving the head to the general area, adjusting the rotation speed and reading the address, and then making minor adjustments to find and access the specific sector.

CD-ROM is appropriate for the distribution of large amounts of data to a large number of users. Because of the expense of the initial writing process, it is not appropriate for individualized applications. Compared with traditional hard disks, the CD-ROM has two advantages:

- The optical disk together with the information stored on it can be mass replicated inexpensively—unlike a magnetic disk. The database on a magnetic disk has to be reproduced by copying one disk at a time using two disk drives.
- The optical disk is removable, allowing the disk itself to be used for archival storage. Most magnetic disks are nonremovable. The information on non-removable magnetic disks must first be copied to tape before the disk drive/disk can be used to store new information.

The disadvantages of CD-ROM are as follows:

- It is read-only and cannot be updated.
- It has an access time much longer than that of a magnetic disk drive, as much as half a second.

Figure 6.11 CD-ROM Block Format

CD Recordable

To accommodate applications in which only one or a small number of copies of a set of data is needed, the write-once read-many CD, known as the CD recordable (CD-R), has been developed. For CD-R, a disk is prepared in such a way that it can be subsequently written once with a laser beam of modest intensity. Thus, with a somewhat more expensive disk controller than for CD-ROM, the customer can write once as well as read the disk.

The CD-R medium is similar to but not identical to that of a CD or CD-ROM. For CDs and CD-ROMs, information is recorded by the pitting of the surface of the medium, which changes reflectivity. For a CD-R, the medium includes a dye layer. The dye is used to change reflectivity and is activated by a high-intensity laser. The resulting disk can be read on a CD-R drive or a CD-ROM drive.

The CD-R optical disk is attractive for archival storage of documents and files. It provides a permanent record of large volumes of user data.

CD Rewritable

The CD-RW optical disk can be repeatedly written and overwritten, as with a magnetic disk. Although a number of approaches have been tried, the only pure optical approach that has proved attractive is called **phase change**. The phase change disk uses a material that has two significantly different reflectivities in two different phase states. There is an amorphous state, in which the molecules exhibit a random orientation and which reflects light poorly; and a crystalline state, which has a smooth surface that reflects light well. A beam of laser light can change the material from one phase to the other. The primary disadvantage of phase change optical disks is that the material eventually and permanently loses its desirable properties. Current materials can be used for between 500,000 and 1,000,000 erase cycles.

The CD-RW has the obvious advantage over CD-ROM and CD-R that it can be rewritten and thus used as a true secondary storage. As such, it competes with magnetic disk. A key advantage of the optical disk is that the engineering tolerances for optical disks are much less severe than for high-capacity magnetic disks. Thus, they exhibit higher reliability and longer life.

Digital Versatile Disk

With the capacious digital versatile disk (DVD), the electronics industry has at last found an acceptable replacement for the analog VHS video tape. The DVD will replace the video tape used in video cassette recorders (VCRs) and, more important for this discussion, replace the CD-ROM in personal computers and servers. The DVD takes video into the digital age. It delivers movies with impressive picture quality, and it can be randomly accessed like audio CDs, which DVD machines can also play. Vast volumes of data can be crammed onto the disk, currently seven times as much as a CD-ROM. With DVD's huge storage capacity and vivid quality, PC games will become more realistic and educational software will incorporate more video. Following in the wake of these developments will be a new crest of traffic over the Internet and corporate intranets, as this material is incorporated into Web sites.

The DVD's greater capacity is due to three differences from CDs (Figure 6.12):

Label

Protective layer (acrylic)

Reflective layer (aluminum)

Polycarbonate substrate (plastic)

1.2 mm thick

Laser focuses on polycarbonate pits in front of reflective layer.

(a) CD-ROM—Capacity 682 MB

Polycarbonate substrate, side 2

Semireflective layer, side 2

Polycarbonate layer, side 2

Fully reflective layer, side 2

Fully reflective layer, side 1

Polycarbonate layer, side 1

Semireflective layer, side 1

Polycarbonate substrate, side 1

1.2 mm thick

Laser focuses on pits in one layer on one side at a time. Disk must be flipped to read other side.

(b) DVD-ROM, double-sided, dual-layer—Capacity 17 GB

Figure 6.12   CD-ROM and DVD-ROM

1. Bits are packed more closely on a DVD. The spacing between loops of a spiral on a CD is 1.6 μm and the minimum distance between pits along the spiral is 0.834 μm. The DVD uses a laser with shorter wavelength and achieves a loop spacing of 0.74 μm and a minimum distance between pits of 0.4 μm. The result of these two improvements is about a seven-fold increase in capacity, to about 4.7 GB.

2. The DVD employs a second layer of pits and lands on top of the first layer. A dual-layer DVD has a semireflective layer on top of the reflective layer, and by adjusting focus, the lasers in DVD drives can read each layer separately. This technique almost doubles the capacity of the disk, to about 8.5 GB. The lower reflectivity of the second layer limits its storage capacity so that a full doubling is not achieved.

3. The DVD-ROM can be two sided whereas data is recorded on only one side of a CD. This brings total capacity up to 17 GB.

As with the CD, DVDs come in writeable as well as read-only versions (Table 6.4).

6.4 MAGNETIC TAPE

Tape systems use the same reading and recording techniques as disk systems. The medium is flexible polyester (similar to that used in some clothing) tape coated with magnetizable material. The coating may consist of particles of pure metal in special binders or vapor-plated metal films The tape and the tape drive are analogous to a home tape recorder system. Tape widths vary from 0.38 cm (0.15 inch) to 1.27 cm (0.5 inch). Tapes used to be packaged as open reels that have to be threaded through a second spindle for use. Today, virtually all tapes are housed in cartridges.

Data on the tape are structured as a number of parallel tracks running lengthwise. Earlier tape systems typically used nine tracks. This made it possible to store data one byte at a time, with an additional parity bit as the ninth track. This was followed by tape systems using 18 or 36 tracks, corresponding to a digital word or double word. The recording of data in this form is referred to as **parallel recording**. Most modern systems instead use **serial recording**, in which data are laid out as a sequence of bits along each track, as is done with magnetic disks. As with the disk, data are read and written in contiguous blocks, called *physical records*, on a tape. Blocks on the tape are separated by gaps referred to as *interrecord* gaps. As with the disk, the tape is formatted to assist in locating physical records.

The typical recording technique used in serial tapes is referred to as **serpentine recording**. In this technique, when data are being recorded, the first set of bits is recorded along the whole length of the tape. When the end of the tape is reached, the heads are repositioned to record a new track, and the tape is again recorded on its whole length, this time in the opposite direction. That process continues, back and forth, until the tape is full (Figure 6.13a). To increase speed, the read-write head is capable of reading and writing a number of adjacent tracks simultaneously (typically 2 to 8 tracks). Data are still recorded serially along individual tracks, but blocks in sequence are stored on adjacent tracks, as suggested by Figure 6.13b. Table 6.5 shows parameters for one system, known as DLTtape.

Table 6.5 DLTtape Drives

	DLT 4000	DLT 8000	SDLT 220
Capacity (GB)	20	40	110
Data rate (MB/s)	1.5	6.0	11.0
Bit density (Kb/cm)	32.3	38.6	51.6
Track density (t/cm)	101	164	317
Media length (m)	549	549	549
Media width (cm)	1.27	1.27	1.27
Number of tracks	128	208	448
Number of tracks read–write simultaneously	2	4	8

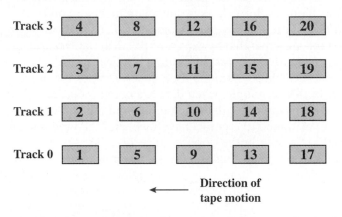

Figure 6.13 Typical Magnetic Tape Features

A tape drive is a *sequential-access* device. If the tape head is positioned at record 1, then to read record *N*, it is necessary to read physical records 1 through *N* − 1, one at a time. If the head is currently positioned beyond the desired record, it is necessary to rewind the tape a certain distance and begin reading forward. Unlike the disk, the tape is in motion only during a read or write operation.

In contrast to the tape, the disk drive is referred to as a *direct-access* device. A disk drive need not read all the sectors on a disk sequentially to get to the desired one. It must only wait for the intervening sectors within one track and can make successive accesses to any track.

Magnetic tape was the first kind of secondary memory. It is still widely used as the lowest-cost, slowest-speed member of the memory hierarchy.

6.5 RECOMMENDED READING AND WEB SITES

[MEE96a] provides a good survey of the underlying recording technology of disk and tape systems. [MEE96b] focuses on the data storage techniques for disk and tape systems. [COME00] is a short but instructive article on current trends in magnetic disk storage technology.

An excellent survey of RAID technology, written by the inventors of the RAID concept, is [CHEN94]. A more detailed discussion is published by the RAID Advisory Board, an association of suppliers and consumers of RAID-related products [MASS97]. A good recent paper is [FRIE96].

[MARC90] gives an excellent overview of the optical storage field. A good survey of the underlying recording and reading technology is [MANS97].

[ROSC99] provides a comprehensive overview of all types of external memory systems, with a modest amount of technical detail on each. [KHUR01] is another good survey.

CHEN94   Chen, P.; Lee, E.; Gibson, G.; Katz, R.; and Patterson, D. "RAID: High-Performance, Reliable Secondary Storage." *ACM Computing Surveys,* June 1994.

COME00   Comerford, R. "Magnetic Storage: The Medium that Wouldn't Die." *IEEE Spectrum*, December 2000.

FRIE96   Friedman, M. "RAID Keeps Going and Going and . . ."*IEEE Spectrum*, April 1996.

KHUR01   Khurshudov, A. *The Essential Guide to Computer Data Storage.* Upper Saddle River, NJ: Prentice Hall, 2001.

MANS97   Mansuripur, M., and Sincerbox, G. "Principles and Techniques of Optical Data Storage." *Proceedings of the IEEE*, November 1997.

MARC90   Marchant, A. *Optical Recording.* Reading, MA: Addison-Wesley, 1990.

MASS97   Massiglia, P. *The RAID Book: A Storage System Technology Handbook.* St. Peter, MN: The Raid Advisory Board, 1997.

MEE96a   Mee, C., and Daniel, E. eds. *Magnetic Recording Technology.* New York: McGraw-Hill, 1996.

MEE96b   Mee, C., and Daniel, E. eds. *Magnetic Storage Handbook.* New York: McGraw-Hill, 1996.

ROSC99   Rosch, W. *Winn L. Rosch Hardware Bible.* Indianapolis, IN: Sams, 1999.

Recommended Web Sites:

- **RAID Advisory Group:** RAID industry group. Information about RAID technology and products.
- **Optical Storage Technology Association:** Good source of information about optical storage technology and vendors, plus extensive list of relevant links.
- **DLTtape:** Good collection of technical information and links to vendors.
- **Data Storage Magazine:** The magazine's Web site contains extensive information on data storage products and vendors.

6.6 KEY TERMS, REVIEW QUESTIONS, AND PROBLEMS

Key Terms

access time	DVD-RW	optical memory
CD	fixed-head disk	pit
CD-ROM	floppy disk	platter
CD-R	gap	RAID
CD-RW	head	removable disk
constant angular velocity (CAV)	land	rotational delay
constant linear velocity (CLV)	magnetic disk	sector
	magnetic tape	seek time
	magnetoresistive	serpentine recording
cylinder	movable-head disk	striped data
DVD	multiple zoned recording	substrate
DVD-ROM		track
DVD-R	nonremovable disk	transfer time

Review Questions

6.1 What are the advantages of using a glass substrate for a magnetic disk?

6.2 How are data written onto a magnetic disk?

6.3 How are data read from a magnetic disk?

6.4 Explain the difference between a simple CAV system and a multiple zoned recording system.

6.5 Define the terms *track*, *cylinder*, and *sector*.

6.6 What is the typical disk sector size?

6.7 Define the terms *seek time*, *rotational delay*, *access time*, and *transfer time*.

6.8 What common characteristics are shared by all RAID levels?

6.9 Briefly define the seven RAID levels.

6.10 Explain the term *striped data*.

6.11 How is redundancy achieved in a RAID system?

6.12 In the context of RAID, what is the distinction between parallel access and independent access?

6.13 What is the difference between CAV and CLV?

6.14 What differences between a CD and a DVD account for the larger capacity of the latter?

6.15 Explain serpentine recording

Problems

6.1 Consider a disk with N tracks numbered from 0 to $(N - 1)$ and assume that requested sectors are distributed randomly and evenly over the disk. We Want to calculate the average number of tracks traversed by a seek.

    a. First, calculate the probability of a seek of length j when the head is currently positioned over track t. *Hint:* this is a matter of determining the total number of combinations, recognizing that all track positions for the destination of the seek are equally likely.

b. Next, calculate the probability of a seek of length K. *Hint:* this involves the summing over all possible combinations of movements of K tracks.

c. Calculate the average number of tracks traversed by a seek, using the formula for expected value

$$E[x] = \sum_{i=0}^{N-1} i \times \Pr[x = i]$$

Hint: Use the equalities: $\sum_{i=1}^{n} i = \dfrac{n(n+1)}{2}$; $\sum_{i=1}^{n} i^2 = \dfrac{n(n+1)(2n+1)}{6}$

d. Show that for large values of N, the average number of tracks traversed by a seek approaches $N/3$.

6.2 Define the following for a disk system:

t_s = seek time; average time to position head over track
r = rotation speed of the disk, in revolutions per second
n = number of bits per sector
N = capacity of a track, in bits
t_A = time to access a sector

Develop a formula for t_A as a function of the other parameters.

6.3 Assume a 10-drive RAID configuration. Fill in the following matrix, which compares the various RAID levels:

RAID Level	Storage Density	Bandwidth Performance	Transaction Performance
0	1		1
1			
2			
3		1	
4			
5			

Each parameter is normalized to the RAID level that delivers the best performance; therefore, the remaining numbers in the matrix should have a value between 0 and 1. Storage density refers to the fraction of disk storage available for user data. Bandwidth performance reflects how fast data can be transferred out of an array. Transaction performance measures how many I/O operations per second an array can perform.

6.4 It should be clear that disk striping can improve data transfer rate when the strip size is small compared to the I/O request size. It should also be clear that RAID 0 provides improved performance relative to a single large disk, because multiple I/O requests can be handled in parallel. However, in this latter case, is disk striping necessary? That is, does disk striping improve I/O request rate performance compared to a comparable disk array without striping?

CHAPTER 7

INPUT/OUTPUT

KEY POINTS

◆ The computer system's I/O architecture is its interface to the outside world. This architecture is designed to provide a systematic means of controlling interaction with the outside world and to provide the operating system with the information it needs to manage I/O activity effectively.

◆ The are three principal I/O techniques: **programmed I/O**, in which I/O occurs under the direct and continuous control of the program requesting the I/O operation; **interrupt-driven I/O**, in which a program issues an I/O command and then continues to execute, until it is interrupted by the I/O hardware to signal the end of the I/O operation; and **direct memory access (DMA)**, in which a specialized I/O processor takes over control of an I/O operation to move a large block of data.

◆ Two important examples of external I/O interfaces are **FireWire** and **Infiniband**.

In addition to the processor and a set of memory modules, the third key element of a computer system is a set of I/O modules. Each module interfaces to the system bus or central switch and controls one or more peripheral devices. An I/O module is not simply a set of mechanical connectors that wire a device into the system bus. Rather, the I/O module contains some "intelligence"; that is, it contains logic for performing a communication function between the peripheral and the bus.

The reader may wonder why one does not connect peripherals directly to the system bus. The reasons are as follows:

- There are a wide variety of peripherals with various methods of operation. It would be impractical to incorporate the necessary logic within the processor to control a range of devices.

- The data transfer rate of peripherals is often much slower than that of the memory or processor. Thus, it is impractical to use the high-speed system bus to communicate directly with a peripheral.

- On the other hand, the data transfer rate of some peripherals is faster than that of the memory or processor. Again, the mismatch would lead to inefficiencies if not managed properly.

- Peripherals often use different data formats and word lengths than the computer to which they are attached.

Thus, an I/O module is required. This module has two major functions (Figure 7.1):

- Interface to the processor and memory via the system bus or central switch
- Interface to one or more peripheral devices by tailored data links

We begin this chapter with a brief discussion of external devices, followed by an overview of the structure and function of an I/O module. Then we look at the various ways in which the I/O function can be performed in cooperation with

Figure 7.1   Generic Model of an I/O Module

the processor and memory: the internal I/O interface. Finally, we examine the external I/O interface, between the I/O module and the outside world.

7.1 EXTERNAL DEVICES

I/O operations are accomplished through a wide assortment of external devices that provide a means of exchanging data between the external environment and the computer. An external device attaches to the computer by a link to an I/O module (Figure 7.1). The link is used to exchange control, status, and data between the I/O module and the external device. An external device connected to an I/O module is often referred to as a *peripheral device* or, simply, a *peripheral*.

We can broadly classify external devices into three categories:

- **Human readable:** Suitable for communicating with the computer user
- **Machine readable:** Suitable for communicating with equipment
- **Communication:** Suitable for communicating with remote devices

Examples of human-readable devices are video display terminals (VDTs) and printers. Examples of machine-readable devices are magnetic disk and tape systems, and sensors and actuators, such as are used in a robotics application. Note that we are viewing disk and tape systems as I/O devices in this chapter, whereas in Chapter 6 we viewed them as memory devices. From a functional point of view, these devices are part of the memory hierarchy, and their use is appropriately discussed in Chapter 6. From a structural point of view, these devices are controlled by I/O modules and are hence to be considered in this chapter.

Communication devices allow a computer to exchange data with a remote device, which may be a human-readable device, such as a terminal, a machine-readable device, or even another computer.

In very general terms, the nature of an external device is indicated in Figure 7.2. The interface to the I/O module is in the form of control, data, and status signals. *Control signals* determine the function that the device will perform, such as send data to the I/O module (INPUT or READ), accept data from the I/O module (OUTPUT or WRITE), report status, or perform some control function particular to the device (e.g., position a disk head). *Data* are in the form of a set of bits to be sent to or received from the I/O module. *Status signals* indicate the state of the device. Examples are READY/NOT-READY to show whether the device is ready for data transfer.

Control logic associated with the device controls the device's operation in response to direction from the I/O module. The *transducer* converts data from electrical to other forms of energy during output and from other forms to electrical during input. Typically, a buffer is associated with the transducer to temporarily hold data being transferred between the I/O module and the external environment; a buffer size of 8 to 16 bits is common.

The interface between the I/O module and the external device will be examined in Section 7.7. The interface between the external device and the environment is beyond the scope of this book, but several brief examples are given here.

Keyboard/Monitor

The most common means of computer/user interaction is a keyboard/monitor arrangement. The user provides input through the keyboard. This input is then trans-

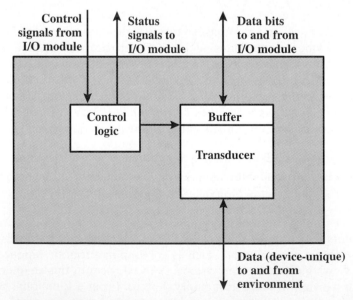

Figure 7.2 Block Diagram of an External Device

Table 7.1 The International Reference Alphabet (IRA)

bit position

b_4	b_3	b_2	b_1	b_7 0 b_6 0 b_5 0	0 0 1	0 1 0	0 1 1	1 0 0	1 0 1	1 1 0	1 1 1
0	0	0	0	NUL	DLE	SP	0	@	P	`	p
0	0	0	1	SOH	DC1	!	1	A	Q	a	q
0	0	1	0	STX	DC2	"	2	B	R	b	r
0	0	1	1	ETX	DC3	#	3	C	S	c	s
0	1	0	0	EOT	DC4	$	4	D	T	d	t
0	1	0	1	ENQ	NAK	%	5	E	U	e	u
0	1	1	0	ACK	SYN	&	6	F	V	f	v
0	1	1	1	BEL	ETB	'	7	G	W	g	w
1	0	0	0	BS	CAN	(	8	H	X	h	x
1	0	0	1	HT	EM	)	9	I	Y	i	y
1	0	1	0	LF	SUB	*	:	J	Z	j	z
1	0	1	1	VT	ESC	+	;	K	[	k	{
1	1	0	0	FF	FS	,	<	L	\	l	|
1	1	0	1	CR	GS	-	=	M	]	m	}
1	1	1	0	SO	RS	.	>	N	^	n	~
1	1	1	1	SI	US	/	?	O	_	o	DEL

mitted to the computer and may also be displayed on the monitor. In addition, the monitor displays data provided by the computer.

The basic unit of exchange is the character. Associated with each character is a code, typically 7 or 8 bits in length. The most commonly used text code is the International Reference Alphabet (IRA).[1] Each character in this code is represented by a unique 7-bit binary code; thus, 128 different characters can be represented. Table 7.1 lists all of the code values. In the table, the bits of each character are labeled from b_7, which is the most significant bit, to b_1, the least significant bit.[2] Characters are of two types: printable and control (Table 7.2). Printable characters are the alphabetic, numeric, and special characters that can be printed on paper or displayed on a screen. For example, the bit representation of the character "K" is $b_7b_6b_5b_4b_3b_2b_1 = 1001011$. Some of the control characters have to do with

---

[1]IRA is defined in ITU-T Recommendation T.50 and was formerly known as International Alphabet Number 5 (IA5). The U.S. national version of IRA is referred to as the American Standard Code for Information Interchange (ASCII).

[2]IRA-encoded characters are almost always stored and transmitted using 8 bits per character. The eighth bit is a parity bit used for error detection. The parity bit is the most significant bit and is therefore labeled b_8.

Table 7.2 IRA Control Characters

Format Control

BS (Backspace): Indicates movement of the printing mechanism or display cursor backward one position.

HT (Horizontal tab): Indicates movement of the printing mechanism or display cursor forward to the next preassigned "tab" or stopping position.

LF (Line feed): Indicates movement of the printing mechanism or display cursor to the start of the next line.

T (Vertical tab): Indicates movement of the printing mechanism or display cursor to the next of a series preassigned printing lines.

FF (Form feed): Indicates movement of the printing mechanism or display cursor to the starting position of the next page, form, or screen.

CR (Carriage return): Indicates movement of the printing mechanism or display cursor to the starting position of the same line.

Transmission Control

SOH (Start of heading): Used to indicate the start of a heading, which may contain address or routing information.

STX (Start of text): Used to indicate the start of the text and so also indicates the end of the heading.

ETX (End of text): Used to terminate the text that was started with STX.

EOT (End of transmission): Indicates the end of a transmission, which may have included one or more "texts" with their headings.

ENQ (Enquiry): A request for a response from a remote station. It may be used as a "WHO ARE YOU" request for a station to identify itself.

ACK (Acknowledge): A character transmitted by a receiving device as an affirmation response to a sender. It is used as a positive response to polling messages.

NAK (Negative acknowledgment): A character transmitted by a receiving device as an negative response to a sender. It is used as a negative response to polling messages.

SYN (Synchronous/idle): Used by a synchronous transmission system to achieve synchronization. When no data are being sent, a synchronous transmission system may send SYN characters continuously.

ETB (End of transmission block): Indicates the end of a block of data for communication purposes. It is used for blocking data where the block structure is not necessarily related to the processing format.

Information Separator

FS (File separator)
GS (Group separator)
RS (Record separator)
US (United separator)

Information separators to be used in an optional manner except that their hierarchy shall be FS (the most inclusive) to US (the least inclusive)

Miscellaneous

NUL (Null): No character. Used for filling in time or filling space on tape when there are no data.

BEL (Bell): Used when there is need to call human attention. It may control alarm or attention devices.

SO (Shift out): Indicates that the code combinations that follow shall be interpreted as outside of the standard character set until a SI character is reached.

SI (Shift in): Indicates that the code combinations that follow shall be interpreted according to the standard character set.

DEL (Delete): Used to obliterate unwanted characters; for example, by overwriting.

SP (Space): A nonprinting character used to separate words, or to move the printing mechanism or display cursor forward by one position.

DLE (Data link escape): A character that shall change the meaning of one or more contiguously following characters. It can provide supplementary controls, or permits the sending of data characters having any bit combination.

DC1, DC2, DC3, DC4 (Device controls): Characters for the control of ancillary devices or special terminal features.

CAN (Cancel): Indicates that the data that precede it in a message or block should be disregarded (usually because an error has been detected).

EM (End of medium): Indicates the physical end of a tape or other medium, or the end of the required or used portion of the medium.

SUB (Substitute): Substituted for a character that is found to be erroneous or invalid.

ESC (Escape): A character intended to provide code extension in that it gives a specified number of continuously following characters an alternate meaning.

controlling the printing or displaying of characters; an example is carriage return. Other control characters are concerned with communications procedures.

For keyboard input, when the user depresses a key, this generates an electronic signal that is interpreted by the transducer in the keyboard and translated into the bit pattern of the corresponding IRA code. This bit pattern is then transmitted to the I/O module in the computer. At the computer, the text can be stored in the same IRA code. On output, IRA code characters are transmitted to an external device from the I/O module. The transducer at the device interprets this code and sends the required electronic signals to the output device either to display the indicated character or perform the requested control function.

Disk Drive

A disk drive contains electronics for exchanging data, control, and status signals with an I/O module plus the electronics for controlling the disk read/write mechanism. In a fixed-head disk, the transducer is capable of converting between the magnetic patterns on the moving disk surface and bits in the device's buffer (Figure 7.2). A moving-head disk must also be able to cause the disk arm to move radially in and out across the disk's surface.

7.2 I/O MODULES

Module Function

The major functions or requirements for an I/O module fall into the following categories:

- Control and timing
- Processor communication
- Device communication
- Data buffering
- Error detection

During any period of time, the processor may communicate with one or more external devices in unpredictable patterns, depending on the program's need for I/O. The internal resources, such as main memory and the system bus, must be shared among a number of activities, including data I/O. Thus, the I/O function includes a **control and timing** requirement, to coordinate the flow of traffic between internal resources and external devices. For example, the control of the transfer of data from an external device to the processor might involve the following sequence of steps:

1. The processor interrogates the I/O module to check the status of the attached device.
2. The I/O module returns the device status.
3. If the device is operational and ready to transmit, the processor requests the transfer of data, by means of a command to the I/O module.
4. The I/O module obtains a unit of data (e.g., 8 or 16 bits) from the external device.
5. The data are transferred from the I/O module to the processor.

If the system employs a bus, then each of the interactions between the processor and the I/O module involves one or more bus arbitrations.

The preceding simplified scenario also illustrates that the I/O module must communicate with the processor and with the external device. **Processor communication** involves the following:

- **Command decoding:** The I/O module accepts commands from the processor, typically sent as signals on the control bus. For example, an I/O module for a disk drive might accept the following commands: READ SECTOR, WRITE SECTOR, SEEK track number, and SCAN record ID. The latter two commands each include a parameter that is sent on the data bus.

- **Data:** Data are exchanged between the processor and the I/O module over the data bus.

- **Status reporting:** Because peripherals are so slow, it is important to know the status of the I/O module. For example, if an I/O module is asked to send data to the processor (read), it may not be ready to do so because it is still working on the previous I/O command. This fact can be reported with a status signal. Common status signals are BUSY and READY. There may also be signals to report various error conditions.

- **Address recognition:** Just as each word of memory has an address, so does each I/O device. Thus, an I/O module must recognize one unique address for each peripheral it controls.

On the other side, the I/O module must be able to perform **device communication**. This communication involves commands, status information, and data (Figure 7.2).

An essential task of an I/O module is **data buffering**. The need for this function is apparent from Figure 7.3. Whereas the transfer rate into and out of main memory or the processor is quite high, the rate is orders of magnitude lower for many peripheral devices and covers a wide range. Data coming from main memory are sent to an I/O module in a rapid burst. The data are buffered in the I/O module and then sent to the peripheral device at its data rate. In the opposite direction, data are buffered so as not to tie up the memory in a slow transfer operation. Thus, the I/O module must be able to operate at both device and memory speeds. Similarly, if the I/O device operates at a rate higher than the memory access rate, then the I/O module performs the needed buffering operation.

Finally, an I/O module is often responsible for **error detection** and for subsequently reporting errors to the processor. One class of errors includes mechanical and electrical malfunctions reported by the device (e.g., paper jam, bad disk track). Another class consists of unintentional changes to the bit pattern as it is transmitted from device to I/O module. Some form of error-detecting code is often used to detect transmission errors. A simple example is the use of a parity bit on each character of data. For example, the IRA character code occupies 7 bits of a byte. The eighth bit is set so that the total number of 1s in the byte is even (even parity) or odd (odd parity). When a byte is received, the I/O module checks the parity to determine whether an error has occurred.

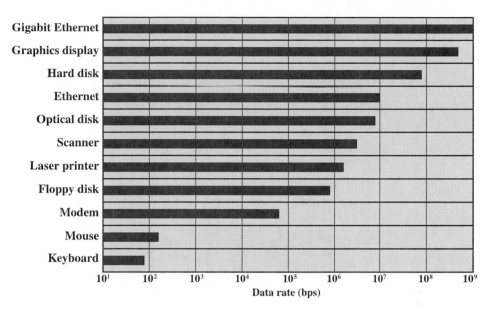

Figure 7.3   Typical I/O Device Data Rates

I/O Module Structure

I/O modules vary considerably in complexity and the number of external devices that they control. We will attempt only a very general description here. (One specific device, the Intel 82C55A, is described in Section 7.4.) Figure 7.4 provides a general block diagram of an I/O module. The module connects to the rest of the computer through a set of signal lines (e.g., system bus lines). Data transferred to and from the module are buffered in one or more data registers. There may also be one or more status registers that provide current status information. A status register may also function as a control register, to accept detailed control information from the processor. The logic within the module interacts with the processor via a set of control lines. The processor uses the control lines to issue commands to the I/O module. Some of the control lines may be used by the I/O module (e.g., for arbitration and status signals). The module must also be able to recognize and generate addresses associated with the devices it controls. Each I/O module has a unique address or, if it controls more than one external device, a unique set of addresses. Finally, the I/O module contains logic specific to the interface with each device that it controls.

An I/O module functions to allow the processor to view a wide range of devices in a simple-minded way. There is a spectrum of capabilities that may be provided. The I/O module may hide the details of timing, formats, and the electromechanics of an external device so that the processor can function in terms of simple read and write commands, and possibly open and close file commands. In its simplest form, the I/O module may still leave much of the work of controlling a device (e.g., rewind a tape) visible to the processor.

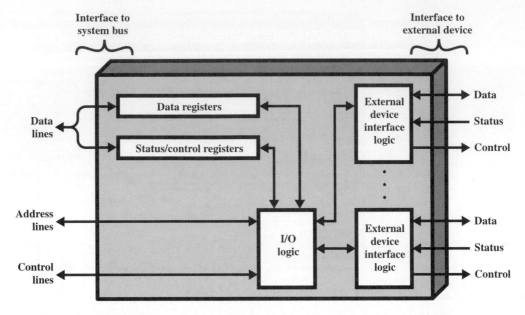

Figure 7.4 Block Diagram of an I/O Module

An I/O module that takes on most of the detailed processing burden, presenting a high-level interface to the processor, is usually referred to as an *I/O channel* or *I/O processor.* An I/O module that is quite primitive and requires detailed control is usually referred to as an *I/O controller* or *device controller.* I/O controllers are commonly seen on microcomputers, whereas I/O channels are used on mainframes.

In what follows, we will use the generic term *I/O module* when no confusion results and will use more specific terms where necessary.

7.3 PROGRAMMED I/O

Three techniques are possible for I/O operations. With *programmed I/O,* data are exchanged between the processor and the I/O module. The processor executes a program that gives it direct control of the I/O operation, including sensing device status, sending a read or write command, and transferring the data. When the processor issues a command to the I/O module, it must wait until the I/O operation is complete. If the processor is faster than the I/O module, this is wasteful of processor time. With *interrupt-driven I/O,* the processor issues an I/O command, continues to execute other instructions, and is interrupted by the I/O module when the latter has completed its work. With both programmed and interrupt I/O, the processor is responsible for extracting data from main memory for output and storing data in main memory for input. The alternative is known as *direct memory access* (DMA). In this mode, the I/O module and main memory exchange data directly, without processor involvement.

Table 7.3 I/O Techniques

	No Interrupts	Use of Interrupts
I/O-to-memory transfer through processor	Programmed I/O	Interrupt-driven I/O
Direct I/O-to-memory transfer		Direct memory access (DMA)

Table 7.3 indicates the relationship among these three techniques. In this section, we explore programmed I/O. Interrupt I/O and DMA are explored in the following two sections, respectively.

Overview of Programmed I/O

When the processor is executing a program and encounters an instruction relating to I/O, it executes that instruction by issuing a command to the appropriate I/O module. With programmed I/O, the I/O module will perform the requested action and then set the appropriate bits in the I/O status register (Figure 7.4). The I/O module takes no further action to alert the processor. In particular, it does not interrupt the processor. Thus, it is the responsibility of the processor periodically to check the status of the I/O module until it finds that the operation is complete.

To explain the programmed I/O technique, we view it first from the point of view of the I/O commands issued by the processor to the I/O module, and then from the point of view of the I/O instructions executed by the processor.

I/O Commands

To execute an I/O-related instruction, the processor issues an address, specifying the particular I/O module and external device, and an I/O command. There are four types of I/O commands that an I/O module may receive when it is addressed by a processor:

- **Control:** Used to activate a peripheral and tell it what to do. For example, a magnetic-tape unit may be instructed to rewind or to move forward one record. These commands are tailored to the particular type of peripheral device.
- **Test:** Used to test various status conditions associated with an I/O module and its peripherals. The processor will want to know that the peripheral of interest is powered on and available for use. It will also want to know if the most recent I/O operation is completed and if any errors occurred.
- **Read:** Causes the I/O module to obtain an item of data from the peripheral and place it in an internal buffer (depicted as a data register in Figure 7.4). The processor can then obtain the data item by requesting that the I/O module place it on the data bus.
- **Write:** Causes the I/O module to take an item of data (byte or word) from the data bus and subsequently transmit that data item to the peripheral.

Figure 7.5a gives an example of the use of programmed I/O to read in a block of data from a peripheral device (e.g., a record from tape) into memory. Data are

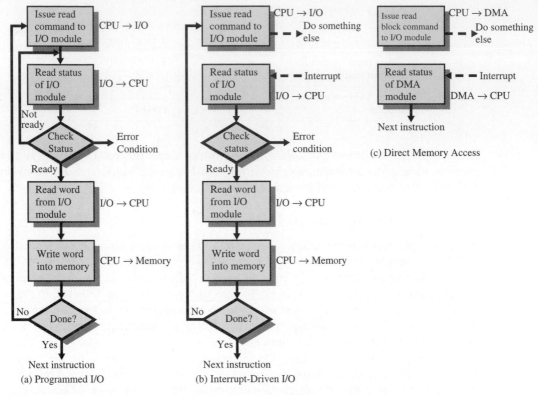

Figure 7.5 Three Techniques for Input of a Block of Data

read in one word (e.g., 16 bits) at a time. For each word that is read in, the processor must remain in a status-checking cycle until it determines that the word is available in the I/O module's data register. This flowchart highlights the main disadvantage of this technique: it is a time-consuming process that keeps the processor busy needlessly.

I/O Instructions

With programmed I/O, there is a close correspondence between the I/O-related instructions that the processor fetches from memory and the I/O commands that the processor issues to an I/O module to execute the instructions. That is, the instructions are easily mapped into I/O commands, and there is often a simple one-to-one relationship. The form of the instruction depends on the way in which external devices are addressed.

Typically, there will be many I/O devices connected through I/O modules to the system. Each device is given a unique identifier or address. When the processor issues an I/O command, the command contains the address of the desired device. Thus, each I/O module must interpret the address lines to determine if the command is for itself.

When the processor, main memory, and I/O share a common bus, two modes of addressing are possible: memory mapped and isolated. With **memory-mapped**

I/O, there is a single address space for memory locations and I/O devices. The processor treats the status and data registers of I/O modules as memory locations and uses the same machine instructions to access both memory and I/O devices. So, for example, with 10 address lines, a combined total of $2^{10} = 1024$ memory locations and I/O addresses can be supported, in any combination.

With memory-mapped I/O, a single read line and a single write line are needed on the bus. Alternatively, the bus may be equipped with memory read and write plus input and output command lines. Now, the command line specifies whether the address refers to a memory location or an I/O device. The full range of addresses may be available for both. Again, with 10 address lines, the system may now support both 1024 memory locations and 1024 I/O addresses. Because the address space for I/O is isolated from that for memory, this is referred to as **isolated I/O**.

Figure 7.6 contrasts these two programmed I/O techniques. Figure 7.6a shows how the interface for a simple input device such as a terminal keyboard might appear to a programmer using memory-mapped I/O. Assume a 10-bit address, with a

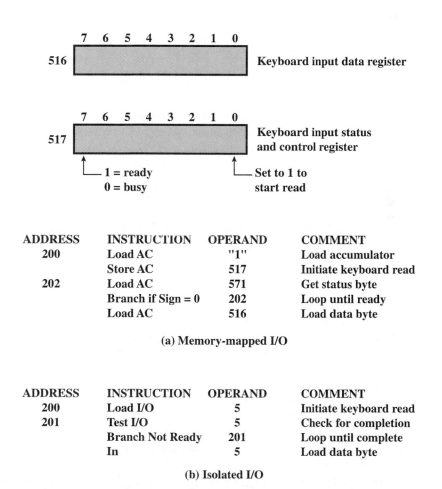

ADDRESS	INSTRUCTION	OPERAND	COMMENT
200	Load AC	"1"	Load accumulator
	Store AC	517	Initiate keyboard read
202	Load AC	571	Get status byte
	Branch if Sign = 0	202	Loop until ready
	Load AC	516	Load data byte

(a) Memory-mapped I/O

ADDRESS	INSTRUCTION	OPERAND	COMMENT
200	Load I/O	5	Initiate keyboard read
201	Test I/O	5	Check for completion
	Branch Not Ready	201	Loop until complete
	In	5	Load data byte

(b) Isolated I/O

Figure 7.6 Memory-Mapped and Isolated I/O

512-bit memory (locations 0–511) and up to 512 I/O addresses (locations 512–1023). Two addresses are dedicated to keyboard input from a particular terminal. Address 516 refers to the data register and address 517 refers to the status register, which also functions as a control register for receiving processor commands. The program shown will read 1 byte of data from the keyboard into an accumulator register in the processor. Note that the processor loops until the data byte is available.

With isolated I/O (Figure 7.6b), the I/O ports are accessible only by special I/O commands, which activate the I/O command lines on the bus.

For most types of processors, there is a relatively large set of different instructions for referencing memory. If isolated I/O is used, there are only a few I/O instructions. Thus, an advantage of memory-mapped I/O is that this large repertoire of instructions can be used, allowing more efficient programming. A disadvantage is that valuable memory address space is used up. Both memory-mapped and isolated I/O are in common use.

7.4 INTERRUPT-DRIVEN I/O

The problem with programmed I/O is that the processor has to wait a long time for the I/O module of concern to be ready for either reception or transmission of data. The processor, while waiting, must repeatedly interrogate the status of the I/O module. As a result, the level of the performance of the entire system is severely degraded.

An alternative is for the processor to issue an I/O command to a module and then go on to do some other useful work. The I/O module will then interrupt the processor to request service when it is ready to exchange data with the processor. The processor then executes the data transfer, as before, and then resumes its former processing.

Let us consider how this works, first from the point of view of the I/O module. For input, the I/O module receives a READ command from the processor. The I/O module then proceeds to read data in from an associated peripheral. Once the data are in the module's data register, the module signals an interrupt to the processor over a control line. The module then waits until its data are requested by the processor. When the request is made, the module places its data on the data bus and is then ready for another I/O operation.

From the processor's point of view, the action for input is as follows. The processor issues a READ command. It then goes off and does something else (e.g., the processor may be working on several different programs at the same time). At the end of each instruction cycle, the processor checks for interrupts (Figure 3.9). When the interrupt from the I/O module occurs, the processor saves the context (e.g., program counter and processor registers) of the current program and processes the interrupt. In this case, the processor reads the word of data from the I/O module and stores it in memory. It then restores the context of the program it was working on (or some other program) and resumes execution.

Figure 7.5b shows the use of interrupt I/O for reading in a block of data. Compare this with Figure 7.5a. Interrupt I/O is more efficient than programmed I/O because it eliminates needless waiting. However, interrupt I/O still consumes a lot of processor time, because every word of data that goes from memory to I/O module or from I/O module to memory must pass through the processor.

Interrupt Processing

Let us consider the role of the processor in interrupt-driven I/O in more detail. The occurrence of an interrupt triggers a number of events, both in the processor hardware and in software. Figure 7.7 shows a typical sequence. When an I/O device completes an I/O operation, the following sequence of hardware events occurs:

1. The device issues an interrupt signal to the processor.
2. The processor finishes execution of the current instruction before responding to the interrupt, as indicated in Figure 3.9.

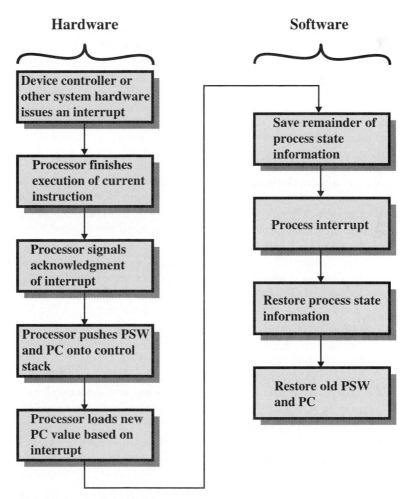

Figure 7.7 Simple Interrupt Processing

3. The processor tests for an interrupt, determines that there is one, and sends an acknowledgment signal to the device that issued the interrupt. The acknowledgment allows the device to remove its interrupt signal.

4. The processor now needs to prepare to transfer control to the interrupt routine. To begin, it needs to save information needed to resume the current program at the point of interrupt. The minimum information required is (a) the status of the processor, which is contained in a register called the program status word (PSW), and (b) the location of the next instruction to be executed, which is contained in the program counter. These can be pushed onto the system control stack.[3]

5. The processor now loads the program counter with the entry location of the interrupt-handling program that will respond to this interrupt. Depending on the computer architecture and operating system design, there may be a single program, one program for each type of interrupt, or one program for each device and each type of interrupt. If there is more than one interrupt-handling routine, the processor must determine which one to invoke. This information may have been included in the original interrupt signal, or the processor may have to issue a request to the device that issued the interrupt to get a response that contains the needed information.

Once the program counter has been loaded, the processor proceeds to the next instruction cycle, which begins with an instruction fetch. Because the instruction fetch is determined by the contents of the program counter, the result is that control is transferred to the interrupt-handler program. The execution of this program results in the following operations:

6. At this point, the program counter and PSW relating to the interrupted program have been saved on the system stack. However, there is other information that is considered part of the "state" of the executing program. In particular, the contents of the processor registers need to be saved, because these registers may be used by the interrupt handler. So, all of these values, plus any other state information, need to be saved. Typically, the interrupt handler will begin by saving the contents of all registers on the stack. Figure 7.8a shows a simple example. In this case, a user program is interrupted after the instruction at location N. The contents of all of the registers plus the address of the next instruction $(N + 1)$ are pushed onto the stack. The stack pointer is updated to point to the new top of stack, and the program counter is updated to point to the beginning of the interrupt service routine.

7. The interrupt handler next processes the interrupt. This includes an examination of status information relating to the I/O operation or other event that caused an interrupt. It may also involve sending additional commands or acknowledgments to the I/O device.

8. When interrupt processing is complete, the saved register values are retrieved from the stack and restored to the registers (e.g., see Figure 7.8b).

---

[3]See Appendix 10A for a discussion of stack operation.

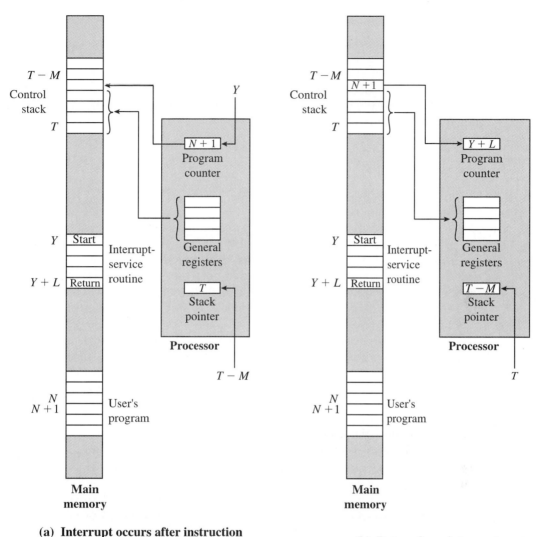

(a) Interrupt occurs after instruction at location N

(b) Return from interrupt

Figure 7.8 Changes in Memory and Registers for an Interrupt

9. The final act is to restore the PSW and program counter values from the stack. As a result, the next instruction to be executed will be from the previously interrupted program.

Note that it is important to save all the state information about the interrupted program for later resumption. This is because the interrupt is not a routine called from the program. Rather, the interrupt can occur at any time and therefore at any point in the execution of a user program. Its occurrence is unpredictable. Indeed, as we will see in the next chapter, the two programs may not have anything in common and may belong to two different users.

Design Issues

Two design issues arise in implementing interrupt I/O. First, because there will almost invariably be multiple I/O modules, how does the processor determine which device issued the interrupt? And second, if multiple interrupts have occurred, how does the processor decide which one to process?

Let us consider device identification first. Four general categories of techniques are in common use:

- Multiple interrupt lines
- Software poll
- Daisy chain (hardware poll, vectored)
- Bus arbitration (vectored)

The most straightforward approach to the problem is to provide **multiple interrupt lines** between the processor and the I/O modules. However, it is impractical to dedicate more than a few bus lines or processor pins to interrupt lines. Consequently, even if multiple lines are used, it is likely that each line will have multiple I/O modules attached to it. Thus, one of the other three techniques must be used on each line.

One alternative is the **software poll**. When the processor detects an interrupt, it branches to an interrupt-service routine whose job it is to poll each I/O module to determine which module caused the interrupt. The poll could be in the form of a separate command line (e.g., TESTI/O). In this case, the processor raises TESTI/O and places the address of a particular I/O module on the address lines. The I/O module responds positively if it set the interrupt. Alternatively, each I/O module could contain an addressable status register. The processor then reads the status register of each I/O module to identify the interrupting module. Once the correct module is identified, the processor branches to a device-service routine specific to that device.

The disadvantage of the software poll is that it is time consuming. A more efficient technique is to use a **daisy chain**, which provides, in effect, a hardware poll. An example of a daisy-chain configuration is shown in Figure 3.25. For interrupts, all I/O modules share a common interrupt request line. The interrupt acknowledge line is daisy chained through the modules. When the processor senses an interrupt, it sends out an interrupt acknowledge. This signal propagates through a series of I/O modules until it gets to a requesting module. The requesting module typically responds by placing a word on the data lines. This word is referred to as a *vector* and is either the address of the I/O module or some other unique identifier. In either case, the processor uses the vector as a pointer to the appropriate device-service routine. This avoids the need to execute a general interrupt-service routine first. This technique is called a *vectored interrupt*.

There is another technique that makes use of vectored interrupts, and that is **bus arbitration**. With bus arbitration, an I/O module must first gain control of the bus before it can raise the interrupt request line. Thus, only one module can raise the line at a time. When the processor detects the interrupt, it responds on the interrupt acknowledge line. The requesting module then places its vector on the data lines.

The aforementioned techniques serve to identify the requesting I/O module. They also provide a way of assigning priorities when more than one device is requesting interrupt service. With multiple lines, the processor just picks the interrupt line with the highest priority. With software polling, the order in which modules are polled determines their priority. Similarly, the order of modules on a daisy chain determines their priority. Finally, bus arbitration can employ a priority scheme, as discussed in Section 3.4.

We now turn to two examples of interrupt structures.

Intel 82C59A Interrupt Controller

The Intel 80386 provides a single Interrupt Request (INTR) and a single Interrupt Acknowledge (INTA) line. To allow the 80386 to handle a variety of devices and priority structures, it is usually configured with an external interrupt arbiter, the 82C59A. External devices are connected to the 82C59A, which in turn connects to the 80386.

Figure 7.9 shows the use of the 82C59A to connect multiple I/O modules for the 80386. A single 82C59A can handle up to 8 modules. If control for more than 8 modules is required, a cascade arrangement can be used to handle up to 64 modules.

The 82C59A's sole responsibility is the management of interrupts. It accepts interrupt requests from attached modules, determines which interrupt has the highest priority, and then signals the processor by raising the INTR line. The processor acknowledges via the INTA line. This prompts the 82C59A to place the appropriate vector information on the data bus. The processor can then proceed to process the interrupt and to communicate directly with the I/O module to read or write data.

The 82C59A is programmable. The 80386 determines the priority scheme to be used by setting a control word in the 82C59A. The following interrupt modes are possible:

- **Fully nested:** The interrupt requests are ordered in priority from 0 (IR0) through 7 (IR7).
- **Rotating:** In some applications a number of interrupting devices are of equal priority. In this mode a device, after being serviced, receives the lowest priority in the group.
- **Special mask:** This allows the processor to inhibit interrupts from certain devices.

The Intel 82C55A Programmable Peripheral Interface

As an example of an I/O module used for programmed I/O and interrupt-driven I/O, we consider the Intel 82C55A Programmable Peripheral Interface. The 82C55A is a single-chip, general-purpose I/O module designed for use with the Intel 80386 processor. Figure 7.10 shows a general block diagram plus the pin assignment for the 40-pin package in which it is housed.

The right side of the block diagram is the external interface of the 82C55A. The 24 I/O lines are programmable by the 80386 by means of the control register. The 80386 can set the value of the control register to specify a variety of operating modes and configurations. The 24 lines are divided into three 8-bit groups (A, B, C). Each group can function as an 8-bit I/O port. In addition, group C is subdivided into 4-bit groups (C_A and C_B), which may be used in conjunction with the A and B I/O ports. Configured in this manner, they carry control and status signals.

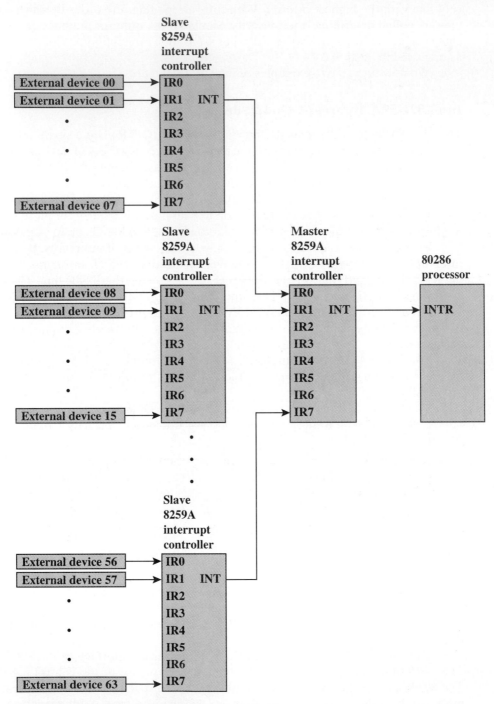

Figure 7.9 Use of the 82C59A Interrupt Controller

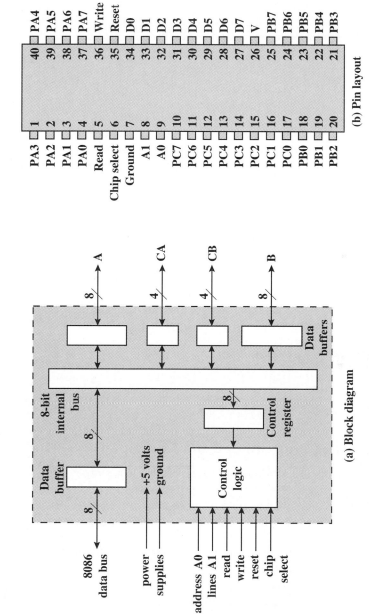

Figure 7.10 The Intel 82C55A Programmable Peripheral Interface

(a) Block diagram

(b) Pin layout

215

The left side of the block diagram is the internal interface to the 80386 bus. It includes an 8-bit bidirectional data bus (D0 through D7), used to transfer data to and from the I/O ports and to transfer control information to the control register. The two address lines specify one of the three I/O ports or the control register. A transfer takes place when the CHIP SELECT line is enabled together with either the READ or WRITE line. The RESET line is used to initialize the module.

The control register is loaded by the processor to control the mode of operation and to define signals, if any. In Mode 0 operation, the three groups of eight external lines function as three 8-bit I/O ports. Each port can be designated as input or output. Otherwise, groups A and B function as I/O ports, and the lines of group C serve as control lines for A and B. The control signals serve two principal purposes: "handshaking" and interrupt request. Handshaking is a simple timing mechanism. One control line is used by the sender as a DATA READY line, to indicate when the data are present on the I/O data lines. Another line is used by the receiver as an ACKNOWLEDGE, indicating that the data have been read and the data lines may be cleared. Another line may be designated as an INTERRUPT REQUEST line and tied back to the system bus.

Because the 82C55A is programmable via the control register, it can be used to control a variety of simple peripheral devices. Figure 7.11 illustrates its use to control a keyboard/display terminal. The keyboard provides 8 bits of input. Two of these bits, SHIFT and CONTROL, have special meaning to the keyboard-handling program executing in the processor. However, this interpretation is transparent to the 82C55A, which simply accepts the 8 bits of data and presents them on the system data bus. Two handshaking control lines are provided for use with the keyboard.

The display is also linked by an 8-bit data port. Again, two of the bits have special meanings that are transparent to the 82C55A. In addition to two handshaking lines, two lines provide additional control functions.

7.5 DIRECT MEMORY ACCESS

Drawbacks of Programmed and Interrupt-Driven I/O

Interrupt-driven I/O, though more efficient than simple programmed I/O, still requires the active intervention of the processor to transfer data between memory and an I/O module, and any data transfer must traverse a path through the processor. Thus, both these forms of I/O suffer from two inherent drawbacks:

1. The I/O transfer rate is limited by the speed with which the processor can test and service a device.
2. The processor is tied up in managing an I/O transfer; a number of instructions must be executed for each I/O transfer (e.g., Figure 7.5).

There is somewhat of a trade-off between these two drawbacks. Consider the transfer of a block of data. Using simple programmed I/O, the processor is dedicated to the task of I/O and can move data at a rather high rate, at the cost of doing nothing else. Interrupt I/O frees up the processor to some extent at the expense of the

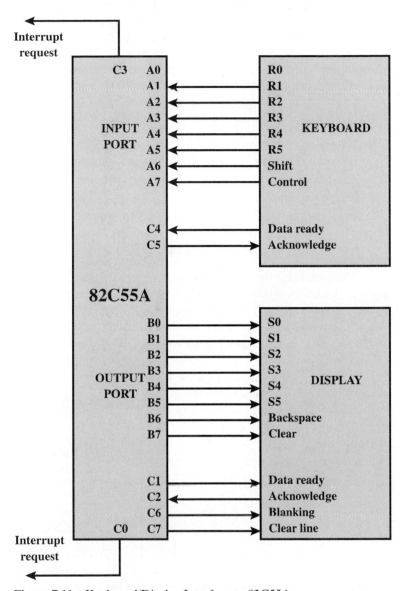

Figure 7.11   Keyboard/Display Interface to 82C55A

I/O transfer rate. Nevertheless, both methods have an adverse impact on both processor activity and I/O transfer rate.

When large volumes of data are to be moved, a more efficient technique is required: direct memory access (DMA).

DMA Function

DMA involves an additional module on the system bus. The DMA module (Figure 7.12) is capable of mimicking the processor and, indeed, of taking over control of the system from the processor. It needs to do this to transfer data to and from memory over the system bus. For this purpose, the DMA module must use the bus only when the processor does not need it, or it must force the processor to suspend operation temporarily. The latter technique is more common and is referred to as *cycle stealing*, because the DMA module in effect steals a bus cycle.

When the processor wishes to read or write a block of data, it issues a command to the DMA module, by sending to the DMA module the following information:

- Whether a read or write is requested, using the read or write control line between the processor and the DMA module
- The address of the I/O device involved, communicated on the data lines
- The starting location in memory to read from or write to, communicated on the data lines and stored by the DMA module in its address register
- The number of words to be read or written, again communicated via the data lines and stored in the data count regis.ter

The processor then continues with other work. It has delegated this I/O operation to the DMA module. The DMA module transfers the entire block of data, one word at a time, directly to or from memory, without going through the processor. When the transfer is complete, the DMA module sends an interrupt signal to the processor. Thus, the processor is involved only at the beginning and end of the transfer (Figure 7.5c).

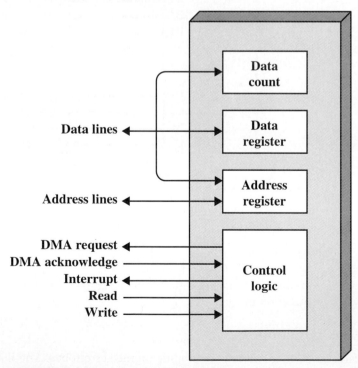

Figure 7.12 Typical DMA Block Diagram

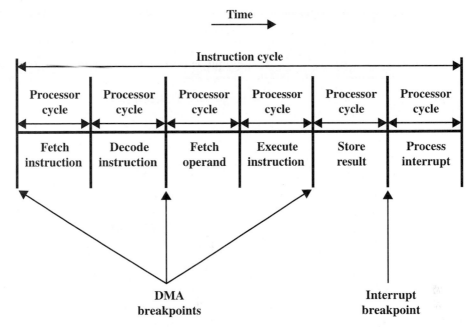

Figure 7.13 DMA and Interrupt Breakpoints during an Instruction Cycle

Figure 7.13 shows where in the instruction cycle the processor may be suspended. In each case, the processor is suspended just before it needs to use the bus. The DMA module then transfers one word and returns control to the processor. Note that this is not an interrupt; the processor does not save a context and do something else. Rather, the processor pauses for one bus cycle. The overall effect is to cause the processor to execute more slowly. Nevertheless, for a multiple-word I/O transfer, DMA is far more efficient than interrupt-driven or programmed I/O.

The DMA mechanism can be configured in a variety of ways. Some possibilities are shown in Figure 7.14. In the first example, all modules share the same system bus. The DMA module, acting as a surrogate processor, uses programmed I/O to exchange data between memory and an I/O module through the DMA module. This configuration, while it may be inexpensive, is clearly inefficient. As with processor-controlled programmed I/O, each transfer of a word consumes two bus cycles.

The number of required bus cycles can be cut substantially by integrating the DMA and I/O functions. As Figure 7.14b indicates, this means that there is a path between the DMA module and one or more I/O modules that does not include the system bus. The DMA logic may actually be a part of an I/O module, or it may be a separate module that controls one or more I/O modules. This concept can be taken one step further by connecting I/O modules to the DMA module using an I/O bus (Figure 7.14c). This reduces the number of I/O interfaces in the DMA module to one and provides for an easily expandable configuration. In all of these cases (Figures 7.14b and c), the system bus that the DMA module shares with the processor and memory is used by the DMA module only to exchange data with memory. The exchange of data between the DMA and I/O modules takes place off the system bus.

(a) Single-bus, detached DMA

(b) Single-bus, integrated DMA-I/O

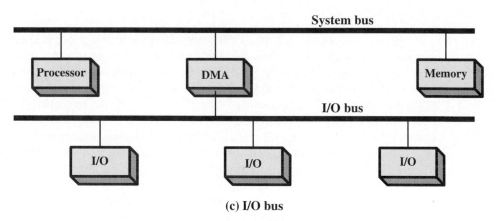

(c) I/O bus

Figure 7.14 Alternative DMA Configurations

7.6 I/O CHANNELS AND PROCESSORS

The Evolution of the I/O Function

As computer systems have evolved, there has been a pattern of increasing complexity and sophistication of individual components. Nowhere is this more evident than in the I/O function. We have already seen part of that evolution. The evolutionary steps can be summarized as follows:

1. The CPU directly controls a peripheral device. This is seen in simple microprocessor-controlled devices.
2. A controller or I/O module is added. The CPU uses programmed I/O without interrupts. With this step, the CPU becomes somewhat divorced from the specific details of external device interfaces.
3. The same configuration as in step 2 is used, but now interrupts are employed. The CPU need not spend time waiting for an I/O operation to be performed, increasing efficiency.
4. The I/O module is given direct access to memory via DMA. It can now move a block of data to or from memory without involving the CPU, except at the beginning and end of the transfer.
5. The I/O module is enhanced to become a processor in its own right, with a specialized instruction set tailored for I/O. The CPU directs the I/O processor to execute an I/O program in memory. The I/O processor fetches and executes these instructions without CPU intervention. This allows the CPU to specify a sequence of I/O activities and to be interrupted only when the entire sequence has been performed.
6. The I/O module has a local memory of its own and is, in fact, a computer in its own right. With this architecture, a large set of I/O devices can be controlled, with minimal CPU involvement. A common use for such an architecture has been to control communication with interactive terminals. The I/O processor takes care of most of the tasks involved in controlling the terminals.

As one proceeds along this evolutionary path, more and more of the I/O function is performed without CPU involvement. The CPU is increasingly relieved of I/O-related tasks, improving performance. With the last two steps (5–6), a major change occurs with the introduction of the concept of an I/O module capable of executing a program. For step 5, the I/O module is often referred to as an *I/O channel*. For step 6, the term *I/O processor* is often used. However, both terms are on occasion applied to both situations. In what follows, we will use the term *I/O channel*.

Characteristics of I/O Channels

The I/O channel represents an extension of the DMA concept. An I/O channel has the ability to execute I/O instructions, which gives it complete control over I/O operations. In a computer system with such devices, the CPU does not execute I/O instructions. Such instructions are stored in main memory to be executed by a special-purpose processor in the I/O channel itself. Thus, the CPU initiates an I/O transfer by instructing the I/O channel to execute a program in memory. The program will specify the device or devices, the area or areas of memory for storage, priority, and actions to be taken for certain error conditions. The I/O channel follows these instructions and controls the data transfer.

Two types of I/O channels are common, as illustrated in Figure 7.15. A *selector channel* controls multiple high-speed devices and, at any one time, is dedicated to the transfer of data with one of those devices. Thus, the I/O channel selects one device and effects the data transfer. Each device, or a small set of devices, is handled by a *controller,* or I/O module, that is much like the I/O modules we have been

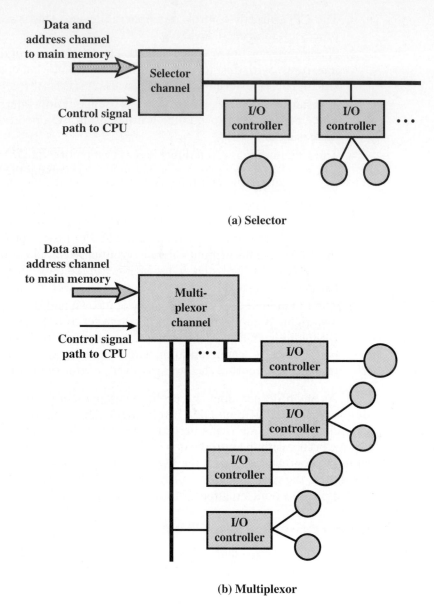

(a) Selector

(b) Multiplexor

Figure 7.15 I/O Channel Architecture

discussing. Thus, the I/O channel serves in place of the CPU in controlling these I/O controllers. A *multiplexor channel* can handle I/O with multiple devices at the same time. For low-speed devices, a *byte multiplexor* accepts or transmits characters as fast as possible to multiple devices. For example, the resultant character stream from three devices with different rates and individual streams $A_1A_2A_3A_4 \ldots, B_1B_2B_3B_4 \ldots$, and $C_1C_2C_3C_4 \ldots$ might be $A_1B_1C_1A_2C_2A_3B_2C_3A_4$, and so on. For high-speed devices, a *block multiplexor* interleaves blocks of data from several devices.

7.7 THE EXTERNAL INTERFACE: FIREWIRE AND INFINIBAND

Types of Interfaces

The interface to a peripheral from an I/O module must be tailored to the nature and operation of the peripheral. One major characteristic of the interface is whether it is serial or parallel (Figure 7.16). In a **parallel interface**, there are multiple lines connecting the I/O module and the peripheral, and multiple bits are transferred simultaneously, just as all of the bits of a word are transferred simultaneously over the data bus. In a **serial interface**, there is only one line used to transmit data, and bits must be transmitted one at a time. A parallel interface has traditionally been used for higher-speed peripherals, such as tape and disk, while the serial interface has traditionally been used for printers and terminals. With a new generation of high-speed serial interfaces, parallel interfaces are becoming much less common.

In either case, the I/O module must engage in a dialogue with the peripheral. In general terms, the dialogue for a write operation is as follows:

1. The I/O module sends a control signal requesting permission to send data.
2. The peripheral acknowledges the request.
3. The I/O module transfers data (one word or a block depending on the peripheral).
4. The peripheral acknowledges receipt of the data.

A read operation proceeds similarly.

Key to the operation of an I/O module is an internal buffer that can store data being passed between the peripheral and the rest of the system. This buffer allows

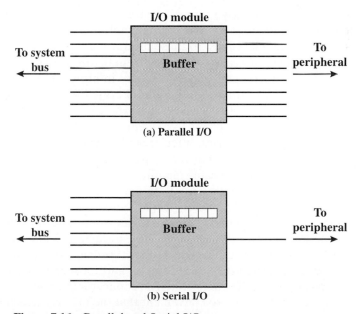

Figure 7.16 Parallel and Serial I/O

the I/O module to compensate for the differences in speed between the system bus and its external lines.

Point-to-Point and Multipoint Configurations

The connection between an I/O module in a computer system and external devices can be either point-to-point or multipoint. A point-to-point interface provides a dedicated line between the I/O module and the external device. On small systems (PCs, workstations), typical point-to-point links include those to the keyboard, printer, and external modem. A typical example of such an interface is the EIA-232 specification (see [STAL00] for a description).

Of increasing importance are multipoint external interfaces, used to support external mass storage devices (disk and tape drives) and multimedia devices (CD-ROMs, video, audio). These multipoint interfaces are in effect external buses, and they exhibit the same type of logic as the buses discussed in Chapter 3. In this section, we look at two key examples: FireWire and InfiniBand.

FireWire Serial Bus

With processor speeds reaching GHz range and storage devices holding multiple gigabits, the I/O demands for personal computers, workstations, and servers are formidable. Yet the high-speed I/O channel technologies that have been developed for mainframe and supercomputer systems are too expensive and bulky for use on these smaller systems. Accordingly, there has been great interest in developing a high-speed alternative to SCSI and other small-system I/O interfaces. The result is the IEEE standard 1394, for a high-performance serial bus, commonly known as FireWire.

FireWire has a number of advantages over older I/O interfaces. It is very high speed, low cost, and easy to implement. In fact, FireWire is finding favor not only for computer systems, but also in consumer electronics products, such as digital cameras, VCRs, and televisions. In these products, FireWire is used to transport video images, which are increasingly coming from digitized sources.

One of the strengths of the FireWire interface is that it uses serial transmission (bit at a time) rather than parallel. Parallel interfaces, such as SCSI, require more wires, which means wider, more expensive cables and wider, more expensive connectors with more pins to bend or break. A cable with more wires requires shielding to prevent electrical interference between the wires. Also, with a parallel interface, synchronization between wires becomes a requirement, a problem that gets worse with increased cable length.

In addition, computers are getting physically smaller even as they expand in computing power and I/O needs. Handheld and pocket-size computers have little room for connectors yet need high data rates to handle images and video.

The intent of FireWire is to provide a single I/O interface with a simple connector that can handle numerous devices through a single port, so that the mouse, laser printer, external disk drive, sound, and local area network hookups can be replaced with this single connector. The connector is inspired by the one used in the Nintendo Gameboy. It is so convenient that the user can reach behind the machine and plug it in without looking.

Figure 7.17   Simple FireWire Configuration

FireWire Configurations

FireWire uses a daisy-chain configuration, with up to 63 devices connected off a single port. Moreover, up to 1022 FireWire buses can be interconnected using bridges, enabling a system to support as many peripherals as required.

FireWire provides for what is known as hot plugging, which makes it possible to connect and disconnect peripherals without having to power the computer system down or reconfigure the system. Also, FireWire provides for automatic configuration; it is not necessary manually to set device Ids or to be concerned with the relative position of devices. Figure 7.17 shows a simple FireWire configuration. With FireWire, there are no terminations, and the system automatically performs a configuration function to assign addresses. Also note that a FireWire bus need not be a strict daisy chain. Rather, a tree-structured configuration is possible.

An important feature of the FireWire standard is that it specifies a set of three layers of protocols to standardize the way in which the host system interacts with the peripheral devices over the serial bus. Figure 7.18 illustrates this stack. The three layers of the stack are as follows:

- **Physical layer:** Defines the transmission media that are permissible under FireWire and the electrical and signaling characteristics of each
- **Link layer:** Describes the transmission of data in the packets
- **Transaction layer:** Defines a request-response protocol that hides the lower-layer details of FireWire from applications

Physical Layer

The physical layer of FireWire specifies several alternative transmission media and their connectors, with different physical and data transmission properties. Data rates from 25 to 400 Mbps are defined. The physical layer converts binary data into electrical signals for various physical media. This layer also provides the arbitration service that guarantees that only one device at a time will transmit data.

Two forms of arbitration are provided by FireWire. The simplest form is based on the tree-structured arrangement of the nodes on a FireWire bus, mentioned earlier. A special case of this structure is a linear daisy chain. The physical layer contains logic that allows all the attached devices to configure themselves so that one node is designated as the root of the tree and other nodes are organized in a parent/child relationship forming the tree topology. Once this configuration is established, the root node acts as a central arbiter and processes requests for bus access in a first-come-first-served fashion. In the case of simultaneous requests, the node with the highest natural priority is granted access. The natural priority is determined by which competing node is closest to the root and, among those of equal distance from the root, which one has the lower ID number.

The aforementioned arbitration method is supplemented by two additional functions: fair arbitration and urgent arbitration. With fairness arbitration, time on the bus is organized into *fairness intervals.* At the beginning of an interval, each node sets an arbitration_enable flag. During the interval, each node may compete for bus access. Once a node has gained access to the bus, it resets its arbitration_enable flag and may not again compete for fair access during this interval. This scheme makes the arbitration more fair, in that it prevents one or more busy high-priority devices from monopolizing the bus.

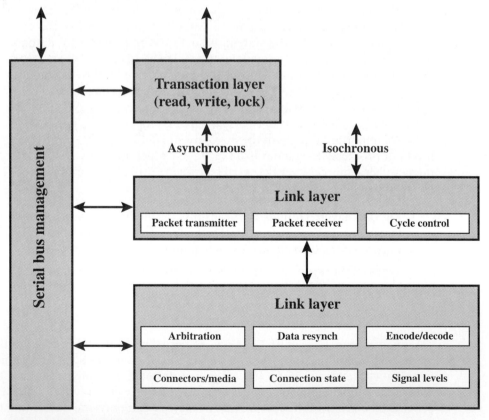

Figure 7.18   FireWire Protocol Stack

In addition to the fairness scheme, some devices may be configured as having *urgent* priority. Such nodes may gain control of the bus multiple times during a fairness interval. In essence, a counter is used at each high-priority node that enables the high-priority nodes to control 75% of the available bus time. For each packet that is transmitted as nonurgent, three packets may be transmitted as urgent.

Link Layer

The link layer defines the transmission of data in the form of packets. Two types of transmission are supported:

- **Asynchronous:** A variable amount of data and several bytes of transaction layer information are transferred as a packet to an explicit address and an acknowledgment is returned.
- **Isochronous:** A variable amount of data is transferred in a sequence of fixed-size packets transmitted at regular intervals. This form of transmission uses simplified addressing and no acknowledgment.

Asynchronous transmission is used by data that have no fixed data rate requirements. Both the fair arbitration and urgent arbitration schemes may be used for asynchronous transmission. The default method is fair arbitration. Devices that desire a substantial fraction of the bus capacity or have severe latency requirements use the urgent arbitration method. For example, a high-speed real-time data collection node may use urgent arbitration when critical data buffers are more than half full.

Figure 7.19a depicts a typical asynchronous transaction. The process of delivering a single packet is called a subaction. The subaction consists of five time periods:

- **Arbitration sequence:** This is the exchange of signals required to give one device control of the bus.
- **Packet transmission:** Every packet includes a header containing the source and destination Ids. The header also contains packet type information, a CRC (cyclic redundancy check) checksum, and parameter information for the specific packet type. A packet may also include a data block consisting of user data and another CRC.
- **Acknowledgment gap:** This is the time delay for the destination to receive and decode a packet and generate an acknowledgment.
- **Acknowledgment:** The recipient of the packet returns an acknowledgment packet with a code indicating the action taken by the recipient.
- **Subaction gap:** This is an enforced idle period to ensure that other nodes on the bus do not begin arbitrating before the acknowledgment packet has been transmitted.

At the time that the acknowledgment is sent, the acknowledging node is in control of the bus. Therefore, if the exchange is a request/response interaction between two nodes, then the responding node can immediately transmit the response packet without going through an arbitration sequence (Figure 7.19b).

For devices that regularly generate or consume data, such as digital sound or video, isochronous access is provided. This method guarantees that data can be delivered within a specified latency with a guaranteed data rate.

To accommodate a mixed traffic load of isochronous and asynchronous data sources, one node is designated as *cycle master*. Periodically, the cycle master issues a cycle_start packet. This signals all other nodes that an isochronous cycle has begun. During this cycle, only isochronous packets may be sent (Figure 7.19c). Each isochronous data source arbitrates for bus access. The winning node immediately transmits a packet. There is no acknowledgment to this packet, and so other isochronous data sources immediately arbitrate for the bus after the previous isochronous packet is transmitted. The result is that there is a small gap between the transmission of one packet and the arbitration period for the next packet, dictated by delays on the bus. This delay, referred to as the isochronous gap, is smaller than a subaction gap.

After all isochronous sources have transmitted, the bus will remain idle long enough for a subaction gap to occur. This is the signal to the asynchronous sources that they may now compete for bus access. Asynchronous sources may then use the bus until the beginning of the next isochronous cycle.

Isochronous packets are labeled with 8-bit channel numbers that are previously assigned by a dialogue between the two nodes that are to exchange isochronous data. The header, which is shorter than that for asynchronous packets, also includes a data length field and a header CRC.

(a) Example asynchronous subaction

(b) Concatenated asynchronous subactions

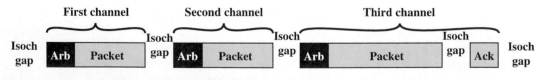

(c) Example isochronous subactions

Figure 7.19 FireWire Subactions

InfiniBand

InfiniBand is a recent I/O specification aimed at the high-end server market.[4] The first version of the specification was released in early 2001 and has attracted numerous vendors. The standard describes an architecture and specifications for data flow between processors and intelligent I/O devices. InfiniBand is intended to replace the PCI bus in servers, to provide greater capacity, increased expandability, and enhanced flexibility in server design. In essence, InfiniBand enables servers, remote storage, and other network devices to be attached in a central fabric of switches and links. The switch-based architecture can connect up to 64,000 servers, storage systems, and networking devices.

Infiniband Architecture

Although PCI is a reliable interconnect method and continues to provide increased speeds, up to 1 Gbps, it is a limited architecture compared to Infiniband. With InfiniBand, it is not necessary to have the basic I/O interface hardware inside the server chassis. With InfiniBand, remote storage, networking, and connections between servers are accomplished by attaching all devices to a central fabric of switches and links. Removing I/O from the server chassis allows greater server density and allows for a more flexible and scalable data center, as independent nodes may be added as needed.

Unlike PCI, which measures distances from a CPU motherboard in centimeters, InfiniBand's channel design enables I/O devices to be placed up to 17 m away from the server using copper, up to 300 m using multimode optical fiber, and up to 10 km with single-mode optical fiber. Transmission rates has high as 30 Gbps can be achieved.

Figure 7.20 illustrates the InfiniBand architecture. The key elements are as follows:

- **Host channel adapter (HCA):** Instead of a number of PCI slots, a typical server needs a single interface to an HCA that links the server to an InfiniBand switch. The HCA attaches to the server at a memory controller, which has access to the system bus and controls traffic between the processor and memory and between the HCA and memory. The HCA uses direct-memory access (DMA) to read and write memory.
- **Target channel adapter (TCA):** A TCA is used to connect storage systems, routers, and other peripheral devices to an InfiniBand switch.
- **InfiniBand switch:** A switch provides point-to-point physical connections to a variety of devices and switches traffic from one link to another. Servers and devices communicate through their adapters, via the switch. The switch's intelligence manages the linkage without interrupting the servers' operation.
- **Links:** The link between a switch and a channel adapter, or between two switches.

---

[4]Infiniband is the result of the merger of two competing projects: Future I/O (backed by Cisco, HP, Compaq, and IBM) and Next Generation I/O (developed by Intel and backed by a number of other companies).

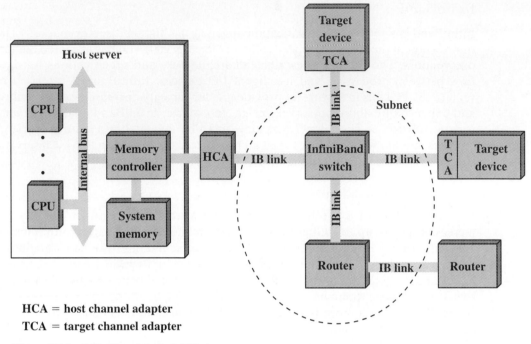

HCA = host channel adapter
TCA = target channel adapter

Figure 7.20 InfiniBand Switch Fabric

- **Subnet:** A subnet consists of one or more interconnected switches plus the links that connect other devices to those switches. Figure 7.20 shows a subnet with a single switch, but more complex subnets are required when a large number of devices are to be interconnected. Subnets allow administrators to confine broadcast and multicast transmissions within the subnet.
- **Router:** Connects InfiniBand subnets, or connects an Infiniband switch to a network, such as a local area network, wide area network, or storage area network.

The channel adapters are intelligent devices that handle all I/O functions without the need to interrupt the server's processor. For example, there is a control protocol by which a switch discovers all TCAs and FCAs in the fabric and assigns logical addresses to each. This is done without processor involvement.

The Infiniband switch temporarily opens up channels between the processor and devices with which it is communicating. The devices do not have to share a channel's capacity, as is the case with a bus-based design such as PCI, which requires that devices arbitrate for access to the processor. Additional devices are added to the configuration by hooking up each device's TCA to the switch.

InfiniBand Operation

Each physical link between a switch and an attached interface (HCA or TCA) can be support up to 16 logical channels, called **virtual lanes**. One lane is reserved for fabric management and the other lanes for data transport. Data are sent in the form of a stream of packets, with each packet containing some portion of the total data to be transferred, plus addressing and control information. Thus, a set of communications protocols are used to manage the transfer of data. A virtual lane is temporarily dedicated to the transfer of data from one end node to another over the InfiniBand fabric. The InfiniBand switch maps traffic from an incoming lane to an outgoing lane to route the data between the desired end points.

Figure 7.21 indicates the logical structure used to support exchanges over InfiniBand. To account for the fact that some devices can send data faster than 'temporarily buffers excess outbound and inbound data. The queues can be located in the channel adapter or in the attached device's memory. A separate pair of queues is used for each virtual lane. The host uses these queues in the following fashion. The host places a transaction, called a work queue entry (WQE) into either the send or receive queue of the queue pair. The two most important WQEs are SEND and RECEIVE. For a SEND operation, the WQE specifies a block of data in the device's memory space for the hardware to send to the destination. A RECEIVE WQE specifies where the hardware is to place data received from another device when that consumer executes a SEND operation. The channel adapter processes each posted WQE in the proper prioritized order and generates a completion queue entry (CQE) to indicate the completion status.

Figure 7.21 also indicates that a layered protocol architecture is used, consisting of four layers:

- **Physical:** The physical-layer specification defines three link speeds (1X, 4X, and 12X) giving transmission rates of 2.5, 10, and 30 Gbps, respectively (Table 7.4). The physical layer also defines the physical media, including copper and optical fiber.
- **Link:** This layer defines the basic packet structure used to exchange data, including an addressing scheme that assigns a unique link address to every device in a subnet. This level includes the logic for setting up virtual lanes and for switching data through switches from source to destination within a subnet. The packet structure includes an error detection code to provide reliability.
- **Network:** The network layer routes packets between different InfiniBand subnets.
- **Transport:** The transport layer provides reliability mechanism for end-to-end transfer of packets across one or more subnets.

Table 7.4   InfiniBand Links and Data Throughput Rates

Link	Signal rate (unidirectional)	Usable capacity (80% of signal rate)	Effective data throughput (send + receive)
1- wide	2.5 Gbps	2 Gbps (250 MBps)	(250 + 250) MBps
4-wide	10 Gbps	8 Gbps (1 GBps)	(1 + 1) GBps
12-wide	30 Gbps	24 Gbps (3 GBps)	(3 + 3) Gbps

Figure 7.21 InfiniBand Communication Protocol Stack

WQE = work queue element
CQE = completion queue entry
QP = queue pair

7.8 RECOMMENDED READING AND WEB SITES

A good discussion of Intel I/O modules and architecture, including the 82C59A and 82C55A, can be found in [BREY00].

FireWire is covered in great detail in [ANDE98]. [WICK97] and [THOM00] provide a concise overviews of FireWire.

InfiniBand is covered in great detail in [FUTR01]. [KAGA01] provides a concise overview.

ANDE98 Anderson, D. *FireWire System Architecture.* Reading, MA: Addison-Wesley, 1998.

BREY00 Brey, B. *The Intel Microprocessors: 8086/8066, 80186/80188, 80286, 80386, 80486, Pentium, Pentium Pro and Pentium II Processors.* Upper Saddle River, NJ: Prentice Hall, 2000.

FUTR01 Futral, W. *InfiniBand Architecture: Development and Deployment.* Hillsboro, OR: Intel Press, 2001.

KAGA01 Kagan, M. "InfiniBand: Thinking Outside the Box Design." *Communications System Design*, September 2001. (www.csdmag.com)

THOM00 Thompson, D. "IEEE 1394: Changing the Way We Do Multimedia Communications." *IEEE Multimedia*, April–June 2000.

WICK97 Wickelgren, I. "The Facts About FireWire." *IEEE Spectrum*, April 1997.

Recommended Web Sites:

- **T10 Home Page:** T10 is a Technical Committee of the National Committee on Information Technology Standards and is responsible for lower-level interfaces. Its principal work is the Small Computer System Interface (SCSI).
- **1394 Trade Association:** Includes technical information and vendor pointers on FireWire.
- **Infiniband Trade Association:** Includes technical information and vendor pointers on Infiniband.

7.9 KEY TERMS, REVIEW QUESTIONS, AND PROBLEMS

Key Terms

cycle stealing	I/O channel	multiplexor channel
direct memory access (DMA)	I/O command	parallel I/O
FireWire	I/O module	peripheral device
InfiniBand	I/O processor	programmed I/O
interrupt	isolated I/O	selector channel
interrupt-driven I/O	memory-mapped I/O	serial I/O

Review Questions

7.1 List three broad classifications of external, or peripheral, devices.

7.2 What is the International Reference Alphabet?

7.3 What are the major functions of an I/O module?

7.4 List and briefly define three techniques for performing I/O.

7.5 What is the difference between memory-mapped I/O and isolated I/O?

7.6 When a device interrupt occurs, how does the processor determine which device issued the interrupt?

7.7 When a DMA module takes control of a bus, and while it retains control of the bus, what does the processor do?

Problems

7.1 In Section 7.3, one advantage and one disadvantage of memory-mapped I/O, compared with isolated I/O, were listed. List two more advantages and two more disadvantages.

7.2 In virtually all systems that include DMA modules, DMA access to main memory is given higher priority than CPU access to main memory. Why?

7.3 Consider a disk system with 960 512-byte sectors per track and assume the disk rotates at 3600 rpm. A processor reads one sector from the disk using interrupt-driven I/O, with one interrupt per byte. If it takes 2.5 (s to process each interrupt, what percentage of the time will the processor spend handling I/O (disregard seek time)?

7.4 Repeat Problem 7.3 using DMA, and assume one interrupt per sector.

7.5 A DMA module is transferring characters to memory using cycle stealing, from a device transmitting at 9600 bps. The processor is fetching instructions at the rate of 1 million instructions per second (1 MIPS). By how much will the processor be slowed down due to the DMA activity?

7.6 A 32-bit computer has two selector channels and one multiplexor channel. Each selector channel supports two magnetic disk and two magnetic tape units. The multiplexor channel has two line printers, two card readers, and 10 VDT terminals connected to it. Assume the following transfer rates:

Disk drive	800 KBytes/s
Magnetic tape drive	200 KBytes/s
Line printer	6.6 KBytes/s
Card reader	1.2 KBytes/s
VDT	1 KBytes/s

Estimate the maximum aggregate I/O transfer rate in this system.

7.7 A computer consists of a processor and an I/O device D connected to main memory M via a shared bus with a data bus width of one word. The processor can execute a maximum of 10^6 instructions per second. An average instruction requires five machine cycles, three of which use the memory bus. A memory read or write operation uses one machine cycle. Suppose that the processor is continuously executing "background" programs that require 95% of its instruction execution rate but not any I/O instructions. Assume that one processor cycle equals one bus cycle. Now suppose the I/O device is to be used to transfer very large blocks of data between M and D.

  a. If programmed I/O is used and each one-word I/O transfer requires the processor to execute two instructions, estimate the maximum I/O data-transfer rate, in words per second, possible through D.

  b. Estimate the same rate if DMA is used.

7.8 A data source produces 7-bit IRA characters, to each of which is appended a parity bit. Derive an expression for the maximum effective data rate (rate of IRA data bits) over an R-bps line for the following:

a. Asynchronous transmission, with a 1.5-unit stop bit

b. Bit synchronous transmission, with a frame consisting of 48 control bits and 128 information bits

c. Same as (b), with a 1024-bit information field

d. Character synchronous, with 9 control characters per frame and 16 information characters

e. Same as (d), with 128 information characters

7.9 The following problem is based on a suggested illustration of I/O mechanisms in [ECKE90] (Figure 7.22):

Two boys are playing on either side of a high fence. One of the boys, named Apple-server, has a beautiful apple tree loaded with delicious apples growing on his side of the fence; he is happy to supply apples to the other boy whenever needed. The other boy, named Apple-eater, loves to eat apples but has none. In fact, he must eat his apples at a fixed rate (an apple a day keeps the doctor away). If he eats them faster than that rate, he will get sick. If he eats them slower, he will suffer malnutrition. Neither boy can talk, and so the problem is to get apples from Apple-server to Apple-eater at the correct rate.

a. Assume that there is an alarm clock sitting on top of the fence and that the clock can have multiple alarm settings. How can the clock be used to solve the problem? Draw a timing diagram to illustrate the solution.

b. Now assume that there is no alarm clock. Instead Apple-eater has a flag that he can wave whenever he needs an apple. Suggest a new solution. Would it be helpful for Apple-server also to have a flag? If so, incorporate this into the solution. Discuss the drawbacks of this approach.

c. Now take away the flag and assume the existence of a long piece of string. Suggest a solution that is superior to that of (b) using the string.

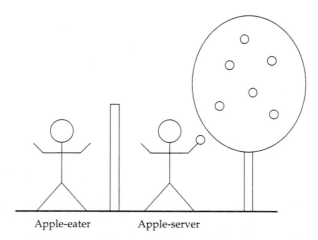

Apple-eater   Apple-server

Figure 7.22 An Apple Problem

7.10 Assume that one 16-bit and two 8-bit microprocessors are to be interfaced to a system bus. The following details are given:

1. All microprocessors have the hardware features necessary for any type of data transfer: programmed I/O, interrupt-driven I/O, and DMA.

2. All microprocessors have a 16-bit address bus.

3. Two memory boards, each of 64 KBytes capacity, are interfaced with the bus. The designer wishes to use a shared memory that is as large as possible.

4. The system bus supports a maximum of four interrupt lines and one DMA line.

Make any other assumptions necessary, and

a. Give the system bus specifications in terms of number and types of lines.

b. Describe a possible protocol for communicating on the bus, i.e., read/write, interrupt, and DMA sequences.

c. Explain how the aforementioned devices are interfaced to the system bus.

Source: [ALEX93]

CHAPTER 8

OPERATING SYSTEM SUPPORT

KEY POINTS

♦ The operating system (OS) is the software that controls the execution of programs on a processor and that manages the processor's resources. A number of the functions performed by the OS, including process scheduling and memory management, can only be performed efficiently and rapidly if the processor hardware includes capabilities to support the OS. Virtually all processors include such capabilities to a greater or lesser extent, including virtual memory management hardware and process management hardware. The hardware includes special-purpose registers and buffers, as well as circuitry to perform basic resource management tasks.

♦ One of the most important functions of the OS is the scheduling of processes, or tasks. The OS determines which process should run at any given time. Typically, the hardware will interrupt a running process from time to time to enable the OS to make a new scheduling decision so as to share processor time fairly among a number of processes.

♦ Another important OS function is memory management. Most contemporary operating systems include a virtual memory capability, which has two benefits: (1) A process can run in main memory without all of the instructions and data for that program being present in main memory at one time, and (2) the total memory space available to a program may far exceed the actual main memory on the system. Although memory management is performed in software, the OS relies on hardware support in the processor, including paging and segmentation hardware.

Although the focus of this text is computer hardware, there is one area of software that needs to be addressed: the computer's operating system. The operating system is a program that manages the computer's resources, provides services for programmers, and schedules the execution of other programs. Some understanding of operating systems is essential to appreciate the mechanisms by which the CPU controls the computer system. In particular, explanations of the effect of interrupts and of the management of the memory hierarchy are best explained in this context.

The chapter begins with an overview and brief history of operating systems. The bulk of the chapter looks at the two operating system functions that are most relevant to the study of computer organization and architecture: scheduling and memory management.

8.1 OPERATING SYSTEM OVERVIEW

Operating System Objectives and Functions

An operating system is a program that controls the execution of application programs and acts as an interface between the user of a computer and the computer hardware. It can be thought of as having two objectives:

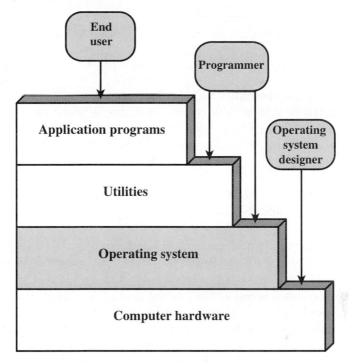

Figure 8.1 Layers and Views of a Computer System

- **Convenience:** An operating system makes a computer more convenient to use.
- **Efficiency:** An operating system allows the computer system resources to be used in an efficient manner.

Let us examine these two aspects of an operating system in turn.

The Operating System as a User/Computer Interface

The hardware and software used in providing applications to a user can be viewed in a layered or hierarchical fashion, as depicted in Figure 8.1. The user of those applications, the end user, generally is not concerned with the computer's architecture. Thus the end user views a computer system in terms of an application. That application can be expressed in a programming language and is developed by an application programmer. If one were to develop an application program as a set of processor instructions that is completely responsible for controlling the computer hardware, one would be faced with an overwhelmingly complex task. To ease this task, a set of systems programs is provided. Some of these programs are referred to as **utilities**. These implement frequently used functions that assist in program creation, the management of files, and the control of I/O devices. A programmer will make use of these facilities in developing an application, and the application, while it is running, will invoke the utilities to perform certain functions. The most important system program is the operating system. The operating system masks the details of the hardware from the programmer and provides the programmer with a convenient interface for using the system. It acts as mediator, making it easier for the programmer and for application programs to access and use those facilities and services.

Briefly, the operating system typically provides services in the following areas:

- **Program creation:** The operating system provides a variety of facilities and services, such as editors and debuggers, to assist the programmer in creating programs. Typically, these services are in the form of utility programs that are not actually part of the operating system but are accessible through the operating system.
- **Program execution:** A number of tasks need to be performed to execute a program. Instructions and data must be loaded into main memory, I/O devices and files must be initialized, and other resources must be prepared. The operating system handles all of this for the user.
- **Access to I/O devices:** Each I/O device requires its own peculiar set of instructions or control signals for operation. The operating system takes care of the details so that the programmer can think in terms of simple reads and writes.
- **Controlled access to files:** In the case of files, control must include an understanding of not only the nature of the I/O device (disk drive, tape drive) but also the file format on the storage medium. Again, the operating system worries about the details. Further, in the case of a system with multiple simultaneous users, the operating system can provide protection mechanisms to control access to the files.
- **System access:** In the case of a shared or public system, the operating system controls access to the system as a whole and to specific system resources. The access function must provide protection of resources and data from unauthorized users and must resolve conflicts for resource contention.
- **Error detection and response:** A variety of errors can occur while a computer system is running. These include internal and external hardware errors, such as a memory error, or a device failure or malfunction; and various software errors, such as arithmetic overflow, attempt to access forbidden memory location, and inability of the operating system to grant the request of an application. In each case, the operating system must make the response that clears the error condition with the least impact on running applications. The response may range from ending the program that caused the error, to retrying the operation, to simply reporting the error to the application.
- **Accounting:** A good operating system will collect usage statistics for various resources and monitor performance parameters such as response time. On any system, this information is useful in anticipating the need for future enhancements and in tuning the system to improve performance. On a multiuser system, the information can be used for billing purposes.

The Operating System as Resource Manager

A computer is a set of resources for the movement, storage, and processing of data and for the control of these functions. The operating system is responsible for managing these resources.

Can we say that it is the operating system that controls the movement, storage, and processing of data? From one point of view, the answer is yes: By managing the computer's resources, the operating system is in control of the computer's basic functions. But this control is exercised in a curious way. Normally, we think of a control mechanism as something external to that which is controlled, or at least as something that is a distinct and separate part of that which is controlled. (For example, a residential heating system is controlled by a thermostat, which is completely distinct from the heat-generation and heat-distribution apparatus.) This is not the case with the operating system, which as a control mechanism is unusual in two respects:

- The operating system functions in the same way as ordinary computer software; that is, it is a program executed by the processor.
- The operating system frequently relinquishes control and must depend on the processor to allow it to regain control.

The operating system is, in fact, nothing more than a computer program. Like other computer programs, it provides instructions for the processor. The key difference is in the intent of the program. The operating system directs the processor in the use of the other system resources and in the timing of its execution of other programs. But in order for the processor to do any of these things, it must cease executing the operating system program and execute other programs. Thus, the operating system relinquishes control for the processor to do some "useful" work and then resumes control long enough to prepare the processor to do the next piece of work. The mechanisms involved in all this should become clear as the chapter proceeds.

Figure 8.2 suggests the main resources that are managed by the operating system. A portion of the operating system is in main memory. This includes the **kernel**, or **nucleus**, which contains the most frequently used functions in the operating system and, at a given time, other portions of the operating system currently in use. The remainder of main memory contains other user programs and data. The allocation of this resource (main memory) is controlled jointly by the operating system and memory-management hardware in the processor, as we shall see. The operating system decides when an I/O device can be used by a program in execution, and controls access to and use of files. The processor itself is a resource, and the operating system must determine how much processor time is to be devoted to the execution of a particular user program. In the case of a multiple-processor system, this decision must span all of the processors.

Types of Operating Systems

Certain key characteristics serve to differentiate various types of operating systems. The characteristics fall along two independent dimensions. The first dimension specifies whether the system is batch or interactive. In an *interactive* system, the user/programmer interacts directly with the computer, usually through a keyboard/display terminal, to request the execution of a job or to perform a transaction. Furthermore, the user may, depending on the nature of the application, communicate with the computer during the execution of the job. A *batch* system is the opposite of interactive. The user's program is batched together with programs

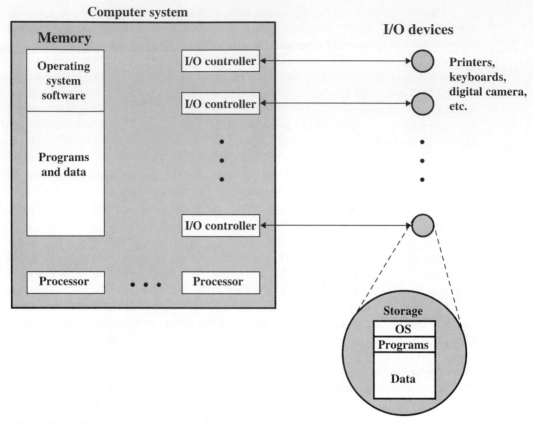

Figure 8.2   The Operating System as Resource Manager

from other users and submitted by a computer operator. After the program is completed, results are printed out for the user. Pure batch systems are rare today. However, it will be useful to the description of contemporary operating systems to examine batch systems briefly.

An independent dimension specifies whether the system employs *multiprogramming* or not. With multiprogramming, the attempt is made to keep the processor as busy as possible, by having it work on more than one program at a time. Several programs are loaded into memory, and the processor switches rapidly among them. The alternative is a *uniprogramming* system that works only one program at a time.

Early Systems

With the earliest computers, from the late 1940s to the mid-1950s, the programmer interacted directly with the computer hardware; there was no operating system. These processors were run from a console, consisting of display lights, toggle switches, some form of input device, and a printer. Programs in processor code were loaded via the input device (e.g., a card reader). If an error halted the program, the error condition was indicated by the lights. The programmer could proceed to examine registers and main memory to determine the cause of the error. If the program proceeded to a normal completion, the output appeared on the printer.

These early systems presented two main problems:

- **Scheduling:** Most installations used a sign-up sheet to reserve processor time. Typically, a user could sign up for a block of time in multiples of a half hour or so. A user might sign up for an hour and finish in 45 minutes; this would result in wasted computer idle time. On the other hand, the user might run into problems, not finish in the allotted time, and be forced to stop before resolving the problem.

- **Setup time:** A single program, called a **job**, could involve loading the compiler plus the high-level language program (source program) into memory, saving the compiled program (object program), and then loading and linking together the object program and common functions. Each of these steps could involve mounting or dismounting tapes, or setting up card decks. If an error occurred, the hapless user typically had to go back to the beginning of the setup sequence. Thus a considerable amount of time was spent just in setting up the program to run.

This mode of operation could be termed serial processing, reflecting the fact that users have access to the computer in series. Over time, various system software tools were developed to attempt to make serial processing more efficient. These include libraries of common functions, linkers, loaders, debuggers, and I/O driver routines that were available as common software for all users.

Simple Batch Systems

Early processors were very expensive, and therefore it was important to maximize processor utilization. The wasted time due to scheduling and setup time was unacceptable.

To improve utilization, simple batch operating systems were developed. With such a system, also called a *monitor,* the user no longer has direct access to the processor. Rather, the user submits the job on cards or tape to a computer operator, who *batches* the jobs together sequentially and places the entire batch on an input device, for use by the monitor.

To understand how this scheme works, let us look at it from two points of view: that of the monitor and that of the processor. From the point of view of the monitor, it is the monitor that controls the sequence of events. For this to be so, much of the monitor must always be in main memory and available for execution (Figure 8.3). That portion is referred to as the **resident monitor**. The rest of the monitor consists of utilities and common functions that are loaded as subroutines to the user program at the beginning of any job that requires them. The monitor reads in jobs one at a time from the input device (typically a card reader or magnetic tape drive). As it is read in, the current job is placed in the user program area, and control is passed to this job. When the job is completed, it returns control to the monitor, which immediately reads in the next job. The results of each job are printed out for delivery to the user.

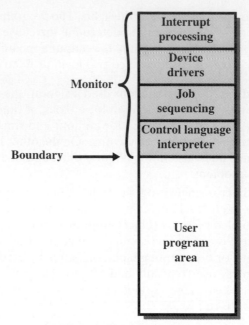

Figure 8.3   Memory Layout for a
Resident Monitor

Now consider this sequence from the point of view of the processor. At a certain point in time, the processor is executing instructions from the portion of main memory containing the monitor. These instructions cause the next job to be read in to another portion of main memory. Once a job has been read in, the processor will encounter in the monitor a branch instruction that instructs the processor to continue execution at the start of the user program. The processor will then execute the instruction in the user's program until it encounters an ending or error condition. Either event causes the processor to fetch its next instruction from the monitor program. Thus the phrase "control is passed to a job" simply means that the processor is now fetching and executing instructions in a user program, and "control is returned to the monitor" means that the processor is now fetching and executing instructions from the monitor program.

It should be clear that the monitor handles the scheduling problem. A batch of jobs is queued up, and jobs are executed as rapidly as possible, with no intervening idle time.

How about the job setup time? The monitor handles this as well. With each job, instructions are included in a **job control language** (JCL). This is a special type of programming language used to provide instructions to the monitor. A simple example is that of a user submitting a program written in FORTRAN plus some data to be used by the program. Each FORTRAN instruction and each item of data is on a separate punched card or a separate record on tape. In addition to FORTRAN and data lines, the job includes job control instructions, which are denoted by the beginning "$". The overall format of the job looks like this:

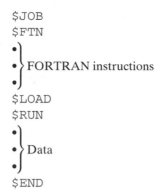

```
$JOB
$FTN
•⎫
•⎬ FORTRAN instructions
•⎭
$LOAD
$RUN
•⎫
•⎬ Data
•⎭
$END
```

To execute this job, the monitor reads the $FTN line and loads the appropriate compiler from its mass storage (usually tape). The compiler translates the user's program into object code, which is stored in memory or mass storage. If it is stored in memory, the operation is referred to as "compile, load, and go." If it is stored on tape, then the $LOAD instruction is required. This instruction is read by the monitor, which regains control after the compile operation. The monitor invokes the loader, which loads the object program into memory in place of the compiler and transfers control to it. In this manner, a large segment of main memory can be shared among different subsystems, although only one such subsystem could be resident and executing at a time.

We see that the monitor, or batch operating system, is simply a computer program. It relies on the ability of the processor to fetch instructions from various portions of main memory in order to seize and relinquish control alternately. Certain other hardware features are also desirable:

- **Memory protection:** While the user program is executing, it must not alter the memory area containing the monitor. If such an attempt is made, the processor hardware should detect an error and transfer control to the monitor. The monitor would then abort the job, print out an error message, and load in the next job.
- **Timer:** A timer is used to prevent a single job from monopolizing the system. The timer is set at the beginning of each job. If the timer expires, an interrupt occurs, and control returns to the monitor.
- **Privileged instructions:** Certain instructions are designated privileged and can be executed only by the monitor. If the processor encounters such an instruction while executing a user program, an error interrupt occurs. Among the privileged instructions are I/O instructions, so that the monitor retains control of all I/O devices. This prevents, for example, a user program from accidentally reading job control instructions from the next job. If a user program wishes to perform I/O, it must request that the monitor perform the operation for it. If a privileged instruction is encountered by the processor while it is executing a user program, the processor hardware considers this an error and transfers control to the monitor.
- **Interrupts:** Early computer models did not have this capability. This feature gives the operating system more flexibility in relinquishing control to and regaining control from user programs.

Read one record from file	0.0015 seconds
Execute 100 instructions	0.0001 seconds
Write one record to file	0.0015 seconds
TOTAL	0.0031 seconds

$$\text{Percent CPU utilization} = \frac{0.0001}{0.0031} = 0.032 = 3.2\%$$

Figure 8.4   System Utilization Example

Processor time alternates between execution of user programs and execution of the monitor. There have been two sacrifices: Some main memory is now given over to the monitor and some processor time is consumed by the monitor. Both of these are forms of overhead. Even with this overhead, the simple batch system improves utilization of the computer.

Multiprogrammed Batch Systems

Even with the automatic job sequencing provided by a simple batch operating system, the processor is often idle. The problem is that I/O devices are slow compared to the processor. Figure 8.4 details a representative calculation. The calculation concerns a program that processes a file of records and performs, on average, 100 processor instructions per record. In this example the computer spends over 96% of its time waiting for I/O devices to finish transferring data! Figure 8.5a illustrates this situation. The processor spends a certain amount of time executing, until it reaches an I/O instruction. It must then wait until that I/O instruction concludes before proceeding.

This inefficiency is not necessary. We know that there must be enough memory to hold the operating system (resident monitor) and one user program. Suppose that there is room for the operating system and two user programs. Now, when one job needs to wait for I/O, the processor can switch to the other job, which likely is not waiting for I/O (Figure 8.5b). Furthermore, we might expand memory to hold three, four, or more programs and switch among all of them (Figure 8.5c). The process is known as **multiprogramming**, or **multitasking**.[1] It is the central theme of modern operating systems.

To illustrate the benefit of multiprogramming, let us take an example. Consider a computer with 256K words of available memory (not used by the operating system), a disk, a terminal, and a printer. Three programs, JOB1, JOB2, and JOB3, are submitted for execution at the same time, with the attributes listed in Table 8.1. We assume minimal processor requirements for JOB2 and JOB3 and continuous disk and printer use by JOB3. For a simple batch environment, these jobs will be executed in sequence. Thus, JOB1 completes in 5 minutes. JOB2 must wait until the 5 minutes is over, and then completes 15 minutes after that. JOB3 begins after 20 minutes and completes at 30 minutes from the time it was initially submitted. The

---

[1]The term *multitasking* is sometimes reserved to mean multiple tasks within the same program that may be handled concurrently by the operating system, in contrast to *multiprogramming*, which would refer to multiple processes from multiple programs. However, it is more common to equate the terms *multitasking* and *multiprogramming*, as is done in most standards dictionaries (e.g., IEEE Std 100-1992, *The New IEEE Standard Dictionary of Electrical and Electronics Terms*).

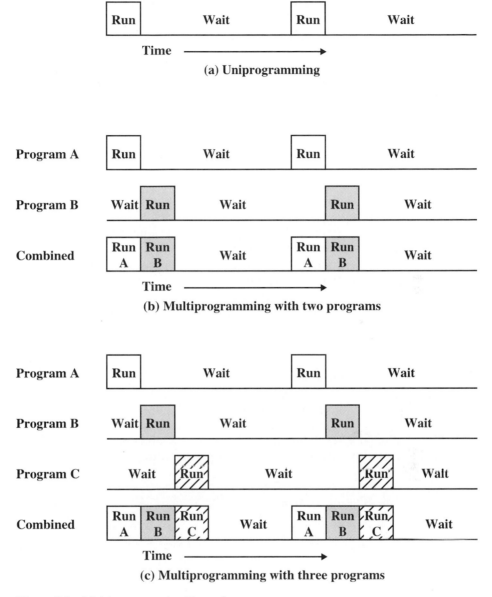

Figure 8.5 Multiprogramming Example

average resource utilization, throughput, and response times are shown in the uni-programming column of Table 8.2. Device-by-device utilization is illustrated in Figure 8.6a. It is evident that there is gross underutilization for all resources when averaged over the required 30-minute time period.

Now suppose that the jobs are run concurrently under a multiprogramming operating system. Because there is little resource contention between the jobs, all three can run in nearly minimum time while coexisting with the others in the computer (assuming that JOB2 and JOB3 are allotted enough processor time to keep

Table 8.1 Sample Program Execution Attributes

	JOB1	JOB2	JOB3
Type of job	Heavy compute	Heavy I/O	Heavy I/O
Duration	5 min	15 min	10 min
Memory required	50K	100K	80K
Need disk?	No	No	Yes
Need terminal?	No	Yes	No
Need printer?	No	No	Yes

their input and output operations active). JOB1 will still require 5 minutes to complete but at the end of that time, JOB2 will be one-third finished, and JOB3 half finished. All three jobs will have finished within 15 minutes. The improvement is evident when examining the multiprogramming column of Table 8.2, obtained from the histogram shown in Figure 8.6b.

As with a simple batch system, a multiprogramming batch system must rely on certain computer hardware features. The most notable additional feature that is useful for multiprogramming is the hardware that supports I/O interrupts and DMA. With interrupt-driven I/O or DMA, the processor can issue an I/O command for one job and proceed with the execution of another job while the I/O is carried out by the device controller. When the I/O operation is complete, the processor is interrupted and control is passed to an interrupt-handling program in the operating system. The operating system will then pass control to another job.

Multiprogramming operating systems are fairly sophisticated compared to single-program, or **uniprogramming**, systems. To have several jobs ready to run, the jobs must be kept in main memory, requiring some form of **memory management**. In addition, if several jobs are ready to run, the processor must decide which one to run, which requires some algorithm for scheduling. These concepts are discussed later in this chapter.

Time-Sharing Systems

With the use of multiprogramming, batch processing can be quite efficient. However, for many jobs, it is desirable to provide a mode in which the user inter-

Table 8.2 Effects of Multiprogramming on Resource Utilization

	Uniprogramming	Multiprogramming
Processor use	22%	43%
Memory use	33%	67%
Disk use	33%	67%
Printer use	33%	67%
Elapsed time	30 min	15 min
Throughput rate	6 jobs/h	12 jobs/h
Mean response time	18 min	10 min

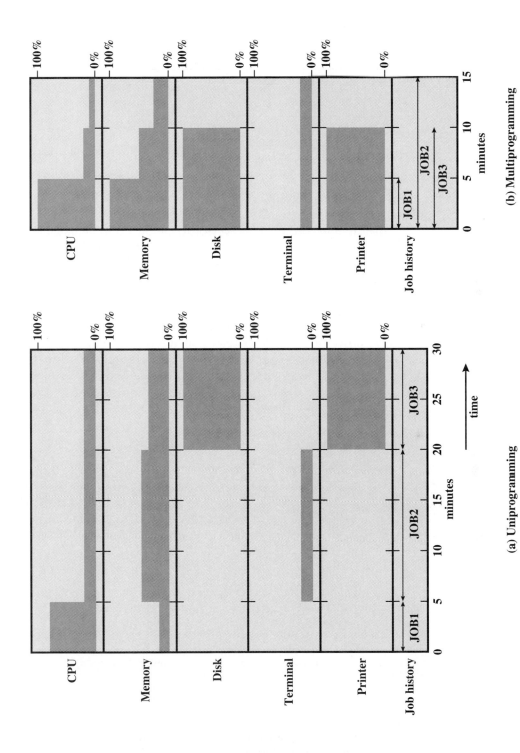

Figure 8.6 Utilization Histograms

249

Table 8.3 Batch Multiprogramming versus Time Sharing

	Batch Multiprogramming	**Time Sharing**
Principal objective	Maximize processor use	Minimize response time
Source of directives to operating system	Job control language commands provided with the job	Commands entered at the terminal

acts directly with the computer. Indeed, for some jobs, such as transaction processing, an interactive mode is essential.

Today, the requirement for an interactive computing facility can be, and often is, met by the use of a dedicated microcomputer. That option was not available in the 1960s, when most computers were big and costly. Instead time sharing was developed.

Just as multiprogramming allows the processor to handle multiple batch jobs at a time, multiprogramming can be used to handle multiple interactive jobs. In this latter case, the technique is referred to as time sharing, because the processor's time is shared among multiple users. In a time-sharing system, multiple users simultaneously access the system through terminals, with the operating system interleaving the execution of each user program in a short burst or quantum of computation. Thus, if there are n users actively requesting service at one time, each user will only see on the average $1/n$ of the effective computer speed, not counting operating system overhead. However, given the relatively slow human reaction time, the response time on a properly designed system should be comparable to that on a dedicated computer.

Both batch multiprogramming and time sharing use multiprogramming. The key differences are listed in Table 8.3.

8.2 SCHEDULING

The key to multiprogramming is scheduling. In fact, four types of scheduling are typically involved (Table 8.4). We will explore these presently. But first, we introduce the concept of *process*. This term was first used by the designers of the Multics operating system in the 1960s. It is a somewhat more general term than *job*. Many definitions have been given for the term *process*, including

Table 8.4 Types of Scheduling

Long-term scheduling	The decision to add to the pool of processes to be executed
Medium-term scheduling	The decision to add to the number of processes that are partially or fully in main memory
Short-term scheduling	The decision as to which available process will be executed by the processor
I/O scheduling	The decision as to which process's pending I/O request shall be handled by an available I/O device

- A program in execution
- The "animated spirit" of a program
- That entity to which a processor is assigned

This concept should become clearer as we proceed.

Long–Term Scheduling

The long-term scheduler determines which programs are admitted to the system for processing. Thus, it controls the degree of multiprogramming (number of processes in memory). Once admitted, a job or user program becomes a process and is added to the queue for the short-term scheduler. In some systems, a newly created process begins in a swapped-out condition, in which case it is added to a queue for the medium-term scheduler.

In a batch system, or for the batch portion of a general-purpose operating system, newly submitted jobs are routed to disk and held in a batch queue. The long-term scheduler creates processes from the queue when it can. There are two decisions involved here. First, the scheduler must decide that the operating system can take on one or more additional processes. Second, the scheduler must decide which job or jobs to accept and turn into processes. The criteria used may include priority, expected execution time, and I/O requirements.

For interactive programs in a time-sharing system, a process request is generated when a user attempts to connect to the system. Time-sharing users are not simply queued up and kept waiting until the system can accept them. Rather, the operating system will accept all authorized comers until the system is saturated, using some predefined measure of saturation. At that point, a connection request is met with a message indicating that the system is full and the user should try again later.

Medium–Term Scheduling

Medium-term scheduling is part of the swapping function, described in Section 8.3. Typically, the swapping-in decision is based on the need to manage the degree of multiprogramming. On a system that does not use virtual memory, memory management is also an issue. Thus, the swapping-in decision will consider the memory requirements of the swapped-out processes.

Short–Term Scheduling

The high-level scheduler executes relatively infrequently and makes the coarse-grained decision of whether or not to take on a new process, and which one to take. The short-term scheduler, also known as the *dispatcher,* executes frequently and makes the fine-grained decision of which job to execute next.

Process States

To understand the operation of the short-term scheduler, we need to consider the concept of a process state. During the lifetime of a process, its status will change a number of times. Its status at any point in time is referred to as a *state.* The term *state* is used because it connotes that certain information exists that defines the status at that point. At minimum, there are five defined states for a process (Figure 8.7):

- **New:** A program is admitted by the high-level scheduler but is not yet ready to execute. The operating system will initialize the process, moving it to the ready state.
- **Ready:** The process is ready to execute and is awaiting access to the processor.
- **Running:** The process is being executed by the processor.
- **Waiting:** The process is suspended from execution waiting for some system resource, such as I/O.
- **Halted:** The process has terminated and will be destroyed by the operating system.

For each process in the system, the operating system must maintain information indicating the state of the process and other information necessary for process execution. For this purpose, each process is represented in the operating system by a *process control block* (Figure 8.8), which typically contains the following:

- **Identifier:** Each current process has a unique identifier.
- **State:** The current state of the process (new, ready, and so on).
- **Priority:** Relative priority level.
- **Program counter:** The address of the next instruction in the program to be executed.
- **Memory pointers:** The starting and ending locations of the process in memory.
- **Context data:** These are data that are present in registers in the processor while the process is executing, and they will be discussed in Part Three. For now, it is enough to say that these data represent the "context" of the process. The context data plus the program counter are saved when the process leaves the ready state. They are retrieved by the processor when it resumes execution of the process.
- **I/O status information:** Includes outstanding I/O requests, I/O devices (e.g., tape drives) assigned to this process, a list of files assigned to the process, and so on.
- **Accounting information:** May include the amount of processor time and clock time used, time limits, account numbers, and so on.

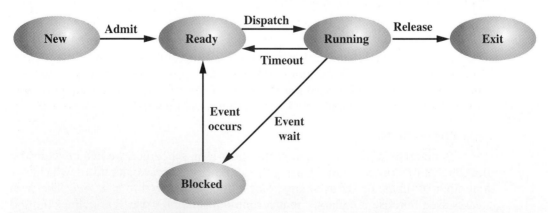

Figure 8.7 Five-State Process Model

Figure 8.8 Process Control Block

When the scheduler accepts a new job or user request for execution, it creates a blank process control block and places the associated process in the new state. After the system has properly filled in the process control block, the process is transferrcd to the ready state.

Scheduling Techniques

To understand how the operating system manages the scheduling of the various jobs in memory, let us begin by considering the simple example in Figure 8.9. The figure shows how main memory is partitioned at a given point in time. The kernel of the operating system is, of course, always resident. In addition, there are a number of active processes, including A and B, each of which is allocated a portion of memory.

We begin at a point in time when process A is running. The processor is executing instructions from the program contained in A's memory partition. At some later point in time, the processor ceases to execute instructions in A and begins executing instructions in the operating system area. This will happen for one of three reasons:

1. Process A issues a service call (e.g., an I/O request) to the operating system. Execution of A is suspended until this call is satisfied by the operating system.
2. Process A causes an *interrupt.* An interrupt is a hardware-generated signal to the processor. When this signal is detected, the processor ceases to execute A and transfers to the interrupt handler in the operating system. A variety of

events related to A will cause an interrupt. One example is an error, such as attempting to execute a privileged instruction. Another example is a timeout; to prevent any one process from monopolizing the processor, each process is only granted the processor for a short period at a time.

3. Some event unrelated to process A that requires attention causes an interrupt. An example is the completion of an I/O operation.

In any case, the result is the following. The processor saves the current context data and the program counter for A in A's process control block and then begins executing in the operating system. The operating system may perform some work, such as initiating an I/O operation. Then the short-term-scheduler portion of the operating system decides which process should be executed next. In this example, B is chosen. The operating system instructs the processor to restore B's context data and proceed with the execution of B where it left off.

This simple example highlights the basic functioning of the short-term scheduler. Figure 8.10 shows the major elements of the operating system involved in the multiprogramming and scheduling of processes. The operating system receives control of the processor at the interrupt handler if an interrupt occurs and at the service-call handler if a service call occurs. Once the interrupt or service call is handled, the short-term scheduler is invoked to pick a process for execution.

Figure 8.9   Scheduling Example

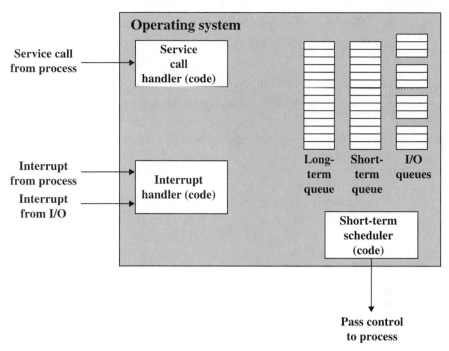

Figure 8.10   Key Elements of an Operating System for Multiprogramming

To do its job, the operating system maintains a number of queues. Each queue is simply a waiting list of processes waiting for some resource. The *long-term queue* is a list of jobs waiting to use the system. As conditions permit, the high-level scheduler will allocate memory and create a process for one of the waiting items. The *short-term queue* consists of all processes in the ready state. Any one of these processes could use the processor next. It is up to the short-term scheduler to pick one. Generally, this is done with a round-robin algorithm, giving each process some time in turn. Priority levels may also be used. Finally, there is an *I/O queue* for each I/O device. More than one process may request the use of the same I/O device. All processes waiting to use each device are lined up in that device's queue.

Figure 8.11 suggests how processes progress through the computer under the control of the operating system. Each process request (batch job, user-defined interactive job) is placed in the long-term queue. As resources become available, a process request becomes a process and is then placed in the ready state and put in the short-term queue. The processor alternates between executing operating system instructions and executing user processes. While the operating system is in control, it decides which process in the short-term queue should be executed next. When the operating system has finished its immediate tasks, it turns the processor over to the chosen process.

As was mentioned earlier, a process being executed may be suspended for a variety of reasons. If it is suspended because the process requests I/O, then it is placed in the appropriate I/O queue. If it is suspended because of a timeout or

Figure 8.11 Queuing Diagram Representation of Processor Scheduling

because the operating system must attend to pressing business, then it is placed in the ready state and put into the short-term queue.

Finally, we mention that the operating system also manages the I/O queues. When an I/O operation is completed, the operating system removes the satisfied process from that I/O queue and places it in the short-term queue. It then selects another waiting process (if any) and signals for the I/O device to satisfy that process's request.

8.3 MEMORY MANAGEMENT

In a uniprogramming system, main memory is divided into two parts: one part for the operating system (resident monitor) and one part for the program currently being executed. In a multiprogramming system, the "user" part of memory is subdivided to accommodate multiple processes. The task of subdivision is carried out dynamically by the operating system and is known as *memory management*.

Effective memory management is vital in a multiprogramming system. If only a few processes are in memory, then for much of the time all of the processes will be waiting for I/O and the processor will be idle. Thus, memory needs to be allocated efficiently to pack as many processes into memory as possible.

Swapping

Referring back to Figure 8.11, we have discussed three types of queues: the long-term queue of requests for new processes, the short-term queue of processes ready to use the processor, and the various I/O queues of processes that are not ready to use the processor. Recall that the reason for this elaborate machinery is that I/O activities are much slower than computation and therefore the processor in a uniprogramming system is idle most of the time.

But the arrangement in Figure 8.11 does not entirely solve the problem. It is true that, in this case, memory holds multiple processes and that the processor can move to another process when one process is waiting. But the processor is so much faster than I/O that it will be common for *all* the processes in memory to be waiting on I/O. Thus, even with multiprogramming, a processor could be idle most of the time.

What to do? Main memory could be expanded, and so be able to accommodate more processes. But there are two flaws in this approach. First, main memory is expensive, even today. Second, the appetite of programs for memory has grown as fast as the cost of memory has dropped. So larger memory results in larger processes, not more processes.

Another solution is *swapping,* depicted in Figure 8.12. We have a long-term queue of process requests, typically stored on disk. These are brought in, one at a time, as space becomes available. As processes are completed, they are moved out of main memory. Now the situation will arise that none of the processes in memory are in the ready state (e.g., all are waiting on an I/O operation). Rather than remain idle, the processor *swaps* one of these processes back out to disk into an *intermediate queue.* This is a queue of existing processes that have been temporarily kicked out of memory. The operating system then brings in another process from the intermediate queue, or it honors a new process request from the long-term queue. Execution then continues with the newly arrived process.

Swapping, however, is an I/O operation, and therefore there is the potential for making the problem worse, not better. But because disk I/O is generally the fastest I/O on a system (e.g., compared with tape or printer I/O), swapping will usually enhance performance. A more sophisticated scheme, involving virtual memory, improves performance over simple swapping. This will be discussed shortly. But first, we must prepare the ground by explaining partitioning and paging.

Partitioning

The simplest scheme for partitioning available memory is to use *fixed-size partitions,* as shown in Figure 8.13. Note that, although the partitions are of fixed size, they need not be of equal size. When a process is brought into memory, it is placed in the smallest available partition that will hold it.

Even with the use of unequal fixed-size partitions, there will be wasted memory. In most cases, a process will not require exactly as much memory as provided by the partition. For example, a process that requires 3M bytes of memory would

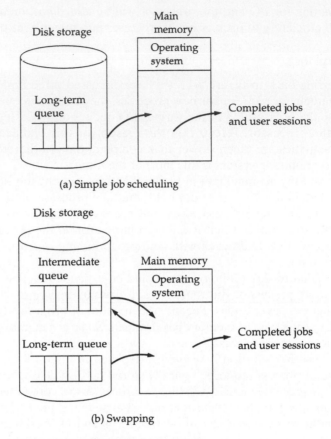

(a) Simple job scheduling

(b) Swapping

Figure 8.12 The Use of Swapping

be placed in the 4M partition of Figure 8.13b, wasting 1M that could be used by another process.

A more efficient approach is to use *variable-size partitions.* When a process is brought into memory, it is allocated exactly as much memory as it requires and no more. An example, using 64 Mbytes of main memory, is shown in Figure 8.14. Initially, main memory is empty, except for the operating system (a). The first three processes are loaded in, starting where the operating system ends and occupying just enough space for each process (b, c, d). This leaves a "hole" at the end of memory that is too small for a fourth process. At some point, none of the processes in memory is ready. The operating system swaps out process 2 (e), which leaves sufficient room to load a new process, process 4 (f). Because process 4 is smaller than process 2, another small hole is created. Later, a point is reached at which none of the processes in main memory is ready, but process 2, in the Ready-Suspend state, is available. Because there is insufficient room in memory for process 2, the operating system swaps process 1 out (g) and swaps process 2 back in (h). As this example shows, this method starts out well, but eventually it leads to a situation in which there are a lot of small holes in memory. As time goes on, memory becomes more and more fragmented, and memory utilization declines. One technique for overcoming this problem is *compaction:* From time to time, the operating system shifts the processes in memory to place all the free memory together in one block. This is a time-consuming procedure, wasteful of processor time.

Before we consider ways of dealing with the shortcomings of partitioning, we must clear up one loose end. If the reader considers Figure 8.14 for a moment, it should become obvious that a process is not likely to be loaded into the same place in main memory each time it is swapped in. Furthermore, if compaction is used, a

(a) Equal-size partitions   **(b) Unequal-size partitions**

Figure 8.13   Example of Fixed Partitioning of a 64-Mbyte Memory

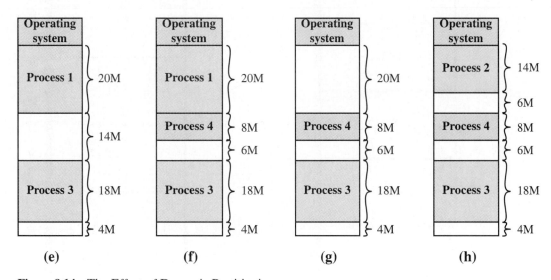

Figure 8.14 The Effect of Dynamic Partitioning

process may be shifted while in main memory. A process in memory consists of instructions plus data. The instructions will contain addresses for memory locations of two types:

- Addresses of data items
- Addresses of instructions, used for branching instructions

But these addresses are not fixed. They will change each time a process is swapped in. To solve this problem, a distinction is made between logical addresses and physical addresses. A **logical address** is expressed as a location relative to the beginning of the program. Instructions in the program contain only logical addresses. A **physical address** is an actual location in main memory. When the processor executes a process, it automatically converts from logical to physical address by adding the current starting location of the process, called its **base address,** to each logical address. This is another example of a processor hardware feature designed to meet an operating system requirement. The exact nature of this hardware feature depends on the memory management strategy in use. We will see several examples later in this chapter.

Paging

Both unequal fixed-size and variable-size partitions are inefficient in the use of memory. Suppose, however, that memory is partitioned into equal fixed-size chunks that are relatively small, and that each process is also divided into small fixed-size chunks of some size. Then the chunks of a program, known as *pages,* could be assigned to available chunks of memory, known as *frames,* or page frames. At most, then, the wasted space in memory for that process is a fraction of the last page.

Figure 8.15 shows an example of the use of pages and frames. At a given point in time, some of the frames in memory are in use and some are free. The list of free frames is maintained by the operating system. Process A, stored on disk, consists of

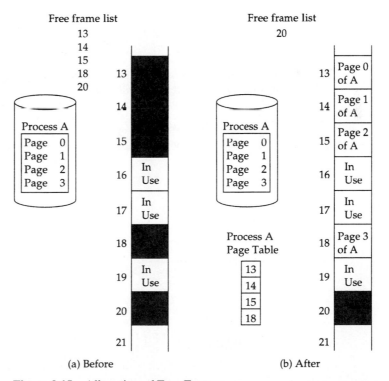

Figure 8.15   Allocation of Free Frames

four pages. When it comes time to load this process, the operating system finds four free frames and loads the four pages of the process A into the four frames.

Now suppose, as in this example, that there are not sufficient unused contiguous frames to hold the process. Does this prevent the operating system from loading A? The answer is no, because we can once again use the concept of logical address. A simple base address will no longer suffice. Rather, the operating system maintains a *page table* for each process. The page table shows the frame location for each page of the process. Within the program, each logical address consists of a page number and a relative address within the page. Recall that in the case of simple partitioning, a logical address is the location of a word relative to the beginning of the program; the processor translates that into a physical address. With paging, the logical-to-physical address translation is still done by processor hardware. The processor must know how to access the page table of the current process. Presented with a logical address (page number, relative address), the processor uses the page table to produce a physical address (frame number, relative address). An example is shown in Figure 8.16.

Figure 8.16 Logical and Physical Addresses

This approach solves the problems raised earlier. Main memory is divided into many small equal-size frames. Each process is divided into frame-size pages: Smaller processes require fewer pages, larger processes require more. When a process is brought in, its pages are loaded into available frames, and a page table is set up.

Virtual Memory

Demand Paging

With the use of paging, truly effective multiprogramming systems came into being. Furthermore, the simple tactic of breaking a process up into pages led to the development of another important concept: virtual memory.

To understand virtual memory, we must add a refinement to the paging scheme just discussed. That refinement is *demand paging,* which simply means that each page of a process is brought in only when it is needed, that is, on demand.

Consider a large process, consisting of a long program plus a number of arrays of data. Over any short period of time, execution may be confined to a small section of the program (e.g., a subroutine), and perhaps only one or two arrays of data are being used. This is the principle of locality, which we introduced in Appendix 4A. It would clearly be wasteful to load in dozens of pages for that process when only a few pages will be used before the program is suspended. We can make better use of memory by loading in just a few pages. Then, if the program branches to an instruction on a page not in main memory, or if the program references data on a page not in memory, a *page fault* is triggered. This tells the operating system to bring in the desired page.

Thus, at any one time, only a few pages of any given process are in memory, and therefore more processes can be maintained in memory. Furthermore, time is saved because unused pages are not swapped in and out of memory. However, the operating system must be clever about how it manages this scheme. When it brings one page in, it must throw another page out. If it throws out a page just before it is about to be used, then it will just have to go get that page again almost immediately. Too much of this leads to a condition known as *thrashing:* The processor spends most of its time swapping pages rather than executing instructions. The avoidance of thrashing was a major research area in the 1970s and led to a variety of complex but effective algorithms. In essence, the operating system tries to guess, based on recent history, which pages are least likely to be used in the near future.

With demand paging, it is not necessary to load an entire process into main memory. This fact has a remarkable consequence: *It is possible for a process to be larger than all of main memory.* One of the most fundamental restrictions in programming has been lifted. Without demand paging, a programmer must be acutely aware of how much memory is available. If the program being written is too large, the programmer must devise ways to structure the program into pieces that can be loaded one at a time. With demand paging, that job is left to the operating system and the hardware. As far as the programmer is concerned, he or she is dealing with a huge memory, the size associated with disk storage.

Because a process executes only in main memory, that memory is referred to as **real memory.** But a programmer or user perceives a much larger memory—that which is allocated on the disk. This latter is therefore referred to as **virtual memory**.

Virtual memory allows for very effective multiprogramming and relieves the user of the unnecessarily tight constraints of main memory.

Page Table Structure

The basic mechanism for reading a word from memory involves the translation of a virtual, or logical, address, consisting of page number and offset, into a physical address, consisting of frame number and offset, using a page table. Because the page table is of variable length, depending on the size of the process, we cannot expect to hold it in registers. Instead, it must be in main memory to be accessed. Figure 8.16 suggests a hardware implementation of this scheme. When a particular process is running, a register holds the starting address of the page table for that process. The page number of a virtual address is used to index that table and look up the corresponding frame number. This is combined with the offset portion of the virtual address to produce the desired real address.

In most systems, there is one page table per process. But each process can occupy huge amounts of virtual memory. For example, in the VAX architecture, each process can have up to $2^{31} = 2$ GBytes of virtual memory. Using $2^9 = 512$-byte pages, that means that as many as 2^{22} page table entries are required *per process*. Clearly, the amount of memory devoted to page tables alone could be unacceptably high. To overcome this problem, most virtual memory schemes store page tables in virtual memory rather than real memory. This means that page tables are subject to paging just as other pages are. When a process is running, at least a part of its page table must be in main memory, including the page table entry of the currently executing page. Some processors make use of a two-level scheme to organize large page tables. In this scheme, there is a page directory, in which each entry points to a page table. Thus, if the length of the page directory is X, and if the maximum length of a page table is Y, then a process can consist of up to $X \times Y$ pages. Typically, the maximum length of a page table is restricted to be equal to one page. We will see an example of this two-level approach when we consider the Pentium II later in this chapter.

An alternative approach to the use of one- or two-level page tables is the use of an inverted page table structure (Figure 8.17). This approach is used on IBM's AS/400 and on all of IBM's RISC products, including the PowerPC.

In this approach, the page number portion of a virtual address is mapped into a hash table using a simple hashing function.[2] The hash table contains a pointer to the inverted page table, which contains the page table entries. With this structure, there is one entry in the hash table and inverted page table for each real memory page rather than one per virtual page. Thus, a fixed proportion of real memory is required for the tables regardless of the number of processes or virtual pages sup-

---

[2] A hash function maps numbers in the range 0 through M into numbers in the range 0 through N, where $M > N$. The output of the hash function is used as an index into the hash table. Since more than one input maps to the same output, it is possible for an input item to map to a hash table entry that is already occupied. In that case, the new item must *overflow* into another hash table location. Typically, the new item is placed in the first succeeding empty space, and a pointer from the original location is provided to chain the entries together. See [STAL01] for a more detailed discussion of hash tables.

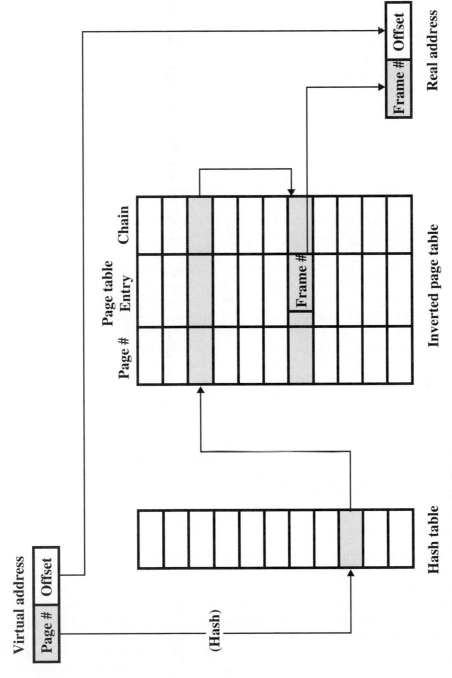

Figure 8.17 Inverted Page Table Structure

265

ported. Because more than one virtual address may map into the same hash table entry, a chaining technique is used for managing the overflow. The hashing technique results in chains that are typically short—either one or two entries.

Translation Lookaside Buffer

In principle, then, every virtual memory reference can cause two physical memory accesses: one to fetch the appropriate page table entry, and one to fetch the desired data. Thus, a straightforward virtual memory scheme would have the effect of doubling the memory access time. To overcome this problem, most virtual memory schemes make use of a special cache for page table entries, usually called a translation lookaside buffer (TLB). This cache functions in the same way as a memory cache and contains those page table entries that have been most recently used. Figure 8.18 is a flowchart that shows the use of the TLB. By the principle of locality, most virtual memory references will be to locations in recently used pages. Therefore, most references will involve page table entries in the cache. Studies of the VAX TLB have shown that this scheme can significantly improve performance [CLAR85, SATY81].

Note that the virtual memory mechanism must interact with the cache system (not the TLB cache, but the main memory cache). This is illustrated in Figure 8.19. A virtual address will generally be in the form of a page number, offset. First, the memory system consults the TLB to see if the matching page table entry is present. If it is, the real (physical) address is generated by combining the frame number with the offset. If not, the entry is accessed from a page table. Once the real address is generated, which is in the form of a tag and a remainder (see Figure 4.17), the cache is consulted to see if the block containing that word is present. If so, it is returned to the processor. If not, the word is retrieved from main memory.

The reader should be able to appreciate the complexity of the processor hardware involved in a single memory reference. The virtual address is translated into a real address. This involves reference to a page table, which may be in the TLB, in main memory, or on disk. The referenced word may be in cache, in main memory, or on disk. In the latter case, the page containing the word must be loaded into main memory and its block loaded into the cache. In addition, the page table entry for that page must be updated.

Segmentation

There is another way in which addressable memory can be subdivided, known as *segmentation.* Whereas paging is invisible to the programmer and serves the purpose of providing the programmer with a larger address space, segmentation is usually visible to the programmer and is provided as a convenience for organizing programs and data, and as a means for associating privilege and protection attributes with instructions and data.

Segmentation allows the programmer to view memory as consisting of multiple address spaces or segments. Segments are of variable, indeed dynamic, size. Typically, the programmer or the operating system will assign programs and data to different segments. There may be a number of program segments for various types

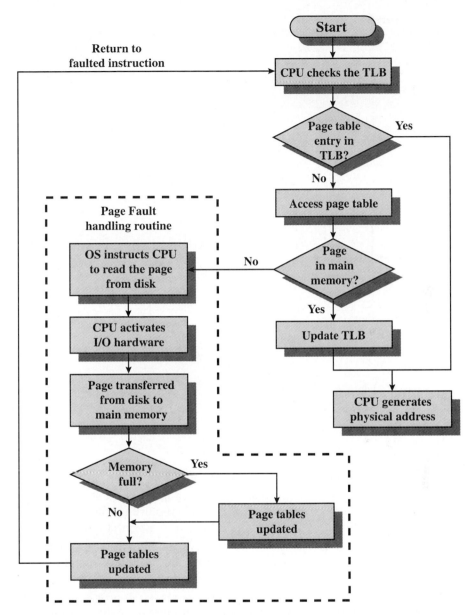

Figure 8.18   Operating of Paging and Translation Lookaside Buffer (TLB) [FURH87]

of programs as well as a number of data segments. Each segment may be assigned access and usage rights. Memory references consist of a (segment number, offset) form of address.

This organization has a number of advantages to the programmer over a non-segmented address space:

Figure 8.19   Translation Lookaside Buffer and Cache Operation

1. It simplifies the handling of growing data structures. If the programmer does not know ahead of time how large a particular data structure will become, it is not necessary to guess. The data structure can be assigned its own segment, and the operating system will expand or shrink the segment as needed.

2. It allows programs to be altered and recompiled independently, without requiring that an entire set of programs be relinked and reloaded. Again, this is accomplished using multiple segments.

3. It lends itself to sharing among processes. A programmer can place a utility program or a useful table of data in a segment that can be addressed by other processes.

4. It lends itself to protection. Because a segment can be constructed to contain a well-defined set of programs or data, the programmer or a system administrator can assign access privileges in a convenient fashion.

These advantages are not available with paging, which is invisible to the programmer. On the other hand, we have seen that paging provides for an efficient form of memory management. To combine the advantages of both, some systems are equipped with the hardware and operating system software to provide both.

8.4 PENTIUM II AND POWERPC MEMORY MANAGEMENT

Pentium II Memory Management Hardware

Since the introduction of the 32-bit architecture, microprocessors have evolved sophisticated memory management schemes that build on the lessons learned with medium- and large-scale systems. In many cases, the microprocessor versions are superior to their larger-system antecedents. Because the schemes were developed by the microprocessor hardware vendor and may be employed with a variety of operating systems, they tend to be quite general purpose. A representative example is the scheme used on the Pentium II. The Pentium II memory-management hardware is essentially the same as that used in the Intel 80386 and 80486 processors, with some refinements.

Address Spaces

The Pentium II includes hardware for both segmentation and paging. Both mechanisms can be disabled, allowing the user to choose from four distinct views of memory:

- **Unsegmented unpaged memory:** In this case, the virtual address is the same as the physical address. This is useful, for example, in low-complexity, high-performance controller applications.
- **Unsegmented paged memory:** Here memory is viewed as a paged linear address space. Protection and management of memory is done via paging. This is favored by some operating systems (e.g., Berkeley UNIX).
- **Segmented unpaged memory:** Here memory is viewed as a collection of logical address spaces. The advantage of this view over a paged approach is that it affords protection down to the level of a single byte, if necessary. Furthermore, unlike paging, it guarantees that the translation table needed (the segment table) is on-chip when the segment is in memory. Hence, segmented unpaged memory results in predictable access times.
- **Segmented paged memory:** Segmentation is used to define logical memory partitions subject to access control, and paging is used to manage the allocation of memory within the partitions. Operating systems such as UNIX System V favor this view.

Segmentation

When segmentation is used, each virtual address (called a logical address in the Pentium II documentation) consists of a 16-bit segment reference and a 32-bit offset. Two bits of the segment reference deal with the protection mechanism, leaving 14 bits for specifying a particular segment. Thus, with unsegmented memory, the user's virtual memory is $2^{32} = 4$ GBytes. With segmented memory, the total virtual memory space as seen by a user is $2^{46} = 64$ terabytes (TBytes). The physical address space employs a 32-bit address for a maximum of 4 GBytes.

The amount of virtual memory can actually be larger than the 64 TBytes. This is because the processor's interpretation of a virtual address depends on which process is currently active. Virtual address space is divided into two parts. One-half of the virtual address space (8K segments × 4 GBytes) is global, shared by all processes; the remainder is local and is distinct for each process.

Associated with each segment are two forms of protection: privilege level and access attribute. There are four privilege levels from most protected (level 0) to least protected (level 3). The privilege level associated with a data segment is its "classification"; the privilege level associated with a program segment is its "clearance." An executing program may only access data segments for which its clearance level is lower than (more privileged) or equal to (same privilege) the privilege level of the data segment.

The hardware does not dictate how these privilege levels are to be used; this depends on the operating system design and implementation. It was intended that privilege level 1 would be used for most of the operating system, and level 0 would be used for that small portion of the operating system devoted to memory management, protection, and access control. This leaves two levels for applications. In many systems, applications will reside at level 3, with level 2 being unused. Specialized application subsystems that must be protected because they implement their own security mechanisms are good candidates for level 2. Some examples are database management systems, office automation systems, and software engineering environments.

In addition to regulating access to data segments, the privilege mechanism limits the use of certain instructions. Some instructions, such as those dealing with memory-management registers, can only be executed in level 0. I/O instructions can only be executed up to a certain level that is designated by the operating system; typically, this will be level 1.

The access attribute of a data segment specifies whether read–write or read-only accesses are permitted. For program segments, the access attribute specifies read/execute or read-only access.

The address translation mechanism for segmentation involves mapping a virtual address into what is referred to as a linear address (Figure 8.20b). A virtual address consists of the 32-bit offset and a 16-bit segment selector (Figure 8.20a). The segment selector consists of the following fields:

- **Table Indicator (TI):** Indicates whether the global segment table or a local segment table should be used for translation.
- **Segment Number:** The number of the segment. This serves as an index into the segment table.
- **Requested Privilege Level (RPL):** The privilege level requested for this access.

Each entry in a segment table consists of 64 bits, as shown in Figure 8.20c. The fields are defined in Table 8.5.

Paging

Segmentation is an optional feature and may be disabled. When segmentation is in use, addresses used in programs are virtual addresses and are converted into linear addresses, as just described. When segmentation is not in use, linear addresses are used in programs. In either case, the following step is to convert that linear address into a real 32-bit address.

Figure 8.20 Pentium Memory-Management Formats

Table 8.5 Pentium II Memory Management Parameters

Segment Descriptor (Segment Table Entry)

Base

Defines the starting address of the segment within the 4-GByte linear address space.

D/B bit

In a code segment, this is the D bit and indicates whether operands and addressing modes are 16 or 32 bits.

Descriptor Privilege Level (DPL)

Specifies the privilege level of the segment referred to by this segment descriptor.

Granularity bit (G)

Indicates whether the Limit field is to be interpreted in units by one byte or 4 KBytes.

Limit

Defines the size of the segment. The processor interprets the limit field in one of two ways, depending on the granularity bit: in units of one byte, up to a segment size limit of 1 MByte, or in units of 4 KBytes, up to a segment size limit of 4 GBytes.

S bit

Determines whether a given segment is a system segment or a code or data segment.

Segment Present bit (P)

Used for nonpaged systems. It indicates whether the segment is present in main memory. For paged systems, this bit is always set to 1.

Type

Distinguishes between various kinds of segments and indicates the access attributes.

Page Directory Entry and Page Table Entry

Accessed bit (A)

This bit is set to 1 by the processor in both levels of page tables when a read or write operation to the corresponding page occurs.

Dirty bit (D)

This bit is set to 1 by the processor when a write operation to the corresponding page occurs.

Page Frame Address

Provides the physical address of the page in memory if the present bit is set. Since page frames are aligned on 4K boundaries, the bottom 12 bits are 0, and only the top 20 bits are included in the entry. In a page directory, the address is that of a page table.

Page Cache Disable bit (PCD)

Indicates whether data from page may be cached.

Page Size bit (PS)

Indicates whether page size is 4 KByte or 4 MByte.

Page Write Through bit (PWT)

Indicates whether write-through or write-back caching policy will be used for data in the corresponding page.

Present bit (P)

Indicates whether the page table or page is in main memory.

Read–Write bit (RW)

For user-level pages, indicates whether the page is read-only access or read–write access for user-level programs.

User/Supervisor bit (US)

Indicates whether the page is available only to the operating system (supervisor level) or is available to both operating system and applications (user level).

To understand the structure of the linear address, you need to know that the Pentium II paging mechanism is actually a two-level table lookup operation. The first level is a page directory, which contains up to 1024 entries. This splits the 4-GByte linear memory space into 1024 page groups, each with its own page table, and cach 4 MBytes in length. Each page table contains up to 1024 entries; each entry corresponds to a single 4-KByte page. Memory management has the option of using one page directory for all processes, one page directory for each process, or some combination of the two. The page directory for the current task is always in main memory. Page tables may be in virtual memory.

Figure 8.20 shows the formats of entries in page directories and page tables, and the fields are defined in Table 8.5. Note that access control mechanisms can be provided on a page or page group basis.

The Pentium II also makes use of a translation lookaside buffer. The buffer can hold 32 page table entries. Each time that the page directory is changed, the buffer is cleared.

Figure 8.21 illustrates the combination of segmentation and paging mechanisms. For clarity, the translation lookaside buffer and memory cache mechanisms are not shown.

Finally, the Pentium II includes a new extension not found on the 80386 or 80486, the provision for two page sizes. If the PSE (page size extension) bit in control register 4 is set to 1, then the paging unit permits the operating system programmer to define a page as either 4 KByte or 4 MByte in size.

When 4-MByte pages are used, there is only one level of table lookup for pages. When the hardware accesses the page directory, the page directory entry (Figure 8.20d) has the PS bit set to 1. In this case, bits 9 through 21 are ignored and bits 22 through 31 define the base address for a 4-MByte page in memory. Thus, there is a single page table.

The use of 4-MByte pages reduces the memory-management storage requirements for large main memories. With 4-KByte pages, a full 4-GByte main memory requires about 4 MBytes of memory just for the page tables. With 4-MByte pages, a single table, 4 KBytes in length, is sufficient for page memory management

PowerPC Memory-Management Hardware

The PowerPC provides a comprehensive set of addressing mechanisms. For 32-bit implementations of the architecture, a paging scheme with a simple segmentation mechanism is implemented. For 64-bit implementations, paging and a more powerful segmentation mechanism are supported. In addition, for both 32-bit and 64-bit processors there is an alternative hardware mechanism, known as block address translation. Briefly, the block addressing scheme is designed to address one drawback of paging mechanisms. With paging, a large number of pages may be frequently referenced by a program. For example, programs that use OS tables or graphics frame buffers may exhibit this behavior. The result may be that frequently used pages are constantly paged in and out. Block addressing enables the processor to map four large blocks of instruction memory and four large blocks of data memory in a way that bypasses the paging mechanism.

A discussion of block addressing is beyond the scope of this chapter. In this subsection, we concentrate on the paging and segmentation mechanisms of the 32-bit PowerPC. The 64-bit scheme is similar.

Figure 8.21   Pentium Memory Address Translation Mechanisms

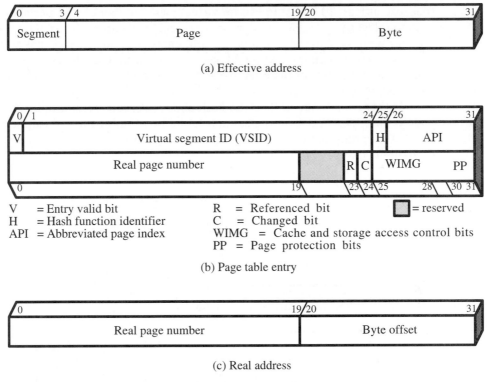

V   = Entry valid bit
H   = Hash function identifier
API = Abbreviated page index

R = Referenced bit
C = Changed bit
WIMG = Cache and storage access control bits
PP = Page protection bits

☐ = reserved

(b) Page table entry

(c) Real address

Figure 8.22   PowerPC 32-Bit Memory-Management Formats

The 32-bit PowerPC makes use of a 32-bit effective address (Figure 8.22a). The address includes a 12-bit byte selector and a 16-bit page identifier. Thus, 2^{12} = 4 KByte pages are used. Up to 2^{16} = 64K pages per segment are allowed. Four bits of the address are used to designate one of 16 segment registers. The contents of these registers are controlled by the operating system. Each segment register includes access control bits and a 24-bit identifier, so that the 32-bit effective address maps into a 52-bit virtual address (Figure 8.23).

The PowerPC makes use of a single inverted page table. The virtual address is used to index into the page table in the following manner. First, a hash code is computed as follows:

$$H(0 \ldots 18) = SID(5 \ldots 23) \oplus VPN(0 \ldots 18)$$

The virtual page number in the virtual address is padded on the left (most significant end) with three binary zeros to form a 19-bit number. Then a bit-by-bit exclusive-or is calculated of that number and the 19 right-most bits of the virtual segment ID to form a 19-bit hash code. The table is organized as *n* groups of 8 entries. From 10 to 19 bits of the hash code (depending on the size of the page table) are used to select one of the groups in the table. The memory-management hardware then scans the eight entries of the group to test for a match with the virtual address.

To do the match, each page table entry includes the virtual segment ID and the left-most 6 bits of the virtual page number, called the abbreviated page index (because at least 10 bits of the 16-bit virtual page number always participate in the hash to select a page table entry group, only an abbreviated form of the virtual page number need be carried in the page table entry to match the virtual address). If there is a match, then the 20-bit real page number from the address is concatenated with the lower 12 bits of the effective address to form the 32-bit physical address to be accessed.

If there is no match, then the hash code is complemented to produce a new page table index that is in the same relative position at the opposite end of the table. This group is then scanned for a match. If no match is found, a page fault interrupt occurs.

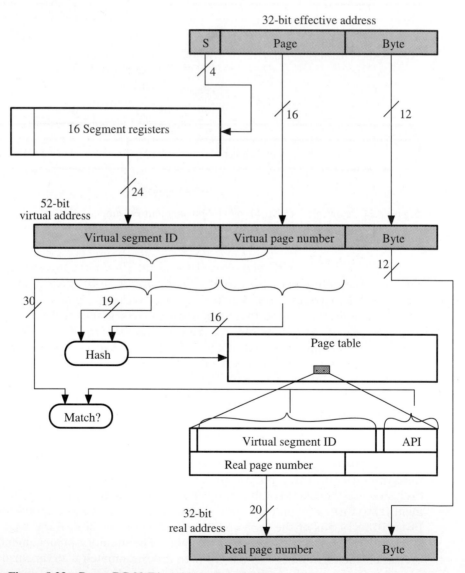

Figure 8.23 PowerPC 32-Bit Address Translation

Table 8.6 PowerPC Memory Management Parameters

Segment Table Entry

Effective Segment ID
Indicates one of 64G effective segments; used to determine entry in segment table.

Entry Valid (V) bit
Indicates whether this is a memory or I/O segment.

Segment Type (T) bit
Indicates whether this is a memory or I/O segment.

Supervisor Key (Ks)
Used with the virtual page number to determine entry in page table.

Page Table Entry

Entry Valid (V) bit
Indicates whether there is valid data in this entry.

Hash Function Identifier (H)
Indicates whether this is a primary or secondary hash entry.

Abbreviated Page Index (API)
Used to match a virtual address uniquely.

Referenced (R) bit
This bit is set to 1 by the processor when a read or write operation to the corresponding page occurs.

Changed (C) bit
This bit is set to 1 by the processor when a write operation to the corresponding page occurs.

WIMG bits
W=0: use write-back policy; W=1: use write-through policy.
I=0: caching not inhibited; I=1: caching inhibited.
M=0: not shared memory; M=1: shared memory.
G=0: not guarded memory; G=1: guarded memory.

Page Protection (PP) bits
Access control bits used with K bits from segment register or segment table entry to define access rights.

Figure 8.22 shows the logic of the address translation mechanism, and Figure 8.23 shows the formats of the effective address, page table entry, and real address. Finally, Table 8.6 defines the parameters in the page table entry.

The 64-bit memory management scheme is designed to be upwardly compatible with the 32-bit implementation. In essence, all effective addresses, general registers, and branch address registers are extended on the left to 64 bits.

8.5 RECOMMENDED READING AND WEB SITES

[STAL01] covers the topics of this chapter in detail.

STAL01 Stallings, W. *Operating Systems, Internals and Design Principles,* 4th edition. Upper Saddle River, NJ: Prentice Hall, 2001.

Recommended Web sites:

- **Operating System Project Information**: Links to OS projects and research
- **ACM Special Interest Group on Operating Systems**: Information on SIGOPS publications and conferences
- **IEEE Technical Committee on Operating Systems and Applications**: Includes an online newsletter and links to other sites
- **Review of Operating Systems**: Comprehensive review of commercial, free, research, and hobby OSs

8.6   KEY TERMS, REVIEW QUESTIONS, AND PROBLEMS

Key Terms

batch system	memory protection	process state
demand paging	multiprogramming	real memory
interactive operating	multitasking	resident monitor
system	nucleus	segmentation
interrupt	operating system (OS)	short-term scheduling
job control language	paging	swapping
(JCL)	page table	thrashing
kernel	partitioning	time-sharing system
logical address	physical address	translation lookaside buffer
long-term scheduling	privileged instruction	(TLB)
medium-term scheduling	process	utility
memory management	process control block	virtual memory

Review Questions

8.1 What is an operating system?

8.2 List and briefly define the key services provided by an operating system.

8.3 List and briefly define the major types of OS scheduling.

8.4 What is the difference between a process and a program?

8.5 What is the purpose of swapping?

8.6 If a process may be dynamically assigned to different locations in main memory, what is the implication for the addressing mechanism?

8.7 Is it necessary for all of the pages of a process to be in main memory while the process is executing?

8.8 Must the pages of a process in main memory be contiguous?

8.9 Is it necessary for the pages of a process in main memory to be in sequential order?

8.10 What is the purpose of a translation lookaside buffer?

Problems

8.1 Suppose that we have a multiprogrammed computer in which each job has identical characteristics. In one computation period, T, for a job, half the time is spent in I/O and the other half in processor activity. Each job runs for a total of N periods. Assume that a simple round-robin priority is used, and that I/O operations can overlap with processor operation. Define the following quantities:

- Turnaround time = actual time to complete a job
- Throughput = average number of jobs completed per time period T
- Processor utilization = percentage of time that the processor is active (not waiting)

Compute these quantities for one, two, and four simultaneous jobs, assuming that the period T is distributed in each of the following ways:

a. I/O first half, processor second half

b. I/O first and fourth quarters, processor second and third quarters

8.2 An I/O-bound program is one that, if run alone, would spend more time waiting for I/O than using the processor. A processor-bound program is the opposite. Suppose a short-term scheduling algorithm favors those programs that have used little processor time in the recent past. Explain why this algorithm favors I/O-bound programs and yet does not permanently deny processor time to processor-bound programs.

8.3 A program computes the row sums

$$C_i = \sum_{j=1}^{n} a_{ij}$$

of an array A that is 100 by 100. Assume that the computer uses demand paging with a page size of 1000 words, and that the amount of main memory allotted for data is five page frames. Is there any difference in the page fault rate if A were stored in virtual memory by rows or columns? Explain.

8.4 Suppose the page table for the process currently executing on the processor looks like the following. All numbers are decimal, everything is numbered starting from zero, and all addresses are memory byte addresses. The page size is 1024 bytes.

Virtual page number	Valid bit	Reference bit	Modify bit	Page frame number
0	1	1	0	4
1	1	1	1	7
2	0	0	0	—
3	1	0	0	2
4	0	0	0	—
5	1	0	1	0

a. Describe exactly how, in general, a virtual address generated by the CPU is translated into a physical main memory address.

b. What physical address, if any, would each of the following virtual addresses correspond to? (Do not try to handle any page faults, if any.)

(i) 1052

(ii) 2221

(iii) 5499

8.5 Give reasons that the page size in a virtual memory system should be neither very small nor very large.

8.6 The following sequence of virtual page numbers is encountered in the course of execution on a computer with virtual memory.

$$3\ 4\ 2\ 6\ 4\ 7\ 1\ 3\ 2\ 6\ 3\ 5\ 1\ 2\ 3$$

Assume that a least recently used page replacement policy is adopted. Plot a graph of page hit ratio (fraction of page references in which the page is in main memory) as a function of main-memory page capacity n for $1 \le n \le 8$. Assume that main memory is initially empty.

8.7 In the VAX computer, user page tables are located at virtual addresses in the system space. What is the advantage of having user page tables in virtual rather than main memory? What is the disadvantage?

8.8 Consider a computer system with both segmentation and paging. When a segment is in memory, some words are wasted on the last page. In addition, for a segment size s and a page size p, there are s/p page table entries. The smaller the page size, the less waste in the last page of the segment, but the larger the page table. What page size minimizes the total overhead?

8.9 A computer has a cache, main memory, and a disk used for virtual memory. If a referenced word is in the cache, 20 ns are required to access it. If it is in main memory but not in the cache, 60 ns are needed to load it into the cache, and then the reference is started again. If the word is not in main memory, 12 ms are required to fetch the word from disk, followed by 60 ns to copy it to the cache, and then the reference is started again. The cache hit ratio is 0.9 and the main-memory hit ratio is 0.6. What is the average time in ns required to access a referenced word on this system?

8.10 Assume a task is divided into four equal-sized segments, and that the system builds an eight-entry page descriptor table for each segment. Thus, the system has a combination of segmentation and paging. Assume also that the page size is 2 KBytes.

a. What is the maximum size of each segment?

b. What is the maximum logical address space for the task?

c. Assume that an element in physical location 00021ABC is accessed by this task. What is the format of the logical address that the task generates for it? What is the maximum physical address space for the system?

8.11 Assume a microprocessor capable of accessing up to 2^{32} bytes of physical main memory. It implements one segmented logical address space of maximum size 2^{31} bytes. Each instruction contains the whole two-part address. External memory management units (MMUs) are used, whose management scheme assigns contiguous blocks of physical memory of fixed size 2^{22} bytes to segments. The starting physical address of a segment is always divisible by 1024. Show the detailed interconnection of the external mapping mechanism that converts logical addresses to physical addresses using the appropriate number of MMUs, and show the detailed internal structure of an MMU (assuming that each MMU contains a 128-entry directly mapped segment descriptor cache) and how each MMU is selected.

8.12 Consider a paged logical address space (composed of 32 pages of 2 KBytes each) mapped into a 1-MByte physical memory space.

a. What is the format of the processor's logical address?

b. What is the length and width of the page table (disregarding the "access rights" bits)?

c. What is the effect on the page table if the physical memory space is reduced by half?

PART THREE

The Central Processing Unit

ISSUES FOR PART THREE

Up to this point, we have viewed the CPU essentially as a "black box" and have considered its interaction with I/O and memory. Part Three examines the internal structure and function of the CPU. The CPU consists of a control unit, registers, the arithmetic and logic unit, the instruction execution unit, and the interconnections among these components. Architectural issues, such as instruction set design and data types, are covered. The part also looks at organizational issues, such as pipelining.

ROAD MAP FOR PART THREE

Chapter 9 Computer Arithmetic

Chapter 9 examines the functionality of the ALU and focuses on the representation of numbers and techniques for implementing arithmetic operations. Processors typically support two types of arithmetic: integer, or fixed point, and floating point. For both cases, the chapter first examines the representation of numbers and then discusses arithmetic operations. The important IEEE 754 floating-point standard is examined in detail.

Chapter 10 Instruction Sets: Characteristics and Functions

From a programmer's point of view, the best way to understand the operation of a processor is to learn the machine instruction set that it executes. The complex topic of instruction set design occupies Chapters 10 and 11. Chapter 10 focuses on the functional aspects of instruction set design. The chapter examines the types of functions that are specified by computer instructions, and then looks specifically at the types of operands (which specify the data to be operated on) and the types of operations (which specify the operations to be performed) commonly found in instruction sets. Then the relationship of processor instructions to assembly language is briefly explained.

Chapter 11 Instruction Sets: Addressing Modes and Formats

Whereas Chapter 10 can be viewed as dealing with the semantics of instruction sets, Chapter 11 is more concerned with the syntax of instruction sets. Specifically, Chapter 11 looks at the way in which memory addresses are specified and at the overall format of computer instructions.

Chapter 12 CPU Structure and Function

Chapter 12 is devoted to a discussion of the internal structure and function of the processor. The chapter describes the use of registers as the CPU's internal memory, and then pulls together all of the material covered so far to provide an overview of CPU structure and function. The overall organization (ALU, control unit, register file) is reviewed. Then the organization of the register file is discussed. The remainder of the chapter describes the functioning of the processor in executing machine instructions. The instruction cycle is examined to show the function and interrelationship of fetch, indirect, execute, and interrupt cycles. Finally, the use of pipelining to improve performance is explored in depth.

Chapter 13 Reduced Instruction Set Computers

The remainder of Part Three looks in more detail at the key trends in CPU design. Chapter 13 describes the approach associated with the concept of a reduced instruction set computer (RISC), which is one of the most significant innovations in computer organization and architecture in recent years. RISC architecture is a dramatic departure from the historical trend in processor architecture. An analysis of this approach brings into focus many of the important issues in computer organization and architecture. The chapter examines the motivation for the use of RISC design and then looks at the details of RISC instruction set design and RISC CPU architecture and compares RISC with the complex instruction set computer (CISC) approach.

Chapter 14 Instruction-Level Parallelism and Superscalar Processors

Chapter 14 examines an even more recent and equally important design innovation: the superscalar processor. Although superscalar technology can be used on any processor, it is especially well suited to a RISC architecture. The chapter also looks at the general issue of instruction-level parallelism.

Chapter 15 The IA-64 Architecture

The IA-64 instruction set architecture is a new approach to providing hardware support for instruction-level parallelism and is significantly different from the approach taken in superscalar architectures. Chapter 15 begins with a discussion of the motivating factors for the new architecture. Next, the chapter looks at the general organization to support the architecture. The chapter then examines in some detail the key features of the IA-64 architecture that promote instruction-level parallelism.

CHAPTER 9

COMPUTER ARITHMETIC

KEY POINTS

♦ The two principal concerns for computer arithmetic are the way in which numbers are represented (the binary format) and the algorithms used for the basic arithmetic operations (add, subtract, multiply, divide). These two considerations apply both to integer and floating-point arithmetic.

♦ Floating-point numbers are expressed as a number (significand) multiplied by a constant (base) raised to some integer power (exponent). Floating-point numbers can be used to represent very large and very small numbers.

♦ Most processors implement the IEEE 754 standard for floating-point representation and floating-point arithmetic. IEEE 754 defines both a 32-bit and a 64-bit format.

We begin our examination of the processor with an overview of the arithmetic and logic unit (ALU). The chapter then focuses on the most complex aspect of the ALU, computer arithmetic. The logic functions that are part of the ALU are described in Chapter 10, and implementations of simple logic and arithmetic functions in digital logic are described in Appendix A of this book.

Computer arithmetic is commonly performed on two very different types of numbers: integer and floating point. In both cases, the representation chosen is a crucial design issue and is treated first, followed by a discussion of arithmetic operations.

This chapter includes a number of examples, each of which is highlighted in a shaded box.

9.1 THE ARITHMETIC AND LOGIC UNIT

The ALU is that part of the computer that actually performs arithmetic and logical operations on data. All of the other elements of the computer system—control unit, registers, memory, I/O—are there mainly to bring data into the ALU for it to process and then to take the results back out. We have, in a sense, reached the core or essence of a computer when we consider the ALU.

An ALU and, indeed, all electronic components in the computer are based on the use of simple digital logic devices that can store binary digits and perform simple Boolean logic operations. For the interested reader, Appendix A explores digital logic implementation.

Figure 9.1 indicates, in general terms, how the ALU is interconnected with the rest of the processor. Data are presented to the ALU in registers, and the results of an operation are stored in registers. These registers are temporary storage locations within the processor that are connected by signal paths to the ALU (e.g., see Figure 2.3). The ALU may also set flags as the result of an operation. For example, an overflow flag is set to 1 if the result of a computation exceeds the length of the register

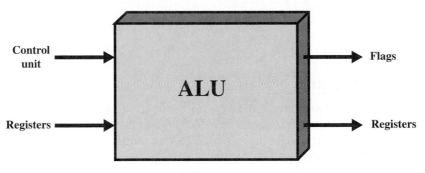

Figure 9.1 ALU Inputs and Outputs

into which it is to be stored. The flag values are also stored in registers within the processor. The control unit provides signals that control the operation of the ALU and the movement of the data into and out of the ALU.

9.2 INTEGER REPRESENTATION

In the binary number system,[1] arbitrary numbers can be represented with just the digits zero and one, the minus sign, and the period, or **radix point**.

$$-1101.0101_2 = -13.3125_{10}$$

For purposes of computer storage and processing, however, we do not have the benefit of minus signs and periods. Only binary digits (0 and 1) may be used to represent numbers. If we are limited to nonnegative integers, the representation is straightforward.

> An 8-bit word can represent the numbers from 0 to 255, including
>
> $$00000000 = 0$$
> $$00000001 = 1$$
> $$00101001 = 41$$
> $$10000000 = 128$$
> $$11111111 = 255$$

In general, if an n-bit sequence of binary digits $a_{n-1}a_{n-2} \ldots a_1a_0$ is interpreted as an unsigned integer A, its value is

---

[1]See Appendix B for a basic refresher on number systems (decimal, binary, hexadecimal).

$$A = \sum_{i=0}^{n-1} 2^i a_i$$

Sign–Magnitude Representation

There are several alternative conventions used to represent negative as well as positive integers, all of which involve treating the most significant (leftmost) bit in the word as a sign bit. If the sign bit is 0, the number is positive; if the sign bit is 1, the number is negative.

The simplest form of representation that employs a sign bit is the sign-magnitude representation. In an n-bit word, the rightmost $n - 1$ bits hold the magnitude of the integer.

> +18= 00010010
> −18= 10010010   (sign magnitude)

The general case can be expressed as follows:

$$\text{Sign Magnitude} \qquad A = \begin{cases} \displaystyle\sum_{i=0}^{n-2} 2^i a_i & \text{if } a_{n-1} = 0 \\ -\displaystyle\sum_{i=0}^{n-2} 2^i a_i & \text{if } a_{n-1} = 1 \end{cases} \tag{9.1}$$

There are several drawbacks to sign-magnitude representation. One is that addition and subtraction require a consideration of both the signs of the numbers and their relative magnitudes to carry out the required operation. This should become clear in the discussion in Section 9.3. Another drawback is that there are two representations of 0:

$$+ 0_{10} = 00000000$$
$$- 0_{10} = 10000000 \quad \text{(sign magnitude)}$$

This is inconvenient, because it is slightly more difficult to test for 0 (an operation performed frequently on computers) than if there were a single representation.

Because of these drawbacks, sign-magnitude representation is rarely used in implementing the integer portion of the ALU. Instead, the most common scheme is twos complement representation.[2]

Twos Complement Representation

Like sign magnitude, twos complement representation uses the most significant bit as a sign bit, making it easy to test whether an integer is positive or negative. It dif-

---

[2]In the literature, the terms *two's complement* or *2's complement* are often used. Here we follow the practice used in standards documents and omit the apostrophe (e.g., IEEE Std 100-1992, *The New IEEE Standard Dictionary of Electrical and Electronics Terms*).

Table 9.1 Characteristics of Twos Complement Representation and Arithmetic

Range	-2^{n-1} through $2^{n-1}-1$
Number of Representations of Zero	One
Negation	Take the Boolean complement of each bit of the corresponding positive number, then add 1 to the resulting bit pattern viewed as an unsigned integer.
Expansion of Bit Length	Add additional bit positions to the left and fill in with the value of the original sign bit.
Overflow Rule	If two numbers with the same sign (both positive or both negative) are added, then overflow occurs if and only if the result has the opposite sign.
Subtraction Rule	To subtract B from A, take the twos complement of B and add it to A.

fers from the use of the sign-magnitude representation in the way that the other bits are interpreted. Table 9.1 highlights key characteristics of twos complement representation and arithmetic, which are elaborated in this section and the next.

Most treatments of twos complement representation focus on the rules for producing negative numbers, with no formal proof that the scheme "works." Instead, our presentation of twos complement integers in this section and in Section 9.3 is based on [DATT93], which suggests that twos complement representation is best understood by defining it in terms of a weighted sum of bits, as we did previously for unsigned and sign-magnitude representations. The advantage of this treatment is that it does not leave any lingering doubt that the rules for arithmetic operations in twos complement notation may not work for some special cases.

Consider an n-bit integer, A, in twos complement representation. If A is positive, then the sign bit, a_{n-1}, is zero. The remaining bits represent the magnitude of the number in the same fashion as for sign magnitude:

$$A = \sum_{i=0}^{n-2} 2^i a_i \qquad \text{for } A \geq 0$$

The number zero is identified as positive and therefore has a 0 sign bit and a magnitude of all 0s. We can see that the range of positive integers that may be represented is from 0 (all of the magnitude bits are 0) through $2^{n-1} - 1$ (all of the magnitude bits are 1). Any larger number would require more bits.

Now, for a negative number A ($A < 0$), the sign bit, a_{n-1}, is one. The remaining $n - 1$ bits can take on any one of 2^{n-1} values. Therefore, the range of negative integers that can be represented is from -1 to -2^{n-1}. We would like to assign the bit values to negative integers in such a way that arithmetic can be handled in a straightforward fashion, similar to unsigned integer arithmetic. In unsigned integer representation, to compute the value of an integer from the bit representation, the weight of the most significant bit is $+2^{n-1}$. For a representation with a sign bit, it turns out that the desired arithmetic properties are achieved, as we will see in Section 9.3, if the weight of the most significant bit is -2^{n-1}. This is the convention used in twos complement representation, yielding the following expression for negative numbers:

$$\textbf{Two Complement} \qquad A = -2^{n-1}a_{n-1} + \sum_{i=0}^{n-2} 2^i a_i \qquad (9.2)$$

In the case of positive integers, $a_{n-1} = 0$, so the term $-2^{n-1}a_{n-1} = 0$. Therefore, Equation (9.2) defines the twos complement representation for both positive and negative numbers.

Table 9.2 compares the sign-magnitude and twos complement representations for 4-bit integers. Although twos complement is an awkward representation from the human point of view, we will see that it facilitates the most important arithmetic operations, addition and subtraction. For this reason, it is almost universally used as the processor representation for integers.

A useful illustration of the nature of twos complement representation is a value box, in which the value on the far right in the box is 1 (2^0) and each succeeding position to the left is double in value, until the leftmost position, which is negated. As you can see in Figure 9.2a, the most negative twos complement number that can be represented is -2^{n-1}; if any of the bits other than the sign bit is one, it adds a positive amount to the number. Also, it is clear that a negative number must have a 1 at its leftmost position and a positive number must have a 0 in that position. Thus, the largest positive number is a 0 followed by all 1s, which equals $2^{n-1} - 1$.

The rest of Figure 9.2 illustrates the use of the value box to convert from twos complement to decimal and from decimal to twos complement.

Table 9.2 Alternative Representations for 4-Bit Integers

Decimal Representation	Sign-Magnitude Representation	Twos Complement Representation	Biased Representation
+8	—	—	1111
+7	0111	0111	1110
+6	0110	0110	1101
+5	0101	0101	1100
+4	0100	0100	1011
+3	0011	0011	1010
+2	0010	0010	1001
+1	0001	0001	1000
+0	0000	0000	0111
−0	1000	—	
−1	1001	1111	0110
−2	1010	1110	0101
−3	1011	1101	0100
−4	1100	1100	0011
−5	1101	1011	0010
−6	1110	1010	0001
−7	1111	1001	0000
−8	—	1000	—

−128	64	32	16	8	4	2	1

(a) An eight-position twos complement value box

−128	64	32	16	8	4	2	1
1	0	0	0	0	0	1	1

−128   +2   +1 = −125

(b) Convert binary 10000011 to decimal

−128	64	32	16	8	4	2	1
1	0	0	0	1	0	0	0

−120 = −128   +8

(c) Convert decimal −120 to binary

Figure 9.2   Use of a Value Box for Conversion between Twos Complement Binary and Decimal

Converting between Different Bit Lengths

It is sometimes desirable to take an n-bit integer and store it in m bits, where $m > n$. In sign-magnitude notation, this is easily accomplished: Simply move the sign bit to the new leftmost position and fill in with zeros.

```
+18  =          00010010    (sign magnitude, 8 bits)
+18  =  0000000000010010    (sign magnitude, 16 bits)
−18  =          10010010    (sign magnitude, 8 bits)
−18  =  1000000000010010    (sign magnitude, 16 bits)
```

This procedure will not work for twos complement negative integers. Using the same example,

```
   +18  =          00010010    (twos complement, 8 bits)
   +18  =  0000000000010010    (twos complement, 16 bits)
   −18  =          11101110    (twos complement, 8 bits)
−32,658  =  1000000001101110    (twos complement, 16 bits)
```

The next to last line is easily seen using the value box of Figure 9.2. The last line can be verified using Equation (9.2) or a 16-bit value box.

Instead, the rule for twos complement integers is to move the sign bit to the new leftmost position and fill in with copies of the sign bit. For positive numbers, fill in with zeros, and for negative numbers, fill in with ones. This is called sign extension.

$$-18 = \qquad\qquad 11101110 \qquad\qquad \text{(twos complement, 8 bits)}$$
$$-18 = 1111111111101110 \qquad\qquad \text{(twos complement, 16 bits)}$$

To see why this rule works, let us again consider an n-bit sequence of binary digits $a_{n-1}a_{n-2}\ldots.a_1a_0$ interpreted as a twos complement integer A, so that its value is

$$A = -2^{n-1}a_{n-1} + \sum_{i=0}^{n-2} 2^i a_i$$

If A is a positive number, the rule clearly works. Now, if A is negative and we want to construct an m-bit representation, with $m > n$. Then

$$A = -2^{m-1}a_{m-1} + \sum_{i=0}^{m-2} 2^i a_i$$

The two values must be equal:

$$-2^{m-1} + \sum_{i=0}^{m-2} 2^i a_i = -2^{n-1} + \sum_{i=0}^{n-2} 2^i a_i$$

$$-2^{m-1} + \sum_{i=n-1}^{m-2} 2^i a_i = -2^{n-1}$$

$$2^{n-1} + \sum_{i=n-1}^{m-2} 2^i a_i = 2^{m-1}$$

$$1 + \sum_{i=0}^{n-2} 2^i + \sum_{i=n-1}^{m-2} 2^i a_i = 1 + \sum_{i=0}^{m-2} 2^i$$

$$\sum_{i=n-1}^{m-2} 2^i a_i = \sum_{i=n-1}^{m-2} 2^i$$

$$=> a_{m-2} = \ldots = a_{n-2} = a_{n-1} = 1$$

In going from the first to the second equation, we require that the least significant $n - 1$ bits do not change between the two representations. Then we get to the next to last equation, which is only true if all of the bits in positions $n - 1$ through $m - 2$ are 1. Thus the sign-extension rule works.

Fixed–Point Representation

Finally, we mention that the representations discussed in this section are sometimes referred to as fixed point. This is because the radix point (binary point) is fixed and assumed to be to the right of the rightmost digit. The programmer can use the same representation for binary fractions by scaling the numbers so that the binary point is implicitly positioned at some other location.

9.3 INTEGER ARITHMETIC

This section examines common arithmetic functions on numbers in twos complement representation.

Negation

In sign-magnitude representation, the rule for forming the negation of an integer is simple: Invert the sign bit. In twos complement notation, the negation of an integer can be formed with the following rules:

1. Take the Boolean complement of each bit of the integer (including the sign bit). That is, set each 1 to 0 and each 0 to 1.
2. Treating the result as an unsigned binary integer, add 1.

This two-step process is referred to as the **twos complement operation**, or the taking of the twos complement of an integer.

$$
\begin{array}{rll}
+18 & = & 00010010 \quad \text{(twos complement)} \\
\text{bitwise complement} & = & 11101101 \\
& + & \underline{\qquad 1} \\
& & 11101110 = -18
\end{array}
$$

As expected, the negative of the negative of that number is itself:

$$
\begin{array}{rll}
-18 & = & 11101110 \quad \text{(twos complement)} \\
\text{bitwise complement} & = & 00010001 \\
& - & \underline{\qquad 1} \\
& & 00010010 = +18
\end{array}
$$

We can demonstrate the validity of the operation just described using the definition of the twos complement representation in Equation (9.2). Again, interpret an n-bit sequence of binary digits $a_{n-1}a_{n-2}\ldots a_1a_0$ as a twos-complement integer A, so that its value is

$$
A = -2^{n-1}a_{n-1} + \sum_{i=0}^{n-2} 2^i a_i
$$

Now form the bitwise complement, $\overline{a_{n-1}}\ \overline{a_{n-2}}\cdots\overline{a_0}$, and, treating this is an unsigned integer, add 1. Finally, interpret the resulting n-bit sequence of binary digits as a twos-complement integer B, so that its value is

$$
B = -2^{n-1}\overline{a_{n-1}} + 1 + \sum_{i=0}^{n-2} 2^i \overline{a_i}
$$

Now, we want $A = -B$, which means $A + B = 0$. This is easily shown to be true:

$$A + B = -(a_{n-1} + \overline{a_{n-1}})2^{n-1} + 1 + \left(\sum_{i=0}^{n-2} 2^i(a_i + \overline{a_i}) \right)$$

$$= -2^{n-1} + 1 + \left(\sum_{i=0}^{n-2} 2^i \right)$$

$$= -2^{n-1} + 1 + (2^{n-1} - 1)$$

$$= -2^{n-1} + 2^{n-1} = 0$$

The preceding derivation assumes that we can first treat the bitwise complement of A as an unsigned integer for the purpose of adding 1, and then treat the result as a twos complement integer. There are two special cases to consider. First, consider $A = 0$. In that case, for an 8-bit representation,

$$
\begin{array}{rcl}
0 & = & 00000000 \quad \text{(twos complement)} \\
\text{bitwise complement} & = & 11111111 \\
& + & \underline{1} \\
& & 100000000 = 0
\end{array}
$$

There is *carry* out of the most significant bit position, which is ignored. The result is that the negation of 0 is 0, as it should be.

The second special case is more of a problem. If we take the negation of the bit pattern of 1 followed by $n - 1$ zeros, we get back the same number. For example, for 8-bit words,

$$
\begin{array}{rcl}
-128 & = & 10000000 \quad \text{(twos complement)} \\
\text{bitwise complement} & = & 01111111 \\
& + & \underline{1} \\
& & 100000000 = -128
\end{array}
$$

Some such anomaly is unavoidable. The number of different bit patterns in an n-bit word is 2^n, which is an even number. We wish to represent positive and negative integers and 0. If an equal number of positive and negative integers are represented (sign magnitude), then there are two representations for 0. If there is only one representation of 0 (twos complement), then there must be an unequal number of negative and positive numbers represented. In the case of twos complement, for an n-bit length, there is a representation for -2^n but not for $+2^n$.

Addition and Subtraction

Addition in twos complement is illustrated in Figure 9.3. The first four examples illustrate successful operations. If the result of the operation is positive, we get a positive number in ordinary binary notation. If the result of the operation is negative, we get a negative number in twos complement form. Note that, in some

```
1001  =  -7              1100  =  -4
+0101  =   5            +0100  =   4
1110  =  -2            10000  =   0

  (a) (-7) + (+5)          (b) (-4) + (+4)


0011  =  3               1100  =  -4
+0100  =  4             +1111  =  -1
0111  =  7             11011  =  -5

  (c) (+3) + (+4)          (d) (-4) + (-1)


0101  =  5               1001  =  -7
+0100  =  4             +1010  =  -6
1001  =  Overflow     10011  =  Overflow

  (e) (+5) + (+4)          (f) (-7) + (-6)
```

Figure 9.3 Addition of Numbers in Twos Complement Respresentation

instances, there is a carry bit beyond the end of the word (indicated by shading), which is ignored.

On any addition, the result may be larger than can be held in the word size being used. This condition is called **overflow**. When overflow occurs, the ALU must signal this fact so that no attempt is made to use the result. To detect overflow, the following rule is observed: If two numbers are added, and they are both positive or both negative, then overflow occurs if and only if the result has the opposite sign. Figures 9.3e and f show examples of overflow. Note that overflow can occur whether or not there is a carry.

Subtraction is also easily handled with the following rule: To subtract one number (subtrahend) from another (minuend), take the twos complement (negation) of the subtrahend and add it to the minuend. Thus, subtraction is achieved using addition, as illustrated in Figure 9.4. The last two examples demonstrate that the overflow rule still applies.

Some insight into twos complement addition and subtraction can be gained by looking at a geometric depiction [BENH92], as shown in Figure 9.5. The circle in the upper half of each part of the figure is formed by selecting the appropriate segment of the number line and joining the endpoints. Note that when the numbers are laid out on a circle, the twos complement of any number is horizontally opposite that number (indicated by dashed horizontal lines). Starting at any number on the circle, we can add positive k (or subtract negative k) to that number by moving k positions clockwise, and we can subtract positive k (or add negative k) from that number by moving k positions counterclockwise. If an arithmetic operation results in traversal of the point where the endpoints are joined, an incorrect answer is given (overflow).

All of the examples of Figures 9.3 and 9.4 are easily traced in the circle of Figure 9.5.

Figure 9.6 suggests the data paths and hardware elements needed to accomplish addition and subtraction. The central element is a binary adder, which is presented two numbers for addition and produces a sum and an overflow indication. The binary adder treats the two numbers as unsigned integers. (A logic implementation of an adder is given in Appendix A.) For addition, the two numbers are presented to the adder from two registers, designated in this case as A and B registers. The result may be stored in one of these registers or in a third. The overflow indication is stored in a 1-bit overflow flag (0 = no overflow; 1 = overflow). For subtraction, the subtrahend (B register) is passed through a twos complementer so that its twos complement is presented to the adder.

Multiplication

Compared with addition and subtraction, multiplication is a complex operation, whether performed in hardware or software. A wide variety of algorithms have been used in various computers. The purpose of this subsection is to give the reader some feel for the type of approach typically taken. We begin with the simpler problem of multiplying two unsigned (nonnegative) integers, and then we look at one of the most common techniques for multiplication of numbers in twos complement representation.

Unsigned Integers

Figure 9.7 illustrates the multiplication of unsigned binary integers, as might be carried out using paper and pencil. Several important observations can be made:

```
         0010 =   2                      0101 =   5
        +1001 =  -7                     +1110 =  -2
         1011 =  -5                     10011 =   3

(a)  M = 2 = 0010              (b)  M = 5 = 0101
     S = 7 = 0111                   S = 2 = 0010
    -S =       1001                -S =       1110


         1011 =  -5                      0101 =   5
        +1110 =  -2                     +0010 =   2
        11001 =  -7                      0111 =   7

(c)  M =-5 = 1011              (d)  M = 5 = 0101
     S = 2 = 0010                   S =-2 = 1110
    -S =       1110                -S =       0010


         0111 =   7                      1010 =  -6
        +0111 =   7                     +1100 =  -4
         1110 = Overflow               10110 = Overflow

(e)  M =   7 = 0111           (f)  M = -6 = 1010
     S = -7 = 1001                  S =  4 = 0100
    -S =       0111                 -S =       1100
```

Figure 9.4 Subtraction of Numbers in Twos Complement Representation (M − S)

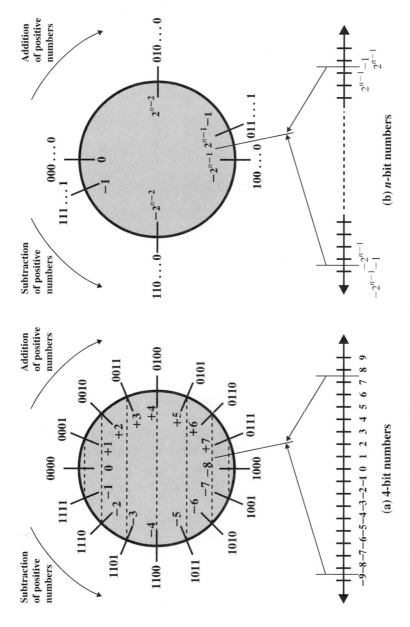

Figure 9.5 Geometric Depiction of Twos Complement Integers

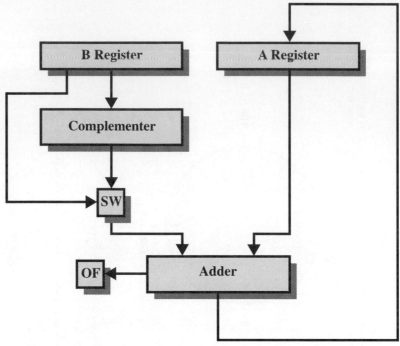

OF = Overflow bit
SW = Switch (select addition or subtraction)

Figure 9.6 Block Diagram of Hardware for Addition and Subtraction

1. Multiplication involves the generation of partial products, one for each digit in the multiplier. These partial products are then summed to produce the final product.
2. The partial products are easily defined. When the multiplier bit is 0, the partial product is 0. When the multiplier is 1, the partial product is the multiplicand.
3. The total product is produced by summing the partial products. For this operation, each successive partial product is shifted one position to the left relative to the preceding partial product.
4. The multiplication of two n-bit binary integers results in a product of up to $2n$ bits in length (e.g., $11 \times 11 = 1001$).

Figure 9.7 Multiplication of Unsigned Binary Integers

Compared with the pencil-and-paper approach, there are several things we can do to make computerized multiplication more efficient. First, we can perform a running addition on the partial products rather than waiting until the end. This eliminates the need for storage of all the partial products; fewer registers are needed. Second, we can save some time on the generation of partial products. For each 1 on the multiplier, an add and a shift operation are required; but for each 0, only a shift is required.

Figure 9.8a shows a possible implementation employing these measures. The multiplier and multiplicand are loaded into two registers (Q and M). A third register, the A register, is also needed and is initially set to 0. There is also a 1-bit C register, initialized to 0, which holds a potential carry bit resulting from addition.

The operation of the multiplier is as follows. Control logic reads the bits of the multiplier one at a time. If Q_0 is 1, then the multiplicand is added to the A reg-

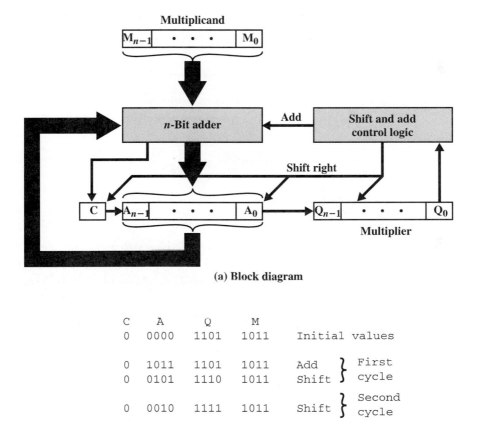

(a) Block diagram

```
C     A      Q      M
0    0000   1101   1011    Initial values

0    1011   1101   1011    Add     } First
0    0101   1110   1011    Shift   } cycle

0    0010   1111   1011    Shift   } Second
                                   } cycle

0    1101   1111   1011    Add     } Third
0    0110   1111   1011    Shift   } cycle

1    0001   1111   1011    Add     } Fourth
0    1000   1111   1011    Shift   } cycle
```

(b) Example from Figure 9.7 (product in A, Q)

Figure 9.8 Hardware Implementation of Unsigned Binary Multiplication

Figure 9.9 Flowchart for Unsigned Binary Multiplication

ister and the result is stored in the A register, with the C bit used for overflow. Then all of the bits of the C, A, and Q registers are shifted to the right one bit, so that the C bit goes into A_{n-1}, A_0 goes into Q_{n-1}, and Q_0 is lost. If Q_0 is 0, then no addition is performed, just the shift. This process is repeated for each bit of the original multiplier. The resulting $2n$-bit product is contained in the A and Q registers. A flowchart of the operation is shown in Figure 9.9, and an example is given in Figure 9.8b. Note that on the second cycle, when the multiplier bit is 0, there is no add operation.

Twos Complement Multiplication

We have seen that addition and subtraction can be performed on numbers in twos complement notation by treating them as unsigned integers. Consider

$$
\begin{array}{r}
1001 \\
+\underline{0011} \\
1100
\end{array}
$$

If these numbers are considered to be unsigned integers, then we are adding 9 (1001) plus 3 (0011) to get 12 (1100). As twos complement integers, we are adding −7 (1001) to 3 (0011) to get −4 (1100).

```
        1001
      × 1101
      00001011    1011 × 1 × 2⁰
      00000000    1011 × 0 × 2¹
      00101100    1011 × 1 × 2²
      01011000    1011 × 1 × 2³
      10001111
```

Figure 9.10 Multiplication of Two Unsigned 4-Bit Integers Yielding and 8-Bit Result

Unfortunately, this simple scheme will not work for multiplication. To see this, consider again Figure 9.7. We multiplied 11 (1011) by 13 (1101) to get 143 (10001111). If we interpret these as twos complement numbers, we have -5 (1011) times -3 (1101) equals -113 (10001111). This example demonstrates that straight-forward multiplication will not work if both the multiplicand and multiplier are negative. In fact, it will not work if either the multiplicand or the multiplier is negative. To justify this statement, we need to go back to Figure 9.7 and explain what is being done in terms of operations with powers of 2. Recall that any unsigned binary number can be expressed as a sum of powers of 2. Thus,

$$1101 = 1 \times 2^3 + 1 \times 2^2 + 0 \times 2^1 + 1 \times 2^0$$
$$= 2^3 + 2^2 + 2^0$$

Further, the multiplication of a binary number by 2^n is accomplished by shifting that number to the left n bits. With this in mind, Figure 9.10 recasts Figure 9.7 to make the generation of partial products by multiplication explicit. The only difference in Figure 9.10 is that it recognizes that the partial products should be viewed as $2n$-bit numbers generated from the n-bit multiplicand.

Thus, as an unsigned integer, the 4-bit multiplicand 1011 is stored in an 8-bit word as 00001011. Each partial product (other than that for 2^0) consists of this number shifted to the left, with the unoccupied positions on the right filled with zeros (e.g., a shift to the left of two places yields 00101100).

Now we can demonstrate that straightforward multiplication will not work if the multiplicand is negative. The problem is that each contribution of the negative multiplicand as a partial product must be a negative number on a $2n$-bit field; the sign bits of the partial products must line up. This is demonstrated in Figure 9.11,

```
    1001   (9)                    1001   (−7)
   ×0011   (3)                   ×0011   (3)
  00001001  1001 × 2⁰         11111001  (−7) × 2⁰ = (−7)
  00010010  1001 × 2¹         11110010  (−7) × 2¹ = (−14)
  00011011  (27)              11101011  (−21)

   (a) Unsigned integers        (b) Twos complement integers
```

Figure 9.11 Comparison of Multiplication of Unsigned and Twos Complement Integers which shows that multiplication of 1001 by 0011. If these are treated as unsigned integers, the multiplication of $9 \times 3 = 27$ proceeds simply. However, if 1001 is interpreted as the twos complement value -7, then each partial product must be a negative twos complement number of $2n$ (8) bits, as shown in Figure 9.11b. Note that this is accomplished by padding out each partial product to the left with binary 1s.

If the multiplier is negative, straightforward multiplication also will not work. The reason is that the bits of the multiplier no longer correspond to the shifts or multiplications that must take place. For example, the 4-bit decimal number -3 is written 1101 in twos complement. If we simply took partial products based on each bit position, we would have the following correspondence:

$$1101 \leftrightarrow -(1 \times 2^3 + 1 \times 2^2 + 0 \times 2^1 + 1 \times 2^0) = -(2^3 + 2^2 + 2^0)$$

In fact, what is desired is $-(2^1 + 2^0)$. So this multiplier cannot be used directly in the manner we have been describing.

There are a number of ways out of this dilemma. One would be to convert both multiplier and multiplicand to positive numbers, perform the multiplication, and then take the twos complement of the result if and only if the sign of the two original numbers differed. Implementers have preferred to use techniques that do not require this final transformation step. One of the most common of these is Booth's algorithm. This algorithm also has the benefit of speeding up the multiplication process, relative to a more straightforward approach.

Booth's algorithm is depicted in Figure 9.12 and can be described as follows. As before, the multiplier and multiplicand are placed in the Q and M registers, respectively. There is also a 1-bit register placed logically to the right of the least significant bit (Q_0) of the Q register and designated Q_{-1}; its use is explained shortly. The results of the multiplication will appear in the A and Q registers. A and Q_{-1} are initialized to 0. As before, control logic scans the bits of the multiplier one at a time. Now, as each bit is examined, the bit to its right is also examined. If the two bits are the same (1–1 or 0–0), then all of the bits of the A, Q, and Q_{-1} registers are shifted to the right 1 bit. If the two bits differ, then the multiplicand is added to or subtracted from the A register, depending on whether the two bits are 0–1 or 1–0. Following the addition or subtraction, the right shift occurs. In either case, the right shift is such that the leftmost bit of A, namely A_{n-1}, not only is shifted into A_{n-2}, but also remains in A_{n-1}. This is required to preserve the sign of the number in A and Q. It is known as an **arithmetic shift**, because it preserves the sign bit.

Figure 9.13 shows the sequence of events in Booth's algorithm for the multiplication of 7 by 3. More compactly, the same operation is depicted in Figure 9.14a. The rest of Figure 9.14 gives other examples of the algorithm. As can be seen, it works with any combination of positive and negative numbers. Note also the efficiency of the algorithm. Blocks of 1s or 0s are skipped over, with an average of only one addition or subtraction per block.

Why does Booth's algorithm work? Consider first the case of a positive multiplier. In particular, consider a positive multiplier consisting of one block of 1s surrounded by 0s (for example, 00011110). As we know, multiplication can be achieved by adding appropriately shifted copies of the multiplicand:

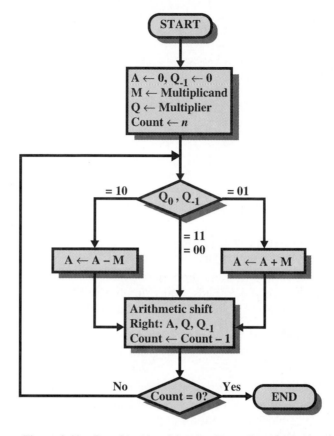

Figure 9.12 Booth's Algorithm for Twos Complement Multiplication

$$M \times (00011110) = M \times (2^4 + 2^3 + 2^2 + 2^1)$$
$$= M \times (16 + 8 + 4 + 2)$$
$$= M \times 30$$

The number of such operations can be reduced to two if we observe that

$$2^n + 2^{n-1} + \ldots + 2^{n-K} = 2^{n+1} - 2^{n-K} \qquad (9.3)$$

$$M \times (00011110) = M \times (2^5 - 2^1)$$
$$= M \times (32 - 2)$$
$$= M \times 30$$

```
  A      Q     Q₋₁   M
0000    0011    0    0111       Initial values

1001    0011    0    0111       A ← A - M ⎫  First
1100    1001    1    0111       Shift     ⎬  cycle
                                          ⎭
                                          ⎫  Second
1110    0100    1    0111       Shift     ⎬  cycle
                                          ⎭
0101    0100    1    0111       A ← A + M ⎫  Third
0010    1010    0    0111       Shift     ⎬  cycle
                                          ⎭
                                          ⎫  Fourth
0001    0101    0    0111       Shift     ⎬  cycle
                                          ⎭
```

Figure 9.13 Example of Booth's Algorithm (7×3)

So the product can be generated by one addition and one subtraction of the multiplicand. This scheme extends to any number of blocks of 1s in a multiplier, including the case in which a single 1 is treated as a block.

$$M \times (01111010) = M \times (2^6 + 2^5 + 2^4 + 2^3 + 2^1)$$
$$= M \times (2^7 - 2^3 + 2^2 - 2^1)$$

Booth's algorithm conforms to this scheme by performing a subtraction when the first 1 of the block is encountered (1–0) and an addition when the end of the block is encountered (0–1).

```
       0111                            0111
     ×0011     (0)                   ×1101     (0)
  11111001     1-0                11111001     1-0
  0000000      1-1                0000111      0-1
  000111       0-1                111001       1-0
  00010101     (21)               11101011     (-21)

     (a) (7) × (3) = (21)             (b) (7) × (-3) = (-21)

       1001                            1001
     ×0011     (0)                   ×1101     (0)
  00000111     1-0                00000111     1-0
  0000000      1-1                1111001      0-1
  111001       0-1                000111       1-0
  11101011     (-21)              00010101     (21)

     (c) (-7) × (3) = (-21)           (d) (-7) × (-3) = (21)
```

Figure 9.14 Examples Using Booth's Algorithm

To show that the same scheme works for a negative multiplier, we need to observe the following. Let X be a negative number in twos complement notation:

$$\text{Representation of } X = \{1x_{n-2}x_{n-3}\ldots x_1x_0\}$$

Then the value of X can be expressed as follows:

$$X = -2^{n-1} + (x_{n-2} \times 2^{n-2}) + (x_{n-3} \times 2^{n-3}) + \ldots + (x_1 \times 2^1) + (x_0 \times 2^0) \qquad (9.4)$$

The reader can verify this by applying the algorithm to the numbers in Table 9.2.

The leftmost bit of X is 1, because X is negative. Assume that the leftmost 0 is in the kth position. Thus, X is of the form

$$\text{Representation of } X = \{111\ldots10x_{k-1}\,x_{k-2}\ldots x_1x_0\} \qquad (9.5)$$

Then the value of X is

$$X = -2^{n-1} + 2^{n-2} + \ldots + 2^{k+1} + (x_{k-1} \times 2^{k-1}) + \ldots + (x_0 \times 2^0) \qquad (9.6)$$

From Equation (9.3), we can say that

$$2^{n-2} + 2^{n-3} + \ldots + 2^{k+1} = 2^{n-1} - 2^{k+1}$$

Rearranging,

$$-2^{n-1} + 2^{n-2} + 2^{n-3} + \ldots + 2^{k+1} = -2^{k+1} \qquad (9.7)$$

Substituting Equation (9.7) into Equation (9.6), we have

$$X = -2^{k+1} + (x_{k-1} \times 2^{k-1}) + \ldots + (x_0 \times 2^0) \qquad (9.8)$$

At last we can return to Booth's algorithm. Remembering the representation of X [Equation (9.5)], it is clear that all of the bits from x_0 up to the leftmost 0 are handled properly, because they produce all of the terms in Equation (9.8) but (-2^{k+1}) and thus are in the proper form. As the algorithm scans over the leftmost 0 and encounters the next 1 (2^{k+1}), a 1–0 transition occurs and a subtraction takes place (-2^{k+1}). This is the remaining term in Equation (9.8).

As an example, consider the multiplication of some multiplicand by (-6). In twos complement representation, using an 8-bit word, (-6) is represented as 11111010. By Equation (9.4), we know that

$$-6 = -2^7 + 2^6 + 2^5 + 2^4 + 2^3 + 2^1$$

which the reader can easily verify. Thus,

$$M \times (11111010) = M \times (-2^7 + 2^6 + 2^5 + 2^4 + 2^3 + 2^1)$$

Using Equation (9.7),

$$M \times (11111010) = M \times (-2^3 + 2^1)$$

which the reader can verify is still $M \times (-6)$. Finally, following our earlier line of reasoning,

$$M \times (11111010) = M \times (-2^3 + 2^2 - 2^1)$$

We can see that Booth's algorithm conforms to this scheme. It performs a subtraction when the first 1 is encountered (1–0), an addition when (01) is encountered, and finally another subtraction when the first 1 of the next block of 1s is encountered. Thus, Booth's algorithm performs fewer additions and subtractions than a more straightforward algorithm.

Division

Division is somewhat more complex than multiplication but is based on the same general principles. As before, the basis for the algorithm is the paper-and-pencil approach, and the operation involves repetitive shifting and addition or subtraction.

Figure 9.15 shows an example of the long division of unsigned binary integers. It is instructive to describe the process in detail. First, the bits of the dividend are examined from left to right, until the set of bits examined represents a number greater than or equal to the divisor; this is referred to as the divisor being able to divide the number. Until this event occurs, 0s are placed in the quotient from left to right. When the event occurs, a 1 is placed in the quotient and the divisor is subtracted from the partial dividend. The result is referred to as a *partial remainder*. From this point on, the division follows a cyclic pattern. At each cycle, additional bits from the dividend are appended to the partial remainder until the result is greater than or equal to the divisor. As before, the divisor is subtracted from this number to produce a new partial remainder. The process continues until all the bits of the dividend are exhausted.

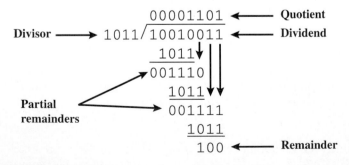

Figure 9.15   Example of Division of Unsigned Binary Integers

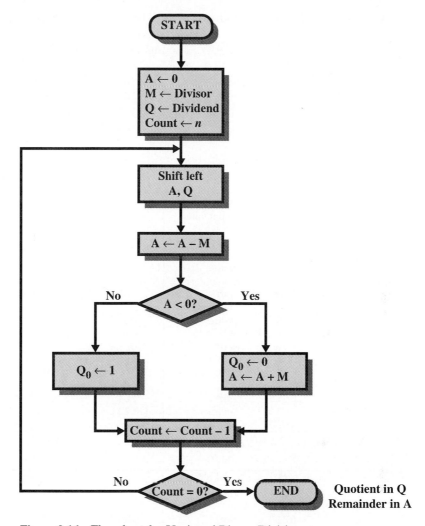

Figure 9.16 Flowchart for Unsigned Binary Division

Figure 9.16 shows a machine algorithm that corresponds to the long division process. The divisor is placed in the M register, the dividend in the Q register. At each step, the A and Q registers together are shifted to the left 1 bit. M is subtracted from A to determine whether A divides the partial remainder.[3] If it does, then Q_0 gets a 1 bit. Otherwise, Q_0 gets a 0 bit and M must be added back to A to restore the previous value. The count is then decremented, and the process continues for n steps. At the end, the quotient is in the Q register and the remainder is in the A register.

---

[3]This is subtraction of unsigned integers. A result that requires a borrow out of the most significant bit is a negative result.

This process can, with some difficulty, be extended to negative numbers. We give here one approach for twos complement numbers. Several examples of this approach are shown in Figure 9.17. The algorithm can be summarized as follows.

1. Load the divisor into the M register and the dividend into the A, Q registers. The dividend must be expressed as a $2n$-bit twos complement number. Thus, for example, the 4-bit 0111 becomes 00000111, and 1001 becomes 11111001.
2. Shift A, Q left 1 bit position.

A	Q	M = 0011	A	Q	M = 1101
0000	0111	Initial value	0000	0111	Initial value
0000	1110	shift	0000	1110	shift
1101		subtract	1101		add
0000	1110	restore	0000	1110	restore
0001	1100	shift	0001	1100	shift
1110		subtract	1110		add
0001	1100	restore	0001	1100	restore
0011	1000	shift	0011	1000	shift
0000		subtract	0000		add
0000	1001	set $Q_0 = 1$	0000	1001	set $Q_0 = 1$
0001	0010	shift	0001	0010	shift
1110		subtract	1110		add
0001	0010	restore	0001	0010	restore

(a) (7)/(3)   (b) (7)/(−3)

A	Q	M = 0011	A	Q	M = 1101
1111	1001	Initial value	1111	1001	Initial value
1111	0010	shift	1111	0010	shift
0010		add	0010		subtract
1111	0010	restore	1111	0010	restore
1110	0100	shift	1110	0100	shift
0001		add	0001		subtract
1110	0100	restore	1110	0100	restore
1100	1000	shift	1100	1000	shift
1111		add	1111		subtract
1111	1001	set $Q_0 = 1$	1111	1001	set $Q_0 = 1$
1111	0010	shift	1111	0010	shift
0010		add	0010		subtract
1111	0010	restore	1111	0010	restore

(c) (−7)/(3)   (d) (−7)/(−3)

Figure 9.17   Examples of Twos Complement Division

3. If M and A have the same signs, perform $A \leftarrow A - M$; otherwise, $A \leftarrow A + M$.
4. The preceding operation is successful if the sign of A is the same before and after the operation.
   a. If the operation is successful or $A = 0$, then set $Q_0 \leftarrow 1$.
   b. If the operation is unsuccessful and $A \neq 0$, then set $Q_0 \leftarrow 0$ and restore the previous value of A.
5. Repeat steps 2 through 4 as many times as there are bit positions in Q.
6. The remainder is in A. If the signs of the divisor and dividend were the same, then the quotient is in Q; otherwise, the correct quotient is the twos complement of Q.

The reader will note from Figure 9.17 that $(-7) \div (3)$ and $(7) \div (-3)$ produce different remainders. This is because the remainder is defined by

$$D = Q \times V + R$$

where

$$D = \text{dividend}$$
$$Q = \text{quotient}$$
$$V = \text{divisor}$$
$$R = \text{remainder}$$

The results of Figure 9.17 are consistent with this formula.

9.4 FLOATING-POINT REPRESENTATION

Principles

With a fixed-point notation (e.g., twos complement) it is possible to represent a range of positive and negative integers centered on 0. By assuming a fixed binary or radix point, this format allows the representation of numbers with a fractional component as well.

This approach has limitations. Very large numbers cannot be represented, nor can very small fractions. Furthermore, the fractional part of the quotient in a division of two large numbers could be lost.

For decimal numbers, one gets around this limitation by using scientific notation. Thus, 976,000,000,000,000 can be represented as 9.76×10^{14}, and 0.0000000000000976 can be represented as 9.76×10^{-14}. What we have done, in effect, is dynamically to slide the decimal point to a convenient location and use the exponent of 10 to keep track of that decimal point. This allows a range of very large and very small numbers to be represented with only a few digits.

This same approach can be taken with binary numbers. We can represent a number in the form

$$\pm S \times B^{\pm E}$$

(a) Format

$$1.1010001 \times 2^{10100} = 0\ 10010011\ 1010001000000000000000 = 1.638125 \times 2^{20}$$
$$-1.1010001 \times 2^{10100} = 1\ 10010011\ 1010001000000000000000 = -1.638125 \times 2^{20}$$
$$1.1010001 \times 2^{-10100} = 0\ 01101011\ 1010001000000000000000 = 1.638125 \times 2^{-20}$$
$$-1.1010001 \times 2^{-10100} = 1\ 01101011\ 1010001000000000000000 = -1.638125 \times 2^{-20}$$

(b) Examples

Figure 9.18 Typical 32-Bit Floating-Point Format

This number can be stored in a binary word with three fields:

- Sign: plus or minus
- Significand S
- Exponent E

The **base** B is implicit and need not be stored because it is the same for all numbers. Typically, it is assumed that the radix point is to the right of the leftmost, or most significant, bit of the significand. That is, there is one bit to the left of the radix point.

The principles used in representing binary floating-point numbers are best explained with an example. Figure 9.18a shows a typical 32-bit floating-point format. The leftmost bit stores the **sign** of the number (0 = positive, 1 = negative). The **exponent** value is stored in the next 8 bits. The representation used is known as a **biased representation**. A fixed value, called the bias, is subtracted from the field to get the true exponent value. Typically, the bias equals ($2^{k-1} - 1$), where k is the number of bits in the binary exponent. In this case, the 8-bit field yields the numbers 0 through 255. With a bias of 127, the true exponent values are in the range -127 to $+128$. In this example, the base is assumed to be 2.

Table 9.2 shows the biased representation for 4-bit integers. Note that when the bits of a biased representation are treated as unsigned integers, the relative magnitudes of the numbers do not change. For example, in both biased and unsigned representations, the largest number is 1111 and the smallest number is 0000. This is not true of sign-magnitude or twos complement representation. An advantage of biased representation is that nonnegative floating-point numbers can be treated as integers for comparison purposes.

The final portion of the word (23 bits in this case) is the **significand**, also called the mantissa.

Any floating-point number can be expressed in many ways.

> The following are equivalent, where the significand is expressed in binary form:
>
> $$0.110 \times 2^5$$
> $$110 \times 2^2$$
> $$0.0110 \times 2^6$$

To simplify operations on floating-point numbers, it is typically required that they be normalized. A **normalized number** is one in which the most significant digit of the significand is nonzero. For base 2 representation, a normalized number is therefore one in which the most significant bit of the significand is one. As was mentioned, the typical convention is that there is one bit to the left of the radix point. Thus, a normalized nonzero number is one in the form

$$\pm 1.bbb \ldots b \times 2^{\pm E}$$

where b is either binary digit (0 or 1). Because the most significant bit is always one, it is unnecessary to store this bit; rather, it is implicit. Thus, the 23-bit field is used to store a 24-bit significand with a value in the half open interval $[1, 2)$. Given a number that is not normalized, the number may be normalized by shifting the radix point to the right of the leftmost 1 bit and adjusting the exponent accordingly.

Figure 9.18b gives some examples of numbers stored in this format. Note the following features:

- The sign is stored in the first bit of the word.
- The first bit of the true significand is always 1 and need not be stored in the significand field.
- The value 127 is added to the true exponent to be stored in the exponent field.
- The base is 2.

With this representation, Figure 9.19 indicates the range of numbers that can be represented in a 32-bit word. Using twos complement integer representation, all of the integers from -2^{31} to $2^{31} - 1$ can be represented, for a total of 2^{32} different numbers. With the example floating-point format of Figure 9.18, the following ranges of numbers are possible:

- Negative numbers between $-(2 - 2^{-23}) \times 2^{128}$ and -2^{-127}
- Positive numbers between 2^{-127} and $(2 - 2^{-23}) \times 2^{128}$

Five regions on the number line are not included in these ranges:

- Negative numbers less than $-(2 - 2^{-23}) \times 2^{128}$, called **negative overflow**
- Negative numbers greater than 2^{-127}, called **negative underflow**
- Zero
- Positive numbers less than 2^{-127}, called **positive underflow**
- Positive numbers greater than $(2 - 2^{-23}) \times 2^{128}$, called **positive overflow**

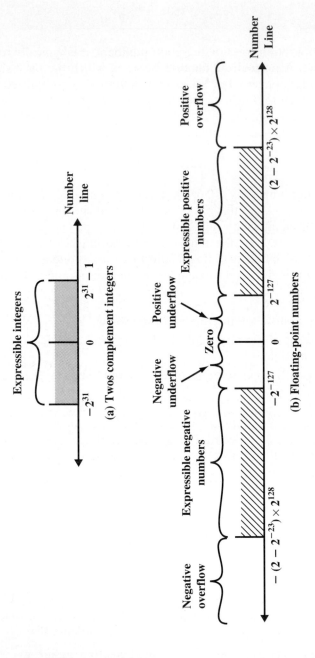

Figure 9.19 Expressible Numbers in Typical 32-Bit Formats

(a) Twos complement integers

Expressible integers

-2^{31} 0 $2^{31} - 1$

Number line

(b) Floating-point numbers

Negative overflow

Expressible negative numbers

Negative underflow

Zero

Positive underflow

Expressible positive numbers

Positive overflow

$-(2 - 2^{-23}) \times 2^{128}$ -2^{-127} 0 2^{-127} $(2 - 2^{-23}) \times 2^{128}$

Number Line

Figure 9.20 Density of Floating-Point Numbers

The representation as presented will not accommodate a value of 0. However, as we shall see, actual floating-point representations include a special bit pattern to designate zero. Overflow occurs when an arithmetic operation results in a magnitude greater than can be expressed with an exponent of 128 (e.g., $2^{120} \times 2^{100} = 2^{220}$). Underflow occurs when the fractional magnitude is too small (e.g., $2^{-120} \times 2^{-100} = 2^{-220}$). Underflow is a less serious problem because the result can generally be satisfactorily approximated by 0.

It is important to note that we are not representing more individual values with floating-point notation. The maximum number of different values that can be represented with 32 bits is still 2^{32}. What we have done is to spread those numbers out in two ranges, one positive and one negative.

Also, note that the numbers represented in floating-point notation are not spaced evenly along the number line, as are fixed-point numbers. The possible values get closer together near the origin and farther apart as you move away, as shown in Figure 9.20. This is one of the trade-offs of floating-point math: Many calculations produce results that are not exact and have to be rounded to the nearest value that the notation can represent.

In the type of format depicted in Figure 9.18, there is a trade-off between range and precision. The example shows 8 bits devoted to the exponent and 23 to the significand. If we increase the number of bits in the exponent, we expand the range of expressible numbers. But because only a fixed number of different values can be expressed, we have reduced the density of those numbers and therefore the precision. The only way to increase both range and precision is to use more bits. Thus, most computers offer, at least, single-precision numbers and double-precision numbers. For example, a single-precision format might be 32 bits, and a double-precision format 64 bits.

So there is a trade-off between the number of bits in the exponent and the number of bits in the significand. But it is even more complicated than that. The implied base of the exponent need not be 2. The IBM S/390 architecture, for example, uses a base of 16 [ANDE67b]. The format consists of a 7-bit exponent and a 24-bit significand.

In the IBM base-16 format,

$$0.11010001 \times 2^{10100} = 0.11010001 \times 16^{101}$$

and the exponent is stored to represent 5 rather than 20.

The advantage of using a larger exponent is that a greater range can be achieved for the same number of exponent bits. But remember, we have not increased the number of different values that can be represented. Thus, for a fixed format, a larger exponent base gives a greater range at the expense of less precision.

IEEE Standard for Binary Floating-Point Representation

The most important floating-point representation is defined in IEEE Standard 754 [IEEE85]. This standard was developed to facilitate the portability of programs from one processor to another and to encourage the development of sophisticated, numerically oriented programs. The standard has been widely adopted and is used on virtually all contemporary processors and arithmetic coprocessors.

The IEEE standard defines both a 32-bit single and a 64-bit double format (Figure 9.21), with 8-bit and 11-bit exponents, respectively. The implied base is 2. In addition, the standard defines two extended formats, single and double, whose exact format is implementation dependent. The extended formats include additional bits in the exponent (extended range) and in the significand (extended precision). The extended formats are to be used for intermediate calculations. With their greater precision, the extended formats lessen the chance of a final result that has been contaminated by excessive roundoff error; with their greater range, they also lessen the chance of an intermediate overflow aborting a computation whose result would have been representable in a basic format. An additional motivation for the single extended format is that it affords some of the benefits of a double format without incurring the time penalty usually associated with higher precision. Table 9.3 summarizes the characteristics of the four formats.

Not all bit patterns in the IEEE formats are interpreted in the usual way; instead, some bit patterns are used to represent special values. Table 9.4 indicates the values assigned to various bit patterns. The extreme exponent values of all zeros (0) and all ones (255 in single format, 2047 in double format) define special values. The following classes of numbers are represented:

(a) Single format

(b) Double format

Figure 9.21   IEEE 754 Formats

Table 9.3 IEEE 754 Format Parameters

Parameter	Format			
	Single	**Single Extended**	**Double**	**Double Extended**
Word width (bits)	32	$\geq$43	64	$\geq$79
Exponent width (bits)	8	$\geq$11	11	$\geq$15
Exponent bias	127	Unspecified	1023	Unspecified
Maximum exponent	127	$\geq$1023	1023	$\geq$16383
Minimum exponent	–126	$\leq$–1022	–1022	$\leq$–16382
Number range (base 10)	10^{-38}, 10^{+38}	Unspecified	10^{-308}, 10^{+308}	Unspecified
Significand width (bits)*	23	$\geq$31	52	$\geq$63
Number of exponents	254	Unspecified	2046	Unspecified
Number of fractions	2^{23}	Unspecified	2^{52}	Unspecified
Number of values	1.98×2^{31}	Unspecified	1.99×2^{63}	Unspecified

* Not including implied bit

- For exponent values in the range of 1 through 254 for single format and 1 through 2046 for double format, normalized nonzero floating-point numbers are represented. The exponent is biased, so that the range of exponents is −126 through +127 for single format and −1022 through +1023. A normalized number requires a 1 bit to the left of the binary point; this bit is implied, giving an effective 24-bit or 53-bit significand (called fraction in the standard).
- An exponent of zero together with a fraction of zero represents positive or negative zero, depending on the sign bit. As was mentioned, it is useful to have an exact value of 0 represented.
- An exponent of all ones together with a fraction of zero represents positive or negative infinity, depending on the sign bit. It is also useful to have a representation of infinity. This leaves it up to the user to decide whether to treat overflow as an error condition or to carry the value ∞ and proceed with whatever program is being executed.
- An exponent of zero together with a nonzero fraction represents a denormalized number. In this case, the bit to the left of the binary point is zero and the true exponent is −126 or −1022. The number is positive or negative depending on the sign bit.
- An exponent of all ones together with a nonzero fraction is given the value NaN, which means *Not a Number*, and is used to signal various exception conditions.

The significance of denormalized numbers and NaNs is discussed in Section 9.5.

9.5 FLOATING-POINT ARITHMETIC

Table 9.5 summarizes the basic operations for floating-point arithmetic. For addition and subtraction, it is necessary to ensure that both operands have the same

Table 9.4 Interpretation of IEEE 754 Floating-Point Numbers

	Single Precision (32 bits)				Double Precision (64 bits)			
	Sign	Biased exponent	Fraction	Value	Sign	Biased exponent	Fraction	Value
Positive zero	0	0	0	0	0	0	0	0
Negative zero	1	0	0	-0	1	0	0	-0
Plus infinity	0	255 (all 1s)	0	∞	0	2047 (all 1s)	0	∞
Minus infinity	1	255 (all 1s)	0	$-\infty$	1	2047 (all 1s)	0	$-\infty$
Quiet NaN	0 or 1	255 (all 1s)	$\neq 0$	NaN	0 or 1	2047 (all 1s)	$\neq 0$	NaN
Signaling NaN	0 or 1	255 (all 1s)	$\neq 0$	NaN	0 or 1	2047 (all 1s)	$\neq 0$	NaN
Positive normalized nonzero	0	$0 < e < 255$	f	$2^{e-127}(1.f)$	0	$0 < e < 2047$	f	$2^{e-1023}(1.f)$
Negative normalized nonzero	1	$0 < e < 255$	f	$-2^{e-127}(1.f)$	1	$0 < e < 2047$	f	$-2^{e-1023}(1.f)$
Positive denormalized	0	0	$f \neq 0$	$2^{e-126}(0.f)$	0	0	$f \neq 0$	$2^{e-1022}(0.f)$
Negative denormalized	1	0	$f \neq 0$	$-2^{e-126}(0.f)$	1	0	$f \neq 0$	$-2^{e-1022}(0.f)$

exponent value. This may require shifting the radix point on one of the operands to achieve alignment. Multiplication and division are more straightforward.

A floating-point operation may produce one of these conditions:

- **Exponent overflow:** A positive exponent exceeds the maximum possible exponent value. In some systems, this may be designated as $+\infty$ or $-\infty$.
- **Exponent underflow:** A negative exponent is less than the minimum possible exponent value (e.g., -200 is less than -127). This means that the number is too small to be represented, and it may be reported as 0.
- **Significand underflow:** In the process of aligning significands, digits may flow off the right end of the significand. As we shall discuss, some form of rounding is required.
- **Significand overflow:** The addition of two significands of the same sign may result in a carry out of the most significant bit. This can be fixed by realignment, as we shall explain.

Addition and Subtraction

In floating-point arithmetic, addition and subtraction are more complex than multiplication and division. This is because of the need for alignment. There are four basic phases of the algorithm for addition and subtraction:

1. Check for zeros.
2. Align the significands.
3. Add or subtract the significands.
4. Normalize the result.

A typical flowchart is shown in Figure 9.22. A step-by-step narrative highlights the main functions required for floating-point addition and subtraction. We assume a format similar to those of Figure 9.21. For the addition or subtraction operation, the two operands must be transferred to registers that will be used by the ALU. If

Table 9.5 Floating-Point Numbers and Arithmetic Operations

Floating Point Numbers	Arithmetic Operations
$X = X_S \times B^{X_E}$ $Y = Y_S \times B^{Y_E}$	$\left.\begin{array}{l} X + Y = (X_S \times B^{X_E - Y_E} + Y_S) \times B^{Y_E} \\ X - Y = (X_S \times B^{X_E - Y_E} - Y_S) \times B^{Y_E} \end{array}\right\} X_E \leq Y_E$ $X \times Y = (X_S \times Y_S) \times B^{X_E + Y_E}$ $\dfrac{X}{Y} = \left(\dfrac{X_S}{Y_S}\right) \times B^{X_E - Y_E}$

Examples:
$X = 0.3 \times 10^2 = 30$
$Y = 0.2 \times 10^3 = 200$
$X + Y = (0.3 \times 10^{2-3} + 0.2) \times 10^3 = 0.23 \times 10^3 = 230$
$X - Y = (0.3 \times 10^{2-3} - 0.2) \times 10^3 = (-0.17) \times 10^3 = -170$
$X \times Y = (0.3 \times 0.2) \times 10^{2+3} = 0.06 \times 10^5 = 6000$
$X \div Y = (0.3 \div 0.2) \times 10^{2-3} = 1.5 \times 10^{-1} = 0.15$

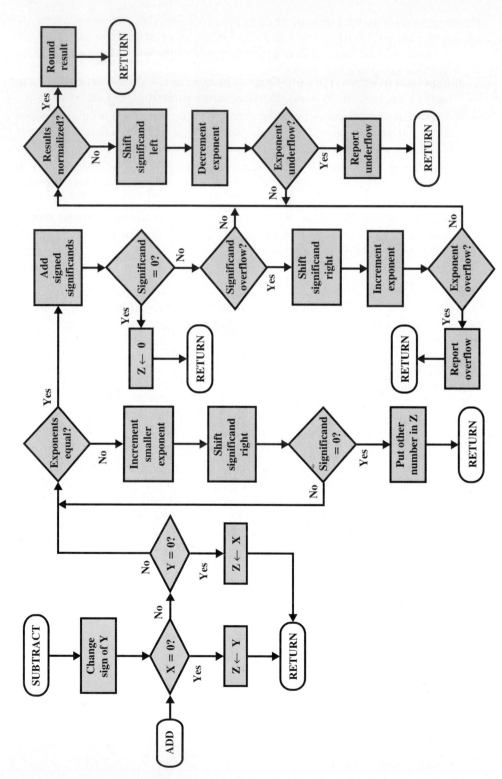

Figure 9.22 Floating-Point Addition and Subtraction ($Z \leftarrow X \pm Y$)

the floating-point format includes an implicit significand bit, that bit must be made explicit for the operation.

Phase 1: Zero check. Because addition and subtraction are identical except for a sign change, the process begins by changing the sign of the subtrahend if it is a subtract operation. Next, if either operand is 0, the other is reported as the result.

Phase 2: Significand alignment. The next phase is to manipulate the numbers so that the two exponents are equal.

To see the need for aligning exponents, consider the following decimal addition:

$$(123 \times 10^0) + (456 \times 10^{-2})$$

Clearly, we cannot just add the significands. The digits must first be set into equivalent positions, that is, the 4 of the second number must be aligned with the 3 of the first. Under these conditions, the two exponents will be equal, which is the mathematical condition under which two numbers in this form can be added. Thus,

$$(123 \times 10^0) + (456 \times 10^{-2}) = (123 \times 10^0) + (4.56 \times 10^0) = 127.56 \times 10^0$$

Alignment may be achieved by shifting either the smaller number to the right (increasing its exponent) or shifting the larger number to the left. Because either operation may result in the loss of digits, it is the smaller number that is shifted; any digits that are lost are therefore of relatively small significance. The alignment is achieved by repeatedly shifting the magnitude portion of the significand right 1 digit and incrementing the exponent until the two exponents are equal. (Note that if the implied base is 16, a shift of 1 digit is a shift of 4 bits.) If this process results in a 0 value for the significand, then the other number is reported as the result. Thus, if two numbers have exponents that differ significantly, the lesser number is lost.

Phase 3: Addition. Next, the two significands are added together, taking into account their signs. Because the signs may differ, the result may be 0. There is also the possibility of significand overflow by 1 digit. If so, the significand of the result is shifted right and the exponent is incremented. An exponent overflow could occur as a result; this would be reported and the operation halted.

Phase 4: Normalization. The final phase normalizes the result. Normalization consists of shifting significand digits left until the most significant digit (bit, or 4 bits for base-16 exponent) is nonzero. Each shift causes a decrement of the exponent and thus could cause an exponent underflow. Finally, the result must be rounded off and then reported. We defer a discussion of rounding until after a discussion of multiplication and division.

Multiplication and Division

Floating-point multiplication and division are much simpler processes than addition and subtraction, as the following discussion indicates.

We first consider multiplication, illustrated in Figure 9.23. First, if either operand is 0, 0 is reported as the result. The next step is to add the exponents. If the exponents are stored in biased form, the exponent sum would have doubled

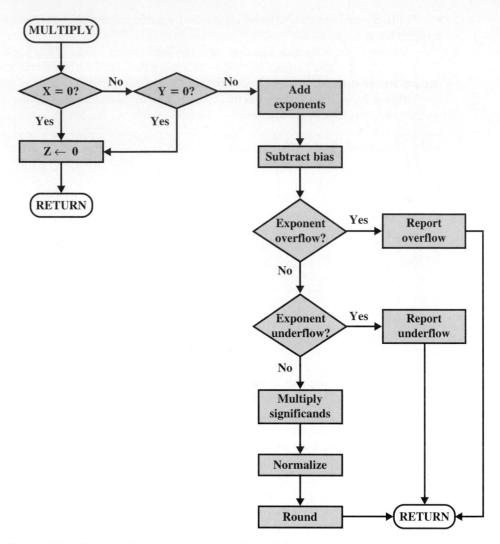

Figure 9.23 Floating-Point Multiplication ($Z \leftarrow X \times Y$)

the bias. Thus, the bias value must be subtracted from the sum. The result could be either an exponent overflow or underflow, which would be reported, ending the algorithm.

If the exponent of the product is within the proper range, the next step is to multiply the significands, taking into account their signs. The multiplication is performed in the same way as for integers. In this case, we are dealing with a sign-magnitude representation, but the details are similar to those for twos complement representation. The product will be double the length of the multiplier and multiplicand. The extra bits will be lost during rounding.

After the product is calculated, the result is then normalized and rounded, as was done for addition and subtraction. Note that normalization could result in exponent underflow.

Finally, let us consider the flowchart for division depicted in Figure 9.24. Again, the first step is testing for 0. If the divisor is 0, an error report is issued, or the result is set to infinity, depending on the implementation. A dividend of 0 results in 0. Next, the divisor exponent is subtracted from the dividend exponent. This removes the bias, which must be added back in. Tests are then made for exponent underflow or overflow.

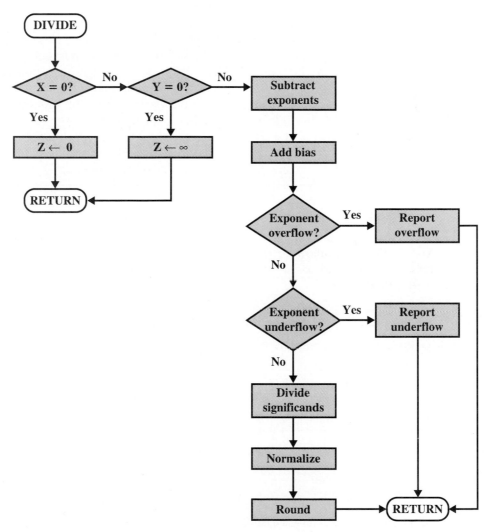

Figure 9.24   Floating-Point Division (Z ← X/Y)

The next step is to divide the significands. This is followed with the usual normalization and rounding.

Precision Considerations

Guard Bits

We mentioned that, prior to a floating-point operation, the exponent and significand of each operand are loaded into ALU registers. In the case of the significand, the length of the register is almost always greater than the length of the significand plus an implied bit. The register contains additional bits, called guard bits, which are used to pad out the right end of the significand with 0s.

The reason for the use of guard bits is illustrated in Figure 9.25. Consider numbers in the IEEE format, which has a 24-bit significand, including an implied 1 bit to the left of the binary point. Two numbers that are very close in value are $X = 1.00 \ldots 00 \times 2^1$ and $Y = 1.11 \ldots 11 \times 2^0$. If the smaller number is to be subtracted from the larger, it must be shifted right 1 bit to align the exponents. This is shown in Figure 9.25a. In the process, Y loses 1 bit of significance; the result is 2^{-22}. The same operation is repeated in part b with the addition of guard bits. Now the least significant bit is not lost due to alignment, and the result is 2^{-23}, a difference of a factor of 2 from the previous answer. When the radix is 16, the loss of precision can be greater. As Figures 9.25c and d show, the difference can be a factor of 16.

Rounding

Another detail that affects the precision of the result is the rounding policy. The result of any operation on the significands is generally stored in a longer register. When the result is put back into the floating-point format, the extra bits must be disposed of.

$x = 1.000\ldots\ldots00 \times 2^1$ $\underline{-y = 0.111\ldots\ldots11 \times 2^1}$ $z = 0.000\ldots\ldots01 \times 2^1$ $\quad = 1.000\ldots\ldots00 \times 2^{-22}$ (a) Binary example, without guard bits	$x = .100000 \times 16^1$ $\underline{-y = .0FFFFF \times 16^1}$ $z = .000001 \times 16^1$ $\quad = .100000 \times 16^{-4}$ (c) Hexadecimal example, without guard bits
$x = 1.000\ldots\ldots00\ 0000 \times 2^1$ $\underline{-y = 0.111\ldots\ldots11\ 1000 \times 2^1}$ $z = 0.000\ldots\ldots00\ 1000 \times 2^1$ $\quad = 1.000\ldots\ldots00\ 0000 \times 2^{-23}$ (b) Binary example, with guard bits	$x = .100000\ 00 \times 16^1$ $\underline{-y = .0FFFFF\ F0 \times 16^1}$ $z = .000000\ 10 \times 16^1$ $\quad = .100000\ 00 \times 16^{-5}$ (d) Hexadecimal example, with guard bits

Figure 9.25 The Use of Guard Bits

A number of techniques have been explored for performing rounding. In fact, the IEEE standard lists four alternative approaches:

- **Round to nearest:** The result is rounded to the nearest representable number.
- **Round toward $+\infty$:** The result is rounded up toward plus infinity.
- **Round toward $-\infty$:** The result is rounded down toward negative infinity.
- **Round toward 0:** The result is rounded toward zero.

Let us consider each of these policies in turn. **Round to nearest** is the default rounding mode listed in the standard and is defined as follows: The representable value nearest to the infinitely precise result shall be delivered; if the two nearest representable values are equally near, the one with its least significant bit 0 shall be delivered.

> If the extra bits, beyond the 23 bits that can be stored, are 10010, then the extra bits amount to more than one-half of the last representable bit position. In this case, the correct answer is to add binary 1 to the last representable bit, rounding up to the next representable number. Now consider that the extra bits are 01111. In this case, the extra bits amount to less than one-half of the last representable bit position. The correct answer is simply to drop the extra bits (truncate), which has the effect of rounding down to the next representable number.

The standard also addresses the special case of extra bits of the form 10000 . . . Here the result is exactly halfway between the two possible representable values. One possible technique here would be to always truncate, as this would be the simplest operation. However, the difficulty with this simple approach is that it introduces a small but cumulative bias into a sequence of computations. What is required is an unbiased method of rounding. One possible approach would be to round up or down on the basis of a random number so that, on average, the result would be unbiased. The argument against this approach is that it does not produce predictable, deterministic results. The approach taken by the IEEE standard is to force the result to be even: If the result of a computation is exactly midway between two representable numbers, the value is rounded up if the last representable bit is currently 1 and not rounded up if it is currently 0.

The next two options, **rounding to plus and minus infinity**, are useful in implementing a technique known as interval arithmetic. Interval arithmetic provides an efficient method for monitoring and controlling errors in floating-point computations by producing two values for each result. The two values correspond to the lower and upper endpoints of an interval that contains the true result. The width of the interval, which is the difference between the upper and lower endpoints, indicates the accuracy of the result. If the endpoints of an interval are not representable, then the interval endpoints are rounded down and up, respectively. Although the width of the interval may vary according to implementation, many algorithms have been designed to produce narrow intervals. If the range between the upper and lower bounds is sufficiently narrow, then a sufficiently accurate result has been obtained. If not, at least we know this and can perform additional analysis.

The final technique specified in the standard is **round toward zero**. This is, in fact, simple truncation: The extra bits are ignored. This is certainly the simplest technique. However, the result is that the magnitude of the truncated value is always less than or equal to the more precise original value, introducing a consistent bias toward zero in the operation. This is a more serious bias than was discussed earlier, because this bias affects every operation for which there are nonzero extra bits.

IEEE Standard for Binary Floating-Point Arithmetic

IEEE 754 goes beyond the simple definition of a format to lay down specific practices and procedures so that floating-point arithmetic produces uniform, predictable results independent of the hardware platform. One aspect of this has already been discussed, namely rounding. This subsection looks at three other topics: infinity, NaNs, and denormalized numbers.

Infinity

Infinity arithmetic is treated as the limiting case of real arithmetic, with the infinity values given the following interpretation:

$$-\infty < (\text{every finite number}) < +\infty$$

With the exception of the special cases discussed subsequently, any arithmetic operation involving infinity yields the obvious result.

For example,

$$
\begin{aligned}
5 + (+\infty) &= +\infty & 5 \div (+\infty) &= +0 \\
5 - (+\infty) &= -\infty & (+\infty) + (+\infty) &= +\infty \\
5 + (-\infty) &= -\infty & (-\infty) + (-\infty) &= -\infty \\
5 - (-\infty) &= +\infty & (-\infty) - (+\infty) &= -\infty \\
5 \times (+\infty) &= +\infty & (+\infty) - (-\infty) &= +\infty
\end{aligned}
$$

Quiet and Signaling NaNs

A NaN is a symbolic entity encoded in floating-point format, of which there are two types: signaling and quiet. A signaling NaN signals an invalid operation exception whenever it appears as an operand. Signaling NaNs afford values for uninitialized variables and arithmetic-like enhancements that are not the subject of the standard. A quiet NaN propagates through almost every arithmetic operation without signaling an exception. Table 9.6 indicates operations that will produce a quiet NaN.

Note that both types of NaNs have the same general format (Table 9.4): an exponent of all ones and a nonzero fraction. The actual bit pattern of the nonzero fraction is implementation dependent; the fraction values can be used to distinguish quiet NaNs from signaling NaNs and to specify particular exception conditions.

Denormalized Numbers

Denormalized numbers are included in IEEE 754 to handle cases of exponent underflow. When the exponent of the result becomes too small (a negative expo-

Table 9.6 Operations that Produce a Quiet NaN

Operation	Quiet NaN Produced by
Any	Any operation on a signaling NaN
Add or subtract	Magnitude subtraction of infinities: $(+\infty) + (-\infty)$ $(-\infty) + (+\infty)$ $(+\infty) - (+\infty)$ $(-\infty) - (-\infty)$
Multiply	$0 \times \infty$
Division	$\dfrac{0}{0}$ or $\dfrac{\infty}{\infty}$
Remainder	x REM 0 or ∞ REM y
Square root	$\sqrt{x}$ where $x < 0$

nent with too large a magnitude), the result is denormalized by right shifting the fraction and incrementing the exponent for each shift, until the exponent is within a representable range.

Figure 9.26 illustrates the effect of the addition of denormalized numbers. The representable numbers can be grouped into intervals of the form $[2^n, 2^{n+1}]$. Within each such interval, the exponent portion of the number remains constant while the fraction varies, producing a uniform spacing of representable numbers within the

(a) 32-Bit format without denormalized numbers

(b) 32-Bit format with denormalized numbers

Figure 9.26 The Effect of IEEE 754 Denormalized Numbers interval. As we get closer to zero, each successive interval is half the width of the preceding interval but contains the same number of representable numbers. Hence the density of representable numbers increases as we approach zero. However, if only normalized numbers are used, there is a gap between the smallest normalized number and 0. In the case of the 32-bit IEEE 754 format, there are 2^{23} representable numbers in each interval, and the smallest representable positive number is 2^{-126}. With the addition of denormalized numbers, an additional 2^{23} numbers are uniformly added between 0 and 2^{-126}.

The use of denormalized numbers is referred to as *gradual underflow* [COON81]. Without denormalized numbers, the gap between the smallest representable nonzero number and zero is much wider than the gap between the smallest representable nonzero number and the next larger number. Gradual underflow fills in that gap and reduces the impact of exponent underflow to a level comparable with roundoff among the normalized numbers.

9.6 RECOMMENDED READING AND WEB SITES

[PARH00] is an excellent treatment of computer arithmetic, covering all of the topics in this chapter in detail. [FLYN01] is a useful discussion that focuses on practical design and implementation issues. For the serious student of computer arithmetic, a very useful reference is the two-volume [SWAR90]. Volume I was originally published in 1980 and provides key papers (some very difficult to obtain otherwise) on computer arithmetic fundamentals. Volume II contains more recent papers, covering theoretical, design, and implementation aspects of computer arithmetic.

For floating-point arithmetic, [GOLD91] is well named: "What Every Computer Scientist Should Know About Floating-Point Arithmetic." Another excellent treatment of the topic is contained in [KNUT98], which also covers integer computer arithmetic. The following more in-depth treatments are also worthwhile: [OVER01, EVEN00, OBER97a, OBER97b, SODE96].

[SCHW99] describes the first IBM S/390 processor to integrate radix-16 and IEEE 754 floating-point arithmetic in the same floating-point unit.

EVEN00 Even, G., and Paul, W. "On the Design of IEEE Compliant Floating-Point Units." *IEEE Transactions on Computers*, May 2000.

FLYN01 Flynn, M., and Oberman, S. *Advanced Computer Arithmetic Design."* New York: Wiley, 2001.

GOLD91 Goldberg, D. "What Every Computer Scientist Should Know About Floating-Point Arithmetic." *ACM Computing Surveys*, March 1991. Available at http://www.validgh.com/

KNUT98 Knuth, D. *The Art of Computer Programming, Volume 2: Seminumerical Algorithms*. Reading, MA: Addison-Wesley, 1998.

OBER97a Oberman, S., and Flynn, M. "Design Issues in Division and Other Floating-Point Operations." *IEEE Transactions on Computers*, February 1997.

OBER97b Oberman, S., and Flynn, M. "Division Algorithms and Implementations." *IEEE Transactions on Computers*, August 1997.

OVER01 Overton, M. *Numerical Computing with IEEE Floating Point Arithmetic.* Philadelphia, PA: Society for Industrial and Applied Mathematics, 2001.

PARH00 Parhami, B. *Computer Arithmetic: Algorithms and Hardware Design.* Oxford: Oxford University Press, 2000.

SCHW99 Schwarz, E., and Krygowski, C. "The S/390 G5 Floating-Point Unit." *IBM Journal of Research and Development*, September/November 1999. (www.)

SODE96 Soderquist, P., and Leeser, M. "Area and Performance Tradeoffs in Floating-Point Divide and Square-Root Implementations." *ACM Computing Surveys*, September 1996.

SWAR90 Swartzlander, E., ed. *Computer Arithmetic, Volumes I and II.* Los Alamitos, CA: IEEE Computer Society Press, 1990.

Recommended Web Site:

- **IEEE 754:** The IEEE 754 documents, related publications and papers, and a useful set of links related to computer arithmetic

9.7 KEY TERMS, REVIEW QUESTIONS, AND PROBLEMS

Key Terms

arithmetic and logic unit (ALU)	guard bits	product
arithmetic shift	minuend	quotient
base	multiplicand	radix point
biased representation	multiplier	remainder
denormalized number	negative overflow	rounding
dividend	negative underflow	sign bit
divisor	normalized number	significand
exponent	ones complement representation	significand overflow
exponent overflow	overflow	significand underflow
exponent underflow	partial product	sign-magnitude representation
fixed-point representation	positive overflow	subtrahend
floating-point representation	positive underflow	twos complement representation

Review Questions

9.1 Briefly explain the following representations: sign-magnitude, twos complement, biased.

9.2 Explain how to determine if a number is negative in the following representations: sign-magnitude, twos complement, biased.

9.3 What is the sign-extension rule for twos complement numbers?

9.4 How can you form the negation of an integer in twos complement representation?

9.5 In general terms, when does the twos complement operation on an *n*-bit integer produce the same integer?

9.6 What is the difference between the twos complement representation of a number and the twos complement of a number?

9.7 If we treat 2 twos complement numbers as unsigned integers for purposes of addition, the result is correct if interpreted as a twos complement number. This is not true for multiplication. Why?

9.8 What are the four essential elements of a number in floating-point notation?

9.9 What is the benefit of using biased representation for the exponent portion of a floating-point number?

9.10 What are the differences among positive overflow, exponent overflow, and significand overflow?

9.11 What are the basic elements of floating-point addition and subtraction?

9.12 Give a reason for the use of guard bits.

9.13 List four alternative methods of rounding the result of a floating-point operation.

Problems

9.1 Another representation of binary integers that is sometimes encountered is **ones complement**. Positive integers are represented in the same way as sign magnitude. A negative integer is represented by taking the Boolean complement of each bit of the corresponding positive number.

  a. Provide a definition of ones complement numbers using a weighted sum of bits, similar to Equations (9.1) and (9.2).

  b. What is the range of numbers that can be represented in ones complement?

  c. Define an algorithm for performing addition in ones complement arithmetic.

9.2 Add columns to Table 9.1 for sign magnitude and ones complement.

9.3 Consider the following operation on a binary word. Start with the least significant bit. Copy all bits that are 0 until the first bit is reached and copy that bit, too. Then take the complement of each bit thereafter. What is the result?

9.4 In Section 9.3, the twos complement operation is defined as follows. To find the twos complement of X, take the Boolean complement of each bit of X, and then add 1.

  a. Show that the following is an equivalent definition. For an n-bit integer X, the twos complement of X is formed by treating X as an unsigned integer and calculating $(2n - X)$.

  b. Demonstrate that Figure 9.2 can be used to support graphically the claim in part a, by showing how a clockwise movement is used to achieve subtraction.

9.5 Find the following differences using twos complement arithmetic:

  a. 111000   **b.** 11001100   **c.** 111100001111   **d.** 11000011
      -110011   - 101110   -110011110011   -11101000

9.6 Is the following a valid alternative definition of overflow in twos complement arithmetic?

  > If the exclusive-OR of the carry bits into and out of the leftmost column is 1, then there is an overflow condition. Otherwise, there is not.

9.7 Compare Figures 9.9 and 9.12. Why is the C bit not used in the latter?

9.8 Given $x = 0101$ and $y = 1010$ in twos complement notation (i.e., $x = 4$, $y = -6$), compute the product $p = x \times y$ with Booth's algorithm.

9.9 Prove that the multiplication of two n-digit numbers in base B gives a product of no more than $2n$ digits.

9.10 Verify the validity of the unsigned binary division algorithm of Figure 9.16 by showing the steps involved in calculating the division depicted in Figure 9.15. Use a presentation similar to that of Figure 9.17.

9.11 The twos complement integer division algorithm described in Section 9.3 is known as the restoring method because the value in the A register must be restored following unsuccessful subtraction. A slightly more complex approach, known as non-restoring, avoids the unnecessary subtraction and addition. Propose an algorithm for this latter approach.

9.12 Under computer integer arithmetic, the quotient J/K of two integers J and K is less than or equal to the usual quotient. True or false?

9.13 Divide -145 by 13 in binary twos complement notation, using 12-bit words. Use the algorithm described in Section 9.3.

9.14 Assume that the exponent e is constrained to lie in the range $0 \le e \le X$, with a bias of q, that the base is b, and that the significand is p digits in length.

   a. What are the largest and smallest positive values that can be written?

   b. What are the largest and smallest positive values that can be written as normalized floating-point numbers?

9.15 Express the following numbers in IEEE 32-bit floating-point format:

   a. -5 **c.** -1.5 **e.** $1/16$

   b. -6 **d.** 384 **f.** $-1/32$

9.16 Express the following numbers in IBM's 32-bit floating-point format, which uses a 7-bit exponent with an implied base of 16:

a. 1.0	**c.** 1/64	**e.** -15.0	**g.** 7.2×10^{75}
b. 0.5	**d.** 0.0	**f.** 5.4×10^{-79}	

9.17 What would be the bias value for

   a. A base-2 exponent (B = 2) in a 6-bit field?

   b. A base-8 exponent (B = 8) in a 7-bit field?

9.18 Draw a number line similar to that in Figure 9.19b for the floating-point format of Figure 9.21b.

9.19 Consider a floating-point format with 8 bits for the biased exponent and 23 bits for the significand. Show the bit pattern for the following numbers in this format:

   a. -720

   b. 0.645

9.20 When people speak about inaccuracy in floating-point arithmetic, they often ascribe errors to cancellation that occurs during the subtraction of nearly equal quantities. But when X and Y are approximately equal, the difference $X - Y$ is obtained exactly, with no error. What do these people really mean?

9.21 Any floating-point representation used in a computer can represent only certain real numbers exactly; all others must be approximated. If A' is the stored value approximating the real value A, then the relative error, r, is expressed as

$$r = \frac{A - A'}{A}$$

Represent the decimal quantity $+0.4$ in the following floating-point format: base = 2; exponent: biased, 4 bits; significand, 7 bits. What is the relative error?

9.22 Numerical values A and B are stored in the computer as approximations A' and B'. Neglecting any further truncation or roundoff errors, show that the relative error of the product is approximately the sum of the relative errors in the factors.

9.23 If $A = 1.427$, find the relative error if A is truncated to 1.42 and if it is rounded to 1.43.

9.24 One of the most serious errors in computer calculations occurs when two nearly equal numbers are subtracted. Consider $A = 0.22288$ and $B = 0.22211$. The computer truncates all values to four decimal digits. Thus $A' = 0.2228$ and $B' = 0.2221$.

   a. What are the relative errors for A' and B'?

   b. What is the relative error for $C' = A' - B'$?

9.25 Show how the following floating-point additions are performed (where significands are truncated to 4 decimal digits).

    a. $0.5566 \times 10^3 + 0.7777 \times 10^3$ **b.** $0.3344 \times 10^2 + 0.8877 \times 10^{-1}$

9.26 Show how the following floating point subtractions are performed (where significands are truncated to 4 decimal digits).

    a. $0.7744 \times 10^{-2} - 0.6666 \times 10^{-2}$ **b.** $0.8844 \times 10^{-2} - 0.2233 \times 10^0$

9.27 Show how the following floating-point calculations are performed (where significands are truncated to 4 decimal digits).

    a. $(0.2255 \times 10^2) \times (0.1234 \times 10^1)$ **b.** $(0.8833 \times 10^3) \div (0.5555 \times 10^5)$

9.28 Express the following octal numbers in hexadecimal notation:

    a. 12   **b.** 5655   **c.** 2550276   **d.** 3726755

9.29 Prove that every real number with a terminating binary representation (finite number of digits to the right of the binary point) also has a terminating decimal representation (finite number of digits to the right of the decimal point).

CHAPTER **10**

INSTRUCTION SETS: CHARACTERISTICS AND FUNCTIONS

KEY POINTS

◆ The essential elements of a computer instruction are the opcode, which specifies the operation to be performed; the source and destination operand references, which specify the input and output locations for the operation; and a next instruction reference, which is usually implicit.

◆ Opcodes specify operations in one of the following general categories: arithmetic and logic operations; movement of data between two registers, register and memory, or two memory locations; I/O; and control.

◆ Operand references specify a register or memory location of operand data. The type of data may be addresses, numbers, characters, or logical data.

◆ A common architectural feature in processors is the use of a stack, which may or may not be visible to the programmer. Stacks are used to manage procedure calls and returns and may be provided as an alternative form of addressing memory. The basic stack operations are PUSH, POP, and operations on the top one or two stack locations. Stacks typically are implemented to grow from higher addresses to lower addresses.

◆ Processors may be categorized as big-endian, little-endian, or bi-endian. A multibyte numerical value stored with the most significant byte in the lowest numerical address is stored in big-endian fashion; if it is stored with the most significant byte in the highest numerical address, that is little-endian fashion. A bi-endian processor can handle both styles.

Much of what is discussed in this book is not readily apparent to the user or programmer of a computer. If a programmer is using a high-level language, such as Pascal or Ada, very little of the architecture of the underlying machine is visible.

One boundary where the computer designer and the computer programmer can view the same machine is the machine instruction set. From the designer's point of view, the machine instruction set provides the functional requirements for the CPU: Implementing the CPU is a task that in large part involves implementing the machine instruction set. From the user's side, the user who chooses to program in machine language (actually, in assembly language; see Section 10.6) becomes aware of the register and memory structure, the types of data directly supported by the machine, and the functioning of the ALU.

A description of a computer's machine instruction set goes a long way toward explaining the computer's CPU. Accordingly, we focus on machine instructions in this chapter and the next.

10.1 MACHINE INSTRUCTION CHARACTERISTICS

The operation of the CPU is determined by the instructions it executes, referred to as *machine instructions* or *computer instructions*. The collection of different instructions that the CPU can execute is referred to as the CPU's *instruction set*.

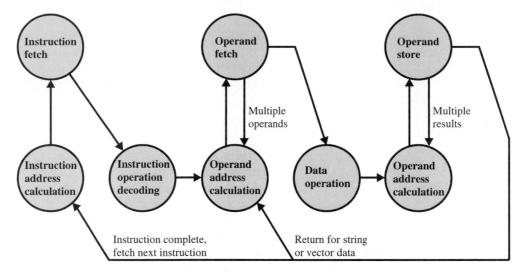

Figure 10.1 Instruction Cycle State Diagram

Elements of a Machine Instruction

Each instruction must contain the information required by the CPU for execution. Figure 10.1, which repeats Figure 3.6, shows the steps involved in instruction execution and, by implication, defines the elements of a machine instruction. These elements are as follows:

- **Operation code:** Specifies the operation to be performed (e.g., ADD, I/O). The operation is specified by a binary code, known as the operation code, or opcode.
- **Source operand reference:** The operation may involve one or more source operands, that is, operands that are inputs for the operation.
- **Result operand reference:** The operation may produce a result.
- **Next instruction reference:** This tells the CPU where to fetch the next instruction after the execution of this instruction is complete.

The next instruction to be fetched is located in main memory or, in the case of a virtual memory system, in either main memory or secondary memory (disk). In most cases, the next instruction to be fetched immediately follows the current instruction. In those cases, there is no explicit reference to the next instruction. When an explicit reference is needed, then the main memory or virtual memory address must be supplied. The form in which that address is supplied is discussed in Chapter 11.

Source and result operands can be in one of three areas:

- **Main or virtual memory:** As with next instruction references, the main or virtual memory address must be supplied.
- **CPU register:** With rare exceptions, a CPU contains one or more registers that may be referenced by machine instructions. If only one register exists, refer-

ence to it may be implicit. If more than one register exists, then each register is assigned a unique number, and the instruction must contain the number of the desired register.

- **I/O device:** The instruction must specify the I/O module and device for the operation. If memory-mapped I/O is used, this is just another main or virtual memory address.

Instruction Representation

Within the computer, each instruction is represented by a sequence of bits. The instruction is divided into fields, corresponding to the constituent elements of the instruction. A simple example of an instruction format is shown in Figure 10.2. As another example, the IAS instruction format is shown in Figure 2.2. With most instruction sets, more than one format is used. During instruction execution, an instruction is read into an instruction register (IR) in the CPU. The CPU must be able to extract the data from the various instruction fields to perform the required operation.

It is difficult for both the programmer and the reader of textbooks to deal with binary representations of machine instructions. Thus, it has become common practice to use a *symbolic representation* of machine instructions. An example of this was used for the IAS instruction set, in Table 2.1.

Opcodes are represented by abbreviations, called *mnemonics,* that indicate the operation. Common examples include

ADD	Add
SUB	Subtract
MPY	Multiply
DIV	Divide
LOAD	Load data from memory
STOR	Store data to memory

Operands are also represented symbolically. For example, the instruction

```
ADD R, Y
```

may mean add the value contained in data location Y to the contents of register R. In this example, Y refers to the address of a location in memory, and R refers to a particular register. Note that the operation is performed on the contents of a location, not on its address.

Thus, it is possible to write a machine-language program in symbolic form. Each symbolic opcode has a fixed binary representation, and the programmer spec-

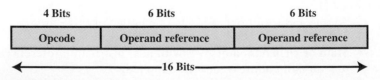

Figure 10.2   A Simple Instruction Format

ifies the location of each symbolic operand. For example, the programmer might begin with a list of definitions:

$$X = 513$$
$$Y = 514$$

and so on. A simple program would accept this symbolic input, convert opcodes and operand references to binary form, and construct binary machine instructions.

Machine-language programmers are rare to the point of nonexistence. Most programs today are written in a high-level language or, failing that, assembly language, which is discussed at the end of this chapter. However, symbolic machine language remains a useful tool for describing machine instructions, and we will use it for that purpose.

Instruction Types

Consider a high-level language instruction that could be expressed in a language such as BASIC or FORTRAN. For example,

$$X = X + Y$$

This statement instructs the computer to add the value stored in Y to the value stored in X and put the result in X. How might this be accomplished with machine instructions? Let us assume that the variables X and Y correspond to locations 513 and 514. If we assume a simple set of machine instructions, this operation could be accomplished with three instructions:

1. Load a register with the contents of memory location 513.
2. Add the contents of memory location 514 to the register.
3. Store the contents of the register in memory location 513.

As can be seen, the single BASIC instruction may require three machine instructions. This is typical of the relationship between a high-level language and a machine language. A high-level language expresses operations in a concise algebraic form, using variables. A machine language expresses operations in a basic form involving the movement of data to or from registers.

With this simple example to guide us, let us consider the types of instructions that must be included in a practical computer. A computer should have a set of instructions that allows the user to formulate any data processing task. Another way to view it is to consider the capabilities of a high-level programming language. Any program written in a high-level language must be translated into machine language to be executed. Thus, the set of machine instructions must be sufficient to express any of the instructions from a high-level language. With this in mind we can categorize instruction types as follows:

- **Data processing:** Arithmetic and logic instructions
- **Data storage:** Memory instructions
- **Data movement:** I/O instructions
- **Control:** Test and branch instructions

Arithmetic instructions provide computational capabilities for processing numeric data. *Logic* (Boolean) instructions operate on the bits of a word as bits rather than as numbers; thus, they provide capabilities for processing any other type of data the user may wish to employ. These operations are performed primarily on data in CPU registers. Therefore, there must be *memory* instructions for moving data between memory and the registers. *I/O* instructions are needed to transfer programs and data into memory and the results of computations back out to the user. *Test* instructions are used to test the value of a data word or the status of a computation. *Branch* instructions are then used to branch to a different set of instructions depending on the decision made.

We will examine the various types of instructions in greater detail later in this chapter.

Number of Addresses

One of the traditional ways of describing processor architecture is in terms of the number of addresses contained in each instruction. This dimension has become less significant with the increasing complexity of CPU design. Nevertheless, it is useful at this point to draw and analyze this distinction.

What is the maximum number of addresses one might need in an instruction? Evidently, arithmetic and logic instructions will require the most operands. Virtually all arithmetic and logic operations are either unary (one operand) or binary (two operands). Thus, we would need a maximum of two addresses to reference operands. The result of an operation must be stored, suggesting a third address. Finally, after completion of an instruction, the next instruction must be fetched, and its address is needed.

This line of reasoning suggests that an instruction could plausibly be required to contain four address references: two operands, one result, and the address of the next instruction. In practice, four-address instructions are extremely rare. Most instructions have one, two, or three operand addresses, with the address of the next instruction being implicit (obtained from the program counter).

Figure 10.3 compares typical one-, two-, and three-address instructions that could be used to compute $Y = (A - B) \div (C + D \times E)$. With three addresses, each instruction specifies two operand locations and a result location. Because we would like to not alter the value of any of the operand locations, a temporary location, T, is used to store some intermediate results. Note that there are four instructions and that the original expression had five operands.

Three-address instruction formats are not common, because they require a relatively long instruction format to hold the three address references. With two-address instructions, and for binary operations, one address must do double duty as both an operand and a result. Thus, the instruction SUB Y, B carries out the calculation $Y - B$ and stores the result in Y. The two-address format reduces the space requirement but also introduces some awkwardness. To avoid altering the value of an operand, a MOVE instruction is used to move one of the values to a result or temporary location before performing the operation. Our sample program expands to six instructions.

Simpler yet is the one-address instruction. For this to work, a second address must be implicit. This was common in earlier machines, with the implied address being a CPU register known as the *accumulator,* or AC. The accumulator contains

Instruction		Comment
SUB	Y, A, B	Y ← A – B
MPY	T, D, E	T ← D × E
ADD	T, T, C	T ← T + C
DIV	Y, Y, T	Y ← Y ÷ T

(a) Three-address instructions

Instruction		Comment
MOVE	Y, A	Y ← A
SUB	Y, B	Y ← Y – B
MOVE	T, D	T ← D
MPY	T, E	T ← T × E
ADD	T, C	T ← T + C
DIV	Y, T	Y ← Y ÷ T

(b) Two-address instructions

Instruction		Comment
LOAD	D	AC ← D
MPY	E	AC ← AC × E
ADD	C	AC ← AC + C
STOR	Y	Y ← AC
LOAD	A	AC ← A
SUB	B	AC ← AC – B
DIV	Y	AC ← AC ÷ Y
STOR	Y	Y ← AC

(c) One-address instructions

Figure 10.3 Programs to Execute Y = (A − B) ÷ (C + D × E)

one of the operands and is used to store the result. In our example, eight instructions are needed to accomplish the task.

It is, in fact, possible to make do with zero addresses for some instructions. Zero-address instructions are applicable to a special memory organization, called a *stack*. A stack is a last-in-first-out set of locations. The stack is in a known location and, often, at least the top two elements are in CPU registers. Thus, zero-address instructions would reference the top two stack elements. Stacks are described in Appendix 10A. Their use is explored further later in this chapter and in Chapter 11.

Table 10.1 summarizes the interpretations to be placed on instructions with zero, one, two, or three addresses. In each case in the table, it is assumed that the address of the next instruction is implicit, and that one operation with two source operands and one result operand is to be performed.

The number of addresses per instruction is a basic design decision. Fewer addresses per instruction result in more primitive instructions, which requires a less complex CPU. It also results in instructions of shorter length. On the other hand,

Table 10.1 Utilization of Instruction Addresses (Nonbranching Instructions)

Number of Addresses	Symbolic Representation	Interpretation
3	OP A, B, C	A ← B OP C
2	OP A, B	A ← A OP B
1	OP A	AC ← AC OP A
0	OP	T ← (T − 1) OP T

AC	=	accumulator
T	=	top of stack
A, B, C	=	memory or register locations
(T −)	=	contents of second element of stack

programs contain more total instructions, which in general results in longer execution times and longer, more complex programs. Also, there is an important threshold between one-address and multiple-address instructions. With one-address instructions, the programmer generally has available only one general-purpose register, the accumulator. With multiple-address instructions, it is common to have multiple general-purpose registers. This allows some operations to be performed solely on registers. Because register references are faster than memory references, this speeds up execution. For reasons of flexibility and ability to use multiple registers, most contemporary machines employ a mixture of two- and three-address instructions.

The design trade-offs involved in choosing the number of addresses per instruction are complicated by other factors. There is the issue of whether an address references a memory location or a register. Because there are fewer registers, fewer bits are needed for a register reference. Also, as we shall see in the next chapter, a machine may offer a variety of addressing modes, and the specification of mode takes one or more bits. The result is that most CPU designs involve a variety of instruction formats.

Instruction Set Design

One of the most interesting, and most analyzed, aspects of computer design is instruction set design. The design of an instruction set is very complex, because it affects so many aspects of the computer system. The instruction set defines many of the functions performed by the CPU and thus has a significant effect on the implementation of the CPU. The instruction set is the programmer's means of controlling the CPU. Thus, programmer requirements must be considered in designing the instruction set.

It may surprise you to know that some of the most fundamental issues relating to the design of instruction sets remain in dispute. Indeed, in recent years, the level of disagreement concerning these fundamentals has actually grown. The most important of these fundamental design issues include the following:

- **Operation repertoire:** How many and which operations to provide, and how complex operations should be
- **Data types:** The various types of data upon which operations are performed
- **Instruction format:** Instruction length (in bits), number of addresses, size of various fields, and so on
- **Registers:** Number of CPU registers that can be referenced by instructions, and their use
- **Addressing:** The mode or modes by which the address of an operand is specified

These issues are highly interrelated and must be considered together in designing an instruction set. This book, of course, must consider them in some sequence, but an attempt is made to show the interrelationships.

Because of the importance of this topic, much of Part Three is devoted to instruction set design. Following this overview section, this chapter examines data types and operation repertoire. Chapter 11 examines addressing modes (which includes a consideration of registers) and instruction formats. Chapter 13 examines the reduced instruction set computer (RISC). RISC architecture calls into question many of the instruction set design decisions made in many contemporary commercial computers.

10.2 TYPES OF OPERANDS

Machine instructions operate on data. The most important general categories of data are

- Addresses
- Numbers
- Characters
- Logical data

We will see, in discussing addressing modes in Chapter 11, that addresses are, in fact, a form of data. In many cases, some calculation must be performed on the operand reference in an instruction to determine the main or virtual memory address. In this context, addresses can be considered to be unsigned integers.

Other common data types are numbers, characters, and logical data, and each of these is briefly examined in this section. Beyond that, some machines define specialized data types or data structures. For example, there may be machine operators that operate directly on a list or a string of characters.

Numbers

All machine languages include numeric data types. Even in nonnumeric data processing, there is a need for numbers to act as counters, field widths, and so forth. An important distinction between numbers used in ordinary mathematics and numbers stored in a computer is that the latter are limited. This is true in two senses. First, there is a limit to the magnitude of numbers representable on a machine and second, in the case of floating-point numbers, a limit to their precision. Thus, the programmer is faced with understanding the consequences of rounding, overflow, and underflow.

Three types of numerical data are common in computers:

- Integer or fixed point
- Floating point
- Decimal

We examined the first two in some detail in Chapter 9. It remains to say a few words about decimal numbers.

Although all internal computer operations are binary in nature, the human users of the system deal with decimal numbers. Thus, there is a necessity to convert from decimal to binary on input and from binary to decimal on output. For applications in which there is a great deal of I/O and comparatively little, comparatively simple computation, it is preferable to store and operate on the numbers in decimal form. The most common representation for this purpose is packed decimal.

With packed decimal, each decimal digit is represented by a 4-bit code, in the obvious way. Thus, $0 = 0000$, $1 = 0001$, . . . , $8 = 1000$, and $9 = 1001$. Note that this is a rather inefficient code because only 10 of 16 possible 4-bit values are used. To form numbers, 4-bit codes are strung together, usually in multiples of 8 bits. Thus, the code for 246 is 0000001001000110. This code is clearly less compact than a straight binary representation, but it avoids the conversion overhead. Negative numbers can be represented by including a 4-bit sign digit at either the left or right end of a string of packed decimal digits. For example, the code 1111 might stand for the minus sign.

Many machines provide arithmetic instructions for performing operations directly on packed decimal numbers. The algorithms are quite similar to those described in Section 9.3 but must take into account the decimal carry operation.

Characters

A common form of data is text or character strings. While textual data are most convenient for human beings, they cannot, in character form, be easily stored or transmitted by data processing and communications systems. Such systems are designed for binary data. Thus, a number of codes have been devised by which characters are represented by a sequence of bits. Perhaps the earliest common example of this is the Morse code. Today, the most commonly used character code in the International Reference Alphabet (IRA), referred to in the United States as the American Standard Code for Information Interchange (ASCII; see Table 7.1). IRA is also widely used outside the United States. Each character in this code is represented by a unique 7-bit pattern; thus, 128 different characters can be represented. This is a larger number than is necessary to represent printable characters, and some of the patterns represent *control* characters. Some of these control characters have to do with controlling the printing of characters on a page. Others are concerned with communications procedures. IRA-encoded characters are almost always stored and transmitted using 8 bits per character. The eighth bit may be set to 0 or used as a parity bit for error detection. In the latter case, the bit is set such that the total number of binary 1s in each octet is always odd (odd parity) or always even (even parity).

Note in Table 7.1 that for the IRA bit pattern 011XXXX, the digits 0 through 9 are represented by their binary equivalents, 0000 through 1001, in the rightmost 4 bits. This is the same code as packed decimal. This facilitates conversion between 7-bit IRA and 4-bit packed decimal representation.

Another code used to encode characters is the Extended Binary Coded Decimal Interchange Code (EBCDIC). EBCDIC is used on IBM S/390 machines. It is an 8-bit code. As with IRA, EBCDIC is compatible with packed decimal. In the case of EBCDIC, the codes 11110000 through 11111001 represent the digits 0 through 9.

Logical Data

Normally, each word or other addressable unit (byte, halfword, and so on) is treated as a single unit of data. It is sometimes useful, however, to consider an n-bit unit as consisting of n 1-bit items of data, each item having the value 0 or 1. When data are viewed this way, they are considered to be *logical* data.

There are two advantages to the bit-oriented view. First, we may sometimes wish to store an array of Boolean or binary data items, in which each item can take on only the values 1 (true) and 0 (false). With logical data, memory can be used most efficiently for this storage. Second, there are occasions when we wish to manipulate the bits of a data item. For example, if floating-point operations are implemented in software, we need to be able to shift significant bits in some operations. Another example: To convert from IRA to packed decimal, we need to extract the rightmost 4 bits of each byte.

Note that, in the preceding examples, the same data are treated sometimes as logical and other times as numerical or text. The "type" of a unit of data is determined by the operation being performed on it. While this is not normally the case in high-level languages, it is almost always the case with machine language.

10.3 PENTIUM AND POWERPC DATA TYPES

Pentium Data Types

The Pentium can deal with data types of 8 (byte), 16 (word), 32 (doubleword), and 64 (quadword) bits in length. To allow maximum flexibility in data structures and efficient memory utilization, words need not be aligned at even-numbered addresses; doublewords need not be aligned at addresses evenly divisible by 4; and quadwords need not be aligned at addresses evenly divisible by 8. However, when data are accessed across a 32-bit bus, data transfers take place in units of doublewords, beginning at addresses divisible by 4. The processor converts the request for misaligned

Table 10.2 Pentium Data Types

Data Type	Description
General	Byte, word (16 bits), doubleword (32 bits), and quadword (64 bits) locations with arbitrary binary contents.
Integer	A signed binary value contained in a byte, word, or doubleword, using twos complement representation.
Ordinal	An unsigned integer contained in a byte, word, or doubleword.
Unpacked binary coded decimal (BCD)	A representation of a BCD digit in the range 0 through 9, with one digit in each byte.
Packed BCD	Packed byte representation of two BCD digits; value in the range 0 to 99.
Near pointer	A 32-bit effective address that represents the offset within a segment. Used for all pointers in a nonsegmented memory and for references within a segment in a segmented memory.
Bit field	A contiguous sequence of bits in which the position of each bit is considered as an independent unit. A bit string can begin at any bit position of any byte and can contain up to $2^{32} - 1$ bits.
Byte string	A contiguous sequence of bytes, words, or doublewords, containing form zero to $2^{32} - 1$ bytes.
Floating point	See Figure 10.4.

values into a sequence of requests for the bus transfer. As with all of the Intel 80x86 machines, the Pentium uses the little-endian style; that is, the least significant byte is stored in the lowest address (see Appendix 10B for a discussion of endianness).

The byte, word, doubleword, and quadword are referred to as general data types. In addition, the Pentium supports an impressive array of specific data types that are recognized and operated on by particular instructions. Table 10.2 summarizes these types.

Figure 10.4 illustrates the Pentium numerical data types. The signed integers are in twos complement representation and may be 16, 32, or 64 bits long. The floating-

Figure 10.4 Pentium Numeric Data Formats

point type actually refers to a set of types that are used by the floating-point unit and operated on by floating-point instructions. The three floating-point representations conform to the IEEE 754 standard.

PowerPC Data Types

The PowerPC can deal with data types of 8 (byte), 16 (halfword), 32 (word), and 64 (doubleword) bits in length. Some instructions require that memory operands be aligned on a 32-bit boundary. In general, however, alignment is not required. One interesting feature of the PowerPC is that it can use either little-endian or big-endian style; that is, the least significant byte is stored in the lowest or highest address (see Appendix 10B for a discussion of endianness).

The byte, halfword, word, and doubleword are general data types. The processor interprets the contents of a given item of data depending on the instruction. The fixed-point processor recognizes the following data types:

- **Unsigned byte:** Can be used for logical or integer arithmetic operations. It is loaded from memory into a general register by zero extending on the left to the full register size.
- **Unsigned halfword:** As for unsigned byte, but for 16-bit quantities.
- **Signed halfword:** Used for arithmetic operations; loaded into memory by sign extending on the left to full register size (i.e., the sign bit is replicated in all vacant positions).
- **Unsigned word:** Used for logical operations and as an address pointer.
- **Signed word:** Used for arithmetic operations.
- **Unsigned doubleword:** Used as an address pointer.
- **Byte string:** From 0 to 128 bytes in length.

In addition, the PowerPC supports the single- and double-precision floating-point data types defined in IEEE 754.

10.4 TYPES OF OPERATIONS

The number of different opcodes varies widely from machine to machine. However, the same general types of operations are found on all machines. A useful and typical categorization is the following:

- Data transfer
- Arithmetic
- Logical
- Conversion
- I/O
- System control
- Transfer of control

Table 10.3 (based on [HAYE98]) lists common instruction types in each category. This section provides a brief survey of these various types of operations,

Table 10.3 Common Instruction Set Operations

Type	Operation Name	Description
Data transfer	Move (transfer)	Transfer word or block from source to destination
	Store	Transfer word from processor to memory
	Load (fetch)	Transfer word from memory to processor
	Exchange	Swap contents of source and destination
	Clear (reset)	Transfer word of 0s to destination
	Set	Transfer word of 1s to destination
	Push	Transfer word from source to top of stack
	Pop	Transfer word from top of stack to destination
Arithmetic	Add	Compute sum of two operands
	Subtract	Compute difference of two operands
	Multiply	Compute product of two operands
	Divide	Compute quotient of two operands
	Absolute	Replace operand by its absolute value
	Negate	Change sign of operand
	Increment	Add 1 to operand
	Decrement	Subtract 1 from operand
Logical	AND	
	OR	
	NOT (Complement)	Perform the specified logical operation bitwise
	Exclusive-OR	
	Test	Test specified condition; set flag(s) based on outcome
	Compare	Make logical or arithmetic comparison of two or more operands; set flag(s) based on outcome
	Set control variables	Class of instructions to set controls for protection purposes, interrupt handling, timer control, etc.
	Shift	Left (right) shift operand, introducing constants at end
	Rotate	Left (right) shift operand, with wraparound end
Transfer of control	Jump (branch)	Unconditional transfer; load PC with specified address
	Jump conditional	Test specified condition; either load PC with specified address or do nothing, based on condition
	Jump to subroutine	Place current program control information in known location; jump to specified address
	Return	Replace contents of PC and other register from known location
	Execute	Fetch operand from specified location and execute as instruction; do not modify PC
	Skip	Increment PC to skip next instruction
	Skip conditional	Test specified condition; either skip or do nothing based on condition
	Halt	Stop program execution
	Wait (hold)	Stop program execution; test specified condition repeatedly; resume execution when condition is satisfied
	No operation	No operation is performed, but program execution is continued
Input/output	Input (read)	Transfer data from specified I/O port or device to destination (e.g., main memory or processor register)
	Output (write)	Transfer data from specified source to I/O port or device
	Start I/O	Transfer instructions to I/O processor to initiate I/O operation
	Test I/O	Transfer status information from I/O system to specified destination
Conversion	Translate	Translate values in a section of memory based on a table of correspondences
	Convert	Convert the contents of a word from one form to another (e.g., packed decimal to binary)

Table 10.4 CPU Actions for Various Types of Operations

Data transfer	Transfer data from one location to another If memory is involved: 　　Determine memory address 　　Perform virtual-to-actual-memory address transformation 　　Check cache 　　Initiate memory read/write
Arithmetic	May involve data transfer, before and/or after Perform function in ALU Set condition codes and flags
Logical	Same as arithmetic
Conversion	Similar to arithmetic and logical. May involve special logic to perform conversion
Transfer of control	Update program counter. For subroutine call/return, manage parameter passing and linkage
I/O	Issue command to I/O module If memory-mapped I/O, determine memory-mapped address

together with a brief discussion of the actions taken by the CPU to execute a particular type of operation (summarized in Table 10.4). The latter topic is examined in more detail in Chapter 12.

Data Transfer

The most fundamental type of machine instruction is the data transfer instruction. The data transfer instruction must specify several things. First, the location of the source and destination operands must be specified. Each location could be memory, a register, or the top of the stack. Second, the length of data to be transferred must be indicated. Third, as with all instructions with operands, the mode of addressing for each operand must be specified. This latter point is discussed in Chapter 11.

The choice of data transfer instructions to include in an instruction set exemplifies the kinds of trade-offs the designer must make. For example, the general location (memory or register) of an operand can be indicated in either the specification of the opcode or the operand. Table 10.5 shows examples of the most common IBM S/390 data transfer instructions. Note that there are variants to indicate the amount of data to be transferred (8, 16, 32, or 64 bits). Also, there are different instructions for register to register, register to memory, and memory to register transfers. In contrast, the VAX has a move (MOV) instruction with variants for different amounts of data to be moved, but it specifies whether an operand is register or memory as part of the operand. The VAX approach is somewhat easier for the programmer, who has fewer mnemonics to deal with. However, it is also somewhat less compact than the IBM S/390 approach, because the location (register versus memory) of each operand must be specified separately in the instruction. We will return to this distinction when we discuss instruction formats, in the next chapter.

In terms of CPU action, data transfer operations are perhaps the simplest type. If both source and destination are registers, then the CPU simply causes data to be

Table 10.5   Examples of IBM S/390 Data Transfer Operations

Operation Mnemonic	Name	Number of Bits Transferred	Description
L	Load	32	Transfer from memory to register
LH	Load halfword	16	Transfer from memory to register
LR	Load	32	Transfer from register to register
LER	Load (short)	32	Transfer from floating-point register to floating-point register
LE	Load (short)	32	Transfer from memory to floating-point register
LDR	Load (long)	64	Transfer from floating-point register to floating-point register
LD	Load (long)	64	Transfer from memory to floating-point register
ST	Store	32	Transfer from register to memory
STH	Store halfword	16	Transfer from register to memory
STC	Store character	8	Transfer from register to memory
STE	Store (short)	32	Transfer from floating-point register to memory
STD	Store (long)	64	Transfer from floating-point register to memory

transferred from one register to another; this is an operation internal to the CPU. If one or both operands are in memory, then the CPU must perform some or all of the following actions:

1. Calculate the memory address, based on the address mode (discussed in Chapter 11).
2. If the address refers to virtual memory, translate from virtual to actual memory address.
3. Determine whether the addressed item is in cache.
4. If not, issue a command to the memory module.

Arithmetic

Most machines provide the basic arithmetic operations of add, subtract, multiply, and divide. These are invariably provided for signed integer (fixed-point) numbers. Often they are also provided for floating-point and packed decimal numbers.

Other possible operations include a variety of single-operand instructions; for example,

- **Absolute:** Take the absolute value of the operand.
- **Negate:** Negate the operand.
- **Increment:** Add 1 to the operand.
- **Decrement:** Subtract 1 from the operand.

The execution of an arithmetic instruction may involve data transfer operations to position operands for input to the ALU, and to deliver the output of the ALU. Figure 3.5 illustrates the movements involved in both data transfer and arithmetic operations. In addition, of course, the ALU portion of the CPU performs the desired operation.

Logical

Most machines also provide a variety of operations for manipulating individual bits of a word or other addressable units, often referred to as "bit twiddling." They are based upon Boolean operations (see Appendix A).

Some of the basic logical operations that can be performed on Boolean or binary data are shown in Table 10.6. The NOT operation inverts a bit. AND, OR, and Exclusive-OR (XOR) are the most common logical functions with two operands. EQUAL is a useful binary test.

These logical operations can be applied bitwise to n-bit logical data units. Thus, if two registers contain the data

$$(R1) = 10100101$$
$$(R2) = 00001111$$

then

$$(R1) \text{ AND } (R2) = 00000101$$

where the notation (X) means the contents of location X. Thus, the AND operation can be used as a *mask* that selects certain bits in a word and zeros out the remaining bits. As another example, if two registers contain

$$(R1) = 10100101$$
$$(R2) = 11111111$$

then

$$(R1) \text{ XOR } (R2) = 01011010$$

With one word set to all 1s, the XOR operation inverts all of the bits in the other word (ones complement).

In addition to bitwise logical operations, most machines provide a variety of shifting and rotating functions. The most basic operations are illustrated in Figure 10.5. With a **logical shift,** the bits of a word are shifted left or right. On one end, the bit shifted out is lost. On the other end, a 0 is shifted in. Logical shifts are useful primarily for isolating fields within a word. The 0s that are shifted into a word displace unwanted information that is shifted off the other end.

Table 10.6   Basic Logical Operations

P	Q	NOT P	P AND Q	P OR Q	P XOR Q	P=Q
0	0	1	0	0	0	1
0	1	1	0	1	1	0
1	0	0	0	1	1	0
1	1	0	1	1	0	1

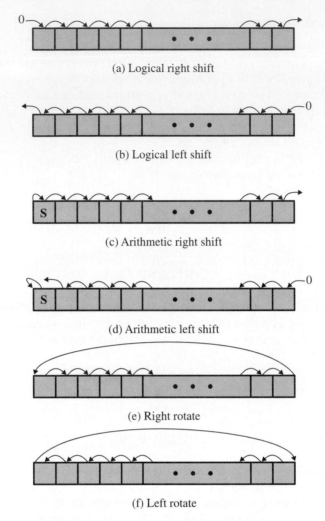

Figure 10.5 Shift and Rotate Operations

As an example, suppose we wish to transmit characters of data to an I/O device 1 character at a time. If each memory word is 16 bits in length and contains two characters, we must *unpack* the characters before they can be sent. To send the two characters in a word,

1. Load the word into a register.
2. AND with the value 1111111100000000. This masks out the character on the right.
3. Shift to the right eight times. This shifts the remaining character to the right half of the register.
4. Perform I/O. The I/O module reads the lower-order 8 bits from the data bus.

The preceding steps result in sending the left-hand character. To send the right-hand character,

1. Load the word again into the register.
2. AND with 0000000011111111.
3. Perform I/O.

The **arithmetic shift** operation treats the data as a signed integer and does not shift the sign bit. On a right arithmetic shift, the sign bit is replicated into the bit position to its right. On a left arithmetic shift, a logical left shift is performed on all bits but the sign bit, which is retained. These operations can speed up certain arithmetic operations. With numbers in twos complement notation, a right arithmetic shift corresponds to a division by 2, with truncation for odd numbers. Both an arithmetic left shift and a logical left shift correspond to a multiplication by 2 when there is no overflow. If overflow occurs, arithmetic and logical left shift operations produce different results, but the arithmetic left shift retains the sign of the number. Because of the potential for overflow, many processors do not include this instruction, including PowerPC and Itanium. Others, such as the IBM S/390, do offer the instruction. Curiously, the Pentium architecture includes an arithmetic left shift but defines it to be identical to a logical left shift.

Rotate, or cyclic shift, operations preserve all of the bits being operated on. One possible use of a rotate is to bring each bit successively into the leftmost bit, where it can be identified by testing the sign of the data (treated as a number).

As with arithmetic operations, logical operations involve ALU activity and may involve data transfer operations. Table 10.7 gives examples of all of the shift and rotate operations discussed in this subsection.

Conversion

Conversion instructions are those that change the format or operate on the format of data. An example is converting from decimal to binary. An example of a more complex editing instruction is the S/390 Translate (TR) instruction. This instruction can be used to convert from one 8-bit code to another, and it takes three operands:

$$TR \ R1, R2, L$$

The operand R2 contains the address of the start of a table of 8-bit codes. The L bytes starting at the address specified in R1 are translated, each byte being replaced

Table 10.7 Examples of Shift and Rotate Operations

Input	Operation	Result
10100110	Logical right shift (3 bits)	00010100
10100110	Logical left shift (3 bits)	00110000
10100110	Arithmetic right shift (3 bits)	11110100
10100110	Arithmetic left shift (3 bits)	10110000
10100110	Right rotate (3 bits)	11010100
10100110	Left rotate (3 bits)	00110101

by the contents of a table entry indexed by that byte. For example, to translate from EBCDIC to IRA, we first create a 256-byte table in storage locations, say, 1000–10FF hexadecimal. The table contains the characters of the IRA code in the sequence of the binary representation of the EBCDIC code; that is, the IRA code is placed in the table at the relative location equal to the binary value of the EBCDIC code of the same character. Thus, locations 10F0 through 10F9 will contain the values 30 through 39, because F0 is the EBCDIC code for the digit 0, and 30 is the IRA code for the digit 0, and so on through digit 9. Now suppose we have the EBCDIC for the digits 1984 starting at location 2100 and we wish to translate to IRA. Assume the following:

- Locations 2100–2103 contain F1 F9 F8 F4.
- R1 contains 2100.
- R2 contains 1000.

Then, if we execute

$$\text{TR R1, R2, 4}$$

locations 2100–2103 will contain 31 39 38 34.

Input/Output

Input/output instructions were discussed in some detail in Chapter 7. As we saw, there are a variety of approaches taken, including isolated programmed I/O, memory-mapped programmed I/O, DMA, and the use of an I/O processor. Many implementations provide only a few I/O instructions, with the specific actions specified by parameters, codes, or command words.

System Control

System control instructions are those that can be executed only while the processor is in a certain privileged state or is executing a program in a special privileged area of memory. Typically, these instructions are reserved for the use of the operating system.

Some examples of system control operations are as follows. A system control instruction may read or alter a control register; we discuss control registers in Chapter 12. Another example is an instruction to read or modify a storage protection key, such as is used in the S/390 memory system. Another example is access to process control blocks in a multiprogramming system.

Transfer of Control

For all of the operation types discussed so far, the next instruction to be performed is the one that immediately follows, in memory, the current instruction. However, a significant fraction of the instructions in any program have as their function changing the sequence of instruction execution. For these instructions, the operation performed by the CPU is to update the program counter to contain the address of some instruction in memory.

There are a number of reasons why transfer-of-control operations are required. Among the most important are the following:

1. In the practical use of computers, it is essential to be able to execute each instruction more than once and perhaps many thousands of times. It may require thousands or perhaps millions of instructions to implement an application. This would be unthinkable if each instruction had to be written out separately. If a table or a list of items is to be processed, a program loop is needed. One sequence of instructions is executed repeatedly to process all the data.

2. Virtually all programs involve some decision making. We would like the computer to do one thing if one condition holds, and another thing if another condition holds. For example, a sequence of instructions computes the square root of a number. At the start of the sequence, the sign of the number is tested. If the number is negative, the computation is not performed, but an error condition is reported.

3. To compose correctly a large or even medium-size computer program is an exceedingly difficult task. It helps if there are mechanisms for breaking the task up into smaller pieces that can be worked on one at a time.

We now turn to a discussion of the most common transfer-of-control operations found in instruction sets: branch, skip, and procedure call.

Branch Instructions

A branch instruction, also called a jump instruction, has as one of its operands the address of the next instruction to be executed. Most often, the instruction is a *conditional branch* instruction. That is, the branch is made (update program counter to equal address specified in operand) only if a certain condition is met. Otherwise, the next instruction in sequence is executed (increment program counter as usual).

There are two common ways of generating the condition to be tested in a conditional branch instruction. First, most machines provide a 1-bit or multiple bit condition code that is set as the result of some operations. This code can be thought of as a short user-visible register. As an example, an arithmetic operation (ADD, SUBTRACT, and so on) could set a 2-bit condition code with one of the following four values: 0, positive, negative, overflow. On such a machine, there could be four different conditional branch instructions:

BRP X   Branch to location X if result is positive.
BRN X   Branch to location X if result is negative.
BRZ X   Branch to location X if result is zero.
BRO X   Branch to location X if overflow occurs.

In all of these cases, the result referred to is the result of the most recent operation that set the condition code.

Another approach that can be used with a three-address instruction format is to perform a comparison and specify a branch in the same instruction. For example,

BRE R1, R2, X   Branch to X if contents of R1 = contents of R2.

Figure 10.6 shows examples of these operations. Note that a branch can be either *forward* (an instruction with a higher address) or *backward* (lower address). The example shows how an unconditional and a conditional branch can be used to create a repeating loop of instructions. The instructions in locations 202 through 210 will be executed repeatedly until the result of subtracting Y from X is 0.

Skip Instructions

Another common form of transfer-of-control instruction is the skip instruction. The skip instruction includes an implied address. Typically, the skip implies that one instruction be skipped; thus, the implied address equals the address of the next instruction plus one instruction-length.

Because the skip instruction does not require a destination address field, it is free to do other things. A typical example is the increment-and-skip-if-zero (ISZ) instruction. Consider the following program fragment:

```
301
  •
  •
  •
309  ISZ  R1
310  BR   301
311
```

In this fragment, the two transfer-of-control instructions are used to implement an iterative loop. R1 is set with the negative of the number of iterations to be performed. At the end of the loop, R1 is incremented. If it is not 0, the program branches back to the beginning of the loop. Otherwise, the branch is skipped, and the program continues with the next instruction after the end of the loop.

Figure 10.6 Branch Instructions

Procedure Call Instructions

Perhaps the most important innovation in the development of programming languages is the *procedure*. A procedure is a self-contained computer program that is incorporated into a larger program. At any point in the program the procedure may be invoked, or *called*. The processor is instructed to go and execute the entire procedure and then return to the point from which the call took place.

The two principal reasons for the use of procedures are economy and modularity. A procedure allows the same piece of code to be used many times. This is important for economy in programming effort and for making the most efficient use of storage space in the system (the program must be stored). Procedures also allow large programming tasks to be subdivided into smaller units. This use of *modularity* greatly eases the programming task.

The procedure mechanism involves two basic instructions: a call instruction that branches from the present location to the procedure, and a return instruction that returns from the procedure to the place from which it was called. Both of these are forms of branching instructions.

Figure 10.7a illustrates the use of procedures to construct a program. In this example, there is a main program starting at location 4000. This program includes a call to procedure PROC1, starting at location 4500. When this call instruction is encountered, the CPU suspends execution of the main program and begins execution of PROC1 by fetching the next instruction from location 4500. Within PROC1, there are two calls to PROC2 at location 4800. In each case, the execution of PROC1 is suspended and PROC2 is executed. The RETURN statement causes the CPU to go back to the calling program and continue execution at the instruction after the corresponding CALL instruction. This behavior is illustrated in Figure 10.7b.

Several points are worth noting:

1. A procedure can be called from more than one location.
2. A procedure call can appear in a procedure. This allows the *nesting* of procedures to an arbitrary depth.
3. Each procedure call is matched by a return in the called program.

Because we would like to be able to call a procedure from a variety of points, the CPU must somehow save the return address so that the return can take place appropriately. There are three common places for storing the return address:

- Register
- Start of called procedure
- Top of stack

Consider a machine-language instruction CALL X, which stands for *call procedure at location X*. If the register approach is used, CALL X causes the following actions:

$$RN \leftarrow PC + \Delta$$
$$PC \leftarrow X$$

(a) Calls and returns   **(b) Execution sequence**

Figure 10.7 Nested Procedures

where RN is a register that is always used for this purpose, PC is the program counter, and Δ is the instruction length. The called procedure can now save the contents of RN to be used for the later return.

A second possibility is to store the return address at the start of the procedure. In this case, CALL X causes

$$X \leftarrow PC + \Delta$$
$$PC \leftarrow X + 1$$

This is quite handy. The return address has been stored safely away.

Both of the preceding approaches work and have been used. The only limitation of these approaches is that they prevent the use of *reentrant* procedures. A reentrant procedure is one in which it is possible to have several calls open to it at the same time. A recursive procedure (one that calls itself) is an example of the use of this feature.

A more general and powerful approach is to use a stack (see Appendix 10A for a definition of the stack). When the CPU executes a call, it places the return address on the stack. When it executes a return, it uses the address on the stack. Figure 10.8 illustrates the use of the stack.

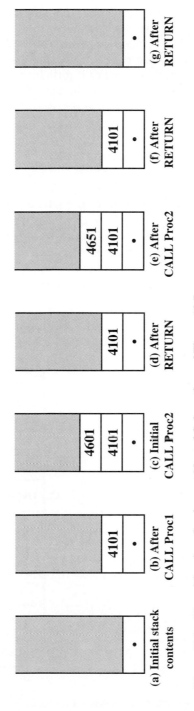

Figure 10.8 Use of Stock to Implement Nested Subroutines of Figure 10.7

In addition to providing a return address, it is also often necessary to pass parameters with a procedure call. These can be passed in registers. Another possibility is to store the parameters in memory just after the CALL instruction. In this case, the return must be to the location following the parameters. Again, both of these approaches have drawbacks. If registers are used, the called program and the calling program must be written to assure that the registers are used properly. The storing of parameters in memory makes it difficult to exchange a variable number of parameters. Both approaches prevent the use of reentrant procedures.

A more flexible approach to parameter passing is the stack. When the processor executes a call, it not only stacks the return address, it stacks parameters to be passed to the called procedure. The called procedure can access the parameters from the stack. Upon return, return parameters can also be placed on the stack. The entire set of parameters, including return address, that is stored for a procedure invocation is referred to as a *stack frame*.

An example is provided in Figure 10.9. The example refers to procedure P in which the local variables x1 and x2 are declared, and procedure Q, which can be called by P and in which the local variables y1 and y2 are declared. In this figure, the return point for each procedure is the first item stored in the corresponding stack frame. Next is stored a pointer to the beginning of the previous frame. This is needed if the number or length of parameters to be stacked is variable.

Figure 10.9 Stock Frame Growth Using Sample Procedures P and Q

10.5 PENTIUM AND POWERPC OPERATION TYPES

Pentium Operation Types

The Pentium provides a complex array of operation types, including a number of specialized instructions. The intent was to provide tools for the compiler writer to produce optimized machine language translation of high-level language programs. Table 10.8 lists the types and gives examples of each. Most of these are the conventional instructions found in most machine instruction sets, but several types of instructions are tailored to the 80x86/Pentium architecture and are of particular interest.

Call/Return Instructions

The Pentium provides four instructions to support procedure call/return: CALL, ENTER, LEAVE, RETURN. It will be instructive to look at the support provided by these instructions. Recall from Figure 10.9 that a common means of implementing the procedure call/return mechanism is via the use of stack frames. When a new procedure is called, the following must be performed upon entry to the new procedure:

- Push the return point on the stack.
- Push the current frame pointer on the stack.
- Copy the stack pointer as the new value of the frame pointer.
- Adjust the stack pointer to allocate a frame.

The CALL instruction pushes the current instruction pointer value onto the stack and causes a jump to the entry point of the procedure by placing the address of the entry point in the instruction pointer. In the 8088 and 8086 machines, the typical procedure began with the sequence

```
PUSH     EBP
MOV      EBP, ESP
SUB      ESP, space_for_locals
```

where EBP is the frame pointer and ESP is the stack pointer. In the 80286 and later machines, the ENTER instruction performs all the aforementioned operations in a single instruction.

The ENTER instruction was added to the instruction set to provide direct support for the compiler. The instruction also includes a feature for support of what are called nested procedures in languages such as Pascal, COBOL, and Ada (not found in C or FORTRAN). It turns out that there are better ways of handling nested procedure calls for these languages. Furthermore, although the ENTER instruction saves a few bytes of memory compared with the PUSH, MOV, SUB sequence (4 bytes versus 6 bytes), it actually takes longer to execute (10 clock cycles versus 6 clock cycles). Thus, although it may have seemed a good idea to the instruction set designers to add this feature, it complicates the implementation of the processor while providing little or no benefit. We will see that, in contrast, a RISC approach

Table 10.8 Pentium Operation Types (with Examples of Typical Operations)

Instruction	Description
Data Movement	
MOV	Move operand, between registers or between register and memory.
PUSH	Push operand onto stack.
PUSHA	Push all registers on stack.
MOVSX	Move byte, word, dword, sign extended. Moves a byte to a word or a word to a doubleword with twos-complement sign extension.
LEA	Load effective address. Loads the offset of the source operand, rather than its value to the destination operand.
XLAT	Table lookup translation. Replaces a byte in AL with a byte from a user-coded translation table. When XLAT is executed, AL should have an unsigned index to the table. XLAT changes the contents of AL from the table index to the table entry.
IN, OUT	Input, output operand from I/O space.
Arithmetic	
ADD	Add operands.
SUB	Subtract operands.
MUL	Unsigned integer multiplication, with byte, word, or double word operands, and word, doubleword, or quadword result.
IDIV	Signed divide.
Logical	
AND	AND operands.
BTS	Bit test and set. Operates on a bit field operand. The instruction copies the current value of a bit to flag CF and sets the original bit to 1.
BSF	Bit scan forward. Scans a word or doubleword for a 1-bit and stores the number of the first 1-bit into a register.
SHL/SHR	Shift logical left or right.
SAL/SAR	Shift arithmetic left or right.
ROL/ROR	Rotate left or right.
SETcc	Sets a byte to zero or one depending on any of the 16 conditions defined by status flags.
Control Transfer	
JMP	Unconditional jump.
CALL	Transfer control to another location. Before transfer, the address of the instruction following the CALL is placed on the stack.
JE/JZ	Jump if equal/zero.
LOOPE/LOOPZ	Loops if equal/zero. This is a conditional jump using a value stored in register ECX. The instruction first decrements ECX before testing ECX for the branch condition.
INT/INTO	Interrupt/Interrupt if overflow. Transfer control to an interrupt service routine.
String Operations	
MOVS	Move byte, word, dword string. The instruction operates on one element of a string, indexed by registers ESI and EDI. After each string operation, the registers are automatically incremented or decremented to point to the next element of the string.
LODS	Load byte, word, dword of string.
High-Level Language Support	
ENTER	Creates a stack frame that can be used to implement the rules of a block-structured high-level language.
LEAVE	Reverses the action of the previous ENTER.

Table 10.8 *continued*

	High-Level Language Support *continued*
BOUND	Check array bounds. Verifies that the value in operand 1 is within lower and upper limits. The limits are in two adjacent memory locations referenced by operand 2. An interrupt occurs if the value is out of bounds. This instruction is used to check an array index.
	Flag Control
STC	Set Carry flag.
LAHF	Load A register from flags. Copies SF, ZF, AF, PF, and CF bits into A register.
	Segment Register
LDS	Load pointer into D segment register.
	System control.
HLT	Halt.
LOCK	Asserts a hold on shared memory so that the Pentium has exclusive use of it during the instruction that immediately follows the LOCK.
ESC	Processor extension escape. An escape code that indicates the succeeding instructions are to be executed by a numeric coprocessor that supports high-precision integer and floating-point calculations.
WAIT	Wait until BUSY# negated. Suspends Pentium program execution until the processor detects that the BUSY pin is inactive, indicating that the numeric coprocessor has finished execution.
	Protection
SGDT	Store global descriptor table.
LSL	Load segment limit. Loads a user-specified register with a segment limit.
VERR/VERW	Verify segment for reading/writing.
	Cache Management
INVD	Flushes the internal cache memory.
WBINVD	Flushes the internal cache memory after writing dirty lines to memory.
INVLPG	Invalidates a translation lookaside buffer (TLB) entry.

to processor design would avoid complex instructions such as ENTER and might produce a more efficient implementation with a sequence of simpler instructions.

Memory Management

Another set of specialized instructions deals with memory segmentation. These are privileged instructions that can only be executed from the operating system. They allow local and global segment tables (called descriptor tables) to be loaded and read, and for the privilege level of a segment to be checked and altered.

The special instructions for dealing with the on-chip cache were discussed in Chapter 4.

Condition Codes

We have mentioned that condition codes are bits in special registers that may be set by certain operations and used in conditional branch instructions. These conditions are set by arithmetic and compare operations. The compare operation in most languages subtracts two operands, as does a subtract operation. The difference is that a compare operation only sets condition codes, whereas a subtract operation also stores the result of the subtraction in the destination operand.

Table 10.9 lists the condition codes used on the Pentium. Each condition, or combinations of these conditions, can be tested for a conditional jump. Table 10.10 shows the combinations of conditions for which conditional jump opcodes have been defined.

Several interesting observations can be made about this list. First, we may wish to test two operands to determine if one number is bigger than another. But this will depend on whether the numbers are signed or unsigned. For example, the 8-bit number 11111111 is bigger than 00000000 if the two numbers are interpreted as unsigned integers ($255 > 0$), but is less if they are considered as 8-bit twos complement numbers ($-1 < 0$). Many assembly languages therefore introduce two sets of terms to distinguish the two cases: If we are comparing two numbers as signed integers, we use the terms *less than* and *greater than;* if we are comparing them as unsigned integers, we use the terms *below* and *above.*

A second observation concerns the complexity of comparing signed integers. A signed result is greater than or equal to zero if (1) the sign bit is zero and there is no overflow (S = 0 AND O = 0), or (2) the sign bit is one and there is an overflow. A study of Figure 9.4 should convince you that the conditions tested for the various signed operations are appropriate (see Problem 10.14).

Pentium MMX Instructions

In 1996, Intel introduced MMX technology into its Pentium product line. MMX is set of highly optimized instructions for multimedia tasks. There are 57 new instructions that treat data in a SIMD (single-instruction, multiple-data) fashion, which makes it possible to perform the same operation, such as addition or multiplication, on multiple data elements at once. Each instruction typically takes a single clock cycle to execute. For the proper application, these fast parallel operations can yield a speedup of two to eight times over comparable algorithms that do not use the MMX instructions [ATKI96].

Table 10.9 Pentium Condition Codes

Status Bit	Name	Description
C	Carry	Indicates carrying or borrowing into the leftmost bit position following an arithmetic operation. Also modified by some of the shift and rotate operations.
P	Parity	Parity of the result of an arithmetic or logic operation. 1 indicates even parity; 0 indicates odd parity.
A	Auxiliary carry	Represents carrying or borrowing between half-bytes of an 8-bit arithmetic or logic operation using the AL register.
Z	Zero	Indicates that the result of an arithmetic or logic operation is 0.
S	Sign	Indicates the sign of the result of an arithmetic or logic operation.
O	Overflow	Indicates an arithmetic overflow after an addition or subtraction.

Table 10.10 Pentium Conditions for Conditional Jump and SETcc Instructions

Symbol	Condition Tested	Comment
A, NBE	C=0 AND Z=0	Above; not below or equal (greater than, unsigned)
AE, NB, NC	C=0	Above or equal; not below (greater than or equal, unsigned); not carry
B, NAE, C	C=1	Below; not above or equal (less than, unsigned); carry set
BE, NA	C=1 OR Z=1	Below or equal; not above (less than or equal, unsigned)
E, Z	Z=1	Equal; zero (signed or unsigned)
G, NLE	[(S=1 AND O=1) OR (S=0 AND O=0)] AND [Z=0]	Greater than; not less than or equal (signed)
GE, NL	(S=1 AND O=1) OR (S=0 AND O=0)	Greater than or equal; not less than (signed)
L, NGE	(S=1 AND O=0) OR (S=0 AND O=1)	Less than; not greater than or equal (signed)
LE, NG	(S=1 AND O=0) OR (S=0 AND O=1) OR (Z=1)	Less than or equal; not greater than (signed)
NE, NZ	Z=0	Not equal; not zero (signed or unsigned)
NO	O=0	No overflow
NS	S=0	Not sign (not negative)
NP, PO	P=0	Not parity; parity odd
O	O=1	Overflow
P	P=1	Parity; parity even
S	S=1	Sign (negative)

The focus of MMX is multimedia programming. Video and audio data are typically composed of large arrays of small data types, such as 8 or 16 bits, whereas conventional instructions are tailored to operate on 32- or 64-bit data. Here are some examples: In graphics and video, a single scene consists of an array of pixels,[1] and there are 8 bits for each pixel or 8 bits for each pixel color component (red, green, blue). Typical audio samples are quantized using 16 bits. For some 3D graphics algorithms, 32 bits are common for basic data types. To provide for parallel operation on these data lengths, three new data types are defined in MMX. Each data type is 64 bits in length and consists of multiple smaller data fields, each of which holds a fixed-point integer. The types are as follows:

- **Packet byte:** Eight bytes packed into one 64-bit quantity
- **Packed word:** Four 16-bit words packed into 64 bits
- **Packed doubleword:** Two 32-bit doublewords packed into 64 bits

Table 10.11 lists the MMX instruction set. Most of the instructions involve parallel operation on bytes, words, or doublewords. For example, the PSLLW instruction

---

[1]A pixel, or picture element, is the smallest element of a digital image that can be assigned a gray level. Equivalently, a pixel is an individual dot in a dot-matrix representation of a picture.

Table 10.11 MMX Instruction Set

Category	Instruction	Description
Arithmetic	PADD [B, W, D]	Parallel add of packed eight bytes, four 16 bit words, or two 32-bit doublewords, with wraparound
	PADDS [B, W]	Add with saturation
	PADDUS [B, W]	Add unsigned with saturation
	PSUB [B, W, D]	Subtract with wraparound
	PSUBS [B, W]	Subtract with saturation
	PSUBUS [B, W]	Subtract unsigned with saturation
	PMULHW	Parallel multiply of four signed 16-bit words, with high-order 16 bits of 32-bit result chosen
	PMULLW	Parallel multiply of four signed 16-bit words, with low-order 16 bits of 32-bit result chosen
	PMADDWD	Parallel multiply of four signed 16-bit words; add together adjacent pairs of 32-bit results
Comparison	PCMPEQ [B, W, D]	Parallel compare for equality; result is mask of 1s if true or 0s if false
	PCMPGT [B, W, D]	Parallel compare for greater than; result is mask of 1s if true or 0s if false
Conversion	PACKUSWB	Pack words into bytes with unsigned saturation
	PACKSS [WB, DW]	Pack words into bytes, or doublewords into words, with signed saturation
	PUNPCKH [BW, WD, DQ]	Parallel unpack (interleaved merge) high-order bytes, words, or doublewords from MMX register
	PUNPCKL [BW, WD, DQ]	Parallel unpack (interleaved merge) low-order bytes, words, or doublewords from MMX register
Logical	PAND	64-bit bitwise logical AND
	PNDN	64-bit bitwise logical AND NOT
	POR	64-bit bitwise logical OR
	PXOR	64-bit bitwise logical XOR
Shift	PSLL [W, D, Q]	Parallel logical left shift of packed words, doublewords, or quadword by amount specified in MMX register or immediate value
	PSRL [W, D, Q]	Parallel logical right shift of packed words, doublewords, or quadword
	PSRA [W, D]	Parallel arithmetic right shift of packed words, doublewords, or quadword
Data Transfer	MOV [D, Q]	Move doubleword or quadword to/from MMX register
State Mgt	EMMS	Empty MMX state (empty FP registers tag bits)

Note: If an instruction supports multiple data types [byte (B), word (W), doubleword (D), quadword (Q)], the data types are indicated in brackets.

performs a left logical shift separately on each of the four words in the packed word operand; the PADDB instruction takes packed byte operands as input and performs parallel additions on each byte position independently to produce a packed byte output.

One unusual feature of the new instruction set is the introduction of saturation arithmetic. With ordinary unsigned arithmetic, when an operation overflows (i.e., a carry out of the most significant bit), the extra bit is truncated. This is referred to as wraparound, because the effect of the truncation can be, for example, to produce an addition result that is smaller than the two input operands. Consider the addition of the two words, in hexadecimal, F000h and 3000h. The sum would be expressed as

```
  F000h   =   1111 0000 0000 0000
+ 3000h   =   0011 0000 0000 0000
             10010 0000 0000 0000  =  2000h
```

If the two numbers represented image intensity, then the result of the addition is to make the combination of two dark shades turn out to be lighter. This is typically not what is intended. With saturation arithmetic, if addition results in overflow or subtraction results in underflow, the result is set to the largest or smallest value representable. For the preceding example, with saturation arithmetic, we have

```
  F000h   =   1111 0000 0000 0000
+ 3000h   =   0011 0000 0000 0000
             10010 0000 0000 0000
              1111 1111 1111 1111  =  FFFFh
```

To provide a feel for the use of MMX instructions, we look at an example, taken from [PELE97]. A common video application is the fade-out, fade-in effect, in which one scene gradually dissolves into another. Two images are combined with a weighted average:

$$\text{Result\_pixel} = \text{A\_pixel} \times \text{fade} + \text{B\_pixel} \times (1 - \text{fade})$$

This calculation is performed on each pixel position in A and B. If a series of video frames is produced while gradually changing the fade value from 1 to 0 (scaled appropriately for an 8-bit integer), the result is to fade from image A to image B.

Figure 10.10 shows the sequence of steps required for one set of pixels. The 8-bit pixel components are converted to 16-bit elements to accommodate the MMX 16-bit multiply capability. If these images use 640×480 resolution, and the dissolve technique uses all 255 possible values of the fade value, then the total number of instructions executed using MMX is 535 million. The same calculation, performed without the MMX instructions, requires 1.4 billion instructions [INTE98].

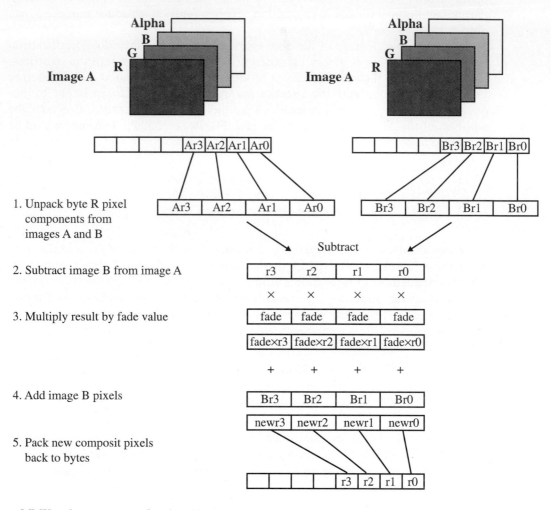

MMX code sequence performing this operation:

```
pxor        mm7, mm7      ;zero out mm7
movq        mm3, fad_val  ;load fade value replicated 4 times
movd        mm0, imageA   ;load 4 red pixel components from image A
movd        mm1, imageB   ;load 4 red pixel components from image B
punpckblw   mm0, mm7      ;unpack 4 pixels to 16 bits
punpckblw   mm1, mm7      ;unpack 4 pixels to 16 bits
psubw       mm0, mm1      ;subtract image B from image A
pmulhw      mm0, mm3      ;multiply the subtract result by fade values
padddw      mm0, mm1      ;add result to image B
packuswb    mm0, mm7      ;pack 16-bit results back to bytes
```

Figure 10.10 Image Compositing on Color Plane Representation [PELE97]

Table 10.12 PowerPC Operation Types (with Examples of Typical Operations)

Instruction	Description
Branch Oriented	
b	Unconditional branch
bl	Branch to target address and place effective address of instruction following the branch into the Link Register
bc	Branch conditional on Count Register and/or on bit in Condition Register
sc	System call to invoke an operating system service
trap	Compare two operands and invoke system trap handler if specified conditions are met
Load/Store	
lwzu	Load word and zero extend to left; update source register
ld	Load doubleword
lmw	Load multiple word; load consecutive words into contiguous registers from the target register through general-purpose register 31
lswx	Load a string of bytes into registers beginning with target register; 4 bytes per register; wrap around from register 31 to register 0
Integer Arithmetic	
add	Add contents of two registers and place in third register
subf	Subtract contents of two registers and place in third register
mullw	Multiply low-order 32-bit contents of two registers and place 64-bit product in third register
divd	Divide 64-bit contents of two registers and place in quotient in third register
Logical and Shift	
cmp	Compare two operands and set four condition bits in the specified condition register field
crand	Condition register AND: two bits of the Condition Register are ANDed and the result placed in one of the two bit positions
and	AND contents of two registers and place in third register
cntlzd	Count number of consecutive 0 bits starting at bit zero in source register and place count in destination register
rldic	Rotate left doubleword register, AND with mask, and store in destination register
sld	Shift left bits in source register and store in destination register
Floating Point	
lfs	Load 32-bit floating-point number from memory, convert to 64-bit format, and store in floating-point register
fadd	Add contents of two registers and place in third register
fmadd	Multiply contents of two registers, add the contents of a third, and place result in fourth register
fcmpu	Compare two floating-point operands and set condition bits
Cache Management	
dcbf	Data cache block flush; perform lookup in cache on specified target address and perform flushing operation
icbi	Instruction cache block invalidate

PowerPC Operation Types

The PowerPC provides a large collection of operation types. Table 10.12 lists the types and gives examples of each. Several features are worth noting.

Branch-Oriented Instructions

The PowerPC supports the usual unconditional and conditional branch capabilities. Conditional branch instructions test a single bit of the condition register for true, false, or don't care and the contents of the count register for zero, nonzero, or don't care. Thus, there are nine separate conditions that can be defined for the conditional branch instruction. If the count register is tested for zero or nonzero, then it is decremented by 1 prior to the test. This is convenient for setting up iteration loops.

Branch instructions can also indicate that the address of the location following the branch is to be placed in the link register, described in Chapter 14. This facilitates call/return processing.

Load/Store Instructions

In the PowerPC architecture, only load and store instructions access memory locations; arithmetic and logical instructions are performed only on registers. This is characteristic of RISC design, and it is explored further in Chapter 13.

There are two features that characterize the different load/store instructions:

- **Data size:** Data can be transferred in units of byte, halfword, word, or doubleword. Instructions are also available for loading or storing a string of bytes into or from multiple registers.
- **Sign extension:** For halfword and word loads, the unused bits to the left in the 64-bit destination register are either filled with zeros or with the sign bit of the loaded quantity.

10.6 ASSEMBLY LANGUAGE

A CPU can understand and execute machine instructions. Such instructions are simply binary numbers stored in the computer. If a programmer wished to program directly in machine language, then it would be necessary to enter the program as binary data.

Consider the simple BASIC statement

$$N = I + J + K$$

Suppose we wished to program this statement in machine language and to initialize I, J, and K to 2, 3, and 4, respectively. This is shown in Figure 10.11a. The program starts in location 101 (hexadecimal). Memory is reserved for the four variables starting at location 201. The program consists of four instructions:

1. Load the contents of location 201 into the AC.
2. Add the contents of location 202 to the AC.
3. Add the contents of location 203 to the AC.
4. Store the contents of the AC in location 204.

This is clearly a tedious and very error-prone process.

A slight improvement is to write the program in hexadecimal rather than binary notation (Figure 10.11b). We could write the program as a series of lines. Each line contains the address of a memory location and the hexadecimal code of the binary value to be stored in that location. Then we need a program that will accept this input, translate each line into a binary number, and store it in the specified location.

For more improvement, we can make use of the symbolic name or mnemonic of each instruction. This results in the *symbolic program* shown in Figure 10.11c. Each line of input still represents one memory location. Each line consists of three fields, separated by spaces. The first field contains the address of a location. For an instruction, the second field contains the three-letter symbol for the opcode. If it is a memory-referencing instruction, then a third field contains the address. To store arbitrary data in a location, we invent a *pseudoinstruction* with the symbol DAT. This is merely an indication that the third field on the line contains a hexadecimal number to be stored in the location specified in the first field.

Address	Contents			
101	0010	0010	0000	0001
102	0001	0010	0000	0010
103	0001	0010	0000	0011
104	0011	0010	0000	0100
201	0000	0000	0000	0010
202	0000	0000	0000	0011
203	0000	0000	0000	0100
204	0000	0000	0000	0000

(a) Binary program

Address	Instruction	
101	LDA	201
102	ADD	202
103	ADD	203
104	STA	204
201	DAT	2
202	DAT	3
203	DAT	4
204	DAT	0

(b) Symbolic program

Address	Contents	Label	Operation	Operand
101	2201	FORMUL	LDA	I
102	1202		ADD	J
103	1203		ADD	K
104	3204		STA	N
201	0002	I	DATA	2
202	0003	J	DATA	3
203	0004	K	DATA	4
204	0000	N	DATA	0

(c) Hexadecimal program

(d) Assembly program

Figure 10.11 Computation of the Formula $N = I + J + K$

For this type of input we need a slightly more complex program. The program accepts each line of input, generates a binary number based on the second and third (if present) fields, and stores it in the location specified by the first field.

The use of a symbolic program makes life much easier but is still awkward. In particular, we must give an absolute address for each word. This means that the program and data can be loaded into only one place in memory, and we must know that place ahead of time. Worse, suppose we wish to change the program some day by adding or deleting a line. This will change the addresses of all subsequent words.

A much better system, and one commonly used, is to use symbolic addresses. This is illustrated in Figure 10.11d. Each line still consists of three fields. The first field is still for the address, but a symbol is used instead of an absolute numerical address. Some lines have no address, implying that the address of that line is one more than the address of the previous line. For memory-reference instructions, the third field also contains a symbolic address.

With this last refinement, we have an *assembly language*. Programs written in assembly language (assembly programs) are translated into machine language by an *assembler*. This program must not only do the symbolic translation discussed earlier, but also assign some form of memory addresses to symbolic addresses.

The development of assembly language was a major milestone in the evolution of computer technology. It was the first step to the high-level languages in use today. Although few programmers use assembly language, virtually all machines provide one. They are used, if at all, for systems programs such as compilers and I/O routines.

10.7 RECOMMENDED READING

A number of textbooks provide good coverage of machine language and instruction set design, including [PATT98], [TANE99], and [HAYE98]. The Pentium instruction set is well covered by [BREY00]. The PowerPC instruction set is covered in [IBM94] and [WEIS94].

BREY00   Brey, B. *The Intel Microprocessors: 8086/8066, 80186/80188, 80286, 80386, 80486, Pentium, Pentium Pro and Pentium II Processors.* Upper Saddle River, NJ: Prentice Hall, 2000.

HAYE98   Hayes, J. *Computer Architecture and Organization, Second Edition.* New York: McGraw-Hill, 1998.

IBM94   International Business Machines, Inc. *The PowerPC Architecture: A Specification for a New Family of RISC Processors.* San Francisco, CA: Morgan Kaufmann, 1994.

PATT98   Patterson, D., and Hennessy, J. *Computer Organization and Design: The Hardware/Software Interface.* San Mateo, CA: Morgan Kaufmann, 1998.

TANE99   Tanenbaum, A. *Structured Computer Organization.* Englewood Cliffs, NJ: Prentice Hall, 1999.

WEIS94   Weiss, S., and Smith, J. *POWER and PowerPC.* San Francisco: Morgan Kaufmann, 1994.

10.8 KEY TERMS, REVIEW QUESTIONS, AND PROBLEMS

Key Terms

accumulator	jump	procedure call
address	little endian	procedure return
arithmetic shift	logical shift	push
bi-endian	machine instruction	reentrant procedure
big endian	operand	reverse Polish notation
branch	operation	rotate
conditional branch	packed decimal	skip
instruction set	pop	stack

Review Questions

10.1 What are the typical elements of a machine instruction?

10.2 What types of locations can hold source and destination operands?

10.3 If an instruction contains four addresses, what might be the purpose of each address?

10.4 List and briefly explain five important instruction set design issues.

10.5 What types of operands are typical in machine instruction sets?

10.6 What is the relationship between the IRA character code and the packed decimal representation?

10.7 What is the difference between an arithmetic shift and a logical shift?

10.8 Why are transfer of control instructions needed?

10.9 List and briefly explain two common ways of generating the condition to be tested in a conditional branch instruction.

10.10 What is meant by the term *nesting of procedures*?

10.11 List three possible places for storing the return address for a procedure return.

10.12 What is a reentrant procedure?

10.13 What is the difference between assembly language and machine language?

10.14 What is reverse Polish notation?

10.15 What is the difference between big endian and little endian?

Problems

10.1 Many CPUs provide logic for performing arithmetic on packed decimal numbers. Although the rules for decimal arithmetic are similar to those for binary operations, the decimal results may require some corrections to the individual digits if binary logic is used.

Consider the decimal addition of two unsigned numbers. If each number consists of N digits, then there are $4N$ bits in each number. The two numbers are to be added using a binary adder. Suggest a simple rule for correcting the result. Perform addition in this fashion on the numbers 1698 and 1786.

10.2 The tens complement of the decimal number X is defined to be $10^N - X$, where N is the number of decimal digits in the number. Describe the use of ten's complement representation to perform decimal subtraction. Illustrate the procedure by subtracting $(0326)_{10}$ from $(0736)_{10}$.

10.3 Compare zero-, one-, two-, and three-address machines by writing programs to compute

$$X = (A + B \times C)/(D - E \times F)$$

for each of the four machines. The instructions available for use are as follows:

0 Address	1 Address	2 Address	3 Address
PUSH M	LOAD M	MOVE (X ← Y)	MOVE (X ← Y)
POP M	STORE M	ADD (X ← X + Y)	ADD (X ← Y + Z)
ADD	ADD M	SUB (X ← X − Y)	SUB (X ← Y − Z)
SUB	SUB M	MUL (X ← X × Y)	MUL (X ← Y × Z)
MUL	MUL M	DIV (X ← X/Y)	DIV (X ← Y/Z)
DIV	DIV M		

10.4 Consider a hypothetical computer with an instruction set of only two n-bit instructions. The first bit specifies the opcode, and the remaining bits specify one of the $2^n - 1$ n-bit words of main memory. The two instructions are

    SUBS X   Subtract the contents of location X from the accumulator, and store the result in location X and the accumulator.

    JUMP X   Place address X in the program counter.

A word in main memory may contain either an instruction or a binary number in twos complement notation. Demonstrate that this instruction repertoire is reasonably complete by specifying how the following operations can be programmed:

a. Data transfer: Location X to accumulator, accumulator to location X

b. Addition: Add contents of location X to accumulator

c. Conditional branch

d. Logical OR

e. I/O Operations

10.5 Many instruction sets contain the instruction NOOP, meaning no operation, which has no effect on the CPU state other than incrementing the program counter. Suggest some uses of this instruction.

10.6 In Section 10.4, it was stated that both an arithmetic left shift and a logical left shift correspond to a multiplication by 2 when there is no overflow, and if overflow occurs, arithmetic and logical left shift operations produce different results, but the arithmetic left shift retains the sign of the number. Demonstrate that these statements are true for 5-bit twos complement integers.

10.7 In what way are numbers rounded using arithmetic right shift (e.g., round toward $+\infty$, round toward $-\infty$, toward zero, away from 0)?

10.8 Suppose a stack is to be used by the CPU to manage procedure calls and returns. Can the program counter be eliminated by using the top of the stack as a program counter?

10.9 Appendix 10A points out that there are no stack-oriented instructions in an instruction set if the stack is to be used only by the CPU for such purposes as procedure handling. How can the CPU use a stack for any purpose without stack-oriented instructions?

10.10 Convert the following formulas from reverse Polish to infix:

a. AB + C + D ×

b. AB/CD/ +

c. ABCDE + × × /

d. ABCDE + F/ + G − H/ × +

10.11 Convert the following formulas from infix to reverse Polish:

a. A + B + C + D + E

b. (A + B) × (C + D) + E

    c. $(A \times B) + (C \times D) + E$

    d. $(A - B) \times (((C - D \times E)/F)/G) \times H$

10.12 Convert the expression $A + B - C$ to postfix notation using Dijkstra's algorithm. Show the steps involved. Is the result equivalent to $(A + B) - C$ or $A + (B - C)$? Does it matter?

10.13 The Pentium architecture includes an instruction called Decimal Adjust after Addition (DAA). DAA performs the following sequence of instructions:

```
if ((AL AND 0FH) > 9) OR (AF = 1) then
        AL  ←  AL + 6;
        AF  ←  1;
else
        AF  ←  0;
endif;
if (AL > 9FH) OR (CF = 1) then
        AL  ←  AL + 60H;
        CF  ←  1;
else
        AF  ←  0;
endif.
```

"H" indicates hexadecimal. AL is an 8-bit register that holds the result of addition of two unsigned 8-bit integers. AF is a flag set if there is a carry from bit 3 to bit 4 in the result of an addition. CF is a flag set if there is a carry from bit 7 to bit 8. Explain the function performed by the DAA instruction.

10.14 The Pentium Compare instruction (CMP) subtracts the source operand from the destination operand; it updates the status flags (C, P, A, Z, S, O) but does not alter either of the operands. The CMP instruction may be followed by a conditional Jump (Jcc) or Set Condition (SETcc) instruction, where cc refers to one of the 16 conditions listed in Table 10.11. Demonstrate that the conditions tested for a signed number comparison are correct.

10.15 Most microprocessor instruction sets include an instruction that tests a condition and sets a destination operand if the condition is true. Examples include the SETcc on the Pentium, the Scc on the Motorola MC68000, and the Scond on the National NS32000.

    a. There are a few differences among these instructions:

- SETcc and Scc operate only on a byte, whereas Scond operates on byte, word, and doubleword operands.
- SETcc and Scond set the operand to integer one if true and to zero if false. Scc sets the byte to all binary ones if true and all zeros if false.

What are the relative advantages and disadvantages of these differences?

    b. None of these instructions set any of the condition code flags, and thus an explicit test of the result of the instruction is required to determine its value. Discuss whether condition codes should be set as a result of this instruction.

    c. A simple IF statement such as IF a > b THEN can be implemented using a numerical representation method, that is, making the Boolean value manifest, as opposed to a *flow of control* method, which represents the value of a Boolean expression by a point reached in the program. A compiler might implement IF a > b THEN with the following 80X86 code:

```
        SUB    CX, CX  ;set register CX to 0
        MOV    AX, B   ;move contents of location B to register AX
        CMP    AX, A   ;compare contents of register AX and location A
        JLE    TEST    ;jump if A ≤ B
        INC    CX      ;add 1 to contents of register CX
TEST    JCXZ   OUT     ;jump if contents of CX equal 0
THEN

OUT
```

The result of (A > B) is a Boolean value held in a register and available later on, outside the context of the flow of code just shown. It is convenient to use register CX for this, because many of the branch and loop opcodes have a built-in test for CX.

Show an alternative implementation using the SETcc instruction that saves memory and execution time. (*Hint:* No additional new 80x86 instructions are needed, other than the SETcc.)

d. Now consider the high-level language statement:

$$A: = (B > C) \text{ OR } (D = F)$$

A compiler might generate the following code:

```
      MOV    EAX, B    ;move contents of location B to register EAX
      CMP    EAX, C    ;compare contents of register EAX and location C
      MOV    BL, 0     ;0 represents false
      JLE    N1        ;jump if B ≤ C
      MOV    BL, 1     ;1 represents false
N1    MOV    EAX, D
      CMP    EAX, F
      MOV    BH, 0
      JNE    N2
      MOV    BH, 1
N2    OR     BL, BH
```

Show an alternative implementation using the SETcc instruction that saves memory and execution time.

10.16 Using the algorithm for converting infix to postfix defined in Appendix 10A, show the steps involved in converting the expression of Figure 10.15 into postfix. Use a presentation similar to Figure 10.17.

10.17 Show the calculation of the expression in Figure 10.17, using a presentation similar to Figure 10.16.

10.18 Redraw the little-endian layout in Figure 10.18 so that the bytes appear as numbered in the big-endian layout. That is, show memory in 64-bit rows, with the bytes listed left to right, top to bottom.

10.19 For the following data structures, draw the big-endian and little-endian layouts, using the format of Figure 10.18, and comment on the results.

a. struct {
```
          double i;   //0x1112131415161718
      } s1;
```

b. struct {
```
          int i;        //0x11121314
          int j;        //0x15161718
      } s2;
```

c. struct {
```
          short i;   //0x1112
          short j;   //0x1314
          short k;   //0x1516
          short l;   //0x1718
      } s3;
```

10.20 The PowerPC architecture specification does not dictate how a processor should implement little-endian mode. It specifies only the view of memory a processor must have when operating in little-endian mode. When converting a data structure from big endian to little endian, processors are free to implement a true byte-swapping

Little-endian address mapping

Byte address								
					11	**12**	**13**	**14**
00	00	01	02	03	04	05	06	07
	21	**22**	**23**	**24**	**25**	**26**	**27**	**28**
08	08	09	0A	0B	0C	0D	0E	0F
	'D'	**'C'**	**'B'**	**'A'**	**31**	**32**	**33**	**34**
10	10	11	12	13	14	15	16	17
			51	**52**		**'G'**	**'F'**	**'E'**
18	18	19	1A	1B	1C	1D	1E	1F
					61	**62**	**63**	**64**
20	20	21	22	23	24	25	26	27

Figure 10.12 PowerPC Little-Endian Structure s in Memory

mechanism or to use some sort of an address modification mechanism. Current PowerPC processors are all default big-endian machines and use address modification to treat data as little-endian.

Consider the structure s defined in Figure 10.18. The layout in the lower-right portion of the figure shows the structure s as seen by the processor. In fact, if structure s is compiled in little-endian mode, its layout in memory is shown in Figure 10.12. Explain the mapping that is involved, describe an easy way to implement the mapping, and discuss the effectiveness of this approach.

10.21 Write a small program to determine the endianness of machine and report the results. Run the program on a computer available to you and turn in the output.

APPENDIX 10A STACKS

Stacks

A *stack* is an ordered set of elements, only one of which can be accessed at a time. The point of access is called the *top* of the stack. The number of elements in the stack, or *length* of the stack, is variable. Items may only be added to or deleted from the top of the stack. For this reason, a stack is also known as a *pushdown list* or a *last-in-first-out (LIFO) list*.

Figure 10.13 shows the basic stack operations. We begin at some point in time when the stack contains some number of elements. A PUSH operation appends one new item to the top of the stack. A POP operation removes the top item from the stack. In both cases, the top of the stack moves accordingly. Binary operations, which require two operands (e.g., multiply, divide, add, subtract), use the top two stack items as operands, pop both items, and push the result back onto the stack. Unary operations, which require only one operand (e.g., logical NOT), use the item on the top of the stack. All of these operations are summarized in Table 10.13.

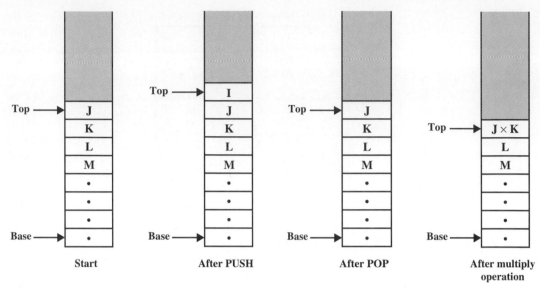

Figure 10.13   Basic Stack Operation

Stack Implementation

The stack is a useful structure to provide as part of a CPU implementation. One use, discussed in Section 10.4, is to manage procedure calls and returns. Stacks may also be useful to the programmer. An example of this is expression evaluation, discussed later in this section.

The implementation of a stack depends in part on its potential uses. If it is desired to make stack operations available to the programmer, then the instruction set will include stack-oriented operations, including PUSH, POP, and operations that use the top one or two stack elements as operands. Because all of these operations refer to a unique location, namely the top of the stack, the address of the operand or operands is implicit and need not be included in the instruction. These are the zero-address instructions referred to in Section 10.1.

If the stack mechanism is to be used only by the CPU, for such purposes as procedure handling, then there will not be explicit stack-oriented instructions in the

Table 10.13   Stack-Oriented Operations

PUSH	Append a new element on the top of the stack.
POP	Delete the top element of the stack.
Unary operation	Perform operation on top element of stack. Replace top element with result.
Binary operation	Perform operation on top two elements of stack. Delete top two elements of stack. Place result of operation on top of stack.

instruction set. In either case, the implementation of a stack requires that there be some set of locations used to store the stack elements. A typical approach is illustrated in Figure 10.14a. A contiguous block of locations is reserved in main memory (or virtual memory) for the stack. Most of the time, the block is partially filled with stack elements and the remainder is available for stack growth.

Three addresses are needed for proper operation, and these are often stored in CPU registers:

- **Stack pointer:** Contains the address of the top of the stack. If an item is appended to or deleted from the stack, the pointer is incremented or decremented to contain the address of the new top of the stack.
- **Stack base:** Contains the address of the bottom location in the reserved block. If an attempt is made to POP when the stack is empty, an error is reported.
- **Stack limit:** Contains the address of the other end of the reserved block. If an attempt is made to PUSH when the block is fully utilized for the stack, an error is reported.

Traditionally, and on most machines today, the base of the stack is at the high-address end of the reserved stack block, and the limit is at the low-address end. Thus, the stack grows from higher addresses to lower addresses.

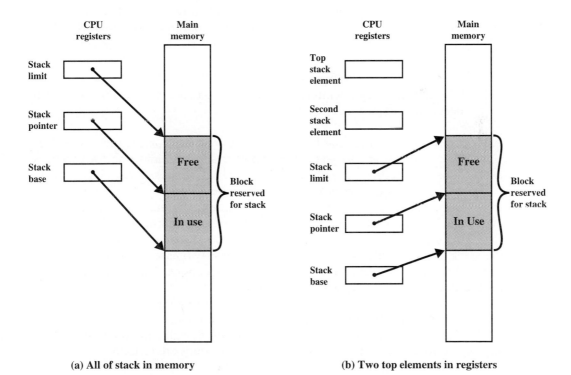

(a) All of stack in memory   (b) Two top elements in registers

Figure 10.14 Typical Stack Organizations

To speed up stack operations, the top two stack elements are often stored in registers, as shown in Figure 10.14b. In this case, the stack pointer contains the address of the third element of the stack.

Expression Evaluation

Mathematical formulas are usually expressed in what is known as *infix* notation. In this form, a binary operation appears between the operands (e.g., a + b). For complex expressions, parentheses are used to determine the order of evaluation of expressions. For example, a + (b × c) will yield a different result than (a + b) × c. To minimize the use of parentheses, operations have an implied precedence. Generally, multiplication takes precedence over addition, so that a + b × c is equivalent to a + (b × c).

An alternative technique is known as *reverse Polish,* or postfix, notation. In this notation, the operator follows its two operands. For example,

a + b	becomes a b +
a + (b × c)	becomes a b c × +
(a + b) × c	becomes a b + c ×

Note that, regardless of the complexity of an expression, no parentheses are required when using reverse Polish.

The advantage of postfix notation is that an expression in this form is easily evaluated using a stack. An expression in postfix notation is scanned from left to right. For each element of the expression, the following rules are applied:

1. If the element is a variable or constant, push it onto the stack.
2. If the element is an operator, pop the top two items of the stack, perform the operation, and push the result.

After the entire expression has been scanned, the result is on the top of the stack.

The simplicity of this algorithm makes it a convenient one for evaluating expressions. Accordingly, many compilers will take an expression in a high-level language, convert it to postfix notation, and then generate the machine instructions from that notation. Figure 10.15 shows the sequence of machine instructions for evaluating f = (a − b)/(c + d × e) using stack-oriented instructions. The figure also shows the use of one-address and two-address instructions. Note that, even though the stack-oriented rules were not used in the last two cases, the postfix notation served as a guide for generating the machine instructions. The sequence of events for the stack program is shown in Figure 10.16.

The process of converting an infix expression to a postfix expression is itself most easily accomplished using a stack. The following algorithm is due to Dijkstra [DIJK63]. The infix expression is scanned from left to right, and the postfix expression is developed and output during the scan. The steps are as follows:

1. Examine the next element in the input.
2. If it is an operand, output it.

	Stack	General Registers	Single Register
	Push a Push b Subtract Push c Push d Push e Multiply Add Divide Pop f	Load R1, a Subtract R1, b Load R2, d Multiply R2, e Add R2, c Divide R1, R2 Store R1, f	Load d Multiply e Add c Store f Load a Subtract b Divide f Store f
Number of instructions	10	7	8
Memory access	10 op + 6 d	7 op + 6 d	8 op + 8 d

Figure 10.15 Comparison of Three Programs to Calculate f = (a − b)/(c + d × e)

3. If it is an opening parenthesis, push it onto the stack.
4. If it is an operator, then
   - If the top of the stack is an opening parenthesis, then push the operator.
   - If it has higher priority than the top of the stack (multiply and divide have higher priority than add and subtract), then push the operator.
   - Else, pop operation from stack to output, and repeat step 4.

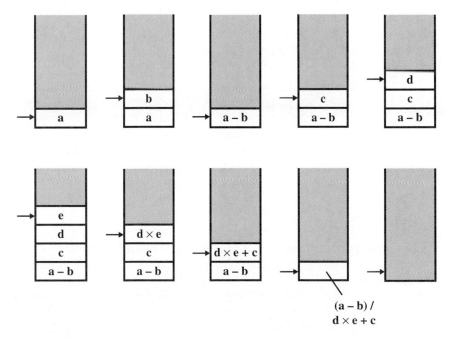

Figure 10.16 Use of Stack to Compute f = (a − b)/(d × e + c)

Input	Output	Stack (top on right)
A + B × C + (D + E) × F	empty	empty
+ B × C + (D + E) × F	A	empty
B × C + (D + E) × F	A	+
× C + (D + E) × F	A B	+
C + (D + E) × F	A B	+ ×
+ (D + E) × F	A B C	+ ×
(D + E) × F	A B C × +	+
D + E) × F	A B C × +	+ (
+ E) × F	A B C × + D	+ (
E) × F	A B C × + D	+ (+
) × F	A B C × + D E	+ (+
× F	A B C × + D E +	+
F	A B C × + D E +	+ ×
empty	A B C × + D E + F	+ ×
empty	A B C × + D E + F × +	empty

Figure 10.17 Conversion of an Expression from Infix to Postfix Notation

5. If it is a closing parenthesis, pop operators to the output until an opening parenthesis is encountered. Pop and discard the opening parenthesis.

6. If there is more input, go to step 1.

7. If there is no more input, unstack the remaining operands.

Figure 10.17 illustrates the use of this algorithm. This example should give the reader some feel for the power of stack-based algorithms.

APPENDIX 10B LITTLE-, BIG- AND BI-ENDIAN

An annoying and curious phenomenon relates to how the bytes within a word and the bits within a byte are both referenced and represented. We look first at the problem of byte ordering, and then consider that of bits.

Byte Ordering

The concept of endianness was first discussed in the literature by Cohen [COHE81]. With respect to bytes, endianness has to do with the byte ordering of multibyte scalar values. The issue is best introduced with an example. Suppose we have the 32-bit hexadecimal value 12345678 and that it is stored in a 32-bit word in byte-addressable memory at byte location 184. The value consists of four bytes, with the least significant byte containing the value 78 and the most significant byte containing the value 12. There are two ways to store this value:

Address	Value
184	12
185	34
186	56
187	78

Address	Value
184	78
185	56
186	34
187	12

The mapping on the left stores the most significant byte in the lowest numerical byte address; this is known as big endian and is equivalent to the left-to-right order of writing in Western culture languages. The mapping on the right stores the least significant byte in the lowest numerical byte address; this is known as little endian and is reminiscent of the right-to-left order of arithmetic operations in arithmetic units.[2] For a given multibyte scalar value, big endian and little endian are byte-reversed mappings of each other.

The concept of endianness arises when it is necessary to treat a multiple-byte entity as a single data item with a single address, even though it is composed of smaller addressable units. Some machines, such as the Intel 80x86, Pentium, VAX, and Alpha, are little-endian machines, whereas others, such as the IBM System 370/390, the Motorola 680x0, Sun SPARC, and most RISC machines, are big endian. This presents problems when data are transferred from a machine of one endian type to the other, and when a programmer attempts to manipulate individual bytes or bits within a multibyte scalar.

The property of endianness does not extend beyond an individual data unit. In any machine, aggregates such as files, data structures, and arrays are composed of multiple data units, each with endianness. Thus, conversion of a block of memory from one style of endianness to the other requires knowledge of the data structure.

Figure 10.18 illustrates how endianness determines addressing and byte order. The C structure at the top contains a number of data types. The memory layout in the lower left results from compilation of that structure for a big-endian machine, and that in the lower right for a little-endian machine. In each case, memory is depicted as a series of 64-bit rows. For the big endian case, memory typically is laid out left to right, top to bottom, whereas for the little-endian case, memory typically is laid out right to left, top to bottom. Note that these layouts are arbitrary. Either scheme could use either left to right or right to left within a row; this is a matter of depiction, not memory assignment. In fact, in looking at programmer manuals for a variety of machines, a bewildering collection of depictions is to be found, even within the same manual.

We can make several observations about this data structure:

- Each data item has the same address in both schemes. For example, the address of the doubleword with hexadecimal value 2122232425262728 is 08.
- Within any given multibyte scalar value, the ordering of bytes in the little-endian structure is the reverse of that for the big-endian structure.

---

[2] The terms *big endian* and *little endian* come from Part I, Chapter 4 of Jonathan Swift's *Gulliver's Travels*. They refer to a religious war between two groups, one that breaks eggs at the big end and the other that breaks eggs at the little end.

```
struct{
    int     a;      //0x1112_1314                      word
    int     pad;    //
    double  b;      //0x2122_2324_2526_2728            doubleword
    char*   c;      //0x3132_3334                      word
    char    d[7];   //'A'.'B','C','D','E','F','G'      byte array
    short   e;      //0x5152                           halfword
    int     f;      //0x6161_6364                      word
} s;
```

		Big-endian address mapping									Little-endian address mapping								

Byte address

Big-endian address mapping:

11	12	13	14				
00	01	02	03	04	05	06	07
21	22	23	24	25	26	27	28
08	09	0A	0B	0C	0D	0E	0F
31	32	33	34	'A'	'B'	'C'	'D'
10	11	12	13	14	15	16	17
'E'	'F'	'G'		51	52		
18	19	1A	1B	1C	1D	1E	1F
61	62	63	64				
20	21	22	23				

Byte address: 00, 08, 10, 18, 20

Little-endian address mapping:

				11	12	13	14
07	06	05	04	03	02	01	00
21	22	23	24	25	26	27	28
0F	0E	0D	0C	0B	0A	09	08
'D'	'C'	'B'	'A'	31	32	33	34
17	16	15	14	13	12	11	10
		51	52		'G'	'F'	'E'
1F	1E	1D	1C	1B	1A	19	18
				61	62	63	64
				23	22	21	20

Byte address: 00, 08, 10, 18, 20

Figure 10.18   Example C Data Structure and Its Endian Maps

- Endianness does not affect the ordering of data items within a structure. Thus, the four-character word c exhibits byte reversal, but the seven-character byte array d does not. Hence, the address of each individual element of d is the same in both structures.

The effect of endianness is perhaps more clearly demonstrated when we view memory as a vertical array of bytes, as shown in Figure 10.19.

There is no general consensus as to which is the superior style of endianness.[3] The following points favor the big-endian style:

- **Character-string sorting:** A big-endian processor is faster in comparing integeraligned character strings; the integer ALU can compare multiple bytes in parallel.
- **Decimal/IRA dumps:** All values can be printed left to right without causing confusion.
- **Consistent order:** Big-endian processors store their integers and character strings in the same order (most significant byte comes first).

The following points favor the little-endian style:

- A big-endian processor has to perform addition when it converts a 32-bit integer address to a 16-bit integer address, to use the least significant bytes.

---

[3]The prophet revered by both groups in the Endian Wars of *Gulliver's Travels* had this to say. "All true Believers shall break their Eggs at the convenient End." Not much help!

	(a) Big endian		(b) Little endian
00	11	00	14
	12		13
	13		12
	14		11
04		04	
08	21	08	28
	22		27
	23		26
	24		25
0C	25	0C	24
	26		23
	27		22
	28		21
10	31	10	34
	32		33
	33		32
	34		31
14	'A'	14	'A'
	'B'		'B'
	'C'		'C'
	'D'		'D'
18	'E'	18	'E'
	'F'		'F'
	'G'		'G'
1C	51	1C	52
	52		51
20	61	20	64
	62		63
	63		62
	64		61

(a) Big endian   **(b) Little endian**

Figure 10.19 Another View of Figure 10.18

- It is easier to perform higher-precision arithmetic with the little-endian style; you don't have to find the least-significant byte and move backward.

The differences are minor and the choice of endian style is often more a matter of accommodating previous machines than anything else.

The PowerPC is a bi-endian processor that supports both big-endian and little-endian modes. The bi-endian architecture enables software developers to choose either mode when migrating operating systems and applications from other machines. The operating system establishes the endian mode in which processes execute. Once a mode is selected, all subsequent memory loads and stores are determined by the memory-addressing model of that mode. To support this hardware feature, 2 bits are maintained in the machine state register (MSR) maintained by the operating system as part of the process state. One bit specifies the endian mode in which the kernel runs; the other specifies the processor's current operating mode. Thus, mode can be changed on a per-process basis.

Bit Ordering

In ordering the bits within a byte, we are immediately faced with two questions:

1. Do you count the first bit as bit zero or as bit one?
2. Do you assign the lowest bit number to the byte's least significant bit (little endian) or to the bytes most significant bit (big endian)?

These questions are not answered in the same way on all machines. Indeed, on some machines, the answers are different in different circumstances. Furthermore, the choice of big- or little-endian bit ordering within a byte is not always consistent with big- or little-endian ordering of bytes within a multibyte scalar. The programmer needs to be concerned with these issues when manipulating individual bits.

Another area of concern is when data are transmitted over a bit-serial line. When an individual byte is transmitted, does the system transmit the most significant bit first or the least significant bit first? The designer must make certain that incoming bits are handled properly. For a discussion of this issue, see [JAME90].

CHAPTER 11

INSTRUCTION SETS: ADDRESSING MODES AND FORMATS

KEY POINTS

◆ An operand reference in an instruction either contains the actual value of the operand (immediate) or a reference to the address of the operand. A wide variety of addressing modes is used in various instruction sets. These include direct (operand address is in address field), indirect (address field points to a location that contains the operand address), register, register indirect, and various forms of displacement, in which a register value is added to an address value to produce the operand address.

◆ The instruction format defines the layout fields in the instruction. Instruction format design is a complex undertaking, including such considerations as instruction length, fixed or variable length, number of bits assigned to opcode and each operand reference, and how addressing mode is determined.

In Chapter 10, we focused on *what* an instruction set does. Specifically, we examined the types of operands and operations that may be specified by machine instructions. This chapter turns to the question of *how* to specify the operands and operations of instructions. Two issues arise. First, how is the address of an operand specified, and second, how are the bits of an instruction organized to define the operand addresses and operation of that instruction?

11.1 ADDRESSING

The address field or fields in a typical instruction format are relatively small. We would like to be able to reference a large range of locations in main memory or, for some systems, virtual memory. To achieve this objective, a variety of addressing techniques has been employed. They all involve some trade-off between address range and/or addressing flexibility, on the one hand, and the number of memory references and/or the complexity of address calculation, on the other. In this section, we examine the most common addressing techniques:

- Immediate
- Direct
- Indirect
- Register
- Register indirect
- Displacement
- Stack

These modes are illustrated in Figure 11.1. In this section, we use the following notation:

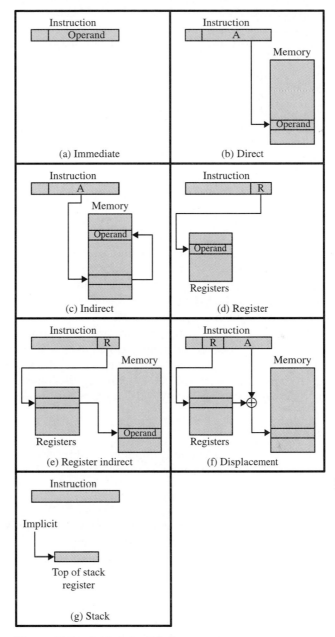

Figure 11.1 Addressing Modes

A = contents of an address field in the instruction
R = contents of an address field in the instruction that refers to a register
EA = actual (effective) address of the location containing the referenced operand
(X) = contents of memory location X or register X

Table 11.1 indicates the address calculation performed for each addressing mode.

Table 11.1   Basic Addressing Modes

Mode	Algorithm	Principal Advantage	Principal Disadvantage
Immediate	Operand = A	No memory reference	Limited operand magnitude
Direct	EA = A	Simple	Limited address space
Indirect	EA = (A)	Large address space	Multiple memory references
Register	EA = R	No memory reference	Limited address space
Register indirect	EA = (R)	Large address space	Extra memory reference
Displacement	EA = A + (R)	Flexibility	Complexity
Stack	EA = top of stack	No memory reference	Limited applicability

Before beginning this discussion, two comments need to be made. First, virtually all computer architectures provide more than one of these addressing modes. The question arises as to how the control unit can determine which address mode is being used in a particular instruction. Several approaches are taken. Often, different opcodes will use different addressing modes. Also, one or more bits in the instruction format can be used as a *mode field*. The value of the mode field determines which addressing mode is to be used.

The second comment concerns the interpretation of the effective address (EA). In a system without virtual memory, the *effective address* will be either a main memory address or a register. In a virtual memory system, the effective address is a virtual address or a register. The actual mapping to a physical address is a function of the paging mechanism and is invisible to the programmer.

Immediate Addressing

The simplest form of addressing is immediate addressing, in which the operand is actually present in the instruction:

$$OPERAND = A$$

This mode can be used to define and use constants or set initial values of variables. Typically, the number will be stored in twos complement form; the leftmost bit of the operand field is used as a sign bit. When the operand is loaded into a data register, the sign bit is extended to the left to the full data word size.

The advantage of immediate addressing is that no memory reference other than the instruction fetch is required to obtain the operand, thus saving one memory or cache cycle in the instruction cycle. The disadvantage is that the size of the number is restricted to the size of the address field, which, in most instruction sets, is small compared with the word length.

Direct Addressing

A very simple form of addressing is direct addressing, in which the address field contains the effective address of the operand:

$$EA = A$$

The technique was common in earlier generations of computers but is not common on contemporary architectures. It requires only one memory reference and no special calculation. The obvious limitation is that it provides only a limited address space.

Indirect Addressing

With direct addressing, the length of the address field is usually less than the word length, thus limiting the address range. One solution is to have the address field refer to the address of a word in memory, which in turn contains a full-length address of the operand. This is known as *indirect addressing:*

$$EA = (A)$$

As defined earlier, the parentheses are to be interpreted as meaning *contents of.* The obvious advantage of this approach is that for a word length of N, an address space of 2^N is now available. The disadvantage is that instruction execution requires two memory references to fetch the operand: one to get its address and a second to get its value.

Although the number of words that can be addressed is now equal to 2^N, the number of different effective addresses that may be referenced at any one time is limited to 2^K, where K is the length of the address field. Typically, this is not a burdensome restriction, and it can be an asset. In a virtual memory environment, all the effective address locations can be confined to page 0 of any process. Because the address field of an instruction is small, it will naturally produce low-numbered direct addresses, which would appear in page 0. (The only restriction is that the page size must be greater than or equal to 2^K.) When a process is active, there will be repeated references to page 0, causing it to remain in real memory. Thus, an indirect memory reference will involve, at most, one page fault rather than two.

A rarely used variant of indirect addressing is multilevel or cascaded indirect addressing:

$$EA = (\ldots (A) \ldots)$$

In this case, one bit of a full-word address is an indirect flag (I). If the I bit is 0, then the word contains the EA. If the I bit is 1, then another level of indirection is invoked. There does not appear to be any particular advantage to this approach, and its disadvantage is that three or more memory references could be required to fetch an operand.

Register Addressing

Register addressing is similar to direct addressing. The only difference is that the address field refers to a register rather than a main memory address:

$$EA = R$$

Typically, an address field that references registers will have from 3 to 5 bits, so that a total of from 8 to 32 general-purpose registers can be referenced.

The advantages of register addressing are that (1) only a small address field is needed in the instruction, and (2) no memory references are required. As was discussed in Chapter 4, the memory access time for a register internal to the CPU is much less than that for a main memory address. The disadvantage of register addressing is that the address space is very limited.

If register addressing is heavily used in an instruction set, this implies that the CPU registers will be heavily used. Because of the severely limited number of registers (compared with main memory locations), their use in this fashion makes sense only if they are employed efficiently. If every operand is brought into a register from main memory, operated on once, and then returned to main memory, then a wasteful intermediate step has been added. If, instead, the operand in a register remains in use for multiple operations, then a real savings is achieved. An example is the intermediate result in a calculation. In particular, suppose that the algorithm for twos complement multiplication were to be implemented in software. The location labeled A in the flowchart (Figure 9.12) is referenced many times and should be implemented in a register rather than a main memory location.

It is up to the programmer to decide which values should remain in registers and which should be stored in main memory. Most modern CPUs employ multiple general-purpose registers, placing a burden for efficient execution on the assembly-language programmer (e.g., compiler writer).

Register Indirect Addressing

Just as register addressing is analogous to direct addressing, register indirect addressing is analogous to indirect addressing. In both cases, the only difference is whether the address field refers to a memory location or a register. Thus, for register indirect address,

$$EA = (R)$$

The advantages and limitations of register indirect addressing are basically the same as for indirect addressing. In both cases, the address space limitation (limited range of addresses) of the address field is overcome by having that field refer to a word-length location containing an address. In addition, register indirect addressing uses one less memory reference than indirect addressing.

Displacement Addressing

A very powerful mode of addressing combines the capabilities of direct addressing and register indirect addressing. It is known by a variety of names depending on the context of its use, but the basic mechanism is the same. We will refer to this as *displacement addressing*:

$$EA = A + (R)$$

Displacement addressing requires that the instruction have two address fields, at least one of which is explicit. The value contained in one address field (value = A) is used directly. The other address field, or an implicit reference based on opcode, refers to a register whose contents are added to A to produce the effective address.

We will describe three of the most common uses of displacement addressing:

- Relative addressing
- Base-register addressing
- Indexing

Relative Addressing

For relative addressing, the implicitly referenced register is the program counter (PC). That is, the current instruction address is added to the address field to produce the EA. Typically, the address field is treated as a twos complement number for this operation. Thus, the effective address is a displacement relative to the address of the instruction.

Relative addressing exploits the concept of locality that was discussed in Chapters 4 and 8. If most memory references are relatively near to the instruction being executed, then the use of relative addressing saves address bits in the instruction.

Base-Register Addressing

For base-register addressing, the interpretation is the following: The referenced register contains a memory address, and the address field contains a displacement (usually an unsigned integer representation) from that address. The register reference may be explicit or implicit.

Base-register addressing also exploits the locality of memory references. It is a convenient means of implementing segmentation, which was discussed in Chapter 8. In some implementations, a single segment-base register is employed and is used implicitly. In others, the programmer may choose a register to hold the base address of a segment, and the instruction must reference it explicitly. In this latter case, if the length of the address field is K and the number of possible registers is N, then one instruction can reference any one of N areas of 2^K words.

Indexing

For indexing, the interpretation is typically the following: The address field references a main memory address, and the referenced register contains a positive displacement from that address. Note that this usage is just the opposite of the interpretation for base-register addressing. Of course, it is more than just a matter of user interpretation. Because the address field is considered to be a memory address in indexing, it generally contains more bits than an address field in a comparable base-register instruction. Also, we shall see that there are some refinements to indexing that would not be as useful in the base-register context. Nevertheless, the method of calculating the EA is the same for both base-register addressing and indexing, and in both cases the register reference is sometimes explicit and sometimes implicit (for different CPU types).

An important use of indexing is to provide an efficient mechanism for performing iterative operations. Consider, for example, a list of numbers stored starting at location A. Suppose that we would like to add 1 to each element on the list. We need to fetch each value, add 1 to it, and store it back. The sequence of effective addresses that we need is A, A + 1, A + 2, . . . , up to the last location on the list. With indexing, this is easily done. The value A is stored in the instruction's address field, and the chosen register, called an *index register,* is initialized to 0. After each operation, the index register is incremented by 1.

Because index registers are commonly used for such iterative tasks, it is typical that there is a need to increment or decrement the index register after each reference to it. Because this is such a common operation, some systems will automatically do this as part of the same instruction cycle. This is known as *autoindexing.* If certain registers are devoted exclusively to indexing, then autoindexing can be invoked implicitly and automatically. If general-purpose registers are used, the autoindex operation may need to be signaled by a bit in the instruction. Autoindexing using increment can be depicted as follows:

$$EA = A + (R)$$
$$(R) \leftarrow (R) + 1$$

In some machines, both indirect addressing and indexing are provided, and it is possible to employ both in the same instruction. There are two possibilities: The indexing is performed either before or after the indirection.

If indexing is performed after the indirection, it is termed *postindexing:*

$$EA = (A) + (R)$$

First, the contents of the address field are used to access a memory location containing a direct address. This address is then indexed by the register value. This technique is useful for accessing one of a number of blocks of data of a fixed format. For example, it was described in Chapter 8 that the operating system needs to employ a process control block for each process. The operations performed are the same regardless of which block is being manipulated. Thus, the addresses in the instructions that reference the block could point to a location (value = A) containing a variable pointer to the start of a process control block. The index register contains the displacement within the block.

With *preindexing,* the indexing is performed before the indirection:

$$EA = (A + (R))$$

An address is calculated as with simple indexing. In this case, however, the calculated address contains not the operand, but the address of the operand. An example of the use of this technique is to construct a multiway branch table. At a particular point in a program, there may be a branch to one of a number of locations depending on conditions. A table of addresses can be set up starting at location A. By indexing into this table, the required location can be found.

Typically, an instruction set will not include both preindexing and postindexing.

Stack Addressing

The final addressing mode that we consider is stack addressing. As defined in Appendix 9A, a stack is a linear array of locations. It is sometimes referred to as a *pushdown list* or *last-in-first-out queue.* The stack is a reserved block of locations. Items are appended to the top of the stack so that, at any given time, the block is partially filled. Associated with the stack is a pointer whose value is the address of the top of the stack. Alternatively, the top two elements of the stack may be in CPU registers, in which case the stack pointer references the third element of the stack (Figure 10.14b). The stack pointer is maintained in a register. Thus, references to stack locations in memory are in fact register indirect addresses.

The stack mode of addressing is a form of implied addressing. The machine instructions need not include a memory reference but implicitly operate on the top of the stack.

11.2 PENTIUM AND POWERPC ADDRESSING MODES

Pentium Addressing Modes

Recall from Figure 8.21 that the Pentium address translation mechanism produces an address, called a virtual or effective address, that is an offset into a segment. The sum of the starting address of the segment and the effective address produces a linear address. If paging is being used, this linear address must pass through a page-translation mechanism to produce a physical address. In what follows, we ignore this last step, because it is transparent to the instruction set and to the programmer.

The Pentium is equipped with a variety of addressing modes intended to allow the efficient execution of high-level languages. Figure 11.2 indicates the logic involved. The segment register determines the segment that is the subject of the reference. There are six segment registers; the one being used for a particular reference depends on the context of execution and the instruction. Each segment register holds the starting address of the corresponding segment. Associated with each user-visible segment register is a segment descriptor register (not programmer visible), which records the access rights for the segment as well as the starting address and limit (length) of the segment. In addition, there are two registers that may be used in constructing an address: the base register and the index register.

Table 11.2 lists the 12 Pentium addressing modes. Let us consider each of these in turn.

For the **immediate mode**, the operand is included in the instruction. The operand can be a byte, word, or doubleword of data.

For **register operand mode**, the operand is located in a register. For general instructions, such as data transfer, arithmetic, and logical instructions, the operand can be one of the 32-bit general registers (EAX, EBX, ECX, EDX, ESI, EDI, ESP, EBP), one of the 16-bit general registers (AX, BX, CX, DX, SI, DI, SP, BP), or one of the 8-bit general registers (AH, BH, CH, DH, AL, BL, CL, DL). For floating-point operations, 64-bit operands are formed by using two 32-bit registers as a pair. There are also some instructions that reference the segment registers (CS, DS, ES, SS, FS, GS).

The remaining addressing modes reference locations in memory. The memory location must be specified in terms of the segment containing the location and the offset from the beginning of the segment. In some cases, a segment is specified explicitly; in others, the segment is specified by simple rules that assign a segment by default.

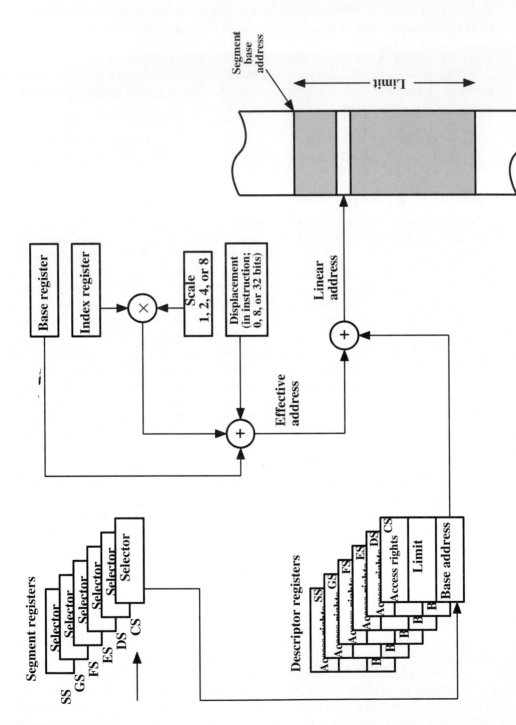

Figure 11.2 Pentium Addressing Mode Calculation

Table 11.2 Pentium II Addressing Modes

Mode	Algorithm
Immediate	Operand = A
Register operand	LA = R
Displacement	LA = (SR) + A
Base	LA = (SR) + (B)
Base with displacement	LA = (SR) + (B) + A
Scaled index with displacement	LA = (SR) + (I) × S + A
Base with index and displacement	LA = (SR) + (B) + (I) + A
Base with scaled index and displacement	LA = (SR) + (I) × S + (B) + A
Relative	LA = (PC) + A

LA = linear address
(X) = contents of X
SR = segment register
PC = program counter
A = contents of an address field in the instruction
R = register
B = base register
I = index register
S = scaling factor

In the **displacement mode**, the operand's offset (the effective address of Figure 11.2) is contained as part of the instruction as an 8-, 16-, or 32-bit displacement. With segmentation, all addresses in instructions refer merely to an offset in a segment. The displacement addressing mode is found on few machines because, as mentioned earlier, it leads to long instructions. In the case of the Pentium, the displacement value can be as long as 32 bits, making for a 6-byte instruction. Displacement addressing can be useful for referencing global variables.

The remaining addressing modes are indirect, in the sense that the address portion of the instruction tells the processor where to look to find the address. The **base mode** specifies that one of the 8-, 16-, or 32-bit registers contains the effective address. This is equivalent to what we have referred to as register indirect addressing.

In the **base with displacement mode**, the instruction includes a displacement to be added to a base register, which may be any of the general-purpose registers. Examples of uses of this mode include the following:

- Used by a compiler to point to the start of a local variable area. For example, the base register could point to the beginning of a stack frame, which contains the local variables for the corresponding procedure.

- Used to index into an array when the element size is not 1, 2, 4, or 8 bytes and which therefore cannot be indexed using an index register. In this case, the displacement points to the beginning of the array, and the base register holds the results of a calculation to determine the offset to a specific element within the array.

- Used to access a field of a record. The base register points to the beginning of the record, while the displacement is an offset to the field.

In the **scaled index with displacement mode**, the instruction includes a displacement to be added to a register, in this case called an index register. The index register may be any of the general-purpose registers except the one called ESP, which is generally used for stack processing. In calculating the effective address, the contents of the index register are multiplied by a scaling factor of 1, 2, 4, or 8, and then added to a displacement. This mode is very convenient for indexing arrays. A scaling factor of 2 can be used for an array of 16-bit integers. A scaling factor of 4 can be used for 32-bit integers or floating-point numbers. Finally, a scaling factor of 8 can be used for an array of double-precision floating-point numbers.

The **base with index and displacement mode** sums the contents of the base register, the index register, and a displacement to form the effective address. Again, the base register can be any general-purpose register and the index register can be any general-purpose register except ESP. As an example, this addressing mode could be used for accessing a local array on a stack frame. This mode can also be used to support a two-dimensional array; in this case, the displacement points to the beginning of the array, and each register handles one dimension of the array.

The **based scaled index with displacement mode** sums the contents of the index register multiplied by a scaling factor, the contents of the base register, and the displacement. This is useful if an array is stored in a stack frame; in this case, the array elements would be 2, 4, or 8 bytes each in length. This mode also provides efficient indexing of a two-dimensional array when the array elements are 2, 4, or 8 bytes in length.

Finally, **relative addressing** can be used in transfer-of-control instructions. A displacement is added to the value of the program counter, which points to the next instruction. In this case, the displacement is treated as a signed byte, word, or doubleword value, and that value either increases or decreases the address in the program counter.

PowerPC Addressing Modes

In common with most RISC machines, and unlike the Pentium and most CISC machines, the PowerPC uses a simple and relatively straightforward set of addressing modes. As Table 11.3 indicates, these modes are conveniently classified with respect to the type of instruction.

Load/Store Architecture

The PowerPC provides two alternative addressing modes for load/store instructions (Figure 11.3). With indirect addressing, the instruction includes a 16-bit displacement to be added to a base register, which may be any of the general-purpose registers. In addition, the instruction may specify that the newly computed effective address is to be fed back to the base register, updating the current contents. The update option is useful for progressive indexing of arrays in loops.

The other addressing technique for load/store instructions is **indirect indexed addressing**. In this case, the instruction references a base register and an index register, both of which may be any of the general-purpose registers. The effective

Table 11.3 PowerPC Addressing Modes

Mode	Algorithm
Load/Store Addressing	
Indirect	EA = (BR) + D
Indirect indexed	EA = (BR) + (IR)
Branch Addressing	
Absolute	EA = I
Relative	EA = (PC) + I
Indirect	EA = (L/CR)
Fixed-Point Computation	
Register	EA = GPR
Immediate	Operand = I
Floating-Point Computation	
Register	EA = FPR

EA   = effective address
(X)   = contents of X
BR   = base register
IR   = index register
L/CR = link or count register
GPR = general-purpose register
FPR = floating-point register
D   = displacement
I   = immediate value
PC   = program counter

address is the sum of the contents of these two registers. Again, the update option causes the base register to be updated to the new effective address.

Branch Addressing

Three branch addressing modes are provided. When **absolute addressing** is used with unconditional branch instructions, the effective address of the next instruction is derived from a 24-bit immediate value within the instruction. The 24-bit value is extended to a 32-bit value by adding two zeros to its least significant end (this is permissible because all instructions must occur on 32-bit boundaries) and sign extending. For conditional branch instructions, the effective address of the next instruction is derived from a 16-bit immediate value within the instruction. The 16-bit value is extended to a 32-bit value by adding two zeros to its least significant end and sign extending.

With **relative addressing**, the 24-bit immediate value (unconditional branch instructions) or 14-bit immediate value (conditional branch instructions) is extended as before. The resulting value is then added to the program counter to define a location relative to the current instruction. The other conditional branch addressing mode is **indirect addressing**. This mode obtains the effective address of the next instruction from either the link register or the count register. Note that in this case

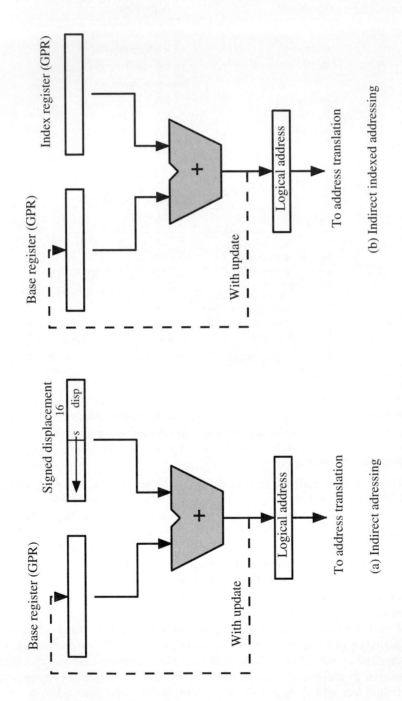

Figure 11.3 PowerPC Memory Operand Addressing Modes

(a) Indirect adressing

(b) Indirect indexed addressing

the count register is used to hold the address for a branch instruction. This register may also be used to hold a count for looping, as explained earlier.

Arithmetic Instructions

For integer arithmetic, all operands must be contained either in registers or as part of the instruction. With register addressing, a source or destination operand is specified as one of the general-purpose registers. With immediate addressing, a source operand appears as a 16-bit signed quantity in the instruction.

For floating-point arithmetic, all operands are in floating-point registers; that is, only register addressing is used.

11.3 INSTRUCTION FORMATS

An instruction format defines the layout of the bits of an instruction, in terms of its constituent parts. An instruction format must include an opcode and, implicitly or explicitly, zero or more operands. Each explicit operand is referenced using one of the addressing modes described in Section 11.1. The format must, implicitly or explicitly, indicate the addressing mode for each operand. For most instruction sets, more than one instruction format is used.

The design of an instruction format is a complex art, and an amazing variety of designs have been implemented. We examine the key design issues, looking briefly at some designs to illustrate points, and then we examine the Pentium and PowerPC solutions in detail.

Instruction Length

The most basic design issue to be faced is the instruction format length. This decision affects, and is affected by, memory size, memory organization, bus structure, CPU complexity, and CPU speed. This decision determines the richness and flexibility of the machine as seen by the assembly-language programmer.

The most obvious trade-off here is between the desire for a powerful instruction repertoire and a need to save space. Programmers want more opcodes, more operands, more addressing modes, and greater address range. More opcodes and more operands make life easier for the programmer, because shorter programs can be written to accomplish given tasks. Similarly, more addressing modes give the programmer greater flexibility in implementing certain functions, such as table manipulations and multiple-way branching. And, of course, with the increase in main memory size and the increasing use of virtual memory, programmers want to be able to address larger memory ranges. All of these things (opcodes, operands, addressing modes, address range) require bits and push in the direction of longer instruction lengths. But longer instruction length may be wasteful. A 64-bit instruction occupies twice the space of a 32-bit instruction but is probably less than twice as useful.

Beyond this basic trade-off, there are other considerations. Either the instruction length should be equal to the memory-transfer length (in a bus system, data-bus length) or one should be a multiple of the other. Otherwise, we will not get an integral number of instructions during a fetch cycle. A related consideration is the memory transfer rate. This rate has not kept up with increases in processor speed. Accordingly, memory can become a bottleneck if the processor can execute instructions faster than it can fetch them. One solution to this problem is to use cache memory (see Section 4.3); another is to use shorter instructions. Thus, 16-bit instructions can be fetched at twice the rate of 32-bit instructions but probably can be executed less than twice as fast.

A seemingly mundane but nevertheless important feature is that the instruction length should be a multiple of the character length, which is usually 8 bits, and of the length of fixed-point numbers. To see this, we need to make use of that unfortunately ill-defined word, *word* [FRAI83]. The word length of memory is, in some sense, the "natural" unit of organization. The size of a word usually determines the size of fixed-point numbers (usually the two are equal). Word size is also typically equal to, or at least integrally related to, the memory transfer size. Because a common form of data is character data, we would like a word to store an integral number of characters. Otherwise, there are wasted bits in each word when storing multiple characters, or a character will have to straddle a word boundary. The importance of this point is such that IBM, when it introduced the System/360 and wanted to employ 8-bit characters, made the wrenching decision to move from the 36-bit architecture of the scientific members of the 700/7000 series to a 32-bit architecture.

Allocation of Bits

We've looked at some of the factors that go into deciding the length of the instruction format. An equally difficult issue is how to allocate the bits in that format. The trade-offs here are complex.

For a given instruction length, there is clearly a trade-off between the number of opcodes and the power of the addressing capability. More opcodes obviously mean more bits in the opcode field. For an instruction format of a given length, this reduces the number of bits available for addressing. There is one interesting refinement to this trade-off, and that is the use of variable-length opcodes. In this approach, there is a minimum opcode length but, for some opcodes, additional operations may be specified by using additional bits in the instruction. For a fixed-length instruction, this leaves fewer bits for addressing. Thus, this feature is used for those instructions that require fewer operands and/or less powerful addressing.

The following interrelated factors go into determining the use of the addressing bits:

- **Number of addressing modes:** Sometimes an addressing mode can be indicated implicitly. For example, certain opcodes might always call for indexing. In other cases, the addressing modes must be explicit, and one or more mode bits will be needed.
- **Number of operands:** We have seen that fewer addresses can make for longer, more awkward programs (e.g., Figure 10.3). Typical instructions on today's machines provide for two operands. Each operand address in the instruction might require its own mode indicator, or the use of a mode indicator could be limited to just one of the address fields.

- **Register versus memory:** A machine must have registers so that data can be brought into the CPU for processing. With a single user-visible register (usually called the accumulator), one operand address is implicit and consumes no instruction bits. However, single-register programming is awkward and requires many instructions. Even with multiple registers, only a few bits are needed to specify the register. The more that registers can be used for operand references, the fewer bits are needed. A number of studies indicate that a total of 8 to 32 user-visible registers is desirable [LUND77, HUCK83]. Most contemporary architectures have at least 32 registers.

- **Number of register sets:** Most contemporary machines have one set of general-purpose registers, with typically 32 or more registers in the set. These registers can be used to store data and can be used to store addresses for displacement addressing. Some architectures, including that of the Pentium, have a collection of two or more specialized sets (such as data and displacement). One advantage of this latter approach is that, for a fixed number of registers, a functional split requires fewer bits to be used in the instruction. For example, with two sets of eight registers, only 3 bits are required to identify a register; the opcode implicitly will determine which set of registers is being referenced.

- **Address range:** For addresses that reference memory, the range of addresses that can be referenced is related to the number of address bits. Because this imposes a severe limitation, direct addressing is rarely used. With displacement addressing, the range is opened up to the length of the address register. Even so, it is still convenient to allow rather large displacements from the register address, which requires a relatively large number of address bits in the instruction.

- **Address granularity:** For addresses that reference memory rather than registers, another factor is the granularity of addressing. In a system with 16- or 32-bit words, an address can reference a word or a byte at the designer's choice. Byte addressing is convenient for character manipulation but requires, for a fixed-size memory, more address bits.

Thus, the designer is faced with a host of factors to consider and balance. How critical the various choices are is not clear. As an example, we cite one study [CRAG79] that compared various instruction format approaches, including the use of a stack, general-purpose registers, an accumulator, and only memory-to-register approaches. Using a consistent set of assumptions, no significant difference in code space or execution time was observed.

Let us briefly look at how two historical machine designs balance these various factors.

PDP-8

One of the simplest instruction designs for a general-purpose computer was for the PDP-8 [BELL78b]. The PDP-8 uses 12-bit instructions and operates on 12-bit words. There is a single general-purpose register, the accumulator.

Despite the limitations of this design, the addressing is quite flexible. Each memory reference consists of 7 bits plus two 1-bit modifiers. The memory is divided into fixed-length pages of $2^7 = 128$ words each. Address calculation is based on

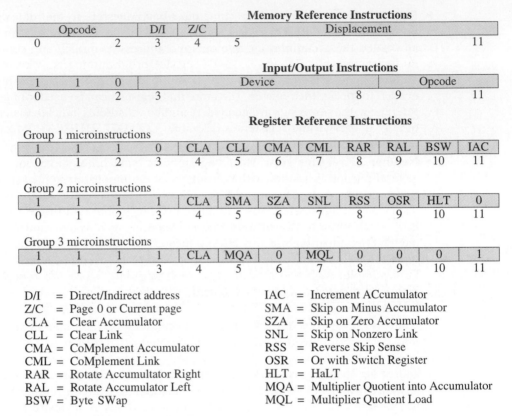

Figure 11.4 PDP-8 Instruction Formats

references to page 0 or the current page (page containing this instruction) as determined by the page bit. The second modifier bit indicates whether direct or indirect addressing is to be used. These two modes can be used in combination, so that an indirect address is a 12-bit address contained in a word of page 0 or the current page. In addition, 8 dedicated words on page 0 are autoindex "registers." When an indirect reference is made to one of these locations, preindexing occurs.

Figure 11.4 shows the PDP-8 instruction format. There are a 3-bit opcode and three types of instructions. For opcodes 0 through 5, the format is a single-address memory reference instruction including a page bit and an indirect bit. Thus, there are only six basic operations. To enlarge the group of operations, opcode 7 defines a register reference or *microinstruction*. In this format, the remaining bits are used to encode additional operations. In general, each bit defines a specific operation (e.g., clear accumulator), and these bits can be combined in a single instruction. The microinstruction strategy was used as far back as the PDP-1 by DEC and is, in a sense, a forerunner of today's microprogrammed machines, to be discussed in Part Four. Opcode 6 is the I/O operation; 6 bits are used to select one of 64 devices, and 3 bits specify a particular I/O command.

The PDP-8 instruction format is remarkably efficient. It supports indirect addressing, displacement addressing, and indexing. With the use of the opcode extension, it supports a total of approximately 35 instructions. Given the constraints of a 12-bit instruction length, the designers could hardly have done better.

PDP-10

A sharp contrast to the instruction set of the PDP-8 is that of the PDP-10. The PDP-10 was designed to be a large-scale time-shared system, with an emphasis on making the system easy to program, even if additional hardware expense was involved.

Among the design principles that were employed in designing the instruction set were [BELL78c].

- **Orthogonality:** Orthogonality is a principle by which two variables are independent of each other. In the context of an instruction set, the term indicates that other elements of an instruction are independent of (not determined by) the opcode. The PDP-10 designers use the term to describe the fact that an address is always computed in the same way, independent of the opcode. This is in contrast to many machines, where the address mode sometimes depends implicitly on the operator being used.
- **Completeness:** Each arithmetic data type (integer, fixed-point, real) should have a complete and identical set of operations.
- **Direct addressing:** Base plus displacement addressing, which places a memory organization burden on the programmer, was avoided in favor of direct addressing.

Each of these principles advances the main goal of ease of programming.

The PDP-10 has a 36-bit word length and a 36-bit instruction length. The fixed instruction format is shown in Figure 11.5. The opcode occupies 9 bits, allowing up to 512 operations. In fact, a total of 365 different instructions are defined. Most instructions have two addresses, one of which is one of 16 general-purpose registers. Thus, this operand reference occupies 4 bits. The other operand reference starts with an 18-bit memory address field. This can be used as an immediate operand or a memory address. In the latter usage, both indexing and indirect addressing are allowed. The same general-purpose registers are also used as index registers.

A 36-bit instruction length is true luxury. There is no need to do clever things to get more opcodes; a 9-bit opcode field is more than adequate. Addressing is also straightforward. An 18-bit address field makes direct addressing desirable. For memory sizes greater than 2^{18}, indirection is provided. For the ease of the pro-

Opcode	Register	I	Index register	Memory address
0 8	9 12	14	17 18	35

I = indirect bit

Figure 11.5 PDP-10 Instruction Format

grammer, indexing is provided for table manipulation and iterative programs. Also, with an 18-bit operand field, immediate addressing becomes attractive.

The PDP-10 instruction set design does accomplish the objectives listed earlier [LUND77]. The PDP-10 instruction set eases the task of the programmer or compiler at the expense of an inefficient utilization of space. This was a conscious choice made by the designers and therefore cannot be faulted as poor design.

Variable-Length Instructions

The examples we have looked at so far have used a single fixed instruction length, and we have implicitly discussed trade-offs in that context. But the designer may choose instead to provide a variety of instruction formats of different lengths. This tactic makes it easy to provide a large repertoire of opcodes, with different opcode lengths. Addressing can be more flexible, with various combinations of register and memory references plus addressing modes. With variable-length instructions, these many variations can be provided efficiently and compactly.

The principal price to pay for variable-length instructions is an increase in the complexity of the CPU. Falling hardware prices, the use of microprogramming (discussed in Part Four), and a general increase in understanding the principles of CPU design have all contributed to making this a small price to pay. However, we will see that RISC and superscalar machines can exploit the use of fixed-length instructions to provide improved performance.

The use of variable-length instructions does not remove the desirability of making all of the instruction lengths integrally related to the word length. Because the CPU does not know the length of the next instruction to be fetched, a typical strategy is to fetch a number of bytes or words equal to at least the longest possible instruction. This means that sometimes multiple instructions are fetched. However, as we shall see in Chapter 12, this is a good strategy to follow in any case.

PDP-11

The PDP-11 was designed to provide a powerful and flexible instruction set within the constraints of a 16-bit minicomputer [BELL70].

The PDP-11 employs a set of eight 16-bit general-purpose registers. Two of these registers have additional significance: One is used as a stack pointer for special-purpose stack operations, and one is used as the program counter, which contains the address of the next instruction.

Figure 11.6 shows the PDP-11 instruction formats. Thirteen different formats are used, encompassing zero-, one-, and two-address instruction types. The opcode can vary from 4 to 16 bits in length. Register references are 6 bits in length. Three bits identify the register, and the remaining 3 bits identify the addressing mode. The PDP-11 is endowed with a rich set of addressing modes. One advantage of linking the addressing mode to the operand rather than the opcode, as is sometimes done, is that any addressing mode can be used with any opcode. As was mentioned, this independence is referred to as *orthogonality*.

PDP-11 instructions are usually one word (16 bits) long. For some instructions, one or two memory addresses are appended, so that 32-bit and 48-bit instructions are part of the repertoire. This provides for further flexibility in addressing.

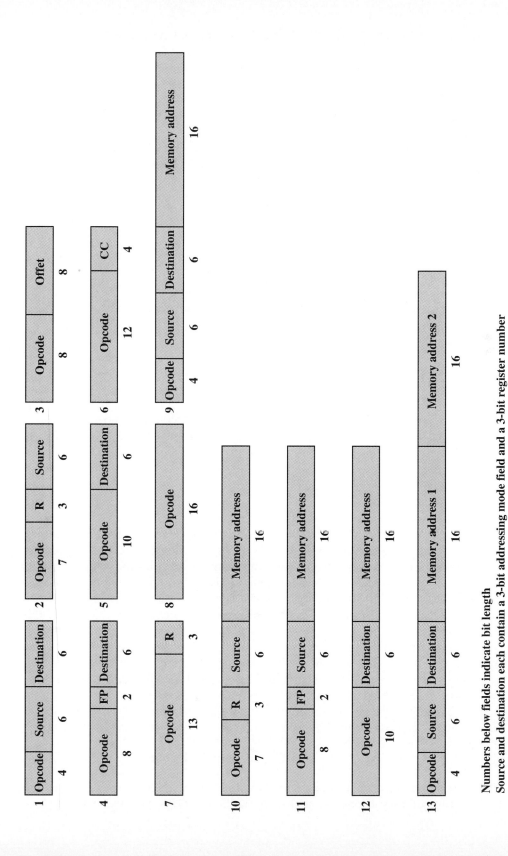

Figure 11.6 Instruction Formats for the PDP-11

Numbers below fields indicate bit length
Source and destination each contain a 3-bit addressing mode field and a 3-bit register number
FP indicates one of four floating-point registers
R indicates one of the general-purpose registers
CC is the condition code field

401

The PDP-11 instruction set and addressing capability are complex. This increases both hardware cost and programming complexity. The advantage is that more efficient or compact programs can be developed.

VAX

Most architectures provide a relatively small number of fixed instruction formats. This can cause two problems for the programmer. First, addressing mode and opcode are not orthogonal. For example, for a given operation, one operand must come from a register and another from memory, or both from registers, and so on. Second, only a limited number of operands can be accommodated: typically up to two or three. Because some operations inherently require more operands, various strategies must be used to achieve the desired result using two or more instructions.

To avoid these problems, two criteria were used in designing the VAX instruction format [STRE78]:

1. All instructions should have the "natural" number of operands.
2. All operands should have the same generality in specification.

The result is a highly variable instruction format. An instruction consists of a 1- or 2-byte opcode followed by from zero to six operand specifiers, depending on the opcode. The minimal instruction length is 1 byte, and instructions up to 37 bytes can be constructed. Figure 11.7 gives a few examples.

The VAX instruction begins with a 1-byte opcode. This suffices to handle most VAX instructions. However, as there are over 300 different instructions, 8 bits are not enough. The hexadecimal codes FD and FF indicate an extended opcode, with the actual opcode being specified in the second byte.

The remainder of the instruction consists of up to six operand specifiers. An operand specifier is, at minimum, a 1-byte format in which the leftmost 4 bits are the address mode specifier. The only exception to this rule is the literal mode, which is signaled by the pattern 00 in the leftmost 2 bits, leaving space for a 6-bit literal. Because of this exception, a total of 12 different addressing modes can be specified.

An operand specifier often consists of just one byte, with the rightmost 4 bits specifying one of 16 general-purpose registers. The length of the operand specifier can be extended in one of two ways. First, a constant value of one or more bytes may immediately follow the first byte of the operand specifier. An example of this is the displacement mode, in which an 8-, 16-, or 32-bit displacement is used. Second, an index mode of addressing may be used. In this case, the first byte of the operand specifier consists of the 4-bit addressing mode code of 0100 and a 4-bit index register identifier. The remainder of the operand specifier consists of the base address specifier, which may itself be one or more bytes in length.

The reader may be wondering, as the author did, what kind of instruction requires six operands. Surprisingly, the VAX has a number of such instructions. Consider

ADDP6 OP1, OP2, OP3, OP4, OP5, OP6

This instruction adds two packed decimal numbers. OP1 and OP2 specify the length and starting address of one decimal string; OP3 and OP4 specify a second string.

Hexadecimal Format	Explanation	Assembler Notation and Description

Figure 11.7 Example of VAX Instructions

These two strings are added and the result is stored in the decimal string whose length and starting location are specified by OP5 and OP6.

The VAX instruction set provides for a wide variety of operations and addressing modes. This gives a programmer, such as a compiler writer, a very powerful and flexible tool for developing programs. In theory, this should lead to efficient machine-language compilations of high-level language programs and, in general, to effective and efficient use of CPU resources. The penalty to be paid for these benefits is the increased complexity of the CPU compared with a processor with a simpler instruction set and format.

We return to these matters in Chapter 13, where we examine the case for very simple instruction sets.

11.4 PENTIUM AND POWERPC INSTRUCTION FORMATS

Pentium Instruction Formats

The Pentium is equipped with a variety of instruction formats. Of the elements described in this subsection, only the opcode field is always present. Figure 11.8 illustrates the general instruction format. Instructions are made up of from zero to four optional instruction prefixes, a 1- or 2-byte opcode, an optional address specifier (which consists of the ModR/m byte and the Scale Index byte), an optional displacement, and an optional immediate field.

Let us first consider the prefix bytes:

- **Instruction prefixes:** The instruction prefix, if present, consists of the LOCK prefix or one of the repeat prefixes. The LOCK prefix is used to ensure exclusive use of shared memory in multiprocessor environments. The repeat prefixes specify repeated operation of a string, which enables the Pentium to process strings much faster than with a regular software loop. There are five different repeat prefixes: REP, REPE, REPZ, REPNE, and REPNZ. When the absolute REP prefix is present, the operation specified in the instruction is executed repeatedly on successive elements of the string; the number of repetitions is specified in register CX. The conditional REP prefix causes the instruction to repeat until the count in CX goes to zero or until the condition is met.

- **Segment override:** Explicitly specifies which segment register an instruction should use, overriding the default segment-register selection generated by the Pentium for that instruction.

- **Address size:** The processor can address memory using either 16- or 32-bit addresses. The address size determines the displacement size in instructions and the size of address offsets generated during effective address calculation. One of these sizes is designated as default, and the address size prefix switches between 32-bit and 16-bit address generation.

- **Operand size:** An instruction has a default operand size of 16 or 32 bits, and the operand prefix switches between 32-bit and 16-bit operands.

The instruction itself includes the following fields:

- **Opcode:** One- or two-byte opcode. The opcode may also include bits that specify if data are byte- or full-size (16 or 32 bits depending on context), direction of data operation (to or from memory), and whether an immediate data field must be sign extended.

- **ModR/m:** This byte, and the next, provide addressing information. The ModR/m byte specifies whether an operand is in a register or in memory; if it is in

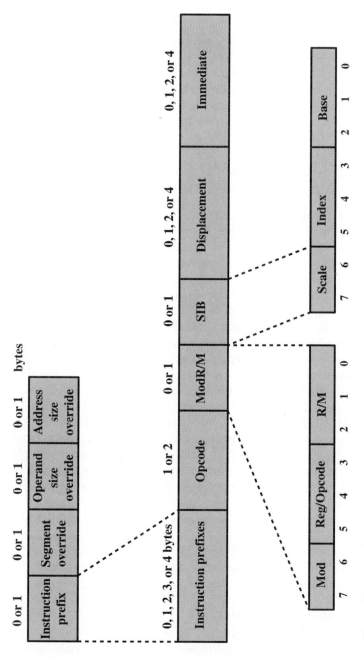

Figure 11.8 Pentium Instruction Format

405

memory, then fields within the byte specify the addressing mode to be used. The ModR/m byte consists of three fields: The Mod field (2 bits) combines with the r/m field to form 32 possible values: 8 registers and 24 indexing modes; the Reg/Opcode field (3 bits) specifies either a register number or three more bits of opcode information; the r/m field (3 bits) can specify a register as the location of an operand, or it can form part of the addressing-mode encoding in combination with the Mod field.

- **SIB:** Certain encoding of the ModR/m byte specifies the inclusion of the SIB byte to specify fully the addressing mode. The SIB byte consists of three fields: The Scale field (2 bits) specifies the scale factor for scaled indexing; the Index field (3 bits) specifies the index register; the Base field (3 bits) specifies the base register.
- **Displacement:** When the addressing-mode specifier indicates that a displacement is used, an 8-, 16-, or 32-bit signed integer displacement field is added.
- **Immediate:** Provides the value of an 8-, 16-, or 32-bit operand.

Several comparisons may be useful here. In the Pentium format, the addressing mode is provided as part of the opcode sequence rather than with each operand. Because only one operand can have address-mode information, only one memory operand can be referenced in an instruction. In contrast, the VAX carries the address-mode information with each operand, allowing memory-to-memory operations. The Pentium instructions are therefore more compact. However, if a memory-to-memory operation is required, the VAX can accomplish this in a single instruction.

The Pentium format allows the use of not only 1-byte, but also 2-byte and 4-byte offsets for indexing. Although the use of the larger index offsets results in longer instructions, this feature provides needed flexibility. For example, it is useful in addressing large arrays or large stack frames. In contrast, the IBM S/370 instruction format allows offsets no greater than 4K bytes (12 bits of offset information), and the offset must be positive. When a location is not in reach of this offset, the compiler must generate extra code to generate the needed address. This problem is especially apparent in dealing with stack frames that have local variables occupying in excess of 4K bytes. As [DEWA90] puts it, "generating code for the 370 is so painful as a result of that restriction that there have even been compilers for the 370 that simply chose to limit the size of the stack frame to 4K bytes."

As can be seen, the encoding of the Pentium instruction set is very complex. This has to do partly with the need to be backward compatible with the 8086 machine and partly with a desire on the part of the designers to provide every possible assistance to the compiler writer in producing efficient code. It is a matter of some debate whether an instruction set as complex as this is preferable to the opposite extreme of the RISC instruction sets.

PowerPC Instruction Formats

All instructions in the PowerPC are 32 bits long and follow a regular format. The first 6 bits of an instruction specify the operation to be performed. In some cases, there is an extension to the opcode elsewhere in the instruction that specifies a particular subcase of an operation. In Figure 11.9, opcode bits are represented by the shaded portion of each format.

← 6 Bits →	← 5 Bits →	← 5 Bits →	← 16 Bits →		
Branch	Long immediate			A	L
Br Conditional	Options	CR bit	Branch displacement	A	L
Br Conditional	Options	CR bit	Indirect through Link or Count Register		L

(a) Branch instructions

CR	Dest bit	Source bit	Source bit	Add, or, Xor, etc.	/

(b) Condition register logical instructions

Ld / st Indirect	Dest register	Base register	Displacement		
Ld / st Indirect	Dest register	Base register	Index register	Size, sign, update	/
Ld / st Indirect	Dest register	Base register	Displacement	XO	

(c) Load/store instructions

Arithmetic	Dest register	Src register	Src register	O	Add, sub, etc.		R
Add, Sub, etc.	Dest register	Src register	Signed immediate value				
Logical	Src register	Dest register	Src register	Add, Or, Xor, etc.			R
And, Or, etc.	Src register	Dest register	Unsigned immediate value				
Rotate	Src register	Dest register	Shift amt	Mask begin	Mask end		R
Rotate or shift	Src register	Dest register	Src register	Shift type or mask			R
Rotate	Src register	Dest register	Shift amt	Mask		XO	S R
Rotate	Src register	Dest register	Src register	Mask		XO	R
Shift	Src register	Dest register	Shift amt	Shift type or mask		S	R

(d) Integer arithmetic, logical, and shift/rotate instructions

Flt sgl / dbl	Dest Register	Src Register	Src Register	Src Register	Fadd, etc.	R

(e) Floating-point arithmetic instructions

A = Absolute or PC Relative   * = 64-bit implementations only
L = Link to Subroutine
O = Record Overflow in XER
R = Record Conditions in CR1
XO = OpCode Extension
S = Part of Shift Amount Field

Figure 11.9   PowerPC Instruction Formats

Note the regular structure of the formats, which eases the job of the instruction decode units. For all load/store, arithmetic, and logical instructions, the opcode is followed by two 5-bit register references, enabling 32 general-purpose registers to be used.

The branch instructions include a link (L) bit that indicates that the effective address of the instruction following the branch instruction is to be placed in the link register. Two forms of the instruction also include a bit (A) that indicates whether the addressing mode is absolute or PC relative. For the conditional branch instructions, the CR bit field specifies the bit to be tested in the condition register. The options field specifies the conditions under which the branch is to be taken. The following conditions may be specified:

- Branch always.
- Branch if count ≠ 0 and condition is false.
- Branch if count ≠ 0 and condition is true.
- Branch if count = 0 and condition is false.
- Branch if count = 0 and condition is true.
- Branch if count ≠ 0.
- Branch if count = 0.
- Branch if condition is false.
- Branch if condition is true.

Most instructions that result in a computation (arithmetic, floating-point arithmetic, logical) include a bit that indicates whether the result of the operation should be recorded in the condition register. As will be shown, this feature is useful for branch prediction processing.

Floating-point instructions have fields for three source registers. In many cases, only two source registers are used. A few instructions involve multiplication of two source registers and then addition or subtraction of a third source register. These composite instructions are included because of the frequency of their use. For example, the inner product that is part of many matrix operations can be implemented using multiply-adds.

11.5 RECOMMENDED READING

The references cited in Chapter 10 are equally applicable to the material of this chapter. [BLAA97] contains a detailed discussion of instruction formats and addressing modes. In addition, the reader may wish to consult [FLYN85] for a discussion and analysis of instruction set design issues, particularly those relating to formats.

BLAA97   Blaauw, G., and Brooks, F. *Computer Architecture: Concepts and Evolution.* Reading, MA: Addison-Wesley, 1997.

FLYN85   Flynn, M.; Johnson, J.; and Wakefield, S. "On Instruction Sets and Their Formats." *IEEE Transactions on Computers,* March 1985.

11.6 KEY TERMS, REVIEW QUESTIONS, AND PROBLEMS

Key Terms

autoindexing	immediate addressing	preindexing
base-register addressing	indexing	register addressing
direct addressing	indirect addressing	register indirect addressing
displacement addressing	instruction format	relative addressing
effective address	postindexing	word

Review Questions

11.1 Briefly define immediate addressing.

11.2 Briefly define direct addressing.

11.3 Briefly define indirect addressing.

11.4 Briefly define register addressing.

11.5 Briefly define register indirect addressing.

11.6 Briefly define displacement addressing.

11.7 Briefly define relative addressing.

11.8 What is the advantage of autoindexing?

11.9 What is the difference between postindexing and preindexing?

11.10 What facts go into determining the use of the addressing bits of an instruction?

11.11 What are the advantages and disadvantages of using a variable-length instruction format?

Problems

11.1 Justify the assertion that a 32-bit instruction is probably much less than twice as useful as a 16-bit instruction.

11.2 Given the following memory values and a one-address machine with an accumulator, what values do the following instructions load into the accumulator?
- Word 20 contains 40.
- Word 30 contains 50.
- Word 40 contains 60.
- Word 50 contains 70.
   a. LOAD IMMEDIATE 20
   b. LOAD DIRECT 20
   c. LOAD INDIRECT 20
   d. LOAD IMMEDIATE 30
   e. LOAD DIRECT 30
   f. LOAD INDIRECT 30

11.3 Let the address stored in the program counter be designated by the symbol X1. The instruction stored in X1 has an address part (operand reference) X2. The operand needed to execute the instruction is stored in the memory word with address X3. An index register contains the value X4. What is the relationship between these various quantities if the addressing mode of the instruction is (a) direct; (b) indirect; (c) PC relative; (d) indexed?

11.4 An address field in an instruction contains decimal value 14. Where is the corresponding operand located for:

a. immediate addressing?

b. direct addressing?

c. indirect addressing?

d. register addressing?

e. register indirect addressing?

11.5 A PC-relative mode branch instruction is stored in memory at address 620_{10}. The branch is made to location 530_{10}. The address field in the instruction is 10 bits long. What is the binary value in the instruction?

11.6 How many times does the CPU need to refer to memory when it fetches and executes an indirect-address-mode instruction if the instruction is (a) a computation requiring a single operand; (b) a branch?

11.7 The IBM 370 does not provide indirect addressing. Assume that the address of an operand is in main memory. How would you access the operand?

11.8 Why was IBM's decision to move from 36 bits to 32 bits per word wrenching, and to whom?

11.9 In [COOK82], the author proposes that the PC-relative addressing modes be eliminated in favor of other modes, such as the use of a stack. What is the disadvantage of this proposal?

11.10 Assume an instruction set that uses a fixed 16-bit instruction length. Operand specifiers are 6 bits in length. There are K two-operand instructions and L zero-operand instructions. What is the maximum number of one-operand instructions that can be supported?

11.11 Design a variable-length opcode to allow all of the following to be encoded in a 36-bit instruction:

- instructions with two 15-bit addresses and one 3-bit register number
- instructions with one 15-bit address and one 3-bit register number
- instructions with no addresses or registers

11.12 Consider the results of Problem 10.3. Assume that M is a 16-bit memory address and that X, Y, and Z are either 16-bit addresses or 4-bit register numbers. The one-address machine uses an accumulator, and the two- and three-address machines have 16 registers and instructions operating on all combinations of memory locations and registers. Assuming 8-bit opcodes and instruction lengths that are multiples of 4 bits, how many bits does each machine need to compute X?

11.13 Is there any possible justification for an instruction with two opcodes?

11.14 The Pentium includes the following instruction:

```
IMUL op1, op2, immediate
```

This instruction multiplies op2, which may be either register or memory, by the immediate operand value, and places the result in op1, which must be a register. There is no other three-operand instruction of this sort in the instruction set. What is the possible use of such an instruction? *Hint:* Consider indexing.

CHAPTER 12

CPU STRUCTURE AND FUNCTION

KEY POINTS

◆ A processor includes both user-visible registers and control/status registers. The former may be referenced, implicitly or explicitly, in machine instructions. User-visible registers may be general purpose or have a special use, such as fixed-point or floating-point numbers, addresses, indexes, and segment pointers. Control and status registers are used to control the operation of the CPU. One obvious example is the program counter. Another important example is a program status word (PSW) that contains a variety of status and condition bits. These include bits to reflect the result of the most recent arithmetic operation, interrupt enable bits, and an indicator of whether the CPU is executing in supervisor or user mode.

◆ Processors make use of instruction pipelining to speed up execution. In essence, pipelining involves breaking up the instruction cycle into a number of separate stages that occur in sequence, such as fetch instruction, decode instruction, determine operand addresses, fetch operands, execute instruction, and write operand result. Instructions move through these stages, as on an assembly line, so that in principle, each stage can be working on a different instruction at the same time. The occurrence of branches and dependencies between instructions complicates the design and use of pipelines.

This chapter discusses aspects of the processor not yet covered in Part Three and sets the stage for the discussion of RISC and superscalar architecture in Chapters 13 and 14.

We begin with a summary of processor organization. Registers, which form the internal memory of the processor, are then analyzed. We are then in a position to return to the discussion (begun in Section 3.2) of the instruction cycle. A description of the instruction cycle and a common technique known as instruction pipelining complete our description. The chapter concludes with an examination of some additional aspects of the Pentium and PowerPC organizations.

12.1 PROCESSOR ORGANIZATION

To understand the organization of the CPU, let us consider the requirements placed on the CPU, the things that it must do:

- **Fetch instruction:** The CPU reads an instruction from memory.
- **Interpret instruction:** The instruction is decoded to determine what action is required.

- **Fetch data:** The execution of an instruction may require reading data from memory or an I/O module.
- **Process data:** The execution of an instruction may require performing some arithmetic or logical operation on data.
- **Write data:** The results of an execution may require writing data to memory or an I/O module.

To do these things, it should be clear that the CPU needs to store some data temporarily. It must remember the location of the last instruction so that it can know where to get the next instruction. It needs to store instructions and data temporarily while an instruction is being executed. In other words, the CPU needs a small internal memory.

Figure 12.1 is a simplified view of a CPU, indicating its connection to the rest of the system via the system bus. A similar interface would be needed for any of the interconnection structures described in Chapter 3. The reader will recall that the major components of the CPU are an *arithmetic and logic unit* (ALU) and a *control unit* (CU). The ALU does the actual computation or processing of data. The control unit controls the movement of data and instructions into and out of the CPU and controls the operation of the ALU. In addition, the figure shows a minimal internal memory, consisting of a set of storage locations, called *registers*.

Figure 12.2 is a slightly more detailed view of the CPU. The data transfer and logic control paths are indicated, including an element labeled *internal CPU bus*. This element is needed to transfer data between the various registers and the

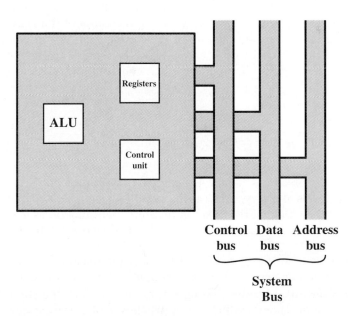

Figure 12.1 The CPU with the System Bus

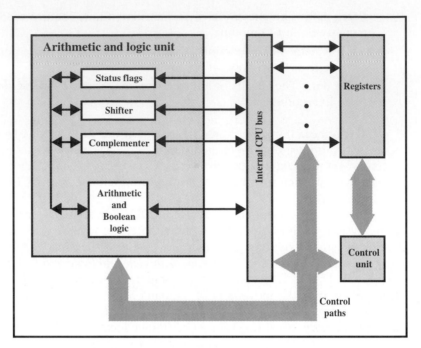

Figure 12.2 Internal Structure of the CPU

ALU, because the ALU in fact operates only on data in the internal CPU memory. The figure also shows typical basic elements of the ALU. Note the similarity between the internal structure of the computer as a whole and the internal structure of the CPU. In both cases, there is a small collection of major elements (computer: CPU, I/O, memory; CPU: control unit, ALU, registers) connected by data paths.

12.2 REGISTER ORGANIZATION

As we discussed in Chapter 4, a computer system employs a memory hierarchy. At higher levels of the hierarchy, memory is faster, smaller, and more expensive (per bit). Within the CPU, there is a set of registers that function as a level of memory above main memory and cache in the hierarchy. The registers in the CPU perform two roles:

- **User-visible registers:** These enable the machine- or assembly-language programmer to minimize main memory references by optimizing use of registers.
- **Control and status registers:** These are used by the control unit to control the operation of the CPU and by privileged, operating system programs to control the execution of programs.

There is not a clean separation of registers into these two categories. For example, on some machines the program counter is user visible (e.g., Pentium), but on many it is not (e.g., PowerPC). For purposes of the following discussion, however, we will use these categories.

User–Visible Registers

A user-visible register is one that may be referenced by means of the machine language that the CPU executes. We can characterize these in the following categories:

- General purpose
- Data
- Address
- Condition codes

General-purpose registers can be assigned to a variety of functions by the programmer. Sometimes their use within the instruction set is orthogonal to the operation. That is, any general-purpose register can contain the operand for any opcode. This provides true general-purpose register use. Often, however, there are restrictions. For example, there may be dedicated registers for floating-point and stack operations.

In some cases, general-purpose registers can be used for addressing functions (e.g., register indirect, displacement). In other cases, there is a partial or clean separation between data registers and address registers. **Data registers** may be used only to hold data and cannot be employed in the calculation of an operand address. **Address registers** may themselves be somewhat general purpose, or they may be devoted to a particular addressing mode. Examples include the following:

- **Segment pointers:** In a machine with segmented addressing (see Section 8.3), a segment register holds the address of the base of the segment. There may be multiple registers: for example, one for the operating system and one for the current process.
- **Index registers:** These are used for indexed addressing and may be autoindexed.
- **Stack pointer:** If there is user-visible stack addressing, then typically the stack is in memory and there is a dedicated register that points to the top of the stack. This allows implicit addressing; that is, push, pop, and other stack instructions need not contain an explicit stack operand.

There are several design issues to be addressed here. An important issue is whether to use completely general-purpose registers or to specialize their use. We have already touched on this issue in the preceding chapter, because it affects instruction set design. With the use of specialized registers, it can generally be implicit in the opcode which type of register a certain operand specifier refers to. The operand specifier must only identify one of a set of specialized registers rather than one out of all the registers, thus saving bits. On the other hand, this specialization limits the programmer's flexibility.

Another design issue is the number of registers, either general purpose or data plus address, to be provided. Again, this affects instruction set design because more registers require more operand specifier bits. As we previously discussed, somewhere between 8 and 32 registers appears optimum [LUND77]. Fewer registers result in more memory references; more registers do not noticeably reduce memory references (e.g., see [WILL90]). However, a new approach, which finds advantage in the use of hundreds of registers, is exhibited in some RISC systems and is discussed in Chapter 13.

Finally, there is the issue of register length. Registers that must hold addresses obviously must be at least long enough to hold the largest address. Data registers should be able to hold values of most data types. Some machines allow two contiguous registers to be used as one for holding double-length values.

A final category of registers, which is at least partially visible to the user, holds **condition codes** (also referred to as *flags*). Condition codes are bits set by the CPU hardware as the result of operations. For example, an arithmetic operation may produce a positive, negative, zero, or overflow result. In addition to the result itself being stored in a register or memory, a condition code is also set. The code may subsequently be tested as part of a conditional branch operation.

Condition code bits are collected into one or more registers. Usually, they form part of a control register. Generally, machine instructions allow these bits to be read by implicit reference, but the programmer cannot alter them.

In some machines, a subroutine call will result in the automatic saving of all user-visible registers, to be restored on return. The CPU performs the saving and restoring as part of the execution of call and return instructions. This allows each subroutine to use the user-visible registers independently. On other machines, it is the responsibility of the programmer to save the contents of the relevant user-visible registers prior to a subroutine call, by including instructions for this purpose in the program.

Control and Status Registers

There are a variety of CPU registers that are employed to control the operation of the CPU. Most of these, on most machines, are not visible to the user. Some of them may be visible to machine instructions executed in a control or operating system mode.

Of course, different machines will have different register organizations and use different terminology. We list here a reasonably complete list of register types, with a brief description.

Four registers are essential to instruction execution:

- **Program counter (PC):** Contains the address of an instruction to be fetched.
- **Instruction register (IR):** Contains the instruction most recently fetched.
- **Memory address register (MAR):** Contains the address of a location in memory.
- **Memory buffer register (MBR):** Contains a word of data to be written to memory or the word most recently read.

Typically, the CPU updates the PC after each instruction fetch so that the PC always points to the next instruction to be executed. A branch or skip instruction will also modify the contents of the PC. The fetched instruction is loaded into an IR, where the opcode and operand specifiers are analyzed. Data are exchanged with memory using the MAR and MBR. In a bus-organized system, the MAR connects directly to the address bus, and the MBR connects directly to the data bus. User-visible registers, in turn, exchange data with the MBR.

The four registers just mentioned are used for the movement of data between the CPU and memory. Within the CPU, data must be presented to the ALU for processing. The ALU may have direct access to the MBR and user-visible registers. Alternatively, there may be additional buffering registers at the boundary to the ALU; these registers serve as input and output registers for the ALU and exchange data with the MBR and user-visible registers.

All CPU designs include a register or set of registers, often known as the *program status word* (PSW), that contain status information. The PSW typically contains condition codes plus other status information. Common fields or flags include the following:

- **Sign:** Contains the sign bit of the result of the last arithmetic operation.
- **Zero:** Set when the result is 0.
- **Carry:** Set if an operation resulted in a carry (addition) into or borrow (subtraction) out of a high-order bit. Used for multiword arithmetic operations.
- **Equal:** Set if a logical compare result is equality.
- **Overflow:** Used to indicate arithmetic overflow.
- **Interrupt enable/disable:** Used to enable or disable interrupts.
- **Supervisor:** Indicates whether the CPU is executing in supervisor or user mode. Certain privileged instructions can be executed only in supervisor mode, and certain areas of memory can be accessed only in supervisor mode.

A number of other registers related to status and control might be found in a particular CPU design. In addition to the PSW, there may be a pointer to a block of memory containing additional status information (e.g., process control blocks). In machines using vectored interrupts, an interrupt vector register may be provided. If a stack is used to implement certain functions (e.g., subroutine call), then a system stack pointer is needed. A page table pointer is used with a virtual memory system. Finally, registers may be used in the control of I/O operations.

A number of factors go into the design of the control and status register organization. One key issue is operating system support. Certain types of control information are of specific utility to the operating system. If the CPU designer has a functional understanding of the operating system to be used, then the register organization can to some extent be tailored to the operating system.

Another key design decision is the allocation of control information between registers and memory. It is common to dedicate the first (lowest) few hundred or thousand words of memory for control purposes. The designer must decide how much control information should be in registers and how much in memory. The usual trade-off of cost versus speed arises.

Example Microprocessor Register Organizations

It is instructive to examine and compare the register organization of comparable systems. In this section, we look at two 16-bit microprocessors that were designed at about the same time: the Motorola MC68000 [STRI79] and the Intel 8086 [MORS78]. Figures 12.3a and b depict the register organization of each; purely internal registers, such as a memory address register, are not shown.

The MC68000 partitions its 32-bit registers into eight data registers and nine address registers. The eight data registers are used primarily for data manipulation and are also used in addressing as index registers. The width of the registers allows 8-, 16-, and 32-bit data operations, determined by opcode. The address registers contain 32-bit (no segmentation) addresses; two of these registers are also used as stack pointers, one for users and one for the operating system, depending on the current execution mode. Both registers are numbered 7, because only one can be used at a time. The MC68000 also includes a 32-bit program counter and a 16-bit status register.

The Motorola team wanted a very regular instruction set, with no special-purpose registers. A concern for code efficiency led them to divide the registers into two functional components, saving one bit on each register specifier. This seems a reasonable compromise between complete generality and code compaction.

The Intel 8086 takes a different approach to register organization. Every register is special purpose, although some registers are also usable as general purpose. The 8086 contains four 16-bit data registers that are addressable on a byte or 16-bit basis, and four 16-bit pointer and index registers. The data registers can be used as general purpose in some instructions. In others, the registers are used implicitly. For example, a multiply instruction always uses the accumulator. The four pointer registers are also used implicitly in a number of operations; each contains a segment offset. There are also four 16-bit segment registers. Three of the four segment registers are used in a dedicated, implicit fashion, to point to the segment of the current instruction (useful for branch instructions), a segment containing data, and a segment containing a stack, respectively. These dedicated and implicit uses provide for compact encoding at the cost of reduced flexibility. The 8086 also includes an instruction pointer and a set of 1-bit status and control flags.

The point of this comparison should be clear. There is, as yet, no universally accepted philosophy concerning the best way to organize CPU registers [TOON81]. As with overall instruction set design and so many other CPU design issues, it is still a matter of judgment and taste.

A second instructive point concerning register organization design is illustrated in Figure 12.3c. This figure shows the user-visible register organization for the Intel 80386 [ELAY85], which is a 32-bit microprocessor designed as an extension of the 8086.[1] The 80386 uses 32-bit registers. However, to provide upward compatibility for programs written on the earlier machine, the 80386 retains the original register organization embedded in the new organization. Given this design constraint, the architects of the 32-bit processors had limited flexibility in designing the register organization.

---

[1]Because the MC68000 already uses 32-bit registers, the MC68020 [MACG84], which is a full 32-bit architecture, uses the same register organization.

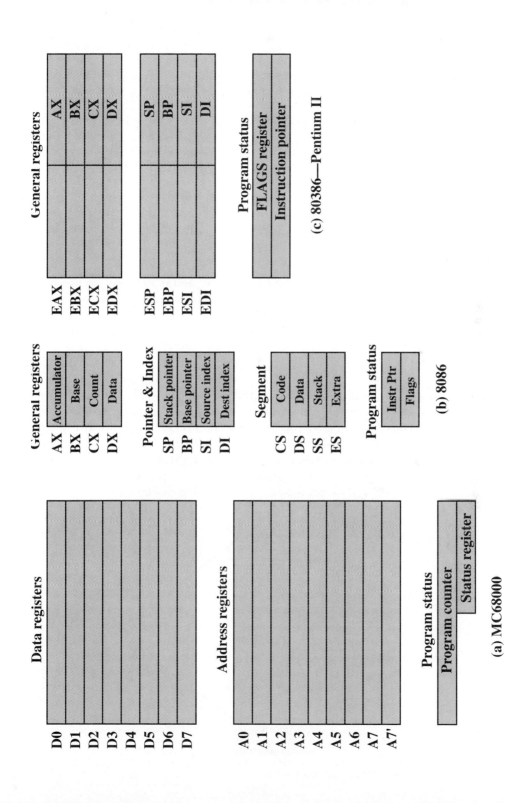

Figure 12.3 Example Microprocessor Register Organizations

419

12.3 INSTRUCTION CYCLE

In Section 3.2, we described the CPU's instruction cycle (Figure 3.9). To recall, an instruction cycle includes the following subcycles:

- **Fetch:** Read the next instruction from memory into the CPU.
- **Execute:** Interpret the opcode and perform the indicated operation.
- **Interrupt:** If interrupts are enabled and an interrupt has occurred, save the current process state and service the interrupt.

We are now in a position to elaborate somewhat on the instruction cycle. First, we must introduce one additional subcycle, known as the indirect cycle.

The Indirect Cycle

We have seen, in Chapter 11, that the execution of an instruction may involve one or more operands in memory, each of which requires a memory access. Further, if indirect addressing is used, then additional memory accesses are required.

We can think of the fetching of indirect addresses as one more instruction subcycle. The result is shown in Figure 12.4. The main line of activity consists of alternating instruction fetch and instruction execution activities. After an instruction is fetched, it is examined to determine if any indirect addressing is involved. If so, the required operands are fetched using indirect addressing. Following execution, an interrupt may be processed before the next instruction fetch.

Another way to view this process is shown in Figure 12.5, which is a revised version of Figure 3.12. This illustrates more correctly the nature of the instruction cycle. Once an instruction is fetched, its operand specifiers must be identified. Each

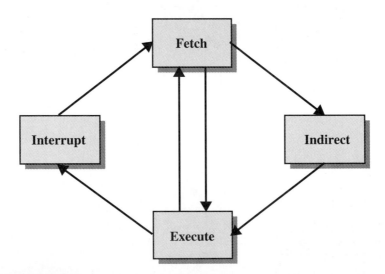

Figure 12.4 The Instruction Cycle

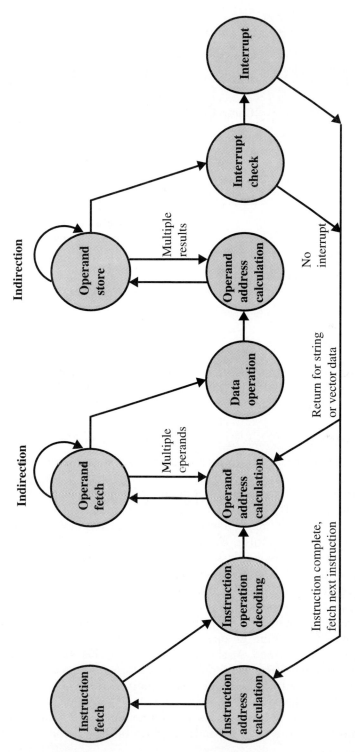

Figure 12.5 Instruction Cycle State Diagram

421

MBR = Memory buffer register
MAR = Memory address register
IR = Instruction register
PC = Program counter

Figure 12.6   Data Flow, Fetch Cycle

input operand in memory is then fetched, and this process may require indirect addressing. Register-based operands need not be fetched. Once the opcode is executed, a similar process may be needed to store the result in main memory.

Data Flow

The exact sequence of events during an instruction cycle depends on the design of the CPU. We can, however, indicate in general terms what must happen. Let us assume that a CPU that employs a memory address register (MAR), a memory buffer register (MBR), a program counter (PC), and an instruction register (IR).

During the *fetch cycle,* an instruction is read from memory. Figure 12.6 shows the flow of data during this cycle. The PC contains the address of the next instruction to be fetched. This address is moved to the MAR and placed on the address bus. The control unit requests a memory read, and the result is placed on the data bus and copied into the MBR and then moved to the IR. Meanwhile, the PC is incremented by 1, preparatory for the next fetch.

Once the fetch cycle is over, the control unit examines the contents of the IR to determine if it contains an operand specifier using indirect addressing. If so, an *indirect cycle* is performed. As shown in Figure 12.7, this is a simple cycle. The rightmost *N* bits of the MBR, which contain the address reference, are transferred to the MAR. Then the control unit requests a memory read, to get the desired address of the operand into the MBR.

The fetch and indirect cycles are simple and predictable. The *execute cycle* takes many forms; the form depends on which of the various machine instructions

Figure 12.7 Data Flow, Indirect Cycle

is in the IR. This cycle may involve transferring data among registers, read or write from memory or I/O, and/or the invocation of the ALU.

Like the fetch and indirect cycles, the *interrupt cycle* is simple and predictable (Figure 12.8). The current contents of the PC must be saved so that the CPU can resume normal activity after the interrupt. Thus, the contents of the PC are transferred to the MBR to be written into memory. The special memory location reserved for this purpose is loaded into the MAR from the control unit. It might, for example, be a stack pointer. The PC is loaded with the address of the interrupt routine. As a result, the next instruction cycle will begin by fetching the appropriate instruction.

Figure 12.8 Data Flow, Interrupt Cycle

12.4 INSTRUCTION PIPELINING

As computer systems evolve, greater performance can be achieved by taking advantage of improvements in technology, such as faster circuitry. In addition, organizational enhancements to the CPU can improve performance. We have already seen some examples of this, such as the use of multiple registers rather than a single accumulator, and the use of a cache memory. Another organizational approach, which is quite common, is instruction pipelining.

Pipelining Strategy

Instruction pipelining is similar to the use of an assembly line in a manufacturing plant. An assembly line takes advantage of the fact that a product goes through various stages of production. By laying the production process out in an assembly line, products at various stages can be worked on simultaneously. This process is also referred to as *pipelining,* because, as in a pipeline, new inputs are accepted at one end before previously accepted inputs appear as outputs at the other end.

To apply this concept to instruction execution, we must recognize that, in fact, an instruction has a number of stages. Figure 12.5, for example, breaks the instruction cycle up into 10 tasks, which occur in sequence. Clearly, there should be some opportunity for pipelining.

As a simple approach, consider subdividing instruction processing into two stages: fetch instruction and execute instruction. There are times during the execution of an instruction when main memory is not being accessed. This time could be used to fetch the next instruction in parallel with the execution of the current one. Figure 12.9a depicts this approach. The pipeline has two independent stages. The first stage fetches an instruction and buffers it. When the second stage is free, the first stage passes it the buffered instruction. While the second stage is executing the instruction, the first stage takes advantage of any unused memory cycles to fetch and buffer the next instruction. This is called *instruction prefetch* or *fetch overlap.*

It should be clear that this process will speed up instruction execution. If the fetch and execute stages were of equal duration, the instruction cycle time would be halved. However, if we look more closely at this pipeline (Figure 12.9b), we will see that this doubling of execution rate is unlikely for two reasons:

1. The execution time will generally be longer than the fetch time. Execution will involve reading and storing operands and the performance of some operation. Thus, the fetch stage may have to wait for some time before it can empty its buffer.
2. A conditional branch instruction makes the address of the next instruction to be fetched unknown. Thus, the fetch stage must wait until it receives the next instruction address from the execute stage. The execute stage may then have to wait while the next instruction is fetched.

Guessing can reduce the time loss from the second reason. A simple rule is the following: When a conditional branch instruction is passed on from the fetch to the

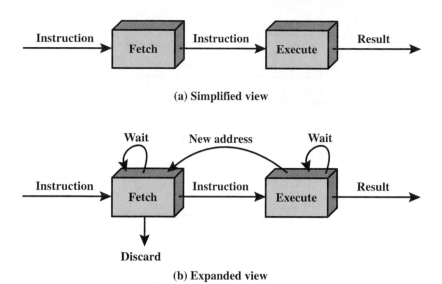

(a) Simplified view

(b) Expanded view

Figure 12.9 Two-Stage Instruction Pipeline

execute stage, the fetch stage fetches the next instruction in memory after the branch instruction. Then, if the branch is not taken, no time is lost. If the branch is taken, the fetched instruction must be discarded and a new instruction fetched.

While these factors reduce the potential effectiveness of the two-stage pipeline, some speedup occurs. To gain further speedup, the pipeline must have more stages. Let us consider the following decomposition of the instruction processing.

- **Fetch instruction (FI):** Read the next expected instruction into a buffer.
- **Decode instruction (DI):** Determine the opcode and the operand specifiers.
- **Calculate operands (CO):** Calculate the effective address of each source operand. This may involve displacement, register indirect, indirect, or other forms of address calculation.
- **Fetch operands (FO):** Fetch each operand from memory. Operands in registers need not be fetched.
- **Execute instruction (EI):** Perform the indicated operation and store the result, if any, in the specified destination operand location.
- **Write operand (WO):** Store the result in memory.

With this decomposition, the various stages will be of more nearly equal duration. For the sake of illustration, let us assume equal duration. Using this assumption, Figure 12.10 shows that a six-stage pipeline can reduce the execution time for 9 instructions from 54 time units to 14 time units.

Several comments are in order: The diagram assumes that each instruction goes through all six stages of the pipeline. This will not always be the case. For example, a load instruction does not need the WO stage. However, to simplify the

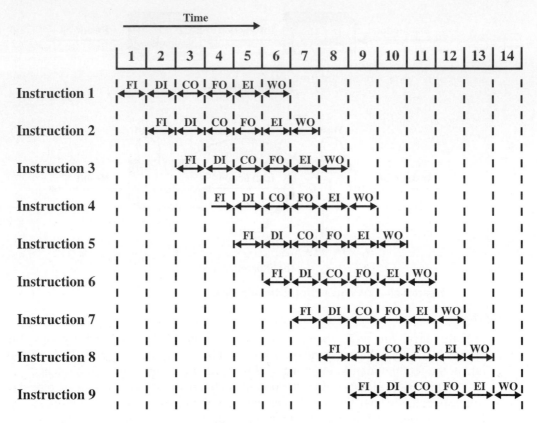

Figure 12.10 Timing Diagram for Instruction Pipeline Operation

pipeline hardware, the timing is set up assuming that each instruction requires all six stages. Also, the diagram assumes that all of the stages can be performed in parallel. In particular, it is assumed that there are no memory conflicts. For example, the FI, FO, and WO stages involve a memory access. The diagram implies that all these accesses can occur simultaneously. Most memory systems will not permit that. However, the desired value may be in cache, or the FO or WO stage may be null. Thus, much of the time, memory conflicts will not slow down the pipeline.

Several other factors serve to limit the performance enhancement. If the six stages are not of equal duration, there will be some waiting involved at various pipeline stages, as discussed before for the two-stage pipeline. Another difficulty is the conditional branch instruction, which can invalidate several instruction fetches. A similar unpredictable event is an interrupt. Figure 12.11 illustrates the effects of the conditional branch, using the same program as Figure 12.10. Assume that instruction 3 is a conditional branch to instruction 15. Until the instruction is executed, there is no way of knowing which instruction will come next. The pipeline, in this example, simply loads the next instruction in sequence (instruction 4) and proceeds. In Figure 12.10, the branch is not taken, and we get the full performance benefit of the enhancement. In Figure 12.11, the branch is taken. This is not determined until the end of time unit 7. At this point, the pipeline must be cleared of instructions that are not useful. During time unit 8, instruction 15 enters the pipeline. No instructions complete during time units 9 through 12; this is the performance penalty incurred because we could not anticipate the branch. Figure 12.12 indicates the logic needed for pipelining to account for branches and interrupts.

Other problems arise that did not appear in our simple two-stage organization. The CO stage may depend on the contents of a register that could be altered by a previous instruction that is still in the pipeline. Other such register and memory conflicts could occur. The system must contain logic to account for this type of conflict.

To clarify pipeline operation, it might be useful to look at an alternative depiction. Figures 12.10 and 12.11 show the progression of time horizontally across the figures, with each row showing the progress of an individual instruction. Figure 12.13 shows same sequence of events, with time progressing vertically down the figure,

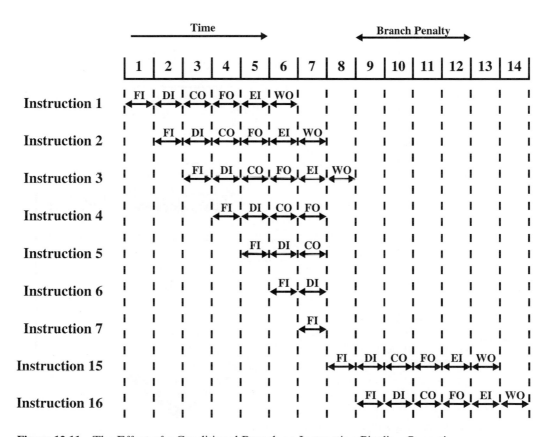

Figure 12.11   The Effect of a Conditional Branch on Instruction Pipeline Operation

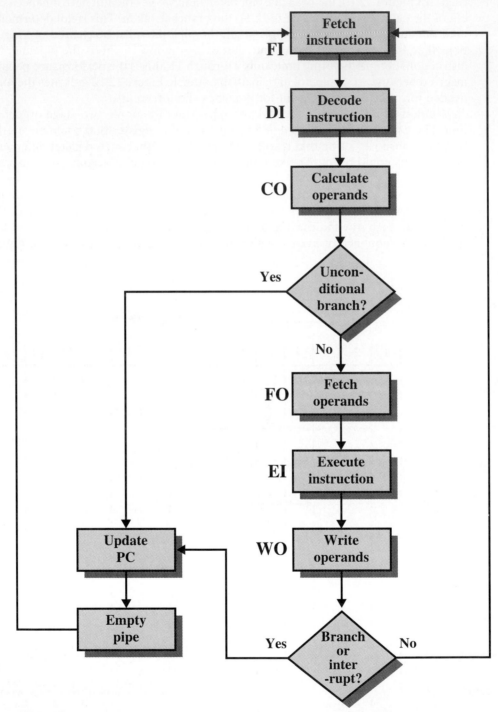

Figure 12.12 Six-Stage CPU Instruction Pipeline

and each row showing the state of the pipeline at a given point in time. In Figure 12.13a (which corresponds to Figure 12.10), the pipeline is full at time 6, with 6 different instructions in various stages of execution, and remains full through time 9; we assume that instruction I9 is the last instruction to be executed. In Figure 12.13b, (which corresponds to Figure 12.11), the pipeline is full at times 6 and 7. At time 7,

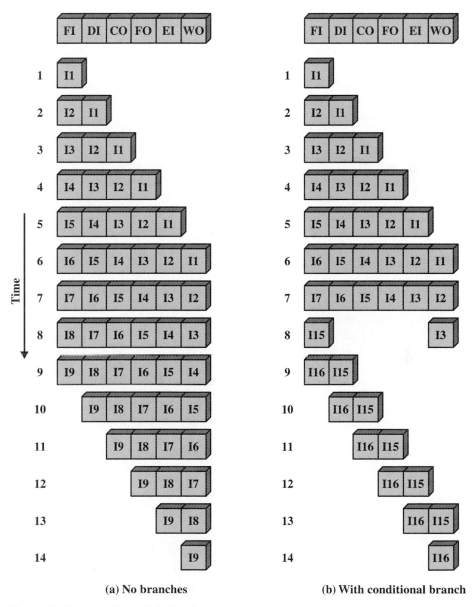

(a) No branches **(b) With conditional branch**

Figure 12.13 An Alternative Pipeline Depiction

instruction 3 is in the execute stage and executes a branch to instruction 15. At this point, instructions I4 through I7 are flushed from the pipeline, so that at time 8, only two instructions are in the pipeline, I3 and I15.

From the preceding discussion, it might appear that the greater the number of stages in the pipeline, the faster the execution rate. Some of the IBM S/360 designers pointed out two factors that frustrate this seemingly simple pattern for high-performance design [ANDE67a], and they remain elements that designer must still consider:

1. At each stage of the pipeline, there is some overhead involved in moving data from buffer to buffer and in performing various preparation and delivery functions. This overhead can appreciably lengthen the total execution time of a single instruction. This is significant when sequential instructions are logically dependent, either through heavy use of branching or through memory access dependencies.

2. The amount of control logic required to handle memory and register dependencies and to optimize the use of the pipeline increases enormously with the number of stages. This can lead to a situation where the logic controlling the gating between stages is more complex than the stages being controlled.

Instruction pipelining is a powerful technique for enhancing performance but requires careful design to achieve optimum results with reasonable complexity.

Pipeline Performance

In this subsection, we develop some simple measures of pipeline performance and relative speedup (based on a discussion in [HWAN93]). The cycle time τ of an instruction pipeline is the time needed to advance a set of instructions one stage through the pipeline; each column in Figures 12.10 and 12.11 represents one cycle time. The cycle time can be determined as

$$\tau = \max_{i}[\tau_i] + d = \tau_m + d \qquad 1 \leq i \leq k$$

where

$$\tau_m = \text{maximum stage delay (delay through stage}$$
$$\text{which experiences the largest delay)}$$
$$k = \text{number of stages in the instruction pipeline}$$
$$d = \text{time delay of a latch, needed to advance signals}$$
$$\text{and data from one stage to the next}$$

In general, the time delay d is equivalent to a clock pulse and $\tau_m \gg d$. Now suppose that n instructions are processed, with no branches. The total time required T_k to execute all n instructions is

$$T_k = [k + (n - 1)]\tau \qquad (12.1)$$

A total of k cycles are required to complete the execution of the first instruction, and the remaining $n - 1$ instructions require $n - 1$ cycles.[2] This equation is easily verified from Figure 12.10. The ninth instruction completes at time cycle 14:

$$14 = [6 + (9 - 1)]$$

The speedup factor for the instruction pipeline compared to execution without the pipeline is defined as

$$S_k = \frac{T_1}{T_k} = \frac{nk\tau}{[k + (n - 1)]\tau} = \frac{nk}{k + (n - 1)} \tag{12.2}$$

Figure 12.14a plots the speedup factor as a function of the number of instructions that are executed without a branch. As might be expected, at the limit $(n \to \infty)$, we have a k-fold speedup. Figure 12.14b shows the speedup factor as a function of the number of stages in the instruction pipeline.[3] In this case, the speedup factor approaches the number of instructions that can be fed into the pipeline without branches. Thus, the larger the number of pipeline stages, the greater the potential for speedup. However, as a practical matter, the potential gains of additional pipeline stages are countered by increases in cost, delays between stages, and the fact that branches will be encountered requiring the flushing of the pipeline,

Dealing with Branches

One of the major problems in designing an instruction pipeline is assuring a steady flow of instructions to the initial stages of the pipeline. The primary impediment, as we have seen, is the conditional branch instruction. Until the instruction is actually executed, it is impossible to determine whether the branch will be taken or not.

A variety of approaches have been taken for dealing with conditional branches:

- Multiple streams
- Prefetch branch target
- Loop buffer
- Branch prediction
- Delayed branch

Multiple Streams

A simple pipeline suffers a penalty for a branch instruction because it must choose one of two instructions to fetch next and may make the wrong choice. A brute-force approach is to replicate the initial portions of the pipeline and allow the

---

[2]We are being a bit sloppy here. The cycle time will only equal the maximum value of τ when all the stages are full. At the beginning, the cycle time may be less for the first one or few cycles.
[3]Note that the x-axis is logarithmic in Figure 12.14a and linear in Figure 12.14b.

(a)

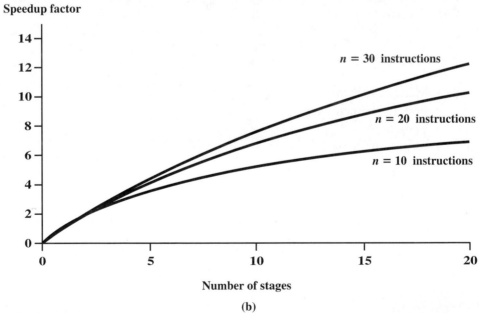

(b)

Figure 12.14   Speedup Factors with Instruction Pipelining pipeline to fetch both instructions, making use of two streams. There are two problems with this approach:

- With multiple pipelines there are contention delays for access to the registers and to memory.
- Additional branch instructions may enter the pipeline (either stream) before the original branch decision is resolved. Each such instruction needs an additional stream.

Despite these drawbacks, this strategy can improve performance. Examples of machines with two or more pipeline streams are the IBM 370/168 and the IBM 3033.

Prefetch Branch Target

When a conditional branch is recognized, the target of the branch is prefetched, in addition to the instruction following the branch. This target is then saved until the branch instruction is executed. If the branch is taken, the target has already been prefetched.

The IBM 360/91 uses this approach.

Loop Buffer

A loop buffer is a small, very-high-speed memory maintained by the instruction fetch stage of the pipeline and containing the n most recently fetched instructions, in sequence. If a branch is to be taken, the hardware first checks whether the branch target is within the buffer. If so, the next instruction is fetched from the buffer. The loop buffer has three benefits:

1. With the use of prefetching, the loop buffer will contain some instruction sequentially ahead of the current instruction fetch address. Thus, instructions fetched in sequence will be available without the usual memory access time.
2. If a branch occurs to a target just a few locations ahead of the address of the branch instruction, the target will already be in the buffer. This is useful for the rather common occurrence of IF–THEN and IF–THEN–ELSE sequences.
3. This strategy is particularly well suited to dealing with loops, or iterations; hence the name *loop buffer*. If the loop buffer is large enough to contain all the instructions in a loop, then those instructions need to be fetched from memory only once, for the first iteration. For subsequent iterations, all the needed instructions are already in the buffer.

The loop buffer is similar in principle to a cache dedicated to instructions. The differences are that the loop buffer only retains instructions in sequence and is much smaller in size and hence lower in cost.

Figure 12.15 gives an example of a loop buffer. If the buffer contains 256 bytes, and byte addressing is used, then the least significant 8 bits are used to index the buffer. The remaining most significant bits are checked to determine if the branch target lies within the environment captured by the buffer.

Among the machines using a loop buffer are some of the CDC machines (Star-100, 6600, 7600) and the CRAY-1. A specialized form of loop buffer is available on the Motorola 68010, for executing a three-instruction loop involving the DBcc (decrement and branch on condition) instruction (see Problem 12.6). A three-word buffer is maintained, and the processor executes these instructions repeatedly until the loop condition is satisfied.

Branch Prediction

Various techniques can be used to predict whether a branch will be taken. Among the more common are the following:

- Predict never taken
- Predict always taken
- Predict by opcode
- Taken/not taken switch
- Branch history table

The first three approaches are static: They do not depend on the execution history up to the time of the conditional branch instruction. The latter two approaches are dynamic: They depend on the execution history.

The first two approaches are the simplest. These either always assume that the branch will not be taken and continue to fetch instructions in sequence, or they always assume that the branch will be taken and always fetch from the branch target. The 68020 and the VAX 11/780 use the predict-never-taken approach. The VAX 11/780 also includes a feature to minimize the effect of a wrong decision. If the fetch of the instruction after the branch will cause a page fault or protection violation, the processor halts its prefetching until it is sure that the instruction should be fetched.

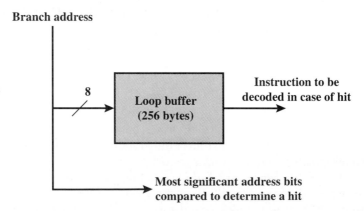

Figure 12.15 Loop Buffer

Studies analyzing program behavior have shown that conditional branches are taken more than 50% of the time [LILJ88], and so if the cost of prefetching from either path is the same, then always prefetching from the branch target address should give better performance than always prefetching from the sequential path. However, in a paged machine, prefetching the branch target is more likely to cause a page fault than prefetching the next instruction in sequence, and so this performance penalty should be taken into account. An avoidance mechanism may be employed to reduce this penalty.

The final static approach makes the decision based on the opcode of the branch instruction. The processor assumes that the branch will be taken for certain branch opcodes and not for others. [LILJ88] reports success rates of greater than 75% with this strategy.

Dynamic branch strategies attempt to improve the accuracy of prediction by recording the history of conditional branch instructions in a program. For example, one or more bits can be associated with each conditional branch instruction that reflect the recent history of the instruction. These bits are referred to as a taken/not taken switch that directs the processor to make a particular decision the next time the instruction is encountered. Typically, these history bits are not associated with the instruction in main memory. Rather, they are kept in temporary high-speed storage. One possibility is to associate these bits with any conditional branch instruction that is in a cache. When the instruction is replaced in the cache, its history is lost. Another possibility is to maintain a small table for recently executed branch instructions with one or more bits in each entry. The processor could access the table associatively, like a cache, or by using the low-order bits of the branch instruction's address.

With a single bit, all that can be recorded is whether the last execution of this instruction resulted in a branch or not. A shortcoming of using a single bit appears in the case of a conditional branch instruction that is almost always taken, such as a loop instruction. With only one bit of history, an error in prediction will occur twice for each use of the loop: once on entering the loop, and once on exiting.

If two bits are used, they can be used to record the result of the last two instances of the execution of the associated instruction, or to record a state in some other fashion. Figure 12.16 shows a typical approach (see Problem 12.5 for other possibilities). Assume that the algorithm starts at the upper left-hand corner of the flowchart. As long as each succeeding conditional branch instruction that is encountered is taken, the decision process predicts that the next branch will be taken. If a single prediction is wrong, the algorithm continues to predict that the next branch is taken. Only if two successive branches are not taken does the algorithm shift to the right-hand side of the flowchart. Subsequently, the algorithm will predict that branches are not taken until two branches in a row are taken. Thus, the algorithm requires two consecutive wrong predictions to change the prediction decision.

The decision process can be represented more compactly by a finite-state machine, shown in Figure 12.17. The finite-state machine representation is commonly used in the literature.

The use of history bits, as just described, has one drawback: If the decision is made to take the branch, the target instruction cannot be fetched until the target address, which is an operand in the conditional branch instruction, is decoded. Greater efficiency could be achieved if the instruction fetch could be initiated as soon as the branch decision is made. For this purpose, more information must be saved, in what is known as a branch target buffer, or a branch history table.

The branch history table is a small cache memory associated with the instruction fetch stage of the pipeline. Each entry in the table consists of three elements: the address of a branch instruction, some number of history bits that record the state of use of that instruction, and information about the target instruction. In most proposals and implementations, this third field contains the address of the target instruction. Another possibility is for the third field to actually contain the target instruction. The trade-off is clear: Storing the target address yields a smaller table but a greater instruction fetch time compared with storing the target instruction [RECH98].

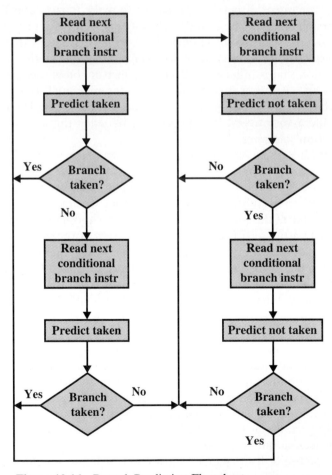

Figure 12.16 Branch Prediction Flowchart

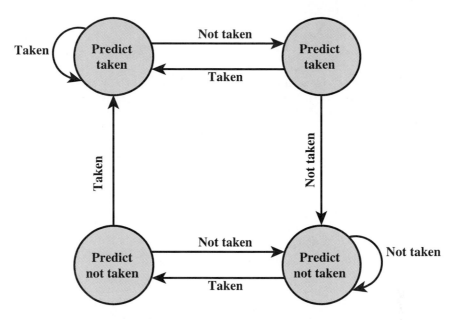

Figure 12.17   Branch Prediction State Diagram

Figure 12.18 contrasts this scheme with a predict-never-taken strategy. With the former strategy, the instruction fetch stage always fetches the next sequential address. If a branch is taken, some logic in the processor detects this and instructs that the next instruction be fetched from the target address (in addition to flushing the pipeline). The branch history table is treated as a cache. Each prefetch triggers a lookup in the branch history table. If no match is found, the next sequential address is used for the fetch. If a match is found, a prediction is made based on the state of the instruction: Either the next sequential address or the branch target address is fed to the select logic.

When the branch instruction is executed, the execute stage signals the branch history table logic with the result. The state of the instruction is updated to reflect a correct or incorrect prediction. If the prediction is incorrect, the select logic is redirected to the correct address for the next fetch. When a conditional branch instruction is encountered that is not in the table, it is added to the table and one of the existing entries is discarded, using one of the cache replacement algorithms discussed in Chapter 4.

One example of an implementation of a branch history table is the Advanced Micro Device AMD29000 microprocessor.

Delayed Branch

It is possible to improve pipeline performance by automatically rearranging instructions within a program, so that branch instructions occur later than actually desired. This intriguing approach is examined in Chapter 13.

(a) Predict never taken strategy

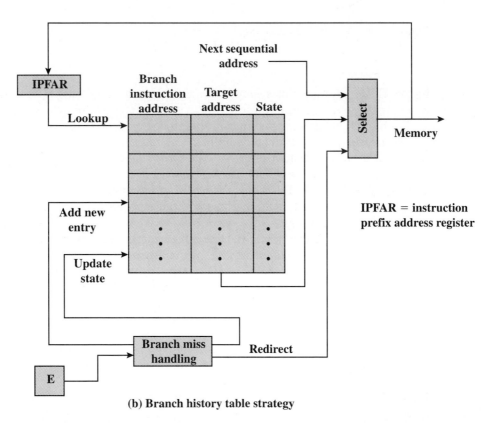

IPFAR = instruction
prefix address register

(b) Branch history table strategy

Figure 12.18 Dealing with Branches

Intel 80486 Pipelining

The 80486 implements a five-stage pipeline:

- **Fetch:** Instructions are fetched from the cache or from external memory and placed into one of the two 16-byte prefetch buffers. The objective of the fetch stage is to fill the prefetch buffers with new data as soon as the old data have been consumed by the instruction decoder. Because instructions are of variable length (from 1 to 11 bytes not counting prefixes), the status of the prefetcher relative to the other pipeline stages varies from instruction to instruction. On average, about five instructions are fetched with each 16-byte load [CRAW90]. The fetch stage operates independently of the other stages to keep the prefetch buffers full.

- **Decode stage 1:** All opcode and addressing-mode information is decoded in the D1 stage. The required information, as well as instruction-length information, is included in at most the first 3 bytes of the instruction. Hence, 3 bytes are passed to the D1 stage from the prefetch buffers. The D1 decoder can then direct the D2 stage to capture the rest of the instruction (displacement and immediate data), which is not involved in the D1 decoding.

- **Decode stage 2:** The D2 stage expands each opcode into control signals for the ALU. It also controls the computation of the more complex addressing modes.

- **Execute:** This stage includes ALU operations, cache access, and register update.

- **Write back:** This stage, if needed, updates registers and status flags modified during the preceding execute stage. If the current instruction updates memory, the computed value is sent to the cache and to the bus-interface write buffers at the same time.

With the use of two decode stages, the pipeline can sustain a throughput of close to one instruction per clock cycle. Complex instructions and conditional branches can slow down this rate.

Figure 12.19 shows examples of the operation of the pipeline. Part a shows that there is no delay introduced into the pipeline when a memory access is required. However, as part b shows, there can be a delay for values used to compute memory addresses. That is, if a value is loaded from memory into a register and that register is then used as a base register in the next instruction, the processor will stall for one cycle. In this example, the processor accesses the cache in the EX stage of the first instruction and stores the value retrieved in the register during the WB stage. However, the next instruction needs this register in its D2 stage. When the D2 stage lines up with the WB stage of the previous instruction, bypass signal paths allow the D2 stage to have access to the same data being used by the WB stage for writing, saving one pipeline stage.

Figure 12.19c illustrates the timing of a branch instruction, assuming that the branch is taken. The compare instruction updates condition codes in the WB stage, and bypass paths make this available to the EX stage of the jump instruction at the same time. In parallel, the processor runs a speculative fetch cycle to the target of the jump during the EX stage of the jump instruction. If the processor determines

Fetch	D1	D2	EX	WB			MOV Reg1, Mem1
	Fetch	D1	D2	EX	WB		MOV Reg1, Reg2
		Fetch	D1	D2	EX	WB	MOV Mem2, Reg1

(a) No data load delay in the pipeline

Fetch	D1	D2	EX	WB			MOV Reg1, Mem1
	Fetch	D1		D2	EX		MOV Reg2, (Reg1)

(b) Pointer load delay

Fetch	D1	D2	EX	WB			CMP Reg1, Imm
	Fetch	D1	D2	EX			Jcc Target
		Fetch	D1	D2	EX		Target

(c) Branch instruction timing

Figure 12.19   80486 Instruction Pipeline Examples

a false branch condition, it discards this prefetch and continues execution with the next sequential instruction (already fetched and decoded).

12.5 THE PENTIUM PROCESSOR

An overview of the Pentium 4 processor organization is depicted in Figure 4.13. In this section, we examine some of the details.

Register Organization

The register organization includes the following types of registers (Table 12.1):

- **General:** There are eight 32-bit general-purpose registers (see Figure 12.3c). These may be used for all types of Pentium instructions; they can also hold operands for address calculations. In addition, some of these registers also serve special purposes. For example, string instructions use the contents of the ECX, ESI, and EDI registers as operands without having to reference these registers explicitly in the instruction. As a result, a number of instructions can be encoded more compactly.

- **Segment:** The six 16-bit segment registers contain segment selectors, which index into segment tables, as discussed in Chapter 8. The code segment (CS) register references the segment containing the instruction being executed. The stack segment (SS) register references the segment containing a user-visible stack. The remaining segment registers (DS, ES, FS, GS) enable the user to reference up to four separate data segments at a time.
- **Flags:** The EFLAGS register contains condition codes and various mode bits.
- **Instruction pointer:** Contains the address of the current instruction.

There are also registers specifically devoted to the floating-point unit:

- **Numeric:** Each register holds an extended-precision 80-bit floating-point number. There are eight registers that function as a stack, with push and pop operations available in the instruction set.
- **Control:** The 16-bit control register contains bits that control the operation of the floating-point unit, including the type of rounding control; single, double, or extended precision; and bits to enable or disable various exception conditions.

Table 12.1   Pentium Processor Registers

(a) Integer Unit

Type	Number	Length (bits)	Purpose
General	8	32	General-purpose user registers
Segment	6	16	Contain segment selectors
Flags	1	32	Status and control bits
Instruction pointer	1	32	Instruction pointer

(b) Floating-Point Unit

Type	Number	Length (bits)	Purpose
Numeric	8	80	Hold floating-point numbers
Control	1	16	Control bits
Status	1	16	Status bits
Tag word	1	16	Specifies contents of numeric registers
Instruction pointer	1	48	Points to instruction interrupted by exception
Data pointer	1	48	Points to operand interrupted by exception

- **Status:** The 16-bit status register contains bits that reflect the current state of the floating-point unit, including a 3-bit pointer to the top of the stack; condition codes reporting the outcome of the last operation; and exception flags.
- **Tag word:** This 16-bit register contains a 2-bit tag for each floating-point numeric register, which indicates the nature of the contents of the corresponding register. The four possible values are valid, zero, special (NaN, infinity, denormalized), and empty. These tags enable programs to check the contents of a numeric register without performing complex decoding of the actual data in the register. For example, when a context switch is made, the processor need not save any floating-point registers that are empty.

The use of most of the aforementioned registers is easily understood. Let us elaborate briefly on several of the registers.

EFLAGS Register

The EFLAGS register (Figure 12.20) indicates the condition of the processor and helps to control its operation. It includes the six condition codes defined in Table 10.8 (carry, parity, auxiliary, zero, sign, overflow), which report the results of an integer operation. In addition, there are bits in the register that may be referred to as control bits:

- **Trap flag (TF):** When set, causes an interrupt after the execution of each instruction. This is used for debugging.
- **Interrupt enable flag (IF):** When set, the processor will recognize external interrupts.
- **Direction flag (DF):** Determines whether string processing instructions increment or decrement the 16-bit half-registers SI and DI (for 16-bit operations) or the 32-bit registers ESI and EDI (for 32-bit operations).
- **I/O privilege flag (IOPL):** When set, causes the processor to generate an exception on all accesses to I/O devices during protected-mode operation.
- **Resume flag (RF):** Allows the programmer to disable debug exceptions so that the instruction can be restarted after a debug exception without immediately causing another debug exception.
- **Alignment check (AC):** Activates if a word or doubleword is addressed on a nonword or nondoubleword boundary.
- **Identification flag (ID):** If this bit can be set and cleared, then this processor supports the CPUID instruction. This instruction provides information about the vendor, family, and model.

In addition, there are 4 bits that relate to operating mode. The nested task (NT) flag indicates that the current task is nested within another task in protected-mode operation. The virtual mode (VM) bit allows the programmer to enable or disable virtual 8086 mode, which determines whether the processor runs as an 8086 machine. The virtual interrupt flag (VIF) and virtual interrupt pending (VIP) flag are used in a multitasking environment.

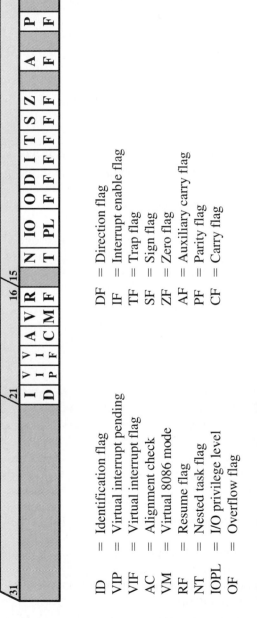

ID	= Identification flag
VIP	= Virtual interrupt pending
VIF	= Virtual interrupt flag
AC	= Alignment check
VM	= Virtual 8086 mode
RF	= Resume flag
NT	= Nested task flag
IOPL	= I/O privilege level
OF	= Overflow flag

DF	= Direction flag
IF	= Interrupt enable flag
TF	= Trap flag
SF	= Sign flag
ZF	= Zero flag
AF	= Auxiliary carry flag
PF	= Parity flag
CF	= Carry flag

Figure 12.20 Pentium II EFLAGS Register

443

Control Registers

The Pentium employs four 32-bit control registers (register CR1 is unused) to control various aspects of processor operation (Figure 12.21). The CR0 register contains system control flags, which control modes or indicate states that apply generally to the processor rather than to the execution of an individual task. The flags are as follows:

- **Protection enable (PE):** Enable/disable protected mode of operation.
- **Monitor coprocessor (MP):** Only of interest when running programs from earlier machines on the Pentium; it relates to the presence of an arithmetic coprocessor.
- **Emulation (EM):** Set when the processor does not have a floating-point unit, and causes an interrupt when an attempt is made to execute floating-point instructions.
- **Task switched (TS):** Indicates that the processor has switched tasks.
- **Extension type (ET):** Not used on the Pentium; used to indicate support of math coprocessor instructions on earlier machines.
- **Numeric error (NE):** Enables the standard mechanism for reporting floating-point errors on external bus lines.
- **Write protect (WP):** When this bit is clear, read-only user-level pages can be written by a supervisor process. This feature is useful for supporting process creation in some operating systems.
- **Alignment mask (AM):** Enables/disables alignment checking.
- **Not Write through (NW):** Selects mode of operation of the data cache. When this bit is set, the data cache is inhibited from cache write-through operations.
- **Cache disable (CD):** Enables/disables the internal cache fill mechanism.
- **Paging (PG):** Enables/disables paging.

When paging is enabled, the CR2 and CR3 registers are valid. The CR2 register holds the 32-bit linear address of the last page accessed before a page fault interrupt. The leftmost 20 bits of CR3 hold the 20 most significant bits of the base address of the page directory; the remainder of the address contains zeros. Two bits of CR3 are used to drive pins that control the operation of an external cache. The page-level cache disable (PCD) enables or disables the external cache, and the page-level writes transparent (PWT) bit controls write through in the external cache.

Nine additional control bits are defined in CR4:

- **Virtual-8086 mode extension (VME):** Enables support for the virtual interrupt flag in virtual-8086 mode.
- **Protected-mode virtual Interrupts (PVI):** Enables support for the virtual interrupt flag in protected mode.
- **Time stamp disable (TSD):** Disables the read from time stamp counter (RDTSC) instruction, which is used for debugging purposes.

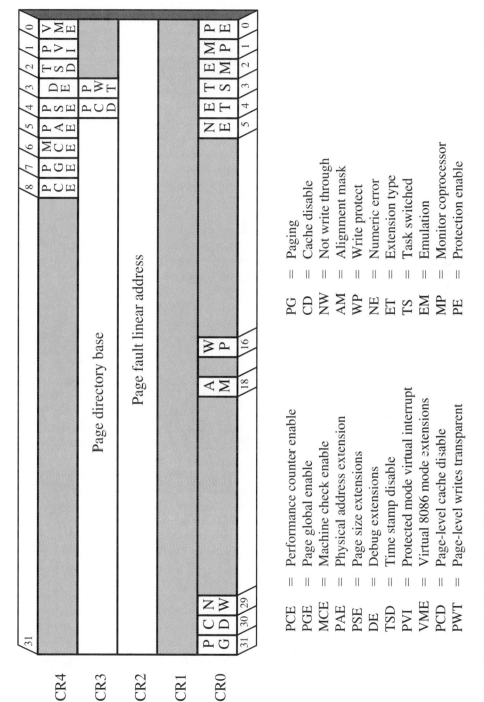

		PCE	=	Performance counter enable		PG	=	Paging
		PGE	=	Page global enable		CD	=	Cache disable
		MCE	=	Machine check enable		NW	=	Not write through
		PAE	=	Physical address extension		AM	=	Alignment mask
		PSE	=	Page size extensions		WP	=	Write protect
		DE	=	Debug extensions		NE	=	Numeric error
		TSD	=	Time stamp disable		ET	=	Extension type
		PVI	=	Protected mode virtual interrupt		TS	=	Task switched
		VME	=	Virtual 8086 mode extensions		EM	=	Emulation
		PCD	=	Page-level cache disable		MP	=	Monitor coprocessor
		PWT	=	Page-level writes transparent		PE	=	Protection enable

Figure 12.21 Pentium II Control Registers

445

- **Debugging extensions (DE):** Enables I/O breakpoints; this allows the processor to interrupt on I/O reads and writes.
- **Page size extensions (PSE):** Enables the use of 4-Mbyte pages when set in the Pentium or 2M-byte pages when set in the Pentium Pro and Pentium.
- **Physical address extension (PAE):** Enables address lines A35 through A32 whenever a special new addressing mode, controlled by the PSE, is enabled for the Pentium Pro and subsequent Pentium architectures (Pentium II through Pentium 4).
- **Machine check enable (MCE):** Enables the machine check interrupt, which occurs when a data parity error occurs during a read bus cycle or when a bus cycle is not successfully completed.
- **Page global enable (PGE):** Enables the use of global pages. When PGE = 1 and a task switch is performed, all of the TLB entries are flushed with the exception of those marked global.
- **Performance counter enable (PCE):** Enables the execution of the RDPMC (read performance counter) instruction at any privilege level. Two performance counters are used to measure the duration of a specific event type and the number of occurrences of a specific event type.

MMX Registers

Recall from Section 10.3 that the Pentium MMX capability makes use of several 64-bit data types. The MMX instructions make use of 3-bit register address fields, so that eight MMX registers are supported. In fact, the processor does not include specific MMX registers. Rather, the processor uses an aliasing technique (Figure 12.22). The existing floating-point registers are used to store MMX values. Specifically, the low-order 64 bits (mantissa) of each floating-point register are used to form the eight MMX registers. Thus, the existing Pentium architecture is easily extended to support the MMX capability. Some key characteristics of the MMX use of these registers are as follows:

- Recall that the floating-point registers are treated as a stack for floating-point operations. For MMX operations, these same registers are accessed directly.
- The first time that an MMX instruction is executed after any floating-point operations, the FP tag word is marked valid. This reflects the change from stack operation to direct register addressing.
- The EMMS (Empty MMX State) instruction sets bits of the FP tag word to indicate that all registers are empty. It is important that the programmer insert this instruction at the end of an MMX code block so that subsequent floating-point operations function properly.
- When a value is written to an MMX register, bits [79:64] of the corresponding FP register (sign and exponent bits) are set to all ones. This sets the value in the FP register to NaN (not a number) or infinity when viewed as a floating-point value. This ensures that an MMX data value will not look like a valid floating-point value.

Figure 12.22   Mapping of MMX Registers to Floating-Point Registers

Interrupt Processing

Interrupt processing within a processor is a facility provided to support the operating system. It allows an application program to be suspended, in order that a variety of interrupt conditions can be serviced and later resumed.

Interrupts and Exceptions

Two classes of events cause the Pentium to suspend execution of the current instruction stream and respond to the event: interrupts and exceptions. In both cases, the processor saves the context of the current process and transfers to a predefined routine to service the condition. An *interrupt* is generated by a signal from hardware, and it may occur at random times during the execution of a program. An *exception* is generated from software, and it is provoked by the execution of an instruction. There are two sources of interrupts and two sources of exceptions:

1. Interrupts
   - **Maskable interrupts:** Received on the processor's INTR pin. The processor does not recognize a maskable interrupt unless the interrupt enable flag (IF) is set.
   - **Nonmaskable interrupts:** Received on the processor's NMI pin. Recognition of such interrupts cannot be prevented.

2. Exceptions

- **Processor-detected exceptions:** Results when the processor encounters an error while attempting to execute an instruction.
- **Programmed exceptions:** These are instructions that generate an exception (INT0, INT3, INT, and BOUND).

Interrupt Vector Table

Interrupt processing on the Pentium uses the interrupt vector table. Every type of interrupt is assigned a number, and this number is used to index into the interrupt vector table. This table contains 256 32-bit interrupt vectors, which is the address (segment and offset) of the interrupt service routine for that interrupt number.

Table 12.2 shows the assignment of numbers in the interrupt vector table; shaded entries represent interrupts, while nonshaded entries are exceptions. The NMI hardware interrupt is type 2. INTR hardware interrupts are assigned numbers in the range of 32 to 255; when an INTR interrupt is generated, it must be accompanied on the bus with the interrupt vector number for this interrupt. The remaining vector numbers are used for exceptions.

If more than one exception or interrupt is pending, the processor services them in a predictable order. The location of vector numbers within the table does not reflect priority. Instead, priority among exceptions and interrupts is organized into five classes. In descending order of priority, these are

- **Class 1:** Traps on the previous instruction (vector number 1)
- **Class 2:** External interrupts (2, 32–255)
- **Class 3:** Faults from fetching next instruction (3, 14)
- **Class 4:** Faults from decoding the next instruction (6, 7)
- **Class 5:** Faults on executing an instruction (0, 4, 5, 8, 10–14, 16, 17)

Interrupt Handling

Just as with a transfer of execution using a CALL instruction, a transfer to an interrupt-handling routine uses the system stack to store the processor state. When an interrupt occurs and is recognized by the processor, a sequence of events takes place:

1. If the transfer involves a change of privilege level, then the current stack segment register and the current extended stack pointer (ESP) register are pushed onto the stack.

2. The current value of the EFLAGS register is pushed onto the stack.

3. Both the interrupt (IF) and trap (TF) flags are cleared. This disables INTR interrupts and the trap or single-step feature.

4. The current code segment (CS) pointer and the current instruction pointer (IP or EIP) are pushed onto the stack.

5. If the interrupt is accompanied by an error code, then the error code is pushed onto the stack.

6. The interrupt vector contents are fetched and loaded into the CS and IP or EIP registers. Execution continues from the interrupt service routine.

To return from an interrupt, the interrupt service routine executes an IRET instruction. This causes all of the values saved on the stack to be restored; execution resumes from the point of the interrupt.

Table 12.2 Pentium Exception and Interrupt Vector Table

Vector Number	Description
0	Divide error; division overflow or division by zero
1	Debug exception; includes various faults and traps related to debugging
2	NMI pin interrupt; signal on NMI pin
3	Breakpoint; caused by INT 3 instruction, which is a 1-byte instruction useful for debugging
4	INTO-detected overflow; occurs when the processor executes INTO with the OF flag set
5	BOUND range exceeded; the BOUND instruction compares a register with boundaries stored in memory and generates an interrupt if the contents of the register is out of bounds.
6	Undefined opcode
7	Device not available; attempt to use ESC or WAIT instruction fails due to lack of external device
8	Double fault; two interrupts occur during the same instruction and cannot be handled serially
9	Reserved
10	Invalid task state segment; segment describing a requested task is not initialized or not valid
11	Segment not present; required segment not present
12	Stack fault; limit of stack segment exceeded or stack segment not present
13	General protection; protection violation that does not cause another exception (e.g., writing to a read-only segment)
14	Page fault
15	Reserved
16	Floating-point error; generated by a floating-point arithmetic instruction
17	Alignment check; access to a word stored at an odd byte address or a doubleword stored at an address not a multiple of 4
18	Machine check; model specific
19–31	Reserved
32–255	User interrupt vectors; provided when INTR signal is activated

Unshaded: exceptions
Shaded: interrupts

12.6 THE POWERPC PROCESSOR

An overview of the PowerPC processor organization is depicted in Figure 4.14. In this section, we examine some of the details of the 64-bit implementation.

Register Organization

Figure 12.23 depicts the user-visible registers for the PowerPC. The fixed-point unit includes

- **General:** There are thirty-two 64-bit general-purpose registers. These may be used to load, store, and manipulate data operands and may also be used for register indirect addressing. Register 0 is treated somewhat differently. For load and store operations and several of the add instructions, register 0 is treated as having a constant value zero regardless of its actual contents.
- **Exception register (XER):** Includes 3 bits that report exceptions in integer arithmetic operations. This register also includes a byte count field that is used as an operand for some string instructions (Figure 12.23a).

The floating-point unit contains additional user-visible registers:

- **General:** There are thirty-two 64-bit general-purpose registers, used for all floating-point operations.
- **Floating-point status and control register (FPSCR):** This 32-bit register contains bits that control the operation of the floating-point unit and bits that record the status resulting from floating-point operations (Table 12.3).

The branch processing unit contains these user-visible registers:

- **Condition register:** Consists of eight 4-bit condition code fields (Figure 12.24b).
- **Link register:** The link register can be used in a conditional branch instruction for indirect addressing of the target address. This register is also used for call/return behavior. If the LK bit in a conditional branch instruction is set, then the address following the branch instruction is placed in the link register, and it can be used for a later return.
- **Count:** The count register can be used to control an iteration loop, as explained in Chapter 10; the count register is decremented each time it is tested in a conditional branch instruction. Another use for this register is indirect addressing of the target address in a branch instruction.

The fields of the condition register have a number of uses. The first 4 bits (CR0) are set for all integer arithmetic instructions for which the Rc bit is set. As Table 12.4 shows, the field indicates whether the result of the operation is positive, negative, or zero. The fourth bit is a copy of the summary overflow bit from the XER. The next field (CR1) is set for all floating-point arithmetic instructions for which the Rc bit is set. In this case, the 4 bits are set equal to the first four bits of the FPSCR (Table 12.3). Finally, the eight condition fields (CR0 through CR7) can

Figure 12.23 PowerPC User-Visible Registers

Table 12.3 PowerPC Floating-Point Status and Control Register

Bit	Definition
0	Exception summary. Set if any exception occurs; remains set until reset by software.
1	Enabled exception summary. Set if any enabled exception has occurred.
2	Invalid operation exception summary. Set if an invalid operation exception has occurred.
3	Overflow exception. Magnitude of result exceeds what can be represented.
4	Underflow exception. Result is to small to be normalized.
5	Zero divide exception. Divisor is zero and dividend is finite nonzero.
6	Inexact exception. Rounded result differs from intermediate result or an overflow occurs with overflow exception disabled.
7:12	Invalid operation exception. 7: signaling NaN; 8: $(\infty - \infty)$; 9: $(\infty \div \infty)$; 10: $(0 \div 0)$; 11: $(\infty \times 0)$; 12: comparison involving NaN.
13	Fraction rounded. Rounding of the result incremented the fraction.
14	Fraction inexact. Rounded result changes fraction or an overflow occurs with overflow exception disabled.
15:19	Result flags. Five-bit code specifies less than, greater than, equal, unordered, quiet NaN, $\pm\infty$, $\pm$normalized, $\pm$denormalized, ± 0
20	Reserved
21:23	Invalid operation exception. 21: software request; 22: square root of a negative number; 23: Integer conversion involving a large number, an infinity, or a NaN.
24	Invalid operation exception enable
25	Overflow exception enable
26	Underflow exception enable
27	Zero divide exception enable
28	Inexact exception enable
29	Non-IEEE mode
30:31	Rounding control. Two-bit code specifies to nearest, toward 0, toward $+\infty$, toward $-\infty$.

Unshaded: status bits
Shaded: control bits

be used with a compare instruction; in each case, the identity of the field is specified in the instruction itself. For both fixed-point and floating-point compare instructions, the first 3 bits of the designated condition field record whether the first operand is less than, greater than, or equal to the second operand. The fourth bit is the summary overflow bit for a fixed-point compare, and an unordered indicator for a floating-point compare.

Interrupt Processing

As with any processor, the PowerPC includes a facility that enables the processor to interrupt the currently executing program to deal with an exception condition.

Types of Interrupts

Interrupts on a PowerPC are classified as those caused by some system condition or event and those caused by the execution of an instruction. Table 12.5 lists the interrupts recognized by the PowerPC.

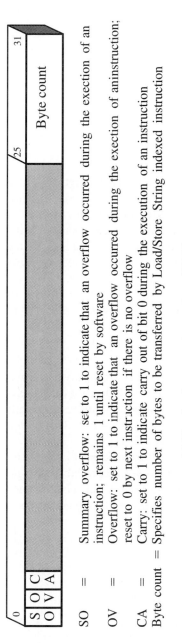

S	O								
O	V					Byte count			

SO = Summary overflow: set to 1 to indicate that an overflow occurred during the exection of an instruction; remains 1 until reset by software

OV = Overflow: set to 1 to indicate that an overflow occurred during the exection of aninstruction; reset to 0 by next instraction if there is no overflow

CA = Carry: set to 1 to indicate carry out of bit 0 during the execution of an instruction

Byte count = Specifies number of bytes to be transferred by Load/Store String indexed instruction

(a) Fixed-point exception register (XER)

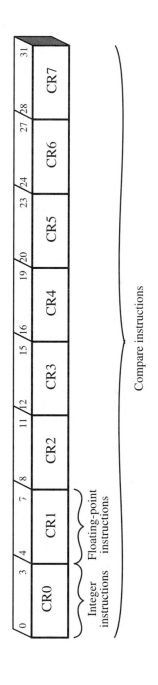

CR0	CR1	CR2	CR3	CR4	CR5	CR6	CR7

Integer instructions

Floating-point instructions

Compare instructions

(b) Condition register

Figure 12.24 PowerPC Register Formats

Table 12.4 Interpretation of Bits in Condition Register

Bit position	CR0 (integer instruction with Rc=1)	CR1 (floating-point instruction with Rc=1)	CRi (fixed-point compare instruction)	CRi (floating-point compare instruction)
i	result < 0	Exception summary	op1 $<$ op2	op1 $<$ op2
$i + 1$	result > 0	Enabled exception summary	op1 $>$ op2	op1 $>$ op2
$i + 2$	result $= 0$	Invalid operation exception summary	op1 $=$ op2	op1 $=$ op2
$i + 3$	Summary overflow	Overflow exception	Summary overflow	Unordered (one operand is a NaN)

Most of the interrupts listed in the table are easily understood. A few warrant further comment. The system reset interrupt happens at power on and when the reset button on the system unit is pressed, and it causes the system to reboot. The machine check interrupt deals with certain anomalies, such as cache parity error and reference to a nonexistent memory location, and may cause the system to enter what is known as a checkstop state; this state suspends processor execution and freezes the contents of registers until a reboot. The floating-point assist enables the processor to invoke software routines to complete operations that cannot be handled directly by the floating-point unit, such as those involving denormalized numbers or unimplemented floating-point opcodes.

Machine State Register

Fundamental to the interruption of a program is the ability to recover the state of the processor at the time of the interrupt. This includes not only the contents of the various registers but also various control conditions relating to execution. These conditions are conveniently summarized in the MSR (Table 12.6). Again, several of the bits in this register warrant further comment.

When the privilege mode bit (bit 49) is set, the processor is operating at a user privilege level. Only a subset of the instruction set is available. When the bit is cleared, the processor operates at supervisor privilege level. This enables all of the instructions and provides access to certain system registers (such as the MSR) not accessible from the user privilege level.

The values of the two floating-point exception bits (bits 52 and 55) define the types of interrupts that the floating-point unit may generate. The interpretation is as follows:

FE0	FE1	Interrupts that will be recognized
0	0	None
0	1	Imprecise nonrecoverable
1	0	Imprecise recoverable
1	1	Precise

Table 12.5 PowerPC Interrupt Table

Entry Point	Interrupt Type	Description
00000h	Reserved	
00100h	System reset	Assertion of the processor's hard or soft reset input signals by external logic
00200h	Machine check	Assertion of TEA# to the processor when it is enabled to recognize machine checks
00300h	Data storage	Examples: data page fault; access rights violation on load/store
00400h	Instruction storage	Code page fault; attempted instruction fetch from I/O segment; access rights violation
00500h	External	Assertion of the processor's external interrupt input signal by external logic when external interrupt recognition is enabled
00600h	Alignment	Unsuccessful attempt to access memory due to mis-aligned operand
00700h	Program	Floating-point interrupt; user attempts to execute privileged instruction; trap instruction executed with specified condition met; illegal instruction
00800h	Floating-point unavailable	Attempt to execute floating-point instruction with floating-point unit disabled
00900h	Decrementer	Exhaustion of the decrementer register when external interrupt recognition is enabled
00A00h	Reserved	
00B00h	Reserved	
00C00h	System call	Execution of a system call instruction
00D00h	Trace	Single-step or branch trace interrupt
00E00h	Floating-point assist	Attempt to execute relatively infrequent, complex floating-point operation (e.g., operation on denormalized number)
00E10h through 00FFFh	Reserved	
01000h through 02FFFh	Reserved (implementation specific)	

Unshaded: interrupts caused by instruction execution
Shaded: interrupts not caused by instruction execution

When the single-step trace bit (bit 53) is set, the processor branches to the trace interrupt handler after the successful completion of each instruction. When the branch trace bit (bit 54) is set, the processor branches to the branch trace interrupt handler after the successful completion of each branch instruction, whether or not the branch was taken.

The instruction address translation (bit 58) and data address translation (bit 59) determine whether real addressing is used or whether the memory-management unit performs address translation.

Table 12.6 PowerPC Machine State Register

Bit	Definition
0	Processor is in 32-bit/64-bit mode
1:44	Reserved
45	Power management enabled/disabled
46	Implementation dependent
47	Defines whether interrupt handlers run in big-endian or little-endian mode
48	External interrupt enabled/disabled
49	Privileged/nonprivileged state
50	Floating-point unit available/unavailable
51	Machine check interrupts enabled/disabled
52	Floating-point exception mode 0
53	Single-step trace enabled/disabled
54	Branch trace enabled/disabled
55	Floating-point exception mode 1
56	Reserved
57	Most significant part of exception address is 000h/FFFh
58	Instruction address translation on/off
59	Data address translation on/off
60:61	Reserved
62	Interrupt is recoverable/nonrecoverable
63	Processor is in big-endian/little-endian mode

Unshaded: copied to SRR1

Shaded: not copied to SRR1

Interrupt Handling

When an interrupt occurs and is recognized by the processor, the following sequence of events takes place:

1. The processor places the address of the instruction to be executed next in the Save/Restore Register 0 (SRR0). This is the address of the currently executing instruction if the interrupt was caused by a failed attempt to execute that instruction; otherwise, it is the address of the next instruction to be executed after the current instruction.

2. The processor copies machine state information from the MSR to the Save/ Restore Register 1 (SRR1). The bits that are depicted as unshaded in Table 12.6 are copied. The remaining bits of SRR1 are loaded with information specific to the interrupt type.

3. The MSR is set to a hardware-defined value specific to the interrupt type. For all interrupt types, address translation is turned off and external interrupts are disabled.

4. The processor then transfers control to the appropriate interrupt handler. The addresses of the interrupt handlers are stored in the Interrupt Table

(Table 12.5). The base address of that table is determined by bit 57 of the MSR.

To return from an interrupt, the interrupt service routine executes an rfi (return from interrupt) instruction. This causes the bit values saved in SRR1 to be restored to the MSR. Execution resumes at the location stored in SRR0.

12.7 RECOMMENDED READING

[PATT01] and [MOSH01] provide excellent coverage of the pipelining issues discussed in this chapter. [HENN91] and [HWAN93] contain detailed discussions of pipelining. [SOHI90] provides an excellent, detailed discussion of the hardware design issues involved in an instruction pipeline.

[EVER01] examines the evolution of branch prediction strategies. [CRAG92] is a detailed study of branch prediction in instruction pipelines. [DUBE91] and [LILJ88] examine various branch prediction strategies that can be used to enhance the performance of instruction pipelining. [KAEL91] examines the difficulty introduced into branch prediction by instructions whose target address is variable.

The Intel 80486 instruction pipeline is described in [TABA91]. [BREY00] provides good coverage of interrupt processing on the Pentium, as does [SHAN95] for the PowerPC.

BREY00   Brey, B. *The Intel Microprocessors: 8086/8066, 80186/80188, 80286, 80386, 80486, Pentium, Pentium Pro and Pentium II Processors.* Upper Saddle River, NJ: Prentice Hall, 2000.

CRAG92   Cragon, H. *Branch Strategy Taxonomy and Performance Models.* Los Alamitos, CA: IEEE Computer Society Press, 1992.

DUBE91   Dubey, P., and Flynn, M. "Branch Strategies: Modeling and Optimization." *IEEE Transactions on Computers,* October 1991.

EVER01   Evers, M., and Yeh, T. "Understanding Branches and Designing Branch Predictors for High-Performance Microprocessors." *Proceedings of the IEEE,* November 2001.

HENN91   Hennessy, J., and Jouppi, N. "Computer Technology and Architecture: An Evolving Interaction." *Computer,* September 1991.

HWAN93   Hwang, K. *Advanced Computer Architecture.* New York: McGraw-Hill, 1993.

KAEL91   Kaeli, D., and Emma, P. "Branch History Table Prediction of Moving Target Branches Due to Subroutine Returns." *Proceedings, 18th Annual International Symposium on Computer Architecture,* May 1991.

LILJ88   Lilja, D. "Reducing the Branch Penalty in Pipelined Processors." *Computer,* July 1988.

MOSH01   Moshovos, A., and Sohi, G. "Microarchitectural Innovations: Boosting Microprocessor Performance Beyond Semiconductor Technology Scaling." *Proceedings of the IEEE,* November 2001.

PATT01   Patt, Y. "Requirements, Bottlenecks, and Good Fortune: Agents for Microprocessor Evolution." *Proceedings of the IEEE,* November 2001.

SHAN95   Shanley, T. *PowerPC System Architecture.* Reading, MA: Addison-Wesley, 1995.

SOHI90   Sohi, G. "Instruction Issue Logic for High-Performance Interruptable, Multiple Functional Unit, Pipelined Computers." *IEEE Transactions on Computers,* March 1990.

TABA91   Tabak, D. *Advanced Microprocessors.* New York: McGraw-Hill, 1991.

12.8 KEY TERMS, REVIEW QUESTIONS, AND PROBLEMS

Key Terms

branch prediction	flag	instruction prefetch
condition code	instruction cycle	program status word (PSW)
delayed branch	instruction pipeline	

Review Questions

12.1   What general roles are performed by CPU registers?

12.2   What categories of data are commonly supported by user-visible registers?

12.3   What is the function of condition codes?

12.4   What is a program status word?

12.5   Why is a two-stage instruction pipeline unlikely to cut the instruction cycle time in half, compared with the use of no pipeline?

12.6   List and briefly explain various ways in which an instruction pipeline can deal with conditional branch instructions.

12.7   How are history bits used for branch prediction?

Problems

12.1   **a.** If the last operation performed on a computer with an 8-bit word was an addition in which the two operands were 2 and 3, what would be the value of the following flags?
- Carry
- Zero
- Overflow
- Sign
- Even parity
- Half-carry

  b. What if the operands were −1 (twos complement) and +1?

12.2   Consider the timing diagram of Figure 12.10. Assume that there is only a two-stage pipeline (fetch, execute). Redraw the diagram to show how many time units are now needed for four instructions.

12.3:   Consider an instruction sequence of length n that is streaming through the instruction pipeline. Let p be the probability of encountering a conditional or unconditional branch instruction, and let q be the probability that execution of a branch instruction I causes a jump to a nonconsecutive address. Assume that each such jump requires the pipeline to be cleared, destroying all ongoing instruction processing, when I emerges from the last stage. Revise Equations 12.1 and 12.2 to take these probabilities into account.

12.4   One limitation of the multiple-stream approach to dealing with branches in a pipeline is that additional branches will be encountered before the first branch is resolved. Suggest two additional limitations or drawbacks.

12.5   Consider the state diagrams of Figure 12.25.

  a. Describe the behavior of each.

  b. Compare these with the branch prediction state diagram in Section 12.4. Discuss the relative merits of each of the three approaches to branch prediction.

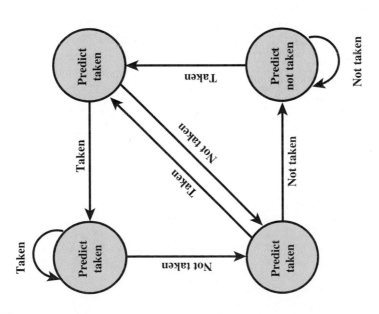

Figure 12.25 State Diagram for Problem 12.5

12.6 The Motorola 680x0 machines include the instruction Decrement and Branch According to Condition, which has the following form:

```
DBcc Dn, displacement
```

where cc is one of the testable conditions, Dn is a general-purpose register, and displacement specifies the target address relative to the current address. The instruction can be defined as follows:

```
if (cc = False)
then begin
    Dn := (Dn) - 1;
    if Dn ≠ -1 then PC := (PC) + displacement end
else PC := (PC) + 2;
```

When the instruction is executed, the condition is first tested to determine whether the termination condition for the loop is satisfied. If so, no operation is performed and execution continues at the next instruction in sequence. If the condition is false, the specified data register is decremented and checked to see if it is less than zero. If it is less than zero, the loop is terminated and execution continues at the next instruction in sequence. Otherwise, the program branches to the specified location. Now consider the following assembly-language program fragment:

```
AGAIN    CMPM.L   (A0)+,(A1)+
         DBNE     D1, AGAIN
         NOP
```

Two strings addressed by A0 and A1 are compared for equality; the string pointers are incremented with each reference. D1 initially contains the number of longwords (4 bytes) to be compared.

a. The initial contents of the registers are A0 = $00004000, A1 = $00005000, and D1 = $000000FF (the $ indicates hexadecimal notation). Memory between $4000 and $6000 is loaded with words $AAAA. If the foregoing program is run, specify the number of times the DBNE loop is executed and the contents of the three registers when the NOP instruction is reached.

b. Repeat (a), but now assume that memory between $4000 and $4FEE is loaded with $0000 and between $5000 and $6000 is loaded with $AAA.

12.7 Redraw Figure 12.19c, assuming that the conditional branch is not taken.

CHAPTER 13

REDUCED INSTRUCTION SET COMPUTERS

KEY POINTS

◆ Studies of the execution behavior of high-level language programs have provided guidance in designing a new type of processor architecture: the reduced instruction set computer (RISC). Assignment statements predominate, suggesting that the simple movement of data should be optimized. There are also many IF and LOOP instructions, which suggests that the underlying sequence control mechanism needs to be optimized to permit efficient pipelining. Studies of operand reference patterns suggest that it should be possible to enhance performance by keeping a moderate number of operands in registers.

◆ These studies have motivated the key characteristics of RISC machines: (1) a limited instruction set with a fixed format, (2) a large number of registers or the use of a compiler that optimizes register usage, and (3) an emphasis on optimizing the instruction pipeline.

◆ The simple instruction set of a RISC lends itself to efficient pipelining because there are fewer and more predictable operations performed per instruction. A RISC instruction set architecture also lends itself to the delayed branch technique, in which branch instructions are rearranged with other instructions to improve pipeline efficiency.

Since the development of the stored-program computer around 1950, there have been remarkably few true innovations in the areas of computer organization and architecture. The following are some of the major advances since the birth of the computer:

- **The family concept:** Introduced by IBM with its System/360 in 1964, followed shortly thereafter by DEC, with its PDP-8. The family concept decouples the architecture of a machine from its implementation. A set of computers is offered, with different price/performance characteristics, that presents the same architecture to the user. The differences in price and performance are due to different implementations of the same architecture.

- **Microprogrammed control unit:** Suggested by Wilkes in 1951, and introduced by IBM on the S/360 line in 1964. Microprogramming eases the task of designing and implementing the control unit and provides support for the family concept.

- **Cache memory:** First introduced commercially on IBM S/360 Model 85 in 1968. The insertion of this element into the memory hierarchy dramatically improves performance.

- **Pipelining:** A means of introducing parallelism into the essentially sequential nature of a machine-instruction program. Examples are instruction pipelining and vector processing.

- **Multiple processors:** This category covers a number of different organizations and objectives.

Table 13.1   Characteristics of Some CISCs, RISCs, and Superscalar Processors

Characteristic	Complex Instruction Set (CISC) Computer			Reduced Instruction Set (RISC) Computer		Superscalar		
	IBM 370/168	VAX 11/780	Intel 80486	SPARC	MIPS R4000	PowerPC	Ultra SPARC	MIPS R10000
Year developed	1973	1978	1989	1987	1991	1993	1996	1996
Number of instructions	208	303	235	69	94	225		
Instruction size (bytes)	2–6	2–57	1–11	4	4	4	4	4
Addressing modes	4	22	11	1	1	2	1	1
Number of general-purpose registers	16	16	8	40–520	32	32	40–520	32
Control memory size (kbits)	420	480	246	—	—	—	—	—
Cache size (kbytes)	64	64	8	32	128	16–32	32	64

To this list must now be added one of the most interesting and, potentially, one of the most important innovations: reduced instruction set computer (RISC) architecture. The RISC architecture is a dramatic departure from the historical trend in processor architecture. An analysis of the RISC architecture brings into focus many of the important issues in computer organization and architecture.

Although RISC systems have been defined and designed in a variety of ways by different groups, the key elements shared by most designs are these:

- A large number of general-purpose registers, and/or the use of compiler technology to optimize register usage
- A limited and simple instruction set
- An emphasis on optimizing the instruction pipeline

Table 13.1 compares several RISC and non-RISC systems.

We begin this chapter with a brief survey of some results on instruction sets, and then examine each of the three topics just listed. This is followed by a description of two of the best-documented RISC designs.

13.1 INSTRUCTION EXECUTION CHARACTERISTICS

One of the most visible forms of evolution associated with computers is that of programming languages. As the cost of hardware has dropped, the relative cost of software has risen. Along with that, a chronic shortage of programmers has driven up software costs in absolute terms. Thus, the major cost in the life cycle of a system is software, not hardware. Adding to the cost, and to the inconvenience, is the element of unreliability: It is common for programs, both system and application, to continue to exhibit new bugs after years of operation.

The response from researchers and industry has been to develop ever more powerful and complex high-level programming languages. These high-level languages (HLLs) allow the programmer to express algorithms more concisely, take care of much of the detail, and often support naturally the use of structured programming or object-oriented design.

Alas, this solution gave rise to another problem, known as the *semantic gap,* the difference between the operations provided in HLLs and those provided in computer architecture. Symptoms of this gap are alleged to include execution inefficiency, excessive machine program size, and compiler complexity. Designers responded with architectures intended to close this gap. Key features include large instruction sets, dozens of addressing modes, and various HLL statements implemented in hardware. An example of the latter is the CASE machine instruction on the VAX. Such complex instruction sets are intended to

- Ease the task of the compiler writer.
- Improve execution efficiency, because complex sequences of operations can be implemented in microcode.
- Provide support for even more complex and sophisticated HLLs.

Meanwhile, a number of studies have been done over the years to determine the characteristics and patterns of execution of machine instructions generated from HLL programs. The results of these studies inspired some researchers to look for a different approach: namely, to make the architecture that supports the HLL simpler, rather than more complex.

To understand the line of reasoning of the RISC advocates, we begin with a brief review of instruction execution characteristics. The aspects of computation of interest are as follows:

- **Operations performed:** These determine the functions to be performed by the processor and its interaction with memory.
- **Operands used:** The types of operands and the frequency of their use determine the memory organization for storing them and the addressing modes for accessing them.
- **Execution sequencing:** This determines the control and pipeline organization.

In the remainder of this section, we summarize the results of a number of studies of high-level-language programs. All of the results are based on dynamic measurements. That is, measurements are collected by executing the program and counting the number of times some feature has appeared or a particular property has held true. In contrast, static measurements merely perform these counts on the source text of a program. They give no useful information on performance, because they are not weighted relative to the number of times each statement is executed.

Operations

A variety of studies have been made to analyze the behavior of HLL programs. Table 4.7, discussed in Chapter 4, includes key results from a number of studies.

There is quite good agreement in the results of this mixture of languages and applications. Assignment statements predominate, suggesting that the simple movement of data is of high importance. There is also a preponderance of conditional statements (IF, LOOP). These statements are implemented in machine language with some sort of compare and branch instruction. This suggests that the sequence control mechanism of the instruction set is important.

These results are instructive to the machine instruction set designer, indicating which types of statements occur most often and therefore should be supported in an "optimal" fashion. However, these results do not reveal which statements use the most time in the execution of a typical program. That is, given a compiled machine-language program, which statements in the source language cause the execution of the most machine-language instructions?

To get at this underlying phenomenon, the Patterson programs [PATT82a], described in Appendix 4A, were compiled on the VAX, PDP-11, and Motorola 68000 to determine the average number of machine instructions and memory references per statement type. The second and third columns in Table 13.2 show the relative frequency of occurrence of various HLL instructions in a variety of programs; the data were obtained by observing the occurrences in running programs, rather than just the number of times that statements occur in the source code. Hence these are dynamic frequency statistics. To obtain the data in columns four and five (machine-instruction weighted), each value in the second and third columns is multiplied by the number of machine instructions produced by the compiler. These results are then normalized so that columns four and five show the relative frequency of occurrence, weighted by the number of machine instructions per HLL statement. Similarly, the sixth and seventh columns are obtained by multiplying the frequency of occurrence of each statement type by the relative number of memory references caused by each statement. The data in columns four through seven provide surrogate measures of the actual time spent executing the various statement types. The results suggest that the procedure call/return is the most time-consuming operation in typical HLL programs.

The reader should be clear on the significance of Table 13.2. This table indicates the relative significance of various statement types in an HLL, when that HLL is compiled for a typical contemporary instruction set architecture. Some other architecture could conceivably produce different results. However, this study produces results that are representative for contemporary complex instruction set com-

Table 13.2 Weighted Relative Dynamic Frequency of HLL Operations [PATT82a]

| | Dynamic Occurrence | | Machine-Instruction Weighted | | Memory-Reference Weighted | |
	Pascal	C	Pascal	C	Pascal	C
ASSIGN	45%	38%	13%	13%	14%	15%
LOOP	5%	3%	42%	32%	33%	26%
CALL	15%	12%	31%	33%	44%	45%
IF	29%	43%	11%	21%	7%	13%
GOTO	—	3%	—	—	—	—
OTHER	6%	1%	3%	1%	2%	1%

puter (CISC) architectures. Thus, they can provide guidance to those looking for more efficient ways to support HLLs.

Operands

Much less work has been done on the occurrence of types of operands, despite the importance of this topic. There are several aspects that are significant.

The Patterson study already referenced [PATT82a] also looked at the dynamic frequency of occurrence of classes of variables (Table 13.3). The results, consistent between Pascal and C programs, show that the majority of references are to simple scalar variables. Further, more than 80% of the scalars were local (to the procedure) variables. In addition, references to arrays/structures require a previous reference to their index or pointer, which again is usually a local scalar. Thus, there is a preponderance of references to scalars, and these are highly localized.

The Patterson study examined the dynamic behavior of HLL programs, independent of the underlying architecture. As discussed before, it is necessary to deal with actual architectures to examine program behavior more deeply. One study, [LUND77], examined DEC-10 instructions dynamically and found that each instruction on the average references 0.5 operand in memory and 1.4 registers. Similar results are reported in [HUCK83] for C, Pascal, and FORTRAN programs on S/370, PDP-11, and VAX. Of course, these figures depend highly on both the architecture and the compiler, but they do illustrate the frequency of operand accessing.

These latter studies suggest the importance of an architecture that lends itself to fast operand accessing, because this operation is performed so frequently. The Patterson study suggests that a prime candidate for optimization is the mechanism for storing and accessing local scalar variables.

Procedure Calls

We have seen that procedure calls and returns are an important aspect of HLL programs. The evidence (Table 13.2) suggests that these are the most time-consuming operations in compiled HLL programs. Thus, it will be profitable to consider ways of implementing these operations efficiently. Two aspects are significant: the number of parameters and variables that a procedure deals with, and the depth of nesting.

Tanenbaum's study [TANE78] found that 98% of dynamically called procedures were passed fewer than six arguments, and that 92% of them used fewer than six local scalar variables. Similar results were reported by the Berkeley RISC team [KATE83], as shown in Table 13.4. These results show that the number of words required per procedure activation is not large. The studies reported earlier indicated that a high proportion of operand references is to local scalar variables. These studies show that those references are in fact confined to relatively few variables.

Table 13.3 Dynamic Percentage of Operands

	Pascal	**C**	**Average**
Integer constant	16%	23%	20%
Scalar variable	58%	53%	55%
Array/structure	26%	24%	25%

Table 13.4 Procedure Arguments and Local Scalar Variables

Percentage of Executed Procedure Calls With	Compiler, Interpreter, and Typesetter	Small Nonnumeric Programs
>3 arguments	0–7%	0–5%
>5 arguments	0–3%	0%
>8 words of arguments and local scalars	1–20%	0–6%
>12 words of arguments and local scalars	1–6%	0–3%

The same Berkeley group also looked at the pattern of procedure calls and returns in HLL programs. They found that it is rare to have a long uninterrupted sequence of procedure calls followed by the corresponding sequence of returns. Rather, they found that a program remains confined to a rather narrow window of procedure-invocation depth. This is illustrated in Figure 4.16, which was discussed in Chapter 4. These results reinforce the conclusion that operand references are highly localized.

Implications

A number of groups have looked at results such as those just reported and have concluded that the attempt to make the instruction set architecture close to HLLs is not the most effective design strategy. Rather, the HLLs can best be supported by optimizing performance of the most time-consuming features of typical HLL programs.

Generalizing from the work of a number of researchers, three elements emerge that, by and large, characterize RISC architectures. First, use a large number of registers or use a compiler to optimize register usage. This is intended to optimize operand referencing. The studies just discussed show that there are several references per HLL instruction, and that there is a high proportion of move (assignment) statements. This, coupled with the locality and predominance of scalar references, suggests that performance can be improved by reducing memory references at the expense of more register references. Because of the locality of these references, an expanded register set seems practical.

Second, careful attention needs to be paid to the design of instruction pipelines. Because of the high proportion of conditional branch and procedure call instructions, a straightforward instruction pipeline will be inefficient. This manifests itself as a high proportion of instructions that are prefetched but never executed.

Finally, a simplified (reduced) instruction set is indicated. This point is not as obvious as the others, but should become clearer in the ensuing discussion.

13.2 THE USE OF A LARGE REGISTER FILE

The results summarized in Section 13.1 point out the desirability of quick access to operands. We have seen that there is a large proportion of assignment statements in HLL programs, and many of these are of the simple form A ← B. Also, there is a significant number of operand accesses per HLL statement. If we couple these results with the fact that most accesses are to local scalars, heavy reliance on register storage is suggested.

The reason that register storage is indicated is that it is the fastest available storage device, faster than both main memory and cache. The register file is physically small, on the same chip as the ALU and control unit, and employs much shorter addresses than addresses for cache and memory. Thus, a strategy is needed that will allow the most frequently accessed operands to be kept in registers and to minimize register-memory operations.

Two basic approaches are possible, one based on software and the other on hardware. The software approach is to rely on the compiler to maximize register usage. The compiler will attempt to allocate registers to those variables that will be used the most in a given time period. This approach requires the use of sophisticated program-analysis algorithms. The hardware approach is simply to use more registers so that more variables can be held in registers for longer periods of time.

In this section, we will discuss the hardware approach. This approach has been pioneered by the Berkeley RISC group [PATT82a]; was used in the first commercial RISC product, the Pyramid [RAGA83]; and is currently used in the popular SPARC architecture.

Register Windows

On the face of it, the use of a large set of registers should decrease the need to access memory. The design task is to organize the registers in such a fashion that this goal is realized.

Because most operand references are to local scalars, the obvious approach is to store these in registers, with perhaps a few registers reserved for global variables. The problem is that the definition of *local* changes with each procedure call and return, operations that occur frequently. On every call, local variables must be saved from the registers into memory, so that the registers can be reused by the called program. Furthermore, parameters must be passed. On return, the variables of the parent program must be restored (loaded back into registers) and results must be passed back to the parent program.

The solution is based on two other results reported in Section 13.1. First, a typical procedure employs only a few passed parameters and local variables (Table 13.4). Second, the depth of procedure activation fluctuates within a relatively narrow range (Figure 4.16). To exploit these properties, multiple small sets of registers are used, each assigned to a different procedure. A procedure call automatically switches the processor to use a different fixed-size window of registers, rather than saving registers in memory. Windows for adjacent procedures are overlapped to allow parameter passing.

The concept is illustrated in Figure 13.1. At any time, only one window of registers is visible and is addressable as if it were the only set of registers (e.g., addresses 0 through $N - 1$). The window is divided into three fixed-size areas. Parameter registers hold parameters passed down from the procedure that called the current procedure and hold results to be passed back up. Local registers are used for local variables, as assigned by the compiler. Temporary registers are used to exchange parameters and results with the next lower level (procedure called by current procedure). The temporary registers at one level are physically the same as the parameter registers at the next lower level. This overlap permits parameters to be passed without the actual movement of data.

To handle any possible pattern of calls and returns, the number of register windows would have to be unbounded. Instead, the register windows can be used to hold the few most recent procedure activations. Older activations must be saved in memory and later restored when the nesting depth decreases. Thus, the actual organization of the register file is as a circular buffer of overlapping windows. Two notable examples of this approach are Sun's SPARC architecture, described in Section 13.7, and the IA-64 architecture used in Intel's Itanium processor, described in Chapter 15.

This organization is shown in Figure 13.2, which depicts a circular buffer of six windows. The buffer is filled to a depth of 4 (A called B; B called C; C called D) with procedure D active. The current-window pointer (CWP) points to the window of the currently active procedure. Register references by a machine instruction are offset by this pointer to determine the actual physical register. The saved-window pointer identifies the window most recently saved in memory. If procedure D now calls procedure E, arguments for E are placed in D's temporary registers (the overlap between w3 and w4) and the CWP is advanced by one window.

If procedure E then makes a call to procedure F, the call cannot be made with the current status of the buffer. This is because F's window overlaps A's window. If F begins to load its temporary registers, preparatory to a call, it will overwrite the parameter registers of A (A.in). Thus, when CWP is incremented (modulo 6) so that it becomes equal to SWP, an interrupt occurs, and A's window is saved. Only the first two portions (A.in and A.loc) need be saved. Then, the SWP is incremented and the call to F proceeds. A similar interrupt can occur on returns. For example, subsequent to the activation of F, when B returns to A, CWP is decremented and becomes equal to SWP. This causes an interrupt that results in the restoration of A's window.

From the preceding, it can be seen that an *N*-window register file can hold only $N - 1$ procedure activations. The value of *N* need not be large. As was mentioned in Appendix 4A, one study [TAMI83] found that, with 8 windows, a save or restore is needed on only 1% of the calls or returns. The Berkeley RISC computers use 8 windows of 16 registers each. The Pyramid computer employs 16 windows of 32 registers each.

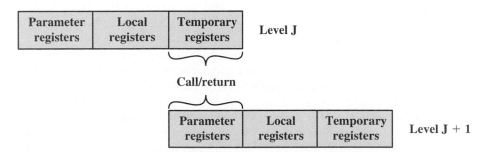

Figure 13.1   Overlapping Register Windows

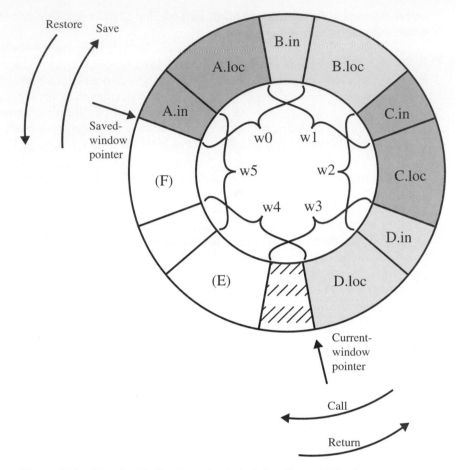

Figure 13.2 Circular-Buffer Organization of Overlapped Windows

Global Variables

The window scheme just described provides an efficient organization for storing local scalar variables in registers. However, this scheme does not address the need to store global variables, those accessed by more than one procedure. Two options suggest themselves. First, variables declared as global in an HLL can be assigned memory locations by the compiler, and all machine instructions that reference these variables will use memory-reference operands. This is straightforward, from both the hardware and software (compiler) points of view. However, for frequently accessed global variables, this scheme is inefficient.

An alternative is to incorporate a set of global registers in the processor. These registers would be fixed in number and available to all procedures. A unified numbering scheme can be used to simplify the instruction format. For example, references to registers 0 through 7 could refer to unique global registers, and references to registers 8 through 31 could be offset to refer to physical registers in the current window. There is an increased hardware burden to accommodate the split in register addressing. In addition, the compiler must decide which global variables should be assigned to registers.

Large Register File versus Cache

The register file, organized into windows, acts as a small, fast buffer for holding a subset of all variables that are likely to be used the most heavily. From this point of view, the register file acts much like a cache memory, although a much faster memory. The question therefore arises as to whether it would be simpler and better to use a cache and a small traditional register file.

Table 13.5 compares characteristics of the two approaches. The window-based register file holds all the local scalar variables (except in the rare case of window overflow) of the most recent $N - 1$ procedure activations. The cache holds a selection of recently used scalar variables. The register file should save time, because all local scalar variables are retained. On the other hand, the cache may make more efficient use of space, because it is reacting to the situation dynamically. Furthermore, caches generally treat all memory references alike, including instructions and other types of data. Thus, savings in these other areas are possible with a cache and not a register file.

A register file may make inefficient use of space, because not all procedures will need the full window space allotted to them. On the other hand, the cache suffers from another sort of inefficiency: Data are read into the cache in blocks. Whereas the register file contains only those variables in use, the cache reads in a block of data, some or much of which will not be used.

The cache is capable of handling global as well as local variables. There are usually many global scalars, but only a few of them are heavily used [KATE83]. A cache will dynamically discover these variables and hold them. If the window-based register file is supplemented with global registers, it too can hold some global scalars. However, it is difficult for a compiler to determine which globals will be heavily used.

With the register file, the movement of data between registers and memory is determined by the procedure nesting depth. Because this depth usually fluctuates within a narrow range, the use of memory is relatively infrequent. Most cache mem-

Table 13.5   Characteristics of Large-Register-File and Cache Organizations

Large Register File	Cache
All local scalars	Recently used local scalars
Individual variables	Blocks of memory
Compiler-assigned global variables	Recently used global variables
Save/restore based on procedure nesting depth	Save/restore based on cache replacement algorithm
Register addressing	Memory addressing

ories are set associative with a small set size. Thus, there is the danger that other data or instructions will overwrite frequently used variables.

Based on the discussion so far, the choice between a large window-based register file and a cache is not clear-cut. There is one characteristic, however, in which the register approach is clearly superior and which suggests that a cache-based system will be noticeably slower. This distinction shows up in the amount of addressing overhead experienced by the two approaches.

Figure 13.3 illustrates the difference. To reference a local scalar in a window-based register file, a "virtual" register number and a window number are used. These can pass through a relatively simple decoder to select one of the physical registers. To reference a memory location in cache, a full-width memory address must be generated. The complexity of this operation depends on the addressing mode. In a set associative cache, a portion of the address is used to read a number of words

(a) Windows-based register file

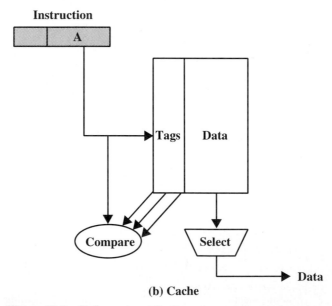

(b) Cache

Figure 13.3 Referencing a Scalar

and tags equal to the set size. Another portion of the address is compared with the tags, and one of the words that were read is selected. It should be clear that even if the cache is as fast as the register file, the access time will be considerably longer. Thus, from the point of view of performance, the window-based register file is superior for local scalars. Further performance improvement could be achieved by the addition of a cache for instructions only.

13.3 COMPILER-BASED REGISTER OPTIMIZATION

Let us assume now that only a small number (e.g., 16–32) of registers is available on the target RISC machine. In this case, optimized register usage is the responsibility of the compiler. A program written in a high-level language has, of course, no explicit references to registers. Rather, program quantities are referred to symbolically. The objective of the compiler is to keep the operands for as many computations as possible in registers rather than main memory, and to minimize load-and-store operations.

In general, the approach taken is as follows. Each program quantity that is a candidate for residing in a register is assigned to a symbolic or virtual register. The compiler then maps the unlimited number of symbolic registers into a fixed number of real registers. Symbolic registers whose usage does not overlap can share the same real register. If, in a particular portion of the program, there are more quantities to deal with than real registers, then some of the quantities are assigned to memory locations. Load-and-store instructions are used to position quantities in registers temporarily for computational operations.

The essence of the optimization task is to decide which quantities are to be assigned to registers at any given point in the program. The technique most commonly used in RISC compilers is known as graph coloring, which is a technique borrowed from the discipline of topology [CHAI82, CHOW86, COUT86, CHOW90].

The graph coloring problem is this. Given a graph consisting of nodes and edges, assign colors to nodes such that adjacent nodes have different colors, and do this in such a way as to minimize the number of different colors. This problem is adapted to the compiler problem in the following way. First, the program is analyzed to build a register interference graph. The nodes of the graph are the symbolic registers. If two symbolic registers are "live" during the same program fragment, then they are joined by an edge to depict interference. An attempt is then made to color the graph with n colors, where n is the number of registers. Nodes that share the same color can be assigned to the same register. If this process does not fully succeed, then those nodes that cannot be colored must be placed in memory, and loads and stores must be used to make space for the affected quantities when they are needed.

Figure 13.4 is a simple example of the process. Assume a program with six symbolic registers to be compiled into three actual registers. Figure 13.4a shows the time sequence of active use of each symbolic register, and part b shows the register interference graph (shading and cross-hatching are used instead of colors). A possible coloring with three colors is indicated. One symbolic register, F, is left uncolored and must be dealt with using loads and stores.

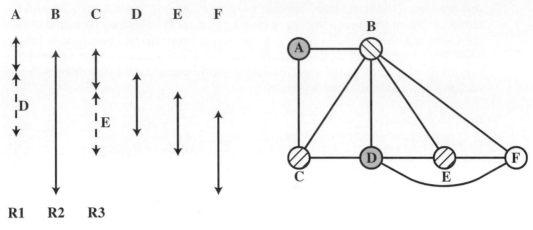

(a) Time sequence of active use of registers

(b) Register interference graph

Figure 13.4 Graph Coloring Approach

In general, there is a trade-off between the use of a large set of registers and compiler-based register optimization. For example, [BRAD91a] reports on a study that modeled a RISC architecture with features similar to the Motorola 88000 and the MIPS R2000. The researchers varied the number of registers from 16 to 128, and they considered both the use of all general-purpose registers and registers split between integer and floating-point use. Their study showed that with even simple register optimization, there is little benefit to the use of more than 64 registers. With reasonably sophisticated register optimization techniques, there is only marginal performance improvement with more than 32 registers. Finally, they noted that with a small number of registers (e.g., 16), a machine with a shared register organization executes faster than one with a split organization. Similar conclusions can be drawn from [HUGU91], which reports on a study that is primarily concerned with optimizing the use of a small number of registers, rather than comparing the use of large register sets with optimization efforts.

13.4 REDUCED INSTRUCTION SET ARCHITECTURE

In this section, we look at some of the general characteristics of and the motivation for a reduced instruction set architecture. Specific examples will be seen later in this chapter. We begin with a discussion of motivations for contemporary complex instruction set architectures.

Why CISC

We have noted the trend to richer instruction sets, which include a larger number of instructions and more complex instructions. Two principal reasons have motivated this trend: a desire to simplify compilers and a desire to improve performance. Underlying both of these reasons was the shift to high-level languages (HLL) on the part of programmers; architects attempted to design machines that provided better support for HLLs.

It is not the intent of this chapter to say that the CISC designers took the wrong direction. Indeed, because technology continues to evolve and because architectures exist along a spectrum rather than in two neat categories, a black-and-white assessment is unlikely ever to emerge. Thus, the comments that follow are simply meant to point out some of the potential pitfalls in the CISC approach and to provide some understanding of the motivation of the RISC adherents.

The first of the reasons cited, compiler simplification, seems obvious. The task of the compiler writer is to generate a sequence of machine instructions for each HLL statement. If there are machine instructions that resemble HLL statements, this task is simplified. This reasoning has been disputed by the RISC researchers ([HENN82], [RADI83], [PATT82b]). They have found that complex machine instructions are often hard to exploit because the compiler must find those cases that exactly fit the construct. The task of optimizing the generated code to minimize code size, reduce instruction execution count, and enhance pipelining is much more difficult with a complex instruction set. As evidence of this, studies cited earlier in this chapter indicate that most of the instructions in a compiled program are the relatively simple ones.

The other major reason cited is the expectation that a CISC will yield smaller, faster programs. Let us examine both aspects of this assertion: that programs will be smaller and that they will execute faster.

There are two advantages to smaller programs. First, because the program takes up less memory, there is a savings in that resource. With memory today being so inexpensive, this potential advantage is no longer compelling. More important, smaller programs should improve performance, and this will happen in two ways. First, fewer instructions means fewer instruction bytes to be fetched. Second, in a paging environment, smaller programs occupy fewer pages, reducing page faults.

The problem with this line of reasoning is that it is far from certain that a CISC program will be smaller than a corresponding RISC program. In many cases, the CISC program, expressed in symbolic machine language, may be *shorter* (i.e., fewer instructions), but the number of bits of memory occupied may not be noticeably *smaller*. Table 13.6 shows results from three studies that compared the size of compiled C programs on a variety of machines, including RISC I, which has a reduced

Table 13.6 Code Size Relative to RISC I

	[PATT82a] 11 C Programs	[KATE83] 12 C Programs	[HEAT84] 5 C Programs
RISC I	1.0	1.0	1.0
VAX-11/780	0.8	0.67	
M68000	0.9		0.9
Z8002	1.2		1.12
PDP-11/70	0.9	0.71	

instruction set architecture. Note that there is little or no savings using a CISC over a RISC. It is also interesting to note that the VAX, which has a much more complex instruction set than the PDP 11, achieves very little savings over the latter. These results were confirmed by IBM researchers [RADI83], who found that the IBM 801 (a RISC) produced code that was 0.9 times the size of code on an IBM S/370. The study used a set of PL/I programs.

There are several reasons for these rather surprising results. We have already noted that compilers on CISCs tend to favor simpler instructions, so that the conciseness of the complex instructions seldom comes into play. Also, because there are more instructions on a CISC, longer opcodes are required, producing longer instructions. Finally, RISCs tend to emphasize register rather than memory references, and the former require fewer bits. An example of this last effect is discussed presently.

So the expectation that a CISC will produce smaller programs, with the attendant advantages, may not be realized. The second motivating factor for increasingly complex instruction sets was that instruction execution would be faster. It seems to make sense that a complex HLL operation will execute more quickly as a single machine instruction rather than as a series of more primitive instructions. However, because of the bias toward the use of those simpler instructions, this may not be so. The entire control unit must be made more complex, and/or the microprogram control store must be made larger, to accommodate a richer instruction set. Either factor increases the execution time of the simple instructions.

In fact, some researchers have found that the speedup in the execution of complex functions is due not so much to the power of the complex machine instructions as to their residence in high-speed control store [RADI83]. In effect, the control store acts as an instruction cache. Thus, the hardware architect is in the position of trying to determine which subroutines or functions will be used most frequently and assigning those to the control store by implementing them in microcode. The results have been less than encouraging. On S/390 systems, instructions such as Translate and Extended-Precision-Floating-Point-Divide reside in high-speed storage, while the sequence involved in setting up procedure calls or initiating an interrupt handler are in slower main memory.

Thus, it is far from clear that a trend to increasingly complex instruction sets is appropriate. This has led a number of groups to pursue the opposite path.

Characteristics of Reduced Instruction Set Architectures

Although a variety of different approaches to reduced instruction set architecture have been taken, certain characteristics are common to all of them:

- One instruction per cycle
- Register-to-register operations
- Simple addressing modes
- Simple instruction formats

Here, we provide a brief discussion of these characteristics. Specific examples are explored later in this chapter.

The first characteristic listed is that there is **one machine instruction per machine cycle**. A *machine cycle* is defined to be the time it takes to fetch two operands from registers, perform an ALU operation, and store the result in a register. Thus, RISC machine instructions should be no more complicated than, and execute about as fast as, microinstructions on CISC machines (discussed in Part Four). With simple, one-cycle instructions, there is little or no need for microcode; the machine instructions can be hardwired. Such instructions should execute faster than comparable machine instructions on other machines, because it is not necessary to access a microprogram control store during instruction execution.

A second characteristic is that most operations should be **register to register**, with only simple LOAD and STORE operations accessing memory. This design feature simplifies the instruction set and therefore the control unit. For example, a RISC instruction set may include only one or two ADD instructions (e.g., integer add, add with carry); the VAX has 25 different ADD instructions. Another benefit is that such an architecture encourages the optimization of register use, so that frequently accessed operands remain in high-speed storage.

This emphasis on register-to-register operations is notable for RISC designs. Contemporary CISC machines provide such instructions but also include memory-to-memory and mixed register/memory operations. Attempts to compare these approaches were made in the 1970s, before the appearance of RISCs. Figure 13.5a illustrates the approach taken. Hypothetical architectures were evaluated on program size and the number of bits of memory traffic. Results such as this one led one researcher to suggest that future architectures should contain no registers at all [MYER78]. One wonders what he would have thought, at the time, of the RISC machine once produced by Pyramid, which contained no less than 528 registers!

What was missing from those studies was a recognition of the frequent access to a small number of local scalars and that, with a large bank of registers or an optimizing compiler, most operands could be kept in registers for long periods of time. Thus, Figure 13.5b may be a fairer comparison.

A third characteristic is the use of **simple addressing modes**. Almost all RISC instructions use simple register addressing. Several additional modes, such as displacement and PC-relative, may be included. Other, more complex modes can be synthesized in software from the simple ones. Again, this design feature simplifies the instruction set and the control unit.

A final common characteristic is the use of **simple instruction formats**. Generally, only one or a few formats are used. Instruction length is fixed and aligned on word boundaries. Field locations, especially the opcode, are fixed. This design feature has a number of benefits. With fixed fields, opcode decoding and register operand accessing can occur simultaneously. Simplified formats simplify the control unit. Instruction fetching is optimized because word-length units are fetched. Alignment on a word boundary also means that a single instruction does not cross page boundaries.

Taken together, these characteristics can be assessed to determine the potential benefits of the RISC approach. These benefits fall into two main categories: those related to performance, and those related to VLSI implementation.

With respect to performance, a certain amount of "circumstantial evidence" can be presented. First, more effective optimizing compilers can be developed. With more-primitive instructions, there are more opportunities for moving functions out of loops, reorganizing code for efficiency, maximizing register utilization, and so forth. It is even possible to compute parts of complex instructions at compile time. For example, the

(a) A ← B + C

Memory-to-memory

8	16	16	16
Add	B	C	A

I = 56, D = 96, M = 152

Register-to-memory

8	4	16
Load	rB	B
Load	rC	B
Add	rA	rB	rC
Store	rA		A

Register-to-memory
I = 104, D = 96, M = 200

(b) A ← B + C; B ← A + C; D ← D − B

Memory-to-memory

8	16	16	16
Add	B	C	A
Add	A	C	B
Sub	B	D	D

I = 168, D = 288, M = 456

Register-to-memory

8	4	4	4
Add	rA	rB	rC
Add	rB	rA	rC
Sub	rD	rD	rB

I = Size of executed instructions
D = Size of executed data
M = I + D = Total memory traffic

Figure 13.5 Two Comparisons of Register-to-Register and Memory-to-Memory Approaches

478

S/390 Move Characters (MVC) instruction moves a string of characters from one location to another. Each time it is executed, the move will depend on the length of the string, whether and in which direction the locations overlap, and what the alignment characteristics are. In most cases, these will all be known at compile time. Thus, the compiler could produce an optimized sequence of primitive instructions for this function.

A second point, already noted, is that most instructions generated by a compiler are relatively simple anyway. It would seem reasonable that a control unit built specifically for those instructions and using little or no microcode could execute them faster than a comparable CISC.

A third point relates to the use of instruction pipelining. RISC researchers feel that the instruction pipelining technique can be applied much more effectively with a reduced instruction set. We examine this point in some detail presently.

A final, and somewhat less significant, point is that RISC processors are more responsive to interrupts because interrupts are checked between rather elementary operations. Architectures with complex instructions either restrict interrupts to instruction boundaries or must define specific interruptible points and implement mechanisms for restarting an instruction.

The case for improved performance for a reduced instruction set architecture is strong, but one could perhaps still make an argument for CISC. A number of studies have been done but not on machines of comparable technology and power. Further, most studies have not attempted to separate the effects of a reduced instruction set and the effects of a large register file. The "circumstantial evidence," however, is suggestive.

The second area of potential benefit, which is more clear-cut, relates to VLSI implementation. When VLSI is used, the design and implementation of the processor are fundamentally changed. Traditional processors, such as the IBM S/390 and the VAX, consist of one or more printed circuit boards containing standardized SSI and MSI packages. With the advent of LSI and VLSI, it is possible to put an entire processor on a single chip. For a single-chip processor, there are two motivations for following a RISC strategy. First, there is the issue of performance. On-chip delays are of much shorter duration than interchip delays. Thus, it makes sense to devote scarce chip real estate to those activities that occur frequently. We have seen that simple instructions and access to local scalars are, in fact, the most frequent activities. The Berkeley RISC chips were designed with this consideration in mind. Whereas a typical single-chip microprocessor dedicates about half of its area to the microcode control store, the RISC I chip devotes only about 6% of its area to the control unit [SHER84].

A second VLSI-related issue is design-and-implementation time. A VLSI processor is difficult to develop. Instead of relying on available SSI/MSI parts, the designer must perform circuit design, layout, and modeling at the device level. With a reduced instruction set architecture, this process is far easier, as evidenced by Table 13.7 [FITZ81]. If, in addition, the performance of the RISC chip is equivalent to comparable CISC microprocessors, then the advantages of the RISC approach become evident.

CISC versus RISC Characteristics

After the initial enthusiasm for RISC machines, there has been a growing realization that (1) RISC designs may benefit from the inclusion of some CISC features

Table 13.7 Design and Layout Effort for Some Microprocessors

CPU	Transistors (thousands)	Design (person-months)	Layout (person-months)
RISC I	44	15	12
RISC II	41	18	12
M68000	68	100	70
Z8000	18	60	70
Intel iAPx-432	110	170	90

and that (2) CISC designs may benefit from the inclusion of some RISC features. The result is that the more recent RISC designs, notably the PowerPC, are no longer "pure" RISC and the more recent CISC designs, notably the Pentium II and later Pentium models, do incorporate some RISC characteristics.

An interesting comparison in [MASH95] provides some insight into this issue. Table 13.8 lists a number of processors and compares them across a number of characteristics. For purposes of this comparison, the following are considered typical of a classic RISC:

1. A single instruction size.
2. That size is typically 4 bytes.
3. A small number of data addressing modes, typically less than five. This parameter is difficult to pin down. In the table, register and literal modes are not counted and different formats with different offset sizes are counted separately.
4. No indirect addressing that requires you to make one memory access to get the address of another operand in memory.
5. No operations that combine load/store with arithmetic (e.g., add from memory, add to memory).
6. No more than one memory-addressed operand per instruction.
7. Does not support arbitrary alignment of data for load/store operations.
8. Maximum number of uses of the memory management unit (MMU) for a data address in an instruction.
9. Number of bits for integer register specifier equal to five or more. This means that at least 32 integer registers can be explicitly referenced at a time.
10. Number of bits for floating-point register specifier equal to four or more. This means that at least 16 floating-point registers can be explicitly referenced at a time.

Items 1 through 3 are an indication of instruction decode complexity. Items 4 through 8 suggest the ease or difficulty of pipelining, especially in the presence of virtual memory requirements. Items 9 and 10 are related to the ability to take good advantage of compilers.

In the table, the first eight processors are clearly RISC architectures, the next five are clearly CISC, and the last two are processors often thought of as RISC that in fact have many CISC characteristics.

Table 13.8 Characteristics of Some Processors

Processor	Number of instruction sizes	Max instruction size in bytes	Number of addressing modes	Indirect addressing	Load/store combined with arithmetic	Max number of memory operands	Unaligned addressing allowed	Max number of MMU uses	Number of bits for integer register specifier	Number of bits for FP register specifier
AMD29000	1	4	1	no	no	1	no	1	8	3[a]
MIPS R2000	1	4	1	no	no	1	no	1	5	4
SPARC	1	4	2	no	no	1	no	1	5	4
MC88000	1	4	3	no	no	1	no	1	5	4
HP PA	1	4	10[a]	no	no	1	no	1	5	4
IBM RT/PC	2[a]	4	1	no	no	1	no	1	4[a]	3[a]
IBM RS/6000	1	4	4	no	no	1	yes	1	5	5
Intel i860	1	4	4	no	no	1	no	1	5	4
IBM 3090	4	8	2[b]	no[b]	yes	2	yes	4	4	2
Intel 80486	12	12	15	no[b]	yes	2	yes	4	3	3
NSC 32016	21	21	23	yes	yes	2	yes	4	3	3
MC68040	11	22	44	yes	yes	2	yes	8	4	3
VAX	56	56	22	yes	yes	6	yes	24	4	0
Clipper	4[a]	8[a]	9[a]	no	no	1	0	2	4[a]	3[a]
Intel 80960	2[a]	8[a]	9[a]	no	no	1	yes[a]	—	5	3[a]

[a] RISC that does not conform to this characteristic.
[b] CISC that does not conform to this characteristic.

481

13.5 RISC PIPELINING

Pipelining with Regular Instructions

As we discussed in Section 12.4, instruction pipelining is often used to enhance performance. Let us reconsider this in the context of a RISC architecture. Most instructions are register to register, and an instruction cycle has the following two stages:

- I: Instruction fetch.
- E: Execute. Performs an ALU operation with register input and output.

For load and store operations, three stages are required:

- I: Instruction fetch.
- E: Execute. Calculates memory address.
- D: Memory. Register-to-memory or memory-to-register operation.

Figure 13.6a depicts the timing of a sequence of instructions using no pipelining. Clearly, this is a wasteful process. Even very simple pipelining can substantially improve performance. Figure 13.6b shows a two-stage pipelining scheme, in which the I and E stages of two different instructions are performed simultaneously. This scheme can yield up to twice the execution rate of a serial scheme. Two problems prevent the maximum speedup from being achieved. First, we assume that a single-port memory is used and that only one memory access is possible per stage. This requires the insertion of a wait state in some instructions. Second, a branch instruction interrupts the sequential flow of execution. To accommodate this with minimum circuitry, a NOOP instruction can be inserted into the instruction stream by the compiler or assembler.

Pipelining can be improved further by permitting two memory accesses per stage. This yields the sequence shown in Figure 13.6c. Now, up to three instructions can be overlapped, and the improvement is as much as a factor of 3. Again, branch instructions cause the speedup to fall short of the maximum possible. Also, note that data dependencies have an effect. If an instruction needs an operand that is altered by the preceding instruction, a delay is required. Again, this can be accomplished by a NOOP.

The pipelining discussed so far works best if the three stages are of approximately equal duration. Because the E stage usually involves an ALU operation, it may be longer. In this case, we can divide into two substages:

- E_1: Register file read
- E_2: ALU operation and register write

Because of the simplicity and regularity of a RISC instruction set, the design of the phasing into three or four stages is easily accomplished. Figure 13.6d shows the result with a four-stage pipeline. Up to four instructions at a time can be under way, and the maximum potential speedup is a factor of 4. Note again the use of NOOPs to account for data and branch delays.

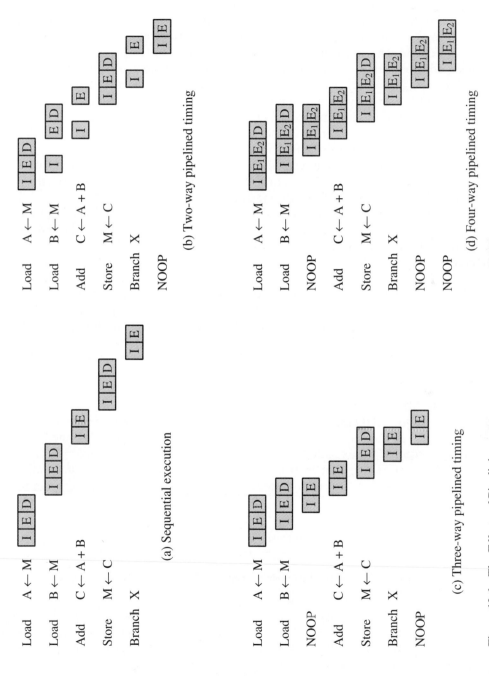

Figure 13.6 The Effects of Pipelining

Optimization of Pipelining

Because of the simple and regular nature of RISC instructions, pipelining schemes can be efficiently employed. There are few variations in instruction execution duration, and the pipeline can be tailored to reflect this. However, we have seen that data and branch dependencies reduce the overall execution rate.

To compensate for these dependencies, code reorganization techniques have been developed. First, let us consider branching instructions. *Delayed branch,* a way of increasing the efficiency of the pipeline, makes use of a branch that does not take effect until after execution of the following instruction (hence the term *delayed*). The instruction location immediately following the branch is referred to as the *delay slot*. This strange procedure is illustrated in Table 13.9. In the column labeled "normal branch," we see a normal symbolic instruction machine-language program. After 102 is executed, the next instruction to be executed is 105. To regularize the pipeline, a NOOP is inserted after this branch. However, increased performance is achieved if the instructions at 101 and 102 are interchanged.

Figure 13.7 shows the result. Figure 13.7a shows the traditional approach to pipelining, of the type discussed in Chapter 12 (e.g., see Figures 12.11 and 12.12). The JUMP instruction is fetched at time 3. At time 4, the JUMP instruction is executed at the same time that instruction 103 (ADD instruction) is fetched. Because a JUMP occurs, which updates the program counter, the pipeline must be cleared of instruction 103; at time 5, instruction 105, which is the target of the JUMP, is loaded. Figure 13.7b shows the same pipeline handled by a typical RISC organization. The timing is the same. However, because of the insertion of the NOOP instruction, we do not need special circuitry to clear the pipeline; the NOOP simply executes with no effect. Figure 13.7c shows the use of the delayed branch. The JUMP instruction is fetched at time 2, before the ADD instruction, which is fetched at time 3. Note, however, that the ADD instruction is fetched before the execution of the JUMP instruction has a chance to alter the program counter. Therefore, during time 4, the ADD instruction is executed at the same time that instruction 105 is fetched. Thus, the original semantics of the program are retained but one less clock cycle is required for execution.

This interchange of instructions will work successfully for unconditional branches, calls, and returns. For conditional branches, this procedure cannot be

Table 13.9   Normal and Delayed Branch

Address	Normal Branch		Delayed Branch		Optimized Delayed Branch	
100	LOAD	X,A	LOAD	X,A	LOAD	X,A
101	ADD	1,A	ADD	1,A	JUMP	105
102	JUMP	105	JUMP	106	ADD	1,A
103	ADD	A,B	NOOP		ADD	A,B
104	SUB	C,B	ADD	A,B	SUB	C,B
105	STORE	A,Z	SUB	C,B	STORE	A,Z
106			STORE	A,Z		

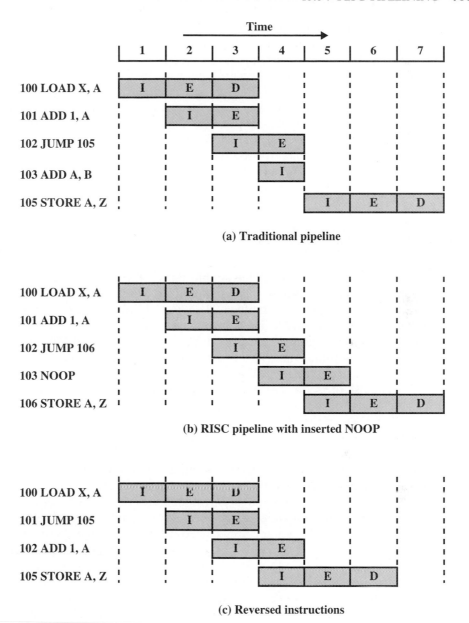

Figure 13.7 Use of the Delayed Branch

blindly applied. If the condition that is tested for the branch can be altered by the immediately preceding instruction, then the compiler must refrain from doing the interchange and instead insert a NOOP. Otherwise, the compiler can seek to insert a useful instruction after the branch. The experience with both the Berkeley RISC and IBM 801 systems is that the majority of conditional branch instructions can be optimized in this fashion ([PATT82a], [RADI83]).

A similar sort of tactic, called the delayed load, can be used on LOAD instructions. On LOAD instructions, the register that is to be the target of the load is locked by the processor. The processor then continues execution of the instruction stream until it reaches an instruction requiring that register, at which point it idles until the load is complete. If the compiler can rearrange instructions so that useful work can be done while the load is in the pipeline, efficiency is increased.

As a final note, we should point out that the design of the instruction pipeline should not be carried out in isolation from other optimization techniques applied to the system. For example, [BRAD91b] shows that the scheduling of instructions for the pipeline and the dynamic allocation of registers should be considered together to achieve the greatest efficiency.

13.6 MIPS R4000

One of the first commercially available RISC chip sets was developed by MIPS Technology Inc. The system was inspired by an experimental system, also using the name MIPS, developed at Stanford [HENN84]. In this section we look at the MIPS R4000. It has substantially the same architecture and instruction set of the earlier MIPS designs: the R2000 and R3000. The most significant difference is that the R4000 uses 64 rather than 32 bits for all internal and external data paths and for addresses, registers, and the ALU.

The use of 64 bits has a number of advantages over a 32-bit architecture. It allows a bigger address space—large enough for an operating system to map more than a terabyte of files directly into virtual memory for easy access. With 1-gigabyte and larger disk drives now common, the 4-gigabyte address space of a 32-bit machine becomes limiting. Also, the 64-bit capacity allows the R4000 to process data such as IEEE double-precision floating-point numbers and character strings, up to eight characters in a single action.

The R4000 processor chip is partitioned into two sections, one containing the CPU and the other containing a coprocessor for memory management. The processor has a very simple architecture. The intent was to design a system in which the instruction execution logic was as simple as possible, leaving space available for logic to enhance performance (e.g., the entire memory-management unit).

The processor supports thirty-two 64-bit registers. It also provides for up to 128 Kbytes of high-speed cache, half each for instructions and data. The relatively large cache (the IBM 3090 provides 128 to 256 Kbytes of cache) enables the system to keep large sets of program code and data local to the processor, off-loading the main memory bus and avoiding the need for a large register file with the accompanying windowing logic.

Instruction Set

Table 13.10 lists the basic instruction set for all MIPS R series processors. Table 13.11 lists the additional instructions implemented in the R4000. All processor instructions are encoded in a single 32-bit word format. All data operations are register to register; the only memory references are pure load/store operations.

The R4000 makes no use of condition codes. If an instruction generates a condition, the corresponding flags are stored in a general-purpose register. This avoids the need for special logic to deal with condition codes as they affect the pipelining mechanism and the reordering of instructions by the compiler. Instead, the mechanisms already implemented to deal with register-value dependencies are employed.

Table 13.10 MIPS R-Series Instruction Set

OP	Description	OP	Description
	Load/Store Instructions		**Multiply/Divide Instructions**
LB	Load Byte	MULT	Multiply
LBU	Load Byte Unsigned	MULTU	Multiply Unsigned
LH	Load Halfword	DIV	Divide
LHU	Load Halfword Unsigned	DIVU	Divide Unsigned
LW	Load Word	MFHI	Move from HI
LWL	Load Word Left	MTHI	Move to HI
LWR	Load Word Right	MFLO	Move from LO
SB	Store Byte	MTLO	Move to LO
SH	Store Halfword		**Jump and Branch Instructions**
SW	Store Word	J	Jump
SWL	Store Word Left	JAL	Jump and Link
SWR	Store Word Right	JR	Jump to Register
	Arithmetic Instructions (ALU Immediate)	JALR	Jump and Link Register
ADDI	Add Immediate	BEQ	Branch on Equal
ADDIU	Add Immediate Unsigned	BNE	Branch on Not Equal
SLTI	Set on Less Than Immediate	BLEZ	Branch on Less Than or Equal to Zero
SLTIU	Set on Less Than Immediate Unsigned	BGTZ	Branch on Greater than Zero
ANDI	AND Immediate	BLTZ	Branch on Less than Zero
ORI	OR Immediate	BGEZ	Branch on Greater Than or Equal to Zero
XORI	Exclusive-OR Immediate	BLTZAL	Branch on Less than Zero and Link
LUI	Load Upper Immediate	BGEZAL	Branch on Greater Than or Equal to Zero and Link
	Arithmetic Instructions (3-operand, R-type)		**Coprocessor instructions**
ADD	Add	LWCz	Load Word to Coprocessor
ADDU	Add Unsigned	SWCz	Store Word to Coprocessor
SUB	Subtract	MTCz	Move to Coprocessor
SUBU	Subtract Unsigned	MFCz	Move from Coprocessor
SLT	Set on Less Than	CTCz	Move Control to Coprocessor
SLTU	Set on Less Than Unsigned	CFCz	Move Control from Coprocessor
AND	AND	COPz	Coprocessor Operation
OR	OR	BCzT	Branch on Coprocessor z True
XOR	Exclusive-OR	BCzF	Branch on Coprocessor z false
NOR	NOR		**Special instructions**
	Shift Instructions	SYSCALL	System Call
SLL	Shift Left Logical	BREAK	Break
SRL	Shift Right Logical		
SRA	Shift Right Arithmetic		
SLLV	Shift Left Logical Variable		
SRLV	Shift Right Logical Variable		
SRAV	Shift Right Arithmetic Variable		

Table 13.11   Additional R4000 Instructions

OP	Description	OP	Description
	Load/Store Instructions		**Exception Instructions**
LL	Load Linked	TGE	Trap if Greater Than or Equal
SC	Store Conditional	TGEU	Trap if Greater Than or Equal Unsigned
SYNC	Sync	TLT	Trap if Less Than
	Jump and Branch Instructions	TLTU	Trap if Less Than Unsigned
BEQL	Branch on Equal Likely	TEQ	Trap if Equal
BNEL	Branch on Not Equal Likely	TNE	Trap if Not Equal
BLEZL	Branch on Less Than or Equal to Zero Likely	TGEI	Trap if Greater Than or Equal Immediate
BGTZL	Branch on Greater Than Zero Likely	TGEIU	Trap if Greater Than or Equal Unsigned Immediate
BLTZL	Branch on Less Than Zero Likely	TLTI	Trap if Less Than Immediate
BGEZL	Branch on Greater Than or Equal to Zero Likely	TLTIU	Trap if Less Than Unsigned Immediate
BLTZAL L	Branch on Less Than Zero and Link Likely	TEQI	Trap if Equal Immediate
BGEZAL L	Branch on Greater Than or Equal to Zero and Link Likely	TNEI	Trap if Not Equal Immediate
BCzTL	Branch on Coprocessor z True Likely		**Coprocessor instructions**
CDzFL	Branch on Coprocessor z False Likely	LDCz	Load Double Coprocessor
		SDCz	Store Double Coprocessor

Further, conditions mapped onto the register files are subject to the same compile-time optimizations in allocation and reuse as other values stored in registers.

As with most RISC-based machines, the MIPS uses a single 32-bit instruction length. This single instruction length simplifies instruction fetch and decode, and it also simplifies the interaction of instruction fetch with the virtual memory management unit (i.e., instructions do not cross word or page boundaries). The three instruction formats (Figure 13.8) share common formatting of opcodes and register references, simplifying instruction decode. The effect of more complex instructions can be synthesized at compile time.

Only the simplest and most frequently used memory-addressing mode is implemented in hardware. All memory references consist of a 16-bit offset from a 32-bit register. For example, the "load word" instruction is of the form

```
lw r2, 128(r3) load word at address 128 offset from register 3 into register 2
```

Each of the 32 general-purpose registers can be used as the base register. One register, r0, always contains 0.

The compiler makes use of multiple machine instructions to synthesize typical addressing modes in conventional machines. Some examples are provided in Table 13.12 [CHOW87]. The table shows the use of the instruction lui (load upper immediate). This instruction loads the upper half of a register with a 16-bit immediate value, setting the lower half to zero.

Instruction Pipeline

With its simplified instruction architecture, the MIPS can achieve very efficient pipelining. It is instructive to look at the evolution of the MIPS pipeline, as it illustrates the evolution of RISC pipelining in general.

The initial experimental RISC systems and the first generation of commercial RISC processors achieve execution speeds that approach one instruction per system clock cycle. To improve on this performance, two classes of processors have evolved to offer execution of multiple instructions per clock cycle: superscalar and super-pipelined architectures. In essence, a superscalar architecture replicates each of the pipeline stages so that two or more instructions at the same stage of the pipeline can be processed simultaneously. A superpipelined architecture is one that makes use of more, and more fine-grained, pipeline stages. With more stages, more instructions can be in the pipeline at the same time, increasing parallelism.

Both approaches have limitations. With superscalar pipelining, dependencies between instructions in different pipelines can slow down the system. Also, overhead logic is required to coordinate these dependencies. With superpipelining, there is overhead associated with transferring instructions from one stage to the next.

Chapter 14 is devoted to a study of superscalar architecture. The MIPS R4000 is a good example of a RISC-based superpipeline architecture.

Operation	Operation code
rs	Source register specifier
rt	Source/destination register specifier
Immediate	Immediate, branch, or address displacement
Target	Jump target address
rd	Destination register specifier
Shift	Shift amount
Function	ALU/shift function specifier

Figure 13.8 MIPS Instruction Formats

Table 13.12 Synthesizing Other Addressing Modes with the MIPS Addressing Mode

Apparent Instruction	Actual Instruction
lw r2, <16-bit offset>	lw r2, <16-bit offset> (r0)
lw r2, <32-bit offset>	lui r1, <high 16 bits of offset> lw r2, <low 16 bits of offset> (r1)
lw r2, <32-bit offset> (r4)	lui r1, <high 16 bits of offset> addu r1, r1, r4 lw r2, <low 16 bits of offset> (r1)

Figure 13.9a shows the instruction pipeline of the R3000. In the R3000, the pipeline advances once per clock cycle. The MIPS compiler is able to reorder instructions to fill delay slots with code 70 to 90% of the time. All instructions follow the same sequence of five pipeline stages:

- Instruction fetch
- Source operand fetch from register file
- ALU operation or data operand address generation
- Data memory reference
- Write back into register file

As illustrated in Figure 13.9a, there is not only parallelism due to pipelining but also parallelism within the execution of a single instruction. The 60-ns clock cycle is divided into two 30-ns stages. The external instruction and data access operations to the cache each require 60 ns, as do the major internal operations (OP, DA, IA). Instruction decode is a simpler operation, requiring only a single 30-ns stage, overlapped with register fetch in the same instruction. Calculation of an address for a branch instruction also overlaps instruction decode and register fetch, so that a branch at instruction i can address the ICACHE access of instruction $i + 2$. Similarly, a load at instruction i fetches data that are immediately used by the OP of instruction $i + 1$, while an ALU/shift result gets passed directly into instruction $i + 1$ with no delay. This tight coupling between instructions makes for a highly efficient pipeline.

In detail, then, each clock cycle is divided into separate stages, denoted as $\phi 1$ $\phi 2$. The functions performed in each stage are summarized in Table 13.13.

The R4000 incorporates a number of technical advances over the R3000. The use of more advanced technology allows the clock cycle time to be cut in half, to 30 ns, and for the access time to the register file to be cut in half. In addition, there is greater density on the chip, which enables the instruction and data caches to be incorporated on the chip. Before looking at the final R4000 pipeline, let us consider how the R3000 pipeline can be modified to improve performance using R4000 technology.

Figure 13.9b shows a first step. Remember that the cycles in this figure are half as long as those in Figure 13.9a. Because they are on the same chip, the instruction

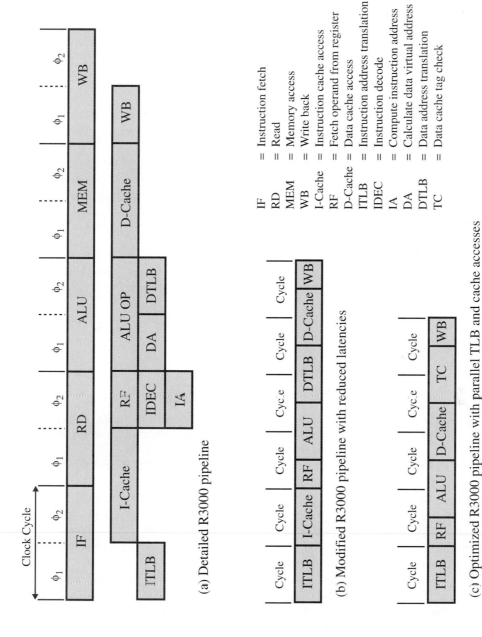

(a) Detailed R3000 pipeline

(b) Modified R3000 pipeline with reduced latencies

(c) Optimized R3000 pipeline with parallel TLB and cache accesses

Figure 13.9 Enhancing the R3000 Pipeline

IF	= Instruction fetch
RD	= Read
MEM	= Memory access
WB	= Write back
I-Cache	= Instruction cache access
RF	= Fetch operand from register
D-Cache	= Data cache access
ITLB	= Instruction address translation
IDEC	= Instruction decode
IA	= Compute instruction address
DA	= Calculate data virtual address
DTLB	= Data address translation
TC	= Data cache tag check

Table 13.13 R3000 Pipeline Stages

Pipeline Stage	Phase	Function
IF	φ1	Using the TLB, translate an instruction virtual address to a physical address (after a branching decision).
IF	φ2	Send the physical address to the instruction address.
RD	φ1	Return instruction from instruction cache. Compare tags and validity of fetched instruction.
RD	φ2	Decode instruction. Read register file. If branch, calculate branch target address.
ALU	φ1 + φ2	If register-to-register operation, the arithmetic or logical operation is performed.
ALU	φ1	If a branch, decide whether the branch is to be taken or not. If a memory reference (load or store), calculate data virtual address.
ALU	φ2	If a memory reference, translate data virtual address to physical using TLB.
MEM	φ1	If a memory reference, send physical address to data cache.
MEM	φ2	If a memory reference, return data from data cache, and check tags.
WB	φ1	Write to register file.

and data cache stages take only half as long; so they still occupy only one clock cycle. Again, because of the speedup of the register file access, register read and write still occupy only half of a clock cycle.

Because the R4000 caches are on-chip, the virtual-to-physical address translation can delay the cache access. This delay is reduced by implementing virtually indexed caches and going to a parallel cache access and address translation. Figure 13.9c shows the optimized R3000 pipeline with this improvement. Because of the compression of events, the data cache tag check is performed separately on the next cycle after cache access.

In a superpipelined system, existing hardware is used several times per cycle by inserting pipeline registers to split up each pipe stage. Essentially, each super-pipeline stage operates at a multiple of the base clock frequency, the multiple depending on the degree of superpipelining. The R4000 technology has the speed and density to permit superpipelining of degree 2. Figure 13.10a shows the optimized R3000 pipeline using this superpipelining. Note that this is essentially the same dynamic structure as Figure 13.9c.

Further improvements can be made. For the R4000, a much larger and specialized adder was designed. This makes it possible to execute ALU operations at twice the rate. Other improvements allow the execution of loads and stores at twice the rate. The resulting pipeline is shown in Figure 13.10b.

The R4000 has eight pipeline stages, meaning that as many as eight instructions can be in the pipeline at the same time. The pipeline advances at the rate of two stages per clock cycle. The eight pipeline stages are as follows:

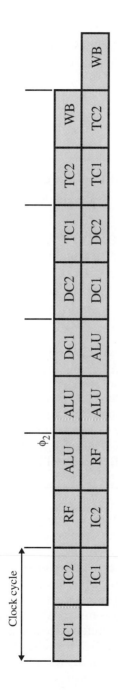

(a) Superpipelined implmentation of the optimized R3000 pipeline

IF = Instruction fetch first half
IS = Instruction fetch second half
RF = Fetch operands from register
EX = Instruction execute
IC = Instruction cache
DC = Data cache
DF = Data cache first half
DS = Data cache second half
TC = Tag check

(b) R4000 pipeline

Figure 13.10 Theoretical R3000 and Actual R4000 Superpipelines

- **Instruction fetch first half:** Virtual address is presented to the instruction cache and the translation lookaside buffer.
- **Instruction fetch second half:** Instruction cache outputs the instruction and the TLB generates the physical address.
- **Register file:** Three activities occur in parallel:
  - Instruction is decoded and check made for interlock conditions (i.e., this instruction depends on the result of a preceding instruction).
  - Instruction cache tag check is made.
  - Operands are fetched from the register file.
- **Instruction execute:** One of three activities can occur:
  - If the instruction is a register-to-register operation, the ALU performs the arithmetic or logical operation.
  - If the instruction is a load or store, the data virtual address is calculated.
  - If the instruction is a branch, the branch target virtual address is calculated and branch conditions are checked.
- **Data cache first:** Virtual address is presented to the data cache and TLB.
- **Data cache second:** Data cache outputs the instruction, and the TLB generates the physical address.
- **Tag check:** Cache tag checks are performed for loads and stores.
- **Write back:** Instruction result is written back to register file.

13.7 SPARC

SPARC (Scalable Processor Architecture) refers to an architecture defined by Sun Microsystems. Sun developed its own SPARC implementation but also licenses the architecture to other vendors to produce SPARC-compatible machines. The SPARC architecture is inspired by the Berkeley RISC I machine, and its instruction set and register organization is based closely on the Berkeley RISC model.

SPARC Register Set

As with the Berkeley RISC, the SPARC makes use of register windows. Each window consists of 24 registers, and the total number of windows is implementation dependent and ranges from 2 to 32 windows. Figure 13.11 illustrates an implementation that supports 8 windows, using a total of 136 physical registers; as the discussion in Section 13.2 indicates, this seems a reasonable number of windows. Physical registers 0 through 7 are global registers shared by all procedures. Each process sees logical registers 0 through 31. Logical registers 24 through 31, referred to as *ins*, are shared with the calling (parent) procedure; and logical registers 8 through 15, referred to as *outs*, are shared with any called (child) procedure. These two portions overlap with other windows. Logical registers 16 through 23, referred to as *locals*, are not shared and do not overlap with other windows. Again, as the discussion of Section 12.1 indicates, the availability of 8 registers for parameter passing should be adequate in most cases (e.g., see Table 13.4).

Physical registers

Logical registers

| | Procedure A | Procedure B | Procedure C |

```
135
 •        Ins
128
127
 •        Locals
120
119
 •        Outs/Ins
112
111
 •        Locals
104
103
 •        Outs/Ins
 96
 95
 •        Locals
 88
 87
 •        Outs
 80
```

Procedure A:
```
R31_C
 •        Ins
R24_C
R23_C
 •        Locals
R16_C
R15_C
 •        Outs
R8_C
```

Procedure B:
```
R31_C
 •        Ins
R24_C
R23_C
 •        Locals
R16_C
R15_C
 •        Outs
R8_C
```

Procedure C:
```
R31_C
 •        Ins
R24_C
R23_C
 •        Locals
R16_C
R15_C
 •        Outs
R8_C
```

```
 7
 •        Globals
 0
```

```
R7
 •        Globals
R0
```

```
R7
 •        Globals
R0
```

```
R7
 •        Globals
R0
```

Figure 13.11 SPARC Register Window Layout with Three Procedures

Figure 13.12 is another view of the register overlap. The calling procedure places any parameters to be passed in its *outs* registers; the called procedure treats these same physical registers as it *ins* registers. The processor maintains a current window pointer (CWP), located in the processor status register (PSR), that points to the window of the currently executing procedure. The window invalid mask (WIM), also in the PSR, indicates which windows are invalid.

With the SPARC register architecture, it is usually not necessary to save and restore registers for a procedure call. The compiler is simplified because the compiler need be concerned only with allocating the local registers for a procedure in an efficient manner and need not be concerned with register allocation between procedures.

Instruction Set

Table 13.14 lists the instructions for the SPARC architecture. Most of the instructions reference only register operands. Register-to-register instructions have three operands and can be expressed in the form

$$R_d \leftarrow R_{S1} \text{ op } S2$$

R_d and R_{S1} are register references; S2 can refer either to a register or to a 13-bit immediate operand. Register zero (R_0) is hardwired with the value 0. This form is well suited to typical programs, which have a high proportion of local scalars and constants.

Figure 13.12   Eight Register Windows Forming a Circular Stack in SPARC

Table 13.14 SPARC Instruction Set

OP	Description	OP	Description
Load/Store Instructions		**Arithmetic Instructions**	
LDSB	Load signed byte	ADD	Add
LDSH	Load signed halfword	ADDCC	Add, set icc
LDUB	Load unsigned byte	ADDX	Add with carry
LDUH	Load unsigned halfword	ADDXCC	Add with carry, set icc
LD	Load word	SUB	Subtract
LDD	Load doubleword	SUBCC	Subtract, set icc
STB	Store byte	SUBX	Subtract with carry
STH	Store halfword	SUBXCC	Subtract with carry, set icc
STD	Store word	MULSCC	Multiply step, set icc
STDD	Store doubleword	**Jump/Branch Instructions**	
Shift Instructions		BCC	Branch on condition
SLL	Shift left logical	FBCC	Branch on floating-point condition
SRL	Shift right logical	CBCC	Branch on coprocessor condition
SRA	Shift right arithmetic	CALL	Call procedure
Boolean Instructions		JMPL	Jump and link
AND	AND	TCC	Trap on condition
ANDCC	AND, set icc	SAVE	Advance register window
ANDN	NAND	RESTORE	Move windows backward
ANDNCC	NAND, set icc	RETT	Return from trap
OR	OR	**Miscellaneous Instructions**	
ORCC	OR, set icc	SETHI	Set high 22 bits
ORN	NOR	UNIMP	Unimplemented instruction (trap)
ORNCC	NOR, set icc	RD	Read a special register
XOR	XOR	WR	Write a special register
XORCC	XOR, set icc	IFLUSH	Instruction cache flush
XNOR	Exclusive NOR		
XNORCC	Exclusive NOR, set icc		

The available ALU operations can be grouped as follows:

- Integer addition (with or without carry)
- Integer subtraction (with or without carry)
- Bitwise Boolean AND, OR, XOR and their negations
- Shift left logical, right logical, or right arithmetic

All of these instructions, except the shifts, can optionally set the four condition codes (ZERO, NEGATIVE, OVERFLOW, CARRY). Signed integers are represented in 32-bit twos complement form.

Only simple load and store instructions reference memory. There are separate load and store instructions for word (32 bits), doubleword, halfword, and byte. For the latter two cases, there are instructions for loading these quantities as signed or unsigned numbers. Signed numbers are sign extended to fill out the 32-bit destination register. Unsigned numbers are padded with zeros.

The only available addressing mode, other than register, is a displacement mode. That is, the effective address of an operand consists of a displacement from an address contained in a register:

$$EA = (R_{S1}) + S2$$
$$\text{or } EA = (R_{S1}) + (R_{S2})$$

depending on whether the second operand is immediate or a register reference. To perform a load or store, an extra stage is added to the instruction cycle. During the second stage, the memory address is calculated using the ALU; the load or store occurs in a third stage. This single addressing mode is quite versatile and can be used to synthesize other addressing modes, as indicated in Table 13.15.

It is instructive to compare the SPARC addressing capability with that of the MIPS. The MIPS makes use of a 16-bit offset, compared with a 13-bit offset on the SPARC. On the other hand, the MIPS does not permit an address to be constructed from the contents of two registers.

Instruction Format

As with the MIPS R4000, SPARC uses a simple set of 32-bit instruction formats (Figure 13.13). All instructions begin with a 2-bit opcode. For most instructions, this

Table 13.15 Synthesizing Other Addressing Modes with SPARC Addressing Modes

Mode	Algorithm	SPARC Equivalent	Instruction Type
Immediate	operand = A	S2	Register to register
Direct	EA = A	R_0 + S2	Load, store
Register	EA = R	R_{S1}, R_{S2}	Register to register
Register indirect	EA = (R)	R_{S1} + 0	Load, store
Displacement	EA = (R) + A	R_{S1} + S2	Load, store

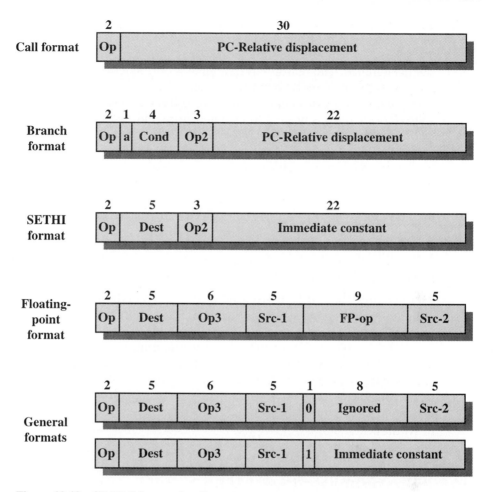

Figure 13.13 SPARC Instruction Formats

is extended with additional opcode bits elsewhere in the format. For the Call instruction, a 30-bit immediate operand is extended with two zero bits to the right to form a 32-bit PC-relative address in twos complement form. Instructions are aligned on a 32-bit boundary so that this form of addressing suffices.

The Branch instruction includes a 4-bit condition field that corresponds to the four standard condition code bits, so that any combination of conditions can be tested. The 22-bit PC-relative address is extended with two zero bits on the right to form a 24-bit twos complement relative address. An unusual feature of the Branch instruction is the annul bit. When the annul bit is not set, the instruction after the branch is always executed, regardless of whether the branch is taken. This is the typical delayed branch operation found on many RISC machines and described in Section 13.5 (see Figure 13.7). However, when the annul bit is set, the instruction following the branch is executed only if the branch is taken. The processor suppresses the effect of that instruction even though it is already in the pipeline. This annul bit is useful because it makes it easier for the compiler to fill the delay slot following a conditional branch. The instruction that is the target of the branch can always be put in the delay slot, because if the branch is not taken, the instruction can be annulled. The reason this technique is desirable is that conditional branches are generally taken more than half the time.

The SETHI instruction is a special instruction used to load or store a 32-bit value. This feature is needed to load and store addresses and large constants. The SETHI instruction sets the 22 high-order bits of a register with its 22-bit immediate operand, and zeros out the low-order 10 bits. An immediate constant of up to 13 bits can be specified in one of the general formats, and such an instruction could be used to fill in the remaining 10 bits of the register. A load or store instruction can also be used to achieve a direct addressing mode. To load a value from location K in memory, we could use the following SPARC instructions:

```
sethi   %hi(K), %r8          ;load high-order 22 bits of address of
                             ;location K into register r8
ld      [%r8 + %lo(K)], %r8  ;load contents of location K into r8
```

The macros %hi and %lo are used to define immediate operands consisting of the appropriate address bits of a location. This use of SETHI is similar to the use of the LUI instruction on the MIPS (Table 13.12).

The floating-point format is used for floating-point operations. Two source and one destination registers are designated.

Finally, all other operations, including loads, stores, arithmetic, and logical operations use one of the last two formats shown in Figure 13.13. One of the formats makes use of two source registers and a destination register, while the other uses one source register, one 13-bit immediate operand, and one destination register.

13.8 RISC VERSUS CISC CONTROVERSY

For many years, the general trend in computer architecture and organization has been toward increasing processor complexity: more instructions, more addressing modes, more specialized registers, and so on. The RISC movement represents a fundamental break with the philosophy behind that trend. Naturally, the appearance of RISC systems, and the publication of papers by its proponents extolling RISC virtues, led to a reaction from those involved in the design of CISC architectures.

The work that has been done on assessing merits of the RISC approach can be grouped into two categories:

- **Quantitative:** Attempts to compare program size and execution speed of programs on RISC and CISC machines that use comparable technology
- **Qualitative:** Examination of issues such as high-level language support and optimum use of VLSI real estate

Most of the work on quantitative assessment has been done by those working on RISC systems [PATT82b, HEAT84, PATT84], and it has been, by and large, favorable to the RISC approach. Others have examined the issue and come away unconvinced [COLW85a, FLYN87, DAVI87]. There are several problems with attempting such comparisons [SERL86]:

- There is no pair of RISC and CISC machines that are comparable in life-cycle cost, level of technology, gate complexity, sophistication of compiler, operating system support, and so on.
- No definitive test set of programs exists. Performance varies with the program.
- It is difficult to sort out hardware effects from effects due to skill in compiler writing.
- Most of the comparative analysis on RISC has been done on "toy" machines rather than commercial products. Furthermore, most commercially available machines advertised as RISC possess a mixture of RISC and CISC characteristics. Thus, a fair comparison with a commercial, "pure-play" CISC machine (e.g., VAX, Pentium) is difficult.

The qualitative assessment is, almost by definition, subjective. Several researchers have turned their attention to such an assessment [COLW85a, WALL85], but the results are, at best, ambiguous, and certainly subject to rebuttal [PATT85b] and, of course, counterrebuttal [COLW85b].

In more recent years, the RISC versus CISC controversy has died down to a great extent. This is because there has been a gradual convergence of the technologies. As chip densities and raw hardware speeds increase, RISC systems have become more complex. At the same time, in an effort to squeeze out maximum performance, CISC designs have focused on issues traditionally associated with RISC, such as an increased number of general-purpose registers and increased emphasis on instruction pipeline design.

13.9 RECOMMENDED READING

Textbooks with good coverage of RISC concepts are [WARD90], [PATT98], and [HENN96]. [KANE92] covers the commercial MIPS machine in detail. [MIRA92] provides a good overview of the MIPS R4000. [BASH91] discusses the evolution from the R3000 pipeline to the R4000 superpipeline. The SPARC is covered in some detail in [DEWA90].

BASH91 Bashteen, A.; Lui, I.; and Mullan, J. "A Superpipeline Approach to the MIPS Architecture." *Proceedings, COMPCON Spring '91,* February 1991.

DEWA90 Dewar, R., and Smosna, M. *Microprocessors: A Programmer's View.* New York: McGraw-Hill, 1990.

HENN96 Hennessy, J., and Patterson, D. *Computer Architecture: A Quantitative Approach.* San Mateo, CA: Morgan Kaufmann, 1996.

KANE92 Kane, G., and Heinrich, J. *MIPS RISC Architecture.* Englewood Cliffs, NJ: Prentice Hall, 1992.

MIRA92 Mirapuri, S.; Woodacre, M.; and Vasseghi, N. "The MIPS R4000 Processor." *IEEE Micro,* April 1992.

PATT98 Patterson, D., and Hennessy, J. *Computer Organization and Design: The Hardware/ Software Interface.* San Mateo, CA: Morgan Kaufmann, 1998.

WARD90 Ward, S., and Halstead, R. *Computation Structures.* Cambridge, MA: MIT Press, 1990.

13.10 KEY TERMS, REVIEW QUESTIONS, AND PROBLEMS

Key Terms

complex instruction set computer (CISC) delayed branch delayed load	high-level language (HLL) reduced instruction set computer (RISC)	register file register window SPARC

Review Questions

13.1 What are some typical distinguishing characteristics of RISC organization?

13.2 Briefly explain the two basic approaches used to minimize register-memory operations on RISC machines.

13.3 If a circular register buffer is used to handle local variables for nested procedures, describe two approaches for handling global variables.

13.4 What are some typical characteristics of a RISC instruction set architecture?

13.5 What is a delayed branch?

Problems

13.1 Considering the call-return pattern in Figure 4.16, how many overflows and underflows (each of which causes a register save/restore) will occur with a window size of
   a. 5?
   b. 8?
   c. 16?

13.2 In the discussion of Figure 13.2, it was stated that only the first two portions of a window are saved or restored. Why is it not necessary to save the temporary registers?

13.3 We wish to determine the execution time for a given program using the various pipelining schemes discussed in Section 13.5. Let

$$N = \text{number of executed instructions}$$
$$D = \text{number of memory accesses}$$
$$J = \text{number of jump instructions}$$

For the simple sequential scheme (Figure 13.6a), the execution time is $2N + D$ stages. Derive formulas for two-stage, three-stage, and four-stage pipelining.

13.4 Consider the following code fragment in a high-level language:

```
for I in 1. . .100 loop
    S ← S + Q(I).VAL
end loop;
```

Assume that Q is an array of 32-byte records and the VAL field is in the first 4 bytes of each record. Using 80x86 code, we can compile this program fragment as follows:

```
        MOV    ECX,1          ;use register ECX to hold I
LP:     IMUL   EAX, ECX, 32   ;get offset in EAX
        MOV    EBX, Q[EAX]    ;load VAL field
        ADD    S, EBX         ;add to S
        INC    ECX            ;increment I
        JNE    LP             ;loop until I = 100
```

This program makes use of the IMUL instruction, which multiplies the second operand by the immediate value in the third operand and places the result in the first operand (see Problem 10.13). A RISC advocate would like to demonstrate that a clever compiler can eliminate unnecessarily complex instructions such as IMUL. Provide the demonstration by rewriting the above 80x86 program without using the IMUL instruction.

13.5 Consider the following loop:

```
S := 0;
for K := 1 to 100 do
      S : = S - K;
```

A straightforward translation of this into a generic assembly language would look something like this:

```
        LD    R1, 0            ;keep value of S in R1
        LD    R2, 1            ;keep value of K in R2
LP      SUB   R1, R1, R2       ;S := S - K
        BEQ   R2, 100, EXIT    ;done if K = 100
        ADD   R2, R2, 1        ;else increment K
        JMP   LP               ;back to start of loop
```

A compiler for a RISC machine will introduce delay slots into this code so that the processor can employ the delayed branch mechanism. The JMP instruction is easy to deal with, because this instruction is always followed by the SUB instruction; therefore, we can simply place a copy of the SUB instruction in the delay slot after the JMP. The BEQ presents a difficulty. We can't leave the code as is, because the ADD instruction would then be executed one too many times. Therefore, a NOP instruction is needed. Show the resulting code.

13.6 Add entries for the following processors to Table 13.8:
   a. Pentium II
   b. PowerPC

13.7 In many cases, common machine instructions that are not listed as part of the MIPS instruction set can be synthesized with a single MIPS instruction. Show this for the following:
   a. Register-to-register move
   b. Increment, decrement
   c. Complement
   d. Negate
   e. Clear

13.8 A SPARC implementation has K register windows. What is the number N of physical registers?

13.9 SPARC is lacking a number of instructions commonly found on CISC machines. Some of these are easily simulated using either register R0, which is always set to 0, or a constant operand. These simulated instructions are called pseudoinstructions and are recognized by the SPARC compiler. Show how to simulate the following pseudoinstructions, each with a single SPARC instruction. In all of these, src and dst refer to registers. *Hint:* A store to R0 has no effect.
   a. MOV src, dst   **d.** NOT dst   **g.** DEC dst
   b. COMPARE src1, src2   **e.** NEG dst   **h.** CLR dst
   c. TEST src1   **f.** INC dst   **i.** NOP

13.10 Consider the following code fragment:

```
if K > 10
      L := K + 1
else
      L := K - 1;
```

A straightforward translation of this statement into SPARC assembler could take the following form:

```
      sethi  %hi(K), %r8              ;load high-order 22 bits of address
                                      ;of location K into register r8
      ld     [%r8 + %lo(K)], %r8      ;load contents of location K into r8
      cmp    %r8, 10                  ;compare contents of r8 with 10
      ble    L1                       ;branch if (r8) ≤ 10
      nop
      sethi  %hi(K), %r9
      ld     [%r9 + %lo(K)], %r9      ;load contents of location K into r9
      inc    %r9                      ;add 1 to (r9)
      sethi  %hi(L), %r10
      st     %r9, [%r10 + %lo(L)]     ;store (r9) into location L
      b      L2
      nop
L1:   sethi  %hi(K), %r11
      ld     [%r11 + %lo(K)], %r12    ;load contents of location K into r12
      dec    %r12                     ;subtract 1 from (r12)
      sethi  %hi(L), %r13
      st     %r12, [%r13 + %lo(L)]    ;store (r12) into location L
L2:
```

The code contains a nop after each branch instruction to permit delayed branch operation.

a. Standard compiler optimizations that have nothing to do with RISC machines are generally effective in being able to perform two transformations on the foregoing code. Notice that two of the loads are unnecessary and that the two stores can be merged if the store is moved to a different place in the code. Show the program after making these two changes.

b. It is now possible to perform some optimizations peculiar to SPARC. The nop after the ble can be replaced by moving another instruction into that delay slot and setting the annul bit on the ble instruction (expressed as ble,a L1). Show the program after this change.

c. There are now two unnecessary instructions. Remove these and show the resulting program.

CHAPTER **14**

INSTRUCTION-LEVEL PARALLELISM AND SUPERSCALAR PROCESSORS

KEY POINTS

◆ A superscalar processor is one in which multiple independent instruction pipelines are used. Each pipeline consists of multiple stages, so that each pipeline can handle multiple instructions at a time. Multiple pipelines introduce a new level of parallelism, enabling multiple streams of instructions to be processed at a time. A superscalar processor exploits what is known as instruction-level parallelism, which refers to the degree to which the instructions of a program can be executed in parallel.

◆ A superscalar processor typically fetches multiple instructions at a time and then attempts to find nearby instructions that are independent of one another and can therefore be executed in parallel. If the input to one instruction depends on the output of a preceding instruction, then the latter instruction cannot complete execution at the same time or before the former instruction. Once such dependencies have been identified, the processor may issue and complete instructions in an order that differs from that of the original machine code.

◆ The processor may eliminate some unnecessary dependencies by the use of additional registers and the renaming of register references in the original code.

◆ Whereas pure RISC processors often employ delayed branches to maximize the utilization of the instruction pipeline, this method is less appropriate to a superscalar machine. Instead, most superscalar machines use traditional branch prediction methods to improve efficiency.

A superscalar implementation of a processor architecture is one in which common instructions—integer and floating-point arithmetic, loads, stores, and conditional branches—-can be initiated simultaneously and executed independently. Such implementations raise a number of complex design issues related to the instruction pipeline.

Superscalar design arrives on the scene hard on the heels of RISC architecture. Although the simplified instruction set architecture of a RISC machine lends itself readily to superscalar techniques, the superscalar approach can be used on either a RISC or CISC architecture.

Whereas the gestation period for the arrival of commercial RISC machines from the beginning of true RISC research with the IBM 801 and the Berkeley RISC I was seven or eight years, the first superscalar machines became commercially available within just a year or two of the coining of the term *superscalar*. The superscalar approach has now become the standard method for implementing high-performance microprocessors.

In this chapter, we begin with an overview of the superscalar approach, contrasting it with superpipelining. Next, we present the key design issues associated with superscalar implementation. Then we look at several important examples of superscalar architecture.

14.1 OVERVIEW

The term *superscalar,* first coined in 1987 [AGER87], refers to a machine that is designed to improve the performance of the execution of scalar instructions. In most applications, the bulk of the operations are on scalar quantities. Accordingly, the superscalar approach represents the next step in the evolution of high-performance general-purpose processors.

The essence of the superscalar approach is the ability to execute instructions independently in different pipelines. The concept can be further exploited by allowing instructions to be executed in an order different from the program order. Figure 14.1 shows, in general terms, the superscalar approach. There are multiple functional units, each of which is implemented as a pipeline, which support parallel execution of several instructions. In this example, two integer, two floating-point, and one memory (either load or store) operations can be executing at the same time.

Many researchers have investigated superscalar-like processors, and their research indicates that some degree of performance improvement is possible. Table 14.1 presents the reported performance advantages. The differences in the results arise from differences both in the hardware of the simulated machine and in the applications being simulated.

Superscalar versus Superpipelined

An alternative approach to achieving greater performance is referred to as superpipelining, a term first coined in 1988 [JOUP88]. Superpipelining exploits the fact that many pipeline stages perform tasks that require less than half a clock cycle. Thus, a doubled internal clock speed allows the performance of two tasks in one external clock cycle. We have seen one example of this approach with the MIPS R4000.

Figure 14.2 compares the two approaches. The upper part of the diagram illustrates an ordinary pipeline, used as a base for comparison. The base pipeline issues one instruction per clock cycle and can perform one pipeline stage per clock cycle. The pipeline has four stages: instruction fetch, operation decode, operation execu-

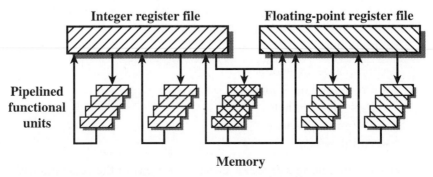

Figure 14.1 General Superscalar Organization [COME95]

Table 14.1   Reported Speedups of Superscalar-Like Machines

Reference	Speedup
[TJAD70]	1.8
[KUCK72]	8
[WEIS84]	1.58
[ACOS86]	2.7
[SOHI90]	1.8
[SMIT89]	2.3
[JOUP89b]	2.2
[LEE91]	7

tion, and result write back. The execution stage is crosshatched for clarity. Note that although several instructions are executing concurrently, only one instruction is in its execution stage at any one time.

The next part of the diagram shows a superpipelined implementation that is capable of performing two pipeline stages per clock cycle. An alternative way of looking at this is that the functions performed in each stage can be split into two nonoverlapping parts and each can execute in half a clock cycle. A superpipeline implementation that behaves in this fashion is said to be of degree 2. Finally, the lowest part of the diagram shows a superscalar implementation capable of executing two instances of each stage in parallel. Higher-degree superpipeline and superscalar implementations are of course possible.

Both the superpipeline and the superscalar implementations depicted in Figure 14.2 have the same number of instructions executing at the same time in the steady state. The superpipelined processor falls behind the superscalar processor at the start of the program and at each branch target.

Limitations

The superscalar approach depends on the ability to execute multiple instructions in parallel. The term **instruction-level parallelism** refers to the degree to which, on average, the instructions of a program can be executed in parallel. A combination of compiler-based optimization and hardware techniques can be used to maximize instruction-level parallelism. Before examining the design techniques used in superscalar machines to increase instruction-level parallelism, we need to look at the fundamental limitations to parallelism with which the system must cope. [JOHN91] lists five limitations:

- True data dependency
- Procedural dependency
- Resource conflicts
- Output dependency
- Antidependency

We examine the first three of these limitations in the remainder of this section. A discussion of the last two must await some of the developments in the next section.

True Data Dependency

Consider the following sequence:

```
add     r1, r2    ;load register r1 with the contents of r2
                   plus the contents of r1
move    r3, r1    ;load register r3 with the contents of r1
```

The second instruction can be fetched and decoded but cannot execute until the first instruction executes. The reason is that the second instruction needs data produced by the first instruction. This situation is referred to as a true data dependency (also called flow dependency or write-read dependency).

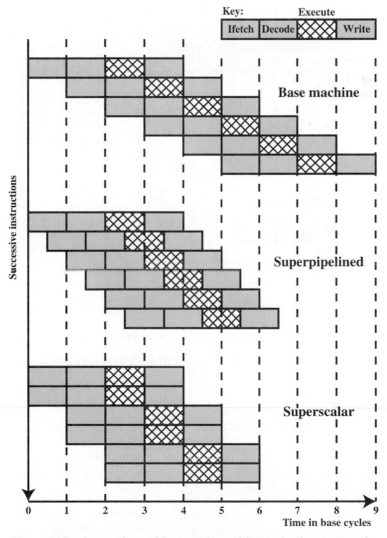

Figure 14.2   Comparison of Superscalar and Superpipeline Approaches

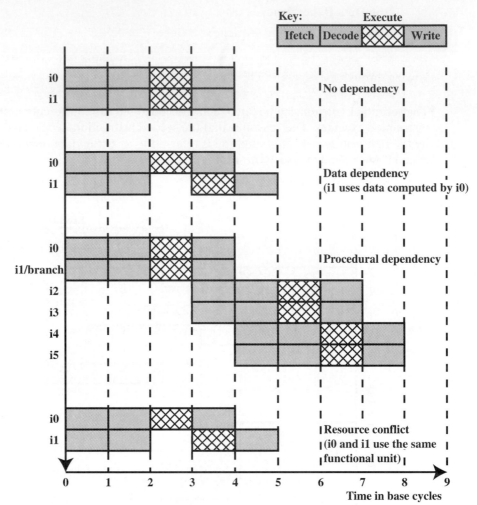

Figure 14.3 Effect of Dependencies

Figure 14.3 illustrates this dependency in a superscalar machine of degree 2. With no dependency, two instructions can be fetched and executed in parallel. If there is a data dependency between the first and second instructions, then the second instruction is delayed as many clock cycles as required to remove the dependency. In general, any instruction must be delayed until all of its input values have been produced.

In a simple scalar pipeline, the aforementioned sequence of instructions would cause no delay. However, consider the following, in which one of the loads is from memory rather than from a register:

```
load    r1, eff     ;load register r1 with the contents of
                     effective memory address eff
move    r3, r1       ;load register r3 with the contents of r1
```

A typical RISC processor takes two or more cycles to perform a load from memory because of the delay of an off-chip memory or cache access. One way to compensate for this delay is for the compiler to reorder instructions so that one or more subsequent instructions that do not depend on the memory load can begin flowing through the pipeline. This scheme is less effective in the case of a superscalar pipeline: The independent instructions executed during the load are likely to be executed on the first cycle of the load, leaving the processor with nothing to do until the load completes.

Procedural Dependencies

As was discussed in Chapter 12, the presence of branches in an instruction sequence complicates the pipeline operation. The instructions following a branch (taken or not taken) have a procedural dependency on the branch and cannot be executed until the branch is executed. Figure 14.3 illustrates the effect of a branch on a superscalar pipeline of degree 2.

As we have seen, this type of procedural dependency also affects a scalar pipeline. Again, the consequence for a superscalar pipeline is more severe, because a greater magnitude of opportunity is lost with each delay.

If variable-length instructions are used, then another sort of procedural dependency arises. Because the length of any particular instruction is not known, it must be at least partially decoded before the following instruction can be fetched. This prevents the simultaneous fetching required in a superscalar pipeline. This is one of the reasons that superscalar techniques are more readily applicable to a RISC or RISC-like architecture, with its fixed instruction length.

Resource Conflict

A resource conflict is a competition of two or more instructions for the same resource at the same time. Examples of resources include memories, caches, buses, register-file ports, and functional units (e.g., ALU adder).

In terms of the pipeline, a resource conflict exhibits similar behavior to a data dependency (Figure 14.3). There are some differences, however. For one thing, resource conflicts can be overcome by duplication of resources, whereas a true data dependency cannot be eliminated. Also, when an operation takes a long time to complete, resource conflicts can be minimized by pipelining the appropriate functional unit.

14.2 DESIGN ISSUES

Instruction–Level Parallelism and Machine Parallelism

[JOUP89a] makes an important distinction between the two related concepts of instruction-level parallelism and machine parallelism. **Instruction-level parallelism** exists when instructions in a sequence are independent and thus can be executed in parallel by overlapping.

As an example of the concept of instruction-level parallelism, consider the following two code fragments [JOUP89b]:

```
Load  R1 ← R2              Add R3 ← R3, "1"
Add   R3 ← R3, "1"         Add R4 ← R3, R2
Add   R4 ← R4, R2          Store [R4] ← R0
```

The three instructions on the left are independent, and in theory all three could be executed in parallel. In contrast, the three instructions on the right cannot be executed in parallel because the second instruction uses the result of the first, and the third instruction uses the result of the second.

Instruction-level parallelism is determined by the frequency of true data dependencies and procedural dependencies in the code. These factors, in turn, are dependent on the instruction set architecture and on the application. Instruction-level parallelism is also determined by what [JOUP89a] refers to as operation latency: the time until the result of an instruction is available for use as an operand in a subsequent instruction. The latency determines how much of a delay a data or procedural dependency will cause.

Machine parallelism is a measure of the ability of the processor to take advantage of instruction-level parallelism. Machine parallelism is determined by the number of instructions that can be fetched and executed at the same time (the number of parallel pipelines) and by the speed and sophistication of the mechanisms that the processor uses to find independent instructions.

Both instruction-level and machine parallelism are important factors in enhancing performance. A program may not have enough instruction-level parallelism to take full advantage of machine parallelism. The use of a fixed-length instruction set architecture, as in a RISC, enhances instruction-level parallelism. On the other hand, limited machine parallelism will limit performance no matter what the nature of the program.

Instruction Issue Policy

As was mentioned, machine parallelism is not simply a matter of having multiple instances of each pipeline stage. The processor must also be able to identify instruction-level parallelism and orchestrate the fetching, decoding, and execution of instructions in parallel. [JOHN91] uses the term **instruction issue** to refer to the process of initiating instruction execution in the processor's functional units and the term **instruction issue policy** to refer to the protocol used to issue instructions.

In essence, the processor is trying to look ahead of the current point of execution to locate instructions that can be brought into the pipeline and executed. Three types of orderings are important in this regard:

- The order in which instructions are fetched
- The order in which instructions are executed
- The order in which instructions update the contents of register and memory locations

The more sophisticated the processor, the less it is bound by a strict relationship between these orderings. To optimize utilization of the various pipeline elements, the processor will need to alter one or more of these orderings with respect to the ordering to be found in a strict sequential execution. The one constraint on the processor is that the result must be correct. Thus, the processor must accommodate the various dependencies and conflicts discussed earlier.

In general terms, we can group superscalar instruction issue policies into the following categories:

- In-order issue with in-order completion
- In-order issue with out-of-order completion
- Out-of-order issue with out-of-order completion

In-Order Issue with In-Order Completion

The simplest instruction issue policy is to issue instructions in the exact order that would be achieved by sequential execution (in-order issue) and to write results in that same order (in-order completion). Not even scalar pipelines follow such a simple-minded policy. However, it is useful to consider this policy as a baseline for comparing more sophisticated approaches.

Figure 14.4a gives an example of this policy. We assume a superscalar pipeline capable of fetching and decoding two instructions at a time, having three separate functional units (e.g., two integer arithmetic and one floating-point arithmetic), and having two instances of the write-back pipeline stage. The example assumes the following constraints on a six-instruction code fragment:

- I1 requires two cycles to execute.
- I3 and I4 conflict for the same functional unit.
- I5 depends on the value produced by I4.
- I5 and I6 conflict for a functional unit.

Instructions are fetched two at a time and passed to the decode unit. Because instructions are fetched in pairs, the next two instructions must wait until the pair of decode pipeline stages has cleared. To guarantee in-order completion, when there is a conflict for a functional unit or when a functional unit requires more than one cycle to generate a result, the issuing of instructions temporarily stalls.

In this example, the elapsed time from decoding the first instruction to writing the last results is eight cycles.

In-Order Issue with Out-of-Order Completion

Out-of-order completion is used in scalar RISC processors to improve the performance of instructions that require multiple cycles. Figure 14.4b illustrates its use on a superscalar processor. Instruction I2 is allowed to run to completion prior to I1. This allows I3 to be completed earlier, with the net result of a savings of one cycle.

With out-of-order completion, any number of instructions may be in the execution stage at any one time, up to the maximum degree of machine parallelism across all functional units. Instruction issuing is stalled by a resource conflict, a data dependency, or a procedural dependency.

In addition to the aforementioned limitations, a new dependency, which we referred to earlier as an **output dependency** (also called **write-write dependency**),

Decode		Execute			Write		Cycle
I1	I2						1
I3	I4	I1	I2				2
I3	I4	I1					3
	I4			I3	I1	I2	4
I5	I6			I4			5
	I6	I5			I3	I4	6
		I6					7
					I5	I6	8

(a) In-order issue and in-order completion

Decode		Execute			Write		Cycle
I1	I1						1
I3	I4	I1	I2				2
	I4	I1		I3	I2		3
I5	I6			I4	I1	I3	4
	I6	I5			I4		5
		I6			I5		6
					I6		7

(b) In-order issue and out-of-order completion

Decode		Window	Execute			Write		Cycle
I1	I2							1
I3	I4	*I1,I2*	I1	I2				2
I5	I6	*I3,I4*	I1		I3	I2		3
		I4,I5,I6		I6	I4	I1	I3	4
		I5		I5		I4	I6	5
						I5		6

(c) Out-of-order issue and out-of-order completion

Figure 14.4 Superscalar Instruction Issue and Completion Policies

arises. The following code fragment illustrates this dependency (op represents any operation):

```
I1:  R3 ← R3 op R5
I2:  R4 ← R3 + 1
I3:  R3 ← R5 + 1
I4:  R7 ← R3 op R4
```

Instruction I2 cannot execute before instruction I1, because it needs the result in register R3 produced in I1; this is an example of a true data dependency, as described in Section 14.1. Similarly, I4 must wait for I3, because it uses a result produced by I3. What about the relationship between I1 and I3? There is no data dependency here, as we have defined it. However, if I3 executes to completion prior to I1, then the wrong value of the contents of R3 will be fetched for the execution of I4. Consequently, I3 must complete after I1 to produce the correct output values. To ensure this, the issuing of the third instruction must be stalled if its result might later be overwritten by an older instruction that takes longer to complete.

Out-of-order completion requires more complex instruction issue logic than in-order completion. In addition, it is more difficult to deal with instruction interrupts and exceptions. When an interrupt occurs, instruction execution at the current point is suspended, to be resumed later. The processor must assure that the resumption takes into account that, at the time of interruption, instructions ahead of the instruction that caused the interrupt may already have completed.

Out-of-Order Issue with Out-of-Order Completion

With in-order issue, the processor will only decode instructions up to the point of a dependency or conflict. No additional instructions are decoded until the conflict is resolved. As a result, the processor cannot look ahead of the point of conflict to subsequent instructions that may be independent of those already in the pipeline and that may be usefully introduced into the pipeline.

To allow out-of-order issue, it is necessary to decouple the decode and execute stages of the pipeline. This is done with a buffer referred to as an **instruction window**. With this organization, after a processor has finished decoding an instruction, it is placed in the instruction window. As long as this buffer is not full, the processor can continue to fetch and decode new instructions. When a functional unit becomes available in the execute stage, an instruction from the instruction window may be issued to the execute stage. Any instruction may be issued, provided that (1) it needs the particular functional unit that is available and (2) no conflicts or dependencies block this instruction.

The result of this organization is that the processor has a lookahead capability, allowing it to identify independent instructions that can be brought into the execute stage. Instructions are issued from the instruction window with little regard for their original program order. As before, the only constraint is that the program execution behaves correctly.

Figures 14.4c illustrates this policy. On each cycle, two instructions are fetched into the decode stage. On each cycle, subject to the constraint of the buffer size, two instructions move from the decode stage to the instruction window. In this example, it is possible to issue instruction I6 ahead of I5 (recall that I5 depends on I4, but I6 does not). Thus, one cycle is saved in both the execute and write-back stages, and the end-to-end savings, compared with Figure 14.4b, is one cycle.

The instruction window is depicted in Figure 14.4c to illustrate its role. However, this window is not an additional pipeline stage. An instruction being in the window simply implies that the processor has sufficient information about that instruction to decide when it can be issued.

The out-of-order issue, out-of-order completion policy is subject to the same constraints described earlier. An instruction cannot be issued if it violates a dependency or conflict. The difference is that more instructions are available for issuing, reducing the probability that a pipeline stage will have to stall. In addition, a new dependency, which we referred to earlier as an **antidependency** (also called **read-**

write dependency), arises. The code fragment considered earlier illustrates this dependency:

```
I1:  R3 ← R3 op R5
I2:  R4 ← R3 + 1
I3:  R3 ← R5 + 1
I4:  R7 ← R3 op R4
```

Instruction I3 cannot complete execution before instruction I2 begins execution and has fetched its operands. This is so because I3 updates register R3, which is a source operand for I2. The term *antidependency* is used because the constraint is similar to that of a true data dependency, but reversed: Instead of the first instruction producing a value that the second instruction uses, the second instruction destroys a value that the first instruction uses.

Register Renaming

When out-of-order instruction issuing and/or out-of-order instruction completion are allowed, we have seen that this gives rise to the possibility of output dependencies and antidependencies. These dependencies differ from true data dependencies and resource conflicts, which reflect the flow of data through a program and the sequence of execution. Output dependencies and antidependencies, on the other hand, arise because the values in registers may no longer reflect the sequence of values dictated by the program flow.

When instructions are issued in sequence and complete in sequence, it is possible to specify the contents of each register at each point in the execution. When out-of-order techniques are used, the values in registers cannot be fully known at each point in time just from a consideration of the sequence of instructions dictated by the program. In effect, values are in conflict for the use of registers, and the processor must resolve those conflicts by occasionally stalling a pipeline stage.

Antidependencies and output dependencies are both examples of storage conflicts. Multiple instructions are competing for the use of the same register locations, generating pipeline constraints that retard performance. The problem is made more acute when register optimization techniques are used (as discussed in Chapter 13), because these compiler techniques attempt to maximize the use of registers, hence maximizing the number of storage conflicts.

One method for coping with these types of storage conflicts is based on a traditional resource-conflict solution: duplication of resources. In this context, the technique is referred to as **register renaming**. In essence, registers are allocated dynamically by the processor hardware, and they are associated with the values needed by instructions at various points in time. When a new register value is created (i.e., when an instruction executes that has a register as a destination operand), a new register is allocated for that value. Subsequent instructions that access that value as a source operand in that register must go through a renaming process: The register references in those instructions must be revised to refer to the register containing the needed value. Thus, the same original register reference in several different instructions may refer to different actual registers, if different values are intended.

Let us consider how register renaming could be used on the code fragment we have been examining:

$$\begin{array}{l}
\text{I1:} \quad R3_b \leftarrow R3_a \text{ op } R5_a \\
\text{I2:} \quad R4_b \leftarrow R3_b + 1 \\
\text{I3:} \quad R3_c \leftarrow R5_a + 1 \\
\text{I4:} \quad R7_b \leftarrow R3_c \text{ op } R4_b
\end{array}$$

The register reference without the subscript refers to the logical register reference found in the instruction. The register reference with the subscript refers to a hardware register allocated to hold a new value. When a new allocation is made for a particular logical register, subsequent instruction references to that logical register as a source operand are made to refer to the most recently allocated hardware register (recent in terms of the program sequence of instructions).

In this example, the creation of register $R3_c$ in instruction I3 avoids the anti-dependency on the second instruction and the output dependency on the first instruction, and it does not interfere with the correct value being accessed by I4. The result is that I3 can be issued immediately; without renaming, I3 cannot be issued until the first instruction is complete and the second instruction is issued.

Machine Parallelism

In the preceding, we have looked at three hardware techniques that can be used in a superscalar processor to enhance performance: duplication of resources, out-of-order issue, and renaming. One study that illuminates the relationship among these techniques was reported in [SMIT89]. The study made use of a simulation that modeled a machine with the characteristics of the MIPS R2000, augmented with various superscalar features. A number of different program sequences were simulated.

Figure 14.5 shows the results. In each of the graphs, the vertical axis corresponds to the mean speedup of the superscalar machine over the scalar machine. The horizontal axis shows the results for four alternative processor organizations. The base machine does not duplicate any of the functional units, but it can issue instructions out of order. The second configuration duplicates the load/store functional unit that accesses a data cache. The third configuration duplicates the ALU, and the fourth configuration duplicates both load/store and ALU. In each graph, results are shown for instruction window sizes of 8, 16, and 32 instructions, which dictates the amount of lookahead the processor can do. The difference between the two graphs is that, in the second, register renaming is allowed. This is equivalent to saying that the first graph reflects a machine that is limited by all dependencies, whereas the second graph corresponds to a machine that is limited only by true dependencies.

The two graphs, combined, yield some important conclusions. The first is that it is probably not worthwhile to add functional units without register renaming. There is some slight improvement in performance, but at the cost of increased hardware complexity. With register renaming, which eliminates antidependencies and output dependencies, noticeable gains are achieved by adding more functional units. Note, however, that there is a significant difference in the amount of gain achievable between using an instruction window of 8 versus a larger instruction

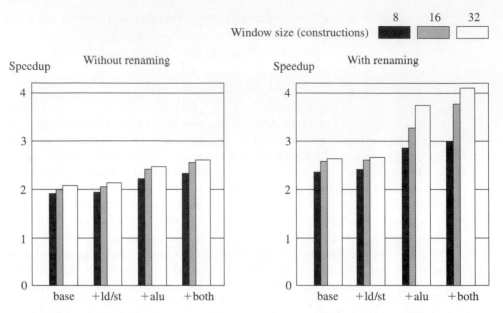

Figure 14.5 Speedups of Various Machine Organizations, without procedural Dependencies

window. This indicates that if the instruction window is too small, data dependencies will prevent effective utilization of the extra functional units; the processor must be able to look quite far ahead to find independent instructions to utilize the hardware more fully.

Branch Prediction

Any high-performance pipelined machine must address the issue of dealing with branches. For example, the Intel 80486 addressed the problem by fetching both the next sequential instruction after a branch and speculatively fetching the branch target instruction. However, because there are two pipeline stages between prefetch and execution, this strategy incurs a two-cycle delay when the branch gets taken.

With the advent of RISC machines, the delayed branch strategy was explored. This allows the processor to calculate the result of conditional branch instructions before any unusable instructions have been prefetched. With this method, the processor always executes the single instruction that immediately follows the branch. This keeps the pipeline full while the processor fetches a new instruction stream.

With the development of superscalar machines, the delayed branch strategy has less appeal. The reason is that multiple instructions need to execute in the delay slot, raising several problems relating to instruction dependencies. Thus, superscalar machines have returned to pre-RISC techniques of branch prediction. Some, like the PowerPC 601, use a simple static branch prediction technique. More sophisticated processors, such as the PowerPC 620 and the Pentium 4, use dynamic branch prediction based on branch history analysis.

Superscalar Execution

We are now in a position to provide an overview of superscalar execution of programs; this is illustrated in Figure 14.6. The program to be executed consists of a linear sequence of instructions. This is the static program as written by the programmer or generated by the compiler. The instruction fetch process, which includes branch prediction, is used to form a dynamic stream of instructions. This stream is examined for dependencies, and the processor may remove artificial dependencies. The processor then dispatches the instructions into a window of execution. In this window, instructions no longer form a sequential stream but are structured according to their true data dependencies. The processor performs the execution stage of each instruction in an order determined by the true data dependencies and hardware resource availability. Finally, instructions are conceptually put back into sequential order and their results are recorded.

The final step mentioned in the preceding paragraph is referred to as *committing*, or *retiring*, the instruction. This step is needed for the following reason. Because of the use of parallel, multiple pipelines, instructions may complete in an order different from that shown in the static program. Further, the use of branch prediction and speculative execution means that some instructions may complete execution and then must be abandoned because the branch they represent is not taken. Therefore, permanent storage and program-visible registers cannot be updated immediately when instructions complete execution. Results must be held in some sort of temporary storage that is usable by dependent instructions and then made permanent when it is determined that the sequential model would have executed the instruction.

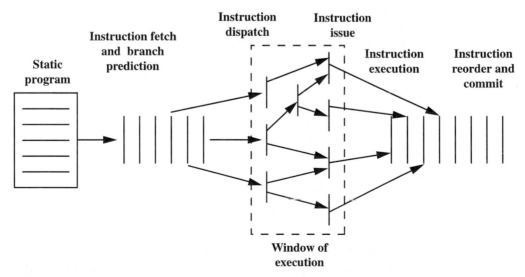

Figure 14.6 Conceptual Depiction of Superscalar Processing [SMIT95]

Superscalar Implementation

Based on our discussion so far, we can make some general comments about the processor hardware required for the superscalar approach. [SMIT95] lists the following key elements:

- Instruction fetch strategies that simultaneously fetch multiple instructions, often by predicting the outcomes of, and fetching beyond, conditional branch instructions. These functions require the use of multiple pipeline fetch and decode stages, and branch prediction logic.
- Logic for determining true dependencies involving register values, and mechanisms for communicating these values to where they are needed during execution.
- Mechanisms for initiating, or issuing, multiple instructions in parallel.
- Resources for parallel execution of multiple instructions, including multiple pipelined functional units and memory hierarchies capable of simultaneously servicing multiple memory references.
- Mechanisms for committing the process state in correct order.

14.3 PENTIUM 4

Although the concept of superscalar design is generally associated with the RISC architecture, the same superscalar principles can be applied to a CISC machine. Perhaps the most notable example of this is the Pentium. The evolution of superscalar concepts in the Intel line is interesting to note. The 80486 was a straightforward traditional CISC machine, with no superscalar elements. The original Pentium had a modest superscalar component, consisting of the use of two separate integer execution units. The Pentium Pro introduced a full-blown superscalar design. Subsequent Pentium models have refined and enhanced the superscalar design.

A general block diagram of the Pentium 4 was shown in Figure 4.13. Figure 14.7, based on one in [CARM00], depicts the same structure in a way more suitable for the pipeline discussion in this section. The operation of the Pentium 4 can be summarized as follows:

1. The processor fetches instructions from memory in the order of the static program.
2. Each instruction is translated into one or more fixed-length RISC instructions, known as micro-operations, or micro-ops.
3. The processor executes the micro-ops on a superscalar pipeline organization, so that the micro-ops may be executed out of order.
4. The processor commits the results of each micro-op execution to the processor's register set in the order of the original program flow.

In effect, the Pentium 4 architecture consists of an outer CISC shell with an inner RISC core. The inner RISC micro-ops pass through a pipeline with at least 20 stages (Figure 14.8); in some cases, the micro-op requires multiple execution stages,

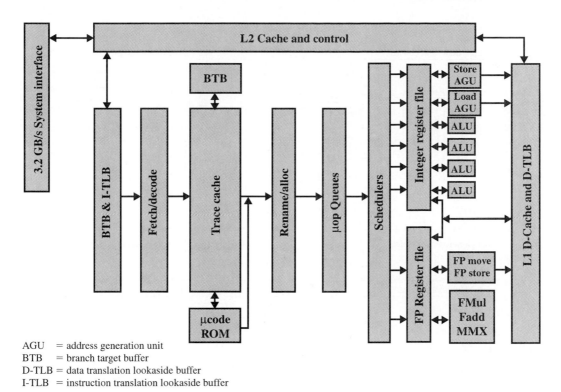

AGU   = address generation unit
BTB   = branch target buffer
D-TLB = data translation lookaside buffer
I-TLB = instruction translation lookaside buffer

Figure 14.7   Pentium 4 Block Diagram

resulting in an even longer pipeline. This contrasts with the five-stage pipeline (Figure 12.18) used on the Intel x86 processors and on the Pentium.

We now trace to operation of the Pentium 4 pipeline, using Figure 14.9 to illustrate its operation.

Front End

Generation of Micro-Ops

The Pentium 4 organization includes an in-order front end (Figure 14.9a) that can be considered outside the scope of the pipeline depicted in Figure 14.8. This front end feeds into an L1 instruction cache, called the trace cache, which is where

1	2	3	4	5	6	7	8	9	10	11	12	13	14	15	16	17	18	19	20
TC Nxt IP		TC Fetch		Drive	Alloc	Rename		Que	Sch	Sch	Sch	Disp	Disp	RF	RF	Ex	Flgs	Br Ck	Drive

TC Next IP = trace cache next instruction pointer   Rename = register renaming   RF = register file
TC Fetch = trace cache fetch   Que = micro-op queuing   Ex = execute
Alloc = allocate   Sch = micro-op scheduling   Flgs = flags
                                                      Disp = Dispatch   Br Ck = branch check

Figure 14.8   Pentium 4 Pipeline

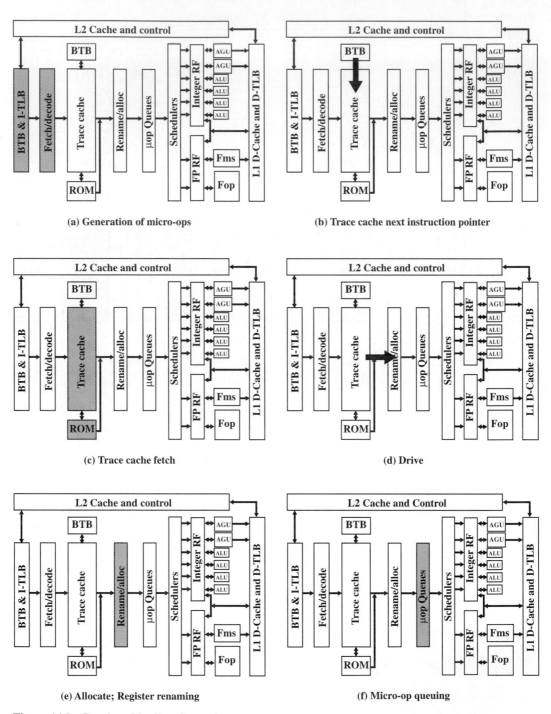

(a) Generation of micro-ops

(b) Trace cache next instruction pointer

(c) Trace cache fetch

(d) Drive

(e) Allocate; Register renaming

(f) Micro-op queuing

Figure 14.9 Pentium Pipeline Operation

(g) Micro-op scheduling

(h) Dispatch

(i) Register file

(j) Execute; flags

(k) Branch check

(l) Branch check result

Figure 14.9 Pentium Pipeline Operation *(continued)*

the pipeline proper begins. Usually, the processor operates from the trace cache; when a trace cache miss occurs, the in-order front end feeds new instructions into the trace cache.

With the aid of the branch target buffer and the instruction lookaside buffer (BTB & I-TLB), the fetch/decode unit fetches Pentium 4 machine instructions from the L2 cache 64 bytes at a time. As a default, instructions are fetched sequentially, so that each L2 cache line fetch includes the next instruction to be fetched. Branch prediction via the BTB & I-TLB unit may alter this sequential fetch operation. The ITLB translates the linear instruction pointer address given it into physical addresses needed to access the L2 cache. Static branch prediction in the front-end BTB is used to determine which instructions to fetch next.

Once instructions are fetched, the fetch/decode unit scans the bytes to determine instruction boundaries; this is a necessary operation because of the variable length of Pentium instructions. The decoder translates each machine instruction into from one to four micro-ops, each of which is a 118-bit RISC instruction. Note for comparison that most pure RISC machines have an instruction length of just 32 bits. The longer micro-op length is required to accommodate the more complex Pentium operations. Nevertheless, the micro-ops are easier to manage than the original instructions from which they derive.

The generated micro-ops are stored in the trace cache.

Trace Cache Next Instruction Pointer

The first two pipeline stages (Figure 14.9b) deal with the selection of instructions in the trace cache and involve a separate branch prediction mechanism from that described in the previous section. The Pentium 4 uses a dynamic branch prediction strategy based on the history of recent executions of branch instructions. A branch target buffer (BTB) is maintained that caches information about recently encountered branch instructions. Whenever a branch instruction is encountered in the instruction stream, the BTB is checked. If an entry already exists in the BTB, then the instruction unit is guided by the history information for that entry in determining whether to predict that the branch is taken. If a branch is predicted, then the branch destination address associated with this entry is used for prefetching the branch target instruction.

Once the instruction is executed, the history portion of the appropriate entry is updated to reflect the result of the branch instruction. If this instruction is not represented in the BTB, then the address of this instruction is loaded into an entry in the BTB; if necessary, an older entry is deleted.

The description of the preceding two paragraphs fits, in general terms, the branch prediction strategy used on the original Pentium model, as well as the later Pentium models, including Pentium 4. However, in the case of the Pentium, a relatively simple 2-bit history scheme is used. The later Pentium models have much longer pipelines (20 stages for the Pentium 4 compared with 5 stages for the Pentium) and therefore the penalty for misprediction is greater. Accordingly, the later Pentium models use a more elaborate branch prediction scheme with more history bits to reduce the misprediction rate.

The Pentium 4 BTB is organized as a four-way set-associative cache with 512 lines. Each entry uses the address of the branch as a tag. The entry also includes the branch destination address for the last time this branch was taken and a 4-bit history field. Thus use of four history bits contrasts with the 2 bits used in the original Pentium and used in most superscalar processors. With 4 bits, the Pentium 4 mechanism can take into account a longer history in predicting branches. The algorithm that is used is referred to as Yeh's algorithm [YEH91]. The developers of this algorithm have demonstrated that it provides a significant reduction in misprediction compared to algorithms that use only 2 bits of history [EVER98].

Conditional branches that do not have a history in the BTB are predicted using a static prediction algorithm, according to the following rules:

- For branch addresses that are not IP relative, predict taken if the branch is a return and not taken otherwise.
- For IP-relative backward conditional branches, predict taken. This rule reflects the typical behavior of loops.
- For IP-relative forward conditional branches, predict not taken.

Trace Cache Fetch

The trace cache (Figure 14.9c) takes the already-decoded micro-ops from the instruction decoder and assembles them in to program-ordered sequences of micro-ops called traces. Micro-ops are fetched sequentially from the trace cache, subject to the branch prediction logic.

A few instructions require more than four micro-ops. These instructions are transferred to microcode ROM, which contains the series of micro-ops (five or more) associated with a complex machine instruction. For example, a string instruction may translate into a very large (even hundreds), repetitive sequence of micro-ops. Thus, the microcode ROM is a microprogrammed control unit in the sense discussed in Part Four. After the microcode ROM finishes sequencing micro-ops for the current Pentium instruction, fetching resumes from the trace cache.

Drive

The fifth stage (Figure 14.9d) of the Pentium 4 pipeline delivers decoded instructions from the trace cache to the rename/allocator module.

Out-of-Order Execution Logic

This part of the processor reorders micro-ops to allow them to execute as quickly as their input operands are ready.

Allocate

The allocate stage (Figure 14.9e) allocates resources required for execution. It performs the following functions:

- If a needed resource, such as a register, is unavailable for one of the three micro-ops arriving at the allocator during a clock cycle, the allocator stalls the pipeline.
- The allocator allocates a reorder buffer (ROB) entry, which tracks the completion status of one of the 126 micro-ops that could be in process at any time.

- The allocator allocates one of the 128 integer or floating-point register entries for the result data value of the micro-op, and possibly a load or store buffer used to track one of the 48 loads or 24 stores in the machine pipeline.
- The allocator allocates an entry in one of the two micro-op queues in front of the instruction schedulers.

The ROB is a circular buffer that can hold up to 126 micro-ops and also contains the 128 hardware registers. Each buffer entry consists of the following fields:

- **State:** Indicates whether this micro-op is scheduled for execution, has been dispatched for execution, or has completed execution and is ready for retirement.
- **Memory Address:** The address of the Pentium instruction that generated the micro-op.
- **Micro-op:** The actual operation.
- **Alias Register:** If the micro-op references one of the 16 architectural registers, this entry redirects that reference to one of the 128 hardware registers.

Micro-ops enter the ROB in order. Micro-ops are then dispatched from the ROB to the Dispatch/Execute unit out of order. The criterion for dispatch is that the appropriate execution unit and all necessary data items required for this micro-op are available. Finally, micro-ops are retired from the ROB in order. To accomplish in-order retirement, micro-ops are retired oldest first after each micro-op has been designated as ready for retirement.

Register Renaming

The rename stage (Figure 14.9e) remaps references to the 16 architectural registers (8 floating-point registers, plus EAX, EBX, ECX, EDX, ESI, EDI, EBP, and ESP) into a set of 128 physical registers. The stage removes false dependencies caused by a limited number of architectural registers while preserving the true data dependencies (reads after writes).

Micro-op Queuing

After resource allocation and register renaming, micro-ops are placed in one of two micro-op queues (Figure 14.9f), where they are held until there is room in the schedulers. One of the two queues is for memory operations (loads and stores) and the other for micro-ops that do not involve memory references. Each queue obeys a FIFO (first-in-first-out) discipline, but no order is maintained between queues. That is, a micro-op may be read out of one queue out of order with respect to micro-ops in the other queue. This provides greater flexibility to the schedulers.

Micro-op Scheduling and Dispatching

The schedulers (Figure 14.9g) are responsible for retrieving micro-ops from the micro-op queues and dispatching these for execution. Each scheduler looks for micro-ops in whose status indicates that the micro-op has all of its operands. If the execution unit needed by that micro-op is available, then the scheduler fetches the micro-op and dispatches it to the appropriate execution unit (Figure 14.9h). Up to six micro-ops can be dispatched in one cycle. If more than one micro-op is available for a given execution unit, then the scheduler dispatches them in sequence from the queue. This is a sort of FIFO discipline that favors in-order execution, but by this time the instruction stream has been so rearranged by dependencies and branches that it is substantially out of order.

Four ports attach the schedulers to the execution units. Port 0 is used for both integer and floating-point instructions, with the exception of simple integer operations and the handling of branch mispredictions, which are allocated to Port 1. In addition, MMX execution units are allocated between these two ports. The remaining ports are for memory loads and stores.

Integer and Floating-Point Execution Units

The integer and floating-point register files are the source for pending operations by the execution units (Figure 14.9i). The execution units retrieve values from the register files as well as from the L1 data cache (Figure 14.9j). A separate pipeline stage is used to compute flags (e.g., zero, negative); these are typically the input to a branch instruction.

A subsequent pipeline stage performs branch checking (Figure 14.9k). This function compares the actual branch result with the prediction. If a branch prediction turns out to have been wrong, then there are micro-operations in various stages of processing that must be removed from the pipeline. The proper branch destination is then provided to the Branch Predictor during a drive stage (Figure 14.9l), which restarts the whole pipeline from the new target address.

14.4 POWERPC

The PowerPC architecture is a direct descendant of the IBM 801, the RT PC, and the RS/6000, the last also referred to as an implementation of the POWER architecture. All of these are RISC machines, but the first in the series to exhibit superscalar features was the RS/6000. The first implementation of the PowerPC architecture, the 601, has a superscalar design quite similar to that of the RS/6000. Subsequent PowerPC models carry the superscalar concept further. In this section, we focus on the 601, which provides a good example of a RISC-based superscalar design. At the end of the section, we briefly consider the 620.

PowerPC 601

Figure 14.10 is a general view of the 601 organization. As with other superscalar machines, the 601 is broken up into independent functional units to enhance opportunities for overlapped execution. In particular, the core of the 601 consists of three independent pipelined execution units: integer, floating-point, and branch processing. Together, these units can execute three instructions at a time, yielding a superscalar design of degree 3.

Figure 14.11 shows a logical view of the 601 architecture, emphasizing the flow of instructions between functional units. The fetch unit can prefetch up to eight instructions at a time from the cache. The cache unit supports a combined instruction/

data cache and is responsible for feeding instructions to the other units and data to the registers. Cache arbitration logic sends the address of the highest-priority access to the cache.

Dispatch Unit

The dispatch unit takes instructions from the cache and loads them into the dispatch queue, which can hold eight instructions at a time. It processes this stream of instructions to feed a steady flow of instructions to the branch processing, integer, and floating-point units. The upper half of the queue simply acts as a buffer to hold instructions until they move into the lower half. Its purpose is to ensure that the dispatch unit is not delayed waiting for instructions from the cache. In the lower half, instructions are dispatched according to the following scheme:

- **Branch processing unit:** Handles all branch instructions. The lowest such instruction in the bottom half of the dispatch queue is issued to the branch processing unit if that unit can accept it.
- **Floating-point unit:** Handles all floating-point instructions. The lowest such instruction in the bottom half of the dispatch queue is issued to the floating-point unit if the instruction pipeline in that unit is not full.
- **Integer unit:** Handles integer instructions, load/stores between the register files and the cache, and integer compare instructions. An integer instruction is only issued after it has filtered to the bottom of the dispatch queue.

Allowing branch and floating-point instructions to be issued out of order from the dispatch queue helps keep the instruction pipelines in the branch processing and floating-point units full, and it moves instructions through the dispatch queue as rapidly as possible.

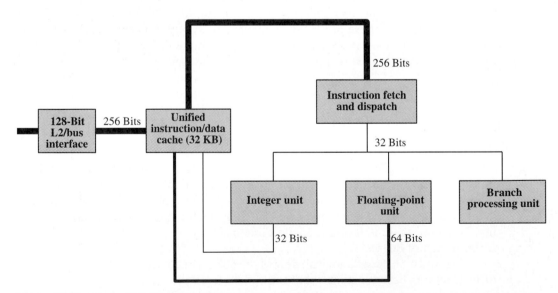

Figure 14.10   PowerPC 601 Block Diagram

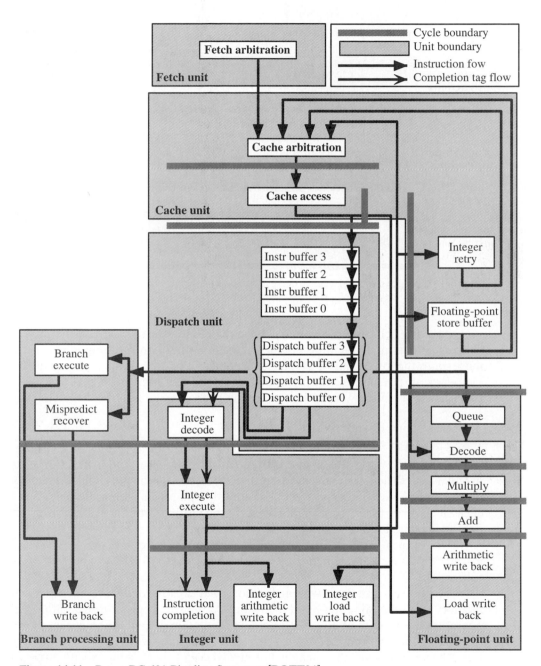

Figure 14.11   PowerPC 601 Pipeline Structure [POTT94]

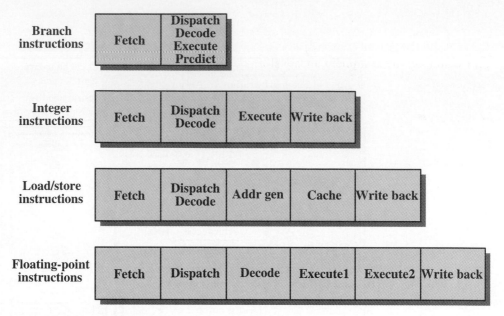

Figure 14.12 PowerPC 601 Pipeline

The dispatch unit also contains logic that enables it to calculate the prefetch address. It continues fetching instructions sequentially until a branch instruction moves into the lower half of the dispatch queue. When the branch processing unit processes an instruction, it may update the prefetch address so that succeeding instructions are fetched from the new address and entered into the dispatch queue.

Instruction Pipelines

Figure 14.12 illustrates the instruction pipelines for the various units. There is a common fetch cycle for all instructions; this occurs before an instruction is dispatched to a particular unit. The second cycle begins with the dispatch of an instruction to a particular unit. This overlaps with other activities within the unit. During each clock cycle, the dispatch unit considers the bottom four entries of the instruction queue and dispatches up to three instructions.

For branch instructions, the second cycle involves decoding and executing instructions as well as predicting branches. The last activity is discussed in the next subsection.

The integer unit deals with instructions that cause a load/store operation with memory (including floating-point load/store), a register–register move, or an ALU operation. In the case of a load/store, there is an address generation cycle followed by sending the resulting address to the cache and, if necessary, a write-back cycle. For other instructions, the cache is not involved and there is an execute cycle followed by a write back to register.

Floating-point instructions follow a similar pipeline, but there are two execute cycles, reflecting the complexity of floating-point operations.

Several additional points are worth noting. The condition register contains eight independent 4-bit condition code fields. This allows multiple condition codes to be retained, which reduces the interlock or dependency between instructions. For example, the compiler can transform the sequence

```
compare
branch
compare
branch
.
.
.
```

to the sequence

```
compare
compare
.
.
.
branch
branch
.
.
.
```

Because each functional unit can send its condition codes to different fields in the condition register, interlocks between instructions caused by sharing of condition codes can be avoided.

The presence of the Save and Restore registers (SRRs) in the branch processor allows it to handle simple interrupts and software interrupts without involving logic in the other functional units. Thus, simple operating system services can be performed rapidly without complicated state manipulation or synchronization between the functional units.

Because the 601 can issue branch and floating-point instructions out of order, controls are needed to ensure proper execution. When a dependency exists (i.e., when an instruction needs an operand that has yet to be computed by a previous instruction), the pipeline in the corresponding unit stalls.

Branch Processing

The key to the high performance of a RISC or superscalar machine is its ability to optimize the use of the pipeline. Typically, the most critical element in the design is how branches are handled. In the PowerPC, branch processing is the responsibility of the branch unit. The unit is designed so that in many cases, branches have no effect on the pace of execution in the other units; these type of branches are referred to as zero-cycle branches. To achieve zero-cycle branching, the following strategies are employed:

1. Logic is provided to scan through the dispatch buffer for branches. Branch target addresses are generated when a branch first appears in the lower half of the queue and no prior branches are pending execution.

2. An attempt is made to determine the outcome of conditional branches. If the condition code has been set sufficiently far in advance, this can be determined. In any case, as soon as a branch instruction is encountered, logic determines if the branch

   a. Will be taken; this is the case for unconditional branches and for conditional branches whose condition code is known and indicates a branch.

   b. Will not be taken; this is the case for conditional branches whose condition code is known and indicates no branch.

   c. Outcome cannot yet be determined. In this case, the branch is guessed to be taken for backward branches (typical of loops) and guessed not to be taken for forward branches. Sequential instructions past the branch instruction are passed to the execution units in a conditional fashion. Once the condition code value is produced in the execution unit, the branch unit either cancels the instructions in the pipeline and proceeds with the fetched target if the branch is taken, or signals for the conditional instructions to be executed. The compiler can use a single bit in the instruction coding to reverse this default behavior.

The incorporation of a branch prediction strategy based on branch history was rejected because the designers felt that a minimal payoff would be achieved.

As an example of the branch prediction effect, consider the program of Figure 14.13 and assume that the branch processor predicts that the conditional branch instruction is not taken (the default case for a forward branch). Figure 14.14a shows the effect on the pipeline if in fact the branch is not taken. In the first cycle, the dispatch queue is loaded with eight instructions. The first six instructions are integer instructions and are dispatched one per cycle to the integer unit. The conditional branch instruction cannot be dispatched until it progresses to the lower half of the dispatch queue, which happens in cycle 5. The branch unit predicts that this branch will not be taken, and so the next instruction in sequence is conditionally dispatched (indicated by a D′). The branch cannot be resolved until the compare instruction executes in cycle 8. At that time, the branch processor confirms that its prediction was correct, and execution continues. There are no delays, and the pipeline is kept full.

Note that no instructions are fetched during cycles 4 through 8. This is because the cache is busy during those cycles with the cache access stage of the five load instructions. Even so, the instruction stream is not delayed, because the dispatch queue can hold eight instructions.

Figure 14.14b shows the result if the prediction is incorrect and the branch is taken. In this case, the three instructions starting at the IF must be flushed, and fetching resumes with instructions starting at ELSE. As a result, the execute stage of the integer pipeline is idle for cycles 9 and 10, resulting in a two-cycle loss because of the incorrect prediction.

PowerPC 620

The 620 is the first 64-bit implementation of the PowerPC architecture. A notable feature of this implementation is that it includes six independent execution units:

- Instruction unit
- Three integer units
- Load/store unit
- Floating-point unit

This organization enables the processor to dispatch up to four instructions simultaneously to the three integer units and one floating-point unit.

The 620 employs a high-performance branch prediction strategy that involves prediction logic, register rename buffers, and reservation stations inside the execution units. When an instruction is fetched, it is assigned a rename buffer to hold instruction results temporarily, such as register stores. Because of the use of rename buffers, the processor can *speculatively execute* instructions based on branch prediction; if the prediction turns out to be incorrect, then the results of the speculative instructions can be flushed without damaging the register file. Once the outcome of a branch is confirmed, temporary results can be written out permanently.

Each unit has two or more reservation stations, which store dispatched instructions that must be held up for the results of other instructions. This feature clears these instructions out of the instruction unit, enabling it to continue dispatching instructions to other execution units.

```
if (a > 0)
          a = a + b + c + d + e;
else
          a = a - b - c - d - e;
```

(a) C code

```
                                    #r1 points to a,
                                    #r1+4 points to b,
                                    #r1+8 points to c,
                                    #r1+12 points to d,
                                    #r1+16 points to e.
        lwz     r8=a(r1)            #load a
        lwz     r12=b(r1,4)         #load b
        lwz     r9=c(r1,8)          #load c
        lwz     r10=d(r1,12)        #load d
        lwz     r11=e(r1,16)        #load e
        cmpi    cr0=r8,0            #compare immediate
        bc      ELSE,cr0/gt=false   #branch if bit false
IF:
        add     r12=r8,r12          #add
        add     r12=r12,r9          #add
        add     r12=r12,r10         #add
        add     r4=r12,r11          #add
        stw     a(r1)=r4            #store
        b       OUT                 #unconditional branch
ELSE:
        subf    r12=r12,r8          #subtract
        subf    r12=r9,r12          #subtract
        subf    r12=r10,r12         #subtract
        subf    r4=r12,r11          #subtract
        stw     a(r1)=r4            #store
OUT:
```

(b) Assembly code

Figure 14.13 Code Example with Conditional Branch [WEIS94]

	1	2	3	4	5	6	7	8	9	10	11	12	13	14	15	16
lwz r8=a(r1)	F	D	E	C	W											
lwz r12=b(r1,4)	F	•	D	E	C	W										
lwz r9=c(r1,8)	F	•	•	D	E	C	W									
lwz r10=d(r1,12)	F	•	•	•	D	E	C	W								
lwz r11=e(r1,16)	F	•	•	•	•	D	E	C	W							
cmpi cr0=r8,0	F	•	•	•	•	•	D	E								
bc ELSE,cr0/gt=false	F	•	•	•	S											
IF: add r12=r8,r12	F	•	•	•	•	•	•	•	D'	E	W					
add r12=r12,r9		F	•	•	•	•	•	•		D	E	W				
add r12=r12,r10		F	•	•	•	•	•	•	•		D	E	W			
add r4=r12,r11									F	•		D	E	W		
stw a(r1)=r4									F	•	•	D	E	C		
b OUT																
ELSE: subf r12=r8,r12																
subf r12=r12,r9																
subf r12=r12,r10																
subf r4=r12,r11																
stw a(r1)=r4																
OUT:																

(a) Correct prediction: Branch was not taken

	1	2	3	4	5	6	7	8	9	10	11	12	13	14	15	16
lwz r8=a(r1)	F	D	E	C	W											
lwz r12=b(r1,4)	F	•	D	E	C	W										
lwz r9=c(r1,8)	F	•	•	D	E	C	W									
lwz r10=d(r1,12)	F	•	•	•	D	E	C	W								
lwz r11=e(r1,16)	F	•	•	•	•	D	E	C	W							
cmpi cr0=r8,0	F	•	•	•	•	•	D	E								
bc ELSE,cr0/gt=false	F	•	•	•	S											
IF: add r12=r8,r12	F	•	•	•	•	•	•	•	D'							
add r12=r12,r9		F	•	•	•	•	•	•								
add r12=r12,r10		F	•	•	•	•	•	•								
add r4=r12,r11																
stw a(r1)=r4																
b OUT																
ELSE: subf r12=r8,r12									F	D	E	W				
subf r12=r12,r9									F	•	D	E	W			
subf r12=r12,r10									F	•	•	D	E	W		
subf r4=r12,r11									F	•	•	•	D	E	W	
stw a(r1)=r4									F	•	•	•	•	D	E	C
OUT:																

(b) Incorrect prediction: Branch was taken

F = fetch   C = cache access
D = dispatch/decode   W = writeback
E = execute/address   S = dispatch

Figure 14.14 Branch Prediction: Not Taken [WEIS94]

The 620 can speculatively execute up to four unresolved branch instructions (versus one for the 601). Branch prediction is based on the use of a branch history table with 2048 entries. Simulations run by the PowerPC designers show that the branch prediction success rate is 90% [THOM94].

14.5 RECOMMENDED READING

[JOHN91] remains a relevant and excellent book-length treatment of superscalar design. Worthwhile survey articles on the subject are [SMIT95] and [SIMA97]. [JOUP89a] examines instruction-level parallelism, looks at various techniques for maximizing parallelism, and compares superscalar and superpipelined approaches using simulation. Two recent papers that provide good coverage of superscalar design issues are [PATT01] and [MOSH01].

[POPE91] provides a detailed look at a proposed superscalar machine. It also provides an excellent tutorial on the design issues related to out-of-order instruction policies. Another look at a proposed system is found in [KUGA91]; this article raises and considers most of the important design issues for superscalar implementation. [LEE91] examines software techniques that can be used to enhance superscalar performance. [WALL91] is an interesting study of the extent to which instruction-level parallelism can be exploited in a superscalar processor.

Volume I of [INTE01a] provides general description of the Pentium 4 pipeline; more detail is provided in [INTE01b].

[POTT94] is a detailed examination of instruction pipelining on the PowerPC 601. [SHAN95] also provides good coverage.

HINT01 Hinton, G., et al. "The Microarchitecture of the Pentium 4 Processor." *Intel Technology Journal*, Q1 2001. http://developer.intel.com/technology/itj/

INTE01a Intel Corp. *IA-32 Intel Architecture Software Developer's Manual (2 volumes)*. Document 245470 and 245471. Aurora, CO, 2001.

INTE01b Intel Corp. *Intel Pentium 4 Processor Optimization Reference Manual*. Document 248966-04. Aurora, CO, 2001. http://developer.intel.com/design/pentium4/manuals/248966.htm

JOHN91 Johnson, M. *Superscalar Microprocessor Design*. Englewood Cliffs, NJ: Prentice Hall, 1991.

JOUP89a Jouppi, N., and Wall, D. "Available Instruction-Level Parallelism for Superscalar and Superpipelined Machines." *Proceedings, Third International Conference on Architectural Support for Programming Languages and Operating Systems*, April 1989.

KUGA91 Kuga, M.; Murakami, K.; and Tomita, S. "DSNS (Dynamically-hazard resolved, Statically-code-scheduled, Nonuniform Superscalar): Yet Another Superscalar Processor Architecture." *Computer Architecture News*, June 1991.

LEE91 Lee, R.; Kwok, A.; and Briggs, F. "The Floating Point Performance of a Superscalar SPARC Processor." *Proceedings, Fourth International Conference on Architectural Support for Programming Languages and Operating Systems*, April 1991.

MOSH01 Moshovos, A., and Sohi, G. "Microarchitectural Innovations: Boosting Microprocessor Performance Beyond Semiconductor Technology Scaling." *Proceedings of the IEEE*, November 2001.

PATT01 Patt, Y. "Requirements, Bottlenecks, and Good Fortune: Agents for Microprocessor Evolution." *Proceedings of the IEEE*, November 2001.

POPE91 Popescu, V., et al. "The Metaflow Architecture." *IEEE Micro*, June 1991.

POTT94 Potter, T., et al. "Resolution of Data and Control-Flow Dependencies in the PowerPC 601." *IEEE Micro*, October 1994.

SHAN95 Shanley, T. *PowerPC System Architecture*. Reading, MA: Addison-Wesley, 1995.

SIMA97 Sima, D. "Superscalar Instruction Issue." *IEEE Micro*, September/October 1997.

SMIT95 Smith, J., and Sohi, G. "The Microarchitecture of Superscalar Processors." *Proceedings of the IEEE*, December 1995.

WALL91 Wall, D. "Limits of Instruction-Level Parallelism." *Proceedings, Fourth International Conference on Architectural Support for Programming Languages and Operating Systems,* April 1991.

14.6 KEY TERMS, REVIEW QUESTIONS, AND PROBLEMS

Key Terms

antidependency	instruction window	register renaming
branch prediction	machine parallelism	resource conflict
in-order issue	out-of-order completion	superpipelined
in-order completion	out-of-order issue	superscalar
instruction issue	output dependency	true data dependency
instruction-level parallelism	procedural dependency	

Review Questions

14.1 What is the essential characteristic of the superscalar approach to processor design?

14.2 What is the difference between the superscalar and superpipelined approaches?

14.3 What is instruction-level parallelism?

14.4 Briefly define the following terms:
- True data dependency
- Procedural dependency
- Resource conflicts
- Output dependency
- Antidependency

14.5 What is the distinction between instruction-level parallelism and machine parallelism?

14.6 List and briefly define three types of superscalar instruction issue policies.

14.7 What is the purpose of an instruction window?

14.8 What is register renaming and what is its purpose?

14.9 What are the key elements of a superscalar processor organization?

Problems

14.1 When out-of-order completion is used in a superscalar processor, resumption of execution after interrupt processing is complicated, because the exceptional condition may have been detected as an instruction that produced its result out of order. The program cannot be restarted at the instruction following the exceptional instruction, because subsequent instructions have already completed, and doing so would cause these instructions to be executed twice. Suggest a mechanism or mechanisms for dealing with this situation.

14.2 Consider the following sequence of instructions, where the syntax consists of an opcode followed by the destination register followed by one or two source registers:

```
 0    ADD     R3, R1, R2
 1    LOAD    R6, [R3]
 2    AND     R7, R5, 3
 3    ADD     R1, R6, R0
 4    SRL     R7, R0, 8
 5    OR      R2, R4, R7
 6    SUB     R5, R3, R4
 7    ADD     R0, R1, R10
 8    LOAD    R6, [R5]
 9    SUB     R2, R1, R6
10    AND     R3, R7, 15
```

Assume the use of a four-stage pipeline: fetch, decode/issue, execute, write back. Assume that all pipeline stages take one clock cycle except for the execute stage. For simple integer arithmetic and logical instructions, the execute stage takes one cycle, but for a LOAD from memory, five cycles are consumed in the execute stage.

If we have a simple scalar pipeline but allow out-of-order execution, we can construct the following table for the execution of the first seven instructions:

Instruction	Fetch	Decode	Execute	Write Back
0	0	1	2	3
1	1	2	4	9
2	2	3	5	6
3	3	4	10	11
4	4	5	6	7
5	5	6	8	10
6	6	7	9	12

The entries under the four pipeline stages indicate the clock cycle at which each instruction begins each phase. In this program, the second ADD instruction (instruction 3) depends on the LOAD instruction (instruction 1) for one of its operands, r6. Because the LOAD instruction takes five clock cycles, and the issue logic encounters the dependent ADD instruction after two clocks, the issue logic must delay the ADD instruction for three clock cycles. With an out-of-order capability, the processor can stall instruction 3 at clock cycle 4, and then move on to issue the following three independent instructions, which enter execution at clocks 6, 8, and 9. The LOAD finishes execution at clock 9, and so the dependent ADD can be launched into execution on clock 10.

a. Complete the preceding table.

b. Redo the table, assuming no out-of-order capability. What is the savings using the capability?

c. Redo the table, assuming a superscalar implementation that can handle two instructions at a time at each stage.

14.3 In the instruction queue in the dispatch unit of the PowerPC 601, instructions may be dispatched out of order to the branch processing and floating-point units, but instructions intended for the integer unit must be dispatched only from the bottom of the queue. Why this limitation?

14.4 Produce a figure similar to Figure 14.14 for the following cases:

a. Branch prediction: taken; correct prediction: branch was taken

b. Branch prediction: taken; incorrect prediction: branch was not taken

14.5 Consider the following assembly language program:

```
I1:   Move R3, R7        /R3 ← (R7)/
I2:   Load R8, (R3)      /R8 ← Memory (R3)/
I3:   Add R3, R3, 4      /R3 ← (R3) + 4/
I4:   Load R9, (R3)      /R9 ← Memory (R3)/
I5:   BLE R8, R9, L3     /Branch if (R9) > (R8)/
```

This program includes write-write, read-write, and write-read dependencies. Show these.

14.6 Figure 14.15 shows an example of a superscalar processor organization. The processor can issue two instructions per cycle if there is no resource conflict and no data dependence problem. There are essentially two pipelines, with four processing stages (fetch, decode, execute, and store). Each pipeline has its own fetch decode and store unit. Four functional units (multiplier, adder, logic unit, and load unit) are available for use in the execute stage and are shared by the two pipelines on a dynamic basis. The two store units can be dynamically used by the two pipelines, depending on availability at a particular cycle. There is a lookahead window with its own fetch and decoding logic. This window is used for instruction lookahead for out-of-order instruction issue.

Consider the following program to be executed on this processor:

```
I1:   Load R1, A          /R1 ← Memory (A)/
I2:   Add R2, R1          /R2 ← (R2) + R(1)/
I3:   Add R3, R4          /R3 ← (R3) + R(4)/
I4:   Mul R4, R5          /R4 ← (R4) + R(5)/
I5:   Comp R6    /R6 ← (R6)/
I6:   Mul R6, R7          /R3 ← (R3) + R(4)/
```

a. What dependencies exist in the program?

b. Show the pipeline activity for this program on the processor of Figure 14.15 using in-order issue with in-order completion policies and using a presentation similar to Figure 14.2.

c. Repeat for in-order issue with out-of-order completion.

d. Repeat for out-of-order issue with out-of-order completion.

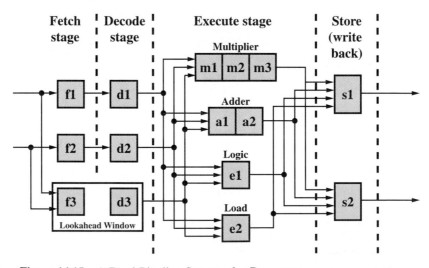

Figure 14.15 A Dual-Pipeline Superscalar Processor

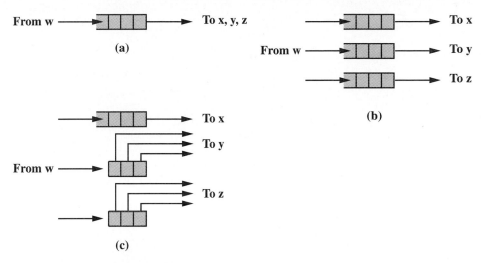

Figure 14.16 Figure for Problem 14.7

14.7 Figure 14.16 is from a paper on superscalar design. Explain the three parts of the figure, and define w, x, y, and z.

CHAPTER **15**

THE IA-64 ARCHITECTURE

KEY POINTS

◆ The IA-64 instruction set architecture is a new approach to providing hardware support for instruction-level parallelism and is significantly different that the approach taken in superscalar architectures.

◆ The most noteworthy features of the IA-64 architecture are hardware support for predicated execution, control speculation, data speculation, and software pipelining.

◆ With **predicated execution**, every IA-64 instruction includes a reference to a 1-bit predicate register and only executes if the predicate value is 1 (true). This enables the processor to speculatively execute both branches of an if statement and only commit after the condition is determined.

◆ With **control speculation**, a load instruction is moved earlier in the program and its original position replaced by a check instruction. The early load saves cycle time; if the load produces an exception, the exception is not activated until the check instruction determines if the load should have been taken.

◆ With **data speculation**, a load is moved before a store instruction that might alter the memory location that is the source of the load. A subsequent check is made to assure that the load receives the proper memory value.

◆ **Software pipelining** is a technique in which instructions from multiple iterations of a loop are enabled to execute in parallel.

With the Pentium 4, the microprocessor family that began with the 8086 and that has been the most successful computer product line ever appears to have come to an end. Intel has teamed up with Hewlett-Packard (HP) to develop a new 64-bit architecture, called IA-64. IA-64 is not a 64-bit extension of Intel's 32-bit x86 architecture, nor is it an adaptation of Hewlett-Packard's 64-bit PA-RISC architecture. Instead, IA-64 is a new architecture that builds on years of research at the two companies and at universities. The architecture exploits the vast circuitry and high speeds available on the newest generations of microchips by a systematic use of parallelism. IA-64 architecture represents a significant departure from the trend to superscalar schemes that have dominated recent processor development.

We begin this chapter with a discussion of the motivating factors for the new architecture. Next, we look at the general organization to support the architecture. We then examine in some detail the key features of the IA-64 architecture that promote instruction-level parallelism. Finally, we look at the IA-64 instruction set architecture and the Itanium organization.

15.1 MOTIVATION

The basic concepts underlying IA-64 are as follows:

- Instruction-level parallelism that is explicit in the machine instructions rather than being determined at run time by the processor
- Long or very long instruction words (LIW/VLIW)
- Branch predication (not the same thing as branch prediction)
- Speculative loading

Intel and HP refer to this combination of concepts as explicitly parallel instruction computing (EPIC). Intel and HP use the term **EPIC** to refer to the technology, or collection of techniques. **IA-64** is an actual instruction set architecture that is intended for implementation using the EPIC technology. The first Intel product based on this IA-64 is referred to as **Itanium**. Other products will follow, based on the same IA-64 architecture.

Table 15.1 summarizes key differences between IA-64 and a traditional superscalar approach.

For Intel, the move to a new architecture, one that is not hardware compatible with the x86 instruction architecture, is a momentous decision. But it is driven by the dictates of the technology. When the x86 family began, back in the late 1970s, the processor chip had tens of thousands of transistors and was an essentially scalar device. That is, instructions were processed one at a time, with little or no pipelining. As the number of transistors increased into the hundreds of thousands in the mid-1980s, Intel introduced pipelining (e.g., Figure 12.18). Meanwhile, other manufacturers were attempting to take advantage of the increased transistor count and increased speed by means of the RISC approach, which enabled more effective pipelining, and later the superscalar/RISC combination, which involved multiple execution units. With the Pentium, Intel made a modest attempt to use superscalar techniques, allowing two CISC instructions to execute at a time. Then, the Pentium Pro and Pentium II through Pentium 4 incorporated a mapping from CISC instruc-

Table 15.1 Traditional Superscalar versus IA-64 Architecture

Superscalar	IA-64
RISC-line instructions, one per word	RISC-line instructions bundled into groups of three
Multiple parallel execution units	Multiple parallel execution units
Reorders and optimizes instruction stream at run time	Reorders and optimizes instruction stream at compile time
Branch prediction with speculative execution of one path	Speculative execution along both paths of a branch
Loads data from memory only when needed, and tries to find the data in the caches first	Speculatively loads data before its needed, and still tries to find data in the caches first

tions to RISC-like micro-operations and the more aggressive use of superscalar techniques. This approach enabled the effective use of a chip with millions of transistors. But for the next generation processor, the one beyond Pentium, Intel and other manufacturers are faced with the need to use effectively tens of millions of transistors on a single processor chip.

Processor designers have few choices in how to use this glut of transistors. One approach is to dump those extra transistors into bigger on-chip caches. Bigger caches can improve performance to a degree but eventually reach a point of diminishing returns, in which larger caches result in tiny improvements in hit rates. Another alternative is to increase the degree of superscaling by adding more execution units. The problem with this approach is that designers are, in effect, hitting a complexity wall. As more and more execution units are added, making the processor "wider," more logic is needed to orchestrate these units. Branch prediction must be improved, out-of-order processing must be used, and longer pipelines must be employed. But with more and longer pipelines, there is a greater penalty for misprediction. Out-of-order execution requires a large number of renaming registers and complex interlock circuitry to account for dependencies. As a result, today's best processors can manage at most to retire six instructions per cycle, and usually less.

To address these problems, Intel and HP have come up with an overall design approach that enables the effective use of a processor with many parallel execution units. The heart of this new approach is the concept of explicit parallelism. With this approach, the compiler statically schedules the instructions at compile time, rather than having the processor dynamically schedule them at run time. The compiler determines which instructions can execute in parallel and includes this information with the machine instruction. The processor uses this information to perform parallel execution. One advantage of this approach is that the EPIC processor does not need as much complex circuitry as an out-of-order superscalar processor. Further, whereas the processor has only a matter of nanoseconds to determine potential parallel execution opportunities, the compiler has orders of magnitude more time to examine the code at leisure and see the program as a whole.

15.2 GENERAL ORGANIZATION

As with any processor architecture, IA-64 can be implemented in a variety of organizations. Figure 15.1 suggests in general terms the organization of an IA-64 machine. The key features are as follows:

- **Large number of registers:** The IA-64 instruction format assumes the use of 256 registers: 128 64-bit registers for integer, logical, and general-purpose use, and 128 82-bit registers for floating-point and graphic use. There are also 64 1-bit predicate registers used for predicated execution, as explained subsequently.
- **Multiple execution units:** A typical commercial superscalar machine today may support four parallel pipelines, using four parallel execution units in both the integer and floating-point portions of the processor. It is expected that IA-64 will be implemented on systems with eight or more parallel units.

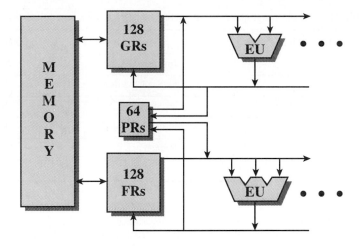

GR = General-purpose or integer register
FR = Floating-point or graphics register
PR = One-bit predicate register
EU = Execution unit

Figure 15.1 General Organization for IA-64 Architecture

The register file is quite large compared with most RISC and superscalar machines. The reason for this is that a large number of registers is needed to support a high degree of parallelism. In a traditional superscalar machine, the machine language (and the assembly language) employs a small number of visible registers, and the processor maps these onto a larger number of registers using register renaming techniques and dependency analysis. Because we wish to make parallelism explicit and relieve the processor of the burden of register renaming and dependency analysis, we need a large number of explicit registers.

The number of execution units is a function of the number of transistors available in a particular implementation. The processor will exploit parallelism to the extent that it can. For example, if the machine language instruction stream indicates that eight integer instructions may be executed in parallel, a processor with four integer pipelines will execute these in two chunks. A processor with eight pipelines will execute all eight instructions simultaneously.

Four types of execution unit are defined in the IA-64 architecture:

- **I-unit:** For integer arithmetic, shift-and-add, logical, compare, and integer multimedia instructions.
- **M-unit:** Load and store between register and memory plus some integer ALU operations.
- **B-unit:** Branch instructions.
- **F-unit:** Floating-point instructions.

Table 15.2   Relationship between Instruction Type and Execution Unit Type

Instruction Type	Description	Execution Unit Type
A	Integer ALU	I-unit or M-unit
I	Non-ALU integer	I-unit
M	Memory	M-unit
F	Floating point	F-unit
B	Branch	B-unit
L + X	Extended	I-unit/B-unit

Each IA-64 instruction is categorized into one of six types. Table 15.2 lists the instruction types and the execution unit types on which they may be executed.

15.3 PREDICATION, SPECULATION, AND SOFTWARE PIPELINING

This section looks at the key features of the IA-64 architecture that support instruction-level parallelism. First, we need to provide an overview of the IA-64 instruction format and, to support the examples in this section, define the general format of IA-64 assembly language instructions.

Instruction Format

IA-64 defines a 128-bit **bundle** that contains three instructions, called **syllables**, and a template field (Figure 15.2a). The processor can fetch instructions one or more bundles at a time; each bundle fetch brings in three instructions. The template field contains information that indicates which instructions can be executed in parallel. The interpretation of the template field is not confined to a single bundle. Rather, the processor can look at multiple bundles to determine which instructions may be executed in parallel. For example, the instruction stream may be such that eight instructions can be executed in parallel. The compiler will reorder instructions so that these eight instructions span contiguous bundles and set the template bits so that the processor knows that these eight instructions are independent.

The bundled instructions do not have to be in the original program order. Further, because of the flexibility of the template field, the compiler can mix independent and dependent instructions in the same bundle. Unlike some previous VLIW designs, IA-64 does not need to insert null-operation (NOP) instructions to fill in the bundles.

Table 15.3 shows the interpretation of the possible values for the 5-bit template field (some values are reserved and not in current use). The template value accomplishes two purposes:

PR = Predicate register
GR = General or floating-point register

Figure 15.2   IA-64 Instruction Format

1. The field specifies the mapping of instruction slots to execution unit types. Not all possible mappings of instructions to units are available.
2. The field indicates the presence of any **stops**. A stop indicates to the hardware that one or more instructions before the stop may have certain kinds of resource dependencies with one or more instructions after the stop. In the table, a heavy vertical line indicates a stop.

Each instruction has a fixed-length 41-bit format (Figure 15.2b). This is somewhat longer than the traditional 32-bit length found on RISC and RISC superscalar machines (although it is much shorter than the 118-bit micro-operation of the Pentium 4). Two factors lead to the additional bits. First, IA-64 makes use of more registers than a typical RISC machine: 128 integer and 128 floating-point registers. Second, to accommodate the predicated execution technique, an IA-64 machine includes 64 predicate registers. Their use is explained subsequently.

Figure 15.2c shows in more detail the typical instruction format. All instructions include a 4-bit major opcode and a reference to a predicate register. Although the major opcode field can only discriminate among 16 possibilities, the interpreta-

Table 15.3 Template Field Encoding and Instruction Set Mapping

Template	Slot 0	Slot 1	Slot 2
00	M-unit	I-unit	I-unit
01	M-unit	I-unit	I-unit
02	M-unit	I-unit	I-unit
03	M-unit	I-unit	I-unit
04	M-unit	L-unit	X-unit
05	M-unit	L-unit	X-unit
08	M-unit	M-unit	I-unit
09	M-unit	M-unit	I-unit
0A	M-unit	M-unit	I-unit
0B	M-unit	M-unit	I-unit
0C	M-unit	F-unit	I-unit
0D	M-unit	F-unit	I-unit
0E	M-unit	M-unit	F-unit
0F	M-unit	M-unit	F-unit
10	M-unit	I-unit	B-unit
11	M-unit	I-unit	B-unit
12	M-unit	B-unit	B-unit
13	M-unit	B-unit	B-unit
16	B-unit	B-unit	B-unit
17	B-unit	B-unit	B-unit
18	M-unit	M-unit	B-unit
19	M-unit	M-unit	B-unit
1C	M-unit	F-unit	B-unit
1D	M-unit	F-unit	B-unit

tion of the major opcode field depends on the template value and the location of the instruction within a bundle (Table 15.3), thus affording more possible opcodes. Typical instructions also include three fields to reference registers, leaving 10 bits for other information needed to fully specify the instruction.

Assembly–Language Format

As with any machine instruction set, an assembly language is provided for the convenience of the programmer. The assembler or compiler then translates each assembly language instruction into a 41-bit IA-64 instruction. The general format of an assembly language instruction is

`[qp] mnemonic[.comp] dest=srcs`

where

qp	Specifies a 1-bit predicate register used to qualify the instruction. If the value of the register is 1 (true) at execution time, the instruction executes and the result is committed in hardware. If the value is false, the result of the instruction is not committed but is discarded. Most IA-64 instructions may be qualified by a predicate but need not be. To account for an instruction that is not predicated, the qp value is set to 0 and predicate register zero always has the constant value of 1.
mnemonic	Specifies the name of an IA-64 instruction.
comp	Specifies one or more instruction completers, separated by periods, which are used to qualify the mnemonic. Not all instructions require the use of a completer.
dest	Specifies one or more destination operands, with the typical case being a single destination.
srcs	Specifies one or more source operands. Most instructions have two or more source operands.

On any line, any characters to the right of a double slash "//" are treated as a comment. Instruction groups and stops are indicated by a double semicolon ";;". An instruction group is defined as a sequence of instructions that have no read after write or write after write dependencies. The processor can issue these without hardware checks for register dependencies. Here is a simple example:

```
ld8 r1 = [r5] ;;    // First group
add r3 = r1, r4     // Second group
```

The first instruction reads an 8-byte value from the memory location whose address is in register r5 and then places that value in register r1. The second instruction adds the contents of r1 and r4 and places the result in r3. Because the second instruction depends on the value in r1, which is changed by the first instruction, the two instructions cannot be in the same group for parallel execution.

Here is a more complex example, with multiple register flow dependencies:

```
ld8 r1 = [r5]       // First group
sub r6 = r8, r9 ;;  // First group
add r3 = r1, r4     // Second group
st8 [r6] = r12      // Second group
```

The last instruction stores the contents of r12 in the memory location whose address is in r6.

We are now ready to look at the four key mechanisms in the IA-64 architecture to support instruction-level parallelism:

- Predication
- Control speculation
- Data speculation
- Software pipelining

Figure 15.3, based on a figure in [HALF97], illustrates the first two of these techniques, which are discussed in this subsection and the next.

Predicated Execution

Predication is a technique whereby the compiler determines which instructions may execute in parallel. In the process, the compiler eliminates branches from the program by using conditional execution. A typical example in a high-level language is an **if-then-else** instruction. A traditional compiler inserts a conditional branch at the **if** point of this construct. If the condition has one logical outcome, the branch is not taken and the next block of instructions is executed, representing the **then** path; at the end of this path is an unconditional branch around the next block, representing the **else** path. If the condition has the other logical outcome, the branch is taken around the **then** block of instructions and execution continues at the **else** block of instructions. The two instruction streams join together after the end of the **else** block. An IA-64 compiler instead does the following (Figure 15.3a):

1. At the **if** point in the program, insert a compare instruction that creates two predicates. If the compare is true, the first predicate is set to true and the second to false; if the compare is false, the first predicate is set to false and the second to true.
2. Augment each instruction in the **then** path with a reference to a predicate register that holds the value of the first predicate, and augment each instruction in the **else** path with a reference to a predicate register that holds the value of the second predicate.
3. The processor executes instructions along both paths. When the outcome of the compare is known, the processor discards the results along one path and commits the results along the other path. This enables the processor to feed instructions on both paths into the instruction pipeline without waiting for the compare operation to complete.

As an example, consider the following source code:

```
if (a&&b)
    j = j + 1;
else
    if (c)
        k = k + 1;
    else
        k = k - 1;
i = i + 1;
```

Source Code:

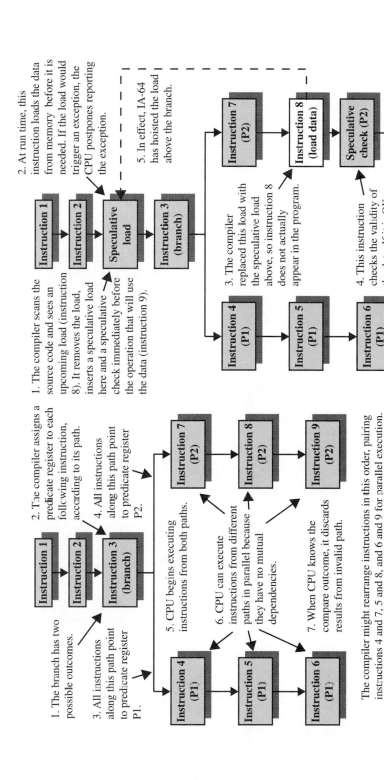

Figure 15.3 IA-64 Predication and Speculative Loading

2. At run time, this instruction loads the data from memory before it is needed. If the load would trigger an exception, the CPU postpones reporting the exception.

5. In effect, IA-64 has hoisted the load above the branch.

Instruction 1 → Instruction 2 → Speculative load → Instruction 3 (branch)

1. The compiler scans the source code and sees an upcoming load (instruction 8). It removes the load, inserts a speculative load here and a speculative check immediately before the operation that will use the data (instruction 9).

Instruction 4 (P1) → Instruction 5 (P1) → Instruction 6 (P1)

Instruction 7 (P2) → Instruction 8 (load data) → Speculative check (P2) → Instruction 9 (P2)

3. The compiler replaced this load with the speculative load above, so instruction 8 does not actually appear in the program.

4. This instruction checks the validity of the data. If it is OK, the CPU does not report an exception.

(b) Speculative loading

2. The compiler assigns a predicate register to each following instruction, according to its path.

4. All instructions along this path point to predicate register P2.

Instruction 1 → Instruction 2 → Instruction 3 (branch)

1. The branch has two possible outcomes.

3. All instructions along this path point to predicate register P1.

Instruction 4 (P1) → Instruction 5 (P1) → Instruction 6 (P1)

Instruction 7 (P2) → Instruction 8 (P2) → Instruction 9 (P2)

5. CPU begins executing instructions from both paths.

6. CPU can execute instructions from different paths in parallel because they have no mutual dependencies.

7. When CPU knows the compare outcome, it discards results from invalid path.

The compiler might rearrange instructions in this order, pairing instructions 4 and 7, 5 and 8, and 6 and 9 for parallel execution.

Instruction 1	Instruction 2	Instruction 3
Instruction 4	Instruction 7	Instruction 5
Instruction 8	Instruction 6	Instruction 9

(a) Predication

Two if statements jointly select one of three possible execution paths. This can be compiled into the following code, using the Pentium assembly language. The program has three conditional branches and one unconditional branch instructions:

Assembly Code:

```
          cmp a, 0          ; compare a with 0
          je L1             ; branch to L1 if a = 0
          cmp b, 0
          je L1
          add j, 1          ; j = j + 1
          jmp L3
     L1:  cmp c, 0
          je L2
          add k, 1          ; k = k + 1
          jmp L3
     L2:  sub k, 1          ; k = k - 1
     L3:  add i, 1          ; i = i + 1
```

In the Pentium assembly language, a semicolon is used to delimit a comment. Figure 15.4 shows a flow diagram of this assembly code. This diagram breaks the assembly language program into separate blocks of code. For each block that

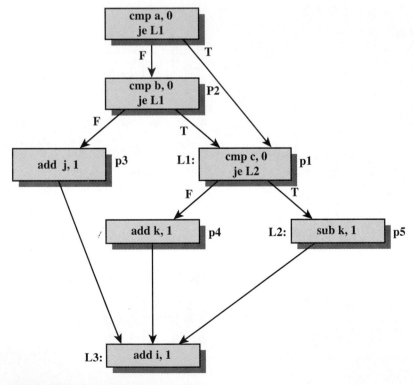

Figure 15.4 Example of Predication

executes conditionally, the compiler can assign a predicate. These predicates are indicated in Figure 15.4. Assuming that all of these predicates have been initialized to false, the resulting IA-64 assembly code is as follows:

Predicated Code:

```
(1)            cmp.eq p1, p2 = 0, a ;;
(2)  (p2)      cmp.eq p1, p3 = 0, b
(3)  (p3)      add j = 1, j
(4)  (p1)      cmp.ne p4, p5 = 0, c
(5)  (p4)      add k = 1, k
(6)  (p5)      add k = -1, k
(7)            add i = 1, i
```

Instruction (1) compares the contents of symbolic register a with 0; it sets the value of predicate register p1 to 1 (true) and p2 to 0 (false) if the relation is true and will set the value of predicate p1 to 0 and p2 to 1 if the relation is false. Instruction (2) is to be executed only if the predicate p2 is true (i.e., if a is true, which is equivalent to a ≠ 0). The processor will fetch, decode, and begin executing this instruction, but only make a decision as to whether to commit the result after it determines whether the value of predicate register p1 is 1 or 0. Note that instruction (2) is a predicate-generating instruction and is itself predicated. This instruction requires three predicate register fields in its format.

Returning to our Pentium program, the first two conditional branches in the Pentium assembly code are translated into two IA-64 predicated compare instructions. If instruction (1) sets p2 to false, the instruction (2) is not executed. After instruction (2) in the IA-64 program, p3 is true only if the outer **if** statement in the source code is true. That is, predicate p3 is true only if the expression (a AND b) is true (i.e., a ≠ 0 AND b ≠ 0). The **then** part of the outer **if** statement is predicated on p3 for this reason. Instruction (4) of the IA-64 code decides whether the addition or subtraction instruction in the outer **else** part is performed. Finally, the increment of i is performed unconditionally. Looking at the source code and then at the predicated code, we see that only one of instructions (3), (5), and (6) is to be executed. In an ordinary superscalar processor, we would use branch prediction to guess which of the three is to be executed and go down that path. If the processor guesses wrong, the pipeline must be flushed. An IA-64 processor can begin execution of all three of these instructions and, once the values of the predicate registers are known, commit only the results of the valid instruction. Thus, we make use of additional parallel execution units to avoid the delays due to pipeline flushing.

Much of the original research on predicated execution was done at the University of Illinois. Their simulation studies indicate that the use of predication results in a substantial reduction in dynamic branches and branch mispredictions and a substantial performance improvement for processors with multiple parallel pipelines (e.g., [MAHL94], [MAHL95]).

Control Speculation

Another key innovation in IA-64 is control speculation, also known as speculative loading. This enables the processor to load data from memory before the program needs it, to avoid memory latency delays. Also, the processor postpones the reporting of exceptions until it becomes necessary to report the exception. The term *hoist* is used to refer to the movement of a load instruction to a point earlier in the instruction stream.

The minimization of load latencies is crucial to improving performance. Typically, early in a block of code, there are a number of load operations that bring data from memory to registers. Because memory, even augmented with one or two levels of cache, is slow compared with the processor, the delays in obtaining data from memory become a bottleneck. To minimize this, we would like to rearrange the code so that loads are done as early as possible. This can be done with any compiler, up to a point. The problem occurs if we attempt to move a load across a control flow. You cannot unconditionally move the load above a branch because the load may not actually occur. We could move the load conditionally, using predicates, so that the data could be retrieved from memory but not committed to an architectural register until the outcome of the predicate is known; or we can use branch prediction techniques of the type we saw in Chapter 14. The problem with this strategy is that the load can blow up. An exception due to invalid address or a page fault could be generated. If this happens, the processor would have to deal with the exception or fault, causing a delay.

How, then, can we move the load above the branch? The solution specified in IA-64 is the control speculation, which separates the load behavior (delivering the value) from the exception behavior (Figure 15.3b). A load instruction in the original program is replaced by two instructions:

- A speculative load (ld.s) executes the memory fetch, performs exception detection, but does not deliver the exception (call the OS routine that handles the exception). This ld.s instruction is hoisted to an appropriate point earlier in the program.
- A checking instruction (chk.s) remains in the place of the original load and delivers exceptions. This chk.s instruction may be predicated so that it will only execute if the predicate is true.

If the ld.s detects an exception, it sets a token bit associated with the target register, known as the *Not a Thing* (NaT) bit. If the corresponding chk.s instruction is executed, and if the NaT bit is set, the chk.s instruction branches to an exception-handling routine.

Let us look at a simple example, taken from [INTE00a, Volume 1]. Here is the original program:

```
(p1) br some_label        // Cycle 0
     ld8 r1 = [r5] ;;     // Cycle 1
     add r2 = r1, r3      // Cycle 3
```

The first instruction branches if predicate p1 is true (register p1 has value 1). Note that the branch and load instructions are in the same instruction group, even though the load should not execute if the branch is taken. IA-64 guarantees that if a branch is taken, later instructions, even in the same instruction group, are not executed. IA-64 implementations may use branch prediction to try to improve efficiency but must assure against incorrect results. Finally, note that the add instruction is delayed by at least a clock period (one cycle) due to the memory latency of the load operation.

The compiler can rewrite this code using a control speculative load and a check:

```
        ld8.s r1 = [r5] ;;          // Cycle -2
                                    // Other instructions
(p1) br some_label                  // Cycle 0
        chk.s r1, recovery          // Cycle 0
        add r2 = r1, r3             // Cycle 0
```

We can't simply move the load instruction above the branch instruction, as is, because the load instruction may cause an exception (e.g., r5 may contain a null pointer). Instead, we convert the load to a speculative load, ld8.s, and then move it. The speculative load doesn't immediately signal an exception when detected; it just records that fact by setting the NaT bit for the target register (in this case, r1). The speculative load now executes unconditionally at least two cycles prior to the branch. The chk.s instruction then checks to see if the NaT bit is set on r1. If not, execution simply falls through to the next instruction. If so, a branch is taken to a recovery program. Note that the branch, check, and add instructions are all shown as being executed in the same clock cycle. However, the hardware ensures that the results produced by the speculative load do not update the application state (change the contents of r1 and r2) unless two conditions occur: The branch is not taken (p1 = 0) and the check does not detect a deferred exception (r1.NaT = 0).

There is one other important point to note about this example. If there is no exception, then the speculative load is an actual load and takes place prior to the branch that it is supposed to follow. If the branch is taken, then a load has occurred that was not intended by the original program. The program, as written, assumes that r1 is not read on the taken-branch path. If r1 is read on the taken-branch path, then the compiler must use another register to hold the speculative result.

Let us look at a more complex example, used by Intel and HP to benchmark predicated programs and to illustrate the use of speculative loads, known as the Eight Queens Problem. The objective is to arrange eight queens on a chessboard so that no queen threatens any other queen. Figure 15.5a shows one solution. The key line of source code, in an inner loop, is the following:

```
if ((b[j] == true) && (a[i + j] == true) && (c[i - j] == true))
```

where $1 \leq i, j \leq 8$.

The queen conflict tracking mechanism consists of three Boolean arrays that track queen status for each row and diagonal. TRUE means no queen is on that row or diagonal; FALSE means a queen is already there. Figures 15.5b and c show the mapping of the arrays to the chess board. All array elements are initialized to TRUE. The B array elements 1–8 correspond to rows 1–8 on the board. A queen in row n sets b[n] to FALSE. C array elements are numbered from −7 to 7 and correspond to the difference between column and row numbers, which defines the diagonals that go down to the right. A queen at column 1, row 1 sets c[0] to FALSE. A queen at column 1, row 8 sets c[−7] to FALSE. The A array elements are numbered 2–16 and correspond to the sum of the column and row. A queen placed in column 1, row 1 sets a[2] to FALSE. A queen placed in column 3, row 5 sets a[8] to FALSE.

The overall program moves through the columns, placing a queen on each column such that the new queen is not attacked by a queen previously placed on either along a row or one of the two diagonals.

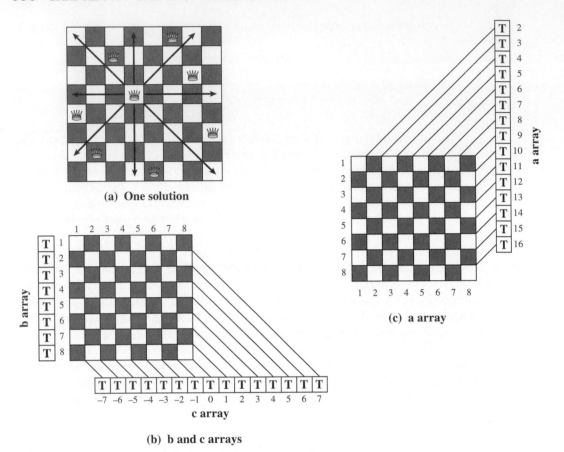

(a) One solution

(b) b and c arrays

(c) a array

Figure 15.5 The Eight Queens Problem

A straightforward Pentium assembly program includes three loads and three branches:

```
             (1)      mov r2, &b[j]        ; transfer contents of location
                                           ; b[j] to register r2
             (2)      cmp r2, 1
             (3)      jne L2
             (4)      mov r4, &a[i + j]
Assembly Code:  (5)   cmp r4, 1
             (6)      jne L2
             (7)      mov r6, &c[i - j]
             (8)      cmp r6, 1
             (9)      jne L2
             (10)L1:  <code for then path>
             (11)L2:  <code for else path>
```

In the preceding program, the notation &x symbolizes an immediate address for location x. Using speculative loads and predicated execution yields the following:

```
(1)              mov r1 = &b[j]           // transfer address of
                                          // b[j] to r1
(2)              mov r3 = &a[i + j]
(3)              mov r5 = &c[i - j + 7]
(4)              ld8 r2 = [r1]            // load indirect via r1
(5)              ld8.s r4 = [r3]
(6)              ld8.s r6 = [r5]
(7)              cmp.eq p1, p2 = 1, r2
(8)       (p2)   br L2
(9)              chk.s r4, recovery_a     // fixup for loading a
(10)             cmp.eq p3, p4 = 1, r4
(11)      (p4)   br L2
(12)             chk.s r6, recovery_b     // fixup for loading b
(13)             cmp.eq p5, p6 = 1, r5
(14)      (p6)   br L2
(15)L1:          <code for then path>
(16)L2:          <code for else path>
```

Code with Speculation and Predication: (corresponds to instructions 1–16 above)

The assembly program breaks down into three basic blocks of code, each of which is a load followed by a conditional branch. The address-setting instructions 4 and 7 in the Pentium assembly code are simple arithmetic calculations; these can be done anytime, so the compiler moves these up to the top. Then the compiler is faced with three simple blocks, each of which consists of a load, a condition calculation, and a conditional branch. There seems little hope of doing anything in parallel here. Furthermore, if we assume that the load takes two or more clock cycles, we have some wasted time before the conditional branch can be executed. What the compiler can do is hoist the second and third loads (instructions 5 and 8 in the Pentium code) above all the branches. This is done by putting a speculative load up top (IA-64 instructions 5 and 6) and leaving a check in the original code block (IA-64 instructions 9 and 12).

This transformation makes it possible to execute all three loads in parallel and to begin the loads early so as to minimize or avoid delays due to load latencies. The compiler can go further by more aggressive use of predication, and eliminate two of the three branches:

```
(1)              mov r1 = &b[j]
(2)              mov r3 = &a[i + j]
(3)              mov r5 = &c[i - j + 7]
(4)              ld8 r2 = [r1]
(5)              ld8.s r4 = [r3]
(6)              ld8.s r6 = [r5]
(7)              cmp.eq p1, p2 = 1, r2
(8)       (p1)   chk.s r4, recovery_a
(9)       (p1)   cmp.eq p3, p4 = 1, r4
(10)      (p3)   chk.s r6, recovery_b
(11)      (p3)   cmp.eq p5, p4 = 1, r5
(12)      (p6)   br L2
(13)L1:          <code for then path>
(14)L2:          <code for else path>
```

Revised Code with Speculation and Predication: (corresponds to instructions 1–14 above)

We already had a compare that generated two predicates. In the revised code, instead of branching on the false predicate, the compiler qualifies execution of both the check and the next compare on the true predicate. The elimination of two branches means the elimination of two potential mispredictions, so that the savings is more than just two instructions.

Data Speculation

In a control speculation, a load is moved earlier in a code sequence to compensate for load latency, and a check is made to assure that an exception doesn't occur if it subsequently turns out that the load was not taken. In data speculation, a load is moved before a store instruction that might alter the memory location that is the source of the load. A subsequent check is made to assure that the load receives the proper memory value. To explain the mechanism, we use an example taken from [INTE00a, Volume 1].

Consider the following program fragment:

```
st8 [r4] = r12        // Cycle 0
ld8 r6 = [r8] ;;      // Cycle 0
add r5 = r6, r7 ;;    // Cycle 2
st8 [r18] = r5        // Cycle 3
```

As written, the code requires four instruction cycles to execute. If registers r4 and r8 do not contain the same memory address, then the store through r4 cannot affect the value at the address contained in r8; under this circumstance, it is safe to reorder the load and store to more quickly bring the value into r6, which is needed subsequently. However, because the addresses in r4 and r8 may be the same or overlap, such a swap is not safe. IA-64 overcomes this problem with the use of a technique known as advanced load.

```
ld8.a r6 = [r8] ;;    // Cycle -2 or earlier; advanced load
                      // other instructions
st8 [r4] = r12        // Cycle 0
ld8.c r6 = [r8]       // Cycle 0; check load
add r5 = r6, r7 ;;    // Cycle 0
st8 [r18] = r5        // Cycle 1
```

Here we have moved the ld instruction earlier and converted it into an advanced load. In addition to performing the specified load, the ld8.a instruction writes its source address (address contained in r8) to a hardware data structure known as the Advanced Load Address Table (ALAT). Each IA-64 store instruction checks the ALAT for entries that overlap with its target address; if a match is found, the ALAT entry is removed. When the original ld8 is converted to an ld8.a instruction and moved, the original position of that instruction is replaced with a check load instruction, ld8.c. When the check load is executed, it checks the ALAT for a matching address. If one is found, no store instruction between the advanced load and the check load has altered the source address of the load, and no action is taken. However, if the check load instruction does not find a matching ALAT entry, then the load operation is performed again to assure the correct result.

We may also want to speculatively execute instructions that are data dependent on a load instruction, together with the load itself. Starting with the same original program, suppose we move up both the load and the subsequent add instruction:

```
        ld8.a r6 = [r8] ;;      // Cycle -3 or earlier; advanced load
                                // other instructions
        add r5 = r6, r7         // Cycle -1; add that uses r6
                                // other instructions
        st8 [r4] = r12          // Cycle 0
        chk.a r6, recover       // Cycle 0; check
back:                           // return point from jump to recover
        st8 [r18] = r5          // Cycle 0
```

Here we use a chk.a instruction rather than an ld8.c instruction to validate the advanced load. If the chk.a instruction determines that the load has failed, it cannot simply reexecute the load; instead, it branches to a recovery routine to clean up:

```
Recover:
        ld8 r6 = [r8] ;;        // reload r6 from [r8]
        add r5 = r6, r7 ;;      // re-execute the add
        br back                 // jump back to main code
```

This technique is effective only if the loads and stores involved have little chance of overlapping.

Software Pipelining

Consider the following loop:

```
L1: ld4 r4 = [r5], 4 ;;     // Cycle 0; load postinc 4
    add r7 = r4, r9 ;;      // Cycle 2
    st4 [r6] = r7, 4        // Cycle 3; store postinc 4
    br.cloop L1 ;;          // Cycle 3
```

This loop adds a constant to one vector and stores the result in another vector (e.g. y[i] = x[i] + c). The ld4 instruction loads 4 bytes from memory. The qualifier ", 4" at the end of the instruction signals that this is the base update form of the load instruction; the address in r5 is incremented by 4 after the load takes place. Similarly, the st4 instruction stores four bytes in memory and the address in r6 is incremented by four after the store. The br.cloop instruction, known as a counted loop branch, uses the Loop Count (LC) application register. If the LC register is greater than zero, it is decremented and the branch is taken. The initial value in LC is the number of iterations of the loop.

Notice that in this program, there is virtually no opportunity for instruction-level parallelism within a loop. Further, the instructions in iteration x are all executed before iteration $x + 1$ begins. However, if there is no address conflict between the load and store (r5 and r6 point to nonoverlapping memory locations), then utilization could be improved by moving independent instructions from iteration $x + 1$ to iteration x. Another way of saying this is that if we unroll the loop code by actually writing out a new set of instructions for each iteration, then there is opportunity to increase parallelism. Let's see what could be done with five iterations:

```
ld4  r32 = [r5], 4 ;;        // Cycle 0
ld4  r33 = [r5], 4 ;;        // Cycle 1
ld4  r34 = [r5], 4           // Cycle 2
add  r36 = r32, r9 ;;        // Cycle 2
ld4  r35 = [r5], 4           // Cycle 3
add  r37 = r33, r9           // Cycle 3
st4  [r6] = r36, 4 ;;        // Cycle 3
ld4  r36 = [r5], 4           // Cycle 3
add  r38 = r34, r9           // Cycle 4
st4  [r6] = r37, 4 ;;        // Cycle 4
add  r39 = r35, r9           // Cycle 5
st4  [r6] = r38, 4 ;;        // Cycle 5
add  r40 = r36, r9           // Cycle 6
st4  [r6] = r39, 4 ;;        // Cycle 6
st4  [r6] = r40, 4 ;;        // Cycle 7
```

This program completes 5 iterations in 7 cycles, compared with 20 cycles in the original looped program. This assumes that there are two memory ports so that a load and a store can be executed in parallel. This is an example of software pipelining, analogous to hardware pipelining. Figure 15.6 illustrates the process. Parallelism is achieved by grouping together instructions from different iterations. For this to work, the temporary registers used inside the loop must be changed for each iteration to avoid register conflicts. In this case, two temporary registers are used (r4 and r7 in the original program). In the expanded program, the register number of each

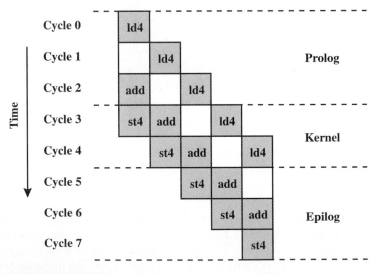

Figure 15.6 Software Pipelining Example

register is incremented for each iteration, and the register numbers are initialized sufficiently far apart to avoid overlap.

Figure 15.6 shows that the software pipeline has three phases. During the **prolog phase**, a new iteration is initiated with each clock cycle and the pipeline gradually fills up. During the **kernel phase**, the pipeline is full, achieving maximum parallelism. For our example, three instructions are performed in parallel during the kernel phase, but the width of the pipeline is four. During the **epilog phase**, one iteration completes with each clock cycle.

Software pipelining by loop unrolling places a burden on the compiler or programmer to assign register names properly. Further, for long loops with many iterations, the unrolling results in a significant expansion in code size. For an indeterminate loop (total iterations unknown at compile time), the task is further complicated by the need to do a partial unroll and then to control the loop count. IA-64 provides hardware support to perform software pipelining with no code expansion and with minimal burden on the compiler. The key features that support software pipelining are as follows:

- **Automatic register renaming:** A fixed-sized area of the predicate and floating-point register files (p16 to p63; fr32 to fr127) and a programmable-sized area of the general register file (maximum range of r32 to r127) are capable of rotation. This means that during each iteration of a software-pipeline loop, register references within these ranges are automatically incremented. Thus, if a loop makes use of general register r32 on the first iteration, it automatically makes use of r33 on the second iteration, and so on.
- **Predication:** Each instruction in the loop is predicated on a rotating predicate register. The purpose of this is to determine whether the pipeline is in prolog, kernel, or epilog phase, as explained subsequently.
- **Special loop terminating instructions:** These are branch instructions that cause the registers to rotate and the loop count to decrement.

This is a relatively complex topic; here, we present an example that illustrates some of the IA-64 software pipelining capabilities. We take the original loop program from this section and show how to program it for software pipelining, assuming a loop count of 200 and that there are two memory ports:

```
        mov lc = 199            // set loop count register to 199,
                                // which equals loop count - 1
        mov ec = 4              // set epilog count register equal
                                // to number of epilog stages + 1
        mov pr.rot = 1<<16;;    // pr16 = 1; rest = 0
L1: (p16) ld4 r32 = [r5], 4     // Cycle 0
    (p17) ---                   // Empty stage
    (p18) add r35 = r34, r9     // Cycle 0
    (p19) st4 [r6] = r36, 4     // Cycle 0
        br.ctop L1 ;;           // Cycle 0
```

We summarize the key points related to this program:

1. The loop body is partitioned into multiple *stages*, with zero or more instructions per stage.
2. Execution of the loop proceeds through three phases. During the prolog phase, a new loop iteration is started each time around, adding one stage to the pipeline. During the kernel phase, one loop iteration is started and one completed each time around; the pipeline is full, with the maximum number of stages active. During the epilog phase, no new iterations are started and one iteration is completed each time around, draining the software pipeline.
3. A predicate is assigned to each stage to control the activation of the instructions in that stage. During the prolog phase, p16 is true and p17, p18, and p19 are false for the first iteration. For the second iteration, p16 and p17 are true; during the third iteration p16, p17, and p18 are true. During the kernel phase, all predicates are true. During the epilog phase, the predicates are turned to false one by one, beginning with p16. The changes in predicate values are achieved by predicate register rotation.
4. All general registers with register numbers greater than 31 are rotated with each iteration. Registers are rotated toward larger register numbers in a wrap-around fashion. For example, the value in register *x* will be located in register *x* + 1 after one rotation; this is achieved not by moving values but by hardware renaming of registers. Thus, in our example, the value that the load writes in r32 is read by the add two iterations (and two rotations) later as r34. Similarly, the value that the add writes in r35 is read by the store one iteration later as r36.

Table 15.4 Loop Trace for Software Pipelining Example

Cycle	Execution Unit/Instruction				State before br.ctop					
	M	I	M	B	P16	P17	P18	P19	LC	EC
0	ld4			br.ctop	1	0	0	0	199	4
1	ld4			br.ctop	1	1	0	0	198	4
2	ld4	add		br.ctop	1	1	1	0	197	4
3	ld4	add	st4	br.ctop	1	1	1	1	196	4
...	...	...	...	...	...	...	...	...	...	...
100	ld4	add	st4	br.ctop	1	1	1	1	99	4
...	...	...	...	...	...	...	...	...	...	...
199	ld4	add	st4	br.ctop	1	1	1	1	0	4
200		add	st4	br.ctop	0	1	1	1	0	3
201		add	st4	br.ctop	0	0	1	1	0	2
202			st4	br.ctop	0	0	0	1	0	1
					0	0	0	0	0	0

5. For the br.ctop instruction, the branch is taken if either LC > 0 or EC > 1. Execution of br.ctop has the following additional effects: If LC > 0, then LC is decremented; this happens during the prolog and kernel phases. If LC = 0 and EC > 1, EC is decremented; this happens during the epilog phase. The instruction also control register rotation. If LC > 0, each execution of br.ctop places a 1 in p63. With rotation, p63 becomes p16, feeding a continuous sequence of ones into the predicate registers during the prolog and kernel phases. If LC = 0, then br.ctop sets p63 to 0, feeding zeros into the predicate registers during the epilog phase.

Table 15.4 shows a trace of the execution of this example.

15.4 IA-64 INSTRUCTION SET ARCHITECTURE

Figure 15.7 shows the set of registers available to application programs. That is, these registers are visible to applications and may be read and, in most cases, written. The register sets include the following:

- **General registers:** 128 general-purpose 64-bit registers. Associated with each register is a NaT bit used to track deferred speculative exceptions, as explained in Section 15.3. Registers r0 through r31 are referred to as static; a program reference to any of these references is literally interpreted. Registers r32 through r127 can be used as rotating registers for software pipelining (discussed in Section 15.3) and for register stack implementation (discussed subsequently in this section). References to these registers are virtual, and the hardware my perform register renaming dynamically.
- **Floating-point registers:** 128 82-bit registers for floating-point numbers. This size is sufficient to hold IEEE 754 double extended format numbers (see Table 9.3). Registers fr0 through fr31 are static, and registers fr32 through fr127 can be used as rotating registers for software pipelining.
- **Predicate registers:** 64 1-bit registers used as predicates. Register pr0 is always set to 1 to enable unpredicated instructions. Registers pr0 through pr15 are static, and registers pr16 through pr63 can be used as rotating registers for software pipelining.
- **Branch registers:** 8 64-bit registers used for branches.
- **Instruction pointer:** Holds the bundle address of the currently executing IA-64 instruction.
- **Current frame marker:** Holds state information relating to the current general register stack frame and rotation information for fr and pr registers.
- **User mask:** A set of single-bit values used for alignment traps, performance monitors, and to monitor floating-point register usage.
- **Performance monitor data registers:** Used to support performance monitor hardware.

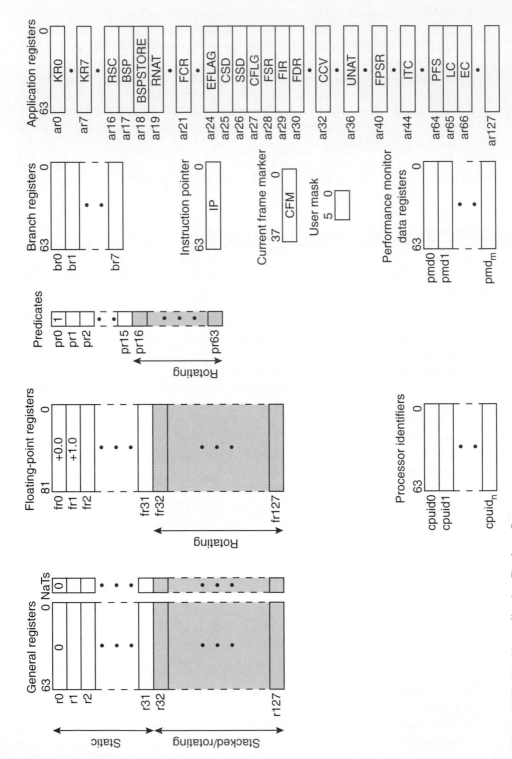

Figure 15.7 IA-64 Application Register Set

- **Processor identifiers:** Describe processor implementation-dependent features.
- **Application registers:** A collection of special-purpose registers. Table 15.5 provides a brief definitsion of each.

Register Stack

The register stack mechanism in IA-64 avoids unnecessary movement of data into and out of registers at procedure call and return. The mechanism automatically provides a called procedure with a new **frame** of up to 96 registers (r32 through r127) upon procedure entry. The compiler specifies the number of registers required by a procedure with the alloc instruction, which specifies how many of these are local (used only within the procedure) and how many are output (used to pass parameters to a procedure called by this procedure). When a procedure call occurs, the IA-64 hardware renames registers so that the local registers from the previous frame are hidden and what were the output registers of the calling procedure now have register numbers starting at r32 in the called procedure. Physical registers in the range r32 through r127 are allocated in a circular-buffer fashion to virtual registers

Table 15.5 IA-64 Application Registers

Kernel registers (KR0-7)	Convey information from the operating system to the application.
Register stack configuration (RSC)	Controls the operation of the register stack engine (RSE).
RSE Backing store pointer (BSP)	Holds the address in memory that is the save location for r32 in the current stack frame
RSE Backing store pointer to memory stores (BSPSTORE)	Holds the address in memory to which the RSE will spill the next value.
RSE NaT collection register (RNAT)	Used by the RSE to temporarily hold NaT bits when it is spilling general registers.
Compare and exchange value (CCV)	Contains the compare value used as the third source operand in the cmpxchg instruction.
User NaT collection register (UNAT)	Used to temporarily hold NaT bits when saving and restoring general registers with the ld8.fill and st8.spill instructions.
Floating-point status register (FPSR)	Controls traps, rounding mode, precision control, flags, and other control bits for floating-point instructions.
Interval time counter (ITC)	Counts up at a fixed relationship to the processor clock frequency.
Previous function state (PFS)	Saves value in CFM register and related information.
Loop count (LC)	Used in counted loops and is decremented by counted-loop-type branches.
Epilog count (EC)	Used for counting the final (epilog) state in modulo-scheduled loops.

associated with procedures. That is, the next register allocated after r127 is r32. When necessary, the hardware moves register contents between registers and memory to free up additional registers when procedure calls occur, and restores contents from memory to registers as procedure returns occur.

Figure 15.8 illustrates register stack behavior. The alloc instruction includes sof (size of frame) and sol (size of locals) operands to specify the required number of registers. These values are stored in the CFM register. When a call occurs, the sol and sof values from the CFM are stored in the sol and sof fields of the previous function state (PFS) application register (Figure 15.9). Upon return these sol and sof values must be restored from the PFS to the CFM. To allow nested calls and returns, previous values of the PFS fields must be saved through successive calls so that they can be restored through successive returns. This is a function of the alloc instruction, which designates a general register to save the current value of the PFS fields before they are overwritten from the CFM fields.

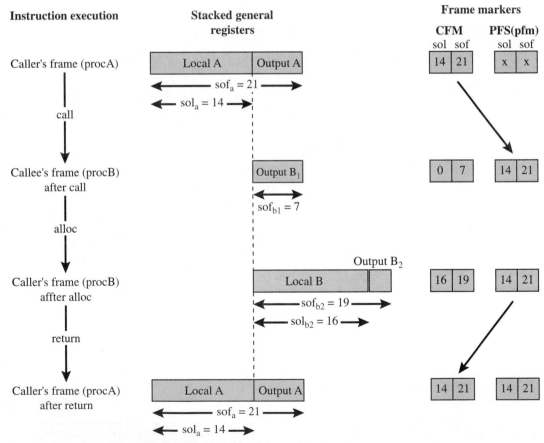

Figure 15.8 Register Stack Behavior on Procedure Call and Return

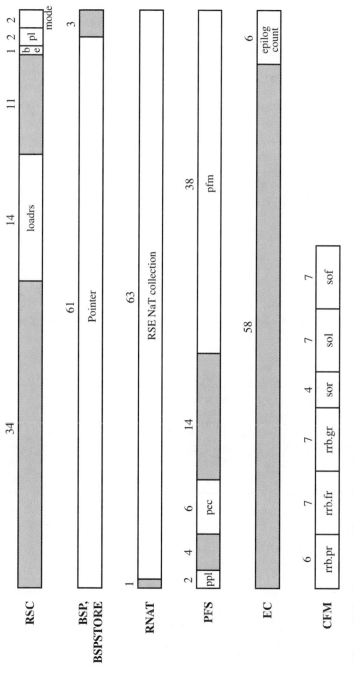

Figure 15.9 Formats of Some IA-64 Registers

Current Frame Marker and Previous Function State

The CFM register describes the state of the current general register stack frame, associated with the currently active procedure. It includes the following fields:

- **sof:** Size of stack frame
- **sol:** Size of locals portion of stack frame
- **sor:** Size of rotating portion of stack frame; this is a subset of the local portion that is dedicated to software pipelining
- **register rename base values:** Values used in performing register rotation general, floating-point and predicate registers

The PFS application register contains the following fields:

- **pfm:** Previous frame marker; contains all of the fields of the CFM
- **pec:** Previous epilog count
- **ppl:** Previous privilege level

15.5 ITANIUM ORGANIZATION

Intel's Itanium processor is the first implementation of the IA-64 instruction set architecture. The Itanium organization blends superscalar features with support for the unique EPIC-related IA-64 features. Among the superscalar features are a six-wide, ten-stage-deep hardware pipeline, dynamic prefetch, branch prediction, and a register scoreboard to optimize for compile time nondeterminism. EPIC-related hardware includes support for predicated execution, control and data speculation, and software pipelining.

Figure 15.10 is a general block diagram of the Itanium organization. The Itanium includes nine execution units: two integer, two floating-point, two memory, and three branch execution units. Instructions are fetched through an L1 instruction cache and fed into a buffer that holds up to eight bundles of instructions. When deciding on functional units for instruction dispersal, the processor views at most two instruction bundles at a time. The processor can issue a maximum of six instructions per clock cycle.

The organization is in some ways simpler than a conventional contemporary superscalar organization. The Itanium does not use reservation stations, reorder buffers, and memory ordering buffers, all replaced by simpler hardware for speculation. The register remapping hardware is simpler than the register aliasing typical of superscalar machines. Register dependency-detection logic is absent, replaced by explicit parallelism directives precomputed by the software.

Using branch prediction, the fetch/prefetch engine can speculatively load an L1 instruction cache to minimize cache misses on instruction fetches. The fetched code is fed into a decoupling buffer that can hold up to eight bundles of code.

Three levels of cache are used. The L1 cache is split into a 16-kbyte instruction cache and a 16-kbyte data cache, each 4-way set associative with a 32-byte

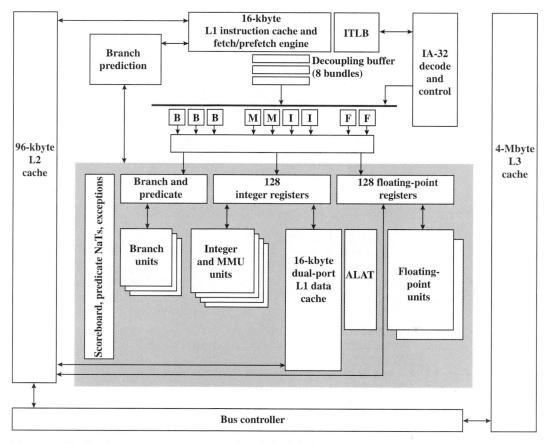

Figure 15.10 Itanium Processor Organization [SHAR00]

line size. The 96-kbyte L2 cache is 6-way set associative with a 64-byte line size. The 4-Mbyte L3 cache is 4-way set associative with a 64-byte line size. The L1 and L2 caches are on the processor chip; the L3 cache is off-chip but on the same package as the processor.

15.6 RECOMMENDED READING AND WEB SITES

[HUCK00] provides an overview of IA-64; another overview is [DULO98]. [SCHL00a] provides a general discussion of EPIC; a more thorough treatment is provided in [SCHL00b]. Two other good treatments are [HWU01] and [KATH01]. [CHAS00] and [HWU98] provide introductions to predicated execution. Volume 1 of [INTE00a] contains a detailed treatment of software pipelining; two articles that provide a good explanation of the topic, with examples, are [JARP01] and [BHAR00].

For an overview of the Itanium processor architecture, see [SHAR00]; [INTE00b] provides a more detailed treatment.

Both [TRIE01] and [MARK00] contain more detailed treatments of the topics of this chapter. Finally, for an exhaustive look at the IA-64 architecture and instruction set, see [INTE00a].

BHAR00 Bharandwaj, J., et al. "The Intel IA-64 Compiler Code Generator." *IEEE Micro*, September/October 2000.

CHAS00 Chasin, A. "Predication, Speculation, and Modern CPUs." *Dr. Dobb's Journal*, May 2000.

DULO98 Dulong, C. "The IA-64 Architecture at Work." *Computer*, July 1998.

HUCK00 Huck, J., et al. "Introducing the IA-64 Architecture." *IEEE Micro*, September/October 2000.

HWU98 Hwu, W. "Introduction to Predicated Execution." *Computer*, January 1998.

HWU01 Hwu, W.; August, D.; and Sias, J. "Program Decision Logic Optimization Using Predication and Control Speculation." *Proceedings of the IEEE*, November 2001.

INTE00a Intel Corp. *Intel IA-64 Architecture Software Developer's Manual (4 volumes).* Document 245317 through 245320. Aurora, CO, 2000.

INTE00b Intel Corp. *Itanium Processor Microarchitecture Reference for Software Optimization.* Aurora, CO, Document 245473. August 2000.

JARP01 Jarp, S. "Optimizing IA-64 Performance." *Dr. Dobb's Journal*, July 2001.

KATH01 Kathail. B.; Schlansker, M.; and Rau, B. "Compiling for EPIC Architectures." *Proceedings of the IEEE*, November 2001.

MARK00 Markstein, P. *IA-64 and Elementary Functions.* Upper Saddle River, NJ: Prentice Hall PTR, 2000.

SCHL00a Schlansker, M.; and Rau, B. "EPIC: Explicitly Parallel Instruction Computing." *Computer*, February 2000.

SCHL00b Schlansker, M.; and Rau, B. *EPIC: An Architecture for Instruction-Level Parallel Processors.* HPL Technical Report HPL-1999-111, Hewlett-Packard Laboratories (www.hpl.hp.com), February 2000.

SHAR00 Sharangpani, H., and Arona, K. "Itanium Processor Microarchitecture." *IEEE Micro*, September/October 2000.

TRIE01 Triebel, W. *Itanium Architecture for Software Developers.* Intel Press, 2001.

Recommended Web Sites:

- **Itanium:** Intel's site for the latest information on IA-64 and Itanium.
- **IMPACT:** This is a site at the University of Illinois, where much of the research on predicated execution has been done. A number of papers on the subject are available.

15.7 KEY TERMS, REVIEW QUESTIONS, AND PROBLEMS

Key Terms

advanced load	execution unit	instruction completer
branch predication	explicitly parallel instruction	instruction group
bundle	computing (EPIC)	Itanium
control speculation	hoist	major opcode
data speculation	IA-64 architecture	NaT bit

predicate register	speculative loading	template field
predication	stack frame	very long instruction word
register stack	stop	(VLIW)
software pipeline	syllable	

Review Questions

15.1 What are the different types of execution units for IA-64?

15.2 Explain the use of the template field in an IA-64 bundle.

15.3 What is the significance of a stop in the instruction stream?

15.4 Define predication and predicated execution.

15.5 How can predicates replace a conditional branch instruction?

15.6 Define control speculation.

15.7 What is the purpose of the NaT bit?

15.8 Define data speculation.

15.9 What is the difference between a hardware pipeline and a software pipeline?

15.10 What is the difference between stacked and rotating registers?

Problems

15.1 Suppose that an IA-64 opcode accepts three registers as operands and produces one register as a result. What is the maximum number of such opcodes that can be defined in one major opcode family?

15.2 At a certain point in an IA-64 program, there are 10 A-type instructions and six floating-point instructions that can be issued concurrently. How many syllables may appear without any stops between them?

15.3 In Problem 15.2,

    a. How many cycles are required for a small IA-64 implementation having one floating-point unit, two integer units, and two memory units?

    b. How many cycles are required for the Itanium organization of Figure 15.10?

15.4 An algorithm that can utilize four floating-point instructions per cycle is coded for IA-64. Should instruction groups contain four floating-point operations? What are the consequences if the machine on which the program runs has fewer than four floating-point units?

15.5 In Section 15.3, we introduced the following constructs for predicated execution:

```
        cmp.crel p2, p3 = a, b
   (p1) cmp.crel p2, p3 = a, b
```

where crel is a relation, such as eq, ne, etc.; p1, p2, and p3 are predicate registers; a is either a register or an immediate operand; and b is a register operand.

Fill in the following truth table:

p1	comparison	p2	p3
not present	0		
not present	1		
0	0		
0	1		
1	0		
1	1		

15.6 For the predicated program in Section 15.3, which implements the flowchart of Figure 15.4, indicate

    a. Those instructions that can be executed in parallel

    b. Those instructions that can be bundled into the same IA-64 instruction bundle

15.7 Consider the following source code segment:

```
for ( i = 0; i < 100; i++ )
      if (A[i] < 50 )
            j = j + 1;
      else
            k = k + 1;
```

    a. Write a corresponding Pentium assembly code segment.

    b. Rewrite as an IA-64 assembly code segment using predicated execution techniques.

15.8 Consider the following C program fragment dealing with floating-point values.

```
a[i] = p * q;
c = a[j];
```

The compiler cannot establish that $i \neq j$, but has reason to believe that it probably is.

    a. Write an IA-64 program using an advanced load to implement this C program. *Hint:* the floating-point load and multiply instructions are ldf and fmpy, respectively.

    b. Recode the program using predication instead of the advanced load.

    c. What are the advantages and disadvantages of the two approaches compared with each other?

15.9 Assume that a stack register frame is created with size equal to SOF = 48. If the size of the local register group is SOL = 16,

    a. How many output registers (SOO) are there?

    b. Which registers are in the local and output register groups?

PART FOUR

The Control Unit

ISSUES FOR PART FOUR

In Part Three, we focused on machine instructions and the operations performed by the processor to execute each instruction. What was left out of this discussion is exactly how each individual operation is caused to happen. This is the job of the control unit.

The control unit is that portion of the processor that actually causes things to happen. The control unit issues control signals external to the processor to cause data exchange with memory and I/O modules. The control unit also issues control signals internal to the processor to move data between registers, to cause the ALU to perform a specified function, and to regulate other internal operations. Input to the control unit consists of the instruction register, flags, and control signals from external sources (e.g., interrupt signals).

ROAD MAP FOR PART FOUR

Chapter 16 Control Unit Operation

In Chapter 16, we turn to a discussion of how processor functions are performed or, more specifically, how the various elements of the processor are controlled to provide these functions, by means of the control unit. It is shown that each instruction cycle is made up of a set of micro-operations that generate control signals. Execution is accomplished by the effect of these control signals, emanating from the control unit to the ALU, registers, and system interconnection structure. Finally, an approach to the implementation of the control unit, referred to as hardwired implementation, is presented.

Chapter 17 Microprogrammed Control

In Chapter 17, we see how the concept of micro-operation leads to an elegant and powerful approach to control unit implementation, known as microprogramming. In essence, a lower-level programming language is developed. Each instruction in the machine language of the processor is translated into a sequence of lower-level control unit instructions. These lower-level instructions are referred to as micro-instructions, and the process of translation is referred to as microprogramming. The chapter describes the layout of a control memory containing a microprogram for each machine instruction is described. The structure and function of the micro-programmed control unit can then be explained.

CHAPTER **16**

CONTROL UNIT OPERATION

KEY POINTS

◆ The execution of an instruction involves the execution of a sequence of sub-steps, generally called cycles. For example, an execution may consist of fetch, indirect, execute, and interrupt cycles. Each cycle is in turn made up of a sequence of more fundamental operations, called micro-operations. A single micro-operation generally involves a transfer between registers, a transfer between a register and an external bus, or a simple ALU operation.

◆ The control unit of a processor performs two tasks: (1) It causes the processor to execute micro-operations in the proper sequence, determined by the program being executed, and (2) it generates the control signals that cause each micro-operation to be executed.

◆ The control signals generated by the control unit cause the opening and closing of logic gates, resulting in the transfer of data to and from registers and the operation of the ALU.

◆ One technique for implementing a control unit is referred to as hardwired implementation, in which the control unit is a combinatorial circuit. Its input logic signals, governed by the current machine instruction, are transferred into a set of output control signals.

In Chapter 10, we pointed out that a machine instruction set goes a long way toward defining the processor. If we know the machine instruction set, including an understanding of the effect of each opcode and an understanding of the addressing modes, and if we know the set of user-visible registers, then we know the functions that the processor must perform. This is not the complete picture. We must know the external interfaces, usually through a bus, and how interrupts are handled. With this line of reasoning, the following list of those things needed to specify the function of a processor emerges:

1. Operations (opcodes)
2. Addressing modes
3. Registers
4. I/O module interface
5. Memory module interface
6. Interrupt processing structure

This list, though general, is rather complete. Items 1 through 3 are defined by the instruction set. Items 4 and 5 are typically defined by specifying the system bus. Item 6 is defined partially by the system bus and partially by the type of support the processor offers to the operating system.

This list of six items might be termed the functional requirements for a processor. They determine what a processor must do. This is what occupied us in Parts

Two and Three. Now, we turn to the question of how these functions are performed or, more specifically, how the various elements of the processor are controlled to provide these functions. Thus, we turn to a discussion of the control unit, which controls the operation of the processor.

16.1 MICRO-OPERATIONS

We have seen that the operation of a computer, in executing a program, consists of a sequence of instruction cycles, with one machine instruction per cycle. Of course, we must remember that this sequence of instruction cycles is not necessarily the same as the *written sequence* of instructions that make up the program, because of the existence of branching instructions. What we are referring to here is the execution *time sequence* of instructions.

We have further seen that each instruction cycle is made up of a number of smaller units. One subdivision that we found convenient is fetch, indirect, execute, and interrupt, with only fetch and execute cycles always occurring.

To design a control unit, however, we need to break down the description further. In our discussion of pipelining in Chapter 12, we began to see that a further decomposition is possible. In fact, we will see that each of the smaller cycles involves a series of steps, each of which involves the processor registers. We will refer to these steps as *micro-operations.* The prefix *micro* refers to the fact that each step is very simple and accomplishes very little. Figure 16.1 depicts the relationship among the various concepts we have been discussing. To summarize, the execution of a program consists of the sequential execution of instructions. Each instruction is executed during an instruction cycle made up of shorter subcycles (e.g., fetch, indirect,

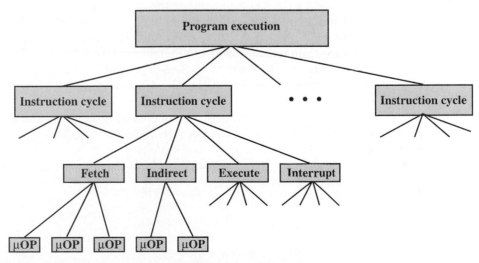

Figure 16.1 Constituent Elements of a Program Execution

execute, interrupt). The performance of each subcycle involves one or more shorter operations, that is, micro-operations.

Micro-operations are the functional, or atomic, operations of a processor. In this section, we will examine micro-operations to gain an understanding of how the events of any instruction cycle can be described as a sequence of such micro-operations. A simple example will be used. In the remainder of this chapter, we then show how the concept of micro-operations serves as a guide to the design of the control unit.

The Fetch Cycle

We begin by looking at the fetch cycle, which occurs at the beginning of each instruction cycle and causes an instruction to be fetched from memory. For purposes of discussion, we assume the organization depicted in Figure 12.6. Four registers are involved:

- **Memory address register (MAR):** Is connected to the address lines of the system bus. It specifies the address in memory for a read or write operation.
- **Memory buffer register (MBR):** Is connected to the data lines of the system bus. It contains the value to be stored in memory or the last value read from memory.
- **Program counter (PC):** Holds the address of the next instruction to be fetched.
- **Instruction register (IR):** Holds the last instruction fetched.

Let us look at the sequence of events for the fetch cycle from the point of view of its effect on the processor registers. An example appears in Figure 16.2. At the beginning of the fetch cycle, the address of the next instruction to be executed is in the program counter (PC); in this case, the address is 1100100. The first step is to move that address to the memory address register (MAR) because this is the only register connected to the address lines of the system bus. The second step is to bring in the instruction. The desired address (in the MAR) is placed on the address bus, the control unit issues a READ command on the control bus, and the result appears on the data bus and is copied into the memory buffer register (MBR). We also need to increment the PC by 1 to get ready for the next instruction. Because these two actions (read word from memory, add 1 to PC) do not interfere with each other, we can do them simultaneously to save time. The third step is to move the contents of the MBR to the instruction register (IR). This frees up the MBR for use during a possible indirect cycle.

Thus, the simple fetch cycle actually consists of three steps and four micro-operations. Each micro-operation involves the movement of data into or out of a register. So long as these movements do not interfere with one another, several of them can take place during one step, saving time. Symbolically, we can write this sequence of events as follows:

$$
\begin{aligned}
t_1: & \quad \text{MAR} \leftarrow (\text{PC}) \\
t_2: & \quad \text{MBR} \leftarrow \text{Memory} \\
& \quad \text{PC} \leftarrow (\text{PC}) + I \\
t_3: & \quad \text{IR} \leftarrow (\text{MBR})
\end{aligned}
$$

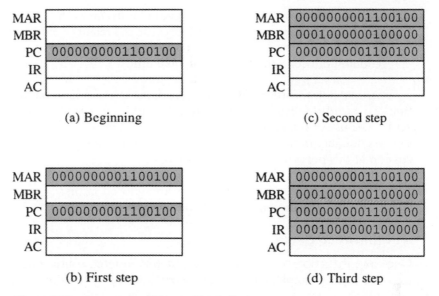

Figure 16.2 Sequence of Events, Fetch Cycle

where *I* is the instruction length. We need to make several comments about this sequence. We assume that a clock is available for timing purposes and that it emits regularly spaced clock pulses. Each clock pulse defines a time unit. Thus, all time units are of equal duration. Each micro-operation can be performed within the time of a single time unit. The notation (t_1, t_2, t_3) represents successive time units. In words, we have

- **First time unit:** Move contents of PC to MAR.
- **Second time unit:** Move contents of memory location specified by MAR to MBR. Increment by *I* the contents of the PC.
- **Third time unit:** Move contents of MBR to IR.

Note that the second and third micro-operations both take place during the second time unit. The third micro-operation could have been grouped with the fourth without affecting the fetch operation:

```
t₁:  MAR ← (PC)
t₂:  MBR ← Memory
t₃:  PC  ← (PC) + I
     IR  ← (MBR)
```

The groupings of micro-operations must follow two simple rules:

1. The proper sequence of events must be followed. Thus (MAR ← (PC)) must precede (MBR ← Memory) because the memory read operation makes use of the address in the MAR.

2. Conflicts must be avoided. One should not attempt to read to and write from the same register in one time unit, because the results would be unpredictable. For example, the micro-operations (MBR ← Memory) and (IR ← MBR) should not occur during the same time unit.

A final point worth noting is that one of the micro-operations involves an addition. To avoid duplication of circuitry, this addition could be performed by the ALU. The use of the ALU may involve additional micro-operations, depending on the functionality of the ALU and the organization of the processor. We defer a discussion of this point until later in this chapter.

It is useful to compare events described in this and the following subsections to Figure 3.5. Whereas micro-operations are ignored in that figure, this discussion shows the micro-operations needed to perform the subcycles of the instruction cycle.

The Indirect Cycle

Once an instruction is fetched, the next step is to fetch source operands. Continuing our simple example, let us assume a one-address instruction format, with direct and indirect addressing allowed. If the instruction specifies an indirect address, then an indirect cycle must precede the execute cycle. The data flow differs somewhat from that indicated in Figure 12.7 and includes the following micro-operations:

$$t_1: \quad \text{MAR} \leftarrow (\text{IR(Address)})$$
$$t_2: \quad \text{MBR} \leftarrow \text{Memory}$$
$$t_3: \quad \text{IR(Address)} \leftarrow (\text{MBR(Address)})$$

The address field of the instruction is transferred to the MAR. This is then used to fetch the address of the operand. Finally, the address field of the IR is updated from the MBR, so that it now contains a direct rather than an indirect address.

The IR is now in the same state as if indirect addressing had not been used, and it is ready for the execute cycle. We skip that cycle for a moment, to consider the interrupt cycle.

The Interrupt Cycle

At the completion of the execute cycle, a test is made to determine whether any enabled interrupts have occurred. If so, the interrupt cycle occurs. The nature of this cycle varies greatly from one machine to another. We present a very simple sequence of events, as illustrated in Figure 12.8. We have

$$t_1: \quad \text{MBR} \leftarrow (\text{PC})$$
$$t_2: \quad \text{MAR} \leftarrow \text{Save\_Address}$$
$$\qquad \text{PC} \leftarrow \text{Routine\_Address}$$
$$t_3: \quad \text{Memory} \leftarrow (\text{MBR})$$

In the first step, the contents of the PC are transferred to the MBR, so that they can be saved for return from the interrupt. Then the MAR is loaded with the address at which the contents of the PC are to be saved, and the PC is loaded with the address of the start of the interrupt-processing routine. These two actions may each be a single micro-operation. However, because most processors provide multiple types and/or levels of interrupts, it may take one or more additional micro-operations to obtain the save_address and the routine_address before they can be transferred to the MAR and PC, respectively. In any case, once this is done, the final step is to store the MBR, which contains the old value of the PC, into memory. The processor is now ready to begin the next instruction cycle.

The Execute Cycle

The fetch, indirect, and interrupt cycles are simple and predictable. Each involves a small, fixed sequence of micro-operations and, in each case, the same micro-operations are repeated each time around.

This is not true of the execute cycle. For a machine with N different opcodes, there are N different sequences of micro-operations that can occur. Let us consider several hypothetical examples.

First, consider an add instruction:

$$\text{ADD R1, X}$$

which adds the contents of the location X to register R1. The following sequence of micro-operations might occur:

$$
\begin{aligned}
t_1&: \quad \text{MAR} \leftarrow (\text{IR(address)}) \\
t_2&: \quad \text{MBR} \leftarrow \text{Memory} \\
t_3&: \quad \text{R1} \leftarrow (\text{R1}) + (\text{MBR})
\end{aligned}
$$

We begin with the IR containing the ADD instruction. In the first step, the address portion of the IR is loaded into the MAR. Then the referenced memory location is read. Finally, the contents of R1 and MBR are added by the ALU. Again, this is a simplified example. Additional micro-operations may be required to extract the register reference from the IR and perhaps to stage the ALU inputs or outputs in some intermediate registers.

Let us look at two more complex examples. A common instruction is increment and skip if zero:

$$\text{ISZ X}$$

The content of location X is incremented by 1. If the result is 0, the next instruction is skipped. A possible sequence of micro-operations is

$$
\begin{aligned}
t_1&: \quad \text{MAR} \leftarrow (\text{IR(address)}) \\
t_2&: \quad \text{MBR} \leftarrow \text{Memory} \\
t_3&: \quad \text{MBR} \leftarrow (\text{MBR}) + 1 \\
t_4&: \quad \text{Memory} \leftarrow (\text{MBR}) \\
&\quad\quad \text{If } ((\text{MBR}) = 0) \text{ then } (\text{PC} \leftarrow (\text{PC}) + \text{I})
\end{aligned}
$$

The new feature introduced here is the conditional action. The PC is incremented if (MBR) = 0. This test and action can be implemented as one micro-operation. Note also that this micro-operation can be performed during the same time unit during which the updated value in MBR is stored back to memory.

Finally, consider a subroutine call instruction. As an example, consider a branch-and-save-address instruction:

$$BSA \quad X$$

The address of the instruction that follows the BSA instruction is saved in location X, and execution continues at location X + I. The saved address will later be used for return. This is a straightforward technique for providing subroutine calls. The following micro-operations suffice:

$$
\begin{aligned}
t_1: \quad & \text{MAR} \leftarrow \text{(IR(address))} \\
& \text{MBR} \leftarrow \text{(PC)} \\
t_2: \quad & \text{PC} \leftarrow \text{(IR(address))} \\
& \text{Memory} \leftarrow \text{(MBR)} \\
t_3: \quad & \text{PC} \leftarrow \text{(PC)} + \text{I}
\end{aligned}
$$

The address in the PC at the start of the instruction is the address of the next instruction in sequence. This is saved at the address designated in the IR. The latter address is also incremented to provide the address of the instruction for the next instruction cycle.

The Instruction Cycle

We have seen that each phase of the instruction cycle can be decomposed into a sequence of elementary micro-operations. In our example, there is one sequence each for the fetch, indirect, and interrupt cycles, and, for the execute cycle, there is one sequence of micro-operations for each opcode.

To complete the picture, we need to tie sequences of micro-operations together, and this is done in Figure 16.3. We assume a new 2-bit register called the *instruction cycle code* (ICC). The ICC designates the state of the processor in terms of which portion of the cycle it is in:

00: Fetch
01: Indirect
10: Execute
11: Interrupt

At the end of each of the four cycles, the ICC is set appropriately. The indirect cycle is always followed by the execute cycle. The interrupt cycle is always followed by the fetch cycle (see Figure 12.4). For both the execute and fetch cycles, the next cycle depends on the state of the system.

Thus, the flowchart of Figure 16.3 defines the complete sequence of micro-operations, depending only on the instruction sequence and the interrupt pattern. Of course, this is a simplified example. The flowchart for an actual processor would be more complex. In any case, we have reached the point in our discussion in which the operation of the processor is defined as the performance of a sequence of micro-operations. We can now consider how the control unit causes this sequence to occur.

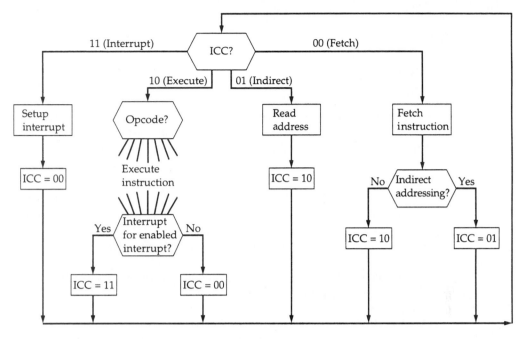

Figure 16.3 Flowchart for Instruction Cycle

16.2 CONTROL OF THE PROCESSOR

Functional Requirements

As a result of our analysis in the preceding section, we have decomposed the be-havior or functioning of the processor into elementary operations, called micro-operations. By reducing the operation of the processor to its most fundamental level, we are able to define exactly what it is that the control unit must cause to happen. Thus, we can define the *functional requirements* for the control unit: those functions that the control unit must perform. A definition of these functional re-quirements is the basis for the design and implementation of the control unit.

With the information at hand, the following three-step process leads to a char-acterization of the control unit:

1. Define the basic elements of the processor.
2. Describe the micro-operations that the processor performs.
3. Determine the functions that the control unit must perform to cause the micro-operations to be performed.

We have already performed steps 1 and 2. Let us summarize the results. First, the basic functional elements of the processor are the following:

- ALU
- Registers
- Internal data paths
- External data paths
- Control unit

Some thought should convince you that this is a complete list. The ALU is the functional essence of the computer. Registers are used to store data internal to the processor. Some registers contain status information needed to manage instruction sequencing (e.g., a program status word). Others contain data that go to or come from the ALU, memory, and I/O modules. Internal data paths are used to move data between registers and between register and ALU. External data paths link registers to memory and I/O modules, often by means of a system bus. The control unit causes operations to happen within the processor.

The execution of a program consists of operations involving these processor elements. As we have seen, these operations consist of a sequence of micro-operations. Upon review of Section 16.1, the reader should see that all micro-operations fall into one of the following categories:

- Transfer data from one register to another.
- Transfer data from a register to an external interface (e.g., system bus).
- Transfer data from an external interface to a register.
- Perform an arithmetic or logic operation, using registers for input and output.

All of the micro-operations needed to perform one instruction cycle, including all of the micro-operations to execute every instruction in the instruction set, fall into one of these categories.

We can now be somewhat more explicit about the way in which the control unit functions. The control unit performs two basic tasks:

- **Sequencing:** The control unit causes the processor to step through a series of micro-operations in the proper sequence, based on the program being executed.
- **Execution:** The control unit causes each micro-operation to be performed.

The preceding is a functional description of what the control unit does. The key to how the control unit operates is the use of control signals.

Control Signals

We have defined the elements that make up the processor (ALU, registers, data paths) and the micro-operations that are performed. For the control unit to perform its function, it must have inputs that allow it to determine the state of the system and outputs that allow it to control the behavior of the system. These are the external specifications of the control unit. Internally, the control unit must have the logic required to perform its sequencing and execution functions. We defer a discussion of the internal operation of the control unit to Section 16.3 and Chapter 17. The remainder of this section is concerned with the interaction between the control unit and the other elements of the processor.

Figure 16.4 is a general model of the control unit, showing all of its inputs and outputs. The inputs are as follows:

- **Clock:** This is how the control unit "keeps time." The control unit causes one micro-operation (or a set of simultaneous micro-operations) to be performed for each clock pulse. This is sometimes referred to as the processor cycle time, or the clock cycle time.
- **Instruction register:** The opcode of the current instruction is used to determine which micro-operations to perform during the execute cycle.
- **Flags:** These are needed by the control unit to determine the status of the processor and the outcome of previous ALU operations. For example, for the increment-and-skip-if-zero (ISZ) instruction, the control unit will increment the PC if the zero flag is set.
- **Control signals from control bus:** The control bus portion of the system bus provides signals to the control unit, such as interrupt signals and acknowledgments.

The outputs are as follows:

- **Control signals within the processor:** These are two types: those that cause data to be moved from one register to another, and those that activate specific ALU functions.
- **Control signals to control bus:** These are also of two types: control signals to memory, and control signals to the I/O modules.

The new element that has been introduced in this figure is the control signal. Three types of control signals are used: those that activate an ALU function, those that activate a data path, and those that are signals on the external system bus or other external interface. All of these signals are ultimately applied directly as binary inputs to individual logic gates.

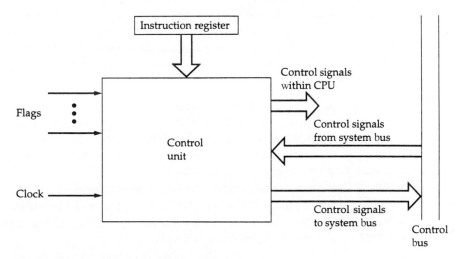

Figure 16.4 Model of the Control Unit

Let us consider again the fetch cycle to see how the control unit maintains control. The control unit keeps track of where it is in the instruction cycle. At a given point, it knows that the fetch cycle is to be performed next. The first step is to transfer the contents of the PC to the MAR. The control unit does this by activating the control signal that opens the gates between the bits of the PC and the bits of the MAR. The next step is to read a word from memory into the MBR and increment the PC. The control unit does this by sending the following control signals simultaneously:

- A control signal that opens gates, allowing the contents of the MAR onto the address bus
- A memory read control signal on the control bus
- A control signal that opens the gates, allowing the contents of the data bus to be stored in the MBR
- Control signals to logic that add 1 to the contents of the PC and store the result back to the PC

Following this, the control unit sends a control signal that opens gates between the MBR and the IR.

This completes the fetch cycle except for one thing: The control unit must decide whether to perform an indirect cycle or an execute cycle next. To decide this, it examines the IR to see if an indirect memory reference is made.

The indirect and interrupt cycles work similarly. For the execute cycle, the control unit begins by examining the opcode and, on the basis of that, decides which sequence of micro-operations to perform for the execute cycle.

A Control Signals Example

To illustrate the functioning of the control unit, let us examine a simple example. Figure 16.5 illustrates the example. This is a simple processor with a single accumulator. The data paths between elements are indicated. The control paths for signals emanating from the control unit are not shown, but the terminations of control signals are labeled C_i and indicated by a circle. The control unit receives inputs from the clock, the instruction register, and flags. With each clock cycle, the control unit reads all of its inputs and emits a set of control signals. Control signals go to three separate destinations:

- **Data paths:** The control unit controls the internal flow of data. For example, on instruction fetch, the contents of the memory buffer register are transferred to the instruction register. For each path to be controlled, there is a gate (indicated by a circle in the figure). A control signal from the control unit temporarily opens the gate to let data pass.
- **ALU:** The control unit controls the operation of the ALU by a set of control signals. These signals activate various logic devices and gates within the ALU.
- **System bus:** The control unit sends control signals out onto the control lines of the system bus (e.g., memory READ).

The control unit must maintain knowledge of where it is in the instruction cycle. Using this knowledge, and by reading all of its inputs, the control unit emits

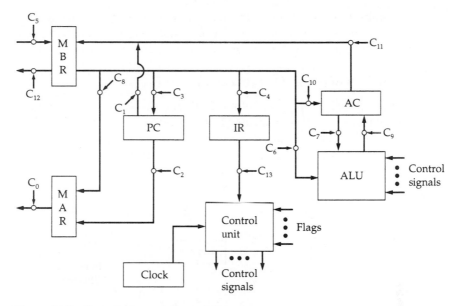

Figure 16.5 Data Paths and Control Signals

a sequence of control signals that causes micro-operations to occur. It uses the clock pulses to time the sequence of events, allowing time between events for signal levels to stabilize. Table 16.1 indicates the control signals that are needed for some of the micro-operation sequences described earlier. For simplicity, the data and control paths for incrementing the PC and for loading the fixed addresses into the PC and MAR are not shown.

It is worth pondering the minimal nature of the control unit. The control unit is the engine that runs the entire computer. It does this based only on knowing the instructions to be executed and the nature of the results of arithmetic and logical

Table 16.1 Micro-Operations and Control Signals

Micro-Operations	Timing	Active Control Signals
Fetch:	t1: MAR ← (PC)	C_2
	t2: MBR ← Memory	C_5, C_R
	PC ← (PC) + 1	
	t3: IR ← (MBR)	C_4
Indirect:	t1: MAR ← (IR(Address))	C_8
	t2: MBR ← Memory	C_5, C_R
	t3: IR(Address) ← (MBR(Address))	C_4
Interrupt:	t1: MBR ← (PC)	C_1
	t2: MAR ← Save-address	
	PC ← Routine-address	
	t3: Memory ← (MBR)	C_{12}, C_W

C_R = Read control signal to system bus.
C_W = Write control signal to system bus.

operations (e.g., positive, overflow, etc.). It never gets to see the data being processed or the actual results produced. And it controls everything with a few control signals to points within the processor and a few control signals to the system bus.

Internal Processor Organization

Figure 16.5 indicates the use of a variety of data paths. The complexity of this type of organization should be clear. More typically, some sort of internal bus arrangement, as was suggested in Figure 12.2, will be used.

Using an internal processor bus, Figure 16.5 can be rearranged as shown in Figure 16.6. A single internal bus connects the ALU and all processor registers. Gates and control signals are provided for movement of data onto and off the bus

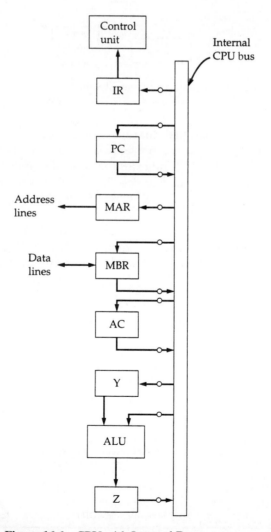

Figure 16.6 CPU with Internal Bus

from each register. Additional control signals control data transfer to and from the system (external) bus and the operation of the ALU.

Two new registers, labeled Y and Z, have been added to the organization. These are needed for the proper operation of the ALU. When an operation involving two operands is performed, one can be obtained from the internal bus, but the other must be obtained from another source. The AC could be used for this purpose, but this limits the flexibility of the system and would not work with a processor with multiple general-purpose registers. Register Y provides temporary storage for the other input. The ALU is a combinatorial circuit (see Appendix A) with no internal storage. Thus, when control signals activate an ALU function, the input to the ALU is transformed to the output. Thus, the output of the ALU cannot be directly connected to the bus, because this output would feed back to the input. Register Z provides temporary output storage. With this arrangement, an operation to add a value from memory to the AC would have the following steps:

$$
\begin{aligned}
t_1: &\quad \text{MAR} \leftarrow \text{(IR(address))} \\
t_2: &\quad \text{MBR} \leftarrow \text{Memory} \\
t_3: &\quad \text{Y} \leftarrow \text{(MBR)} \\
t_4: &\quad \text{Z} \leftarrow \text{(AC)} + \text{(Y)} \\
t_5: &\quad \text{AC} \leftarrow \text{(Z)}
\end{aligned}
$$

Other organizations are possible, but, in general, some sort of internal bus or set of internal buses is used. The use of common data paths simplifies the interconnection layout and the control of the processor. Another practical reason for the use of an internal bus is to save space. Especially for microprocessors, which may occupy only a 1/4-inch square piece of silicon, space occupied by interregister connections must be minimized.

The Intel 8085

To illustrate some of the concepts introduced thus far in this chapter, let us consider the Intel 8085. Its organization is shown in Figure 16.7. Several key components that may not be self-explanatory are as follows:

- **Incrementer/decrementer address latch:** Logic that can add 1 to or subtract 1 from the contents of the stack pointer or program counter. This saves time by avoiding the use of the ALU for this purpose.
- **Interrupt control:** This module handles multiple levels of interrupt signals.
- **Serial I/O control:** This module interfaces to devices that communicate 1 bit at a time.

Table 16.2 describes the external signals into and out of the 8085. These are linked to the external system bus. These signals are the interface between the 8085 processor and the rest of the system (Figure 16.8).

The control unit is identified as having two components labeled (1) instruction decoder and machine cycle encoding and (2) timing and control. A discussion of the first component is deferred until the next section. The essence of the control unit is the timing and control module. This module includes a clock and accepts as inputs

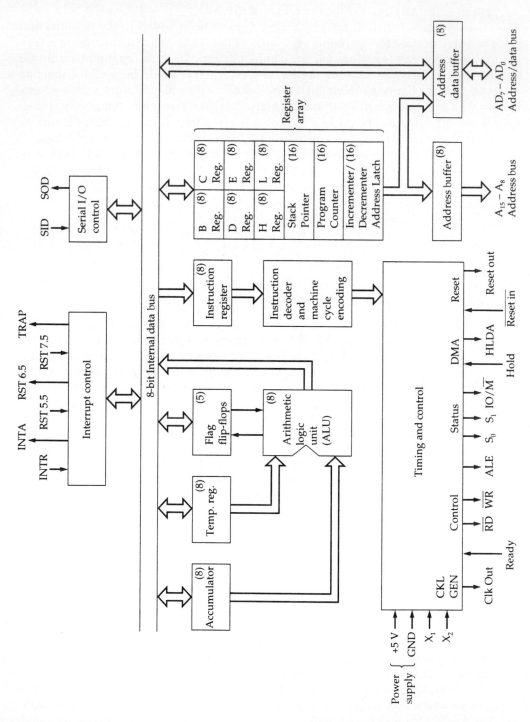

Figure 16.7 Intel 8085 CPU Block Diagram

Table 16.2   Intel 8085 External Signals

Address and Data Signals

High Address (A15–A8)

The high-order 8 bits of a 16-bit address.

Address/Data (AD7–AD0)

The lower-order 8 bits of a 16-bit address or 8 bits of data. This multiplexing saves on pins.

Serial Input Data (SID)

A single-bit input to accommodate devices that transmit serially (one bit at a time).

Serial Output Data (SOD)

A single-bit output to accommodate devices that receive serially.

Timing and Control Signals

CLK (OUT)

The system clock. Each cycle represents one T state. The CLK signal goes to peripheral chips and synchronizes their timing.

X1, X2

These signals come from an external crystal or other device to drive the internal clock generator.

Address Latch Enabled (ALE)

Occurs during the first clock state of a machine cycle and causes peripheral chips to store the address lines. This allows the address module (e.g., memory, I/O) to recognize that it is being addressed.

Status (S0, S1)

Control signals used to indicate whether a read or write operation is taking place.

IO/M

Used to enable either I/O or memory modules for read and write operations.

Read Control (RD)

Indicates that the selected memory or I/O module is to be read and that the data bus is available for data transfer.

Write Control (WR)

Indicates that data on the data bus is to be written into the selected memory or I/O location.

Memory and I/O Initiated Symbols

Hold

Requests the CPU to relinquish control and use of the external system bus. The CPU will complete execution of the instruction presently in the IR and then enter a hold state, during which no signals are inserted by the CPU to the control, address, or data buses. During the hold state, the bus may be used for DMA operations.

Hold Acknowledge (HOLDA)

This control unit output signal acknowledges the HOLD signal and indicates that the bus is now available.

READY

Used to synchronize the CPU with slower memory or I/O devices. When an addressed device asserts READY, the CPU may proceed with an input (DBIN) or output (WR) operation. Otherwise, the CPU enters a wait state until the device is ready.

Interrupt-Related Signals

TRAP

Restart Interrupts (RST 7.5, 6.5, 5.5)

Interrupt Request (INTR)

These five lines are used by an external device to interrupt the CPU. The CPU will not honor the request if it is in the hold state or if the interrupt is disabled. An interrupt is honored only at the completion of an instruction. The interrupts are in descending order of priority.

Interrupt Acknowledge

Acknowledges an interrupt.

CPU Initialization

RESET IN

Causes the contents of the PC to be set to zero. The CPU resumes execution at location zero.

RESET OUT

Acknowledges that the CPU has been reset. The signal can be used to reset the rest of the system.

Voltage and Ground

VCC

+5 volt power supply

VSS

Electrical ground

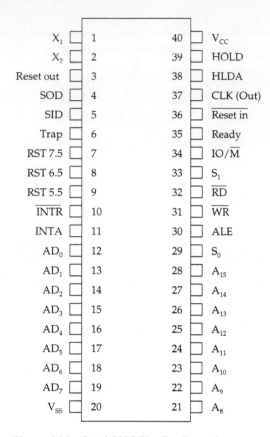

Figure 16.8 Intel 8085 Pin Configuration

the current instruction and some external control signals. Its output consists of control signals to the other components of the processor plus control signals to the external system bus.

The timing of processor operations is synchronized by the clock and controlled by the control unit with control signals. Each instruction cycle is divided into from one to five *machine cycles;* each machine cycle is in turn divided into from three to five *states.* Each state lasts one clock cycle. During a state, the processor performs one or a set of simultaneous micro-operations as determined by the control signals.

The number of machine cycles is fixed for a given instruction but varies from one instruction to another. Machine cycles are defined to be equivalent to bus accesses. Thus, the number of machine cycles for an instruction depends on the number of times the processor must communicate with external devices. For example, if an instruction consists of two 8-bit portions, then two machine cycles are required to fetch the instruction. If that instruction involves a 1-byte memory or I/O operation, then a third machine cycle is required for execution.

Figure 16.9 gives an example of 8085 timing, showing the value of external control signals. Of course, at the same time, the control unit generates internal control

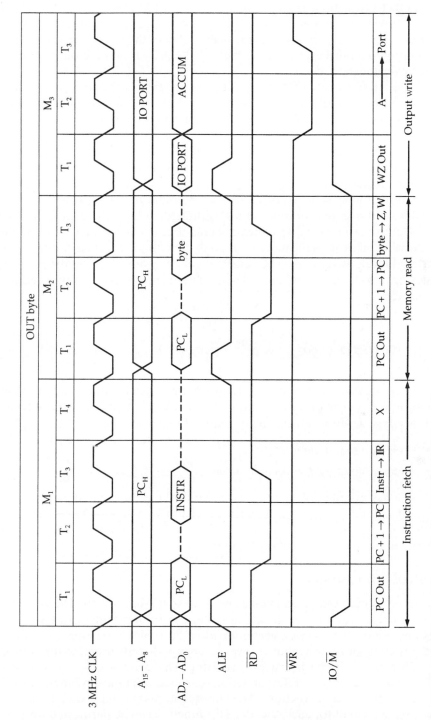

Figure 16.9 Timing Diagram for Intel 8085 OUT Instruction

signals that control internal data transfers. The diagram shows the instruction cycle for an OUT instruction. Three machine cycles (M_1, M_2, M_3) are needed. During the first, the OUT instruction is fetched. The second machine cycle fetches the second half of the instruction, which contains the number of the I/O device selected for output. During the third cycle, the contents of the AC are written out to the selected device over the data bus.

The Address Latch Enabled (ALE) pulse signals the start of each machine cycle from the control unit. The ALE pulse alerts external circuits. During timing state T_1 of machine cycle M_1, the control unit sets the IO/M signal to indicate that this is a memory operation. Also, the control unit causes the contents of the PC to be placed on the address bus (A_{15} through A_8) and the address/data bus (AD_7 through AD_0). With the falling edge of the ALE pulse, the other modules on the bus store the address.

During timing state T_2, the addressed memory module places the contents of the addressed memory location on the address/data bus. The control unit sets the Read Control (RD) signal to indicate a read, but it waits until T_3 to copy the data from the bus. This gives the memory module time to put the data on the bus and for the signal levels to stabilize. The final state, T_4, is a *bus idle* state during which the processor decodes the instruction. The remaining machine cycles proceed in a similar fashion.

16.3 HARDWIRED IMPLEMENTATION

We have discussed the control unit in terms of its inputs, output, and functions. We now turn to the topic of control unit implementation. A wide variety of techniques have been used. Most of these fall into one of two categories:

- Hardwired implementation
- Microprogrammed implementation

In a hardwired implementation, the control unit is essentially a combinatorial circuit. Its input logic signals are transformed into a set of output logic signals, which are the control signals. This approach is examined in this section. Microprogrammed implementation is the subject of Chapter 17.

Control Unit Inputs

Figure 16.4 depicts the control unit as we have so far discussed it. The key inputs are the instruction register, the clock, flags, and control bus signals. In the case of the flags and control bus signals, each individual bit typically has some meaning (e.g., overflow). The other two inputs, however, are not directly useful to the control unit.

First consider the instruction register. The control unit makes use of the opcode and will perform different actions (issue a different combination of control signals) for different instructions. To simplify the control unit logic, there should be a unique logic input for each opcode. This function can be performed by a *decoder,* which takes an encoded input and produces a single output. In general, a decoder will have n binary inputs and 2^n binary outputs. Each of the 2^n different input patterns will activate a single unique output. Table 16.3 is an example. The decoder for a control unit will typically have to be more complex than that, to account for variable-length opcodes. An example of the digital logic used to implement a decoder is presented in Appendix A.

The clock portion of the control unit issues a repetitive sequence of pulses. This is useful for measuring the duration of micro-operations. Essentially, the period of the clock pulses must be long enough to allow the propagation of signals along data paths and through processor circuitry. However, as we have seen, the control unit emits different control signals at different time units within a single instruction cycle. Thus, we would like a counter as input to the control unit, with a different control signal being used for T_1, T_2, and so forth. At the end of an instruction cycle, the control unit must feed back to the counter to reinitialize it at T_1.

With these two refinements, the control unit can be depicted as in Figure 16.10.

Control Unit Logic

To define the hardwired implementation of a control unit, all that remains is to discuss the internal logic of the control unit that produces output control signals as a function of its input signals.

Table 16.3 A Decoder with Four Inputs and Sixteen Outputs

I1	I2	I3	I4	O1	O2	O3	O4	O5	O6	O7	O8	O9	O10	O11	O12	O13	O14	O15	O16
0	0	0	0	0	0	0	0	0	0	0	0	0	0	0	0	0	0	0	1
0	0	0	1	0	0	0	0	0	0	0	0	0	0	0	0	0	0	1	0
0	0	1	0	0	0	0	0	0	0	0	0	0	0	0	0	0	1	0	0
0	0	1	1	0	0	0	0	0	0	0	0	0	0	0	0	1	0	0	0
0	1	0	0	0	0	0	0	0	0	0	0	0	0	0	1	0	0	0	0
0	1	0	1	0	0	0	0	0	0	0	0	0	0	1	0	0	0	0	0
0	1	1	0	0	0	0	0	0	0	0	0	0	1	0	0	0	0	0	0
0	1	1	1	0	0	0	0	0	0	0	0	1	0	0	0	0	0	0	0
1	0	0	0	0	0	0	0	0	0	0	1	0	0	0	0	0	0	0	0
1	0	0	1	0	0	0	0	0	0	1	0	0	0	0	0	0	0	0	0
1	0	1	0	0	0	0	0	0	1	0	0	0	0	0	0	0	0	0	0
1	0	1	1	0	0	0	0	1	0	0	0	0	0	0	0	0	0	0	0
1	1	0	0	0	0	0	1	0	0	0	0	0	0	0	0	0	0	0	0
1	1	0	1	0	0	1	0	0	0	0	0	0	0	0	0	0	0	0	0
1	1	1	0	0	1	0	0	0	0	0	0	0	0	0	0	0	0	0	0
1	1	1	1	1	0	0	0	0	0	0	0	0	0	0	0	0	0	0	0

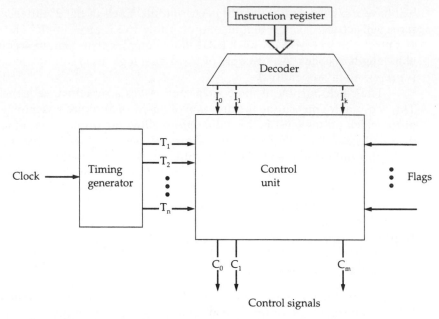

Figure 16.10   Control Unit with Decoded Inputs

Essentially, what must be done is, for each control signal, to derive a Boolean expression of that signal as a function of the inputs. This is best explained by example. Let us consider again our simple example illustrated in Figure 16.5. We saw in Table 16.1 the micro-operation sequences and control signals needed to control three of the four phases of the instruction cycle.

Let us consider a single control signal, C_5. This signal causes data to be read from the external data bus into the MBR. We can see that it is used twice in Table 16.1. Let us define two new control signals, P and Q, that have the following interpretation:

```
PQ = 00    Fetch Cycle
PQ = 01    Indirect Cycle
PQ = 10    Execute Cycle
PQ = 11    Interrupt Cycle
```

Then the following Boolean expression defines C_5:

$$C_5 = \overline{P} \cdot \overline{Q} \cdot T_2 + \overline{P} \cdot Q \cdot T_2$$

That is, the control signal C_5 will be asserted during the second time unit of both the fetch and indirect cycles.

This expression is not complete. C_5 is also needed during the execute cycle. For our simple example, let us assume that there are only three instructions that read from memory: LDA, ADD, and AND. Now we can define C_5 as

$$C_5 = \overline{P} \cdot \overline{Q} \cdot T_2 + \overline{P} \cdot Q \cdot T_2 + P \cdot \overline{Q} \cdot (LDA + ADD + AND) \cdot T_2$$

This same process could be repeated for every control signal generated by the processor. The result would be a set of Boolean equations that define the behavior of the control unit and hence of the processor.

To tie everything together, the control unit must control the state of the instruction cycle. As was mentioned, at the end of each subcycle (fetch, indirect, execute, interrupt), the control unit issues a signal that causes the timing generator to reinitialize and issue T_1. The control unit must also set the appropriate values of P and Q to define the next subcycle to be performed.

The reader should be able to appreciate that in a modern complex processor, the number of Boolean equations needed to define the control unit is very large. The task of implementing a combinatorial circuit that satisfies all of these equations becomes extremely difficult. The result is that a far simpler approach, known as *microprogramming*, is usually used. This is the subject of the next chapter.

16.4 RECOMMENDED READING

A number of textbooks treat the basic principles of control unit function; two particularly clear treatments are in [HAYE98] and [MANO01].

HAYE98   Hayes, J. *Computer Architecture and Organization.* New York: McGraw-Hill, 1998.
MANO01   Mano, M. *Logic and Computer Design Fundamentals.* Upper Saddle River, NJ: Prentice Hall, 1901.

16.5 KEY TERMS, REVIEW QUESTIONS, AND PROBLEMS

Key Terms

control bus	control signal	hardwired implementation
control path	control unit	microoperations

Review Questions

16.1   Explain the distinction between the written sequence and the time sequence of an instruction.
16.2   What is the relationship between instructions and micro-operations?
16.3   What is the overall function of a processor's control unit?
16.4   Outline a three-step process that leads to a characterization of the control unit.
16.5   What basic tasks does a control unit perform?
16.6   Provide a typical list of the inputs and outputs of a control unit.
16.7   List three types of control signals.
16.8   Briefly explain what is meant by a hardwired implementation of a control unit.

Problems

16.1   Your ALU can add its two input registers, and it can logically complement the bits of either input register, but it cannot subtract. Numbers are to be stored in twos complement representation. List the micro-operations your control unit must perform to cause a subtraction.

16.2   Show the micro-operations and control signals in the same fashion as Table 16.1 for the processor in Figure 16.5 for the following instructions:

- Load Accumulator
- Store Accumulator
- Add to Accumulator
- AND to Accumulator
- Jump
- Jump if AC = 0
- Complement Accumulator

16.3   Assume that propagation delay along the bus and through the ALU of Figure 16.6 are 20 and 100 ns, respectively. The time required for a register to copy data from the bus is 10 ns. What is the time that must be allowed for

a. transferring data from one register to another?

b. incrementing the program counter?

16.4   Write the sequence of micro-operations required for the bus structure of Figure 16.6 to add a number to the AC when the number is

a. an immediate operand

b. a direct-address operand

c. an indirect-address operand

16.5   A stack is implemented as shown in Figure 10.14. Show the sequence of micro-operations for

a. popping

b. pushing the stack

CHAPTER 17

MICROPROGRAMMED CONTROL

KEY POINTS

- An alternative to a hardwired control unit is a microprogrammed control unit, in which the logic of the control unit is specified by a microprogram. A microprogram consists of a sequence of instructions in a microprogramming language. These are very simple instructions that specify micro-operations.

- A microprogrammed control unit is a relatively simple logic circuit that is capable of (1) sequencing through microinstructions and (2) generating control signals to execute each microinstruction.

- As in a hardwired control unit, the control signals generated by a microinstruction are used to cause register transfers and ALU operations.

The term *microprogram* was first coined by M. V. Wilkes in the early 1950s [WILK51]. Wilkes proposed an approach to control unit design that was organized and systematic and avoided the complexities of a hardwired implementation. The idea intrigued many researchers but appeared unworkable because it would require a fast, relatively inexpensive control memory.

The state of the microprogramming art was reviewed by *Datamation* in its February 1964 issue. No microprogrammed system was in wide use at that time, and one of the papers [HILL64] summarized the then-popular view that the future of microprogramming "is somewhat cloudy. None of the major manufacturers has evidenced interest in the technique, although presumably all have examined it."

This situation changed dramatically within a very few months. IBM's System/360 was announced in April, and all but the largest models were microprogrammed. Although the 360 series predated the availability of semiconducter ROM, the advantages of microprogramming were compelling enough for IBM to make this move. Since then, microprogramming has become an increasingly popular vehicle for a variety of applications, one of which is the use of microprogramming to implement the control unit of a processor. That application is examined in this chapter.

17.1 BASIC CONCEPTS

Microinstructions

The control unit seems a reasonably simple device. Nevertheless, to implement a control unit as an interconnection of basic logic elements is no easy task. The design must include logic for sequencing through micro-operations, for executing micro-operations, for interpreting opcodes, and for making decisions based on ALU flags. It is difficult to design and test such a piece of hardware. Furthermore, the design is relatively inflexible. For example, it is difficult to change the design if one wishes to add a new machine instruction.

An alternative, which is quite common in contemporary CISC processors, is to implement a microprogrammed control unit.

(a) Horizontal microinstruction

(b) Vertical microinstruction

Figure 17.1 Typical Microinstruction Formats

Consider again Table 16.1. In addition to the use of control signals, each micro-operation is described in symbolic notation. This notation looks suspiciously like a programming language. In fact it is a language, known as a *microprogramming language.* Each line describes a set of micro-operations occurring at one time and is known as a *microinstruction.* A sequence of instructions is known as a *micropro-gram,* or *firmware.* This latter term reflects the fact that a microprogram is midway between hardware and software. It is easier to design in firmware than hardware, but it is more difficult to write a firmware program than a software program.

How can we use the concept of microprogramming to implement a control unit? Consider that for each micro-operation, all that the control unit is allowed to do is generate a set of control signals. Thus, for any micro-operation, each control line emanating from the control unit is either on or off. This condition can, of course, be represented by a binary digit for each control line. So we could construct a *control word* in which each bit represents one control line. Then each micro-operation would be represented by a different pattern of 1s and 0s in the control word.

Suppose we string together a sequence of control words to represent the sequence of micro-operations performed by the control unit. Next, we must recognize that the sequence of micro-operations is not fixed. Sometimes we have an indirect cycle; sometimes we do not. So let us put our control words in a memory, with each word having a unique address. Now add an address field to each control word, indicating the location of the next control word to be executed if a certain condition is true (e.g., the indirect bit in a memory-reference instruction is 1). Also, add a few bits to specify the condition.

The result is known as a *horizontal microinstruction,* an example of which is shown in Figure 17.1a. The format of the microinstruction or control word is as follows. There is one bit for each internal processor control line and one bit for each system bus control line. There is a condition field indicating the condition under which there should be a branch, and there is a field with the address of the microinstruction to be executed next when a branch is taken. Such a microinstruction is interpreted as follows:

1. To execute this microinstruction, turn on all the control lines indicated by a 1 bit; leave off all control lines indicated by a 0 bit. The resulting control signals will cause one or more micro-operations to be performed.
2. If the condition indicated by the condition bits is false, execute the next microinstruction in sequence.
3. If the condition indicated by the condition bits is true, the next microinstruction to be executed is indicated in the address field.

Figure 17.2 shows how these control words or microinstructions could be arranged in a *control memory*. The microinstructions in each routine are to be executed sequentially. Each routine ends with a branch or jump instruction indicating where to go next. There is a special execute cycle routine whose only purpose is to signify that one of the machine instruction routines (AND, ADD, and so on) is to be executed next, depending on the current opcode.

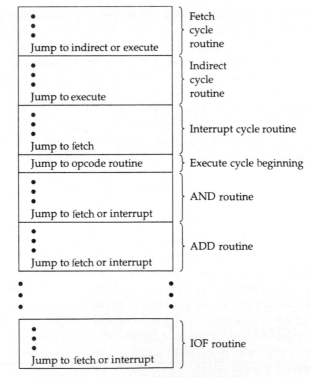

Figure 17.2 Organization of Control Memory

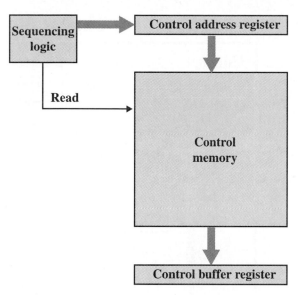

Figure 17.3   Control Unit Microarchitecture

The control memory of Figure 17.2 is a concise description of the complete operation of the control unit. It defines the sequence of micro-operations to be performed during each cycle (fetch, indirect, execute, interrupt), and it specifies the sequencing of these cycles. If nothing else, this notation would be a useful device for documenting the functioning of a control unit for a particular computer. But it is more than that. It is also a way of implementing the control unit.

Microprogrammed Control Unit

The control memory of Figure 17.2 contains a program that describes the behavior of the control unit. It follows that we could implement the control unit by simply executing that program.

Figure 17.3 shows the key elements of such an implementation. The set of microinstructions is stored in the *control memory.* The *control address register* contains the address of the next microinstruction to be read. When a microinstruction is read from the control memory, it is transferred to a *control buffer register.* The left-hand portion of that register (see Figure 17.1a) connects to the control lines emanating from the control unit. Thus, *reading* a microinstruction from the control memory is the same as *executing* that microinstruction. The third element shown in the figure is a sequencing unit that loads the control address register and issues a read command.

Let us examine this structure in greater detail, as depicted in Figure 17.4. Comparing this with Figure 16.4, we see that the control unit still has the same inputs (IR, ALU flags, clock) and outputs (control signals). The control unit functions as follows:

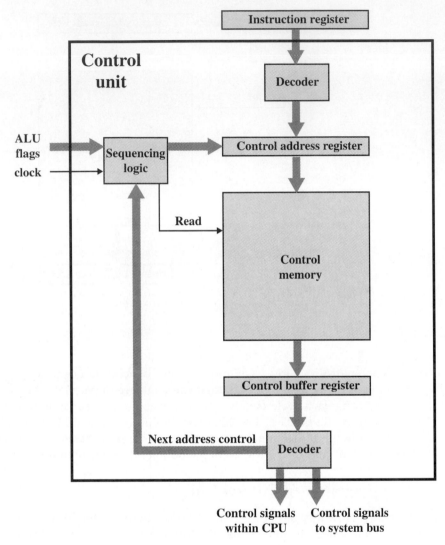

Figure 17.4 Functioning of Microprogrammed Control Unit

1. To execute an instruction, the sequencing logic unit issues a READ command to the control memory.
2. The word whose address is specified in the control address register is read into the control buffer register.
3. The content of the control buffer register generates control signals and next-address information for the sequencing logic unit.
4. The sequencing logic unit loads a new address into the control address register based on the next-address information from the control buffer register and the ALU flags.

All this happens during one clock pulse.

The last step just listed needs elaboration. At the conclusion of each microinstruction, the sequencing logic unit loads a new address into the control address register. Depending on the value of the ALU flags and the control buffer register, one of three decisions is made:

- **Get the next instruction:** Add 1 to the control address register.
- **Jump to a new routine based on a jump microinstruction:** Load the address field of the control buffer register into the control address register.
- **Jump to a machine instruction routine:** Load the control address register based on the opcode in the IR.

Figure 17.4 shows two modules labeled *decoder*. The upper decoder translates the opcode of the IR into a control memory address. The lower decoder is not used for horizontal microinstructions but is used for *vertical microinstructions* (Figure 17.1b). As was mentioned, in a horizontal microinstruction every bit in the control field attaches to a control line. In a vertical microinstruction, a code is used for each action to be performed [e.g., MAR ← (PC)], and the decoder translates this code into individual control signals. The advantage of vertical microinstructions is that they are more compact (fewer bits) than horizontal microinstructions, at the expense of a small additional amount of logic and time delay.

Wilkes Control

As was mentioned, Wilkes first proposed the use of a microprogrammed control unit in 1951 [WILK51]. This proposal was subsequently elaborated into a more detailed design [WILK53]. It is instructive to examine this seminal proposal.

The configuration proposed by Wilkes is depicted in Figure 17.5. The heart of the system is a matrix partially filled with diodes. During a machine cycle, one row of the matrix is activated with a pulse. This generates signals at those points where a diode is present (indicated by a dot in the diagram). The first part of the row generates the control signals that control the operation of the processor. The second part generates the address of the row to be pulsed in the next machine cycle. Thus, each row of the matrix is one microinstruction, and the layout of the matrix is the control memory.

At the beginning of the cycle, the address of the row to be pulsed is contained in Register I. This address is the input to the decoder, which, when activated by a clock pulse, activates one row of the matrix. Depending on the control signals, either the opcode in the instruction register or the second part of the pulsed row is passed into Register II during the cycle. Register II is then gated to Register I by a clock pulse. Alternating clock pulses are used to activate a row of the matrix and to transfer from Register II to Register I. The two-register arrangement is needed because the decoder is simply a combinatorial circuit; with only one register, the output would become the input during a cycle, causing an unstable condition.

This scheme is very similar to the horizontal microprogramming approach described earlier (Figure 17.1a). The main difference is this: In the previous description, the control address register could be incremented by one to get the next address. In the Wilkes scheme, the next address is contained in the microinstruction.

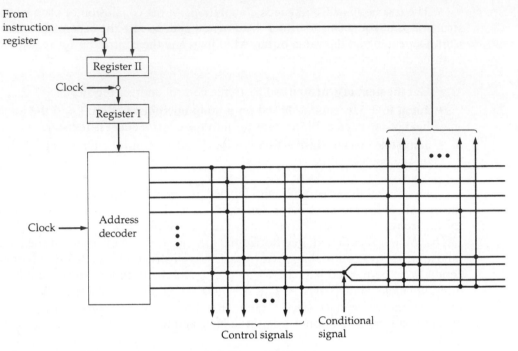

Figure 17.5 Wilkes's Microprogrammed Control Unit

To permit branching, a row must contain two address parts, controlled by a conditional signal (e.g., flag), as shown in the figure.

Having proposed this scheme, Wilkes provides an example of its use to implement the control unit of a simple machine. This example, the first known design of a microprogrammed processor, is worth repeating here because it illustrates many of the contemporary principles of microprogramming.

The processor of the hypothetical machine includes the following registers:

A multiplicand
B accumulator (least-significant half)
C accumulator (most-significant half)
D shift register

In addition, there are three registers and two 1-bit flags accessible only to the control unit. The registers are as follows:

E serves as both a memory address register (MAR) and temporary storage
F program counter
G another temporary register; used for counting

Table 17.1 lists the machine instruction set for this example. Table 17.2 is the complete set of microinstructions, expressed in symbolic form, that implements

Table 17.1 Machine Instruction Set for Wilkes Example

Order	Effect of Order
$A\,n$	$C(Acc) + C(n)$ to Acc_1
$S\,n$	$C(Acc) - C(n)$ to Acc_1
$H\,n$	$C(n)$ to Acc_2
$V\,n$	$C(Acc2) \times C(n)$ to Acc, where $C(n) \geq 0$
$T\,n$	$C(Acc1)$ to n, 0 to Acc
$U\,n$	$C(Acc1)$ to n
$R\,n$	$C(Acc) \times 2^{-(n+1)}$ to Acc
$L\,n$	$C(Acc) \times 2^{n+1}$ to Acc
$G\,n$	IF $C(Acc) < 0$, transfer control to n; if $C(Acc) \geq 0$, ignore (i.e., proceed serially)
$I\,n$	Read next character on input mechanism into n
$O\,n$	Send $C(n)$ to output mechanism

Notation: Acc = accumulator
Acc_1 = most significant half of accumulator
Acc_2 = least significant half of accumulator
n = storage location n
$C(X)$ = contents of X (X = register or storage location)

the control unit. Thus, a total of 38 microinstructions is all that is required to define the system completely.

The first full column gives the address (row number) of each microinstruction. Those addresses corresponding to opcodes are labeled. Thus, when the opcode for the add instruction (A) is encountered, the microinstruction at location 5 is executed. Columns 2 and 3 express the actions to be taken by the ALU and control unit, respectively. Each symbolic expression must be translated into a set of control signals (microinstruction bits). Columns 4 and 5 have to do with the setting and use of the two flags (flip-flops). Column 4 specifies the signal that sets the flag. For example, $(1)C_s$ means that flag number 1 is set by the sign bit of the number in register C. If column 5 contains a flag identifier, then columns 6 and 7 contain the two alternative microinstruction addresses to be used. Otherwise, column 6 specifies the address of the next microinstruction to be fetched.

Instructions 0 through 4 constitute the fetch cycle. Microinstruction 4 presents the opcode to a decoder, which generates the address of a microinstruction corresponding to the machine instruction to be fetched. The reader should be able to deduce the complete functioning of the control unit from a careful study of Table 17.2.

Advantages and Disadvantages

The principal advantage of the use of microprogramming to implement a control unit is that it simplifies the design of the control unit. Thus, it is both cheaper and less error-prone to implement. A *hardwired* control unit must contain complex logic for sequencing through the many micro-operations of the instruction cycle. On the other hand, the decoders and sequencing logic unit of a microprogrammed control unit are very simple pieces of logic.

Table 17.2 Microinstructions for Wilkes Example

Notation: $A, B, C, \ldots$ stand for the various registers in the arithmetical and contol register units. C to D indicates that the switching circuits connect the output of register C to the input register D; $(D + A)$ to C indicates that the output register of A is connected to the one input of the adding unit (the output of D is permanently connected to the other input), and the output of the adder to register C. A numerical symbol n in quotes (e.g., 'n') stands for the source whose output is the number n in units of the least significant digit.

		Arithmetical Unit	Control Register Unit	Conditional Flip-Flop Set	Conditional Flip-Flop Use	Next Micro-instruction 0	Next Micro-instruction 1
	0		F to G and E			1	
	1		$(G$ to '1'$)$ to F			2	
	2		Store to G			3	
	3		G to E			4	
	4		E to decoder			—	
A	5	C to D				16	
S	6	C to D				17	
H	7	Store to B				0	
V	8	Store to A				27	
T	9	C to Store				25	
U	10	C to Store				0	
R	11	B to D	E to G			19	
L	12	C to D	E to G			22	
G	13		E to G	$(1)C_5$		18	
I	14	Input to Store				0	
O	15	Store to Output				0	
	16	$(D + \text{Store})$ to C				0	
	17	$(D - \text{Store})$ to C				0	
	18				1	0	1
	19	D to B (R)*	$(G - $ '1'$)$ to E			20	
	20	C to D		$(1)E_5$		21	
	21	D to C (R)			1	11	0
	22	D to C (L)†	$(G - $ '1'$)$ to E			23	
	23	B to D		$(1)E_5$		24	
	24	D to B (L)			1	12	0
	25	'0' to B				26	
	26	B to C				0	
	27	'0' to C	'18' to E			28	

Table 17.2 *(continued)*

	Arithmetical Unit	Control Register Unit	Conditional Flip-Flop		Next Micro-instruction	
			Set	Use	0	1
28	*B* to *D*	*E to G*	(1)B_1		29	
29	*D* to *B (R)*	(*G* − '1') to *E*			30	
30	*C* to *D (R)*		(2)E_5	1	31	32
31	*D* to *C*			2	28	33
32	(*D* + *A*) to *C*			2	28	33
33	*B* to *D*		(1)B_1		34	
34	*D* to *B (R)*				35	
35	*C* to *D (R)*			1	36	37
36	*D* to *C*				0	
37	(*D* − *A*) to *C*				0	

*Right shift. The switching circuits in the arithmetic unit are arranged so that the least significant digit of the register *C* is placed in the most significant place of register *B* during right shift micro-operations, and the most significant digit of register *C* (sign digit) is repeated (thus making the correction for negative numbers).

† Left shift. The switching circuits are similarly arranged to pass the most significant digit of register *B* to the least significant place of register *C* during left shift micro-operations.

The principal disadvantage of a microprogrammed unit is that it will be somewhat slower than a hardwired unit of comparable technology. Despite this, microprogramming is the dominant technique for implementing control units in contemporary CISC, due to its ease of implementation. RISC processors, with their simpler instruction format, typically use hardwired control units. We now examine the microprogrammed approach in greater detail.

17.2 MICROINSTRUCTION SEQUENCING

The two basic tasks performed by a microprogrammed control unit are as follows:

- **Microinstruction sequencing:** Get the next microinstruction from the control memory.
- **Microinstruction execution:** Generate the control signals needed to execute the microinstruction.

In designing a control unit, these tasks must be considered together, because both affect the format of the microinstruction and the timing of the control unit. In this section, we will focus on sequencing and say as little as possible about format and timing issues. These issues are examined in more detail in the next section.

Design Considerations

Two concerns are involved in the design of a microinstruction sequencing technique: the size of the microinstruction and the address-generation time. The first concern is obvious; minimizing the size of the control memory reduces the cost of that component. The second concern is simply a desire to execute microinstructions as fast as possible.

In executing a microprogram, the address of the next microinstruction to be executed is in one of these categories:

- Determined by instruction register
- Next sequential address
- Branch

The first category occurs only once per instruction cycle, just after an instruction is fetched. The second category is the most common in most designs. However, the design cannot be optimized just for sequential access. Branches, both conditional and unconditional, are a necessary part of a microprogram. Furthermore, microinstruction sequences tend to be short; one out of every three or four microinstructions could be a branch [SIEW82]. Thus, it is important to design compact, time-efficient techniques for microinstruction branching.

Sequencing Techniques

Based on the current microinstruction, condition flags, and the contents of the instruction register, a control memory address must be generated for the next microinstruction. A wide variety of techniques have been used. We can group them into three general categories, as illustrated in Figures 17.6 to 17.8. These categories are based on the format of the address information in the microinstruction:

- Two address fields
- Single address field
- Variable format

The simplest approach is to provide two address fields in each microinstruction. Figure 17.6 suggests how this information is to be used. A multiplexer is provided that serves as a destination for both address fields plus the instruction register. Based on an address-selection input, the multiplexer transmits either the opcode or one of the two addresses to the control address register (CAR). The CAR is subsequently decoded to produce the next microinstruction address. The address-selection signals are provided by a branch logic module whose input consists of control unit flags plus bits from the control portion of the microinstruction.

Although the two-address approach is simple, it requires more bits in the microinstruction than other approaches. With some additional logic, savings can be achieved. A common approach is to have a single address field (Figure 17.7). With this approach, the options for next address are as follows:

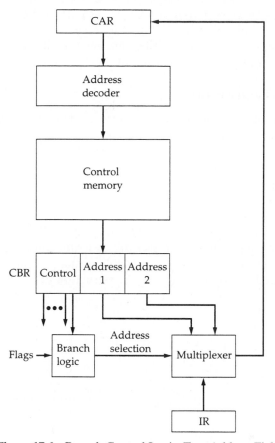

Figure 17.6 Branch Control Logic, Two Address Fields

- Address field
- Instruction register code
- Next sequential address

The address-selection signals determine which option is selected. This approach reduces the number of address fields to one. Note, however, that the address field often will not be used. Thus, there is some inefficiency in the microinstruction coding scheme.

Another approach is to provide for two entirely different microinstruction formats (Figure 17.8). One bit designates which format is being used. In one format, the remaining bits are used to activate control signals. In the other format, some bits drive the branch logic module, and the remaining bits provide the address. With the first format, the next address is either the next sequential address or an address derived from the instruction register. With the second format, either a conditional or unconditional branch is being specified. One disadvantage of this approach is that one entire cycle is consumed with each branch microinstruction. With the other approaches, address generation occurs as part of the same cycle as control signal generation, minimizing control memory accesses.

The approaches just described are general. Specific implementations will often involve a variation or combination of these techniques.

Address Generation

We have looked at the sequencing problem from the point of view of format considerations and general logic requirements. Another viewpoint is to consider the various ways in which the next address can be derived or computed.

Table 17.3 lists the various address generation techniques. These can be divided into explicit techniques, in which the address is explicitly available in the microinstruction, and implicit techniques, which require additional logic to generate the address.

We have essentially dealt with the explicit techniques. With a two-field approach, two alternative addresses are available with each microinstruction. Using either a single address field or a variable format, various branch instructions can be implemented. A conditional branch instruction depends on the following types of information:

- ALU flags
- Part of the opcode or address mode fields of the machine instruction

Figure 17.7 Branch Control Logic, Single Address Field

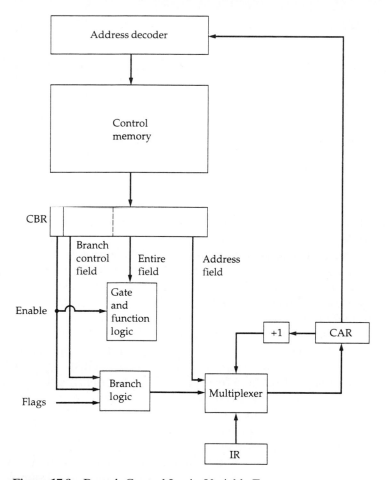

Figure 17.8 Branch Control Logic, Variable Format

- Parts of a selected register, such as the sign bit
- Status bits within the control unit

Several implicit techniques are also commonly used. One of these, mapping, is required with virtually all designs. The opcode portion of a machine instruction must be mapped into a microinstruction address. This occurs only once per instruction cycle.

Table 17.3 Microinstruction Address Generation Techniques

Explicit	Implicit
Two-field	Mapping
Unconditional branch	Addition
Conditional branch	Residual control

Figure 17.9 IBM 3033 Control Address Register

A common implicit technique is one that involves combining or adding two portions of an address to form the complete address. This approach was taken for the IBM S/360 family [TUCK67] and used on many of the S/370 models. We will use the IBM 3033 as an example.

The control address register on the IBM 3033 is 13 bits long and is illustrated in Figure 17.9. Two parts of the address can be distinguished. The highest-order 8 bits (00–07) normally do not change from one microinstruction cycle to the next. During the execution of a microinstruction, these 8 bits are copied directly from an 8-bit field of the microinstruction (the BA field) into the highest-order 8 bits of the control address register. This defines a block of 32 microinstructions in control memory. The remaining 5 bits of the control address register are set to specify the specific address of the microinstruction to be fetched next. Each of these bits is determined by a 4-bit field (except one is a 7-bit field) in the current microinstruction; the field specifies the condition for setting the corresponding bit. For example, a bit in the control address register might be set to 1 or 0 depending on whether a carry occurred on the last ALU operation.

The final approach listed in Table 17.3 is termed *residual control*. This approach involves the use of a microinstruction address that has previously been saved in temporary storage within the control unit. For example, some microinstruction sets come equipped with a subroutine facility. An internal register or stack of registers is used to hold return addresses. An example of this approach is taken on the LSI-11, which we now examine.

LSI-11 Microinstruction Sequencing

The LSI-11 is a microcomputer version of a PDP-11, with the main components of the system residing on a single board. The LSI-11 is implemented using a microprogrammed control unit [SEBE76].

The LSI-11 makes use of a 22-bit microinstruction and a control memory of 2K 22-bit words. The next microinstruction address is determined in one of five ways:

- **Next sequential address:** In the absence of other instructions, the control unit's control address register is incremented by 1.
- **Opcode mapping:** At the beginning of each instruction cycle, the next microinstruction address is determined by the opcode.
- **Subroutine facility:** Explained presently.

- **Interrupt testing:** Certain microinstructions specify a test for interrupts. If an interrupt has occurred, this determines the next microinstruction address.
- **Branch:** Conditional and unconditional branch microinstructions are used.

A one-level subroutine facility is provided. One bit in every microinstruction is dedicated to this task. When the bit is set, an 11-bit return register is loaded with the updated contents of the control address register. A subsequent microinstruction that specifies a return will cause the control address register to be loaded from the return register.

The return is one form of unconditional branch instruction. Another form of unconditional branch causes the bits of the control address register to be loaded from 11 bits of the microinstruction. The conditional branch instruction makes use of a 4-bit test code within the microinstruction. This code specifies testing of various ALU condition codes to determine the branch decision. If the condition is not true, the next sequential address is selected. If it is true, the 8 lowest-order bits of the control address register are loaded from 8 bits of the microinstruction. This allows branching within a 256-word page of memory.

As can be seen, the LSI-11 includes a powerful address sequencing facility within the control unit. This allows the microprogrammer considerable flexibility and can ease the microprogramming task. On the other hand, this approach requires more control unit logic than do simpler capabilities.

17.3 MICROINSTRUCTION EXECUTION

The microinstruction cycle is the basic event on a microprogrammed processor. Each cycle is made up of two parts: fetch and execute. The fetch portion is determined by the generation of a microinstruction address, and this was dealt with in the preceding section. This section deals with the execution of a microinstruction.

Recall that the effect of the execution of a microinstruction is to generate control signals. Some of these signals control points internal to the processor. The remaining signals go to the external control bus or other external interface. As an incidental function, the address of the next microinstruction is determined.

The preceding description suggests the organization of a control unit shown in Figure 17.10. This slightly revised version of Figure 17.4 emphasizes the focus of this section. The major modules in this diagram should by now be clear. The sequencing logic module contains the logic to perform the functions discussed in the preceding section. It generates the address of the next microinstruction, using as inputs the instruction register, ALU flags, the control address register (for incrementing), and the control buffer register. The last may provide an actual address, control bits, or both. The module is driven by a clock that determines the timing of the microinstruction cycle.

The control logic module generates control signals as a function of some of the bits in the microinstruction. It should be clear that the format and content of the microinstruction will determine the complexity of the control logic module.

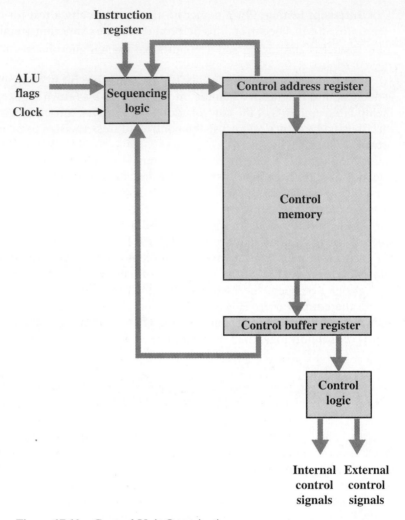

Figure 17.10   Control Unit Organization

A Taxonomy of Microinstructions

Microinstructions can be classified in a variety of ways. Distinctions that are commonly made in the literature include the following:

- Vertical/horizontal
- Packed/unpacked
- Hard/soft microprogramming
- Direct/indirect encoding

All of these bear on the format of the microinstruction. None of these terms has been used in a consistent, precise way in the literature. However, an examination of these pairs of qualities serves to illuminate microinstruction design alternatives. In the following paragraphs, we first look at the key design issue underlying all of these pairs of characteristics, and then we look at the concepts suggested by each pair.

In the original proposal by Wilkes [WILK51], each bit of a microinstruction either directly produced a control signal or directly produced one bit of the next address. We have seen, in the preceding section, that more complex address sequencing schemes, using fewer microinstruction bits, are possible. These schemes require a more complex sequencing logic module. A similar sort of trade-off exists for the portion of the microinstruction concerned with control signals. By encoding control information, and subsequently decoding it to produce control signals, control word bits can be saved.

How can this encoding be done? To answer that, consider that there are a total of K different internal and external control signals to be driven by the control unit. In Wilkes's scheme, K bits of the microinstruction would be dedicated to this purpose. This allows all of the 2^K possible combinations of control signals to be generated during any instruction cycle. But we can do better than this if we observe that not all of the possible combinations will be used. Examples include the following:

- Two sources cannot be gated to the same destination (e.g., C_2 and C_8 in Figure 16.5).
- A register cannot be both source and destination (e.g., C_5 and C_{12} in Figure 16.5).
- Only one pattern of control signals can be presented to the ALU at a time.
- Only one pattern of control signals can be presented to the external control bus at a time.

So, for a given processor, all possible allowable combinations of control signals could be listed, giving some number $Q < 2^K$ possibilities. These could be encoded with $\log_2 Q$ bits, with $(\log_2 Q) < K$. This would be the tightest possible form of encoding that preserves all allowable combinations of control signals. In practice, this form of encoding is not used, for two reasons:

- It is as difficult to program as a pure decoded (Wilkes) scheme. This point is discussed further presently.
- It requires a complex and therefore slow control logic module.

Instead, some compromises are made. These are of two kinds:

- More bits than are strictly necessary are used to encode the possible combinations.
- Some combinations that are physically allowable are not possible to encode.

The latter kind of compromise has the effect of reducing the number of bits. The net result, however, is to use more than $\log_2 Q$ bits.

In the next subsection, we will discuss specific encoding techniques. The remainder of this subsection deals with the effects of encoding and the various terms used to describe it.

Based on the preceding, we can see that the control signal portion of the microinstruction format falls on a spectrum. At one extreme, there is one bit for each control signal; at the other extreme, a highly encoded format is used. Table 17.4

Table 17.4 The Microinstruction Spectrum

Characteristics	
Unencoded	Highly encoded
Many bits	Few bits
Detailed view of hardware	Aggregated view of hardware
Difficult to program	Easy to program
Concurrency fully exploited	Concurrency not fully exploited
Little or no control logic	Complex control logic
Fast execution	Slow execution
Optimize performance	Optimize programming
Terminology	
Unpacked	Packed
Horizontal	Vertical
Hard	Soft

shows that other characteristics of a microprogrammed control unit also fall along a spectrum and that these spectra are, by and large, determined by the degree-of-encoding spectrum.

The second pair of items in the table is rather obvious. The pure Wilkes scheme will require the most bits. It should also be apparent that this extreme presents the most detailed view of the hardware. Every control signal is individually controllable by the microprogrammer. Encoding is done in such a way as to aggregate functions or resources, so that the microprogrammer is viewing the processor at a higher, less detailed level. Furthermore, the encoding is designed to ease the microprogramming burden. Again, it should be clear that the task of understanding and orchestrating the use of all the control signals is a difficult one. As was mentioned, one of the consequences of encoding, typically, is to prevent the use of certain otherwise allowable combinations.

The preceding paragraph discusses microinstruction design from the microprogrammer's point of view. But the degree of encoding also can be viewed from its hardware effects. With a pure unencoded format, little or no decode logic is needed; each bit generates a particular control signal. As more compact and more aggregated encoding schemes are used, more complex decode logic is needed. This, in turn, may affect performance. More time is needed to propagate signals through the gates of the more complex control logic module. Thus, the execution of encoded microinstructions takes longer than the execution of unencoded ones.

Thus, all of the characteristics listed in Table 17.4 fall along a spectrum of design strategies. In general, a design that falls toward the left end of the spectrum is intended to optimize the performance of the control unit. Designs toward the right end are more concerned with optimizing the process of microprogramming. Indeed, microinstruction sets near the right end of the spectrum look very much like machine instruction sets. A good example of this is the LSI-11 design, described later in this section. Typically, when the objective is simply to implement a control unit, the design will be near the left end of the spectrum. The IBM 3033 design, discussed presently, is in this category. As we shall discuss later, some systems permit a variety of users to construct different microprograms using the same microinstruction facility. In the latter cases, the design is likely to fall near the right end of the spectrum.

We can now deal with some of the terminology introduced earlier. Table 17.4 indicates how three of these pairs of terms relate to the microinstruction spectrum. In essence, all of these pairs describe the same thing but emphasize different design characteristics.

The degree of packing relates to the degree of identification between a given control task and specific microinstruction bits. As the bits become more *packed,* a given number of bits contains more information. Thus, packing connotes encoding. The terms *horizontal* and *vertical* relate to the relative width of microinstructions. [SIEW82] suggests as a rule of thumb that vertical microinstructions have lengths in the range of 16 to 40 bits, and that horizontal microinstructions have lengths in the range of 40 to 100 bits. The terms *hard* and *soft* microprogramming are used to suggest the degree of closeness to the underlying control signals and hardware layout. Hard microprograms are generally fixed and committed to read-only memory. Soft microprograms are more changeable and are suggestive of user microprogramming.

The other pair of terms mentioned at the beginning of this subsection refers to direct versus indirect encoding, a subject to which we now turn.

Microinstruction Encoding

In practice, microprogrammed control units are not designed using a pure un-encoded or horizontal microinstruction format. At least some degree of encoding is used to reduce control memory width and to simplify the task of microprogramming.

The basic technique for encoding is illustrated in Figure 17.11a. The microinstruction is organized as a set of fields. Each field contains a code, which, upon decoding, activates one or more control signals.

Let us consider the implications of this layout. When the microinstruction is executed, every field is decoded and generates control signals. Thus, with N fields, N simultaneous actions are specified. Each action results in the activation of one or more control signals. Generally, but not always, we will want to design the format so that each control signal is activated by no more than one field. Clearly, however, it must be possible for each control signal to be activated by at least one field.

Now consider the individual field. A field consisting of L bits can contain one of 2^L codes, each of which can be encoded to a different control signal pattern. Because only one code can appear in a field at a time, the codes are mutually exclusive, and, therefore, the actions they cause are mutually exclusive.

The design of an encoded microinstruction format can now be stated in simple terms:

- Organize the format into independent fields. That is, each field depicts a set of actions (pattern of control signals) such that actions from different fields can occur simultaneously.
- Define each field such that the alternative actions that can be specified by the field are mutually exclusive. That is, only one of the actions specified for a given field could occur at a time.

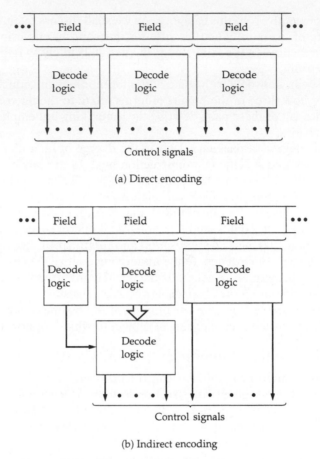

Figure 17.11 Microinstruction Encoding

Two approaches can be taken to organizing the encoded microinstruction into fields: functional and resource. The *functional encoding* method identifies functions within the machine and designates fields by function type. For example, if various sources can be used for transferring data to the accumulator, one field can be designated for this purpose, with each code specifying a different source. *Resource encoding* views the machine as consisting of a set of independent resources and devotes one field to each (e.g., I/O, memory, ALU).

Another aspect of encoding is whether it is direct or indirect (Figure 17.11b). With indirect encoding, one field is used to determine the interpretation of another field. For example, consider an ALU that is capable of performing eight different arithmetic operations and eight different shift operations. A 1-bit field could be used to indicate whether a shift or arithmetic operation is to be used; a 3-bit field would indicate the operation. This technique generally implies two levels of decoding, increasing propagation delays.

Figure 17.12 is a simple example of these concepts. Assume a processor with a single accumulator and several internal registers, such as a program counter and a temporary register for ALU input. Figure 17.12a shows a highly vertical format. The

(a) Vertical microinstruction repertoire

Field definition
1 - Register transfer
2 - Memory operation
3 - Sequencing operation
4 - ALU operation
5 - Register selection
6 - Constant

(b) Horizontal microinstruction format

Figure 17.12 Alternative Microinstruction Formats for a Simple Machine first 3 bits indicate the type of operation, the next 3 encode the operation, and the final 2 select an internal register. Figure 17.12b is a more horizontal approach, although encoding is still used. In this case, different functions appear in different fields.

LSI-11 Microinstruction Execution

The LSI-11 [SEBE76] is a good example of a vertical microinstruction approach. We look first at the organization of the control unit, then at the microinstruction format.

LSI-11 Control Unit Organization

The LSI-11 is the first member of the PDP-11 family that was offered as a single-board processor. The board contains three LSI chips, an internal bus known as the *microinstruction bus* (MIB), and some additional interfacing logic.

Figure 17.13 depicts, in simplified form, the organization of the LSI-11 processor. The three chips are the data, control, and control store chips. The data chip contains an 8-bit ALU, twenty-six 8-bit registers, and storage for several condition codes. Sixteen of the registers are used to implement the eight 16-bit general-purpose registers of the PDP-11. Others include a program status word, memory address register (MAR), and memory buffer register. Because the ALU deals with only 8 bits at a time, two passes through the ALU are required to implement a 16-bit PDP-11 arithmetic operation. This is controlled by the microprogram.

The control store chip or chips contain the 22-bit-wide control memory. The control chip contains the logic for sequencing and executing microinstructions. It

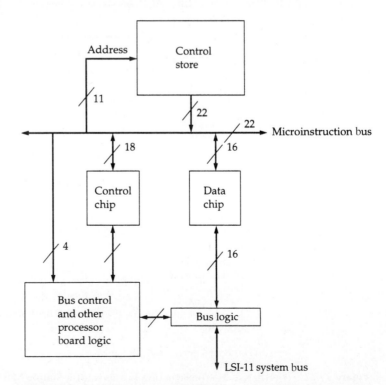

Figure 17.13 Simplified Block Diagram of the LSI-11 Processor

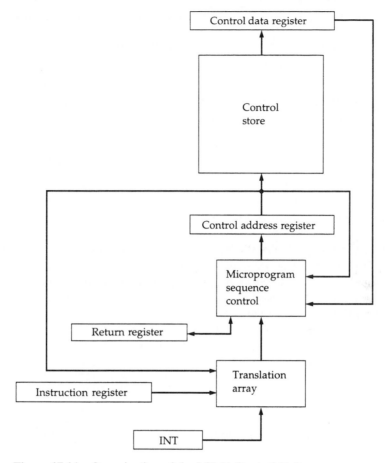

Figure 17.14 Organization of the LSI-11 Control Unit

contains the control address register, the control data register, and a copy of the machine instruction register.

The MIB ties all the components together. During microinstruction fetch, the control chip generates an 11-bit address onto the MIB. Control store is accessed, producing a 22-bit microinstruction, which is placed on the MIB. The low-order 16 bits go to the data chip, while the low-order 18 bits go to the control chip. The high-order 4 bits control special processor board functions.

Figure 17.14 provides a still simplified but more detailed look at the LSI-11 control unit: The figure ignores individual chip boundaries. The address sequencing scheme described in Section 17.2 is implemented in two modules. Overall sequence control is provided by the microprogram sequence control module, which is capable of incrementing the microinstruction address register and performing unconditional branches. The other forms of address calculation are carried out by a separate translation array. This is a combinatorial circuit that generates an address based on the microinstruction, the machine instruction, the microinstruction program counter, and an interrupt register.

The translation array comes into play on the following occasions:

- The opcode is used to determine the start of a microroutine.
- At appropriate times, address mode bits of the microinstruction are tested to perform appropriate addressing.
- Interrupt conditions are periodically tested.
- Conditional branch microinstructions are evaluated.

LSI-11 Microinstruction Format

The LSI-11 uses an extremely vertical microinstruction format, which is only 22 bits wide. The microinstruction set strongly resembles the PDP-11 machine instruction set that it implements. This design was intended to optimize the performance of the control unit within the constraint of a vertical, easily programmed design. Table 17.5 lists some of the LSI-11 microinstructions.

Figure 17.15 shows the 22-bit LSI-11 microinstruction format. The high-order 4 bits control special functions on the processor board. The translate bit enables the translation array to check for pending interrupts. The load return register bit is used at the end of a microroutine to cause the next microinstruction address to be loaded from the return register.

The remaining 16 bits are used for highly encoded micro-operations. The format is much like a machine instruction, with a variable-length opcode and one or more operands.

Table 17.5   Some LSI-11 Microinstructions

Arithmetic Operations	General Operations
Add word (byte, literal)	MOV word (byte)
Test word (byte, literal)	Jump
Increment word (byte) by 1	Return
Increment word (byte) by 2	Conditional jump
Negate word (byte)	Set (reset) flags
Conditionally increment (decrement) byte	Load G low
Conditionally add word (byte)	Conditionally MOV word (byte)
Add word (byte) with carry	**Input/Output Operations**
Conditionally add digits	Input word (byte)
Subtract word (byte)	Input status word (byte)
Compare word (byte, literal)	Read
Subtract word (byte) with carry	Write
Decrement word (byte) by 1	Read (write) and increment word (byte) by 1
Logical Operations	Read (write) and increment word (byte) by 2
AND word (byte, literal)	Read (write) acknowledge
Test word (byte)	Output word (byte, status)
OR word (byte)	
Exclusive-OR word (byte)	
Bit clear word (byte)	
Shift word (byte) right (left) with (without) carry	
Complement word (byte)	

(a) Format of the full LSI-11 microinstruction

Unconditional jump microinstruction format

Conditional jump microinstruction format

Literal microinstruction format

Register microinstruction format

(b) Format of the encoded part of the LSI-11 microinstruction

Figure 17.15 LSI-11 Microinstruction Format

IBM 3033 Microinstruction Execution

The standard IBM 3033 control memory consists of 4K words. The first half of these (0000–07FF) contain 108-bit microinstructions, while the remainder (0800–0FFF) are used to store 126-bit microinstructions. The format is depicted in Figure 17.16. Although this is a rather horizontal format, encoding is still extensively used. The key fields of that format are summarized in Table 17.6.

The ALU operates on inputs from four dedicated, non-user-visible registers, A, B, C, and D. The microinstruction format contains fields for loading these registers from user-visible registers, performing an ALU function, and specifying a user-visible register for storing the result. There are also fields for loading and storing data between registers and memory.

The sequencing mechanism for the IBM 3033 was discussed in Section 17.2.

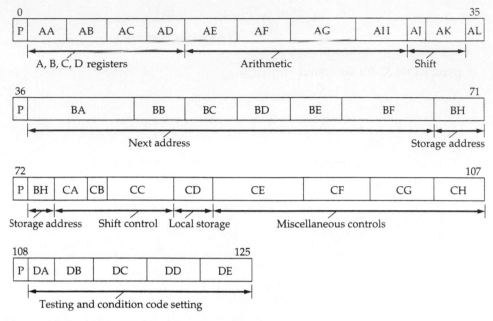

Figure 17.16   IBM 3033 Microinstruction Format

Table 17.6   IBM 3033 Microinstruction Control Fields

ALU Control Fields	
AA(3)	Load A register from one of data registers
AB(3)	Load B register from one of data registers
AC(3)	Load C register from one of data registers
AD(3)	Load D register from one of data registers
AE(4)	Route specified A bits to ALU
AF(4)	Route specified B bits to ALU
AG(5)	Specifies ALU arithmetic operation on A input
AH(4)	Specifies ALU arithmetic operation on B input
AJ(1)	Specifies D or B input to ALU on B side
AK(4)	Route arithmetic output to shifter
CB(1)	Activate shifter
CC(5)	Specifies logical and carry functions
CE(7)	Specifies shift amount
CA(3)	Load F register

Sequencing and Branching Fields	
AL(1)	End operation and perform branch
BA(8)	Set high-order bits (00–07) of control address register
BB(4)	Specifies condition for setting bit 8 of control address register
BC(4)	Specifies condition for setting bit 9 of control address register
BD(4)	Specifies condition for setting bit 10 of control address register
BE(4)	Specifies condition for setting bit 11 of control address register
BF(4)	Specifies condition for setting bit 12 of control address register

17.4 TI 8800

The Texas Instruments 8800 Software Development Board (SDB) is a microprogrammable 32-bit computer card. The system has a writable control store, implemented in RAM rather than ROM. Such a system does not achieve the speed or density of a microprogrammed system with a ROM control store. However, it is useful for developing prototypes and for educational purposes.

The 8800 SDB consists of the following components (Figure 17.17):

- Microcode memory
- Microsequencer
- 32-bit ALU
- Floating-point and integer processor
- Local data memory

Figure 17.17   TI 8800 Block Diagram

Two buses link the internal components of the system. The DA bus provides data from the microinstruction data field to the ALU, the floating-point processor, or the microsequencer. In the latter case, the data consists of an address to be used for a branch instruction. The bus can also be used for the ALU or microsequencer to provide data to other components. The System Y bus connects the ALU and floating-point processor to local memory and to external modules via the PC interface.

The board fits into an IBM PC-compatible host computer. The host computer provides a suitable platform for microcode assembly and debug.

Microinstruction Format

The microinstruction format for the 8800 consists of 128 bits broken down into 30 functional fields, as indicated in Table 17.7. Each field consists of one or more bits, and the fields are grouped into five major categories:

- Control of board
- 8847 floating-point and integer processor chip
- 8832 registered ALU
- 8818 microsequencer
- WCS data field

As indicated in Figure 17.17, the 32 bits of the WCS data field are fed into the DA bus to be provided as data to the ALU, floating-point processor, or microsequencer. The other 96 bits (fields 1–27) of the microinstruction are control signals that are fed directly to the appropriate module. For simplicity, these other connections are not shown in Figure 17.17.

The first six fields deal with operations that pertain to the control of the board, rather than controlling an individual component. Control operations include the following:

- Selecting condition codes for sequencer control. The first bit of field 1 indicates whether the condition flag is to be set to 1 or 0, and the remaining 4 bits indicate which flag is to be set.
- Sending an I/O request to the PC/AT.
- Enabling local data memory read/write operations.
- Determining the unit driving the system Y bus. One of the four devices attached to the bus (Figure 17.17) is selected.

The last 32 bits are the data field, which contain information specific to a particular microinstruction.

The remaining fields of the microinstruction are best discussed in the context of the device that they control. In the remainder of this section, we discuss the microsequencer and the registered ALU. The floating-point unit introduces no new concepts and is skipped.

Microsequencer

The principal function of the 8818 microsequencer is to generate the next microinstruction address for the microprogram. This 15-bit address is provided to the microcode memory (Figure 17.17).

Table 17.7   TI 8800 Microinstruction Format

Field Number	Number of Bits	Description
		Control of Board
1	5	Select condition code input
2	1	Enable/disable external I/O request signal
3	2	Enable/disable local data memory read/write operations
4	1	Load status/do no load status
5	2	Determine unit driving Y bus
6	2	Determine unit driving DA bus
		8847 Floating Point and Integer Processing Chip
7	1	C register control: clock, do not clock
8	1	Select most significant or least significant bits for Y bus
9	1	C register data source: ALU, multiplexer
10	4	Select IEEE or FAST mode for ALU and MUL
11	8	Select sources for data operands: RA registers, RB registers, P register, 5 register, C register
12	1	RB register control: clock, do not clock
13	1	RA register control: clock, do not clock
14	2	Data source confirmation
15	2	Enable/disable pipeline registers
16	11	8847 ALU function
		8832 Registered ALU
17	2	Write enable/disable data output to selected register: most significant half, least significant half
18	2	Select register file data source: DA bus, DB bus, ALU Y MUX output, system Y bus
19	3	Shift instruction modifier
20	1	Carry in: force, do not force
21	2	Set ALU configuration mode: 32, 16, or 8 bits
22	2	Select input to 5 multiplexer: register file, DB bus, MQ register
23	1	Select input to R multiplexer: register file, DA bus
24	6	Select register in file C for write
25	6	Select register in file B for read
26	6	Select register in file A for write
27	8	ALU function
		8818 Microsequencer
28	12	Control input signals to the 8818
		WCS Data Field
29	16	Most significant bits of writable control store data field
30	16	Least significant bits of writable control store data field

The next address can be selected from one of five sources:

1. The microprogram counter (MPC) register, used for repcat (reuse same address) and continue (increment address by 1) instructions.
2. The stack, which supports microprogram subroutine calls as well as iterative loops and returns from interrupts.
3. The DRA and DRB ports, which provide two additional paths from external hardware by which microprogram addresses can be generated. These two ports are connected to the most significant and least significant 16 bits of the DA bus, respectively. This allows the microsequencer to obtain the next instruction address from the WCS data field of the current microinstruction or from a result calculated by the ALU.
4. Register counters RCA and RCB, which can be used for additional address storage.
5. An external input onto the bidirectional Y port to support external interrupts.

Figure 17.18 is a logical block diagram of the 8818. The device consists of the following principal functional groups:

- A 16-bit microprogram counter (MPC) consisting of a register and an incrementer
- Two register counters, RCA and RCB, for counting loops and iterations, storing branch addresses, or driving external devices
- A 65-word by 16-bit stack, which allows microprogram subroutine calls and interrupts
- An interrupt return register and Y output enable for interrupt processing at the microinstruction level
- A Y output multiplexer by which the next address can be selected from MPC, RCA, RCB, external buses DRA and DRB, or the stack

Registers/Counters

The registers RCA and RCB may be loaded from the DA bus, either from the current microinstruction or from the output of the ALU. The values may be used as counters to control the flow of execution and may be automatically decremented when accessed. The values may also be used as microinstruction addresses to be supplied to the Y output multiplexer. Independent control of both registers during a single microinstruction cycle is supported with the exception of simultaneous decrement of both registers.

Stack

The stack allows multiple levels of nested calls or interrupts, and it can be used to support branching and looping. Keep in mind that these operations refer to the control unit, not the overall processor, and that the addresses involved are those of microinstructions in the control memory.

Six stack operations are possible:

1. Clear, which sets the stack pointer to zero, emptying the stack
2. Pop, which decrements the stack pointer

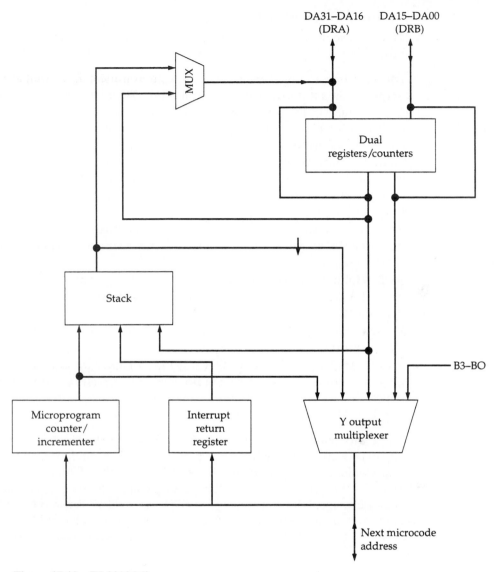

Figure 17.18 TI 8818 Microsequencer

3. Push, which puts the contents of the MPC, interrupt return register, or DRA bus onto the stack and increments the stack pointer

4. Read, which makes the address indicated by the read pointer available at the Y output multiplexer

5. Hold, which causes the address of the stack pointer to remain unchanged

6. Load stack pointer, which inputs the seven least significant bits of DRA to the stack pointer

Control of Microsequencer

The microsequencer is controlled primarily by the 12-bit field of the current microinstruction, field 28 (Table 17.7). This field consists of the following subfields:

- **OSEL (1 bit):** Output select. Determines which value will be placed on the output of the multiplexer that feeds into the DRA bus (upper left-hand corner of Figure 17.18). The output is selected to come from either the stack or from register RCA. DRA then serves as input to either the Y output multiplexer or to register RCA.
- **SELDR (1 bit):** Select DR bus. If set to 1, this bit selects the external DA bus as input to the DRA/DRB buses. If set to 0, selects the output of the DRA multiplexer to the DRA bus (controlled by OSEL) and the contents of RCB to the DRB bus.
- **ZEROIN (1 bit):** Used to indicate a conditional branch. The behavior of the microsequencer will then depend on the condition code selected in field 1 (Table 17.7).
- **RC2–RC0 (3 bits):** Register controls. These bits determine the change in the contents of registers RCA and RCB. Each register can either remain the same, decrement, or load from the DRA/DRB buses.
- **S2–S0 (3 bits):** Stack controls. These bits determine which stack operation is to be performed.
- **MUX2–MUX0:** Output controls. These bits, together with the condition code if used, control the Y output multiplexer and therefore the next microinstruction address. The multiplexer can select its output from the stack, DRA, DRB, or MPC.

These bits can be set individually by the programmer. However, this is typically not done. Rather, the programmer uses mnemonics that equate to the bit patterns that would normally be required. Table 17.8 lists the 15 mnemonics for field 28. A microcode assembler converts these into the appropriate bit patterns.

As an example, the instruction INC88181 is used to cause the next microinstruction in sequence to be selected, if the currently selected condition code is 1. From Table 17.8, we have

$$\text{INC88181} = 000000111110$$

which decodes directly into

- **OSEL = 0:** Selects RCA as output from DRA output MUX; in this case the selection is irrelevant.
- **SELDR = 0:** As defined previously; again, this is irrelevant for this instruction.
- **ZEROIN = 0:** Combined with the value for MUX, indicates no branch should be taken.
- **R = 000:** Retain current value of RA and RC.
- **S = 111:** Retain current state of stack.
- **MUX = 110:** Choose MPC when condition code = 1, DRA when condition code = 0.

Table 17.8 TI 8818 Microsequencer Microinstruction Bits (Field 28)

Mnemonic	Value	Description
RST8818	000000000110	Reset instruction
BRA88181	011000111000	Branch to DRA instruction
BRA88180	010000111110	Branch to DRA instruction
INC88181	000000111110	Continue instruction
INC88180	001000001000	Continue instruction
CAL88181	010000110000	Jump to subroutine at address specified by DRA
CAL88180	010000101110	Jump to subroutine at address specified by DRA
RET8818	000000011010	Return from subroutine
PUSH8818	000000110111	Push interrupt return address onto stack
POP8818	100000010000	Return from interrupt
LOADDRA	000010111110	Load DRA counter from DA bus
LOADDRB	000110111110	Load DRB counter from DA bus
LOADDRAB	000110111100	Load DRA/DRB
DECRDRA	010001111100	Decrement DRA counter and branch if not zero
DECRDRB	010101111100	Decrement DRB counter and branch if not zero

Registered ALU

The 8832 is a 32-bit ALU with 64 registers that can be configured to operate as four 8-bit ALUs, two 16-bit ALUs, or a single 32-bit ALU.

The 8832 is controlled by the 39 bits that make up fields 17 through 27 of the microinstruction (Table 17.7); these are supplied to the ALU as control signals. In addition, as indicated in Figure 17.17, the 8832 has external connections to the 32-bit DA bus and the 32-bit system Y bus. Inputs from the DA can be provided simultaneously as input data to the 64-word register file and to the ALU logic module. Input from the system Y bus is provided to the ALU logic module. Results of the ALU and shift operations are output to the DA bus or the system Y bus. Results can also be fed back to the internal register file.

Three 6-bit address ports allow a two-operand fetch and an operand write to be performed within the register file simultaneously. An MQ shifter and MQ register can also be configured to function independently to implement double-precision 8-bit, 16-bit, and 32-bit shift operations.

Fields 17 through 26 of each microinstruction control the way in which data flow within the 8832 and between the 8832 and the external environment. The fields are as follows:

17. **Write Enable.** These two bits specify write 32 bits, or 16 most significant bits, or 16 least significant bits, or do not write into register file. The destination register is defined by field 24.

18. **Select Register File Data Source.** If a write is to occur to the register file, these two bits specify the source: DA bus, DB bus, ALU output, or system Y bus.

19. **Shift Instruction Modifier.** Specifies options concerning supplying end fill bits and reading bits that are shifted during shift instructions.

20. **Carry In.** This bit indicates whether a bit is carried into the ALU for this operation.

21. **ALU Configuration Mode.** The 8832 can be configured to operate as a single 32-bit ALU, two 16-bit ALUs, or four 8-bit ALUs.

22. **S Input.** The ALU logic module inputs are provided by two internal multiplexers referred to as the S and R multiplexers. This field selects the input to be provided by the S multiplexer: register file, DB bus, or MQ register. The source register is defined by field 25.

23. **R Input.** Selects input to be provided by the R multiplexer: register file or DA bus.

24. **Destination Register.** Address of register in register file to be used for the destination operand.

25. **Source Register.** Address of register in register file to be used for the source operand, provided by the S multiplexer.

26. **Source Register.** Address of register in register file to be used for the source operand, provided by the R multiplexer.

Finally, field 27 is an 8-bit opcode that specifies the arithmetic or logical function to be performed by the ALU. Table 17.9 lists the different operations that can be performed.

Table 17.9   TI 8832 Registered ALU Instruction Field (Field 27)

Group 1		Function
ADD	H#01	R + S + Cn
SUBR	H#02	(NOT R) + S + Cn
SUBS	H#03	R = (NOT S) + Cn
INSC	H#04	S + Cn
INCNS	H#05	(NOT S) + Cn
INCR	H#06	R + Cn
INCNR	H#07	(NOT R) + Cn
XOR	H#09	R XOR S
AND	H#0A	R AND S
OR	H#0B	R OR S
NAND	H#0C	R NAND S
NOR	H#0D	R NOR S
ANDNR	H#0E	(NOT R) AND S

Table 17.9 *(continued)*

Group 2		Function
SRA	H#00	Arithmetic right single precision shift
SRAD	H#10	Arithmetic right double precision shift
SRL	H#20	Logical right single precision shift
SRLD	H#30	Logical right double precision shift
SLA	H#40	Arithmetic left single precision shift
SLAD	H#50	Arithmetic left double precision shift
SLC	H#60	Circular left single precision shift
SLCD	H#70	Circular left double precision shift
SRC	H#80	Circular right single precision shift
SRCD	H#90	Circular right double precision shift
MQSRA	H#A0	Arithmetic right shift MQ register
MQSRL	H#B0	Logical right shift MQ register
MQSLL	H#C0	Logical left shift MQ register
MQSLC	H#D0	Circular left shift MQ register
LOADMQ	H#E0	Load MQ register
PASS	H#F0	Pass ALU to Y (no shift operation)
Group 3		**Function**
SET1	H#08	Set bit 1
Set0	H#18	Set bit 0
TB1	H#28	Test bit 1
TB0	H#38	Test bit 0
ABS	H#48	Absolute value
SMTC	H#58	Sign magnitude/twos complement
ADDI	H#68	Add immediate
SUBI	H#78	Subtract immediate
BADD	H#88	Byte add R to S
BSUBS	H#98	Byte subtract S from R
BSUBR	H#A8	Byte subtract R from S
BINCS	H#B8	Byte increment S
BINCNS	H#C8	Byte increment negative S
BXOR	H#D8	Byte XOR R and S
BAND	H#E8	Byte AND R and S
BOR	H#F8	Byte OR R and S

Table 17.9 *(continued)*

Group 4		Function
CRC	H#00	Cyclic redundancy character accum.
SEL	H#10	Select S or R
SNORM	H#20	Single length normalize
DNORM	H#30	Double length normalize
DIVRF	H#40	Divide remainder fix
SDIVQF	H#50	Signed divide quotient fix
SMULI	H#60	Signed multiply iterate
SMULT	H#70	Signed multiply terminate
SDIVIN	H#80	Signed divide initialize
SDIVIS	H#90	Signed divide start
SDIVI	H#A0	Signed divide iterate
UDIVIS	H#B0	Unsigned divide start
UDIVI	H#C0	Unsigned divide iterate
UMULI	H#D0	Unsigned multiply iterate
SDIVIT	H#E0	Signed divide terminate
UDIVIT	H#F0	Unsigned divide terminate
Group 5		Function
LOADFF	H#0F	Load divide/BCD flip-flops
CLR	H#1F	Clear
DUMPFF	H#5F	Output divide/BCD flip-flops
BCDBIN	H#7F	BCD to binary
EX3BC	H#8F	Excess_3 byte correction
EX3C	H#9F	Excess_3 word correction
SDIVO	H#AF	Signed divide overflow test
BINEX3	H#DF	Binary to excess_3
NOP32	H#FF	No operation

As an example of the coding used to specify fields 17 through 27, consider the instruction to add the contents of register 1 to register 2 and place the result in register 3. The symbolic instruction is

```
CONT11 [17], WELH, SELRYFYMX, [24], R3, R2, R1, PASS+ADD
```

The assembler will translate this into the appropriate bit pattern. The individual components of the instruction can be described as follows:

- CONT11 is the basic NOP instruction.
- Field [17] is changed to WELH (write enable, low and high), so that a 32-bit register is written into
- Field [18] is changed to SELRFYMX to select the feedback from the ALU Y MUX output.
- Field [24] is changed to designate register R3 for the destination register.
- Field [25] is changed to designate register R2 for one of the source registers.
- Field [26] is changed to designate register R1 for one of the source registers.
- Field [27] is changed to specify an ALU operation of ADD. The ALU shifter instruction is PASS; therefore, the ALU output is not shifted by the shifter.

Several points can be made about the symbolic notation. It is not necessary to specify the field number for consecutive fields. That is,

```
CONT11 [17], WELH, [18], SELRFYMX
```

can be written as

```
CONT11 [17], WELH, SELRFYMX
```

because SELRFYMX is in field 18.

ALU instructions from Group 1 of Table 17.9 must always be used in conjunction with Group 2. ALU instructions from Groups 3–5 must not be used with Group 2.

17.5 APPLICATIONS OF MICROPROGRAMMING

Since the introduction of microprogramming, and especially since the late 1960s, the applications of microprogramming have become increasingly varied and widespread. As early as 1971, most if not all of the contemporary uses of microprogramming were in evidence [FLYN71]. Subsequent surveys discuss essentially the same set of applications (e.g., [RAUS80]). The set of current applications for microprogramming includes

- Realization of computers
- Emulation
- Operating system support
- Realization of special-purpose devices
- High-level language support
- Microdiagnostics
- User tailoring

This chapter has been devoted to a discussion of *realization of computers*. The microprogrammed approach offers a systematic technique for control unit implementation. A related technique is *emulation* [MALL75]. Emulation refers to the use of a microprogram on one machine to execute programs originally written for another. The most common use of emulation is to aid users in migrating from one computer to another. This is frequently done by a vendor to make it easier for existing customers to trade in older machines for newer ones, thus making a switch to another vendor unattractive. Users are often surprised to find out how long this transition tool stays around. One observer [MALL83] noted that it was still possible in 1983 to find an IBM System/370 emulating an IBM 1401 that was physically replaced over a decade and a half earlier.

Another fruitful use of microprogramming is in the area of *operating system support*. Microprograms can be used to implement primitives that replace important portions of operating system software. This technique can simplify the task of operating system implementation and improve operating system performance.

Microprogramming is useful as a vehicle for implementing *special-purpose devices* that may be incorporated into a host computer. A good example of this is a data communications board. The board will contain its own microprocessor. Because it is being used for a special purpose, it makes sense to implement some of its functions in firmware rather than software to enhance performance.

High-level language support is another fruitful area for the application of microprogramming techniques. Various functions and data types can be implemented directly in firmware. The result is that it is easier to compile the program into an efficient machine language form. In effect, the machine language is tailored to meet the needs of the high-level language (e.g., FORTRAN, COBOL, Ada).

Microprogramming can be used to support the monitoring, detection, isolation, and repair of system errors. These features are known as *microdiagnostics* and can significantly enhance the system maintenance facility. This approach allows the system to reconfigure itself when failure is detected; for example, if a high-speed multiplier is malfunctioning, a microprogrammed multiplier can take over.

A general category of application is *user tailoring*. A number of machines provide a *writable control store*, that is, a control memory implemented in RAM rather than ROM, and allow the user to write microprograms. Generally, a very vertical, easy-to-use microinstruction set is provided. This allows the user to tailor the machine to the desired application.

17.6 RECOMMENDED READING

There are a number of books devoted to microprogramming. Perhaps the most comprehensive is [LYNC93]. [SEGE91] presents the fundamentals of microcoding and the design of microcoded systems by means of a step-by-step design of a simple 16-bit processor. [CART96] also presents the basic concepts using a sample machine. [PARK89] and [TI90] provide a detailed description of the TI 8800 Software Development Board.

CART96 Carter, J. *Microprocesser Architecture and Microprogramming.* Upper Saddle River, NJ: Prentice Hall, 1996.

LYNC93 Lynch, M. *Microprogrammed State Machine Design.* Boca Raton, FL: CRC Press, 1993.

PARK89 Parker, A., and Hamblen, J. *An Introduction to Microprogramming with Exercises Designed for the Texas Instruments SN74ACT8800 Software Development Board.* Dallas, TX: Texas Instruments, 1989.

SEGE91 Segee, B., and Field, J. *Microprogramming and Computer Architecture.* New York: Wiley, 1991.

TI90 Texas Instruments Inc. *SN74ACT880 Family Data Manual.* SCSS006C, 1990.

17.7 KEY TERMS, REVIEW QUESTIONS, AND PROBLEMS

Key Terms

control memory	microinstruction encoding	microprogrammed control
control word	microinstruction execution	unit
firmware	microinstruction	microprogramming language
hard microprogramming	sequencing	soft microprogramming
horizontal	microinstructions	unpacked microinstruction
microinstruction	microprogram	vertical microinstruction

Review Questions

17.1 What is the difference between a hardwired implementation and a microprogrammed implementation of a control unit?

17.2 How is a horizontal microinstruction interpreted?

17.3 What is the purpose of a control memory?

17.4 What is a typical sequence in the execution of a horizontal microinstruction?

17.5 What is the difference between horizontal and vertical microinstructions?

17.6 What are the basic tasks performed by a microprogrammed control unit?

17.7 What is the difference between packed and unpacked microinstructions?

17.8 What is the difference between hard and soft microprogramming?

17.9 What is the difference between functional and resource encoding?

17.10 List some common applications of microprogramming.

Problems

17.1 Describe the implementation of the multiply instruction in the hypothetical machine designed by Wilkes. Use narrative and a flowchart.

17.2 Assume a microinstruction set that includes a microinstruction with the following symbolic form:

```
IF (AC₀ = 1) THEN CAR ← (C₀₋₆) ELSE CAR ← (CAR) + 1
```

AC_0 is the sign bit of the accumulator and C_{0-6} are the first seven bits of the microinstruction. Using this microinstruction, write a microprogram that implements a Branch Register Minus (BRM) machine instruction, which branches if the AC is negative. Assume that bits C_1 through C_n of the microinstruction specify a parallel set of micro-operations. Express the program symbolically.

17.3 A simple processor has four major phases to its instruction cycle: fetch, indirect, execute, and interrupt. Two 1-bit flags designate the current phase in a hardwired implementation.

a. Why are these flags needed?

b. Why are they not needed in a microprogrammed control unit?

17.4 Consider the control unit of Figure 17.7. Assume that the control memory is 24 bits wide. The control portion of the microinstruction format is divided into two fields. A micro-operation field of 13 bits specifies the micro-operations to be performed. An address selection field specifies a condition, based on the flags, that will cause a microinstruction branch. There are eight flags.

    a. How many bits are in the address selection field?

    b. How many bits are in the address field?

    c. What is the size of the control memory?

17.5 How can unconditional branching be done under the circumstances of the previous problem? How can branching be avoided. That is, describe a microinstruction that does not specify any branch, conditional or unconditional.

17.6 We wish to provide 8 control words for each machine instruction routine. Machine instruction opcodes have 5 bits, and control memory has 1024 words. Suggest a mapping from the instruction register to the control address register.

17.7 An encoded microinstruction format is to be used. Show how a 9-bit micro-operation field can be divided into subfields to specify 46 different actions.

17.8 A processor has 16 registers, an ALU with 16 logic and 16 arithmetic functions, and a shifter with 8 operations, all connected by an internal processor bus. Design a microinstruction format to specify the various micro-operations for the processor.

Parallel Organization

The final part of the book looks at the increasingly important area of parallel organization. In a parallel organization, multiple processing units cooperate to execute applications. Whereas a superscalar processor exploits opportunities for parallel execution at the instruction level, a parallel processing organization looks for a grosser level of parallelism, one that enables work to be done in parallel, and cooperatively, by multiple processors. A number of issues are raised by such organizations. For example, if multiple processors, each with its own cache, share access to the same memory, hardware or software mechanisms must be employed to ensure that both processors share a valid image of main memory; this is known as the cache coherence problem. This design issue, and others, is explored in Part Five.

Chapter 18 Parallel Processing

Chapter 18 provides an overview of parallel processing considerations. Then the chapter looks at three approaches to organizing multiple processors: symmetric multiprocessors (SMP), clusters, and nonuniform memory access (NUMA) machines. SMPs and clusters are the two most common ways of organizing multiple processors to improve performance and availability. NUMA systems are a more recent concept that have not yet achieved widespread commercial success but that show considerable promise. Finally, Chapter 18 looks at the specialized organization known as a vector processor.

CHAPTER 18

PARALLEL PROCESSING

KEY POINTS

♦ A traditional way to increase system performance is to use multiple processors that can execute in parallel to support a given workload. The two most common multiple-processor organizations are symmetric multiprocessors (SMPs) and clusters. More recently, nonuniform memory access (NUMA) systems have been introduced commercially.

♦ An SMP consists of multiple similar processors within the same computer, interconnected by a bus or some sort of switching arrangement. The most critical problem to address in an SMP is that of cache coherence. Each processor has its own cache and so it is possible for a given line of data to be present in more than one cache. If such a line is altered in one cache, then both main memory and the other cache have an invalid version of that line. Cache coherence protocols are designed to cope with this problem.

♦ A cluster is a group of interconnected, whole computers working together as a unified computing resource that can create the illusion of being one machine. The term *whole computer* means a system that can run on its own, apart from the cluster.

♦ A NUMA system is a shared-memory multiprocessor in which the access time from a given processor to a word in memory varies with the location of the memory word.

♦ A special-purpose type of parallel organization is the vector facility, which is tailored to the processing of vectors or arrays of data.

Traditionally, the computer has been viewed as a sequential machine. Most computer programming languages require the programmer to specify algorithms as sequences of instructions. Processors execute programs by executing machine instructions in a sequence and one at a time. Each instruction is executed in a sequence of operations (fetch instruction, fetch operands, perform operation, store results).

This view of the computer has never been entirely true. At the micro-operation level, multiple control signals are generated at the same time. Instruction pipelining, at least to the extent of overlapping fetch and execute operations, has been around for a long time. Both of these are examples of performing functions in parallel. This approach is taken further with superscalar organization, which exploits instruction-level parallelism. With a superscalar machine, there are multiple execution units within a single processor, and these may execute multiple instructions from the same program in parallel.

As computer technology has evolved, and as the cost of computer hardware has dropped, computer designers have sought more and more opportunities for parallelism, usually to enhance performance and, in some cases, to increase availability. After an overview, this chapter looks at three of the most prominent approaches to parallel organization. First, we examine symmetric multiprocessors (SMPs), one of the earliest and still the most common example of parallel organization. In an SMP organization, multiple processors share a common memory. This organization raises the issue of cache coherence, to which a separate section is devoted. Then we describe clusters, which consist of multiple independent computers organized in a cooperative fashion. Clusters have become increasingly common to support workloads that are beyond the capacity of a single SMP. The third approach to the use of multiple processors that we examine is that of nonuniform memory access (NUMA) machines. The NUMA approach is relatively new and not yet proven in the marketplace, but is often considered as an alternative to the SMP or cluster approach. Finally, this chapter looks at hardware organizational approaches to vector computation. These approaches optimize the ALU for processing vectors or arrays of floating-point numbers. They are common on the class of systems known as *supercomputers*.

18.1 MULTIPLE PROCESSOR ORGANIZATIONS

Types of Parallel Processor Systems

A taxonomy first introduced by Flynn [FLYN72] is still the most common way of categorizing systems with parallel processing capability. Flynn proposed the following categories of computer systems:

- **Single instruction, single data (SISD) stream:** A single processor executes a single instruction stream to operate on data stored in a single memory. Uniprocessors fall into this category.
- **Single instruction, multiple data (SIMD) stream:** A single machine instruction controls the simultaneous execution of a number of processing elements on a lockstep basis. Each processing element has an associated data memory, so that each instruction is executed on a different set of data by the different processors. Vector and array processors fall into this category.
- **Multiple instruction, single data (MISD) stream:** A sequence of data is transmitted to a set of processors, each of which executes a different instruction sequence. This structure is not commercially implemented.
- **Multiple instruction, multiple data (MIMD) stream:** A set of processors simultaneously execute different instruction sequences on different data sets. SMPs, clusters, and NUMA systems fit into this category.

With the MIMD organization, the processors are general purpose; each is able to process all of the instructions necessary to perform the appropriate data transformation. MIMDs can be further subdivided by the means in which the processors communicate (Figure 18.1). If the processors share a common memory, then each processor accesses programs and data stored in the shared memory, and processors communicate with each other via that memory. The most common form of such system is known as a **symmetric multiprocessor (SMP)**, which we examine in Section 18.2. In an SMP, multiple processors share a single memory or pool of memory by means of a shared bus or other interconnection mechanism; a distinguishing feature is that the memory access time to any region of memory is approximately the same for each processor. A more recent development is the **nonuniform memory access (NUMA)** organization, which is described in Section 18.5. As the name suggests, the memory access time to different regions of memory may differ for a NUMA processor.

A collection of independent uniprocessors or SMPs may be interconnected to form a **cluster**. Communication among the computers is either via fixed paths or via some network facility.

Parallel Organizations

Figure 18.2 illustrates the general organization of the taxonomy of Figure 18.1. Figure 18.2a shows the structure of an SISD. There is some sort of control unit (CU) that provides an instruction stream (IS) to a processing unit (PU). The processing unit operates on a single data stream (DS) from a memory unit (MU). With an SIMD, there is still a single control unit, now feeding a single instruction stream to multiple PUs. Each PU may have its own dedicated memory (illustrated in Figure 18.2b), or there may be a shared memory. Finally, with the MIMD, there are multiple control units, each feeding a separate instruction stream to its own PU. The MIMD may be a shared-memory multiprocessor (Figure 18.2c) or a distributed-memory multicomputer (Figure 18.2d).

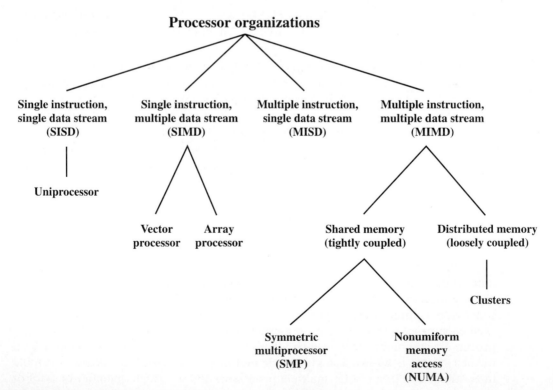

Figure 18.1 A Taxonomy of Parallel Processor Architectures

Figure 18.2 Alternative Computer Organizations

The design issues relating to SMPs, clusters, and NUMAs are complex, involving issues relating to physical organization, interconnection structures, interprocessor communication, operating system design, and application software techniques. Our concern here is primarily with organization, although we touch briefly on operating system design issues.

18.2 SYMMETRIC MULTIPROCESSORS

Until fairly recently, virtually all single-user personal computers and most workstations contained a single general-purpose microprocessor. As demands for performance increase and as the cost of microprocessors continues to drop, vendors have introduced systems with an SMP organization. The term *SMP* refers to a computer hardware architecture and also to the operating system behavior that reflects that architecture. An SMP can be defined as a standalone computer system with the following characteristics:

1. There are two or more similar processors of comparable capability.
2. These processors share the same main memory and I/O facilities and are interconnected by a bus or other internal connection scheme, such that memory access time is approximately the same for each processor.

3. All processors share access to I/O devices, either through the same channels or through different channels that provide paths to the same device.

4. All processors can perform the same functions (hence the term *symmetric*).

5. The system is controlled by an integrated operating system that provides interaction between processors and their programs at the job, task, file, and data element levels.

Points 1 to 4 should be self-explanatory. Point 5 illustrates one of the contrasts with a loosely coupled multiprocessing system, such as a cluster. In the latter, the physical unit of interaction is usually a message or complete file. In an SMP, individual data elements can constitute the level of interaction, and there can be a high degree of cooperation between processes.

The operating system of an SMP schedules processes or threads across all of the processors. An SMP organization has a number of potential advantages over a uniprocessor organization, including the following:

- **Performance:** If the work to be done by a computer can be organized so that some portions of the work can be done in parallel, then a system with multiple processors will yield greater performance than one with a single processor of the same type (Figure 18.3).

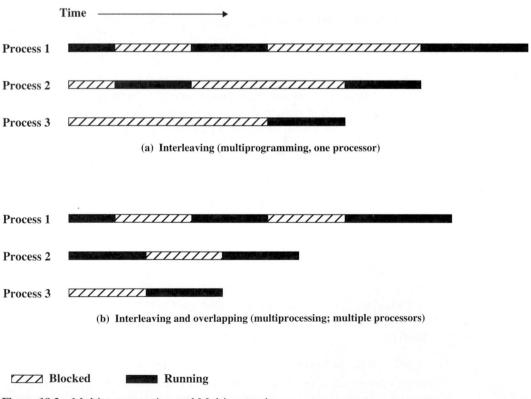

(a) Interleaving (multiprogramming, one processor)

(b) Interleaving and overlapping (multiprocessing; multiple processors)

Blocked   Running

Figure 18.3   Multiprogramming and Multiprocessing

- **Availability:** In a symmetric multiprocessor, because all processors can perform the same functions, the failure of a single processor does not halt the machine. Instead, the system can continue to function at reduced performance.
- **Incremental growth:** A user can enhance the performance of a system by adding an additional processor.
- **Scaling:** Vendors can offer a range of products with different price and performance characteristics based on the number of processors configured in the system.

It is important to note that these are potential, rather than guaranteed, benefits. The operating system must provide tools and functions to exploit the parallelism in an SMP system.

An attractive feature of an SMP is that the existence of multiple processors is transparent to the user. The operating system takes care of scheduling of threads or processes on individual processors and of synchronization among processors.

Organization

Figure 18.4 depicts in general terms the organization of a multiprocessor system. There are two or more processors. Each processor is self-contained, including a con-

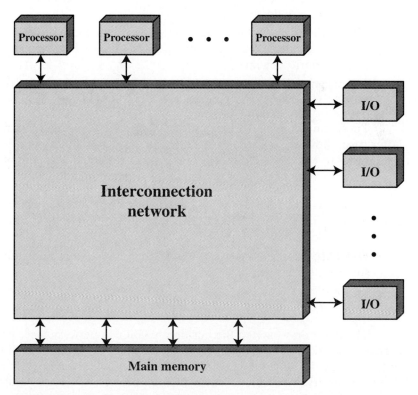

Figure 18.4 Generic Block Diagram of a Tightly Coupled Multiprocessor

trol unit, ALU, registers, and, typically, one or more levels of cache. Each processor has access to a shared main memory and the I/O devices through some form of interconnection mechanism. The processors can communicate with each other through memory (messages and status information left in common data areas). It may also be possible for processors to exchange signals directly. The memory is often organized so that multiple simultaneous accesses to separate blocks of memory are possible. In some configurations, each processor may also have its own private main memory and I/O channels in addition to the shared resources.

Organizational approaches for an SMP can be classified as follows:

- Time-shared or common bus
- Multiport memory
- Central control unit

Time-Shared Bus

The time-shared bus is the simplest mechanism for constructing a multiprocessor system (Figure 18.5). The structure and interfaces are basically the same as for a single-processor system that uses a bus interconnection. The bus consists of control, address, and data lines. To facilitate DMA transfers from I/O processors, the following features are provided:

- **Addressing:** It must be possible to distinguish modules on the bus to determine the source and destination of data.
- **Arbitration:** Any I/O module can temporarily function as "master." A mechanism is provided to arbitrate competing requests for bus control, using some sort of priority scheme.
- **Time sharing:** When one module is controlling the bus, other modules are locked out and must, if necessary, suspend operation until bus access is achieved.

These uniprocessor features are directly usable in an SMP organization. In this latter case, there are now multiple processors as well as multiple I/O processors all attempting to gain access to one or more memory modules via the bus.

The bus organization has several advantages compared with other approaches:

- **Simplicity:** This is the simplest approach to multiprocessor organization. The physical interface and the addressing, arbitration, and time-sharing logic of each processor remain the same as in a single-processor system.
- **Flexibility:** It is generally easy to expand the system by attaching more processors to the bus.
- **Reliability:** The bus is essentially a passive medium, and the failure of any attached device should not cause failure of the whole system.

The main drawback to the bus organization is performance. All memory references pass through the common bus. Thus, the bus cycle time limits the speed of the system. To improve performance, it is desirable to equip each processor with a cache memory. This should reduce the number of bus accesses dramatically. Typ-

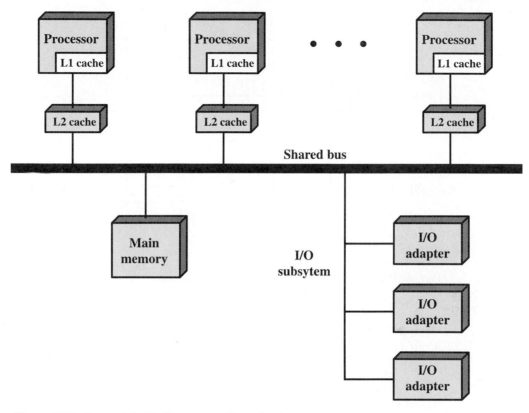

Figure 18.5 Symmetric Multiprocessor Organization

ically, workstation and PC SMPs have two levels of cache, with the L1 cache internal (same chip as the processor) and the L2 cache either internal or external.

The use of caches introduces some new design considerations. Because each local cache contains an image of a portion of memory, if a word is altered in one cache, it could conceivably invalidate a word in another cache. To prevent this, the other processors must be alerted that an update has taken place. This problem is known as the *cache coherence* problem and is typically addressed in hardware rather than by the operating system. We address this issue in Section 18.3.

Multiport Memory

The multiport memory approach allows the direct, independent access of main memory modules by each processor and I/O module (Figure 18.6). Logic associated with memory is required for resolving conflicts. The method often used to resolve conflicts is to assign permanently designated priorities to each memory port. Typically, the physical and electrical interface at each port is identical to what would be seen in a single-port memory module. Thus, little or no modification is needed for either processor or I/O modules to accommodate multiport memory.

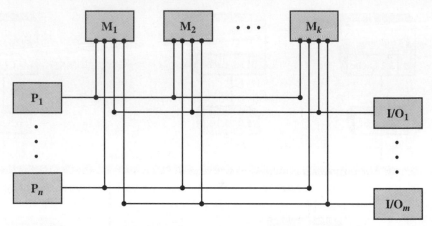

Figure 18.6   Multiport Memory

The multiport memory approach is more complex than the bus approach, requiring a fair amount of logic to be added to the memory system. It should, however, provide better performance because each processor has a dedicated path to each memory module. Another advantage of multiport is that it is possible to configure portions of memory as "private" to one or more processors and/or I/O modules. This feature allows for increasing security against unauthorized access and for the storage of recovery routines in areas of memory not susceptible to modification by other processors.

One other point: A write-through policy should be used for cache control because there is no other convenient means to alert other processors to a memory update.

Central Control Unit

The central control unit funnels separate data streams back and forth between independent modules: processor, memory, I/O. The controller can buffer requests and perform arbitration and timing functions. It can also pass status and control messages between processors and perform cache update alerting.

Because all the logic for coordinating the multiprocessor configuration is concentrated in the central control unit, interfaces from I/O, memory, and processor remain essentially undisturbed. This provides the flexibility and simplicity of interfacing of the bus approach. The key disadvantages of this approach are that the control unit is quite complex and that it is a potential performance bottleneck.

The central control unit structure was once quite common for multiple processor mainframe systems, such as large-scale members of the IBM S/370 family. It is rarely seen today.

Multiprocessor Operating System Design Considerations

An SMP operating system manages processor and other computer resources so that the user perceives a single operating system controlling system resources. In fact, such a configuration should appear as a single-processor multiprogramming system. In both the SMP and uniprocessor cases, multiple jobs or processes may be active at one time, and it is the responsibility of the operating system to schedule their execution and to allocate resources. A user may construct applications that use multiple processes or multiple threads within processes without regard to whether a single processor or multiple processors will be available. Thus a multiprocessor operating system must provide all the functionality of a multiprogramming system plus additional features to accommodate multiple processors. Among the key design issues are the following:

- **Simultaneous concurrent processes:** OS routines need to be reentrant to allow several processors to execute the same IS code simultaneously. With multiple processors executing the same or different parts of the OS, OS tables and management structures must be managed properly to avoid deadlock or invalid operations.
- **Scheduling:** Any processor may perform scheduling, so conflicts must be avoided. The scheduler must assign ready processes to available processors.
- **Synchronization:** With multiple active processes having potential access to shared address spaces or shared I/O resources, care must be taken to provide effective synchronization. Synchronization is a facility that enforces mutual exclusion and event ordering.
- **Memory management:** Memory management on a multiprocessor must deal with all of the issues found on uniprocessor machines, as is discussed in Chapter 8. In addition, the operating system needs to exploit the available hardware parallelism, such as multiported memories, to achieve the best performance. The paging mechanisms on different processors must be coordinated to enforce consistency when several processors share a page or segment and to decide on page replacement.
- **Reliability and fault tolerance:** The operating system should provide graceful degradation in the face of processor failure. The scheduler and other portions of the operating system must recognize the loss of a processor and restructure management tables accordingly.

A Mainframe SMP

Most PC and workstation SMPs use a bus interconnection strategy as depicted in Figure 18.5. It is instructive to look at an alternative approach, which is used for a recent implementation of the IBM S/390 mainframe family [MAK97]. Figure 18.7 depicts the overall organization of the S/390 SMP. This family of systems spans a range from a uniprocessor with one main memory card to a high-end system with ten processors and four memory cards. The configuration includes one or two additional processors that serve as I/O processors. The key components of the configuration are as follows:

- **Processor unit (PU):** This is a CISC microprocessor, in which the most frequently used instructions are hardwired and the rest are executed by firmware. Each PU includes a 64-KB L1 cache that is unified (combined data and instruc-

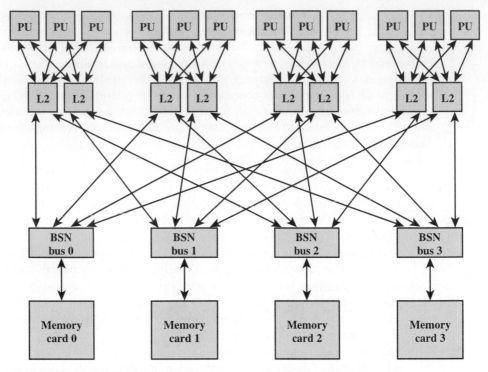

Figure 18.7 IBM S/390 Organization

tion). The L1 cache size was chosen to fit on the PU chip and to achieve a one-cycle access.

- **L2 cache:** Each L2 cache contains 384 kB. The L2 caches are arranged in clusters of two, with each cluster supporting three PUs and providing access to the entire main memory space.
- **Bus-switching network adapter (BSN):** The BSNs interconnect the L2 caches and the main memory. Each BSN also includes a level 3 (L3) cache whose size is 2 MB.
- **Memory card:** Each card holds 8 GB of memory, for a total of 32 GB capacity.

There are a number of interesting features in the S/390 SMP configuration, which we discuss in turn:

- Switched interconnection
- Shared L2 caches
- L3 cache

Switched Interconnection

A single shared bus is a common arrangement on SMPs for PCs and workstations (Figure 18.5). With this arrangement, the single bus becomes a bottleneck affecting the scalability (ability to scale to larger sizes) of the design. The S/390 copes with this problem in two ways. First, main memory is split into four separate cards, each with its own storage controller that can handle memory accesses at high speeds. The average traffic load to main memory is cut by a factor of 4, because of the four independent paths to four separate parts of memory. Second, the connection from processors (actually from L2 caches) to a single memory card is not in the form of a shared bus but rather point-to-point links, where each link connects a group of three processors via an L2 cache to a BSN. The BSN, in turn, performs the function of a switch that can route data among its five links (four L2 links, one memory card). With respect to the four L2 links, the BSN connects the four physical links to one logical data bus. Thus, an incoming signal on any of the four L2 links is echoed back to the remaining three L2 links; this feature is required to support cache coherence.

Note that although there are four separate memory cards, each PU and each L2 cache has only has two physical ports in the direction of main memory. This is because each L2 cache only caches data from half the main memory. A pair of caches is required to service all of main memory, and each PU must connect to both caches in a pair.

Shared L2 Caches

In a typical two-level cache scheme for an SMP, each processor has a dedicated L1 cache and a dedicated L2 cache. In recent years, interest in the concept of a shared L2 cache has been growing. In an earlier version of its S/390 SMP, known as generation 3 (G3), IBM made use of dedicated L2 caches. In its later versions (G4 and G5), a shared L2 cache is used. Two considerations dictated this change:

1. In moving from G3 to G4, IBM doubled the speed of the microprocessors. If the G3 organization was retained, a significant increase in bus traffic would occur. At the same time, it was desired to reuse as many G3 components as possible. Without a significant bus upgrade, the BSNs would become a bottleneck.
2. Analysis of typical S/390 workloads revealed a large degree of sharing of instructions and data among processors.

These considerations led the S/390 G4 design team to consider the use of one or more L2 caches, each of which was shared by multiple processors (each processor having a dedicated on-chip L1 cache). At first glance, sharing an L2 cache might seem a bad idea. Access to memory from processors should be slower because the processors must now contend for access to a single L2 cache. However, if a sufficient amount of data is in fact shared by multiple processors, then a shared cache can increase throughput rather than retard it. Data that are shared and found in the shared cache are obtained more quickly than if they must be obtained over the bus.

One approach considered by the S/390 G4 design time was a single large fully shared cache, used by all processors. While this would have provided improved system performance via higher cache efficiency, this design approach would have required a complete redesign of the existing system bus organization. But performance analysis indicated that introducing cache sharing on each of the existing BSN buses would generate a large percentage of the advantage of shared caches while reducing bus traffic. The value of shared caching was confirmed by performance measurements that showed that the shared cache improved cache hit rates signifi-

Table 18.1   Typical Cache Hit Rate on S/390 SMP Configuration

Memory Subsystem	Access Penalty (PU cycles)	Cache Size	Hit Rate (%)
L1 cache	1	32 KB	89
L2 cache	5	256 KB	5
L3 cache	14	2 MB	3
Memory	32	8 GB	3

cantly over the dedicated cache scheme used in the G3 organization [MAK97]. Studies of the value of shared caches on smaller-scale microprocessor SMPs confirm the value of this approach (e.g., [NAYF96]).

L3 Cache

Another interesting feature of the S/390 SMP is the use of a third level of cache (L3).[1] The L3 caches are located in the BSNs, and therefore each L3 cache provides a buffer between L2 caches and one memory card. The L3 cache reduces latency for the data not kept in the L1 and L2 caches of the requesting processor. It provides the data much more quickly than a main memory access if the requested cache line is already shared by other processors but was not recently used by the requesting processor.

Table 18.1 shows performance results for this three-level cache system for a typical S/390 commercial workload with heavy memory and bus load [DOET97].[2] The storage access penalty is the latency between the data request to the cache hierarchy and the first returned 16-byte data block. The L1 cache produces a hit rate of 89%, so that the remaining 11% of memory references must be resolved at the L2, L3, or memory level. Of this 11%, 5% are resolved at the L2 level, and so on. With three levels of cache, only 3% of references require a memory access. Without the third level, the rate of main memory access doubles.

18.3 CACHE COHERENCE AND THE MESI PROTOCOL

In contemporary multiprocessor systems, it is customary to have one or two levels of cache associated with each processor. This organization is essential to achieve reasonable performance. It does, however, create a problem known as the *cache coherence* problem. The essence of the problem is this: Multiple copies of the same data can exist in different caches simultaneously, and if processors are allowed to

---

[1]IBM's literature refers to this cache as an L2.5 cache. There seems no particular advantage to this term, because in fact this cache constitutes a third level of caching.

[2]The data are for a G3 system, which uses dedicated L2 caches. However, the results are suggestive of the performance to be expected with shared L2 caches, as found on G4 and G5 S/390s.

update their own copies freely, an inconsistent view of memory can result. In Chapter 4 we defined two common write policies:

- **Write back:** Write operations are usually made only to the cache. Main memory is only updated when the corresponding cache line is flushed from the cache.
- **Write through:** All write operations are made to main memory as well as to the cache, ensuring that main memory is always valid.

It is clear that a write-back policy can result in inconsistency. If two caches contain the same line, and the line is updated in one cache, the other cache will unknowingly have an invalid value. Subsequent reads to that invalid line produce invalid results. Even with the write-through policy, inconsistency can occur unless other caches monitor the memory traffic or receive some direct notification of the update.

In this section, we will briefly survey various approaches to the cache coherence problem and then focus on the approach that is most widely used: the MESI (modified/exclusive/shared/invalid) protocol. A version of this protocol is used on both the Pentium 4 and PowerPC implementations.

For any cache coherence protocol, the objective is to let recently used local variables get into the appropriate cache and stay there through numerous reads and write, while using the protocol to maintain consistency of shared variables that might be in multiple caches at the same time. Cache coherence approaches have generally been divided into software and hardware approaches. Some implementations adopt a strategy that involves both software and hardware elements. Nevertheless, the classification into software and hardware approaches is still instructive and is commonly used in surveying cache coherence strategies.

Software Solutions

Software cache coherence schemes attempt to avoid the need for additional hardware circuitry and logic by relying on the compiler and operating system to deal with the problem. Software approaches are attractive because the overhead of detecting potential problems is transferred from run time to compile time, and the design complexity is transferred from hardware to software. On the other hand, compile-time software approaches generally must make conservative decisions, leading to inefficient cache utilization.

Compiler-based coherence mechanisms perform an analysis on the code to determine which data items may become unsafe for caching, and they mark those items accordingly. The operating system or hardware then prevents noncacheable items from being cached.

The simplest approach is to prevent any shared data variables from being cached. This is too conservative, because a shared data structure may be exclusively used during some periods and may be effectively read-only during other periods. It is only during periods when at least one process may update the variable and at least one other process may access the variable that cache coherence is an issue.

More efficient approaches analyze the code to determine safe periods for shared variables. The compiler then inserts instructions into the generated code to enforce cache coherence during the critical periods. A number of techniques have been developed for performing the analysis and for enforcing the results; see [LILJ93] and [STEN90] for surveys.

Hardware Solutions

Hardware-based solutions are generally referred to as cache coherence protocols. These solutions provide dynamic recognition at run time of potential inconsistency conditions. Because the problem is only dealt with when it actually arises, there is more effective use of caches, leading to improved performance over a software approach. In addition, these approaches are transparent to the programmer and the compiler, reducing the software development burden.

Hardware schemes differ in a number of particulars, including where the state information about data lines is held, how that information is organized, where coherence is enforced, and the enforcement mechanisms. In general, hardware schemes can be divided into two categories: directory protocols and snoopy protocols.

Directory Protocols

Directory protocols collect and maintain information about where copies of lines reside. Typically, there is a centralized controller that is part of the main memory controller, and a directory that is stored in main memory. The directory contains global state information about the contents of the various local caches. When an individual cache controller makes a request, the centralized controller checks and issues necessary commands for data transfer between memory and caches or between caches themselves. It is also responsible for keeping the state information up to date; therefore, every local action that can affect the global state of a line must be reported to the central controller.

Typically, the controller maintains information about which processors have a copy of which lines. Before a processor can write to a local copy of a line, it must request exclusive access to the line from the controller. Before granting this exclusive access, the controller sends a message to all processors with a cached copy of this line, forcing each processor to invalidate its copy. After receiving acknowledgments back from each such processor, the controller grants exclusive access to the requesting processor. When another processor tries to read a line that is exclusively granted to another processor, it will send a miss notification to the controller. The controller then issues a command to the processor holding that line that requires the processor to do a write back to main memory. The line may now be shared for reading by the original processor and the requesting processor.

Directory schemes suffer from the drawbacks of a central bottleneck and the overhead of communication between the various cache controllers and the central controller. However, they are effective in large-scale systems that involve multiple buses or some other complex interconnection scheme.

Snoopy Protocols

Snoopy protocols distribute the responsibility for maintaining cache coherence among all of the cache controllers in a multiprocessor. A cache must recognize when a line that it holds is shared with other caches. When an update action is performed on a shared cache line, it must be announced to all other caches by a broadcast mechanism. Each cache controller is able to "snoop" on the network to observe these broadcasted notifications, and react accordingly.

Snoopy protocols are ideally suited to a bus-based multiprocessor, because the shared bus provides a simple means for broadcasting and snooping. However, because one of the objectives of the use of local caches is to avoid bus accesses, care must be taken that the increased bus traffic required for broadcasting and snooping does not cancel out the gains from the use of local caches.

Two basic approaches to the snoopy protocol have been explored: write invalidate and write update (or write broadcast). With a write-invalidate protocol, there can be multiple readers but only one writer at a time. Initially, a line may be shared among several caches for reading purposes. When one of the caches wants to perform a write to the line, it first issues a notice that invalidates that line in the other caches, making the line exclusive to the writing cache. Once the line is exclusive, the owning processor can make cheap local writes until some other processor requires the same line.

With a write-update protocol, there can be multiple writers as well as multiple readers. When a processor wishes to update a shared line, the word to be updated is distributed to all others, and caches containing that line can update it.

Neither of these two approaches is superior to the other under all circumstances. Performance depends on the number of local caches and the pattern of memory reads and writes. Some systems implement adaptive protocols that employ both write-invalidate and write-update mechanisms.

The write-invalidate approach is the most widely used in commercial multiprocessor systems, such as the Pentium 4 and PowerPC. It marks the state of every cache line (using two extra bits in the cache tag) as modified, exclusive, shared, or invalid. For this reason, the write-invalidate protocol is called MESI. In the remainder of this section, we will look at its use among local caches across a multiprocessor. For simplicity in the presentation, we do not examine the mechanisms involved in coordinating among both level 1 and level 2 locally as well as at the same time coordinating across the distributed multiprocessor. This would not add any new principles but would greatly complicate the discussion.

The MESI Protocol

To provide cache consistency on an SMP, the data cache often supports a protocol known as MESI. For MESI, the data cache includes two status bits per tag, so that each line can be in one of four states:

- **Modified:** The line in the cache has been modified (different from main memory) and is available only in this cache.
- **Exclusive:** The line in the cache is the same as that in main memory and is not present in any other cache.
- **Shared:** The line in the cache is the same as that in main memory and may be present in another cache.
- **Invalid:** The line in the cache does not contain valid data.

Table 18.2 MESI Cache Line States

	M Modified	E Exclusive	S Shared	I Invalid
This cache line valid?	Yes	Yes	Yes	No
The memory copy is . . .	out of date	Valid	Valid	—
Copies exist in other caches?	No	No	Maybe	Maybe
A write to this line . . .	Does not go to bus	Does not go to bus	Goes to bus and updates cache	Goes directly to bus

Table 18.2 summarizes the meaning of the four states. Figure 18.8 displays a state diagram for the MESI protocol. Keep in mind that each line of the cache has its own state bits and therefore its own realization of the state diagram. Figure 18.8a shows the transitions that occur due to actions initiated by the processor attached to this cache. Figure 18.8b shows the transitions that occur due to events that are snooped on the common bus. This presentation of separate state diagrams for processor-initiated and bus-initiated actions helps to clarify the logic of the MESI protocol. At any time a cache line is in a single state. If the next event is from the attached processor, then the transition is dictated by Figure 18.8a and if the next event is from the bus, the transition is dictated by Figure 18.8b. Let us look at these transitions in more detail.

Read Miss

When a read miss occurs in the local cache, the processor initiates a memory read to read the line of main memory containing the missing address. The processor inserts a signal on the bus that alerts all other processor/cache units to snoop the transaction. There are a number of possible outcomes:

- If one other cache has a clean (unmodified since read from memory) copy of the line in the exclusive state, it returns a signal indicating that it shares this line. The responding processor then transitions the state of its copy from exclusive to shared, and the initiating processor reads the line from main memory and transitions the line in its cache from invalid to shared.
- If one or more caches have a clean copy of the line in the shared state, each of them signals that it shares the line. The initiating processor reads the line and transitions the line in its cache from invalid to shared.
- If one other cache has a modified copy of the line, then that cache blocks the memory read and provides the line to the requesting cache over the shared bus. The responding cache then changes its line from modified to shared.[3]

---

[3]In some implementations, the cache with the modified line signals the initiating processor to retry. Meanwhile, the processor with the modified copy seizes the bus, writes the modified line back to main memory, and transitions the line in its cache from modified to shared. Subsequently, the requesting processor tries again and finds that one or more processors have a clean copy of the line in the shared state, as described in the preceding point.

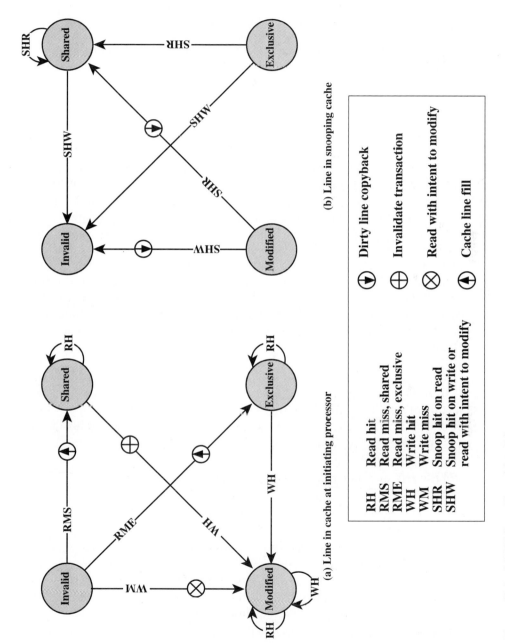

(a) Line in cache at initiating processor

(b) Line in snooping cache

RH	Read hit
RMS	Read miss, shared
RME	Read miss, exclusive
WH	Write hit
WM	Write miss
SHR	Snoop hit on read
SHW	Snoop hit on write or read with intent to modify

⊕ Dirty line copyback

⊕ Invalidate transaction

⊗ Read with intent to modify

⊖ Cache line fill

Figure 18.8 MESI State Transition Diagram

- If no other cache has a copy of the line (clean or modified), then no signals are returned. The initiating processor reads the line and transitions the line in its cache from invalid to exclusive.

Read Hit

When a read hit occurs on a line currently in the local cache, the processor simply reads the required item. There is no state change: The state remains modified, shared, or exclusive.

Write Miss

When a write miss occurs in the local cache, the processor initiates a memory read to read the line of main memory containing the missing address. For this purpose, the processor issues a signal on the bus that means *read-with-intent-to-modify* (RWITM). When the line is loaded, it is immediately marked modified. With respect to other caches, two possible scenarios precede the loading of the line of data.

First, some other cache may have a modified copy of this line (state = modify). In this case, the alerted processor signals the initiating processor that another processor has a modified copy of the line. The initiating processor surrenders the bus and waits. The other processor gains access to the bus, writes the modified cache line back to main memory, and transitions the state of the cache line to invalid (because the initiating processor is going to modify this line). Subsequently, the initiating processor will again issue a signal to the bus of RWITM and then read the line from main memory, modify the line in the cache, and mark the line in the modified state.

The second scenario is that no other cache has a modified copy of the requested line. In this case, no signal is returned, and the initiating processor proceeds to read in the line and modify it. Meanwhile, if one or more caches have a clean copy of the line in the shared state, each cache invalidates its copy of the line, and if one cache has a clean copy of the line in the exclusive state, it invalidates its copy of the line.

Write Hit

When a write hit occurs on a line currently in the local cache, the effect depends on the current state of that line in the local cache:

- **Shared:** Before performing the update, the processor must gain exclusive ownership of the line. The processor signals its intent on the bus. Each processor that has a shared copy of the line in its cache transitions the sector from shared to invalid. The initiating processor then performs the update and transitions its copy of the line from shared to modified.
- **Exclusive:** The processor already has exclusive control of this line, and so it simply performs the update and transitions its copy of the line from exclusive to modified.
- **Modified:** The processor already has exclusive control of this line and has the line marked as modified, and so it simply performs the update.

L1-L2 Cache Consistency

We have so far described cache coherency protocols in terms of the cooperate activity among caches connected to the same bus or other SMP interconnection facility. Typically, these caches are L2 caches, and each processor also has an L1 cache that does not connect directly to the bus and that therefore cannot engage in a snoopy protocol. Thus, some scheme is needed to maintain data integrity across both levels of cache and across all caches in the SMP configuration.

The strategy is to extend the MESI protocol (or any cache coherence protocol) to the L1 caches. Thus, each line in the L1 cache includes bits to indicate the state. In essence, the objective is the following: For any line that is present in both an L2 cache and its corresponding L1 cache, the L1 line state should track the state of the L2 line. A simple means of doing this is to adopt the write-through policy in the L1 cache; in this case the write through is to the L2 cache and not to the memory. The L1 write-through policy forces any modification to an L1 line out to the L2 cache and therefore makes it visible to other L2 caches. The use of the L1 write-through policy requires that the L1 content must be a subset of the L2 content. This in turn suggests that the associativity of the L2 cache should be equal to or greater than that of the L1 associativity. The L1 write-through policy is used in the IBM S/390 SMP.

If the L1 cache has a write-back policy, the relationship between the two caches is more complex. There are several approaches to maintaining coherence. For example, the approach used on the Pentium II is described in detail in [SHAN98].

18.4 CLUSTERS

One of the hottest new areas in computer system design is clustering. Clustering is an alternative to symmetric multiprocessing as an approach to providing high performance and high availability and is particularly attractive for server applications. We can define a cluster as a group of interconnected, whole computers working together as a unified computing resource that can create the illusion of being one machine. The term *whole computer* means a system that can run on its own, apart from the cluster; in the literature, each computer in a cluster is typically referred to as a *node*.

[BREW97] lists four benefits that can be achieved with clustering. These can also be thought of as objectives or design requirements:

- **Absolute scalability:** It is possible to create large clusters that far surpass the power of even the largest standalone machines. A cluster can have dozens of machines, each of which is a multiprocessor.
- **Incremental scalability:** A cluster is configured in such a way that it is possible to add new systems to the cluster in small increments. Thus, a user can start out with a modest system and expand it as needs grow, without having to go through a major upgrade in which an existing small system is replaced with a larger system.
- **High availability:** Because each node in a cluster is a standalone computer, the failure of one node does not mean loss of service. In many products, fault tolerance is handled automatically in software.

- **Superior price/performance:** By using commodity building blocks, it is possible to put together a cluster with equal or greater computing power than a single large machine, at much lower cost.

Cluster Configurations

In the literature, clusters are classified in a number of different ways. Perhaps the simplest classification is based on whether the computers in a cluster share access to the same disks. Figure 18.9a shows a two-node cluster in which the only interconnection is by means of a high-speed link that can be used for message exchange to coordinate cluster activity. The link can be a LAN that is shared with other noncluster computers or it can be a dedicated interconnection facility. In the latter case, one or more of the computers in the cluster will have a link to a LAN or WAN so that there is a connection between the server cluster and remote client systems. Note that in the figure, each computer is depicted as being a multiprocessor. This is not necessary but does enhance both performance and availability.

Figure 18.9 Cluster Configurations

In the simple classification depicted in Figure 18.9, the other alternative is a shared-disk cluster. In this case, there generally is still a message link between nodes. In addition, there is a disk subsystem that is directly linked to multiple computers within the cluster. In this figure, the common disk subsystem is a RAID system. The use of RAID or some similar redundant disk technology is common in clusters so that the high availability achieved by the presence of multiple computers is not compromised by a shared disk that is a single point of failure.

A clearer picture of the range of cluster options can be gained by looking at functional alternatives. Table 18.3 provides a useful classification along functional lines, which we now discuss.

A common, older method, known as **passive standby**, is simply to have one computer handle all of the processing load while the other computer remains inactive, standing by to take over in the event of a failure of the primary. To coordinate the machines, the active, or primary, system periodically sends a "heartbeat" message to the standby machine. Should these messages stop arriving, the standby assumes that the primary server has failed and puts itself into operation. This approach increases availability but does not improve performance. Further, if the only information that is exchanged between the two systems is a heartbeat message, and if the two systems do not share common disks, then the standby provides a functional backup but has no access to the databases managed by the primary.

Table 18.3   Clustering Methods: Benefits and Limitations

Clustering Method	Description	Benefits	Limitations
Passive Standby	A secondary server takes over in case of primary server failure.	Easy to implement.	High cost because the secondary server is unavailable for other processing tasks.
Active Secondary	The secondary server is also used for processing tasks.	Reduced cost because secondary servers can be used for processing.	Increased complexity.
Separate Servers	Separate servers have their own disks. Data are continuously copied from primary to secondary server.	High availability.	High network and server overhead due to copying operations.
Servers Connected to Disks	Servers are cabled to the same disks, but each server owns its disks. If one server fails, its disks are taken over by the other server.	Reduced network and server overhead due to elimination of copying operations.	Usually requires disk mirroring or RAID technology to compensate for risk of disk failure.
Servers Share Disks	Multiple servers simultaneously share access to disks.	Low network and server overhead. Reduced risk of downtime caused by disk failure.	Requires lock manager software. Usually used with disk mirroring or RAID technology.

The passive standby is generally not referred to as a cluster. The term *cluster* is reserved for multiple interconnected computers that are all actively doing processing while maintaining the image of a single system to the outside world. The term **active secondary** is often used in referring to this configuration. Three classifications of clustering can be identified: separate servers, shared nothing, and shared memory.

In one approach to clustering, each computer is a **separate server** with its own disks and there are no disks shared between systems (Figure 18.9a). This arrangement provides high performance as well as high availability. In this case, some type of management or scheduling software is needed to assign incoming client requests to servers so that the load is balanced and high utilization is achieved. It is desirable to have a failover capability, which means that if a computer fails while executing an application, another computer in the cluster can pick up and complete the application. For this to happen, data must constantly be copied among systems so that each system has access to the current data of the other systems. The overhead of this data exchange ensures high availability at the cost of a performance penalty.

To reduce the communications overhead, most clusters now consist of servers connected to common disks (Figure 18.9b). In variation on this approach, called **shared nothing**, the common disks are partitioned into volumes, and each volume is owned by a single computer. If that computer fails, the cluster must be reconfigured so that some other computer has ownership of the volumes of the failed computer.

It is also possible to have multiple computers share the same disks at the same time (called the **shared disk** approach), so that each computer has access to all of the volumes on all of the disks. This approach requires the use of some type of locking facility to ensure that data can only be accessed by one computer at a time.

Operating System Design Issues

Full exploitation of a cluster hardware configuration requires some enhancements to a single-system operating system.

Failure Management

How failures are managed by a cluster depends on the clustering method used (Table 18.3). In general, two approaches can be taken to dealing with failures: highly available clusters and fault-tolerant clusters. A highly available cluster offers a high probability that all resources will be in service. If a failure does occur, such as a system goes down or a disk volume is lost, then the queries in progress are lost. Any lost query, if retried, will be serviced by a different computer in the cluster. However, the cluster operating system makes no guarantee about the state of partially executed transactions. This would need to be handled at the application level.

A fault-tolerant cluster ensures that all resources are always available. This is achieved by the use of redundant shared disks and mechanisms for backing out uncommitted transactions and committing completed transactions.

The function of switching applications and data resources over from a failed system to an alternative system in the cluster is referred to as **failover**. A related function is the restoration of applications and data resources to the original system once it has been fixed; this is referred to as **failback**. Failback can be automated, but this is desirable only if the problem is truly fixed and unlikely to recur. If not, automatic failback can cause subsequently failed resources to bounce back and forth between computers, resulting in performance and recovery problems.

Load Balancing

A cluster requires an effective capability for balancing the load among available computers. This includes the requirement that the cluster be incrementally scalable. When a new computer is added to the cluster, the load-balancing facility should automatically include this computer in scheduling applications. Middleware mechanisms need to recognize that services can appear on different members of the cluster and may migrate from one member to another.

Parallelizing Computation

In some cases, effective use of a cluster requires executing software from a single application in parallel. [KAPP00] lists three general approaches to the problem:

- **Parallelizing compiler:** A parallelizing compiler determines, at compile time, which parts of an application can be executed in parallel. These are then split off to be assigned to different computers in the cluster. Performance depends on the nature of the problem and how well the compiler is designed.
- **Parallelized application:** In this approach, the programmer writes the application from the outset to run on a cluster, and uses message passing to move data, as required, between cluster nodes. This places a high burden on the programmer but may be the best approach for exploiting clusters for some applications.
- **Parametric computing:** This approach can be used if the essence of the application is an algorithm or program that must be executed a large number of times, each time with a different set of starting conditions or parameters. A good example is a simulation model, which will run a large number of different scenarios and then develop statistical summaries of the results. For this approach to be effective, parametric processing tools are needed to organize, run, and manage the jobs in an orderly manner.

Cluster Computer Architecture

Figure 18.10 shows a typical cluster architecture. The individual computers are connected by some high-speed LAN or switch hardware. Each computer is capable of operating independently. In addition, a middleware layer of software is installed in each computer to enable cluster operation. The cluster middleware provides a unified system image to the user, known as a **single-system image**. The middleware is also responsible for providing high availability, by means of load balancing and responding to failures in individual components. [HWAN99] lists the following as desirable cluster middleware services and functions:

- **Single entry point:** A user logs onto the cluster rather than to an individual computer.

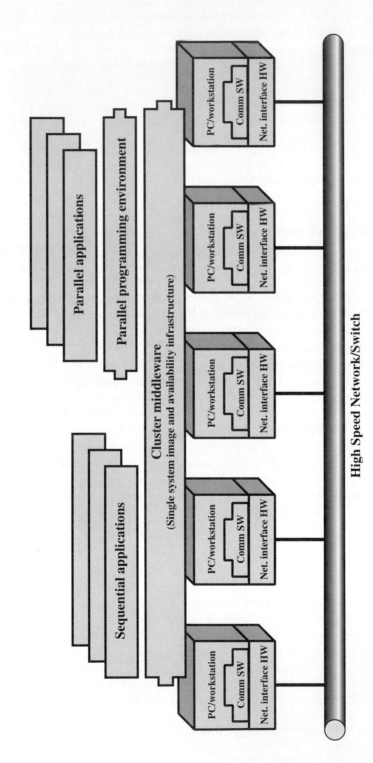

Figure 18.10 Cluster Computer Architecture [BUYY99a]

- **Single file hierarchy:** The user sees a single hierarchy of file directories under the same root directory.
- **Single control point:** There is a default workstation used for cluster management and control.
- **Single virtual networking:** Any node can access any other point in the cluster, even though the actual cluster configuration may consist of multiple interconnected networks. There is a single virtual network operation.
- **Single memory space:** Distributed shared memory enables programs to share variables.
- **Single job-management system:** Under a cluster job scheduler, a user can submit a job without specifying the host computer to execute the job.
- **Single user interface:** A common graphic interface supports all users, regardless of the workstation from which they enter the cluster.
- **Single I/O space:** Any node can remotely access any I/O peripheral or disk device without knowledge of its physical location.
- **Single process space:** A uniform process-identification scheme is used. A process on any node can create or communicate with any other process on a remote node.
- **Checkpointing:** This function periodically saves the process state and intermediate computing results, to allow rollback recovery after a failure.
- **Process migration:** This function enables load balancing.

The last four items on the preceding list enhance the availability of the cluster. The remaining items are concerned with providing a single system image.

Returning to Figure 18.10, a cluster will also include software tools for enabling the efficient execution of programs that are capable of parallel execution.

Clusters versus SMP

Both clusters and symmetric multiprocessors provide a configuration with multiple processors to support high-demand applications. Both solutions are commercially available, although SMP schemes have been around far longer.

The main strength of the SMP approach is that an SMP is easier to manage and configure than a cluster. The SMP is much closer to the original single-processor model for which nearly all applications are written. The principal change required in going from a uniprocessor to an SMP is to the scheduler function. Another benefit of the SMP is that it usually takes up less physical space and draws less power than a comparable cluster. A final important benefit is that the SMP products are well established and stable.

Over the long run, however, the advantages of the cluster approach are likely to result in clusters dominating the high-performance server market. Clusters are far superior to SMPs in terms of incremental and absolute scalability. Clusters are also superior in terms of availability, because all components of the system can readily be made highly redundant.

18.5 NONUNIFORM MEMORY ACCESS

In terms of commercial products, the two common approaches to providing a multiple-processor system to support applications are SMPs and clusters. For some years, another approach, known as nonuniform memory access (NUMA), has been the subject of research and commercial NUMA products are now available.

Before proceeding, we should define some terms often found in the NUMA literature.

- **Uniform memory access (UMA):** All processors have access to all parts of main memory using loads and stores. The memory access time of a processor to all regions of memory is the same. The access times experienced by different processors are the same. The SMP organization discussed in Sections 18.2 and 18.3 is UMA.
- **Nonuniform memory access (NUMA):** All processors have access to all parts of main memory using loads and stores. The memory access time of a processor differs depending on which region of main memory is accessed. The last statement is true for all processors; however, for different processors, which memory regions are slower and which are faster differ.
- **Cache-coherent NUMA (CC-NUMA):** A NUMA system in which cache coherence is maintained among the caches of the various processors.

A NUMA system without cache coherence is more or less equivalent to a cluster. The commercial products that have received much attention recently are CC-NUMA systems, which are quite distinct from both SMPs and clusters. Usually, but unfortunately not always, such systems are in fact referred to in the commercial literature as CC-NUMA systems. This section is concerned only with CC-NUMA systems.

Motivation

With an SMP system, there is a practical limit to the number of processors that can be used. An effective cache scheme reduces the bus traffic between any one processor and main memory. As the number of processors increases, this bus traffic also increases. Also, the bus is used to exchange cache-coherence signals, further adding to the burden. At some point, the bus becomes a performance bottleneck. Performance degradation seems to limit the number of processors in an SMP configuration to somewhere between 16 and 64 processors. For example, Silicon Graphics' Power Challenge SMP is limited to 64 R10000 processors in a single system; beyond this number performance degrades substantially.

The processor limit in an SMP is one of the driving motivations behind the development of cluster systems. However, with a cluster, each node has its own private main memory; applications do not see a large global memory. In effect, coherency is maintained in software rather than hardware. This memory granularity affects performance and, to achieve maximum performance, software must be tailored to this environment. One approach to achieving large-scale multiprocessing while retaining the flavor of SMP is NUMA. For example, the Silicon Graphics Origin NUMA system is designed to support up to 1024 MIPS R10000 processors [WHIT97] and the Sequent NUMA-Q system is designed to support up to 252 Pentium II processors [LOVE96].

The objective with NUMA is to maintain a transparent systemwide memory while permitting multiple multiprocessor nodes, each with its own bus or other internal interconnect system.

Organization

Figure 18.11 depicts a typical CC-NUMA organization. There are multiple independent nodes, each of which is, in effect, an SMP organization. Thus, each node contains multiple processors, each with its own L1 and L2 caches, plus main memory. The node is the basic building block of the overall CC-NUMA organization. For example, each Silicon Graphics Origin node includes two MIPS R10000 processors; each Sequent NUMA-Q node includes four Pentium II processors. The nodes are interconnected by means of some communications facility, which could be a switching mechanism, a ring, or some other networking facility.

Each node in the CC-NUMA system includes some main memory. From the point of view of the processors, however, there is only a single addressable memory, with each location having a unique systemwide address. When a processor initiates a memory access, if the requested memory location is not in that processor's cache, then the L2 cache initiates a fetch operation. If the desired line is in the local portion of the main memory, the line is fetched across the local bus. If the desired line is in a remote portion of the main memory, then an automatic request is sent out to fetch that line across the interconnection network, deliver it to the local bus, and then deliver it to the requesting cache on that bus. All of this activity is automatic and transparent to the processor and its cache.

In this configuration, cache coherence is a central concern. Although implementations differ as to details, in general terms we can say that each node must maintain some sort of directory that gives it an indication of the location of various portions of memory and also cache status information. To see how this scheme works, we give an example taken from [PFIS98]. Suppose that processor 3 on node 2 (P2-3) requests a memory location 798, which is in the memory of node 1. The following sequence occurs:

1. P2-3 issues a read request on the snoopy bus of node 2 for location 798.
2. The directory on node 2 sees the request and recognizes that the location is in node 1.
3. Node 2's directory sends a request to node 1, which is picked up by node 1's directory.
4. Node 1's directory, acting as a surrogate of P2-3, requests the contents of 798, as if it were a processor.
5. Node 1's main memory responds by putting the requested data on the bus.
6. Node 1's directory picks up the data from the bus.
7. The value is transferred back to node 2's directory.

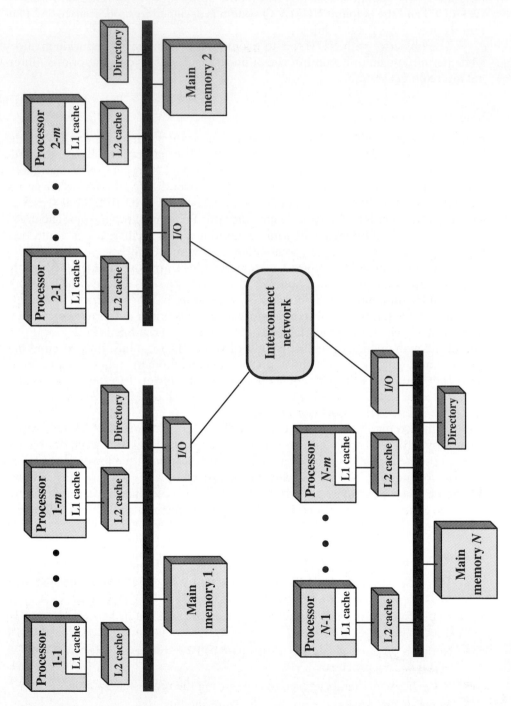

Figure 18.11 CC-NUMA Organization

8. Node 2's directory places the data back on node 2's bus, acting as a surrogate for the memory that originally held it.

9. The value is picked up and placed in P2-3's cache and delivered to P2-3.

The preceding sequence explains how data are read from a remote memory using hardware mechanisms that make the transaction transparent to the processor. On top of these mechanisms, some form of cache coherence protocol is needed. Various systems differ on exactly how this is done. We make only a few general remarks here. First, as part of the preceding sequence, node 1's directory keeps a record that some remote cache has a copy of the line containing location 798. Then, there needs to be a cooperative protocol to take care of modifications. For example, if a modification is done in a cache, this fact can be broadcast to other nodes. Each node's directory that receives such a broadcast can then determine if any local cache has that line and, if so, cause it to be purged. If the actual memory location is at the node receiving the broadcast notification, then that node's directory needs to maintain an entry indicating that that line of memory is invalid and remains so until a write back occurs. If another processor (local or remote) requests the invalid line, then the local directory must force a write back to update memory before providing the data.

NUMA Pros and Cons

The main advantage of a CC-NUMA system is that it can deliver effective performance at higher levels of parallelism than SMP, without requiring major software changes. With multiple NUMA nodes, the bus traffic on any individual node is limited to a demand that the bus can handle. However, if many of the memory accesses are to remote nodes, performance begins to break down. There is reason to believe that this performance breakdown can be avoided. First, the use of L1 and L2 caches is designed to minimize all memory accesses, including remote ones. If much of the software has good temporal locality, then remote memory accesses should not be excessive. Second, if the software has good spatial locality, and if virtual memory is in use, then the data needed for an application will reside on a limited number of frequently used pages that can be initially loaded into the memory local to the running application. The Sequent designers report that such spatial locality does appear in representative applications [LOVE96]. Finally, the virtual memory scheme can be enhanced by including in the operating system a page migration mechanism that will move a virtual memory page to a node that is frequently using it; the Silicon Graphics designers report success with this approach [WHIT97].

There are disadvantages to the CC-NUMA approach as well. Two in particular are discussed in detail in [PFIS98]. First, a CC-NUMA does not transparently look like an SMP; software changes will be required to move an operating system and applications from an SMP to a CC-NUMA system. These include page allocation, already mentioned, process allocation, and load balancing by the operating system. A second concern is that of availability. This is a rather complex issue and depends on the exact implementation of the CC-NUMA system; the interested reader is referred to [PFIS98].

18.6 VECTOR COMPUTATION

Although the performance of mainframe general-purpose computers continues to improve relentlessly, there continue to be applications that are beyond the reach of the contemporary mainframe. There is a need for computers to solve mathematical problems of physical processes, such as occur in disciplines including aerodynamics, seismology, meteorology, and atomic, nuclear, and plasma physics.

Typically, these problems are characterized by the need for high precision and a program that repetitively performs floating-point arithmetic operations on large arrays of numbers. Most of these problems fall into the category known as *continuous-field simulation*. In essence, a physical situation can be described by a surface or region in three dimensions (e.g., the flow of air adjacent to the surface of a rocket). This surface is approximated by a grid of points. A set of differential equations defines the physical behavior of the surface at each point. The equations are represented as an array of values and coefficients, and the solution involves repeated arithmetic operations on the arrays of data.

Supercomputers were developed to handle these types of problems. These machines are typically capable of hundreds of millions of floating-point operations per second and cost in the 10 to 15 million dollar range. In contrast to mainframes, which are designed for multiprogramming and intensive I/O, the supercomputer is optimized for the type of numerical calculation just described.

The supercomputer has limited use and, because of its price tag, a limited market. Comparatively few of these machines are operational, mostly at research centers and some government agencies with scientific or engineering functions. As with other areas of computer technology, there is a constant demand to increase the performance of the supercomputer. Thus, the technology and performance of the supercomputer continues to evolve.

There is another type of system that has been designed to address the need for vector computation, referred to as the *array processor*. Although a supercomputer is optimized for vector computation, it is a general-purpose computer, capable of handling scalar processing and general data processing tasks. Array processors do not include scalar processing; they are configured as peripheral devices by both mainframe and minicomputer users to run the vectorized portions of programs.

Approaches to Vector Computation

The key to the design of a supercomputer or array processor is to recognize that the main task is to perform arithmetic operations on arrays or vectors of floating-point numbers. In a general-purpose computer, this will require iteration through each element of the array. For example, consider two vectors (one-dimensional arrays) of numbers, A and B. We would like to add these and place the result in C. In the example of Figure 18.12, this requires six separate additions. How could we speed up this computation? The answer is to introduce some form of parallelism.

Several approaches have been taken to achieving parallelism in vector computation. We illustrate this with an example. Consider the vector multiplication $C = A \times B$, where A, B, and C are $N \times N$ matrices. The formula for each element of C is

$$\begin{bmatrix} 1.5 \\ 7.1 \\ 6.9 \\ 100.5 \\ 0 \\ 59.7 \end{bmatrix} + \begin{bmatrix} 2.0 \\ 39.7 \\ 1000.003 \\ 11 \\ 21.1 \\ 19.7 \end{bmatrix} = \begin{bmatrix} 3.5 \\ 46.8 \\ 1006.903 \\ 111.5 \\ 21.1 \\ 79.4 \end{bmatrix}$$
$$A \quad + \quad B \quad = \quad C$$

Figure 18.12   Example of Vector Addition

$$c_{i,j} = \sum_{k=1}^{N} a_{i,k} \times b_{k,j}$$

where A, B, and C have elements $a_{i,j}$, $b_{i,j}$, and $c_{i,j}$, respectively. Figure 18.13a shows a FORTRAN program for this computation that can be run on an ordinary scalar processor.

One approach to improving performance can be referred to as *vector processing*. This assumes that it is possible to operate on a one-dimensional vector of data. Figure 18.13b is a FORTRAN program with a new form of instruction that allows

```
        DO 100 I = 1, N
        DO 100 J = 1, N
        C(I, J) = 0.0
        DO 100 K = 1, N
        C(I, J) = C(I, J) + A(I, K) + B(K, J)
100     CONTINUE
```

(a) Scalar processing

```
        DO 100 I = 1, N
        C(I, J) = 0.0 (J = 1, N)
        DO 100 K = 1, N
        C(I, J) = C(I, J) + A(I, K) + B(K, J) (J = 1, N)
100     CONTINUE
```

(b) Vector processing

```
        DO 50 J = 1, N − 1
        FORK 100
50      CONTINUE
        J = N
100     DO 200 I = 1, N
        C(I, J) = 0.0
        DO 200 K = 1, N
        C(I, J) = C(I, J) + A(I, K) + B(K, J)
200     CONTINUE
```

(c) Parallel processing

Figure 18.13   Matrix Multiplication $(C = A \times B)$

vector computation to be specified. The notation (J = 1, N) indicates that operations on all indices J in the given interval are to be carried out as a single operation. How this can be achieved is addressed shortly.

The program in Figure 18.13b indicates that all the elements of the *i*th row are to be computed in parallel. Each element in the row is a summation, and the summations (across K) are done serially rather than in parallel. Even so, only N2 vector multiplications are required for this algorithm as compared with N3 scalar multiplications for the scalar algorithm.

Another approach, *parallel processing,* is illustrated in Figure 18.13c. This approach assumes that we have *N* independent processors that can function in parallel. To utilize processors effectively, we must somehow parcel out the computation to the various processors. Two primitives are used. The primitive FORK *n* causes an independent process to be started at location *n*. In the meantime, the original process continues execution at the instruction immediately following the FORK. Every execution of a FORK spawns a new process. The JOIN instruction is essentially the inverse of the FORK. The statement JOIN N causes *N* independent processes to be merged into one that continues execution at the instruction following the JOIN. The operating system must coordinate this merger, and so the execution does not continue until all *N* processes have reached the JOIN instruction.

The program in Figure 18.13c is written to mimic the behavior of the vector processing program. In the parallel processing program, each column of *C* is computed by a separate process. Thus, the elements in a given row of *C* are computed in parallel.

The preceding discussion describes approaches to vector computation in logical or architectural terms. Let us turn now to a consideration of types of processor organization that can be used to implement these approaches. A wide variety of organizations have been and are being pursued. Three main categories stand out:

- Pipelined ALU
- Parallel ALUs
- Parallel processors

Figure 18.14 illustrates the first two of these approaches. We have already discussed pipelining in Chapter 12. Here the concept is extended to the operation of the ALU. Because floating-point operations are rather complex, there is opportunity for decomposing a floating-point operation into stages, so that different stages can operate on different sets of data concurrently. This is illustrated in Figure 18.15a. Floating-point addition is broken up into four stages (see Figure 9.22): compare, shift, add, and normalize. A vector of numbers is presented sequentially to the first stage. As the processing proceeds, four different sets of numbers will be operated on concurrently in the pipeline.

It should be clear that this organization is suitable for vector processing. To see this, consider the instruction pipelining described in Chapter 12. The processor goes through a repetitive cycle of fetching and processing instructions. In the absence of branches, the processor is continuously fetching instructions from sequential locations. Consequently, the pipeline is kept full and a savings in time is

(a) Pipelined ALU

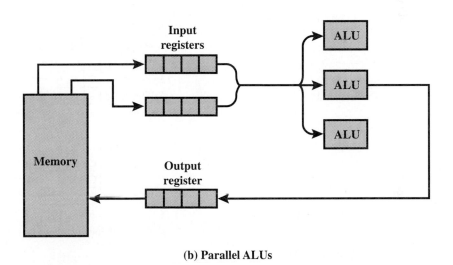

(b) Parallel ALUs

Figure 18.14 Approaches to Vector Computation

achieved. Similarly, a pipelined ALU will save time only if it is fed a stream of data from sequential locations. A single, isolated floating-point operation is not speeded up by a pipeline. The speedup is achieved when a vector of operands is presented to the ALU. The control unit cycles the data through the ALU until the entire vector is processed.

The pipeline operation can be further enhanced if the vector elements are available in registers rather than from main memory. This is in fact suggested by Figure 18.14a. The elements of each vector operand are loaded as a block into a vector

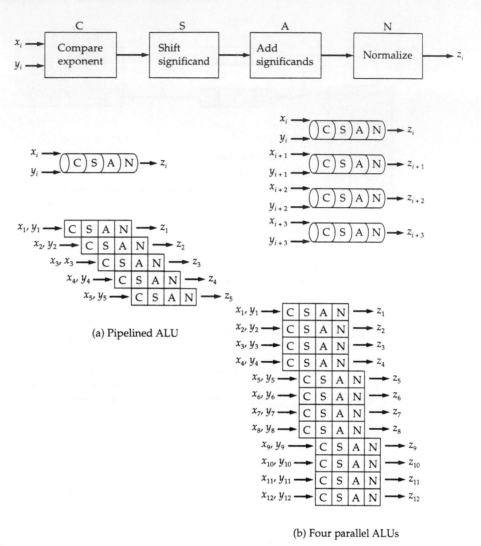

(a) Pipelined ALU

(b) Four parallel ALUs

Figure 18.15 Piplined Processing

register, which is simply a large bank of identical registers. The result is also placed in a vector register. Thus, most operations involve only the use of registers, and only load and store operations and the beginning and end of a vector operation require access to memory.

The mechanism illustrated in Figure 18.15 could be referred to as *pipelining within an operation*. That is, we have a single arithmetic operation (e.g., $C = A + B$) that is to be applied to vector operands, and pipelining allows multiple vector elements to be processed in parallel. This mechanism can be augmented with *pipelining across operations*. In this latter case, there is a sequence of arithmetic vector operations, and instruction pipelining is used to speed up processing. One approach to this, referred to as **chaining**, is found on the Cray supercomputers. The basic rule for chaining is this: A vector operation may start as soon as the first element of the operand vector(s) is available and the functional unit (e.g., add, subtract, multiply, divide) is free. Essentially, chaining causes results issuing from one functional unit to be fed immediately into another functional unit and so on. If vector registers are used, intermediate results do not have to be stored into memory and can be used even before the vector operation that created them runs to completion.

For example, when computing $C = (s \times A) + B$, where A, B, and C are vectors and s is a scalar, the Cray may execute three instructions at once. Elements fetched for a load immediately enter a pipelined multiplier, the products are sent to a pipelined adder, and the sums are placed in a vector register as soon as the adder completes them:

1. Vector load $A \rightarrow$ Vector Register (VR1)
2. Vector load $B \rightarrow$ VR2
3. Vector multiply $s \times$ VR1 $\rightarrow$ VR3
4. Vector add   VR3 + VR2 $\rightarrow$ VR4
5. Vector store   VR4 $\rightarrow$ C

Instructions 2 and 3 can be chained (pipelined) because they involve different memory locations and registers. Instruction 4 needs the results of instructions 2 and 3, but it can be chained with them as well. As soon as the first elements of vector registers 2 and 3 are available, the operation in instruction 4 can begin.

Another way to achieve vector processing is by the use of multiple ALUs in a single processor, under the control of a single control unit. In this case, the control unit routes data to ALUs so that they can function in parallel. It is also possible to use pipelining on each of the parallel ALUs. This is illustrated in Figure 18.15b. The example shows a case in which four ALUs operate in parallel.

As with pipelined organization, a parallel ALU organization is suitable for vector processing. The control unit routes vector elements to ALUs in a round-robin fashion until all elements are processed. This type of organization is more complex than a single-ALU CPI.

Finally, vector processing can be achieved by using multiple parallel processors. In this case, it is necessary to break the task up into multiple processes to be executed in parallel. This organization is effective only if the software and hardware for effective coordination of parallel processors is available.

We can expand our taxonomy of Section 18.1 to reflect these new structures, as shown in Figure 18.16. Computer organizations can be distinguished by the presence of one or more control units. Multiple control units imply multiple processors. Following our previous discussion, if the multiple processors can function cooperatively on a given task, they are termed *parallel processors.*

The reader should be aware of some unfortunate terminology likely to be encountered in the literature. The term *vector processor* is often equated with a pipelined ALU organization, although a parallel ALU organization is also designed

Figure 18.16 A Taxonomy of Computer Organizations

for vector processing, and, as we have discussed, a parallel processor organization may also be designed for vector processing. *Array processing* is sometimes used to refer to a parallel ALU, although, again, any of the three organizations is optimized for the processing of arrays. To make matters worse, *array processor* usually refers to an auxiliary processor attached to a general-purpose processor and used to perform vector computation. An array processor may use either the pipelined or parallel ALU approach.

At present, the pipelined ALU organization dominates the marketplace. Pipelined systems are less complex than the other two approaches. Their control unit and operating system design are well developed to achieve efficient resource allocation and high performance. The remainder of this section is devoted to a more detailed examination of this approach, using a specific example.

IBM 3090 Vector Facility

A good example of a pipelined ALU organization for vector processing is the vector facility developed for the IBM 370 architecture and implemented on the high-end 3090 series [PADE88, TUCK87]. This facility is an optional add-on to the basic system but is highly integrated with it. It resembles vector facilities found on super-computers, such as the Cray family.

The IBM facility makes use of a number of vector registers. Each register is actually a bank of scalar registers. To compute the vector sum $C = A + B$, the vectors A and B are loaded into two vector registers. The data from these registers are passed through the ALU as fast as possible, and the results are stored in a third vector register. The computation overlap, and the loading of the input data into the registers in a block, results in a significant speeding up over an ordinary ALU operation.

Organization

The IBM vector architecture, and similar pipelined vector ALUs, provides increased performance over loops of scalar arithmetic instructions in three ways:

- The fixed and predetermined structure of vector data permits housekeeping instructions inside the loop to be replaced by faster internal (hardware or microcoded) machine operations.
- Data-access and arithmetic operations on several successive vector elements can proceed concurrently by overlapping such operations in a pipelined design or by performing multiple-element operations in parallel.

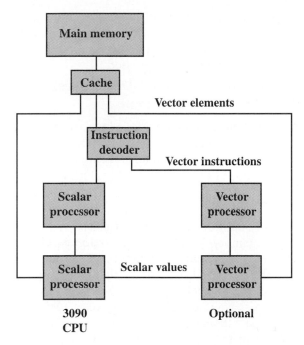

Figure 18.17 IBM 3090 with Vector Facility

- The use of vector registers for intermediate results avoids additional storage reference.

Figure 18.17 shows the general organization of the vector facility. Although the vector facility is seen to be a physically separate add-on to the processor, its architecture is an extension of the System/370 architecture and is compatible with it. The vector facility is integrated into the System/370 architecture in the following ways:

- Existing System/370 instructions are used for all scalar operations.
- Arithmetic operations on individual vector elements produce exactly the same result as do corresponding System/370 scalar instructions. For example, one design decision concerned the definition of the result in a floating-point DIVIDE operation. Should the result be exact, as it is for scalar floating-point division, or should an approximation be allowed that would permit higher-speed implementation but could sometimes introduce an error in one or more low-order bit positions? The decision was made to uphold complete compatibility with the System/370 architecture at the expense of a minor performance degradation.
- Vector instructions are interruptible, and their execution can be resumed from the point of interruption after appropriate action has been taken, in a manner compatible with the System/370 program-interruption scheme.
- Arithmetic exceptions are the same as, or extensions of, exceptions for the scalar arithmetic instructions of the System/370, and similar fix-up routines can

be used. To accommodate this, a vector interruption index is employed that indicates the location in a vector register that is affected by an exception (e.g., overflow). Thus, when execution of the vector instruction resumes, the proper place in a vector register is accessed.

- Vector data reside in virtual storage, with page faults being handled in a standard manner.

This level of integration provides a number of benefits. Existing operating systems can support the vector facility with minor extensions. Existing application programs, language compilers, and other software can be run unchanged. Software that could take advantage of the vector facility can be modified as desired.

Registers

A key issue in the design of a vector facility is whether operands are located in registers or memory. The IBM organization is referred to as *register-to-register,* because the vector operands, both input and output, can be staged in vector registers. This approach is also used on the Cray supercomputer. An alternative approach, used on Control Data machines, is to obtain operands directly from memory. The main disadvantage of the use of vector registers is that the programmer or compiler must take them into account for good performance. For example, suppose that the length of the vector registers is K and the length of the vectors to be processed is $N > K$. In this case, a vector loop must be performed, in which the operation is performed on K elements at a time and the loop is repeated N/K times. The main advantage of the vector register approach is that the operation is decoupled from slower main memory and instead takes place primarily with registers.

The speedup that can be achieved using registers is demonstrated in Figure 18.18 [PADE88]. The FORTRAN routine multiplies vector A by vector B to produce vector C, where each vector has a real part (AR, BR, CR) and an imaginary part (AI, BI, CI). The 3090 can perform one main-storage access per processor, or clock, cycle (either read or write), has registers that can sustain two accesses for reading and one for writing per cycle, and produces one result per cycle in its arithmetic unit. Let us assume the use of instructions that can specify two source operands and a result.[4] Part a of the figure shows that, with memory-to-memory instructions, each iteration of the computation requires a total of 18 cycles. With a pure register-to-register architecture (part b), this time is reduced to 12 cycles. Of course, with register-to-register operation, the vector quantities must be loaded into the vector registers prior to computation and stored in memory afterward. For large vectors, this fixed penalty is relatively small. Figure 18.18c shows that the ability to specify both storage and register operands in one instruction further reduces the time to 10 cycles per iteration. This latter type of instruction is included in the vector architecture.[5]

---

[4]For the 370/390 architecture, the only three-operand instructions (register and storage instructions, RS) specify two operands in registers and one in memory. In part a of the example, we assume the existence of three-operand instructions in which all operands are in main memory. This is done for purposes of comparison and, in fact, such an instruction format could have been chosen for the vector architecture.

[5]Compound instructions, discussed subsequently, afford a further reduction.

FORTRAN ROUTINE:

```
        DO 100 J = 1, 50
        CR(J) = AR(J) * BR(J) – AI(J) * BI(J)
100     CI(J) = AR(J) * BI(J) + AI(J) * BR(J)
```

Operation	Cycles
AR(J) * BR(J) → T1(J)	3
AI(J) * BI(J) → T2(J)	3
T1(J) – T2(J) → CR(J)	3
AR(J) * BI(J) → T3(J)	3
AI(J) * BR(J) → T4(J)	3
T3(J) + T4(J) → CI(J)	3
TOTAL	18

(a) Storage to storage

Operation	Cycles
AR(J) → V1(J)	1
V1(J) * BR(J) → V2(J)	1
AI(J) → V3(J)	1
V3(J) * BI(J) → V4(J)	1
V2(J) – V4(J) → V5(J)	1
V5(J) → CR(J)	1
V1(J) * BI(J) → V6(J)	1
V4(J) * BR(J) → V7(J)	1
V6(J) + V7(J) → V8(J)	1
V8(J) → CI(J)	
TOTAL	10

(c) Storage to register

Vi = Vector registers
AR, BR, AI, BI = Operands in memory
Ti = Temporary locations in memory

Operation	Cycles
AR(J) → V1(J)	1
BR(J) → V2(J)	1
V1(J) * V2(J) → V3(J)	1
AI(J) → V4(J)	1
BI(J) → V5(J)	1
V4(J) * V5(J) → V6(J)	1
V3(J) – V6(J) → V7(J)	1
V7(J) → CR(J)	1
V1(J) * V5(J) → V8(J)	1
V4(J) * V2(J) → V9(J)	1
V8(J) + V9(J) → V0(J)	1
V0(J) → CI(J)	
TOTAL	12

(b) Register to register

Operation	Cycles
AR(J) → V1(J)	1
V1(J) * BR(J) → V2(J)	1
AI(J) → V3(J)	1
V2(J) – V3(J) * BI(J) → V2(J)	1
V2(J) → CR(J)	1
V1(J) * BI(J) → V4(J)	1
V4(J) + V3(J) * BR(J) → V5(J)	1
V5(J) → CI(J)	
TOTAL	8

(d) Compound instruction

Figure 18.18   Alternative Programs for Vector Calculation

Figure 18.19 illustrates the registers that are part of the IBM 3090 vector facility. There are sixteen 32-bit vector registers. The vector registers can also be coupled to form eight 64-bit vector registers. Any register element can hold an integer or floating-point value. Thus, the vector registers may be used for 32-bit and 64-bit integer values, and 32-bit and 64-bit floating-point values.

The architecture specifies that each register contains from 8 to 512 scalar elements. The choice of actual length involves a design trade-off. The time to do a vector operation consists essentially of the overhead for pipeline startup and register filling plus one cycle per vector element. Thus, the use of a large number of register elements reduces the relative startup time for a computation. However, this efficiency must be balanced against the added time required for saving and restoring vector reg-

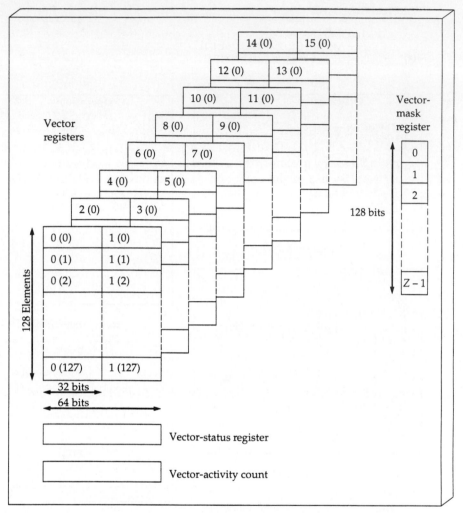

Figure 18.19 Registers of the IBM 3090 Vector Facility

isters on a process switch and the practical cost and space limits. These considerations led to the use of 128 elements per register in the current 3090 implementation.

Three additional registers are needed by the vector facility. The vector-mask register contains mask bits that may be used to select which elements in the vector registers are to be processed for a particular operation. The vector-status register contains control fields, such as the vector count, that determine how many elements in the vector registers are to be processed. The vector-activity count keeps track of the time spent executing vector instructions.

Compound Instructions

As was discussed previously, instruction execution can be overlapped using chaining to improve performance. The designers of the IBM vector facility chose not to include this capability for several reasons. The System/370 architecture would have to be extended to handle complex interruptions (including their effect on virtual memory management), and corresponding changes would be needed in the software. A more basic issue was the cost of including the additional controls and register access paths in the vector facility for generalized chaining.

Instead, three operations are provided that combine into one instruction (one opcode) the most common sequences in vector computation, namely multiplication followed by addition, subtraction, or summation. The storage-to-register MULTIPLY-AND-ADD instruction, for example, fetches a vector from storage, multiplies it by a vector from a register, and adds the product to a third vector in a register. By use of the compound instructions MULTIPLY-AND-ADD and MULTIPLY-AND-SUBTRACT in the example of Figure 18.18, the total time for the iteration is reduced from 10 to 8 cycles.

Unlike chaining, compound instructions do not require the use of additional registers for temporary storage of intermediate results, and they require one less register access. For example, consider the following chain:

$$A \rightarrow VR1$$
$$VR1 + VR2 \rightarrow VR1$$

In this case, two stores to the vector register VR1 are required. In the IBM architecture there is a storage-to-register ADD instruction. With this instruction, only the sum is placed in VR1. The compound instruction also avoids the need to reflect in the machine-state description the concurrent execution of a number of instructions, which simplifies status saving and restoring by the operating system and the handling of interrupts.

The Instruction Set

Table 18.4 summarizes the arithmetic and logical operations that are defined for the vector architecture. In addition, there are memory-to-register load and register-to-memory store instructions. Note that many of the instructions use a three-operand format. Also, many instructions have a number of variants, depending on the location of the operands. A source operand may be a vector register (V), storage (S), or a scalar register (Q). The target is always a vector register, except for comparison, the result of which goes into the vector-mask register. With all these variants, the total number of opcodes (distinct instructions) is 171. This rather large number, however, is not as expensive to implement as might be imagined. Once the machine provides the arithmetic units and the data paths to feed operands from storage, scalar registers, and vector registers to the vector pipelines, the major hardware cost has been incurred. The architecture can, with little difference in cost, provide a rich set of variants on the use of those registers and pipelines.

Most of the instructions in Table 18.4 are self-explanatory. The two summation instructions warrant further explanation. The accumulate operation adds together the elements of a single vector (ACCUMULATE) or the elements of the product of two vectors (MULTIPLY-AND-ACCUMULATE). These instructions present an interesting design problem. We would like to perform this operation as rapidly as possible, taking full advantage of the ALU pipeline. The difficulty is that

Table 18.4 IBM 3090 Vector Facility: Arithmetic and Logical Instructions

Operation	Data Types Floating Point — Long	Short	Binary or Logical	Operand Locations			
Add	FL	FS	BI	$V+V \rightarrow V$	$V+S \rightarrow V$	$Q+V \rightarrow V$	$Q+S \rightarrow V$
Subtract	FL	FS	BI	$V-V \rightarrow V$	$V-S \rightarrow V$	$Q-V \rightarrow V$	$Q-S \rightarrow V$
Multiply	FL	FS	BI	$V \times V \rightarrow V$	$V \times S \rightarrow V$	$Q \times V \rightarrow V$	$Q \times S \rightarrow V$
Divide	FL	FS	—	$V/V \rightarrow V$	$V/S \rightarrow V$	$Q/V \rightarrow V$	$Q/S \rightarrow V$
Compare	FL	FS	BI	$V \cdot V \rightarrow V$	$V \cdot S \rightarrow V$	$Q \cdot V \rightarrow V$	$Q \cdot S \rightarrow V$
Multiply and Add	FL	FS	—		$V+V \times S \rightarrow V$	$V+Q \times V \rightarrow V$	$V+Q \times S \rightarrow V$
Multiply and Subtract	FL	FS	—		$V-V \times S \rightarrow V$	$V-Q \times V \rightarrow V$	$V-Q \times S \rightarrow V$
Multiply and Accumulate	FL	FS	—	$P+V \rightarrow V$	$P+ \cdot S \cdot V$		
Complement	FL	FS	BI	$-V \rightarrow V$			
Positive Absolute	FL	FS	BI	$|V| \rightarrow V$			
Negative Absolute	FL	FS	BI	$-|V| \rightarrow V$			
Maximum	FL	FS	—			$Q \cdot V \rightarrow Q$	
Maximum Absolute	FL	FS	—			$Q \cdot V \rightarrow Q$	
Minimum	FL	FS	—			$Q \cdot V \rightarrow Q$	
Shift Left Logical	—	—	LO	$\cdot V \rightarrow V$			
Shift Right Logical	—	—	LO	$\cdot V \rightarrow V$			
And	—	—	LO	$V \& V \rightarrow V$	$V \& S \rightarrow V$	$Q \& V \rightarrow V$	$Q \& S \rightarrow V$
OR	—	—	LO	$V | V \rightarrow V$	$V | S \rightarrow V$	$Q | V \rightarrow V$	$Q | S \rightarrow V$
Exclusive-OR	—	—	LO	$V \oplus V \rightarrow V$	$V \oplus S \rightarrow V$	$Q \oplus V \rightarrow V$	$Q \oplus S \rightarrow V$

Explanation:

Data Types
FL Long floating point
FS Short floating point
BI Binary integer
LO Logical

Operand Locations
V Vector register
S Storage
Q Scalar (general or floating-point register)
P Partial sums in vector register
· Special operation

the sum of two numbers put into the pipeline is not available until several cycles later. Thus, the third element in the vector cannot be added to the sum of the first two elements until those two elements have gone through the entire pipeline. To overcome this problem, the elements of the vector are added in such a way as to produce four partial sums. In particular, elements 0, 4, 8, 12, . . . , 124 are added in that order to produce partial sum 0; elements 1, 5, 9, 13, . . . , 125 to partial sum 1; elements 2, 6, 10, 14, . . . , 126 to partial sum 2; and elements 3, 7, 11, 15, . . . , 127 to partial sum 4. Each of these partial sums can proceed through the pipeline at top speed, because the delay in the pipeline is roughly four cycles. A separate vector register is used to hold the partial sums. When all elements of the original vector have been processed, the four partial sums are added together to produce the final result. The performance of this second phase is not critical, because only four vector elements are involved.

18.7 RECOMMENDED READING

[CATA94] surveys the principles of multiprocessors and examines SPARC-based SMPs in detail. SMPs are also covered in some detail in [STON93] and [HWAN93].

[MILE00] is an overview of cache coherence algorithms and techniques for multiprocessors, with an emphasis on performance issues. Another survey of the issues relating to cache coherence in multiprocessors is [LILJ93]. [TOMA93] contains reprints of many of the key papers on the subject.

[PFIS98] is essential reading for anyone interested in clusters; the book covers the hardware and software design issues and contrasts clusters with SMPs and NUMAs; the book also contains a solid technical description of SMP and NUMA design issues. A thorough treatment of clusters can be found in [BUYY99a] and [BUYY99b]. [WEYG01] is a less technical survey of clusters, with good commentary on various commercial products.

Good discussions of vector computation can be found in [STON93] and [HWAN93].

BUYY99a Buyya, R. *High Performance Cluster Computing: Architectures and Systems.* Upper Saddle River, NJ: Prentice Hall, 1999.

BUYY99b Buyya, R. *High Performance Cluster Computing: Programming and Applications.* Upper Saddle River, NJ: Prentice Hall, 1999.

CATA94 Catanzaro, B. *Multiprocessor System Architectures.* Mountain View, CA: Sunsoft Press, 1994.

HWAN93 Hwang, K. *Advanced Computer Architecture.* New York: McGraw-Hill, 1993.

LILJ93 Lilja, D. "Cache Coherence in Large-Scale Shared-Memory Multiprocessors: Issues and Comparisons." *ACM Computing Surveys,* September 1993.

MILE00 Milenkovic, A. "Achieving High Performance in Bus-Based Shared-Memory Multiprocessors." *IEEE Concurrency*, July–September 2000.

PFIS98 Pfister, G. *In Search of Clusters.* Upper Saddle River, NJ: Prentice Hall, 1998.

STON93 Stone, H. *High-Performance Computer Architecture.* Reading, MA: Addison-Wesley, 1993.

TOMA93 Tomasevic, M., and Milutinovic, V. *The Cache Coherence Problem in Shared-Memory Multiprocessors: Hardware Solutions.* Los Alamitos, CA: IEEE Computer Society Press, 1993.

WEYG01 Weygant, P. *Clusters for High Availability.* Upper Saddle River, NJ: Prentice Hall, 2001.

18.8 KEY TERMS, REVIEW QUESTIONS, AND PROBLEMS

Key Terms

active standby	MESI protocol	symmetric multiprocessor
cache coherence	multiprocessor	(SMP)
cluster	nonuniform memory	uniform memory access
directory protocol	access (NUMA)	(UMA)
failback	passive standby	uniprocessor
failover	snoopy protocol	vector facility

Review Questions

18.1 List and briefly define three types of computer system organization.

18.2 What are the chief characteristics of an SMP?

18.3 What are some of the potential advantages of an SMP compared with a uniprocessor?

18.4 What are some of the key OS design issues for an SMP?

18.5 What is the difference between software and hardware cache coherent schemes?

18.6 What is the meaning of each of the four states in the MESI protocol?

18.7 What are some of the key benefits of clustering?

18.8 What is the difference between failover and failback?

18.9 What are the differences among UMA, NUMA, and CC-NUMA?

Problems

18.1 Let α be the percentage of program code that can be executed simultaneously by n processors in a computer system. Assume that the remaining code must be executed sequentially by a single processor. Each processor has an execution rate of x MIPS.

 a. Derive an expression for the effective MIPS rate when using the system for exclusive execution of this program, in terms of n, α, and x.

 b. If $n = 16$ and $x = 4$ MIPS, determine the value of α that will yield a system performance of 40 MIPS.

18.2 A multiprocessor with eight processors has 20 attached tape drives. There are a large number of jobs submitted to the system that each require a maximum of four tape drives to complete execution. Assume that each job starts running with only three tape drives for a long period before requiring the fourth tape drive for a short period toward the end of its operation. Also assume an endless supply of such jobs.

 a. Assume the scheduler in the OS will not start a job unless there are four tape drives available. When a job is started, four drives are assigned immediately and are not released until the job finishes. What is the maximum number of jobs that can be in progress at once? What are the maximum and minimum number of tape drives that may be left idle as a result of this policy?

 b. Suggest an alternative policy to improve tape drive utilization and at the same time avoid system deadlock. What is the maximum number of jobs that can be in progress at once? What are the bounds on the number of idling tape drives?

18.3 Can you foresee any problem with the write-once cache approach on bus-based multiprocessors? If so, suggest a solution.

18.4 Consider a situation in which two processors in an SMP configuration, over time, require access to the same line of data from main memory. Both processors have a cache and use the MESI protocol. Initially, both caches have an invalid copy of the line.

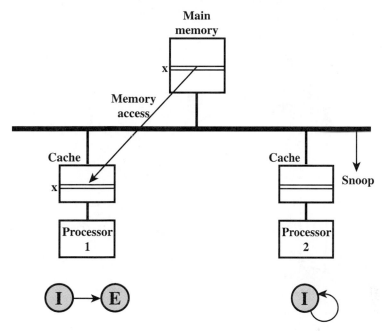

Figure 18.20 MESI Example: Processor 1 Rads Line x

Figure 18.20 depicts the consequence of a read of line x by Processor P1. If this is the start of a sequence of accesses, draw the subsequent figures for the following sequence:

1. P2 reads x.

2. P1 writes to x (for clarity, label the line in P1's cache x').

3. P1 writes to x (label the line in P1's cache x").

4. P2 reads x.

18.5 Figure 18.21 shows the state diagrams of two possible cache coherence protocols. Deduce and explain each protocol, and compare each to MESI.

18.6 Consider an SMP with both L1 and L2 caches using the MESI protocol. As explained in Section 18.3, one of four states is associated with each line in the L2 cache. Are all four states also needed for each line in the L1 cache? If so, why? If not, explain which state or states can be eliminated.

18.7 Table 18.1 shows the performance of a three-level cache arrangement for the IBM S/390. The purpose of this problem is to determine whether the inclusion of the third level of cache seems worthwhile. Determine the access penalty (average number of PU cycles) for a system with only an L1 cache, and normalize that value to 1.0. Then determine the normalized access penalty when both an L1 and L2 cache are used, and the access penalty when all three caches are used. Note the amount of improvement in each case and state your opinion on the value of the L3 cache.

18.8 The following code segment needs to be executed 64 times for the evaluation of the vector arithmetic expression: $D(I) = A(I) + B(I) \times C(I)$ for $0 \le I \le 63$.

```
Load   R1, B(I)      /R1 ← Memory (α + I)/
Load   R2, C(I)      /R2 ← Memory (β + I)/
Multiply R1, R2      /R1 ← (R1) × (R2)/
Load   R3, A(I)      /R3 ← Memory (γ + I)/
Add    R3, R1        /R3 ← (R3) + (R1)/
Load   D1, R3        /Memory (θ + I) ← (R3)/
```

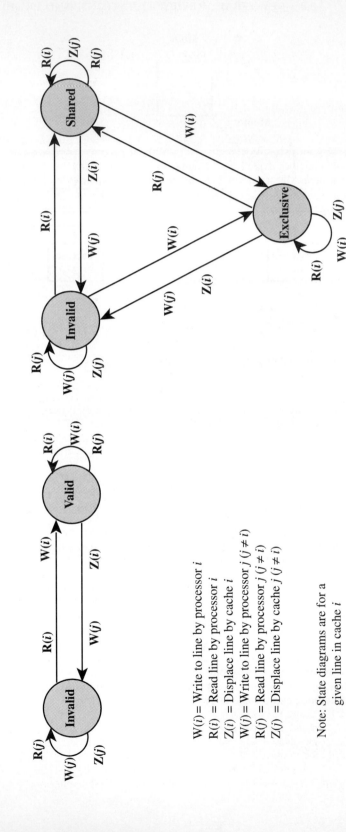

$W(i)$ = Write to line by processor i
$R(i)$ = Read line by processor i
$Z(i)$ = Displace line by cache i
$W(j)$ = Write to line by processor j $(j \neq i)$
$R(j)$ = Read line by processor j $(j \neq i)$
$Z(j)$ = Displace line by cache j $(j \neq i)$

Note: State diagrams are for a
given line in cache i

Figure 18.21 Two Cache Coherence Protocols

where R1, R2, and R3 are processor registers, and α, α, γ, θ are the starting main memory addresses of arrays B(I), C(I), A(I), and D(I), respectively. Assume four clock cycles for each Load or Store, two cycles for the Add, and eight cycles for the Multiplier on either a uniprocessor or a single processor in an SIMD machine.

a. Calculate the total number of processor cycles needed to execute this code segment repeatedly 64 times on a SISD uniprocessor computer sequentially, ignoring all other time delays.

b. Consider the use of an SIMD computer with 64 processing elements to execute the vector operations in six synchronized vector instructions over 64-component vector data and both driven by the same-speed clock. Calculate the total execution time on the SIMD machine, ignoring instruction broadcast and other delays.

c. What is the speedup gain of the SIMD computer over the SISD computer?

18.9 Produce a vectorized version of the following program:

```
            DO 20 I = 1, N
            B(I, 1) = 0
            DO 10 J = 1, M
            A(I) = A(I) + B(I, J) × C(I, J)
     10     CONTINUE
            D(I) = E(I) + A(I)
     20     CONTINUE
```

18.10 An application program is executed on a nine-computer cluster. A benchmark program took time T on this cluster. Further, it was found that 25% of T was time in which the application was running simultaneously on all nine computers. The remaining time, the application had to run on a single computer.

a. Calculate the effective speedup under the aforementioned condition as compared with executing the program on a single computer. Also calculate α, the percentage of code that has been parallelized (programmed or compiled so as to use the cluster mode) in the preceding program.

b. Suppose that we are able to effectively use 18 computers rather than 9 computers on the parallelized portion of the code. Calculate the effective speedup that is achieved.

18.11 The following FORTRAN program is to be executed on a computer, and a parallel version is to be executed on a 32-computer cluster.

```
L1:             DO 10 I = 1, 1024
L2:                 SUM(I) = 0
L3:                 DO 20 J = 1, I
L4:     20              SUM(I) = SUM(I) + I
L5:     10      CONTINUE
```

Suppose lines 2 and 4 each take two machine cycle times, including all processor and memory-access activities. Ignore the overhead caused by the software loop control statements (lines 1, 3, 5) and all other system overhead and resource conflicts.

a. What is the total execution time (in machine cycle times) of the program on a single computer?

b. Divide the I-loop iterations among the 32 computers as follows: Computer 1 executes the first 32 iterations (I = 1 to 32), processor 2 executes the next 32 iterations, and so on. What are the execution time and speedup factor compared with part (a)? (Note that the computational workload, dictated by the J-loop, is unbalanced among the computers.)

c. Explain how to modify the parallelizing to facilitate a balanced parallel execution of all the computational workload over 32 computers. By a balanced load is meant an equal number of additions assigned to each computer with respect to both loops.

d. What is the minimum execution time resulting from the parallel execution on 32 computers? What is the resulting speedup over a single computer?

APPENDIX A

DIGITAL LOGIC

T he operation of the digital computer is based on the storage and processing of binary data. Throughout this book, we have assumed the existence of storage elements that can exist in one of two stable states and of circuits that can operate on binary data under the control of control signals to implement the various computer functions. In this appendix, we suggest how these storage elements and circuits can be implemented in digital logic, specifically with combinational and sequential circuits. The appendix begins with a brief review of Boolean algebra, which is the mathematical foundation of digital logic. Next, the concept of a gate is introduced. Finally, combinational and sequential circuits, which are constructed from gates, are described.

A.1 BOOLEAN ALGEBRA

The digital circuitry in digital computers and other digital systems is designed, and its behavior is analyzed, with the use of a mathematical discipline known as *Boolean algebra*. The name is in honor of an English mathematician George Boole, who proposed the basic principles of this algebra in 1854 in his treatise, *An Investigation of the Laws of Thought on Which to Found the Mathematical Theories of Logic and Probabilities.* In 1938, Claude Shannon, a research assistant in the Electrical Engineering Department at M.I.T., suggested that Boolean algebra could be used to solve problems in relay-switching circuit design [SHAN38]. Shannon's techniques were subsequently used in the analysis and design of electronic digital circuits. Boolean algebra turns out to be a convenient tool in two areas:

- **Analysis:** It is an economical way of describing the function of digital circuitry.
- **Design:** Given a desired function, Boolean algebra can be applied to develop a simplified implementation of that function.

As with any algebra, Boolean algebra makes use of variables and operations. In this case, the variables and operations are logical variables and operations. Thus, a variable may take on the value 1 (TRUE) or 0 (FALSE). The basic logical operations are AND, OR, and NOT, which are symbolically represented by dot, plus sign, and overbar:

$$A \text{ AND } B = A \cdot B$$
$$A \text{ OR } B = A + B$$
$$\text{NOT } A = \overline{A}$$

The operation AND yields true (binary value 1) if and only if both of its operands are true. The operation OR yields true if either or both of its operands are true. The unary operation NOT inverts the value of its operand. For example, consider the equation

$$D = A + (\overline{B} \cdot C)$$

D is equal to 1 if A is 1 or if both B = 0 and C = 1. Otherwise D is equal to 0.

Several points concerning the notation are needed. In the absence of parentheses, the AND operation takes precedence over the OR operation. Also, when no

Table A.1 Boolean Operators

P	Q	NOT P	P AND Q	P OR Q	P XOR Q	P NAND Q	P NOR Q
0	0	1	0	0	0	1	1
0	1	1	0	1	1	1	0
1	0	0	0	1	1	1	0
1	1	0	1	1	0	0	0

ambiguity will occur, the AND operation is represented by simple concatenation instead of the dot operator. Thus,

$$A + B \cdot C = A + (B \cdot C) = A + BC$$

all mean "Take the AND of B and C; then take the OR of the result and A."

Table A.1 defines the basic logical operations in a form known as a *truth table,* which simply lists the value of an operation for every possible combination of values of operands. The table also lists three other useful operators: XOR, NAND, and NOR. The exclusive-or (XOR) of two logical operands is 1 if and only if exactly one of the operands has the value 1. The NAND function is the complement (NOT) of the AND function, and the NOR is the complement of OR:

$$A \text{ NAND } B = \text{NOT}(A \text{ AND } B) = \overline{AB}$$
$$A \text{ NOR } B = \text{NOT}(A \text{ OR } B) = \overline{A + B}$$

As we shall see, these three new operations can be useful in implementing certain digital circuits.

Table A.2 summarizes key identities of Boolean algebra. The equations have been arranged in two columns to show the complementary, or dual, nature of the AND and OR operations. There are two classes of identities: basic rules (or *postulates*), which are stated without proof, and other identities that can be derived from

Table A.2 Basic Identities of Boolean Algebra

Basic Postulates		
$A \cdot B = B \cdot A$	$A + B = B + A$	Commutative laws
$A \cdot (B + C) = (A \cdot B) + (A \cdot C)$	$A + (B \cdot C) = (A + B) \cdot (A + C)$	Distributive laws
$1 \cdot A = A$	$0 + A = A$	Identity elements
$A \cdot \overline{A} = 0$	$A + \overline{A} = 1$	Inverse elements

Other Identities		
$0 \cdot A = 0$	$1 + A = 1$	
$A \cdot A = A$	$A + A = A$	
$A \cdot (B \cdot C) = (A \cdot B) \cdot C$	$A + (B + C) = (A + B) + C$	Associative laws
$\overline{A \cdot B} = \overline{A} + \overline{B}$	$\overline{A + B} = \overline{A} \cdot \overline{B}$	DeMorgan's theorem

the basic postulates. The postulates define the way in which Boolean expressions are interpreted. One of the two distributive laws is worth noting because it differs from what we would find in ordinary algebra:

$$A + (B \cdot C) = (A + B) \cdot (A + C)$$

The two bottommost expressions are referred to as DeMorgan's theorem. We can restate them as follows:

$$A \text{ NOR } B = \overline{A} \text{ AND } \overline{B}$$
$$A \text{ NAND } B = \overline{A} \text{ OR } \overline{B}$$

The reader is invited to verify the expressions in Table A.2 by substituting actual values (1s and 0s) for the variables A, B, and C.

A.2 GATES

The fundamental building block of all digital logic circuits is the gate. Logical functions are implemented by the interconnection of gates.

A gate is an electronic circuit that produces an output signal that is a simple Boolean operation on its input signals. The basic gates used in digital logic are AND, OR, NOT, NAND, and NOR. Figure A.1 depicts these five gates. Each gate is defined in three ways: graphic symbol, algebraic notation, and truth table. The symbology used here and throughout the appendix is the IEEE standard, IEEE Std 91. Note that the inversion (NOT) operation is indicated by a circle.

Each gate has one or two inputs and one output. When the values at the input are changed, the correct output signal appears almost instantaneously, delayed only by the propagation time of signals through the gate (known as the *gate delay*). The significance of this is discussed in Section A.3.

In addition to the gates depicted in Figure A.1, gates with three, four, or more inputs can be used. Thus, $X + Y + Z$ can be implemented with a single OR gate with three inputs.

Typically, not all gate types are used in implementation. Design and fabrication are simpler if only one or two types of gates are used. Thus, it is important to identify *functionally complete* sets of gates. This means that any Boolean function can be implemented using only the gates in the set. The following are functionally complete sets:

- AND, OR, NOT
- AND, NOT
- OR, NOT
- NAND
- NOR

It should be clear that AND, OR, and NOT gates constitute a functionally complete set, because they represent the three operations of Boolean algebra. For the AND and NOT gates to form a functionally complete set, there must be a way

Name	Graphic Symbol	Algebraic Function	Truth Table
AND	A ———⊐ F B	$F = A \cdot B$ or $F = AB$	A B | F 0 0 | 0 0 1 | 0 1 0 | 0 1 1 | 1
OR	A ———⊐ F B	$F = A + B$	A B | F 0 0 | 0 0 1 | 1 1 0 | 1 1 1 | 1
NOT	A ——▷○— F	$F = \overline{A}$ or $F = A'$	A | F 0 | 1 1 | 0
NAND	A ———○ F B	$F = (\overline{AB})$	A B | F 0 0 | 1 0 1 | 1 1 0 | 1 1 1 | 0
NOR	A ———○ F B	$F = (\overline{A + B})$	A B | F 0 0 | 1 0 1 | 0 1 0 | 0 1 1 | 0

Figure A.1 Basic Logic Gates

to synthesize the OR operation from the AND and NOT operations. This can be done by applying DeMorgan's theorem:

$$A + B = \overline{\overline{A} \cdot \overline{B}}$$

A OR B = NOT((NOT A) AND (NOT B))

Similarly, the OR and NOT operations are functionally complete because they can be used to synthesize the AND operation.

Figure A.2 shows how the AND, OR, and NOT functions can be implemented solely with NAND gates, and Figure A.3 shows the same thing for NOR gates. For this reason, digital circuits can be, and frequently are, implemented solely with NAND gates or solely with NOR gates.

With gates, we have reached the most primitive level of computer science and engineering. An examination of the transistor combinations used to construct gates departs from that realm and enters the realm of electrical engineering. For our purposes, however, we are content to describe how gates can be used as building blocks to implement the essential logical circuits of a digital computer.

Figure A.2 The Use of NAND Gates

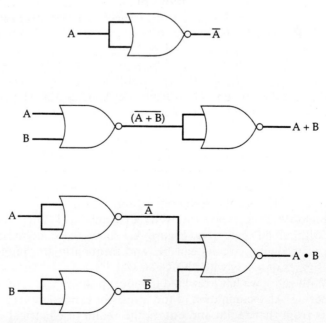

Figure A.3 The Use of NOR Gates

A.3 COMBINATIONAL CIRCUITS

A combinational circuit is an interconnected set of gates whose output at any time is a function only of the input at that time. As with a single gate, the appearance of the input is followed almost immediately by the appearance of the output, with only gate delays.

In general terms, a combinational circuit consists of n binary inputs and m binary outputs. As with a gate, a combinational circuit can be defined in three ways:

- **Truth table:** For each of the 2^n possible combinations of input signals, the binary value of each of the m output signals is listed.
- **Graphical symbols:** The interconnected layout of gates is depicted.
- **Boolean equations:** Each output signal is expressed as a Boolean function of its input signals.

Implementation of Boolean Functions

Any Boolean function can be implemented in electronic form as a network of gates. For any given function, there are a number of alternative realizations. Consider the Boolean function represented by the truth table in Table A.3. We can express this function by simply itemizing the combinations of values of A, B, and C that cause F to be 1:

$$F = \overline{A}B\overline{C} + \overline{A}BC + AB\overline{C} \qquad (A.1)$$

There are three combinations of input values that cause F to be 1, and if any one of these combinations occurs, the result is 1. This form of expression, for self-evident reasons, is known as the *sum of products* (SOP) form. Figure A.4 shows a straightforward implementation with AND, OR, and NOT gates.

Another form can also be derived from the truth table. The SOP form expresses that the output is 1 if any of the input combinations that produce 1 is true.

Table A.3 Boolean Function of Three Variables

A	B	C	F
0	0	0	0
0	0	1	0
0	1	0	1
0	1	1	1
1	0	0	0
1	0	1	0
1	1	0	1
1	1	1	0

Figure A.4 Sum-of-Products Implementation of Table A.3

We can also say that the output is 1 if none of the input combinations that produce 0 is true. Thus

$$F = (\overline{\overline{A}\overline{B}\overline{C}}) \cdot (\overline{\overline{A}B\overline{C}}) \cdot (\overline{A\overline{B}\overline{C}}) \cdot (\overline{A\overline{B}C}) \cdot (\overline{ABC})$$

This can be rewritten using a generalization of DeMorgan's theorem:

$$\overline{(X \cdot T \cdot Z)} = \overline{X} + \overline{Y} + \overline{Z}$$

Thus,

$$F = (\overline{\overline{A}} + \overline{\overline{B}} + \overline{\overline{C}}) \cdot (\overline{\overline{A}} + \overline{B} + \overline{\overline{C}}) \cdot (\overline{A} + \overline{\overline{B}} + \overline{\overline{C}}) \cdot (\overline{A} + \overline{\overline{B}} + \overline{C}) \cdot (\overline{A} + \overline{B} + \overline{C})$$

$$= (A + B + C) \cdot (A + B + \overline{C}) \cdot (\overline{A} + B + C) \cdot (\overline{A} + B + \overline{C}) \cdot (\overline{A} + \overline{B} + \overline{C}) \qquad \text{(A.2)}$$

This is in the *product of sums* (POS) form, which is illustrated in Figure A.5. For clarity, NOT gates are not shown. Rather, it is assumed that each input signal and its complement are available. This simplifies the logic diagram and makes the inputs to the gates more readily apparent.

Thus, a Boolean function can be realized in either SOP or POS form. At this point, it would seem that the choice would depend on whether the truth table contains more 1s or 0s for the output function: The SOP has one term for each 1, and the POS has one term for each 0. However, there are other considerations:

- It is generally possible to derive a simpler Boolean expression from the truth table than either SOP or POS.

- It may be preferable to implement the function with a single gate type (NAND or NOR).

The significance of the first point is that, with a simpler Boolean expression, fewer gates will be needed to implement the function. Three methods that can be used to achieve simplification are as follows:

- Algebraic simplification
- Karnaugh maps
- Quine–McKluskey tables

Algebraic Simplification

Algebraic simplification involves the application of the identities of Table A.2 to reduce the Boolean expression to one with fewer elements. For example, consider again Equation (A.1). Some thought should convince the reader that an equivalent expression is

$$F = \bar{A}B + B\bar{C} \qquad (A.3)$$

Or, even simpler,

$$F = B(\bar{A} + \bar{C})$$

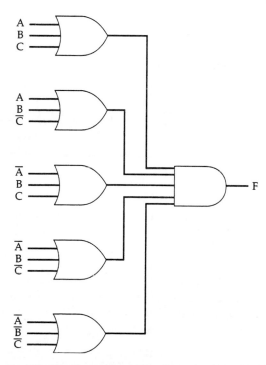

Figure A.5   Product-of-Sums Implementation of Table A.3

Figure A.6 Simplified Implementation of Table A.3

This expression can be implemented as shown in Figure A.6. The simplification of Equation (A.1) was done essentially by observation. For more complex expression, some more systematic approach is needed.

Karnaugh Maps

For purposes of simplification, the Karnaugh map is a convenient way of representing a Boolean function of a small number (up to four to six) of variables. The map is an array of 2^n squares, representing the possible combinations of values of n binary variables. Figure A.7a shows the map of four squares for a function of two variables. It is convenient for later purposes to list the combinations in the order 00, 01, 11, 10. Because the squares corresponding to the combinations are to be used

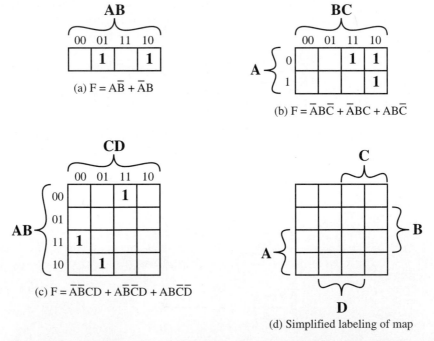

Figure A.7 The Use of Karnaugh Maps to Represent Boolean Functions

for recording information, the combinations are customarily written above the squares. In the case of three variables, the representation is an arrangement of eight squares (Figure A.7b), with the values for one of the variables to the left and for the other two variables above the squares. For four variables, 16 squares are needed, with the arrangement indicated in Figure A.7c.

The map can be used to represent any Boolean function in the following way. Each square corresponds to a unique product in the sum-of-products form, with a 1 value corresponding to the variable and a 0 value corresponding to the NOT of that variable. Thus, the product $A\bar{B}$ corresponds to the fourth square in Figure A.7a. For each such product in the function, 1 is placed in the corresponding square. Thus, for the two-variable example, the map corresponds to $A\bar{B} + \bar{A}B$. Given the truth table of a Boolean function, it is an easy matter to construct the map: For each combination of values of variables that produce a result of 1 in the truth table, fill in the corresponding square of the map with 1. Figure A.7b shows the result for the truth table of Table A.3. To convert from a Boolean expression to a map, it is first necessary to put the expression into what is referred to as *canonical* form: Each term in the expression must contain each variable. So, for example, if we have Equation (A.3), we must first expand it into the full form of Equation (A.1) and then convert this to a map.

The labeling used in Figure A.7d emphasizes the relationship between variables and the rows and columns of the map. Here the two rows embraced by the symbol A are those in which the variable A has the value 1; the rows not embraced by the symbol A are those in which A is 0; similarly for B, C, and D.

Once the map of a function is created, we can often write a simple algebraic expression for it by noting the arrangement of the 1s on the map. The principle is as follows. Any two squares that are adjacent differ in only one of the variables. If two adjacent squares both have an entry of one, then the corresponding product terms differ in only one variable. In such a case, the two terms can be merged by eliminating that variable. For example, in Figure A.8a, the two adjacent squares correspond to the two terms $\bar{A}B\bar{C}D$ and $\bar{A}BCD$. Thus, the function expressed is

$$\bar{A}B\bar{C}D + \bar{A}BCD = \bar{A}BD$$

This process can be extended in several ways. First, the concept of adjacency can be extended to include wrapping around the edge of the map. Thus, the top square of a column is adjacent to the bottom square, and the leftmost square of a row is adjacent to the rightmost square. These conditions are illustrated in Figures A.8b and c. Second, we can group not just 2 squares but 2^n adjacent squares (that is, 4, 8, etc.). The next three examples in Figure A.8 show groupings of 4 squares. Note that in this case, two of the variables can be eliminated. The last three examples show groupings of 8 squares, which allow three variables to be eliminated.

We can summarize the rules for simplification as follows:

1. Among the marked squares (squares with a 1), find those that belong to a unique largest block of either 1, 2, 4, or 8 and circle those blocks.
2. Select additional blocks of marked squares that are as large as possible and as few in number as possible, but include every marked square at least once. The

results may not be unique in some cases. For example, if a marked square combines with exactly two other squares, and there is no fourth marked square to complete a larger group, then there is a choice to be made as two which of the two groupings to choose. When you are circling groups, you are allowed to use the same 1 value more than once.

3. Continue to draw loops around single marked squares, or pairs of adjacent marked squares, or groups of four, eight, and so on, in such a way that every marked square belongs to at least one loop; then use as few of these blocks as possible to include all marked squares.

Figure A.9a, based on Table A.3, illustrates the process. If any isolated 1s remain after the groupings, then each of these is circled as a group of 1s. Finally, before going from the map to a simplified Boolean expression, any group of 1s that

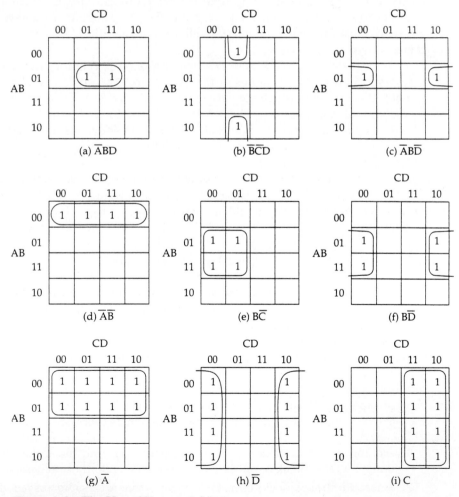

Figure A.8 The Use of Karnaugh Maps

Figure A.9 Overlapping Groups

is completely overlapped by other groups can be eliminated. This is shown in Figure A.9b. In this case, the horizontal group is redundant and may be ignored in creating the Boolean expression.

One additional feature of Karnaugh maps needs to be mentioned. In some cases, certain combinations of values of variables never occur, and therefore the corresponding output never occurs. These are referred to as "don't care" conditions. For each such condition, the letter "d" is entered into the corresponding square of the map. In doing the grouping and simplification, each "d" can be treated as a 1 or 0, whichever leads to the simplest expression.

An example, presented in [HAYE98], illustrates the points we have been discussing. We would like to develop the Boolean expressions for a circuit that adds 1 to a packed decimal digit. Recall from Section 9.2 that with packed decimal, each decimal digit is represented by a 4-bit code, in the obvious way. Thus, $0 = 0000$, $1 = 0001, \ldots, 8 = 1000$, and $9 = 1001$. The remaining 4-bit values, from 1010 to 1111, are not used. This code is also referred to as Binary Coded Decimal (BCD).

Table A.4 shows the truth table for producing a 4-bit result that is one more than a 4-bit BCD input. The addition is modulo 10. Thus, $9 + 1 = 0$. Also, note that six of the input codes produce "don't care" results, because those are not valid BCD inputs. Figure A.10 shows the resulting Karnaugh maps for each of the output variables. The d squares are used to achieve the best possible groupings.

The Quine–McKluskey Method

For more than four variables, the Karnaugh map method becomes increasingly cumbersome. With five variables, two 16×16 maps are needed, with one map con-

Table A.4 Truth Table for the One-Digit Packed Decimal Incrementer

	Input					Output			
Number	A	B	C	D	Number	W	X	Y	Z
0	0	0	0	0	1	0	0	0	1
1	0	0	0	1	2	0	0	1	0
2	0	0	1	0	3	0	0	1	1
3	0	0	1	1	4	0	1	0	0
4	0	1	0	0	5	0	1	0	1
5	0	1	0	1	6	0	1	1	0
6	0	1	1	0	7	0	1	1	1
7	0	1	1	1	8	1	0	0	0
8	1	0	0	0	9	1	0	0	1
9	1	0	0	1	0	0	0	0	0
Don't care condition {	1	0	1	0		d	d	d	d
	1	0	1	1		d	d	d	d
	1	1	0	0		d	d	d	d
	1	1	0	1		d	d	d	d
	1	1	1	0		d	d	d	d
	1	1	1	1		d	d	d	d

sidered to be on top of the other in three dimensions to achieve adjacency. Six variables requires the use of four 16×16 tables in four dimensions! An alternative approach is a tabular technique, referred to as the Quine–McKluskey method. The method is suitable for programming on a computer to give an automatic tool for producing minimized Boolean expressions.

The method is best explained by means of an example. Consider the following expression:

$$ABCD + AB\bar{C}D + AB\bar{C}\bar{D} + A\bar{B}CD + \bar{A}BCD + \bar{A}BC\bar{D} + \bar{A}B\bar{C}D + \bar{A}B\bar{C}D$$

Let us assume that this expression was derived from a truth table. We would like to produce a minimal expression suitable for implementation with gates.

The first step is to construct a table in which each row corresponds to one of the product terms of the expression. The terms are grouped according to the number of complemented variables. That is, we start with the term with no complements, if it exists, then all terms with one complement, and so on. Table A.5 shows the list for our example expression, with horizontal lines used to indicate the grouping. For clarity, each term is represented by a 1 for each uncomplemented variable and a 0 for each complemented variable. Thus, we group terms according to the number of 1s they contain. The index column is simply the decimal equivalent and is useful in what follows.

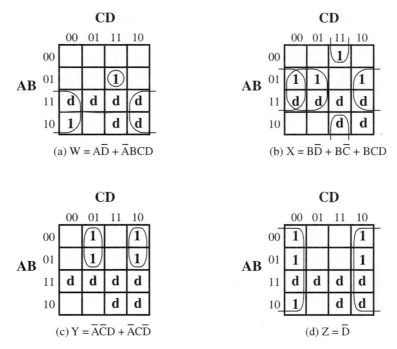

Figure A.10 Karnaugh Maps for the Incrementer

The next step is to find all pairs of terms that differ in only one variable, that is, all pairs of terms that are the same except that one variable is 0 in one of the terms and 1 in the other. Because of the way in which we have grouped the terms, we can do this by starting with the first group and comparing each term of the first group with every term of the second group. Then compare each term of the second group with all of the terms of the third group, and so on. Whenever a match is found,

Table A.5 First Stage of Quine–McKluskey Method
(for F = ABCD + ABC$\overline{\text{D}}$ + AB$\overline{\text{C}}$$\overline{\text{D}}$ + A$\overline{\text{B}}$CD + $\overline{\text{A}}$BCD + $\overline{\text{A}}$BC$\overline{\text{D}}$ + $\overline{\text{A}}$B$\overline{\text{C}}$D + $\overline{\text{A}}$$\overline{\text{B}}$$\overline{\text{C}}$D)

Product Term	Index	A	B	C	D	
$\overline{\text{A}}$$\overline{\text{B}}$$\overline{\text{C}}$D	1	0	0	0	1	✔
$\overline{\text{A}}$B$\overline{\text{C}}$D	5	0	1	0	1	✔
$\overline{\text{A}}$BC$\overline{\text{D}}$	6	0	1	1	0	✔
AB$\overline{\text{C}}$$\overline{\text{D}}$	12	1	1	0	0	✔
$\overline{\text{A}}$BCD	7	0	1	1	1	✔
A$\overline{\text{B}}$CD	11	1	0	1	1	✔
ABC$\overline{\text{D}}$	13	1	1	0	1	✔
ABCD	15	1	1	1	1	✔

Table A.6 Last Stage of Quine–McKluskey Method
(for $F = ABCD + AB\overline{C}D + AB\overline{C}\,\overline{D} + A\overline{B}CD + \overline{A}BCD + \overline{A}BC\overline{D} + \overline{A}B\overline{C}D + \overline{A}\,\overline{B}\,\overline{C}D$)

	$ABCD$	$AB\overline{C}D$	$AB\overline{C}\,\overline{D}$	$A\overline{B}CD$	$\overline{A}BCD$	$\overline{A}BC\overline{D}$	$\overline{A}B\overline{C}D$	$\overline{A}\,\overline{B}\,\overline{C}D$
BD	X	X			X		X	
$\overline{A}\,\overline{C}D$							[X]	(×)
$\overline{A}BC$					[X]	(×)		
$AB\overline{C}$		[X]	(×)					
ACD	[X]			(×)				

place a check next to each term, combine the pair by eliminating the variable that differs in the two terms, and add that to a new list. Thus, for example, the terms $\overline{A}BC\overline{D}$ and $\overline{A}BCD$ are combined to produce $\overline{A}BC$. This process continues until the entire original table has been examined. The result is a new table with the following entries:

$$\overline{A}\,\overline{C}D \qquad AB\overline{C} \qquad ABD\ \checkmark$$
$$\qquad B\overline{C}D\ \checkmark \qquad ACD$$
$$\qquad \overline{A}BC \qquad BCD\ \checkmark$$
$$\qquad \overline{A}BD\ \checkmark$$

The new table is organized into groups, as indicated, in the same fashion as the first table. The second table is then processed in the same manner as the first. That is, terms that differ in only one variable are checked and a new term produced for a third table. In this example, the third table that is produced contains only one term: BD.

In general, the process would proceed through successive tables until a table with no matches was produced. In this case, this has involved three tables.

Once the process just described is completed, we have eliminated many of the possible terms of the expression. Those terms that have not been eliminated are used to construct a matrix, as illustrated in Table A.6. Each row of the matrix corresponds to one of the terms that has not been eliminated (has no check) in any of the tables used so far. Each column corresponds to one of the terms in the original expression. An X is placed at each intersection of a row and a column such that the row element is "compatible" with the column element. That is, the variables present in the row element have the same value as the variables present in the column element. Next, circle each X that is alone in a column. Then place a square around each X in any row in which there is a circled X. If every column now has either a squared or a circled X, then we are done, and those row elements whose Xs have been marked constitute the minimal expression. Thus, in our example, the final expression is

$$AB\overline{C} + ACD + \overline{A}BC + \overline{A}\,\overline{C}D$$

In cases in which some columns have neither a circle nor a square, additional processing is required. Essentially, we keep adding row elements until all columns are covered.

Let us summarize the Quine–McKluskey method to try to justify intuitively why it works. The first phase of the operation is reasonably straightforward. The process eliminates unneeded variables in product terms. Thus, the expression $ABC + AB\bar{C}$ is equivalent to AB, because

$$ABC + AB\bar{C} = AB(C + \bar{C}) = AB$$

After the elimination of variables, we are left with an expression that is clearly equivalent to the original expression. However, there may be redundant terms in this expression, just as we found redundant groupings in Karnaugh maps. The matrix layout assures that each term in the original expression is covered and does so in a way that minimizes the number of terms in the final expression.

NAND and NOR Implementations

Another consideration in the implementation of Boolean functions concerns the types of gates used. It is often desirable to implement a Boolean function solely with NAND gates or solely with NOR gates. Although this may not be the minimum-gate implementation, it has the advantage of regularity, which can simplify the manufacturing process. Consider again Equation (A.3):

$$F = B(\bar{A} + \bar{C})$$

Because the complement of the complement of a value is just the original value,

$$F = B(\bar{A} + \bar{C}) = \overline{\overline{(\overline{A}B)} + \overline{(B\bar{C})}}$$

Applying DeMorgan's theorem,

$$F = \overline{(\overline{A}B)} \cdot \overline{(B\bar{C})}$$

which has three NAND forms, as illustrated in Figure A.11.

Multiplexers

The multiplexer connects multiple inputs to a single output. At any time, one of the inputs is selected to be passed to the output. A general block diagram representa-

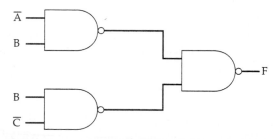

Figure A.11   NAND Implementation of Table A.3

Figure A.12 4-to-1 Multiplexer Representation

tion is shown in Figure A.12. This represents a 4-to-1 multiplexer. There are four input lines, labeled D0, D1, D2, and D3. One of these lines is selected to provide the output signal F. To select one of the four possible inputs, a 2-bit selection code is needed, and this is implemented as two select lines labeled S1 and S2.

An example 4-to-1 multiplexer is defined by the truth table in Table A.7. This is a simplified form of a truth table. Instead of showing all possible combinations of input variables, it shows the output as data from line D0, D1, D2, or D3. Figure A.13 shows an implementation using AND, OR, and NOT gates. S1 and S2 are connected to the AND gates in such a way that, for any combination of S1 and S2, three of the AND gates will output 0. The fourth AND gate will output the value of the selected line, which is either 0 or 1. Thus, three of the inputs to the OR gate are always 0, and the output of the OR gate will equal the value of the selected input gate. Using this regular organization, it is easy to construct multiplexers of size 8-to-1, 16-to-1, and so on.

Multiplexers are used in digital circuits to control signal and data routing. An example is the loading of the program counter (PC). The value to be loaded into the program counter may come from one of several different sources:

- A binary counter, if the PC is to be incremented for the next instruction
- The instruction register, if a branch instruction using a direct address has just been executed
- The output of the ALU, if the branch instruction specifies the address using a displacement mode

Table A.7 4-to-1 Multiplexer Truth Table

S2	S1	F
0	0	D0
0	1	D1
1	0	D2
1	1	D3

Figure A.13 Multiplexer Implementation

These various inputs could be connected to the input lines of a multiplexer, with the PC connected to the output line. The select lines determine which value is loaded into the PC. Because the PC contains multiple bits, multiple multiplexers are used, one per bit. Figure A.14 illustrates this for 16-bit addresses.

Decoders

A decoder is a combinational circuit with a number of output lines, only one of which is asserted at any time, dependent on the pattern of input lines. In general, a decoder has n inputs and 2^n outputs. Figure A.15 shows a decoder with three inputs and eight outputs.

Figure A.14 Multiplexer Input to Program Counter

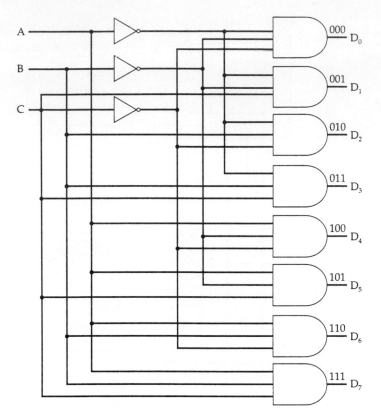

Figure A.15 Decoder with 3 Inputs and $2^3 = 8$ Outputs

Decoders find many uses in digital computers. One example is address decoding. Suppose we wish to construct a 1K-byte memory using four 256×8–bit RAM chips. We want a single unified address space, which can be broken down as follows:

Address	Chip
0000–00FF	0
0100–01FF	1
0200–02FF	2
0300–03FF	3

Each chip requires 8 address lines, and these are supplied by the lower-order 8 bits of the address. The higher-order 2 bits of the 10-bit address are used to select one of the four RAM chips. For this purpose, a 2-to-4 decoder is used whose output enables one of the four chips, as shown in Figure A.16.

With an additional input line, a decoder can be used as a demultiplexer. The demultiplexer performs the inverse function of a multiplexer; it connects a single input to one of several outputs. This is shown in Figure A.17. As before, n inputs are decoded to produce a single one of 2^n outputs. All of the 2^n output lines are ANDed with a data input line. Thus, the n inputs act as an address to select a particular output line, and the value on the data input line (0 or 1) is routed to that output line.

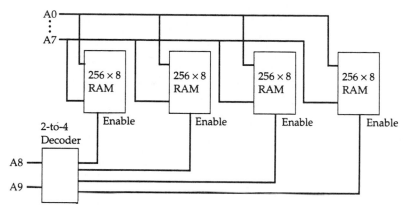

Figure A.16 Address Decoding

The configuration in Figure A.17 can be viewed in another way. Change the label on the new line from *Data Input* to *Enable.* This allows for the control of the timing of the decoder. The decoded output appears only when the encoded input is present *and* the enable line has a value of 1.

Programmable Logic Array

Thus far, we have treated individual gates as building blocks, from which arbitrary functions can be realized. The designer could pursue a strategy of minimizing the number of gates to be used by manipulating the corresponding Boolean expressions.

As the level of integration provided by integrated circuits increases, other considerations apply. Early integrated circuits, using small-scale integration (SSI), provided from one to ten gates on a chip. Each gate is treated independently, in the building-block approach described so far. Figure A.18 is an example of some SSI chips. To construct a logic function, a number of these chips are laid out on a printed circuit board and the appropriate pin interconnections are made.

Increasing levels of integration made it possible to put more gates on a chip and to make gate interconnections on the chip as well. This yields the advantages of

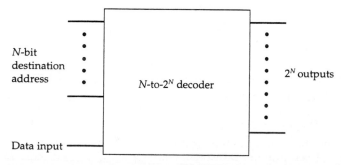

Figure A.17 Implementation of a Demultiplexer Using a Decoder

Figure A.18 Some SSI Chips. Pin layouts from *The TTL Data Book for Design Engineers*, copyright © 1976 Texas Instrument Incorporated.

decreased cost, decreased size, and increased speed (because on-chip delays are of shorter duration than off-chip delays). A design problem arises, however. For each particular logic function or set of functions, the layout of gates and interconnections on the chip must be designed. The cost and time involved in such custom chip design is high. Thus, it becomes attractive to develop a general-purpose chip that can be readily adapted to specific purposes. This is the intent of the *programmable logic array* (PLA).

The PLA is based on the fact that any Boolean function (truth table) can be expressed in a sum-of-products (SOP) form, as we have seen. The PLA consists of a regular arrangement of NOT, AND, and OR gates on a chip. Each chip input is passed through a NOT gate so that each input and its complement are available to each AND gate. The output of each AND gate is available to each OR gate, and the output of each OR gate is a chip output. By making the appropriate connections, arbitrary SOP expressions can be implemented.

Figure A.19a shows a PLA with three inputs, eight gates, and two outputs. Most larger PLAs contain several hundred gates, 15 to 25 inputs, and 5 to 15 outputs. The connections from the inputs to the AND gates, and from the AND gates to the OR gates, are not specified.

PLAs are manufactured in two different ways to allow easy programming (making of connections). In the first, every possible connection is made through a fuse at every intersection point. The undesired connections can then be later removed by blowing the fuses. This type of PLA is referred to as a *field-programmable logic array*. Alternatively, the proper connections can be made during chip fabrication by using an appropriate mask supplied for a particular interconnection pattern. In either case, the PLA provides a flexible, inexpensive way of implementing digital logic functions.

Figure A.19b shows a design that realizes two Boolean expressions.

Read-Only Memory

Combinational circuits are often referred to as "memoryless" circuits, because their output depends only on their current input and no history of prior inputs is retained. However, there is one sort of memory that is implemented with combinational circuits, namely *read-only memory* (ROM).

Recall that a ROM is a memory unit that performs only the read operation. This implies that the binary information stored in a ROM is permanent and was created during the fabrication process. Thus, a given input to the ROM (address lines) always produces the same output (data lines). Because the outputs are a function only of the present inputs, the ROM is in fact a combinational circuit.

A ROM can be implemented with a decoder and a set of OR gates. As an example, consider Table A.8. This can be viewed as a truth table with four inputs and four outputs. For each of the 16 possible input values, the corresponding set of values of the outputs is shown. It can also be viewed as defining the contents of a 64-bit ROM consisting of 16 words of 4 bits each. The four inputs specify an address, and the four outputs specify the contents of the location specified by the address. Figure A.20 shows how this memory could be implemented using a 4-to-16 decoder and four OR gates. As with the PLA, a regular organization is used, and the interconnections are made to reflect the desired result.

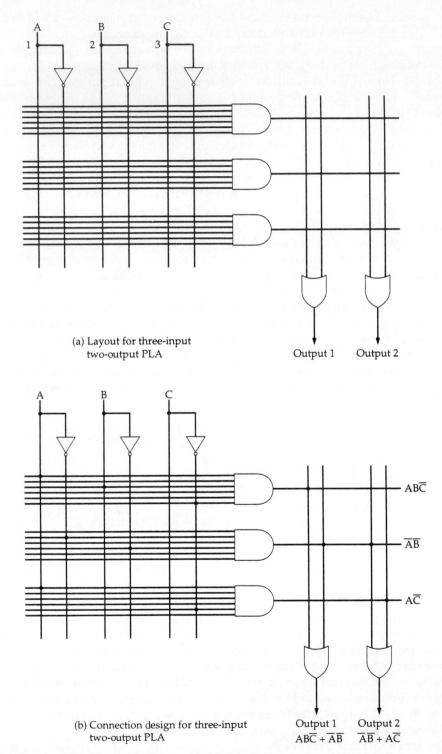

(a) Layout for three-input
two-output PLA

Output 1   Output 2

(b) Connection design for three-input
two-output PLA

Output 1   Output 2
$AB\overline{C} + \overline{A}\,\overline{B}$ $\overline{A}\,\overline{B} + A\overline{C}$

Figure A.19   An Example of a Programmable Logic Array

Table A.8 Truth Table for a ROM

Input				Output			
0	0	0	0	0	0	0	0
0	0	0	1	0	0	0	1
0	0	1	0	0	0	1	1
0	0	1	1	0	0	1	0
0	1	0	0	0	1	1	0
0	1	0	1	0	1	1	1
0	1	1	0	0	1	0	1
0	1	1	1	0	1	0	0
1	0	0	0	1	1	0	0
1	0	0	1	1	1	0	1
1	0	1	0	1	1	1	1
1	0	1	1	1	1	1	0
1	1	0	0	1	0	1	0
1	1	0	1	1	0	1	1
1	1	1	0	1	0	0	1
1	1	1	1	1	0	0	0

Adders

So far, we have seen how interconnected gates can be used to implement such functions as the routing of signals, decoding, and ROM. One essential area not yet addressed is that of arithmetic. In this brief overview, we will content ourselves with looking at the addition function.

Binary addition differs from Boolean algebra in that the result includes a carry term. Thus,

0	0	1	1
+ 0	+ 1	+ 0	+ 1
0	1	1	10

However, addition can still be dealt with in Boolean terms. In Table A.9a, we show the logic for adding two input bits to produce a 1-bit sum and a carry bit. This truth table could easily be implemented in digital logic. However, we are not interested in performing addition on just a single pair of bits. Rather, we wish to add two n-bit numbers. This can be done by putting together a set of adders so that the carry from one adder is provided as input to the next. A 4-bit adder is depicted in Figure A.21.

For a multiple-bit adder to work, each of the single-bit adders must have three inputs, including the carry from the next-lower-order adder. The revised truth table appears in Table A.9b. The two outputs can be expressed:

$$\text{Sum} = \overline{A}\overline{B}C + \overline{A}B\overline{C} + ABC + A\overline{B}\overline{C}$$
$$\text{Carry} = AB + AC + BC$$

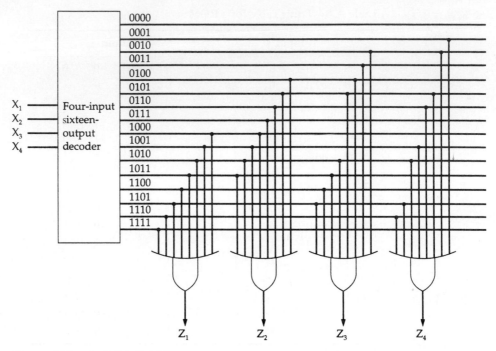

Figure A.20   A 64-Bit ROM

Figure A.22 is an implementation using AND, OR, and NOT gates.

Thus we have the necessary logic to implement a multiple-bit adder such as shown in Figure A.23. Note that because the output from each adder depends on the carry from the previous adder, there is an increasing delay from the least significant to the most significant bit. Each single-bit adder experiences a certain amount

Table A.9   Binary Addition Truth Tables

(a) Single-Bit Addition				(b) Addition with Carry Input				
A	**B**	**Sum**	**Carry**	C_{in}	**A**	**B**	**Sum**	C_{out}
0	0	0	0	0	0	0	0	0
0	1	1	0	0	0	1	1	0
1	0	1	0	0	1	0	1	0
1	1	0	1	0	1	1	0	1
				1	0	0	1	0
				1	0	1	0	1
				1	1	0	0	1
				1	1	1	1	1

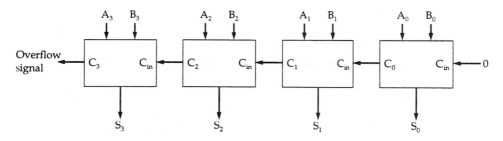

Figure A.21 4-Bit Adder

of gate delay, and this gate delay accumulates. For larger adders, the accumulated delay can become unacceptably high.

 If the carry values could be determined without having to ripple through all the previous stages, then each single-bit adder could function independently, and delay would not accumulate. This can be achieved with an approach known as *carry lookahead*. Let us look again at the 4-bit adder to explain this approach.

 We would like to come up with an expression that specifies the carry input to any stage of the adder without reference to previous carry values. We have

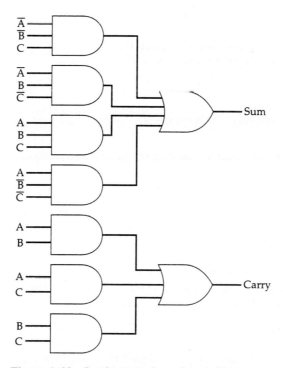

Figure A.22 Implementation of an Adder

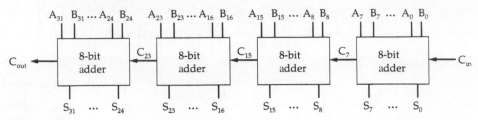

Figure A.23 Construction of a 32-Bit Adder Using 8-Bit Adders

$$C_0 = A_0B_0 \tag{A.4}$$

$$C_1 = A_1B_1 + A_1A_0B_0 + B_1A_0B_0 \tag{A.5}$$

Following the same procedure, we get

$$C_2 = A_2B_2 + A_2A_1B_1 + A_2A_1A_0B_0 + A_2B_1A_0B_0 + B_2A_1B_1 + B_2A_1A_0B_0 + B_2B_1A_0B_0$$

This process can be repeated for arbitrarily long adders. Each carry term can be expressed in SOP form as a function only of the original inputs, with no dependence on the carries. Thus, only two levels of gate delay occur regardless of the length of the adder.

For long numbers, this approach becomes excessively complicated. Evaluating the expression for the most significant bit of an n-bit adder requires an OR gate with $n - 1$ inputs and n AND gates with from 2 to $n + 1$ inputs. Accordingly, full carry lookahead is typically done only 4 to 8 bits at a time. Figure A.23 shows how a 32-bit adder can be constructed out of four 8-bit adders. In this case, the carry must ripple through the four 8-bit adders, but this will be substantially quicker than a ripple through thirty-two 1-bit adders.

A.4 SEQUENTIAL CIRCUITS

Combinational circuits implement the essential functions of a digital computer. However, except for the special case of ROM, they provide no memory or state information, elements also essential to the operation of a digital computer. For the latter purposes, a more complex form of digital logic circuit is used: the sequential circuit. The current output of a sequential circuit depends not only on the current input, but also on the past history of inputs. Another and generally more useful way to view it is that the current output of a sequential circuit depends on the current input and the current state of that circuit.

In this section, we examine some simple but useful examples of sequential circuits. As will be seen, the sequential circuit makes use of combinational circuits.

Flip-Flops

The simplest form of sequential circuit is the flip-flop. There are a variety of flip-flops, all of which share two properties:

- The flip-flop is a bistable device. It exists in one of two states and, in the absence of input, remains in that state. Thus, the flip-flop can function as a 1-bit memory.
- The flip-flop has two outputs, which are always the complements of each other. These are generally labeled Q and $\bar{Q}$.

The S–R Latch

Figure A.24 shows a common configuration known as the S–R flip-flop or S–R latch. The circuit has two inputs, S (Set) and R (Reset), and two outputs, Q and $\bar{Q}$, and consists of two NOR gates hooked together in a feedback arrangement.

First, let us show that the circuit is bistable. Assume that both S and R are 0 and that Q is 0. The inputs to the lower NOR gate are Q = 0 and S = 0. Thus, the output $\bar{Q}$ = 1 means that the inputs to the upper NOR gate are $\bar{Q}$ = 1 and R = 0, which has the output Q = 0. Thus, the state of the circuit is internally consistent and remains stable as long as S = R = 0. A similar line of reasoning shows that the state Q = 1, $\bar{Q}$ = 0 is also stable for R = S = 0.

Thus, this circuit can function as a 1-bit memory. We can view the output Q as the "value" of the bit. The inputs S and R serve to write the values 1 and 0, respectively, into memory. To see this, consider the state Q = 0, $\bar{Q}$ = 1, S = 0, R = 0. Suppose that S changes to the value 1. Now the inputs to the lower NOR gate are S = 1, Q = 0. After some time delay Δt, the output of the lower NOR gate will be $\bar{Q}$ = 0 (see Figure A.25). So, at this point in time, the inputs to the upper NOR gate become R = 0, $\bar{Q}$ = 0. After another gate delay of Δt, the output Q becomes 1. This is again a stable state. The inputs to the lower gate are now S = 1, Q = 1, which maintain the output Q = 0. As long as S = 1 and R = 0, the outputs will remain Q = 1, $\bar{Q}$ = 0. Furthermore, if S returns to 0, the outputs will remain unchanged.

The R output performs the opposite function. When R goes to 1, it forces Q = 0, $\bar{Q}$ = 1 regardless of the previous state of Q and $\bar{Q}$. Again, a time delay of $2\Delta t$ occurs before stability is re-established (Figure A.25).

The S–R latch can be defined with a table similar to a truth table, called a *characteristic table*, which shows the next state or states of a sequential circuit as a function of current states and inputs. In the case of the S–R latch, the state can be defined by the value of Q. Table A.10a shows the resulting characteristic table. Observe that the inputs S = 1, R = 1 are not allowed, because these would produce an inconsistent output (both Q and $\bar{Q}$ equal 0). The table can be expressed more

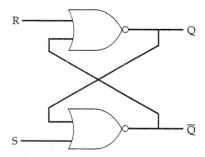

Figure A.24 The S–R Latch Implemented with NOR Gates

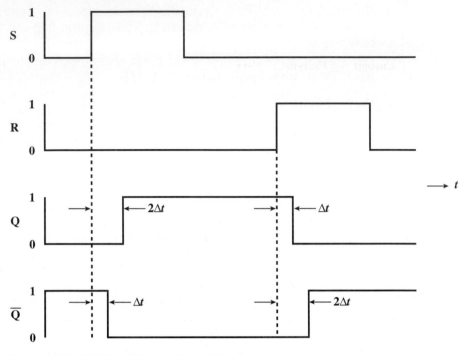

Figure A.25 NOR S–R Latch timing Diagram

compactly, as in Table A.10b. An illustration of the behavior of the S–R latch is shown in Table A.10c.

Clocked S–R Flip-Flop

The output of the S–R latch changes, after a brief time delay, in response to a change in the input. This is referred to as asynchronous operation. More typically, events in the digital computer are synchronized to a clock pulse, so that changes occur only when a clock pulse occurs. Figure A.26 shows this arrangement. This device is referred to as a *clocked S–R flip-flop*. Note that the R and S inputs are passed to the NOR gates only during the clock pulse.

D Flip-Flop

One problem with S–R flip-flop is that the condition R = 1, S = 1 must be avoided. One way to do this is to allow just a single input. The D flip-flop accomplishes this. Figure A.27 shows a gate implementation and the characteristic table of the D flip-flop. By using an inverter, the nonclock inputs to the two AND gates are guaranteed to be the opposite of each other.

The D flip-flop is sometimes referred to as the data flip-flop because it is, in effect, storage for one bit of data. The output of the D flip-flop is always equal to the most recent value applied to the input. Hence, it remembers and produces the last input. It is also referred to as the delay flip-flop, because it delays a 0 or 1 applied to its input for a single clock pulse.

Table A.10 The S–R Latch

(a) Characteristic Table				(b) Simplified Characteristic Table		

Current Inputs	Current State	Next State		S	R	Q_{n+1}
SR	Q_n	Q_{n+1}		0	0	Q_n
00	0	0		0	1	0
00	1	1		1	0	1
01	0	0		1	1	—
01	1	0				
10	0	1				
10	1	1				
11	0	—				
11	1	—				

(c) Response to Series of Inputs

t	0	1	2	3	4	5	6	7	8	9
S	1	0	0	0	0	0	0	0	1	0
R	0	0	0	1	0	0	1	0	0	0
Q_{n+1}	1	1	1	0	0	0	0	0	1	1

J–K Flip-Flop

Another useful flip-flop is the J–K flip-flop. Like the S–R flip-flop, it has two inputs. However, in this case all possible combinations of input values are valid. Figure A.28 shows a gate implementation of the J–K flip-flop, and Figure A.29 shows its characteristic table (along with those for the S–R and D flip-flops). Note that the first three combinations are the same as for the S–R flip-flop. With no input, the output is stable. The J input alone performs a set function, causing the output

Figure A.26 Clocked S–R Flip-Flop

D	Q_{n+1}
0	0
1	1

Figure A.27   D Flip-Flop

to be 1; the K input alone performs a reset function, causing the output to be 0. When both J and K are 1, the function performed is referred to as the toggle function: the output is reversed. Thus, if Q is 1 and 1 is applied to J and K, then Q becomes 0. The reader should verify that the implementation of Figure A.28 produces this characteristic function.

Registers

As an example of the use of flip-flops, let us first examine one of the essential elements of the CPU: the register. As we know, a register is a digital circuit used within

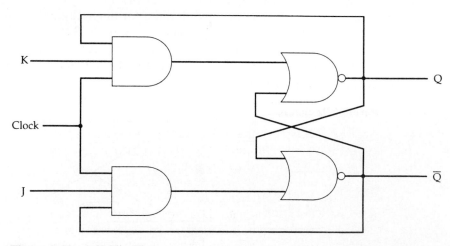

Figure A.28   J–K Flip-Flop

Name	Graphic Symbol	Characteristic Table
S–R		$S \quad R \;\mid\; Q_{n+1}$ $0 \quad 0 \;\mid\; Q_n$ $0 \quad 1 \;\mid\; 0$ $1 \quad 0 \;\mid\; 1$ $1 \quad 1 \;\mid\; -$
J–K		$J \quad K \;\mid\; Q_{n+1}$ $0 \quad 0 \;\mid\; Q_n$ $0 \quad 1 \;\mid\; 0$ $1 \quad 0 \;\mid\; 1$ $1 \quad 1 \;\mid\; \overline{Q_n}$
D		$D \;\mid\; Q_{n+1}$ $0 \;\mid\; 0$ $1 \;\mid\; 1$

Figure A.29   Basic Flip-Flops

the CPU to store one or more bits of data. Two basic types of registers are commonly used: parallel registers and shift registers.

Parallel Registers

A parallel register consists of a set of 1-bit memories that can be read or written simultaneously. It is used to store data. The registers that we have discussed throughout this book are parallel registers.

The 8-bit register of Figure A.30 illustrates the operation of a parallel register. S–R latches are used. A control signal, labeled *input data strobe*, controls writing into the register from signal lines, D11 through D18. These lines might be the output of multiplexers, so that data from a variety of sources can be loaded into the register. Output is controlled in a similar fashion. As an extra feature, a reset line is

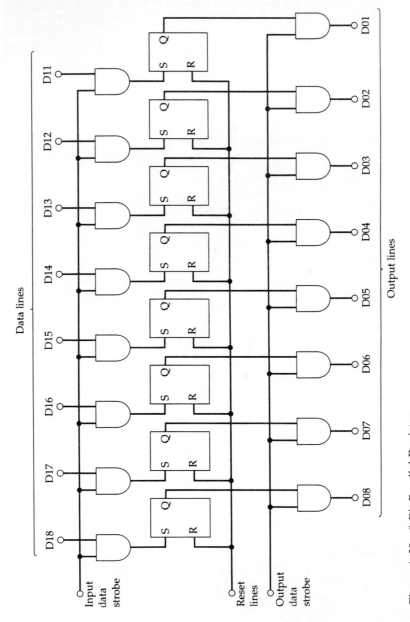

Figure A.30 8-Bit Parallel Register

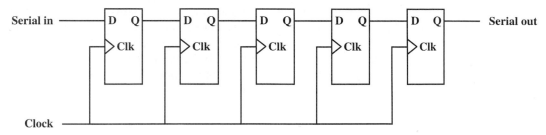

Figure A.31   5-Bit Shift Register

available that allows the register to be easily set to 0. Note that this could not be accomplished as easily with a register constructed from D flip-flops.

Shift Register

A shift register accepts and/or transfers information serially. Consider, for example, Figure A.31, which shows a 5-bit shift register constructed from clocked D flip-flops. Data are input only to the leftmost flip-flop. With each clock pulse, data are shifted to the right one position, and the rightmost bit is transferred out.

Shift registers can be used to interface to serial I/O devices. In addition, they can be used within the ALU to perform logical shift and rotate functions. In this latter capacity, they need to be equipped with parallel read/write circuitry as well as serial.

Counters

Another useful category of sequential circuit is the counter. A counter is a register whose value is easily incremented by 1 modulo the capacity of the register. Thus, a register made up of n flip-flops can count up to 2^n-1. When the counter is incremented beyond its maximum value, it is set to 0. An example of a counter in the CPU is the program counter.

Counters can be designated as asynchronous or synchronous, depending on the way in which they operate. Asynchronous counters are relatively slow because the output of one flip-flop triggers a change in the status of the next flip-flop. In a synchronous counter, all of the flip-flops change state at the same time. Because the latter type is much faster, it is the kind used in CPUs. However, it is useful to begin the discussion with a description of an asynchronous counter.

Ripple Counter

An asynchronous counter is also referred to as a ripple counter, because the change that occurs to increment the counter starts at one end and "ripples" through to the other end. Figure A.32 shows an implementation of a 4-bit counter using J–K flip-flops, together with a timing diagram that illustrates its behavior. The timing diagram is idealized in that it does not show the propagation delay that occurs as the signals move down the series of flip-flops. The output of the leftmost flip-flop (Q_0) is the least significant bit. The design could clearly be extended to an arbitrary number of bits by cascading more flip-flops.

In the illustrated implementation, the counter is incremented with each clock pulse. The J and K inputs to each flip-flop are held at a constant 1. This means that, when there is a clock pulse, the output at Q will be inverted (1 to 0; 0 to 1). Note that the change in state is shown as occurring with the falling edge of the clock pulse; this is known as an edge-triggered flip-flop. Using flip-flops that respond to the transition in a clock pulse rather than the pulse itself provides better timing control in complex circuits. If one looks at patterns of output for this counter, it can be seen that it cycles through 0000, 0001, . . . , 1110, 1111, 0000, and so on.

Synchronous Counters

The ripple counter has the disadvantage of the delay involved in changing value, which is proportional to the length of the counter. To overcome this disadvantage, CPUs make use of synchronous counters, in which all of the flip-flops of the counter change at the same time. In this subsection, we present a design for a 3-bit synchronous counter. In doing so, we illustrate some basic concepts in the design of a synchronous circuit.

For a 3-bit counter, three flip-flops will be needed. Let us use J–K flip-flops. Label the uncomplemented output of the three flip-flops A, B, C, respectively, with C representing the least significant bit. The first step is to construct a truth table

(a) Sequential circuit

(b) Timing diagram

Figure A.32 Ripple Counter

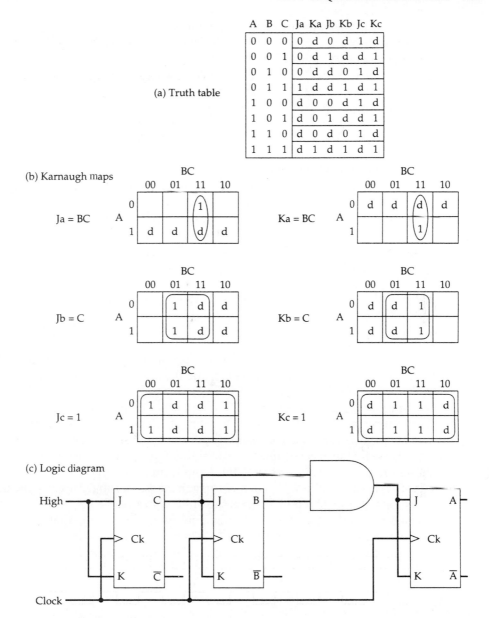

Figure A.33 Design of a Synchronous Counter

that relates the J–K inputs and outputs, to allow us to design the overall circuit. Such a truth table is shown in Figure A.33a. The first three columns show the possible combinations of outputs A, B, and C. They are listed in the order that they will appear as the counter is incremented. Each row lists the current value of A, B, C and the inputs to the three flip-flops that will be required to reach the next value of A, B, C.

To understand the way in which the truth table of Figure A.33a is constructed, it may be helpful to recast the characteristic table for the J–K flip-flop. Recall that this table was presented as follows:

J	K	Q_{n+1}
0	0	Q_n
0	1	0
1	0	1
1	1	$\overline{Q}_{n+1}$

In this form, the table shows the effect that the J and K inputs have on the output. Now consider the following organization of the same information:

Q_n	J	K	Q_{n+1}
0	0	d	0
0	1	d	1
1	d	1	0
1	d	0	1

In this form, the table provides the value of the next output when the inputs and the present output are known. This is exactly the information needed to design the counter or, indeed, any sequential circuit. In this form, the table is referred to as an excitation table.

Let us return to Figure A.33a. Consider the first row. We want the value of A to remain 0, the value of B to remain 0, and the value of C to go from 0 to 1 with the next application of a clock pulse. The excitation table shows that to maintain an output of 0, we must have inputs of J = 0 and don't care for K. To effect a transition from 0 to 1, the inputs must be J = 1 and K = d. These values are shown in the first row of the table. By similar reasoning, the remainder of the table can be filled in.

Having constructed the truth table of Figure A.33a, we see that the table shows the required values of all of the J and K inputs as functions of the current values of A, B, and C. With the aid of Karnaugh maps, we can develop Boolean expressions for these six functions. This is shown in part b of the figure. For example, the Karnaugh map for the variable Ja (the J input to the flip-flop that produces the A output) yields the expression Ja = BC. When all six expressions are derived, it is a straightforward matter to design the actual circuit, as shown in part c of the figure.

A.5 PROBLEMS

A.1 Construct a truth table for the following Boolean expressions:
  a. $ABC + \overline{A}\overline{B}\overline{C}$
  b. $ABC + A\overline{B}\overline{C} + \overline{A}\overline{B}\overline{C}$
  c. $A(B\overline{C} + \overline{B}C)$
  d. $(A + B)(A + C)(\overline{A} + \overline{B})$

A.2 Simplify the following expressions according to the commutative law:
  a. $A \cdot \overline{B} + \overline{B} \cdot A + C \cdot D \cdot E + \overline{C} \cdot D \cdot E + E \cdot \overline{C} \cdot D$
  b. $A \cdot B + A \cdot C + B \cdot A$
  c. $(L \cdot M \cdot N)(A \cdot B)(C \cdot D \cdot E)(M \cdot N \cdot L)$
  d. $F \cdot (K + R) + S \cdot V + W \cdot \overline{X} + V \cdot S + \overline{X} \cdot W + (R + K) \cdot F$

A.3 Apply DeMorgan's theorem to the following equations:
   a. $F = \overline{V + A + L}$
   b. $F = \overline{A} + \overline{B} + \overline{C} + \overline{D}$
A.4 Simplify the following expressions:
   a. $A = S \cdot T + V \cdot W + R \cdot S \cdot T$
   b. $A = T \cdot U \cdot V + X \cdot Y + Y$
   c. $A = F \cdot (E + F + G)$
   d. $A = (P \cdot Q + R + S \cdot T)T \cdot S$
   e. $A = \overline{\overline{D \cdot \overline{D} \cdot E}}$
   f. $A = Y \cdot (W + X + \overline{\overline{Y} + \overline{Z}}) \cdot Z$
   g. $A = (B \cdot E + C + F) \cdot C$
A.5 Construct the operation XOR from the basic Boolean operations AND, OR, and NOT.
A.6 Given a NOR gate and NOT gates, draw a logic diagram that will perform the three-input AND function.
A.7 Write the Boolean expression for a four-input NAND gate.
A.8 A combinational circuit is used to control a seven-segment display of decimal digits, as shown in Figure A.34. The circuit has four inputs, which provide the four-bit code used in packed decimal representation ($0_{10} = 0000, \ldots, 9_{10} = 1001$). The seven outputs define which segments will be activated to display a given decimal digit. Note that some combinations of inputs and outputs are not needed.
   a. Develop a truth table for this circuit.
   b. Express the truth table in SOP form.
   c. Express the truth table in POS form.
   d. Provide a simplified expression.
A.9 Design an 8-to-1 multiplexer.
A.10 Add an additional line to Figure A.15 so that it functions as a demultiplexer.

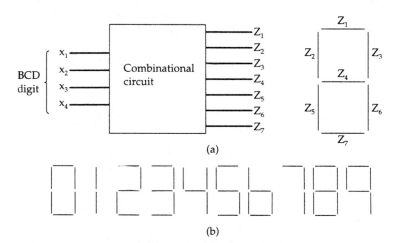

(a)

(b)

Figure A.34   Seven-Segment LED Display Example

A.11 The Gray code is a binary code for integers. It differs from the ordinary binary representation in that there is just a single bit change between the representations of any two numbers. This is useful for applications such as counters or analog-to-digital converters where a sequence of numbers is generated. Because only one bit changes at a time, there is never any ambiguity due to slight timing differences. The first eight elements of the code are as follows:

Binary Code	Gray Code
000	000
001	001
010	011
011	010
100	110
101	111
110	101
111	100

Design a circuit that converts from binary to Gray code.

A.12 Design a 5×32 decoder using four 3×8 decoders (with enable inputs) and one 2×4 decoder.

A.13 Implement the full adder of Figure A.22 with just five gates. (*Hint:* Some of the gates are XOR gates.)

A.14 Consider Figure A.22. Assume that each gate produces a delay of 10 ns. Thus, the sum output is valid after 30 ns and the carry output after 0 ns. What is the total add time for a 32-bit adder:

a. Implemented without carry lookahead, as in Figure A.21?

b. Implemented with carry lookahead and using 8-bit adders, as in Figure A.23?

APPENDIX B

NUMBER SYSTEMS

B.1 THE DECIMAL SYSTEM

In everyday life we use a system based on decimal digits (0, 1, 2, 3, 4, 5, 6, 7, 8, 9) to represent numbers and refer to the system as the decimal system. Consider what the number 83 means. It means eight tens plus three:

$$83 = (8 \times 10) + 3$$

The number 4728 means four thousands, seven hundreds, two tens, plus eight:

$$4728 = (4 \times 1000) + (7 \times 100) + (2 \times 10) + 8$$

The decimal system is said to have a **base**, or **radix**, of 10. This means that each digit in the number is multiplied by 10 raised to a power corresponding to that digit's position:

$$83 = (8 \times 10^1) + (3 \times 10^0)$$
$$4728 = (4 \times 10^3) + (7 \times 10^2) + (2 \times 10^1) + (8 \times 10^0)$$

The same principle holds for decimal fractions but negative powers of 10 are used. Thus, the decimal fraction 0.256 stands for 2 tenths plus 5 hundredths plus 6 thousandths:

$$0.256 = (2 \times 10^{-1}) + (5 \times 10^{-2}) + (6 \times 10^{-3})$$

A number with both an integer and fractional part has digits raised to both positive and negative powers of 10:

$$472.\,256 = (4 \times 10^2) + (7 \times 10^1) + (2 \times 10^0) + (2 \times 10^{-1}) + (5 \times 10^{-2}) + (6 \times 10^{-3})$$

In general, for the decimal representation of $X = \{\ldots d_2 d_1 d_0 . d_{-1} d_{-2} d_{-3} \ldots\}$, the value of X is

$$X = \sum_i d_i \times 10^i$$

B.2 THE BINARY SYSTEM

In the decimal system, 10 different digits are used to represent numbers with a base of 10. In the binary system, we have only two digits, 1 and 0. Thus, numbers in the binary system are represented to the base 2.

To avoid confusion, we will sometimes put a subscript on a number to indicate its base. For example, 83_{10} and 4728_{10} are numbers represented in decimal notation or, more briefly, decimal numbers. The digits 1 and 0 in binary notation have the same meaning as in decimal notation:

$$0_2 = 0_{10}$$
$$1_2 = 1_{10}$$

To represent larger numbers, as with decimal notation, each digit in a binary number has a value depending on its position:

$$10_2 = (1 \times 2^1) + (0 \times 2^0) = 2_{10}$$
$$11_2 = (1 \times 2^1) + (1 \times 2^0) = 3_{10}$$
$$100_2 = (1 \times 2^2) + (0 \times 2^1) + (0 \times 2^0) = 4_{10}$$

and so on. Again, fractional values are represented with negative powers of the radix:

$$1001.101 = 2^3 + 2^0 + 2^{-1} + 2^{-3} = 9.625_{10}$$

In general, for the binary representation of $Y = \{ \ldots b_2 b_1 b_0 . b_{-1} b_{-2} b_{-3} \ldots \}$, the value of Y is

$$Y = \sum_i b_i \times 2^i$$

B.3 CONVERTING BETWEEN BINARY AND DECIMAL

It is a simple matter to convert a number from binary notation to decimal notation. In fact, we showed several examples in the previous subsection. All that is required is to multiply each binary digit by the appropriate power of 2 and add the results.

To convert from decimal to binary, the integer and fractional parts are handled separately.

Integers

For the integer part, recall that in binary notation, an integer represented by

$$b_{m-1} b_{m-2} \ldots b_2 b_1 b_0 \qquad\qquad b_i = 0 \text{ or } 1$$

has the value

$$(b_{m-1} \times 2^{m-1}) + (b_{m-2} \times 2^{m-2}) + \ldots + (b_1 \times 2^1) + b_0$$

Suppose it is required to convert a decimal integer N into binary form. If we divide N by 2, in the decimal system, and obtain a quotient N_1 and a remainder R_0, we may write

$$N = 2 \times N_1 + R_0 \qquad\qquad R_0 = 0 \text{ or } 1$$

Next, we divide the quotient N_1 by 2. Assume that the new quotient is N_2 and the new remainder R_1. Then

$$N_1 = 2 \times N_2 + R_1 \qquad\qquad R_1 = 0 \text{ or } 1$$

so that

$$N = 2(2N_2 + R_1) + R_0 = (N_2 \times 2^2) + (R_1 \times 2^1) + R_0$$

If next

$$N_2 = 2N_3 + R_2$$

we have

$$N = (N_3 \times 2^3) + (R_2 \times 2^2) + (R_1 \times 2^1) + R_0$$

Because $N > N_1 > N_2 \ldots$ continuing this sequence will eventually produce a quotient $N_{m-1} = 1$ (except for the decimal integers 0 and 1, whose binary equivalents are 0 and 1, respectively) and a remainder R_{m-2}, which is 0 or 1. Then

$$N = (1 \times 2^{m-1}) + (R_{m-2} \times 2^{m-2}) + \ldots + (R_2 \times 2^2) + (R_1 \times 2^1) + R_0$$

which is the binary form of N. Hence, we convert from base 10 to base 2 by repeated divisions by 2. The remainders and the final quotient, 1, give us, in order of increasing significance, the binary digits of N. Figure B.1 shows two examples.

Fractions

For the fractional part, recall that in binary notation, a number with a value between 0 and 1 is represented by

$$0.b_{-1}b_{-2}b_{-3} \ldots \qquad\qquad b_i = 0 \text{ or } 1$$

and has the value

$$(b_{-1} \times 2^{-1}) + (b_{-2} \times 2^{-2}) + (b_{-3} \times 2^{-3}) \ldots$$

This can be rewritten as

$$2^{-1} \times (b_{-1} + 2^{-1} \times (b_{-2} + 2^{-1} \times (b_{-3} + \ldots$$

This expression suggests a technique for conversion. Suppose we want to convert the number F $(0 < F < 1)$ from decimal to binary notation. We know that F can be expressed in the form

$$F = 2^{-1} \times (b_{-1} + 2^{-1} \times (b_{-2} + 2^{-1} \times (b_{-3} + \ldots$$

If we multiply F by 2, we obtain:

$$2 \times F = b_{-1} + 2^{-1} \times (b_{-2} + 2^{-1} \times (b_{-3} + \ldots$$

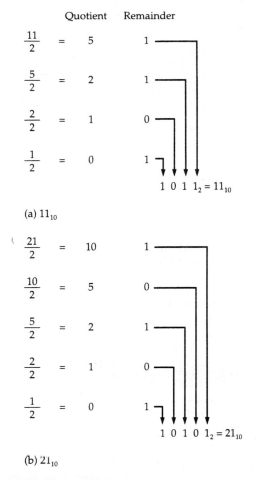

(a) 11_{10}

(b) 21_{10}

Figure B.1 Examples of Converting from Decimal Notation to Binary Notation for Integral Numbers

From this equation, we see that the integer part of $(2 \times F)$, which must be either 0 or 1 because $0 < F < 1$, is simply b_{-1}. So we can say $(2 \times F) = b_{-1} + F_1$, where $0 < F_1 < 1$ and where

$$F_1 = 2^{-1} \times (b_{-2} + 2^{-1} \times (b_{-3} + 2^{-1} \times (b_{-4} + \dots$$

To find b_{-2}, we repeat the process. Therefore, the conversion algorithm involves repeated multiplication by 2. At each step, the fractional part of the number from the previous step is multiplied by 2. The digit to the left of the decimal point in the product will be 0 or 1 and contributes to the binary representation, starting with the most significant digit. The fractional part of the product is used as the multiplicand in the next step. Figure B.2 shows two examples.

This process is not necessarily exact; that is, a decimal fraction with a finite number of digits may require a binary fraction with an infinite number of digits. In

(a) $0.81_{10} = 0.110011_2$ (approximate)

(b) $0.25_{10} = 0.01_2$ (exact)

Figure B.2 Examples of Converting from Decimal
Notation to Binary Notation for Fractional Numbers

such cases, the conversion algorithm is usually halted after a prespecified number of steps, depending on the desired accuracy.

B.4 HEXADECIMAL NOTATION

Because of the inherent binary nature of digital computer components, all forms of data within computers are represented by various binary codes. However, no matter how convenient the binary system is for computers, it is exceedingly cumbersome for human beings. Consequently, most computer professionals who must spend time working with the actual raw data in the computer prefer a more compact notation.

What notation to use? One possibility is the decimal notation. This is certainly more compact than binary notation, but it is awkward because of the tediousness of converting between base 2 and base 10.

Instead, a notation known as hexadecimal has been adopted. Binary digits are grouped into sets of four. Each possible combination of four binary digits is given a symbol, as follows:

0000 = 0	1000 = 8
0001 = 1	1001 = 9
0010 = 2	1010 = A
0011 = 3	1011 = B
0100 = 4	1100 = C
0101 = 5	1101 = D
0110 = 6	1110 = E
0111 = 7	1111 = F

Because 16 symbols are used, the notation is called **hexadecimal**, and the 16 symbols are the **hexadecimal digits**.

A sequence of hexadecimal digits can be thought of as representing an integer in base 16. Thus,

$$2C_{16} = (2_{16} \times 16^1) + (C_{16} = 16^0)$$
$$= (2_{10} \times 16^1) + (12_{10} \times 16^0) = 44$$

Hexadecimal notation is used not only for representing integers. It is also used as a concise notation for representing any sequence of binary digits, whether they represent text, numbers, or some other type of data. The reasons for using hexadecimal notation are as follows:

1. It is more compact than binary notation.
2. In most computers, binary data occupy some multiple of 4 bits, and hence some multiple of a single hexadecimal digit.
3. It is extremely easy to convert between binary and hexadecimal.

As an example of the last point, consider the binary string 110111100001. This is equivalent to

1101	1110	0001	$= DE1_{16}$
D	E	1	

This process is performed so naturally that an experienced programmer can mentally convert visual representations of binary data to their hexadecimal equivalent without written effort.

B.5 PROBLEMS

B.1 Convert the following binary numbers to their decimal equivalents:
   a. 001100   **b.** 000011   **c.** 011100   **d.** 111100   **e.** 101010
B.2 Convert the following binary numbers to their decimal equivalents:
   a. 11100.011   **b.** 110011.10011   **c.** 1010101010.1
B.3 Convert the following decimal numbers to their binary equivalents:
   a. 64   **b.** 100   **c.** 111   **d.** 145   **e.** 255
B.4 Convert the following decimal numbers to their binary equivalents:
   a. 34.75   **b.** 25.25   **c.** 27.1875
B.5 Express the following octal numbers in hexadecimal notation:
   a. 12   **b.** 5655   **c.** 2550276   **d.** 76545336   **e.** 3726755
B.6 Convert the following hexadecimal numbers to their decimal equivalents:
   a. C   **b.** 9F   **c.** D52   **d.** 67E   **e.** ABCD
B.7 Convert the following hexadecimal numbers to their decimal equivalents:
   a. F.4   **b.** D3.E   **c.** 1111.1   **d.** 888.8   **e.** EBA.C
B.8 Convert the following decimal numbers to their hexadecimal equivalents:
   a. 16   **b.** 80   **c.** 2560   **d.** 3000   **e.** 62,500
B.9 Convert the following decimal numbers to their hexadecimal equivalents:
   a. 204.125   **b.** 255.875   **c.** 631.25   **d.** 10000.00390625

B.10 Convert the following hexadecimal numbers to their binary equivalents:

   a. E **b.** 1C **c.** A64 **d.** 1F.C **e.** 239.4

B.11 Convert the following binary numbers to their decimal equivalents:

   a. 1001.1111 **b.** 110101.011001 **c.** 10100111.111011

B.12 Prove that every real number with a terminating binary representation (finite number of digits to the right of the binary point) also has a terminating decimal representation (finite number of digits to the right of the decimal point).

APPENDIX C

PROJECTS FOR TEACHING COMPUTER ORGANIZATION AND ARCHITECTURE

Many instructors believe that research or implementation projects are crucial to the clear understanding of the concepts of computer organization and architecture. Without projects, it may be difficult for students to grasp some of the basic concepts and interactions among components. Projects reinforce the concepts introduced in the book, give students a greater appreciation of the inner workings of a processor, and can motivate students and give them confidence that they have mastered the material.

In this text, I have tried to present the concepts as clearly as possible and have provided numerous homework problems to reinforce those concepts. Many instructors will wish to supplement this material with projects. This appendix provides some guidance in that regard and describes support material available in the instructor's manual. The support material covers three types of projects:

- Research projects
- Simulation projects
- Reading/report assignments

C.1 RESEARCH PROJECTS

An effective way of reinforcing basic concepts from the course and for teaching students research skills is to assign a research project. Such a project could involve a literature search as well as a Web search of vendor products, research lab activities, and standardization efforts. Projects could be assigned to teams or, for smaller projects, to individuals. In any case, it is best to require some sort of project proposal early in the term, giving the instructor time to evaluate the proposal for appropriate topic and appropriate level of effort. Student handouts for research projects should include the following:

- A format for the proposal
- A format for the final report
- A schedule with intermediate and final deadlines
- A list of possible project topics

The students can select one of the listed topics or devise their own comparable project. The instructor's manual includes a suggested format for the proposal and final report as well as a list of possible research topics.

C.2 SIMULATION PROJECTS

An excellent way to obtain a grasp of the internal operation of a processor and to study and appreciate some of the design trade-offs and performance implications is by simulating key elements of the processor. Two useful tools that are useful for this purpose are SimpleScalar and SMPCache.

Compared with actual hardware implementation, simulation provides two advantages for both research and educational use:

- With simulation, it is easy to modify various elements of an organization, to vary the performance characteristics of various components, and then to analyze the effects of such modifications.
- Simulation provides for detailed performance statistics collection, which can be used to understand performance trade-offs.

SimpleScalar

SimpleScalar [BURG97, MANJ01a, MANJ01b] is a set of tools that can be used to simulate real programs on a range of modern processors and systems. The tool set includes compiler, assembler, linker, and simulation and visualization tools. Simple-Scalar provides processor simulators that range from an extremely fast functional simulator to a detailed out-of-order issue, superscalar processor simulator that supports nonblocking caches and speculative execution. The instruction set architecture and organizational parameters may be modified to create a variety of experiments.

The instructor's manual for this book includes a concise introduction to SimpleScalar for students, with instructions on how to load and get started with SimpleScalar. The manual also includes some suggested project assignments.

SimpleScalar is a portable software package the runs on most UNIX platforms. The SimpleScalar software can be downloaded from the SimpleScalar Web site. It is available at no cost for noncommercial use.

SMPCache

SMPCache is a trace-driven simulator for the analysis and teaching of cache memory systems on symmetric multiprocessors [RODR01]. The simulation is based on a model built according to the architectural basic principles of these systems. The simulator has a full graphic and friendly interface. Some of the parameters that they can be studied with the simulator are: program locality; influence of the number of processors, cache coherence protocols, schemes for bus arbitration, mapping, replacement policies, cache size (blocks in cache), number of cache sets (for set associative caches), number of words by block (memory block size)

The instructor's manual for this book includes a concise introduction to SimpleScalar for students, with instructions on how to load and get started with SimpleScalar. The manual also includes some suggested project assignments.

SimpleScalar is a portable software package the runs on PC systems with Windows. The SimpleScalar software can be downloaded from the SimpleScalar Web site. It is available at no cost for noncommercial use.

C.3 READING/REPORT ASSIGNMENTS

Another excellent way to reinforce concepts from the course and to give students research experience is to assign papers from the literature to be read and analyzed.

The instructor's manual includes a suggested list of papers, one or two per chapter, to be assigned. All of the papers are readily available either via the Internet or in any good college technical library. The manual also includes a suggested assignment wording.

GLOSSARY

Some of the terms in this glossary are from the *American National Dictionary for Information Systems* (1996). These are indicated in the glossary by an asterisk.

Absolute Address* An address in a computer language that identifies a storage location or a device without the use of any intermediate reference.

Accumulator The name of the CPU register in a single-address instruction format. The accumulator, or AC, is implicitly one of the two operands for the instruction.

Address Bus That portion of a system bus used for the transfer of an address. Typically, the address identifies a main memory location or an I/O device.

Address Space The range of addresses (memory, I/O) that can be referenced.

Arithmetic and Logic Unit (ALU)* A part of a computer that performs arithmetic operations, logic operations, and related operations.

ASCII American Standard Code for Information Interchange. ASCII is a 7-bit code used to represent numeric, alphabetic, and special printable characters. It also includes codes for *control characters,* which are not printed or displayed but specify some control function.

Assembly Language* A computer-oriented language whose instructions are usually in one-to-one correspondence with computer instructions and that may provide facilities such as the use of macroinstructions. Synonymous with *computer-dependent language.*

Associative Memory* A memory whose storage locations are identified by their contents, or by a part of their contents, rather than by their names or positions.

Asynchronous Timing A technique in which the occurrence of one event on a bus follows and depends on the occurrence of a previous event.

Autoindexing A form of indexed addressing in which the index register is automatically incremented or decremented with each memory reference.

Base* In the numeration system commonly used in scientific papers, the number that is raised to the power denoted by the exponent and then multiplied by the mantissa to determine the real number represented (e.g., the number 10 in the expression $2.7 \times 10^2 = 270$).

Base Address* A numeric value that is used as a reference in the calculation of addresses in the execution of a computer program.

Binary Operator* An operator that represents an operation on two and only two operands.

Bit* In the pure binary numeration system, either of the digits 0 and 1.

Block Multiplexor Channel A multiplexer channel that interleaves blocks of data. See also *byte multiplexor channel.* Contrast with *selector channel.*

Branch Prediction A mechanism used by the processor to predict the outcome of a program branch prior to its execution.

Buffer* Storage used to compensate for a difference in rate of flow of data, or time of occurrence of events, when transferring data from one device to another.

Bus A shared communications path consisting of one or a collection of lines. In some computer systems, CPU, memory, and I/O components are connected by a common bus. Since the lines are shared by all components, only one component at a time can successfully transmit.

Bus Arbitration The process of determining which competing bus master will be permitted access to the bus.

Bus Master A device attached to a bus that is capable of initiating and controlling communication on the bus.

Byte Eight bits. Also referred to as an *octet.*

Byte Multiplexor Channel* A multiplexer channel that interleaves bytes of data. See also *block multiplexor channel.* Contrast with *selector channel.*

Cache Coherence Protocol A mechanism to maintain data validity among multiple caches so that every data access will always acquire the most recent version of the contents of a main memory word.

Cache Line A block of data associated with a cache tag and the unit of transfer between cache and memory.

Cache Memory* A special buffer storage, smaller and faster than main storage, that is used to hold a copy of instructions and data in main storage that are likely to be needed next by the processor and that have been obtained automatically from main storage.

CD-ROM Compact Disk Read-Only Memory. A nonerasable disk used for storing computer data. The standard system uses 12-cm disks and can hold more than 550 Mbytes.

Central Processing Unit (CPU) That portion of a computer that fetches and executes instructions. It consists of an arithmetic and logic unit (ALU), a control unit, and registers. Often simply referred to as a *processor.*

Cluster   A group of interconnected, whole computers working together as a unified computing resource that can create the illusion of being one machine. The term *whole computer* means a system that can run on its own, apart from the cluster.

Combinational Circuit*   A logic device whose output values, at any given instant, depend only on the input values at that time. A combinational circuit is a special case of a sequential circuit that does not have a storage capability. Synonymous with *combinatorial circuit.*

Compact Disk (CD)   A nonerasable disk that stores digitized audio information.

Computer Instruction*   An instruction that can be recognized by the processing unit of the computer for which it is designed. Synonymous with *machine instruction.*

Computer Instruction Set*   A complete set of the operators of the instructions of a computer together with a description of the types of meanings that can be attributed to their operands. Synonymous with *machine instruction set.*

Conditional Jump*   A jump that takes place only when the instruction that specifies it is executed and specified conditions are satisfied. Contrast with *unconditional jump.*

Condition Code   A code that reflects the result of a previous operation (e.g., arithmetic). A CPU may include one or more condition codes, which may be stored separately within the CPU or as part of a larger control register. Also known as a *flag.*

Control Bus   That portion of a system bus used for the transfer of control signals.

Control Registers   CPU registers employed to control CPU operation. Most of these registers are not user visible.

Control Storage   A portion of storage that contains microcode.

Control Unit   That part of the CPU that controls CPU operations, including ALU operations, the movement of data within the CPU, and the exchange of data and control signals across external interfaces (e.g., the system bus).

Daisy Chain*   A method of device interconnection for determining interrupt priority by connecting the interrupt sources serially.

Data Bus   That portion of a system bus used for the transfer of data.

Data Communication   Data transfer between devices. The term generally excludes I/O.

Decoder*   A device that has a number of input lines of which any number may carry signals and a number of output lines of which not more than one may carry a signal, there being a one-to-one correspondence between the outputs and the combinations of input signals.

Demand Paging*   The transfer of a page from auxiliary storage to real storage at the moment of need.

Direct Access* The capability to obtain data from a storage device or to enter data into a storage device in a sequence independent of their relative position, by means of addresses that indicate the physical location of the data.

Direct Address* An address that designates the storage location of an item of data to be treated as operand. Synonymous with *one-level address*.

Direct Memory Access (DMA) A form of I/O in which a special module, called a *DMA module*, controls the exchange of data between main memory and an I/O module. The CPU sends a request for the transfer of a block of data to the DMA module and is interrupted only after the entire block has been transferred.

Disabled Interrupt A condition, usually created by the CPU, during which the CPU will ignore interrupt request signals of a specified class.

Diskette* A flexible magnetic disk enclosed in a protective container. Synonymous with *flexible disk*.

Disk Pack* An assembly of magnetic disks that can be removed as a whole from a disk drive, together with a container from which the assembly must be separated when operating.

Disk Stripping A type of disk array mapping in which logically contiguous blocks of data, or strips, are mapped round-robin to consecutive array members. A set of logically consecutive strips that maps exactly one strip to each array member is referred to as a stripe.

Dynamic RAM A RAM whose cells are implemented using capacitors. A dynamic RAM will gradually lose its data unless it is periodically refreshed.

Emulation* The imitation of all or part of one system by another, primarily by hardware, so that the imitating system accepts the same data, executes the same programs, and achieves the same results as the imitated system.

Enabled Interrupt A condition, usually created by the CPU, during which the CPU will respond to interrupt request signals of a specified class.

Erasable Optical Disk A disk that uses optical technology but that can be easily erased and rewritten. Both 3.25-inch and 5.25-inch disks are in use. A typical capacity is 650 Mbytes.

Error-Correcting Code* A code in which each character or signal conforms to specific rules of construction so that deviations from these rules indicate the presence of an error and in which some or all of the detected errors can be corrected automatically.

Error-Detecting Code* A code in which each character or signal conforms to specific rules of construction so that deviations from these rules indicate the presence of an error.

Execute Cycle That portion of the instruction cycle during which the CPU performs the operation specified by the instruction opcode.

Fetch Cycle   That portion of the instruction cycle during which the CPU fetches from memory the instruction to be executed.

Firmware*   Microcode stored in read-only memory.

Fixed-Point Representation System*   A radix numeration system in which the radix point is implicitly fixed in the series of digit places by some convention upon which agreement has been reached.

Flip-Flop*   A circuit or device containing active elements, capable of assuming either one of two stable states at a given time. Synonymous with *bistable circuit, toggle.*

Floating-Point Representation System*   A numeration system in which a real number is represented by a pair of distinct numerals, the real number being the product of the fixed-point part, one of the numerals, and a value obtained by raising the implicit floating-point base to a power denoted by the exponent in the floating-point representation, indicated by the second numeral.

G   Prefix meaning *billion.*

Gate   An electronic circuit that produces an output signal that is a simple Boolean operation on its input signals.

General-Purpose Register*   A register, usually explicitly addressable, within a set of registers, that can be used for different purposes, for example, as an accumulator, as an index register, or as a special handler of data.

Global Variable   A variable defined in one portion of a computer program and used in at least one other portion of that computer program.

High-Performance Computing (HPC)   A research area dealing with super-computers and the software that runs on supercomputers. The emphasis is on scientific applications, which may involve heavy use of vector and matrix computation, and parallel algorithms.

Immediate Address*   The contents of an address part that contains the value of an operand rather than an address. Synonymous with *zero-level address.*

Indexed Address*   An address that is modified by the content of an index register prior to or during the execution of a computer instruction.

Indexing   A technique of address modification by means of index registers.

Index Register*   A register whose contents can be used to modify an operand address during the execution of computer instructions; it can also be used as a counter. An index register may be used to control the execution of a loop, to control the use of an array, as a switch, for table lookup, or as a pointer.

Indirect Address*   An address of a storage location that contains an address.

Indirect Cycle   That portion of the instruction cycle during which the CPU performs a memory access to convert an indirect address into a direct address.

Input-Output (I/O)   Pertaining to either input or output, or both. Refers to the movement of data between a computer and a directly attached peripheral.

Instruction Address Register* A special-purpose register used to hold the address of the next instruction to be executed.

Instruction Cycle The processing performed by a CPU to execute a single instruction.

Instruction Format The layout of a computer instruction as a sequence of bits. The format divides the instruction into fields, corresponding to the constituent elements of the instruction (e.g., opcode, operands).

Instruction Register* A register that is used to hold an instruction for interpretation.

Integrated Circuit (IC) A tiny piece of solid material, such as silicon, upon which is etched or imprinted a collection of electronic components and their interconnections.

Interrupt* A suspension of a process, such as the execution of a computer program, caused by an event external to that process, and performed in such a way that the process can be resumed. Synonymous with *interruption.*

Interrupt Cycle That portion of the instruction cycle during which the CPU checks for interrupts. If an enabled interrupt is pending, the CPU saves the current program state and resumes processing at an interrupt-handler routine.

Interrupt-Driven I/O A form of I/O. The CPU issues an I/O command, continues to execute subsequent instructions, and is interrupted by the I/O module when the latter has completed its work.

I/O Channel A relatively complex I/O module that relieves the CPU of the details of I/O operations. An I/O channel will execute a sequence of I/O commands from main memory without the need for CPU involvement.

I/O Controller A relatively simple I/O module that requires detailed control from the CPU or an I/O channel. Synonymous with *device controller.*

I/O Module One of the major component types of a computer. It is responsible for the control of one or more external devices (peripherals) and for the exchange of data between those devices and main memory and/or CPU registers.

I/O Processor An I/O module with its own processor, capable of executing its own specialized I/O instructions or, in some cases, general-purpose machine instructions.

Isolated I/O A method of addressing I/O modules and external devices. The I/O address space is treated separately from main memory address space. Specific I/O machine instructions must be used. Compare *memory-mapped* I/O.

K Prefix meaning $2^{10} = 1024$. Thus, 2 kb = 2048 bits.

Local Variable A variable that is defined and used only in one specified portion of a computer program.

Locality of Reference The tendency of a processor to access the same set of memory locations repetitively over a short period of time.

M   Prefix meaning $2^{20} = 1,048,576$. Thus, 2 Mb = 2,097,152 bits.

Magnetic Disk*   A flat circular plate with a magnetizable surface layer, on one or both sides of which data can be stored.

Magnetic Tape*   A tape with a magnetizable surface layer on which data can be stored by magnetic recording.

Mainframe   A term originally referring to the cabinet containing the central processor unit or "main frame" of a large batch machine. After the emergence of smaller minicomputer designs in the early 1970s, the traditional larger machines were described as mainframe computers, mainframes. Typical characteristics of a mainframe are that it supports a large database, has elaborate I/O hardware, and is used in a central data processing facility.

Main Memory*   Program-addressable storage from which instructions and other data can be loaded directly into registers for subsequent execution or processing.

Memory Address Register (MAR)*   A register, in a processing unit, that contains the address of the storage location being accessed.

Memory Buffer Register (MBR)   A register that contains data read from memory or data to be written to memory.

Memory Cycle Time   The inverse of the rate at which memory can be accessed. It is the minimum time between the response to one access request (read or write) and the response to the next access request.

Memory-Mapped I/O   A method of addressing I/O modules and external devices. A single address space is used for both main memory and I/O addresses, and the same machine instructions are used both for memory read/write and for I/O.

Microcomputer*   A computer system whose processing unit is a microprocessor. A basic microcomputer includes a microprocessor, storage, and an input/output facility, which may or may not be on one chip.

Microinstruction*   An instruction that controls data flow and sequencing in a processor at a more fundamental level than machine instructions. Individual machine instructions and perhaps other functions may be implemented by microprograms.

Micro-Operation   An elementary CPU operation, performed during one clock pulse.

Microprocessor*   A processor whose elements have been miniaturized into one or a few integrated circuits.

Microprogram*   A sequence of microinstructions that are in special storage where they can be dynamically accessed to perform various functions.

Microprogrammed CPU   A CPU whose control unit is implemented using microprogramming.

Microprogramming Language   An instruction set used to specify microprograms.

Multiplexer   A combinational circuit that connects multiple inputs to a single output. At any time, only one of the inputs is selected to be passed to the output.

Multiplexor Channel   A channel designed to operate with a number of I/O devices simultaneously. Several I/O devices can transfer records at the same time by interleaving items of data. See also *byte multiplexor channel, block multiplexor channel.*

Multiprocessor*   A computer that has two or more processors that have common access to a main storage.

Multiprogramming*   A mode of operation that provides for the interleaved execution of two or more computer programs by a single processor.

Multitasking*   A mode of operation that provides for the concurrent performance or interleaved execution of two or more computer tasks. The same as multiprogramming, using different terminology.

Nonuniform Memory Access (NUMA) Multiprocessor   A shared-memory multiprocessor in which the access time from a given processor to a word in memory varies with the location of the memory word.

Nonvolatile Memory   Memory whose contents are stable and do not require a constant power source.

Nucleus   That portion of an operating system that contains its basic and most frequently used functions. Often, the nucleus remains resident in main memory.

Ones Complement Representation   Used to represent binary integers. A positive integer is represented as in sign magnitude. A negative integer is represented by reversing each bit in the representation of a positive integer of the same magnitude.

Opcode   Abbreviated form for *operation code.*

Operand*   An entity on which an operation is performed.

Operating System*   Software that controls the execution of programs and that provides services such as resource allocation, scheduling, input/output control, and data management.

Operation Code*   A code used to represent the operations of a computer. Usually abbreviated to opcode.

Orthogonality   A principle by which two variables or dimensions are independent of one another. In the context of an instruction set, the term is generally used to indicate that other elements of an instruction (address mode, number of operands, length of operand) are independent of (not determined by) opcode.

Page*   In a virtual storage system, a fixed-length block that has a virtual address and that is transferred as a unit between real storage and auxiliary storage.

Page Fault   Occurs when the page containing a referenced word is not in main memory. This causes an interrupt and requires the operating system to bring in the needed page.

Page Frame* An area of main storage used to hold a page.

Parity Bit* A binary digit appended to a group of binary digits to make the sum of all the digits either always odd (odd parity) or always even (even parity).

Peripheral Equipment (IBM) In a computer system, with respect to a particular processing unit, any equipment that provides the processing unit with outside communication. Synonymous with *peripheral device.*

Pipeline A processor organization in which the processor consists of a number of stages, allowing multiple instructions to be executed concurrently.

Predicated Execution A mechanism that supports the conditional execution of individual instructions. This makes it possible to execute speculatively both branches of a branch instruction and retain the results of the branch that is ultimately taken.

Process A program in execution. A process is controlled and scheduled by the operating system.

Process Control Block The manifestation of a process in an operating system. It is a data structure containing information about the characteristics and state of the process.

Processor* In a computer, a functional unit that interprets and executes instructions. A processor consists of at least an instruction control unit and an arithmetic unit.

Processor Cycle Time The time required for the shortest well-defined CPU microoperation. It is the basic unit of time for measuring all CPU actions. Synonymous with *machine cycle time.*

Program Counter Instruction address register.

Programmable Logic Array (PLA)* An array of gates whose interconnections can be programmed to perform a specific logical function.

Programmable Read-Only Memory (PROM) Semiconductor memory whose contents may be set only once. The writing process is performed electrically and may be performed by the user at a time later than original chip fabrication.

Programmed I/O A form of I/O in which the CPU issues an I/O command to an I/O module and must then wait for the operation to be complete before proceeding.

Program Status Word (PSW) An area in storage used to indicate the order in which instructions are executed, and to hold and indicate the status of the computer system. Synonymous with *processor status word.*

Random-Access Memory (RAM) Memory in which each addressable location has a unique addressing mechanism. The time to access a given location is independent of the sequence of prior access.

Read-Only Memory (ROM) Semiconductor memory whose contents cannot be altered, except by destroying the storage unit. Nonerasable memory.

Redundant Array of Independent Disks (RAID)   A disk array in which part of the physical storage capacity is used to store redundant information about user data stored on the remainder of the storage capacity. The redundant information enables regeneration of user data in the event that one of the array's member disks or the access path to it fails.

Registers   High-speed memory internal to the CPU. Some registers are user visible; that is, available to the programmer via the machine instruction set. Other registers are used only by the CPU, for control purposes.

Scalar*   A quantity characterized by a single value.

Secondary Memory   Memory located outside the computer system itself, including disk and tape.

Selector Channel   An I/O channel designed to operate with only one I/O device at a time. Once the I/O device is selected, a complete record is transferred one byte at a time. Contrast with *block multiplexor channel, multiplexor channel.*

Semiconductor   A solid crystalline substance, such as silicon or germanium, whose electrical conductivity is intermediate between insulators and good conductors. Used to fabricate transistors and solid-state components.

Sequential Circuit   A digital logic circuit whose output depends on the current input plus the state of the circuit. Sequential circuits thus possess the attribute of memory.

Sign-Magnitude Representation   Used to represent binary integers. In an N-bit word, the leftmost bit is the sign (0 = positive, 1 = negative) and the remaining $N - 1$ bits comprise the magnitude of the number.

Solid-State Component*   A component whose operation depends on the control of electric or magnetic phenomena in solids (e.g., transistor crystal diode, ferrite core).

Speculative Execution   The execution of instructions along one path of a branch. If it later turns out that this branch was not taken, then the results of the speculative execution are discarded.

Stack*   A list that is constructed and maintained so that the next item to be retrieved is the most recently stored item in the list, last-in-first-out (LIFO).

Static RAM   A RAM whose cells are implemented using flip-flops. A static RAM will hold its data as long as power is supplied to it; no periodic refresh is required.

Superpipelined Processor   A processor design in which the instruction pipeline consists of many very small stages, so that more than one pipeline stage can be executed during one clock cycle and so that a large number of instructions may be in the pipeline at the same time.

Superscalar Processor   A processor design that includes multiple-instruction pipelines, so that more than one instruction can be executing in the same pipeline stage simultaneously.

Symmetric Multiprocessing (SMP)   A form of multiprocessing that allows the operating system to execute on any available processor or on several available processors simultaneously.

Synchronous Timing   A technique in which the occurrence of events on a bus is determined by a clock. The clock defines equal-width time slots, and events begin only at the beginning of a time slot.

System Bus   A bus used to interconnect major computer components (CPU, memory, I/O).

Truth Table*   A table that describes a logic function by listing all possible combinations of input values and indicating, for each combination, the output value.

Twos Complement Representation   Used to represent binary integers. A positive integer is represented as in sign magnitude. A negative number is represented by taking the Boolean complement of each bit of the corresponding positive number, then adding 1 to the resulting bit pattern viewed as an unsigned integer.

Unary Operator*   An operator that represents an operation on one and only one operand.

Unconditional Jump*   A jump that takes place whenever the instruction that specified it is executed.

Uniprocessing   Sequential execution of instructions by a processing unit, or independent use of a processing unit in a multiprocessing system.

User-Visible Registers   CPU registers that may be referenced by the programmer. The instruction-set format allows one or more registers to be specified as operands or addresses of operands.

Vector*   A quantity usually characterized by an ordered set of scalars.

Very Long Instruction Word   Refers to the use of instructions that contain multiple operations. In effect, multiple instructions are contained in a single word. Typically, a VLIW is constructed by the compiler, which places operations that may be executed in parallel in the same word.

Virtual Storage*   The storage space that may be regarded as addressable main storage by the user of a computer system in which virtual addresses are mapped into real addresses. The size of virtual storage is limited by the addressing scheme of the computer system and by the amount of auxiliary storage available, and not by the actual number of main storage locations.

Volatile Memory   A memory in which a constant electrical power source is required to maintain the contents of memory. If the power is switched off, the stored information is lost.

REFERENCES

Abbreviations

ACM   Association for Computing Machinery

IEEE   Institute of Electrical and Electronics Engineers

ABBO00   Abbot, D. *PCI Bus Demystified.* Eagle Rock, VA: LLH Technology Publishing, 2000.

ACOS86   Acosta, R.; Kjelstrup, J.; and Torng, H. "An Instruction Issuing Approach to Enhancing Performance in Multiple Functional Unit Processors." *IEEE Transactions on Computers,* September 1986.

ADAM91   Adamek, J. *Foundations of Coding.* New York: Wiley, 1991.

AGAR89   Agarwal, A. *Analysis of Cache Performance for Operating Systems and Multiprogramming.* Boston: Kluwer Academic Publishers, 1989.

AGER87   Agerwala, T., and Cocke, J. *High Performance Reduced Instruction Set Processors.* Technical Report RC12434 (#55845). Yorktown, NY: IBM Thomas J. Watson Research Center, January 1987.

ALEX93   Alexandridis, N. *Design of Microprocessor-Based Systems.* Englewood Cliffs, NJ: Prentice Hall, 1993.

ANDE67a   Anderson, D.; Sparacio, F.; and Tomasulo, F. "The IBM System/360 Model 91: Machine Philosophy and Instruction Handling." *IBM Journal of Research and Development,* January 1967.

ANDE67b   Anderson, S., et al. "The IBM System/360 Model 91: Floating-Point Execution Unit." *IBM Journal of Research and Development,* January 1967. Reprinted in [SWAR90, Volume 1].

ANDE98   Anderson, D. *FireWire System Architecture.* Reading, MA: Addison-Wesley, 1998.

ATKI96   Atkins, M. "PC Software Performance Tuning." *IEEE Computer,* August 1996.

AZIM92   Azimi, M.; Prasad, B.; and Bhat, K. "Two Level Cache Architectures." *Proceedings COMPCON '92,* February 1992.

BAEN97 Baentsch, M., et al. "Enhancing the Web's Infrastructure: From Caching to Replication." *Internet Computing*, March/April 1997.

BAIL93 Bailey, D. "RISC Microprocessors and Scientific Computing." *Proceedings, Supercomputing '93*, 1993.

BASH81 Bashe, C.; Bucholtz, W.; Hawkins, G.; Ingram, J.; and Rochester, N. "The Architecture of IBM's Early Computers." *IBM Journal of Research and Development,* September 1981.

BASH91 Bashteen, A.; Lui, I.; and Mullan, J. "A Superpipeline Approach to the MIPS Architecture." *Proceedings, COMPCON Spring '91,* February 1991.

BELL70 Bell, C.; Cady, R.; McFarland, H.; Delagi, B.; O'Loughlin, J.; and Noonan, R. "A New Architecture for Minicomputers—The DEC PDP-11." *Proceedings, Spring Joint Computer Conference,* 1970.

BELL71a Bell, C., and Newell, A. *Computer Structures: Readings and Examples.* New York: McGraw-Hill, 1971.

BELL78a Bell, C.; Mudge, J.; and McNamara, J. *Computer Engineering: A DEC View of Hardware Systems Design.* Bedford, MA: Digital Press, 1978.

BELL78b Bell, C.; Newell, A.; and Siewiorek, D. "Structural Levels of the PDP-8." In [BELL78a].

BELL78c Bell, C.; Kotok, A.; Hastings, T.; and Hill, R. "The Evolution of the DEC System-10." *Communications of the ACM,* January 1978.

BENH92 Benham, J. "A Geometric Approach to Presenting Computer Representations of Integers." *SIGCSE Bulletin*, December 1992.

BETK97 Betker, M.; Fernando, J.; and Whalen, S. "The History of the Microprocessor." *Bell Labs Technical Journal*, Autumn 1997.

BHAR00 Bharandwaj, J., et al. "The Intel IA-64 Compiler Code Generator." *IEEE Micro*, September/October 2000.

BLAA97 Blaauw, G., and Brooks, F. *Computer Architecture: Concepts and Evolution.* Reading, MA: Addison-Wesley, 1997.

BLAH83 Blahut, R. *Theory and Practice of Error Control Codes.* Reading, MA: Addison-Wesley, 1983.

BOHR98 Bohr, M. "Silicon Trends and Limits for Advanced Microprocessors." *Communications of the ACM*, March 1998.

BRAD91a Bradlee, D.; Eggers, S.; and Henry, R. "The Effect on RISC Performance of Register Set Size and Structure Versus Code Generation Strategy." *Proceedings, 18th Annual International Symposium on Computer Architecture,* May 1991.

BRAD91b Bradlee, D.; Eggers, S.; and Henry, R. "Integrating Register Allocation and Instruction Scheduling for RISCs." *Proceedings, Fourth International Conference on Architectural Support for Programming Languages and Operating Systems,* April 1991.

BREW97   Brewer, E. "Clustering: Multiply and Conquer." *Data Communications*, July 1997.

BREY00   Brey, B. *The Intel Microprocessors: 8086/8066, 80186/80188, 80286, 80386, 80486, Pentium, Pentium Pro and Pentium II Processors.* Upper Saddle River, NJ: Prentice Hall, 2000.

BURG97   Burger, D., and Austin, T. "The SimpleScalar Tool Set, Version 2.0." *Computer Architecture News*, June 1997.

BURK46   Burks, A.; Goldstine, H.; and von Neumann, J. *Preliminary Discussion of the Logical Design of an Electronic Computer Instrument.* Report prepared for U.S. Army Ordnance Dept., 1946, reprinted in [BELL71a].

BUYY99a   Buyya, R. *High Performance Cluster Computing: Architectures and Systems.* Upper Saddle River, NJ: Prentice Hall, 1999.

BUYY99b   Buyya, R. *High Performance Cluster Computing: Programming and Applications.* Upper Saddle River, NJ: Prentice Hall, 1999.

CART96   Carter, J. *Microprocesser Architecture and Microprogramming.* Upper Saddle River, NJ: Prentice Hall, 1996.

CATA94   Catanzaro, B. *Multiprocessor System Architectures.* Mountain View, CA: Sunsoft Press, 1994.

CHAI82   Chaitin, G. "Register Allocation and Spilling via Graph Coloring." *Proceedings, SIGPLAN Symposium on Compiler Construction*, June 1982.

CARM00   Carmean, D. "Inside the High-Performance Intel Pentium 4 Processor Microarchitecture." *Intel Developer Forum*, Fall 2000. ftp://download.intel.com/ design/id /all2000/presentations/pda/pda_s01_cd.pdf.

CHAS00   Chasin, A. "Predication, Speculation, and Modern CPUs." *Dr. Dobb's Journal*, May 2000.

CHEN94   Chen, P.; Lee, E.; Gibson, G.; Katz, R.; and Patterson, D. "RAID: High-Performance, Reliable Secondary Storage." *ACM Computing Surveys,* June 1994.

CHOW86   Chow, F.; Himmelstein, M.; Killian, E.; and Weber, L. "Engineering a RISC Compiler System." *Proceedings, COMPCON Spring '86,* March 1986.

CHOW87   Chow, F.; Correll, S.; Himmelstein, M.; Killian, E.; and Weber, L. "How Many Addressing Modes Are Enough?" *Proceedings, Second International Conference on Architectural Support for Programming Languages and Operating Systems,* October 1987.

CHOW90   Chow, F., and Hennessy, J. "The Priority-Based Coloring Approach to Register Allocation." *ACM Transactions on Programming Languages,* October 1990.

CLAR85   Clark, D., and Emer, J. "Performance of the VAX-11/780 Translation Buffer: Simulation and Measurement." *ACM Transactions on Computer Systems,* February 1985.

CLEM00   Clements, A. "The Undergraduate Curriculum in Computer Architecture." *IEEE Micro*, May/June 2000.

COHE81   Cohen, D. "On Holy Wars and a Plea for Peace." *Computer*, October 1981.

COLW85a   Colwell, R.; Hitchcock, C.; Jensen, E.; Brinkley-Sprunt, H.; and Kollar, C. "Computers, Complexity, and Controversy." *Computer,* September 1985.

COLW85b   Colwell, R.; Hitchcock, C.; Jensen, E.; and Sprunt, H. "More Controversy About 'Computers, Complexity, and Controversy.' " *Computer,* December 1985.

COME95   Comerford, R. "An Overview of High Performance." *IEEE Spectrum*, April 1995.

COME00   Comerford, R. "Magnetic Storage: The Medium that Wouldn't Die." *IEEE Spectrum*, December 2000.

COOK82   Cook, R., and Dande, N. "An Experiment to Improve Operand Addressing." *Proceedings, Symposium on Architecture Support for Programming Languages and Operating Systems,* March 1982.

COON81   Coonen, J. "Underflow and Denormalized Numbers." *IEEE Computer,* March 1981.

COUT86   Coutant, D.; Hammond, C.; and Kelley, J. "Compilers for the New Generation of Hewlett-Packard Computers." *Proceedings, COMPCON Spring '86,* March 1986.

CRAG79   Cragon, H. "An Evaluation of Code Space Requirements and Performance of Various Architectures." *Computer Architecture News,* February 1979.

CRAG92   Cragon, H. *Branch Strategy Taxonomy and Performance Models.* Los Alamitos, CA: IEEE Computer Society Press, 1992.

CRAW90   Crawford, J. "The i486 CPU: Executing Instructions in One Clock Cycle." *IEEE Micro,* February 1990.

CRIS97   Crisp, R. "Direct RAMBUS Technology: The New Main Memory Standard." *IEEE Micro*, November/December 1997.

DATT93   Dattatreya, G. "A Systematic Approach to Teaching Binary Arithmetic in a First Course." *IEEE Transactions on Education,* February 1993.

DAVI87   Davidson, J., and Vaughan, R. "The Effect of Instruction Set Complexity on Program Size and Memory Performance." *Proceedings, Second International Conference on Architectural Support for Programming Languages and Operating Systems,* October 1987.

DENN68   Denning, P. "The Working Set Model for Program Behavior." *Communications of the ACM,* May 1968.

DEWA90   Dewar, R., and Smosna, M. *Microprocessors: A Programmer's View.* New York: McGraw-Hill, 1990.

DIJK63 Dijkstra, E. "Making an ALGOL Translator for the X1." in *Annual Review of Automatic Programming, Volume 4.* Pergamon, 1963.

DOET97 Doetting, G., et al. "S/390 Parallel Enterprise Server Generation 3: A Balanced System and Cache Structure." *IBM Journal of Research and Development*, July/September 1997.

DOWD98 Dowd, K., and Severance, C. *High Performance Computing.* Sebastopol, CA: O'Reilly, 1998.

DUBE91 Dubey, P., and Flynn, M. "Branch Strategies: Modeling and Optimization." *IEEE Transactions on Computers*, October 1991.

DULO98 Dulong, C. "The IA-64 Architecture at Work." *Computer*, July 1998.

ECKE90 Eckert, R. "Communication Between Computers and Peripheral Devices—An Analogy." *ACM SIGCSE Bulletin*, September 1990.

ELAY85 El-Ayat, K., and Agarwal, R. "The Intel 80386—Architecture and Implementation." *IEEE Micro*, December 1985.

EVEN00 Even, G., and Paul, W. "On the Design of IEEE Compliant Floating-Point Units." *IEEE Transactions on Computers*, May 2000.

EVER98 Evers, M., et al. "An Analysis of Correlation and Predictability: What Makes Two-Level Branch Predictors Work." *Proceedings, 25th Annual International Symposium on Microarchitecture*, July 1998.

EVER01 Evers, M., and Yeh, T. "Understanding Branches and Designing Branch Predictors for High-Performance Microprocessors." *Proceedings of the IEEE*, November 2001.

FARM92 Farmwald, M., and Mooring, D. "A Fast Path to One Memory." *IEEE Spectrum*, October 1992.

FITZ81 Fitzpatrick, D., et al. "A RISCy Approach to VLSI." *VLSI Design*, 4th quarter, 1981. Reprinted in *Computer Architecture News*, March 1982.

FLYN71 Flynn, M., and Rosin, R. "Microprogramming: An Introduction and a Viewpoint." *IEEE Transactions on Computers*, July 1971.

FLYN72 Flynn, M. "Some Computer Organizations and Their Effectiveness." *IEEE Transactions on Computers*, September 1972.

FLYN85 Flynn, M.; Johnson, J.; and Wakefield, S. "On Instruction Sets and Their Formats." *IEEE Transactions on Computers*, March 1985.

FLYN87 Flynn, M.; Mitchell, C.; and Mulder, J. "And Now a Case for More Complex Instruction Sets." *Computer*, September 1987.

FLYN01 Flynn, M., and Oberman, S. *Advanced Computer Arithmetic Design.* New York: Wiley, 2001.

FRAI83 Frailey, D. "Word Length of a Computer Architecture: Definitions and Applications." *Computer Architecture News*, June 1983.

FRIE96   Friedman, M. "RAID Keeps Going and Going and..." *IEEE Spectrum*, April 1996.

FURH87   Furht, B., and Milutinovic, V. "A Survey of Microprocessor Architectures for Memory Management." *Computer,* March 1987.

FUTR01   Futral, W. *InfiniBand Architecture: Development and Deployment.* Hillsboro, OR: Intel Press, 2001.

GIFF87   Gifford, D., and Spector, A. "Case Study: IBM's System/360-370 Architecture." *Communications of the ACM,* April 1987.

GOLD91   Goldberg, D. "What Every Computer Scientist Should Know About Floating-Point Arithmetic." *ACM Computing Surveys*, March 1991. Available at http://www.validgh.com/

HAND98   Handy, J. *The Cache Memory Book.* San Diego: Academic Press, 1993.

HALF97   Halfhill, T. "Beyond Pentium II." *Byte*, December 1997.

HAYE98   Hayes, J. *Computer Architecture and Organization.* New York: McGraw-Hill, 1998.

HEAT84   Heath, J. "Re-evaluation of RISC I." *Computer Architecture News,* March 1984.

HENN82   Hennessy, J., et al. "Hardware/Software Tradeoffs for Increased Performance." *Proceedings, Symposium on Architectural Support for Programming Languages and Operating Systems,* March 1982.

HENN84   Hennessy, J. "VLSI Processor Architecture." *IEEE Transactions on Computers,* December 1984.

HENN91   Hennessy, J., and Jouppi, N. "Computer Technology and Architecture: An Evolving Interaction." *Computer,* September 1991.

HENN96   Hennessy, J., and Patterson, D. *Computer Architecture: A Quantitative Approach.* San Mateo, CA: Morgan Kaufmann, 1996.

HIDA90   Hidaka, H.; Matsuda, Y.; Asakura, M.; and Kazuyasu, F. "The Cache DRAM Architecture: A DRAM with an On-Chip Cache Memory." *IEEE Micro,* April 1990.

HIGB90   Higbie, L. "Quick and Easy Cache Performance Analysis." *Computer Architecture News,* June 1990.

HILL64   Hill, R. "Stored Logic Programming and Applications." *Datamation,* February 1964.

HILL89   Hill, M. "Evaluating Associativity in CPU Caches." *IEEE Transactions on Computers,* December 1989.

HINT01   Hinton, G., et al. "The Microarchitecture of the Pentium 4 Processor." *Intel Technology Journal*, Q1 2001. http://developer.intel.com/technology/itj/

HUCK83   Huck, T. *Comparative Analysis of Computer Architectures.* Stanford University Technical Report No. 83-243, May 1983.

HUCK00 Huck, J., et al. "Introducing the IA-64 Architecture." *IEEE Micro*, September/October 2000.

HUGU91 Huguet, M., and Lang, T. "Architectural Support for Reduced Register Saving/Restoring in Single-Window Register Files." *ACM Transactions on Computer Systems,* February 1991.

HUTC96 Hutcheson, G., and Hutcheson, J. "Technology and Economics in the Semiconductor Industry." *Scientific American*, January 1996.

HWAN93 Hwang, K. *Advanced Computer Architecture.* New York: McGraw-Hill, 1993.

HWAN99 Hwang, K, et al. "Designing SSI Clusters with Hierarchical Checkpointing and Single I/O Space." *IEEE Concurrency*, January-March 1999.

HWU98 Hwu, W. "Introduction to Predicated Execution." *Computer*, January 1998.

HWU01 Hwu, W.; August, D.; and Sias, J. "Program Decision Logic Optimization Using Predication and Control Speculation." *Proceedings of the IEEE*, November 2001.

IBM94 International Business Machines, Inc. *The PowerPC Architecture: A Specification for a New Family of RISC Processors.* San Francisco, CA: Morgan Kaufmann, 1994.

IBM01 International Business Machines, Inc. *64 Mb Synchronous DRAM.* IBM Data Sheet 364164, January 2001.

IEEE85 Institute of Electrical and Electronics Engineers. *IEEE Standard for Binary Floating-Point Arithmetic.* ANSI/IEEE Std 754-1985, 1985.

INTE98 Intel Corp. *Pentium Pro and Pentium II Processors and Related Products.* Aurora, CO, 1998.

INTE00a Intel Corp. *Intel IA-64 Architecture Software Developer's Manual (4 volumes).* Document 245317 through 245320. Aurora, CO, 2000.

INTE00b Intel Corp. *Itanium Processor Microarchitecture Reference for Software Optimization.* Aurora, CO, Document 245473. August 2000.

INTE01a Intel Corp. *IA-32 Intel Architecture Software Developer's Manual (2 volumes).* Document 245470 and 245471. Aurora, CO, 2001.

INTE01b Intel Corp. *Intel Pentium 4 Processor Optimization Reference Manual.* Document 248966-04. Aurora, CO, 2001. http://developer.intel.com/design/pentium4/manuals/248966.htm.

JAME90 James, D. "Multiplexed Buses: The Endian Wars Continue." *IEEE Micro*, September 1983.

JARP01 Jarp, S. "Optimizing IA-64 Performance." *Dr. Dobb's Journal*, July 2001.

JOHN91 Johnson, M. *Superscalar Microprocessor Design.* Englewood Cliffs, NJ: Prentice Hall, 1991.

JOUP88   Jouppi, N. "Superscalar versus Superpipelined Machines." *Computer Architecture News,* June 1988.

JOUP89a   Jouppi, N., and Wall, D. "Available Instruction-Level Parallelism for Superscalar and Superpipelined Machines." *Proceedings, Third International Conference on Architectural Support for Programming Languages and Operating Systems,* April 1989.

JOUP89b   Jouppi, N. "The Nonuniform Distribution of Instruction-Level and Machine Parallelism and Its Effect on Performance." *IEEE Transactions on Computers,* December 1989.

JTF01   Joint Task Force on Computing Curricula. *Computing Curricula 2001 Computer Science.* IEEE Computer Society and ACM, August 2001.

KAEL91   Kaeli, D., and Emma, P. "Branch History Table Prediction of Moving Target Branches Due to Subroutine Returns." *Proceedings, 18th Annual International Symposium on Computer Architecture,* May 1991.

KAGA01   Kagan, M. "InfiniBand: Thinking Outside the Box Design." *Communications System Design*, September 2001. (www.csdmag.com)

KANE92   Kane, G., and Heinrich, J. *MIPS RISC Architecture.* Englewood Cliffs, NJ: Prentice Hall, 1992.

KAPP00   Kapp, C. "Managing Cluster Computers." *Dr. Dobb's Journal*, July 2000.

KATE83   Katevenis, M. *Reduced Instruction Set Computer Architectures for VLSI.* Ph.D. dissertation, Computer Science Department, University of California at Berkeley, October 1983. Reprinted by MIT Press, Cambridge, MA, 1985.

KATH01   Kathail. B.; Schlansker, M.; and Rau, B. "Compiling for EPIC Architectures." *Proceedings of the IEEE*, November 2001.

KATZ89   Katz, R.; Gibson, G.; and Patterson, D. "Disk System Architecture for High Performance Computing." *Proceedings of the IEEE*, December 1989.

KEET01   Keeth, B., and Baker, R. *DRAM Circuit Design: A Tutorial.* Piscataway, NJ: IEEE Press, 2001.

KHUR01   Khurshudov, A. *The Essential Guide to Computer Data Storage.* Upper Saddle River, NJ: Prentice Hall, 2001.

KNUT71   Knuth, D. "An Empirical Study of FORTRAN Programs." *Software Practice and Experience,* vol. 1, 1971.

KNUT98   Knuth, D. *The Art of Computer Programming, Volume 2: Seminumerical Algorithms*. Reading, MA: Addison-Wesley, 1998.

KUCK72   Kuck, D.; Muraoka, Y.; and Chen, S. "On the Number of Operations Simultaneously Executable in Fortran-like Programs and Their Resulting Speedup." *IEEE Transactions on Computers,* December 1972.

KUGA91   Kuga, M.; Murakami, K.; and Tomita, S. "DSNS (Dynamically-hazard resolved, Statically-code-scheduled, Nonuniform Superscalar): Yet Another Superscalar Processor Architecture." *Computer Architecture News,* June 1991.

LEE91 Lee, R.; Kwok, A.; and Briggs, F. "The Floating Point Performance of a Superscalar SPARC Processor." *Proceedings, Fourth International Conference on Architectural Support for Programming Languages and Operating Systems,* April 1991.

LILJ88 Lilja, D. "Reducing the Branch Penalty in Pipelined Processors." *Computer,* July 1988.

LILJ93 Lilja, D. "Cache Coherence in Large-Scale Shared-Memory Multiprocessors: Issues and Comparisons." *ACM Computing Surveys,* September 1993.

LOVE96 Lovett, T., and Clapp, R. "Implementation and Performance of a CC-NUMA System." *Proceedings, 23rd Annual International Symposium on Computer Architecture*, May 1996.

LUND77 Lunde, A. "Empirical Evaluation of Some Features of Instruction Set Processor Architectures." *Communications of the ACM,* March 1977.

LYNC93 Lynch, M. *Microprogrammed State Machine Design.* Boca Raton, FL: CRC Press, 1993.

MACG84 MacGregor, D.; Mothersole, D.; and Moyer, B. "The Motorola MC68020." *IEEE Micro*, August 1984.

MAHL94 Mahlke, S., et al. "Characterizing the Impact of Predicated Execution on Branch Prediction." *Proceedings, 27th International Symposium on Microarchitecture*, December 1994.

MAHL95 Mahlke, S., et al. "A Comparison of Full and Partial Predicated Execution Support for ILP Processors." *Proceedings, 22nd International Symposium on Computer Architecture*, June 1995.

MAK97 Mak, P., et al. "Shared-Cache Clusters in a System with a Fully Shared Memory." *IBM Journal of Research and Development*, July/September 1997.

MALL75 Mallach, E. "Emulation Architecture." *Computer,* August 1975.

MALL83 Mallach, E., and Sondak, N. *Advances in Microprogramming.* Dedham, MA: Artech House, 1983.

MANJ01a Manjikian, N. "More Enhancements of the SimpleScalar Tool Set." *Computer Architecture News*, September 2001.

MANJ01b Manjikian, N. "Multiprocessor Enhancements of the SimpleScalar Tool Set." *Computer Architecture News*, March 2001.

MANO01 Mano, M. *Logic and Computer Design Fundamentals.* Upper Saddle River, NJ: Prentice Hall, 2001.

MARC90 Marchant, A. *Optical Recording.* Reading, MA: Addison-Wesley, 1990.

MARK00 Markstein, P. *IA-64 and Elementary Functions.* Upper Saddle River, NJ: Prentice Hall PTR, 2000.

MASH95 Mashey, J. "CISC vs. RISC (or what is RISC really)." *USENET comp.arch newsgroup, article 46782,* February 1995.

MASS97   Massiglia, P. *The RAID Book: A Storage System Technology Handbook.* St. Peter, MN: The Raid Advisory Board, 1997.

MAYB84   Mayberry, W., and Efland, G. "Cache Boosts Multiprocessor Performance." *Computer Design,* November 1984.

MCEL85   McEliece, R. "The Reliability of Computer Memories." *Scientific American*, January 1985.

MEE96a   Mee, C., and Daniel, E. eds. *Magnetic Recording Technology.* New York: McGraw-Hill, 1996.

MEE96b   Mee, C., and Daniel, E. eds. *Magnetic Storage Handbook.* New York: McGraw-Hill, 1996.

MILE00   Milenkovic, A. "Achieving High Performance in Bus-Based Shared-Memory Multiprocessors." *IEEE Concurrency*, July–September 2000.

MIRA92   Mirapuri, S.; Woodacre, M.; and Vasseghi, N. "The MIPS R4000 Processor." *IEEE Micro,* April 1992.

MOOR65   Moore, G. "Cramming More Components Onto Integrated Circuits." *Electronics Magazine*, April 19, 1965.

MORS78   Morse, S.; Pohlman, W.; and Ravenel, B. "The Intel 8086 Microprocessor: A 16-bit Evolution of the 8080." *Computer,* June 1978.

MOSH01   Moshovos, A., and Sohi, G. "Microarchitectural Innovations: Boosting Microprocessor Performance Beyond Semiconductor Technology Scaling." *Proceedings of the IEEE*, November 2001.

MOTO01   Motorola, Inc. *PowerPC MPC7410 RISC Microprocessor Hardware Specifications.* Denver, CO: 2001. www.motorola.com

MYER78   Myers, G. "The Evaluation of Expressions in a Storage-to-Storage Architecture." *Computer Architecture News,* June 1978.

NAYF96   Nayfeh, B.; Olukotun, K.; and Singh, J. "The Impact of Shared Cache Clustering in Small-Scale Shared-Memory Multiprocessors." *Proceedings of the Second International Symposium on High Performance Computer Architecture*, 1996.

NOVI93   Novitsky, J.; Azimi, M.; and Ghaznavi, R. "Optimizing Systems Performance Based on Pentium Processors." *Proceedings COMPCON '92,* February 1993.

OBER97a   Oberman, S., and Flynn, M. "Design Issues in Division and Other Floating-Point Operations." *IEEE Transactions on Computers*, February 1997.

OBER97b   Oberman, S., and Flynn, M. "Division Algorithms and Implementations." *IEEE Transactions on Computers*, August 1997.

OVER01   Overton, M. *Numerical Computing with IEEE Floating Point Arithmetic.* Philadelphia, PA: Society for Industrial and Applied Mathematics, 2001.

PADE81   Padegs, A. "System/360 and Beyond." *IBM Journal of Research and Development,* September 1981.

PADE88   Padegs, A.; Moore, B.; Smith, R.; and Buchholz, W. "The IBM System/370 Vector Architecture: Design Considerations." *IEEE Transactions on Communications,* May 1988.

PARH00   Parhami, B. *Computer Arithmetic: Algorithms and Hardware Design.* Oxford: Oxford University Press, 2000.

PARK89   Parker, A., and Hamblen, J. *An Introduction to Microprogramming with Exercises Designed for the Texas Instruments SN74ACT8800 Software Development Board.* Dallas, TX: Texas Instruments, 1989.

PATT82a   Patterson, D., and Sequin, C. "A VLSI RISC." *Computer,* September 1982.

PATT82b   Patterson, D., and Piepho, R. "Assessing RISCs in High-Level Language Support." *IEEE Micro,* November 1982.

PATT84   Patterson, D. "RISC Watch." *Computer Architecture News,* March 1984.

PATT85a   Patterson, D. "Reduced Instruction Set Computers." *Communications of the ACM.* January 1985.

PATT85b   Patterson, D., and Hennessy, J. "Response to 'Computers, Complexity, and Controversy.' " *Computer,* November 1985.

PATT88   Patterson, D.; Gibson, G.; and Katz, R. "A Case for Redundant Arrays of Inexpensive Disks (RAID)." *Proceedings, ACM SIGMOD Conference of Management of Data,* June 1988.

PATT98   Patterson, D., and Hennessy, J. *Computer Organization and Design: The Hardware/Software Interface.* San Mateo, CA: Morgan Kaufmann, 1998.

PATT01   Patt, Y. "Requirements, Bottlenecks, and Good Fortune: Agents for Microprocessor Evolution." *Proceedings of the IEEE*, November 2001.

PEIR99   Peir, J.; Hsu, W.; and Smith, A. "Functional Implementation Techniques for CPU Cache Memories." *IEEE Transactions on Computers*, February 1999.

PELE97   Peleg, A.; Wilkie, S.; and Weiser, U. "Intel MMX for Multimedia PCs." *Communications of the ACM*, January 1997.

PFIS98   Pfister, G. *In Search of Clusters.* Upper Saddle River, NJ: Prentice Hall, 1998.

POPE91   Popescu, V., et al. "The Metaflow Architecture." *IEEE Micro,* June 1991.

POTT94   Potter, T., et al. "Resolution of Data and Control-Flow Dependencies in the PowerPC 601." *IEEE Micro,* October 1994.

PRES01   Pressel, D. "Fundamental Limitations on the Use of Prefetching and Stream Buffers for Scientific Applications." *Proceedings, ACM Symposium on Applied Computing*, March 2001.

PRIN91   Prince, B. *Semiconductor Memories.* New York: Wiley, 1991.

PRIN99   Prince, B. *High Performance Memories: New Architecture DRAMs and SRAMs, Evolution and Function.* New York: Wiley, 1999.

PRZY88 Przybylski, S.; Horowitz, M.; and Hennessy, J. "Performance Trade-offs in Cache Design." *Proceedings, Fifteenth Annual International Symposium on Computer Architecture,* June 1988.

PRZY90 Przybylski, S. "The Performance Impact of Block Size and Fetch Strategies." *Proceedings, 17th Annual International Symposium on Computer Architecture,* May 1990.

RADI83 Radin, G. "The 801 Minicomputer." *IBM Journal of Research and Development,* May 1983.

RAGA83 Ragan-Kelley, R., and Clark, R. "Applying RISC Theory to a Large Computer." *Computer Design,* November 1983.

RAUS80 Rauscher, T., and Adams, P. "Microprogramming: A Tutorial and Survey of Recent Developments." *IEEE Transactions on Computers,* January 1980.

RECH98 Reches, S., and Weiss, S. "Implementation and Analysis of Path History in Dynamic Branch Prediction Schemes." *IEEE Transactions on Computers,* August 1998.

RODR01 Rodriguez, M.; Perez, J.; and Pulido, J. "An Educational Tool for Testing Caches on Symmetric Multiprocessors." *Microprocessors and Microsystems,* June 2001.

ROSC99 Rosch, W. *Winn L. Rosch Hardware Bible.* Indianapolis, IN: Sams, 1999.

SATY81 Satyanarayanan, M., and Bhandarkar, D. "Design Trade-Offs in VAX-11 Translation Buffer Organization." *Computer,* December 1981.

SCHA97 Schaller, R. "Moore's Law: Past, Present, and Future." *IEEE Spectrum,* June 1997.

SCHL00a Schlansker, M.; and Rau, B. "EPIC: Explicitly Parallel Instruction Computing." *Computer,* February 2000.

SCHL00b Schlansker, M.; and Rau, B. *EPIC: An Architecture for Instruction-Level Parallel Processors.* HPL Technical Report HPL-1999-111, Hewlett-Packard Laboratories (www.hpl.hp.com), February 2000.

SCHW99 Schwarz, E., and Krygowski, C. "The S/390 G5 Floating-Point Unit." *IBM Journal of Research and Development,* September/November 1999.

SEBE76 Sebern, M. "A Minicomputer-compatible Microcomputer System: The DEC LSI-11." *Proceedings of the IEEE,* June 1976.

SEGE91 Segee, B., and Field, J. *Microprogramming and Computer Architecture.* New York: Wiley, 1991.

SERL86 Serlin, O. "MIPS, Dhrystones, and Other Tales." *Datamation,* June 1, 1986.

SHAN38 Shannon, C. "Symbolic Analysis of Relay and Switching Circuits." *AIEE Transactions,* vol. 57, 1938.

SHAN95a   Shanley, T., and Anderson, D. *PCI Systems Architecture.* Richardson, TX: Mindshare Press, 1995.

SHAN95b   Shanley, T. *PowerPC System Architecture.* Reading, MA: Addison-Wesley, 1995.

SHAN98   Shanley, T. *Pentium Pro and Pentium II System Architecture.* Reading, MA: Addison-Wesley, 1998.

SHAR97   Sharma, A. *Semiconductor Memories: Technology, Testing, and Reliability.* New York: IEEE Press, 1997.

SHAR00   Sharangpani, H., and Arona, K. "Itanium Processor Microarchitecture." *IEEE Micro*, September/October 2000.

SHER84   Sherburne, R. *Processor Design Tradeoffs in VLSI.* PhD thesis, Report No. UCB/CSD 84/173, University of California at Berkeley, April 1984.

SIEW82   Siewiorek, D.; Bell, C.; and Newell, A. *Computer Structures: Principles and Examples.* New York: McGraw-Hill, 1982.

SIMA97   Sima, D. "Superscalar Instruction Issue." *IEEE Micro*, September/October 1997.

SIMO69   Simon, H. *The Sciences of the Artificial.* Cambridge, MA: MIT Press, 1969.

SMIT82   Smith, A. "Cache Memories." *ACM Computing Surveys,* September 1992.

SMIT87   Smith, A. "Line (Block) Size Choice for CPU Cache Memories." *IEEE Transactions on Communications,* September 1987.

SMIT89   Smith, M.; Johnson, M.; and Horowitz, M. "Limits on Multiple Instruction Issue." *Proceedings, Third International Conference on Architectural Support for Programming Languages and Operating Systems,* April 1989.

SMIT95   Smith, J., and Sohi, G. "The Microarchitecture of Superscalar Processors." *Proceedings of the IEEE*, December 1995.

SODE96   Soderquist, P., and Leeser, M. "Area and Performance Tradeoffs in Floating-Point Divide and Square-Root Implementations." *ACM Computing Surveys*, September 1996.

SOHI90   Sohi, G. "Instruction Issue Logic for High-Performance Interruptable, Multiple Functional Unit, Pipelined Computers." *IEEE Transactions on Computers,* March 1990.

STAL00   Stallings, W. *Data and Computer Communications,* 5th edition. Upper Saddle River, NJ: Prentice Hall, 1997.

STAL01   Stallings, W. *Operating Systems, Internals and Design Principles,* 4th edition. Upper Saddle River, NJ: Prentice Hall, 2001.

STEN90   Stenstrom, P. "A Survey of Cache Coherence Schemes of Multiprocessors." *Computer,* June 1990.

STEV64   Stevens, W. "The Structure of System/360, Part II: System Implementation." *IBM Systems Journal,* Vol. 3, No. 2, 1964. Reprinted in [SIEW82].

STON93   Stone, H. *High-Performance Computer Architecture.* Reading, MA: Addison-Wesley, 1993.

STRE78   Strecker, W. "VAX-11/780: A Virtual Address Extension to the DEC PDP-11 Family." *Proceedings, National Computer Conference,* 1978.

STRE83   Strecker, W. "Transient Behavior of Cache Memories." *ACM Transactions on Computer Systems,* November 1983.

STRI79   Stritter, E., and Gunter, T. "A Microprocessor Architecture for a Changing World: The Motorola 68000." *Computer,* February 1979.

SWAR90   Swartzlander, E., editor. *Computer Arithmetic, Volumes I and II.* Los Alamitos, CA: IEEE Computer Society Press, 1990.

TABA91   Tabak, D. *Advanced Microprocessors.* New York: McGraw-Hill, 1991.

TAMI83   Tamir, Y., and Sequin, C. "Strategies for Managing the Register File in RISC." *IEEE Transactions on Computers,* November 1983.

TANE78   Tanenbaum, A. "Implications of Structured Programming for Machine Architecture." *Communications of the ACM,* March 1978.

TANE99   Tanenbaum, A. *Structured Computer Organization.* Englewood Cliffs, NJ: Prentice Hall, 1999.

THOM94   Thompson, T., and Ryan, B. "PowerPC 620 Soars." *Byte,* November 1994.

THOM00   Thompson, D. "IEEE 1394: Changing the Way We Do Multimedia Communications." *IEEE Multimedia,* April–June 2000.

TI90   Texas Instruments Inc. *SN74ACT880 Family Data Manual.* SCSS006C, 1990.

TJAD70   Tjaden, G., and Flynn, M. "Detection and Parallel Execution of Independent Instructions." *IEEE Transactions on Computers,* October 1970.

TOMA93   Tomasevic, M., and Milutinovic, V. *The Cache Coherence Problem in Shared-Memory Multiprocessors: Hardware Solutions.* Los Alamitos, CA: IEEE Computer Society Press, 1993.

TOON81   Toong, H., and Gupta, A. "An Architectural Comparison of Contemporary 16-Bit Microprocessors." *IEEE Micro,* May 1981.

TRIE01   Triebel, W. *Itanium Architecture for Software Developers.* Intel Press, 2001.

TUCK67   Tucker, S. "Microprogram Control for System/360." *IBM Systems Journal,* No. 4, 1967.

TUCK87   Tucker, S. "The IBM 3090 System Design with Emphasis on the Vector Facility." *Proceedings, COMPCON Spring '87,* February 1987.

VOEL88   Voelker, J. "The PDP-8." *IEEE Spectrum,* November 1988.

VOGL94   Vogley, B. "800 Megabyte Per Second Systems Via Use of Synchronous DRAM." *Proceedings, COMPCON '94,* March 1994.

VONN45   Von Neumann, J. *First Draft of a Report on the EDVAC.* Moore School, University of Pennsylvania, 1945. Reprinted in *IEEE Annals on the History of Computing,* No. 4, 1993.

VRAN80   Vranesic, Z., and Thurber, K. "Teaching Computer Structures." *Computer,* June 1980.

WALL85   Wallich, P. "Toward Simpler, Faster Computers." *IEEE Spectrum,* August 1985.

WALL91   Wall, D. "Limits of Instruction-Level Parallelism." *Proceedings, Fourth International Conference on Architectural Support for Programming Languages and Operating Systems,* April 1991.

WANG99   Wang, G., and Tafti, D. "Performance Enhancement on Microprocessors with Hierarchical Memory Systems for Solving Large Sparse Linear Systems." *International Journal of Supercomputing Applications*, vol. 13, 1999.

WARD90   Ward, S., and Halstead, R. *Computation Structures.* Cambridge, MA: MIT Press, 1990.

WEIN75   Weinberg, G. *An Introduction to General Systems Thinking.* New York: Wiley, 1975.

WEIS84   Weiss, S., and Smith, J. "Instruction Issue Logic in Pipelined Supercomputers." *IEEE Transactions on Computers,* November 1984.

WEIS94   Weiss, S., and Smith, J. *POWER and PowerPC.* San Francisco: Morgan Kaufmann, 1994.

WEYG01   Weygant, P. *Clusters for High Availability.* Upper Saddle River, NJ: Prentice Hall, 2001.

WHIT97   Whitney, S., et al. "The SGI Origin Software Environment and Application Performance." *Proceedings, COMPCON Spring '97*, February 1997.

WICK97   Wickelgren, I. "The Facts About FireWire." *IEEE Spectrum*, April 1997.

WILK51   Wilkes, M. "The Best Way to Design an Automatic Calculating Machine." *Proceedings, Manchester University Computer Inaugural Conference,* July 1951.

WILK53   Wilkes, M., and Stringer, J. "Microprogramming and the Design of the Control Circuits in an Electronic Digital Computer." *Proceedings of the Cambridge Philosophical Society,* April 1953. Reprinted in [SIEW82].

WILL90   Williams, F., and Steven, G. "Address and Data Register Separation on the M68000 Family." *Computer Architecture News,* June 1990.

YEH91   Yeh, T., and Patt, Y. "Two-Level Adaptive Training Branch Prediction." *Proceedings, 24th Annual International Symposium on Microarchitecture,* 1991.

ZHAN01   Zhang, Z.; Zhu, Z.; and Zhang, X. "Cached DRAM for ILP Processor Memory Access Latency Reduction." *IEEE Micro*, July–August 2001.

INDEX

INDEX

Action
Replays

Action Replays

ARCHIE MACPHERSON

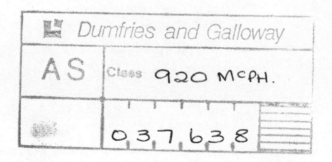

Dumfries and Galloway

AS | Class 920 McPH.

037,638

CHAPMANS

Chapmans Publishers Ltd
141–143 Drury Lane
London WC2B 5TB

BRITISH LIBRARY CATALOGUING IN PUBLICATION DATA
Macpherson, Archie
Action replays.
I. Title
791.445
ISBN 1–85592–564–8

First published by Chapmans 1991

Photoset in Linotron Ehrhardt by
Rowland Phototypesetting Ltd
Bury St Edmunds, Suffolk
Printed and bound in Great Britain by
Butler and Tanner Ltd, Frome, Somerset

To the family, especially for
tolerating the absences

Acknowledgements

I would like to thank John Burrowes, formerly of the Scottish *Daily Record* and author of several fine books, for his early advice on the manuscript. Pat Woods, librarian and researcher, ferreted to excellent effect for me. I am indebted also to Kevin McAra for his editing of the manuscript and his sensible suggestions. I could not have progressed much without the help of countless numbers of people from within BBC Television who were sources of both inspiration and verification for the narrative.

Contents

Illustrations

Introduction

The torch was about a quarter of a mile away when I first saw it. The carrier was completely hidden by an entourage consisting of motor-cyclists, a press and television car and a halo of accompanying runners. So the flame coming from his torch seemed to have an existence of its own. It danced and wavered like a firefly in the mellow Korean evening. The torch burned in a way that reminded me of Leerie the lamplighter piercing the gloom of Edinburgh. It was perhaps an odd thought to have but then the situation was far from ordinary. To be standing in running gear which did nothing to hide the ballast of over-indulgence on a road just outside a Korean city called Chongju was not what I had bargained for even a few days before.

The Olympic flame was heading my way and in my hand I held the oil-filled torch. In a few moments it would be fired into frenzy by the tongue of fire steadily nearing, sending me along the road lined by smiling, disciplined Korean faces. They were taking time out from their slavish commitment to their economic miracle to acknowledge the flame as it made its slow but inevitable progress towards the capital, Seoul, where the 1988 Olympic Games would commence three days later.

The distance I had to run was only one kilometre. I turned and looked ahead and saw a road apparently stretching to infinity and briefly wondered if I would make it. For all the number of times I had appeared in front of a camera I felt that this would leave me more isolated and vulnerable than I had ever been, even though I

I

was not involved in a direct broadcast. Nerves were weakening the legs, like a sudden onset of flu. It wasn't going to be a long run, I kept telling myself. One kilometre was a minute fraction of the global relay which had started on Mount Olympus many weeks before but each section would be shown on television. We had our own BBC unit there to record the moment. I had to speak a piece to camera just before the other runner was to reach me and there would only be one single, solitary chance to get it right. When I turned back the flame now seemed an inferno and was no more than twenty yards away. For the first time I could see the runner. He was a squat Korean with a smile as broad as the 38th parallel. I suddenly realised that after our flames had embraced we would never meet again.

In broadcasting terms it had taken me over two decades to reach Korea. Travelling the world now is relatively easy but the first assignment seemed like a journey to the ends of the earth even though it was only to Hamilton on a red bus. It was on an October day in 1962. The bus wheezed its way through Lanarkshire, halting clumsily at innumerable bus-stops like an elderly asthmatic calling in for sustaining whiffs of oxygen then lurching on its way again with triumphant coughs sending tremors throughout the interior. These buses always suggested the imminence of breakdown and I found myself wondering if it would be no bad thing if it did.

Lumbering towards the first professional engagement in broad-casting was like heading towards a blind date. I was in that early stage of paralysis which, in polite company, is described as stage fright. The mind was wandering. As the bus crossed Bothwell Bridge before crawling up past Hamilton Racecourse I found myself thinking of the battle fought there by the Covenanters of the 18th century and of how incredibly stupid men were to fight each other in the name of religion. These thoughts of a travelling atheist might seem wholly irrelevant now but in the struggle to stay on an even keel it seemed a healthy idea to be contemplating in a superior way the agonies of my ancestors. They put the apprehensions of a baptism in broadcasting into a more acceptable perspective. Only momentarily though. Something like panic intervened again and was not eased by observing the jumbled normality of the bus or the indifference of pedestrians about their business.

Hearts supporters passing in the opposite direction on their way to Hampden for the League Cup Final with Kilmarnock that very same afternoon looked out of the windows of their special buses with undisguised superiority. This merely emphasised the strange feeling of tranquillity inside Douglas Park for I was a follower of fashion and had not seen a football crowd of less than twenty thousand for years. There was a disconcerting air of privacy surrounding the fixture between Hamilton and Stenhousemuir in the Scottish Second Division. I wondered if this is how a foreign correspondent might feel on his first look at an alien setting.

The day was windy, the showers were occasional and heavy. Douglas Park was a stubborn piece of Lanarkshire dreariness that properly reflected the domestic plainness of football within the boundaries of a steel county. I found my seat and was disappointed to discover that the press there were not sectioned off or separated as I thought that exalted species always had a right to be. The homogeneity of the stand was a massive disappointment to me. No press box, indeed! It was like an novice entering his new church and discovering the altar missing.

However, I sat down beside a man bulky in his heavy overcoat and scarf. I was glad I did not have to disturb him to get to my seat for he was sitting at his phone in a manner I was later to recognise as the local correspondent's territorial crouch, like Fagin hoarding his cash. He was in the middle of an unforced drawling discourse which he was addressing to the empty pitch but which was being avidly listened to by other shapes, whose notebooks lay on the ledges in front of them like hymn books.

'What a bastard Kennedy is,' he was saying. 'What right has he to be sending ships out to stop the Russians on the high seas? The Americans have got rockets in Turkey, right on the Russian border.'

Someone mumbled assent; a disciple not quite believing but too scared to take issue. It was not exactly what I had expected. After all I had hoped that in coming to watch Hamilton Academicals play Stenhousemuir it might be easy to put up the shutters against the spine-chilling possibilities of the Cuban crisis. I had anticipated that football, this intensely human game with global appeal, might remind us of the joys of living and of the enduring primacy of the species. But after twenty minutes of a wind-swept anonymous game which left the pages of my notebook pallidly blank I have to admit thoughts of Armageddon began to infiltrate the mind.

I recalled that Pat Arrowsmith of CND had taken off with friends to the western extremity of Ireland to Macgillycuddy's Reeks at the first whiff of the Cuban confrontation claiming that in view of the prevailing winds it would be the safest place in Europe when the buttons were pressed. Not staying to fry with the rest of us had seemed cowardly but on reflection I began to envy Pat in her cabin 'of clay and wattles made' as we sat there at Douglas Park, in the front line.

'Who are you here for?' It was the man with the phone. He had barely turned his head in my direction but the eyes had summed me up. I toyed with the idea of a quick riposte: 'For the mortgage.' But something instinctively told me that the man had been hewn out of a quarry somewhere on Tinto Hill and that he would respect attempts at humour as tolerantly as a Wee Free minister listening to Bernard Manning. I choked back the words. And then I said it.

'For the BBC.' I regretted uttering it with so much emphasis as it implied I was on the pensionable staff and that Lord Reith was my great-uncle. In fact I was merely a trialist who might last only one broadcast. But it had an effect. The man stirred. He looked at my notebook and then back at me. 'The BBC?' There was no doubting the disbelief in the voice. 'Do you intend using a phone?' he asked. It was evident that if I wished to see the end of the game I couldn't exactly say, 'Yes, yours, when you're not looking.' I tried to put his territorial apprehensions at ease. 'I won't need a phone,' I replied. 'They're sending a car for me. I'm doing a live report from the studio ... in Glasgow.' I knew as soon as I said it that it was a mistake. It sounded hopelessly superior. James the chauffeur coming to pick me up at twenty to five sort of thing.

'A car?' he muttered with a shake of the head and something of a crimped smile around the lips. He made it sound like outrageous decadence. He was the first in a long line of licence-holders who would attempt to induce guilt at the Corporation's extravagant use of public funds. He didn't speak another word to me but every now and again looked down at something I tried to scribble in the notebook. On one occasion I felt like asking him the identity of a player, much as he repeatedly did with his other colleagues, but I sensed I was being left to my own devices. It was a day in which the feeling of impotence increased as the light of a late October afternoon diminished. Elsewhere, the world's fate was being decided.

The match ended in a 1–0 win for Hamilton. The car turned up exactly on time to whisk me back to the Queen Margaret Drive studios in Glasgow. On the way I wrote feverishly in the notebook, preparing to tell the world what Hamilton and Stenhousemuir had contributed to a very important Saturday afternoon indeed for mankind. I infused the match with a life it hadn't possessed. Not distorting, merely embellishing, I thought. Fortunately I didn't myself hear the report. My body went into a sort of trance as I sat down in front of the mike, which reared up at me like a hooded cobra about to strike.

It went tolerably well for they invited me back and continued to do so through five World Cups, three Olympic games, numerous occasions when I left the spittle of ecstasy on the surface of the commentator's lip-microphone, occasional conflicts, blazing arguments, huffs, panics, and triumphs. But the craft first touched upon in Hamilton remains the same. It is about observation and recording and interpreting. It is about trying to balance one's ambitions and inadequacies against the rigorous expectations of one's superiors, amongst whom you have to count the public. It is about selfishness and making a constant mistress of the suitcase. It is about sharing in folly and conceit and the massaging of ego.

Travelling the world from one event to another I have tended to view sport as part of the natural vegetation without which the planet could not survive. This prejudiced standpoint causes me no hardship. The power of access to places and events first conferred on me some considerable time ago has produced images which I can transmit in my mind whenever I choose. It is probably time, though, to offer the schedule to others. The selection is unaffected by what Fred Friendly, the great American producer, called 'the distant drummer of the ratings leading us all on'. These are simply the pictures which stuck and are in deeper focus than others.

That is why it is important to start at the first football field that made any sense to me, for old habits die hard. You would not have called it a stadium, but we thought it was, we from Shettleston in the East End of Glasgow. There I could claim, years before I went into broadcasting, that I had seen the debut of a star, a real live genuine solid-gold football personality. It made its mark.

But I have much to be thankful for from that first assignment to Hamilton. I am grateful, above all, to Mr Nikita Khrushchev for asking his captains on the ships heading for Cuba to please turn round and go home and take their rockets with them. Had he not, Saturdays might never have been the same again.

1

Home Ground

The first stop after getting out of the cradle was Shettleston Juniors. Sometimes I paid to get in. Sometimes I didn't. If you were good at it you could climb in over the back of Greenfield Park from the railway line and if you were caught by the polis (often while onlookers voiced that Glaswegian humanitarian plea, 'Leave the wean alane!') they simply led you round the ground and let you out again. It was not a bad risk to take although I never much fancied a life of delinquency having seen too often the boys from the local remand home. They were paraded in their brown uniforms to the cinema and swimming baths but never to the football park, which suggested that falling into trouble carried harsh penalties.

I paid distinctly more attention to match reports on the 'Town' as they were called, than I did to biblical text. I told adults dutifully that Jesus was central to my life. But in fact he was way down the league. He did not keep me awake at night, or send me to bed holding back tears or make me think that the key to life was a sixpence entry money and ninety minutes of triumph. The imagination was more engaged by the likes of 'Doc' McManus, a Shettleston player who came from that tradition of Scottish inside-forward who owed a great deal to stunted growth, a fondness for the bevvy, a disdain of sprinting any more than six yards and a body swerve in which the heavily endowed backside and torso seemed to part company for a fraction of a second.

I always thought he had been specially obtained for Junior

football from a knacker's yard in the Gallowgate. His lumpiness, reminiscent of a discarded couch, was part of what we liked most about him. He would put his arms out and roll his way towards a defence like a man reluctantly leaving a pub for his work but he occasionally found holes there with deft little touches. Then, he seemed to be defying nature and proving that football's geniuses do not need anatomical symmetry. Greenfield Park was, if not a second home, at the very least an outhouse of the extended family which allowed Shettleston to flourish as a stable, warm and civilised community.

The 'Town' did not own their ground then. It belonged to the adjacent bottle works at a time before plastic containers abominably usurped glass and brought its demise. The works formed a palisade to what might have been called the Kop end of Greenfield Park. It was of course not the only employer in the area. Further to the west for example was the Forge where they had made some of the shells and bombs which, so I was fondly told, helped us to win the war. A huge proportion of the local men worked there. But the football park clung to the bottle works and it helped form for me a strong image of work and play entangled inseparably. Men in dungarees walked to the pub for a drink then straight to the match. It was not an age for much pausing in between. The aroma of honest sweat permeated the queues for football matches. Men went not for gentle relaxation nor to abscond from pressure but simply to take it on in another sphere. Getting away from it all happened at the Glasgow Fair; football was a stimulant not an anaesthetic.

Considering what is on offer now for the working man, life had almost a plodding sameness about it. There was work, football, cinema, the 'dugs' and the pub. For most men, that is. But it had stability and the course of life was linear and true. Or so it seemed. Greenfield Park was right in the middle of Shettleston though boundaries in the East End were ill-defined. Football was certainly the most distinct way in which you could be recognised as belonging to either Parkhead, Tollcross, Bridgeton or Shettleston. Identities were largely blurred until familiarity with a particular football ground was established. I had no problems with the extent of this parish. To me the pull of the 'Town' went as far as the eye could see. North over the nearby railway line was the relatively modern development of Carntyne sloping cleanly to the sky. The eye was also inevitably drawn to the bulky profile of Barlinnie Prison sulking on the horizon.

From the terracings we threatened the jail to many and complained bitterly of the lack of justice involved in their freedom. One man who played for Petershill, a club from a more effete part of the city, was linked almost continually with Barlinnie by our supporters. He had clearly committed some unforgivable misdemeanour in the past and even when he appeared before kick-off the crowd were turned into a baying mob. A child molester could not have been given a less gracious welcome.

I never discovered what his original offence had been. There was nothing else for me to do but to shout and bawl abuse for how could so many of my neighbours be wrong. The swearing was good too since there was nothing quite as emancipating as letting rip with words that you might only have furtively whispered amongst your pals. Coming from a non-swearing family I took boldness to extreme and let vent with such lurid remarks as would have made my mother wish she had committed infanticide. The man, it must be said on reflection, did not seem ever to bother much but kicked everything in sight and played with a leering Bela Lugosi smile on his face.

My father's connection with the club had been one of the main reasons I had such an affection for it. He had gone into baking after school but by that stage of the late Forties had given up professional football. It was still a delight for me to sift through the pile of memorabilia including team sheets, letters from managers, contracts and listen to him recount how he would work night shift in the bakery and then go straight to the match to play. His only training in the week was a one hour rub-down with liniment by my mother. How many men, after all, could play on ash-pitches without having had any sleep, be fast enough to have run at Powderhall and also make perfect doughnuts in a small pot of fat on the kitchen hob? It all seemed noble. Consequently, missing a game at Greenfield Park felt like letting the family down. The addiction I developed for that tiny little patch of ground helped me come to terms with emotions which might have lain dormant and perhaps overwhelmed me at some stage of my life. I had the good fortune to run the whole gamut of them over and over again watching Shettleston Juniors before I moved into my teens.

However, I seem not to have been in an over-wrought state the day Tommy Docherty made his debut there. I cannot claim to have been conscious of the emergence of one of football's all-time stars and colourful personalities. But, as Max Boyce would say, 'I was there!' I do know that whilst most of us were tolerant there was a group who stood just to the east of the pavilion who were not too easily pleased. I swear they would have thought Pele better employed selling bananas in the fruit-market, Beckenbauer a poof and Maradona too wee. They were what critic Frank Rich is to Broadway or General Schwarzkopf to waffling questioners. They could destroy a reputation in a sentence. They enjoyed it. Having disposed of their aggression on the terracings the cat and the wife were probably safe on return from an awful game. Docherty would have known what a critical gallery he faced for he was brought up no more than a couple of hundred yards away from the Park in the 'Bowery', which as its name implies did not feature Palladian architecture.

Decades later when he came to the BBC studios for me to meet him personally for the first time and to interview him he breezed into the building with the cockiness of the man who used to act street saint for the Dead End Kids. For he was always Cagney to me. Nothing could alter that image, not all the years. He had decorated and embellished the quick-witted pugnacious style for it suited the image and it paid off for him in the south.

He had come back to Scotland to manage the national team and had already amassed in England a reputation for speaking his mind in ill-timed circumstances. When he made his point he always managed a decorous little smile but his eyelids flickered nervously, hinting at other meanings. I tried him out with the Shettleston Juniors debut story. He was impressed. He mentioned the Town with a reasonable reverence. His accent of course had undergone various vowel transplants for you cannot reside in England without submitting to some of its ways. Suddenly in almost mid-sentence he broke off his reverie and said, 'Two hundred pounds!'

'I beg your pardon?' I asked politely.

'Two hundred pounds. That'll do.'

'Do for what?' I responded naively.

'The interview,' he said and smiled endearingly at the secretary who had suddenly stopped typing.

'The interview?'

'Two Hundred Pounds,' he added with a little more emphasis, the eyelids blinking irreverently.

'For the Interview?'

'Or I don't do it,' he said mildly and then turned to the secretary to remark, 'Warm for this time of the year, isn't it, dear?'

'But Tommy,' I protested, 'we have set rates for interviews. The BBC tries to be meticulously fair about how it dispenses its money and I am sure you'll understand we are offering you the best platform for your views that you'll get anywhere and given the challenge of the job you face and the need to develop a healthy relationship between you, us, the SFA and the public . . .'

'Two hundred pounds,' he said.

I felt a slight tremor of panic and tried not to show it. We had an entire fully manned studio waiting downstairs for the entrance of the great man and his interview, which was going to be no longer than five minutes. Everything had been set up through me without any money having been mentioned and suddenly I was confronted with a man who clearly was not going to budge. Two hundred pounds even by today's standards still represents something of a handsome bounty but in the early Seventies it was like the gifts of the Magi.

As I left him to find the producer who alone could settle these things I wondered about that slim figure, hair neatly shedded, dapper in movement, sharp in action who had played with such obvious distinction on that Saturday afternoon at Greenfield Park. I had been in on the birth of a marvellous player after all. That in itself had seemed to me to promise kinship. But here I was, held to ransom by this great fellow Shettlestonian.

'The Doc wants two hundred notes or else he won't go on,' I told the producer in the gallery above the studio.

'Jesus H. Christ!' he hissed. (I had recently loaned him *The Catcher in the Rye*.) 'We can't pay two hundred. He won't go on? Look, go back and humour him! I'll have to make a few phone calls. Good God, we've billed him to go on tonight. Go on, humour him!'

Humouring the Doc would have been like trying to raise the level of the North Sea with a garden hose. When I went back to my office I had to restrain myself from laughing. There he was lounging back on a soft chair, whistling, scanning the secretary's *Woman's Own*, the only reading matter available, and putting on such an act of nonchalance as would have made you think he had demanded nothing more outrageous than milk in his coffee. I warmed to that. The healthy East End tradition of dissent was still very much alive. I had visions of BBC apparatchiks scurrying along corridors of power in London shouting, 'Docherty's asked for two hundred' and convening special meetings. I knew, and he knew that I knew, that he was going to get what he wanted. After about half-an-hour the producer phoned me. 'I don't want to create any precedent by this but get him along here and get the bloody thing done!'

As I put the phone down the Doc simply stood up and started walking towards the door. 'Where's the studio?' he asked. 'What was that you were saying about Shettleston? Good wee club the Town. Still got a soft spot for it. Learned a wee bit about the game there you know . . .'

When he sat down opposite me in the studio, two hundred pounds richer, I could see clearly in my mind's eye the youthful figure in the white shirt, as if when the chat were finished he would go to the dressing room, change and run out to play.

That day at Greenfield Park he had quite simply grabbed the eye not just because of his performance, the precise details of which are now lost to memory, but because of the circumstances. A boy sitting beside me dangling his legs over the barrier said with obvious pride, 'Docherty's goin' to the Cellic.' To say as much was to create more than usual interest for if you knew anybody was bound for either Rangers or Celtic you invested him with qualities which more often than not bore little relation to reality. A simple pass from such a lad would be like an exquisite gem. A header would be the perfection of timing, and so on. Potential Old Firm players came and went and most disappeared without trace like the children of Hamelin, never to wear a blue or green and white first-team jersey. But the most important aspect was that they played together, there at Greenfield. The boy, prepared to give Docherty the benefit of the doubt even before he had seen him kick a ball, wore a tiny religious medallion round his neck. We noticed these things. But here tribal identities which could otherwise lead to discomfort were rendered null and void by loyalty to the Town. Here it didn't really matter but just outside on the streets it did, to a greater or lesser degree.

To me religion then was just a way of validating the separation of people. After all we couldn't school together and nobody seemed to mind. Indeed, the policy was extolled on both sides. We couldn't be buried together or go to funerals together or, in most cases, socialise with each other. As we understood it the Catholics did all this according to diktat. The Protestants did it with voluntary exhilaration. But at that time just after the war there were no great examinations of this. Everybody had been concerned with getting rid of the Tories and making the great new socialist society work. Religious divisions were natural, and that was that.

The only feeling of tension probably came when the Orange Walk swung down Shettleston Road; a gloating, raucous, tuneful and resplendent arterial pulse pumping between dark-walled tenements as if it would never come to an end. My grandmother thought it a refined expression of Protestantism to stay indoors and react as if it wasn't happening and to take the progeny with her to play cards, but not for money because she was a Methodist. 'You're not watching the Walk,' my mother would say with the same kind of distaste she used when catching me with a girlie magazine once. I suspect that those reservations about the marchers also contained the feeling that, like the SAS, their methods might not inspire public approval but it was useful nevertheless to have them on one's side.

To me it was a game which adults played which harmed no one and indeed I thought the distaste misplaced. The Walk was colourful and if your elementary freedoms were limited because you could not cross the road in its path at least the marshal did not ask your religion before he broke your bones. The lead cane he carried was quite non-sectarian. If you were the other kind you simply stayed away or watched from afar until it passed. That of course was over-simplifying its effect. Its very existence was at least technically an affront to a large section of the community although, in truth, most Catholics took it with a smile on their faces and treated it as a freakish side-show. They simply dusted themselves down when it was all over and the following day you would not have guessed so much as a single flute had passed along Shettleston Road.

The fact is the bigotry which existed had little to do with the Orange Walk. There was no need for an annual cacophony of Protestant triumphalism to prolong and deepen the feelings of superiority the majority felt for the minority. That Catholics were alien to the basic traditions of Scottish life was simply taken for granted. Friendships did flourish across the barriers but, at the same time, they had an uncanny atmosphere of mutual constraint. Each party gauged just how far they could encroach on the fields of the other. I remember an elderly woman school-teacher of mine being roused by a letter from a priest in the *Glasgow Herald* and telling me solemnly, 'Glasgow was a Whig Presbyterian city. That is its roots and so it shall stay. Do you know that churches rang the bells of triumph and bonfires of celebration were burned in the city when the people heard that Bonnie Prince Charlie and his Jacobites had been defeated at Culloden?'

No, I hadn't known. I had thought he had been on our side. I felt this statement confused all sorts of issues. By comparison, Rangers and Celtic were much easier to understand. There was certainly no merging at their games, which sanctified the apartheid. Mutual hostility and ancient beliefs in religious superiority were considered not only proper and natural but lay like a sacred trust outside the area of any rational explanation. Only the ignorant could not understand that. To be very young and to be there was to be in awe of the sheer magnitude of arrogant conviction which solidified on the terracings. It had a terrible splendour.

The allegiances to Rangers and Celtic permeated the entire city and owed nothing to geography. You might have said the entire East End had a working-class unity which was honourably resistant to religious ghettos. Of course it was understood that by and large the district of Bridgeton was Orange and Garngad was Green, and there were odd little pockets where the identity was clearly aligned one way or the other. For instance, one street just off Shettleston Road was simply and irrevocably tagged 'Little Dublin'. The name was meant to contain insult as well as identity. But the religious spread was largely indiscriminate although people were unfailingly aware of the differences. You would know precisely, and no mistaking, how many Catholics and Protestants lived up a particular close. The Protestants were especially obsessed by the numbers game, fearful of the geometric progression of the Catholic birth-rate and used the word 'swamp' with such intensity that it still connotes to me crowded maternity wards.

So, Greenfield Park was exceptional. We could not be educated together. We rarely played in each other's groups. You watched Rangers or Celtic depending on accident of birth. But with not the slightest demur we could rub shoulders together to watch junior football. The white shirt of Shettleston Juniors was the shirt of neutrality. It was that important.

I remember most of all the start of the season and the evening football and the park crowded and the ball bouncing awkwardly on a pitch that for most of the time I went there was largely bare of grass. I recall men of thick unathletic legs and dumpy shin-guards who feared nothing and smote the ball with a vengeance. I recall glowing with triumph after a victory and mixing with the men streaming out of the ground, sharing their contentment and heading for the fish and chip shop where we would queue for an eternity mulling over the game and then walk homewards eating a poke of chips which had been salted and vinegared beyond redemption. I recall the despair of defeat in the Scottish Junior Cup which made a death in the family seem like an endowment.

And if it wasn't Greenfield Park for football it came through the wireless. We would huddle over it listening to a range of voices. Out of them emerged one which gave me a new cause for living: Peter Thomson. Being a commentator seemed like not a bad way of passing one's time.

2

Radio Times

Peter's voice was part of the family. His famous Wembley commentary remains a burnished relic of the great days of radio sports broadcasting. It rang with pleasure and defiance from the depths of the south that Saturday in 1949 as goal followed goal. They were described in detail so clear that when you listen to it again in the archives you can still see Mason's inside of foot passing, Houliston's header, Lawrie Reilly flashing through a defence. He created entire personalities just by mentioning their names. His language was economical, ungarnished besides the likes of the flamboyant Raymond Glendenning, but the more effective for all that. He could strike terror into the heart by incanting, 'And here comes Matthews to Lawton to Finney.' It was a Scots father warning you of the approach of Cumberland's cavalry.

No other game meant quite as much to me in those days as that Wembley international. It came from one of those larynxes which sounded golden and rich in vowel. When the final whistle sounded that day we hugged each other round the backyard and then rushed to the front road to wait for tram-cars. We lifted our hands with the fingers up denoting the score, 3–1, and the first tram-driver to pass us, bereft of such modern devices as transistor radios and ignorant of the dawning of the new age of Scottish supremacy at Wembley, greeted the news with a large beam on his face. His tram went wobbling off into the distance towards Glasgow and he rang the foot bell with relish, the sound carrying the good news to that slender and freakish minority who had not huddled over their wirelesses that afternoon and who had not been intoxicated by the good-natured sonority of Peter's voice.

I met him for the first time in the middle of September 1962. He was gently but deeply spoken, wore very heavy glasses and was quite Magooish in a way for when he took them off there was a blinking naivety to the eyes that suggested he would walk straight into the nearest wall. It is awkward to make contact with a man who is a public figure and whose familiarity as such simply increases his strangeness. All the tiny mental calculations I had made about him in preparation for the meeting didn't seem quite right. Smaller, quieter, more nervous, hesitant. I think he was actually proud that he had excited such public interest in his day. It wasn't vanity for he was as modest as anyone I have ever met in television or radio although, in common with everybody else, he liked to be recognised publicly. I think he never escaped from the need for public recognition to help counter his deep feeling of insecurity which I believe constantly plagued him. He was almost the definitive example of how a lad with hardly any academic credentials could join the Corporation and get to the top of his own area. But I always felt he suffered an inferiority complex amongst other broadcasting luminaries, some of whom rather looked down on him while at the same time envying Peter's popularity.

He was making the transition from radio to television but clearly he was more at home in the claustrophobic ambience of the groundfloor radio studios at Queen Margaret Drive in Glasgow which housed his cronies. That is a word which might have a certain pejorative sense but Peter had to like the broadcasters he gathered around him. They were, firstly and foremost, friends. They did have to have a certain ability at the microphone but essentially I do not imagine that anyone who could not get on with Peter socially could have lasted. This led to outrageous sycophancy to which he was deliberately myopic but the Saturday get-together in that sound radio studio to broadcast everything from top class football all the way through the Highland League via shinty and road races round Mull and other parts had a Pickwickian, clubbable feel to it and I suspect Peter enjoyed that aspect as much as the broadcasting itself.

There was not a real journalist among them and I found this

17

strange. There would be the occasional use of John Blair, who wrote for the *Sunday People*, Percy Huggins of the *Evening Times* and athletics writer Dunky Wright, but no more than that. In his use of part-timers like myself, from a wide variety of professions, he had created a gulf between broadcasting and journalism which led to outright hostility between the two areas. He did not seem to mind this in the least but it bothered me grievously for there was little doubt in my mind when I entered the portals of Queen Margaret Drive that I would attempt to embark on a career and not simply supplement my teaching income. I found little evidence of such burning ambition in any of the others I came across weekly and the cosiness of it all made me uncomfortable at times.

I wanted to know how to get on in this business. Some of the advice was breathtakingly frank. They sent me to Firhill to do a report for radio in one of my first outings. I learned early on that Firhill was something of a free-speech zone. You could say virtually anything you liked about Partick Thistle, there was hardly any come-back. People could safely give public support to them without being hounded for it. Others of course had to harbour private allegiances to the two major Glasgow Clubs, like the love that dare not speak its name. I sat beside Jameson Clark the actor, who did a lot of freelance work in both radio and television then. That day hunched within his overcoat and with his soft hat pulled to the back of his head he might have been playing the part of the hardened hack wearily mulling over in his mind the threadworn clichés of his craft before the game started. But in fact he was never other than the couthy approachable man who made you feel completely at ease even if you were a newcomer. So began a conversation that was to last on and off for about fifteen years. That day he lectured me and the words stuck.

'Listen,' he said. 'Keep as many interests going as you can. Don't get too ambitious just for television. Let me admit something to you. I sometimes waken up in the middle of the night in a cold sweat. Drenched. Just thinking about what's to come next for me when I can't guarantee that I'll get another piece of work in my life again. I've no guarantees. Nothing. In the news room I've just to wait and see what happens every day. Whiles I draw a blank. And someday they'll turn their back on me. Maybe next week for all I know. You never can tell. Cinema comes along once in a while but even there, sooner or later, they'll cast somebody else in the part you think you should have got and that'll be that. You've got to have guarantees. Whatever you do, get guarantees. If you're freelance like me you can be very vulnerable. Be warned.'

I tried hard not to take that to heart for I wanted to believe that once I had got my foot in the door nothing could stop me. Surely Jameson Clark, who at one time in the films played every kind of Scot short of the lead in *Greyfriars Bobby*, didn't have cold sweats?

However, having written short stories for the BBC before approaching Peter to get into sport I had obviously convinced him I was a cross between Guy de Maupassant and Jim Baxter. Such is the brimming confidence when opportunity stares you in the face early on. I was off and running. Every week I was at some ground to report a game. Normally it would be a match of no great significance and I would come to recognise that stratum of journalists who worked painstakingly in the middle regions of the game. Some were older and resolutely beyond any change. Others, younger like myself, were bursting with ambition and biding their time for the day when the Old Firm clamour would not merely be a distant sound of battle but the real thing, with the political shrapnel of the occasion making them the hardened correspondents they all wished to be.

Peter took great comfort from having these people around him but underneath his usually phlegmatic appearance he was a profoundly uneasy man. 'It is difficult to recall some games,' he told me not long after I started to work for him. 'I got so uptight about them sometimes I didn't know whether I was at Hampden Park or Wembley when I was working. All I could do was concentrate on the match. It just got so I wanted the game finished, over and done with. I just wanted out of it, away from it all.'

This feeling of desperation never really surfaced in his commentaries which were models of sure, simple statement. He certainly treated the 'phoney' commentator with disdain. He vividly recalled for me the occasions he observed the Canadian commentator Stewart MacPherson, who attained a formidable reputation in the UK just after the war, arriving at the Outside Broadcast position with pre-arranged phrases written out on cards. These were slipped in at 'appropriate' moments during a broadcast. 'If you're going to do this,' he said wryly, 'don't write them out on cards for people to see. Memorise them. Or better still, try and be spontaneous. That, I suppose, is what we are here for.'

According to Peter, Glendenning described one of the famous goals at Hampden Park, Billy Steel's thirty-yarder for Britain against the Rest of Europe in 1947 as they were centring the ball to restart the game. He was expressing both criticism and admiration for the famous English commentator who could both be so behind the play yet salvage himself with a seamless verbal patch-up. He was in effect warning me, without expressing it in a deliberately censorious way, of the ethics of sound radio broadcasting, of the awesome power of the commentator. That person had a duty to be accurate and honest and yet he might also have the ability to create images and events of his own, as his tongue and ego got the better of him. It was a Scottish puritanical observation, much too concerned with guilt, and for me seemed to make the possibility of the twinning of inspired rhapsodising and objectivity an impossible ideal. But the more I got to know Peter the more I realised that broadcasting had become a bed of nails for him. At times he looked and sounded a tortured man. The pressures which grew through his sound radio experiences intensified cruelly when he had to make the transition to television.

Whilst I gained the impression that everybody in broadcasting had rubbed their hands in anticipation of this new challenge I sensed, even though I entered the scene some years after the revolution had started, that the deeper feelings were of regret. This was a period of transition from the medium which had forged the BBC's reputation to something which was as yet untamed and volatile, and clearly at times beyond the discreet and careful control of the sound radio programme. After all, Peter Thomson had been a pioneer of radio and here he was like a wagon master having reached the coast with his charges being asked to head for the unknown again with barely a rest. Few of his contemporaries were equipped for such a dramatic change. In many ways they suffered the same sort of fate, in inverted form, bequeathed Hollywood by the *Jazz Singer.* Voices became handicaps in the movies. So, on TV, faces and presentation very often did not suit the new medium.

Nothing was hidden. Looking straight at the television camera either in a studio or out of doors without the aid of script, which one could crouch over in a radio studio, was like facing a firing squad. The transition produced victims.

One man who coped well was George Davidson. He was the ex-sea captain whose almost imperious voice had virtually shoved Peter's off the air in commentating on football. George looked authoritative in the studio and sounded almost professorial behind the mike. He was of enormous value to me, not so much in strict broadcasting terms but in the way he seemed to be able to ride above crisis like the veritable mariner in the storm. I have been with him when he was harangued by supporters and he treated it with the verbal disdain of a headmaster quelling a rebellious class of kids. In his days at sea, he had been in the first boat to land in Yokohama after the great earthquake of 1923. He used that experience to try and enlighten me as to the demands of broadcasting.

'You know,' he said to me once, 'I have been virtually assaulted by supporters, insulted by the occasional manager, made mistakes in front of camera, been criticised by the public for all kinds of things and yet it is nothing. I am surrounded by people who worry about the slightest thing, they are obsessed with broadcasting and don't know what the real world is. After seeing the bodies piled up in heaps in that city that day and the maimed and the barely surviving crawling in the streets it does give you a kind of perspective on life. We can become too self-obsessed. Broadcasting is not easy. But it's only as difficult as you make it yourself. Keep a sense of perspective and don't put up the shutters around you in here. There are other things in life more important.'

The most important thing for me then and there though was to make it. To where in broadcasting I was not sure, but I had now got it into my system. Even after only a few weeks a new impetus had been added to life. I was afflicted by Saturday afternoon fever.

It is about five-fifteen. We have returned from the games we have been reporting. Papers are strewn about the table, on the middle of which is the microphone, the object of all our desires. On the immediate outside of the studio, through the glass in the production suite, Peter Thomson paces up and down, his hand interminably in his pocket worming away nervously at his balls. A voice is linking the items, ponderously but with great sense of diction. It belongs to the small Toulouse Lautrec figure of Andy Cowan Martin, whose physique does not immediately suggest the power of voice or the capacity to lower tumblers of the gold stuff after programmes. He was once about to make an announcement when he handed the piece of paper hurriedly to his co-presenter who had one look then shoved it to the reporter who after a hurried glance passed it back to Andy who simply threw it to the floor without a word. He had vowed never to try to announce the result of the dreaded Buchan Firkin Trophy which was to him 2–1 on for a spoonerism.

We are relaxed. These are friends together. In the insulated studio the impression is that nobody is listening anyway. We have our notes in front of us. They have been changed several times. Adjectives have been strewn around, metaphors normally revolving round strength, endurance and character are curlicues on our pages. We launch into it and are finished after about ninety seconds but hungering for more.

Only a few yards away is the television studio. We arrive breathless seeking to know how the game finished because invariably we have to leave half-way through the second half to get back in time. Someone wearing headphones greets you without a smile for this is grim business bringing the news in. The door is squeezed open noiselessly. Dark shapes are silhouetted against the crescent of light which dominates the back of the studio where sits Peter Thomson tense and so smothered in make-up an audition for a Japanese Noh play seems imminent. There is no evidence of camaraderie. In the artificial division of harsh light and bulky darkness the impression gathers that you are about to be cross-examined by a public prosecutor. You are ushered to the set beside Peter. He is too involved to acknowledge your presence and when you hear his words of introduction, slow and deliberate, the feeling deepens that you have had no preparation and that sentences are cruel obstacles in the way of your ultimate escape. A red light goes on, a hand waves under a camera and you are on.

Those almost off-the-cuff reports in the early days still represent to me the hardest of all the television challenges. When the lights flooded on after the programme the sense of relief would gush through the studio. Whereas the radio experience suggested travelling in a well-upholstered limousine in some considerable comfort, television was like shooting the rapids in a leaky canoe.

About a month or so after I had started regular reporting Peter sat in his office assessing me. 'People will start recognising you in the streets,' he said. It was a sort of coded way of saying he thought I would be around for a while. 'You get used to it.' I didn't really believe that sentiment then and still don't now. One way or the other that sort of distant recognition produces a self-consciousness that is as comfortable as a hair-shirt.

'Just smile a bit more and you'll be all right,' he went on. Smile? It was an effort of mind merely to breathe in front of a camera let alone get brain and muscle co-ordination for a smile.

'Not too many big words,' he said, smiling. It was the gentlest of reprimands. I had used the phrase 'peripheral vision' about one player. My phrase had come straight from the coaching manual of one Walter Winterbottom of the FA and I thought I was being clever. I was being told very nicely I was being a smart arse. 'What are your ambitions?' he suddenly asked. Well, I couldn't resist. 'To do a commentary at Wembley,' I replied. He looked away and tilted his head as he had a habit of doing then looked back straight at me, with a wry smile bending his mouth. 'You never know,' he said.

Not long after that I was invited to London by the sports editor there, Angus Mackay, who on the strength of a few radio broadcasts offered me a job at the time Eamonn Andrews was leaving *Sports Report* to go to ITV. My head was greatly turned by this but I recall most of all from that whirlwind visit Brian Moore, who was still involved with radio broadcasting, turning to me out of earshot of Mackay and saying with great deliberation, 'You'd be mad to come here. If you don't suit you could be back to Scotland in a few weeks' time, right out of a job. This can be a very cruel place.'

It can be and probably was and I didn't accept. I did not need to agonise all that much for another seed had been sown, television commentary. Peter had used the offer of this to keep me in Scotland. More than that though, I had gone with George Davidson to Celtic Park just before the London visit to watch as he commentated on film. This was a close observation of a new technique and a new power. I certainly wanted a bit of this. I especially liked the way he had developed a rapport with the crowd, some of whom detested him, whilst others loved him. I saw him then not just as a commentator but a catalyst. I marvelled at this. I felt myself becoming infected with this new possibility of becoming a figure of some controversy. The lure was infinitely stronger than the distant attraction of Portland Place, W1.

3

·Camera Capers

It was the year Nelson Mandela was put in prison. It was the year Baxter broke his leg in Vienna and was never quite the same player again. I prefer to think of 1964 though as the start of the Mack Sennett period of television for me. It was still the age of black and white film even for the coverage of a football match and most times we were able to get images on a screen which looked as if they had been sent to the Shettleston 'steamie', put through a wringer and hung out to dry before being seen by the viewer. In those days technology was still dependent on the Good Fairy of the North to get us on the programme in time and in one piece.

We worked off tiny little platforms mostly tucked unobtrusively against grandstands at the back of enclosures. The vantage points were roughly equivalent to that of a worm emerging from subterranean safety before being plucked out by the early bird. Even Eisenstein or Cecil B De Mille would have found it hard to make anything of a film camera down there. Nor did they have to deliver the goods every week to a Saturday night audience. It clearly possessed a tolerance level then which makes your urbane viewer now seem like a cynical shark.

I was introduced to my first film unit one Saturday in August of that year on the little postage stamp platform at Fir Park, Motherwell. We were strangers. All five of us. As it was the cameraman just happened to be Eddie McConnel, one of the most respected documentary film-makers in the country. I remembered an award-winning film he had made about a drunk coming to terms with wakening up in the centre of Glasgow. His actor had been Phil McCall and one of the shots had stuck in my mind; a low angle view along the steps of the Commercial Library just off Queen Street, with a bottle in the foreground. His ability to handle the camera at that low angle, I thought, would stand him in good stead at Fir Park where there was a fair chance of some exciting shots of the players' studs, from below. But of course that had been a perfectly framed static shot. What was a respected documentary maker doing here?

'Earning a living,' Eddie told me before the camera rolled. I could tell he was also a philosopher. Apart from being there to do my first commentary for television I was coming face to face with the realities of surviving in the film industry in Scotland. Football would help finance Eddie for other projects. With that end in mind he kept his eye glued to the viewfinder for ninety minutes trying to spot the ball. Four years later he was to make *The Celtic Story*.

Although it was always referred to as the 'unit' the main feature of the coverage of football then was how disjointed everything was. We were all separated from the studios for the whole afternoon so they had no idea what was coming back to them. We employed drivers to speed canisters of film back to Queen Margaret Drive so that they could be developed as quickly as possible. Some had the intrepid spirit of the Pony Express in their bones. Others would dally along the taverns or bookies of Great Western Road, thus sending the film-processors apoplectic. On one occasion, coming all the way back from Easter Road with a can which contained the only goal of the first half, the driver absconded altogether. He was never seen again and since he was known for humming 'The Sash' as he traipsed the highways and byways of the land we could only assume he was carrying a goal for Hibs against Rangers. He had sacrificed himself and the can of film for the cause. Another became a friend of goalkeepers. He didn't wait for us in the car-park but instead boldly watched the game from behind the net along with the photographers. Unlike them, he had nothing much else to do and would regularly confer with goalkeepers. A goalkeeper once asked him to put a bet on for him during a game. Walking round the track, out into the street through the tunnel, up the street to the bookies and back again, he duly did so as play raged on.

But as we sat there together on those Saturdays on these platforms each of us would never know for certain what was actually going on to film let alone how or when it would get back to the studios. I lifted up the mike just before kick-off that first day hoping that somebody would say something in the way of guidance of when to start and stop. All Peter had said that morning was, 'Remember it's not radio. Don't overdo it!' I no longer had the supreme advantage of radio's immediacy. Here we would have to cover the equivalent of the Grand National before reaching the public, if at all.

I launched into it though. Ten minutes of the Motherwell–Hibs game had elapsed when suddenly there was a violent tap on the shoulder. It was the sound man. 'Stop,' he said abruptly. I also saw Eddie pull back from his camera and a flurry of activity exploding round the camera as his assistant pulled frantically at the hump of the magazine of film. 'Fault?' I asked with a sudden, falling heart. 'No. Change,' the sound man said. 'Changing the film.'

It is here I have to admit to a technical blindness which has afflicted me all my broadcasting life. Somehow I have always wanted to remain quite distant from anything to do with television's innards. I want the large intestine to function with regularity but I do not necessarily want a working knowledge of the process. Perhaps I ought to put it down to that day when I felt it was better not to get involved, not to fret, but just to let skill, expertise and sheer fate take over. As the unit only had one camera and as the film only lasted ten minutes they had to take out the old magazine and put in the new and do it pretty bloody quick, for the rules of association football did not allow for stoppage whilst cameramen changed reels.

Nobody had prepared me for this. It did occur to me to ask, 'Yes, but what happens if a goal is scored while you're changing mags?' I didn't, though, for it would have betrayed ignorance of the whole process and in any case a cameraman or his assistant involved in this is as easily lured into idle conversation as a man grappling with a lion. I simply put down the mike and watched this feverish activity as Motherwell and Hibs quite inconsiderately tried to score goals against each other.

They seemed to take an eternity, the unit that is. As they fumbled to get the casing snapped shut a Motherwell player took a ball in that inimitable stride of his and from ten yards struck for goal. It soared towards Motherwell Bridge Works well over the bar. A Motherwell supporter just in front of us shouted, 'Ya mug.' I felt like shouting, 'Stay there, ya beauty.'

I struggled with this new medium, all the time thinking, 'What's going to happen after another ten minutes?' That in itself was discomfiting but the essential unrest came from the practice of restraint. On radio you treat your larynx and the listener to a veritable avalanche of words. Here, I knew I had to practise, although was not at all sure that I was managing, the art of verbal contraception, of shielding myself and the listener from the possible birth of irritation. Alas, no foolproof method of control has yet been devised for this.

The gods were kind to us that day, or so we thought. The studio had already started the editing of the film before the first half had ended so by the time we returned they were well into shaping the game for the evening transmission. I stood for the first time at the back of the BBC building overlooking the Kelvin, examining the first examples of our work. The film was edited in negative which I found most disconcerting. Faces were black, jerseys were white. The sound track was separate, so the editor was working with two ribbons of celluloid which he had to keep in 'sync'. Juggling these different elements made it difficult to concentrate especially as he was working from a hand-cranked machine with a viewing screen not much bigger than a credit card. This would be about the same 'window' as the cameraman had at the actual game except he had to keep his eye fixed on it and pull a camera-head around at the same time to follow the ball. Even standing there peering at the tiny screen I could barely make out any spherical object at all. My admiration for Eddie increased as I realised he missed little and I also began to appreciate that only one tiny slip, an eye watering, a hair in the works, a slip of the hand, a sneeze and the programme could be made to look ridiculous. He was far and away the most important element in our coverage.

Then the sound came. Peter Thomson had come down to the cutting room desperately anxious for me to have succeeded. When a producer picks out a potential broadcaster and puts him up front he is, to a great extent, staking his reputation on him. He certainly doesn't want to be let down and made a fool of. Conversely, if he has found a star, his stock rises. Sometimes, because of that, he is not entirely objective in appraising the early results. He is invariably optimistic. The film editor took the sound reel off the small hand-cranked machine, put it on some other contraption and we listened.

My voice sounded as if it were coming from a catacomb. It had more of the timbre of the basso profundo of grand opera than league football commentary. It didn't relate. There was a long, horrible moment when we all stood around listening without anybody wishing to volunteer a comment. After a while Peter said, 'Could you stop it for a moment?' and then added, 'Who was the sound man?' Right away I could see he was being defensive of me. It was somebody else's fault. But it wasn't of course and I think he knew it. I suddenly realised that the voice was a pure mimicking of his own, that I was trying to do a 'Peter Thomson'. Imitation might be the sincerest form of flattery but in this instance it sounded like pure pantomime and I could see that Peter was disturbed.

Worried or not he put it out that night and frankly in a succeeding television generation it would never have seen the light of day, so droning was the voice. I didn't watch the programme: I had seen and heard enough in the film-cutting room. A friend said to me the following week, 'I thought at one stage you sounded like Paul Robeson.' He was, I think, trying to be kind.

As the weeks went by and I got over the trauma of hearing my voice on film for the first time I got slightly cuter about it all and tried to save any eloquence for those moments when I knew it was more likely to be used; for example immediately after a goal had been scored or at kick-off. What I had to take into account, though, was that the film would pass through many tests before it would reach the screen. It would have to be processed firstly. This was either handled by an outside company or within the BBC itself. Wherever it went there was absolutely no guarantee that it would come out unscathed or indeed come out at all. Much of our film looked like chopped liver. This had nothing to do with lack of professionalism within the system but much to do with the hazards of rushing it on to the screen.

But collectively we knew there were constraints we had to work within, some of which existed during the actual commentary. You had never to talk over a goal-kick. You had never to breathe a word during a throw-in. You had not to open your mouth as a player was being treated for an injury. You had to shut up instantly whenever you had identified a free-kick. You had not to ramble on after kick-off unless there was a quick goal. All these were clearly recognisable edit points through which the editor could slice the razor and make neat joins. If you were not talking over the goalkeeper kicking the ball upfield the editor, if he so wished, could make the ball land ten minutes later by inserting a cutaway shot of a player simply looking vacantly into space. Crowd shots were the best means of editing though. They simply filmed the crowd standing on the terracing and could use them over and over again. Sometimes they didn't match. You would see a ball rolling over the touchline for one team to claim a throw-in and the next shot would be of the crowd hugging and kissing each other. Only at Firhill was that edit not thought unusual. When we had problems with sound we would simply lay on some other stuff from the library stock. One night we showed Hibs scoring at Easter Road, followed by cheering and a distinct choir in the background singing 'We'll Guard Old Derry's Walls'. As you can imagine, the culture shock in Auld Reekie was immense.

With all of this in mind it was an accomplishment merely to get through a commentary and see the end product on the air at all let alone being concerned with the niceties of style. Frequently, Peter had to go on and face the public to make apologies for some sort of breakdown and the man must have been near to tears on some occasions although he put a brave face on it. One night I was lending some support in the background when the film came in from Celtic Park after an Old Firm game. Celtic had won 1–0.

'Jesus Christ,' Peter said just as he was about to go on for a rehearsal of the opening. 'We've not got the Celtic goal. It's lost.' 'Lost? Where?' I said as I saw his features dissolve into those of a man getting his first taste of the thumb-screw. 'God knows. God knows,' he repeated in a demented way. Technical mishaps were far from unique but this was somewhat different. An Old Firm game? A Celtic goal? The only goal of the game? Not going to be shown? As we would say in the trade, 'Batten down the hatches.'

Celtic did not trust the BBC then. In a way, you could hardly blame them for their circumspection. In the famous 7–1 victory over Rangers in the 1957 League Cup Final a technician in London, tele-recording the match all the way down the line from Hampden, put a dust cover over the lens at half-time when the score was 2–1 and forgot to take it off at the re-start of the second half so Celtic's other five goals and the cavalry charge of white horses into the riotous Rangers end could not be shown. Try telling that to a Celtic supporter. Then think of what it must have been like for Peter Thomson to have had to explain it away to Bob Kelly, the Celtic chairman. The game in its entirety has never been seen publicly although a private amateur film was subsequently uncovered and I am surprised Celtic did not commission Carl Davis to put it to music.

That night, after a po-faced Peter Thomson had calmly announced that Celtic had won but, sorry, their goal could not be shown for technical reasons, I experienced the violent reaction of the public for the first time. Each call I took either started, concluded or was interspersed with the soubriquet 'Orange bastard'. It is the characteristic of these calls that they do not really expect a rational explanation. It is the letting-off of steam that is the most important issue. I was reminded that man does not live by bread alone but thrives also on the imagined plottings of the establishment.

As it happened, we discovered much later that that particular piece of film had been chewed up in processing. But it has to be said that there was a liberality to the 'buggeration factor', which then was as virulent as Asian flu. When we went to Hampden Park on an October evening in 1965 to cover the Rangers–Kilmarnock League Cup semi-final it seemed like any other night. It was not to be though. Going into Hampden Park then was considerably worse than it is now which means it was horrendous. I believe the lights have since been upgraded but then the luminosity was that of a ghost-train tunnel at the carnival. To pass through the underbelly of the stand to get to the back of the enclosure required the courage of a pot-holer and the directional sense of a Bedouin finding the last water hole in Arabia. You had to grope your way alongside the men's toilet, which was dark and sinister enough to make Joe Orton water at the mouth. Once out in the open with a decided sense of relief you were pinned up against the bottom of the stand just behind where the players' dug-out is now.

What followed was the apotheosis of the age of technical blunderdom. Firstly, Eddie was not there and that caused anxiety since in his place was a young fresh-faced kid who looked as if he had only photographed his sister's wedding or Masonic harmony. I was aware early on of a jerkiness to the lad's movement that suggested he might have been finding the ball elusive. What unnerved me slightly was that while he was pointing the camera on one occasion at the Rangers' goal the ball was still in the Kilmarnock penalty area. Still, even at a football match one ought to expect some poetic licence. But the game did not require an aspiring Ingmar Bergman. We just needed the ball. At all times the ball. Alas we were not to get it as often as we would have liked.

The camera suddenly jammed. He rushed to the other one. It jammed as well. Rangers scored, then almost immediately added another as two cameras hung in a kind of post-coital droop incapable, it appeared, of any more. The 53,900 crowd, who were perhaps amusing themselves with the thought that they could hurry home and see the highlights later that night, were blissfully unaware that the filming of the game had been entrusted to Dad's Army. We managed to get one camera going. Then Rangers got a penalty just before half-time. This was surely it. Our first capture of the night. George McLean took it and scored. The cameraman looked relieved enough and when half-time came we sent the film winging back to the studio. The game ended 6–4 to Rangers with Tommy McLean getting a hat-trick for Kilmarnock in the last twenty minutes.

But when we got back to the studios we were met by a doleful Peter Thomson. 'How could they have missed a penalty? How could they?' he moaned. For when the film was transmitted the penalty looked as if it had been shot from the wrong end of a telescope and when the camera jerked towards goal the ball was already being kicked back up the field for the centre. Peter admirably and coolly used up his whole year's quotas of apologies as he tried to explain to the viewers why, when the score was 6–4, we had made it look something like 3–1 or, for those who didn't have twenty-twenty vision, 0–0. A young trainee cameraman helped us that night, not, I hasten to say, that he filmed any of the fiasco. His name was Bill Forsyth. In later years I was to remind him of that as he went on to win laurels for his wry film-making. 'At least we could see the ball in *Gregory's Girl*,' I ventured. Like me he could see the funny side of it but, then, neither of us had had to face the public directly.

We were slaughtered mostly by Rangers' supporters after that. For the first, and certainly not the last, time in my life in answering a call I was called an 'Effing Tim'. A newspaper, I think the *Sunday Mail*, published a letter from a viewer comparing our coverage to 'filming with a Brownie whilst jumping on a Trampoline'. It was time to hide but it was difficult to do so. Certainly not from one particular member of the public who did not let much pass him.

It was a couple or so weeks after that I heard his voice directed towards me for the first time. 'Heh, you,' it rasped. 'They say you're a teacher. You couldn't count at the Rangers game, could you? You'll have to get your arithmetic right before you watch us. What about that fiasco? Where did you get your cameras? The Barras?'

He was standing on the steps of the entrance to the Central Hotel in Glasgow. He was wearing a black woollen coat which emphasised the breadth of his shoulders. And his name was Stein.

4

Please Can I Go to Lisbon?

He was off out of sight into the interior of the hotel even before I could open my mouth in reply. It was a classic Jock Stein manoeuvre. Hit, destroy, depart. I was to experience and witness it for another couple of decades as he towered above every other influence on my career. It was 1965, the year Churchill had died, and I now recall the words Harold Wilson used in tribute of the great man:

> For now the noises of hooves thundering over the veldt, the clamour of hustings in a score of contests, the urgent warnings of the Nazis . . . all are silent.

I think of that first meeting with Stein and of the crowded, turbulent, magnificent, depressing, tumultuous, incandescent years that followed; and of the day in 1985 when I sat down in a deserted BBC studio in Cardiff trying to think of words which were adequate to his passing; and of how, preposterous though it may seem to those who are strangers to football or who simply did not like Stein, Churchillian analogies kept offering themselves.

The brand new Celtic manager of 1965, who had been with the club only a few months and had led them to a Scottish Cup win, was then bristling with vitality and bore the impression of a man for whom the immediate future couldn't come quickly enough. At that stage his relationship with the BBC and myself was foul. Within the sports corridors of the Beeb in Scotland he was

regarded as almost being the Great Satan. It took years before he
ceased to be my nemesis. Later, though, he would give invaluable
advice at critical junctures in my professional life and work with
relish with me on several outstanding broadcasting occasions.
There was never any intimate relationship for he was both man
and citadel and resisted with ease almost everybody I know who
attempted to slip into his private fief. Few managed it and many
who claimed that achievement were really deluding themselves.
But at least I shared a great deal of his public life. The transition
from outright animosity to a tolerable level of personal friendship
took me on a long and exacting course, mostly over rocky terrain
but at least ending in a pleasant amble that quite literally carried
us round the world together.

It's difficult to convey the impact of that first meeting, however
brief. It got into the bones and stayed there. The sudden onslaught,
very often delivered, as it had been then, with a smile on his face,
became renowned throughout the media. It left you feeling as if
you had just developed a very bad hangover without the preceding
pleasures. He had dismissed me contemptuously, although he did
not know me personally. He did so because I came from the Peter
Thomson stable and in Stein's eyes that automatically made you
an Ibrox lackey. 'If the man at the top of the house is like that then
you're all the same,' he once barked at me in the early days. Then,
of course, he knew I was a teacher. I wasn't really part of the
game. He hardly thought much of some of the most experienced
journalists who were barnacularly attached to him then so what
chance of credibility did I have? But I certainly was not part of the
media who danced attendance on managers daily or weekly so
there was little opportunity of developing any kind of bond with
anybody in football, let alone this man I had never met before. But
he was the first to make me acutely aware that I was, in football's
province, an 'outsider'. I was still very much in that category by
the time Celtic had qualified for the final of the European Cup in
1967.

I flew to Lisbon with a suitcase the size of a garden shed, a
plastic bag with two litres of duty free whisky, the *Michelin Guide*
to Portugal, the BBC medical officer's tips on hygiene and com-
municable diseases in the Iberian Peninsula, a good-luck card

from a couple of pupils in the school I was headmaster of at the time, Kenneth Wolstenholme and a small bottle of phenobarbitone. It was difficult to say as we lifted off from Heathrow which was going to be the most helpful.

Certainly the suitcase contained enough gear for a fortnight's stay when it was only going to be a couple of nights. The whisky I had vowed not to touch until I got back home. The Michelin was a typical 'I-have-never-been-abroad-before-on-an-assignment-like-this' sort of gesture and tilted me more towards the tourist category rather than that of broadcasting journalist. The medical officer's strictures neither terrified nor elucidated.

The card from the children really told me that when I got back home I would have to come down to earth very quickly. Kenneth Wolstenholme I had never met before, but he was polite if distant when we met in the lounge at Heathrow where he took me to the VIP lounge ('Please come in, Mr Wolstenholme. How nice to see you. Champagne I suppose? Where are we going to this time? Lisbon? What's on? Oh, Celtic! In the European Cup final? Are they really? Now what can I get *you* to drink, sir?') and I felt more like a batman trailing in the wake of his public recognition. The feeling of inferiority was accentuated when we boarded the plane and separated, he to first-class, myself to the back.

Perhaps I could have done without all of them bar the phenobarbitone. Only armed assault would have taken that small bottle away from me and even then I would have gone down fighting. It was a lifeline, or so it seemed to me. With much apparently prospering for me – a headmastership in my twenties, a constant commentating role, more writing of educational scripts for schools broadcasting and now a trip to commentate on the European Cup final – it might have seemed that life had taken on a lustrous pink glow. The world, in fact, had developed a dingy monochrome appearance as gloom followed me like a swarm of harvest flies.

It's difficult to know when or how this started but that I suppose is the nature of depression; you disappear up your own backside if you try to work it out logically. Events were happening around me which I barely recognised, even though I was supposed to be part of them. I recalled Peter Thomson telling me about his mental disorientation under pressure and sometimes in a broadcast not being able to identify at a particular moment in time where he actually was. I wondered if all this was some kind of occupational disease: that obsession with broadcasting brought an emotional torture which the body wasn't too willing to put up with and caused it to send less than amorous messages up the spinal cord to the cerebellum. Or perhaps it had nothing to do with that. There was confusion.

I was living a private life of lacerating self-doubt, instinctive mistrust of people and the sure certainty that I was terminally ill. Apart from that everything was fine. I had suddenly become a devotee of *Black's Medical Dictionary*, sneaking into the public library at Baillieston ostensibly to meander through the fiction section but in reality to flick through the pages of the dictionary with a deep sense of foreboding and guilt to determine whether the headache I had was the beginning of migraine or an inoperable brain tumour. I believed the odds heavily stacked on the latter. In a period of a year I assumed I had every disease from leukaemia to Parkinson's. Even a stitch in the side running for a bus conveyed the idea of a colostomy to follow. A tiny little blemish on the skin meant melanoma was nigh. I had taken on hypochondria with the dedication of a religious zealot.

'You are doing far too much,' the doctor said when I went to see him about the amputation which I believed would be the inevitable outcome of a nasty corn on my right toe. 'Here,' he said. 'Take these! They'll be a help.' He gave me those tiny little white pills which, then if not now, doctors tended to hand out like Smarties at a children's birthday party.

There seemed to be thousands of them in the bottle but, to any hypochondriac worth his salt, that only indicated that they had given me up for lost and were trying to tranquillise me against the inevitable outcome. He might as well have been handing me strychnine. The pills had the effect of drying the mouth up completely. He hadn't warned me about that so after stuffing myself with them one fine day I set off for Ibrox to do a sound report for Glasgow and London and, when I came to speak, discovered to my horror that my mouth felt as if it had just been stuffed with an old sock. Lips, tongue, cheeks and even teeth seemed afflicted with the drought of Death Valley. The words were dying before

37

any sound got past the epiglottis and the report sounded like a man whose teeth had snared the tongue like a gin-trap.

A commiserating voice from London enquired up the line, 'Are you pissed, Arch?' Afterwards the doctor did say in the most nonchalant way, 'Oh, yes! You did notice that effect. I wondered!' I was about to ask him if, realising what I actually did for a living, he would recommend a blindfold for shortsightedness. However, I was too much in debt to medical science during this period to mock its practitioners. Pure faith in medical solutions, as I had, only led to this ambivalent mistrust of anybody putting his pen to a prescription. I would be more careful in the future. It took me about a year to get through this and in retrospect 'hypochondria' is but a term I use to make light of something deep-rooted and infinitely more like a nightmare.

So Lisbon might have seemed the perfect antidote, better than anything dreamed up by the lads in the Swiss labs. The sun didn't let us down but shone with a clarity that took us out of our north-European stiffness as soon as we left the airport. We had arrived in a ruthless dictatorship but we were not disposed to look for evidence of it although I distinctly remember the heavy-set, dark-jowled, solemn, corpulent police with their fat holsters. It occurred to me that authoritarianism bred indolence amongst the security men. The system might have become so rigid, and habitual to its citizens, that the police just stood around and got fat with nothing more to do than look threatening. The air of menace they exuded contrasted sharply with the freshness of the coastline between Lisbon and Cascais, the plush holiday resort which lies about three miles outside the city.

At least the dictatorship had the advantage of an immediate coastline which easily drugged the visitor into indifference to Dr Salazar's peculiar notion of civilised behaviour. We relished the invading blueness of the Atlantic and a marbled hotel, polished and gleaming with pride, humming with greatly practised and highly efficient subservience. It was only a mile from Celtic's base. All of this made it easy for me, however fleetingly, to dissolve into background and camouflage myself from the problems continually dogging me. The mood did not last all that long for things were not going to work out during this forthcoming broadcast. The whole atmosphere changed after my first chat with Wolstenholme that evening.

It had been agreed that a Scottish commentator was required for such an occasion. Since George Davidson was unavailable Peter Thomson asked me if I would travel. 'You will assist Ken on commentary,' Peter assured me. 'You will split up each half between you. Straight down the middle. Can you be released to do it?'

I said yes without really knowing whether it would be possible or not. This sudden turn of events only compounded the tension I felt trying to occupy two roles. There was no way I was going to turn this opportunity down and I immediately began concocting contingency plans for the possibility of the Director of Education saying no. I could hardly claim time off for my grandmother's funeral when the whole of the UK was going to be listening to me in Lisbon. Nor could I simply resign. There wasn't enough time. The final was only a couple of weeks away. It was not that two to three days away from Swinton was going to disrupt the education service. It was just the awareness that I was cheating on myself, that despite having thrown myself into my teaching job I was really looking in another direction. Nor could I bear the thought of the Education authorities turning a request down. I decided to play my political card.

I knew that a straightforward letter to the Education offices in Hamilton might get short shrift. But I also knew that a large number of the ruling Labour group in Lanarkshire were Celtic supporters. I let it be known to our local councillor that I had been asked to go to Lisbon and, quite correctly, that if I didn't Scotland would not have a commentator at the greatest club match in the history of Scottish football. I knew the call had taken the trick when Jimmy Hamilton, my MP, called to say he would do all he could for me. Jimmy, one of the most likeable of men, sat every week in the directors' box at Celtic Park. I was told simply to write for formal permission for release and it looked plain sailing. But they did ask me why the BBC thought it so necessary that I attend this match. I duly passed on Peter Thomson's explanation, little realising the difficulty I was eventually to face as a result. It was accepted. I was granted three days' leave.

So that first night in a little fish restaurant in Cascais I sat with Wolstenholme and had lobster and champagne as if it were part of my daily diet. Being abroad for the first time with the BBC, and not knowing what might be accepted on expenses, I was a trifle tentative to start with but I had vowed after watching Wolstenholme being escorted into first-class on the flight that I would not act the country bumpkin. 'Another bottle, Ken?' I heard myself saying, fists clenched apprehensively under the table. No need to record the reply. But he waited until near the end of the meal before he broke the news.

'Has anybody explained what is happening tomorrow?' he asked.

'In what sense?' I replied.

'Well, you see, I was on the phone to London this afternoon and they thought they'd let you know what they wanted you to do. I had to pass it on to you.'

'I'm doing half of each half.'

'Well, not exactly,' he went on after a sip. 'What they want you to do is summarise.'

'Summarise?'

'Yes, I'll bring you in for a minute before kick-off, then a minute after the half-time whistle and a minute at the end of the game. Perhaps a little more if it goes to extra-time.'

Christ! Was I hearing right?

'What? Are you sure?'

'Absolutely sure. That's been agreed.'

'By whom?'

'London,' he said tersely.

'And Scotland?'

'I don't know about Scotland. I know that's what Ginger has agreed.'

'Ginger' was a coded message. Brian 'Ginger' Cowgill was the dominant force in BBC sports broadcasting then and a man not to be taken lightly. In full spate in a television gallery Cowgill was an awesome sight, with his blunt north of England, stentorian delivery sending underlings jumping through any hoop the master indicated. He had, in fact, created a nervous tension within sports output that greatly added to its professionalism. Only a department continually on its toes would suffice. It was reflected in the sharp,

brilliantly-honed voices of Coleman and Wolstenholme and lent
BBC network output a distinction and authority which has never
been surpassed. Cowgill helped establish the foundations of that
before leaving to join ITV some years later. He scared the hell out
of most of us. It wasn't likely that I would be phoning him from
Cascais to complain.

Nevertheless, I felt shattered. To get to Lisbon I had just done a
deal with my MP, had the backing of councillors, and the understanding of the local education authority. The explanation had been
that I was to be the indispensable Scottish voice sharing commentary. Now I had come all this way, through that process, to be told I
was to do about four minutes' work. It was like a brickie arriving with
the tools only to be told he was now the tea-boy.

I had a sleepless night, especially as the sea-front at Cascais
also attracts rasping motor-cyclists as much as it does seagulls. I
was beginning to panic. I put in a call to Peter Thomson in Glasgow. Phoning from Portugal in that era was an operation involving
the mangling of the English language and rising doubt about the
sanity of the human race. After four hours I got through to him
and gave him the whole 'cri de coeur' bit.

'How am I going to face up to my employers and my colleagues
in Lanarkshire after travelling all this way just to do a couple of
minutes or so. That was not the agreement. It is very embarrassing.
Do you understand that?' I shouted down the line, not angrily but
just so he could hear me. 'I will be crucified!'

His normal depth of voice seemed to disappear around the Bay
of Biscay and the tinny reply sounded like, 'I'll see what I can do.
They are bastards, you should know that! I will try and get in touch
before kick-off!'

I believed him. I went to the pre-match lunch in one of the
most beautiful restaurants in the world just outside Cascais. The
Amoexes is set on a rocky promontory beside a horseshoe curve
of golden beach and the surf pounded all around us. I watched
Wolstenholme mix with the other European commentators and
envied him his cosmopolitan confidence but felt rather smug in
the knowledge that political wheels were turning within the BBC
and I would gain full restitution of rights. It was then he strolled
up to me with a glass of wine in one hand and a canapé in the

other and almost nonchalantly declared, 'Oh, by the way, I meant to say, London passed on a message this morning. If there is a replay, which would be on Thursday, could you stay on and do it for them by yourself as I have another commitment? Think you could manage that?'

Was I the only man who arrived in the stadium that afternoon hoping inwardly, in the most selfish way, for a draw? Probably. I had no idea how I was going to cope but not even the threat of a sacking, which might even then have been imminent, would hold me back.

The Portuguese television people had built tiny cubicles which were both to shelter us from the sun and to section us off from the many other commentators sharing that area. They had also installed huge television monitors on the bench in front of us. Neither of us was tiny and we could barely squeeze into the space allotted. I had found Wolstenholme very pleasant company but I did not fancy our bodies being virtually intertwined for almost two hours. What is more, we could not budge the monitor from in front of us and the only view I could get of the pitch was by half-rising out of my seat in a sort of constipated lavatorial pose. Then, a slot of about letter-box size was opened to me. By adjusting my head I could view certain selected areas but at no time that afternoon was I able to see the entire playing area. What is more the sun was changing its angle and by kick-off I realised that it would be shining straight at the screen of the monitor making it almost impossible to make out the play on it. Thus it was under the worst possible broadcasting circumstances we prepared for this historic game.

About twenty minutes or so before the teams came out I put it straight to Wolstenholme.

'I take it that everything has been worked out and I'll be sharing commentary?' I asked in a matter of fact tone.

He shrugged.

'What I told you last night stands,' he replied innocently. 'I've been instructed only to bring you in as I said. Sorry. Nothing I can do about it. London's instructions.'

'Four minutes' worth in total?' I stressed in an almost contemptuous tone.

He shrugged again.

'Perhaps you could talk over the line to London,' he said. 'They might listen to you.'

I knew this was the last thing they would do and I realised that Peter Thomson and BBC Scotland had been put in their place. Yet now I find it difficult to find fault in this, other than in the second-hand manner by which I was informed. Professionally speaking, Wolstenholme was a network football commentator of the highest calibre, perhaps the best they ever had. I had never been involved in a live commentary before and I could well imagine 'Ginger' Cowgill's reaction to news that 'his' audience was being entrusted to a Scottish voice he had never heard within the BBC. After my original enthusiasm to do well, though, I was now quite inconsolable. Right up till then I had been reciting my broadcasting catechism with fond remembrance of the rule of verbal contraception, my head saturated with facts which I had passed on the night before to Wolstenholme, my voice like a greyhound in the trap ready to be let loose for a sprint to glory. I am sure great poets have had words for that particular agony of denial, of unconsummated desire. I simply felt knackered.

The game worked wonders. I forgot my own selfish introspection. Even when they were one down you could feel a Celtic victory in the air like the tangy aroma of a woodfire, unseen, but somewhere in the vicinity. I got cramp trying to see the game through this tiny space in front of me. At the same time I was listening to Wolstenholme steer his expert way through one of the great games of all time. How I envied him! So near yet so far. When the final whistle went he made his own buoyant comments and then turned, handed over the mike to me and shrugged his shoulders in a heavy, sleepy sort of movement, almost as if to say, 'What more can one add?'

I had only spoken twice so far during the game. One minute's worth of less than sparkling wisdom. Now with the ecstasy of victory in its first throes I tried to match the occasion. I was determined to make this sound like an oratorical masterpiece. Now when I listen to it, it sounds like a schoolboy shouting at his mates across the playground: slightly hysterical, the style and substance of little merit. I had added nothing to this momentous day other

43

than a soprano-like postscript. There are few fates worse than falling into the role of token Scot.

What did not occur to me then is that the Celtic supporting councillors back home, my MP, and whole swathes of the population couldn't have cared less at that particular moment if Humpty Dumpty had done the commentary. Celtic had won.

The engineer who had helped us throughout the broadcast told me in a matter of fact way that London had been in touch and that they would now like to interview Jock Stein. I was to go down and bring him to the commentary position. I looked from our position half-way up the terracing onto the seething mass of invading supporters who now covered the pitch below. My God, I recall thinking. Where is he? I knew for a start that at that stage in our relationship Stein would not have given me an interview if we had been alone on a desert island together, but I had to make the effort. Down I went and joined the swirling mass of supporters who had engulfed players and management and the pitch resembled a Corryvreckan of jubilation with Stein in the middle trying to control the tide.

I got within about ten yards of him but there was no hope of getting nearer. On his face was not the slightest indication of triumph or satisfaction. Indeed he looked angry. He was trying to push supporters away with a ferocity that would have been the envy of a night-club bouncer. At one stage he attempted to prise Tommy Gemmell free from a group who looked as if they would suffocate the player. Gemmell looked on the point of exhaustion and even in the circumstances of spontaneous and understandable jubilation it seemed the Celtic supporters' enthusiasm was about to get out of hand. Stein continued to fight and push and struggle and get angrier. I recall him throwing one supporter off his feet with a mighty sweep of his arm.

The shirt was almost torn off my back and I knew as he managed to help his players fight free of the throng that my task was hopeless. I went back and reported this to London who did not take too kindly to failing to get the first British manager to win the European Cup for live interview. But as I tried to collect my senses in this curious mix of personal disillusionment and infectious celebration an English-speaking Portuguese liaison officer asked me if I wouldn't mind coming to the public address microphone to ask the crowd if they would please get off the pitch so the presentation of the trophy could proceed. It would help if the plea came from a Scottish voice. Why not?

It wasn't until I actually got to the cubicle I realised that I had as much chance of success with this as going into the 'Sarry Heid' of a Saturday evening to ask the clientele if they would mind giving up the bevvy and join the AA. I spoke. I shouted. I pleaded. And I enjoyed it I suppose because it was the longest period I had spent with a microphone all afternoon. But it was just another of my lost causes that day, for the Celtic supporters were now beatifying the pitch. It was theirs and would be for eternity. They were oblivious to all except the texture of Portuguese grass, which they embraced and dug up, pausing only momentarily to watch an exhausted Billy McNeill climb up to the presidential box to receive the European Cup.

Later, that same trophy, full of champagne, was presented to the teetotal Jock Stein in the dressing room and he raised it to his lips to drink, then decided against it. 'Why should I?' he said in a display of self-control that reminded everyone that a superb afternoon in Lisbon and his own acquisition of 'immortality' would be less important to him if he were to step out of character. This was emphasised later that night in the heart of Lisbon.

We went there to the UEFA banquet. Up the narrow winding hill in the centre of the city and into a restaurant that was packed and noisy and uncomfortable. It had been liberally gate-crashed by about half the Portuguese nation and the scene was chaotic as people fought for seats. Stein sat at the top table, not at all comfortably. He looked dour. There is little doubt he could be the life and soul of the party if he wanted to be. Nobody had a sharper wit. But he was essentially a man of anti-climax. On numerous occasions I was to see the incongruity of this almost sad demeanour in the middle of euphoria; tense, unable to unburden himself, smouldering, as if he could create victory yet not understand the language of it. That night, if you were to have come upon the scene and compared him to Helenio Herrera, the Inter manager, you might not have been able to discern who had triumphed that afternoon. The only difference was that whilst Herrera sat in deep contemplation and looked thoroughly morose (and no wonder) Stein was tense, fidgety and fit to burst.

I was sitting some distance from the top table in the middle of a raucous debate between Bill Shankly and some Dutch journalists who had never forgiven the 'Shanks' for some of the insulting things he had said about Ajax prior to a European game. 'You are nothing but a very big loud-mouth,' was one of the kinder comments being made to the Scot. As the UEFA officials tried to get some order to make speeches so the hubbub grew. The Inter players were sitting in abject dejection at a table just behind me, their sullenness as thick as the smoky atmosphere. But I thought I might get some sort of comment from Herrera so I got up and squeezed my way towards their table. I never reached it. As I passed by the table where most of the Celtic players were sitting I paused to congratulate Ronnie Simpson. I had only managed to say a few words when the massive figure descended and a hand gripped my shoulder. The very large hand indeed of Jock Stein.

'Don't talk to my players,' he barked at me, almost incoherent with rage.'You are only a guest here. You never talk to my players at the best of times so you're not talking to them now. Sit on your arse!'

Even at the height of this unique triumph he could not relax his vigilance towards the 'enemy'. Victory was no antidote to the old suspicions lingering constantly in his mind. Indeed, it seemed to have heightened them. The look of contempt on his face would have turned a bull-mastiff to jelly. He pushed his way back to the top table and in the general rowdiness of the restaurant I hoped that the confrontation hadn't been noticed. I now felt bitterly angry and realised that if I were to be much longer in broadcasting this would have to be resolved.

On that glorious day I felt like a complete alien within a celebrating family. They with their cup, me with my phenobarbitone.

Taking on Mr Stein

In 1969 Neil Armstrong bounced on to the moon with his well-rehearsed tribute to mankind's ability to look further than its navel. A new age of pushing back frontiers seemed to have dawned but the relationship between Celtic Football Club and BBC Scotland had, conversely, sunk into a primeval swamp. It was based on ignorance. We didn't really know each other and not an effort was being made to rectify this.

Peter Thomson, frankly, was terrified of Stein. I did not look upon him as an avuncular figure myself at that time and when I was in his presence I always put myself on red alert for sudden swoops. But the issue was avoided. In all the time I worked with him during the Stein era I cannot once recall Peter Thomson setting foot inside Celtic Park. I had always believed that this bizarre situation had to be sorted out at the top but I knew it would not be. Then, things changed. And it started with a man who wouldn't have known Celtic from Inverness Clachnacuddin if they had run on to a field together. He was Alasdair Milne, who had become Controller of BBC Scotland and was later to be Director General.

He offered me a job. I was now Peter's first substitute to introduce 'Sportsreel' on occasional Saturday evenings. I preferred this to commentary simply because it seemed so much easier and I was carrying the banner for the entire output. I was also still teaching and the accumulation of pressures to keep both ends up was taking its steady toll. Something had to give. Milne's offer of a full-time job came as a relief therefore. It was when I stepped into the BBC for my first full-time contractual position that I vowed, whatever the cost inside the BBC, I would strike up new relationships with the press and with the man who held us in almost continual contempt.

When I commentated on my first Scottish Cup Final in 1969 I realised that that task was not going to be simple and straight-forward. It would have been an exacting commitment at the best of times but I went to Hampden that day knowing that a major row had broken with Celtic and, according to one of my colleagues who had spoken to me the previous evening, Stein was 'looking for blood!' At Hampden, when the teams arrived the procedure was to go through the enclosure out on to the track and then up the stairs to the dressing room area where you could approach the managers for the team numbers. Without them, most of our cameramen would have been shooting in the dark. For at an out-side broadcast the quickest way for commentator, director and cameraman to keep up with each other is for the director's secre-tary, if required, to shout numbers rather than names through the headphones. 'Rangers 6. On to Celtic 8' and so on. The procedure of 'getting the teams' was no academic exercise but of the utmost importance. The quicker we had that information the better.

I had just missed Stein. He had had his brisk walk out on the pitch as usual with the players and had gone inside to the dressing room. A message was then passed out to us that we would not receive any help from anybody with his club that day. No teams, no numbers. In fact we did get them from another source in time for kick-off which made the apparent petulance all the more irrelevant. All managers, and that includes perhaps the greatest of them, have the propensity both to enter a stadium like a gladiator and also to behave, at the same time, like a spoiled child demanding more pocket money. Stein's message was clear. He wanted nothing to do with us.

What had incensed him was a review of that league season which we had broadcast prior to the Cup final. Celtic had won the league all right but in so doing they had also been beaten twice by Rangers in the process. We had shown these games properly as part of the summary of the season. Stein had been so enraged by seeing them included that he had phoned immediately after the programme from Seamill, unknown to me, claiming we had distorted events and that some English people watching the programme in his company at the hotel had concluded that Rangers, not Celtic, had won the championship.

So he shunned us.

Celtic won that day in the very first couple of minutes when Billy McNeill headed in a Bobby Lennox corner when he should have been marked by Alex Ferguson. They won in a canter 4–0. He told our stage manager, who tried to grab him on the track immediately after the final whistle, where to stick an interview. What he did do though was accept an invitation to talk straight down the television line to *Grandstand*'s David Coleman. As he waited to go on I was sitting in the television area in the enclosure watching the television monitor replaying the first Celtic goal. I saw a broad smile cross Stein's face and he said wryly to Coleman, before the actual transmission, 'Macpherson sounded sick there.' There were, it has to be said, people working with me in the BBC who couldn't have cared less about this situation.

The wishful thinkers or the divine-right-of-Rangers-to-rule brigade believed Stein was nothing more than a temporary phenomenon anyway and that he would be put in his place before long. I instinctively felt he was as temporary as a Californian Redwood. But here was Stein cultivating BBC London and by-passing his own patch. He was rubbing it in to us. Sam Leitch, ex-*Daily Mirror* and once Sportswriter of the Year, who was then working for BBC London, warned me not long after that, 'I don't care what your own views on the big man are. He goes over the top, all right. But you know he came from the other side. He knows what it's been like to look down on people. I come from King's Park so I know what it's all about. He knows what goes on in some Protestant minds up there. He's trying to change that whole scene. But how can you get anywhere in this business if we know down here in London he won't even talk to you! I know it's not your particular responsibility but if nobody else is going to sort it out then you'll have to do it yourself!'

Leitch was right to point up the practicalities. Celtic were going over the barricades. Rangers were merely digging in behind them.

Celtic clearly had a man who embraced the future with clarity of vision, great self-confidence and ruthless ambition. Rangers were bogged down by their past and simply did not know how to react to this. Celtic had a manager whose personality would have emerged distinctly in a throng of celebrities. Rangers had Davie White, a decent little man of honest intent shrouded in anonymity. For BBC Scotland not to have access to Celtic in these circumstances would have been like a trader setting up in the market place with an empty stall. The objective was not to prove our altruism to Celtic. We were simply being thoroughly unprofessional in not trying to cope, even though there was a danger of some of my colleagues interpreting any move on our part as succumbing to naked intimidation.

Rangers themselves were aware that Stein was beginning to sway opinion within the media. But there was little they could do about it. Their efforts at reaching the minds of those communicators in the business were puerile by comparison. It was like comparing a faded hoarding on a derelict building to a sparkling television advert.

I had publicly supported the Davie White appointment when Rangers, albeit crudely, got rid of Scot Symon. At least they realised that Symon, even with Rangers at the top of the league at the time, did not fit the future. In retrospect it was the footballing equivalent of the dispatch of Margaret Thatcher to the back benches. When I interviewed that honourable little man Ian McMillan, of the deft touch, about this matter he launched a totally uncharacteristic attack on Symon, claiming he was not fit to lead a team in the modern game. He cited the lack of pre-match tactics in the European Cup semi-final against Eintracht in 1960, where Rangers lost twelve goals over the two ties, as the prime example. I bumped into Symon by accident three days later in a restaurant in Perth and he advanced on me ominously. 'If my wife had got hold of you on Saturday night,' he said, 'she would have torn the eyes out of your head.' And then he added, 'However, you are entitled to your opinion.'

He uttered the last statement with such dignity I thought I was going to weep. The mix of sudden guilt, justified or not, and the sight of the retreating, greying figure walking out of the restaurant reminded me suddenly of the essential transience of figures in the game, even those of the stature of a great Rangers manager whose time was so clearly up.

Davie White was swamped by circumstance. Against any other opponent he might have survived. I saw him with Stein once at a function at the BBC and you could see he was in awe of the other man. Perhaps he wasn't aware of it himself but he moved circumspectly in his presence. Stein, in a fit of sudden ecumenism that night but calculated, I believe, to be heard by some of the press, claimed that he would never go out of his way to 'savage' White if they were to appear in a television interview together. He wouldn't have, of course, but in that more public setting of television he nevertheless possessed the ability to put people away with a subtle wit that was quieter but more lethal than any overt display of aggression. There was never any doubt that White would not last long. He didn't. By the autumn of 1969 the press was obsessed with the question of who would lead Rangers' revival against Stein. This was something which both greatly amused and irked the Celtic manager. When we travelled to Hamburg for the West Germany–Scotland World Cup qualifying game around that time he was in the official Scottish party.

In the magnificently chandeliered Reichshof Hotel, with the heavily carpeted staircase down which the fräuleins of the Third Reich must have made grand entries, the speculation was not just about how Scotland could qualify for the World Cup finals in Mexico but also of how much longer White would last and of whether Stein was domestically unstoppable. Other questions were asked, like, 'What did your bill cost you last night?' In the company I was keeping, and to which I subscribed with little protest, passing an evening in the art galleries and museums of this Hanseatic League city was not a preferred nocturnal activity. We found ourselves pleasantly enough diverted by the proliferation of entertainment which flourished around the Reeperbahn and which can easily take the mind off such compelling subjects as whether Willi Schultz would be fit enough to play for West Germany or the likelihood of Scotland using the sweeper system. There were certain machismo obligations to attend to which lent one the proper credentials over and above the holding of a union card. I undertook then and there to be indented into the custom of ensuring that the evening before a game did not entail you turning into a hotel-room-bound Trappist monk, cramming yourself with largely irrelevant statistics.

On the other hand, lest some misinterpret this as an irrelevance or indeed irresponsibility, some of the best discussions I have had on football have taken place in rather dingy and bizarre settings in the middle of the night when the tongues have loosened and the jackets are off, metaphorically speaking. We got involved in such a one that night.

We had trawled, my senior companion and I, through some lurid places and had ended up wiser but poorer in a bierkeller of some relative respectability. In other words, the waitresses in this one wore clothes. It was there a kind of 'Stop Stein' conversation began at the centre of which was a journalist from the *Daily Express* called Willie Waddell. Two other prominent journalists, the SFA doctor and myself suddenly became embroiled in an argument about the decline of Rangers. The doctor, revealing an impassioned interest in Rangers, took it upon himself to turn the tide of the increasingly turbulent argument into a plea to Waddell to demand the Ibrox job. This was taken up with some surprising eagerness by the other journalists who looked at any moment as if they would go down on bended knee. Waddell himself was not only unmoved by all of this but quite vehement in his denial of any interest in the post. At the same time he heaped scorn on Rangers, almost as if they were beyond redemption.

This was hardly surprising since the club looked as if they were moving into a fantasy world in which things would work out well for them by natural law. What they needed of course was not only a new footballing brain but strength of character. That became clear to me in a personal way when Waddell, despite his protestations that night, became manager a few weeks later. I interviewed the Rangers chairman John Lawrence, who sat in the studio with me and pleasantly forgot the name of the manager he had just sacked.

'He was a very nice fellow, David . . . eh David . . . eh!'

'White!' I had to remind him.

Now they were going to get a spokesman of some considerable

strength. But that evening in Germany demonstrated to me that Old Firm politics preoccupied minds in a way which made Scottish international football pale into insignificance. We had hardly talked about Scotland's very important game. One way or the other it was Stein who was dominating everybody's mind, either negatively or positively.

The following morning there he was sitting in the lobby, the familiar black coat on, bristling with confidence. As I walked up to him he put on that by now familiar smile which told you something was about to come forth. 'I hear you were all trying to get *the job* for Waddell last night,' he said. In later years he was to use that same sarcasm when he admitted to me that Willie Allison, Rangers' PRO, had unofficially tapped him for *the job* when he was still with Celtic. It may even have happened around the time we were in Hamburg.

What surprised me was that between the wee sma' hours discussion and breakfast time he had learned about it. Had he been hiding in the shadows, furtively taking notes? No, he had not. He was demonstrating, as he would so often do, that he had a network of informants which the CIA would have envied. He seemed not at all perturbed though, just highly amused.

'You're all worried men,' he added, the smile becoming more taunting. 'And you're all trying to get the other wee man the sack. What kind of people are you, eh?'

His defence of White was not all that surprising for he had been angered by Waddell himself after he had written an attack on the Rangers' manager under the heading 'The Boy David' which had amounted to a journalistic slaughter. Stein had expressed his views to the press in no uncertain manner. He no doubt did have a certain amount of genuine sympathy for White. But this display of displeasure was also an indication of Stein's burgeoning self-confidence and of an ability to command an audience on issues which did not have a direct bearing on Celtic Football Club. It was also, of course, true that White's remaining at Ibrox was unlikely to give him an ulcer.

The conversation didn't last long although I tried to engage him on the subject of his apparent paranoia about the BBC in Scotland. He exercised his apparent prerogative, ending a conversation whenever he wanted and rising to walk off as if it had never started in the first place.

That night in the vast openness of the stadium in Hamburg I broadcast live on TV for the first time from abroad. Scotland, drawing 2–2 with under half-an-hour to go, lost 3–2; 'Stan' Libuda ripping Scotland apart, Tommy Gemmell almost ripping Helmut Haller apart and being sent off. I felt more like a member of the travellers' club after that trip. I was anxious to be seen as a member of the travelling corps now that I had joined the BBC, for there was decided hostility directed towards the broadcaster from at least certain members of the press.

Television was still feeling its way forward in football coverage. If football clubs were suspicious, newspapers persistently clobbered us for having the potential to kill off football. So, some of the older members of the Fourth Estate were delighted by the war of attrition taking place between Stein and myself. On that trip, and others, I learned to identify the professional gloater, someone smirking in the background or nodding assent as Stein waded in and I tried to counter. Sycophancy in the reign of terror was rife. It was imperative to come to terms with Stein without being seen to be enslaved, as some clearly were. I knew that he would virtually dictate the copy that certain writers put out. In a way it was a tribute to the man's immensely powerful presence that in such a relatively short space of time he had almost all of the media by the short and curlies. If you wanted your share of the goodies from him you had to play ball. He, of course, had a lot to offer. If you missed out you were obviously in trouble.

When I returned from Hamburg I told Peter Thomson that I was going to Celtic Park to have it out with the manager. 'No way!' he said. 'I wouldn't approve of that. We'll bide our time. He'll need us before we need him.'

That was all very well to state within the confines of a BBC office but for the outrider like myself, who was being ambushed every now and again, it was scant comfort. I had got on well with Peter initially but I realised I couldn't accept this philosophy. He was my mentor and on this issue, which he regarded as vital, I could hardly be seen to be out of step. At the same time, I knew this wouldn't last.

Stein actually tried to stop me from travelling on the official team plane to the quarter-final of the European Cup against Fiorentina in 1970 but was over-ruled by the chairman, Bob Kelly. He was, however, far too contented to bother about any particular individual joining the party to Milan for the final itself in the merry month of May. In truth, I believe he, and the rest of the Celtic players for that matter, thought they had actually won the Cup by beating Leeds in the famous game at Hampden Park in the semi-final.

We stayed in Varese in a hotel on top of a hill and hardly ever during our stay there would you have thought that Celtic were approaching a European Cup final. In Lisbon I saw the manager pounce on a player sitting in the Palacio Hotel in Estoril simply because he had his head exposed to the sun coming through the window. And that was his reserve goalkeeper! In this sumptuous hotel north of Milan there were times when you might have deduced the players were on an end of season jaunt. Nobody at the time queried Celtic's approach to any great degree. It certainly raised some eyebrows to see the manager allowing the players' representative to hold meetings with them and strike deals there and then in the hotel. Stein himself seemed to have unburdened a great deal of the tension he normally stored up on these occasions. The exception was the night before the game when he strode into the large foyer, saw me sitting with Hugh McIlvanney of the *Observer* and thought he would have some banter.

'How are Feyenoord going to play in midfield?' he asked me abruptly. I had been caught cold.

'If you tell me how you're going to play it, I'll tell you their plan,' I said, trying feebly to appeal to his sense of humour.

I might as well have kicked him in the groin.

'You mean to say that you've come all this way and you don't know Feyenoord's midfield . . .'

'I know their names,' I pled. 'But how they'll play it . . .'

'You should be up all night thinking about this game,' he barked and looked around for sympathy which, of course, he got. 'I'll kick every ball tonight. I'll go through it over and over again. I can see everybody's face, I can see their build, I can see the way they run. You should be the same, thinking it out, all the possibilities.'

This was more like him – impassioned and part brutal with a languishing audience. It was as if he had come out of a dream. Perhaps the sight of the men who were going to be writing or commenting on him on the morrow had summoned up his Lisbon self. In that identity he spent every second immersed in trying to arrange the future, and anguished by the fact that not even he could guarantee that.

They lost. People have become very clever about this game and have laid the blame largely on Stein for misreading Feyenoord. He certainly underrated them and every player I have talked to from that team would admit it. On the other hand hardly anybody says that Feyenoord were quite simply the better side. They were technically far superior and in Ove Kindvall they had one of the most exciting traditional centre-forwards in the game, the sort of player Jock Stein loved. Of all the famous Argentinians in their World Cup winning team in 1978 the attacker, Luque, appealed to him most of all. Kindvall scored the winner a few minutes from the end of extra-time.

Perhaps Lisbon had been burning far too brightly in people's minds. This setting under floodlights in a gaunt bowl of a place seemed inappropriate to Celtic. They had procured an identity of triumph associated uniquely with blue skies, sweat, brilliantly green grass, trees and the sun gleaming off a trophy. This wet, drab night in northern, industrial Italy, however reminiscent of Glasgow, felt quite alien to me. I am sure it was for everyone associated with the club. Perhaps their memories helped beat them even before they started.

I got back to the hotel before the rest of the media by chance in picking up a convenient taxi. Frankly the last man I wanted to see that night was Stein. And yet there he was sitting in the foyer in his favourite position, in a large chair in the corner so that he could see everything that moved. Jim Steele, the physiotherapist, was with him. The players had vanished. The hotel was like a morgue. I went straight up to him.

'I'm sorry about that,' I said. What, after all, do you say in these circumstances?

'They were a better team than us,' he said softly, his face drawn and tired. 'Look at their support too. They outnumbered us. The

Dutch have got more money than us. They can afford to travel to a place like this. How did the broadcast go, by the way? Would you like a drink of champagne? There are bottles of the stuff over there. Help yourself.'

From defeat came the first sympathetic conversation I had had with him. It was not the occasion to exploit it or expand it any further. I would have been very wrong to read too much into it in any case.

In the following season Celtic played Rangers in the Scottish Cup final. In the game on the Saturday Derek Johnstone scored the equaliser for Rangers to make it 1–1 with only seconds remaining. It went to a replay where Jimmy Johnstone was outstanding and Celtic won 2–1. I was there to do the interviews. Weeks earlier Celtic had played Aberdeen in an important league game at Pittodrie. I had invited in some people to watch it in the studios at Queen Margaret Drive. That match ended in a 1–1 draw. The audience watching with me that afternoon were of mixed persuasion. Inevitably, when Aberdeen scored there was a positive reaction from those present who did not go to Celtic Park regularly. By the time the Cup final had come around I had forgotten about that game and that audience. Others hadn't.

When I approached the Celtic dressing room door at Hampden not long after the final whistle on the Wednesday night I could hear the natural sounds of jubilation from within. I had to bang on it for anybody to hear. The door was opened and there, just inside, was Stein, naked but for a towel wrapped round him. He wasn't smiling.

'Could you come out for interview?' I asked.

'Well, well, well. Look who it is,' he said cheerily enough. Then added, withdrawing the smile quickly, 'You know what you lot are? A bunch of bigots! I heard about it all. All of you standing up there at the studios cheering when Aberdeen scored against us at Pittodrie. You're nothin' but a bloody bunch of bigots!'

The door was slammed in my face. He had just won the Cup but he had stored up this wrath and not even in the moment of triumph was he going to stifle it. It fair took the breath away, largely because, as I was walking away from the dressing room, I was still trying to work out what he was talking about. It wasn't until I had got back on to the running track beside the camera that I remembered the occasion and realised that the spy network had been in operation. He had accepted a highly selective interpretation of events, probably because it accorded with the general anti-Celtic conspiracy theory. I knew this state of affairs could go on no longer.

Two days later I went to Parkhead. I didn't tell Peter Thomson nor did I tell Stein in advance but presented myself at the front door and asked to see him. He was out with some of the younger players and came back in and was surprised to see me sitting waiting for him in the hall when he came back. We went into the boardroom and he stood in his mud-caked black tracksuit with his back to the main road, a photograph of John F Kennedy just over his right shoulder. I can't remember exactly what I was doing when Kennedy was assassinated, as many can, but I will always remember the day he looked down on two Protestants about to confront one another about the running sore of sectarianism.

It's not that I rushed at him, for frankly, to use W C Fields' phrase, I would rather have been in Philadelphia. The conversation wasn't a long one. I kicked it off by saying that he had got us wrong and that we were no worse or better than anybody else he had to deal with and that, in any case, he listened to too much gossip about us. I put it to him that he would be as well speaking his mind about me and the BBC here and now, so that I could answer any allegations or criticisms.

'Where's your boss?' he asked.

'I've taken it on myself to talk to you,' I answered.

'He's the man who employs you all,' he said. 'He doesn't employ many Celtic supporters, does he?'

'You mean Catholics, don't you?'

'All right, Catholics? How many have you got up there?'

It's not that he wanted numbers. It was a point he was making. I gave him the stock answer.

'I don't know anybody's religion,' I said. That was a mistake.

He laughed in disbelief and I remember he turned away and waved at me dismissively.

'All right,' I added. 'I suppose none. At a guess!'

'It would be a good guess,' he said, laughing now, and I felt a thawing. 'Look,' he said and straightened up and put both hands out like a man about to accept a hank of wool for unfolding. It was a posture I saw him adopt on countless occasions. It always prefaced a fit of real candour and not some of the feigned and controlled outbursts of which, I believe, he was the master.

'You know as well as I do how this club has been treated in the past. Are you really going to tell me it has had a square deal in the press compared to the other lot? Some of them come in here and butter me up and I just have to take it, but all they're doing is patronising Celtic. How many of you really genuinely mean it when you wish us good luck?'

He didn't wait for an answer.

'Very few. What you do is your own business but you want to get away from some of the old-fashioned habits.'

What followed I can recall so well I can virtually hear the little puffs of breath in between.

'You're starting out. If you've got any sense you'll see this is where the real action is going to be. We're going to be in Europe for a long time to come. You've got to get your feet in this club and not treat it like it was inferior or else you're going to be left behind. We've all got to forget the old boyhood stuff. That's for your own sake I say that. Times have changed. If you want to come to any training session at Celtic Park at any time give me a ring in advance. Now, I'm away to have a shower.'

And with that he pushed himself away from the wall and made for the door with a slight limp, breaking into song as he did so. I heard him singing Sinatra's 'Strangers in the Night' at the top of his voice in the dressing room as I made my way out.

It was hardly a great leap forward for mankind but at least he and I now seem to have recognised that we dwelt on the same planet.

6

One Disaster after Another

Those of us who experienced the times of Stein, and particularly the early years, must have come as near as anyone could to experiencing the power of the absolutist reign of the Sun King, Louis XIV at Versailles in the 17th century. To become a courtier at Parkhead and enjoy Stein's patronage bestowed on you the sort of privileges enjoyed by the fawning aristocracy of those distant times and with it the feeling of attributed power. Rejection by him also carried the distant fear that your very professional life would not be worth a damn.

Rangers were painfully aware of his dominance but could do nothing about it. They had re-introduced Waddell to Ibrox but that entailed not just some flag-flying and the installation of a spiritual leader but also having to beat Stein on the park. That was proving to be the hard bit. There was still this stubborn assumption amongst the Ibrox loyalists that the deity would see the Protestants through to a rightful ascendancy in the end. To listen to the average Rangers supporter then, when Stein seemed invincible, was like hearing the forlorn plea of a Palestinian for his rights to a homeland.

By this time I had begun to feel a growing adherence to the BBC and often found the company at Queen Margaret Drive sophisticated and stimulating. I should record, though, that all of us in our different ways were driven daily by harshly practical considerations. In my case, I was advised to concentrate my energies on Rangers and Celtic. As the newcomer I tried to resist this and to broaden our focus. Peter riposted that a Saturday night audience wanted the Old Firm as the staple diet and get them they would. The audience figures were his legions in support of his view and anybody who disagreed was a smart arse who really ought to be off doing documentaries on 'Weaving Traditions in the Borders' and subjects like that. Peter, of course, was entirely right. I was too callow to realise that a programme enjoying popularity was also fulfilling a public service.

It was an imbalanced scene I was surveying at the beginning of the Seventies. Celtic were far out in front of Rangers. Stein was looking back contemptuously over his shoulder at them. But then came a period of eighteen months which changed the course of the Ibrox club's history and into which I was sucked willy-nilly as a broadcaster. It produced traumas that are beyond repair. The events began on a chilly winter's afternoon when, presciently, Glasgow was wearing a sombre mask.

We were in the ground floor studio listening to the sound commentary when we heard the news that Celtic had scored in the last minute against Rangers at Ibrox, to go one up. At the height of the Stein era there was nothing terribly surprising in that except that on this occasion they had left it later than we had assumed they would. I walked out of the studio to prepare my script for the late afternoon television programme which was Scotland's fifteen minute contribution to *Grandstand*. I was mentally composing a headline of sorts as I paced slowly out of the ground floor with a piece of paper and a pen in my hand. I had barely got to the end of the corridor, literally a few yards, when I heard a yell which, within the natural calm of a quiet BBC building partially deserted on this public holiday, almost stopped the heart. Peter Thomson came racing out of the studio, bouncing up and down.

'You're never going to believe it,' he shouted. 'Rangers have equalised! Colin Stein!' and rushed past me. I tore up my thoughts and immediately imagined that in the press box at Ibrox there would have been a massive journalistic double-take like mine. Copy would now be in the process of a total re-write.

We had a late afternoon programme to do and we had to go about it as if the pulses were unaffected, hoping we could appear to be calm and self-possessed. We went through our programme and thought we had smoothed out the news crisply and unsensationally, although two goals in the last minute of an Old Firm game is what you dream about for headlines. You gloat over it as if you yourself had created the news in the first place. We felt quite pleased with ourselves. Indeed, we thought that it was going to be a smooth day and we looked forward to later that night when we would celebrate the New Year with a few drams.

But the year was 1971 and the day was 2 January.

I can't precisely recall at what particular time we heard about deaths. It was about five fifteen. Frank Bough, with a slight look of puzzlement on his face, near the end of *Grandstand*, simply said, 'I believe that twenty-two people have died in an incident at Ibrox.' We stopped talking and writing and could not take this in. First came the inaction of bewilderment, the walking around bumping into people who were also unwilling to accept this as fact. Then came the rush to phones to call God-knows-who. It was the pretence of purpose. The information we were getting was sketchy but before Bough went off the air he did chillingly allude to the fact that the casualty figure might be much worse.

It was decided the best thing to do was for me to take a taxi and get to Ibrox to find out at first hand. We were unable to make contact with our radio or television people for reasons which became clearer later on. The stadium loomed up, a spectral hulk in the chilling mist. There was an eerie calm near the front entrance. Stein was just stepping out when I got there and I recall a journalist asking him if he had any comment to make about the game.

'In the name of God,' he said. 'This is no time to be talking about football. There are far more important things to think about now.'

Inside I had a glimpse of Willie Waddell hurtling up the marble staircase, his face tight and mute with incomprehension. The scene under the stand was one of bizarre tidiness with a neat linear arrangement of dead bodies where one had, I suppose, expected to find chaos. A man asked me if I had a fag. I don't know who he was. Relative, supporter, first-aid man?

'It's no' real, is it?' he said in bewilderment.

In truth, it wasn't. I knew I was refusing to accept this and that

I was actually making an effort to be solemn and grave at the same time, like an interloper on a family tragedy. The reality came more easily from the mouths of others.

'Sixty-six confirmed dead' the police inspector told me.

I returned to Queen Margaret Drive with these appalling statistics to be confronted by a Corporation which didn't quite know what to do. Risk at a football match consisted perhaps of getting a toe trod on, or pneumonia in bad weather, or somebody peeing down your leg. But sixty-six dead seemed to belong in the environment of the airport, or the mine, or the tanker at sea. And therein lay the reason for our confusion in the sports area. We could not duck out and simply leave it to our news colleagues, who by now had set their professional ball rolling.

News departments, both in London and Glasgow, were incensed that there were no pictures available. This might seem ludicrous when you consider that the BBC had a full outside broadcast unit in the stadium which had covered the game that afternoon. This was the festive season, though, and they had packed up and gone with more than the usual speed, not knowing of a single death. Indeed some members of the crew who were only a couple of hundred yards away from where it happened knew nothing about it until much later that night. The accident occurred on the terracing steps in the north-east corner right at the end of the game and it took many minutes for the news of what was happening to filter back across to the other side of the stadium. By the time that had happened the cameras had departed. It was understandable.

But to the disaster experts in television news departments nothing is understandable if there is no access to pictures when cameras are in the vicinity. So, the fur was flying without there being any legitimate reason for it. 'You bloody people can't do anything right, can you?' a broad anonymous London voice said on the phone to me from their news department. 'We're sending people up right away!'

I little cared about that information. But I did care about our response. Senior BBC executives together with the News Editor and Peter Thomson met with me three hours before we were due to go on the air. I kicked off the discussion by suggesting that we drop the programme altogether and put on something in its stead. This, admittedly, was going to prove difficult. There was no immediate package to replace it and we did not want simply to put on an English sports programme. We were stricken by uncertainty. I stuck to my line, though, that we could not put out the programme. The opposition to that view was beginning to grow and it was noticeable that Peter, my editor, was taking no part in the discussion at all, but leaving me to make the running. I knew I was heading for trouble.

The senior BBC executives were among the most charming men I ever met within the Corporation but there was a decided edge to our conversation that night. They were in effect telling me that I was too closely bound up with the tragedy to make any objective judgement and that we had to remain dispassionate. For my part, I was beginning to think that this distancing from the event was producing not good judgement, but insensitivity.

'How many people were at the match?' I was asked.

'Eighty thousand or thereabouts,' I replied.

'Sixty-six dead out of eighty thousand isn't all that many really!' came the retort.

To this day I have preferred to allow that remark to be shrouded in anonymity for I do think that we owed it to each other to admit afterwards that we had become, by different routes, emotionally unstable. I was livid.

'If they had been miners, or people come down with an airliner, you would have been moving heaven and earth to have the whole schedules altered and outside-broadcasts brought in. But because they are just football supporters sixty-six out of eighty thousand isn't all that many!'

The argument then descended into a slanging match for a few moments until Bob Coulter, the Controller of BBC Scotland, admonished us with a patrician, 'Come, come! From now on I'll do the talking. We'll put a programme on the air. But what's going to be in it?'

They compromised. The Old Firm game of January 1971 has, to this day, never been seen on television. We broadcast highlights of the English 'Match of the Day' and I interviewed the Lord Provost, Sir Donald Liddell and Sir James Robertson, the Chief

Superintendent of Police. It is the only programme I have ever wanted to avoid. We were weeping before we went on and during the programme Donald Liddell's tears flowed constantly. This made it difficult for me to control myself. I had to keep nipping my thigh hard to keep some semblance of order in what I was doing, and doing with the deepest reluctance. Nobody else in the BBC had seen the bodies. That had made its deep impact on me. I had, after all, been too affected by that sight for me to make objective judgements.

But of course in the final analysis that did not matter. They were right to put on a programme of sorts. They were right to reflect something of the grief. They were right to remain, in their own context, as clinical as the surgeons who at that very moment were operating on some of the survivors. Later that night, though, while trying to ward off nightmares, I recognised that I had probably done myself no good by speaking up so vigorously. I also knew that it was the end for Peter Thomson, who had contributed nothing to the debate in the office but had been quite overwhelmed by the event.

Waddell wasn't. On the Monday we doorstepped him. Journalists from around the world had arrived to put Ibrox under siege, waiting for the first statements. BBC London had indeed sent their own men. John Simpson, who has more recently distinguished himself with his war reports from Baghdad, was on one of his first broadcasting assignments. He asked me if I would point out Willie Waddell when the time came. There has been repeated criticism through the years of BBC London muscling in on events which occur in Scotland which could be covered by local correspondents. This seemed a perfect instance of this.

However, experience has taught me that one of the most important corner stones of creating even news programmes is building up identity and authority. You establish your own men or women and you persist with them on the basis of their own expertise. Being English and not knowing who Waddell was by sight was much less important than knowing what to ask and how. In the scramble to get hold of Waddell, as he came out to face the world for the first time that freezing cold morning, Simpson was to the forefront, barking his questions well above the cacophony of noise that erupted on the front steps of the main entrance at Ibrox Stadium.

Throughout the entire year to come Waddell was to face up to horrendous problems and managed to maintain a rugged indomitable dignity which held the club together. There was nobody on the Ibrox board to match him as the world seemed to fall in upon the club. Its board consisted of very successful Glasgow businessmen from the 'Wee Arra Peepul' school of thought and suffered the consequent myopia and inarticulacy which rendered them quite unsuitable to face up to all of this. Joe Beattie, the police superintendent put in charge of the original investigation, went straight to Ibrox on the night of the disaster and recalled to me how one Rangers director had greeted him in the boardroom like a long lost friend. The man then regaled the company, to some merriment, with amusing stories of how they had played football together at Ashfield and of how they weren't really up to scratch and what a great time was had by all in the good old days. Beattie remembers thinking immediately that the reality of sixty-six bodies lying just under their feet on the running track had still not seeped into the boardroom. On the other hand, it might have been said that it was a night when many rational people trying to come to terms with the disaster were turned into headless chickens.

Waddell, however, faced the world full square and the directors lined up eagerly behind him. From his obsessive drive to create order out of what, at least initially, appeared to be chaos emerged the character who was eventually to rule Ibrox with a rod of iron. Cometh the hour, as they say. His every interview carried strength and understanding. It was extremely difficult to try to make anything of football for a long, long time. The first commentary I did at Ibrox afterwards was like watching a silent movie.

Life had to go on, however, and Waddell could not shake off Stein. The Celtic manager was at the height of his powers, coaxing, cajoling, bullying, exhorting and able to give his club the momentum of a runaway train. Derailments occasionally happened but he was good at repairs. He was also seeing Rangers off, despite Waddell moving to Ibrox. We must never underrate Stein's passionate desire to do so. He would, from time to time, say that the Old Firm needed each other. But that particular sentiment rings of sanctimony. It implies that the football parish for them is extremely limited.

In reality, Stein's vision was limitless. He could not have survived without his excursions to Europe. It meant freedom to him. It meant throwing off the shackles of traditional values and joining a commune of the élite to which he felt he rightly belonged. For, although he had the gently expressed touch of the common man at crucial times, he most certainly enjoyed being part of the aristocracy of achievers. He didn't need Rangers for that.

About then he gave an interview to Arthur Montford of STV in which he expressed the view that footballing success came in cycles and that 'Rangers' turn will come again'. This implied that nature took a hand in these things. Stein would have allowed nature no such wanton liberty. He was to Rangers' existence what an avalanche would be to a Swiss hamlet. He wanted to bury them.

Waddell led the club out of the despair which followed the accident on Stairway 13 simply to face the comparatively trivial, but nonetheless endemic depression felt by the large community of Rangers supporters. They were beginning to suffer Celtic's success as a chronic ailment, akin to colitis. Any cure offered only temporary remission before the agony returned all over again. The effect was especially severe for those who had grown up with Struth and Symon, believing that bloodstock would lend the species supremacy.

Accordingly, it was not simply a European Cup Winner's Cup final they all sallied forth to in Barcelona the following year but an occasion in which they might rid themselves of this pervasive influence back in Glasgow. To many Rangers supporters the final in Spain could be seen as an exorcism.

We made our plans to cover this game thinking that, having now taken on board two European finals, everything would fall into place easily. Of course it didn't. To our utter astonishment we could not work out an agreement to broadcast the match live. It was to be shown as a 'deferred relay'. That is, transmitted in its entirety but only immediately after the final whistle. It seems odd now that such a situation could have been tolerated but we travelled to Barcelona with a sense of anti-climax, for as broadcasters our natural habitat for such an event is in the 'live' zone.

We went in advance of the official Rangers party to make a film for showing immediately prior to the broadcast. Anybody listening to radio would have found it odd for us to be previewing the match on television whilst it was actually being played. It was the first time I had been involved in filming in any depth, although it was eventually to become my stock-in-trade. I took a liking to it there and then and I suppose I have to thank Barcelona for that.

Film-makers could set up permanent base around the grand harbour, where there is an atmosphere of constant wheeling and dealing between sea and land. You fear that moving away from the fat, squatting ships and the constant hubbub around the ferries might provide an anti-climax. But it does not. Just across the road from the Med is the Ramblas. This broad avenue mixes the tranquillity of its tree-covered spine with the sheer fanaticism of its traffic and invites comparison with the stark contrast set at the corrida where genteel ladies sit courteously and watch the gorings in the ring. It runs to the heart of the city but, most importantly, its congested and narrow side streets are filled with enough attractions and temptations. There is a constant sense of menace and impropriety. Which is why we took the camera in.

The night we moved off the beaten track, the American navy had done the same. An aircraft carrier had berthed in the harbour and the entire strike force of the Fourth fleet, or whatever, seemed to be on shore leave. They were pointing their missiles in other directions that evening with the consequence that their truculent dealings with the ladies in the doorways would not have endeared them to the Daughters of the American Revolution. They certainly were not behaving as Gene Kelly did in *Anchors Aweigh*. Two sailors who got completely out of hand were brusquely separated from the others by a couple of burly Guardia Civil. Arms up their backs, they were bundled down a tiny little alley and the last I saw of them batons were striking them about the head. I had always understood that the American Shore Patrol was the only body allowed to handle these guardians of democracy but the Spanish police that night were not waiting for diplomatic notes to be interchanged before meting out summary justice.

In all of this we should have seen something, a portent, a clue. The booze, the haphazard nature of the city, the atavistic nature of the police, the somnolent heat; all of these ought to have hinted at a possible confrontation for the lads from Larkhall, Dunipace and other parts who might not make the right kind of cultural adjustments. It's easy enough to say that now, yet even in hindsight our innocence of the potential for disaster looks unhealthily close to stupidity. We went into Los Caracoles restaurant for a filming conference. A good restaurant is one of the most effective settings for beating down differences of opinion amongst a film crew. If you can get the cameramen drunk, all the better, for the following day they cannot remember what it is they have agreed to do for you. 'But I swear you did say you would go on the top of the crane and swing down to the water level on the harness and get a close up of the propeller of the ferry going out! Didn't he, lads?' Sometimes it worked.

This restaurant is now a kind of tourist trap but then it was a genuine cathedral of Catalan cooking. You walk through the kitchen to get to your table in one of the tiny alcoves which honeycomb this magnificent old building. The famous original owner Boffuril, now deceased, was sitting there in all his resplendent corpulence, breathing heavily and also shouting out the orders to the chefs through his microphone. It was as noisy inside as it was out. It was while sitting there, wolfing down the sucking-pig, that my producer John Coleman said to me of the city, 'The Rangers supporters will have a ball here.' That must now go down as one of the finest examples of dramatic irony since the about to be assassinated King Duncan in Macbeth uttered, 'This castle hath a pleasant seat'.

A few days later Rangers arrived. They were staying in the Don Jaime hotel, half an hour's drive from the stadium, on a hilltop in Castelldefels. The receptionist proudly told us that the film actor, George Sanders, had committed suicide in one of their rooms a few weeks before. She made it sound as if the Spanish Tourist Board had sponsored it. Still, everything was promising. The hotel looked directly into the eyes of the sea, the players had that right mix of taut expectancy and almost insolent disregard for the perilous situation they were in. They had won nothing that season and were now following in the European footsteps of Celtic. The weather was idyllic, the mosquitoes seemed only to bite the bad guys in the media and we also heard that the Russians had injuries and were worried. No European tie would be legitimate without such rumours but we set off anyway, two days before the game, to watch Moscow Dynamo train.

We weren't allowed in. Not at first anyway, for it is the prime rule of filming never to give up. The tiny Spaniards manning the gate explained that it was under instructions from 'them'. They pointed at two large figures in tracksuits standing on the edge of the track. These were the days when no Russian side left their country without a heavy escort from the KGB. They bulged with heavily-armoured arrogance. If a smile ever broke over their faces when they were on duty you could only think they were looking over your shoulder at something which amused them, like a lorry running down a blind child. We bribed one of the Spaniards with enough pesetas to buy him a smallholding in Majorca and he let us slip through another gate on the understanding that we would not take in the camera.

In fact the cameraman slipped an overcoat over his arm, covering the camera which he jammed under his armpit and held tightly with his right hand. Since we were not requiring sound the idea was to start rolling it mute with the lens poked through one of the sleeves. Overcoats in Barcelona in May are usually food for moths in attics so I felt we might just as well have put up a placard reading 'We have a camera hidden under here!' Nonetheless, we filmed the Russians for posterity employing the method James Bond would have used to reveal a Scud missile site outside Omsk. The fact of the matter is that there was nothing of any importance to record. Training sessions are normally of unremitting boredom and all of them bear a sameness that can be very deceiving, as I was later to find out more dramatically in Argentina. What I did notice was that the players were downbeat. Russian sportsmen and women can look inordinately dour at times but I detected something more than that, a lack of sympathy with this setting they now found themselves in. They knew they would be playing with hardly any support in the stadium in front of an antagonistic crowd who simply refused to think that Rangers could be beaten. Moscow Dynamo looked as if their souls had refused to come west with them.

We arrived for the game early on a pleasant summer's evening and, to our astonishment, discovered the pitch was already covered by Rangers supporters. They were still trying to get used to the strange fact that one of the greatest stadiums in the whole of Europe scarcely had a security system. Getting onto the pitch was probably easier here than on Glasgow Green.

That might well have preoccupied us if we had not discovered that our commentary position in this huge bowl which towered above us was in fact only three rows away from the pitch side and amongst the supporters. They were already drinking. This was not a surprising fact given that a bottle of the hard stuff cost them no more than a postage stamp would back home. Those on the pitch were slowly ushered back by the police in a manner which now bears some special consideration for it was going to turn out to be a key element in the events which followed.

The police were all tiny men by comparison with the Glasgow 'polis'. If you can imagine your average Spanish welterweight and put a uniform on him you might get the picture. But they were sturdy and dapper with gun-holsters blistering their hips and truncheons rigidly appended to them like spare walking-sticks. But at that moment they struck a false posture of geniality which utterly deceived everybody including the Rangers supporters, who must have been convinced that they were a soft touch. It was at this extremely early hour, before the floodlights were required and the players walked onto the pitch, things went seriously wrong. We had not allowed, none of us, for the fact that Franco's police had one method for all circumstances, suppression. At that stage, though, they looked no more than park wardens ushering children from a flower-bed.

The game went well for Rangers. The Russians played, not surprisingly, as if the whole occasion was too much for them. They had come emotionally neutral to a setting which required passion. It was a case of surly technicians versus a tribe on the warpath. The tribe was three up before their legs began to wobble. Then, the Russians' greater fitness and athleticism took its toll on a Rangers defence which seemed about to draw its last breath and conceded two goals.

With twenty minutes to go and the crowd around us in turmoil a Rangers supporter with a bottle of Fundador came and sat on my knee. My producer tried to extricate him but it was no easy matter. He was trying to pour me a drink, which was decent of him, but I was still chuntering on. The drink was slopping out of the bottle all over the pair of us and soon I was beginning to reek like a distillery. Colleague Bill Malcolm, who was attempting to do his own job, was now standing and had the man round the neck to drag him away.

He never fully left us for the rest of the game and the tumbler of brandy was still occasionally pushed under my face. From then until full-time events were interpreted by me with one eye on the field and another on the invitation to oblivion. The Rangers supporters, particularly those on the opposite side of the stadium from us, had invaded the field after the second and third goals and just before the end of the game, when they mistook a referee's decision for the final whistle. The police stood by and ignored all. This, coming on top of their casual initial approach to the night, seemed now to have completed their offer of *carte blanche* to the Scots. The fans were determined to out-Lisbon Celtic with their pitch celebrations. When the game ended 3–2, with Rangers near total exhaustion, the character of the evening suddenly changed.

The following events are not at all blurred by the passing of time. What occurred was so out of kilter with the benign preamble to the evening and the impassivity of the police, which made their presence almost superfluous, that it stamped itself clearly on the mind. Nor did it take you by surprise with its speed. The character of the Barcelona riot, as it then became tagged, unfolded itself in a slow, avoidable, almost choreographed way. From the ringside seat we had, you could not make too many mistakes about what you saw and heard.

A few minutes after the end of the match, the crowd, in a considerable frenzy, had advanced right across the pitch to the main stand where they waited for the Cup presentation. At that stage it was not much different from Lisbon. But the ceremony which in fact was supposed to be at pitch level couldn't take place because of the congestion around the touchline. The police had by then merely retreated until they were standing, their backs to us in the stand, within touching distance. It would not have taken too much re-organising to have brought the Rangers captain to the middle of the stand and presented the cup there. Instead, they waited for some time for calm and order, which they were not going to get, and then ushered him down the steep steps of the tunnel which led to the dressing rooms for the first ever subterranean presentation of a football trophy.

The crowd, having come all this way, still felt entitled to public acclamation of the triumph. The authorities tried to cap the gusher. If the supporters had simply been allowed then to protest vocally, or carouse on the pitch, Barcelona would have been forgotten by the following week. Disastrously, the police decided to act.

It started slowly with the thin line of light brown uniforms pressing against the crowd, their batons held with both hands in front of them, like drum majors in a slow march. The crowd ebbed and flowed a little under this pressure without retreating any considerable distance. It was stale-mate. So it should have remained. We were still actively recording and I was involved in commentating on this although viewers back home had not yet seen even the start of the game. I was becoming conscious of an agitation right in front of us. There, a martinet of a Spanish policeman, of some rank, was barking at his men. I remember him raising his arm and giving a signal that was a bit like one-handed tic-tac, a magician's sleight of wrist wiggle.

It was not as if it all happened then in unison. The action was on cue but some were faster than others. It was ragged to start with and I saw a baton flailing just to my right. It seemed to strike a supporter on the shoulder and I have this image of him dropping to his knee and suddenly cowering. Then it became like a threshing machine as the whirl of batons advanced on a crowd whose front rank could not escape this onslaught because of the pressure of those at the back. They couldn't see the touchline, did not know what was happening and weren't budging.

In this jam a terrible price was being paid by those at the front. The batons were slashing recklessly and supporters who had stumbled just in front of me were being openly kicked. I saw two of the police taking turns hitting a man on the ground. I recall how one of them was using the backhand technique in an almost nonchalant way like a Wimbledon player in a casual warm-up.

By this time, the Rangers supporters were in full flight back across the pitch, some stumbling and being hacked mercilessly, the rest getting to the safety of the enclosure on the other side. Then, my attention was diverted by something which still seems to me of some significance. As soon as the first real assault had taken place the Spanish television director turned his main camera away from the high shot of the pitch in a very quick pan to a view of the brightly-lit streets outside the stadium. It remained there. Not a single television picture was taken of the police in action. The reason for this was to fall into place later on.

From being a reckless, but nevertheless jovial crowd, the Rangers support had been turned into a wounded beast, licking its sores, insulted, angered and seeking revenge. We thought it was all over but, to our astonishment, we then saw supporters going into the seating area and smashing the wooden seats with their feet until they had some fragment from which they could improvise a missile or a spear. Having regrouped in a remarkably spontaneous way, which might have drawn praise from a Field Marshal if moral judgement on all of this was suspended, they mounted a counter-attack.

The police broke ranks and retreated at more than a jog trot as a flood of red, white and blue swept back across the field carrying fragments of the Nou Camp with them. The fans were a ragged army, stupidly caught up in their own hurt pride, venting their frustration suicidally on the malicious puppets in uniform who had caused it all. First they drove the police back to our side of the stadium. Then they would retreat under another onslaught of batons and boots. Objectively speaking, the supporters were giving as good as they got. Hand-to-hand combat was going on all over the pitch, bits of seats flew through the air, supporters wielded pieces of wood like machetes, while the police swung madly away with their batons in an increased tempo. By this time, on the principle that war correspondents do not actually need to report from the trenches themselves, Bill and I had climbed from the pitch-side and sought safety high up in the stand.

'Any moment now the guns could come out, for God's sake,' a man said gently beside me. He turned out to be Reuter's correspondent in the area. I recall his words vividly.

'What you're seeing down there is the Fascist police in action,' he went on. 'That is the only way they can handle any disturbance. They are the experts in ruthless suppression. They are not even local police. They are not Catalans. That is why they are so hated in this city. They are Franco's men. They are recruited from Castile or Murcia. Anywhere but from Catalonia. They are principally in this area to maintain a dictatorship. They have regarded these supporters from their very first invasion like an assault on the Caudillo, Franco himself. That is how they are conditioned to act. Respond to command, don't think. These supporters simply do not understand that their lives could now be at risk.'

The height that we had gained had miniaturised the battle. It now looked like the Munchkins versus the Subbuteo Invaders. Unbridled violence now appeared no more threatening than a *son et lumière* spectacle. I wondered if this really was the sort of detachment achieved by the war correspondent. I also thought of how much odder it was to be spectating on a full-scale battle from the high safety of the top tier of the stand and being lectured at the same time on the iniquities which had befallen the Catalonians since the revolution. But it made much more sense than some of the thoughts expressed immediately afterwards.

It occurred to me then that the television director had turned his cameras away not by command but through the general convention of obliging the autocracy. The media, as part of the system, knew how to handle insurrection – by turning a blind eye. Of course, the Rangers supporters hadn't picked a fight with Franco. Theirs had been conflict on a different level. They had been turned into a street gang. It has been suggested that this was their own intrinsic response to provocation; that only they would have responded in such a way. It is a theory that dangles irresistibly in front of you, awaiting confirmation from outside the prejudiced Old Firm context.

All the same, those of us who have subsequently seen much trouble around Europe originating from gratuitous violence, and taking place in all manner of environments, can now look back on Barcelona and at least appreciate more clearly the logic of events. It was police batons which started the battle, the supporters finished it. Perhaps they should have gone meekly to the exits and made off home. But somehow I do not think it is in the nature of the Scot to take a battering without some aggressive reaction. So, the battle had been lamentably predictable from the moment the first supporter was felled.

We watched it come to an end, running out of steam as even the angriest lost the taste for more. People were bundled away and downstairs I saw a supporter receiving a mauling from two small men in uniform who, as they pummelled him with their batons, digging him in the ribs and twisting his arms even though he was as lethal as a rag doll by now, looked as impassive as two ledger clerks rubber-stamping a series of documents. I was actually no longer horrified by this and that is a sure sign you have had enough.

We hailed a taxi and returned to the Don Jaime hotel where, by now, the team were well advanced in their celebrations. They simply were not aware of the scale of the disaster and it would have been churlish to intervene with the bad news. Waddell only intermittently looked like a man who had won a European trophy. He knew full well the implications of what had gone on. The following day the Scottish morning newspapers had arrived at Barcelona airport and the team sat stunned in the aircraft just before take-off, looking at front pages which resembled reports from Vietnam rather than summaries of sporting achievements. Alex Miller, one of the reserves, picked his head up from reading the news and said to me with a distinct expression of disbelief, 'Will they take the cup off us?' It had sunk in.

But perhaps 'sunk' is too mild an expression. No detailed inquest could possibly have taken place into the causes of the riot in the time available. The emphasis was being placed naturally enough on the conduct of the Rangers supporters. In other words, on the aftermath of the assault by the police. The riot was not fully described. Scandalously, it never officially was. When we made efforts to try to rationalise and apportion blame fairly we were condemned by the public. There was one special reason for that. We had not shown the riot. Letters and phone calls poured in on us. We were accused of hiding the truth, of toadying to 'that' club, of being cowardly. In fact, we were discovering that trying to tell the truth was not enough.

We could not back up anything I said later, in introducing

programmes and discussing the matter with a variety of people, because we simply did not have the pictures. The Spanish director had seen to that. Any effort on my part to try to drive this point home was greeted with aggressive scepticism.

A prominent Celtic director told me solemnly, 'If it had been our supporters you would have shown the scenes, more than likely.' I was stunned by this, although I was to hear equally stupid remarks being made to me from the other camp in my time. In other words, we hadn't given at least some of the public what they desperately wanted to see: the Rangers supporters in disgrace. I knew, of course, that had it been Celtic in identical circumstances, the same adverse reaction would have come from the other side.

We had come back from Spain, with a reputation deformed by a riot, to a society still disfigured by its own introspection. Only eighteen months or so after having experienced a suspension of suspicion within the city's two footballing communities, through the cruel means of a disaster, fighting on a foreign field had restored the normal service of recrimination. Perhaps we ought to have expected nothing less.

What we then hoped was that some lessons would have been learned from the scale and nature of those two sad episodes, not just for Rangers but for others too. Waddell's dour dedication to rebuilding the club in all ways, and particularly in a straightforward business sense, was successful, given that its reputation had been reduced almost to rubble. Although their traditions made them vulnerable to universal condemnation and sometimes led them to a bunker mentality, they did learn vital lessons about their economic well-being. They also at least veered towards a tentative ending to their social myopia. Ironically their great rivals, replete with every success at that time, saw fit to close their eyes to the future.

We now know which of the two great Glasgow clubs gradually acquired the closer resemblance to that ancien régime of the French which 'learned nothing and forgot nothing'.

1974 *Weltmeisterschaft*

As the Germans had once tried to kill me I had taken a long time to agree with the idea of rapprochement. My notion of vengeance does not extend to setting fire to their towels and deck chairs in Majorca, but even yet I bridle slightly at the sound of the thick accent suddenly rasping its way into my presence. This awful prejudice was slightly diluted by the coming of Hildegard Neff to the silver screen in the Sixties. Her voice and presence temporarily eased my squeamishness at the sound of the 'Horst Wessel Song' or the sight of the scars that nation had left on others.

This irrational distaste sprang from the night they came to bomb Clydebank and I was taken out as a child in arms to a half-completed bomb shelter which actually had no roof. Looking upwards, I heard adult voices trying to distinguish amongst the stars, the lights of any German planes, the flares, and the searchlights. On its way westward one bastard dropped a bomb in the garden of a house only a hundred yards away but it failed to explode. I also, therefore, do not go along with the notion of German infallibility. I am thankful for the slovenliness in the Ruhr factories but think the near miss was too close to comfort and I cannot accord their race an accolade simply because they also produced Wagner and Beckenbauer.

To carry these old thoughts around with you in the Seventies, when the Germans were enjoying a resurgence of their supremacy in almost all sports, was like harbouring a heresy. So, what then was I to do about this Dr Wilfrid Gerhardt, who was standing in front of me in his office smiling and extending a genuine hand of friendship?

'Welcome to Frankfurt,' he said. It was 1974 and, by now, they were richer than us anyway and Wilfrid Gerhardt was no Dr Strangelove. He was an extremely pleasant and urbane gentleman who spoke the kind of superb English which rather humbles you, the more so since he was able to switch to fluent Spanish and French on the phone during interruptions to our conversation. He was also Secretary to the West German Football Association. The following night the draw was to be made for the World Cup Finals and Scotland were there for the first time since Sweden in 1958.

He was politely explaining to me the method of the draw which, in turn, I would need to explain to viewers. World Cup draws, you must understand, are not all that simple. What I admired about this man, whom I was to meet repeatedly over the years, was not just his command of language but of himself. He was extremely calm and relaxed, in rather hectic circumstances, and personified the great sophistication of the German footballing system. He was briefing me not just on the draw but about the stadia which would be used that summer. I was now a member of the Scottish Sports Council and with plans being mooted for a new Hampden (yes, even then!) I had a notion of bringing a study of them to a council meeting.

'You must go to Dortmund,' he said. 'You never know, perhaps Scotland will be drawn to play there. It is the sort of stadium which represents the best way forward for our game because it has been built principally for football. There is an intimacy to the ground as a result. No running track to distance you from the play, just a place to watch closely in comfort with the emphasis on good facilities for the customer.'

It was on the tip of my tongue to tell him it sounded like Cappielow but, even with his mastery of our tongue, the allusion might have been lost on him. The following night, in the main broadcasting hall of the Hessicher Rundfunk Television Company, the draw was made and, sure enough, our first game turned out to be in Dortmund, against Zaire. This neat coincidence seemed to augur well for the coming summer, with an apparently easy first game in a stadium I wanted to examine closely and with the Germans assuring us that this would be the best organised tournament of them all. This is a claim made dutifully before every World Cup finals and, as then, the actuality is invariably rather different from the boast.

That night we toasted our good luck with Willie Ormond, the Scottish team manager. If the meek really were to inherit the earth then Willie could have laid claim to most of the northern hemisphere. He was quite the nicest man I have ever met in football, apart from Celtic's Jimmy McGrory and Willie Thornton of Rangers. These three men seemed remarkably unadapted to football management. They didn't wear humanity like a suit which could be hung on a peg and forgotten when the brute necessity of commanding men arose. It was in their veins. It is possible that they did lose their temper and became aggressive at some stage or other. After all, I can hardly lay claim to knowing every detail of their personal or professional lives. To conceive of them doing so, however, is like trying to imagine the minister telling blue jokes in the middle of a Sunday sermon. They were all driven to management because they had been successful players but they did not have the armament to ward off 'the slings and arrows of outrageous fortune'.

I had first met Ormond up in Perth, when he was manager of St Johnstone. We sat one night in a hotel where a burn rushes madly underneath you in the lounge. He liked sitting chatting with a drink in his hand and, although some would have it that his favourite pastime ultimately became his obsession, I only had experience of mutually pleasant conviviality, with his gentle nature fired up into anecdote. He recounted to me that night his real fear of flying which originated in a horrendous attempt at a take off in Yugoslavia in winter when he had St Johnstone on a European trip.

'I could see we weren't making it,' he said. 'The branches of the trees were brushing against the wings and the whole plane was shuddering. I thought this was going to be it. I don't think I even prayed. I was too terrified to think of anything. Then, somehow or other, the pilot swung the plane round and I kept my eyes shut. But we landed. We got off the plane and I remember they told us they were going to have another go at taking off in about an hour.

"Not on your bloody life," I thought. But I knew I had to get back somehow so I went into the lounge and drank it dry. I was paralytic when I went back on and I remember bugger-all about anything else until we landed back in Edinburgh.'

There was a self-deprecatory flavour to much of what Ormond said about himself, which in itself was endearing, but in the run-up to the summer of that year you constantly wondered how this homely little man could possibly measure up to the stature of his rivals. Men like Rinus Michels of Holland, Miljan Miljanic of Yugoslavia, Helmut Schoen of West Germany, and Mario Zagalo of Brazil all had impressive international pedigrees. But at least he was there. The night Scotland qualified he brought back thirty-three-year-old Denis Law to play against Czechoslovakia and although the Czechs scored first it was a night of voluptuary appreciation of the Scottish 2–1 victory. Scottish Television were covering the game and as a Czech bore down on Bremner, commentator Arthur Montford cried out 'Watch your legs, Billy.' In that now famous declamation one sensed the communal nature of that evening at Hampden. We all wanted to lay on hands and help eleven men levitate to a level we had originally thought beyond them.

Naturally, the thought of going to a World Cup for the first time turned us into virtual kids although, compared to the hysteria which was to follow the next time, en route to Argentina, we were almost gripped by inertia. Television broadcasting had now established itself in colour and only snobs declared they would retain black and white. When we made the change I am sure the first sight of us, revealed in full Pre-Raphaelite hues must have shocked many to the core.

I did receive a call from a rather sardonic member of the public who complained that the colour could not possibly be accurate as it did not show up my 'blue' nose. I wondered at the time if it had been Jock Stein, with false voice, again sending me up and to this day I have never been quite sure. Make-up girls would spend a long time pondering my face before deciding that perhaps it ought to retain its natural vampirish sallowness. Thus, I was consigned to a pat or two with powder-puff and left looking for years after as if I suffered from pernicious anaemia.

Peter Thomson was on the way out so the World Cup was to be his major swan-song. It was to be the last time I was to work under anybody, in the rest of my career with BBC Scotland, who had not only an innate love of football but who, despite his unbending distaste for Stein, possessed an instinctive understanding of the political undercurrents. Lamentably, they were to be too often disregarded as unimportant in succeeding years. My only regret was that after I had arranged for Stein to be part of a studio panel for the first time, so confirming his change of relationship with BBC Scotland, Peter did not show up on the night. I considered it something of a personal triumph that I had persuaded Stein to identify himself with us. In the same year he had answered, '*Sportsreel*' when the Aberdeen match programme asked him for his favourite comedy show. Peter was allowing me leeway in helping to prepare programmes and make decisions about our contributors but he nevertheless felt that having Stein in the studio was nothing more than grovelling sycophancy. I found the necessity of having him seen with us to be infinitely more important than tittle-tattle about subservience to the Celtic manager. I discovered its true value, in the most practical way, when we eventually got to Germany for the Finals themselves that summer.

We did not go direct but, momentously, via Belgium and Norway. Relationships between the media and the entire SFA party, including officials, Ormond and the players, ranged from ragged to rancid. The Jimmy Johnstone rowing boat incident, which occurred prior to the England match, before Scotland left for the Finals, was much played up in the newspapers. It had been a good story after all: Jimmy out on a boat without oars heading in the general direction of Manhattan, the players in stitches on the shore and the Celtic star trying with difficulty to see the funny side of it. It is not your 'We have a player with a slight thigh strain' stuff which is sometimes all there is to deal in before a major game. This was *Drop the Dead Donkey* material and was greedily mawed by everybody in the press bar the *War Cry*, who were not accredited for the World Cup anyway. Ormond and the players did not like this. It smacked of disloyalty, not to say downright treachery. At the end of the England match at Hampden, won 2–0 by Scotland, the players looked skywards, not to acknowledge divine support but to catch the eye of the busily-working media. Their body language on the pitch below then sent the blatant message, 'You are a bunch of wankers.' Water off a duck's back though. We all loved this stuff.

So off we set to Belgium that morning from Glasgow Airport, the heroes at the front of the plane, the vampires and vultures at the back. I've often wondered if the carriers British Airways sensed the division. They certainly brought the mediation to end all mediation. Out came the bottles. By the time the plane had nosed its way to the first layer of cirro-cumulus, and was still apparently at an angle, we each had a bottle of champagne. The players were not excluded. It might seem hypocritical to criticise the amount of booze downed on that relatively short flight since none of the media on board were actually championing the cause of abstention. Yet, it has to be taken as a real factor in the entire World Cup trip which was to last another four weeks in total.

It seemed to consecrate the drifting, meandering and generally undisciplined nature of the tour. Apart from the abstemious secretary of the SFA, Willie Allan, there were few who left the plane who did not now see dull Belgium as Judy suddenly saw Technicolor Oz after the monochrome of Kansas. We were, in fact, heading for the World Cup like bus trippers bound for Blackpool and the September weekend.

Needless to say when the players lined up against Belgium in the warm-up game two days later they hardly looked like frisking lambs. Now, athletes, footballers in particular, have wonderful recuperative powers after a night on the tiles. Stein used to recall receiving a phone call from a sneak accusing Jimmy Johnstone of having stayed up all night and saying he had just been decanted from some pub in Glasgow. Stein prepared a welcome party for him that morning consisting of Willie Wallace and Bobby Lennox, the two fastest men at the club. He told them to put a pallid looking Johnstone through the hoop. The outcome? The manager simply shrugged his shoulders and said, 'The wee man was brilliant. He did everything asked of him and came back for more. What could I say to him?'

We could say, however, that on the performance that day in the little stadium in Bruges Scotland looked like a pub team playing in borrowed boots on Glasgow Green. They looked hungover. We had a sharp, sudden intake of breath to rouse us from our slumbers. This rabble to play Brazil in a couple of weeks' time? Never! It was then we began to give serious thought to the leadership of the party both on and off the field. By the time we travelled to Oslo, for the last game before heading for Frankfurt, the trip was disintegrating into something which Feydeau or Brian Rix would have adored.

The setting was a students' hostel. We had been told in advance that it was a hotel but in fact it was part of the university whose students' quarters were used during the summer for tourist accommodation. The rooms were like tiny cells into which you could manage a suitcase and yourself plus, perhaps, the odd termite. Everything, bar the soap in the bathroom, was made of wood. I do not exclude the mattress from this description. The sophisticates within the Scottish party, accustomed to five-star comfort, thought they had landed up in an Outward Bound school and were not amused. Footballers normally live in the lap of luxury when they travel abroad; the best hotels, the best food. It is a boring cycle admittedly of hanging around, training and hanging around once more. At least, however, they have beds where they can lie without having to hang their feet out of the window, as a rule. Here, the claustrophobia of rooms obviously built for masochistic wood fetishists only compounded the misery that had originated with the appalling display in Belgium. Austerity was in. Surliness was blossoming. Anarchy was spreading. And some of us began to contemplate the unthinkable, that perhaps the players should turn round and go back home while the going was good, before Rivelino and his mates could get at them.

The ensuing days I sub-divide into two distinct categories:

1 The Great Bremner-Johnstone Affair.
2 The Bans.

The Great Bremner–Johnstone Affair

There were certain consolations living in this student area. The beer was good and cheaper than elsewhere, although still expensive enough. The atmosphere of the howfs, with their student life, was relaxed. We all spent some time in them, including the players. But a curfew of sorts had been set by Willie Ormond, although thankfully this did not extend to the media. We sat there one night, looking dispassionately at the leggy, languid Norwegian blondes and yearning for nothing but our own student days, when we spied Billy Bremner and Jimmy Johnstone. They were in fine fettle. It was past midnight.

I had been joined on the trip by John Motson, from London, with a film crew who were now to make some preview programmes with me. We were sipping our way through those apparently bottomless glasses of beer when the two players spotted us and made straight for our group. They were singing. There was nothing wrong with that and indeed I have never been much in favour of treating footballers like schoolboys. They turned out to be good company and in a few minutes we discovered nothing more startling than that Jimmy Johnstone could sing better than Billy Bremner, although knowing the little Leeds man's conviction about himself I was not going to be awarding him 'null pwann'.

Of course, there was more to it. This was a gesture of outright rebellion. It was an act by a captain, Bremner, who obviously didn't give a damn for the manager and who knew that Ormond wasn't the kind of personality who would shed blood. That assumption was proved correct. They regaled us with more songs, to the great delight of the Norwegian students. If they were studying anthropology it must have been a highly educational half-hour. Then, Willie Ormond suddenly appeared at the top of the steps leading down to the cellar. He took one long look at his two players, turned on his heel and left. If it had been Stein or Waddell or Wallace the two of them would have been picked up by the neck like a couple of dachshunds and not released until they were in their rooms.

As it was, the SFA and Celtic doctor, Dr Fitzsimmons appeared on the scene five minutes later, whispered in the players' ears, put his arm round their shoulders and ushered them out of the room. They went peacefully. He had been sent down to perform the fireman's act. It was a scene which, in fact, symbolised the reversal of power roles. Willie Ormond was not an insignificant figure in

Germany, of course, but he was certainly subordinate to Bremner in terms of influence amongst the players and that, as it turned out, was no bad thing.

By the morning the place was rife with rumours of the incident in the night. So began the debate, even before any official SFA statement was made, as to whether it would be right to send the two players home as an act of support for the manager. The manager might have been crudely challenged by the pair but in essence this stemmed from his own liberal attitude towards behaviour. In the days before a game in the home internationals he had allowed players to visit pubs, so long as they were back by a certain time. As he had also avoided a confrontation with the pair this time but had sent somebody to do it for him, I didn't think he deserved much support.

On the other hand, coming after the farce on the Clyde, the debacle in Belgium and the constant press criticism of the general indiscipline some kind of purge seemed a sensible idea. We were bewildered largely because of our own naivety. Apart from a journalist or two and perhaps a couple of officials, none of us had prepared for a World Cup before. We assumed that players would approach this task like men studying for the priesthood, or soldiers doing bayonet drill before going over the top. We believed it was the time for asceticism. I think most of us would have thought a player seen licking a stamp was acting like a footloose libertine.

In this nervy atmosphere, bullets were fired off willingly by the press. After all, there was nothing else to write about except sunsets on boring old fiords. To a journalist this incident was like finding caviar in a bacon sandwich. Bremner and Johnstone were pulverised on the front pages back home. The tension in the entire squad of players, officials and media was growing. The notorious pair themselves were actually preparing to fly home. The SFA cloistered themselves to determine their response. We believed the whole fate of the World Cup campaign hinged on this fateful decision. Bickering started amongst those whose duty it was to report the whole affair as conflicting views were offered. They ranged from banning them *sine die* to, in one specific and caustic suggestion, awarding the twosome the Willie Ormond Award for Late Night Drinking. These divisions were hardly healed when the announcement was made that the players would remain with the party.

The general view was that the SFA had blundered again and that they should have sacrificed the players in the interests of morale and the establishment of some code of inflexible conduct. Bremner and Johnstone, not unaware of what had been written and said about them, looked sullen and embittered. Care was taken about walking along corridors in case you found yourself alone with either of them. In that circumstance Norway might have experienced its first incidence of mugging.

The television people like myself were slightly withdrawn from all of this. It was not our prior obligation to ferret out news or banner headlines. We were merely filming largely innocuous interviews for use in previews just before the tournament started. Consequently, we were perceived for a time to be as harmless as inter-round card carriers during a title fight. This was the wrong assumption to make about us for there is little doubt anything newsworthy would have been passed on in the usual commercial way to my colleagues. You suffered sharp little intakes of breath when a Scottish player beside you called a pressman in the vicinity 'vermin', as if we on TV were above it all. However, this could have been called the honeymoon period. There was to be an aftermath to the Johnstone–Bremner affair which continued the conflict and drew us in as well.

The Bans

The director with the film unit was a pugnacious little Londoner called Bob Abrahams. His true television idiom was film-making, particularly those short films which encapsulated so much information about people and places. Give him four minutes and he could link Peer Gynt, the trolls and cod with the newly designed World Cup trophy. He carried a street-fighter's instinct with him to the corridors of the BBC which helped him to endure so long. He was probably one of the few men in London who would dare tell Ronnie Kray to his face he was a poof and not rush to exile. He was very much the man's man and was popular with the Scottish players, with whom he had struck up an affinity that was also professionally useful. With no England in Germany the BBC were expending all their energies on people who, at the start, were quite foreign to them.

We had been given free rein to move amongst the squad in their rooms, much to the disgust of some pressmen who perhaps did not appreciate that we were paying through the nose to the players' pool for the privilege. One evening a roomful of players besieged by events, and not wishing to arouse any more hostility by breaking curfew, sent Bob for a carry-out of lager. He duly did this out of sympathy for footballers who were looking, by the day, more and more bedraggled. He slipped off to the howf, gathered the nectar, took the lift back upstairs and walked straight into Willie Ormond, about to head in the opposite direction. Bob said, 'Good evening' and walked on.

That deft attempt at normality did not work. Wrath descended upon us and despite the access money which television had liberally paid we were now tarred. We had become part of the fraternity of wolves snapping at the heels of innocent victims. We were detrimental to Scottish chances in Germany. We were banned. We were no longer given the access to the players' area of the campus. We were looked at suspiciously by everyone, except by those who had asked for the lager and others who, no doubt, would ask a favour again. The ban also gave us a curious kinship with the press who, in a show of solidarity, revealed themselves to be tickled pink by our shared plight.

The late John Mackenzie, the 'Voice of Football' of the *Daily Express*, in full view of the others in the reception area as we waited for a morning press-conference, was taken aside by Willie Allan. After a short, mumbled conference John returned and said with a wry smile, 'I've been banned.' He had been told that, because of his communiqués, he was no longer welcome in the official SFA party and that, perforce, he could not travel on the flight to Germany with the rest of us.

Willie Allan, dapper and officious, carried out his duties with a sanguine unconcern about folks' opinion of him. He could be a soft-spoken hatchet man when he wanted to be and his instinct for the administration of SFA business was acute. Errors of judgement by the SFA were borne with an equanimity which sometimes gave him the appearance of a man wearing a blindfold and heading straight for the precipice.

John Mackenzie was not in the slightest perturbed. Indeed you could see he was suffused with the glow of anticipation at what his editor might do about this back in Glasgow. Vibrations of envy were coming from other journalists who thought they fully deserved to be banned every bit as much as Mackenzie. They were probably now thinking that being allowed to travel with Scotland to Germany might be interpreted by their editors as a dereliction of duty. Banning can raise one from either mediocrity or anonymity overnight to that highly-treasured level of notoriety. So, Willie Allan had done nothing more than confer on John Mackenzie the impromptu Norwegian Order of Merit for efforts above and beyond the call of duty.

However, the others were not to be disappointed. It became more democratic after that. We sallied forth dutifully to a training session at the tiny little national stadium in Oslo, arriving just ahead of the team bus, and ascertained where the players were to alight and enter. What then followed might have been scripted by Chaplin, Keaton or Mack Sennett.

The media trudged after the players into the pavilion and made for the passageway to the pitch only to be confronted by a large Norwegian who announced ponderously, 'You are not allowed into training. Mr Ormunn has instructed!'

As we had anticipated an evening of unremitting tedium these words fell on our ears like caresses. The late James Sanderson of the *Daily Mirror* – snappily dressed as always, hair slicked down to perfection, shirt sleeves well in advance of jacket sleeve, tinkling slightly with gold about his person, cigar simmering in right hand – was in the first stages of pink, incandescent rage. But he, like others, had come alive. They could not have asked for more. We waited eagerly for 'Mr Ormunn'.

After about an hour, someone spotted the team bus rolling down the street to a different exit at the other end of the stadium. We rushed out of the pavilion and ran, cameras, pencils, notebooks clanking along, to cram round a small door. Just as the group of about twenty of us had drawn breath in relief, the bus suddenly reversed quickly back up the street to the entrance we had just left. We turned and scurried after it but just as we reached it again it changed direction and started off back down to the other entrance. Expletives rent the air. We scrambled down the street again thinking that scoops might yet have some connection with basic physical fitness.

Ormond was eaten alive when he emerged. He had eventually realised he would have to dig his way out of the stadium to avoid us. Now, he was shaking either with rage or nerves and spat out a great deal of uncharacteristic venom towards us, explaining that he would no longer put up with unfair and inaccurate reporting of the trip. The ban would continue until further notice. An ordinary evening had been turned into a treasure trove for those eager to have their credentials withdrawn like Mackenzie. They dutifully sent the wires humming back to Scotland, the reports replete with scorn and abuse. It was about then Hugh Taylor of the *Daily Record* wrote above his copy the superbly descriptive, succinct heading, 'The Tour de Farce'. This alone would have warranted him being thrown off the Lorelei into the Rhine by the SFA International Committee when we got to Germany.

We slunk into Frankfurt feeling as if the whole journey was quite unnecessary and that we would be back home pretty quickly. Travelling from the airport to the hotel, the television stage manager, who organised outside broadcasts, pointed out the former headquarters of the Gestapo in the Sachsenring.

'That's where they took all the major political prisoners,' he declared. 'Every diabolical torture known to man went on there.'

Not quite, I thought. The Gestapo's victims, so far as I know, had never been on a football trip to Norway. I felt it was going to take us a while to recover from all these traumas and time was in short supply. The players headed for the Taunus Mountains and all the television personnel entered a glass and concrete edifice on the outskirts of the city called the Arabella Hotel. It was besieged by perpendicular columns of glass and concrete office blocks, so giving the illusion that you were looking out of your room into a gigantic mirror. The whole area was devoted to the architecture of commerce, harsh, rectangular, teutonically tall and soulless. By about six o'clock of an evening when all the surrounding buildings decanted their staff it was like coming across some eerie Druidic meeting place. After a few days the hotel itself seemed as congenial as Colditz.

Sam Leitch, the World Cup editor back in London, had advised us not to fraternise with the enemy in the hotel. Not the remnants of the SS, of course, but ITV who, led by Sir Alf Ramsey and Billy Wright, were staging a considerable challenge to the BBC's expected supremacy of coverage. Nothing was to be given away indiscreetly. Careless talk in the bar could cost professional lives. Sam was serious. Don't mix! The bar being about the size of a lounge in a doll's house, this became impractical. After we had been plied with drinks we discovered all that the lads in ITV really wanted to know was where the action was in town. We did, however, send them on some wild goose chases.

Stein was there. He had travelled to Germany to work with the BBC as a match analyst. He had his closest friend, Tony Queen, the Glasgow bookmaker, with him. Stein gobbled up the information we gave him about the trip thus far. Privately, he could hardly disguise his contempt for the manner in which things had been handled up till then. Publicly, throughout the tournament, he remained respectful of Ormond. We travelled together the following day, after arriving in Frankfurt, to Erbismuhle, the quaint little village in the mountains in which sat the ski-lodge housing the Scottish team. Security was intense. Following the Black September attack on the Israeli athletes during the Munich Olympics two years earlier the Germans were taking no chances and had spent a considerable amount on protecting the teams. The security force were all plain-clothes men who smiled a lot but were meticulous in their policing.

They refused to believe that Jock Stein, David Coleman, myself and a film crew were not Palestinian terrorists at first and frisked us as rigorously. The team looked slightly more relaxed in a setting that reminded one of the lodge in which the film *The Lady Vanishes* starts. It was all Bavarian hunting-style, although far from Bavaria and redolent of 'lederhosen' and matronly waitresses carrying brimming-over tankards. They, however, had been replaced by a rather more chic cast. We had to travel an hour-and-a-half every day after that to this charming spot just to keep in touch with the news. There was still a gulf separating manager from media but the main concern was whether morale had been shattered beyond repair. This, of course, was not put to the test until the night we all went to Dortmund for the Zaire match.

It had been stingingly hot during the day. When we arrived I went with Stein and Tony Queen to the Scottish team hotel in the city, not far from the stadium. It is my contention that Jock Stein's influence in Germany went well beyond that of temporary BBC broadcaster. I was made aware of the fact forcibly that late afternoon. We sat in the lounge tolerating that agonising no-man's land of time when nothing much else can be done in preparation for the match and you resort to eating salted peanuts as your only mental exercise.

Even in the cool of the air-conditioned hotel the nerves were still preparing for shock. It was our first World Cup in a considerable time and although we were playing a team from a continent still undistinguished in football, people were still casting up Belfast Celtic in New York, and Paraguay in Switzerland to us as examples of the Scottish tendency to self-destruct. Just as we were ruminating on that Billy Bremner joined us. He flopped down on a leather sofa, looking pale and tired. He launched into an account of all that had gone on in Norway and Belgium although, not surprisingly, in a selective manner. He made it plain that he was happy neither with the general reporting nor the managerial style thus far. He did not specify too much but it was abundantly clear he was baring his soul.

Stein listened to this patiently for some time, then, suddenly, he heaved himself up from the seat he was on until his back was erect and I could see the flush developing on his face, the sure sign of anger. The big fist suddenly stretched across the table towards Bremner until it was only inches from his face.

'Don't bloody well lie down to all of this,' he snapped. 'The answer is in your own hands. You're experienced enough to get things going on the park. You get your players geed up. Never mind about anybody else. Use your own influence. Don't be moaning about everything, just get on with it and stick it right up the press. Just tell the players to remember everything that has been said about them and get them to go out and stuff it right up them.

Bloody well right up them. Get out there tonight and show us you're in a different league from these pygmies you're playing. Go on, stick it right up all your critics. Think of their faces just before kick-off, think, "We're going to stuff everybody tonight." Get out there and show us.'

He sat back after this rapid tirade. Bremner, who might well have been expecting tea and sympathy, had received a psychological kick in the pants. Its suddenness had struck forcibly home for he probably hadn't been talked to like that on the entire tour so far. The vacuum of authority had been filled, if only for a fleeting moment. There was no doubt that I had experienced a proxy team talk which would find its way back to the dressing room. Stein acted with great restraint thereafter during the tournament but it is also clear he became the father-confessor figure to certain prominent players who went to him with their worries. We should not, therefore, underestimate what he did for Scottish morale in Germany, even if he was being paid by the BBC.

At 2–0 that night Scotland put on the brake and, ever after, Bremner has been blamed for it. I regard this criticism as glibly simplistic. The Zaire team would have been content to run like stags all night in this, their first World Cup match. It cannot be proven by those who seem to know better what the score would have been had Scotland played flat out for the ninety minutes in extreme humidity. It might not have been many more. It is easy to quote the Yugoslavian 9–0 victory over them as an indication of a misreading of the situation that night. Zaire, I think, had given all they could in their first game.

On top of that, the Scottish team had just finished the most disastrous trip they had ever undertaken. The desire to grasp two points and leave it at that is not too surprising. Dortmund, far from being the disaster it has been interpreted as in retrospect, was the foundation for taking as much as we could from the rest of the tournament. Scotland had reclaimed some of their pride. And, as the Brazil match was to prove conclusively, they had rediscovered how to fire themselves up at the right time.

That was back in Frankfurt in the Waldstadion. Prior to the match, I interviewed Ormond at the hotel before we journeyed down from the hills to the city. He was nervous but pleasant and slightly detached, as if he was unaware everybody expected an annihilation. I somehow could not picture him taking on the Brazilians. What we eventually produced that night was not down principally to him but to the proper application by the senior professionals in the side, led by Bremner.

We had been told by the German television authorities that BBC Scotland could not have a television commentary position at this match because one had already been allocated to London for David Coleman. A political battle ensued which was won in Glasgow and when we got there that night we discovered that there were at least ten empty commentary positions in the stand. This duplication of BBC effort was to dog our footsteps in every major event involving a Scottish team and I suppose will never be satisfactorily resolved.

It was, debatably, the best performance by a Scottish team against class opposition in any World Cup. I recall the Davie Hay twenty-five-yarder which just went over the bar. I still remain stunned thinking of Bremner, acting on reflex, jabbing the ball past the post from right in front of goal. I admire the way they refused to succumb to reputations like Rivelino's and largely tamed the 'Europeanised' Brazilians, who had come to the Continent thinking, mistakenly, they had to change character to gain success. Brazilian international football has never recovered from that metamorphosis.

We simply were not good enough to beat Yugoslavia. We had now forgotten the Nordic mess and thought we were on the verge of greatness. I was built up for it as I have never been before. When Yugoslavia scored with two minutes to go I felt they had destroyed me personally. The equaliser had a cruel futility to it. I was to become more experienced in coping with disappointment but desolation is what I experienced then. I know my colleague in STV, Arthur Montford, in disgust, sped back to the hotel without talking to anybody, jumped in his car and headed for the North Sea Ferry. Unfortunately, I didn't have my car with me.

We returned by air. Glasgow Airport was thronged by thousands who treated the players like conquering heroes. After all, they hadn't lost a game. Willie Ormond, shedding tears, cut exactly the figure the nation wanted to see. Strube's little man in Scottish guise. The amiable little guy who had cheated fate and come through a test of character was back amongst his ain folk. He has been given great credit for the performances in Germany. His principal asset was his eye for a player. He was not the driving force you need to be at that level. Frankly, despite the initial disciplinary problems he provoked, Bremner's assertion of his own idiosyncratic personality on the Scottish squad had been vital. Without it, Ormond would have been seen as a disaster and the airport would have been deserted on our return.

In any case, this euphoria owed much to a decided sense of relief. After the traumas which preceded Germany and which prompted thoughts of imminent national disgrace, we had been resurrected. But as I look back, I appreciate now that the scenes at the airport were unhealthy. For that day the seeds of self-delusion were being sown. The bitter harvest was to be reaped in Argentina four years later.

8

Bitter Lessons

Scene: The television production gallery somewhere about five o'clock of a Saturday evening.

'Who comes next? . . . Bill McLaren? . . . Is he there yet? Edinburgh Studio! . . . Is Bill there yet? . . . What do you mean you don't bloody know? . . . Go out and bloody look for him or else drag Alistair Dewar back . . . We'll have to go on to Aberdeen, Archie . . . Aberdeen are you receiving us? . . . Whose tea cup is that . . . Get it out of there . . . Three minutes left . . . We'll never get to the Highland League results . . . What a damn pity, hee, hee, hee! . . . Go on to your second last page . . . No! No! Don't! . . . Ad lib the English results . . . and we have Bill McLaren . . . No we don't have Bill McLaren . . . He must be stuck in Princes Street . . . Ad Lib, Archie . . . Ad lib . . . Listen to the countdown . . . Ten-nine-eight-seven . . . Remember we're back tonight don't forget the trail . . . the trail, say it . . . Sportscene 10.30 . . . say the trail for Christ sake . . . four-three-two-one . . . We're off the air. Jesus!'

Something like that. It was the crammed, jumpy kind of programme, like being on the dodgems and not knowing how it was going to work out apart from the inevitable bumps. It was a repeating tale of the unexpected which led inevitably to a flirtation with mishap. Particularly that late afternoon programme. But broadcasting sometimes is less frenetic. Sitting much later on a Saturday evening in the studio after a more than adequate script preparation and with the auto-cue, your umbilical cord to coherence, clearly

96

and distinctly in front of you, the red-light suddenly going on stimulates rather than unnerves you. You simply say the words with a smile. That is broadcasting by auto-pilot. Whereas, the scramble to get news and views on the air in our late afternoon slot was as tidy as the Calgary Stampede.

As you talked to the public so a constant barrage of instructions could be passed on to you by means of the 'deaf-aid', a little plastic pod inserted in your ear. They could communicate directly and consequently dangle you like an electronic puppet. In the earlier days, though, when that technology was still being developed, they simply rang you up on the phone on the desk. I sometimes took more calls than the Samaritan service on a bad night.

So, we live on edge as broadcasters, fearing all the while the unknown, and the mistakes occur more often than not when you adopt, as is so easy to do, the 'look-no-hands' approach. The thought of the slip of the lip is never very far from our minds. I once introduced a programme by coolly announcing, 'The two games tonight are from Hambley and Wemden.' With our adrenaline bubbling over, we really ought to expect the mishap.

Errors are inerasable. They stick with you like reputation. In a live broadcast near one New Year's Eve I discussed sporting values with Hugh McIlvanney, Ian McLauchlan and Peter Alliss. The latter was waxing lyrical about how values, in general, had descended so low that an old woman of eighty couldn't walk down the street for fear of rape nowadays. McIlvanney, wishing to lighten the subject somewhat, said, *sotto voce*, 'Depends what she looks like.' Humour of that sort is sometimes not quickly appreciated and fearing a rush of protest from the switchboard I rushed in where angels fear to tread. I found myself interrupting to get quickly and diplomatically on to the next subject by saying, 'Don't knock it till you've tried it!'

As I moved heedlessly on, the heavens opened and the switchboard lady in Broadcasting House was bombarded by a nation indignant at what I had taken to be a flippant remark of no consequence. We had been invited, as a family, to Kilconquhar in Fife for the first few days of January, immediately after the programme. It is a beautiful spot but I felt inundated with resentment. My anguish had turned the East Neuk of Fife into Siberia. Blunders

97

like the one I had committed clung to me much more tenaciously than I would care to admit in public. I suffered the pangs of hell as I saw people looking at me at the functions I attended. I could almost hear them saying to one another, 'Dreadful fellow that. Speaking like that about old ladies.'

I wanted to rush up and explain that it wasn't like that at all. I really didn't want old ladies raped no matter how seductive they looked. Why didn't anybody understand me? Ah, the public! If only we could do without them, I thought. No one should imagine that such classic broadcasting non sequiturs are confined to those in front of the cameras whose egos have been bruised. I always comforted myself that others in the business could exceed that. Hugh Moran, who was the Industrial Correspondent at one stage, was once asked indignantly by a BBC admin type, 'Do you think we're here to help you make programmes?'

In the mid and latter part of the Seventies there was hardly a sports programme produced in Scotland that I wasn't part of. In the dual role of presenter and commentator there was not much pause for reflection, especially as my links with London were becoming stronger as well. It was about then I began a long and happy association with *Grandstand*. In the final analysis, though, it was, ironically, to prove a handicap to me in BBC Scotland. Perhaps the most challenging type of broadcast I have ever done was standing at the edge of a Scottish football pitch speaking live to London.

This happened virtually every week on *Football Focus*. The editors of *Grandstand* have come and gone – Alan Hart, Sam Leitch, Mike Murphy, John Philips – but the voice that guided me along the tightrope over the abyss of the live report was the producer Martin Hopkins. He was the voice in the ear telling me when they were about to come to me and above all giving me the crucial countdowns as I spoke to camera. I never had a script. I worked off memory and would give London the cue words earlier in the morning so they knew when to run the pictures that I would be leading into. As soon as I hit the right word, Martin would very coolly start the count until the pictures came up and I would shut up. If there was some problem and the pictures were not there at the last second, then this soothing voice would merely put you back on course for a bit of ad libbing, which you always had to be prepared to do. It didn't matter what the weather was like, the show never closed.

At Easter Road one day I launched into my first piece, which Martin cottoned on to when the cue word was mentioned, and right on the dot the pictures came up. As they did so, the weather changed in the most dramatic way. Suddenly a gale-like monsoon blew up from over Calton Hill and an umbrella was thrust at me by one of our assistants. I grabbed at it but it twisted in my hand and I wrestled with it the way a deep-sea diver might fight with a giant octopus, the spokes going in all directions. In the space of a minute the weather had gone from bright sunshine to blizzard. It was one of the few times that Hopkins was beside himself. He struggled to fight against the mirth which had taken over the production gallery in London.

When eventually they came back to me for my introduction to the next item the viewers must have thought I had been transplanted, in about that space of sixty seconds, to Reykjavik. I had to try to recall what I was supposed to say and still prevent myself from blowing away and as I did so I knew I had forgotten the cue words. I meandered into waffle whilst at the same time trying to rack my brains for what they might be. Of course I had given them to London but they didn't know that I had forgotten them. Down there at Television Centre they waited and waited as I waded verbally on, trying to keep myself on my feet and the umbrella from blowing into the North Sea. For the first time I could remember on the programme I was panicking. I still didn't want to admit in public that I was lost although I suppose I should have.

Then, Martin twigged. If he hadn't I might still have been speaking through *Dr Who* at tea-time. 'Ah!' he said softly, without a hint of flurry, 'I think the words you are searching for are, "inevitably Easter Road . . ."' and then chuckled slightly. Saved! I took breath and garbled them into a sentence and as the umbrella was about to win the fight the pictures came up. It was the only occasion in about fifteen years' connection with *Football Focus* that we didn't get it quite right. I credit Hopkins with being able to sit inside the performer's head, realising that there is sometimes

agony being experienced. Not everybody in his area has that inclination or ability.

I had decided that the main style of presentation on that programme would not be pontification but would allow a little whimsy.
This suited the style of both Mike Murphy and especially his
successor as editor of *Grandstand*, my fellow Scot John Philips.
Philips eschews the obvious. His idiosyncratic approach to devising
the programme has produced some of the most individual interpretations of sporting events in an area where much is routine. Since
the eye is used to more predictable accounts not everybody appreci-
ates the way he diverges. He is a kind of Edward de Bono of
sports broadcasting. One kaleidoscopic lunch-time survey of sport
previewed what we were to see on the afternoon of the Grand
National. It moved in and out of Aintree, to other venues, to other
sports, with no linking script, allowing the pictures to explain why
each leap had been made. The sequence was underpinned by a
musical motif. The venerable old flagship of BBC sports presentation was pushed towards a kind of television pointillism.

If it jarred with some, it stimulated others. Sports coverage has
been blessed by great technological advance, to the extent that we
can all be privy to the worm's eye view at the foot of the stumps
in a Test match. In too many cases, there has, however, been no
comparable leap in its aesthetic. The conservatism of the emphasis
on plain good coverage of events has led too often to a disregard
for the imaginative exploration of the sporting character. In that
sense, you might regard Philips as a redoubtable maverick.

My input fitted his philosophy and vice versa. We always tried
to venture outside the boundaries of conventional presentation.
One lunch time I turned up as usual to deliver the piece from
Tannadice and discovered that the North Pole had spread to
Dundee. The pitch was buried in snow with no chance of the game
being played. Bill Malcolm, my producer, reading the situation
brilliantly both in terms of the weather and the flavour we wanted,
had got his men to build a snowman. They put my distinctive
sheepskin coat and bonnet with scarf on it and when London
came over to us they saw it rather than me. Just off camera, I
ventriloquised my words for the snowman. It was a risky thing to
attempt. This was before trivia was institutionalised by the Saint

and Greavsie. It perhaps ran counter to the solid, authoritative nature of *Football Focus* then. It seemed to work all the same. London solemnly thanked me for the services I had rendered through several seasons and bade me adieu. They were now putting the snowman on contract.

The public were increasingly taking a hand in my life though. Criticism did not pass through me quickly but persisted like an unidentified virus which even a good overnight sweat won't budge. I discovered this earlier, in 1969, when the home internationals went into an end of season package and I was asked to do all three matches 'live'. It was not a happy experience. In the first game at Wrexham I arrived to discover that BBC network and ITV had actually constructed their television platforms on top of scaffolding which stretched right along the track in front of the centre stand. The ticket holders paying handsomely for the privilege were going to have to watch the game through a fretwork. This was an outrageous piece of arrogance by both channels who, having paid each home association the princely sum for those days of £30,000, felt they could virtually re-write the laws of the game.

As I was about to climb up the ladder before the game a technician asked me who I was with. When I told him BBC Scotland he shook his head and said, 'You're there!' and pointed to the back of the stand. So, I was pigeon-holed in the very last row of the stand looking not only at the game through this aluminium web in front of me but also over the heads of the irate stand patrons. They had never experienced this before and were rising from time to time throughout the game to hurl insults at my colleagues from both BBC network and ITV, David Coleman and Brian Moore, who were sitting like monarchs of all they surveyed with a superb view of the pitch. My tiny little television monitor from which I deduced what was happening on the field of play was like a crumb from the master's table.

It was an almost impossible task. I felt like a negro in Alabama when, once upon a time, they had to sit at the rear of even an empty bus. Identification of players had been a nightmare and if you are not coping with that fluency is impossible, a feeling for the game is beyond you. It was a struggle and a failure.

There is one thought that must never pass through your mind

in broadcasting and that is, 'It can only get better.' As I travelled back from Wales that self-comforting sentiment was in mind as I mentally prepared for the Scotland–Northern Ireland game which had been switched from Belfast because of the start of the troubles there. I could not have been more wrong. On that date Glasgow was hit by a storm. It didn't stop raining for twenty-four hours, ninety minutes of which was the international match. Only 7,483 certifiable souls turned up at Hampden (the lowest international crowd on record this century) while the rest sanely remained at home taking the opportunity of watching it live on television and, perhaps less sanely, with the sound up listening to me.

In the mud of Hampden that night the game began to resemble the Eton Wall Game with clusters of shadowy players pursuing an object that was elusive not just to them but to the commentator in his position low down behind the Hampden dug-out. Within ten minutes the bedraggled players were caked in mud and their jersey numbers disappeared. Even the Scottish players looked indistinguishable from each other, so you can imagine the Pelmanistic nightmare I was having with the Irish. Eventually you could barely tell them from the Scots in the far from ideal floodlights at Hampden.

It is one of the clichés of television that as the viewers can actually see the game anyway it can speak for itself. If in doubt, shut up! This is simply not true. Viewers need a voice not just for information but also to bounce off, or agonise about, or vilify, or perhaps even be amused by. The American attempts at cutting out the ball by ball commentaries ended in failure. The much-hated commentators suddenly found new friends. The public wanted them back. It was like the Boston Strangler being suddenly perceived as the kindly neighbourhood traffic warden.

The fear of rebuke for talking too much must never predominate or you become utterly stifled. At the same time, the ability to slip into a silence is certainly one of the prime assets in a television commentator's make-up. But that is utterly different from abdicating responsibility by hiding behind the silence and 'shutting up', which is what I did that night. The game was crying out for excess and damn the consequences, simply because it was making no pattern to the viewer. Wit and a bit of wisdom would have helped but as the rain dripped off the end of my nose I froze and lapsed into incommunicable silence. The game didn't speak for itself, it mumbled incoherently. I was panned for it. I spied a solitary spectator on the East Terracing of Hampden without umbrella, shivering and bedraggled. It summed up the misery of a damp desolate stadium. I chose to use one word to describe this. 'Drookit'. It was thrown back at me by a correspondent of a newspaper who thought it aptly described my commentary.

Peter Thomson at the time was supportive and told me that he had had his disasters, but I was inconsolable. I travelled to Wembley at the end of that same week, for my first-ever broadcast there, having sleepless nights about it. A famous commentator took me to a club in Soho where the nipples were bigger than the guns of Navarone. For a fleeting moment or two sitting in this seedy setting, disillusioned by the cultural choice of this man whom I had assumed was going to show me round the Tate, I forgot about the morrow. I thought realising my ambition to commentate at Wembley would be an experience of such transcendental significance that I would be floating in nirvana. As England clinically demolished us, the whole experience was as uplifting as being stranded at Crewe Junction overnight. If you bring the news of a Scottish disaster to the public you are too often associated with it, almost as if you were an accessory after the fact. If only I could have sounded uplifting, like Thomson himself when he described that great 3−1 win in 1949. If only I could have sent inspirational sounds throughout the land I might well have benefited from it personally as a by-product. But there is nothing you can do about a 4−1 defeat by the Auld Enemy. Two decades later, I was asked during a broadcast to cheer the nation up when Scotland were playing miserably in Genoa. I had the good sense to recognise the basic phoniness of such a request and refused. There and then as a novice I might just have succumbed to such pressure and sounded even more idiotic than I had in the previous two games. The commentary in itself, I think, had been adequate but linked with the result and combined with the previous two efforts that week I was hardly regarded by the public as an infant prodigy in the business.

That is why retreating from football occasionally acted as good therapy. The Commonwealth Games in Edinburgh in 1970 was a case in point. There, I reported on a wide range of sports on radio and came into contact with, amongst others, a curmudgeonly old soul called Harold Abrahams. He had good cause to recall Edinburgh with mixed memories and at the end of his broadcasting career with radio he seemed keener to involve people in arguments about the tea being cold in the office, or where his pen had gone and how the Edinburgh weather was foul. At least some of his sentiments were not wildly inaccurate. But when I asked him if he would record some recollections of Eric Liddell for Radio Scotland he simply waved me away like a star denying a boy an autograph.

It was Lachie Stewart who made that diversion into another area eminently worth while by demonstrating the durability of what we thought was a fast vanishing breed, the true amateur, by winning the 10,000 metres on a dreich Edinburgh Saturday afternoon. This little dental mechanic who made model boats for bottles in his spare time had destroyed one of the world's first 'shamateurs', Ron Clarke. The lean and lanky Australian always ran brilliantly against the clock and broke record after record at middle distance but he had never won a gold medal at the top level. He couldn't run in a high class competitive race, apparently, but as this was to be his last ever effort and as his times were way in front of everybody else, he was not only expected to win but world athletic sentiment outside of Scotland was also clearly on his side. He lost.

At the crowded press conference afterwards most people had forgotten that it was little Lachie who was wearing the gold medal round his neck. All the questions were directed towards Clarke. To one concerning his retiral and his reasons for taking up athletics in the first place he gave vent to a philosophical explanation about how he felt life itself to be challenging, about how his sport extended his horizons and opened up his mind to the greater realities of living, and so on. Then suddenly somebody remembered that it was Lachie who had actually won the race and asked him similarly why he had taken up athletics. He looked up and replied, 'Because I got fed up going to the pictures.' The sentence came as a sudden gush of spring water in a parched field. Surrounded, as we often were, by the cynicism of professional football, and in the immediate vicinity of the pomposity of an athlete taking his running shoes a little too seriously, Stewart became an instant hero to those of us who battled daily with the spurious in search of a true original.

His breed became slowly extinct during the Seventies, though. There was little chance of him being an inspirational model to others, not when George Best was in vogue, linking his genius on the field to the rewards offered by the Marbella Club and an endless succession of blondes. Continuing after his triumph to make dentures by day and mini-*Cutty Sarks*, squeezed by leger-demain into small bottles by night, did not seem an adequate reward for the enormous effort which Lachie put into his triumph. Sport, increasingly, was being seen as a vehicle for improving life-style. It was an adjunct to the list of other social aids which the upwardly mobile sought after.

Ryder Cup golfer Harry Bannerman could certainly have moved on to higher education. His ex-headmaster, walking round the course with him, once asked Harry why he hadn't gone for his degree. Harry said, 'Wait a minute,' took out a three iron and smote the ball over two hundred yards to within a couple of feet of the hole. 'I see,' said the old teacher and changed the topic of conversation.

The footballer, never myopic when currency is on the horizon, had turned predator. In 1974 the World Cup Squad had taken their breakfast knives to rip off the distinctive stripes from their boots before a training session to be filmed by us because the sponsor Adidas had refused to pay money to everybody in the squad and only to those who actually played in the games. When Hibs won the Drybrough Cup Final against Celtic in 1972 I hauled Eddie Turnbull, the Hibs manager, out of a rejoicing dressing room, still flushed with triumph, still rabbiting on about how splen-did a victory it had been. We wired him up, got a voice level from him, got a countdown on the tape about to run to a recording when suddenly it dawned on him that he was about to be on television. 'How much am I getting for this?' he asked. 'I really have no idea,' I said. 'Well, you can stuff it up your arse then,' he replied, ripping off the mike and storming off up the tunnel.

Agents began to appear even then. Nothing wrong with the principle of having an agent. I have one myself. Except that some of the ones I met had as much money sense and deftness of touch as slaughterers at an abattoir. When we approached the possibility of qualifying for Argentina in the late Seventies that breed moved into top gear. A trend was being set. The backhander was now passé. It was all up front and it was into the outstretched palm.

It is not that Lachie Stewart was a better person than those in, or even distantly connected with, professional sport who were about to plunder the market. It is just that those nine words of explanation of why he took up athletics – 'Because I got fed up going to the pictures' – registered with me as a voice from some less complicated age, a reflection of an antique virtue that was doomed to be an anachronism. Whatever else I was to hear and see in the Seventies, the sound of those words remained with me, as if I wanted to cling on to some personal link with a past that had little contemporary meaning, just as I could never forget, even if I wanted to, the sound of a peerie being whipped in a Glasgow street.

9

Politics in Play

Sanctuary was hard to find in the late Seventies. However hard they tried, it was difficult for people in sport to elude the political tentacles which drew them into messes of other people's making. It was inevitable that the world's great controversies would impinge on sport but many of its administrators continued to believe it had a special immunity, that it could opt out of reality as it wished. This sterile philosophy was easy to justify so long as you kept your eyes selectively shut. Some of us found it difficult.

We had gone to Czechoslovakia in 1976. There, sport was supposed to be a means of demonstrating the purity of the communist system to the rest of the world. As Scotland were to play a crucial World Cup qualifying game against them, we decided to make a documentary about their whole sporting organisation, which regularly produced outstanding performers in a wide range of activities. The idea was to travel there a couple of months before the game, film what we wanted and transmit the programme the night before the match. At that time Czechoslovakia was one of the hard-line communist countries and also, because of its car, glass and beer industries, one of the most prosperous. After the usual rigmarole with their embassy about visas and documentation to film around Prague, which frustrated us no end, we flew into the city. With a relative smoothness which surprised us we made contact with our film unit and our marvellous interpreter, Yarka, who probably spoke English better than any of us. She assured us that we would be permitted to go anywhere and look at anything we wanted. We politely smiled our gratitude at that, although after the experience of our first night in the Alkron Hotel, just off Wenceslas Square, we felt that they might think us easily duped.

There were three of us: Malcolm Kellard, the sports editor, Bill Malcolm, the producer, and myself. Although the hotel was empty they had put us into a suite which housed only one single and one double bed. If the hotel had been crammed we would have put up with that but repeated requests for a switch of rooms were met by that characteristically implacable eastern European look of helplessness. We were to get used to this. Squeezed as we were into that tiny space in this huge empty hotel, we quite naturally reached the conclusion that an arrangement had been made to 'bug' the room and that we could not possibly be moved. It seemed the only explanation. Now, *Three Men and a Bug* has a sort of Jerome K. Jerome ring to it but we could not think of any other explanation. After all we were here to make a film and perhaps they might think we were less interested in muscles than we were in munitions. This country being blessed with marvellous glass, our suspicions centred on the magnificent crystal chandelier suspended from the centre of the suite. It might, in retrospect, have seemed a trifle obvious but it was to that object that we directed our remarks in loud, theatrical voices. At first painfully artificial (try to think of yourself being bugged!) we then resorted to jokes of such unambiguous filth that whoever had the earphones on in the basement was actually going to get enough material to establish himself as a stand-up comedian in the Workers Commune Club in Bratislava. Alternatively, in a fit of communist puritanism, he would wrench the headset off and slope back home. One way or the other they were going to find out they were wasting their time. Later Yarka was to admit to me that we had been listened to, although, by the contrite and apologetic look on her face, the 'listeners' had obviously not told her any of the jokes.

This early frustration was matched by the fact that we could not get the proper film stock. We almost gave up and went home but I argued that we were dealing with a system that went its own ponderous way and we must have patience. But we were blessed with great technicians. The Czech film industry is world-renowned and we ended up with a cameraman and a sound man who had both worked with Milos Forman before he had gone into exile to Hollywood to make such works as *One Flew Over the Cuckoo's Nest*, which has itself been seen as an allegory on the communist system and the durability of the human spirit. They both spoke creditable English. The cameraman was distinctly Russian orientated and kept reprimanding the sound man for criticising Russian films. The little sound man would say, 'I hate Russky films. All psycholgie. Nothing but psycholgie and war!' The tall gaunt cameraman would, in English, so that we would be aware of his inclination, cajole him and talk about the 'war when twenty million Russian lives were lost to save the world'. I was to hear that stark and truthful remark trotted out on innumerable occasions behind the Iron Curtain by people at functions who would suddenly pop up to tell you how marvellous the system was. We worked together well, except that we had no clapper board to put the film into synchronisation and Bill Malcolm had to stand in front of camera and clap his hands and shout out the number of the takes before every shot or else the editor back in Scotland would have been lost. Bill was probably the first man in film-making history to suffer bruising of the hands on a job. Then, one day, the first touch of the sinister.

We had gone to the vast Spartakiad Stadium to reflect the kernel of the entire system. Every four years the nation's gymnasts, from village and city, would take part in mass exercises in one of the most gigantic displays anywhere in world sport. To stand in the middle of its sandy surface was like being in a desert. When we had finished our exterior shots we went inside to watch some of the young gymnasts being put through their paces by an instructress whom I recognised immediately. The Golden Girl of the Mexico Olympics of 1968, Vera Caslavska, the winner of four gold medals. She had got married in Mexico City during the Games. I asked Yarka if she would arrange an interview with her. She went down into the gym and talked to this beautiful and still lithe blonde who, during the conversation with our interpreter, looked up and smiled shyly at us as if in assent to the request. Yarka returned and said it had been arranged for two days' time, a Saturday morning. When we duly showed up with our cameras she wasn't there. In her place was another, rather statuesque lady who had won a gold at a previous Olympics. When I asked where Vera had gone, Yarka apologised and told me that, unfortunately, the Gymnastic Association had requested her to hold some tests for children in another part of the city. They passed on a message from Vera saying she was very apologetic but that she was sure we would understand that her job came first. Of course we did. Until that same evening.

We were in the hotel restaurant. We had ordered a meal from a menu the size of the *Daily Record* and been told, as usual, that of the twenty thousand dishes on display only the pork was available, but that it did come four different ways. We were entertaining Yarka both for her brilliant translations during interviews and for her charm and general serenity during those periods of filming when the affable can give way so easily to the irascible. But she got slightly tiddly on the excellent and very reasonably priced Russian champagne. She suddenly went quiet for a spell and then, late into the evening, turned and whispered to me, 'I am ashamed! Very ashamed of myself!' Then she fell quiet again.

'Why?' I asked.

'I told you a lie,' she said quietly. 'About Vera Caslavska. She was not allowed to meet you. She is, what you say, persona non grata. She is in disgrace. When she came back from the Mexico Olympics she showed her support for Dubcek and the political changes he was trying to establish by presenting him with her four gold medals. That was not forgotten when the changes took place and there was the clamp down. She is in permanent disgrace now and is not allowed to speak to anybody from the western media. She would have liked to so much. Please do not breathe a word to anybody about this. I could not have forgiven myself if I had allowed you to leave without telling you the truth about that.'

I felt a slight chill running up the spine. A great athlete gives the leader of a country her Olympic medals and is now considered to be a villain? It did not seem credible but then the Prague Spring which offered so much hope for change in Czechoslovakia and was ruthlessly suppressed seemed far off. This beautiful city was now dour, dull and resigned to it all. The budding of hope that came with Dubcek belonged to another and forgotten age. Yarka was deeply upset about this.

'I am very ashamed for myself and my country,' she went on. 'There is so much of this.'

The genuine pity that I felt for her was compounded two days later when we went to film the famous Rude Pravo Road Race which was run annually through the streets of Prague and won on this occasion by the Finn Lasse Viren, the man who went in for the Dracula-like blood transfusions before each Olympics to notable effect. But it was not this running skeleton who haunted me afterwards but another figure.

'Do you recognise that face?' Yarka asked me as we filmed the dignitaries' stand near the crowded finishing line. There he was, walking slowly and almost painfully amongst the top brass of the party and army shaking hands like a fawning beggar, smiling like a clockwork doll. It was Emil Zatopek, the great Czech middle distance runner of the early Fifties, the man with the head-bobbing, pained running expression who had great clashes on the British tracks with the likes of Chris Chataway. He would always be regarded as one of the finest runners of all time.

'He is another one,' Yarka said.

'Another what?'

'In disgrace. He did the same as Vera. He showed his support for Dubcek. One day he was a Master of Sport, a distinguished man in our sports system. The next he was a clerk licking stamps and tying string. That is what he now does in a small office. You see he is with these men trying to get back into favour. But it's no use. There is no way back for him.'

Zatopek shook his last hand on the platform then, bald head gleaming in the sharp autumn sun, shuffled down the stairs out of sight. I was beginning to dislike Czechoslovakia a great deal. We had come mentally prepared to be fighting to disentangle ourselves from a miasmic bureaucracy but were ill-equipped to respond to this malevolence. We did in fact portray Zatopek as the disgraced hero and expressed, in the context of a pointedly non-political film, a diversionary comment on his plight.

Our hands were not completely free. We had been offered the co-operation of the Czech television service on the condition that when we returned for the coverage of the international match we would show them the finished documentary. This would not have affected our ultimate transmission but, as they had apparently given us the help upon which we were totally dependent, to make a film about sport we wanted to play fair with them. I was worried though about bringing back the completed version for them to view because in the delicate situation we found ourselves you could never ensure their complete acceptance.

We completed our film. We reflected on the importance they attached to developing sport and how much that meant in an international arena. We looked at how they nurtured their young talent and showed the work at a special football school in the city. We even recorded recreational activities for the general population, having been taken by one of the party apparatchiks to a 'trim' park where people could exercise freely.

We wanted to film an interview with a young family we saw walking through the park; a mother, father and daughter of about six. But we desisted when they asked for money. We had obviously bumped into a capitalist 'cell'. Yarka transcribed all the interviews painstakingly into English so that we would have no misinterpretations in our scripting back in Glasgow. However, to be as meticulous as we possibly could, I approached Glasgow University to find out if someone could check the language for us. Down to the studios came a professor who had been born and brought up in Prague. His name was Dr Emil Soukoup.

Silver-haired, urbane, mild-mannered Dr Soukoup sat in front of the viewing screen in the editing room listening to the interviews and watching the panorama of his native city unfold. His expressions varied from extreme sadness to chuckling hilarity, especially as he checked the speech with the written translations Yarka had provided. Having looked through every foot of film he turned to me.

'Oh, dear!' he cried. 'They make it sound so simple don't they? All they told you was what they wanted you to hear, nothing more. And I think we could beef up the translations a little more. Oh, dear! What a sad place!'

He had a beautifully modulated, 'mittel-European' accent which made me think he would be ideal as the voice speaking in English on the film over the Czech voices. When I suggested this to him he resisted, saying he could not possibly, he of all people, no of course not! But in truth it did not take all that much arm twisting to get him to change his mind because I think he was emotionally pulled into the documentary, as if it was providing a vicarious trip back to his beloved city. We had not asked him too much about himself since we were simply interested in translation and it was his ability in linguistics that impressed us.

'I have never been back since I left some years ago,' he explained to us. 'I am a refugee who was lucky enough to get a job in languages. I have been very fortunate. But I would not go back. I hate and despise what they have done to my country.'

So, he put his voice on the film for us and, the job completed, we set out to return to Prague. We took with us a video recording of our programme but some instinct of mine was at work. I advised my producer to hold on to the tape until we were leaving the country again, as our stay was only three days. Each day Yarka came to the hotel or phoned us to ask for the tape and for three days we played a cat and mouse game with her. It is difficult to know now how we managed to elude these requests but we did one way or the other, feigning forgetfulness or saying that one or other of us had had it in mind to come to the television station but that something had cropped up. She wasn't exactly the dumbest girl in the world and must have known that something was afoot, although, having developed a genuine friendship with us, I think she did not want to push this too much. It was not as if we had pilloried their country or their political system but, on Dr Soukoup's advice, we had altered certain translations and I had certainly changed my script in accordance with his interpretations of some of the things said to us. It queried rather than criticised and in that sense was, in my view, only mildly admonitory. And yet I felt uneasy about it.

We commentated on Czechoslovakia beating Scotland 2–0, retired despondently to our hotel, where we sought succour in the plum brandy, and generally made ourselves scarce until the following morning, just half-an-hour before the bus left for the airport, when we met Yarka and presented her with the tape. We said our farewells and my producer and I admitted to each other that there was a sense of relief at having got this off our hands. We were eager to get home, out of this frigid country. We did not reckon on the weather though. SFA Secretary, Ernie Walker marched into the lounge of the hotel just ten minutes after Yarka had left to announce that there was fog at the airport and that we could be delayed up to four or five hours. Bill Malcolm and I could scarcely believe this.

'Are you thinking what I'm thinking?' Bill asked me.

Yes, I had been. They would have plenty of time to look at the video and we still would be in the country. We thought of making ourselves scarce, going for a walk. The trouble about walking in the old town of Prague, in the twisting maze of streets, is that even with the keenest sense of direction you could so easily get lost. We considered it but, then, I had had enough. Perhaps we were being over-sensitive about this whole episode anyway. We were not.

About an hour-and-a-half later we saw two, black top-grade Skoda limousines swinging into the square beside the hotel. Out of the first stepped Yarka. She was followed by three men who did not actually come into the hotel but stood outside the swing-doors. I rose to meet her. I put out my hand but unsmilingly she suddenly broke into that chilling formalese which was so uncharacteristic of her, but so typical of the robotic communist attempts at communication by ordinance.

'I would like to thank you for coming to my country, Mr Macpherson,' she clipped. It was as if they had given her some injection so that she could talk to us in the manner befitting a female of the party, like Ninotchka. 'But we are very unhappy with the film. The English is not good. Some of the things said are distorted. We are very unhappy. Who was the man who voiced the translation?'

This didn't seem to be Yarka but some clone. At the same time a little voice in my head told me to act dumb.

'Oh, it was an actor we picked up,' I replied. 'He put on a fake sort of accent for us to make it sound middle-European. He was good at it.'

She was not taken in but did not try to contradict me.

'I think we know the voice, you know,' she said softly. 'He said things which did not please us. Certain inflections of meaning in the translation. We are unhappy with the English. Is there no more light you can shed on this?'

'No,' I lied, feeling both remorse and anger that this delightful lady had apparently been lobotomised to party conformity.

'Good-bye,' she said suddenly, turned and walked to the door.

I followed trying to think of some apology but felt quite defeated by the circumstances. At the door she stopped and merely said, 'They were very angry but I spoke up for you. You know it could have been worse. But I think it will be difficult for you to come back to my country. They will not trust you.'

And off she went in her black car leaving me distraught. I felt as if I had cheated her personally and was also disturbed by her sudden change of personality. Certainly the men had been watching her from the door. Yet I wasn't sure that accounted for it. It was difficult to grasp why this relatively innocuous filming exercise was concluding like one of John Le Carré's bleak endings.

It was possible that, after all, she was a party hack stringing us along all the time. I wanted to doubt that but I would never know for sure, which was the unkindest cut of all.

When we returned to Glasgow, after sweating for a time in Prague airport, and suspicious of even the lavatory attendants, I made straight for Dr Soukoup. I took him to lunch.

'Who are you?' I asked bluntly.

I told him what had happened.

'I am sorry,' he apologised. 'I did not want to say too much. And you did not ask too much. I was in politics in Czechoslovakia. I was political secretary to the Foreign Minister Jan Masaryk. As you probably know he was in the last government to be democratically elected before the communists took over in 1948. You know of course that Jan died in Wenceslas Square. He fell from a balcony. Many people claim he was pushed. Not physically he wasn't. Perhaps the pressure of events had overcome him and in that sense he was pushed. He knew a communist coup was on hand and there seemed nothing that could be done to save democracy. I was the first to reach the body in the square.

'If he had been pushed he would have resisted and his body would have landed in a contorted mess on the street. But as it was, there were clear signs that he had fallen like a man in some kind of trance. His thigh bones went clean through his shoulder blades. A classic suicide, you would say. I knew I was then in serious danger myself. So I did as much as I could with his body, went home, gathered my belongings, got into my car and drove over the border and I have never been back. Now I teach and occasionally I broadcast from a station in Rome into Czechoslovakia, telling the truth. I think they would really like to get their hands on me.'

He told this with a certain reluctance, as if it ought to have been confined within a strictly familial conversation. Perhaps he is now back in Prague teaching at the university. Perhaps Yarka is working for a West German branch of a multi-national company now taking executives round the city. I saw them both as victims of a brutal political system and myself innocently drawn into the convoluted mess of their lives. All because I wanted to know what made a Czechoslovakian athlete tick. In truth, whilst their national football team did enjoy a certain moderate success it gradually began to resemble a mechanical toy needing regular winding up by a toy-maker reluctant to do so. It reflected the dehydrated spirit of a country which had essentially lost its self-esteem.

But the 'free' world offered its major problems as well as we discovered when, in preparation for a possible qualification for the finals in Argentina, the SFA decided to take on a South American tour consisting of games in Chile, Argentina and Brazil. Although it was the second leg of the trip I cannot think of South American football or what the people were then suffering without first recalling our entry into Argentina.

The welcome party in Buenos Aires consisted largely of grim-faced men with pistols, machine-guns, rifles, and armoured cars. Cheery sorts who looked as if a body a day kept the blues away. We knew that there had been a reputation of animosity from time to time between the SFA and the media but we did not think it had reached the ears of the Argentinians. Yet, arriving, as we were, at the International Airport just outside the capital city, we assumed they thought hostilities were about to break out in the arrival lounge, thus necessitating the presence of a peace force. As we shuffled from the terminal I sought out somebody who could speak English and discovered a large man who kept sweeping his eyes round the curious crowds gazing at the Scottish party. I asked him why there was a show of force.

'The Montoneros,' he said heavily, without looking at me. 'They threaten violence.'

Anybody who could have contemplated threatening violence against this gorilla would have been deranged. He kept his right hand in his jacket, Napoleon-like; not, I supposed, to assist in philosophical meditation. There were many others like him around. The airport looked as if it were under siege and yet here we were in the year of our Lord 1977, simply coming to a country to play football. It didn't seem that the month of May was a merry one in Argentina.

'Montoneros?' I asked.

'Bad. Verr, verr bad,' he replied moving off. Our interpreters told us later that they were the guerrilla group fighting the military dictatorship in Argentina and that they had promised to disrupt the World Cup the following year, bringing hand-grenades rather than ricketies to provide background noise. It wasn't as if we had flown into this tense South American country totally naive about the political situation. It is just that such a dimension seemed to lie outwith our own interest. Reading about it didn't quite prepare us for looking down the barrel of a gun or seeing the military hardware surrounding us. There were two buses for the group from the airport, as is normal. But the separation of media from players and officials followed a different order.

'Yours is the first bus,' a suave gentleman told us. 'You will lead the way in the convoy.'

Convoy? Sure enough there was an armoured car just in front of the leading bus and, beside it and between the two buses, large cars and behind that again another armoured car. But the media bus travelling first to the hotel seemed an outrageous breach of the normal protocol, although Ernie Walker did not seem to be objecting all that much. I learned from the loose-tongued interpreter the reason for this.

'Well, you see,' he said. 'If the Montoneros were to attack they would perhaps bomb the first bus in the convoy, thinking it was the team and officials. That is why they are putting the press up front.'

Was there a smile on Ernie's face? Were we to be decoys? It might just have been occurring to the SFA that the Montoneros could once and for all rid them of a company of men who hung round their necks like lead weights at times. We had never been decoys before and we took to it with that jocular fortitude that the Scot shows in time of great stress, although we stopped short of gaily putting our names in a hat and having a sweep on when the first strike would be. Our journey into the city though left us no time to reflect on this bizarre scenario for we did not simply leave the airport, we were catapulted from it.

We took off from the airport and onto the frenetic roads of Buenos Aires at ninety miles an hour. Sirens wailing, we stopped for nothing. Just in front of us the plain-clothed state thugs were leaning out of their windows, waving revolvers at passers-by and shouting to warn them from crossing our paths. Cars sped out of our way up onto pavements, brakes screeching, horns blasting as the convoy seemed to leap at Buenos Aires' jugular. So far this was working a treat, sobering up those who had been a bit heavy on the Chilean vino on the trip over the Andes, and putting a bomb-throwing Montonero shouting, 'Libre Argentina' right out of our heads. Then out of the window up ahead I saw an old man crossing the road, hobbling slightly and leaning on a walking stick. The gangsters in the car in front were screaming at him. I swear I detected a little touch of defiance in him as he just about got out of the way but did not leave the road and stared stolidly at us as we approached.

As the car got to him I saw the policeman leaning further out of the window and swiping at him with the barrel of the revolver. The old man dropped like a stone as the bus sped by. It all happened in a blur, almost as if it had been a mirage, but from our side of the bus we could look back and see him lying in the road behind us.

We had barely recovered from that when the assault troops in front started to hammer on the roofs of cars with their bare fists to get them out of the way as we neared the city centre, leaving big dents, in some cases, on the bodywork. As we swung through the traffic into the bewildering maze of streets the police continued to lash out at cars and people until we eventually swept into the hotel forecourt screeching and coming to rest like a runaway train halted inches from the buffers. I felt drained. What kind of country was this we had come to? What kind of animals were these men purportedly lending us protection? I sensed we had come to an evil place. The incident with the old man had been one thing but what kind of tyranny was this when police molested cars as if they were people? Was not even that potent icon of Buenos Aires sacred?

This was Argentina and to a great extent the journey from the airport summarised much of what South America was in the Seventies. We were in a large military camp which was unable to comprehend the changes that had taken place in the mother countries of Spain and Portugal. It was generally governed by the men in silly uniforms with decorative braid as subtle as neon lighting. Playing football and holding a World Cup would be one of the ways of anaesthetising the population against rebellious, rousing ideas. It could even endear them to the rest of the world. In the long run it didn't work but for a while sport was used as a temporary buttress supporting a wall with little foundation.

When this tour, with its first stop in Chile, had been originally mooted, it provoked outrage, particularly amongst the political left and trade unions. In 1973, Salvador Allende, the first-ever democratically elected Marxist president in the western world, had been killed in a coup brought about by the Chilean generals led by Pinochet. Those opponents of the new regime were herded into the national football stadium and many were taken from this temporary concentration camp to be slaughtered. Chile was now a ruthless dictatorship. This did not deter the SFA from electing to arrange an international match against them some four years later.

Soon after the coup, in 1973, the Soviet Union had refused to play a World Cup decider qualifying match in that very stadium. They had sent a message to FIFA declaring that 'Soviet sportsmen cannot at present play at a stadium stained with the blood of Chilean patriots'. FIFA asked Chile if the game could be held in another ground. This was rebuffed and as the Soviet Union would not budge they were eliminated from the World Cup.

One is not sure how many telexes of protest about blood spillage and unjust internment were sent to the Gulags in Siberia from the Soviet FA. Perhaps they never got round to it. It was also suggested that since the game between the sides in Moscow had ended in a 0–0 draw the Soviets had little stomach to travel all that way for almost certain elimination.

However, to be totally fair, they had offered to play in any other venue than the notorious National Stadium. So, even though their stance smacked of hypocrisy, they had at least decided that sport was not possible in absolutely any context. That in itself seemed to me to be indisputable. The SFA though pushed ahead with their arrangements despite the Labour government's strong disapproval or, perhaps, even because of it, for there is nobody more obdurate than a sports official scorned by a politician. The trip was settled and agreed. The unions were incensed and threatened to withdraw any labour associated with departure from airports.

I had made my own position clear departmentally within the BBC. I did not think the SFA should have arranged this match but when it became clear that they would go ahead, my employers made it equally clear to me that they would like me to report and commentate on the trip, although they would not take me to task if I refused to go. There was no chance of my refusing. I wanted, at first hand, to see this country and Argentina. Journalistically, it would have been madness to have spurned the opportunity. I did want to see this stadium and I did want to talk to people. That, at least, is what I told myself over and over again.

We arrived there debauched by jet-lag having travelled all the way for something like twenty-six hours in a plane that seemed to have been designed for flights round Arran. After those cramped confines, with our knees practically up to our chins, there was little of the bounding investigative zeal left in anybody by the time we found our beds in the hotel. I surveyed the tranquil scene out of my bedroom on that first morning mentally composing a telephone report which I was due to give within the hour back to Scotland.

The Andes loomed up above us like they were about to topple in at any moment. The mountain range would come and go like a reluctant apparition as the mist flirted with them. The city itself was overhung with smog very much like Los Angeles but the physical stillness of this large bowl, scooped out of the foothills, was unsettling given the turbulent political background we had heard so much about. Imbued with passion on the subject, I was not to be taken in by this idyllic scene. So, when the call came, I launched into my two-way chat with the studio presenter by examining the political soul of this country, discussing what we might see in this stadium of shame and talking of how we would try to identify the true suffering of this nation and asserting that the eyes of the world would be on this tour. Back came the retort, 'Yes, but will Scotland be playing 4–2–4 or 4–3–3?' There was no answer to that.

That same morning, as the players and others lounged around the swimming pool, resting after the ordeal of the long flight, a silver-haired gentleman turned up and casually wandered amongst the group, sounding impeccably English. He looked like a retired colonel or a British textile manufacturer of whom there were many all down that side of the South American continent. I did not pay much attention to him until he wandered near a group of players which included Kenny Dalglish.

I then heard him pontificating about life in Chile, of how marvellous it was for everybody and of how it would be important for the players to go back home and tell the people the truth about the situation and of how everybody had distorted the facts and that in reality the people were settled and happy. I have no way of knowing if Kenny has subsequently studied political philosophy. At that stage in his career though, he was merely interested in penalty box play and not the downfall of a Marxist in Chile and the CIA's involvement in such. But Kenny has always had, and will never lose, his Glasgow street instinct for spotting a phoney when he sees one. He immediately did so here.

'You're talking a load of crap!' he told the dignified figure posturing near the sun-lounger. 'We'll make up our own minds about what we see here. We don't need you to tell us.'

The man seemed to crumple under that blast, as others have since at some of Kenny's subsequent press conferences as a manager, and sidled away in the same manner he had insinuated himself. He had obviously been sent with a message for all of us. He looked and sounded sinisterly simplistic and his demolition by Kenny was quite the most marvellous come-uppance I have ever seen anybody getting, considering he thought he had come into the midst of a bunch of simpletons.

The head of the Chilean FA, General Gordon, also happened to be head of the local police and the following day he invited the entire Scottish group to a barbecue in the Prince of Wales Country Club. This was a middle-class enclave guarded by men with guns and comprising a magnificent golf course and a whole variety of sporting and leisure facilities in a stunning setting with the Andes monstrously big above us and the streams and trees of the complex giving the impression of utter tranquillity.

The people there were at pains to tell us that if Allende had stayed in power all of what we could see would have been at risk. They did not go so far as to say that they supported his killing, or that they admired General Pinochet, but they made it clear the economy would have been ruined and anarchy would have ensued. My attempts to try and broaden the argument to the lack of support Allende got from the international community, especially the United States, whose complicity in the downfall of the President had been strongly indicated, were met with polite scorn. We didn't really know the true facts. It was all very well for us to criticise, and so on.

I pointed out that travelling through Santiago we were besieged by people begging in the streets, women and children, obviously starving. We were told that that sort of thing was quite common throughout South America and we would simply get used to it. It is certainly true I have seen it now throughout that continent. But I have never got used to it. I felt that this crowd of well-heeled British expatriates with their Chilean middle-class counterparts enjoyed not just a major recreational facility in this place but asylum as well. Outside there was a threatening world held at bay by a ruthless and convenient dictator. If the suppression was out of sight, then it didn't really matter.

But we saw the other side. Later that night a little man with a broad Scottish accent presented himself at the hotel. He was wearing a rather crumpled jacket over an open-necked shirt and was tieless. It looked as if he had walked all the way from home seeking autographs. He was in fact from Shotts and he was a Catholic priest. His name was Father Jimmy Small. This man had been in a mission in Santiago for years and was part of the worker-priest movement which was flourishing in South America. He invited us the following day to the mission for lunch which, he warned us in advance, would be very simple in nature. He took us down just before midday and outside the simple hacienda-type building he pointed to the distinct marks on the yellow, plastered wall.

'These are bullet holes,' he said. 'You will see such all over Santiago.' We had in fact noticed the scooped marks in the centre of the city where, it was pointed out to us, Allende had supposedly been gunned down. 'But we regard these as a reminder of how dangerous our situation is. These were some of the bullets they fired at Dr Sheila Cassidy the night they came to capture her.'

Sheila Cassidy's experience had become a *cause célèbre* back in the UK when eventually she had been able to get away. Her testimony about the scale of torture going on in Chile did much to lend credence to the criticism of the Pinochet regime. She had in fact been in captivity, and been cruelly tortured, but that night had gained asylum in the mission.

'They killed her housekeeper though,' the priest said. 'It is a sad country. We are watched all the time. Right now they will have us under surveillance.'

We looked round almost sheepishly.

'Oh, you won't see them,' he said. 'But I can assure you they will be taking photographs of all of us. They regard us as enemies, the way they did Sheila Cassidy. All she was doing was ministering to the poor. That was her crime. Ours is in extending our mission into helping to feed the poor. There is no good serving the soul if people are dying on you needlessly because of starvation.'

The meal was simple. Mince, bread and mineral water. We sat amongst a gathering of about twenty foreign priests from all over the world, all of them engaged in what became fashionably described as 'liberation theology'. This consisted of taking the view that you could not, in South America, separate the social conditions of the tragically deprived and under-nourished classes from their spiritual nourishment. A political stance had to be taken against the totalitarian or inefficient political systems. This was bound to cause tensions within those societies as well as within the church. But these men had seen too much of the horrific conditions of the people not to take a hard line against Pinochet. Nor could they bother too much at that time about what the Vatican thought.

'We are delighted to see you,' the little priest said. 'It is good that you came to Chile. But you must come to see the "poblaciones". These are our parishes. The poverty may sicken you.'

It did. The conditions were so appalling that the priests working there could not possibly wear their normal vestments. Rickets was the main disease of children, malnutrition was rife, sanitation well nigh non-existent and at that moment whether Scotland played 4–2–4 or 4–3–3 the following night seemed of colossal irrelevance. But that after all is why we were here. In a sense I was grateful for the SFA's impassivity on the matter. This little segment of the visit to Chile had certainly made an enormous impact on me but it also reinforced my view that turning one's back on a political system because one didn't approve could simply lead to ignorance.

The National Stadium sent a chill through the bones not only because of the reverberating echoes of all that had happened there but because, on the night of the game, a mist had enveloped it. A match of stunning insignificance became a guessing game of identity and, as hardly anybody had turned up to watch, it seemed less an international and more an inter-departmental works competition. The mist got so bad that from the commentary position we could not see that Scotland had substituted their goalkeeper at half-time.

But they won 4–2, easily, and the thin, miserable Chilean crowd seemed like party hacks drummed up for the occasion. The whole affair was, after all, quite squalid. The natural plumage of this part of the world ought to have been gloriously multi-coloured but we were now seeing it like Whitechapel on one of the nights Jack the Ripper loved. It was appropriate. We had visited a political cess-pit and although I tried to record the fact in my reports it has to be said that back in Scotland nobody was all that much interested. They wanted me to conjure up stories about the players which quite frankly didn't exist on a relatively plain-sailing tour. Politics and sport don't mix, they just shadow each other and occasionally collide like two ships in a fog. The fog of that last night in Chile clung to me long after. Call it a metaphor for the awful condition the continent was in.

The brief visit to Argentina underlined the impression. The peso kept changing in value. Beggars walked through fashionable areas in Buenos Aires like Florida, the main shopping centre. There I stopped a man to ask him the way to a hotel and it turned out, freakishly enough, that his name was McWhirter. He was of Scottish descent, several generations back, but had never actually met a European. When I questioned him about the police and social conditions he told me in his broken English that it wasn't safe to speak even in a shopping promenade about the state of the country.

This atmosphere of apprehension never changed even when we arrived at Boca Juniors Stadium for the match against Argentina and a brown paper parcel was seen just below our commentary position half-an-hour before the game. The police emptied that section of the stand and, guns flourishing again, waited until a bomb squad had arrived on the scene. The 'bomb' turned out to be a parcel of sandwiches left by one of the stadium attendants.

The only real scare that night was that we had a technical conundrum which I couldn't work out at the time. During the live transmission I apologised for the fact that there were no slow-motion replays and pointed out that the production was by Argentina television. I had been looking at my monitor for the first twenty minutes and none had appeared. Suddenly I heard the voice of my producer in Glasgow saying to me down my earpiece in the perfect communications we had with them, 'What do you mean there are no replays! We're seeing them here.'

What then followed might have appealed to those who adore *Monty Python*. For there I was in Argentina listening to my producer in Glasgow giving me his commentary on the replays all the way to Buenos Aires for me to repeat them blindly all the way back again to the unknowing Scottish viewers. After all the tensions of the trip it seemed an appropriate touch of the bizarre. Scotland drew 1–1 that night and we left the city the following day with horns blaring again, armoured escort in attendance, and the feeling that the world was in a 'state o' chassis'.

From Prague all the way over the Andes to Chile and back again to Argentina we had experienced political oppression of one sort or the other. Through it all we plied our own sporting trade with the apparent insouciance of a besieged colonial group in their compound, playing croquet as the masses batter at the gates.

10

The Argentina Experience

Strangers on a train gave me the news about Peter Thomson. I got on the subway at Hillhead and was minding my own business when I overheard them talking about the newspaper report of his death in 1977. I had forgotten just how powerful an influence his voice had on people. Indeed I had forgotten him altogether. That peculiar aroma of the Glasgow Subway used to have an aphrodisiacal tang to it after a night out along Byres Road. Now it seemed like the incense of a requiem.

It was not so much the sadness of hearing about this but of knowing that Peter had not been able to cope with leaving the BBC two years previously. Anytime I saw him after that he seemed a crushed man. He had tragically lost his wife and, in terms that he would have understood himself, was like a studio without electrical power, inert, dark, directionless. I remember, previous to this night, thinking that I could not allow myself to become so umbilically tied to the job that separation would mean some fatal wounding. I felt I had to resist that. Binding your life to the institution would be foolish. You were fixing your gaze on a date clearly and distinctly etched on a headstone. But it is still the easy option for some, and the only choice for many.

The stilling of Peter's voice broke my last tangible link with the age of 'The McFlannels', 'Aunt' Kathleen Garscadden, 'Down At the Mains', austerity, ration-books, Attlee, Crosby, Ben Hogan and playing 'wee-heedies' up a close.

We had moved off in another direction after he had left.

Malcolm Kellard, from Ireland, had taken his place, with the emphasis on more stylish presentation both on and off screen. I suppose I greeted him like someone jealously preserving his own status. I had staked my ground and no one, not even this talented import, was going to make me budge. I underrated his charm and over-rated his intention. He wanted to change things, probably took me for granted as the bearer of everything he needed to know and imbibe about the Scottish football scene, but there was nothing more sinister in it than that. He knew how to handle the BBC system much better than I could, largely because I was not wholly interested in it. I still tended to regard the work outside the building as more important to both the Corporation and myself than coping with the complexities, ambiguities and subtleties of 'getting on' within the institution. Not that this attitude of mine was much appreciated at the time.

It was not, however, a great period of upheaval within either my own area or throughout the BBC. The problems which arose were mostly about facilities and local expense. Alasdair Milne once took time off from discussing really weighty matters to ask me why, in the name of heaven, we could not get a new camera position at Tynecastle, where the pillars got in the way and drove him to distraction. As we tailed off that conversation he added, 'By the way, I get letters in saying you are biased in your commentaries. Don't worry about that. We pay you to express your views. I wouldn't expect anything else.' He was sharp, direct and stimulating.

We knew of course that the criticism was not just about what was said but how we projected ourselves. Throughout the Seventies we were castigated by the public for our poor camera work. Letters would appear in the press and comments would be made to me personally about how the English were better at it than we were. I felt sorry for our cameramen who, ironically enough, were mostly English. It was not shoddy camera work. It was lack of equipment. Whereas we normally covered a game with two cameras, network had the luxury of double or treble the number. They could place cameras behind the goal and at pitch level whilst we were lucky to hoist a couple on to a central platform on the halfway-line. We were two-dimensional by comparison and it showed painfully.

One night at Hampden Park in 1975 we lost a goal altogether because of this. Romania scored against Scotland from a long midfield pass into the penalty area that our minimal number of cameras could not quite lock-on to. The technique of commentary involves you in keeping an eye on the game and the other on the television monitor beside you so that you are reporting on what the viewer will see at home eventually. It stands to reason, doesn't it? Except that reason does not always prevail in this business. Sometimes you merely have to watch the play itself to ensure proper identification especially when danger threatens a defence in the penalty area. So I took my eye off the monitor momentarily to describe this quite brilliant goal. I did so with enthusiasm.

In those days we did not have immediate replays available to us. We had to visualise the goal immediately after and repeat the commentary in the hope that the words would fit the picture which would be not so much an instant replay, more a second edit 'pasted' on later. So when I looked back down at the monitor all I saw were men hugging each other in celebration. I thought nothing of that and continued. I left the stadium that night not realising anything was amiss because the producer had not the heart to tell me that he had missed the goal altogether.

I went back with some friends to a favourite hostelry in the East End and we set ourselves up to watch the recorded highlights of the game in the bar. Eventually we reached the point where I was lyrically describing a goal that simply was not coming up on the screen. All we saw was a Romanian in midfield admiring his own telling pass, then a quick cut to consenting adults embracing in the penalty area. If you have never been in an East-End bar in Glasgow when silence suddenly falls and about forty pairs of eyes turn towards you, glasses suspended just below the lips, then you will not know what icy terror really means. I left hurriedly without explanation.

Mishaps like that put our credibility continually on the line and unfortunately tended to detract from excellent productions on other occasions. The public by and large do not write or phone in to praise but to criticise or condemn. We were noticed for our gaffes. Competence is synonymous with anonymity. On the other hand we felt that being the BBC we were held under greater scrutiny than our rivals. This might seem unbearably arrogant but nevertheless there was an element of truth in it.

However, criticisms were never in my experience taken lightly. But they were mostly transient. We had not yet encountered the new 'philosophers' of the right and the attacks on the whole concept of a licence-based system. In defence of its uncommercial integrity we faced up to nothing more daunting than the threat of football going off the screens because of the advent of shirt advertising. The 'Long-Room' Colonel Blimp fundamentalists in our ranks believed such a thing would never be allowed. My own view was that it ought to happen and that the sole criterion should be aesthetic. When all this came to pass I could not bring myself to remind people of their faith in the BBC not budging on the issue. Instead I respected the Corporation for the way it showed it could adapt without throwing overboard its main principles.

We duly paid attention to our competitors, STV, but perhaps rather complacently assumed that in a straight contest with them we would always come out with three times the audience. This seemed to be borne out by the viewing figures for the Scottish Cup Final when we were in straight opposition. We enjoyed this in-built Establishment 'special occasion' advantage, without always meriting it. STV, in their own way, projected the Cup final just as well as we did and, I know, felt sorely aggrieved at not commanding bigger audiences. So when the World Cup of 1978 came round we felt confident that in a head-on clash with commercial television the BBC would hold its normal advantage. Indeed, on the night Scotland played Wales at Anfield in the deciding game we drew the biggest ever audience for live football up till then. Not a man, woman or child in Scotland seemed to miss that match. It was not simply the importance of the occasion which proved compulsive but also the way in which a national state-of-the-art passion had been designed by one man, Ally MacLeod.

My first sighting of Ally MacLeod was in one of his first games for Third Lanark at Cathkin. Being a left winger he was, for half the match, near the enclosure where we used to stand and looked the kind of pimply boy who might still be delivering the papers or the milk. His schoolboyish enthusiasm was the very feature which made him so noticeable. He rushed at defences with an apparently unco-ordinated whirl of legs and arms that seemed part combine harvester on the move, part irate man escaping from a swarm of bees. It was the football of impetuous youth which quickly endeared him to people. Not much changed through the years. The fountain of youth danced away behind even some of his darker moments when he led the crusade to Argentina. But, of course, it is with that period of his life he will be irrevocably associated.

But I can never think of Argentina or Ally without firstly recalling the occupation of Liverpool on the evening of 12 October, 1977. That night saw the full flourishing of the dubious emotion I had recognised at Glasgow Airport three years earlier on our return from Germany. It had seemed then that it could turn into unjustified and uncontrollable frenzy. The Welsh had relinquished the right to play this game on their own soil and, selling their birthright to Mammon, decided that Anfield would swell the coffers more. Knowing the pride the Welsh engender normally in their sport, particularly on the rugby field, where toughened veterans can be reduced to tears by the singing of the national anthem even before somebody has kicked them in a loose maul, this transplantation into England was not just tatty but lent the whole affair a spurious quality. For me, it spoiled the eventual triumph to a great extent.

The area around Anfield resembled a kind of medieval fair with pickpockets plundering the great and the mighty just outside the main entrance, people shouting and bartering for tickets, and others making arrangements about how they were going to travel to Argentina. Everywhere there was singing, drinking, and waving of banners. The final congestion just inside the main gates was claustrophobic. It was the carousal of confidence. It was the kind I have never enjoyed hearing from Scottish people. It was blatant and aggressive and intimidatory.

'I hope to God we win,' Jock Stein said to me on the television platform as we tried to settle down just before kick-off. 'If we don't I think they'll take Liverpool apart.'

He didn't need to coax me towards that conclusion. The platform at Anfield affords you a sweeping and high view of the stadium and looking round it you could see the Welsh had been confined to a small enclave on the stand side of the Kop. Everywhere else was a mass of Scottish banners and tumultuous bragging of inevitable supremacy. It was not healthy. They were not there to support possible success, they were demanding it. I am convinced that on that very night in Liverpool Stein crystallised his views on how vulnerable Scottish players are on these occasions when the gauntlet is thrown down not just by the opposition but by their own supporters.

He could see the potential for the hysteria spreading on to the pitch, quite indiscriminate in its effect. It did as much harm to ourselves as to the opposition. He was to be plagued by that image throughout his own subsequent management of the national team. Certainly the previous May at Wembley, when Scotland had won 2–1 on Ally MacLeod's managerial debut, the atmosphere had been like a grand family party which had gone slightly over the top.

One's official face had to engage in formal 'tut-tutting' over the damage to property, the pitch being stripped of some of its assets and the goalposts being divested of their cross-bar. Once MacLeod had managed to persuade the security people that he was after all the Scottish team manager and they had allowed him to walk down the tunnel, he arrived in the dressing room to discover five supporters who had dodged the strict security which Ally himself had just experienced. They were, fully clothed, swimming around in the large bath with the Scottish players.

But it wasn't a case of the Visigoths taking it out on Rome. This was a mass of men out to enjoy themselves and, having been given little opportunity for delirium in the past, not quite able to handle it in a way that would suit the text book. It was the sense of decorum which was offended then. It wasn't an intimation of the imminent demise of civilisation. But that was the turning point. From that date onwards the whole nature of the outing to London changed.

It had always been a rather jolly middle-aged or family outing, with more damage being done by the wives in the shops of Oxford Street than the men in the pubs of north London, and the banners and flags were emblematic decorations and nothing more. Now, the style changed. More people got their hands on tickets. The average age of the bulk of the support seemed to drop dramatically

Above: The first 'star' I ever beheld. Tommy Docherty's tongue took over when his legs had lost the appetite for this.

Left: A tangled memory. Staircase 13 at Ibrox where 66 died and the television cameras went home without knowing it.

Above: Jock Stein's reign held players, supporters and media in sway.

Below: A profile of bewilderment. Ally MacLeod in Argentina sharing disillusionment with the press.

Right: Who's that with Willie Ormond? Scotland's little man became an unexpected and reluctant hero.

Above: A Catholic with Protestants. The morning when Souness's capture of his club's first recognised Catholic, ex-Celt Maurice Johnston, turned Glasgow topsy-turvy.

Left: The impassive Ben Johnson before turning Seoul into a frenzy and journalists into sleuths.

Below: Bobby Charlton, scourge of the Scots on the field, but friend and adviser to a Scottish commentator in many foreign places.

until you could see masses of teenagers, apparently drugged on some crude idea of nationalism, marauding their way through London and turning Trafalgar Square and Piccadilly Circus, before they were inevitably barricaded, into large-scale latrines.

You could tell that some perfectly decent Londoners were concluding that nothing much had changed since the Roman legions had tried to colonise the northern parts. Along with this new arrogant swagger emerged a bitter anti-English trend which to me, at any rate, had a fascistic ring to it.

There was a recrudescence of the Bannockburn image, a battle which certainly played its part in making me proud of our heritage but which considerably lessened in impact the more you saw its meaning hijacked by people who wouldn't have known a skean dhu from a declaration of independence. To be in central London on the Wembley of 1979, the year after Argentina, was like being present when an invading army ransacked a city.

I saw large plate shop windows smashed in recklessly, cars turned over on their sides and a sizeable element displaying gratuitous hatred in a manner that seemed to denote nothing more than the malevolent side of a massive inferiority complex. Had the English, as they certainly were to achieve in other places in Europe, embarked on the same ploys north of the border the Scottish nation would have arisen and driven them into the sea. We could hardly complain, then, when this conduct provoked such outrage in London. Neither can we ignore the fact that, although behaviour was to improve dramatically with the demise of the Wembley weekend, in the excursions from 1977 to 1981 some of our kith and kin established the procedure for converting the football supporter into urban terrorist.

Ally MacLeod had been confident about Anfield of course. But then there was nothing in his make-up, certainly then, which suggested he could think in any other way. His disposition was almost inevitably sunny, his attitude genial, his tongue and body-language irrepressibly ebullient. All this ideally suited the current mood of a swelling support which did not want a diet of realism but rather the heady words of the super-optimist, who stoked their fantasies like a parent spoon-feeding the family. He knew exactly when to reach towards the open mouths.

Immediately after the game, for example, when we did some interviews, he indulged in some whimsical remarks about the English and their inability to qualify for the finals. Perfect timing, I thought. It had nothing to do with the performance of the night nor with our own chances in Argentina but it was like cocking a snook at the bigger nation and we all laughed with him.

The study of the happenings in and around Argentina is not solely about considering a man propelled by delusions of grandeur, as some people might have interpreted it. We all fitted perfectly into the grand scheme of things and contributed, all of us, to a monumental downfall, and then looked innocently around for someone to blame.

Ally was in perpetual over-drive, the supporters were a charging army which verged sometimes more towards Nuremberg than Mount Florida, and the media latched on, euphoric and largely quiescent.

The writing was, in fact, on the wall that very night. Of course, we could not see that at the time. We were fortunate to beat Wales. The Scottish players looked as if their very bone marrow had been sucked out of them by the cacophony which continued unabated and which was proving to be counter-productive. It was the Welsh who were inspired by all of this and had not Alan Rough, always looking edgy throughout the game, made a superb save from John Toshack in the second half history would have told a different story. A penalty eased the pressure and little did I realise at the time that the handling offence would be shown like a piece of evidence in a national court case, seeking somebody's forensic footballing skills to solve the matter.

There was never any doubt between Jock Stein and myself on the platform at the time that there had been a handling offence. Watch it as I have over and over again, with the intensity of a Nessie hunter looking at some deep-water evidence, I have never really deduced whose hand it actually was. That goal did it and when Kenny scored that magnificent header for the second my voice and emotions united to sweep my larynx skywards, right over the top. I heard the replay during that year's Sports Review of the Year in London and hid under the seat in embarrassment at the thrust of my voice, which sounded like someone in the throes of the agony/ecstasy of premature ejaculation. I have deliberately avoided it ever since; the recording that is.

The sound I emitted came from an almost hysterical relief. Relief that Liverpool would be left intact by supporters whose jingoism had always sounded threatening but who could now sublimate their aggression by thinking of how they might cross the Atlantic. Our thoughts turned to the commercial potential. Ally and I were signed up by a brewery firm to travel around the country to meet the fans and to have open-ended discussion about footballing matters. Over a couple of months we criss-crossed Scotland, meeting 'Ally's Army' face to face. It was a formidable experience.

Ally himself was like a bounding gazelle, leaping from venue to venue with an inexhaustible vigour which seemed to be tapped into the true energy source, the adulation of the fans. They would quite literally be standing on table tops chanting his name. And that was just at the start of the night. It would be easy in hindsight to admit to being worried by all of this. It wasn't as strong a feeling as that. However, I felt uneasy about the uncritical enthusiasm which, perhaps rightly, he had no wish to dampen. But more than that, his weakness, in truth, was that he encouraged it.

One night, in a hotel packed to the doors with almost hysterical people doting on his every word, I ventured the opinion, as the chairman, that perhaps a few of his players might have peaked too soon before Argentina. Moreover, I said, some of them, like Bruce Rioch and Don Masson, were no chickens and we might not get the best out of them in the summer. I stopped short of actually saying what I really meant, which is that they might be over the hill ever so slightly. I was howled down. Ally criticised that view, but pleasantly. However, he did nothing to prevent me getting a roasting from supporters who thought I had been floored by him.

My view stemmed not from some unique perspicacity. This was a perfectly straightforward observation which simply was not being aired at the time and it centred on what was to be one of the most telling factors in the World Cup. But, as I sat there taking considerable stick, it did pass through my mind, and I admitted as much to colleagues shortly after, that if Ally were to fall in Argentina he would fall with a helluva clatter and that some of the very people treating him like a demi-god might not wish to pick up the bits.

Against the background of this rising hysteria we made plans to try to show the public something of Scotland's opponents. We learned that Argentina were to play Peru, Scotland's group opponents, in a friendly in Lima. This seemed an ideal opportunity to combine a look at the host nation in action along with an inspection of largely unknown Peruvian players. To this day I will never understand why Ally did not travel to see this game. He had been relying on observation of tapes of Peru in action and whilst that can provide much information it is never as satisfactory as seeing them in the flesh, if only to cover the tracks politically, in case accusations are made that the homework wasn't good enough. I suspect he regretted not doing so in the light of subsequent events.

We were not prepared for what we found in Peru. We encountered poverty at its most extreme in the faces of the Indians who seemed to portray the notion that living was merely a process of slowly dying. All over the city you would see what appeared to be bundles of rags awaiting collection for a gigantic jumble-sale. But what you were looking at were people, whole families huddled together sleeping on the pavements and, when they awoke, simply begging. One very rich Peruvian I talked to admitted that he didn't even notice the Indians any longer. To him they had become invisible, which perhaps was the only antidote to perpetually agonising over them, I suppose.

The poor played football. Out of their shanty towns they would come to the long dusty pitches which ran for mile after mile stretching out from the outskirts of the city for as far as the eye could see. It was certainly much less romantic than Copacabana's beach games but it had something of the natural quality of that as the youngsters performed miracles of control on hard, powdery surfaces. The sun rose and set on these games which suggested to me that they were helping to stave off the effects of a life constricted by horrendous poverty.

We were surprised to be greeted by a battery of cameras at the airport. Unknown to my producer and myself the air company who had flown us to Lima had told the press for promotional purposes that we were coming to 'spy' on Peru for Ally MacLeod. After this had been explained to me I hammed it up to the full. Such celebrity status in a foreign country, I felt, could only help. I was not wrong. They took us to a television studio where, with the help of an interpreter, I solemnly told the Peruvian nation that I would be scrutinising every detail of their side and would duly report back to my mentor Mr MacLeod.

Our only problem was the cameraman and the camera. For reasons of economy we thought we would hire a film crew in Lima, which, admittedly, is not as well endowed with such as, say, downtown Burbank. We did not expect a lot and not a lot is what we got. The cameraman looked like Leo Carrillo, who used to play the 'Cisco Kid', but he certainly wasn't as proficient as the Kid. He had a camera which I imagine must have dated back to the D. W. Griffith period or thereabouts. It had to be plugged into a wall for most of the time which as you might surmise did not make life easy. We faced the nightmarish problem of coming all this way, spending all that money to produce duff film.

By the time we came to film the Peru–Argentina game we had given up in despair. We knew even as they were out there playing in a rather lacklustre friendly that to take anything usable back would be miraculous. We suffered and watched and interviewed the managers, including Menotti the Argentinian, quite the gloomiest man I have ever met, assessed the Peruvians who looked slick, fast and skilful without holding any special menace, and at the same time tried to recover from the destructive effect of a drink called pisco sour which is like taking milk but does to your inside what eating raw cactus would do. We left the cameraman to his own devices and hoped for the best. As we were the only crew there any film was going to be much sought after when we returned to the UK.

However, our cameraman lived up to our expectations of him. He could not have filmed a flower growing with the camera bolted to the spot. All we could salvage on our return were little fragments that added up to virtually nothing. It had been an almost total waste of time. 'El Espion' had produced, as we say in the trade, a 'turkey'. I have to say that it had passed through our minds to play up the 'El Espion' angle for viewer consumption and imply criticism of Ally for not availing himself of the opportunity to see both sides. After watching the shreds we had brought back we kept our mouths tightly shut. That, of course, was a disaster on a minor scale compared to what was to follow. As we moved into the last phase of our preparation for the Finals we thought we had prepared for everything.

Cordoba was to be our base in Argentina. We arrived there in late May, which was their autumn, and immediately were struck by how hospitable the people were. They seemed to exist in a compartment within the military dictatorship whose intrusion was, probably at different levels, both insidious and brutal. Restaurants were always busy, the food and wine were cheap, theatres and cinemas normally packed. The population willingly opened their doors to us. Still you could not totally hide the military presence. There was one day when we visited the stadium for the first time and saw a line of about twenty men in the frisking position, with their hands flat against a wall and the legs straddled with a solitary soldier guarding them with a gun. They were still there in that same position two hours later. We never discovered why they were being treated that way but, as I was told they were the groundsmen, it did lead me to think that the penalties for not cutting the grass properly were rather severe in this country.

An hour away from Cordoba, deeper into the hills, was the little town of Alta Gracia which was to house the Scottish party. We went there to record their arrival, for which the entire town turned out. The welcome was a mix of genuine delight and curiosity. They hardly ever saw Europeans there and certainly not those fair-skinned types from the north of Europe so the rapturous acclaim as the team left their bus gave way to the more lasting habit of gawping. The hotel was a rambling building of Spanish colonial style but which carried a certain resemblance to a kind of run-down Gleneagles. The bull-necked, wide-girthed guards at the gate gave us a taste of security the likes of which made the German system for the World Cup seem like open-house. The fears were that it was not an accreditation pass we would need to gain access but a flame-thrower.

One wrong step and they might have blown your head off. Which is what made the first news story of the stay so juicy; players strolling off for a walk, going towards the casino, climbing back over the fence under the possibility of attack by the very trigger-happy guards there to defend them against the Montoneros. Great stuff. News Editors back home abed could think themselves accursed they were not there and eventually gobbled this story up with the greatest of relish. It splashed and the echoes were heard in Alta Gracia amongst the Scottish officials who looked upon the incident as a possible, but not outrageous, breach of discipline. The manner in which the story was handled in Scotland puzzled some of us but it indicated that any honeymoon between the official party and the media was now over.

There was an underlying vexation to all of this. The journey between the hotel and Cordoba was taking two hours out of the day and whilst this was not the greatest hardship we have ever had to face it still seemed a burden when you were travelling all that way for pre-ordained conferences from which not all that much emerged. It created an unnecessary tension. There were these early hints that the course of events was not running as smoothly as we had anticipated.

Ally got tenser than I had ever seen him, which was of course not at all surprising, but the alfresco interviews added nothing to the advancement of knowledge in the world. Film-wise we did try to indicate that the distant Andes lent enchantment, etc, etc. In short the pre-tournament anodyne guff was typical. But Ally was changing. He was snappier and more suspicious than normal, although still perfectly accessible. There was distinctly less bombast though.

The stadium in Cordoba was probably the worst kind for football, both for those spectating and those reporting or commentating. It was one of those pestilential all-purpose grounds which are fine for the social welfare of a community wishing to encourage and develop a wide range of sporting talents but wretched for creating the right kind of atmosphere for a football match. The players were so distant from those of us at the back of the stand that they looked like Subbuteo pieces on a table. We calculated that the television platform was about forty yards away from the touchline and very high indeed. It was going to be a nightmare of identification. In fact it was not. The nightmare took a different form.

I have to confess that Peru's victory over Scotland is now something of a void in my mind, not because I was traumatised by the result but because I suppose I have blotted it out deliberately to avoid the pain of the broadcasting disaster I suffered. From our little 'goldfish bowl' commentating position we reckoned that things were not going to be easy. The players were too far away and behind the glass all contact with the atmosphere of the stadium would be cut off. If that happens to a commentator it is like the loss of an oxygen supply to a space-walker. A commentator has to be a party of the first part, that is wholly engaged and absorbed in wilful participation. From behind almost sound-proof glass he might as well be in his own living room.

But we were poised and ready. After all we had been preparing for this for almost a year, had we not? I lifted the mike to my lips as the teams came out to warm up, so that I could make initial contact with our studio people back in Glasgow, who were primed up for the occasion just as much as we were. But there was nothing. No contact. The line remained silent.

As I had experienced this sort of thing before from abroad I refused to panic. I left my colleagues to do that for me. But when the whistle blew for the start of the game and there was still no contact made with Glasgow I suffered the first of a series of pangs of acute anguish. After about twenty minutes we gave up because our network colleagues informed us that there was no line back to Scotland for the simple reason it had not been booked in advance!

This simple explanation fell on me like an axe on the nape of the neck. The crass incompetence left me almost too weak for anger. As the viewers had probably been handed a bonus in receiving David Coleman instead of me I felt quite humiliated. I watched the rest of the game through a red mist. I knew others had had their problems before from abroad but I nevertheless felt almost emasculated. After all it had been brought about through lack of proper planning. So I did not absorb the full agony of that game, although I think I can still recall Cubillas' magnificent outside of right-foot free-kick strike that effectively sank Scotland.

I did not wait to say much after the game, lest utterances would have led to more serious infractions. I simply went back to the hotel, dumped my notes which now looked as useful as last week's newspapers, and went out to wander through Cordoba on my own. There were many twisting alleyways in that lovely old faded city and I definitely had it in mind to drop into one of the many splendid little bars and stay there until I had drunk my way into oblivion. Except as fate would have it I heard the sound of accordion tango music and much as Tam O'Shanter on his wild dark night was lured to Kirk Alloway I followed the strains of the music until I found myself in a brightly lit tango hall.

I was wearing a special casual Scottish World Cup jacket and when I was recognised as a Scot the people there greeted me like a hero. They knew nothing about my own problem but they did realise what had happened to Scotland that day and they clearly possessed that finest of humanitarian instincts, knowing how to console a depressed football man. It was a marvellously therapeutic night. I was away from the constant talk of football, from Scotland's disaster, from my own indignity and I didn't have to get stupidly drunk. These warm-hearted people sobered me up in fact and gave me a sense of perspective on what had occurred that afternoon. The sense of futility, of wasted time and effort that had dogged me since I had left the stadium drained away.

At the height of the Falklands crisis I thought of those people and of how they had wined and dined me as an honoured guest, rather than a total stranger, and felt confident that their basic nature would be unmoved by what was portrayed to us then as national hysteria. The Argentinians when they expressed themselves as a crowd or a mob were obsessively 'pro patria' and raucously obnoxious at times. They took to the streets like that every time Argentina won during the World Cup in a way comparable to the 'Malvinas' demonstrations. But beneath that there was a more controlled, decently proud people. I discovered them that night.

But of course there was no real hiding place. We had to face up to the reality that we were on the brink of a possible disaster, for Peru had exposed our apparent lack of ability to handle the pace of such as Oblitas, Munante and Cubillas. We were therefore grateful for the breathing space of playing Iran. I travelled to watch them training two days later and thought I had seen nothing quite so slip-shod as their manner of going about things. They looked clumsy in their ball control, indisciplined in their relationship with their coach and like a rabble training for a game in the Tehran and District League. But I was fooling myself. I was looking for the wrong things.

It was not that they were hiding anything. It was just that I failed to recognise one of the increasingly important factors in world football and certainly in World Cup finals, fitness. They were tall, strong, bristling with athleticism, and had borne much less of a burden than our own players whose draining league season had allowed no time for recuperation before the World Cup. I was blind to that and in my previews I spoke with confidence.

Then came Willie Johnston. The news that he had taken a proscribed drug came not so much as a bombshell but more of a stiletto stuck in the ribs. I heard about it when my guard was lowered. We were enjoying the hospitality of some expatriate group in our hotel and wolfing the canapés when one of my colleagues took a phone call and came back to whisper softly in my ear that Willie Johnston had failed a drugs test. Coming after the unexpected Peruvian result I suppose my first thought apart from finding it difficult to believe was, 'What have we all done to deserve this?' It was nothing to how it was taken up in Alta Gracia.

Ally told me years afterwards that nobody from the SFA International Committee was in the hotel when the telegram arrived informing them of Johnston's failed test. He went straight to Dr Fitzsimmons' room to find out the medical background to the reported use of this banned substance. He walked straight in on the Celtic doctor, an extremely devout man, who was at prayer. All Ally could say was, 'You'd better say one for me, Doc. Look what I've got here!'

This engulfed the entire Scottish party in a media blitz from which they barely recovered. That formal barrier of restrained fury mixed with diplomatic niceties which the SFA put up meant that the separation of themselves from the media was even clearer.

Whilst they dealt promptly and correctly with the ignorant stupidity of Johnston by sending him packing, you got the impression that Ernie Walker and company were now preparing for a long siege. The game against Iran did not help. At least they had managed to establish a line for my commentary back to Scotland and we leapt eagerly into the fray. Allan Herron of the *Sunday Mail* was at my side. Never before have I felt the gradual encroachment of gloom so remorselessly envelop us as it did that day. The Scottish players seemed to have lost all sense of purpose and the inner voice was shrieking for mercy for them.

The 1–1 draw, with the assistance of Eskandarian's own goal, embarrassed us in a way which bit deeply. The following day we went to a press conference at the team's hotel. It was a pleasant, crisp autumnal day. A mass of people awaited the appearance of the manager who, almost sheepishly, came forward to his chair on the grass outside the reception area. As he did so, a dog appeared from somewhere. It jumped and frolicked around him as if they had been buddies for some time. Ally patted it and it nuzzled his hand. As he sat down he stroked the dog and said to the packed throng around him, 'Well, at least I've got one friend here today.' Nobody laughed.

I had never seen Ally bitter before but that day he occasionally converted that touch of whimsy that was always in him into a kind of sardonic defence of what had gone on. He was restrained, though, because apart from any consideration of his tactical approach he felt he had been badly let down. That he had been by Johnston was quite evident and I do believe that even if the Scottish manager had been a representative of the US Drug Enforcement Agency Johnston would still have unwittingly carried on swallowing the things. But ever since Argentina Ally has been haunted by one event about which he still remains deeply embittered.

He had been at pains to allow access to himself by the press on a non-exclusive basis. The *Scottish Daily Express* then offered him £25,000 for an exclusive interview. He apparently refused to give an exclusive interview, but when the interview appeared the newspaper was claiming that very exclusivity. The rest of the press corps were quite understandably incensed. Ally still insists on his innocence and is convinced the episode turned certain of the big guns in the Scottish press against him. He has always felt that he would have been spared some of the ultimate personal savaging if he had not been seen to hand out a personal favour to one newspaper.

I was a mere spectator to all of this because all I was after, apart from being involved in commentary, was the occasional interview in which, as so often, nothing much was said. The hostility crowded in on him. Of course, it is obvious that the media do not pick teams, despite what people think, nor play the actual games. They could not materially alter the course of events so it might sound like resorting to some paltry excuse to bring up matters like a single interview and what it meant to relationships. However, in the totality of a World Cup campaign whose smallest nuance of behaviour can affect people and re-route the emotions in odd directions, it certainly mattered to MacLeod and his critics.

The players had been badly affected by some wildly irresponsible reports one of which suggested that they had drunk the hotel dry and had sent out a 'drinks trolley', whatever that might have been, for more of the same. That particular report went out on television and was considered so damaging that on return to Scotland Ernie Walker perused the film with the SFA lawyers, at the BBC, with a view to possible legal action. It was considered by Ernie eventually as just not worth the trouble. He wanted to bury Argentina as quickly as he could and not stir the embers with litigation.

It is perfectly possible that some players did a bit of drinking. I personally see nothing wrong with that. The Dutch who got to the final were allowed amazing social liberties in contrast to the Scots. But I have yet to hear a shred of evidence about the bacchanalian orgies which were now widely understood to have been held in the Scottish camp. Much of this reporting originated from the local press which could not tell the difference between a drunk supporter, with their identikit Scottish gear, and a Scottish player. They duly waded in with some outrageously inaccurate reporting. So not only were Scotland and MacLeod now being put to the sword but you felt that all everybody wanted was to get out of Argentina as quickly as possible. But we had to go to Mendoza first.

This town lay in the very foothills of the Andes and seemed to me to be on the fringe of civilisation. It was at the centre of the Argentinian vineyards so there were immediate consolations. You can go off a place very quickly though. On the very first night in the grotty hotel we had been consigned to I found the hall-porter ransacking my case and trying to shove some miniatures of whisky into his pocket. As he whined his apologies on his knees (he was only about four feet two) he wished all good luck and blessings to be heaped upon me and my family and victory to Scotland against Holland the following night. What finally won me over was the promise not to be presented with a bill for any wine for the remainder of the stay. But it was still unsettling and seemed to fit the picture of the gradual disintegration of this trip.

The stadium though was quite magnificent. Built into a hill, the pitch, whether by optical illusion or not, seemed to be below ground level and was circled by trees and loomed over by the Andes. It looked the perfect setting for some sort of climax. There was a kind of demob feeling about us all. This was the end, thank God. Jock Stein was in the London studio as the pundit during my commentary, on which Allan Herron assisted. Stein once told me how he had reacted to it.

'It was an amazing transformation,' he said. 'You sounded at first as if you were at a funeral. Then you got slightly more enthusiastic. Then you sounded as if you were both at a wedding. And at the end you were almost back to your funeral again.'

Nobody could have put it better. That is how the course of the game went. Dejection, followed by promise, coming upon elation, and finally sadness. There were something like thirty commentators in a row along the front of the stand and just to my left was ITV's Hugh Johns with the cotton-wool inevitably in his ears to drown out the noise of any other commentator and with the fixed tiny binoculars to his specs to aid sightings.

When Archie Gemmill scored his famous goal I experienced something I have not seen before or since. To a man every commentator rose from his seat in a concerted explosion of delight and wonderment. It was a goal of perfect commentating symmetry with a distinct beginning, middle and end. 'Will he do it? Can he get there? Yes, he's scored.' Brief but indelibly registered as the most perfect goal I have ever had to describe. But of course it wasn't enough. A victory over Holland by 3–2 now seemed hollow. I went to a club with a London cameraman and we tried the wine.

I had had only two hours of sleep when the phone rang the

following morning. It was Buenos Aires. The editor Alan Hart was not amused. A report had just been put out that Ally MacLeod was resigning that very day. Why didn't I know anything about it and why had I allowed myself to be scooped? Of course I did not know about it and I was sure Ally wasn't quitting. I advised Alan Hart that I would stake my reputation on it. Now, staking your reputation on matters is not really a very clever idea out in the field, especially when you have been out of touch with things for even a few hours. As soon as I had said it I began to panic. Suppose Ally had had enough!

I beat a hasty retreat to the rather ramshackle hotel the Scottish team were in and joined the now bedraggled media corps waiting for the gates to open. The problem was that I had a deadline to beat for the BBC wanted a straight report to camera on this matter within the hour to be beamed back to Buenos Aires. I had come prepared. I bribed one of the thugs with the guns at the gate with a bottle of whisky to see if he could slip me in to get hold of Ally.

I was of course breaking every regulation in the book but my neck was on the line. He ushered me through and I waited in the large reception area to find out if Ally would be annoyed at suddenly being confronted by me. In fact he wasn't, for when I virtually bumped into him coming round a corner in the hotel and asked him outright about this report he uttered the sweetest word I had heard in the entire trip. 'Rubbish!' So he was sticking to his task after all. I duly made my report and then rejoined my colleagues to mull and brood over the outcome of this sad period.

To those of us close to football, Argentina was more traumatic than we cared to admit, certainly in public. We went there armed with fantasies, hooked on an inadequate appreciation of our own abilities, and unable to come to terms with a foreign field. We emerged tattered. The brutal assessment was that we were not good enough, nor were we likely to get any better. That thought bit deeply.

So it is too glib to focus the inquest purely on Ally. His fall was going to resound more loudly than most because he chose to perform on the high-wire of publicity from which there could be only one direction to go with almost any slip. Hardly anybody called for restraint during that period though. You could point to certain technical considerations, like the fact that he did not really get his homework right because he did not study the opposition as he should have. He himself admits a major mistake came in the Iran game.

'I should have played Graeme Souness in that match,' he told me long afterwards. 'If I had we could have qualified for the final stages. It was a bad mistake on my part.'

I suspect though that he had got the best out of his players long before they arrived in Argentina. They had lost their bounce. He also could have done with Masson scoring from the penalty spot when the score was 1–1 in the game with Peru. But more fascinating than these inquests is how little is said about certain reactions to all of this. The spectacle of the likes of Lou Macari and Don Masson, even before they had left the country, hawking their stories around the press did not enhance the professional footballer in anybody's eyes. Many of us in the media, and I include myself prominently in the matter, had enjoyed and, by our virtually complete silence, encouraged the circus barker's approach. The idea of winning the World Cup was sold to the Scottish punter when it never was and never will be a real possibility. So, Ally was not a one-man band. We helped make him and then poured scorn on him for our own misdemeanours in the whole affair. Not too many of us should be proud about that.

Then the public turned against him in a way which I think besmirched our reputation as a tolerant people. I will long remember the faces of hate which screamed at him as he walked from the pitch after the Iran game. If they had been able to get over the barrier in the Cordoba Stadium they would have torn him alive. They contented themselves with the more civilised aggression of spitting. These ugly faces, without one redeeming feature about them, were recorded by television and used in a sequence for one of the most damning visual comments ever used about a manager and given a certain self-indulgent spice by an English producer.

MacLeod did not warrant the continual torrent of oaths from the people who, a month previously, had sworn by him. I hope those who mouthed venom and those like the restaurateur who put up a public notice in his premises advising people that Ally MacLeod did not eat there might now feel some sense of shame.

He was not a war criminal. He was a failed football manager in a nation which produces that category with predictable regularity. I think the passing of time has shown us that clearly.

On the very last day I was in Argentina Alan Sharp, who in between being a Scottish punter writes novels and Hollywood film-scripts, growled to me from beneath his wide-brimmed hat about that paradoxical victory over Holland.

'We didn't win. We just discovered a new way of losing.'

It seemed a fair summary. Scottish initiative had landed a bridge too far.

11

The Last of Stein

'The bull stands no chance!' So Jock Stein in 1982 dismissed in a sentence the ancient and enduring Iberian obsession for the duel in the sand. 'It's no contest. That's why it's no use.' Even though he had managed a club side which had slaughtered much that had got in its way, he liked to think of sport as an engagement with the unpredictable, that there was no such thing as an absolute certainty where humans were concerned.

After all hadn't Thistle beaten them famously in the 1971 League Cup final when it was barely worth while putting a bet on Celtic? Hadn't Kai Johansen materialised like an avenging warrior, just when his team were looking like overwhelming Rangers, and put them to the sword in the 1966 Cup final replay at Hampden one night? Hadn't he made a mistake about Feyenoord? He disliked the notion of the certainty, if only because his addiction to horse-racing had shown him that it was a preposterous concept even when you gave animals their own head.

Except here in Spain where they stabbed the animal first and stuck things in its neck before a man polished it off, hiding the sword underneath a cape. As Stein himself contemptuously put it, the animal was a foregone loser. It was not a sentiment that would have found favour with Hemingway, even though I suspect Stein and Hemingway, as men of action, would have got on famously.

The Scottish manager was in Malaga looking at hotels just after the draw for the World Cup finals and he had been grabbed by an oily tourist rep extolling the virtues of the Costa Del Sol, including the bull fights. Stein, when wishing to rid himself of somebody, did not mind being undiplomatic and on this occasion the man had given him the opportunity to launch an attack on the 'corrida'.

I suppose at the back of his mind too was the thought that, amidst the initial reaction to the group draw which placed us with Brazil and Russia, he was going to have to counter the most pessimistic forecasts which saw Scotland as that vulnerable bull inevitably suffering a death in the afternoon under the hot Spanish sun. The analogy wasn't hard to make. Stein had now deliberately begun to play down the pessimism. He stayed like that for most of the following months, except when another factor infiltrated his mind.

The Falklands were invaded in April of that year and it affected us all, even if only distantly. It was too soon to determine immediately if the World Cup was going to be cancelled or badly disrupted or the British teams withdrawn. But long before the start in June the South Atlantic confrontation was intruding on the best-laid plans.

I had heard that Stein was planning to go to New Zealand to see the 'dark horses' of the tournament who had surprised everybody by qualifying for the finals. When I talked to him about this he admitted that all he wanted to do was cover his political rear so that he could not be blamed for not doing his homework, as Ally MacLeod had been. When I put it to him that I could interest BBC London in making a film of his stay in New Zealand he perked up a little, realising that it would at least provide some company on the long trip. The BBC bought the idea solely on the basis of my guaranteeing that Stein was, surprisingly to them, taking the trouble to travel out there to see rather insipid opposition. They were, however, keen on the idea of Stein facing the Maori War Chant, the geysers and watching football played on sacred rugby pitches.

I did realistically think though that his travelling all the way to New Zealand by himself to see a couple of duff games was a somewhat masochistic over-reaction to the attitude of the previous manager. After about a month of planning, including establishing our film contacts in Auckland, receiving permission from the New

Zealand FA to film their two games, arranging a travel package with PanAm with the emphasis on non-transferable flights and imbued with some great ideas for using the marvellous New Zealand countryside as a contrast to Stein's industrial Lanarkshire environment, we were prepared to go. Then came the British response to the invasion of Port Stanley. The night before we were due to fly down to London for our connection to San Francisco, Stein phoned me at home.

'I don't think we should go,' he said.

My heart sank.

'This war could get nasty and they'll end up cancelling the World Cup or we'll withdraw. Something's bound to happen. I think it'll be a waste of time to go away out there now.'

After my initial shock I sensed that what he was trying to do was bounce the notion off me for my response and that frankly the war was giving him a convenient way out of a tiring journey that he all along hadn't wanted to make. I argued the point that if we didn't go, the fact would sooner or later be picked up by the press and he'd have some explaining to do. After all, at that early stage we were barely sparring with Argentina.

This of course was not the Jock Stein of his Celtic days who by and large would not have cared a toss about what might be written about him and, in any case, would deal with any journalistic insult with a wrath of biblical proportions. This was a man of more measured response to situations, tending to ration out his titanic aggression carefully and, in an astonishing way, given what we knew of him in his prime as a club manager, actually avoiding conflicts he would once have relished.

Two years previously, for instance, we had sat down to dinner in a Swiss hotel after the draw for the groups for the World Cup preliminary stage. Stein, Ernie Walker, the secretary, and some other SFA officials, including the President, Tommy Younger, myself and my producer settled down for a pleasant evening of good banter. It did not turn out that way. Towards the end, after some wine had been taken, it turned sour. To everybody's astonishment Younger, the most affable of men normally, turned on Stein.

Quietly but forcibly he tore his international record to date to shreds. Everybody was embarrassed, not least the two BBC people who should not have been privy to any of this. It was clear Younger had been stoking this up, although it seemed an odd setting to chose. No matter how much an acutely discomfited Ernie Walker tried to cap it, the well of frustration was now blowing wildly out of control from the mouth of the SFA President. At one stage Younger said, 'You have a worse record than Willie Ormond and Ally MacLeod and they both got the sack!'

As Stein sat there quietly I looked for the signs of the famous flush on the face, that journalists' early warning system interpreted unfailingly as the first sign of the retaliatory strike. But there was nothing there. At one stage he very quietly said, 'Tam, maybe we shouldn't be talking about these things in front of our guests here.' But that was all. He was taking this with barely any dissent. Certainly Younger was uttering much of the consensus view of Stein at that stage for his record then was nothing to boast about.

Stein also had a case to put. He was embarked on changing the entire approach of Scottish international football, which, up until then, could have been said to be a reflection of the spirit of the fiery cross. Stein wanted to put that light on the 'peep'. He was after a more cerebral attitude, cooler, less reliant on terracing acoustics. Whether or not it was succeeding or whether he was on the right tack, were highly debatable matters but that, at any rate, is what his philosophy was at that particular time. But there he sat saying virtually nothing. I was beginning to think his self-restraint would become one of the seven wonders of the modern world for if it had been the Stein of Parkhead the other diners in that elegant restaurant would have been entertained to a Lanarkshire 'rap' of venomous intent.

Whilst Ernie Walker silently fumed in the background Stein showed no sign of retaliation. This worried me. It was too quiescent, too much like an SFA official toeing the party line, and it was a role he didn't play well. King Lear might have suited him but certainly not the Bob Cratchit he now seemed. There is no doubt that he had been eminently qualified to take on the national team manager's job. Sometimes we avoid the obvious in these circumstances and the fact went barely without comment on his appointment that in no way were the SFA getting the same man who had endowed Celtic Park with greatness. The simple fact of the matter is that Jock Stein badly needed the SFA job.

He was in excruciating exile in England when conjecture about Ally MacLeod's future was at its peak. Ally, by this time, had been largely traumatised into a husk of his former self, bitter and anguished. His attempts to re-enact his previous ebullience had the hamminess of a rep company's worst actor. Relations with the press were strained, largely because he must have realised that most people wanted rid of him. Only a split vote in the International Committee kept him in his job in the immediate aftermath of Argentina. It was simply a matter of time. Stein, meanwhile, had left Celtic and was now with Leeds but seeking any possible way to get his hands on the Scottish job.

He had uttered genuine sympathy for Ally immediately after the World Cup, which was more humanitarian than professional, for his instinctive support for the Scottish manager could not have extinguished his notion that it was now the post for him. I simply could not see Stein bearing his situation in Leeds too long. He was not in the first flush of youth and he was instinctively a home bird. Friends who would go on holiday with him, particularly to Menorca, a favourite place of his, will tell you that he could not get home quickly enough to Glasgow nevertheless. There was little chance of Stein taking root in England and as the clamour for a change of manager for Scotland rose in intensity people started to work for him behind the scenes.

I was approached by a journalist who asked me to phone Stein one morning. I tracked him down to a hotel in the Midlands where he was staying with the Leeds team prior to an evening game. The call was put through to his room and I could visualise him lying back watching the racing on television. His voice had the sonority of a very unhappy man, deep, tired and almost mournful. There was no doubt about the point of the call. He wanted me to break cover and tout for him publicly in such a way as to indicate that he would take the job if asked. He knew that I was going on *Sportsnight*'s network programme that very night to conjecture about Scotland's future, thus confirming that he certainly had not lost all his faculties, particularly in knowing everything that was going on in the media world. He virtually wrote the script for me, advising what he thought could be said of his delicate position with Leeds and of how he had to be very careful about any of his own personal comments on the matter. He sounded in a grim and determined mood. He desperately wanted the job.

This was right up my street. I duly obliged by telling my colleagues in London what I was about to say that night about Stein so they put me right at the top of the programme. I launched into an unambiguous declaration of Stein's avowed aim to become Scottish team manager, saying that he was the right man for the job as his country needed him, that one word from the SFA would bring him back home and that it would be dereliction of duty on their part if they did not act. This is the stuff that hacks are made of, of course. But I wallowed in it. We were in a kind of no-man's land in international football at that stage anyway so that myself and others had started broadsides on a need for a change of sorts.

The following morning, lying in bed, I heard a radio interview with Stein which must have taken place well after his game the previous night and after the *Sportsnight* transmission. He was being quizzed about his future and about my report on the programme. He stated naturally that he had not seen this report but that he was not responsible for what others tried to make up and that his prime concern was the future welfare of Leeds United. 'Archie Macpherson was just flying a kite,' he concluded. Beautiful! The Machiavellian Stein was back on his best form. Anybody not knowing him might have thought they had been duped by *Sportsnight*. But in a way it was paradoxically satisfying to know that you had been drawn like others into his masterly intrigue. Even if the SFA had shown great reluctance to take him on, which was not the case anyway, we were stirring the public towards inevitable support for him. He was appointed in October 1978.

'I can adjust,' he said to me in his tiny garret-like room in that antiseptic office block of the SFA. It was like a dethroned king occupying the broom cupboard. There he sat, where once he massively filled every nook and cranny of Celtic Park, looking squashed by fate. He agreed terms with the world by fully appreciating the greatest virtue of this move. He was back home. 'People say that I won't be able to put up with not being in daily contact with a team. But it's all about adjusting. You can't look back, you've got to look ahead.'

It was perhaps not the most subtle remark he had ever made but it fitted genuinely enough to his circumstances. Like others, I thought there might have been potential for a personality clash between himself and the secretary Ernie Walker, himself of strong character, but, in fact, the two men, although of contrasting personalities, had a great deal in common. They were both intelligent to a degree greatly in excess of the job requirements, they were both West of Scotland punters whose search for the true meaning of life could not possibly exclude the influence of ninety minutes at a football match, they were both men's men who were pulled towards an admiration of strength in others. So they dovetailed in the most remarkable way, given, I suspect, that Stein resigned himself quickly to the fact that Walker set the whole tone and style of the SFA.

Four years on, Stein had gone through the most undistinguished period of his career. The results were patchy and questions about his apparent loss of touch were being aired, but discreetly, for his past club record was insulating him from the full rebuke of the media. They had long memories and needed to be told neither about his ability to handle men on a football field nor of his strength in annihilating his critics. Many people, in short, were still in awe of him. That is why Younger's broadside on him, unreciprocated, took the breath from me. I knew there had been mutterings about him and that the undistinguished way we finally clinched the point for Spain in a dour draw in Belfast did nothing to inspire great confidence. But this reaction to all of that was decidedly downbeat.

Now he didn't want to go to New Zealand and the BBC, having committed a lot of money to this enterprise, were not going to be too happy after my initial encouragement of the project. We talked for about half-an-hour on the phone before, with extreme reluctance, he agreed he would go ahead. When we eventually set out we were re-routed to Seattle because of some mechanical fault on the scheduled flight and after a wait of four hours without sleep picked up a flight to San Francisco. We arrived there feeling as if we had come by wagon-train through the Rockies. Stein was pale, drawn and obviously fed-up. I went to my room, turned on the television and flopped on the bed. Within about ten seconds the famous American anchorman Dan Rather flashed on to the screen with words which went through me like a rapier.

'Good evening. The war in the South Atlantic has taken a sinister turn with the sinking of the *SS Belgrano* and the reported loss of 99 lives.'

That message did not have much therapeutic value on my body, brutalised by jet-lag and lack of sleep. It was like trying to lull yourself into a slumber to the words of Edgar Allan Poe. A feeling of horror and revulsion swept over me. But I had no time to reflect on my own about it for within a couple of minutes I heard a loud knocking on the door and Stein appeared, shirtless, hair awry, looking almost angered.

'Did you hear that?' he asked in some amazement. 'C'mon, we're getting to hell out of here back home. Maggie'll nuke them next. I told you it could get right out of hand. Get on the phone and get us a flight back home tomorrow.'

I hadn't been expecting this and frankly I was in no mood to argue with him. There and then I made a decision just to agree with his idea and then take it up again in the morning after we had had some sleep. I wasn't caring any longer one way or the other myself. It is just that we were at a halfway house and it was probably as quick to fly back over the Pacific anyway. It wasn't easy to sleep that night. But in the morning, as it so often does, the world seemed to have taken on a different complexion.

The Californian sun was sharp and warm. The people in the hotel treated us like royalty, as they did everybody for that matter. The breakfast was huge and life-enhancing and a cheery friend of Stein's turned up. He was brimming with optimism about Scotland in the World Cup and offering to drive us round San Francisco to sight-see. The previous evening seemed light years away. I was beginning to feel that having brought him this far I would be able to manage the second half of the journey after all. He didn't mention giving up, so we toured the city then went back to our hotel to pack up before continuing our trip across the Pacific. He seemed more content. But as we were driving to the airport the taxi driver hearing our accents started to talk about the war again and then said, 'Pity about you losing a ship.'

'No, it was one of theirs,' Stein interrupted.

'I just heard you lost a ship called the *Sheffield*. Yeah, that's what you call it,' the driver went on. 'The Argies got it!'

I tried not to look at Stein who just whispered a curse. I simply strode into the airport when we were set down and made for the check-in desk. I didn't get far. The large hand pulled on my shoulder.

'I don't think I could face up to this,' he said. 'We could have a world war on our hands. People are getting killed and we're going to be fartin' about amongst the Maoris. It'll look bad, us out there making films and young men getting maimed and slaughtered. It's bad.'

He slumped down on a bench waiting for me to respond. I knew he simply wanted me to cave in but I was now at the end of my tether.

'I'm going on,' I said wearily. 'With or without you. I'll do something out there. I'll make up some kind of story.'

By this time, I suppose, my voice had the tone of Little Orphan Annie. I left him sitting there, booked in, walked into the departure lounge, had a very large whisky, slumped in a seat and waited. Ten minutes later, through he came, limping heavily, and heaved himself down beside me.

'I couldn't let you go on your own,' he said. For the first time I noticed that he was not only looking extremely tired but that his face was like an ashen mask. I have never been too happy about that, looking back. All I had needed to do was agree with him and we could have turned back. The trip to New Zealand meant precious little to him, other than protecting himself, but meant a lot more to me. I was getting him into what I thought could be an interesting film for us both and I selfishly hoped for a few plaudits for myself.

He certainly did not need that sapping, punishing journey especially as, in retrospect, I realise it took more out of him than even he thought it possibly could. The stay in New Zealand offered more than just some pretty shots of us gazing at geysers, or being bemused by the rolling eyes and tongues of the Maoris, or hearing Stein say some diplomatic things about the athletic Kiwis. It was on this trip he opened up to me in a way he never had before.

I had spent a lot of time with him in his last few years with Celtic, particularly after his car accident, when we joined forces to tour Scotland in a kind of mobile chat show sponsored by a brewery. He was brilliant at that. There was no sign of showmanship about him yet by dint of his genuine, authentic views on football he had the audiences eating out of his hand. He didn't pander to them in any way. Indeed because all had not gone as smoothly on the field for him as had been expected he was not swept along by the adulation of the people who turned up to listen to him.

Whereas Ally on the previous tour could have talked in Sanskrit and they would have chaired him round the community afterwards, Stein contented himself with lectures which at times sounded like Socratic dialogues. He argued and questioned his way logically through his philosophy of the game and defended his current policies. He interspersed this with a brilliant wit which sometimes verged on the malicious and could destroy someone who had come out on these occasions like a young gunfighter, ready to cut down the fastest draw in the business. They stood little chance against him. There was nobody he could fail to put away.

He always drove me to these outings and it has to be said, quite frankly, sometimes drove with a demoniacal urgency as if he had heard his house was on fire. He always gave the impression of being pursued by past events and hounded by thoughts of the future. Perhaps it was this which produced his constant restlessness, which he imposed on other people in the most autocratic way. If he wanted to up and go and the rest of the company wanted to stay on for a drink then we upped and went at his command. If he was the star turn then the star turn had to have his way regardless of the difficulties.

We stayed overnight once in Elgin after regaling a packed audience with thoughts on how we must put out of our minds the excesses of Argentina. Stein had agreed to this trip on the condition that the sponsor provided a private aircraft which they duly did. To his astonishment and disgust we then discovered that there were no such things as night flights out of Inverness on a Sunday night. Air-traffic controllers there went to their beds like anyone else. He had expected to be home in Glasgow that same evening. There was little overnight consolation in Elgin for Scotland's leading insomniac, who cursed his lot in life that he had taken on such a trip.

Nor was there much the following morning when I awoke to discover everything was covered in a thick hoar frost which extended to Inverness airport and the little Piper Aztec plane, which looked like a frosted favour for a giant wedding cake. When he was told the plane couldn't take off because of icing on the wings he was livid. Celtic were not playing well at the time and he was obsessed with the need to get back for Monday morning training.

He insisted the pilot try something, because he wanted to push on. No democratic vote was taken when the pilot suggested that if we were really pushed he would try a farmer's fertiliser which he thought might act as a de-icer. I certainly did not want to fly in a plane that had to be fertilised before take off. I protested and told him that not even the Wright Brothers would go up under such circumstances. 'Get the fertiliser on!' Stein shouted at the pilot.

It was as far as I know the first recorded instance of a man crop-spraying a plane. Miraculously it worked and we soared into the air only to be told by the pilot that fog had descended right across the Clyde Valley which meant we had to turn back or take a chance on landing in Edinburgh.

'No way,' Stein shouted against the din of the engine. 'Have a go at Glasgow! It's only a wee plane!'

I protested that fog took no account of the size of a plane, which could hardly be able to sneak in under its cover. The sponsor, crammed into the seat behind us, was beginning to regret he had taken on this trip in the first place. Stein looked out of the window whistling. Then the pilot thought of something.

'We could try Cumbernauld!' he shouted at us.

'Cumbernauld!' we all exclaimed as one, even Stein. But the pilot assured us that there was a landing field there for small planes and that he would contact the control there. Control? I envisaged an old woman at a phone. We swooped down towards Mother Earth, all of us suffering this communal cataract which blurred everything below. Basically I do not like flying, even though I have gone several times around the world by plane. I mistrust those who seem to make light of it, as Stein often did, and interpret that as a sign of their own unease. I therefore had to believe the big man was peeing himself like the rest of us. As we went for it, we could only see the tops of high rise flats peeking through the fluffy carpet of fog.

'Look for them signalling to us,' the pilot said peering down. 'I think I can see the strip just down there.'

We all looked. All I could see was a kind of moth-eaten veil through which there was a suggestion of ground but nothing more definite than that. I was beginning not to believe all of this. Cumbernauld? It was all going to end in Cumbernauld? I realised I had been unkind in some of the things I had said about its town centre but I was thinking I hardly deserved this.

We were about to try blind-flying without instruments just to accommodate the big man getting back in time for training? I was on the verge of screaming a protest when Stein suddenly pulled his face back from the window, tapped the pilot on the shoulder and said, 'Can you sign-write in the sky? Because if you can you spell out to them down there, "You-must-be-effing-joking!"' And he burst out laughing whilst the rest of us offered a silent prayer of thanks that Celtic Football Club were going to have to do without Mr Stein for training that morning. We landed safely, but on wobbly legs, in Edinburgh.

So, in a modest way, perhaps he did owe me one and thus agreed to New Zealand. It was there I felt I got closer to the private Stein than I ever had before. Perhaps not in the country itself, where we wandered around listlessly, trying to make up some pictorial excuse for having gone there to film, but even more so on the long hauls over the Pacific. There was the slightly droning noise of the engines in the background, the resistance to sleep we shared, which not even the normally soporific effect of the in-flight movies could dent, and the dim light of the aircraft announcing that you really should be asleep. In the midst of it sat this huge hulk, wanting to see the night through and this horrible journey eased, whispering beside you willingly about his career and his thoughts on people who had influenced his life. I knew I was beside a man trying desperately to come to terms with the fact that he was growing old.

This 'closeness' you could only use as a relative expression.

Stein encouraged few intimacies and indeed he would slam the portcullis down on anybody thinking of wantonly invading his privacy. Even some of those claiming to be his close friends found themselves bundled out of his presence with a few stark epithets on occasions. He was a complex man, carrying a mass of contradictions which seemed nevertheless to add to his substance, not subtract from it. He was gregarious, yet sullen and bitter, hostile to attention at times. He could have the company dancing to his command and turn within seconds to a man fleeing from it all as quickly as he could. He could be brilliantly philosophical in defeat and also like a man feeling persecuted. Tony Queen, perhaps his closest friend, told me that on a Saturday night after a Celtic defeat, Stein 'was the loneliest man in the world'.

Sometimes you would feel you had penetrated all his reservations and could take him on a level of your own choosing. But the next time you met him it was as if he barely knew you. He hated sycophants but occasionally used them to further himself in the most sanguine way. He liked admiration but could choke the phoniness of gush with breathtaking abruptness.

But twenty-six thousand feet above the Pacific, surprisingly, he needed somebody to talk to. He took some time to tell me about the period of returning to Scotland to play for Celtic and the effect it had on people in his old community. Of how his best pal for years came to the house to see his mother and father but would not go upstairs to speak to him even though he knew he was in, because he was now a Celtic man. He spoke of how his mother would always wish him good luck before playing against Rangers but his father never. Of how a man simply attempting to ply his trade had come back to be treated by some as a pariah.

It had bitten more deeply into him than I had ever supposed and I was surprised to hear him reveal it as such. He spoke to me sardonically of how Willie Allison, the Rangers PRO, at one stage not long after the winning of the European Cup, advised him that the 'call' would come from Ibrox for him. He had savoured that particularly but was denied the ultimate satisfaction of knocking it back in public. He talked at length about lying in the hospital after his serious car accident fighting off death, which he defined as 'like looking at a window-box of flowers. I don't know why but that's what I kept seeing.'

He kept up this introspection throughout our trip until I said to him he should get it all down on paper and that there was a great deal about him that people would want to know behind his public face.

'It's not time yet,' he said. 'Anyway they just want me to tell all I know and dig up some dirt about folk. I'm not interested in that.'

By the time, many weeks later, we all assembled in Spain I was one of the mob again, seeking as much as anybody else in the World Cup media brawl and getting no more than my fair share of news or opinions or comment from him. The portcullis was down once more.

Stein underplayed himself in Spain. He tried to be downbeat and cooler and hammered into the theme of not reliving Argentina. But I think he spent a lot of time, much more than he ought to or needed to, in combating the media. He was obsessed with outwitting them. He had not liked some of the things which had been written and said about the performances in the lead-up to the finals and whilst he had always been a brilliantly capable politician he seemed preoccupied by trying to find out what the media was thinking and saying. He would try and grill people about that. We were seeing the defensive Stein, a man holding down a job, not the man with the acute sense of mission we had known at Parkhead. The SFA knew they had hired an older man.

The Scottish squad stayed down in a golf hotel at Sotogrande, which entailed a long drive from the Torremolinos area along one of the most dangerous coast roads in the world. The SFA had allocated separate times for access to daily newspapers, Sunday press and radio and television. We all queued up and sat sedately with him or the players when our turn came. Stein spent much of his time with me criticising members of the press. He had always enjoyed a good gossip but this time he had targeted people in a way which suggested that he was thinking beyond the World Cup to when he would have to face inquests and that, inherently, he did not deep down believe that Scotland stood much chance of qualifying.

New Zealand certainly caused us some disquiet in the first

match but my abiding recollection of that night was the people of Malaga coming out on to the streets afterwards and cheering the Scottish bus through the streets. We had been expecting 6–0, we had only managed 5–2. But the Spaniards had wanted an entertaining game and they had got it.

During the Soviet Union–Brazil game I commentated on, a voice from London interrupted and told me to be quiet for a few moments while an important announcement was to be made. Then a news-reader said quite simply, 'The government have announced that the Argentinian forces in the Falklands have unconditionally surrendered.' I thought of Dan Rather and Stein and the suspense in San Francisco and I was glad at least part of the world was getting itself sorted out although not even the South Atlantic Expeditionary Force would have been of much use to Scotland in Spain, as it turned out.

There was the last game in Malaga. Scotland conceded to the USSR one of those goals which belongs in a Walt Disney 'Goofy' instructional film on how to cause the maximum embarrassment with the minimum of effort. Not even Souness's well-drilled daisy-cutter near the end could conceal the misery we all felt.

A Russian in front of me, and perhaps a journalist or someone with the official party, had been raising his arms and waving them about until he was blocking our view. Attempts at persuasion failed. In my frustration with the match I eventually punched him hard on the back, put my mike away from my mouth and bawled at him to bugger off. He stood up. He was at least seven feet tall and had the kind of build one associates with lumberjacks and Sherman tanks. He bunched his right fist into a massive piece of malevolent intent and towered above me.

Billy McNeill did all that any human being could do to help me under the circumstances by sliding under his seat in helpless laughter. Quick thinking persuaded me to put my mike to my mouth again promptly, which I did with my voice rising with great passion on the subject of another night of humiliation for us. I kept one eye on the play and another on the fist until I was convinced he was impressed with how tragic my voice was to the Scottish nation and I saw him sit down again with a massive thud.

There are times when a commentator has to do what a commentator has to do. So I spent the last few minutes of that game talking largely against a spine as big as the Urals.

Elements do intrude on a World Cup, apart from the goals, which help the recollections gel but nobody could mention Seville without thinking of Brazil and David Narey. It was not so much the scoring of the goal, about which we all enthused, as the fitting contribution it made to a night which resuscitated our belief in the compelling virtue of football as a life-enhancer. The air of fiesta never deserted the Scottish supporters as they watched Brazil's inevitable 4−1 victory engineered by the strutting Socrates and the flowing Falcao.

I knew, though, as soon as I heard Jimmy Hill, sitting in his presentation seat on top of a block of flats outside the ground watching the game on a television monitor, describe Narey's strike as a 'toe-poke' that it would not be taken lying down by our people. It was to be construed as some monstrous cultural insult, like calling the Clyde-built *Queen Elizabeth* a paddle steamer. Hill, whom I regard as an amiable and extremely sociable man, has developed the knack of arousing resentment in people more readily than other pundits.

I admire him for that. Hill, especially in his earlier days, hooked on to things that aroused you, made you think. He attacked the middle-age spread of the living rooms by provoking the armchair critic to sometimes violent reaction. Ignore him you could not. He was certainly no studio wallflower. He loved the attention of the Scottish supporters forever after. On match days that he attended or watched from the studio, that I can vouch for, no man could have been prouder of being singled out for mob abuse. The 'Jimmy Hill's a Poof' banner frequently seen amongst Scottish fans was not only singularly inaccurate but was to Jimmy simply an eccentric sign of endearment.

But after that comment the relationship between Stein and Hill was never the same. Stein, in fact, was looking for blood and became unusually anti-English, unusual in the sense that he never wished to be seen to be stupidly nationalistic and did value their football. But on this occasion he told me that if Hill approached him he would chew him up and that had it been an English goal it would never have been interpreted in such a dismissive way. Hill himself complained of a gross over-reaction and, in truth, there was something to that. He has always insisted that 'toe-pokes' can be the product of great skill. I agree with him in the sense of his own definition and for the very fact that Dave Narey proved it. If it was one.

Seville saved us from ourselves and our World Cup morbidity. We took defeat like a unique honour. The Brazilians suited the warmth of the night, the pulse of the drums and their limbs seemed elastic and brilliant. There was nothing much we could do about it. Looking back, perhaps we witnessed the last of the great Brazilian sides, at least for many generations. Their awful country has driven their significant professionals to Europe where, in the less amenable climate, something of their spontaneous genius seems to be atrophying. We were all glad to say 'We were there!' So was Stein. He himself did not suffer much from this tournament. He had failed, certainly.

But he hadn't been put to the sword. And, unlike the bull, he was going to get another chance.

His spirit was still buoyant enough over the next three years but he was tiring perceptibly. Qualification for Mexico was draining him. I thought that he was not only involved in achieving success but in trying desperately to prove, perhaps to himself above all, that he still had the capacity to absorb all the pressure. The terrible truth was that he had not. Players in the dressing room began to notice he was forgetful of certain elements of preparation which would have been exhaustively covered in a previous era. There was no great surprise in this. He couldn't outfox nature.

The last time I spoke to him was in the Council Chambers of the SFA the week before travelling to Cardiff for the Wales match in November 1985. He had just held a press conference, after which he was speaking to people individually. Just in front of me he had taken to task a journalist for something that had been said about him years before. It made me smile. He never forgot and he never missed. But it was reprimand without sting. It seemed merely a reminder, no more. He looked drawn but nobody ever pointed these things out to him. Not in public anyway. He talked to me about his son George trying to get over from his job in

Switzerland to see this important game. There was nothing much more to it than that.

I did not see him being carried dying up the tunnel that night at Ninian Park. Neither did the SFA secretary Ernie Walker and Graeme Souness. They had both left their seats and gone down to the tea-room many minutes before the final whistle because the tension of watching Scotland hold on for their 1–1 draw had become intolerable. I knew how they both felt for I had escaped early as well, but for the added reason that I was not on official duty that night and had to speak at a corporate hospitality dinner in Cardiff Castle later. I was on the prawn cocktail when I heard he had died.

I took part in seven obituary programmes on both radio and television over the next forty-eight hours. I churned it out so mechanically eventually that I lost any of the sense of grief I had originally felt. It is the way of journalism.

Stein had grown out of the sour earth of the Old Firm patch to blossom into a patriarchical figure venerated even by those Rangers men who years before regarded him with repugnance. That notable achievement must not confuse us about the roots of his greatness, which stemmed from the impact he made as Celtic manager. I prefer to recall him as the younger man coming straight at me like a gale blowing, eyes flashing, mouth pursed ready to strike terror into the very soul. It's the warrior I remember most of all. For, as that, he was quite simply the best, in the best of all possible times.

12

The Celluloid Olympics

Lionel Richie walked to centre stage dressed in white, his voice suddenly embalming the 90,000 crowd in a respectful hush which intensified the casual cabaret tones of the singer, who was helping to bring the Olympic Games of 1984 in Los Angeles to an end. True to the nature of Tinseltown, the finale had sewn sequins onto the Olympic fabric. His rendition of *All Night Long* simpered into the velvety night as if he was entertaining late-night diners at the Coconut Grove on Wilshire Boulevard.

Beside me most of the British press corps were on their feet, standing on their cubicle desks, arms linked like the line-up from *Chorus Line*, swaying back and forward with the rest of the crowd in time to the music, although admittedly adding tiny trills of their own. It was difficult to relate this to the rather pompous and over-blown ceremonies normally associated with Olympic gatherings.

To get the British media to leave their instruments of communication for an impromptu public 'knees-up' is a rare achievement at any time and one which says much for the seductive quality of marrying the spirit of Baron de Coubertin to that of Busby Berkeley. From the opening ceremony, when fifty grand pianos strummed Gershwin and ladies who looked to be recruited straight from the Ziegfeld Follies, rather than from the 'Babe' Zaharias Memorial Club, wafted down a white staircase, these Games were to be unlike any other.

I had gone to the Olympics as part of BBC's network team with

167

the principal assignment of capturing some of the essence of the character of the Games by filming the more 'off-beat' stories. I had missed out on Russia. BBC London invited me to the Moscow Olympics in 1980 but when Mrs Thatcher denounced the immorality of holding Games in a capital city of a nation occupying Afghanistan the BBC dutifully played ball and cut down the size of the team. I was one of the first casualties. My resulting exclusion from the team I am sure shook the Kremlin to its foundations. It certainly disappointed me.

I had good cause to go to Moscow on a personal basis for we had gone round the world in pursuit of Allan Wells to make a documentary about his preparations for these Games. We caught up with him in Melbourne and discovered a quiet, slightly dour man, monkish in the sort of contemplative way of sprinters, backed by an exuberant wife who seemed to have a Svengali-like and productive influence on him. Her vocal encouragements of him as he ran have made some of the most stimulating sports 'cut-away' shots of all time.

The documentary was of no great note in itself but it did indicate that, under Malcolm Kellard and a sympathetic management at that time, BBC Scotland's sports department was putting itself about. There had been a tendency in the past to allow ourselves to think that only our network sports colleagues in the south could attempt certain ventures. Although I did not believe Kellard was on the same wavelength as myself when it came to domestic sport, and especially football, I could not commend more the spirit of adventure that had been released by his coming.

With the arrival of James Hunter as Head of Television, Kellard's individuality seemed restricted and his trotting up and downstairs for instructions from his direct superior became a rather pathetic example of the means he had to adopt to keep his department moving. Until then, though, we flourished in imaginative ways. We did the unthinkable and travelled to Rome on the tenth anniversary of the Lisbon Lions victory, with Billy McNeill as my co-commentator, to cover the Liverpool–Borussia Moenchengladbach European Cup Final in 1977, rather than simply take the network broadcast. This piece of independent thinking in an area usually dominated by the south was greeted back in Scotland by a solemn piece in the *Glasgow Herald* asking 'Was Archie's Journey Really Necessary?' It made us despair.

My own feeling then, and it hasn't changed all that much, is that anything from the south is considered intrinsically superior by the vast bulk of the Scottish viewing public. LA was to prove that to me.

It is a city I had to get to know quickly for my basic job was to report on a widely varied basis. I had to find out where all the venues were. I started off doing that armed with the statutory local warning about impossible traffic, possible muggers and highly probable smog.

My first sight of the Colosseum in broad daylight was a disappointment. Like many other sports centres which I had only previously seen on film or in photographs it proved the camera is selective and short-sighted. What these views didn't show was that the principal stadium for the Games was surrounded by the encroaching urban decay of the town. As a general rule the more Hispanic faces you saw around you the greater the distance you were from Beverly Hills and the WASP communities in the canyons leading out of the city. The Colosseum, in that sense, might have been in Mexico.

You could see that the whole metropolitan area in fact was not so much a melting-pot but a series of apparently incompatible racial segments which defied that immediate analysis by merging in a mysteriously seamless way. I do not include the district of Watts in that description though. Barry Davies, the commentator, and I went by car to Long Beach one day to look at some of the indoor facilities there. Coming back we took a wrong turning and ended up driving through what might have been an impoverished town somewhere in the Third World. Whether or not we were influenced by our preconception of the place, we felt distinctly threatened as squads of people, perhaps of saintly intent (we were not inclined to dally to find out), gazed at us as if they wished the car would stall.

That's how it seemed as you travelled around looking for venues like needles in hay stacks. It is not until you have to move round the greater area of LA that you realise you are so easily swallowed up in this huge urban sprawl. There is all of twenty-six miles of

Sunset Boulevard for instance and to move from the athletics stadium to Anaheim for the wrestling and judo was like a whole day's journey given you could read the freeway signs correctly and if you couldn't you would end up in Pasadena whether you liked it or not.

Even more importantly there was no communal or municipal link with the Games. Normally in an Olympic city you would find expressions of sheer gratitude or pride or even bombast connected with the festival. But not in LA for the Games did not belong to the civic authorities or the people but to the sponsors. These were the first commercially self-sustaining Olympics and you really did not see any evidence of the Games being there at all until you were practically on the doorstep of the particular venues. Perhaps the apotheosis of crass subjugation to the dollar sign was seen in the fact that the American nation watching on television did not see the entry of the flame into the stadium but were on a commercial at the time.

My own professional efforts nearing the opening of the Games were distinctly stodgy. I had firstly been sent to reflect on how the Great American Breakfast was the last thing any athlete would wish to contemplate during their stay in Tinseltown and, because of a camera fault and the essential cut-away shots for editing purposes, I ate the equivalent of three breakfasts in the most famous breakfast eatery in LA, an undistinguished little café which people queued to get into. This amounted to something like six pancakes smothered in syrup, six eggs, three waffles, and hash potatoes. So far I had been in at the tail end of planning for our build-up to the start of the Games and, about three days before the opening ceremony, I hadn't really achieved all that much. I could end up as irrelevant to the action as some of the tramps who trundled around Lafayette and MacArthur Parks pushing their supermarket trolleys like women of old going to the 'steamie' with their prams. I was going to have to come up with something special.

One night I sat in my room watching the late movie. It was Bob Hope in *The Cat and the Canary*, debatably his funniest film without Crosby. The last time I had seen it was in the Palaceum Cinema just off Shettleston Road when I was still in short-trousers. I was in the middle of enjoying it when it occurred to me that I had met somebody two years previously who had claimed not just to have known Hope but to have been sponsor of his annual Desert Classic golf tournament. I had been at Gleneagles making a film about its attraction for Americans and the professional on the course, Ian Marchbanks, pointed me in the direction of a little man who came to Scotland every year on a golfing pilgrimage. He turned out to be a delightful individual of many anecdotes connected with golf, not least of which was his association with Bob Hope. His name was Jack Hennessy and although he represented the cognac people in California he was not of the original family.

But he was the organiser of the Desert Classic, so he said. After I had interviewed him on film about his liking for Scotland he gave me a warm invite to LA any time and offered me his business card. Now Americans by and large are extremely open people with a propensity for generous invitations to the bosom of the household. They seem to do it with a natural ease that might be mistaken for the rather mechanical and automatic utterance, 'Have a nice day!' Generally speaking, you do not put them to the test.

I mothballed his business card. But that night, as Bob Hope and Paulette Goddard were shrieking their way through the spooky film, I was upturning every little piece of my baggage to find that small piece of pasteboard with his name on it. I was going to put him to the test. I found it buried in a pile of brief-case flotsam and jetsam that had collected through the years and the following morning I phoned him. Within a couple of hours, he was down to take me to lunch at the Lakeside Country Club in North Hollywood in his solid white Cadillac. There was no getting away from the fact that Jack Hennessy was a man of some substance. But it wasn't just his hospitality I was after. As we drove up through Burbank and past the Universal Studios complex I was wondering if he really did know Bob Hope after all.

John Mortimer once described Hollywood as 'suburbia of the soul'. Six weeks wasn't long enough to experience that sort of seediness or to divine the misery that is hidden behind the sumptuous hoardings of sybaritic living. Perhaps I could have gone off the place quickly but as it was I lapped up the environment in the simplest way, as a tourist might do, hoping to bump into celebrities.

Naive I suppose, but if you've been brought up in cinema it seemed a natural inclination. So, with Jack Hennessy in the Lakeside Club, I was introduced to Hollywood.

The Club had boasted Howard Hughes as a member, which means it had more amenities than just hot and cold running water. The centrepiece was a magnificent championship golf course, for from the Thirties onwards golf had become an obsession amongst the stars, many of whom had been or were members. Crosby, Bogart, Hope, Gable, Buddy Rogers, Weismuller, and many others including hundreds of directors and producers from the studios had based themselves there.

The bar in the club was famous. It was there that Bogart, Sydney Greenstreet, Peter Lorre and Mary Astor would retire to every night during the filming of *The Maltese Falcon*. They told me Bogart, in fact, normally stayed there all night and went straight onto the lot, often without sleep, which, apart from his own abilities, partly explained that brilliantly rumpled and acerbic performance. In the bar Jack introduced me to a gentleman called simply Norm who had devised and owned *Looney Tunes* and had been the creator of Woody Woodpecker. We sometimes forget that the ability to sketch in Hollywood had created millionaires outside of Disney and Norm was one. He also happened to be pleasantly crotchety at the age of seventy. When I asked him how the ordinary members in the club reacted to the depth of celebrities around he snorted, 'Doesn't make a damn difference.' He had a huge mane of white hair and a glass of bourbon inevitably just under his chin, which drooped a lot towards the counter. 'Nobody bothers anybody here,' he said. 'We talk business amongst ourselves but golf is golf. When you're out there with your partner it doesn't matter a damn if they're queuing up to see you all over the world. Miss a putt in a foursome and you're just another asshole.

'Why, the most unpopular man in the club was Bogart. What a misfit he was! Nobody wanted to go on the course with him. People thought he cheated, kicked his ball in the rough and all that, and when he'd been on his binges he'd come down here with a hangover the size of Santa Monica pier and be the most miserable sonofabitch in the ENTIRE country. One day a guy in the industry was told he'd been drawn in a foursome with Bogey. He pulled

out! Almost unheard of! When he was asked for his official explanation he just told the committee, "If I want to play with a prick,
I'll play with my own!"'

Perhaps in that 'suburbia of the soul' Norm was the local gossip
columnist. He himself was at pains to tell everybody I was with
the BBC and one gent told me how marvellous it was to meet
somebody from the organisation which had helped the great broadcaster Ed Murrow during the war in London and how much he
respected their standards of objectivity and technical excellence.
Carried away by all of this, I offered him an invite down to the
International Television Centre where, if he so wished, he could
examine our operation. When I asked him what he did for a living
he explained that he was a producer.

'What have you produced?' I asked.

'*Butch Cassidy and the Sundance Kid, The Sting, Slaughterhouse
Five* . . . and I'm off to have a look at the rushes of something by
a guy called John Le Carré . . . Do you know him? . . . I'm doing
that with George Roy Hill. He's directing. It's called *The Little
Drummer Girl*. It's a swine of a book to film but I think George
has cracked it!'

I didn't think it was worthwhile the man coming down to see us
after all.

Eventually I broached the subject.

'Do you see Bob Hope much?' I asked Jack.

'Now and again,' he said. 'Do you want to meet him?'

Did I want to meet him! I tried as best as I possibly could to
remain very British and cool and slightly casual.

'Possible?' I asked languidly.

'Just wait and I'll see if he's in town,' Jack replied.

He went to a wall phone in the large dining room and started
to dial. I was sufficiently far enough away only to pick up fragments
of the conversation but I was getting the gist.

'Hi, where you been . . . just had lunch with a Scot . . . met
him at Gleneagles . . . yeah, he loves golf . . . Arch is his name
. . . Arch . . . with the BBC television company . . . yeah the good
old BBC company . . . over here for the Olympics . . . you wanna
talk to him?'

He beckoned me over. OK, it was just a phone call, but it wasn't all that usual, I was saying to myself. It's just Bob Hope on the other end of the line, no need to get carried away. It's not his autograph you're after.

'Hello,' I said.

'Hi, Arch!' the voice replied.

I suppose a pilgrim throwing himself on a shrine after a lifetime's struggle to reach the sacred spot would be so absorbed in the moment that he would be oblivious to those non-believers who might care to mock. That is how I suppose I would try to justify the juvenile weak-kneed feeling I had hearing that voice on the other end of the line. I had grown up with him, watching him grow older, thinking him the veritable citadel of ham, perhaps decreasingly funny, but always in my mind stuck in the Forties in canisters of black and white film and consequently indestructible. Now he was a two-worded voice on the other end of the line.

'Hi, Bob!' I said as if to an old pal.

I can't remember too much about the conversation because I was mentally preparing to ask him the most vital question of all. But we did talk about how much he liked Scotland and the difficulty of playing Carnoustie and of how he loved the Royal and Ancient and of how he was preparing for an autumn tour of the UK. Now I wanted him for interview.

What the BBC had lacked in LA up till then was some connection with showbiz or the film industry to add some glitter to the major Olympic Preview which was being prepared. There had been some talk about getting Michael Caine and having a barbecue at 'his place' in Beverly Hills but somehow it was beginning to peter out, no doubt because there was an agent involved.

Now Hollywood agents can be a cross between a vulture and a snake and are very difficult people to work with. I had once tried to secure Rod Stewart for an interview when I heard he was coming back from LA and was told that his agent would require the cost of a private plane to get him from London to Glasgow, an overnight suite in a hotel, not just for himself I hasten to add, and a hefty sum that could float a company on the Stock Exchange. Needless to say, Rod probably heard nothing at all about this for these people act as financial 'bouncers' as well. So to arrange a Hollywood celebrity interview was as easy as asking for some free real estate in Malibu. We were in fact getting nowhere.

So I had to make the plunge.

'I was wondering if you wouldn't mind giving us a few words for BBC television. I am sure the people back home would love it. Just any thoughts you have on the Olympics coming to Los Angeles. We'd all be deeply grateful.'

It was just on the right side of grovelling. There was a pause. 'When?' the voice asked.

I was taken aback. It seemed like interest. And then again I wished he hadn't asked that for I simply did not know. I gave myself all of 1.8 seconds to find a hypothetical time.

'Tomorrow afternoon, say about three o'clock?'

'Well I'm kinda busy right now. I'm getting my new Olympic suit fitted. They say I've put on a little bit behind. Slackening it off for me.'

I felt a kind of dangling disappointment.

'Could you bring a camera out to me?'

Could we bring a camera out to him! If it was the last thing I ever did.

'Of course,' I said.

'Then make it three o'clock and bring old Jack out with you. I haven't seen him for a while. See you.'

Just like that. But as soon as I put the phone down I realised I had a problem. There was simply no way of knowing whether I would get a camera unit or not. The coverage of the Olympics is a huge logistical nightmare which requires the most meticulous planning even down to the daily allocation of the three camera units we had with us in LA. The executive producer Alec Weeks ran it properly, like a general leading a battalion, with a stern attention to detail. It was entirely possible he would not release a unit if it was going to cover some mainstream athletics story, not even for a Bob Hope interview. I was gambling on the fact that it was the sort of portion of Tinseltown we badly needed.

Old Norm grunted his approval of Hope.

'Hope has his critics,' he growled. 'He's good on the course and he's not as mean as some folks say. Not in the same way as Bing.

He was the meanest of them all in my book. One night Crosby was down on the Strip, probably with some babes, and Dixie and the family were in the house when suddenly it went on fire. Fire brigade was called and they got word down to Bing. He came racing back in a cab and when he got there the flames had taken over. What does he do? Without asking about the family he dives into the house past the firemen who try to stop him but can't and comes back out a minute later with a shoe. Out of the shoe he's counting some bucks. Something like fifty bucks he had stashed away in a shoe under the bed. A man who could have bought the White House was willing to risk his life for fifty bucks. He was the meanest man in the ENTIRE country! Hey, ask Hope what he thought of *Looney Tunes!*'

I had other things in mind. I went back to our base with my fingers crossed. The International Broadcasting Centre for the Olympics was based just off Hollywood Boulevard in the old Columbia Pictures Studios, now used principally for television. I returned to this chilling, air-conditioned aircraft hangar of a building with the news I had Hope for interview. They wouldn't believe me at first. Indeed some of them casting an envious eye on what I apparently had achieved quite clearly did not want to believe me.

'How much?'

It was the question on everyone's lips when eventually it had sunk in that we did have him on offer. This found me very vulnerable again because I simply did not know.

'We can't proceed until we know how much. It could cost us an arm and a leg and the Games haven't even started yet. Get an idea of how much.'

Of course I thought this was a bad idea and tried to convince them that Hope was actually a friend of a friend.

'Nobody in Hollywood does things for a friend of a friend. Nobody does anything for free. Who's kidding who?'

I was being mauled. But I stuck it out.

'You can have my guts for garters if we're stung,' I said. 'I've got a feeling this is a favour.'

I could see they weren't buying this wholly but with a certain reservation they agreed to proceed. They allocated me Martin Mathewson, quite the best sports cameraman I have worked with, and indeed this was the beginning of a kind of partnership which would see us filming around the world together. Hope's house was in North Hollywood not far from the original Crosby home. Outside his main drive there were three large Chrysler limousines, part of his own personal fleet which he is given by the car company for personal appearances. The house had been added to through the years, from the original villa type, and was now a curious hybrid of mock-Tudor and Spanish hacienda.

Hope was still out when we got there so Jack Hennessy took us right through the house showing us the various sections that had been put on through the years and the *objets d'art* collected. Then we walked outside to the poolside and looked over his own personal golf course. It consisted of four par-four holes which he constantly practised on we were told. We set up the camera near his first tee with the pool in the background and only about ten minutes later than he had agreed, he arrived.

He came out from the French windows with a six-iron in his hand swinging it back and forward gently like a pendulum. Even before he could open his mouth our cameraman suddenly said, 'Excuse me, Mr Hope. Your shirt is white. The light will bounce off it badly and distort the picture. Could you change for us?'

He stopped in his tracks. I would not like to give the impression I was totally in awe of the man but I did freeze and expect him to tell us not to darken his doorstep ever again.

'Hey,' he said. 'I thought you were going to be regular guys. I've only got two shirts. I'll go back in and see if it's still at the laundry.'

At which point he turned, walked back inside and rejoined us ten minutes later with a multi-coloured vertical stripe shirt which I hoped would content our cameraman for the rest of his living days. But we were after all dealing with a consummate professional. To introduce the item we asked him if he would walk with me from his house to the couple of seats we had arranged for the interview. For various reasons we had to ask him to do it four times after which he did exactly the same leg cross position, swept his hat off exactly the same way and placed his golf club across his knee with the same meticulous precision. Even though it was but a humble interview the old habits of working on the set with Paramount were coming out in him.

I noticed that he was older looking than I had expected which is a bit like stating the obvious except that the young 'Lemon Drop Kid' Hope is indelibly stamped on the mind. The creases below the eyes seemed as if they had been stuck on to re-enact the ending of the *Road To Utopia*, where he appeared in the octogenerian trio of Hope, Crosby and Lamour. He was deaf in one ear so he made a blatant appeal to have me speak to his 'good' side. But he was bristling with good humour and made disparagingly jocular remarks about LA, its smog, its traffic, its muggings, the normal sort of thing; but right up our street.

He gave us exactly the brief summary of Hollywood and its interest in the Games that we wanted. When we had finished and we were sitting together as the cameraman set up some separate shots of the two of us I happened to ask him where his wife was. He pointed out to me that she was in fact in London at that very time. I had an idea. Would he like to deliver a message to his wife straight to camera and tell her she could see the full interview on *Olympic Grandstand* at a specific time? There was a little method in this madness. If he did this the BBC would have Bob Hope being used to plug one of their programmes. He jumped at the idea. Indeed he revelled in it. The assistant cameraman used his walkie-talkie back to base to ascertain what the starting time was for this special Opening Ceremony *Grandstand* and we turned the camera on Hope.

'OK,' he said. 'Roll 'em.'

We started the camera.

'Hi, Dolores,' he bubbled. 'How's London? Behaving yourself? Look at me. I'm being a good boy. I've taken out the garbage, haven't had the boys over for cards, kept out of the pool hall. I'll be behaving myself until you get back. Oh, and by the way. You can see all of this tonight on *Olympic Grandstand* starting just after twelve o'clock. Don't forget, watch *Olympic Grandstand* on BBC 1 tonight just after twelve. See you!'

Not once did he do it but twice to suit the sound man, for an aircraft had passed overhead the first time. I was now, ever so slightly, not believing this. At any moment, I thought, an agent is going to appear from behind the bunker on the green just ahead of us flourishing a contract as big as a mallet and I am going to be clobbered not just here but back at base too. Or else I was going to wake up. Was Bob Hope not only doing an interview for us but actually promoting a BBC programme? Well, yes he was! Not only that but he thanked us profusely for letting him talk to his wife and then strolled off back inside with that casual straight-backed grace that pled for someone to play in the background, 'Thanks For The Memory'.

There was no agent, no mention of money, no shocks but simply a star who had done a friend a favour which had been passed on to me. I blessed the day that I had met Jack Hennessy on the golf course at Gleneagles. All the same, it is never wise to think you are home and dry with these items until they actually hit the air and I was not to know that even though I returned to Hollywood Boulevard with the tape, guarding it like a gold ingot, there was trouble to come.

I deposited the tape with the assistant producer, who had accompanied me to Hope's house, having agreed the structure of the edit and the separation of the brief promotion. I then went off to have a look at some of the teams practising basketball at the Forum out beside Hollywood Park Racetrack and returned near midnight to view the final article. The large edit suite was virtually empty and there was only one video-tape editor left. She showed me what had been done to the Hope piece. Many of his quips had been left out and there was no sign of the plug for *Grandstand*. They had been dropped.

'Dropped!' I shouted. 'By whose instructions?'

As I went into ranting and raving mode, I could not get out of the poor girl the reason why it had been done. All that effort for a slack, unjustifiably brief edit. It struck me as the work of a very lazy man indeed, who simply wanted to get the job done and out of the way so he could get out for the night. I knew too that our main editors back in the office would not have known about that for it was late and, what made matters worse, it had been packaged and was sitting waiting there now to be transmitted on the first satellite time booked for early in the morning LA time back to London. It seemed beyond repair.

I went looking for blood but luckily, I suppose, did not find it, even though I scoured the bars near the hotel. The man in question could not be found. I had good reason to claim at least a tiny little scoop, against the rub of the green, as it were, and here it was now being thrown down the drain. I did not sleep much that night. I felt abused in a kind of way. I had gone after recognition for what I was capable of getting out there and now it was thrown almost in the trash can.

I was first up the next day in the hotel in Wilshire and waited for somebody to come downstairs, anybody, so I could tell my story. As luck would have it first down was Jim Reside, a fellow Scot who is a man for decision-making if ever there was one. He was in a senior position in charge of all production output from the television gallery in the complex.

'If I had to tell you that I have Bob Hope promoting *Grandstand* but that it's been dropped, along with other good bits from his full interview, on the package going back on the bird [*satellite*] what would you say?' I asked.

'Get in the car!' was all he replied.

Because of the time difference between LA and London, by the time we reached the studios we had only about half-an-hour to hit the afternoon *Grandstand* programme. The special Olympic Opening Ceremony edition was to start just after midnight. If we wanted Hope's message to Dolores, which was in effect a blatant plug for the later programme, to go out before the end of the afternoon edition we had somehow to get the original and unedited tape and send it out via the satellite, with precious little warning, to the editor in London. John Philips, the editor there, took it in his stride.

He was told by Reside what we were going to try to attempt and he passed on the message to Desmond Lynam, in front of camera, that a very late piece indeed might be arriving from LA. We searched and eventually found the tape as the hands of the clock began moving towards the end of the programme. Sending a piece by satellite requires precision co-ordination between the sender and receiver and everybody has to have their wits about them or else it could be a fiasco. We were not sure in sending the raw material unedited that it would not spill beyond the end of the programme and therefore be unusable.

In the UK *Grandstand*'s viewers were watching the very exciting final of the World Bowls Championships from Aberdeen. Exactly one minute from the end of the programme, the sweat pouring from me even in the air-conditioned production suite, I heard John Philips announce, 'We've got Hope! He's referring to *Olympic Grandstand*, Des. Lead us into it in about thirty seconds.'

Lynam, with only a moment's warning and barely thirty seconds remaining of the programme, picked it up beautifully. 'Well,' he said. 'I was going to mention what we had on tonight. But we bumped into somebody in Hollywood who can probably do it better than I can. I think you'll know him.'

Cut to Hope.

'Hi, Dolores . . .'

We had done it with seconds to spare.

I felt limp all day after that. The fight to get Hope on the air had seemed so unnecessary. That night in London, though, before they came live to the Olympic Stadium they transmitted the entire interview which was a dainty and appropriate morsel to set before the public prior to an event which was part-Olympic, part-Hollywood.

After that I had gained the confidence of the editorial minds in London and I found it easier to suggest items and to be given a unit to go out and create some colour. The day after the opening I went back to Lakeside where they produced a panel of Hollywood men associated with cinema who aired their views on how they thought the opening had been organised. Amongst them was Buddy Rogers, who had acted in the very first film to have won an Academy Award and who had married America's first sweetheart of the screen, Mary Pickford. He had that special attribute of many Californian men in their late seventies, he only looked twenty-six.

He represented a line stretching back to silent cinema and he gushed with pride in his country and its ability to still be the land of the free, unlike the Russians who had refused to come to LA as a reprisal for the Americans refusing to go to Moscow as a protest about the invasion of Afghanistan. On the theme of this merry-go-round of protest Jack Hennessy passed on a red, white and blue hat to me that day which Bob Hope had asked him to give me and which I still possess. It had a buttoned-down brim. When you snap it open the white lettering reads, 'F—— Russia!'

This crude political message from one of the popularisers of the American right simply suggested to me that it would not be a bad idea to record some Soviet press sentiments on these games. I tracked the Tass correspondent down to the huge press-centre in downtown LA and he graciously and in impeccable English told me how he regretted his nation hadn't come but that they could not have their safety guaranteed whilst here. Americans could not even guarantee their own safety. After all, just prior to the Games a man had walked into a McDonald's near San Diego and slaughtered over a dozen people for no apparent reason. It was difficult to reply to that. When I asked him if he was harassed he said he wasn't sure but couldn't care less and only worried about the appalling ignorance of even the American press who continually would ask him what time the curfew was in Moscow. When I took the recording back to base one English producer looked at it solemnly, then asked, 'What time is the curfew in Moscow anyway?'

I then began to mount interview after interview with sportsmen and women in a whole variety of sports although I obviously wanted to continue constructing 'colour' pieces in the sure knowledge that in the remorseless slog of the transmission of event after event, the viewer would like the relaxation of the off-beat report. Of course I would have loved to have been in the main stadium churning out athletic commentary. But the BBC just happens to have the strongest athletic commentating team in the world even though Coleman, Pickering and Storey and Foster were suffering in the immediate aftermath of the loss of the major athletics contract in the UK to ITV. At least I was being given the opportunity to lend a distinctive and personal imprint to these film reports and frankly I indulged to the utmost.

I took a Welsh weightlifter to the Universal Studios to try and re-enact a King Kong scene then placed him in the famous Gold's Gym down near Venice Beach. He had one look round the massive men pumping the iron and said in a voice of disdain from the valleys, 'Cream puffs!'

'What?' I asked.

'They're all poofs here. You can tell a mile away. I'd rather mix with King Kong, if you don't mind.'

Gay muscledom didn't look much different from any other kind of muscledom to me but I took his word for it.

We filmed on Santa Monica beach with British wrestlers and brought the LAPD down on our necks. A large crowd gathered to see us filming and the police came roaring in thinking there was a riot shaping on the sands. It turned out to be our version of the *Sands of Iwo Jima*. We went in on the quite unfashionable British hockey team to film them doing their laundry and other domestic chores, little realising they would turn out to be one of the hits of the Games.

Then I shared a bath with Terry Wogan.

In Hollywood we were always led to believe that the bizarre is merely the mundane. Isn't this the place, after all, where Groucho Marx once hired the entire Los Angeles Symphony Orchestra to come into his living room to play the 1812 Overture to annoy the neighbours upstairs because they had refused to allow him to join a quintet they had formed? That sort of thing. Nothing of such lunacy had we reflected but we wanted to. So I don't know that I can proudly proclaim that what happened with Wogan was a seminal incident in the history of broadcasting, but, to our mutual satisfaction, it was at least different.

It wasn't just your ordinary bath. It was a jacuzzi. That wasn't even ordinary either for it was in the back of a stretch-limousine. I am still unsure as to why Wogan and I actually ended up in it other than that we were easy prey to a streak of the absurd in the work we were doing.

There has been no radio broadcaster more skilled in developing the idiosyncrasies of individuals in his chat than Terry who could spin out a theme over a period of days which, because of the long periods of broadcasting he was committed to, was absolutely necessary for the programme. He had occasionally broadcast comments about me, on the times I passed the caravan he was broadcasting from, which were nippily dabbed with fun. So we decided to confront him on camera about his work and have a go ourselves. But as it was also his birthday, the radio lads had hired this extraordinary limousine with the jacuzzi for his delectation. It was too good to resist. We both went in. What I did not realise was that he was broadcasting live to the UK whilst I was filming him and the ribald comments that were being made must have spiced up a dreary night for some of the souls staying up to listen to his programme.

It was a duel of sorts. I was trying to get my words in before he could ask me questions. The bath bubbled, the crowd around us grew, photographers rushed from all parts. Was this what nymphettes did at Cannes for attention? Later that night, watching the tape with the pair of us sitting partially submerged in this foam, asking each other questions but giving no answers, I had the feeling that although we looked like a couple of cheap publicity-seeking wallies we had entered into the kindred spirit of Groucho. It was candy-floss broadcasting which all of us, perhaps reluctantly, admit we like in small doses.

We were now churning it out as the Games progressed but in truth not knowing what was hitting the screens back home and what wasn't. At first I deeply cared whether something was used or not but experience tells you simply to get it back to base and hope for the best. Although I had probably hit a jackpot getting Hope it had only been an interview after all. I needed another specially shaped item to convey something of Americana and of our reaction to it in this unique Olympic environment. As the Games went on it looked as if it would elude me. But there it was staring me in the face all this time and I couldn't see it. It was Bob Abrahams, the editor at base, who recognised it.

'Think it's about time you did something about baseball?' he asked one day.

Baseball was merely a demonstration sport but it was drawing capacity crowds to the Dodgers Stadium out near the Hollywood Bowl. The stadium is a man-made canyon with enough car-parking space to satisfy the entire human race, it would seem. The Dodgers of course used to belong to Brooklyn. Now they are on a hillside in LA. That sporting nomadism is pure distilled Americana in its own right, but I wanted to feel the popcorn culture myself and suck through a straw the mystique surrounding this American obsession.

So we took ourselves firstly to the press box where we sought an interpreter. He turned up in a rather coincidental manner. In short, he was the first man in the box I asked. I wanted him to sit with me in the crowd and simply talk me through the whole rigmarole as the cameras filmed us. As I spoke to him his features seemed familiar. I hate and detest asking anybody, particularly in LA of all places, 'Haven't I seen you somewhere before?' So I asked him, 'Haven't I seen you somewhere before?' rather than beat about the bush.

I was glad I did for he turned out to be the kind of man who just lived now for that very question to be asked. He had been the original television Mike Hammer in Mickey Spillane's detective series. I cast my mind back to flickery black and white video and visualised him perfectly beneath the brim of his hat. Now he had turned sports reporter to earn a living. From being a well-known, if B movie actor, to sports reporter could be construed as one of the worst forms of falling on hard times. He was small and had a voice that was pure Bronx, 'de boids and de bees' variety. Absolutely perfect. So off we trotted down into the crowd just behind first base.

We sat together and when they started to run the camera I acted the total innocent as he gave me the wholly incomprehensible jargon of the baseball aficionado. We took a shot of the scoreboard which was a jumble of statistics as digestible as computer hieroglyphics. It seemed to be going fine until I felt a tap on my shoulder. I turned to see a large lady wearing an Olympic stewardess's uniform standing over us.

'Excuse me, sir,' she said with emphasised politeness. 'Do you all have tickets for this PAR-TIC-ULAR area?'

As she had deliberately interrupted filming I was rather put out and showed it. I pointed to the Olympic accreditation card I was wearing which granted me access to every venue and explained to her what we were doing.

'But do you have tickets for this PAR-TIC-ULAR area? You need tickets for this PAR-TIC-ULAR area. These passes will not do here!' she repeated like an android, as I always thought many of these Olympic volunteers were anyway. Again, I tried to explain. She insisted though that we would have to move and since she was getting in the way of the camera there was nothing for it but to go. The crowd had been looking on at this stage with interest but no involvement. But we were determined to get our way. We waited until she had gone down a mid-stand tunnel and we crept back in again to the delight of some of the people around us and started up again. We were in the middle of the discourse when the voice boomed above us.

'I am sorry, sir. But I must ask you to leave!' It was her again. I pled with her. She stood her ground and by this time hundreds of people around us were now watching this scene rather than the baseball.

'If you don't go I will have to call the police!' she said.

That did it, the crowd began to respond.

'Hey, bud!' one large man behind me said. 'If you hold my popcorn I'll bop her one on the nose for you.'

I was now slightly regretting this. I didn't want a scene, but, on the other hand, I was angry about it. I was resigned to going when I saw her calling in three large policemen who started to wend their way through the crowd towards us. She said quite bluntly, 'That's them!'

It was just about then that a woman rose up a few seats from us and from the bottom of her heart gave us the founding fathers' stuff.

'What's going on here!' she shouted. 'I thought this was the land of the free not a police state. What did we fight the last war for? To watch some guys just doin' their jobs getting slung out the Dodgers Stadium?' There was a shout of assent and applause from the crowd who were now standing up in a multitude around us. The unknown lady seemed to be inspired by this response.

'These guys are our guests! They're Brits! They fought alongside us during the war! Have you bums ever heard of the London Blitz! These people suffered for our freedom and now they'll go back home thinking America's a dictatorship. You should be ashamed of yourselves, you bums!'

This brought the house down. People stood and cheered her to the echo. The police had one look at this response, took the stewardess by the elbow and just escorted her out of harm's way, then turned and saluted us with a quick snap of the elbow. The crowd responded to this too and well-wishers pushed forward to slap us on the back. Somebody stuck a baseball cap on my head and another gave me a bag of popcorn and, dressed as the All-American punter, I finished the item which we had started over an hour earlier with that piece of American pragmatic hokum 'If you can't beat 'em . . . join 'em'. The crowd rose to that sentiment and short of being given my green card there and then I had become at least a temporary American.

We took the tape back, edited it carefully to the rodeo music of Aaron Copland and the item was shown at least three times during the rest of the Games period.

I had been well down the Olympic cast. But at least I hadn't been left as a face on the cutting-room floor. LA had been good for me, which is why I looked at the *Los Angeles Herald*'s headline the morning after the final ceremony with some regret. It simply said, 'That's A Wrap!'

13

Face Value

Public identity has its mixed blessings. I tried not to take myself too seriously as a so-called television personality but it's honestly difficult to resist the temptation if, for the flimsiest of reasons, people do attribute to you some special status simply because of the electronic face popping up more regularly than the window-cleaner. The responses of course varied.

There were the threats. The first one I had on my life I took very seriously indeed. It was received with the gravity of some-one egotistical enough to imagine that people would actually waste valuable gunpowder on him. It came from a throaty gentleman with a glottal stop who sounded so convincing on the phone that it made the skin creep. 'Bomb you into f—— eternity' was the most poetic of the phrases used. I had apparently offended him in criticising Rangers, against whom he thought I was plotting. A Papish plot to boot, just to give it its proper roundness.

Late on a Saturday night, answering phone calls after the pro-gramme in the loneliness of the office could make a message from the Samaritans sound like a warning from the Mafia. Sometimes in a perverse way I enjoyed these calls for at least it made you aware that somebody out there was paying attention. The routine of the programme, especially if it went smoothly, could easily make you imagine that the only people privy to the broadcast were the handful in the studio and the production gallery. A little private soirée, in fact.

Of course death threats were greeted, rightly as it so happens, with a kind of 'Ho-hum' sort of attitude by even those nearest and dearest. On one occasion at the BBC, though, I received a large brown parcel which whilst not ticking, rattled. I was swooped upon by a large ex-military man of hawkish appearance from admin who proceeded to place the parcel in an empty office and to open it with longish tongs from behind the fortress of a standard BBC filing cabinet, thus confirming the British military's outstanding capacity for improvisation. The parcel contained a free sample of beer. We promised to keep this revelation to a minimum of sensible people but before hours had elapsed the building was agog with the stories of this unnecessary act of valour and the red faces which went with it. I remember actually vowing to risk obliteration in future rather than face the indignity of anti-climax.

There was an assumption even by those in the business that being the face on the screen made you the sort of property which might fall under the control of a Public Works Department, with access available to everyone except on Boxing Days and Easter Sundays.

Whilst it would be untrue to say that I did not occasionally wallow in the glow of public recognition I was, throughout, always tentative about it. I feared let-downs. An old lady on a train between Dundee and Stonehaven once paid me such glowing tributes I almost burst into tears of gratitude. It was only when she alighted in that north-eastern town and bade me good-bye that I realised she had mistaken me for Donny B. MacLeod. It was as if the Open Championship had been wrested from your grasp because you hadn't filled in the score-card correctly. A journalist entertained me to lunch and superbly engineered the loosening of the tongue by amongst other things offering his appreciation of all my talents and a week later produced an article of finely-honed ridicule.

I could never relax my apprehension of the imminence of back-lash. This was the indiscriminate aspect of my relationship with the public but there was another which needed more consider-ation, more care. I was frequently inundated with requests from charities for some sort of recognition or presence. This was very

189

difficult to cope with. You had to be very selective or else life would have become quite unbearable. On top of that there were the formal requests to speak to groups of one kind or another and I found this much more intriguing. It was then I realised that television was a useful passport to areas normally denied others.

I realised the appropriateness of what I had once taken to be a cravenly stupid and superior remark made to me by someone in administration when he said, 'I hope you realise that to be on the box is a privilege not to be abused.' In the sense that being on telly was something which had been worked on rather than bestowed on me as a favour, he was quite wrong. But in knowing that television can confer powers of entry that would undo the most ingenious Yale lock, he was absolutely right. I discovered the truth of it in the most telling ways.

In the mid-Seventies I was invited to visit that building which had so dominated my childhood skyline, Barlinnie Prison. The only reason given was that I was a 'well-known personality'. Intrigued, I accepted. After the numerous outer perimeter security checks I was taken through various inner-courtyard doors to what appeared to be a kind of temporary, detached structure that initially, and perhaps mistakenly, reminded me of Army barracks. A tall man in uniform with lots of keys on his person opened the door for me and closed it behind me. I was in the Special Unit.

I only knew vaguely about this Unit. I did know that it contained only murderers who were providing constant problems to the system. This was an attempt at rehabilitation. That is why I was so taken aback. I was in a bright, spacious room which had the strange impact of making me feel I was walking into a modern, open-ended primary school classroom. It had neither the trappings nor the stale stench of prison. About six men, mostly in shirts and jeans, were lounging around the room, casually engaged in reading or writing. The tension which I had felt entering the place contrasted with the rather indolent, sprawling scene in front of me. A slight figure with auburn hair approached me and gripped my hand in a firm, markedly positive handshake.

'Nice to see you. My name's Jimmy Boyle. Can I show you around?'

You cannot live in Glasgow without certain names ringing in the ears with the timbre of undiminished and constant threat. Boyle's name was once a monosyllabic obscenity. Even the police feared him. He had murdered and slashed and been seen as a hit man of classical iciness. At that very instant, grasping the hand, looking at the benign face but hearing the name, I realised the huge problem facing Boyle, his companions and the Unit. Not even an enlightened penal system can live down reputations. As one respected crime reporter said to me on my return after describing my visit, 'That man will never change. He's a beast and he always will be! He shouldn't be allowed out.' I somehow felt listening to him that he was almost disappointed in Boyle's transformation, as if the prisoner was on the verge of leaving a club to which both belonged. The apostate from the razor showed me through the cells.

I cannot imagine anybody who stumbled accidentally on Gauguin's work on his Polynesian island could have been more stunned than I was in walking into Boyle's cell. It glowed in a profusion of colour. Paintings, murals, and sculptures were cramped into the relatively tiny space like a secret hoard of art. Boyle himself explained his work to me although, in all honesty, by this time, even if Vasari had materialised through the walls to offer analysis, I could not have taken anything in. I felt quite overwhelmed by this.

No cell door was shut and the half-a-dozen inmates and the prison officers mixed communally in the central area. Eventually they sat in a semi-circle around me and I talked about broadcasting and sport. There was no doubting who was the dominant personality in this unconventional arrangement. Boyle was the paterfamilias of the entire establishment including, from where I was observing, the prison officers, who were not slow to recognise what he had to say. When he interrupted me to say it was time for a tea-break an officer upped and put the kettle on and then passed round the cups.

I wondered there and then whether the strength of this experiment was based on Boyle's own vivid personality, or whether rehabilitation entailed a kind of role reversal or whether, despite all their back-up, the officers could not forget he was the violent man with a murderous reputation the Krays would have been proud of. The fact that the Unit is still vigorously in existence would answer some of these views but in terms of its reputation at that time the Special Unit was The House That Jimmy Built.

He overshadowed even Larry Winters, who achieved post-humous fame through the film they made about him, *Silent Scream*. I remember Winters from that visit as a quiet, softish-looking man, gently asking intelligent questions about television, but only when it seemed Boyle was not wishing to hold the floor. The evening wore on until Boyle announced that it was getting close to lights out. He made a little decorous speech of thanks to me and invited me back some time. I left deeply impressed. However, when I made it clear to friends and colleagues I would do everything in my power to publicise what was going on there and give the whole concept any support I could I was met largely with cynicism.

They felt it was a bit of a showcase, a gratuitous attempt to appease those who wanted some modernisation of the penal system and that those men were beyond rehabilitation anyway. Perhaps I got a bit carried away but since they had shown a great knowledge of sport and of watching television I suggested that in the spirit of the whole experimentation we could mount some broadcast from there. This would demonstrate the Unit's usefulness by recognising what was going on in a revolutionary way. The idea was squashed very quickly. Nobody wanted anything to do with this. If Barlinnie wanted to play around with murderers and give them clay and tubes with oil-paint to toy with then let them get on with it. It had nothing to do with real life.

Wherever I could I drummed out the message of the Special Unit. I went back twice, once to talk, once to see their art exhibition which of course was dominated by Boyle. On that occasion he seemed more moody, withdrawn and slightly testy. This wasn't surprising. They were now becoming slightly freakish and being constantly gawped at as an exotic species kept in a special tank. I had, however, become a sort of unofficial spokesman for them. I ran into constant flak about this. 'You're being conned, hood-winked by them!' one ex-crime journalist asserted to me one day. He then proceeded to tell me in detail what Boyle is reputed to have done to his victims and I found myself visualising the face again and felt again the firmness of the press of flesh of his handshake.

But the grisly description did not fit the reality of the present and I would not budge. 'If he gets out, he'll do it all over again,' my colleague assured me. 'You can't cure these people.' But I continued to speak up in support of this experimentation. Boyle was released from the prison system on 1 November, 1982. I cannot claim to have directly helped in this, as other journalists close to him did, but at least I had added a new element of support which could have done no harm. The last time I talked to him was in Carnaby Street in London some five years later, when he was trawling through the shops like any other tourist. He seemed at ease although, perhaps through my own experience of meeting him inside, I felt he was a man who would forever now be constantly on guard against the world, not the other way round.

When Larry Winters died of a drugs overdose in the unit on 11 September, 1977 people rushed to tell me, 'I told you so!' All I felt was pity for the man, not disillusionment. I was constantly asked how I felt about the families of their victims. I didn't really have an answer to that. All I knew was that I hoped men would come through this experience successfully and that there could be nothing intrinsically wrong with any civilising process.

I have never been one for deliberately collecting memorabilia. Some things of course just simply cling. Others you stumble over in the course of moving house or cleaning out an old drawer. I have even infuriated my family by coming back from major events without a single photograph taken. I prefer the mind's eye. But one article I did preserve. It was a Christmas card. It was signed by five murderers. They had designed it themselves in the Unit. The script lettering of greetings was impeccable. But on the front of the large card was the delicate painting of a vase full of flowers, reaching appropriately for the sun.

I became quite obdurate about wanting to be of use to some cause even though the reasons for any celebrity I had were flimsy. In the earlier part of the year of Winters' death I welcomed an invitation which came to my office to visit the State Hospital at Carstairs, which houses some of the most vicious of murderers and the criminally insane, and to which it is said some people wished to send Jimmy Boyle in the first place. I was shown around by a large man with a gentle disposition, the Chief Male Nurse, a Mr Oswald, and one of his assistants, Neil McLelland. This hospital, it has to be said, has a permanent chill to it for an outsider, even on a gentle spring day, which it was then. You cannot avoid this feeling as a newcomer. I put it down then to prejudice and wished to rid myself of it but it was hard going. It was clear they wished to demonstrate to me that within the obvious constraints of security the place was not all that bad, indeed in many respects quite normal. That was hard going to accept also, but I was trying.

A month later a deputation came to the BBC with a proposal that I head an 'outsiders' committee to attempt to dispel the fear and dread the place instilled in society, by helping to arrange more public visitations, particularly from well-known personalities, to speak to selected patients and nurses. I felt that I might in fact be doing something useful here, proving my worth to society rather than just identifying footballers. I leaped at it enthusiastically.

To establish the scheme my wife and myself were invited to their sports day to present prizes that summer of 1977. The nurses did not seem put out too much when I asked when I arrived why there were no javelin or pole vault events. Some of the patients liked the quip too. Although there was quite clearly careful supervision, such was the informality, and the lack of official uniforming, that it was almost impossible to say who was nurse and who was patient. The sheer normality of the place was perhaps the most off-putting aspect of all. I was firstly introduced to a handsome, dark-haired lady whom I took to be a nursing-matron of sorts and who explained the day's events to me.

She had in fact killed her months-old baby by pushing it down the lavatory pan. I talked to a short gentleman called Ian Simpson who was charming and intelligent, on the assumption that he was on the psychiatric staff. I was told later he was the man who had killed a couple of foreign tourists in Loch Lomondside, buried them, travelled to England, come across a serious road accident, turned his collar round to pretend he was a priest and acted out the last rites to the victims.

I found myself playing out this game of hide and seek. Who were the patients? What had they done? They were our viewers after all. They certainly shared that with the outside world. By the end of the afternoon I had been totally sold on the current hospital philosophy which was, within reason, to allow the world into this place and to lower those unnecessary barriers.

In November of that year, on St Andrew's Day, as I was in the process of establishing names and events that might fit into a visitation calendar two inmates called Robert Moan and Thomas McCulloch, armed with axes, made an escape from Carstairs. Ian Simpson tried to stop them. They chopped off his head. Neil McLelland, the nursing officer I had befriended, got in their way and was bludgeoned to death. Outside they were challenged by a local policeman. They brutally murdered him. Carstairs in a few short hours had gone beyond the pale again.

I felt quite ill on hearing this. I had trumpeted the ways of this enlightened regime led by Oswald. Now I felt like some dilettante do-gooder made to look extremely naive. A decent, honourable attempt to bridge the gap between the abnormal and its onlookers had failed. To have uttered any justification, immediately afterwards, for what the nursing staff had tried to achieve with the likes of myself would have sounded like a bleat in a storm. However humane you wish to be you don't let the criminally insane get their hands on axes, full stop, end of argument. Perhaps, I thought at the time, I should stick to opening garden fêtes or church bazaars. Sometimes they paid you for doing such.

Thoughts of all that came chillingly back when I sat aloft, in the eyrie called the Hampden Park commentary area, in 1980 watching the battle ebbing and flowing underneath me, bottles flying through the air, and men and children being felled. I learned later of a friend and press-photographer colleague Eric Craig ending

195

up with brain surgery in Killearn Hospital after being hit by a missile from a supporter. And all because Celtic had beaten Rangers in a Scottish Cup Final. I recalled the Carstairs killings and wondered about the precarious quality of the emotions. Why should we be so smug and secure, us, on this side of the security fence. This reflection gave my description of the clashes on the pitch a touch of bitterness and disgust.

Indeed a colleague, producer Nevin McGhee, said afterwards to me, quite fairly and accurately, that I had described the riot on the park better than the game itself. A *Scotsman* newspaper editorial picked up my words on the Monday morning, little knowing the memory which the riot had sparked off.

As time progressed I grew more cautious as to when and how I would take the 'telly' face into public view. But you could not always insulate yourself. After the heavy 5–1 defeat by England at Wembley in 1975 I was sitting with some rather affluent friends in a huge limousine in the insufferably congested car park outside the ground when some Scottish supporters spotted me. Linking me to the black, shiny car, to some cigars glowing in the interior and to a uniformed chauffeur they jumped to a rather surprising conclusion.

'It's the SFA!' someone screamed and we were immediately surrounded by as genteel a bunch as put paid to General Gordon at Khartoum. They began to rock the limousine whilst screaming for their money back, having wasted it coming all that way to watch such crap, and that us lot wouldn't be sleeping in the corridor of the train on the way back home like them and were we not ashamed of ourselves? They lifted the car up until we were spilling across the interior like the earliest upset in the *Poseidon Adventure*. I tried to tell them that Ernie Walker had already left and that my friends were English, although that might not have helped. We were rescued by the police who suddenly swooped out of nowhere. I was left with some friends vowing never to go again to a Scotland game with the man with the recognisable face. I would have disembowelled myself for anonymity there and then.

Or would I? In the darker moments this is what I would have preferred. But recognition did mean something. Very few of the human race would not want to be singled out from the mass but the television ego is sometimes hyper-active, hoping that upon your entry heads will turn. It doesn't matter all that much if it is done admiringly so long as it happens. With it comes the feeling, despite your rational self trying to deny so, that you could not possibly face the day when even your next door neighbour wouldn't know you from Adam.

At one stage in my career when I was interested in moving behind the camera into production I applied for a job on BBC staff which would have put an end to television appearances. It was only when I was about seven-eighths of the way through the process that I had one of those cold sweats that Jimmy Clark had talked about, not over the precariousness of my current role as presenter but at its total disappearance, at my own volition. I was preparing to kill myself off, I concluded.

Whilst a significant section of the population would not have been prepared to stand in my way it is something I realised inwardly I could not face up to. I didn't do it. I knew it was illogical to let this electronic alter ego be so possessive but only ten years into the business I had no fears that it could be my very own Dorian Gray. Television immortality is a very seductive notion. We are in the business to stay there and dig ourselves in, without too much difficulty, I thought at the time. And anonymity is simply over the trenches in no-man's land where you're sure to meet a sticky end. No more trying to charge out if you have any sense.

There was very little tranquil socialising indeed. Virtually always the subject of television, my own role, something I had said or opined on would be brought up by complete strangers butting into my life, sometimes viciously. At first the technique I employed was simply to take it all with a benign smile on the face, for after all this was an occupational hazard, was it not? However, tiring of having to listen at times to lengthy harangues, I decided to be more positive rather than being a passive target.

This consisted of slightly narrowing the eyes, stepping nearer the critic and in a voice something like Jack Palance's as he stood in front of the saloon in *Shane* saying menacingly, 'What was that you said?' This had a variety of effects ranging from those who could have been no more dumbfounded had I unzipped my fly in front of them, to those who simply stepped even further forward and repeated what they had said in a louder voice. But it either halted in their tracks those who wished to bombard me or at least truncated the vitriol. People generally did not like 'the face' answering back.

Whilst I had always wanted to 'switch' identity occasionally and enter into other fields of broadcasting I was finding it difficult. You are easily typecast. 'Why is a football commentator wanting to move into current affairs?', or 'You want to interview people outside sport? Really? How pretentious!' That generally was the attitude I faced. I suppose to some it seemed like the clown-wanting-to-play-Hamlet syndrome so normally any venture on my part in that kind of direction was greeted with polite bemused rejection. One producer though, David Martin, was prepared to back me in a series of celebrity interviews for a programme called *Three's Company* in which I would chat to two famous people who had something or other in common.

I found this plain sailing despite my own fears of coming a cropper on it. Two occasions stick out. The first was when Andrew Neil, the editor of the *Sunday Times*, and John Junor, then the editor of the *Sunday Express*, crossed swords. Before the pro-gramme it had become clear that Junor disliked Neil. Indeed he had told our researcher that he found Neil to be something of a young upstart. And he treated him like that, in the dressing-room area before the recording and during the programme. Neil was talking about death threats to himself on the air and Junor inter-jected with an acerbic, 'Who would want to kill *you*?' The under-currents of antagonism surfaced, producing a very articulate slanging match.

I was inundated with letters congratulating me for this great piece of television. But really it was easy television. All I had done was act as a kind of referee who wanted to encourage this clash. Compared to what I had to do in my own sports area which more often than not entailed trying to draw water from stone this was like stumbling on a new oil well. Similarly, when I had poor Terry Waite and Jean Waddell, the Tehran nurse, together, all I had to do was sit admiringly as they nestled into a discussion about hostages and solitary confinement. All I did was nudge occasionally. Yet again, letters came to me expressing admiration for how sensitively I had handled this. What disappointed me about that particular interview was that I could not get the other side of Terry's character revealed. Far from being the gentle giant, he took over the company, in the Ubiquitous Chip restaurant afterwards, downed large whiskies with great finesse, hardly stopped talking about his views on life and emerged as a very tough personality indeed. This was clearly a man of great steel.

To receive anything remotely like praise for a programme was, however, something of a unique experience for me, coming from a region of controversy and ingrained footballing hatreds. I had hoped for a more permanent route into this sort of work but circumstances dictated otherwise. Television itself could also mock that rather vacuous abstraction, the 'television personality'. A producer asked me if I wouldn't mind taking part in a kind of self-deprecatory meeting with a Scottish punter which might illustrate and confirm at long last the transience of the influence of television on the average man in the street. This great sociological study was to take place in a programme called *Scotch and Wry* and the punter was to be Rikki Fulton.

Fulton is a solemn man. I swear it. At least he is when I'm around. He was even more solemn after he attempted his sketch with me. To watch him come alive at a rehearsal was like watching a body suddenly possessed by a comic genie. The lines of script were his very soul. The problem was that I very rarely worked with specific scripts on television. Much of my work was now in the outside-broadcast area, which lent itself to the spontaneity I loved. It was not that I intended to make a Feste the Clown from a short sketch but I thought I would enter into what I assumed would be the spirit of the occasion and throw in an unscripted line or two in response to Rikki's slightly inebriated man, fascinated by thinking he recognised the face from the box. He was to stumble up to me and tell me what a great fan he was of mine but, like the old lady on the train in Stonehaven, it was to be a case of mistaken identity.

'It is you, isn't it? Tell me, it is you, isn't it?' he said tottering towards me with that glazed look of punter wonderment I had seen so often come over the faces of those in awe of the person from the screen. I can't now remember my line but I managed it, with an embellishment. I added another line. You can perhaps visualise Rikki's face freezing into immobility, his jaw slightly hanging, his eyes in doleful bewilderment. No face can do it like Rikki's face. I was reminded there and then of those physiognomic sculptures when he played the Scottish version of Molière's *The Miser*, which gave the impression that Rikki's face even when asleep was a comic masterpiece. He had stopped. I thought this was part of the sketch and waited for him to continue. He just stood there gazing. The producer, Gordon Menzies, wandered in.

'Where did that line come from?' he asked politely.

'I made it up,' I replied like a schoolboy caught saying a naughty word.

'Made it up? Made it up?' When a man says a thing like that twice it spells reprimand. Rikki was still silent yet his immobile, puzzled but eloquent face was saying clearly and distinctly, 'Who is this eejit we've got here?'

'I think we should stick to the script,' Menzies said. 'Let's try it again.'

I suddenly realised I was not in a sketch with a comedian simply limbering up but with a comedy actor precisely honing his perform-ance, however brief this interlude with me was to be. This was acting by a man who would be indulging in something like fifteen different sketches in the space of an hour, so there could be no fooling around. This was serious business. Came the night. I was more nervous than I ought to have been but then I didn't like sticking to scripts. My whole body was telling me that. I also knew I was going on to record perhaps the most popular light entertainment programme that BBC Scotland had ever produced. As Gus Macdonald of Scottish Television said of it, 'The only way we could beat *Scotch and Wry* in the ratings was if we could persuade Rangers and Celtic to play a game live against it.'

We went on in front of the studio audience. Up came the party scene with Rikki stumbling on across the floor towards me as the inebriated reveller spotting his favourite television personality.

'It is you, isn't it? Tell me, it is you, isn't it?'

It wasn't impish. It wasn't that I wanted deliberately to introduce the buggeration factor. But it just came. I did it again. I threw in an impromptu response, a one-liner that came from off the top of the head in the way I had been used to adding words with Des Lynam or Bob Wilson. In a display of superb professionalism Rikki allowed himself only a fleeting second of being thunderstruck. For one moment I thought he was going to call everything to a halt or that the producer would run on the set and change the party scene into a public mugging. But he was playing a stumbling drunk anyway which helped him to cover up the little hiatus that followed my additional words. But only he and I and the producer in the gallery would have noticed the stumble, the bewilderment. Beneath Rikki's Hogmanay mask was a professional staring contemptuously at a ham. The punch-line in the sketch of course was that he thought I was Bamber Gascoigne!

In his acceptance speech for his Award as Television Personality of the Year he gave me a tongue in the cheek scolding for my love of the impromptu. At least I think it was tongue in cheek. But for years afterwards that sketch simply would not go away. *Scotch and Wry* sold the biggest number of video recordings around the world for the BBC that year. In Toronto airport a Canadian customs officer of Scottish origin looked at me and said, 'It is you, isn't it? Tell me, it's you, isn't it?' In Sheffield a worker on a building site shouted the same after me. In London a taxi driver smiled and said 'Hi, Bamber!' On his very first meeting with me Jonathan Powell, Controller BBC 1, said, 'It is you, isn't it?' Little boys in the street were shouting it after me. I had been reduced to a catch phrase. It was as if Rikki was getting his revenge.

That little sketch I suppose summed up the recurring dilemma of the face on the box. It gives only clues to real identity and nothing much more. I had the good fortune to let that superficiality work sometimes to my advantage by simply intriguing people into opening doors for me. Sometimes it worked positively against me. They say of the fat man that there is a thin man inside fighting to get out, so with people constantly in front of the camera there is the struggle to emerge into the light three-dimensionally and not to be summed up merely as a figment of the horizontal and vertical holds. But we cannot ever escape from the figure of our own making and the tantalising notion that our existence, our very being, is wholly dependent on the living room and someone's hand on the switch.

14

Taking Risks

The eruption from Alex Ferguson came suddenly, without warning. He was in the main passageway at Easter Road when he launched into a tirade against me for something I had said about his goalkeeper. I cannot remember what it was I had said, nor did it seem important even then, for the row wandered up other alleys into quite lurid personal abuse as if we had forgotten what it was all about in the first place. However, I think I would have preferred to have been sued for every penny I owned, for whatever view I had expressed, rather than to have stood with the spittle of rage flecking our two faces. This was just before he left to go south in 1986. I had been very friendly with Ferguson, often publicly expressing my admiration for his talents. We seemed to get on well together and I remember distinctly being the first journalist to reach him on the pitch in Gothenburg where, both of us slicked with rain, we hugged. Now this.

In a sense the actual incident was less important than the warning it contained. In the business of expressing views you lay minefields of your own which remain quite uncharted. You feel as if you are striding through life comfortably, then bang!

I had staunchly defended him against some criticism which he inevitably sustained during and after the Mexico World Cup in 1986. It had been an anti-climax in all sorts of ways, not least of which was the absence of Stein. Ferguson was in a temporary position with other ambitions in mind. Ernie Walker, not surprisingly, was missing the man who had become his close friend. On the evidence of what I saw there was no gelling of the two. On one occasion Walker banned all television units from the Scottish team hotel. Ferguson got round that by simply coming outside the gates to talk to us in outright defiance of the secretary.

The Aberdeen manager had already proved he was of independent mind in his successful club role and could not take kindly to being tied to anybody's petticoats. He knew that the Scottish team manager's job was a thankless task. Stein described it once to me quite simply as 'impossible' and only took it the second time round, after his temporary flirtation with it in the Sixties, because it was a route back to Scotland. Living up to the wildly inflated expectations of the public was hard enough in its own way but when you are reliant on a chain of contacts with clubs throughout the UK you can very often dangle hopelessly with the same chain round your neck. Ferguson realised that very well. Stein had jealously guarded his own authority as manager which meant that he did not really tap the tactical genius of Jim McLean, as he should have, when he was assistant. Ferguson wanted, and achieved, more of a say. But he had no desire to take the job permanently.

Scotland's three games in the competition were stupendously ordinary and whilst there was much controversy over whether Souness should have been picked for the last one, against Uruguay, it was a simple case of many people being wise after the event in my view. For up in the steamy hot city of Queretaro against West Germany, in his last ever game for his country, Souness's legs seemed to go.

That particular afternoon contained so many of the ingredients of anti-climax to which I had now become accustomed that I remember it mostly for having to keep Pierre Littbarski, the German player, and Gordon Strachan company for a couple of hours with a camera unit after the game whilst they waited for their natural juices to gather so they could pee and present a sample for drug-testing because our editor, news-wise, hoped one of them would fail it. We had to stay there all night if necessary, until it happened. It says much for the deflated and tedious mood of the evening that the sound of one of them eventually passing urine into a flask elated us as much as if we had heard a fruit-machine ejaculating in Vegas.

The lesson though I had learned from my relationship with Ferguson was that you never take friendships too far in football for one day there might be the unexpected reckoning. Managers of course do wish to intimidate from time to time. It is as much part of their apparel as their padded sports jackets. That is why we all wondered how this entirely new man, Andy Roxburgh, would perform both as manager of a side and in the handling of his relationships with us. He proved articulate and friendly except on one occasion when obviously highly strung before a game with England at Hampden he accused me of trying to wreck a training session at Girvan because I had arrived with the English commentator Barry Davies whom Roxburgh thought would be on a spying mission for Bobby Robson. This unlikely interpretation of our presence came from a man experiencing a new form of pressure; a man employed to bring a fresh approach to the job. But the protest from him that particular morning sounded depressingly familiar.

Between the two World Cups of Mexico in 1986 and Italy in 1990 broadcasting was taking on a new look for me and life began to get stormier. We had decided to take the presentation of *Sportscene* to the actual outside broadcast itself; that is, to introduce the programme from the pitch or the commentary platform, either before the game or immediately afterwards. This meant recording it. The advantages were as obvious as the disadvantages. In the first place, an introduction with the crowd in the background and the teams coming on to the pitch gave the programme a look of immediacy and urgency, thus eliminating the need for a bland studio introduction. The very first programme we recorded this way was at Celtic Park, which happens to have one of the best commentary positions in the country, for you can swing a camera round easily to have the platform in vision itself.

Consequently it looked good especially at the start of the season in the fine light. Ibrox, where the existing commentary position is too low to allow the proper panoramic view of the pitch and does less than justice to the magnificent stadium, is nevertheless spectacular when you turn a camera on anybody presenting from the platform. Aberdeen was fine too, others were passable. The visual possibilities and the pitching of *Sportscene* into the midst of the action pushed the programme into new territory. This meant I both presented the programme, commentated and also contrived to summarise the Scottish results for one minute straight to camera for the network audience on *Grandstand* immediately after the game, and I mean immediately.

I had no knowledge of the news from the other Scottish games for obvious reasons but the system was that somebody back in the office would phone me with a summary. I would take quick notes, the camera would swing round to me and, once in position, Des Lynam would introduce me. Very often I would be told to truncate the report to either 45 seconds or even half-a-minute, on the spot. This was only about five minutes after I had stopped commentary. I would then rush down to the press conference to find out if anything useful was being said and then beat a quick retreat back to the presentation area again. The recording would then take place, but not in an untrammelled way.

We had a specific deadline of six o'clock. Given all that I had to do before it, it was often after half-past-five before I was in a position to start thinking of an impromptu script. But there were to be no concessions. It had to be done by six o'clock, or else. I am not sure precisely what 'or else' meant for although we over-ran by a few seconds on several occasions we always managed our recording, even if there were frequent slips. If there is one thing I have always loathed doing, it is recording pieces to camera. I would rather go 'live' in a howling gale, or amidst enemy fire than record. Somehow there is always what my late and dear colleague Donny MacLeod called 'that impish little voice' telling you not to worry and that if you don't get it right first time, you can always do it again. If it does talk to you then it can be fatal. Not only did it talk to me during that period it almost became a chatterbox.

Coming on top of finishing a commentary which completely absorbs the mind, rushing to get material for network information, obtaining statements or interviews from managers, receiving news to record for the late programme and then standing in front of a camera with men standing behind it looking at their watches and ready to pull the plug at six o'clock, the voice frequently told me, 'Sorry, pal! You're not going to make it tonight!'

So occasionally it was a struggle. But the disadvantages were not just personal but affected the programme as a whole as well. Firstly, if you record something at six o'clock at night and do not transmit it until about ten o'clock you may miss some very dramatic news. The worst instance of this was a Saturday in May 1985 when, on a lovely spring afternoon after a game to match, and with the season about to finish anyway, in a kind of end-of-term buoyancy I introduced the programme by saying how wonderful it was to have seen such a fine game of football and how everything was coming up roses, or words to that effect. It was bright and effervescent. That night, the national news which almost invariably came before *Sportscene*, ended its transmission with the most horrific football stadium pictures ever recorded. People rushed from the flames of the Bradford City grandstand and a solitary man passed across the scene like a walking inferno. I followed on immediately after that looking and sounding as if the world had just had one of its most tranquil days ever. We simply had had no knowledge of this disaster when we had put everything on tape at half-past-five that afternoon. There was nothing we could do about it. Not only did I look and sound extremely foolish, but grossly insensitive as well.

It might have been gratifying to think of the revamping of *Sportscene* as specifically geared to utilising my abilities in those various areas. But that of course would be quite inaccurate. It did have its intrinsic value but it was also very much a cost-cutting exercise. It eliminated the need to use a studio on late Saturday evenings and by shutting up the sports shop at six o'clock it also excluded the need to go into weekend extra payments. When an attempt at savings was perhaps the prime purpose you can hardly feel comfortable in your own mind that, in fact, it is the best thing for yourself. It clearly wasn't. Yet, I suppose doing everything in the programme appealed to the ego which, when you are so much up front, prefers great exposure to common sense. This one man band exercise had its severe drawbacks especially in our climate.

One late winter's afternoon at Tannadice my jaw simply froze. It went beyond central command. I was ceasing to function. It was difficult enough to speak at all that day let alone impart information to the public. A correspondent actually wrote to the *Glasgow Herald* asking for someone to take mercy on me as my red nose and general Worzel Gummidge appearance by late on a winter's afternoon drove him to charitable thoughts about me which normally he was reluctant to feel. I think he was suggesting some sort of mercy killing. Although the sting in the tail of his letter was to note how skimpy the Beeb were to handle their programmes that way. It was becoming clear that the occasions on which it could be said this system worked were being outnumbered by those when it clearly did not.

We were now of course well into the Thatcher days by the mid-Eighties. We were in the era of value for money studies and, as it so happens, while the BBC was being sifted through by the experts so another institution was being examined in exactly the same way and I enjoyed the unique position of being part of both of them at the one time. In 1985 I became Rector of the University of Edinburgh.

I am not sure if BBC Scotland realised that new dimension I had taken on for in the entire three years I was in office nobody there ever mentioned the fact to me. My colleagues from London certainly did and on one occasion would have liked to set me against the campus in a football story they planned with Johnny Haynes, who was then domiciled in the capital. I thought the better of it and kept the role at a distance from broadcasting.

The other candidates in the election were Margo MacDonald, the ex-SNP MP, Teddy Taylor MP, and Richard Demarco. I had also been told to prepare for student apathy on the matter of the Rectorship, so with mixed feelings I turned up for the first public meeting at Pollock Halls of Residence. It was mobbed. For one moment I thought I would be too scared to say anything at all. If Margo enjoyed my being in the contest she certainly camouflaged it well, for in the entire campaign she spoke but a few words to me and, at times, I thought her attitude came across too obviously as disdain. She certainly did not look happy even though I certainly had done her no harm as far as I could make out. One of my supporters had a theory.

'She thinks you're an amateur, you see,' he said, this lad who is probably now a leading light in industry. 'Perhaps it's beneath her to be competing against the likes of yourself.'

If that's what Margo actually did think then she was not far wrong. I was an amateur but if she only knew at the time, her uncommunicative attitude towards me actually gave me a bigger incentive to get through this thing well than probably any other factor. Indeed a local newspaper, rooting for her, deplored my presence and in advocating her qualities wrote, 'The nearest Archie Macpherson has been to academia has been in watching Hamilton Academicals.' One of my students studying law advised me that this could be libellous but having had worse things said about me in the media I thought I would try to turn the comment on its head. In my first speeches I regularly referred to the fact that a single afternoon watching Hamilton Academicals told you more about the human condition than a term studying Sigmund Freud. What were the problems of the Rat Man compared to an Accies supporter?

Moving from meeting to meeting taught me a lot too about the student condition. Some were friendly, some hostile, some inquisitorial. I turned up to speak to the Labour Group for what I thought would be a cosy evening amongst people from my own tradition, but I was grilled. A small woman, a mature student, took out a piece of paper when question time came up. Hers was: 'Can you tell me your views on the following: Abortion, possession of nuclear weapons, the armed struggle of ANC, student grants, siting of nuclear bases in Scotland and devolution?'

And she proceeded to tick off every reply as I tried to wade my way through it all as if she was giving me marks. I had the tremor of a D minus in my voice.

Then came the most dramatic interjection of the entire election. It came from a demure young lady with a tongue obviously dipped in vitriol.

'Can you tell me if you are, or have ever been, a member of the Orange Order?' she asked without blinking.

'I beg your pardon?' was all I could bring myself to reply. She repeated it. I looked round this austere room and every face groomed in conscientious socialism was now looking for an answer. They were taking this seriously. Should I?

'I cannot believe you are asking me that question seriously,' I said. 'Can't we discuss something that has some relevance rather than this fantasy!'

'Answer, yes or no!' the demure young lady insisted.

'I came into this University in the hope of taking part in serious discussions about education. Now you're making preposterous suggestions.'

'Answer, yes or no!'

I refused to be coerced by her so the meeting broke up in some disarray with the chairman, a nice lad from Glasgow, trying to thank me for my presence although I was making for the exit mentally noting not to go wooing the Labour group again. Afterwards my supporters, offering no shred of evidence by the way, suggested this was a rumour being put about by Margo's supporters. They smelled skulduggery. Whatever or whoever it was, it didn't work.

I won the election . . . and three days later I chaired the University Court.

I found that the next three years added a discipline to my life that was in stark contrast to the freelance television journalist's existence of hopping from one assignment to the other. It had come at the onset of difficult times for universities which were being assailed by government to make swingeing cuts in expenditure. The Jarratt Report, like the Peat Marwick study of broadcasting, investigated the University of Edinburgh and the entire UK university system to find out how cost effective the institutions were.

My sympathies lay with those people who perceived a university education as that which helped open the mind, exercised the imagination, encouraged value judgements and, quite simply, prepared you for living. The change of emphasis, enforced from the very top of government, to balancing the books and converting the university into something like a training college which would help you get a job with ICI or GEC or whoever, no matter how important that is, was a negation of much that Edinburgh had represented as a distinguished seat of learning. The whole nature of the humanities-based university seemed under threat. It is not that savings could not be made, but that the enforced cuts were, by necessity, quite brutal.

As I chaired the University Court, listening to the repeated gloom of the Principal Sir John Burnett reciting the harsh facts of life to the professors gathered round him, under the magisterial gaze of the Raeburn portraits surrounding the room, I could not help but think that hardly anybody outside the four walls would hear all of this. The public are noticeably deaf about education as a subject until it hits them in some direct way, and that is very seldom. Carnage was going on, blood was flowing yet the crisis repeatedly seemed to be contained in an exclusive debating chamber. Protests were made of course. I took part in demonstrations, helped out during the lecturers' strike, half-way through my period of office, spoke all over the UK and in North America to try to encourage fund-raising activities. Unless people had prior experience of the university system, however, you felt that provoking widespread concern would be as easy as encouraging the Cabinet of the day to fund the expansion of Greek as a subject.

The public of course were interested in the broadcasting licensing fee, always. It was perpetually cast up to me that the public's money was being wasted or frittered away or misused. Money is misused or wasted or frittered away at some time or other in all sorts of public and private businesses and it would be preposterous to imagine otherwise. All the same, in my own sphere of sport, we were not unduly influenced by the occasional hysterical outbursts against BBC overspending. In Seoul there was an attempt to embarrass the Corporation over the accommodation it had picked for the troops.

When you walked into our hotel you might have been led to believe that extravagance was the norm for us. It was a truly splendid establishment which I think probably led to a shortage of marble in the Korean countryside. At a reception for the media there some of the press from more modest lodgings, eyes goggling, saw a news story. They sniffed. One smoothie who, to my utter astonishment was briefly employed by the BBC a year or so later, quizzed me at some length about what sort of rooms we had, what they all cost and whether penthouses were involved. Even as you dodge and evade questions or answer them honestly you realise the story is going to be written quite independently of the truth. And so it was duly splashed back in London.

There were lurid tales about sumptuous living off the licence fee, the apotheosis of which was that Coleman had a suite to

himself with butler. Leaving aside the fact that Coleman didn't
need a butler, with the help he had on hand in the BBC, what they
had studiously ignored was the expense of all this. The executive
producer Martin Hopkins had negotiated a discount deal with the
hotel right at the outset, and at a favourable exchange rate, which
led to one of the most reasonable arrangements ever made for a
huge broadcasting party abroad. But we were an easy and convenient target.

We knew we were now in the middle of fundamental changes
in the broadcasting world. Satellite had arrived and, whilst there
was a general feeling amongst my colleagues in sport that it would
never succeed, many talented people in the Corporation and ITV
moved off to join them. Money was being splashed around as
if the tiny sphere circumnavigating the earth also minted pound
notes.

Of course the one very effective way to get at the BBC, apart
from allowing the gradual erosion of the real value of the licence
fee, is to ensure that the competition to it is overwhelming. That,
sadly, has been the trend. The Corporation has safeguarded many
of its commitments to sport because of the general acceptance of
the high quality of its coverage. But not always. They lost the
Rugby World Cup contract to ITV without any due consideration
being given to quality. With the best will in the world, commercial
television has no real track record in that area and they didn't have
Bill McLaren, a fact that cannot be overestimated. So, that ought
to be a warning that new options have arrived.

In a truly free and untrammelled market BBC Television would
struggle to maintain its presence as the major purveyor of sport.
Such is its handicapped financial state. It is when major events
like Wimbledon, or the Open Championship, or boxing title fights
disappear from the public service screens, because of the more
powerful purse of other interests, that people will wake up to the
reality that the superb sports coverage by the Corporation has
largely been taken for granted. It would be sorely missed but, by
then, it could be too late to do anything about it. Only if government kept major events as special areas of public interest and
allowed a natural involvement by the BBC could they survive, but
that seems an impossibility. The Corporation is fighting a rear-

guard action which will diminish the quality of sports broadcasting if they lose in the long run.

The University and the BBC therefore seemed to echo each other throughout that period. You could easily have superimposed the voices of one on the institution of the other without noticing much difference as both sets of values came under siege from similar forces.

It was during my period of office at Edinburgh that I almost brought a newspaper out on strike. Because of a dispute between the football authorities and the two television channels *Sportscene* went off the air. We went virtually the entire season without our regular work. Buffeted around by circumstances beyond my control I was beginning to think that life on a limited contract was as fruitful as driving down the M74 with one's eyes closed. Then one day in the middle of this awful period I got a phone call from Endell Laird, editor of the *Sunday Mail*, who asked me if I would report a football match for his newspaper. As a member of the National Union of Journalists I took this on in all innocence and accepted it as a perfectly legitimate task. At the same time I was asked by *Grandstand* if I could cover a game, travel back to the studio in Glasgow and report on it to camera. The problem was that I had to leave the game ten minutes before the match was over. As I attempted to do both, I simply ran into big trouble.

I took on that commitment one Saturday but the next week brought a reaction. On the Friday night I was in the University of Edinburgh at a function as Rector and was called to the phone. It was someone from the NUJ connected with the *Sunday Mail*. He was extremely affable in tone but his message was unmistakable and uncompromising. He told me that because someone was having to cover the part of the game report that I could not complete for the *Mail*, as a result of my early exit, I was in effect encroaching on the work rights of staff reporters. In truth, I had no knowledge, one way or the other, that it was causing upheaval and tried to tell him that. He was sympathetic but went on to deliver an ultimatum. I had to give a guarantee that I would report properly for the *Sunday Mail*, that is, the full game without leaving before the end to do *Grandstand*, or else face the consequences. They included the suggestion 'the paper might not reach the streets that night'.

I recall that sentence vividly enough. I was beginning to feel this was some sort of nightmare. However, I was fully to blame for both being naive and not having come to a proper arrangement balancing my two commitments. As a trade-unionist myself, and having already gone on strike action within days of joining the BBC, being considered some kind of 'scab' made my blood curdle. I simply told him that I would only do the report for the *Sunday Mail* under the normal conditions.

I put down the phone and contacted the editor of *Grandstand*, John Philips, at home and explained the position to him. I was in a quandary but as a legitimate exercise as a freelance I wanted to try to fit both reports in and told him that the union were so serious they might even stop the production of the paper. He did not believe this at first, as I hadn't. Eventually he saw the dilemma I was in and, against his nature, because he preferred me to be in vision for my reports, he agreed that it could be done by telephone with a slide photograph of myself put up on the screen. I was determined to show that I could practise my trade properly without giving the impression of tramping over anybody. I managed both reports that following day. But the residue of anger against me by some people who were quick to see this as an attempt to muscle in on a situation showed itself. I walked in to the *Daily Record* offices one day on some matter not long after that and heard a voice, largely anonymous, floating over the office towards me, 'He must be in for his blood money!'

It only saddened me. I had gone on the verge of falling out with a union of which I was a dedicated member. I had obviously angered colleagues I had known for some time, unwittingly. I'd had to push my relationship with *Grandstand* to the limit to get them to change their normal custom of reporting, just to help me out of a dilemma. The whole arrangement, purely temporary, came to a halt only a few weeks after that anyway. If any blood had been spilled in this whole episode I suspect I was minus a few pints myself.

Flexibility is the main asset of any contract and although it was clear from that episode I wasn't going to be able to wander into any area without a bit more careful thought I had to seek alternatives if only because BBC Scotland offered none. Thankfully the work came from the south. One of the most enjoyable films I was ever involved in was travelling to the Isles of Scilly one December to film their football league. They played League championship, Cup and League Cup games throughout the season, but there were only two teams on the island! The means by which they contrived all this formed the basis of a slightly tongue in cheek story about how football holds sway in even the strangest outposts.

We put this out on New Year's Day on *Grandstand* and showed how we filmed in a small four-seater aircraft to reveal the lighthouse keeper of Wolf Rock trying to get off his work to play in the important cup-tie. The flower farmer, a kind of laird, organised the two teams so that nobody would run away with titles and cups. We showed how the local bobby had to have his wife look after crime on the island whilst he was off playing. That sort of thing. Lo and behold as soon as it went out in *Grandstand* I began to hear murmurs that I was turning my back on Scotland. After all, weren't the Old Firm playing then, and shouldn't we be previewing their game? Even the stone-age people in Papua New Guinea had heard about the Old Firm and there is always a creative case to be made for avoiding sacred cows from time to time.

I didn't realise how strongly people actually felt about my continuing and increasing involvement in network broadcasting until one journalist described me as 'BBC London's pet Jock'. The thinly veiled jibe thereby implied the kind of relationship that one might see in the ghillie taking the patronising English gentry off to the shoot. What they didn't realise was that throughout my career many of the significant producers who had employed me were Scots themselves, and that the Caledonian broadcasting community in London was extremely strong, although I would obviously not call them the Scottish Mafia. They are much more powerful than that. It was a Scot who had helped me in a critical moment in Los Angeles and it was the same Scot, Jim Reside, who asked me to go to the Winter Olympics in Calgary, Canada in 1988.

This was a different venture altogether from the summer Olympics. The Winter Games have a micro-identity which makes them appear arcane to the less-experienced eye like mine. People were sliding down a hill whether on their feet, or on their backs on objects like large shovels or on elongated machines which look like scooped-out cigar-tubes and which have to be pushed into activity (then hysterically guided down an insanely steep and twisting track), or jumping into space bent like someone suffering an attack of the cramp to land on two feet on skis. It requires specialised judgement to appreciate all this properly. To that extent I was an outsider, required to bring the outsider's viewpoint to events and reports. And like all my other colleagues in the media sent there to do the same we were saved by one man, Eddie Edwards.

Every Games needs a moment in time or an individual to synthesise the profusion of feelings which their size and scope stimulate and for which they will always be identified. There was Fanny Blankers-Koen in London, Mary Rand in Tokyo, the Black Panther salute in Mexico. Moving about a Games is a bit like wandering, shopping in a bazaar with so much on offer that the senses are confused. You can be left with a strangely bloated but unfulfilled sensation. There was much to admire and be impressed by but the Calgary Games were turning out to be as bland as the city itself.

It sits in the middle of the prairie signalling itself to the Rockies with the universal stamp of progress; high rise glass and aluminium office blocks in an extravagant city centre which seemed always to be looking for people. Even in an Olympic period it appeared too vast for what it was supposed to serve. The Games were spread around the outskirts. When we arrived the temperatures were about fifteen to twenty degrees below freezing but an astonishing phenomenon occurred. The Chinook wind blew in from the Rockies. This has a sudden, thawing influence which sweeps over the mountains. By the time it hits the prairie it has the dramatic effect of a blow-torch being pointed at snow. Winter disappeared almost overnight, as in twenty-four hours the temperatures soared to ten degrees above freezing. It was like conjuring up spring by magic. The prairie turned from white to saddened brown and the environment, with the top winter athletes caged in by this freakish whim of nature, took on an air of unreality.

But you cannot make the weather the top event. It is always a non-starter in news and serves to remind people that you have nothing much else to talk about. But talk about the weather we did for there was little else to report as we skedaddled around this gushingly friendly town to find some reportorial gold. It came largely through myopia.

I am sure that Eddie the Eagle's courage stemmed partially from the fact that he could not see all that far through his thick bottle-glass spectacles. This lessened the shock of standing at the top of the ski jump looking into space. If you have never done this (standing looking down, not jumping) you cannot possibly imagine the surge of terror which goes through you from deep within the bowels. You do not think of it as a sport but more a ritual challenge devised by some primitive tribe to introduce youth to manhood. Eddie seemed fragile and in grave danger as he stood blinkingly at the top of the ramp. But when his first leap was so far behind the others and he looked like a lad who ought to have been mending the window-sash for you, carrying the crazy aspirations of all we ordinary people to achieve the impossible, the Canadians took him to their hearts. We took him to our headlines. Both the Games and the media needed something different to stimulate a particular identity for Calgary and it was coming, for the first time in Olympic history, from the example of bumbling mediocrity.

He became a hero. Ron Pickering, commentating previously on him in an event before he arrived in Canada, watched him fly through the air with the elegance of a flying hat-stand. When Edwards landed on the slope, wobbling and tottering to keep his balance, Pickering could not resist the triumphal but sardonic exclamation, 'The Eagle has landed!'

The phrase stuck. Other commentators picked it up. The world press followed as the Canadian crowds, starved of anything unusual in the Games, like the media, chanted his name and made of him the unlikeliest hero since Tom Thumb. A community crazed with the pin-swapping tendency and idiosyncratic tee-shirts purchasing suddenly became prey to the Eddie the Eagle entrepreneurs. His tee-shirt became the hottest property in town. Manufactured overnight, people queued to get it. We queued up for his interview. The Mayor paid a special visit and was photographed with him, probably for potential electioneering purposes. And the other British competitors fumed. After all, Eddie had done nothing. His definitive accomplishment was always to finish last. The refreshing by-product was to reverse the conventional North American attitude which helps mythologise only the successful. Now we had adoration of the failed. At least it was different. Then one day we were told an important announcement was to be made about his future at a hotel in town that night.

We scurried round with our film unit. So did the rest of the world. I had managed to get ahead of the mob and was directed through to back stage to meet the man who said he was going to sign Eddie up in an important business deal. This had stemmed from the fact that the American television company ABC, losing money hand over foot with their coverage of the Games, desperately flew Eddie all the way back during the Games to make an appearance on the Johnny Carson Show. This ultimate media canonisation was to open the financial floodgates for him, so it was said. The man I met was wearing a tuxedo, as they would say out there, with rings on his fingers bigger than knuckle-dusters, and smoking a large cigar. Behind him were six lissome girl dancers limbering up for a floor-show. They certainly did not look to me like amateurs.

'We are up here from Las Vegas with our little show and we're gonna make Eddie the Eagle a star,' the man told me. 'We're gonna put Eddie on the stage here tonight with these lovely ladies and he is gonna dance with them.' I felt slightly sick. Sick for Eddie and sick for having to go along with all of this. Indeed the man's partner, behind his back, looked at me and said, 'Care to vomit?'

It was exploitation that might just denude Eddie very quickly of his short-sighted charm overnight, as the Chinook pared the hills of snow and ice. We expected to be allowed in with the cameras to film this unique Olympic happening, a competing athlete taking part in cabaret. Then, as we prepared to walk in with our unit, four 'heavies' stood in our way and blocked the entrance. We did not try to use force against them. If you can visualise the men who came to that room to shoot Burt Lancaster in Hemingway's *The Killers* you will probably realise why. We waited outside the room for three hours for a little man who desisted at the last minute from getting up to dance with the girls and had merely been presented on stage. He had provoked a media circus which was now beginning to question its own sanity in pursuing this any further. However, in circumstances like these, the interest and fever are self-propagating. Although we all knew this was a con and Eddie was of no merit, either on the slopes or off, we were worried about who might steal an exclusive with the little man who had captivated the nation. So Eddie's very insignificance was indemnified by the interest of the people like ourselves who had helped create him. Nobody, in short, was going to ignore him.

He walked out to a battle. I have been in the presence of Muhammad Ali, Pele, Maradona, John McEnroe, to name but a few, as they faced the press but there was nothing like this. At least twenty different camera crews physically fought with each other to get close to him. I personally was hauled back by a large Austrian gentleman as solid as the Jungfrau but I stamped on his foot and pushed in on Eddie. A punch was thrown at me. I dug an elbow back into somebody's ribs behind me and in the confusion of mêlée and attempt at restraint we became one amoebic swirl. It became too difficult to strike out.

Eddie's minders, and yes he had them by now, pushed us back and held on to him. The little man looked pale and confused and I felt we didn't need any words from him. His look portrayed the bewildered stare of the hunted animal. It was as if, in the middle of the scrum, he had suddenly realised he had now pushed his minimal status to the limit and that it was time to retreat from the edge of this precipice. Perhaps, after all, it had been worth it to be in the middle of a chaotic pummelling just to capture the look on that face.

The entire media retreated from that squalid scene that night more than a little shame-faced. We were too embarrassed to talk about it much for it must have been the first time in the history of the Olympics that the event had been upstaged by a man who was as remote from the laurel wreath as Calgary was from genuine sophistication. It was time to worry about the Games. It was time to reflect on how the introspection of organisers and athletes can make them forget that the public and media wish for spectacle, colourful characters and touches of the extraordinary. We had to realise that even the most significant athletic achievement will not register if it does not spark the imagination. That is why later on in Seoul the world's media poured scorn and vilification on Ben Johnson but at the same time warmed to the excitement of the hunt and to the injection of controversy. The Games were now vulnerable to all of that.

So Eddie had dabbed a little colour on the Calgary Games which had been splendidly mounted, contained some fine athletic achievement but had been as flat and predictable as the prairie. 'The Eagle' had provided the third dimension.

I went back to continue my work on both sides of the border but within BBC Scotland I was now, like Eddie, looking into space without being able to see an appropriate landing spot.

15

End Game

The last commentary I broadcast for BBC Scotland was in Turin. It is not a city I have ever much cared for because it seems even more sprawling than Los Angeles, more constricted by traffic than Mexico City and more incoherently planned than the old city of Jerusalem. In short, it hasn't got much going for it as far as I'm concerned. Any misery I felt in having to commentate on such a mediocre event as the Scotland–Brazil match, which the game certainly had turned out to be, was compounded when I afterwards drove the Director General of the BBC Michael Checkland and his wife back to our hotel.

Their car had failed to arrive but their geniality was stretched, I am sure, almost beyond diplomatic endurance by the fact that I got hopelessly lost in this disjointed city. The hotel at last emerged from the damp bleakness of the night, but at least a couple of hours later than we had hoped, which left us feeling limp and hard done by.

Being by now well familiarised with the ways of World Cup self-pity I was probably more at ease with this situation than some of my companions who had never before experienced this now almost copyrighted Scottish experience of plummeting emotionally from something like the sublime to the ridiculous within the time-span of a few days. All the same, I was preoccupied with my own position in broadcasting and was ill-prepared to indulge in inquests over the Scottish squad when, at the same time, I was questioning my own future.

There were few redeeming features in the World Cup in Italy for me. Indeed when Maurice Johnston missed his chance in front of goal late on in the Brazilian game, which would have meant so much to the cause, I felt not a shred of disillusionment realising that yet again the Gods had written this to end in the normality of anti-climax. In a sense I was privately relieved that I would not now be subjected to a prolonged stay in Italy, in an atmosphere of increasing mistrust which I felt had been engendered for me within the BBC Scotland group out there. My destiny, in any case, would be determined by a man not in Italy, but back in Glasgow. From a couple of thousand miles away he had intervened in a broadcast which, apart from its overt meaning, also conveyed to me a message of confrontation. It happened in Genoa.

Genoa has not attained its present girth without some extreme physical effort and ingenious engineering. It is corseted by sea and mountain and, from the vantage point of one who would not have known how to fit Lego blocks together, the achievement of linking the city to the rest of Italy seems something of a miracle. You don't want to be a sufferer from claustrophobia though. You bore your way in and out of the city in any direction by a series of tunnels which gives the immediate effect of disorienting you but, despite that, it works. From our base in Rapallo, a holiday resort of considerable elegance, we would drive almost daily through a chain of these tunnels into Genoa which was to house two of Scotland's games in the section. The rectangular Luigi Ferraris Stadium looked as if it had been dumped down temporarily and left for someone to collect later and deposit somewhere more in keeping with its style and modernity. Amongst the rather traditional and flaking Italian tenements it was as out of place as a hotel in a necropolis. Inside, it was constructed superbly to create the feeling of intimacy for the game, not unlike the very first World Cup stadium I had visited in Dortmund in Germany. I took one long look and thought it would be absolutely perfect. But you can go off a place quickly.

I had an uneasy feeling early in the Scotland–Costa Rica meeting. Nothing more than that. If you have covered as many games as I have, particularly at that level, you get an instinctive sense for how a game might evolve. That is not to say you can predict the score but you can perceive certain trends, some of which can worry you. I occasionally like to speak to others at half-time in a game to bounce thoughts off them, for you can be isolated in a commentary position. I went down to the press area and spoke to the freelance journalist Ray Hepburn. I didn't need to ask him. He just looked at me and said, 'This is dreadful. The worst. I feel a disaster coming on!'

Back I went, feeling, if anything, that perhaps it would work out after all. Surely we couldn't have another Iran! Costa Rica scored. Scotland slumped. Their legs seemed to have gone and their heads weren't any better. As a commentator with some four World Cups already behind me the sense of déjà vu was almost overwhelming. Knowing that the Scottish public had suffered considerably in the past, and would not wish to be charitable about the possible defeat from a Third World country, it was hardly the time to interpret all this with a broad grin on one's face. Remember, we were not playing Brazil, but a nation which, at least before the World Cup, was considered probably the poorest team in the tournament. So the game was being evaluated in that particular light by me as I criticised what I was seeing, just like the rest of the Scottish nation back home.

Then came the message from Glasgow, two thousand miles away. It came directly into my headphones. The voice said, 'I'm sorry about this but I have to pass on a message to you from Jim Hunter. It's not from me remember. He says,' and there was a deliberate pause, '"Be more encouraging of Scotland. They are going through a crisis!"'

It was from the Head of Television in Scotland. I looked at my producer Mike Abbott who looked back in some considerable astonishment at me. Back in Glasgow Gordon Brown, the ex-British Lion rugby player who had been watching the game in the BBC studios, told me he almost fell off his seat in astonishment when he heard that this message had been passed on.

It is difficult to convey now the impact that that intervention had on me. Here I was being interrupted, for the first time in my career in mid-commentary, by a message from a man on the other side of Europe, completely divorced from the atmosphere in the stadium, which is an important factor in capturing the real essence of a game, telling me in which direction the commentary ought to develop. It must only have been for a few moments but at the time it seemed like an eternity. I stopped in my tracks as the game raged on.

'Encourage?' I said to Mike Abbott. Now you do not need to be a member of Mensa to realise that commentators can hardly encourage players on the field; not unless he intended me to put down the mike and start singing 'Flower of Scotland' with the punters. And, if he meant me to make more encouraging noises for the viewers back home, then you need not rack your memories to recall that we were all of us watching as pathetic a performance as we had turned in against Iran in Argentina, in other words the very nadir of Scotland's international fortunes. I couldn't alter the course of events.

Nor could I offer a very astute viewing audience some false optimism when not a shred of evidence existed that Scotland could salvage themselves. You can only kid the people for so long and the Scottish public, having had more than their fair share of World Cup disappointment, I knew, would be in no mood for any more apologetic waffle. I had often wondered, in fact, if Hunter had all along preferred the bland to the cutting edge anyway. It all seemed to be coming out now. It was almost as if, in some stupidly national-istic way, someone covering Culloden had to make it sound as if it were a ceilidh.

I thought that the instruction was inane and almost an object lesson in how to be professionally irresponsible.

I also thought that the impact was enormous, throwing the pro-ducer and me off course completely. I asked him simply to pass a message back saying I refused to adopt that tone or line, call it what you like. No self-respecting commentator can do a commentary by long-distance diktat. I could have dodged this and said nothing. But the source of the message I saw as a challenge. I preferred to be absolutely honest in my response even though I knew that honesty would be no asset in dealing with him. I feared that he would seek retribution in some way, whatever else he might have had in mind for me. Even though my judgement on the game was proved to be absolutely right, and the critical tone I had adopted was in fact praised by people, I believed that all that would be an irrelevance in the final inquest. I had offended against Holy Writ.

In conversations afterwards with experienced broadcasters we reached the view that it was probably the first time a senior BBC figure had actively encouraged a commentator to be biased. For if you step outside the field of objectivity into so-called 'encouraging' you are taking sides. The fact that it was Scotland I had to be biased for is quite irrelevant. Commentators are normally hounded by the public for being biased. There is enough of that without being pushed into it from the rear.

So we retreated to our hotel in Rapallo, a short distance down the Italian Riviera, licking our wounds, with my tongue busier at it than anybody else. I had to accept that the consequences of the interruption to commentary and my reaction to it might be considerable and it soured the rest of the World Cup for me. My colleagues in journalism were largely incredulous when I recounted the incident to them but it was difficult for me to communicate the underlying nature of that intervention. Coming from James Hunter, the Head of Television in BBC Scotland, it capped years of long-distance irritation which I could now stand no longer.

You can become easily obsessed by feuds or disputes or continual locking of horns with individuals which fall into the conveniently described category of 'personality clash'. I had my fair quota of such during my career with adversaries ranging from floor managers all the way through to such as Hunter. The only type of person I probably did not have a run-in with were make-up ladies although I did object once to a heavy-handed woman who insisted I would look infinitely better with a touch of eye shadow. My stand on that was based on the worry that I might get fond of it.

Rows can flare up on preposterously insignificant matters which in retrospect leave you feeling embarrassed. In a live situation, or trying to beat a deadline, they can proliferate in a way which can almost make them seem an indispensable part of the broadcasting ensemble. But this was not a row. I saw this as a reminder of an influence bearing down on me that would not go away – an authority flexing its muscles. I carried a feeling of resentment with me through the rest of the tournament, although the game against Sweden acted as a purgative which almost cleared me of any bile.

I was involved with a 'live' broadcast. I was prepared to inflict critical damage on the Scottish side if I felt it was appropriate, although I warned myself not to go over the top, to prove my independence of mind from the man back in Glasgow. But events were on my side. It was a marvellous game to be involved in. The mood of the Scottish side was one of defiance.

Commentators of course like to feel the audience is enjoying what they are watching. Scotland two up at one stage in that game suggested to me a nation watching in some wonderment, and in the early stages of euphoria. But there is an even better commentating situation and that is when anxiety is heaped on top of that, when grown men move out of the room for fear of events being over-turned by fluke or divine intervention and can barely stand the pressure. Ernie Walker, who is not known to flinch in some of the great disputes he has presided over as secretary of the SFA, was a well-known 'walker' at games. He would leave his seat and go into the depths of the stand because he could not bear to watch if Scotland were battling against the clock. With a few paltry minutes to go, and with Sweden having pulled back to 2−1 and Scotland hanging on grimly, I knew I had an audience bathed in emotional sweat and prepared to eat out of the commentating hand.

I finished the game feeling as if I had been present at a banquet. Never before in the World Cup had a match given me so much satisfaction to cover. I felt, foolishly as it turned out, that I had driven the Costa Rica experience into oblivion. You can never tell whether your commentary has been adequate to the occasion and it is extremely dangerous to indulge in private celebration. But, in the face of increasing doubts about the rather distant relationship with some of the BBC Scotland staff in Genoa, I enjoyed a moment or two of quiet purring. It had gone as well as could have been expected.

I did feel as relaxed as Andy Roxburgh the following day. My own particular idea of trauma during the Costa Rica game had been but a passing hot-flush compared to the agony he must have suffered. He was incapable, as most humans are, of totally concealing great pain. But he did better than most. His articulate dignity was not without its occasional snappiness but that was to be expected in the melting-pot of the World Cup. Even the angel

Gabriel could be turned into a profane loud-mouth there. Roxburgh's meticulous preparation was almost obsessive and gave rise to thoughts that it was all organisational structure without any real substance. But he had chosen the route of careful groundwork, knowing that even if he had everything calculated in advance right down to the last corn-plaster required, it would all hinge on how his players responded to another eleven men over ninety minutes. He had on board enough helpers to crew an ocean-going liner. His forward planning therefore made the other national managers who preceded him look almost amateurish in comparison but it also incurred the risk of a special kind of embarrassment if it failed.

I had watched Roxburgh at close quarters in Mexico during the World Professional Youth Finals in 1983 and had formed the impression that his excellence in that area was really going to anchor him at that level for good. It was not an unfair judgement, but simply one based on the clear benefits his coaching and educational insights bestowed on impressionable young men. He led well, he taught well. There was an air of the 'lad o'pairts' become popular dominie about him and his handling of the youngsters was both refreshing and impressive. But there was no trace of Billy the Kid about him. You could not imagine him, then and there, with the whiff of cordite in the nostrils, taking on some of the tougher hombres who populate dressing rooms in senior football.

There is little doubt that others saw it that way too and indulged in some rampant scepticism on his appointment. I do not exclude myself from that category for the appointment came unexpectedly and with the firm image of Roxburgh as youth coach ensconced in the mind. That this was intrinsically unfair and that there was an over-reaction to it is quite clear. It is also not too surprising that Roxburgh himself occasionally over-reacted both to this feeling of not fully being accepted and the new pressure on him.

At one point, I wrote a tongue-in-cheek piece in the *Sunday Mail* about how time might be against him in his efforts to qualify Scotland for the World Cup finals and received almost by return a letter of stinging rebuke from him for what I had briefly written on the subject. This was followed up by a lengthy denunciation of me from the hand of Ernie Walker who accused me almost of being a Quisling, in having let down a man who had offered nothing but friendship over the years. I had done nothing of the kind of course. I had merely fulfilled my function by writing a piece of criticism, however flippant the terms. It seemed perfectly in order.

I have always seen friendship with people in other, and sometimes conflicting, areas of football as very relevant but never a reason for suspending critical judgement. Any association which will not permit that is not worthy of being termed a bond between people. I was disturbed by this episode largely because Ernie Walker had been at pains to make it clear that the SFA, in opting for Roxburgh, were adopting a new and refreshing approach to national team management. I suspect that, in the informal chat amongst managers and media, the sifting out process of those 'for' and 'against' certain people still reaches a paranoid level at times.

Our relationship afterwards was proper and formal and my steadily increasing admiration for his staying powers, despite people like me who initially thought he could not measure up to the stature of his immediate predecessors, was amply expressed in different ways. I was pleased for him after the victory over Sweden even though I still felt that the chances of Scotland qualifying for the final phase were marginal.

The evening of the Brazil match turned out to be damp and grey. It made a stark contrast to the previous time the two countries had met in Seville on a warm sunny evening where there was an irresistible mood of fiesta. When you are huddling in doorways to avoid the monsoon, as many supporters were that evening, the samba hides as well. The stadium, too, was vast and impersonal. It may have looked impressive in an architects' magazine and indeed it was spectacular in concept. But football was as remote there as it was close in Genoa. The game was markedly different from the meeting with Sweden.

Firstly, the Brazilians were sub-standard. We had hyped them as we dutifully do at a World Cup but in reality they were as far removed from the Brazil of legendary renown as Rio is from Reykjavik. When we had gone to the delightful town of Asti, where they put the bubbles in the wine, virtually every Brazilian commentator or journalist who spoke English to us at the training camp there denounced the tactics of the manager Lazaroni. They were even more 'Europeanised' than their squad of 1974 and the home-based Brazilian media detested the fact that so many of their players were now resident in clubs around the Continent. There was unrest. So much so that at one of the press conferences I attended the Italian police had to be called to protect the manager from harassment by his own journalists.

I suspect they played against us that night without wishing to break too much sweat. The Scottish team were not good enough, even against instantly forgettable Brazilians. The following day we returned to Rapallo down the coast and there at least some of us thought that we did not want to prolong this with a route into the second phase by courtesy of games in other sections. Two days after the match in Turin we were on a flight back home. The remnants of the excellently-behaved Scottish support were not in any great state of anguish or anger. Most of them were sullenly resigned to it all. They had proved resilient. The 'spitters' of Argentina were now a defunct species.

The route for me though was back to London not Glasgow. Even though I knew I would have to face up to the consequences of the long-distance confrontation during the Costa Rica game my first priority was to return to my contract work for network sport at Television Centre. I had gone to London seeking not fame and fortune, but enough cash to pay the mortgage. No matter how much I tried, I could not obtain any more work in Scotland other than a Saturday afternoon commentary. Fortunately, and perhaps surprisingly, my colleagues in the south were actually delighted with this state of affairs. They gave me an entirely new broadcasting platform but simply could not understand why I needed to be in this peripatetic role, criss-crossing the border every week. Sometimes I dashed by taxi from Glasgow Airport on a Saturday afternoon to get into the commentary position in time for the three o'clock kick-off. It was exhausting, frightening and far from ideal.

One Saturday, in a taxi, we could see a terrible traffic-jam on the motorway leading to Ibrox for the game I had to cover. We went off it and then got snarled up in trying to take a circuitous route to avoid the jam, now congealed around us somewhere in the new Gorbals area. I had vowed, because of the professional circumstances I had found myself in, not to allow anything to prevent me adhering to the contractual obligations, other than illness. I knew I was now on the verge of missing the start of the game for the first time in my life.

I got out, after having paid the man, and ran. I got through the worst of the heavy traffic but the breath was giving out. Suddenly I heard a ribald comment about my appearance. I was leaning against traffic lights and a man sitting at the front of a Rangers supporters bus contrived mock concern about my health. What then followed was the reaching out of arms and I was hauled on to the bus. With some easing of traffic ahead, it took off for Ibrox at speed.

'Gie us the Sash, Archie!' was the first cry from the interior as I slumped back wondering if the lungs had gone on vacation. I could not have given them 'Three Blind Mice'. I always am glad to join in the spirit of occasions but it is better not to commit oneself, even idly and innocently, to identification with any of the predominant colours in the city. That is why I declined the request, just as, on the television platform at Celtic Park, I have not yet succumbed to the chant, 'Archie, Archie, cross yersel!'

They took me almost all of the rest of the way and with gratitude I sped from the bus, ran down Edmiston Drive, swept through the enclosure door, climbed the iron steps, crashed down on the seat on the platform, put on the headphones and feeling like Pheidippides at the end of his run, shattered but slightly triumphant, just as the teams were running out, heard the director's voice say rather sarcastically in my ear, 'Glad you could make it!'

This was no way to prepare for a commentary, but there was nothing I could do about it and before long I saw that London had obvious blessings. The immediate and very personal one was that, at the very least, in London I was enjoying something of a renaissance. On Breakfast Television I had built up a useful rapport with Jeremy Paxman who, if he wasn't eating up politicians for breakfast, was quite willing to indulge in sardonic skirmishes with me as the nation munched its cornflakes. I relished this and with the inevitable challenge of trying to make sports reporting more generally accessible to a wider audience than merely the enthusiast

I felt as much in top gear as I ever had. I hadn't looked forward to getting up at five o'clock every morning to do all of this but once I had got into the habit it came easily. The reward was to be able to drive easily through London at that time of the morning, on the wrong side of the road if you so desired, because of the astonishing emptiness. It was like seeing a city under strict curfew. Earth hath nothing more fair to show than Shepherd's Bush Green without a single vehicle in sight.

Although I had worked on network television for years this new role took me to areas I had never touched before. I was asked to unravel the mysteries of croquet at the Hurlingham Club, almost wept with emotion after having done a film at Cheltenham and stood in the sleet watching Desert Orchid win in that famous finish in the Gold Cup in 1989, sat in the Long Room at Lord's discussing the fortunes of English cricket with Mike Gatting, chattered away on the gin-palaces at Cowes, previewed rugby-league Cup finals, linked the programme live from Wimbledon, and, one famous morning, shared a unique Scottish ensemble in studio with Kirsty Wark, Sally Magnusson and weatherman Francis Wilson.

Looking back to Scotland I simply could not understand what was happening there. Faces in sport came and went. We had a season of lunch-time inserts into *Grandstand* but that series disappeared out of sight eventually. So too did Bob Patience. He had established 'Saint and Greavsie' in the south and, having returned to set up as an independent producer, he had been asked to organise the new afternoon series. He would have been an ideal choice to take over the whole of sports output but the snag was that he would have been determined, quite rightly, to have his own way. Judging by what I saw as a lack of real departmental autonomy, since the inception of Hunter as Head of Television, he would not have been allowed such professional leeway.

I was told that Hunter desired changes then but the most curious of all concerned Dougie Donnelly. An approach was made to Gordon Hewitt who, as it so happens, is a mutual friend of Dougie and myself to find out if he would be available to present either the new lunch-time programme or Saturday evening *Sportscene*. Many years previous to this I had brought Gordon into broadcasting and encouraged Peter Thomson to use him because I felt he had screen presence of considerable value. He had by now become a very successful economist, running his own consultancy business and constantly travelling the world. The first reason for refusing was that his business life would have made it impossible. But even had he been in a position to do so he made it clear that he would not have taken this further if it meant affecting Dougie's position. Being, in any case, a man of considerable honour he telephoned Dougie personally to let him know that he had been approached by the BBC but on no account would he take on anything that would affect Dougie's standing. He would not let any offer of a job get in the way of their friendship. Gordon turned the offer down. He later told me that he could not fathom why they would have thought of possibly replacing Dougie on the main programme. It is no wonder that this information almost shattered Dougie Donnelly. It simply made no sense. There was certainly nothing wrong with considering Gordon Hewitt but as Dougie had established himself professionally, built up a following, and was hardly a geriatric, why this?

I tried to discern a rationale behind it all. It is too simplistic to believe that television has simply to ring the changes from time to time. Somehow or other, and admittedly it is not easy, managers in television must go by instinct in shaping television presentation. They do use quality assessment polls which give popularity ratings for programmes or individuals. These are undoubtedly useful but can hardly be anything other than guides. It depends on what we mean by 'good' or 'average' or 'poor'. For example, Sir Robin Day, whose acerbic manner served the public interest by puncturing political egos but at the same time made him appear to be a television bruiser, was disliked by many people. That, in itself, might have affected any rating. Hugh McIlvanney once brilliantly summed him up to me by saying, 'He seemed to have a thousand things wrong about him and yet he added up to exactly the right person for that sort of role.' The opposite would be blandness but it would not be Sir Robin Day. The selection of people to sit in front of a camera requires not just census returns but an instinct for assessing impact on the public. Swapping one face for another just for the sake of it is actually opting out of accountability to the public, falling back on that laziest of all television dictums: 'Time for a change!'

It is introducing the philosophy of Max Factor to television and indulging purely in whim, juggling with people whilst the public remain untouched, unconsulted and mystified in the background. You need only look at the longevity of people in network sport – Coleman, Maskell, Wilson, Carpenter, Walker – to see the value of rooting personalities stably in the minds of the viewing public and allowing their authority to mature. The possible replacing of Dougie Donnelly by Gordon Hewitt would have been nothing other than a cosmetic exercise which, without the slightest criticism of Gordon, would have meant no seminal change of policy in sports presentation. It did reflect to me this unpredictable current which ran through a sports department dominated by Hunter.

I knew I was dealing with a man who had disliked my attempts to retain independence of view. You have to take this as a matter of course in our business, except that I knew after the World Cup the relationship with Hunter had reached its climax.

I went to see him for the last time. I noticed when I walked into his office a tape marked 'Scotland v Costa Rica' was lying on a desk. I expected him to be poring over the match for I had asked him by letter if we could talk about what had happened in Genoa. Within about a couple of sentences or so he told me he had an unpleasant task to perform and that was to tell me that he would not be renewing my contract when it expired in a few months' time. It did not come as a shock and I sensed surprise growing in him. He actually offered the view that I must be stunned. I am not sure whether he was expecting me to be prostrate with grief and was therefore hugely disappointed. This turn of events left me with a curiously contrasting and euphoric feeling that soon I would be rid of him, whatever other regrets I would have.

He told me that this was a decision made by the sports department and that he had nothing to do with it. I challenged that but he pleaded innocence and said they had only sent him to tell me the news because I was a 'heavyweight'. I simply could not accept that, having previously believed that during all these years each decision of any importance made about me was either inspired or endorsed by him.

233

Attitude came up. I had not attended the World Cup Press Conference prior to the tournament, which was held at Hampden Park. I had to point out to him that I had a contract to work in London and was doing precisely that when the conference was being held and had actually negotiated with the BBC press office to get back later that day after filming. He admitted that what he had quoted was probably not a good example of the wrong attitude. I cannot remember him getting round to telling me what he really had meant. 'Difficult person to work with sometimes,' came up. I ventured that if that were a criterion to be used universally in the BBC the institution could be depopulated overnight. I found it a patchy litany and wondered whether, even if he had made up his mind about what he was going to do, he was still almost seeking to justify himself. Then came a curious switch.

'What are you going to say about this in public?' he asked me.

'The truth!' I replied.

'Couldn't we be economical with the truth?' he suddenly said.

I thought I hadn't heard properly. But no, he had said it. 'Economical with the truth'. I pondered that many weeks after. Was it because he thought it was such an insignificant matter that he felt free to say virtually anything he wanted? Or was it because he was genuinely disturbed about something? Or was I making too much of that in my own mind because of the circumstances, for after all those words had become the rather modish catch-phrase of moral sleaze, a kind of wine-bar note of decadence that one ought not to take too seriously. I would not have thought it would represent some consensus BBC modus operandi. I certainly hope not. I was even more shocked when he quickly added, 'You see I got into the front page of the *Glasgow Herald* twice recently in such matters and I want to avoid that again if I can!'

I remember thinking that I had not up till then considered an appearance on the front page of the *Herald* as being synonymous with public ignominy. Before I left his office he expressed the hope that my departure could be handled with dignity. I was left to wonder how one squared 'economy with the truth' with dignity. On balance I thought it better not even to try.

At a time like that you imagine fancifully it would be right to make a fuss, that it would be productive to throw yourself on the mercy of the public after having been so much the public animal for so long. It is hard to cage the ego. Of course no such court of justice exists. It is also doubtful what the verdict would be even if it did. However, you do feel you want to be heard somehow or other. But there seemed such an imperturbable certainty and determination to what Hunter was doing that I doubt if pleading even the most emotional case would have made a difference.

I believed it was right to say nothing and hold my silence until such time as I thought something sensible and more meaningful could be said, outside the context of mudslinging. I resisted the temptations dangled in front of me by various newspapers to 'come clean'. The news did in fact make page one of the *Herald*, which noted my imminent departure alongside an exasperatingly anodyne comment of praise by Hunter, which I read the way Trotsky must have viewed sentimental overtures from Stalin. I did note with a wistful satisfaction that when Hunter left the BBC a year later his departure was also noted by the *Herald*, but only on page five.

Before I left, he had already made his contacts to get another commentator. When I phoned my lawyer who also happens to be Jock Brown, then STV's commentator, he told me, after I had explained what had happened, and much to my great surprise, that in fact they had approached him. A go-between, a mutual acquaintance of ours, had been used to sound him out and he went on to tell me that he thought the reason I was leaving BBC Scotland was to go to London to work. I thought it best under the circumstances not to wait around for the expiry of my contract but to seek release from it, even though it was going to cost me a considerable amount of money. I wanted to put this muddy situation well behind me. I kept my London contract, which I treasured, and was released from the BBC Scotland element.

Leaving BBC Scotland after over twenty-three years was not painless. It was a bit like leaving the church which you've been in since the cradle and which nurtured you carefully. It might even have been too protective at times. You can begin to be deluded by that rather atheistic notion that there is no such thing as life after the BBC. Ultimately, I suppose, when anyone puts his name to a contract he must realise he becomes, by that very act, a terminal case. Nobody in that category is exempt, not even through longevity. That is the brutal and quite uneconomical truth.

16

Keeping up with Souness

Not time yet to roll the closing credits. The game's still on and you're still a player. I offered myself that little piece of gimcrack philosophy walking away from Queen Margaret Drive. When the offers came in from Caledonian Television, Scottish Television and Radio Clyde I knew that at least some others shared my own sentiments. These contacts meant I could remain in Scottish sports broadcasting rather than end up in rather uncomfortable exile in London. To accept the offers though I had to give up my Television Centre-based contract. Although I tried hard to hold on to it, the powers-that-be thought there would be a clash of interests involved. To renounce such a contract is the equivalent, in our profession, of committing infanticide. I felt the work there had given me a new dimension in the profession but I was also aware that you cannot, at that stage in life, walk easily away from your own identity. For better or for worse my voice was my living and it would not have sounded the same without football.

I had missed the Glasgow football voice penetrating the ear anyway. Sometimes you would wish to run screaming from it. But that feeling was a bit like getting away from the family for a while in the knowledge that you are going back again. The thought of not ever working again in Glasgow actually appalled me. Getting into the scene again properly as opposed to being a sort of weekend guest gave me an opportunity to look closer at one of the most interesting phenomena in European football, the rise of Rangers under Graeme Souness.

He was indisputably the most significant figure I have met in football since Stein. They both commanded attention by their sheer physical presence. When they spoke you found it hard to disregard the substance. But they were not the same kind of men in other equally important aspects. Stein belonged in Scotland. Souness did not. Stein understood the West of Scotland psyche, Souness did not. Stein succeeded in conquering the media, Souness did not. Stein won a European Cup with local lads. Souness did not. But Souness helped prevent Scottish football from sliding into a kind of League of Ireland mediocrity. In England they couldn't believe all that was happening under him. It annoyed me to know of English visitors who would mount the marble staircase at Ibrox, pay sycophantic lip-service to his achievements, and then belittle them on the way down again. Unlike Stein, Souness did not appear to have a real working knowledge of what Hemingway charmingly called 'the shit detector'.

I had known Souness as a player many years before he became Rangers' manager. But of all the conversations I had with him the one which stands out is the first he had with me in his new position. It was not in Glasgow though. It was in a setting which made it difficult to apply all of his thinking to that segment of Scottish society who massed in Govan every other week and who felt they had now acquired a new Messiah.

The Pueblo Indians of Santa Fé, New Mexico barter their goods in one of the arcaded passageways of the pink-adobe style central square of the town with a panache that owes more to the spirit of Woolworths than that of The Great Manitou. They were probably unaware that the new manager of Glasgow Rangers was in their midst. It did not seem likely that the beads and bracelets, the rings and leather pouches on display on the pavements would hold much attraction for the matt-tanned man who was with the Scottish football squad in town for altitude preparation before the World Cup in Mexico in 1986. Indian artefacts would hardly be to Graeme Souness's taste.

After all, he had just come from the country of Gucci where a successful footballer, as he still was, could rightly achieve rewards that would make the Elysian Fields appear to be on this side of eternity. As Sante Fé seemed to have attracted a reasonably mixed bag of the human race – artists seeking space and light, settlers from New York who thought you needed a passport to get into New Mexico in the first place, gays with sweet pinkish little restaurants, architects who designed houses out in the brush that looked like landlocked lighthouses, and bland-looking nuclear scientists from Los Alamos just up the trail a bit – it seemed perfectly in order for this place to try and rid itself of the cow-town image once and for all. It had the chance to accept a man with a cosmopolitanised Scottish accent in a blue tracksuit who vowed out there in the Wild West that he would sign a Catholic footballer for a famous and staunchly Protestant club.

It was there in the hotel on the hill looking across to where one supposes the cattle-herders used to bring in prime stock that Graeme Souness talked to me for the first time of his recent appointment and of the path in front of him. He knew it would make the Santa Fé trail seem like a stroll along Princes Street. He wasn't detailing anything but he was eager to talk about Glasgow, about the Rangers–Celtic thing, about the obsession with religious identity in the city. It was the tone of the rather removed exile who must have known something of the environment from his childhood but who, having come from Edinburgh and never having played senior football in Scotland before acquiring credentials that were now impeccably European, was having to brush up on the patois of the Glasgow rivalry. The contrast with his predecessor could not have been more stark.

Jock Wallace, who had been sacked from Ibrox the previous month, was essentially a man of the people and without that umbilical connection with the hearts of the loyalists he might not have lasted as long as he did. He was a good big man with a much softer and more sensitive side to him than he cared to project to the masses. They preferred to see him as the jungle-fighter and a leader of the Walk. He thrived on this but he also created staunch friends across the religious divide because paradoxically he was one of the least bitter men in a city where bitterness has more varieties than Alpine flora.

Some of the most insufferable bigots I have met are more suited to the dark corner and the sibilant whisper. Wallace's trumpetings of his Protestantism had, to me at any rate, a theatricality to them

239

that suggested he had to be heard by his patrons at the back of the hall. He would be wiping off the grease-paint once the performance was over. He was desperate to get back to Rangers and in his final days at Motherwell, in 1983, he phoned me and asked if I could contact the Rangers chairman John Paton to tell him that he was ready, willing and able to take the call. Sadly, what I could not tell him was that Rangers were not interested. I knew that with John Greig reaching the terminal stages of his period as manager at Ibrox the club were far more interested in the man in the granite city than anybody else.

Alex Ferguson was never offered the job by Rangers in the official sense but he was most certainly 'tapped'. He sat with me one day in the little cubby hole at Pittodrie, opposite the dressing rooms, agonising over the prospect, however distant, of going back to Govan. He did not really like the idea. The son of a Celtic-supporting father, he used to go to Ibrox without parental approval. As a supporter and player he became as obsessed with the club as Jock Wallace ever had been. He would have been the perfect choice for the job. But he had changed.

'How could I go back and not sign Catholics,' he told me. 'What would I tell my friends who are Catholics? "You lot aren't good enough for us." I just couldn't do it.'

One night just after that the phone rang late at home. When I picked it up I heard singing. At first I couldn't recognise the voice, but the song was 'The Sash My Father Wore'. At the end of the well-known refrain, the singing stopped and the voice simply said, 'I got it, son!' It was Jock Wallace's way of letting me know the Ibrox job was his. Much as I liked the man I could not help but feel that the Rangers board were playing to the crowd and thinking with their hearts not their heads. This was confirmation that the Protestant ascendancy would remain. And who in the rest of European football would give a tuppenny-toss about that?

More locally, and in no way less significantly, I am extremely doubtful if anybody at Celtic Park lost any sleep over that appointment. But there is little doubt that some insomnia was experienced there after that morning Souness made his first appearance in front of the media in the Blue Room in a slightly ill-fitting Rangers blazer. For the Wallace style did not work a second time round as

Rangers manager. He lacked the steely grip of Willie Waddell round his jugular. That interplay of character was missing. He had certainly left Ibrox because of monumental rows with Waddell, some of which could be heard after matches as far away as Arran. Achievement in Wallace's second term had been minimal and the crowds disappeared. Two versions of the 'Sash' were heard; one sung and the other, the echo coming back from a half-deserted stadium. If Souness had been asked that day for a rendering of the traditional airs someone would have had to write the words out for him. Something special was happening.

In the brash New Mexico sunshine sitting by the poolside he looked brimmingly fit, ready for the task, and, as I listened to him talking, I could not help but think that the Rangers supporters, nay the entire city of Glasgow, with its preoccupation with the Old Firm, did not know what was about to hit them. Compared to what had just gone before this was Armani replacing off-the-peg. It was a wonderfully frank and refreshing conversation. Indeed I would go so far as to say it was something I had wanted to hear for years but thought I never would.

He made it clear to me that his travels had made him contemptuous of the football parochialism of a city such as Glasgow. He knew it could be a hard place with entrenched views but he had his as well. This was stirring stuff. Particularly the bits about religion. He would not recognise the conventions. He was unhurried and casual in the way he expressed himself but there was no detracting from its seriousness. There is such a structured calm about Souness at times that it is difficult to know if you are touching any of his inner feelings. There is a suggestion of great depth there without the actual seismic proof.

Certainly, at that time people were still bemused by the suddenness and audacity of his appointment. However, they had so far heard only from him the dutiful utterances of a man who had obviously gone to Ibrox for more than the promise of a free yearly ticket on the Glasgow underground. Yet his life in Italy had not been weighing him down. He had been living well in a villa only a Mercedes' gentle purr away from the importunings of the Italian Riviera. Glasgow certainly has its intrinsic charm but we can hardly say the grape flourishes on the vine there. Why go where the westerlies can still be unkind? Souness had always given the impression that life-style was as important as his profession so the move, at the same time as it shocked, also aroused a cynicism which effectively placed Souness in the 'carpet-bagging' mould.

The 'nudge-nudge, wink-wink' brigade went underground almost on the day he arrived but they surfaced again in the following years in the less subtle mode of muggers of reputation. Whatever maulings he received, and deserved, in the time he was at Ibrox I never perceived him as one who exploited his position and used it out of mere selfishness as a staging-post to further his career.

'People will have to change I'm afraid,' he said distinctly. But did he mean it? Could this man, so far removed from the actual sectarian bitterness of the West of Scotland, which is yet as tangible as the 'stour' from Dixon's Blazes used to be, actually mean this? I think my excitement at the prospect of such a confrontation led me to blind my eyes to the other possibility which was ultimately to prove correct. For all that he knew it wasn't going to be easy, for all the backing he was going to receive inside the club, for all the admiration he might engender from outside, Graeme Souness really had no idea what he was letting himself in for. Nor, ultimately, was he fully able to cope. It is one thing to talk with good intentions. It is another to live with your actions. I warmed to his sentiments at the time though. Indeed, such was my weariness at the prospect of another inevitable disappointment in the forthcoming World Cup that I regarded the conversation in Santa Fé with Souness as probably of greater significance than anything that was to occur later the following month in the land of Montezuma's revenge.

We had good relations thereafter. When he spoke to me he always opened out frankly. He never uttered a view without at first explaining in detail why he reached his conclusions. He never rubbished any of his players to me although, when he was disappointed and angry, he would talk his opinions through sensibly and realistically. I was impressed by him. It was to become decidedly unpopular to say so even amongst some of his own supporters but that impression of clarity and purpose he exuded, despite his apparent obstinacies and mistakes, is not something I am required to dismiss from mind and won't. Nobody, not even the critics who speedily flourished around him, could deny, especially in those heady early days of the revolution when anything seemed possible, that he was driven obsessively by the job to the point where he would virtually sacrifice his marriage. His first chairman, David Holmes, himself underrated just how possessed the man was even before his very first season. The proof was in the hunting of an English internationalist.

Souness wanted Terry Butcher. He wanted him badly. He told me in one of our earlier conversations in his office that when he had played in England he had early deduced that you could have the best football-playing team in the land but if you didn't have a defence you had nothing. He negotiated and, with Holmes, agreed the figure that would be offered for Butcher. Holmes went on holiday considering the deal done and since he treasured peace and quiet only his close family knew the whereabouts of the villa near Marbella.

He was only there a couple of days or so when the door-bell rang and there was his new manager outside with a taxi, engine running. He wanted to talk. Could he pay off the taxi? Holmes was astonished that he had tracked him down to where he was in the first place and sent the taxi off. After a swim in the Holmes's pool Souness opened out. He had hit a major snag over Butcher. He needed another fifty thousand pounds. If he didn't get it the deal would be off. Firstly Holmes had been impressed by the resourcefulness of the man in finding him in Spain. But he wasn't going to allow this piece of enterprise to affect his thinking on the limits applicable to even the Ibrox budget. He had set a figure and that was that, even though the outside world believed that Rangers could sign any sort of cheque. So he had to shrug his shoulders regretfully. Nothing doing. But Holmes had to admit he was bowled over by the sheer doggedness of Souness on the matter, for after persevering with his point of view on the importance of Butcher he simply said to the chairman, 'Give me the fifty thousand and I'll give you the championship.'

If that now sounds slightly stagey we can satisfy ourselves that some historic moments have been accompanied by utterances which sound either banal or preposterous including the supposed famous plea of Bosworth Field, 'A horse! A horse! My kingdom for a horse!' Suffice to say that King Richard got less out of his plea than Souness did his, for the chairman, struck by the audacity, stretched out his hand and shook away fifty thousand pounds. Souness of course delivered his part of the deal some time later.

It was a touch of swank that poses the question of just how much latitude you can permit such self-assuredness. I think arrogance, the kind which we say to ourselves we think we admire, all depends on context. Stein, in a hotel in Cadiz before a game with Spain in Seville in 1985, was quite unperturbed that the interview which I had jointly arranged with himself and his captain Souness was overdue by about an hour. Graeme had not appeared. When he did saunter into sight he took his time strolling around the tables talking to other players and journalists who immediately dropped what they were doing to listen to him. Stein, sitting patiently beside me said, 'Class. The man's got class!'

He said that with genuine admiration.

'There's no substitute for that,' Stein went on. 'On and off the park he's got it and we badly need it. You won't push that man around!'

What had seemed outrageous lack of consideration to us had appeared to his manager to be the epitome of the arrogance and self-possession he desperately required from someone to lead others, less capable, into the cauldron of the stadium in Seville. He liked the man's demeanour, his effortless disdain. But it all depended on the time and the place and the angle from which you were looking as you made up your mind. If I hadn't had the access I occasionally did to him, from some of his press conferences it would be easy to conclude that he was nothing more than an ignorant boor. No doubt many people within Ibrox, from where they stood, revelled in the way he frequently handled the aftermaths of games. But too often they were merely exercises in contemptuous brevity. You might have concluded that his understanding of the collective noun for the press was 'arseholes'. The reluctance with which he spoke to them was compounded by distaste. It was particularly difficult to miss in the 'Now-you-see-me-now-you-don't' routine.

You watched in dismay. As one who was in support of all he

was trying to do, I simply had to wonder why. Why this? His dislike for the press became intense.

It is not that other managers haven't drawn the line in the sand and come chasing after you across it. I have seen Jock Stein clear a room of media, as a cannon-shot would remove a flock of roosting pigeons. He once so harangued one of my BBC commentating colleagues, in the passageway between the dressing rooms at Hampden, that the poor man took months to recover. The argument Alex Ferguson and I had in the tunnel at Easter Road was eventually broken up by a large Leith policeman. Jim McLean has made it clear to me on occasions, in his uniquely blunt way, that I would not exactly win his commendation as Commentator of the Year. I have seen Bobby Robson treat his press conferences as if he were in a can of worms. Abrasions are a constant factor. Helluva rows far from rare.

But, no, this seemed to me to be different with Souness. This was like someone sniffing conspiracy, feeling that most people were against him, out to get the club. He gave the distinct impression anyway that he simply did not care what people thought of his attitude. Stuff everybody. That's what came across loud and clear at times. In public life there is really no value in only being privately congenial.

I tried once to give him a small piece of advice about his television interviewing technique for he had a habit of cutting across your voice before you finished the question, making you look foolish or giving the impression that he was bullish and insensitive, which he never really was on those occasions. It was simply his eagerness to get out what he wanted to say. But since it happened so frequently it came across badly. People put the wrong interpretation on it. Even when Stein was at his most truculent with us, he was a different man when the cameras rolled. He knew he had an audience, that he was up front and his personal views on the interviewer, or indeed the question, were less important than communicating with the audience. Souness was less aware of that and I am not sure that what I pointed out to him ever really registered. When he had set his mind on things I doubt if he would have listened to Saatchi and Saatchi.

He certainly would have needed them to explain away some of

the incidents on the field. On 29 August 1987 Celtic played Rangers at Parkhead and Souness was sent off for fouling Billy Stark. I looked at the tackle on the tape back at the BBC that night and could find no redeeming feature about it whatsoever. If the referee had not sent him off he ought to have been sacked. Yet I was not aware that, on the back of this refereeing decision, Souness had made his mind up to leave Rangers there and then because he felt people were out to get him. I thought it was a gross over-reaction of the worst self-pitying kind. When he had gone back to the dressing room, David Holmes had found him in a great state of distress and anger. He poured out his resentment and made it clear that he could carry on no longer in Scottish football and that he was finished with Rangers. Holmes was taken aback both by the sentiment and the power with which it was expressed. It was done in such a way that he hoped that a cooling down would occur. But later that night, in the chairman's home, Souness made it clear he wanted to go. Holmes knew that he was dealing with a strongly determined man and whilst he had, and still has, the greatest admiration for his player-manager, he decided to relent and told him that he would not stand in his way. That night David Holmes thought Rangers had lost Souness.

We have to ask ourselves now, and in light of subsequent events leading to his ultimate departure, what would have happened then and there if a job of note had been available for him somewhere else? Was it merely expedient to hang on? Was the quest to transform Rangers really and truly over long before any of us imagined? It's an intriguing thought for it was increasingly obvious now that he felt the whole rigmarole of being player-manager, working in Glasgow, and coping with some people who refused to hang on his every word and others who were sly and treacherous, was getting too much.

On Monday morning he went back to Ibrox, though. But I am sure he was an irrevocably changed man, not just because of the incident on the field, but because he felt there were insidious forces acting against him and Rangers. Of course there were. There were people who were deeply envious of how Rangers were transforming themselves. There were those who traditionally would have liked to see Rangers disappear like the Glasgow trams.

There were people who had been offended by Souness's reactions to them, ranging from the off-handed to the downright belligerent, and wanted revenge. But so what? Wasn't this exactly what men in his position have always had to face up to? Wasn't the eventually beleaguered Billy McNeill to show him how to cope with the rack upon which all Old Firm managers eventually land with considerable courage and dignity? Haven't people talked face to face with Celtic managers and then gone behind their backs to speak of their religion as if they were vermin? What have they had to put up with through the years? 'This is Glasgow, for God's sake!' you felt like screaming at him.

He was steadily misreading the environment. He had imagined initially he could rise above the inanities of the bitternesses and tribal loyalties but he couldn't. In the first year at Ibrox he sat comfortably in his large office and told me with conviction that he would not mind if Celtic beat Rangers four times in the season so long as the club ended up with the title and that people had to stop thinking that the Old Firm match was a life or death affair. Interesting new theory this. Quite admirable. But worth a stoning in Larkhall. It would also bring on a sharp dose of scepticism in those who supported the revolution at Ibrox but did not want Rangers' Lion Rampant replaced by the white flag. The Souness revolution surely was not to mean putting up with indignity as well? This almost charming innocence of his in this matter did not last of course. Exactly a year later he told me that he had made a mistake about that and that he now knew what the Old Firm meant in the city and that he wanted players who would fight for the club because he had never before experienced so much hatred as he did in Glasgow.

I would note this as the beginning of the end for him. He was not giving any conscious thought to abandoning the task in any way but the idealist I had conversed with in Santa Fé, with dreams of elevating a great club to a level that would release them from their parochial past and dignify them with a new non-sectarian future, had gone. Now he was to take the jacket off and go in there slugging with the old rivals as if to the streets of Glasgow born. It is said that at one team talk before an Old Firm game he said to the players he would not speak about football but instead showed them a photograph of the Queen and told them that's who they were playing for. Jock Wallace could not have done it better.

Paradoxically, it is in that context I have always viewed the Maurice Johnston signing. Judging from the quite stupendous over-reaction to the acquisition of Rangers' first Catholic in modern times you would have thought that Ibrox was about to evolve into a Jesuit seminary. I believe his coming to Ibrox was of much less social significance. Rangers were not setting out on the Via Dolorosa to a state of spiritual bliss. Souness was simply stuffing Celtic, taking from their very bosom one of their most talented sons. It was a piece of good business and brilliant show-manship but really did little to further the cause of ecumenism. When he stood there that day being interviewed by everybody except the *Osservatore Romano* Souness actually did mean it when he said he had simply signed a good player. There was nothing much more to it than that. Maurice himself looked as bewildered as the rest of us that morning and, as we surveyed this delightful, bubbling personality, with the harum-scarum tendencies and a taste for a good vintage we put well to the backs of our minds the thought that the first Catholic in the inner sanctum hardly had a life-style which accorded to the principles of Thomas Aquinas. He would not be going straight from the Blue Room to confession. Since we had waited all those years for it to happen, but had thought it less likely a phenomenon than the Second Coming, we laid aside certain technicalities of religious description and wallowed in an orgy of cant.

Of course it took a certain courage to bring Johnston there but it was not the courage required for the beginning of a whole new moral order. It seemed to me then, and still does now, that Rangers, having been condemned for their sectarianism, could successfully stem criticism and not be held to account by the rather finicky comment that their new signing probably attended fewer masses than the average worshipper. Rangers' critics probably would have preferred the litmus test to be the signing of an Italian player with six weans whose piety was revealed by the prominence of rosary beads. But here they were being pre-empted.

On the basis of 'Once a Catholic always a Catholic' Mo Johnston qualified. And as the odds were on Rangers continuing to be a successful team it was likely that Souness could ride out any Orange storm over a short period. It was a very shrewd and useful exercise indeed.

There was a developing view within Ibrox which I feel was hardening some of their older resolves then that there were elements at Celtic Park who would like to have seen an all-Catholic club. To hear those views expressed was like listening to the echoes of days past. It did not matter whether this was fantasy or fact, it simply indicated that you cannot lift up the tram-lines and pack away into a museum the different rickety vehicles of sectarianism as we nostalgically did with our trams. Nothing upgrades and modernises itself so much as bigotry. The continuing rivalry between these two clubs proves it.

Celtic have never articulated their position on this of course but it would be extremely surprising if it was not part of a hidden agenda to have an all-Catholic club. Those skilled in the 'Kremlinology' of the Old Firm would eagerly tell you the trend is there. Then they settle down to the old numbers game of 'Spot the Protestant'. In a sense, like Rangers, Celtic are entitled to run their own business as they so wish. Perhaps they even had the further entitlement of responding in their own particular fashion after years of being told by another institution that to be Catholic was to be inferior. As a prominent supporter said to me when talking about fund-raising for the financially struggling club in North America, 'It's Catholic money we are looking for!' There is no doubt that Celtic have enjoyed a greater community identity than any other club in the world but it would be a perversion of that unique relationship, and the final triumph for the bigots of all persuasions, if Celtic used Rangers as their role model and brought on to the market their own style of laager mentality. The adoption as manager, in June 1991, of Republic of Ireland internationalist Liam Brady, as articulate and friendly a man as you would ever wish to meet, nevertheless seemed to be confirmation in the darker recesses of the Glasgow mind that the old battalions were being assembled. I myself sensed a polarisation as extreme as there had ever been in my broadcasting involvement.

Souness certainly wearied of this background then became caught up in his own personal troubles, which compounded the normal hassles and seemed to me to demonstrate his unyielding nature. He told me he had received a reprimanding letter from Ernie Walker of the SFA about some comments of his which had appeared in the press. The rebuke seemed to Souness to be well beyond the representation made by an organisation and more that of a criticism from an individual. I could tell he was looking for blood for he told me he would answer along those very lines and put Ernie in his place. That, I knew, would not be the easiest of tasks. Nor was it wise. There is a time when you ignore confrontation, let it slip past you, and feel the better for it. Easy enough to say, particularly in retrospect, but valid nevertheless.

It seemed not to be in his nature and, whatever the protestations to the contrary, I am perfectly satisfied Souness was now a target figure. He had to take much of the blame on himself for allowing that situation to develop but his suspicions were only partly paranoiac. I was told from a very reliable source that one of the members of the SFA referees' committee, about to call Souness to attendance for one of his track-side transgressions said, 'We're going to sort him out once and for all.' Even supposing Souness deserved everything heaped upon him by his own actions, that remark did not suggest the dispassionate atmosphere in which the SFA ought to operate.

It was during the spell of publicity surrounding the departure of his seminal signing, Terry Butcher, that I wondered why Souness was tolerating the job any longer and said so distinctly during a Radio Clyde broadcast. The furore which the splitting up of manager and player caused might be said to be quite simply the dropping of a player who was decidedly out of form. It seems to me, despite what happened behind the scenes in the personal row, that the manager had been more than loyal to the man by continuing to play him when he ought to have been rested. Of course Butcher was no mere mortal. He was a folk hero of considerable proportions amongst the Rangers fraternity.

If you link this with what happened when Graham Roberts, a player of great popularity, was shown the door and the long-lasting love-hate relationship he had with another player, Ally McCoist, who is almost as popular amongst the Rangers supporters as King Billy's white horse, you can see Souness did not feel compelled to ingratiate himself with anybody. He could have played the popular card by abdicating from his own assessments of these matters but he chose not to. I admired him for that. He had come to the club in the first place to help rid it of its populist tradition and make it face up to harsh realities. He was running the club his own way. But at the same time he was losing touch with the terracings.

He was now, quite wrongly in my view, being perceived purely as an arrogant dictator. I cannot think of another example of such a successful manager held in such contempt by so many of his own supporters. This ingratitude I believe stemmed from their long held suspicion that this 'openness' he promised for the club would take away their birthright, their long held identity, their pride, their reason to hate. Many of them could not abide the Mo Johnston signing although the player's quality has stifled criticism. This was the street philosophy which I believe Souness felt, eventually, he could not defeat. It wasn't the specific reason why he left Ibrox but in turning matters over in his mind it could not have offered him any sort of consolation.

Perhaps he should have taken evening classes on the subject. I would have lectured him free of charge. The hostility, the bitterness and suspicion of the football scene I have worked in over the years distinguishes this part of the world from any other. Trust is a notable casualty of our environment. Very few take you at your face value and mostly actions and words are interpreted through the sieve of someone's fundamental perception of you. The nature of the judgement can be summarised, rather more poetically, in the phrase, 'Which foot does he kick with?' The criticism has therefore ranged far and wide, from a globular spittle from a Rangers supporter landing on my black raincoat like a crushed tarantula, to a pompous letter from a Celtic director telling me that, by his count, I was using the first names of Rangers players more than of the Celtic players and warning of dire consequences if I didn't mend my ways.

There were the crank calls threatening violence, the letters of sinister quality, including one from a group calling themselves the Bridgeton Loyalists, advising me that my time on this earth would be limited if I did not desist from impugning the Sons of William. There were the frequent snubs by both Rangers and Celtic players, managers, and directors, spiced with occasions when they displayed great courtesy. But from certain individuals there was always suspicion, bitterness having its subtle manifestations.

I had looked on this divisive scene from a special angle years before, when I was the headmaster of a primary school in Lanarkshire. I admit that I had by then developed a distaste for organised religion of any sort, although acknowledging the right of parents to have religious education in the curriculum of state schools as part of the Christian tradition we all emerged from. There was a falling roll in our school and we had empty classes. The nearby Catholic school was over-flowing and out of common sense, and not untouched by the feeling of contempt for the stupidity of all of this, I suggested informally to a local councillor that some children could be transferred to the empty rooms in our school. It would be an example. Oh, no it wouldn't! I had simply opened up a hornet's nest. Some of our parents thought I had suggested housing sex-criminals. The other side treated it with haughty disdain. The classrooms remained empty. That was me told off in no uncertain manner.

Leave it alone! Leave it be! Leaving it alone produces much of what we disapprove of in the Old Firm phenomenon. For whatever the compelling reasons for church schools one of the prices we pay for the segregation is the children's continuing ignorance of one another. The school experience is, or ought to be, about a sharing of lives. Community separation simply solidifies the battalions. The more they are separated the harder they'll hate. It is a complicated situation which forbids an easy solution. But whilst it is there, those who pour ridicule on the crass bigotries ought to recognise one of its strongest sources.

There seems no way round this. A prominent Celtic supporter and friend of several directors of the club sadly concluded to me in discussion of the status of the Old Firm game in a European football context, 'All we have left is bigotry. That's what makes us all turn up and watch this match. Nothing much more.' The remark seemed chillingly irreproachable judging by the standard on show and the disproportionate interest aroused. It is as if we who could not do without the Old Firm match grudgingly have to accept something of value coming from sectarianism.

Supposing the hatred vanished, the bitterness disappeared? Could we contemplate a city lobotomised, its passion lost, the gain a twee encounter of the nature of Liverpool v Everton? Those of us brought up on prime Aberdeen Angus cannot easily change to a soya substitute. What a terrible price to pay, I hear my ancient voice saying, for becoming civilised.

Rangers had Englishmen, one acknowledged Catholic, another prominent one whom the club wished to keep secret, cups and leagues, triumphs, the occasional disasters and a manager who had not finally won his fans over. As he himself was later to admit he had all of the Celtic support hating him and half of his own people. Although that sounds as if there was no way but out, he did turn down the Liverpool job immediately after Kenny Dalglish resigned and made it clear he was staying at Rangers. But then came a row with a tea-lady at Perth which produced some undignified scenes and apologies exchanged afterwards between the respective chairmen. Then a disagreement with Rangers' strong-minded owner David Murray about the nature of a transfer deal for the Hibernian goalkeeper Andy Goram. That was enough. He was off.

On the last day, at the press conference strongly chaired by Murray, Souness was calm but slightly tense. When he made his brief statement about leaving because circumstances made it impossible for him to do the job in the way he would like, he was looking straight at Murray. Pronounced mention was made of the fact that he was still on good terms with the chairman and that the pair would be dining together on the following Saturday evening. They never did and the truth of the matter is that Murray felt badly hurt by what happened. The relationship was at breaking point. Souness left the room almost at a trot. His eagerness to get out of the stadium as soon as possible was underlined by the fact that he had agreed to be interviewed for a possible documentary on him. When we went downstairs to the camera crew, he had gone.

So, too, I think had the notion that he had been a success. The statistics will certainly tell you he was, but in his declared aim to change the historical nature of the club he was not. He turned his back on something which had really only started. I had supported him to such an extent that, in the many arguments I had, mostly with Rangers supporters, about his objectives and methods and tactics I had become something of an apologist who had, at the same time, to be a contortionist to keep faith. No doubt his departure rather exposes as hollow much of what I believed him to be about. I was left with a sense of personal let-down after having backed the most interesting man to have entered the claustrophobic climate of Glasgow since Stein. It was finally proved he wasn't of the same mettle.

I had been carried away with the image created for me in New Mexico that day in 1986 when Souness sounded like a crusader, the harbinger of a new order. 'Bliss was it in that dawn to be alive,' sort of thing. Or perhaps, after all, with Santa Fé lying 7,000 feet above sea-level the headiness I had felt was merely due to the rarefied air.

17

Body and Seoul

It was the morning after the very long night of the sakes. Soft, velvety rice-wine sometimes makes for heavy landings, which meant that I was far from appreciative about being wakened by the telephone. It pierced and I fumbled and got it to my ear. It was the morning of Tuesday, 27 September in Seoul in 1988. The voice at the other end of the line was polite but firm.

'Ben Johnson has been tested positive for drugs. Would you go out to the village and see if you can get any pictures of him or any interviews with anybody. Yes, I know it sounds incredible but alas it is true!'

Even fully alert, which I was not, it would have been difficult to take in. At that time, and in that state, I was not into forming moral judgements but only able to reflect on how unkind life was. A major figure in the Games had not only taken drugs but was letting the news break at an ungodly hour, thus souring for me the few fleeting hours of freedom given over to licentious eating and drinking the previous night. Ben Johnson on drugs? Perhaps somebody had got it all wrong.

There had been rumours of course. I had heard them back in Los Angeles four years previously and Carl Lewis was not slow to drop hints. Did Johnson really think he could pocket the gold medal in the Blue Riband event on the back of drugs? Then, incredulity took over as I wondered if the lads had known I'd had a heavy night and just wanted to get me out of bed at the crack of dawn. There would be a message for me at reception saying, 'Nice to have you up, Arch!'

Even as I stumbled downstairs into the marbled magnificence of our hotel and then outside to the Alka Seltzer sharpness of the cool morning I was refusing to believe this. In the taxi going through the uncannily empty streets of the normally traffic-atrophied Korean capital, disbelief mixed readily with drowsiness. I reached the village and saw the crowds of journalists and reporters and television crews queuing up in the incredibly disorganised and infuriatingly slow bureaucratic quagmire called the security office. I knew then that something was stirring and it was not a complaint about the village catering. Indeed the place was buzzing with the Johnson story and that special irate quality of the journalistic beast on the prowl had crept into the voices of those trying to gain access to the village quickly lest stories were lost. They were being held up by the statutory smiling morons who are now an indispensable part of the Olympic scene as inspectors of credentials and purveyors of frustration.

As Olympic villages go, the one in Seoul was a city. Walking up the broad main avenue to it was like walking into Castlemilk in its infancy. The honeycomb of blocks of flats was housing the biggest-ever assembly of Olympic athletes and it was never less than stimulating to visit as the various nationalities merged together in gaudy, clamorous unity. The restaurant was always thronged as a central meeting place, although many people gave up trying to eat there as there were always queues, even early in the morning. That day, though, a pall had descended. The area seemed listless and quieter, distinctly so. The advancing tide of media were causing no ripples for the place looked as if it would take an earthquake to wake it from this stupor.

People were numbed already that early Tuesday morning. I doubt if a single piece of news, with the exception of the act of terrorism in Munich, has made such an immediate impact on such a vast gathering of athletes. Johnson had cheated. He had let them all down. He had created almost immediately a new form of Olympic Games – the Games of mistrust, of doubt and suspicion, the unclean Games. Nothing could remove that stain. I got the feeling up there that morning, listening to groups of people talking about him with some aggrieved incredulity, that a deadly virus had been let loose. There is little doubt in my mind that the mood and atmosphere changed in Seoul. The Games took on a graver aspect.

But, of course, that morning there was no sign of Johnson. Philip Marlowe couldn't have found him. Indeed as we were racing round the village trying to make sense of all of this he was, as we were later to learn, being shoved through customs at Seoul Airport on his way out of the country minus his gold medal. And there was no sign of any Canadian in the village. Normally they were very demonstrative and colourful. But only a couple of hours after the breaking of the news they had taken down all the banners which were splashed along the balconies of their apartments and they were behind locked doors. The Maple Leaf had contracted Dutch Elm disease overnight.

We could extract nothing from their representatives, who refused to make any comment. So we made for the British Team Headquarters where the BBC had installed a remote control camera which was operated by technicians in the International Broadcasting Centre on the other side of Seoul. The balcony was small, the technology of global dimension. With the help of surely the nicest press-officer known to mankind, Caroline Searle of the British Olympic Association, we managed to persuade Linford Christie to get up out of bed and give us his reaction. This, as it turned out, had its ironic element.

'He's a disgrace,' Linford told me as I took him up to the small balcony where the camera was. 'The man should be hounded out of this business.'

I turned on the lighting switch, the engineer several miles away in the centre of Seoul pressed the right button, the camera jerked into life and swung round towards Linford and his brooding face was seen live back in London. His two-way interview was deeply critical of Johnson. It was also quite impressive, for his tone was of a man betrayed. He sounded as if he had appointed himself as a kind of ad hoc spokesman not just for all the Games' athletes but particularly for that esoteric clan, the sprinters. In their obsession with shortening space and time they have cultivated their own strange ethic.

257

Indeed, I recall the great aerobics guru Dr Kenneth Cooper who set America off jogging telling me almost dismissively of sprinters that in his cardiac lab in Texas he had tested for endurance a fifty-year-old woman and Hasely Crawford, who won the gold medal for the 100 metres in Montreal, and the woman beat him hands down. 'They have a special kind of fitness,' he said. 'They cannot really be models for the rest of us. They are a unique species. Being fit and capable for what they do does not make them necessarily fit for life as a whole.'

This enclave they create for themselves can lead to bitchiness. Stories circulated in Los Angeles about Carl Lewis's sexual preferences and there was an even more scurrilous one about his attitude to cocaine. They were put about with relish inside his own fraternity. Lewis himself had long murmured suspicions about Johnson's abilities and whether they were aided or not. So, Linford was talking of Johnson as if he had just been defrocked from a sort of priesthood of the cult of brevity. Indeed he pointedly said that people like himself would now be unfairly tarred with the same brush. It was a plea for the innocents. Those words stuck. I associate them now with the look on the face of the late Ron Pickering, the BBC athletics commentator, some two nights later when, going into his hotel room very late on, he told me grimly, 'Say nothing about this at the moment but I hear a British athlete has been tested positive!' And I remember the pause, a long one. 'I think it's Linford.'

He got out the malt whisky and we let it soften the blow. Like all big men, Pickering looked particularly devastated when he displayed shock. He sat massively on his chair, wondering over and over again what this was all about, sounding alternately pessimistic and optimistic. 'I'm sure if it is him it won't amount to anything serious.' If he said that once he said it fifty times in the space of the next couple of hours.

Pickering was a man of sharp intellect and towering passion. The lucidity of his arguments over such matters as sporting boycotts of South Africa or the cheating of drug-taking athletes was supplemented by an almost evangelistic fervour which inevitably won him both admirers and detractors. Some of his criticisms came out like biblical denunciations but, although he always gave the impression of possessing a Calvinistic regret that a code of ethics was being swamped by current political and social immoralities, he never was, as his critics tried to portray him, a pompous pontificator. I saw him essentially as a man's man. He could hold his booze with the best, converse on your terms as well as his and was one of the best dispensers of the risqué joke in the business.

Although it was still only a rumour, I knew that Ron had got information from somewhere and that he feared the imminent disintegration of the Games. 'If this is true,' he told me that night, 'I will never believe what another athlete says about drugs so long as I live. How could anybody?'

Certainly the Johnson disclosure had stunned us but what Ron had just told me about Linford seemed like confirmation that the disease was virulent. He had warned me not to mention any names but to keep on the alert for something sensational. When I got back to my room in the wee small hours I found a message informing me the word was out that an unnamed British athlete had failed a test. Everybody was now really on edge. From having come to cover a sporting festival we were now all on battle stations. But our discomfort was as nothing compared to what was happening within the British Olympic Association.

Two days after the Johnson news broke, they were hosting a party for their sponsors without whom there would have been precious little team there in the first place. The evening was going smoothly and although these poor officials needed another canapé orgy like they needed a drug scandal they were going through the diplomatic motions of keeping everybody happy. The function was obviously a jolly affair, but only for so long. Back in the almost deserted British Team headquarters an envelope was hand-delivered to the remaining official there who took receipt of it and might have pigeon-holed it until the morning. However, he had the presence of mind to act on what was stamped on the outside. 'Seoul Medical Commission. Urgent.' There is urgent and there is urgent, but during a major sports event if you have any business prompted by the medical authorities it is, given the worry about drugs, as well to act quickly. Otherwise, at the very least, rumour gets out of hand. The quicker you ascertain the truth the better

259

for any possible defence. It also gives you the chance to keep it under wraps.

The official took the note to the party. There, it was read in a quiet corner. It told them that Linford Christie had failed his A test. Caroline Searle admits she wanted to scream. Dick Palmer, the Head of the British delegation and the soul of rectitude and diplomacy, showed the classical British skill at underplaying a crisis by proceeding with his socialising and encouraging the others to do likewise. At the same time, he wished that the ground would open up and swallow him. They were particularly devastated in view of the high moral tone of Linford's denunciation of Ben Johnson. Eventually the news seeped out and Linford was besieged by the media.

To this day, some of the British officials are convinced that a person in the laboratories, or in the Medical Commission itself, was bribed by someone in the media to disclose this finding. Linford himself was determined to get out and about. Even though he knew that he was in the centre of a controversy he chose to go down to the relay training at the practice track, where the media were awaiting. The fact that so many people were acting as if he must be guilty outraged him. He was now to be hounded, though.

He wanted to keep his head held high and not to go skulking in a dark corner out of the way. On one occasion I actually thought he was going to lash out physically at a group of hacks but he controlled himself. Linford was like a man straining to get away from his blocks but held back because the gun has yet to sound. The tension was building, the mood was grim, and Caroline Searle, representing the BOA in her first Olympics, was facing up to a constant barrage of media questions whenever she appeared in public. Her renowned equanimity held but her face was visibly paling and she looked as if she had hardly slept for days. And yet it was all so needless.

Linford had taken ginseng, which is a famous Korean product. Its name is derived from the aromatic root which, ironically enough, is called in the original Mandarin 'Jen Man', meaning it resembles human legs. This was a normal practice of his. He had been taking it for years. Ginseng is merely a root, not a substance banned by the IOC. But he had bought some which had been corrupted in some way and which contained a pseudo-Ephedrine, a stimulant which is most definitely on the proscribed list. Fifteen American athletes had tested positive for this very substance only a few months before and the medical officers of the BOA had expressly warned the sports' governing bodies of its dangers. In this instance Linford had bought ginseng which must have been 'spiked' for extra effect and it slipped under the guard.

In the post-Ben Johnson period of hysteria Linford was treated like a common criminal by some of the media. The acute embarrassment felt by the British officials, who were still looking around to see who they could blame, was less painful than that of a man whose reputation and integrity now looked gravely at risk. He knew that previous to the Johnson disclosures two British Modern Pentathletes had been found positive for taking illegal substances, but they had been cleared after their explanation was found adequate. There had been little publicity attached to that. The sprint silver-medallist, though, was to be a special case. He also accrued much more publicity than the wretched judo athlete Kerrith Brown who had taken Furosomide, a diuretic, to help with a knee swelling. It has weight-enhancing properties and is consequently a banned substance. Brown was certainly technically more culpable than Linford, in that he must have known of the dangers, and was ultimately disqualified.

There was no real elation amongst the British medical people on the eventual clearing of Linford when he appeared in front of the Medical Commission, for they knew what the future was going to hold in store for every athlete from then on. As one doctor told me, 'We'll have to ban athletes from visiting the chemist's during Games for if they want to cure the common cold they're going to be in trouble. Ephedrine is in every respectable cough mixture. There is a veritable stimulant jungle out there which we'll have to carve our way through very carefully.'

Pickering was more forthright.

'They're still cheating,' he told me later. 'There are still people out there who should be put behind bars for what they're doing, the pedlars as well as the athletes.'

In the face of this it would have to be concluded that there was something amateurish about the checks and warnings which were supposed to exist amongst the British team. Pickering knew better than anybody that the anabolic and hormone growth treatments which athletes engaged in throughout the year could be less easily detected at the Games and, Orwellian though it might sound, the problem would have to be combated throughout the world by a 'flying-squad', spot-testing for the use of these substances. Without that we would still be watching cheats rising to the Olympic rostrum.

For it was the ones who got away with it that people were eventually talking about all over Seoul. There were beanfeasts of conjecture. 'How could she have so improved her performances over six months? Look at her muscles now, anyway!' That was the favourite comment. Some of the most prominent names turned up in conversation. But, then, nobody could actually prove anything. Triumph therefore was compromised by doubt and suspicion. People simply could not be sure any longer. Ben Johnson had left not only his gold medal behind but also a considerable psychosis.

This was all some eighteen months before the World Cup in Italy but I felt that somehow Korea represented the apogee in my relationship with BBC Scotland. Yet, although I was so exotically remote, I was never able to quell the unease I felt about not sitting on a platform on a Saturday afternoon at the edge of a Scottish football pitch, regardless of weather. Whatever the attractions of broadcasting in network on an occasion such as the Olympic Games, if you go desperately seeking football results from a land six thousand miles away at the same time as you are juggling with a totally alien project, you are still rooted to your own soil. My work in Korea made me ponder more seriously than I had previously just how far I could go in balancing these elements. I had to reflect on my willingness to work in this way. I knew that some people in Scotland saw it as an inevitable drift away from my stereotyped role. Professionally it always seemed extremely odd to me that nobody in BBC Scotland ever discussed my work on my return. It was as if I had never attended the three Olympics.

It was in Korea that I began to wonder if I had reached the

outer limits of broadcasting credibility. Was I, in trying to marry the different elements, losing the absolutely essential feature, for a broadcaster, of clear-cut identity? Apart from that, the Olympic Games in Korea remain vividly in the mind because they contained so many surprises, not the least of which was the capacity of the people there to host them so spectacularly.

We had gone there querying the IOC's decision to take the Games to the divided peninsula. How could those orientals possibly follow Los Angeles anyway? What presumption, one thought! Their opening ceremony, in fact, stunned the senses and made the LA display seem like watching the death throes of American burlesque in a seedy theatre in Hoboken. It was that good. The sheer range of varying cultural displays, cemented by the underlying presence of Korean aggression and meticulous organisation, took us unawares.

Of course they would forever after be identified as the 'Drugs' Games because of the Johnson affair. But that unjustifiably constricts the achievement of these people in making the Games work splendidly. There were many people around to let us know that all this was a phoney show, that too much had been sacrificed to foot the bill. Probably. But no Olympics can be staged now without some dislocation of normality. Perhaps the people who appreciated this less than anybody, and to everybody's surprise, were the Americans. The Koreans hated them. This mood sprang initially from the growing dissatisfaction with having an American Army stationed heavily in their country. Although it was serving a defensive role against the eccentric regime in the north it was now being perceived as superfluous to requirements.

As we were later to see for ourselves, at Panmunjom, the uniformed pantomimical confrontation of eyeball-to-eyeball glowering between the Americans and the North Koreans, within a few feet of each other, made a Punch and Judy show seem as meaningful as *King Lear*. Anyway, the Russians and the Chinese together had warned the North Koreans not to indulge in any hanky-panky during the Games and the only danger to person was if you happened upon a violent student demonstration in Seoul itself. These apparently took place at times convenient to the foreign press. It was a sort of phone-a-riot phenomenon.

The Koreans were not slow to tell us they disliked the Yanks for talking their culture down. One charming woman university professor who figured prominently in the feminist movement in a strongly male-dominated society said to me, 'At the end of the day all that the Americans have introduced to us from their culture is AIDS.'

If this sounded, and probably was, harsh it nevertheless indicated that the Koreans perceived the Americans as an occupying force who could not imbibe the local ways and made their only venture into the culture by entering the shops and prostitutes of the famous downtown Seoul area, Itaewon. All this seemed to be confirmed by NBC, who nightly during the Games trivialised anything Korean, probably innocently, but quite insensitively. 'Hey, getta load of this,' one male presenter would say to the inevitable female co-host. 'I can use these chop-sticks now. Me likee!' She would reply, 'Yes and last night I went to a restaurant and do you know what I had? Kimche. You know, that pickled cabbage that tastes like old socks.' And, with a grimace, 'Well, I did try!'

Jesus wept, you would say to yourself watching this. Their insensitivity reached a climax when a Korean boxer refused to get out of the ring after a verdict went against him. He sat there unbudgeable until the shame of the whole episode was brought home to him. It was an isolated disgrace for which the Koreans sincerely apologised. But the American media in particular waded in as if the entire Korean nation was in insurrection against the ideals of the Olympic movement. I went to a special reunion held by the President of the Olympics for those who had been connected with the torch-run and he was besieged by American journalists who simply would not let this matter drop and harassed the man.

The President dealt with this brilliantly. He would occasionally emit that sloughing adenoidal noise which seems to be endemic in the Orient and in which mucus is obviously being cleared from deep in the tubes. It sounds like a personal drain being unplugged and can be very off-putting at times but I felt that here was a Korean trait being thrown back in the face of the Yankee intruders. It echoed throughout the plush Presidential Suite in the Olympic offices like a thunderstorm. Other than that, with a cool use of colloquial English and sounding as if he had graduated from Harvard Business School, he tried to explain that the boxer had not committed a crime but had indeed offended against etiquette and that, of course, he would be made aware of that. He seemed to take no great offence as the Americans totted up what they thought were the failings of the Games. A Dutch journalist beside me quietly bemoaned, 'They have a hamburger mentality. The Games are not for them, they are for everybody.'

Their arrogance was met more forcibly by the Korean people who began to give them the cold shoulder. Some of my friends in NBC television took the full brunt of the backlash because, while transmitting throughout Korea to their own troops, they had also been picked up by the locals. Having given the impression yet again that only Americans were involved in the Games, they had to stop wearing their distinctive blazers for fear of being shunned in shops and restaurants. But, like anybody else, they knew a good story when they saw one, and they joined the throng chasing after Royalty the day Mark's horse broke down.

I still think of that day I pursued Mark and Anne as some sort of watershed in my broadcasting career, almost as if I could say to myself, 'Now I've done everything.' For this took me into my Nigel Dempster mode for the first and probably last time. There was I, a student of the half-time pie and Bovril and the ululations of ranting football managers, about to assess a Royal relationship.

It was a case of drop everything and head for the hills for not only had we heard that Captain Mark Phillips' horse had gone lame but also knew that the Princess Royal was to be there to see the eventing. With the conjecture mounting by the day about the frailty of their marriage we felt, as did every other television unit in the business, that if we could only get them together somehow, showing some cordiality (a touch, a smile even) it might clear the air. After all, they hadn't been seen together for some considerable time and we knew that as soon as Mark lost interest in the Games he would head for one end of the world and she the other. Now we knew he was out. We got in a fast car and headed out of the city. Nobody was interested all that much in the event or the horses. After all, one remembers Charlton Heston from the chariot race in *Ben Hur*, not the animals.

What we got after waiting around all day for the specially desired 'togetherness' shot was the sight of them walking towards camera without so much as looking at each other as they went towards the Princess Royal's limousine for the so-called farewell scene. They barely spoke. They simply split up and went in opposite directions. Later, viewing the pictures in the editing suite, I felt as if I had just confirmed the end of a relationship. And I also paused to wonder just how easily the media snoopers on Royalty lived with themselves.

It had also taken me further out of my natural habitat than I had ever gone and whilst the feeling of being a minimalist Court reporter did not last long its contrast with other work had been stimulating. If you are reporting during Olympic Games anyway you have to be prepared for a mad whirligig of an existence, hopping from one extreme to another and prepared to grab anything. For great is the broadcasting maw during that period and it needs constant filling.

By now, we were feeling the Games were suffering from elephantiasis. We did not intend to make that a theme of any of our filming yet I hope that it came across as such in our collection. They have spread and fructified to over-ripeness. The entry of the athletes during the opening ceremony is fast becoming a re-creation of the Boers' Great Trek or Mao's Great March. It has now exceeded its boundaries of self-glorification and requires radical surgery. It is not merely a case of stopping growth but of severe pruning. Heaven only knows how that can be achieved given the self-propagating nature of the beast. The mind boggles at certain recreations/sports lining up for acceptance. Regardless of the different sort of athleticism involved it would be difficult for example to reject the claims of ballroom-dancing whilst synchronised swimming so defies objective assessment. Aesthetic equilibrium on the dance-floor is no less exacting or fairer to judge than holding your breath and smiling like Esther Williams for some seconds.

Other categories are excluded on the same fine-line basis but are beating at the door. They must be resisted and others weeded out. If they continue to expand, world championships in the different events could take over as the leaner but more meaningful competitions (as some already are) and the Games would be a sort of World Youth Festival. Their glamour will then appeal more to those who simply want to get on the stage rather than those who chase excellence. Consequently they will be diminished.

The Korean experience was sometimes emotional though, genuinely so. You can feel you are hard-boiled enough to avoid the lump in the throat and that, by and large, you can do without such a manner of feeling anyway. But it comes to all of us. It's probably better to admit it when it does. As I do now.

It was perhaps because I was sitting nearest the editor that I was asked if I would help carry the Olympic flame on one of the stages of the relay on its way up the Korean peninsula. The organisers wanted media representatives to take part in this enterprise. I was too coy to ask just how far I would have to run but if I was going to collapse in the effort, then, having helped to carry the sacred flame, the ancient Greek gods and goddesses would surely see me all right on the other side. Looking at myself in the pristine white running gear they had handed me, though, I decided Terpsichore would have rather overdosed on hemlock than have consorted with me.

Middle age does not necessarily creep up on you. It can also jump out and surprise you in one blinding leap as horrific as a Stephen King spectre coming out of the dark, the more vengeful for your impertinence in ignoring it for so long. The mirror I was staring at in the hotel reflected all those lunches and late nights and years of simply believing in nothing changing. Funny how that torch forced me to look at myself that way. And I hadn't even seen it yet, just the gear that was made for youth but which was now helping me to cut an odd figure.

When we arrived in Chongju we could find no one who spoke English. English-speakers in Korea, despite the long American presence, are like London taxis, only there when you don't really need them. Try miming, 'I am here to carry the Olympic torch on its way to Seoul.' It's not funny for one who could only ever do *Gone With the Wind* when he played charades. Eventually we found a student who had some idea of what we were about and we found the spot where the torch was to be picked up. It was near a crossroads just outside the town. They told me I was to run only one kilometre like everybody else. This seemed bearable. But I had to face up to constructing something for the camera out of the handover, the run and the finish. We agreed that I would start speaking at a certain moment and the camera, having picked up the incoming runner some distance down the road, would then reveal me waiting for him. The words would have to start at the right time and finish just as the runner reached me and above all there would only be one chance to get it right. I hate recording things but on this occasion I could hardly ask the torch officials if we could please try it again. I felt genuinely scared about messing the whole thing up.

That afternoon, looking at the river on one side of us and the low houses on the other and the deserted road along which only an occasional lorry passed there was the feel of a little town too preoccupied with its daily load to be bothered by the fleeting visit of a travelling flame. But when we arrived at the spot half-an-hour before the handover in the early evening the transformation was enormous. Tens of thousands of people were bordering the road straight in front of me leading to the edge of the town. I felt the same sort of stagefright I had experienced all those years before, setting out to broadcast for the first time. I desperately wanted to get the words of commentary right if I never did anything else again in my life. It was a sort of audition. It was to prove one's worth in handling a situation that could easily be overloaded with significance until simply cloyed. It had to breathe naturally and television, in a recorded situation, very rarely allows you to achieve that.

We saw the flame. The cameraman started to record. I awaited the signal from him and I started to speak. When you do these things you sometimes cannot hear exactly what you are saying but the sensor within the broadcaster still registers a flaw, particularly a fatal one. It is an instinctive ability to be able to think of something else whilst the mouth is on auto-pilot. The sensor detected nothing untoward in what I was saying as I stared the camera straight in the eye for the last few seconds. Then I turned to look up the road as my last words fitted the gasping entry of the incoming runner.

Thank God I got that bit right. The small ceremony of the anonymous bartering of flames took but a few seconds and off I went with the sudden realisation that the oil-filled torch seemed to weigh a ton in my right hand.

Half-way down the route, with the people greeting the flame and me as if we had relieved the town from a siege, I was glad the weight of the torch was forcing me to lower it bit by bit so that the smoke blown back by the slight breeze was getting into my eyes. They had already been affected by something more than smoke. I felt that since I was on camera the whole way and had to conclude the run with another chat to the lens I had to have an excuse for the amazing stirring of emotions I felt. I was finding self-control almost impossible as this wave of genuine warmth and appreciation of the presence of the torch surged towards me from the thousands packing the streets. It was the torch and the people who were leading me. Not the reverse. I was sharing, not appearing. It could have been Shettleston Road and that oft-conjured fantasy of the Junior Cup being borne aloft and brought home to Greenfield Park. I imagined this is how the East End community would have reacted, just like this. It made me feel as if I were coming home.

I reached the other runner, tilted the flame towards his torch, ignited the fuel and away he went. I turned to camera to make my final statement and tried to pretend that it was shortage of breath that was causing the hesitancy and not that embarrassing tightness round the throat. When I had finished, presence of mind was beginning to return and I thought that by fading away into the descending gloom I could simply take the torch into my eternal possession. However, a blazing torch is not the easiest thing to stick up your jumper and escape with. I had only walked several paces from the camera when I was seized by three very muscular men who promptly grabbed it from me. I tried to mime the fact that I thought the torch was mine to keep but they were having none of it. They waved me away impatiently and snuffed the torch out somehow. It and they then vanished.

A week later, however, I was invited to a reception where they presented me with the same torch. They had not cleaned it. It was scarred and, indeed, almost deformed in part by the inferno that it had contained. It looked aged, almost beyond repair. But I knew that with fuel and a light it would spark into life despite appearances.

Like when I lift a microphone.

INDEX

(For individual football games, Cup Finals and World Cups, *see*: Football Events)

Index